PREMATURE OBSOLESCENCE

PREMATURE OBSOLESCENCE

In Search of an Improved Legal Framework

Anaïs Michel

INTERSENTIA
Cambridge – Antwerp – Chicago

Intersentia Ltd
8 Wellington Mews | Wellington Street
Cambridge | CB1 1HW | United Kingdom
Tel.: +44 1223 736 170
Email: mail@intersentia.co.uk
www.larcier-intersentia.com

Distribution for the UK and the rest of the world (incl. Eastern Europe):
NBN International
1 Deltic Avenue, Rooksley
Milton Keynes MK13 8LD
United Kingdom
Tel.: +44 1752 202 301 | Fax: +44 1752 202 331
Email: orders@nbninternational.com

Distribution for Europe:
Lefebvre Sarrut Belgium NV
Hoogstraat 139/6
1000 Brussels
Belgium
Tel.: +32 3 680 15 50 | Fax: +32 3 658 71 21
Email: mail@intersentia.be

Distribution for the USA and Canada:
Independent Publishers Group
Order Department
814 North Franklin Street
Chicago, IL60610
USA
Tel.: +1 800 888 4741 (toll free) | Fax: +1312 337 5985
Email: orders@ipgbook.com

Premature Obsolescence. In Search of an
Improved Legal Framework

Cover design: Danny Juchtmans / www.dsigngraphics.be
Cover image: EDUIN / pixabay

ISBN 978-1-83970-375-1 (hardcover)
ISBN 978-1-83970-379-9 (PDF)
D/2023/7849/73
NUR 822

British Library Cataloguing in Publication Data. A catalogue record for this book is available from the British Library.

TABLE OF CONTENTS

ACKNOWLEDGEMENTS

"All that is gold does not glitter,
Not all those who wander are lost (...)"
– J.R.R. Tolkien

Writing a doctoral thesis is an adventure that I never thought I would embark on. It all started thanks to a collaborative project between two prestigious Belgian universities: UCLouvain, where I obtained the degree of Master in Law and which nurtured a true passion for law, and KU Leuven, which gave me the key skills to thrive in this discipline. In addition to these two universities, I am especially grateful to the Research Foundation Flanders (FWO), which funded my research.

During this adventure, I realised that far from being a tough and lonely task, writing a PhD thesis is a tremendous opportunity to meet and strengthen ties with amazing and inspiring people. I have had the companionship of many wonderful people on the journey that has resulted in this book. Although words are not enough to express my gratitude, the following paragraphs aim to acknowledge all the brilliant minds that contributed to this outcome.

My first word of thanks goes to my supervisor, Prof. Dr. Bert Keirsbilck, who instilled in me his passion for law and brought out the best in me. I could always count on him to critically review every page I sent him (down to the smallest comma) and to involve me in all the projects he deemed beneficial for my research. In addition to sharing his experience and his expertise in economic law and other disciplines, he taught me one of the most beautiful life lessons: with rigor, perseverance, and self-confidence, anything is possible. My co-supervisor, Prof. Dr. Anne-Lise Sibony, also greatly contributed to the completion of this project. I thank her for her insightful comments and thorny questions that helped me refine the text of this book, as well as for the continuous kindness and support she gave me. Thank you both for the valuable time you set aside for me.

I appreciate the willingness of Prof. Dr. Evelyne Terryn and Prof. Dr. Geert Van Calster to be members of my supervisory committee and PhD jury. Many thanks for your assistance through every step of my research project, as well as for all the side projects and opportunities you gave me. I would also like to thank Prof. Dr. Alain Strowel, who believed in the project from the very start and agreed to be a member of my PhD jury. Thank you to Prof. Dr. Vanessa Mak, another member of my PhD jury, for her substantial contribution to the better understanding and further development of civil law and for providing me with food for thought on a wide array of topics discussed in this book. I am also very grateful to Prof. Dr. Bernard Tilleman, for having agreed to preside over my PhD defence. Thank you for all the support that you have given me throughout the journey and, more generally, for initiating these very symbolic projects jointly supervised by KU Leuven and UCLouvain. In addition, I wish to acknowledge Prof. Dr. Yves De Cordt, without whom this amazing adventure would not have started, and Dr. Christophe Verdure, who was a member of my supervisory committee as well as a sympathetic ear during these six years of doctoral studies and thanks to whom I became the editorial secretary of the DCCR journal, another project dear to my heart. I also owe a debt of gratitude to all the professors and scholars who crossed my path during my PhD and who, through their wise words, writings, advice and criticism, have fuelled my thoughts.

Also very importantly, I would like to thank all my colleagues who made this journey easier and funnier. My first thanks go to those who witnessed and guided my first steps at the KU Leuven and helped me discover the rich and diverse Flemish culture: Eveline Vanthorre, Charline De Coster, Stijn Aerts, Jonas Lambrechts and Dorien De Wachter. Thank you to all the members of the Consumer Competition Market (CCM) for their support, advice, and good cheer, with special thanks to Harry Slachmuylders, Elisa Paredis, Elias Van Gool, Lennard Michaux, Christof Koolen, Zeno Vanhoyland and Dario Hug, who proofread this work. I have also learned a lot from Jozefien Vanherpe, Friso Bostoen, Pim Jansen and Richard Steppe, who were true models and great coaches. I was equally delighted to share this journey with the members of the Centre de recherche interdisciplinaire Droit, Entreprise et Société (CRIDES) and the Centre Charles De Visscher pour le droit international et européen (CeDIE) who welcomed me with open arms in these excellent forums, where I had fruitful and pleasant discussions. A sincere word of thanks also goes to my new colleagues at the FPS Economy, who encouraged me during the final leg of this journey.

I also feel extremely lucky to be surrounded by all these people that I get to call friends, who I met at school, during my studies, in Brussels or elsewhere. Though for lack of space, I cannot name you all, I hope you realise how important you are in my life. Your kindness kept me motivated along the way. So, from the bottom of my heart, thank you.

My heartfelt thanks go out to my family. Cyril, Lison and Merlin, as the older sister, I have always tried to set a good example for you, but I have realised that in the end you are the ones who impact and inspire me the most. I am immensely proud of you. I would also like to express my deep gratitude to my parents. Your encouragement, trust, and unconditional love have allowed me to overcome challenges and fully realise myself. I know I can count on you in any situation, and this provides me with an invaluable sense of security and confidence. A huge thank to Émilie, Freddy, Marisa and Alister, who are just as supportive as my parents. I also truly appreciated the unwavering support I received from the rest of my family.

Most of all, I would like to thank the man who changed my life, my best friend, the love of my life, Jack. Since you became a part of my life, I have been filled with indescribable happiness. Thank you for your unfailing support and patience. I cannot wait to see what the future holds for us.

INTRODUCTION

A. DEFINITION OF THE PROBLEM

1. THE PHENOMENON OF PREMATURE OBSOLESCENCE

1. PREMATURE OBSOLESCENCE, DECREASING PRODUCT LIFETIME AND THROWAWAY CULTURE – The phenomenon of premature obsolescence of products relates to the fact that products do not last as long as they should or could. There are nowadays growing and widespread suspicions about the diminishing lifetime of consumer products. An increasing number of empirical studies confirm these suspicions, at least for certain goods.[1] For example, in Germany, an increasing number of large household appliances, like washing machines, are replaced within the first 5 years of ownership.[2] Moreover, it has been reported that one-third of appliances are discarded while still working.[3] That accurately reflects what is critically called the 'throwaway society'. This pejorative term condemns today's excessive production and overconsumption of short-lived and disposable items.

2. PREMATURE OBSOLESCENCE IS TYPICAL FOR THE LINEAR ECONOMY – In industrialised countries, the current economic system encourages economic actors – namely producers, other businesses in the contractual chain and consumers – to use more materials and more energy for higher satisfaction, without developing the capacity to absorb and reuse waste and by-products.[4]

---

1 F. Wang et al., 'Enhancing E-waste estimates: improving data quality by multivariate input/output analysis', 33 *Waste Manage* (2013) p. 2397 at p. 2407; H. Wieser, N. Tröger, *Die Nutzungsdauer und Obsoleszenz von Gebrauchsgütern im Zeitalter der Beschleunigungs – Eine Empirische Untersuchung in Österreichischen Haushalten* (Arbeiterkammer Wien 2015); S. Prakash, G. Dehoust, M. Gsell, T. Schleicher, R. Stamminger, *Einfluss der Nutzungsdauer von Produkten auf ihre Umweltwirkung – Schaffung einer Informationsgrundlage und Entwicklung von Strategien gegen "Obsoleszenz"* (Umweltbundesamt 2016).

2 S. Prakash et al., *Einfluss der Nutzungsdauer von Produkten auf ihre Umweltwirkung – Schaffung einer Informationsgrundlage und Entwicklung von Strategien gegen "Obsoleszenz"* (Umweltbundesamt Study 2016) p. 43.

3 See T. Cooper, 'Inadequate Life? Evidence of Consumer Attitudes to Product Obsolescence', 27 *J. Consum. Policy* (2004) p. 437. According to this study, 33% of discarded appliances were reported to be 'still functioning', just over one in five (21%) were considered 'in need of repair', and slightly less than one-half (46%) 'broken beyond repair'.

4 N. Benqué, C. du Tertre, P. Vuidel, *Trajectoire vers l'économie de fonctionnalité et de la coopération, dans une perspective de développement durable* (Atemis 2014) p. 2.

Among the drivers propelling this model to dominance, there is the availability of relatively cheap and abundant natural resources (notwithstanding post-Covid price increases) and energy, as well as various technological and social innovations, ranging from engines and electricity to assembly lines for the mass production of goods.[5] This linear economy, more commonly referred to as 'take-make-use-dispose', is generally identified as the root and support of the phenomenon of premature obsolescence. There appears to be a growing consensus that we should move towards a circular economy.

2. TYPES OF PREMATURE OBSOLESCENCE

3. Five types of premature obsolescence – Premature obsolescence comes in various forms. In this book, five main types of product obsolescence are distinguished.[6]

4. Material and functional obsolescence – Generally, people and media understand the phenomenon of premature obsolescence as being limited to (intentional) *material* and *functional* obsolescence. Material obsolescence relates to practices that includes the introduction of functional defects into the product and the impossibility of disassembling it. One of the best-known examples of intentional material obsolescence is the so-called 'Phoebus cartel' formed by the leading light-bulb companies in 1924 to shorten the life span of light bulbs from 2500 to 1000 hours. Functional obsolescence relates to the incompatibility of the product's hardware with later or competing software versions. When intentional, these practices of material and functional obsolescence are typical examples of what is called 'planned obsolescence'. Some stakeholders – especially from the business community – cast doubt on the existence of these types of intentional obsolescence.[7]

5. Indirect, economic and psychological obsolescence – Beyond material and functional obsolescence, premature obsolescence can be described in broader terms. Producers can also accelerate the obsolescence of their products by restricting the availability of spare parts or accessories (*indirect obsolescence*), by making products economically worthless or not worth repairing (*economic obsolescence*) or no longer attractive in the consumer's mind (*psychological obsolescence*). Besides being more frequently encountered, these types of

[5] European Environmental Agency (EEA), *Circular by design: Products in the circular economy* (European Union 2017) p. 13.

[6] For a more detailed explanation of this choice of typology, see *infra* (n° 98).

[7] See e.g. DigitalEurope's reaction of 8 February 2016 to the Circular Economy Package, p. 3; F. Meszaros, *Are our household appliances durable? – Essay on durability* (CECED 2017) (English summary available on: <https://www.applia.hu/en/durability/>).

obsolescence, and especially psychological obsolescence, attest that consumers' attitudes contribute to decreasing product life spans. Thus, by contrast to the narrative suggesting consumers are victims of 'evil' manufacturers, scholars now accept that the rapid obsolescence of products results from the behaviour of both producers and consumers.[8]

3. IS PREMATURE OBSOLESCENCE ALWAYS A PROBLEM?

6. From phenomenon to problem – The premature obsolescence of consumer products has different impacts from an economic, social and environmental perspective. It is interesting to note that, contrary to preconceived ideas, premature obsolescence is not merely negative. Premature obsolescence can have positive and negative impacts, although the second outweighs the first by far, as explained below.

7. Positive impacts of the phenomenon of premature obsolescence – First, from an economic perspective, the accelerating obsolescence of products can stimulate economic growth[9], boost competition, generate long-term sales by reducing the time between repeat purchases, and drive technological advances.[10] It has also been claimed that premature obsolescence strengthens the producer's incentives to provide adequate quality in other dimensions (e.g. product performance) that would offset the short product lifetime and ensure consumer satisfaction.[11] Consumers benefit from these developments. It enables them to replace less advanced products with better-performing ones, while those who cannot afford the best have access to lower quality products.[12]

Second, the premature replacement of products can be desirable from an environmental point of view. Redesigning products into more durable ones

---

8 See among others T. K. Aladeojebi, 'Planned obsolescence', 4 *International Journal of Scientific & Engineering Research* (2013) pp. 1505–1506; C. Déméné, A. Marchand, 'L'obsolescence des produits électroniques: des responsabilités partagées', 10 *The Ethics Forum* (2015) p. 17 at p. 19; J.L. Rivera, A. Lallmahomed, 'Environmental implications of planned obsolescence and product lifetime: a literature review', 9 *International Journal of Sustainable Engineering* (2016) pp. 123–124.

9 See B. London, *Ending the depression through planned obsolescence* (1932), available on: <https://upload.wikimedia.org/wikipedia/commons/2/27/London_%281932%29_Ending_the_depression_through_planned_obsolescence.pdf>. For further details on this contribution, see n° 10 and n° 47.

10 A. Fishman N. Gandal, O. Shy, 'Planned obsolescence as an engine of technological progress', 141 *Journal of Industrial Economics* (1993) p. 361 at p. 370.

11 R. Strausz, 'Planned obsolescence as an incentive device for unobservable quality', 119 *The Economic Journal* (2009) p. 1405 at p. 1421.

12 European Parliament (EP), *Planned obsolescence: Exploring the issue* (European Union 2016) p. 2.

might require more energy and resources compared to products with shorter life spans.[13] Moreover, in certain cases, replacing an old device with a more efficient version is more eco-friendly, when one considers optimizing rather than maximizing the product's lifespan. This argument is nonetheless only valid for inefficient durable products that mainly pollute or use energy in the use phase.[14] Finally, it is noteworthy that premature obsolescence is not necessarily problematic if the end-of-life of products is well organised.[15] As pointed out by P. Boot, A. Hare and R. Ho, "*the more deliberate we are about both recognizing the inevitable obsolescence of all products and applying that recognition to appropriate planning for obsolescence, the better prepared our products will be at the time of their predictable demise*".[16]

8. Premature obsolescence as a problem – However, the negative consequences of the mass production and consumption of goods with short life spans are manifold. The most preoccupying side effects of premature obsolescence relate to the environment, as it puts the very continuity of human life on earth at risk.[17] It is well known that every product bears an impact on the environment during its lifecycle. Products – and especially electrical and electronic ones – are associated with huge negative environmental impacts during the extraction of raw materials, production, distribution and use, as well as at the end of their lifecycle. Fast-paced product replacement, combined with rapid population growth and the increasing number of households with fewer persons[18], exacerbates flows of resources and wastes from and to the environment.[19] The integrity of natural ecosystems that are essential for humanity's survival is threatened by resource depletion and scarcity, climate change, pollution, waste, and a wide range of other environmental-related impacts.[20] According to a 2019 report issued by the European Commission

---

13 T. Cooper, 'The significance of product longevity', in T. Cooper, *Longer lasting products: Alternatives to the throwaway society* (Gower 2010) p. 20.

14 See e.g. the case of refrigerators, as mentioned in C. Bakker, C. Schuit, *The long view – Exploring product lifetime extension* (United Nations Environment Programme 2017) p. 27.

15 See C. Montalvo et al., *A longer lifetime for products: benefits for consumers and companies* (European Union 2016) p. 17; A. Zeeuw van der Laan, Aurisicchio M., 'Planned obsolescence in the circular economy', in C. Bakker and R. Mugge (eds.), *Product Lifetimes And The Environment 2017 – Conference Proceedings* (IOS Press 2017) p. 446 at p. 452. The second paper gives the example of Fuji disposable cameras, which are designed in a way that each component is optimally reused and its materials recycled after the camera housing is returned.

16 P. Boot, A. Hare and R. Ho, 'Up-front thinking for the optimization of product life', in B. Burns (ed.), *EcoSuss* (Carleton University Press 2008) p. 256.

17 K. Pope, *Understanding planned obsolescence – Unsustainability through production, consumption and waste generation* (Kogan Page 2017) p. 58.

18 See D.H. Meadows, D.L. Meadows, J. Randers, W.W. Behrens III, *The limits to growth* (Universe 1972).

19 EEA, *The European environment – state and outlook 2010* (SOER 2010) p. 9 at p. 17.

20 E. Hertwich, E. van der Voet, S. Suh, A. Tukker et al., *Assessing the Environmental Impacts of Consumption and Production: Priority Products and Materials* (UNEP 2010).

(EC), the ecological footprint of our current consumption patterns represents a significant and increasing share of the total ecological footprint.[21] In that respect, it is appalling that electricity consumption by households has risen, despite many appliances becoming more energy-efficient.[22]

Beyond environmental concerns, the premature obsolescence of consumer products creates other serious problems. On the consumer side, a short product lifetime contributes to an increase in credit purchases and consumer indebtedness, especially amongst the most vulnerable groups.[23] In other words, premature obsolescence affects the purchasing power of consumers, especially the ones with the lowest incomes. Furthermore, consumers are permanently discontented with the quality of products, leading to an erosion of trust in the market.[24] On the business side, there is the threat of exhaustion of many conventional resources in the foreseeable future, as well as the prospect of a price increase and the associated vulnerabilities in the supply of raw materials and energy.[25] Many companies have begun to notice that the linear economy increases their exposure to risks, most notably higher resource prices and supply disruptions. As reported by the Ellen MacArthur Foundation, "*more and more businesses feel squeezed between these rising and less predictable prices in resource markets on the one hand and high competition and stagnating demand for certain sectors on the other*".[26] Besides economic considerations, premature obsolescence tarnishes the producers' reputation in consumers' eyes.

4. GROWING INTEREST IN PREMATURE OBSOLESCENCE

9. Five waves of interest – There are nowadays heated discussions on the topic of premature obsolescence of products. Yet, it should be noted that the concept and the related issues are far from being new. Public awareness and interest in product longevity and obsolescence has gradually increased over the years and spread throughout the world in different waves.

---

21 S. Sala, A. Beylot, S. Corrado, E. Crenna, E. Sanyé-Mengual, M. Secchi, *Indicators and assessment of the environmental impact of EU consumption – JRC Science for Policy Report* (European Commission 2019).

22 EEA, *Environmental Indicator Report 2014. Environmental Impacts of Production-Consumption systems in Europe* (European Union 2014) p. 77.

23 European Parliament (EP), *Planned obsolescence: Exploring the issue* (European Union 2016) p. 3.

24 *Ibid.*

25 F. Bonciu, 'The European Economy: From a linear to a circular economy', 14 *Romanian Journal of European Affairs* (2014) pp. 88–89.

26 Ellen MacArthur Foundation, *Towards the circular economy: Economic and business rationale for an accelerated transition* (2013) p. 6, <https://www.ellenmacarthurfoundation.org/publications>.

10. First wave (stressing the positive impacts) – Economic and socio-political arguments dominated earlier discussions on premature obsolescence. One of the most well-known authors of this first wave is B. London, who is generally credited as the one who coined the terms 'planned obsolescence'. In his striking 1932 pamphlet entitled 'Ending the depression through planned obsolescence', he suggested the American government legally mandate product obsolescence. This, he explained, would ensure full employment and the excess production could be sold and exported so as to foster economic recovery.[27] The concept of 'planned obsolescence' was then popularized in 1954 by B. Stevens, an American industrial designer. In a famous talk, he defined 'planned obsolescence' as "*instilling in the buyer the desire to own something a little newer, a little better, a little sooner than is necessary*".[28] The first wave indeed corresponds to the beginning of the modern consumer society, where consumers replace products that are still fully functioning. Economic arguments on planned obsolescence were further developed afterwards, suggesting that strategies of planned obsolescence were the most profitable to balance technological innovation with businesses' rights to maximize profits.

11. Second wave (stressing the negative impacts) – A few decades later, the phenomenon additionally triggered social and environmental concerns. This shift in perspective was initiated by V. Packard in 1960, with his book entitled 'The Waste Makers'.[29] V. Packard argued that "*American society overemphasize[d] consumption, especially the quantity rather than the quality of what it consume[d], and that it therefore sacrifice[d] culture, prudence, and a proper concern for the future.*[30] The blame was laid at the door of the business community, especially of the marketers and advertisers.

12. Third wave, through the environmental lens – The strongest revival of interest in premature obsolescence occurred with the growing discussions on sustainable consumption and production in the 80s, as well as with the emergence of the idea of a circular economy especially over the last decade. A circular economy consists in "*turn[ing] goods that are at the end of their service life into resources for others, closing loops in industrial ecosystems and minimizing waste*".[31] Several principles are at the heart of a circular economy, like designing out waste, relying on energy from renewable sources and considering waste as

---

27 B. London, *Ending the depression through planned obsolescence* (1932), available on: <https://upload.wikimedia.org/wikipedia/commons/2/27/London_%281932%29_Ending_the_depression_through_planned_obsolescence.pdf>.

28 G. Adamson, *Industrial Strength Design: How Brooks Stevens Shaped Your World* (MIT Press for the Milwaukee Art Museum 2003) p. 4.

29 V. Packard, *The Waste Makers* (David MacKay 1960).

30 A. Rees, 'The Waste-Makers and the String-Savers', 34 *The Journal of Business* (1961) p. 367.

31 W. Stahel, *Circular economy* (Macmillan 2016) p. 435.

'food'.[32] From that perspective, practices causing the rapid obsolescence of products are seen as part of the problem.

13. Fourth wave, with ever-growing concerns in civil society – The surge of interest in premature obsolescence swept beyond academia. Grassroots discussions on the topic have been prompted by the publication of texts such as 'Beyond Recycling'[33] in the UK and 'Eternally Yours'[34] in the Netherlands and by the broadcast of thought-provoking documentaries like 'The Light Bulb Conspiracy' in 2010.[35] A wide range of initiatives have been taken by both citizens and businesses in the quest to fight premature obsolescence and, more generally, improve the relationship between human activities and the environment. These initiatives include, among others, awareness-raising tools and campaigns, voluntary labels and standards, initiatives encouraging and facilitating direct reuse, repair, refurbishment, remanufacturing, recycling, but also product sharing. A new generation of consumers seems prepared to prefer access over ownership for a variety of goods, like cars, machinery, and even articles of daily use.[36] Non-profit organisations were formed within this context of proactivity, such as the French association *Halte à l'Obsolescence Programmée* (HOP).[37]

14. Fifth wave, leading to a policy shift and numerous legislative initiatives – The concepts of planned and premature obsolescence permeated laws and policies. With sustainable development and circular economy as new leading policies, many law makers from around the world, including the EU and its Member States, have paid increasing attention to product obsolescence. At EU level, the major initiatives related to premature obsolescence are undoubtedly the two circular economy action plans issued by the EC.[38] These action plans invite

32 Ellen MacArthur Foundation, *Towards the circular economy: Economic and business rationale for an accelerated transition* (2013) pp. 22–23, available on: <https://www.ellenmacarthurfoundation.org/publications>.

33 T. Cooper, *Beyond recycling – The longer life option* (The New Economics Foundation 1994).

34 E. van Hinte, *Eternally Yours – Time in Design* (Rotterdam: OIOpublishers 2004).

35 C. Dannoritzer, *The Light Bulb Conspiracy* (2010).

36 Ellen MacArthur Foundation, *Towards the circular economy: Economic and business rationale for an accelerated transition*, 2013, p. 11, <https://www.ellenmacarthurfoundation.org/publications>.

37 *Halte à l'Obsolescence Programmée* (Stop planned obsolescence) is an organization dedicated to fighting planned obsolescence, which conducts awareness campaigns, issues articles, reports and policy recommendations on the topic, takes legal actions against companies suspected of planned obsolescence. For further information, see <https://www.halteobsolescence.org/>.

38 See Communication from the Commission of 2 December 2015 to the European Parliament, the Council, the European Economic and Social Committee and the Committee of the Regions on Closing the loop – EU action plan for circular economy, COM(2015) 614 final; Communication from the Commission of 11 March 2020 to the European Parliament, the Council, the European Economic and Social Committee and the Committee of the Regions

the EU institutions, all levels of government, and stakeholders to work together towards this long-term goal and to foster sustainable consumption, including through the promotion of longer-lasting products. Along with these policy actions, a wide range of studies have been carried out and could contribute to the adoption of legislative proposals as well as to ongoing debates on existing regulations.[39] The active engagement in the transition towards a sustainable and circular economy is also noticeable at national level. Examples of national initiatives include the Belgian Circular Economy Action Plan from 2021[40], which contains measures against premature obsolescence, but also the French Energy Transition for Green Growth Act from 2015[41], which introduced the concept of planned obsolescence into the French Consumer Code.

5. A FRAGMENTED LEGAL FRAMEWORK

15. A THREE-TIERED LEGAL FRAGMENTATION – While the concept of premature obsolescence (and its variants) appears more and more in legal documents, the approach against this issue remains fragmented. The mechanisms to prevent and combat the premature obsolescence of products are scattered across multiple instruments, resulting in a three-tiered legal fragmentation. Firstly, both the EU and its Member States have devoted efforts to promote product sustainability (supranational/national). Secondly, the premature obsolescence of products has been addressed directly and indirectly through various types of laws, which either have a general scope or concern only specific products (general/sector-specific). Thirdly, a wide range of legal norms shapes the product throughout its whole lifecycle, while others shape the relationship producers-consumers

---

on A new Circular Economy Action Plan – For a cleaner and more competitive Europe, COM(2020) 98 final.

39 See e.g. S. Boulos, A. Sousanoglou, L. Evans, J. Lee, N. King, C. Facheris, F. Iraldo, B. Nucci, M. Donelli, *The durability of products – Standards assessment for the circular economy under the Eco-Innovation Action Plan* (EC 2015); SIRCOME agency, the University of South Brittany and the University of South Bohemia, *The Influence of Lifespan Labelling on Consumers – ILLC study* (EESC 2016); C. Montalvo, D. Peck, E. Rietveld, *A longer lifetime for products: benefits for consumers and companies* (European Union 2016); K. Tonner, R. Malcolm, *How an EU lifespan guarantee model could be implemented across the European Union (study)* (European Parliament 2017); LE Europe, VVA Europe, Ipsos, ConPolicy, Trinomics, *Behavioural study on consumers' engagement in the circular economy* (European Commission 2018); J.S. Marcus, G. Zachmann, S. Gardner, S. Tagliapietra, E. Lykogianni, *Promoting product longevity – How can the EU product safety and compliance framework help promote product durability and tackle planned obsolescence, foster the production of more sustainable products, and achieve more transparent supply chains for consumers?* (European Parliament 2020).

40 See P.-Y. Dermagne, Z. Khattabi, *Plan d'action fédéral pour une économie circulaire 2021–2024* (SPF Economie et SPF Santé publique, sécurité de la chaine alimentaire et environnement 2021).

41 Loi n° 2015–992 du 17 août 2015 relative à la transition énergétique pour la croissance verte, JORF n°0189 du 18 août 2015, p. 14263 (hereafter 'Energy Transition Act').

surrounding it (intervention at various stages of the supply chain or stages of the transaction). These measures are of various types (preventive/coercive, product-/consumer-oriented, self-regulatory/legislative measures).

16. THE PERSONAL COMPUTER MARKET AS AN EXAMPLE – As an example, there is a wide panoply of EU and national rules regulating computers. At the design and production stage, the Ecodesign Directive[42] and its implementing regulations shape products to make them easy to maintain, repair, upgrade, reuse, disassemble and recycle. Computers are, for example, subject to mandatory requirements on the extraction of key components and critical raw materials, the availability of a functionality for secure data deletion, and the provision of the latest available version of the firmware.[43] Harmonised standards have been introduced in support of these specific ecodesign requirements.[44] The marketing and pre-contractual stage is regulated by EU labelling rules[45], the Unfair Commercial Practices Directive ('UCPD')[46], and the Consumer Rights Directive ('CRD')[47], which all harmonise and regulate information disclosed about computers. Additional information requirements regarding computers are imposed by some Member States, like in France with the newly established reparability index.[48] At the use stage, the legislation on consumer sales and

42 Directive 2009/125/EC of the European Parliament and of the Council of 21 October 2009 establishing a framework for the setting of eco-design requirements for energy-related products (recast), OJ L 285, 31.10.2009, p. 10–35 (hereafter 'Ecodesign Directive').

43 Commission Regulation (EU) 2019/424 of 15 March 2019 laying down ecodesign requirements for servers and data storage products pursuant to Directive 2009/125/EC of the European Parliament and of the Council and amending Commission Regulation (EU) No 617/2013, OJ L 74, 18.3.2019, p. 46–66.

44 Commission Implementing Decision of 6 January 2016 on a standardisation request to the European standardisation organisations as regards computers and computer servers, in support of the implementation of Commission Regulation (EU) No 617/2013 of 26 June 2013, implementing Directive 2009/125/EC of the European Parliament and of the Council with regard to ecodesign requirements for computers and computer servers (M/545), C(2015) 9354 final.

45 Regulation (EU) 2017/1369 of the European Parliament and of the Council of 4 July 2017 setting a framework for energy labelling and repealing Directive 2010/30/EU, OJ L 198, 28.7.2017, p. 1–23; Regulation (EC) No 66/2010 of the European Parliament and of the Council of 25 November 2009 on the EU Ecolabel, OJ L 27, 30.1.2010, p. 1–19.

46 Directive 2005/29/EC of the European Parliament and of the Council of 11 May 2005 concerning unfair business-to-consumer commercial practices in the internal market and amending Council Directive 84/450/EEC, Directives 97/7/EC, 98/27/EC and 2002/65/EC of the European Parliament and of the Council and Regulation (EC) No 2006/2004 of the European Parliament and of the Council, OJ L 149, 11.6.2005, p. 22–39.

47 Directive 2011/83/EU of the European Parliament and of the Council of 25 October 2011 on consumer rights, amending Council Directive 93/13/EEC and Directive 1999/44/EC of the European Parliament and of the Council and repealing Council Directive 85/577/EEC and Directive 97/7/EC of the European Parliament and of the Council, OJ L 304, 22.11.2011, p. 64–88.

48 Art. 16 de la Loi n° 2020–105 du 10 février 2020 relative à la lutte contre le gaspillage et à l'économie circulaire, JORF n°0035 du 11 février 2020.

guarantees, amended by the Sale of Goods Directive ('SGD')[49], lays down the minimum two-year guarantee period and the principle of conformity with the contract, which confers rights on consumers in case the computer does not match the quality or performance expected. Moreover, the 2019 Digital Content Directive ('DCD')[50] grants consumers the right to call upon the trader to supply conform digital content or digital service so that their computers remain functional. At the end-of-life stage, waste rules, which include the Batteries Directive[51], the Waste Framework Directive ('WFD')[52] and the Directive on waste electrical and electronic equipment ('WEEE Directive')[53], encourage producers to make sustainable computers (e.g. the obligation to equip laptops with removable batteries)[54] and give information related to them to other operators in the supply chain (e.g. the general obligation for manufacturers to provide independent operators with information to repair products).[55] The legal fragmentation has been accentuated by self-regulation, such as 'The Blue Angel' (*der Blaue Engel*) in Germany which, among others, adds rules on the availability of spare parts, on product design, and requires information on product durability.[56]

B. OBJECTIVES AND RESEARCH QUESTIONS

17. ALL-ENCOMPASSING AND IN-DEPTH LEGAL ANALYSIS OF PREMATURE OBSOLESCENCE – Whereas the premature obsolescence of products can be analysed through the lens of various disciplines (e.g. economics, engineering, psychology), this book is confined to exploring the issue from a legal perspective. In other words, the aim is not to bring forward technological or economic

---

49 Directive (EU) 2019/771 of the European Parliament and of the Council of 20 May 2019 on certain aspects concerning contracts for the sale of goods, amending Regulation (EU) 2017/2394 and Directive 2009/22/EC, and repealing Directive 1999/44/EC, OJ L 136, 22.5.2019, p. 28–50, which amended Directive 1999/44/EC of the European Parliament and of the Council of 25 May 1999 on certain aspects of the sale of consumer goods and associated guarantees, OJ L 171, 7.7.1999, p. 12–16 (hereafter 'Consumer Sales Directive').

50 Directive (EU) 2019/770 of the European Parliament and of the Council of 20 May 2019 on certain aspects concerning contracts for the supply of digital content and digital services, OJ L 136, 22.5.2019, p. 1–27.

51 Directive 2006/66/EC of the European Parliament and of the Council of 6 September 2006 on batteries and accumulators and waste batteries and accumulators and repealing Directive 91/157/EEC, OJ L 266, 26.9.2006, p. 1–14.

52 Directive 2008/98/EC of the European Parliament and of the Council of 19 November 2008 on waste and repealing certain Directives, OJ L 312, 22.11.2008, p. 3–30.

53 Directive 2012/19/EU of the European Parliament and of the Council of 4 July 2012 on waste electrical and electronic equipment, OJ L 197, 24.7.2012, p. 38–71.

54 Art. 11 of the Batteries Directive.

55 Art. 15 of the WEEE Directive.

56 Basic Award Criteria of the German Ecolabel Blue Angel from January 2017 for computers and keyboards, RAL-UZ 78, available on: <https://www.blauer-engel.de/en/products/electric-devices/computers-and-keyboards>.

alternatives, but rather to shed light on the panoply of legal rules tackling premature obsolescence and promoting product (environmental) sustainability as well as to evaluate it critically.[57]

18. MAIN OBJECTIVES – Starting from the observation that premature obsolescence has significant negative impacts[58], this legal research aims at (i) defining the concept of premature obsolescence; (ii) identifying and describing the multiple legal rules addressing premature obsolescence; (iii) evaluating these multiple legal rules; and (iv) where necessary, proposing policy recommendations. Although premature obsolescence may have positive impacts as well (as briefly discussed above)[59], this research will not examine in detail the possible advantages or disadvantages of premature obsolescence. Rather, the overriding aim of this book is to identify and assess the legal framework tackling the issue. Yet it can be noted that the EU and national law makers adopt rules to reduce premature obsolescence as it is deemed that detriment to consumers and the environment outweigh potential benefits. Based on this objective factor, the book analyses the concerned rules while assuming in this analysis that premature obsolescence should be reduced.

19. CENTRAL AND SUB- QUESTIONS – These four objectives lead to the central question: How do EU and national legal rules tackle premature obsolescence, and if necessary, how could the legal framework be improved? To answer the central question, three sub- research questions are addressed:

i. What is premature obsolescence and which practices fall within this concept? (descriptive and explanatory)
ii. How do existing legal rules at EU and national levels tackle premature obsolescence? (descriptive)
iii. Should the fragmented legal framework governing premature obsolescence be improved, and if so, how? (evaluative and normative)

20. FIRST SUB-QUESTION – The first sub-question will be answered in the first chapter of this book. This chapter describes and explains the concept of 'premature obsolescence' and distinguishes it from 'planned obsolescence'. Defining 'premature obsolescence' in a clear and well-delineated way will prove challenging, especially due to the lack of a commonly accepted definition of this multifaceted phenomenon. The second challenge will be to determine and explain the main types of premature obsolescence. On top of this, other concepts

57 This book focuses on the environmental aspects of sustainability (i.e. with a reduced environmental impact), leaving other non-environmental aspects, such as social and ethical concerns (e.g. child labour, general working conditions, animal welfare, etc.) out of the scope.
58 See *supra*, n° 8.
59 See *supra*, n° 7.

related to strategies that contribute to curbing these practices will also be defined, e.g. the concepts of 'durability', 'repairability', etc.

21. SECOND SUB-QUESTION – To answer the second sub-question, this book will identify and explore the panoply of legal rules adopted by the EU, the selected Member States (Belgium, France and Germany), and the self-regulatory organisations, to trigger product sustainability. Due to the legal fragmentation[60], the complex network of rules will be examined, taking into account the different levels of authorities and the various legal branches.[61] Particular focus will be placed on EU legislation. The thorough analysis of EU law will be enriched, where relevant, by references to national implementing measures and purely national initiatives adopted in the selected Member States. To complete the picture, self-regulation, which contributes to preventing and combating premature obsolescence, will also be part of the analysis.

22. THIRD SUB-QUESTION – Based on the outcome of the two previous queries, the third sub-question firstly consists in evaluating the current legal framework, in relation to four criteria: necessity, effectiveness, consistency and coherence. These criteria are particularly relevant when facing a fragmented legal framework.[62] Against this background, the second part of the developments relating to this question is devoted to (possible) policy recommendations (e.g. to complete, adapt or abolish existing rules), with an indication of their advantages as well as their possible weaknesses and side effects.

C. METHODOLOGY

1. PRELIMINARY REMARKS

23. INTRADISCIPLINARY STUDY – For a complete overview of the legal landscape on premature obsolescence, it is necessary to conduct an intradisciplinary study. The applicable norms are scattered across different yet complementary and interdependent legal branches.[63] While the product-based aspect of premature obsolescence is dealt with by rules governing the design and production stage (environmental law), its consumer-based aspect is regulated by rules governing the marketing and (pre)contractual stage (consumer (contract) law). It is only

60 See *supra*, n° 15–16.
61 See *infra*, n° 27–31.
62 For further explanation of these four criteria, see n° 33–35.
63 On the interaction between environmental law and consumer law, see for ex. T. Wilhelmsson, 'Consumer law and the environment: from consumer to citizen', 21 *J. Consum. Policy* (1998) p. 45 at p. 70.

through an integrated approach involving all these fields of law that the topic can be accurately addressed.

24. Interdisciplinary perspective – While remaining fully within the legal sphere, this research uses notions and findings from behavioural sciences (e.g. psychology and behavioural economics) as well as empirical studies. For instance, research into behaviour is particularly helpful for identifying factors that influence consumers' purchasing decisions.[64] Rather than adding to the knowledge of these disciplines, the aim is to utilise their insights to gain a clearer understanding of premature obsolescence and to explore the concrete implications of the law on actual human behaviour.[65]

2. FIRST SUB-QUESTION: A LITERATURE REVIEW

25. Defining premature obsolescence through a literature review – To answer the first sub- research question, a literature review will be done to delve into both the historical and current context of premature obsolescence. It consists in scrutinizing national and international documents, scholarly journals, legislation, and jurisprudence and selecting the most relevant information for a comprehensive but concise summary on the concept. The final purpose is to formulate a working definition, which would facilitate drawing the line between practices that fall within the category of premature obsolescence and those that do not. The working definition of premature obsolescence will serve as a basis for the evaluation of the legal framework in the next chapters. The task will be to check whether the existing rules curb all aspects of the phenomenon described in this first chapter, and thus whether additional rules are necessary and whether the effectiveness, consistency and coherence of the legal framework need improvement.[66]

26. Methodology used for the literature review – As rightly pointed out by L.G. Anthopoulos, a rigorous literature study requires defining the domain (the disciplinary field in which the literature search is conducted), the sources (publication outlets from that domain to be included in the search), and the search strategy (search terms applied to extract relevant articles).[67]

64 K. Umpfenbach, *Influences on consumer behaviour. Policy implications beyond nudging* (European Commission and Ecologic Institute 2014).

65 C. Jolls, C.R. Sustein, R.H. Thaler, 'A behavioral approach to law and economics', 50 *Stanford Law Review* (1998) p. 1471 at p. 1476.

66 For further explanation of the evaluative assessment, see n° 33–35.

67 L.G. Anthopoulos, 'Understanding the Smart City Domain: A Literature Review', in M.P. Rodríguez Bolívar (ed.), *Transforming City Governments for Successful Smart Cities* (Springer International Publishing 2015) p. 9 at p. 21, as cited in M. Zallio, D. Berry, 'Design and

As regards the domain, due to the multidisciplinary nature of the topic, the literature review will result in the analysis of a large number of works in various disciplines, including law, social and behavioural sciences, engineering and economics. As regards the sources, since the topic of premature obsolescence is widely disseminated, a broad range of sources will be considered, such as books, scientific and journal articles (peer-reviewed or not), reports, conference proceedings, research papers, dictionaries, media articles as well as online blogs. As regards the search strategy, it has been noted that various terms can be linked to the topic of product obsolescence and more generally to limited product lifetime. Some of the terms investigated are: 'obsolescence', 'planned obsolescence', 'premature obsolescence', 'built-in obsolescence', including the same terms in other languages, like '*obsolescence programmée*'. These terms will be searched on search engines, academic databases, and research platforms. The analysis of the literature will generate a taxonomy that will shed light on this complex issue. The first stage of the literature review will be integrative, meaning that the aim is to find common ideas and concepts from the reviewed materials.[68]

3. SECOND SUB-QUESTION: AN ANALYSIS OF THE LEGAL FRAMEWORK

27. Analysing the legal rules tackling premature obsolescence – A descriptive method will be employed to answer the second sub-question. After the first chapter dedicated to the concepts of planned and premature obsolescence, the structure of the book will follow the different stages of the product lifecycle as measures can be taken at every stage to resist, postpone and reverse premature obsolescence.[69] Each chapter corresponds to one stage of the product lifecycle and describes the various legal measures that can influence product lifetime at that stage. Since both the EU and its Member States have devoted effort to promote product sustainability, the book identifies and describes, for every stage of the product lifecycle, (i) the various EU rules tackling premature obsolescence, (ii) the implementing national rules transposing these EU rules into Belgian, French and German law and (iii) purely national initiatives adopted in these selected Member States.

Planned Obsolescence. Theories and Approaches for Designing Enabling Technologies', 20 *The Design Journal* (2017) S3753.

68 The adjective 'integrative' was used to describe literature reviews in C.S.G. Khoo, J.C. Na, K. Jaidka, 'Analysis of the macro-level discourse structure of literature reviews', 35 *Online Information Review* (2011) p. 255 at p. 271, as cited in M. Zallio, D. Berry, 'Design and Planned Obsolescence. Theories and Approaches for Designing Enabling Technologies', 20 *The Design Journal* (2017) S3753.

69 See *infra*, n° 152 *et seq.*

28. EU LAW – Although no EU legislation makes explicit reference to premature obsolescence, the wide body of EU law comprises several EU legal instruments – from various legal branches – that contribute to the quality and sustainability of products.[70] These instruments regulate the whole lifecycle of products that circulate on the EU market. Various EU product requirements shape goods before being placed on the market by obliging producers to conceive and produce their products in a sustainable way. In that regard, the Ecodesign Directive empowers the EC to set mandatory requirements for specific energy-related products, which integrate environmental aspects into product design and information supply.[71] These product requirements include, for example, minimum durability for hoses and motors of vacuum cleaners.[72] A lot of implementing regulations taken on the basis of this Directive have contributed to the development of standards for products.[73] At the marketing and pre-contractual stage, some EU rules, including the EU labelling rules, the UCPD, and the CRD, allow for better information on products to help consumers take cost-effective and eco-friendly purchasing decisions and to incentivize producers to make sustainable goods. At the use stage, the principle of conformity laid down in the SGD deters producers from shortening product lifetimes. If the product does not match the expected quality or performance, consumers are entitled to claim repair, replacement, price reduction or the rescission of the contract within two years of delivery. Remedies are also granted by the DCD in case of lack of supply or lack of conformity of the digital content or the digital service. At the end-of-life stage, there are directives on waste, such as the Batteries Directive, the WFD and the WEEE Directive. Other EU legal branches play a role when it comes to product quality, such as competition rules as well as rules on the free movement of goods and services.

29. BELGIAN LAW – Belgium is among the Member States that are proactive in the fight against premature obsolescence. In October 2016, an Action Plan on Circular Economy was adopted, with the view of putting into place by 2019 a set of measures improving existing product requirements, communication on

---

70 This has already been highlighted by the EC. See e.g. Joint answer from 8 July 2011 on planned obsolescence given by Mr Potočnik on behalf of the Commission, replying to written questions E-001284/11, E-002875/11, E-004273/11.

71 Art. 15 of the Ecodesign Directive.

72 Annex II, pts 7–8 to Commission Regulation (EU) No 666/2013 of 8 July 2013 implementing Directive 2009/125/EC of the European Parliament and of the Council with regard to ecodesign requirements for vacuum cleaners, OJ L 192, 13.7.2013, p. 24–34.

73 Regulation (EU) No 1025/2012 of the European Parliament and of the Council of 25 October 2012 on European standardisation, amending Council Directives 89/686/EEC and 93/15/EEC and Directives 94/9/EC, 94/25/EC, 95/16/EC, 97/23/EC, 98/34/EC, 2004/22/EC, 2007/23/EC, 2009/23/EC and 2009/105/EC of the European Parliament and of the Council and repealing Council Decision 87/95/EEC and Decision No 1673/2006/EC of the European Parliament and of the Council, OJ L 316, 14.11.2012, p. 12–33.

sustainable consumption and consumer protection.[74] Belgium had already been considered as a pioneer in the fight against planned obsolescence with the 2012 Senate Resolution.[75] After several legislative proposals lapsed on grounds of the dissolution of Parliament[76] or were rejected[77], three legislative proposals are still on the table of the Belgian Parliament.[78] These propose various amendments to Belgian consumer law, and mainly to Book VI 'Market practices and consumer protection' of the Economic Law Code and the rules on consumer sales in the Civil Code. These suggest, among others, integrating a definition of the practice, extending the minimum guarantee period and the presumption of non-conformity granted by the rules on consumer sales and guarantees, strengthening consumer information on products (e.g. information on spare parts and lifetime expectancy), improving the availability of spare parts, sanctioning producers when planned obsolescence is detected, and providing economic and fiscal support to the circular economy, such as lower VAT on repair and selling spare parts services. The Federal Government reiterated its commitment to shift towards a more sustainable economy in October and December 2021.[79] A draft law on the 'repair index' has also recently been submitted and should soon be debated by the Federal Government.[80]

---

74 K. Peeters and M.C. Marghem, *Ensemble, faisons tourner l'économie en développant l'économie circulaire en Belgique* (Cabinet de l'Énergie, de l'Environnement et du Développement durable 2016).

75 Proposition de résolution en vue de lutter contre l'obsolescence programmée des produits liés à l'énergie, *Doc. lég.*, Sénat, 2011–2012, 1er février 2012, n° 5 – 1251/4.

76 Proposition de loi modifiant la loi du 6 avril 2010 relative aux pratiques du marché et à la protection du consommateur, concernant l'information des consommateurs en matière d'obsolescence de biens de consommation *Doc. parl.*, Ch., 2011–2012, 14 février 2012, n° 2060/001; Proposition de loi modifiant la loi du 9 février 1994 relative à la sécurité des produits et des services, visant la prévention de l'obsolescence, *Doc. parl.*, Ch., 2011–2012, 14 février 2012, n° 2061/001; Proposition de loi modifiant l'article 1649*quater*, §4, du Code civil, relatif à la protection des consommateurs en cas de vente de biens de consommation en ce qui concerne le défaut de conformité, *Doc. parl.*, Sénat, 2011–2012, 12 juin 2012, n° 1665/1; Proposition de loi relative à la lutte contre l'obsolescence organisée et au soutien à l'économie circulaire, *Doc. parl.*, Ch., 2015–2016, 11 avril 2016, n° 1749/001; Proposition de loi relative à l'obsolescence programmée, *Doc. parl.*, Ch., 2015–2016, 20 avril 2016, n° 1783/001.

77 Proposition de loi modifiant le Code civil et le Code de droit économique, visant à lutter contre l'obsolescence programmée, *Doc. parl.*, Ch., 2015–2016, 22 janvier 2016, n° 1603/001.

78 Proposition de loi visant à lutter contre l'obsolescence programmée et à soutenir l'économie de la réparation, *Doc. parl.*, Ch., 2019, 19 juillet 2019, n° 0193/001; Proposition de loi modifiant le Code civil et le Code de droit économique, visant à lutter contre l'obsolescence programmée et l'obsolescence prématurée et à augmenter les possibilités de réparation, *Doc. parl.*, Ch., 2019–2020, 19 novembre 2019, n° 0771/001; Proposition de loi visant à lutter contre l'obsolescence organisée et à soutenir l'économie circulaire, *Doc. parl.*, Ch., 2019–2020, 7 janvier 2020, n° 0914/001.

79 See P.-Y. Dermagne, Note de Politique Générale – Economie, Ch., 2021–2022, 29 octobre 2021, n° 2294/005; P.-Y. Dermagne, Z. Khattabi, *Plan d'action fédéral pour une économie circulaire 2021–2024* (SPF Economie et SPF Santé publique, sécurité de la chaine alimentaire et environnement 2021).

80 See the press release issued on 13 September 2022 on the website of the Belgian Minister of the Climate, the Environment, Sustainable Development and Green Deal Zakia Khattabi:

30. French law – Rather than merely transposing EU law, France has devoted a great deal of effort to shifting towards a greener and more circular economy. This has generated a myriad of initiatives promoting longer product lifetime, which have contributed to bringing to the forefront the issue of premature obsolescence beyond France at EU level and in other Member States. One of the most well-known new French provisions is the introduction of the criminal offence of 'planned obsolescence' into the French Consumer Code by the Energy Transition Act (2015).[81] This legislation has, however, not been without criticism.[82] Not only is the legal definition of 'planned obsolescence' called into question, but also the compatibility of the total ban with EU law, especially with the UCPD and its black list (Annex I).[83] The French Consumer Code had earlier been modified by the Hamon Law (2014)[84], which (i) extended to two years the presumption of non-conformity, (ii) set out information requirements regarding the availability period of essential spare parts, and (iii) imposed the provision of spare parts within two months of a request by a seller/repairer. The Anti-Waste Law (2020), which contains several provisions specifically aimed at *"acting against planned obsolescence"*[85], complemented and reinforced these measures by, *inter alia*, strengthening information and provision obligations related to spare parts, by establishing reparability and durability indexes for electrical and electronic equipment, and by prohibiting producers from making repair impossible by independent/DIY repairers and from limiting access of professionals to information, spare parts or any other instruments allowing repair.[86] Several sustainability aspects were also tackled by the Law that aims to reduce the environmental footprint of digital technology (2021), including the user awareness about the environmental impact of digital technology, the limited lifetime of devices, and the emergence and development of ecologically sound digital practices.[87] The combination of

<https://khattabi.belgium.be/en/pr-zakia-khattabi-introduces-law-forcing-manufacturers-and-sellers-inform-consumers-about>.

81 Loi n° 2015-992 du 17 août 2015 relative à la transition énergétique pour la croissance verte, JORF n°0189 du 18 août 2015, p. 14263 (hereafter 'Energy Transition Act').

82 See N. Dupont, 'Durabilité des produits et disponibilité des pièces détachées: où en est-on?', 1 *La Semaine Juridique Entreprise et Affaires* (2016) p. 34 at p. 38.

83 The UCPD is of maximum harmonization, which prevents Member States from adding prohibited practices to the blacklist contained in Annex I. Several Member States have already been sanctioned for this kind of violation of EU law. See ECJ 17 January 2013, C-206/11, *Köck*, *EU:C:2013:14*.

84 Loi n° 2014-344 du 17 mars 2014 relative à la consommation, JORF n°0065 du 18 mars 2014, p. 5400 (hereafter 'Hamon Law').

85 See Ministère de la Transition Ecologique et Solidaire, *The Anti-Waste Law in the daily lives of the French people, What does that mean in practice?* (2020), p. 5, available on: <https://circulareconomy.europa.eu/platform/sites/default/files/anti-waste_law_in_the_daily_lives_of_french_people.pdf>.

86 Loi n° 2020-105 du 10 février 2020 relative à la lutte contre le gaspillage et à l'économie circulaire, JORF n°0035 du 11 février 2020 (hereafter 'Anti-Waste Law').

87 Loi n° 2021-1485 du 15 novembre 2021 visant à réduire l'empreinte environnementale du numérique en France, JORF n°0266 du 16 novembre 2021 (hereafter 'Law on the Environmental Footprint of Digital Technology').

these features allows a study of French law to provide meaningful insights for the development and improvement of the rules tackling premature obsolescence.

31. German law – There is currently no German law specifically dedicated to premature obsolescence or any concrete project to put such rules into place.[88] Yet, it is noteworthy that Germany is a pioneer in waste law, as demonstrated by the newly established duty of care (*Obhutspflicht*), which requires distributors in case of distance sales to ensure that products remain usable if returned by the customer and do not become waste.[89] Moreover, in December 2021, the German government committed to implement the right to repair in Germany.[90] A range of self-regulatory initiatives have also been taken[91], the best known being 'The Blue Angel' (*der Blaue Engel*), which is the oldest environmental label worldwide for products and services and which guarantees the respect of high eco-friendly standards. A similar seal for clothes, called the 'Green Button' (*Grüner Knopf*), has been introduced by the Federal Ministry for Economic Cooperation and Development (*Bundesministerium für wirtschaftliche Zusammenarbeit und Entwicklung*).[92] In addition to these measures, several essential studies on premature obsolescence have been issued and workshops have been organised by legislative key stakeholder groups.[93] These studies and workshops have

---

88 It is interesting to note that various legislative proposals promoted longer product lifetime through different means but were finally rejected. The first proposal (Antrag BT-Drucks. 17/13096), submitted in April 2013, focused on consumer rights, calling for the introduction of a minimum period for the use of products (e.g. information on this period, list of products with their corresponding period of use, better after sales services, two-year guarantee period). The second proposal (Antrag BT-Drucks. 17/13917), submitted in June 2013, aimed to improve product requirements (e.g. product reparability, collection, reuse and recycling). In December 2016, a third proposal (Antrag BT-Drucks. 18/9179) suggested similar measures, but again failed due to the votes of the opposition. In 2020, 2021 and 2022, four other legislative proposals dedicated to WEEE and the right to repair were also rejected (see Antrag BT-Drucks. 19/16412; Antrag BT-Drucks. 19/16419; Antrag BT-Drucks. 19/28429; Antrag BT-Drucks. 20/1338).

89 §23 Absatz 2 Nummer 11 Gesetz zur Förderung der Kreislaufwirtschaft und Sicherung der umweltverträglichen Bewirtschaftung von Abfällen (Kreislaufwirtschaftsgesetz) vom 24.02.2012 (BGBl. I S. 212). An English version of this Law is available on: <https://www.bmuv.de/fileadmin/Daten_BMU/Download_PDF/Abfallwirtschaft/kreislaufwirtschaftsgesetz_en_bf.pdf>.

90 Sozialdemokratischen Partei Deutschlands (SPD), Bundnis 90/Die Grünen und den Freiein Demokraten (FDP), *Koalitionsvertrag 2021–2025 – Mehr Fortschritt wagen Bündnis für Freiheit, Gerechtigkeit und Nachhaltigkeit* (2021), especially p. 89. See also the call made by several organisations involved in the repair sector in Runder Tisch Reparatur e.V. et al., *Neue Bundesregierung muss Recht auf Reparatur wirksam umsetzen: Der Teufel liegt im Detail* (2022), available on: <https://runder-tisch-reparatur.de/wp-content/uploads/2022/02/Umsetzung-Recht-auf-Reparatur-2022_Feb.pdf>.

91 T. Hohmuth, ‚Murks? Nein, danke?! Rechtliche Aspekte zum Umgang mit dem Phänomen "geplante Obsoleszenz"', *Zeitschrift zum Innovations- und Technikrecht* (2014) p. 74 at p. 85.

92 For more information, see <https://www.gruener-knopf.de/>.

93 Concerning studies, see S. Schridde, C. Kreiss, J. Winter, *Geplante Obsoleszenz: Entstehungsursachen – Konkrete Beispiele – Schadensfolgen – Handlungsprogramm* (Arge Regio 2014); S. Schlacke, K. Tonner, E. Gawel, *Stärkung eines nachhaltigen*

contributed to the fight against premature obsolescence not only at national level but also at EU level, by formulating further strategies against the environmental impacts of the different types of premature obsolescence. For example, the German Federal Ministry of the Environment took up the idea of a guarantee statement obligation for manufacturers regarding the durability of their products in its 'Environmental Digital Agenda' and announced its intention of trying to foster the implementation of this idea at EU level.[94] German consumer associations are also very active in the field.[95] One of their laudable initiatives is the *Verbraucherzentrale Bundesverband e. V.*'s web presentation for consumer education on sustainable consumption and consumer law.[96] This initiative can contribute to improving consumer skills, although some doubts can be raised on its widespread effect.[97]

4. THIRD SUB-QUESTION: AN EVALUATION OF THE LEGAL FRAMEWORK AND POLICY RECOMMENDATIONS

32. Evaluating the legal rules and making policy recommendations with the help of four criteria – As indicated above[98], this book will evaluate the existing and proposed measures against premature obsolescence and assess whether the current legal framework should be improved, and

Konsums im Bereich Produktnutzung durch Anpassungen im Zivil- und öffentlichen Recht (Umweltbundesamt Study 2015); S. Prakash et al., *Einfluss der Nutzungsdauer von Produkten auf ihre Umweltwirkung – Schaffung einer Informationsgrundlage und Entwicklung von Strategien gegen "Obsoleszenz"* (Umweltbundesamt Study 2016); I. Oehme, A. Jacob, *Strategies against obsolescence Ensuring a minimum product lifetime and improving product service life as well as consumer information* (Umweltbundesamt 2017); F. Keimeyer, P. Gailhofer, M. Gsell, K. Graulich, S. Prakash, C.-S. Scherf, T. Brönneke, R. Gildeggen, R. Schmitt, *Weiterentwicklung von Strategien gegen Obsoleszenz einschließlich rechtlicher Instrumente – Abschlussbericht* (Umweltbundesamt 2020). Concerning workshops, see T. Brönneke, A. Wechsler, *Obsoleszenz interdisziplinär – Vorzeitiger Verschleiß aus Sicht von Wissenschaft und Praxis* (Nomos 2015), which summarizes the results of a 2014 workshop organised by the Polytechnic Pforzheim.

94 Bundesministerium für Umwelt, Naturschutz und nukleare Sicherheit (BMU), *Umweltpolitische Digitalagenda* (2 March 2020) p. 39, available on: <www.bmu.de/fileadmin/Daten_BMU/Download_PDF/Digitalisierung/digitalagenda_bf.pdf>.

95 See L. Reisch, A. Oehler, T. Brönneke, K.-H. Fezer, J. Stellpflug, *Qualität statt vorzeitiger Verschleiß – Diskussionspapier zur eingebauten Obsoleszenz bei Konsumgütern* (Verbraucher Kommission 2014); J. Gurkmann, 'Consumer Protection in Germany – the View of the Vzbv', 8 *EuCML* (2019) p. 125 at p. 127. See also the publications issued by the association 'Runder Tisch Reparatur', available on: <https://runder-tisch-reparatur.de/category/publikation/>.

96 For more information, see <https://www.verbraucherbildung.de/>.

97 See B. Schinkels, 'Information Obligations and Disinformation of Consumers: German Law Report', in G. Straetmans (ed.), *Information Obligations and Disinformation of Consumers* (Springer International Publishing 2019) pp. 154–155.

98 See *supra*, n° 18 and n° 22.

if so, how. Four closely intertwined criteria will be used, namely necessity, effectiveness, consistency and coherence.

33. Necessity – A legal norm is necessary if there are certain issues to address and no existing norm with the same purpose, scope and outcome. It is closely linked to the principle of subsidiarity[99], which questions whether the EU act would provide clear added value or whether similar changes could be achieved at national level. This criterion of necessity is essential when facing legal fragmentation, as non-necessary norms add nothing but instead reduce clarity and legal certainty.

34. Effectiveness – A legal norm is effective if it "*achieves, to the best degree, the objectives or other intended effects*"[100], having regard to its substance and its enforcement. Since objectives of laws and policies closely relate to the interests at stake in cases of premature obsolescence, the effectiveness has to be evaluated against the interests of consumers (e.g. reasonable costs, good quality, freedom of choice, reliable and accessible information), businesses (e.g. economic benefits, no barrier to trade, freedom of design, intellectual property) and the environment (e.g. reasonable use of resources, waste treatment). It is important to note that these interests cannot all be met in their entirety at the same time. For example, although consumers often consider the ecological nature of goods or services to be important, consumer and environmental protection often conflict.[101] Since the preservation of the environment is the long-term interest of both consumers and businesses, environmental protection should be given priority in case of conflict of interests. In that sense, all economic actors should be considered as 'citizens', capable of adopting environmentally responsible behaviours with a long-term perspective, even at the cost of other interests attached to their own position in the market place.[102] As a result, the legal framework/proposed solutions should strike a fair balance between all the interests at stake, while giving a particular emphasis to product sustainability and tilting the balance towards environmental protection if interests conflict.

---

99 Art. 5(3) TEU.

100 D.A. Dukelow and B. Nuse, *Dictionary of Canadian Law* (Carswell Legal Pubns 1995).

101 See C. Kye, *EU environmental law and policy and EU consumer law: converging and diverging trends* (Story Scientia 1995); T. Wilhelmsson, 'Consumer Law and the Environment: From Consumer to Citizen', 21 *J. Consum. Policy* (1998) p. 45; K. Tonner, 'Sustainable consumption, consumer policy and the law', in C. Verdure (ed.), *Environmental law and consumer protection* (Larcier 2011) p. 9 at p. 24.

102 T. Wilhelmsson, 'Consumer Law and the Environment: From Consumer to Citizen', 21 *J. Consum. Policy* (1998) p. 61; J. Lewis, S. Inthorn, K. Wahl-Jorgensen, *Citizens or Consumers? What the Media Tell Us About Political Participation* (Open University Press 2005); E. Terryn, 'A Right to Repair: Towards Sustainable Remedies in Consumer Law', *E.R.P.L.* (2019) p. 873.

35. Consistency and coherence – A norm is deemed consistent if it does not contradict other norms, and coherent if it establishes positive connections with them[103], forming *"a united whole"*.[104] These criteria will be used to investigate the articulation between the different EU legal instruments as well as between EU and national rules. The test will be based on (a) the legal basis under which measures were adopted, (b) the competences granted to the EU (principle of conferral), and (c) the degree of harmonisation required by EU rules.

D. THEORETICAL IMPORTANCE AND SOCIETAL IMPACT

36. Importance to the field – As explained above, premature obsolescence has three main negative impacts.[105] The environment is directly affected by the rapid obsolescence of products, causing *inter alia* resource depletion, pollution, and greenhouse-gas emissions. Despite all the legal instruments put in place, the environment has been deteriorating at an alarming rate.[106] Arguably, premature obsolescence, as well as the rules addressing it, considerably influences consumers' daily life, as their choices are shaped by accessible information, the range and prices of existing products. Consumers increasingly demonstrate their dissatisfaction (e.g. the platform 'trop-vite usé' (worn-out too quickly) created by the Belgian consumer organisation *Test-Achats*[107] or the recent wave of legal cases within the EU)[108] and their desire for better protection.[109] Producers are also deeply concerned, as legislation on premature obsolescence entails far-

103 C. Tietje, 'The Concept of Coherence in the TEU and the CFSP', 2 *Eur. Foreign Aff. Rev.* (1997) p. 212.

104 P. Koutrakos, *Trade, Foreign Policy and Defence in EU Constitutional Law* (Hart Publishing 2001) p. 39.

105 See n° 8.

106 According to the estimates of the United Nations, if the current trends continue by 2050, humankind would need three Earths. See United Nations, *Sustainable development goals – Goal 12: ensure sustainable consumption and production patterns* (2014), available on: <https://www.un.org/sustainabledevelopment/sustainable-consumption-production/>, as well as United Nations, *World Population Prospects 2019 – Highlights* (2019).

107 See <https://www.test-achats.be/trop-vite-use>.

108 See, among others, Tribunal de grande instance de Nanterre 17 september 2017, Plainte au Procureur de la République, *HOP v. X* (France); Autorita Garante della Concorrenza e del Mercato, 25 septembre 2018, *Apple* (Italy); or the class action initiated by *Test-Achats* against Apple before the Brussels Commercial Court (<https://www.test-achats.be/apple>).

109 See the 2013 Eurobarometer, where over 90% of citizens asked for clear labelling indicating product useful lifespan: TNS Political & Social, *Flash Eurobarometer 367 – Attitudes of Europeans towards building the single market for green products* (European Commission 2013) p. 106.

reaching changes in their product and business strategies.[110] They are torn between the current economic conditions which encourage them to achieve high sales levels and profitability[111], and the legal framework which increasingly requires sustainability. Finally, the topic represents a major issue for the EU and its Member States. More fundamentally, restricting consumption with an environmental impact lies at the heart of their environmental commitments laid down in the Paris Agreement (2016).[112]

37. Scientific and societal impact – This research increases theoretical knowledge on the topic. Not only does it shed light on the concept of premature obsolescence, but the original 'holistic' approach to this research also enriches the academic and practical understanding of the legal framework. In addition, this research has strong practical importance. It is intended to contribute to the adoption of legislative proposals[113], as well as to ongoing debate on existing regulations (e.g. the EC's legislative proposals on 'Empowering consumers for the green transition'[114], on 'Sustainable Products'[115], on 'Substantiating green claims'[116] and on 'Promoting the repair of goods').[117] Beyond policy makers, society at large may benefit from the study, which strives to clarify the legal maze consumers and producers have to deal with. It raises consumer awareness about their rights and gives producers guidance on avoiding practices qualified as premature obsolescence.

---

110 C. Dalhammar, 'Industry attitudes towards ecodesign standards for improved resource efficiency', 123 *J. Clean. Prod.* (2016) p. 155 at p. 166.

111 P. A. Grout, I.-U. Park, 'Competitive Planned Obsolescence', 36 *The RAND Journal of Economics* (2005) p. 596 at p. 612; N. Maycroft, *Consumption, planned obsolescence and waste* (Lincoln School of Art and Design 2009).

112 Circle Economy and Ecofys, *Implementing Circular Economy Globally Makes Paris Targets Achievable* (2016), available on: <https://www.circle-economy.com/resources/implementing-circular-economy-globally-makes-paris-targets-achievable>.

113 See *infra* on the Belgian legislative proposals (n° 31); see also calls from various EU institutions and organisations (n° 69).

114 Proposal for a Directive of the European Parliament and of the Council amending Directives 2005/29/EC and 2011/83/EU as regards empowering consumers for the green transition through better protection against unfair practices and better information, COM(2022) 143 final.

115 Proposal for a Regulation of the European Parliament and of the Council establishing a framework for setting ecodesign requirements for sustainable products and repealing Directive 2009/125/EC, COM(2022) 142 final.

116 Proposal for a Directive of the European Parliament and of the Council on substantiation and communication of explicit environmental claims (Green Claims Directive), COM(2023) 166 final (hereafter 'Proposal for a Green Claims Directive').

117 Proposal for a Directive of the European Parliament and of the Council on common rules promoting the repair of goods and amending Regulation (EU) 2017/2394, Directives (EU) 2019/771 and (EU) 2020/1828, COM(2023) 155 final (hereafter 'Proposal for a Directive on common rules promoting repair').

E. DELINEATION OF THE SCOPE OF THE RESEARCH

38. A FOCUS ON NON-FOOD AND MOVABLE GOODS – Although premature obsolescence can affect all goods, including immovable property and other related goods from the real estate sector[118], this book focuses on non-food movables, such as white and brown goods[119], small appliances, furniture and clothes. It should be noted that in this book, the terms 'goods' and 'products' are considered as synonymous and are thus used interchangeably.[120] A particular focus is given to electronic and electrical appliances, which are generally considered as products with the biggest environmental impacts (as these require the use of rare materials and manufacturing processes of high quality), and thus the most problematic when becoming prematurely obsolete.

39. WITH CONSIDERATION FOR SERVICES – Restricting the focus on goods would, however, make the analysis of this book incomplete. Given the new product trends[121], services should be taken into consideration to some extent when dealing with the topic of premature obsolescence. New kinds of goods, including goods that incorporate or are inter-connected with digital content or a digital service, are omnipresent on the market. In parallel, sales of consumer goods are increasingly bundled with ancillary services or replaced by alternatives with no transfer of ownership (such as product-lease and product-as-a-service) or based on new ways of consuming goods through a collaborative economy. These alternatives not only change consumption patterns but can also be seen as part of the solution to limited product lifetime. The 'functional economy'[122], which

118 For a critical overview of the challenges and opportunities existing in the real estate sector in terms of sustainability, see B. Verheye, 'Belgian Property Law and the Circular Economy – Challenges and Opportunities', in B. Keirsbilck, E. Terryn (eds.), *Consumer Protection in a Circular Economy* (Intersentia 2019) p. 243 at p. 286.

119 'White goods' are "*large domestic appliances that are conventionally white, such as refrigerators and washing machines*", whereas 'brown goods' are "*electrical merchandise such as radios, televisions, and hi-fi units, conventionally housed in brown casings*". See Oxford English Dictionary 2006 (3rd edition).

120 This contrasts with some legal instruments, where the notion of 'product' encompasses 'goods' and 'services' (e.g. Art. 2(c) UCPD).

121 A detailed analysis of these trends has been carried out by the European Environmental Agency in EEA, *Circular by design: Products in the circular economy* (European Union 2017) p. 16 at p. 25.

122 A 'functional economy' (or service-oriented economy) is an economy where there is a shift from selling products to offering 'products-as-a-service' or, from a consumer perspective, from buying products to using products ('access-based-consumption'). See among others R. Oliva, R. Kallenberg, 'Managing the transition from products to services', 14 *International Journal of Service Industry Management* (2003) p. 160 at p. 172; S.J. Lawson, M.R. Gleim, R. Perren and J. Hwang, 'Freedom from ownership: An exploration of access-based consumption', 69 *Journal of Business Research* (2016) p. 2615 at p. 2623; F. Zoll, 'From a Product-Based Economy to Services? Legal Aspects of an Economy in Transition', in B.

includes for example the pay-per-use contracts for tires created by *Michelin* or the lighting services proposed by *Philips*[123], encourages producers to make sustainable choices regarding their products (e.g. by using more sustainable resources, making products easier to repair, etc.) as they remain the owner and have thus a vested interest in making products last.[124] The same reasoning can be held for the collaborative economy as it allows individuals to use existing products more intensively, for example through platforms for ridesharing or sharing tools with neighbours, or may allow them to resell their goods, such as electronics or clothes.

40. A FOCUS ON B2C TRANSACTIONS – This book only deals with cases of premature obsolescence occurring in B2C transactions, i.e. for consumer goods bought for private use, although the boundary between B2C, C2C and B2B is becoming increasingly blurred.[125] The term 'consumer' refers to any natural person who is acting for purposes that are outside that person's economic activity (trade, business, craft or profession). This definition corresponds to the common core used in most EU legal instruments that will be analysed in this book.[126] The terms 'manufacturer' and 'producer' are used interchangeably to refer to the entity responsible for placing a particular consumer product on the market. Similarly, the words 'retailer' and 'seller' are used interchangeably to refer to the person who sells a product to a consumer. On occasion, the word 'trader' is used when it is not important whether the consumer is dealing with a producer, a seller or any other business in the contractual chain. Contrary to what some scholars have argued, such a narrow focus on B2C transactions is not justified by the fact that differences exist between B2B and B2C transactions concerning product obsolescence and quality.[127] Rather, it is justified because premature obsolescence presents more challenges to consumers than it does to businesses. In most cases, consumers are still the weaker party in comparison to businesses that determine the price, quality and availability of goods. In spite of this focus, it should be noted that arguments and ideas developed in this book

---

Keirsbilck, E. Terryn (eds.), *Consumer Protection in a Circular Economy* (Intersentia 2019) p. 149 at p. 158.

123 For more examples, see H. Slachmuylders, 'Building back better after Covid-19 – the role of circular business models', *CCM Blog*, 10 June 2021, available on: <https://law.kuleuven.be/ccm/blog/?p=162>.

124 Although not all 'servitisation' automatically leads to increased sustainability, see i.a. A. Tukker, 'Eight types of product-service-system: Eight ways to sustainability? Experiences from Suspronet', *Business Strategy and the Environment* (2004) p. 246 at p. 260.

125 See e.g. the situations involving prosumers, SME's and independent workers. The distinction between private and professional use is also becoming less evident with regard to new technological developments (e.g. smartphones, cloud technologies and connected devices).

126 R. Manko, *The notion of 'consumer' in EU law* (European Parliament 2013) p. 1.

127 S. Schridde, C. Kreiss, J. Winter, *Geplante Obsoleszenz: Entstehungsursachen – Konkrete Beispiele – Schadensfolgen – Handlungsprogramm* (Arge Regio 2014) p. 16.

may be relevant in the context of B2B transactions, where professionals acquire goods that are used as part of their business activity.

41. Between public and private law – In its legal analysis, this book will cross the boundaries between public and private law. As mentioned above[128], the fight against premature obsolescence is part of the broader strategy of sustainable consumption. Since the transition towards sustainable consumption involves the combination of consumer, environmental and product law[129], legal instruments that contribute to tackling premature obsolescence will be found in these branches of law. The scope of this book will, nonetheless, be confined to EU law and the national legislation of the selected Member States. Although international economic law is of relevance for the topic of premature obsolescence, it falls outside the scope of this research. International economic law is indeed a broad and complex field of law that deserves special attention on its various rules, principles and aspects through specific research. This should not prevent making reference to international anecdotes and cases, where it is deemed relevant for this book.

42. Product safety and liability rules is left out of the scope – By contrast with what was initially planned in the research project, the legislation on product safety and liability, which includes the General Product Safety Directive[130], Product Liability Directive[131], as well as sectoral safety legislation[132], will not be analysed in this book. These legal instruments were initially

128 See *supra*, n° 14.

129 K. Tonner, 'Consumer Protection and Environmental Protection: Contradictions and Suggested Steps Towards Integration', 23 *J. Consum. Policy* (2000) p. 63 at p. 78; K. Tonner, 'Sustainable Consumption, Consumer Policy and the Law', in C. Verdure (ed.), *Environmental law and consumer protection* (Larcier 2011) p. 9 at p. 24.

130 Directive 2001/95/EC of the European Parliament and of the Council of 3 December 2001 on general product safety, OJ L 11, 15.1.2002, p. 4–17.

131 Council Directive 85/374/EEC of 25 July 1985 on the approximation of the laws, regulations and administrative provisions of the Member States concerning liability for defective products, OJ L 210, 7.8.1985, p. 29–33.

132 See e.g. Directive 2006/42/EC of the European Parliament and of the Council of 17 May 2006 on machinery, and amending Directive 95/16/EC (recast), OJ L 157, 9.6.2006, p. 24–86; Directive 2009/48/EC of the European Parliament and of the Council of 18 June 2009 on the safety of toys, OJ L 170, 30.6.2009, p. 1–37; Directive 2014/35/EU of the European Parliament and of the Council of 26 February 2014 on the harmonisation of the laws of the Member States relating to the making available on the market of electrical equipment designed for use within certain voltage limits, OJ L 96, 29.3.2014, p. 357–374; Regulation (EU) 2019/2144 of the European Parliament and of the Council of 27 November 2019 on type-approval requirements for motor vehicles and their trailers, and systems, components and separate technical units intended for such vehicles, as regards their general safety and the protection of vehicle occupants and vulnerable road users, amending Regulation (EU) 2018/858 of the European Parliament and of the Council and repealing Regulations (EC) No 78/2009, (EC) No 79/2009 and (EC) No 661/2009 of the European Parliament and of the Council and Commission Regulations (EC) No 631/2009, (EU) No 406/2010, (EU) No 672/2010, (EU) No 1003/2010, (EU) No 1005/2010, (EU) No 1008/2010, (EU) No 1009/2010, (EU) No 19/2011, (EU) No 109/2011, (EU) No 458/2011, (EU) No 65/2012, (EU) No 130/2012, (EU) No

considered as the mechanisms that they establish may dissuade producers from making low quality products. While the product safety legislation could prevent damages *ex ante* by requiring producers to place only durable products on the market, the product liability legislation could compensate consumers *ex-post* for damages suffered from a defective product. Amendments could be envisaged within the framework of the review of the overall product safety and liability framework in light of the emerging technologies[133], including Artificial Intelligence.[134] However, the preliminary research revealed that these legal instruments were not well suited to tackling premature obsolescence.[135] Although extending the mechanisms of product safety rules to cover product sustainability aspects is worthy of consideration[136], the existing ecodesign legal framework makes this idea superfluous.[137] Product liability rules are not the most promising instruments. First, it may be particularly difficult for the consumer to prove the actual harm in cases of premature obsolescence. Second, other layers of protection provided by contractual obligations and guarantees reduce the need to invoke this legislation.[138] Therefore, product safety and liability rules were excluded from the scope of the research.

347/2012, (EU) No 351/2012, (EU) No 1230/2012 and (EU) 2015/166, OJ L 325, 16.12.2019, p. 1–40.

133 Two important steps have been taken in that area of law: first, the Proposal for a Regulation of the European Parliament and the Council on general product safety, amending Regulation (EU) No 1025/2012 of the European Parliament and of the Council, and repealing Council Directive 87/357/EEC and Directive 2001/95/EC of the European Parliament and of the Council, COM(2021) 346 final, and second, the Proposal for a Directive of the European Parliament and of the Council on liability for defective products, COM(2022) 495 final. The EC has also adopted a proposal specifically dedicated to Artificial Intelligence: see Proposal for a Regulation of the European Parliament and the Council laying down harmonised rules on Artificial Intelligence (Artificial Intelligence Act) and amending certain Union legislative acts, COM(2021)206 final. See also the European Parliament Resolution of 16 February 2017 with recommendations to the Commission on Civil Law Rules on Robotics, 2015/2103(INL), as well as the Report from the Commission of 19 February 2020 to the European Parliament and the Council on the safety and liability implications of Artificial Intelligence, the Internet of Things and robotics, COM(2020) 64 final.

134 'Artificial Intelligence' (AI) means "*the capacity of computers or other machines to exhibit or simulate intelligent behaviour*" (Oxford English Dictionary 2006 (3rd ed.)).

135 See also J.S. Marcus, G. Zachmann, S. Gardner, S. Tagliapietra, E. Lykogianni, *Promoting product longevity – How can the EU product safety and compliance framework help promote product durability and tackle planned obsolescence, foster the production of more sustainable products, and achieve more transparent supply chains for consumers?* (EP 2020) pp. 33–34.

136 T. Brönneke, 'Premature Obsolescence: Suggestions for Legislative Counter-measures in German and European Sales & Consumer Law', 14 *Journal for European Environmental & Planning Law* (2017) p. 371. See also in Belgium: Art. 10–21 of the Proposition de loi visant à lutter contre l'obsolescence organisée et à soutenir l'économie circulaire, *Doc. parl.*, Ch., 2019–2020, 7 janvier 2020, n° 0914/001.

137 For further details on the ecodesign legal framework, see Chapter II on the design and production stage.

138 For further details on the contractual obligations and the guarantees, see Chapter III on the use stage.

43. Competition law – Equally, competition law will not be investigated. While it cannot be ruled out that competition law can also play a role in addressing the premature obsolescence of products, this is marginal and will be left outside the scope of this analysis.[139]

First, Article 101 TFEU prohibits agreements between undertakings, decisions by associations of undertakings and concerted practices which have as their object or effect the prevention, restriction, or distortion of competition. Consequently, this provision could sanction undertakings that, as in the Phoebus cartel case[140], reach an agreement aimed to lessen the quality of products to shorten products' life spans and increase the number of products sold. However, if the intention of the cartel is not only to worsen the quality but also to significantly reduce the price of products to make them available to a wider public, it will be almost impossible to prove an infringement of Article 101 TFEU.[141] Another contribution of competition law to environmental protection takes the form of competition rules not being applied, as demonstrated by the EC's decision approving an agreement to improve energy efficiency of washing machines[142], or the Draft Guidelines 'Sustainability Agreements' issued in June 2020 by the Dutch competition authority (*Autoriteit Consument & Markt*).[143]

Second, Article 102 TFEU could cover cases where dominant players abuse their position on the market by adopting strategies of premature obsolescence. For example, an undertaking with a monopolistic position could engage in tying practices, obstruct its competitors from entering the market and reduce the durability of its products to reap all the profits. This would go against its 'special responsibility' not to hinder competition on the market.[144] Other practices could be considered abusive, such as cases where the undertaking no longer produces essential spare parts, stops releasing updates that are necessary for the good functioning of the product or significantly increases repair or upgrade costs. However, Article 102 TFEU only applies if the dominant position of the undertaking is established.[145] And even in this case, it remains challenging to prove that strategies of premature obsolescence are anticompetitive, especially when considering the possible trade-offs between innovation and product

---

139 For a similar conclusion on the contribution of competition law to the implementation of the right to repair, see L. Van Acker, 'The repair economy: unexpected support from competition law?', *CCM Blog*, 16 March 2022, available on: <https://law.kuleuven.be/ccm/blog/?p=306>.

140 See *supra*, n° 4.

141 J. Malinauskaite, F.B. Erdem, 'Planned Obsolescence in the Context of a Holistic Legal Sphere and the Circular Economy', 41 *Oxford Journal of Legal Studies* (2021) p. 736.

142 Commission Decision of 24 January 1999 relating to a proceeding under Article 81 of the EC Treaty and Article 53 of the EEA Agreement, Case IV.F.1/36.718.CECED.

143 Autoriteit Consument & Markt (ACM), *Draft Guidelines on Sustainability agreements – Opportunities within competition law*, available on: <https://www.acm.nl/sites/default/files/documents/2020-07/sustainability-agreements%5B1%5D.pdf>.

144 ECJ 9 November 1983, Case 322/81, *Michelin v Commission, EU:C:1983:313*, para 57.

145 R. Whish, D. Bailey, *Competition law* (Oxford university press 2018) p. 187 *et seq.*

quality.[146] Hence, while amendments to competition rules could be envisaged[147], competition law is not the most promising way to deal with premature obsolescence.

[146] M. Maggiolino, 'Planned Obsolescence: A Strategy in Search of Legal Rules', 50 *International Review of Intellectual Property and Competition Law* (2019) p. 406; J. Malinauskaite, F.B. Erdem, 'Planned Obsolescence in the Context of a Holistic Legal Sphere and the Circular Economy', 41 *Oxford Journal of Legal Studies* (2021) p. 738; L. Bisschop, Y. Hendlin, J. Jaspers, 'Designed to break: planned obsolescence as corporate environmental crime', 78 *Crime, Law and Social Change* (2022) p. 280.

[147] N. Petit, '*"Problem Practices" in EU Competition Law*', in *CCP Annual Conference on "Problem Markets"* (University of Liege 2014), available on: <https://antitrustlair.files.wordpress.com/2014/07/problem-practices-ccp-nicolas-petit.pdf>.

CHAPTER I

FROM PLANNED TO PREMATURE OBSOLESCENCE: CONCEPTS AND DEFINITIONS

A. INTRODUCTION

44. Focus on concepts and definitions – In the dictionary, the word 'obsolescence' is defined as *"the process or fact of becoming obsolete or outdated, or of falling into disuse"*.[148] Every product inevitably becomes obsolete after a certain period of use. In that sense, product obsolescence marks the end of the product use cycle and, if irreversible, can even mark the end of the product lifetime itself. Although the lifetime of products is limited and their obsolescence unavoidable, certain products become obsolete (too) prematurely, without it being the result of normal wear and tear. According to some scholars, the media and popular discourses, the obsolescence of these products is due to deliberate actions and decisions taken by businesses. Many concepts have been coined to describe the premature ageing of products, including 'planned obsolescence' and 'premature obsolescence'. At the beginning of this book, it is crucial to shed light on the context in which the concept of 'planned obsolescence' emerged, to explain why 'premature obsolescence' is a better concept and to define that latter concept that is at the heart of this book.

45. Overview of the first chapter – The first section of this chapter will analyse the history and evolution of the different understandings of 'planned obsolescence' and similar concepts, including in academic literature, popular discourse, media as well as in EU and national laws and policies. This section aims to unravel the various concepts and definitions that have been developed to describe the early ageing of products. Based on this literature review, a definition of the closely intertwined concepts of 'product lifetime', 'product use cycle', 'product obsolescence', 'waste', 'recovery', 'product optimal lifetime', 'product sustainability' and 'premature obsolescence' will be presented in the second section. This second section will also clarify the different types and causes of premature obsolescence. The third section will be dedicated to other

[148] Oxford English Dictionary 2006 (3rd edition).

related concepts such as 'durability', 'maintenance', 'upgrades', 'reuse', 'repair', 'refurbishment', 'remanufacturing' and 'recycling'. The definitions of 'premature obsolescence' and of the related concepts given in this chapter will serve as a basis for evaluating how the law addresses the issue. In a nutshell, this chapter lays the conceptual foundations upon which this book is built.

B. THE (INAPPROPRIATE) CONCEPT OF PLANNED OBSOLESCENCE

1. EMERGENCE OF THE CONCEPT

46. Historical examples – The first well-known example of planned obsolescence dating back to the years following the industrial revolution is the so-called 'Phoebus cartel'.[149] This cartel was formed by the leading light bulb companies in 1924 to lower the lifespan of light bulbs from 2500 to 1000 hours. After having realised the risks of a saturated market with long-lasting light bulbs, these companies had made light bulbs deliberately more fragile. Competitors would be closely monitored (and if necessary, fined) to ensure strict adherence to product degradation.[150] Another example of planned obsolescence from the 1920s concerns the automobile industry. A.P. Sloan, chairman and CEO of *General Motors*, adopted the commercial strategy that consisted in introducing a new car model each year and stimulating the replacement rate of cars.[151] Such practices were taking place in a society of 'conspicuous consumption', as coined by the economist T. Veblen, where people would buy many goods and services, especially expensive ones, to publicly display economic status.[152] The triumph of this 'artificial' obsolescence was seen by some historians as part of the explanation of how H. Ford forfeited his dominant share of the car market.[153] In addition to these cases, certain products became prematurely obsolete due to technological progress, as shown by the emergence of the electric starter motor, which made cars manufactured with the previous technology obsolete[154], or by the production of stereos that replaced old phonographs.[155]

---

149 The Phoebus cartel is an illustrative example of intentional material obsolescence (see n° 4). For further comments on this type of obsolescence, see n° 101 and n° 103.

150 See M. Krajewski, *The Great Lightbulb Conspiracy* (IEEE Spectrum 2014), available on: <https://spectrum.ieee.org/tech-history/dawn-of-electronics/the-great-lightbulb-conspiracy>.

151 This strategy shows the psychological dimension of product obsolescence. For further comments on psychological obsolescence, see n° 120–123.

152 T. Veblen, *The theory of the leisure class: An economic study in the evolution of institutions* (Macmillan 1899).

153 G. Slade, *Made to break – technology and obsolescence in America* (Harvard University Press 2006) p. 33.

154 K. Pope, *Understanding planned obsolescence – Unsustainability through production, consumption and waste generation* (Kogan Page 2017) p. 45.

155 V. Packard, *The Waste Makers* (David MacKay 1960).

47. First terminologies – Though limited, literature on the topic of product obsolescence dating back to these years can be found. This literature corresponds to the beginning of the first wave of interest in the topic, as mentioned above.[156] In 1928, F. J. George coined the term 'progressive obsolescence' to assert the need to induce people to buy a greater variety of goods, not to use them, but to activate commerce and discard them after a short period of time.[157] With his publication, F. J. George aimed to emphasize the role of advertising and design practices used in the context of annual model change in supporting the economy.[158] The same approach was followed by the American real estate broker B. London. In the 1930s, the post-war political and economic context, with the Great Depression, brought a new perspective on planned obsolescence.[159] With its pamphlet entitled 'Ending the depression through planned obsolescence'[160], B. London suggested the American government legally fix product death to assure employment and to sell the excess of production, and thus to foster economic recovery. The government would assign a lease of life to products and at the end of it, the products would be brought to certain governmental agencies and destroyed, in exchange for coupons to purchase new goods. Without using the term 'planned obsolescence', L. Kelley shared a similar idea in his article published in 1936 and entitled 'Outmoded durability: if merchandise does not wear out faster, factories will be idle, people unemployed'.[161] Hence, in its infancy, the concepts related to the phenomenon of planned obsolescence were portrayed positively from an economic perspective.

48. Obsolescence in the 50s and 60s – The public debate on product obsolescence started in the 1950s, a period that is generally acknowledged as the beginning of modern consumer society.[162] During these years, the idea

156 See *supra*, n° 10.

157 F.J. George, 'Is progressive obsolescence the path toward increased consumption?', *Advertising & Selling*, 5 September 1928, pp. 19–20, as cited in G. Slade, *Made to break – technology and obsolescence in America* (Harvard University Press 2006) p. 58.

158 G. Slade, *Made to break – technology and obsolescence in America* (Harvard University Press 2006) p. 58.

159 B. Burns, 'Re-evaluating obsolescence and planning for it', in T. Cooper, *Longer lasting products: Alternatives to the throwaway society* (Gower 2010) p. 42.

160 B. London, *Ending the depression through planned obsolescence* (1932), available on: <https://upload.wikimedia.org/wikipedia/commons/2/27/London_%281932%29_Ending_the_depression_through_planned_obsolescence.pdf>.

161 L. Kelley, 'Outmoded durability: if merchandise does not wear out faster, factories will be idle, people unemployed', *Printer's Ink*, 9 January 1936, as cited in K. Pope, *Understanding planned obsolescence – Unsustainability through production, consumption and waste generation* (Kogan Page 2017) p. 50.

162 See e.g. N. Whiteley, 'Toward a Throwaway Culture: Consumerism, "Style Obsolescence" and Cultural Theory in the 1950s and 1960s', 10 *Oxford Art Journal* (1987) p. 3 at p. 27. For other references, see F. Trentmann, 'The Long History of Contemporary Consumer Society – Chronologies, Practices, and Politics in Modern Europe', 49 *Archiv für Sozialgeschichte* (2009) p. 107.

that 'goods enable people to find themselves' gained ground, with support from technology, advertising, and a new generation of cultural leaders.[163] It is in this context that the concept of 'planned obsolescence' was popularized by B. Stevens, an American industrial designer, at an advertising conference in 1954. In his talk, he defined 'planned obsolescence' as "*instilling in the buyer the desire to own something a little newer, a little better, a little sooner than is necessary*".[164] The controversy was prompted by frustrations among some industrialists at a perceived decline in the quality of products.[165] During this period, the theoretical study of product obsolescence was further elaborated by scholars. Among them was P.M. Gregory, who distinguished two cases of 'purposeful obsolescence': (1) cases where manufacturers produce goods with a shorter physical life than the industry is capable of producing under existing technological and cost conditions and (2) cases where manufacturers or sellers induce the public to replace goods which still retain substantial physical usefulness.[166] J.W. Newman focused on 'psychological obsolescence' caused by "*the strategy of persuading the public that style is an important element in the desirability of one's product*". As a consequence, the older style is obsolete because it no longer satisfies the physical needs of the consumer.[167] Overall, these studies outline the fact that planned obsolescence was also seen positively from a societal and individual perspective in its early days.

49. Obsolescence and consumerism[168] – One of the most notable contributions on the topic of 'planned obsolescence' was made by V. Packard in 1960 with his book entitled 'The Waste Makers'.[169] In this book, V. Packard brought a new perspective on planned obsolescence (corresponding to the second wave of interest)[170], referring to it to criticise consumerist culture and express his concerns about waste and American moral decay.[171] He defined 'planned obsolescence' as "*a strategy to influence either the shape of the product*

---

163 F. Trentmann, *Empire of things: How We Became a World of Consumers, from the Fifteenth Century to the Twenty-First* (Harper 2016) p. 376.

164 G. Adamson, *Industrial Strength Design: How Brooks Stevens Shaped Your World* (MIT Press for the Milwaukee Art Museum 2003) p. 4.

165 M. Mayer, 'Planned obsolescence: Rx for tired markets?', 73 *Dun's Review and Modern Industry* (1959) p. 40 at p. 80, cited in V. Packard, *The Waste Makers* (David MacKay 1960).

166 P.M. Gregory, 'A Theory of Purposeful Obsolescence', 14 *Southern Economic Journal* (1947) p. 24 at p. 45.

167 J.W. Newman, *Motivation Research and Marketing Management* (Harvard University School of Business Administration 1957) p. 237.

168 'Consumerism' is here understood as the "*doctrine advocating a continual increase in the consumption of goods as a basis for a sound economy*" and leading to "*(excessive) emphasis on or preoccupation with the acquisition of consumer goods*", as defined in Oxford English Dictionary 2006 (3rd ed.).

169 V. Packard, *The Waste Makers* (David MacKay 1960).

170 See *supra*, n° 11.

171 F. Trentmann, *Empire of things: How We Became a World of Consumers, from the Fifteenth Century to the Twenty-First* (Harper 2016) p. 730.

or the mental attitude of the consumer" and distinguished three 'ramifications of planned obsolescence'.[172] The first ramification is 'obsolescence of function', whereby "*an existing product becomes outmoded when a product is introduced that performs the function better*". The second ramification is 'obsolescence of quality', which corresponds to the case where it is planned that the product "*breaks down or wears out at a given time, usually not too distant*". For this type of planned obsolescence, V. Packard identified complementary strategies, including the unavailability, complexity, and high costs of necessary spare parts and the lack of repair information.[173] The third ramification is 'obsolescence of desirability', whereby "*a product that is still sound in terms of quality or performance becomes "worn out" in our minds because a styling or other change makes it seem less desirable*". This contribution was followed by other criticisms of mass consumerism, including the one voiced by J. Baudrillard who portrayed consumers as victims of advertising that transformed the product into a system of values.[174] Since then, the coincidence between the emergence of 'planned obsolescence' and consumer society was further stressed.[175]

50. Planned obsolescence from an economic perspective – Since the 1970s, the notion of planned obsolescence became the focus of a growing number of economic studies.[176] In these studies, planned obsolescence is defined as the most profitable strategy to balance technological innovation with businesses' rights to maximize profits.[177] In other words, planning or designing a product with a shortened useful lifetime allows producers to increase their profits by selling more products, which maximizes economic outputs. Producers are therefore encouraged to produce cheap short-lived devices of low quality

---

172 V. Packard, *The Waste Makers* (David MacKay 1960), especially chapter 6.

173 See chapter 2 of V. Packard, *The Waste Makers* (David MacKay 1960).

174 J. Baudrillard, *La société de consommation* (Denoël 1970).

175 See e.g. C. Behrends, *Consequences of Planned Obsolescence for Consumer Culture and the promotional self – Analysing ads* (GRIN Verlag 2004); N. Maycroft, *Consumption, planned obsolescence and waste* (Lincoln School of Art and Design 2009); K. Pope, *Understanding planned obsolescence – Unsustainability through production, consumption and waste generation* (Kogan Page 2017) p. 9 at p. 80; M. Zallio, D. Berry, 'Design and Planned Obsolescence. Theories and Approaches for Designing Enabling Technologies', 20 *The Design Journal* (2017) S3751; A. Girard, C. Thorpe, F. Durif, E. Robinot, 'Obsolescence of Home Appliances and Electronics: What Is the Role of the Consumer?', *Équiterre* (2018) pp. 13–14.

176 See e.g. P.L. Swan, 'Optimum Durability, Second-Hand Markets, and Planned Obsolescence', 80 *Journal of Political Economy* (1972) p. 575 at p. 585; J. Bulow, 'An economic theory of planned obsolescence', 101 *Q. J. Econ.* (1986) p. 729 at p. 749; M. Waldman, 'A New Perspective on Planned Obsolescence', 108 *Q. J. Econ.* (1993) p. 273 at p. 283; A. Fishman N. Gandal, O. Shy, 'Planned obsolescence as an engine of technological progress', 141 *Journal of Industrial Economics* (1993) p. 361 at p. 370; J.P. Choi, 'Network Externality, Compatibility Choice, and Planned Obsolescence', 42 *The Journal of Industrial Economics* (1994) p. 167 at p. 182; M. Waldman, 'Planned Obsolescence and the R&D Decision', 27 *The RAND Journal of Economics* (1996) p. 583 at p. 595.

177 This economic perspective prolongs the first wave of interest, stressing the positive impacts of planned obsolescence (see n° 10).

and not easily repairable, to promote rapid technological developments, to stimulate consumption through marketing practices, and to strongly protect their intellectual property (IP) rights. This economic literature was mostly confined to the economic implications of manipulating product lifetime from a monopolist's point of view. These theories of planned obsolescence only applied to certain types of goods, namely experience goods[178], as such a strategy was not relevant for other goods, like credence goods[179], for which quality is an important competition parameter, or search goods[180], for which consumers are well-informed.

2. REVIVAL OF INTEREST DUE TO ENVIRONMENTAL CONCERNS

51. ENVIRONMENTAL CONCERNS ABOUT PLANNED OBSOLESCENCE – The growing discussions on the environmental impacts of current production and consumption patterns have sparked a new wave of academic interest in the topic of planned obsolescence (corresponding to the third wave of interest).[181] This wave started 50 years ago, as embodied by the report 'The Limits to Growth' on exponential economic and population growth with a finite supply of resources.[182] In the 80s, the Organisation for Economic Co-operation and Development (OECD) issued a report on the environmental benefits of product durability and product life extension.[183] In its report, the OECD drew attention to the development of 'non-repairable' and 'non-maintainable' versions of durable goods (e.g. ballpoint pens and disposable razors), to some manufacturing techniques shortening product life spans (e.g. light bulbs), and to the influence of consumers through their purchasing, retention and discarding decisions.[184]

---

178 According to the Search, Experience, Credence (SEC) classification of goods and services, which is used by economists and marketers, 'experience goods' are those that can be accurately evaluated only after the product has been purchased and experienced.

179 According to the SEC classification, 'credence goods' are those that are difficult or impossible to evaluate even after consumption has occurred. Evaluation difficulties may arise because the consumer lacks the knowledge or technical expertise to make a realistic evaluation or, alternatively because the cost of information-acquisition may outweigh the value of the information available.

180 According to the SEC classification, 'search goods' are those with attributes that can be evaluated prior to purchase or consumption. Consumers rely on prior experience, direct product inspection and other information search activities to locate information that assists in the evaluation process.

181 See *supra*, n° 12.

182 D.H. Meadows, D.L. Meadows, J. Randers, W.W. Behrens III, *The Limits to Growth* (Universe 1972).

183 OECD, *Product Durability and Product Life Extension: Their Contribution to Solid Waste Management* (1982).

184 T. Cooper, 'The significance of product longevity', in T. Cooper, *Longer lasting products: Alternatives to the throwaway society* (Gower 2010) pp. 6–7.

But the strongest revival of interest in the topic of planned obsolescence came a decade later, with the ideas of 'sustainable development' and 'circular economy'.

52. The rise of the concept of sustainable development – Due to increasing environmental concerns, most industrialised countries became strongly committed and attracted by alternatives to the dominant linear economy.[185] One major step was taken in 1992 by the United Nations (UN) with the adoption of Agenda 21.[186] This comprehensive action plan suggests ways for governments and NGOs to promote sustainable development at global, national and local levels. 'Sustainable development' had been earlier defined by the so-called Brundtland Commission as "*development that meets the needs of the present without compromising the ability of future generations to meet their own needs*".[187] This concept not only aims to mitigate the human footprint on the environment, but also includes non-environmental dimensions, like humanitarian and basic social, economic, and cultural rights.[188] Among the main objectives of Agenda 21 is the transition towards more sustainable consumption patterns.[189] Sustainable consumption was subsequently integrated into UN consumer protection guidelines[190], and reaffirmed in 2015 in the Sustainable Development Goal 12 entitled 'Responsible production and consumption'.[191]

53. The rise of the concept of the circular economy (as opposed to the linear economy) – In this drive for sustainability, the idea of circular economy emerged. According to the definition given by W.R. Stahel, who can be considered as one of the pioneers of the concept, a circular economy consists of "*manag[ing] stocks of manufactured assets, such as infrastructure, buildings, vehicles, equipment and consumer goods, to maintain their value and utility as high as possible for as long as possible; and stocks of resources at their highest purity and value*".[192] The concept of circular economy is generally considered

185 China was one of the first countries to take actions because of the huge environmental, human health and social problems posed by its very rapid and continuous economic development patterns and its growing population. See P. Ghisellini, C. Cialani, S. Ulgiati, 'A review on circular economy: the expected transition to a balanced interplay of environmental and economic systems', 114 *J. Clean. Prod.* (2016) p. 12.

186 UN Conference on Environment & Development, *Agenda 21* (1992).

187 UN World Commission on Environment and Development, *Our Common Future* (1987) p. 41.

188 This contrasts with this book, which confines the concept of 'sustainability' to its strict sense, focusing on environmental aspects. See *supra*, n° 17.

189 See chapter 4 of the Agenda 21, p. 18 at p. 22.

190 Resolutions and decisions adopted by the UN Economic and Social Council at the 10th meeting of its resumed organizational session for 1999 and at its substantive session of 1999, E/1999/INF/2/Add.2, p. 14 at p. 23.

191 Resolution adopted by the UN General Assembly of 25 September 2015 on Transforming our world: the 2030 Agenda for Sustainable Development, A/RES/70/1.

192 W.R. Stahel, *The Circular Economy: A User's Guide* (Routledge 2019) p. 6.

as an alternative paradigm to the take-make-use-dispose linear economy and a pathway towards sustainable development.[193] Although its theoretical foundation can be traced back to the early 90s[194], the idea of circular economy was propagated with the publication of the book 'Cradle to Cradle' written by M. Braungart and W. McDonough in 2002.[195] The Ellen MacArthur Foundation, a charity that works with business, academia, policymakers and institutions to accelerate the transition to a circular economy[196], has helped popularize the move to a circular economy with businesses.[197]

54. A GROWING BODY OF LITERATURE, IN VARIOUS DISCIPLINES... – These new concepts led to an expanding body of literature on planned obsolescence in all academic disciplines. The phenomenon remained an attractive subject for economic research[198], with the flourishing of new analyses of the issue.[199] But besides economic literature, other disciplines started to take a great interest in planned obsolescence, including engineering, computer science, social and behavioural sciences, marketing, and many others.[200] Following the trend in other scientific disciplines, there has also been an increasing amount of legal literature on planned obsolescence over the past few years.[201] These studies

---

193 See e.g. F. Bonciu, 'The European Economy: From a linear to a circular economy', 14 *Romanian Journal of European Affairs* (2014) p. 78 at p. 91. See also the public policies at the EU and national level (n° 64).

194 R.U. Ayres, 'Industrial metabolism; theory and policy,' in B.R. Allenby and D.J. Richards (eds.), *The Greening of Industrial Ecosystems* (National Academy Press 1994) p. 23 at p. 37, as cited in N.M.P. Bocken, I. de Pauw, C. Bakker, B. van der Grinten, 'Product design and business model strategies for a circular economy', 33 *Journal of Industrial and Production Engineering* (2016) p. 308.

195 M. Braungart, W. McDonough, *Cradle to cradle: remaking the way we make the things* (North Point Press 2002).

196 For further information, see <https://www.ellenmacarthurfoundation.org/>.

197 See e.g. Ellen MacArthur Foundation, *Towards the circular economy: Economic and business rationale for an accelerated transition* (2013).

198 A. Fishman, R. Rob, 'Product Innovation by a Durable-Good Monopoly', 31 *The RAND Journal of Economics* (2000) p. 237 at p. 252; A. Utaka, 'Planned Obsolescence and Marketing Strategy', 21 *Managerial and Decision Economics* (2000) p. 339 at p. 344; P.A. Grout, I.-U. Park, 'Competitive Planned Obsolescence', 36 *The RAND Journal of Economics* (2005) p. 596 at p. 612; R. Strausz, 'Planned Obsolescence as an Incentive Device for Unobservable Quality', 119 *The Economic Journal* (2009) p. 1405 at p. 1421; C.-H. Miao, 'Tying, Compatibility and Planned Obsolescence', 58 *The Journal of Industrial Economics* (2010) p. 579 at p. 606.

199 See V.V. Agrawal, S. Kavadias, L. B. Toktay, 'The Limits of Planned Obsolescence for Conspicuous Durable Goods', 18 *M&SOM* (2016) p. 216 at p. 226. In this paper, the authors argue that in the presence of consumers who value exclusivity, firms benefit from designing products with higher durability in conjunction with a high-price, low-volume introduction strategy.

200 The interdisciplinary nature of research on product obsolescence can be noted in T. Cooper (ed.), *Longer lasting products: Alternatives to the throwaway society* (Gower 2010) as well as in T. Brönneke, A. Wechsler (eds.), *Obsoleszenz interdisziplinär – Vorzeitiger Verschleiß aus Sicht von Wissenschaft und Praxis* (Nomos 2015).

201 See among others A. Hamann, 'Obsolescence programmée: le droit en panne?', 102 *D.C.C.R.* (2014) p. 41 at p. 82; D. Raes, "L'obsolescence programmée à l'épreuve de l'obligation

mostly take the perspective of separate legal domains, such as environmental, consumer, contract or competition laws. The extensive multidisciplinary literature on planned obsolescence led to different theories and approaches to address this issue, from the late 90s until today.[202] The topic attracted even more attention with the emergence of new technologies, since certain devices – in particular IoT-based and smart products -[203] were deemed to be more prone to becoming obsolete in a shorter time, thus leading to an even further increase of environmental concerns.[204] The notions relating to the rapid obsolescence of products has greatly evolved, from a technical, economic concept to a powerful advocacy tool in favour of sustainable products.

55. ...WITH AN ALMOST EXCLUSIVE FOCUS ON PLANNED OBSOLESCENCE – Among this recent literature, several scholars have echoed the ideas earlier formulated by V. Packard[205], describing the obsolescence of products as the result of producer intent. According to these scholars, 'planned obsolescence' refers to a deliberate action taken by certain profit-oriented manufacturers and manipulative engineers to artificially shorten the lifetime of products, in order

d'information du vendeur, de la notion de conformité et de la garantie des vices cachés" in *Liber Amicorum François Glansdorf et Pierre Legros* (Bruylant 2014) p. 235 at p. 318; E. Maitre-Ekern and C. Dalhammar,'Regulating planned obsolescence: a review of legal approaches to increase product durability and reparability in Europe', 25 *Review of European Community & International Environmental Law* (2016) p. 378 at p. 394; S. Wrbka, 'Warranty law in cases of planned obsolescence – The Austrian situation', 6 *EuCML* (2017) p. 67 at p. 76; M. Langhendries, Le coût de la panne: droit et obsolescence programmée, 71 *Revue du Droit des Technlogies de l'Information* (2018) p. 55 at p. 86; C. Hess, *Geplante Obsoleszenz – Rechtliche Zulässigkeit in der Lebensdauerplanung von technischen Gebrauchgütern* (Nomos 2018); L.A. DiMatteo, S. Wrbka, 'Planned Obsolescence and Consumer Protection: The Unregulated Extended Warranty and Service Contract Industry', 28 *Cornell Journal of Law and Public Policy* (2019) p. 483 at p. 544; J. Malinauskaite, F.B. Erdem, 'Planned Obsolescence in the Context of a Holistic Legal Sphere and the Circular Economy', 41 *Oxford Journal of Legal Studies* (2021) p. 719 at p. 749.

202 For a detailed analysis of the quantity of published works on the theme of planned obsolescence and related, see M. Zallio, D. Berry, 'Design and Planned Obsolescence. Theories and Approaches for Designing Enabling Technologies', 20 *The Design Journal* (2017) S3754. See also J.L. Rivera, A. Lallmahomed, 'Environmental implications of planned obsolescence and product lifetime: a literature review', 9 *International Journal of Sustainable Engineering* (2016) p. 119 at p. 129.

203 'Internet of things' (IoT) means "*a proposed development of the internet in which many everyday objects are embedded with microchips giving them network connectivity, allowing them to send and receive data*", as defined in Oxford English Dictionary 2006 (3rd ed.). A 'smart device' is "*an electronic device, generally connected to other devices or networks via different wireless protocols such as Bluetooth, Zigbee, NFC, Wi-Fi, LiFi, 5G, etc., that can operate to some extent interactively and autonomously*" (see <https://en.wikipedia.org/wiki/Smart_device>).

204 See e.g. M. Zallio, D. Berry, 'Design and Planned Obsolescence. Theories and Approaches for Designing Enabling Technologies', 20 *The Design Journal* (2017) S3750; J. Bachér et al., *Electronic products and obsolescence in a circular economy* (European Topic Centre Waste and Materials in a Green Economy 2020), especially p. 10.

205 See *supra*, n° 49.

to increase product replacement rate, at the expense of consumers and to the detriment of the environment. This category of scholars includes N. Maycroft[206], as well as S. Latouche.[207] The reasoning based on the monocausal attribution of responsibility has also more recently been followed by K. Pope, who wrote that with the boost in productivity generated by technological advances, producers look for solutions to the problem of growing industrial production outpacing consumption. To avoid overproduction without producing less but through selling more, "*many businesspeople began to feel great fascination with the practice of planned obsolescence of quality*".[208] This short-sighted view can also be found in legal scholarship, as exemplified in the paper written by D. Raes, which defines 'planned obsolescence' (*obsolescence programmée*) as "*a practice followed by a manufacturer which consists in designing, producing or marketing a product while deliberately shortening its lifetime, either through the choice of materials, through specific manufacturing processes or through the introduction of an electronic device in the product that makes it stop working after a certain period of use*".[209] Along the same line, M. Maggiolino states that "*[o]ne might think – perhaps naively – that the life span of a product depends on uncontrolled factors such as fate or the wear and tear of its materials. As a matter of fact, the truth is that it is often the result of entrepreneurial choices*".[210] Although some of these scholars do not describe product obsolescence as directly intentional, explaining producers' actions through an economic paradigm, it is still the producer who artificially reduces the durability of goods and, consequently, induces consumers to purchase substitute products.

56. Recent research taking into account consumer influence on product lifetime – By contrast, a significant body of research gradually went beyond the idea of intent and put a wider and more complex perspective on the phenomenon, developing consumer behaviour theories and helping

---

206 N. Maycroft, *Consumption, planned obsolescence and waste* (Lincoln School of Art and Design 2009).

207 S. Latouche, *Bon pour la casse: Les déraisons de l'obsolescence programmée* (Les liens qui libèrent 2012).

208 K. Pope, *Understanding planned obsolescence – Unsustainability through production, consumption and waste generation* (Kogan Page 2017) p. 51 at p. 57. Along the same line, see J. Guiltinan, 'Creative destruction and Destructive Creations: Environmental Ethics and Planned Obsolescence', 89 *Journal of Business Ethics* (2009) p. 21.

209 D. Raes, "L'obsolescence programmée à l'épreuve de l'obligation d'information du vendeur, de la notion de conformité et de la garantie des vices cachés" in *Liber Amicorum François Glansdorf et Pierre Legros* (Bruylant 2014) p. 240: "*L'obsolescence programmée ou désuétude planifiée est une pratique qui consiste pour un fabricant à concevoir, produire, fabriquer ou commercialiser un produit en veillant à en limiter délibérément la durée de vie, que ce soit par le choix des matériaux, par l'utilisation de procédés de fabrication particuliers ou encore par l'insertion dans le produit d'un dispositif électronique programmé pour faire cesser son fonctionnement après un certain temps ou un certain usage.*" (free translation).

210 M. Maggiolino, 'Planned Obsolescence: A Strategy in Search of Legal Rules', 50 *International Review of Intellectual Property and Competition Law* (2019) p. 405 at p. 407.

better understand consumers' influence on product lifetime.[211] These studies exposed and examined cases where the products, though still functioning, were prematurely replaced and discarded by consumers.[212] It was found that causes of rapid product replacement were rather complex and that consumer decisions were not necessarily motivated by the declining performance or irreparable technical failure of the product. J. van Nes and J. Cramer identified a typology for replacement motives, which includes wear and tear, improved utility, improved expression, and new desires.[213] Based on this reasoning, a wide array of typologies of product obsolescence have been elaborated in the multidisciplinary literature.[214] Building on earlier work, T. Cooper categorised product obsolescence to differentiate the failure of a product to function due to objective reasons ('absolute obsolescence') from the disuse of a functional product due to additional subjective reasons ('relative obsolescence').[215] Within the concept

211 See among others M. DeBell, R. Dardis, 'Extending Product Life: Technology Isn't the Only Issue', 6 *Advances in Consumer Research* (1979) p. 381 at p. 385; G.D. Harrell, D.M. McConocha, 'Personal Factors Related to Consumer Product Disposal Tendencies', 26 *Journal of Consumer Affairs* (1992) p. 397 at 417; E. Heiskanen, *Conditions for Product Life Extension – Working Paper* (National Consumer Research Centre 1996); B. Granberg, *The Quality Re-evaluation Process: Product Obsolescence in a Consumer-Producer Interaction Framework* (The Swedish Environmental Protection Agency 1997); T. Cooper, 'Inadequate Life? Evidence of Consumer Attitudes to Product Obsolescence', 27 *J. Consum. Policy* (2004) p. 421 at p. 449; R. Grewal, 'The Timing of Repeat Purchase of Consumer Durable Goods: The Role of Functional Bases of Consumer Attitudes', 41 *Journal of Marketing Research* (2004) p. 101 at p. 115; N. van Nes, J. Cramer, 'Influencing product lifetime through product design', 14 *Business Strategy and Environment* (2005) p. 286 at p. 299; J. Guiltinan, 'Creative destruction and Destructive Creations: Environmental Ethics and Planned Obsolescence', 89 *Journal of Business Ethics* (2009) pp. 22–23; S. Evans, T. Cooper, 'Consumer influences on product life-spans', in T. Cooper, *Longer lasting products: Alternatives to the throwaway society* (Gower 2010) p. 319 at p. 350; T. K. Aladeojebi, 'Planned obsolescence', 4 *International Journal of Scientific & Engineering Research* (2013) pp. 1505–1506; C. Déméné, A. Marchand, 'L'obsolescence des produits électroniques: des responsabilités partagées', 10 *The Ethics Forum* (2015) p. 17 at p. 19; J.L. Rivera, A. Lallmahomed, 'Environmental implications of planned obsolescence and product lifetime: a literature review', 9 *International Journal of Sustainable Engineering* (2016) pp. 123–124; E. Gawel, W. Bretschneider, 'Die Nutzungs- und Lebensdauer von Konsumprodukten als Gegenstand staatlicher Nachhaltigkeitssteuerung', 39 *Zeitschrift für Umweltpolitik und Umweltrecht* (2016) p. 1 at p. 36; F. Echegaray, 'Consumers' reactions to product obsolescence in emerging markets: the case of Brazil', 134 *J. Clean. Prod.* (2016) p. 191 at p. 203; L. Hennies, R. Stamminger, 'An empirical survey on the obsolescence of appliances in German households', 112 *Resources, Conservation and Recycling* (2016) p. 73 at p. 82; C. Bakker, C. Schuit, *The long view – Exploring product lifetime extension* (United Nations Environment Programme 2017), especially pp. 21–23; A. Girard et al., 'Obsolescence of Home Appliances and Electronics: What Is the Role of the Consumer?', *Équiterre* (2018).

212 The findings of these studies shed light on the current 'throwaway society'. See *supra*, n° 1.

213 N. van Nes, J. Cramer, 'Product lifetime optimization: a challenging strategy towards more sustainable consumption patterns', 14 *J. Clean. Prod.* (2006) p. 1307 at p. 1318.

214 For a critical overview of some key typologies, see C. Déméné, A. Marchand, 'L'obsolescence des produits électroniques: des responsabilités partagées', 10 *The Ethics Forum* (2015), especially p. 9 at p. 14.

215 T. Cooper, 'Inadequate life? Evidence of consumer attitudes to product obsolescence', 27 *J. Consum. Policy* (2004) p. 421 at p. 449.

of relative obsolescence, he distinguished cases when consumers are no longer attracted to products or satisfied by them ('psychological obsolescence'), when there are financial factors that cause products to be considered no longer worth keeping ('economic obsolescence') and when the functional qualities of existing products are inferior to newer models ('technological obsolescence').[216] Although these categories lack nuance, mainly allocating responsibility for relative obsolescence to consumers and absolute obsolescence to producers, they nonetheless reflect reality more accurately. B. Burns added a social dimension to these categories, distinguishing between 'aesthetic obsolescence' (i.e. products that have become outmoded), 'social obsolescence' (i.e. products that have become obsolete due to a social response), 'technological obsolescence' and 'economic obsolescence'.[217] All these studies emphasized that planned obsolescence is only one aspect of the problem, next to other cases of premature obsolescence.

57. No 'planned' but 'avoidable' obsolescence – Over the last few years, some scholars have called the concept of 'planned obsolescence' into question. Following their reasoning, this term is inappropriate as the limited lifetime of products is not due to the economic actors, but rather to the current economic model and the associated 'material culture'.[218] T. Brönneke argued that the adjective 'planned' should be replaced with 'avoidable' to describe the issue of product obsolescence. The suggested term avoids imputing to producers any intent to limit product lifetime and allows changing the focus onto the conditions encouraging the existence of practices that cause the premature obsolescence of products. According to T. Brönneke, there is no need to allocate responsibility.[219] Instead of 'avoidable obsolescence', the German consumer organisation (*Verbraucher Kommission*) agreed to use the term 'negligent obsolescence' (*fahrlässiger Obsoleszenz*).[220] Along the same line, E. Poppe and J. Longmuß developed a new definition of 'planned obsolescence' based on

---

216 *Ibid.*, p. 426.

217 B. Burns, 'Re-evaluating obsolescence and planning for it', in T. Cooper, *Longer lasting products: Alternatives to the throwaway society* (Gower 2010) p. 45 at p. 50.

218 M. Jaeger-Erben, M. Proske, 'What's hot what's not: the social construction of product obsolescence and its relevance for strategies to increase functionality', in C. Bakker and R. Mugge (eds.), *Product Lifetimes And The Environment 2017 – Conference Proceedings* (IOS Press 2017) p. 183; M. Jaeger-Erben, 'Eine Frage der Kultur? Gesellschaftliche Treiber von Obsoleszenz', in E. Poppe, J. Longmuß (eds.), *Geplante Obsoleszenz Hinter den Kulissen der Produktentwicklung* (Transcript 2019) p. 171 at p. 190.

219 T. Brönneke, 'Premature obsolescence and European law – Possibilities with regard to the Reform of the Consumer Sales Directive', in *Polytechnic Pforzheim Conference Proceedings* (Hochschule Pforzheim 2014) p. 1, available on: <www.beuc.eu/documents/files/FC/durablegoods/conference/presentations/Bronneke_SustainableConsumption_EN.pdf>.

220 L. Reisch, A. Oehler, T. Brönneke, K.-H. Fezer, J. Stellpflug, *Qualität statt vorzeitiger Verschleiß – Diskussionspapier zur eingebauten Obsoleszenz bei Konsumgütern* (Verbraucher Kommission 2014) p. 4.

three dimensions, namely the form (absolute or relative obsolescence), time (premature or delayed obsolescence) and intention (intended and unintended consequences of obsolescence).[221] More than enriching the concept of planned obsolescence, these criticisms demonstrate how controversial the term 'planned obsolescence' can be, especially due to the serious doubts on its existence.

3. GROWING INTEREST BEYOND ACADEMIA

58. 'PLANNED OBSOLESCENCE' AS A POPULAR BUZZWORD – Far from remaining within the academic sphere, the debate on planned obsolescence sparked off in the media and in popular discourses.[222] As mentioned above, this surge of interest beyond academia was prompted by the publication of texts such as 'Beyond Recycling'[223] in the UK and 'Eternally Yours'[224] in the Netherlands. Thought-provoking documentaries, like 'The Light Bulb Conspiracy' in 2010[225], and television shows, like the French television show 'Cash Investigation: La mort programmée de nos appareils' (Cash Investigation: The planned death of our devices) broadcasted in June 2012[226], intensified the debate and contributed to increasing use of 'planned obsolescence' as a buzzword.[227] In addition, several popular science books on planned obsolescence fed the debate[228], including the book 'Made to break' written by the Canadian freelance writer G. Slade.[229] The use of the term 'planned obsolescence' became even more pervasive in newspapers and other mass media after the adoption of the French law

221 J. Longmuss and E. Poppe, 'Planned obsolescence: who are those planners?', in C. Bakker and R. Mugge (eds.), *Product Lifetimes And The Environment 2017 – Conference Proceedings* (IOS Press 2017) p. 219; E. Poppe, J. Longmuß, 'Zu Begriff und Theorie der geplanten Obsoleszenz', in E. Poppe, J. Longmuß (eds.), *Geplante Obsoleszenz Hinter den Kulissen der Produktentwicklung* (Transcript 2019) p. 23 at p. 31.

222 This corresponds to the fourth wave of interest in the topic of planned obsolescence (see n° 13).

223 T. Cooper, *Beyond recycling – The longer life option* (The New Economics Foundation 1994).

224 E. van Hinte, *Eternally Yours – Time in Design* (OIOpublishers 2004).

225 C. Dannoritzer, *The Light Bulb Conspiracy* (2010).

226 See <https://www.youtube.com/watch?v=NljCDGhFjFc&ab_channel=CashInvestigation>.

227 M. Jaeger-Erben, M. Proske, 'What's hot what's not: the social construction of product obsolescence and its relevance for strategies to increase functionality', in C. Bakker and R. Mugge (eds.), *Product Lifetimes And The Environment 2017 – Conference Proceedings* (IOS Press 2017) p. 181.

228 See e.g. J. Reuß, C. Dannoritzer, *Kaufen für die Müllhalde: Das Prinzip der Geplanten Obsoleszenz* (Orange-Press 2013); C. Kreiß, *Geplanter Verschleiß: Wie die Industrie uns zu immer mehr und immer schnellerem Konsum antreibt – und wie wir uns dagegen wehren können* (Europa Verlag 2014); S. Schridde, *Murks? Nein danke!: Was wir tun können, damit die Dinge besser werden* (Oekom 2014).

229 G. Slade, *Made to break – technology and obsolescence in America* (Harvard University Press 2006). In this book (p. 5), G. Slade defines 'planned obsolescence' as "*the assortment of techniques used to artificially limit the durability of a manufactured good in order to stimulate repetitive consumption*".

prohibiting 'planned obsolescence'[230] as well as cases condemning companies for practices considered as planned obsolescence.[231]

59. Popular focus on planned obsolescence sensu stricto – The mass media and blogosphere generally confine the issue of the rapid obsolescence of products to a restricted and incomplete definition. In most articles, blog posts and documentaries, 'planned obsolescence' is described as a deliberate action taken by certain manufacturers and designers to artificially shorten the lifetime of products by integrating predetermined weak points, in order to increase product replacement rate, at the expense of consumers. Some of them even compare the phenomenon of premature obsolescence to a fight between product suppliers, on the one hand, and consumers, on the other. In this scenario, producers are the guilty ones, accused of deliberately planning the obsolescence of their products to force consumers to buy new ones.[232] Following this line of thought, it is alleged that practices of material and functional obsolescence are ubiquitous in current industrialised society. In these articles, various cases of suspected (and mostly unsubstantiated) planned obsolescence are reported, including lights bulbs, nylon stockings, smartphone batteries, printers and video games. The abovementioned 'Phoebus cartel' is often given as the most striking evidence to support the claim of a broad conspiracy against consumers.[233] Although the approach followed by certain media is more nuanced, like in *The Economist*, which defines 'planned obsolescence' as the result of "*the working of the competitive and technological forces in a free society – forces that lead to ever-*

230 For more details on the French legislation on planned obsolescence, see *infra* on the French legislation on 'planned obsolescence' (n° 73–77).

231 See e.g. D. Schrieberg, 'Landmark French Lawsuit Attacks Epson, HP, Canon and Brother For 'Planned Obsolescence', *Forbes*, 26 September 2017, available on: <www.forbes.com/sites/davidschrieberg1/2017/09/26/landmark-french-lawsuit-attacks-epson-hp-canon-and-brother-for-planned-obsolescence/?sh=6249016f1b36>.

232 For a similar analysis, see M. Jaeger-Erben, M. Proske, 'What's hot what's not: the social construction of product obsolescence and its relevance for strategies to increase functionality', in C. Bakker and R. Mugge (eds.), *Product Lifetimes And The Environment 2017 – Conference Proceedings* (IOS Press 2017) p. 182.

233 See e.g. Welt, 'Hersteller sorgen mit perfiden Tricks für Umsatz' [Manufacturers ensure turnover with perfidious tricks], 29 August 2013, <www.welt.de/wirtschaft/webwelt/article119505169/Hersteller-sorgen-mit-perfiden-Tricks-fuer-Umsatz.html>; Pauline, 'Obsolescence programmée: vos appareils condamnés à mort' [Planned obsolescence: your devices condemned to death], *Consoglobe*, 10 Mars 2016, <www.consoglobe.com/obsolescence-programmee-appareils-cg/3>; Positivr, 'Obsolescence programmée: le top 5 des produits les plus touchés' [Planned obsolescence: the top 5 most affected products], 27 September 2017, <https://positivr.fr/obsolescence-programmee-top-5-produits/>; P. Galouise, 'Top 8 des objets les plus touchés par l'obsolescence programmée' [The top 8 most affected products by planned obsolescence:], 8 March 2018, <www.topito.com/top-objets-obsolescence-programmee>; W. Poritz, 'Planned Obsolescence and Your Right to Repair', 31 August 2020, <https://sustainablebrands.com/read/defining-the-next-economy/planned-obsolescence-and-your-right-to-repair>.

improving goods and services"[234], the responsibility is still solely attributed to manufacturers.[235]

60. Consumer perceptions and dissatisfaction – The ideas elaborated and conveyed by the media have echoed in consumers' minds and given a new breath of life to the notion of 'planned obsolescence' in popular conversations. The diagram on Google trends bears witness to the renewed interest in the topic, showing an increase in the number of searches for the word 'obsolescence programmée' from 2004 onwards (see Figure 1).[236] More and more consumers seem convinced that products do not last as long as they should.[237] In France, a survey published in 2014 by *60 millions de consommateurs* showed that 92% of respondents were convinced that household or high-tech appliances are deliberately designed not to last.[238] Similar perceptions were observed within the framework of the 2018 behavioural study issued by the EC, where some participants shared their impression that newer generations of products were less durable than products that were produced some years ago, notably due to planned obsolescence.[239] Consumer dissatisfaction with goods has also been reflected in the context of the new platform 'trop-vite usé' (worn-out too quickly) created by the Belgian consumer organisation *Test-Achats*, which has recorded no less than 11000 complaints since its creation in November 2016.[240] According to studies, these consumer perceptions stem from past experiences, but also from the belief that practices of planned obsolescence are ubiquitous and commonly used across all industries.[241] The growing and widespread suspicion among

234 The Economist, 'Planned obsolescence', 23 March 2009, <https://www.economist.com/news/2009/03/23/planned-obsolescence>, which is based on T. Hindle, *Guide to Management Ideas and Gurus* (Profile Books Ltd 2008) p. 147–148.

235 This popular view contrasts with the recent development in the literature (see n° 56–57).

236 See <https://trends.google.com/trends/explore?date=all&q=obsolescence%20programm%C3%A9e>.

237 See T. Cooper, 'Inadequate life? Evidence of consumer attitudes to product obsolescence' 27 *J. Consum. Policy* (2004) p. 421 at p. 449, H. Wieser, N. Tröger and R. Hübner, 'The consumers' desired and expected product lifetimes', in T. Cooper, N. Braithwaite, M. Moreno and G. Salvia (eds.), *Product Lifetimes and the Environment (PLATE) Conference proceedings* (Nottingham Trent University: CADBE 2015) p. 388 at p. 392; F. Echegaray, 'Consumers' reactions to product obsolescence in emerging markets: the case of Brazil', 134 *J. Clean. Prod.* (2016) p. 191 at p. 203; A. Girard et al., 'Obsolescence of Home Appliances and Electronics: What Is the Role of the Consumer?', *Équiterre* (2018) p. 8.

238 60 millions de consommateurs, 'La méfiance des consommateurs gagne du terrain', 6 May 2014, <https://www.60millions-mag.com/2014/05/06/la-mefiance-des-consommateurs-gagne-du-terrain-7929>.

239 LE Europe, VVA Europe, Ipsos, ConPolicy, Trinomics, *Behavioural study on consumers' engagement in the circular economy* (European Commission 2018) p. 65 and p. 180.

240 See <https://www.test-achats.be/trop-vite-use>.

241 H. Wieser, N. Tröger, *Die Nutzungsdauer und Obsoleszenz von Gebrauchgütern im Zeitalter der Beschleunigung – Eine empirische Untersuchung in österreichischen Haushalten* (Vienna Arbeiterkammer 2015) pp. 10–11; H. Wieser, N. Tröger and R. Hübner, 'The consumers' desired and expected product lifetimes', in T. Cooper, N. Braithwaite, M. Moreno and

consumers about the decreasing lifetime of products has been reinforced by the media, which has a significant influence on public discourse.

Figure 1. Google trends for 'obsolescence programmée' (2004 – present)

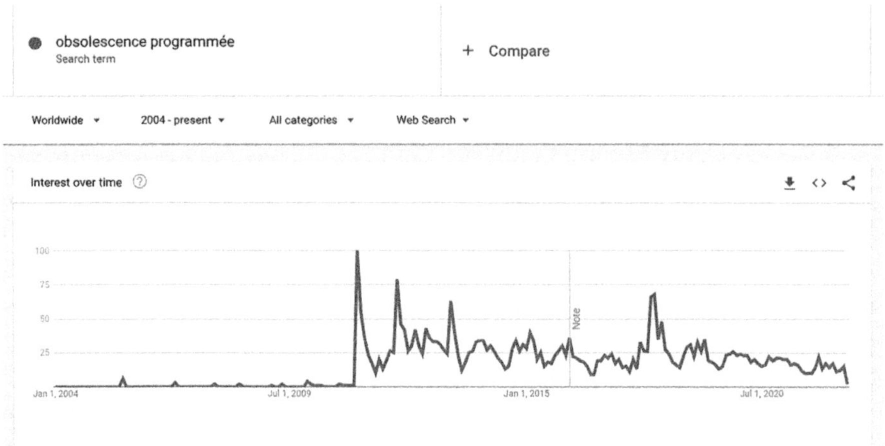

61. CITIZEN- AND COMMUNITY-LED INITIATIVES AGAINST PLANNED OBSOLESCENCE – Numerous endeavours are being made by a variety of stakeholders to curb planned obsolescence and prolong product lifetime. There are, first of all, citizen-led initiatives, which accumulate growing success across the world. One of the most prominent examples is the network of *Repair Cafés*, which consists of a space where people meet to socialize and repair diverse consumer goods, ranging from clothes and bicycles to household appliances.[242] Home-based repair has also developed with the support of networked learning initiatives, like *iFixit*, a Californian company formed in 2003 which publishes free online repair manuals for consumer electronics and sells repair parts on its wiki-based site[243], or *Tournevie*, a non-profit organization in Brussels which has an affordable and ecological tool library and which organizes 'tool training' courses.[244] Through such initiatives, consumers can gain the knowledge and skills necessary to mend defective or broken goods and prolong their lifetime. In addition, public actions and events have been organised[245], and petitions against

G. Salvia (eds.), *Product Lifetimes and the Environment (PLATE) Conference proceedings* (Nottingham Trent University: CADBE 2015) p. 392;

242 Having originated in 2009 in the Netherlands, there were over 1500 *Repair Cafés* operating in more than 30 countries by 2020. See <https://www.repaircafe.org/en/>.

243 *IFixit* has more than one million members and to date has produced nearly 70,000 *iFixit* manuals. See <https://www.ifixit.com/>.

244 See <https://www.tournevie.be/>.

245 See e.g. the Maintenance and Repair Day (www.choixresponsable.fr/journee-nationale-de-lentretien-et-de-la-reparation-de-lelectromenager/); the workshop organised by La Fabrique Ecologique (https://www.lafabriqueecologique.fr/comment-agir-vraiment-contre-

planned obsolescence have been launched.[246] Far from being isolated, these grassroots, often community-led, movements are extending and consolidating their networks in the form of partnerships or non-profit organizations, such as the French organisation *Halte à l'Obsolescence Programmée* (HOP).[247] Other environmental NGOs and consumer associations have written on the topic and taken action, including *Greenpeace*[248], *Les Amis de la Terre*[249] and the *Centre européen de la consommation*.[250]

62. Reactions from the business side – Not only manufacturers' representatives, but also other actors and organisations, have repeatedly and vehemently rejected the allegations of planned obsolescence.[251] According to them, if cases of planned obsolescence were to be found, they would remain exceptional and far from representing reality, since many firms strive for product quality and durability. Moreover, some companies emphasized the need to distinguish between alleged practices of planned obsolescence and cases of unintended obsolescence, which result from given circumstances that are beyond the control of companies and their staff.[252] In that regard, business representatives have already highlighted the importance of striking a fair

lobsolescence-programmee-aller-vers-une-consommation-plus-soutenable/) or the festival organised by ARC (https://arc-culture.be/event/obsolescence_diy_2018/).

246 See e.g. the petition demanding universal access in Europe to affordable spare parts for smartphones and other electronics (https://repair.eu/smartphones/) and the petition demanding Apple to stop practices of planned obsolescence (https://www.change.org/p/tim-cook-apple-stop-%C3%A0-l-obsolescence-programm%C3%A9e).

247 *Halte à l'Obsolescence Programmée* (Stop planned obsolescence) is an organization dedicated to fighting planned obsolescence, which conducts awareness campaigns, issues articles, reports and policy recommendations on the topic, takes legal actions against companies suspected of planned obsolescence. For further information, see <https://www.halteobsolescence.org/>.

248 A. Manhart, M. Blepp, C. Fischer, K. Graulich, S. Prakash, R. Priess, T. Schleicher, M. Tür, *Resource Efficiency in the ICT Sector* (Greenpeace 2016).

249 M. Fabre, W. Winkler, *L'obsolescence programmée, symbole de la société du gaspillage – Le cas des produits électriques et électroniques* (Les Amis de la Terre 2010); C. Lecomte, *Obsolescence des produits high-tech: Comment les marques limitent la durée de vie de nos biens* (Les Amis de la Terre 2012); A. Dufour, M. Peyraut, *Guide éco-citoyen de la réparation – Stop au coup de la panne* (Les Amis de la Terre 2018).

250 Centre Européen de la Consommation, *L'obsolescence programmée ou les dérives de la société de consommation* (2013).

251 At EU level, see e.g. DigitalEurope's reaction of 8 February 2016 to the Circular Economy Package, p. 3; F. Meszaros, *Are our household appliances durable? – Essay on durability* (CECED 2017) (English summary available on: <https://www.applia.hu/en/durability/>). At the French level, see e.g. B. Héger, *De l'obsolescence programmée, du recyclage insuffisant et de toutes ces sortes* (Altande 2020). At the German level, see e.g. J. Longmuss and E. Poppe, 'Planned obsolescence: who are those planners?', in C. Bakker and R. Mugge (eds.), *Product Lifetimes And The Environment 2017 – Conference Proceedings* (IOS Press 2017) p. 220.

252 J. Longmuss and E. Poppe, 'Planned obsolescence: who are those planners?', in C. Bakker and R. Mugge (eds.), *Product Lifetimes And The Environment 2017 – Conference Proceedings* (IOS Press 2017) p. 220.

balance between companies' and consumers' responsibilities when assessing the causes of rapid product replacement.[253]

63. Business initiatives against planned obsolescence – Interestingly, several companies have undertaken initiatives towards more sustainable products and/or business models.[254] Among these initiatives, there is the *Fairphone*, a modular smartphone that is designed and produced with a lower environmental impact.[255] A second notable example is the washing machine *L'Increvable* (the indestructible), created by the French designer J. Phedyaeff and built to last 50 years, which comes as an assembly kit.[256] In this non-exhaustive list of initiatives, one can also mention the French consortium *SEB*, which committed to provide spare parts for 10 years for the small appliances it produces.[257] More recently, the company *Vanden Borre*, distributor on the Belgian market for audio, TV, multimedia and household appliances, launched a repair abonnement for large household appliances.[258] More and more commitments to promoting sustainable products are being made by businesses, as shown by the *Club de la Durabilité* (durability club)[259] or by the Green Consumption Pledge initiative.[260]

4. INCREASING ATTENTION OF POLICYMAKERS AT EU AND NATIONAL LEVELS

64. Towards sustainable development and a circular economy – In recent years, the concept of planned obsolescence has started to permeate EU and national policies, creating a fifth wave of interest in the topic.[261] Just as has been the case in the academic field, the ideas of sustainable development and circular economy serve as vectors in the fight against planned obsolescence.[262] Although the UN instruments promoting sustainable development are non-

[253] See the presentation given by E. Bertrand (Eurochambres) on 30 November 2018 at the EESC Conference on Tackling premature obsolescence in Europe (highlights available on: <https://www.eesc.europa.eu/en/agenda/our-events/events/tackling-premature-obsolescence-europe>).

[254] See also Ellen MacArthur Foundation, *Towards the circular economy: Economic and business rationale for an accelerated transition* (2013) p. 28.

[255] For further information, see <https://www.fairphone.com/en/>.

[256] See <https://www.lincrevable.com/en/>.

[257] See <https://www.seb.fr/produits-reparables>.

[258] For further information, see <https://www.vandenborre.be/fr/info/service-vanden-borre-life>.

[259] HOP, *Durabilité des produits – Le temps de l'action* (2020) p. 24 at p. 34.

[260] See <https://ec.europa.eu/info/policies/consumers/consumer-protection/green-consumption-pledge-initiative_en>.

[261] See *supra*, n° 14.

[262] See *supra*, n° 51–53.

binding, they are intertwined with the binding UN treaties on climate change[263], and thus provide a stepping stone for the EU and its Member States to develop new policies related to sustainable consumption and production, including policies aimed at curbing planned obsolescence.[264] Indeed, since planned obsolescence contributes to increasing resource consumption, waste and pollution, it contradicts the goals of sustainable development and is thus part of the issue that should be solved to reach these goals.[265] In addition to the concept of sustainable development, the transition towards a circular economy has been seen as a panacea for sustainability issues, including planned obsolescence.[266] Accordingly, the circular economy would allow tackling the accelerating obsolescence of products by lengthening product lifetime and by looping products and their materials back into the system to be reused or recovered.[267] The fight against planned obsolescence is therefore part of the longer-term project of shifting towards a circular economy. The EU and its Member States have been actively engaged in the promotion of a more sustainable economy. Their commitment and willingness to shift towards a more sustainable and circular economy have led to major legal developments and proposals on the topic of planned obsolescence, as described in the following paragraphs.

a) *Emergence of the concept at EU level*

65. First reference to planned obsolescence by the EESC – The European Economic and Social Committee (EESC) was the first EU institution to issue an opinion on product lifetimes and consumer information to combat planned obsolescence.[268] In its 2013 opinion, the EESC distinguished 'planned obsolescence', defined as "*designing a product to have a shorter life, if necessary by designing it to run only for a limited number of operations*"[269], from other types of obsolescence, namely 'indirect', 'incompatibility' and 'style' obsolescence.[270] On the basis of this distinction, the EESC called for a total ban on products with

---

263 See UN Kyoto Protocol 2005, available on: <https://unfccc.int/resource/docs/convkp/kpeng.pdf>; UN Paris Agreement 2015, available on: <https://unfccc.int/sites/default/files/english_paris_agreement.pdf>.

264 For concrete examples of innovative policies adopted in Europe to promote sustainable consumption, see G. Scholl, F. Rubik, H. Kalimo, K. Biedenkopf, Ó. Söebech, 'Policies to promote sustainable consumption: innovative approaches in Europe', 34 *Natural Resources Forum* (2010) p. 39 at p. 50.

265 R. Kurz, 'Quality, obsolescence and unsustainable innovation', 28 *Ekonomski vjesnik* (2015) p. 515.

266 For further comments on the circular economy policy at EU level, see S. Eisenriegler (ed.), *The Circular Economy in the European Union – An Interim Review* (Springer 2020).

267 See *infra* on the strategies against premature obsolescence (n° 141 *et seq.*).

268 Opinion of the EESC of 17 October 2013 on Towards more sustainable consumption: industrial product lifetimes and restoring trust through consumer information, CCMI/112.

269 *Ibid.*, p. 4, pt. 2.4.

270 *Ibid.*, pp. 4–5.

built-in defects deliberately designed to end product lifetime and required the EU to curb the most flagrant cases of planned obsolescence, referring to printers with prematurely limited lifetime as an illustrative example.[271] An emphasis was also laid on the absence of a definitive consensus between the various definitions of planned obsolescence and on the need to find an overarching one.[272]

66. The broad definition of planned obsolescence given by BEUC – The publication of the EESC opinion was followed in 2015 by a policy paper written by the European consumer organisation BEUC.[273] In this paper, 'planned obsolescence' was defined as "*a wide range of techniques that certain manufacturers might use to shorten the functional lifespan of products and force consumers to make premature replacements in order to continue selling in saturated markets*".[274] While BEUC asserted the existence of deliberate acts to limit product lifetime, it stressed the sometimes heavy burden of proof accompanying these cases. In addition to those blatant cases, BEUC reported that "*certain manufacturers seem to knowingly accept that their poor quality products fail early as this saves them in production costs*".[275] In the non-exhaustive list of these other cases of planned obsolescence, BEUC included design features that do not allow repair, upgradeability and interoperability with other devices; programmed failure of a device after limited usage; unavailability of spare parts and high costs of repair; marketing strategies that suggest to consumers that in order to stay trendy they should buy new products and replace existing ones very quickly even though the 'old' ones are still fully functional.[276] To illustrate its definition, BEUC made reference to smartphones which, in its words, is "*[a]n area of special concern related to short lasting electronic devices*".[277]

67. An initial focus on planned obsolescence sensu stricto – In 2015, when the legislation on planned obsolescence was under debate at the French Parliament[278], the European Parliament (EP) urged the EC to develop measures against planned obsolescence.[279] Shortly after, the EC considered, for the first time, practices of 'planned obsolescence' in its Action Plan 'Closing the loop'.[280]

271 *Ibid.*, p. 1, pt. 1.2.
272 *Ibid.*, p. 5, pt. 2.5.
273 BEUC Policy Paper of 18 August 2015 on Durable goods: More sustainable products, better consumer rights, BEUC-X-2015-069.
274 *Ibid.*, p. 4.
275 *Ibid.*, p. 4.
276 *Ibid.*, p. 4.
277 *Ibid.*, p. 5.
278 See *infra*, n° 70 *et seq.*
279 European Parliament Resolution of 9 July 2015 on resource efficiency: moving towards a circular economy, (2014/2208(INI)), pt. 26.
280 Communication from the Commission of 2 December 2015 to the European Parliament, the Council, the European Economic and Social Committee and the Committee of the Regions on Closing the loop – EU action plan for circular economy, COM(2015) 614 final, p. 7.

In this plan, the EC requested to *'prepare an independent testing programme under Horizon 2020 to help the identification of issues related to possible planned obsolescence'*.[281] This gave birth to the PROMPT project, which stands for 'Premature Obsolescence multi-stakeholder product testing programme'.[282] In 2016, the EC followed up and introduced a new section specifically dedicated to 'planned obsolescence' in the updated version of the UCPD Guidance. In this document, this notion was defined as *"a commercial policy involving deliberately planning or designing a product with a limited useful life so that it will become obsolete or non-functional after a certain period of time"*.[283] Hence, at the outset, EU institutions confined the problem to planned obsolescence *sensu stricto*.

68. Followed by a broadened focus on premature obsolescence – The focus was further broadened to cover the other types of premature obsolescence than planned obsolescence, as perfectly illustrated by the ongoing PROMPT project.[284] With the involvement of many stakeholders[285], this project aims to develop an integral testing programme for electric and electronic consumer products that takes into account the main issues of product failures and premature obsolescence, i.e. product durability, reliability, adaptability, upgradability and reparability, user behaviour and market. This programme could then enable testing bodies, consumer organisations or product designers to identify the various cases of 'premature obsolescence' through the assessment of product characteristics. The outcomes of the testing programme could also lead to more standardisation requests. Meanwhile, PROMPT has already issued some results from their research on premature obsolescence in several papers.[286]

---

281 *Ibid.*, p. 8.

282 European Commission Decision of 27 October 2017 on Horizon 2020 – Work Programme 2018 – 2020, C(2017)7124, p. 28. For further information, see *infra*, n° 68.

283 European Commission Guidance from 25 May 2016 on the Implementation/Application of Directive 2005/29/EC on Unfair Commercial Practices, SWD(2016) 163 final, pp. 82–83.

284 For updated information on the PROMPT project, see <https://cordis.europa.eu/project/id/820331>.

285 The consortium comprises different consumer, test, repair and research organisations, including *Test-Achats* (Belgium), *iFixit* (Germany), *Union fédérale des consommateurs* (France) and *Stiftung Warentest* (Germany). For the full list of participants, see <https://cordis.europa.eu/project/id/820331>.

286 See for ex. R. van den Berge, T. Thysen, *State-of-the-art knowledge on user, market and legal issues related to premature obsolescence* (PROMPT 2020); T. Dobs, D. Sánchez, K. Schischke, O. Wittler, M. Schneider-Ramelow, 'Assessment of the influencing parameters of the tumble test for robustness testing of smartphones', in *Electronics Goes Green 2020+ – Conference Proceedings* (Fraunhofer IZM 2020) p. 515 at p. 520; S. Dangal, R. van den Berge, B. Pozo Arcos, J. Faludi, R. Balkenende, 'Perceived Capabilities and Barriers for Do-It-Yourself Repair', in C. Fitzpatrick et al. (eds.), *4th international Product Lifetimes and the Environment (PLATE) conference proceedings* (Limerick 2021) p. 132 at p. 137; T. Thysen, A. Berwald, 'Consumers' experiences with premature obsolescence – Insights from seven EU countries', in C. Fitzpatrick et al. (eds.), *4th international Product Lifetimes and the Environment (PLATE) conference proceedings* (Limerick 2021) p. 614 at p. 619. For the complete list of

69. Omnipresence of the concept in the EU political agenda – The issue of product obsolescence is now high on the agenda and is omnipresent in EC documents. Under the Juncker Commission, the New Deal for Consumers from April 2018 complemented the Circular Economy Package in the field of sustainable consumption, with an emphasis on better enforcement of rules, effective tools for redress, and better consumer knowledge of their rights, including against practices of planned obsolescence.[287] In its 2019 European Green Deal, the Von der Leyen Commission announced that it would analyse measures to curb the built-in obsolescence of devices, in particular for electronics.[288] As a result, four ambitious legislative proposals are now on the table (i.e. the legislative proposals on 'Empowering consumers for the green transition',[289] on 'Sustainable Products',[290] on 'Substantiating green claims'[291] and on 'Promoting the repair of goods'[292]). In the new Circular Economy Package from March 2020, the EC used the broader notion of 'premature obsolescence' and suggested measures to encourage businesses to offer, and allow consumers to choose, reusable, durable and repairable products, as well as measures to promote reliable, comparable and verifiable information.[293] The EC confirmed its commitment to fighting 'early obsolescence'[294] in its more recent

papers issued within the framework of the PROMPT project, see <https://prompt-project.eu/results/research-on-premature-obsolescence/>.

287 Communication from the Commission to the European Parliament, the Council and the European Economic and Social Committee on A New Deal for Consumers, COM(2018) 183 final, p. 15.

288 Communication from the Commission of 11 December 2019 to the European Parliament, the European Council, the Council, the European Economic and Social Committee and the Committee of the Regions on The European Green Deal, COM(2019) 640 final, p. 8.

289 Proposal for a Directive of the European Parliament and of the Council amending Directives 2005/29/EC and 2011/83/EU as regards empowering consumers for the green transition through better protection against unfair practices and better information, COM(2022) 143 final.

290 Proposal for a Regulation of the European Parliament and of the Council establishing a framework for setting ecodesign requirements for sustainable products and repealing Directive 2009/125/EC, COM(2022) 142 final.

291 Proposal for a Directive of the European Parliament and of the Council on substantiation and communication of explicit environmental claims (Green Claims Directive), COM(2023) 166 final.

292 Proposal for a Directive of the European Parliament and of the Council on common rules promoting the repair of goods and amending Regulation (EU) 2017/2394, Directives (EU) 2019/771 and (EU) 2020/1828, COM(2023) 155 final.

293 Communication from the Commission of 11 March 2020 to the European Parliament, the Council, the European Economic and Social Committee and the Committee of the Regions on A new Circular Economy Action Plan – For a cleaner and more competitive Europe, COM(2020) 98 final, pp. 4–5.

294 'Early obsolescence' is defined as the situation where *"a product cannot be used for the expected purpose and break earlier than expected"*. See Communication from the Commission of 13 November 2020 to the European Parliament and the Council and the Council on New Consumer Agenda – Strengthening consumer resilience for sustainable recovery, COM(2020) 696 final, p. 5.

Consumer Agenda from November 2020.[295] The UCPD Guidance, including its section on 'planned obsolescence', was also amended in December 2021.[296] Besides EC documents, the topic remains of ongoing interest for other EU actors. In its most recent Resolution from November 2020, the EP called on the EC to tackle practices of premature obsolescence *"which effectively shorten the lifetime of a product to increase its replacement rate and unduly constrain the reparability of products, including software"*.[297] Along the same line, BEUC recommended *"banning specific practices that could lead to early product failures, limit the possibility of repair or mislead consumers about product durability"*.[298]

b) Emergence of the concept at national level

(1) French legislation on 'planned obsolescence'

70. Planned obsolescence considered as a criminal offence – With the adoption of the 2014 Energy Transition for Green Growth Act[299], France became the first country worldwide to legally define and outlaw practices of 'planned obsolescence' (*obsolescence programmée*).[300] Article L. 441-2 of the French Consumer Code, which was introduced by this Act and subsequently amended in 2021[301], defines 'planned obsolescence' as *"the set of techniques, including software-related ones, by which the person responsible for placing the product on the market seeks to deliberately reduce the lifetime of this product"*.[302]

---

295 Communication from the Commission of 13 November 2020 to the European Parliament and the Council and the Council on New Consumer Agenda – Strengthening consumer resilience for sustainable recovery, COM(2020) 696 final, p. 9.

296 See the Commission Notice of 17 December 2021 on Guidance on the interpretation and application of Directive 2005/29/EC of the European Parliament and of the Council concerning unfair business-to-consumer commercial practices in the internal market, OJ C 526, 29.12.2021, p. 1–129, and more specifically p. 104 at p. 107.

297 European Parliament Resolution of 25 November 2020 on Towards a more sustainable single market for business and consumers, 2020/2021(INI), pt. 6 *et seq.*

298 BEUC Policy Paper of 28 June 2021 on Durable and repairable products – Changes needed for a successful path towards the green transition, BEUC-X-2021-061, p. 21.

299 Loi n° 2015-992 du 17 août 2015 relative à la transition énergétique pour la croissance verte, JORF n°0189 du 18 août 2015, p. 14263 (hereafter 'Energy Transition Act').

300 It is noteworthy that legislative proposals aiming to curb planned obsolescence had already been put on the table before the adoption of the Energy Transition Act, with other definitions and sanctions. See Proposition de loi n°429 visant à lutter contre l'obsolescence programmée et à augmenter la durée de vie des produits, déposée au Sénat le 18 mars 2013; Proposition de loi n°2314 visant à lutter contre l'obsolescence programmée, déposée à l'Assemblée Nationale le 22 octobre 2014.

301 Art. 5 and 6 of the Law on the Environmental Footprint of Digital Technology. This Law removed the last part of the definition, which required the aim of stimulating product replacement, and added a reference to software-related techniques.

302 Article L. 441-2 of the French Consumer Code: *"Est interdite la pratique de l'obsolescence programmée qui se définit par le recours à des techniques, y compris logicielles, par lesquelles le responsable de la mise sur le marché d'un produit vise à en réduire délibérément la durée de vie"*. (free translation).

If someone is caught pursuing such a strategy, they could be held guilty of a criminal offence, with up to two years imprisonment and a € 300,000 fine or up to 5% of the average annual turnover.[303] The Energy Transition Act was adopted as part of the French Waste Prevention Programme 2014–2020[304], which was required by Article 29 of the Directive 2008/98/EC and supported by Articles 4 and 22 of the Directive 2012/19/EU. In this Waste Prevention Programme, the fight against planned obsolescence was described as indispensable to prevent waste and foster the shift towards a green and circular economy. The lack of a commonly shared definition of this complex and multifaceted phenomenon had been pointed out.[305]

71. Origins and evolution of the definition – The definition contained in Article L. 441-2 of the French Consumer Code is the result of a compromise reached by the two Chambers of the French Parliament, the National Assembly and the Senate, after months of intense discussions.[306] The 2012 study commissioned by the French Environmental Agency ADEME (*Agence de la transition écologique*) gave a major impulse to the adoption of Article L. 441-2 and served as a basis for the definition.[307] In this study, 'planned obsolescence' (*obsolescence programmée*) is defined as "*a stratagem by which the normative lifetime of a good would be intentionally reduced since its conception, thus limiting its period of use for reasons of economic model*".[308] The normative lifetime of a product corresponds to the average lifetime of a product as measured in

303 Art. L. 454-6 §1-2 of the French Consumer Code.

304 See Ministère de l'Écologie, du Développement durable et de l'Énergie, *Programme national de prévention des déchets 2014-2020* (République Française 2014).

305 See Ministère de l'Écologie, du Développement durable et de l'Énergie, *Programme national de prévention des déchets 2014-2020* (République Française 2014) p. 38.

306 See also E. Maitre-Ekern and C. Dalhammar,'Regulating planned obsolescence: a review of legal approaches to increase product durability and reparability in Europe', 25 *Review of European Community & International Environmental Law* (2016) p. 387.

307 S. Mugdal et al., *Etude sur la durée de vie des équipements électriques et électroniques* (ADEME 2012). See also the following ADEME studies on product lifetime and obsolescence: E. Fangeat, C. Chauvin, *Allongement de la durée de vie des produits* (ADEME 2016); D. Kreziak, I. Prim-Allaz and E. Robinot, *Des tiroirs pleins de téléphones remplacés: consommateurs et objets à obsolescence perçue* (ADEME 2017), as well as practical guides for consumers on how to adopt an eco-friendly behaviour and how to prolong product lifetime: ADEME, *Garanties, réparations, réutilisation... Comment faire durer ses objets?* (2019), available on: <https://www.ademe.fr/sites/default/files/assets/documents/fiche-comment-faire-durer-ses-objets.pdf>; ADEME, *Consommer responsable – Les bons réflexes, de l'achat à la fin de vie des produits* (2019), available on: <https://www.ademe.fr/sites/default/files/assets/documents/guide-pratique-consommer-responsable.pdf>.

308 S. Mugdal et al., *Etude sur la durée de vie des équipements électriques et électroniques* (ADEME 2012) p. 15: "*La notion d' "obsolescence programmée" dénonce un stratagème par lequel un bien verrait sa durée normative sciemment réduite dès sa conception, limitant ainsi sa durée d'usage pour des raisons de modèles économiques.*" (free translation).

specific test conditions or as standardized.[309] Moreover, 'planned obsolescence' is described as one type of obsolescence among others, emphasizing that the obsolescence of products is not always planned.[310] The 2017 report issued by the French Government confirms this initial reasoning, stating that the notion of 'planned obsolescence' must be distinguished from other cases of obsolescence that do not depend on producers' decisions and actions, but are rather due to current production and consumption models.[311] These latter cases include 'functional obsolescence' (*obsolescence fonctionnelle*), whereby a product no longer meets the new expected uses, for technical (e.g. incompatibility with new equipment), regulatory and/or economic reasons. Obsolescence can also originate from product developments (*obsolescence d'évolution*), which is caused by consumers' changing needs and desires following developments in product design and functionality. Finally, products can be obsolete due to an accident, improper use, or because they are (almost) impossible to repair.

72. Emerging case law on planned obsolescence – Since its adoption, three claims have been brought on the basis of Article L. 441-2 of the French Consumer Code. In 2017, the consumer association *HOP* asserted that printer manufacturers (including *Epson*)[312], as well as *Apple*[313], had adopted practices of planned obsolescence. Against *Epson*, the association put forward two techniques arguably used to shorten the lifetime of its printers or the related ink cartridges. *Epson* would make its machines prematurely stop printing by falsely claiming (1) that ink cartridges are empty or (2) that the printer absorber pad is full. Pointing out the design and the high repair and purchase costs of printers and cartridges[314], HOP accused *Epson* of materially and economically planning the obsolescence of its products and suspected a cartel agreement with other printer manufacturers.[315] Against *Apple*, HOP alleged that the firm strongly encouraged its customers to update their smartphones with the operating system IOS 11.2, which would reduce the smartphone performance. The slowdowns

309 See S. Mugdal et al., *Etude sur la durée de vie des équipements électriques et électroniques* (ADEME 2012) p. 11.

310 S. Mugdal et al., *Etude sur la durée de vie des équipements électriques et électroniques* (ADEME 2012), pp. 14–15.

311 Rapport du Gouvernement au Parlement sur l'obsolescence programmée, sa définition juridique et ses enjeux économiques, en application de l'article 8 de la loi du 17 mars 2014 relative à la consommation, avril 2017, pp. 10–11.

312 Tribunal de grande instance de Nanterre 17 September 2017, Plainte au Procureur de la République, *HOP v. X*. In its claim, the association explains that its investigation focused on Epson due to a lack of staff and financial means, although it alleges that the identified practices of planned obsolescence might be followed by other printer manufacturers.

313 Tribunal de grande instance de Paris 27 décembre 2017, Plainte au Procureur de la République, *HOP v. Apple France*.

314 Tribunal de grande instance de Nanterre 17 septembre 2017, Plainte au Procureur de la République, *HOP v. X*, p. 2 at p. 5.

315 Tribunal de grande instance de Nanterre 17 septembre 2017, Plainte au Procureur de la République, *HOP v. X*, p. 14.

caused by these updates would hamper the normal use of smartphones and force consumers to buy new ones. Consumer purchasing decisions would then be blocked by intensive marketing and Apple's own data transfer system. This second case involved software, technical and stylistic obsolescence.[316] Whereas the *Epson* case is still in the preliminary investigation phase (carried out by the DGCCRF), Apple settled with the French authorities for over 25 million euros.[317] In addition to these two claims, the consumer association *UFC-Que choisir* lodged a complaint against *Nintendo* with the Public Prosecutor of the Republic for Nanterre.[318] *Nintendo* was accused of making its joysticks prematurely obsolete. A call has been launched to consumers who encountered problems with those products.[319] Legal proceedings will only be instituted if investigations are successful. If suspicions are confirmed, the court may issue an injunction against the companies requiring them to pay a fine and stop their forbidden behaviour. If, on the contrary, it is proven that the companies did not follow such strategies, they would be cleared and serve as an example.

(2) Belgian legislative proposals related to planned obsolescence

73. Belgium as a pioneer – Belgium is considered a pioneer in the fight against planned obsolescence with the adoption of the 2012 Senate Resolution on the topic.[320] In the explanatory memorandum of this Resolution, 'planned obsolescence' was defined as "*developing and marketing a product while determining in advance when it will expire*".[321] In 2016, measures against planned

---

316 Tribunal de grande instance de Paris 27 décembre 2017, Plainte au Procureur de la République, *HOP v. Apple France*, p. 6.

317 See the settlement (*transaction pénale*) agreed by French public prosecutor, DGCCRF and Apple, communicated on 7 February 2020, available on: <economie.gouv.fr/dgccrf/transaction-avec-le-groupe-apple-pour-pratique-commerciale-trompeuse>. In the field of criminal procedural law, a settlement is an alternative to prosecution. The public prosecutor may, in certain cases, propose to the alleged offender to pay a sum of money defined by him. If he accepts, the alleged offender will not be prosecuted. If he refuses or fails to comply with the penal transaction, the public prosecutor may prosecute him before the criminal courts. For certain offences, the DGCCRF can propose to the public prosecutor the implementation of a penal transaction. For further explanation, see DGCCRF, *Les contrôles de la DGCCRF – Pouvoirs d'enquête et de sanction* (2021) p. 28, available on: <https://www.economie.gouv.fr/files/2021-05/controles-dgccrf-pouvoirs-enquete-sanction.pdf>.

318 Tribunal de grande instance de Nanterre 22 Septembre 2020, Plainte au Procureur de la République, *UFC-Que choisir v. Nintendo*.

319 See the press release issued by the association UFC-Que choisir, 'Nintendo Switch – L'UFC-Que Choisir dénonce l'obsolescence programmée des manettes Joy-Con', 22 September 2020, available on: <https://www.quechoisir.org/nos-combats-switch-nintendo-l-ufc-que-choisir-denonce-l-obsolescence-programmee-des-manettes-joy-cons-n72823/>.

320 Proposition de résolution en vue de lutter contre l'obsolescence programmée des produits liés à l'énergie, *Doc. lég.*, Sénat, 2011–2012, 1er février 2012, n° 5 – 1251/4.

321 Explanatory memorandum to Proposition de résolution en vue de lutter contre l'obsolescence programmée des produits liés à l'énergie, *Doc. lég.*, Sénat, 2010–2011, 7 octobre 2011, n° 5 – 1251/1, p. 1.

obsolescence were put forward in the Belgian Circular Economy Action Plan.[322] This policy action plan was shortly followed by a study on the topic of planned obsolescence commissioned by the Belgian government in 2017.[323] This study outlined a series of measures against planned obsolescence to be taken at EU and national levels and analysed the feasibility and impacts of these measures.

74. A WIDE ARRAY OF LEGISLATIVE PROPOSALS – A multitude of legislative proposals has been tabled since 2012, all suggesting amendments to the existing legislation with the view of curbing premature obsolescence and shifting towards a circular economy. Three former proposals date back to the period immediately after the adoption of the 2012 Resolution on planned obsolescence.[324] These first proposals mostly focused on blatant cases of planned obsolescence, whereby the producer artificially reduced the product lifetime, referring to the Phoebus cartel as an illustrative example in their explanatory memorandum.[325] Interestingly, one of the proposals excluded practices from the definition of 'planned obsolescence' if countervailing benefits exist for consumers (e.g. a significantly lower price compared to a long-lasting product).[326] Shortly afterwards, three other proposals were issued after the adoption of the French legislation on planned obsolescence but were also not adopted.[327] In these legislative proposals, the influence of French law was conspicuous. They all put forward different types of measures to prevent and combat planned obsolescence, including a clear

322 K. Peeters and M.C. Marghem, *Ensemble, faisons tourner l'économie en développant l'économie circulaire en Belgique* (Cabinet de l'Énergie, de l'Environnement et du Développement durable 2016) p. 34, and more specifically measures 10 and 11.

323 RDC Environment, *L'obsolescence programmée: politiques et mesures belges de protection du consommateur* (2017).

324 Proposition de loi modifiant la loi du 6 avril 2010 relative aux pratiques du marché et à la protection du consommateur, concernant l'information des consommateurs en matière d'obsolescence de biens de consommation *Doc. parl.*, Ch., 2011–2012, 14 février 2012, n° 2060/001; Proposition de loi modifiant la loi du 9 février 1994 relative à la sécurité des produits et des services, visant la prévention de l'obsolescence, *Doc. parl.*, Ch., 2011–2012, 14 février 2012, n° 2061/001; Proposition de loi modifiant l'article 1649*quater*, §4, du Code civil, relatif à la protection des consommateurs en cas de vente de biens de consommation en ce qui concerne le défaut de conformité, *Doc. parl.*, Sénat, 2011–2012, 12 juin 2012, n° 1665/1.

325 See the explanatory memorandum to Proposition de loi modifiant la loi du 6 avril 2010 relative aux pratiques du marché et à la protection du consommateur, concernant l'information des consommateurs en matière d'obsolescence de biens de consommation *Doc. parl.*, Ch., 2011–2012, 14 février 2012, n° 2060/001, p. 3, and to Proposition de loi modifiant la loi du 9 février 1994 relative à la sécurité des produits et des services, visant la prévention de l'obsolescence, *Doc. parl.*, Ch., 2011–2012, 14 février 2012, n° 2061/001, p. 4.

326 See the explanatory memorandum to Proposition de loi modifiant la loi du 9 février 1994 relative à la sécurité des produits et des services, visant la prévention de l'obsolescence, *Doc. parl.*, Ch., 2011–2012, 14 février 2012, n° 2061/001, p. 8.

327 Proposition de loi modifiant le Code civil et le Code de droit économique, visant à lutter contre l'obsolescence programmée, *Doc. parl.*, Ch., 2015–2016, 22 janvier 2016, n° 1603/001; Proposition de loi relative à la lutte contre l'obsolescence organisée et au soutien à l'économie circulaire, *Doc. parl.*, Ch., 2015–2016, 11 avril 2016, n° 1749/001; Proposition de loi relative à l'obsolescence programmée, *Doc. parl.*, Ch., 2015–2016, 20 avril 2016, n° 1783/001.

prohibition of it by the introduction of a definition in the Economic Law Code, with the support of sanctions.[328] Two of these proposals copied almost verbatim the French legal definition.[329]

75. THREE LEGISLATIVE PROPOSALS STILL PENDING – Today, three legislative proposals related to the topic are pending before the Belgian Parliament.[330] Striking similarities to French law can be observed in some provisions of these proposals, sometimes differing only in their wording and the sanctions attached to the breach of law. These legislative proposals tie in with the Resolution on circular economy issued in March 2018 by one of the chambers of the Belgian Parliament (*Chambre des représentants*).[331] In this Resolution, the Belgian Federal Government was asked to take clear, coherent and effective measures to promote a circular economy and fight against blatant cases of planned obsolescence, including measures that oblige the availability of spare parts for a minimum period of time at reasonable costs, better information for consumers on product lifetime and possibilities of repairing the product, and which ensure the proper enforcement of the legal guarantee. This Resolution confirms the first request of the Chamber made in 2012.[332] Since then, the importance of the transition towards a circular economy and the fight against premature obsolescence in Belgian policies has been reiterated.[333]

(3) German initiatives against planned obsolescence

76. NO SPECIFIC GERMAN LEGISLATION ON PLANNED OBSOLESCENCE – The topic of planned obsolescence has also been given considerable attention

---

328 Sanctions were either from the Civil Code (nullity of the contract and full reimbursement) or the Criminal Code (from € 500 to 100,000 fine and from one to five years of imprisonment).

329 See Art. 3 of the Proposition de loi modifiant le Code civil et le Code de droit économique, visant à lutter contre l'obsolescence programmée, *Doc. parl.*, Ch., 2015–2016, 22 janvier 2016, n° 1603/001; Art. 3 of the Proposition de loi relative à l'obsolescence programmée, *Doc. parl.*, Ch., 2015–2016, 20 avril 2016, n° 1783/001.

330 Proposition de loi visant à lutter contre l'obsolescence programmée et à soutenir l'économie de la réparation, *Doc. parl.*, Ch., 2019, 19 juillet 2019, n° 0193/001; Proposition de loi modifiant le Code civil et le Code de droit économique, visant à lutter contre l'obsolescence programmée et l'obsolescence prématurée et à augmenter les possibilités de réparation, *Doc. parl.*, Ch., 2019–2020, 19 novembre 2019, n° 0771/001; Proposition de loi visant à lutter contre l'obsolescence organisée et à soutenir l'économie circulaire, *Doc. parl.*, Ch., 2019–2020, 7 janvier 2020, n° 0914/001.

331 Proposition de résolution visant le développement de l'économie circulaire et la lutte contre l'obsolescence programmée, *Doc. lég.*, Ch., 2017–2018, 11 janvier 2018, n° 2884/001.

332 Proposition de résolution en vue de lutter contre l'obsolescence programmée des produits liés à l'énergie, *Doc. lég.*, Sénat, 2011–2012, 1er février 2012, n° 5 – 1251/4.

333 See P.-Y. Dermagne, Note de Politique Générale – Economie, Ch., 2021–2022, 29 octobre 2021, n° 2294/005. See also P.-Y. Dermagne, Z. Khattabi, *Plan d'action fédéral pour une économie circulaire 2021–2024* (SPF Economie et SPF Santé publique, sécurité de la chaine alimentaire et environnement 2021).

in Germany. Like in Belgium, several legislative proposals against planned obsolescence were submitted over the past few years.[334] Although finally rejected, they were characteristic examples of legislation promoting a longer product lifetime.[335]

77. But an active engagement in the promotion of sustainable consumption – In spite of this absence of specific legislation on the topic, Germany is particularly engaged in the promotion of sustainable consumption. This engagement is reflected in the German Programme for Sustainable Consumption, which was drawn up by the Federal Ministry for the Environment, Nature Conservation, Building and Nuclear Safety (*Bundesministerium für Umwelt, Naturschutz, Bau und Reaktorsicherheit* or *BMUB*) and adopted by the Federal Cabinet in 2016.[336] This programme aims to strengthen successful existing instruments and approaches and launch new projects (such as measures to counter obsolescence). In parallel, there is the German Resource Efficiency Program, which was initially adopted in 2012[337], and which must be updated every four years, together with a report submitted by the German government

334 Antrag vom 17.04.2013 zum Ressourcenschutz durch Vorgabe einer Mindestnutzungsdauer für technische Produkte, BT-Drucks. 17/13096; Antrag vom 12.06.2013 zum Geplanten Verschleiß stoppen und die Langlebigkeit von Produkten sichern, BT-Drucks. 17/13917; Antrag vom 14.07.2016 zum Längere Lebensdauer für technische Geräte, BT-Drucks. 18/9179; Antrag vom 09.01.2020 'Elektroschrott – Wertstoffkreisläufe schließen', BT-Drucks. 19/16412; Antrag vom 09.01.2020 'Elektroschrott reduzieren – Recht auf Reparatur', BT-Drucks. 19/16419; Antrag vom 13.04.2021 'Elektro– und Elektronikgeräte effizienter nutzen – Langlebigkeit, Reparatur, Sammlung und Recycling verbessern', BT-Drucks. 19/28429; Antrag vom 05.04.2022 'Rohstoffversorgung sicherer machen – Stoffkreisläufe schließen', BT-Drucks. 20/1338.

335 The first proposal (Antrag BT-Drucks. 17/13096) was consumer-focused. Among the proposed measures, it prescribed the prohibition of intentional built-in obsolescence. Referring to the case of printers with the smart chip, this proposal aimed to put an end to any "*technically unjustifiable predetermined breaking points and artificially induced – planned – functional losses*". The explanatory memorandum of this proposal also raised the issue of Apple-iPads with prematurely defective batteries, which cannot be replaced without considerable costs. The second proposal (Antrag BT-Drucks. 17/13917) was mainly intended to improve product requirements (e.g. extension of ecodesign requirements, improvement of product reparability, collection, reuse and recycling). This second proposal also insisted on examining the possibilities given by EU legislation to curb product obsolescence and strengthening these rules. The third proposal (BT-Drucks. 18/9179) had a similar content to the previous proposals and was followed by a recommendation of the German Committee for the Environment, Nature Conservation, Building and Nuclear Safety. See Beschlussempfehlung und Bericht des Ausschusses für Umwelt, Naturschutz, Bau und Reaktorsicherheit vom 14.12.2016, 18/10666. In 2020, 2021 and 2022, four other legislative proposals dedicated to WEEE and the right to repair were also rejected (see Antrag BT-Drucks. 19/16412; Antrag BT-Drucks. 19/16419; Antrag BT-Drucks. 19/28429; Antrag BT-Drucks. 20/1338).

336 BMUB, *Nationales Programm für nachhaltigen Konsum – Gesellschaftlicher Wandel durch einen nachhaltigen Lebensstil* (2019).

337 See <https://www.bmu.de/themen/wasser-ressourcen-abfall/ressourceneffizienz/deutsches-ressourceneffizienzprogramm>.

to the Bundestag on developments in resource efficiency.[338] In addition to these policy actions, the German Environmental Agency (*Umweltbundesamt* or *UBA*) issued several studies that encourage German and EU law makers to take actions against the premature obsolescence of products.[339] In its study from 2016, the *Umweltbundesamt* draws a distinction between material, functional, economic and psychological obsolescence.[340]

5. CRITICISM OF THE CONCEPT OF PLANNED OBSOLESCENCE

a) *The definition of planned obsolescence*

78. Lack of consensus – The previous parts of this section revealed that a wide array of notions has been used to define the phenomenon relating to the rapid obsolescence of products, let alone the variants in other languages. There are not only different understandings of the phenomenon, but also different terms associated with it. Even when strictly focusing on the concept of 'planned obsolescence', which is the most commonly used term in the literature and public debates, it can be observed that the same notion can mean different things to different people and is fraught with diverse normative, ideological and political implications. This lack of consensus makes it necessary, for the sake of clarity, to provide a definition of the concept.

79. Definition of planned obsolescence – According to the dictionary, the word 'planned' means "*designed, projected, or arranged in accordance with a plan; that is the result of a plan or planning*".[341] As a result, 'planned obsolescence' refers to cases whereby the obsolescence of the product is purposely planned or at least desired, as reflected in the various definitions of 'planned obsolescence'

338 BMUB, *German Resource Efficiency Programme II – Programme for the sustainable use and conservation of natural resources* (2016); BMUB, *Deutsches Ressourceneffizienzprogramm III 2020 – 2023 – Programm zur nachhaltigen Nutzung und zum Schutz der natürlichen Ressourcen* (2020), available on: <https://www.bmu.de/download/deutsches-ressourcen effizienzprogramm-progress-iii>.

339 See S. Schlacke, K. Tonner, E. Gawel, *Stärkung eines nachhaltigen Konsums im Bereich Produktnutzung durch Anpassungen im Zivil- und öffentlichen Recht* (Umweltbundesamt Study 2015); S. Prakash et al., *Einfluss der Nutzungsdauer von Produkten auf ihre Umweltwirkung – Schaffung einer Informationsgrundlage und Entwicklung von Strategien gegen "Obsoleszenz"* (Umweltbundesamt Study 2016); F. Keimeyer et al., *Weiterentwicklung von Strategien gegen Obsoleszenz einschließlich rechtlicher Instrumente – Abschlussbericht* (Umweltbundesamt 2020).

340 S. Prakash et al., *Einfluss der Nutzungsdauer von Produkten auf ihre Umweltwirkung – Schaffung einer Informationsgrundlage und Entwicklung von Strategien gegen "Obsoleszenz"* (Umweltbundesamt Study 2016).

341 Oxford English Dictionary 2006 (3rd edition).

given by the literature. In this book, 'planned obsolescence' is defined as a business strategy by which the lifetime of products is deliberately shortened, in order to increase their replacement rate. Although planned obsolescence is often conceptualised too narrowly as being confined to cases of material and functional obsolescence, practices of planned obsolescence can be of various types, including indirect, economic and psychological obsolescence.[342]

> *Key definition*
>
> 'Planned obsolescence' means a business strategy by which the lifetime of products is deliberately shortened, in order to increase their replacement rate.

b) A biased and restrictive concept

80. A CONTROVERSIAL CONCEPT THAT SHOULD NOT BE THE EXCLUSIVE FOCUS – As mentioned throughout the previous parts of this section, the concept of planned obsolescence has been increasingly dogged by controversy over the past few years. Criticisms came not only from the business side[343], but also from the academic sector[344], as well as policymakers.[345] These criticisms are to be considered valid. Of course, the influence of manufacturers, product designers, sellers and retailers on product lifetime should not be denied. Practices linked to design, advertising, fashion, and technological change can indeed have a significant impact on the early obsolescence of products. Certain producers and sellers might even apply strategies and techniques of obsolescence for the purpose of shortening the period of use of products and thus making end-users replace old products with new ones faster than they would ordinarily do.[346] However, in the light of the more comprehensive and nuanced description of the phenomenon given by the recent literature, the problem should not be reduced to cases of planned obsolescence. In this regard, the concept of planned obsolescence can be challenged for being (1) biased and (2) restrictive.

81. BIASED CONCEPT OF PLANNED OBSOLESCENCE – The concept of planned obsolescence can, first, be criticised as being biased. Through the lens of the media and the man in the street, planned obsolescence constitutes the cause and the symbol of today's overconsumption and excessive production of short-lived and disposable items.[347] This radical view points towards producers and

342 For a detailed description of the different types of obsolescence, see n° 98 *et seq.*
343 See *supra*, n° 62–63.
344 See *supra*, n° 56–57.
345 See *supra*, n° 64.
346 See also S. Wrbka, 'Warranty Law in cases of planned obsolescence – The Austrian situation', 6 *EuCML* (2017) p. 67.
347 See *supra*, n° 59–60.

designers as the instigators of product obsolescence, with a predominant focus on material and functional obsolescence. However, the criticisms levelled by the industry sector and echoed by several scholars with regard to 'planned obsolescence' show how vehement the discussions about the existence of such practices can be.

82. THE (QUESTIONABLE) ACT OF PLANNING – Besides the lack of concrete evidence of producers' intent[348], certain aspects relating to the planning of product obsolescence are controversial. First and foremost, the word 'plan' appears inappropriate as in some cases, planning product obsolescence is aimed to delay obsolescence and prolong product lifetime.[349] Second, contrary to what has been alleged by some scholars[350], it is not so simple, from an engineering and design perspective, to determine the 'death date' of a product in advance. Product lifetime is indeed one of the parameters that is considered by producers at the conception stage and that serves as an orientation for the product designers and developers.[351] Yet, products do not always meet the targeted lifespan. Different reasons can explain the difficulties in planning product lifetime, including developing and producing conditions, the rising complexity of products, time constraints due to increasing speed of innovation cycles (leading to short-cycle testing and simulation) and high-cost pressure.[352] These conditions can induce producers to make decisions that ultimately lead to unintentional forms of premature obsolescence. Last but not least, it does not seem to be in the interests of producers, in today's highly competitive economic environment, to risk their reputation by adopting such strategies.[353] This is without mentioning products for which such strategies are inconceivable (e.g. credence goods).[354] Hence, although it is acknowledged that manufacturers and designers have their share

[348] S. Prakash et al., *Einfluss der Nutzungsdauer von Produkten auf ihre Umweltwirkung – Schaffung einer Informationsgrundlage und Entwicklung von Strategien gegen "Obsoleszenz"* (Umweltbundesamt Study 2016) p. 49 at p. 51; RDC Environment, *L'obsolescence programmée: politiques et mesures belges de protection du consommateur* (2017) pp. 37–38.

[349] B. Röper, R. Marfeld, *Gibt es geplanten Verschleiss? Untersuchungen zur Obsoleszenzthese* (Schwartz Verlag 1976), cited in E. Poppe, J. Longmuß, 'Zu Begriff und Theorie der geplanten Obsoleszenz', in E. Poppe, J. Longmuß (eds.), *Geplante Obsoleszenz Hinter den Kulissen der Produktentwicklung* (Transcript 2019) p. 23.

[350] N. Maycroft, *Consumption, planned obsolescence and waste* (Lincoln School of Art and Design 2009) p. 18 at p. 24; K. Pope, *Understanding planned obsolescence – Unsustainability through production, consumption and waste generation* (Kogan Page 2017) p. 58.

[351] S. Prakash et al., *Einfluss der Nutzungsdauer von Produkten auf ihre Umweltwirkung – Schaffung einer Informationsgrundlage und Entwicklung von Strategien gegen "Obsoleszenz"* (Umweltbundesamt Study 2016) p. 49.

[352] J. Longmuss and E. Poppe, 'Planned obsolescence: who are those planners?', in C. Bakker and R. Mugge (eds.), *Product Lifetimes And The Environment 2017 – Conference Proceedings* (IOS Press 2017) pp. 219–220. See *infra*, n° 126–128.

[353] A. Girard et al., 'Obsolescence of Home Appliances and Electronics: What Is the Role of the Consumer?', *Équiterre* (2018) pp. 12–13.

[354] See *supra*, n° 50.

of responsibility in the limited lifetime of certain products and should devote more efforts to developing sustainable ones, there are serious doubts about the existence of planned obsolescence.

83. Restrictive concept of planned obsolescence – Second, the concept of 'planned obsolescence' is also one-sided and thus restrictive. As B. Burns pointed out, "*[m]ost people encountering the word 'obsolescence' might assume that the word 'planned' has either been omitted as a prefix or is simply an understood component.*"[355] This terminological confusion is mainly due to the media where 'planned obsolescence' has become a buzzword.[356] Yet, practices of planned obsolescence, whether they exist or not, represent only one aspect of the phenomenon that can shorten product lifespan. In other words, the concept of 'planned obsolescence' does not reflect the core of the problem.

84. The influence of consumers on product lifetime – As emphasized by a growing body of literature[357], product lifetime (and obsolescence) is also influenced by consumers' decisions pertaining to the purchase, use, repair and discarding of the product. Consequently, the causes of product obsolescence relate to both the business and consumer sides and lead to various types of obsolescence. Whether the economic actors are responsible or whether this is the result of the current economic model and the associated material culture does not matter.[358] The most important question to ask is: how can products with a limited lifetime be useful, practical, or simply the easiest way for various actors in today's society?[359] In other words, what are the framework conditions that encourage the premature obsolescence of products? The complex network of causes and types of premature obsolescence will be described in following section of this chapter.[360]

c) *Negative impacts of the concept*

85. Lack of perspective – Narrowing the focus on planned obsolescence in the legal and public debates may, first, create a gap between the theory and the reality and could ultimately lead to actions limited to improving the system instead of carrying out the fundamental changes that are required. By failing to take into account the socio-economic context of the phenomenon,

355 B. Burns, 'Re-evaluating obsolescence and planning for it', in T. Cooper, *Longer lasting products: Alternatives to the throwaway society* (Gower 2010) p. 39.
356 See *supra*, n° 58.
357 See *supra*, n° 56.
358 See *supra*, n° 57.
359 M. Jaeger-Erben, 'Eine Frage der Kultur? Gesellschaftliche Treiber von Obsoleszenz', in E. Poppe, J. Longmuß (eds.), *Geplante Obsoleszenz Hinter den Kulissen der Produktentwicklung* (Transcript 2019) p. 186.
360 See *supra*, n° 98–140.

regulatory measures like bans on planned obsolescence could be deemed ineffective. It is certainly important to prevent and sanction producers who implement practices of planned obsolescence. Yet, merely outlawing 'planned obsolescence' is not sufficient to effectively tackle the complex and multifaceted phenomenon of premature obsolescence. In addition to prohibitions, one should not forget the need to take complementary measures to fight all the facets of the phenomenon.[361] If not, there is a risk that practices that accelerate obsolescence are not prevented, but even integrated and justified within a circular economy framework.[362]

86. Impacts on perceptions – A second impact of the use of the concept is that it strengthens the negative connotation of product obsolescence and exacerbates the terminological confusion between planned obsolescence and other cases of premature obsolescence. It is however crucial to pay attention to the type of messages that are relayed through the media or even legislation as they contribute to shaping the perceptions of what is normal.[363] For any sensible analysis of phenomena, especially socially contested ones like premature obsolescence, one needs to remain attentive to how it is perceived and constructed in public discourses, especially in this case where producers are far from being solely responsible.[364] As highlighted by S. Mandl, N. Tröger, "*the accusations on both sides (throw-away society vs. planned obsolescence) do not do justice, however, to the complexity of the use period or the lifespan of durable consumer goods. These approaches refer solely to factual actions, but assiduous attention must also be paid to what perceptions accompany them and to which factors support the underlying attitudes*".[365]

87. Consumer perceptions – The focus on planned obsolescence can lead to misunderstanding of the issue and have different effects on consumers.

361 See also E. Maitre-Ekern and C. Dalhammar,'Regulating planned obsolescence: a review of legal approaches to increase product durability and reparability in Europe', 25 *Review of European Community & International Environmental Law* (2016) p. 378 at p. 394; A. Michel, 'Est-il pertinent de définir légalement et de pénaliser les pratiques d'obsolescence prématurée? – Analyse de la loi française au regard des récentes décisions italiennes contre Apple et Samsung', in A. Bailleux (ed.), *Le droit en transition. Les clés juridiques d'une prospérité sans croissance* (Presses de l'Université Saint-Louis 2020) p. 245 at p. 284.

362 H. Wieser, 'Beyond Planned Obsolescence: Product Lifespans and the Challenges to a Circular Economy', 25 *GAIA* (2016) p. 157.

363 S. Mandl, N. Tröger, 'Possibilities for and Limitations to Consumer Action in the Circular Economy. Perspectives on Prolonging the Use Period for Durable Consumer Goods', in S. Eisenriegler (ed.), *The Circular Economy in the European Union – An Interim Review* (Springer 2020) p. 91.

364 M. Jaeger-Erben, M. Proske, 'What's hot what's not: the social construction of product obsolescence and its relevance for strategies to increase functionality', in C. Bakker and R. Mugge (eds.), *Product Lifetimes And The Environment 2017 – Conference Proceedings* (IOS Press 2017) p. 181.

365 *Ibid.*

First, the allegations on planned obsolescence feed the scepticism and mistrust of consumers on the market.[366] As rightly pointed out by A. Girard et al., the strongly contrasting views of stakeholders on this issue have had the effect of "*sowing confusion in consumers' minds about the existence of planned obsolescence*".[367] Yet, consumer trust is "*an important component of healthy societies and flourishing economies*".[368] Second, focusing on planned obsolescence creates 'consumer apathy' when it comes to product lifetime.[369] The clear linear attribution of responsibility and power over product lifetime to producers, coupled with the generalised feeling of mistrust, can evoke a denial of responsibility among consumers who neither feel responsible nor capable of influencing their products' lifespan.[370] Surveys reveal that the majority of consumers allocate the sole responsibility for limited product lifespans to producers and do not question their own behaviour.[371] Consequently, embodying the concept of planned obsolescence in the law can contribute to consumers lowering their expectations about product lifetime and viewing earlier replacement purchases as inevitable. This can ultimately trigger a vicious circle, where lower expectations influence the way consumers deal with products and lead to shorter product lifetimes.

88. Producer perceptions – The use of the words 'planned obsolescence' can also hamper the dialogue on the issue with the business side.[372] As already explained, the concept is highly contested by businesses, especially producers, as 'planned obsolescence' is deemed provocative towards the industry sector.[373] The tensions associated with the term 'planned obsolescence' are clearly visible in a French judgment delivered in 2018, where a company was condemned for defamatory publication on Facebook.[374] The company had accused the other

366 Brook Lyndhurst, *Public understanding of product lifetimes and durability* (DEFRA 2011), especially p. 63 at p. 67.

367 A. Girard et al., 'Obsolescence of Home Appliances and Electronics: What Is the Role of the Consumer?', *Équiterre* (2018) p. 13.

368 S.I. Becher, A.-L. Sibony, 'Confronting Product Obsolescence', 27 *Colum. J. Eur. L.* (2021) p. 110.

369 C. Bakker, C. Schuit, *The long view – Exploring product lifetime extension* (United Nations Environment Programme 2017) p. 23.

370 M. Jaeger-Erben, M. Proske, 'What's hot what's not: the social construction of product obsolescence and its relevance for strategies to increase functionality', in C. Bakker and R. Mugge (eds.), *Product Lifetimes And The Environment 2017 – Conference Proceedings* (IOS Press 2017) p. 182.

371 SIRCOME agency, the University of South Brittany and the University of South Bohemia, *The Influence of Lifespan Labelling on Consumers – ILLC study* (EESC 2016) pp. 5–6; A. Girard et al., 'Obsolescence of Home Appliances and Electronics: What Is the Role of the Consumer?', *Équiterre* (2018) p. 8.

372 The lack of dialogue has already been noticed, as shown in T. Libaert, 'Consommation et controverse: le cas de l'obsolescence programmée', 73 *Hermès, La Revue* (2015) p. 156.

373 See *supra*, n° 64.

374 CA Lyon (1re ch. civ.), 27 Novembre 2018, n° 17/03622.

company of planned obsolescence, which had damaged its reputation. However, terms with negative connotations cause considerable difficulties for those who want to move forward and change laws and policies. At the same time, lower expectations on product lifetime also permeate business strategy and ensure that shorter product lifetime is assumed and that sales targets are geared to those assumptions.

d) *The need for a neutral and general concept*

89. From planned obsolescence ... – It follows from the previous paragraphs that the concept of 'planned obsolescence' is not without flaws. Because the concept of 'planned obsolescence' is biased and restrictive, it is not appropriate to restrict the focus on it in this book. On the one hand, the purpose of this book is not to confirm or rebut the allegations of planned obsolescence, but rather to describe the phenomenon of shortening product lifetime based on empirical facts and statements in a way that is as neutral as possible. On the other hand, the concept of 'planned obsolescence' does not reflect the complexity of the phenomenon and merely focuses on one of its aspects. Yet, one of the main objectives of this book is to understand the various types and explain the different causes of product obsolescence.[375] Considering the heated debate surrounding the concept of planned obsolescence, it seems necessary to find another concept that is both neutral and general to describe the phenomenon in a way that reflects all its complexity.

90. ... to premature obsolescence – Unlike the concept of 'planned obsolescence', the concept of 'premature obsolescence' meets the conditions of neutrality and generality that need to be satisfied in order to serve as a conceptual basis for this book. The obsolescence of a product is 'premature' if it "*occur[s] (...) before the usual, proper, or appointed time*" or, in other words, if it is "*too early*".[376] By contrast with the concept of 'planned obsolescence'[377], the concept of 'premature obsolescence' does not explicitly refer to intent and allows encompassing cases of planned obsolescence, together with other cases where the obsolescence of products occurs too early. The concept of premature obsolescence has already occurred in some sources, including legal documents. Among the most relevant sources, there is the PROMPT project funded by the EU's Horizon 2020 research and innovation programme.[378] Because the concept of 'premature obsolescence' is deemed sufficiently neutral and general for the purpose of this study, this book will henceforth use it instead of 'planned

---

375 See *supra*, n° 18.
376 Oxford English Dictionary 2006 (3rd ed.).
377 See *supra*, n° 79.
378 See *supra*, n° 68.

obsolescence'. The concept of planned obsolescence will be integrated into the more fitting concept of premature obsolescence.

C. THE CONCEPTS OF PRODUCT LIFETIME AND PREMATURE OBSOLESCENCE

1. THE CONCEPT OF PRODUCT LIFETIME (AND RELATED CONCEPTS)

91. Urgent need for a definition of product lifetime – Before delving deeper into the concept of premature obsolescence, it is important to define 'product lifetime' as this concept is at the heart of the definition of 'premature obsolescence'.[379] A wide array of definitions of 'product lifetime' exists in the literature. Scholars draw a distinction, among others, between useful, actual, normative, service, designed, technical, functional, replacement, economic, expected and optimal product lifetime.[380] No definitive consensus has been reached on the concepts and definition related to product lifetime.

92. Definition of product lifetime, use cycles and obsolescence – After having unravelled all the existing concepts and definitions related to product lifetime, two concepts were deemed relevant for this book, namely 'product lifetime' and 'use cycles'. As rightly pointed out by M.C. Den Hollander, C.A. Bakker and H.J. Hultink, products have only one lifetime.[381] Accordingly, 'product lifetime' is "*the duration of the period that starts at the moment a product is released for use after manufacture and ends at the moment a product becomes obsolete beyond recovery at product level*".[382] Following this approach, product lifetime can comprise one or more use cycles (see Figure 2). A 'product use cycle'

379 See the definition of 'premature obsolescence' (n° 97).

380 See e.g. T. Cooper, 'The significance of product longevity', in T. Cooper, *Longer lasting products: Alternatives to the throwaway society* (Gower 2010) p. 8 at p. 11; S. Murakami, M. Oguchi, T. Tasaki, I. Daigo and S. Hashimoto, 'Lifespan of Commodities, Part I: The Creation of a Database and Its Review', 14 *Journal of Industrial Ecology* (2010) p. 598 at p. 612; M. Oguchi, S. Murakami, T. Tasaki, I. Daigo and S. Hashimoto, 'Lifespan of Commodities, Part II: Methodologies for Estimating Lifespan Distribution of Commodities', 14 *Journal of Indiustrial Ecology* (2010) p. 613 at p. 626; S. Mugdal, B. Tinetti, T. Faninger, S. Lockwood, G. Anderson, *Etude sur la durée de vie des équipements électriques et électroniques* (ADEME 2012) pp. 11–12; E. Fangeat, C. Chauvin, *Allongement de la durée de vie des produits* (ADEME 2016) pp. 12–13; J. Bachér et al., *Electronic products and obsolescence in a circular economy* (European Topic Centre Waste and Materials in a Green Economy 2020) p. 11 at p. 14.

381 M.C. Den Hollander, C.A. Bakker, H.J. Hultink, 'Product design in a circular economy; development of a typology of key concepts and terms', 21 *Journal of Industrial Ecology* (2017) p. 519.

382 *Ibid.*

corresponds to "*the duration of the period that starts at the moment a product is [acquired] for use after manufacture or recovery and ends at the moment a product becomes obsolete*".[383] The concept of product use cycles denotes how long a product is used and encompasses both the duration in operation and the duration on stand-by (including maintenance and repair carried out by the user). Product obsolescence marks the end of the use cycle and, if irreversible, can even mark the end of the product lifetime itself (see Figure 2). Once a product is irreversibly obsolete, it becomes waste. It is noteworthy that product obsolescence is not always irreversible but can, in certain cases, be reversed by a recovery operation.[384]

Figure 2. Product lifetime and its different stages

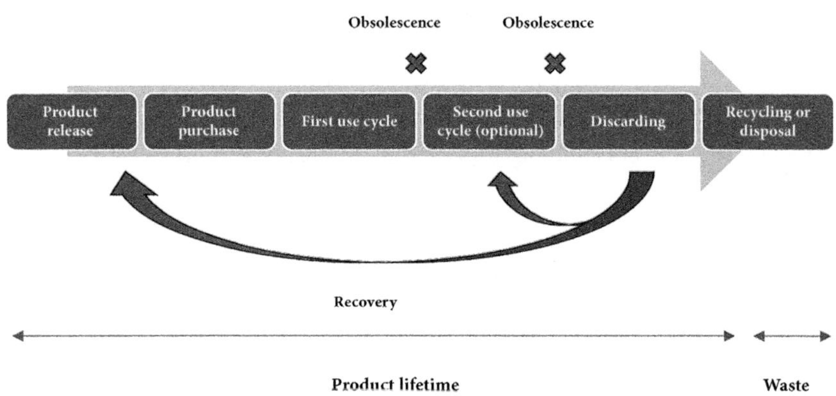

93. Optimal product lifetime and product sustainability – Research has already been carried out on the optimal product lifetime, although the amount of literature on this topic remains limited and focuses on product design.[385] The 'optimal product lifetime' can in theory be obtained by combining different factors, including the environmental impacts of the product, consumer

383 M.C. Den Hollander, C.A. Bakker, H.J. Hultink, 'Product design in a circular economy; development of a typology of key concepts and terms', 21 *Journal of Industrial Ecology* (2017) p. 519. The word 'acquired' seemed more appropriate than the word 'released' used in the original definition.

384 It should be noted that the meaning of the terms 'waste' and 'recovery' differ from the ones contained in the Waste Framework Directive (2008/98/EC), as explained in Chapter V on the end-of-life stage. For further information on the ways of recovering obsolete products or parts, see Section D of this chapter (n° 141 *et seq.*).

385 See e.g. N. van Nes, J. Cramer, 'Product lifetime optimization: a challenging strategy towards more sustainable consumption patterns', 14 *J. Clean. Prod.* (2006) p. 1307 at p. 1318; C. Vezzoli, E. Manzini, *Design for Environmental Sustainability* (Springer 2008) p. 131 at p. 158; R. Kurz, 'Quality, obsolescence and unsustainable innovation', 28 *Ekonomski vjesnik* (2015) p. 511 at p. 522.

satisfaction, emerging technological evolution, and societal progress.[386] In this book, the focus will lie on the environment[387], meaning that the optimal product lifespan will correspond to the point in time where the environmental impacts that arise from producing and using a product equal the embedded impacts of a (more energy efficient) replacement product.[388] When the product lifetime reaches its optimum, the product can be considered as 'sustainable'.[389]

94. Extended product lifetime is not always optimal – It should be noted that the 'optimal product lifetime' does not always correspond to an extended product lifetime as a longer product lifetime, which comprises one or more use cycles, is not *per se* beneficial for the environment.[390] For example, it is sometimes less harmful to the environment to replace rapidly outdated products if they consume more energy and resources at the use stage compared to newer versions.[391] Such cases are nonetheless quite rare in practice. Lifecycle assessment helps determine the optimal replacement moment of a product, though it does not bring a clear-cut answer.[392] This illustrates the sometimes uneasy balance to strike between, on the one hand, innovation and efficiency, and on the other, product sustainability. Yet, for most products, the environmental benefits achieved through innovation and efficiency do not outweigh the benefits of lifetime extension.[393] The latter will generally be

---

386 T. Cooper, 'The significance of product longevity', in T. Cooper, *Longer lasting products: Alternatives to the throwaway society* (Gower 2010) p. 19 at p. 22; J. Bachér et al., *Electronic products and obsolescence in a circular economy* (European Topic Centre Waste and Materials in a Green Economy 2020) p. 12.

387 See *supra*, n° 34.

388 C. Bakker, F. Wang, J. Huisman, M. den Hollander, 'Products that go round: exploring product life extension through design', 69 *J. Clean. Prod.* (2014) p. 12.

389 As already emphasized, this book focuses on eco-friendly aspects of sustainability, meaning with a reduced environmental impact, leaving other non-environmental aspects, such as social and ethical concerns (e.g. child labour, general working conditions, animal welfare, etc.), outside of the scope.

390 See also M. Proske, 'How to address obsolescence in LCA studies – Perspectives on product use-time for a smartphone case study', 376 *J. Clean. Prod.* (2022) 134283.

391 See e.g. W. Dewulf, J.R. Duflou, 'The environmentally optimized lifetime: a crucial concept in life cycle engineering', in G. Seliger et al. (eds.), *Proceedings of the global conference on sustainable product development and life cycle engineering* (Berlin Uni Edition 2004) p. 59 at p. 62; I. Rüdenauer, C.O. Gensch, *Eco-efficiency analysis of washing machines. Refinement of task 4: further use versus substitution of washing machines in stock* (Oeko-Institut 2005); C. Dalhammar, 'Industry attitudes towards ecodesign standards for improved resource efficiency', 123 *J. Clean. Prod.* (2016) p. 158.

392 C. Bakker, C. Schuit, *The long view – Exploring product lifetime extension* (United Nations Environment Programme 2017) p. 38 at p. 40.

393 Extending product lifespans is also likely to be beneficial from an economic and social perspective and may lead to greater consumer satisfaction, as rightly pointed out in T. Cooper, 'The significance of product longevity', in T. Cooper, *Longer lasting products: Alternatives to the throwaway society* (Gower 2010) p. 19 at p. 22. Longer-lasting products can, for example, be economically beneficial for consumers, for whom it is in principle more economical in the long term to repair the product instead of buying a new one. See

desirable from an environmental point of view.[394] Indeed, extending the lifetime of products or parts of products allows avoiding (or at least postponing) the purchase of substitute products and ultimately avoids all the environmental repercussions it entails (e.g. energy and materials consumption, CO_2 emissions, and residual waste and hazardous substances caused by resource extraction, production, packaging, transport, distribution and the likely disposal of the replaced good).[395]

Key definition

'Product lifetime' means the duration of the period that starts the moment a product is released for use after manufacture and ends the moment a product becomes obsolete beyond recovery at product level.

'Product use cycle' means the duration of the period that starts the moment a product is acquired for use after manufacture or recovery and ends the moment a product becomes obsolete.

'Product obsolescence' means the event that marks the end of the use cycle and, if irreversible, the end of the product lifetime.

'Waste' means a product that is irreversibly obsolete.

S. Prakash et al., *Einfluss der Nutzungsdauer von Produkten auf ihre Umweltwirkung – Schaffung einer Informationsgrundlage und Entwicklung von Strategien gegen "Obsoleszenz"* (Umweltbundesamt Study 2016) p. 52.

394 For concrete examples, see S. Kagawa et al., 'The economic and environmental consequences of automobile lifetime extension and fuel economy improvement: Japan's case', 20 *Economic System Research* (2008) p. 3 at p. 28; S. Boulos et al. (Ricardo-AEA), *The durability of products – Standards assessment for the circular economy under the Eco-Innovation Action Plan* (European Commission 2015) p. 3; S. Prakash et al., *Einfluss der Nutzungsdauer von Produkten auf ihre Umweltwirkung – Schaffung einer Informationsgrundlage und Entwicklung von Strategien gegen "Obsoleszenz"* (Umweltbundesamt Study 2016) pp. 51–52; P. Tecchio, F. Ardente, F. Mathieux, *Analysis of durability, reusability and reparability: Application to dishwashers and washing machines – JRC Technical Report* (European Commission 2016); C. Bakker, C. Schuit, *The long view – Exploring product lifetime extension* (United Nations Environment Programme 2017) p. 24 at p. 40; F. Alfieri, M. Cordella, J. Sanfelix, N. Dodd, 'An approach to the assessment of durability of energy-related products', 69 *Procedia CIRP* (2018) p. 878 at p. 891; M. Cordella, J. Sanfelix, F. Alfieri, 'Development of an approach for assessing the reparability and upgradability of energy-related products', 69 *Procedia CIRP* (2018) p. 888 at p. 892; EEB, *Coolproducts don't cost the earth – full report* (2019). For a good summary, see also C. Bakker, C. Schuit, *The long view – Exploring product lifetime extension* (United Nations Environment Programme 2017) p. 24 at p. **40**.

395 According to the European Environmental Bureau (EEB), "*extending the lifetime of all washing machines, notebooks, vacuum cleaners and smartphones in the EU by just one year would save around 4 million tonnes of carbon dioxide (CO_2) annually by 2030, the equivalent of taking over 2 million cars off the roads for a year.*" See EEB, *Coolproducts don't cost the Earth – Full report* (2019) p. 5.

'Recovery' means the operation allowing to reverse product obsolescence.

'Optimal product lifetime' corresponds to the point in time where the environmental impacts that arise from producing and using a product equal the embedded impacts of a (more energy efficient) replacement product.

'Product sustainability' is the ability of a product to reach the optimal product lifetime.

2. THE CONCEPT OF PREMATURE OBSOLESCENCE

a) *The definition of premature obsolescence*

95. No commonly accepted definition – There is no commonly accepted definition of the concept of premature obsolescence. Even research has not reached a consensus on the definition and typologies of premature obsolescence, the causes of which are complex and interrelated. As a result, a constellation of definitions can be found in the diverse sources dedicated to the topic. It is therefore important, for the purpose of studying the phenomenon from a legal perspective, to establish a definition that accurately describes and explains all the facets of premature obsolescence.

96. Premature obsolescence and decreasing product lifetime – A few scientific studies[396], as well as consumer testing magazines[397], provided empirical evidence of the (sometimes slight) decline in the lifetime of certain consumer products through a comparison between the median lifetime of these products over the years. However, it is important to note that other studies have reported the opposite, namely the increasing lifetime of certain products. For instance, an increase in the average lifetime of automobiles[398], as well as

396 F. Wang et al., 'Enhancing E-waste estimates: improving data quality by multivariate input/output analysis', 33 *Waste Manage* (2013) p. 2397 at p. 2407; H. Wieser, N. Tröger, *Die Nutzungsdauer und Obsoleszenz von Gebrauchsgütern im Zeitalter der Beschleunigungs – Eine Empirische Untersuchung in Österreichischen Haushalten* (AK-Wien 2015); S. Prakash, G. Dehoust, M. Gsell, T. Schleicher, R. Stamminger, *Einfluss der Nutzungsdauer von Produkten auf ihre Umweltwirkung – Schaffung einer Informationsgrundlage und Entwicklung von Strategien gegen "Obsoleszenz"* (Umweltbundesamt 2016); J. Bachér et al., *Electronic products and obsolescence in a circular economy* (European Topic Centre Waste and Materials in a Green Economy 2020).

397 See e.g. *Which?* (United Kingdom), *Test Achats* (Belgium) or *Stiftung Warentest* (Germany). Which articles?

398 Y. Adachi, I. Daigo, H. Yamada and Y. Matsuno, 'Development of a dynamic model for CO_2 emissions from gasoline vehicles in their use stage', 11 *Development Engineering* (2005) p. 19 at p. 29; M. Oguchi, S. Murakami, T. Tasaki, I. Daigo and S. Hashimoto, 'Lifespan of

of mobile phones[399], has been observed in Japan. These differences stem from the fact that product obsolescence can be due to (a combination of) different causes, which can significantly vary depending, among other things, on the type of products, on consumer behaviour as well as on countries and their cultural context. This makes the tasks of measuring and comparing product lifetime over the years – and thus proving the shrinking product lifetime, particularly difficult. Hence, as rightly pointed out by T. Cooper, even if claims on decreasing product lifetime could be substantiated, it would be unwise to draw general conclusions.[400] It seems therefore inappropriate to assimilate premature obsolescence with decreasing product lifetime.

97. Definition of premature obsolescence – In view of the foregoing, 'premature obsolescence' can be defined as *"all practices that reduce product lifetime so that the product does not reach its optimal lifetime (from an environmental point of view), without it being the result of normal wear and tear"*. Because product lifetime extension is beneficial in most cases[401], this book will regard product obsolescence as too premature if the lifetime of the product could have been longer from an environmental perspective. By contrast with the definition associated with the concept of 'planned obsolescence'[402], there is no mention of intent behind the practice and no emphasis on the responsibility of one particular actor. This makes the definition more neutral, although definitions are never (totally) neutral.[403] The (vague) wording of this definition also allows covering a vast range of cases and potential future cases of premature obsolescence.[404]

> *Key definition*
>
> 'Premature obsolescence' means all practices that reduce product lifetime so that the product does not reach its optimal lifetime (from an environmental point of view), without it being the result of normal wear and tear.

commodities, Part II: Methodologies for estimating lifespan distribution of commodities', 14 *Journal of Industrial Ecology* (2010) p. 613 at p. 626.

399 S. Murakami, H. Ohsugi, R. Murakami-Suzuki, A. Mukaida and H. Tsujimura, 'Average life span of mobile phones and in-use and hibernating stocks in Japan', 5 *Journal of Life Cycle Assessment, Japan* (2009) p. 138 at p. 144.

400 T. Cooper, 'The significance of product longevity', in T. Cooper, *Longer lasting products: Alternatives to the throwaway society* (Gower 2010) pp. 10–11.

401 See *supra*, n° 94.

402 See *supra*, n° 79.

403 V. Champeil-Desplats, *Méthodologies du droit et des sciences du droit* (Dalloz 2016), especially p. 302 *et seq.*

404 P. Anesa, 'Defining legal vagueness: a contradiction in terms?', 8 *Polemos* (2014) p. 201.

b) *Types of premature obsolescence*

(1) The choice of typology

98. Five main types of premature obsolescence – Different practices shorten the lifetime of products and cause their premature obsolescence. These practices can occur at every stage of the product lifetime. After having identified and evaluated the wide array of typologies developed in literature[405], the typology used by the *Umweltbundesamt* seems to be the most suitable to describe the different manifestations of the phenomenon of premature obsolescence as it accurately reflects the different facets of the phenomenon in a clear and well-delineated way. Taking this typology as a basis, this book distinguishes five types of premature obsolescence, namely material, functional, psychological, economic and indirect obsolescence (See Figure 3). Whereas the first four categories correspond to the classification made in the German study, cases of indirect obsolescence, which were encompassed within the category of economic obsolescence in this study, form a distinct category in this book. The introduction of 'indirect obsolescence' as a distinct category is justified by the fact that in these cases, premature obsolescence (mainly) occurs due to the conditions surrounding the product rather than economic reasons.[406] This typology not only fits with the idea of shared responsibility between the different actors but also allows covering all kinds of practices that can shorten the lifetime of the very diverse consumer goods. Some products will indeed be more prone to some types of premature obsolescence compared to others. This classification will be used throughout the book. This will allow undertaking a useful analysis of the phenomenon as well as of the legislative measures that already tackle – or that should be taken to tackle – some practices of premature obsolescence.

99. Different types, yet inextricably linked – It is worth emphasizing that these categories of premature obsolescence are far from being watertight but are in fact inextricably linked. In other words, there is no clear-cut borderline between the different types of obsolescence in practice. In certain cases, products are prematurely obsolete due to a variety of reasons, which pertain to one or more of these categories. As rightly pointed out in the German study, "*the types of obsolescence are linked and jointly influence product lifetime – pinpointing any one specific cause is difficult*".[407] For example, whether a product without an updated operating system is still functional depends on the owner's subjective judgement. Likewise, while some practices exclusively belong to one category,

405 See *supra* on the concept of planned obsolescence (n° 46 *et seq.*).

406 For further explanation, see *infra* on indirect obsolescence (n° 112–116).

407 S. Prakash et al., *Einfluss der Nutzungsdauer von Produkten auf ihre Umweltwirkung – Schaffung einer Informationsgrundlage und Entwicklung von Strategien gegen "Obsoleszenz"* (Umweltbundesamt Study 2016) p. 45.

others combine elements of different categories, making it difficult to determine within which category the practice falls. One could think, as an example, of practices linked to technological progress, which could lead to the functional and psychological obsolescence of products.

100. Not always irreversible – It should be acknowledged that certain types of obsolescence do not automatically lead to the end-of-life of the concerned product. Depending on the case, the state of obsolescence may be reversed through direct reuse, repair, refurbishment or remanufacturing, giving the product (or its parts or components) a new lease of life and starting a new use cycle.[408] Whereas material, functional and indirect obsolescence will generally lead to the end-of-life of the product (preceded or not by a period of 'hibernation')[409], cases of economic and psychological obsolescence could lead to a state of obsolescence that is only temporary. Hence, some types of obsolescence are more irreversible than others.

Figure 3. Typology of premature obsolescence

Types of obsolescence	Definition	Reversibility
Material	Obsolete due to the failure of one of its parts or components.	Irreversible
Functional	Obsolete due to software-induced factors.	Irreversible
Indirect	Obsolete due to external factors hindering its good functioning and/or its repair.	Irreversible
Economic	Obsolete due to economic factors.	Reversible
Psychological	Obsolete because no longer attractive or satisfying in consumers' eyes.	Reversible

In the following paragraphs, each type of premature obsolescence will be defined in greater detail and illustrated with examples.

(2) Material obsolescence

101. Definition of material obsolescence – Limited product lifetime can first be attributed to the material obsolescence of the product. This type of premature obsolescence encompasses *practices that have a direct influence on product quality*. In other words, the product can no longer be used due to the failure of one of its parts or components. For many decades, material obsolescence has been a hotly debated topic. Certain producers have been suspected of deliberately developing techniques or materials of inferior quality,

408 See *infra* on the concepts related to reversing obsolescence (n° 150–154).

409 See *infra* on the concept of hibernating products (n° 157).

anticipating breakage or wear to reduce the durability of their products.[410] These allegations correspond to the 'obsolescence of quality' as described by V. Packard.[411] Intentional cases of material obsolescence are generally the ones that people and the media exclusively acknowledge when discussing the topic. So far, no evidence has been provided on the current existence of such deliberate practices.[412] Yet, material obsolescence goes beyond the restrictive view, which focuses on producer intent and in-built obsolescence, and covers practices that are adopted deliberately or not by the producer and aggravated by the consumer.

102. Example: obsolescence by notification[413] – Blatant cases of material obsolescence include techniques that consist of designing products with an electronic device that makes them stop working after a certain period of use. As an example, printer producers have been suspected of deliberately producing their devices with smart ink cartridges, which disabled themselves after a specific number of prints or a certain ink level. The printer producer *HP* was sued on the basis of these suspicions before the Northern District Court of California in 2010. No court decision was ultimately issued as it ended with a settlement between the parties.[414] In 2017, a similar claim was lodged by the French consumer association *HOP* against *Epson* and other printer producers.[415] In its claim, *HOP* relied primarily on Article L. 441-2 of the French Consumer Code outlawing 'planned obsolescence' which had been newly adopted at that time. Following this claim, a preliminary investigation has been launched and is still being conducted by the French General Directorate for Competition policy, Consumer affairs and Fraud control (*Direction générale de la consommation, de la concurrence et de la répression des fraudes* or *DGCCRF*). If conclusive evidence comes to light, legal proceedings could follow.

---

410 See e.g. K. Pope, *Understanding planned obsolescence – Unsustainability through production, consumption and waste generation* (Kogan Page 2017) p. 52. For further examples, see *infra* on the concept of planned obsolescence (n° 49 *et seq.*).

411 V. Packard, *The Waste Makers* (David MacKay 1960), especially chapter 6.

412 See e.g. S. Prakash et al., *Einfluss der Nutzungsdauer von Produkten auf ihre Umweltwirkung – Schaffung einer Informationsgrundlage und Entwicklung von Strategien gegen "Obsoleszenz"* (Umweltbundesamt Study 2016) p. 49 at p. 51; RDC Environment, *L'obsolescence programmée: politiques et mesures belges de protection du consommateur* (2017), especially p. 37–38; J. Longmuss and E. Poppe, 'Planned obsolescence: who are those planners?', in C. Bakker and R. Mugge (eds.), *Product Lifetimes And The Environment 2017 – Conference Proceedings* (IOS Press 2017) p. 217 at p. 221.

413 Centre Européen de la Consommation, *L'obsolescence programmée ou les dérives de la société de consommation* (2013) p. 4.

414 Northern District Court of California 26 August 2010, Stipulation of Settlement No. C05-3580 JF, *HP Inkjet Printer Litigation.*

415 Tribunal de grande instance de Nanterre 17 September 2017, Plainte au Procureur de la République, *HOP v. X.* See also HOP, *Imprimantes: cas d'école de l'obsolescence programmée*, September 2017, <https://www.halteobsolescence.org/wp-content/uploads/2017/09/Rapport-HOP-final.pdf>.

103. Example: obsolescence due to specific wear parts – Product lifetime can also be materially reduced due to specific wear parts introduced into the product, which break and thus create a functional defect after a short period of time. A well-known example is the strategy pursued by the Phoebus cartel, which engineered light bulbs with more fragile bulbs so they would burn out faster.[416] Nowadays, this kind of material obsolescence can affect smartphones, which can have a deficient mechanical and electronic robustness depending on some of their components, such as the display assembly, battery, audio control and power button cable or the screen protector.[417] Wear parts have been identified in other consumer products, such as clothes and white goods.[418]

104. Example: obsolescence due to special manufacturing techniques – Material obsolescence can also result from practices whereby the producer conceives their products with special manufacturing techniques so that defective parts cannot be (easily) removed and replaced without risking breaking the product. If a defect occurs, such techniques make repair (almost) impossible for the consumer, who is then forced to replace the whole product. In other words, the obsolescence of some product parts leads to the obsolescence of the whole product. One of the most characteristic examples of this category of material obsolescence pertains to electronic devices. As reported by the platform *iFixit*, several smartphones, tablets and laptops on the market are produced with a battery or screen bonded with industrial strength glue or with non-standard screws, with small components soldered to main components or with long and thin ribbon cables connecting different parts of the device.[419] As a consequence, when the performance of a product part becomes inadequate, which can frequently occur with weaker parts, consumers have no choice but to get another smartphone.[420] Unfortunately, these issues do not exclusively concern electronic products. For example, furniture repairs have become increasingly difficult due to the increased use of adhesives, staples, and poor-quality composite materials.[421]

105. Justifications invoked by producers – Whereas some of these techniques could be seen as a strategy to shorten product lifetime, material obsolescence can also be the result of the manufacturer's decisions to use

---

416 See *supra*, n° 46.

417 S. Prakash et al., *Einfluss der Nutzungsdauer von Produkten auf ihre Umweltwirkung – Schaffung einer Informationsgrundlage und Entwicklung von Strategien gegen "Obsoleszenz"* (Umweltbundesamt Study 2016) p. 46.

418 See e.g. the concrete examples given in S. Schridde, C. Kreiss, J. Winter, *Geplante Obsoleszenz: Entstehungsursachen – Konkrete Beispiele – Schadensfolgen – Handlungsprogramm* (Arge Regio 2014) p. 25 at p. 49.

419 For concrete examples, see: <https://www.ifixit.com/Right-to-Repair/Repairable-Products>.

420 Stiftung Warentest, 'Geplante Obsoleszenz: Gerade gekauft und schon wieder hin?', *9 Stiftung Warentest* (2013) p. 63.

421 RREUSE, *Improving product reparability: Policy options at EU level* (2015) p. 2.

components, fittings, or manufacturing techniques of poor or sub-optimal quality, without these being driven by the need to accelerate product lifetime and boost sales. In practice, manufacturers can invoke economic, technical, safety, aesthetic, financial or IP reasons – all credible – to justify the practices being criticised. For example, *Epson* gave security and technical reasons to justify two techniques considered as 'planned obsolescence' by *HOP*.[422] Similarly, *Apple* justified the sealed battery of its smartphones on aesthetic and security purposes.[423] Beyond these allegations, there is also the fact that, due to fast-changing technology, products and components may not be sufficiently checked for adherence to lifetime requirements during production, this real-time stress exposure is beyond benchmark lifetime requirements implemented in production or that high competitive pressure creates volatility in the availability and quality of components.[424] Although it is difficult to draw the line between intentional and non-intentional cases, understanding 'material obsolescence' in its broad sense allows covering and tackling both types. Material obsolescence, be it with or without intent, remains problematic and should be combatted.

(3) Functional obsolescence

106. Definition of functional obsolescence – In addition to cases of material obsolescence, some devices that are still technically functioning can become prematurely obsolete due to the *introduction onto the market of a product with additional and/or improved functionalities*. This type of obsolescence corresponds to the 'obsolescence of function' coined by V. Packard[425], though here with a special focus on software-induced factors.[426] Functional

---

422 According to *Epson*, (1) the ink cartridges still have some ink although declared empty to preserve the print head (otherwise leading to high risk of the ink being paler or uneven on the page and then defective print head) and (2) the printer absorber pad is declared full so that no ink goes in the device. See V. Fagot, 'Obsolescence programmée: le fabricant d'imprimantes Epson livre sa défense', *Le Monde*, 26 March 2018, available on: <www.lemonde.fr/economie/article/2018/03/26/obsolescence-programmee-le-fabricant-d-imprimantes-epson-livre-sa-defense_5276539_3234.html>.

423 See Apple Patent Application Publication from 1st December 2011 on Integrated Embedded Battery, US 2011/0292598 A1, where it is explained that the iPhone chassis has no gaps, and the equipment is as thin and light as possible so as to reduce chances of moisture and dirt getting inside. See also C. Welch, 'Apple explains why iPhones now show an ominous warning after 'unauthorized' battery replacements', *The Verge*, 14 August 2019, available on: <https://www.theverge.com/2019/8/14/20805744/apple-iphone-battery-replacements-ios-safety-statement-unauthorized>.

424 S. Prakash et al., *Einfluss der Nutzungsdauer von Produkten auf ihre Umweltwirkung – Schaffung einer Informationsgrundlage und Entwicklung von Strategien gegen "Obsoleszenz"* (Umweltbundesamt Study 2016) p. 53. See also n° 133 *et seq.*

425 V. Packard, *The Waste Makers* (David MacKay 1960), especially chapter 6.

426 The other cases whereby the product becomes obsolete due to the introduction of a product that performs the function better, but not because of software-induced factors, pertain in this book to the category of indirect obsolescence (n°112–116).

obsolescence is caused by technological progress and changes in standardisation landscape (e.g. new data formats, new functions, new transmission standards, etc.), which place increasingly demanding requirements on both hardware and software.[427] This consequently poses problems of incompatibility between the hardware of existing products and the software that needs to run on top of it. Digitalisation and the expanding 'Internet of Things' (IoT)[428] increase the number of goods subject to this risk of functional obsolescence. Although this type of obsolescence may be justified in the context of technological innovations and improvements[429], some practices should be avoided and sanctioned.

107. Example: obsolescence due to new updates of the operating system – The functional obsolescence of devices can relate to the development and installation of a new operating system (OS)[430], which implies too heavy modifications for the hardware performance of old or competing ICT devices.[431] As a result, OS updates may affect the hardware performance of the device, leading to its earlier replacement. The device can, for instance, become slower, and some of its functionalities may not be usable anymore. Empirical studies show that typical reasons for functional obsolescence are a technically limited memory or limited battery lifespan.[432] As an illustrative example of this type of functional obsolescence, one can refer to the *Samsung* and *Apple* cases, where the updated OS had reduced the smartphone performance because the battery was not powerful enough.[433] This is even more problematic when updates are irreversible once installed so that the consumer cannot downgrade the OS and return to the previous OS version. Updating the OS may also affect the hardware performance of an electronic device if it fails. This is called 'bricking' a device: due to system-level damage caused by an update error, the device may no longer boot or function and thus becomes a 'brick'. Bricking may be caused

---

427 'Hardware' refers to "*the physical portion of a computer system, including electrical, electronic, electromechanical, and mechanical components (such as a disk drive, CPU, keyboard, etc.)*", whereas 'software' consists of "*programs designed to enable a computer to perform a particular task or series of tasks*". See Oxford English Dictionary 2006 (3rd ed.).

428 For a definition of the 'Internet of Things', see *supra*, footnote n° 202.

429 A. Fishman N. Gandal, O. Shy, 'Planned obsolescence as an engine of technological progress', 141 *Journal of Industrial Economics* (1993) p. 361 at p. 370.

430 An 'operating system' is "*the low-level software that supports a computer's basic functions, such as scheduling tasks, controlling peripherals and allocating storage. It is typically loaded automatically when a computer is switched on by means of a bootstrap routine. It provides the basic interface for the computer when no applications are running*". See Oxford English Dictionary 2006 (3rd ed.).

431 The abbreviation 'ICT' stands for "*information and communications technology*".

432 Stiftung Warentest, 'Geplante Obsoleszenz: Gerade gekauft und schon wieder hin?', 9 *Stiftung Warentest* (2013) p. 62; H. Wieser, N. Tröger, *Die Nutzungsdauer und Obsoleszenz von Gebrauchgütern im Zeitalter der Beschleunigung – Eine empirische Untersuchung in österreichischen Haushalten* (Vienna: Arbeiterkammer 2015) p. 58.

433 Autorita Garante della Concorrenza e del Mercato, 25 septembre 2018, *Apple*; Autorita Garante della Concorrenza e del Mercato, 25 septembre 2018, *Samsung*.

by an invalid update or an update that does not finish successfully.[434] It should be noted that the more foundational an update is, the greater the potential of bricking a device. An OS update, as well as a firmware update[435], is therefore more likely to cause bricking than an application update. Further issues of premature obsolescence can be caused by 'bloatware' – often unnecessary software that comes bundled with the OS and that takes up excessive space – as well as redundant programmes, malicious or obsolete software and viruses.[436]

108. Example: obsolescence due to new software updates – Electronic devices can also become functionally obsolete if they can no longer run the updated version of the software. The evolution of software technologies can lead to new applications and software, which quickly push older devices to their limits due to the new content and functions. As a result, updating software or installing new updated software is no longer possible due to the characteristics and restrictions of old or competing devices. For instance, with increasing demands for the higher processing capacity of new applications, existing phones gradually slow down and lose performance until eventually, they are unable to operate effectively. Some applications also require a specific operating system on the phone. This kind of functional obsolescence is particularly pervasive in the video game sector.[437] The new software is unable to run on the computer hardware as it places a too high demand on hardware performance. Another striking example of functional obsolescence caused by updated software concerns televisions. The development of new TV formats has led in recent years to older devices lacking the necessary hardware chips (transmitter and receiver chips) to be able to handle the corresponding new formats or to render the transmitted content in the desired quality.[438] In all these cases, consumers have the choice between "*using obsolete software with functional hardware or non-obsolete software with unwanted, new hardware*".[439] But most consumers decide to replace the hardware or even the whole original equipment, although it has not yet reached its technical end-of-life. Consumers justify this choice by

---

434 A befitting example is the connected combination microwave and oven sold by *AEG*, which became unusable after update. This update "*used an incorrect software image intended for a steam oven" as the device thinks it is a steam oven*". See N. Flaherty, 'OTA update failure shows perils of connected home', *eeNews Europe*, 28 March 2022, available on: <https://www.eenewseurope.com/en/ota-update-failure-shows-perils-of-connected-home/>.

435 'Firmware' is "*a permanent form of software built into certain kinds of computer*" (see Oxford English Dictionary 2006 (3rd ed.)).

436 E. Oldyrevas, C. McAlister, *Long live the machine – How ecodesign & energy labelling can prevent premature obsolescence of laptops* (Ecos 2020) p. 11.

437 J. Newman, *Best before: Videogames, Supersession and Obsolescence* (Routledge 2012).

438 S. Prakash et al., *Einfluss der Nutzungsdauer von Produkten auf ihre Umweltwirkung – Schaffung einer Informationsgrundlage und Entwicklung von Strategien gegen "Obsoleszenz"* (Umweltbundesamt Study 2016) p. 46.

439 N. Maycroft, *Consumption, planned obsolescence and waste* (Lincoln School of Art and Design 2009) p. 23.

the fact that certain functions do not satisfy their needs anymore as compared to newer and numerous functions that are available on the market with new products.[440] It should be noted that the use of up-to-date and supported software is sometimes required by the law to protect data.[441]

109. Example: obsolescence due to discontinued updates of the operating system – Technological developments can, moreover, induce producers to stop releasing updates for the OS of their devices. The producer can decide to stop updating the operating system or the driver for the current operating system.[442] The consequences of such a decision are twofold. First and foremost, the absence of updates may raise security issues.[443] The discontinuation of support for older operating systems can lead to scenarios where security-relevant updates for operating systems and software are no longer available, impeding protection against viruses and other malware.[444] Second, an 'outdated' OS can become incompatible with updated software. Some applications, once updated, may no longer work on devices that no longer receive updates for their OS. In other words, the discontinuation of the OS can limit the functionality of the software that needs to run on top of the device. A lack of software support for older operating systems can thus significantly hamper its use on newer hardware.[445] In such a scenario, consumers have the possibility of rooting their devices. Rooting essentially allows consumers to update the OS, even on older devices and even if the manufacturer does

---

440 This is closely linked to 'psychological obsolescence' (see *infra*, especially n° 122).

441 See e.g. the German IT Security Act (*IT-Sicherheitsgesetz*), which makes it mandatory to keep critical software infrastructure (including websites) secure, including by using updated, supported versions. The role of legislation on software security is also visible through the EU Cybersecurity Certification Framework, as explained in R. van der Veer, M. Valkema, F. Guasconi, P. Drogkaris, *Advancing Software Security in the EU – The role of the EU cybersecurity certification framework* (ENISA 2020). For a world-wide example, see the UN Regulation No. 156 on Uniform provisions concerning the approval of vehicles with regards to software updates and software updates management systems, OJ L 82, 9.3.2021, p. 60–74, applicable to passenger cars since January 2021.

442 A 'driver' is a piece of software which allows a computer to control a particular piece of hardware or peripheral device (see Oxford English Dictionary 2006 (3rd ed.)). In other words, it provides a software interface to hardware devices, enabling operating systems and other computer programs to access hardware functions without needing to know precise details about the hardware being used (see <https://en.wikipedia.org/wiki/Device_driver#cite_note-dev1-1>).

443 These security issues are more conspicuous within the business context. See for example the Mobile Device Guidance written by the British Cyber Security Centre, which provides advice to organisations who are unable to fully migrate away from obsolete products before the end of their support dates, available on: <https://www.ncsc.gov.uk/collection/mobile-device-guidance/managing-the-risks-from-obsolete-products>.

444 'Malware' means "*programs written with the intent of being disruptive or damaging to (the user of) a computer or other electronic device*", including viruses, worms, spyware, etc. (see Oxford English Dictionary 2006 (3rd ed.)).

445 A. Manhart et al., *Resource Efficiency in the ICT Sector* (Greenpeace 2016) p. 37.

not allow this. Rooting could nonetheless result in voiding the commercial guarantee.[446] Another option for consumers facing discontinued OS updates of their owned device is to install the new OS. However, this option is not always possible. This type of functional obsolescence has occurred in the notebook sector. The OS *Windows 7* was no longer updated, developed and secured. Consequently, *Windows 10* needed to be installed on the hardware, but an update to *Windows 10* could be limited due to higher requirements for random-access memory (RAM) and storage.

110. Example: obsolescence due to discontinued updates of the firmware – Firmware is a permanent form of software, inextricably linked to the device and which cannot be obtained from any alternative provider, as opposed to software. As rightly explained by E. Oldyrevas and C. McAlister, the manufacturer is responsible for providing firmware (BIOS) updates such as bug and security fixes to ensure the proper functioning of the device.[447] Moreover, firmware and OS updates contribute to prolonging the lifetime of the device by facilitating the installation of upgraded components.[448] If firmware updates are discontinued, the device becomes vulnerable. Software and hardware incompatibilities may occur, causing the premature obsolescence of the device.

111. Example: obsolescence of devices tethered to external IT infrastructure – Functional obsolescence can also occur when the device needs a constant connection to the companies' servers. If the servers are shut down, the device no longer functions. This category of devices includes, for example, smart watches or automating lights.[449] Similarly, IoT devices that depend on online services can become bricked if the manufacturer discontinues the service.

---

446 Copyright law may support such legal consequences. In that regard, the Copyright Directive (2001/29/EC) includes exceptions to allow breaking technological protection measures for non-copyright-infringing purposes, such as to run alternative software, but member states vary on the implementation of the directive.

447 E. Oldyrevas, C. McAlister, *Long live the machine – How ecodesign & energy labelling can prevent premature obsolescence of laptops* (Ecos 2020) p. 11.

448 *Ibid.*

449 For a concrete example, see the story of the smart home company *Insteon*, whose servers were shut down, rendering all users smart home-less: R. Amadeo, 'Shameful: Insteon looks dead – just like its users' smart homes', *Ars Technica*, 18 April 2022, available on: <https://arstechnica.com/gadgets/2022/04/shameful-insteon-looks-dead-just-like-its-users-smart-homes/>. It should be noted that the company is now up and running again, but users need to buy a subscription to use their own devices: M. Humphries, 'Insteon Smart Home Hubs Start Coming Back Online', *PC Mag*, 13 June 2022, available on: <https://www.pcmag.com/news/insteon-smart-home-hubs-start-coming-back-online>. See also the blogpost issued by *Insteon*: <https://www.insteon.com/blog/2022/6/9/subscription-letter>.

(4) Indirect obsolescence

112. Definition of indirect obsolescence – Other more 'indirect' causes can make products obsolete after a relatively short period or limited usage. By contrast with material and functional obsolescence, indirect obsolescence is *caused by factors surrounding the product in question, rather than by its design, quality or performance*. The product, although still in working condition, can no longer be used as some of these external factors hinder its good functioning and/or its repair (or more generally its reuse). Like functional obsolescence, some cases of indirect obsolescence are the result of rapid technological advancements and design changes, which are sometimes supported by regulatory standards adopted for safety or energy efficiency reasons. These cases of indirect obsolescence result almost automatically in an irreversible state of obsolescence.

113. Example: obsolescence due to a lack of consumables – Indirect obsolescence occurs if the consumables relating to and compatible with the concerned product are no longer available. Consumables are goods that are intended to be consumed, such as ink cartridges, Polaroid film, or batteries. The unavailability of consumables is particularly problematic as these goods are necessary for the functioning of the main product. As an example, if the producer stops making ink cartridges compatible with the printer, the latter becomes obsolete, and consumers are forced to purchase a new and upgraded printer. This is all the truer if consumables from other brands are not compatible with or recognised by the main product. This can occur when the producer has 'doped' the software system of the product ('software doping by discrimination').[450]

114. Example: obsolescence due to unavailable or incompatible accessories – Likewise, another example of indirect obsolescence is where accessories relating to and compatible with it are made (almost) unavailable by the producers, including due to rapid changes in product design. Accessories are associated products that complement the main product, like phone chargers or headphones. Although accessories are generally not as necessary as consumables, some of them could still lead to product obsolescence if no longer available. The phone charger is an illustrative example. For the rest, even though not essential for the functioning of the product, some accessories are perceived as essential by consumers, which may induce them to buy the new version of the product in order to enjoy all accessories. Conversely, accessories become obsolete if no longer compatible with the new versions of the product as

[450] G. Barthe, P.R. D'Argenio, B. Finkbeiner, H. Hermanns, 'Facets of Software Doping', in T. Margaria, B. Steffen (eds), *Leveraging Applications of Formal Methods, Verification and Validation: Discussion, Dissemination, Applications. ISoLA 2016. Lecture Notes in Computer Science* (Springer 2016) pp. 603–604.

well as with products from other brands, though they still function. This issue of physical incompatibility between associated products, which causes their indirect obsolescence, frequently occurs in the ICT sector. For instance, industry standards regarding the interfaces between the computer and peripheral devices may change.[451]

115. Example: obsolescence due to a lack of spare parts – Among the factors that can lead to the indirect obsolescence of products, there is also the non-availability of spare parts. Spare parts are "*functionally identical or compatible and functionally improved components or modules that may be exchanged during repair in the course of the product lifecycle to replace faulty, failed or worn-out parts*".[452] Those parts are typically the ones that may wear or break down within the scope of the ordinary use of a product. Hence, when the producer decides to stop producing or commercializing them, for example, because it costs too much money and effort to stock and manage spare parts[453], such a decision prevents consumers from repairing their defective product. Producers may also decide to only provide authorised repairers with original spare parts. Repairers who are not authorised may consequently be compelled to use copy parts, which can compromise warranties and commercial guarantees. This is only in the case where no 'software doping' prevents the product from functioning with these copy parts.[454] Producers mainly justify such restrictions by their concerns that they would be forced to support warranties on products that contain incorrectly installed components giving high failure rates and incurring high costs to them.[455] The lack of availability of spare parts has already been reported for a variety of consumer products, including domestic fridges and ovens.[456] When the supply of replacement parts is discontinued, or when they are difficult to find, consumers generally decide to shelve the product and purchase a substitute one.

---

451 N. Maycroft, *Consumption, planned obsolescence and waste* (Lincoln School of Art and Design 2009) p. 23.

452 This definition is given in Basic Award Criteria of the German Ecolabel Blue Angel from January 2017 for computers and keyboards, RAL-UZ 78, p. 10, available on: <https://www.blauer-engel.de/en/products/electric-devices/computers-and-keyboards>.

453 The management of spare parts requires to stock and ship an important number of different items with a proportionally lower value, while tracking each item to match the right spare part to each product.

454 G. Barthe, P.R. D'Argenio, B. Finkbeiner, H. Hermanns, 'Facets of Software Doping', in T. Margaria, B. Steffen (eds), *Leveraging Applications of Formal Methods, Verification and Validation: Discussion, Dissemination, Applications. ISoLA 2016. Lecture Notes in Computer Science* (Springer 2016) pp. 603–604.

455 D. Watson, C. Gylling, B. Bauer, N. Tojo, H. Throne-Holst., *Circular Business Models in the Mobile Phone Industry* (TemaNord 2017) pp. 47–48.

456 S. Boulos et al. (Ricardo-AEA), *The durability of products – Standard assessment for the circular economy under the Eco-Innovation Action Plan – Appendices* (European Union 2015) p. 87.

116. EXAMPLE: OBSOLESCENCE DUE TO THE NON-EXISTENCE OF MAINTENANCE AND REPAIR SERVICES AND THE BARRIERS TO REUSE – Other factors can hinder reuse (including repair) and thus lead to the irreversible obsolescence of the product. First of all, not all producers provide for maintenance and repair services, leaving as only alternatives 'do-it-yourself' (DIY) repair and independent repairers. And these alternatives may encounter various barriers. Among them, there is the lack of access to tools, service and repair manuals, and diagnostic software. If one of these elements is not supplied by the producer, repair may be jeopardised, and the obsolete product discarded. It is interesting to note that the confidentiality of some technical information is, to a certain extent, supported by the legislation on intellectual property rights.[457] These barriers are sometimes reinforced by other mechanisms, such as commercial guarantees stipulating that they no longer apply if the product is dismantled by a third party, or mechanisms of authentication installed in the product and preventing repair outside the authorized repair network. The latter mechanism includes, for example, cases where all the parts of a smartphone are connected and the motherboard would not recognise the spare parts in case of repair outside the authorised network[458], as well as cases where the smartphone has a micro-controller that only authorized technicians can properly configure and where the OS hides the usual battery health stats and displays a warning if it does not detect the right micro-controller.[459] The direct consequence of these obstacles is the decline of repair shops, making the road towards repair longer and harder.[460] Hence, reuse is not only hindered when the maintenance and repair services supplied by the producer are non-existent or discontinued but also because of the many barriers to the alternatives.

(5) Economic obsolescence

117. DEFINITION OF ECONOMIC OBSOLESCENCE – The lifetime of products can also prematurely end if they are *perceived as economically worthless or not worth repairing*, especially when compared to the purchase price of a new product. This is what is called the 'economic obsolescence' of the product. In these cases, premature obsolescence depends on an appreciation of the price-quality ratio of the old and the new products, taking the residual value of the old product and the

---

457 See along the same line, K. Wiens, 'The Shady World of Repair Manuals: Copyrighting for Planned Obsolescence', *Wired*, 11 December 2012, available on: <https://www.wired.com/2012/11/cease-and-desist-manuals-planned-obsolescence/>.

458 See K. Purdy, 'Is This the End of the Repairable iPhone?', *iFixit*, 29 October 2020, available on: <https://www.ifixit.com/News/45921/is-this-the-end-of-the-repairable-iphone>.

459 C. Welch, 'Apple explains why iPhones now show an ominous warning after 'unauthorized' battery replacements', *The Verge*, 14 August 2019, available on: <https://www.theverge.com/2019/8/14/20805744/apple-iphone-battery-replacements-ios-safety-statement-unauthorized>.

460 RREUSE, *Improving product reparability: Policy options at EU level* (2015) pp. 2–3.

costs of use, maintenance, repair and replacement into consideration. This type of obsolescence can be influenced by the producers and sellers[461], though the final decision belongs to the consumer. Like cases of indirect obsolescence, the obsolete product still functions, but other (financial) reasons are constraining or urging the consumer to get another product.

118. Example: obsolescence due to the costs of use, maintenance and repair – The costs for the use and the necessary maintenance and repair of a product can be perceived as disproportionate when compared to the costs and advantages associated with the purchase of a brand-new and updated product. Several factors can tilt the balance in favour of product replacement. First, repair costs can be high due to the sophisticated product design, the insufficient availability of spare parts at a reasonable cost, the need for special tools, and the labour-intensive work involved in the repair services, which require more and more skills to follow technological breakthroughs.[462] For example, it has been observed that the replacement costs of a broken screen for certain smartphones can be higher than, or at least not proportionate to, the price of a new device.[463] Some manufacturers have even been accused of artificially increasing the price of spare parts.[464] Second, the average selling price of many consumer goods has fallen in real terms due to reduced production costs, thereby making replacement by modern product versions increasingly attractive.[465] The gap between the repair costs and the purchase price of a new product is even narrower if consumers benefit from a discount, e.g. when returning their old product, or if they save money on the energy bill because the new product is more energy-efficient. This is without mentioning other factors influencing consumer behaviour in favour of replacement.[466] All in all, the gap is so narrow that it almost makes no sense to repair components prone to failure, whereas consumers could enjoy a brand-new and up-to-date product.

---

461 While the different prices and costs involved are in principle established through the market mechanism, producers and sellers are still able to play with these prices and costs as a commercial strategy.

462 These factors demonstrate how close economic obsolescence can be to material and indirect obsolescence.

463 See T. Morgan, 'How to repair your smartphone', *Which?*, 22 February 2021, available on: <https://www.which.co.uk/reviews/mobile-phones/article/mobile-phone-repair-cheapest-way-to-fix-iphone-or-android-aLUet6v2LdtY>. See also M. Cordella, F. Alfieri, J. Sanfelix, *Guidance for the Assessment of Material Efficiency: Application to Smartphones – JRC Technical Report* (European Commission 2020) p. 75, where it has been reported that "*the repair of a screen can cost up to 40% of the product price and the trend is towards more expensive repairs for more recent models*".

464 See the claim brought by HOP, which accused Renault and PSA of artificially increasing the price of spare parts of vehicles, reported in HOP, 'Automobile: le prix des pièces détachées gonflé artificiellement', 31 May 2018, <https://www.halteobsolescence.org/automobile-le-prix-des-pieces-detachees-gonfle-artificiellement/>.

465 T. Cooper, 'The significance of product longevity', in T. Cooper, *Longer lasting products: Alternatives to the throwaway society* (Gower 2010) p. 18.

466 See *infra* on the causes of premature obsolescence on the consumer side (n°138–147).

119. Example: obsolescence due to purchase subsidy mechanisms – Another typical example of practices causing the economic obsolescence of products can be found in the mobile phone sector. One strategy followed by some operators is to bundle the mobile phone subscription with a 'free' brand-new phone. According to a *Stiftung Warentest* investigation[467], an increasing number of consumers change their mobile phone after periods of less than 3 years because they regularly receive a new phone through their contract (e.g. supposedly low purchase prices of most smartphones hidden in monthly overall contract costs).[468] However, while some service contracts lead to a shortened replacement cycle, it has been shown that this remains limited to a minority of cases. In all other cases, contract holders decided to keep their old phones despite a new one being available.[469]

(6) Psychological obsolescence

120. Definition of psychological obsolescence – Last but not least, there are cases of psychological obsolescence, whereby the product is *no longer attractive or satisfying in consumers' eyes*, resulting in the purchase of a new product, even if the owned one is still fully functioning. While this type of obsolescence primarily stems from consumers' minds and behaviours, marketing strategies can have a strong influence on consumer demand and preferences.[470] Marketing strategies can consist of using targeted and personalised marketing techniques (including online) and playing with product reviews and ratings, product design, brands, and promotional offers (e.g. credit card points, store loyalty programs, gift cards). Such strategies prompt consumers to constantly re-evaluate product qualities, leading to the devaluation of existing products and the purchase of marketed ones.[471] The existence of psychological obsolescence was pointed out in the middle of the 20th century, notably by B. Stevens and P.M. Gregory.[472] V. Packard referred to 'obsolescence of desirability'.[473] Although the term 'psychological' may be deemed ambiguous[474], it allows encapsulating

---

467 *Stiftung Warentest* is a German consumer organisation and foundation involved in investigating and comparing goods and services (<https://www.test.de/>).

468 A. Manhart, M. Blepp, C. Fischer, K. Graulich, S. Prakash, R. Priess, T. Schleicher, M. Tür, *Resource Efficiency in the ICT Sector* (Greenpeace 2016) p. 38.

469 H. Wieser, N. Tröger, 'Exploring the inner loops of the circular economy: Replacement, repair, and reuse of mobile phones in Austria', 172 *J. Clean. Prod.* (2018) p. 3046.

470 B.L. Bayus, 'Accelerating the Durable Replacement Cycle with Marketing Mix Variables', 5 *J. Prod. Innov. Manag.* (1988) p. 216 at p. 226.

471 J. Spinney, K. Burningham, G. Cooper, N. Green and D. Uzzell, 'What I've found is that your related experiences tend to make you dissatisfied': Psychological obsolescence, consumer demand and the dynamics and environmental implications of de-stabilization in the laptop sector', 12 *Journal of Consumer Culture* (2012) p. 347 at p. 370.

472 See *supra*, n° 48.

473 V. Packard, *The Waste Makers* (David MacKay 1960), especially chapter 6.

474 See B. Burns, 'Re-evaluating obsolescence and planning for it', in T. Cooper, *Longer lasting products: Alternatives to the throwaway society* (Gower 2010) p. 45.

various practices and elements that influence consumers' minds, as opposed to 'style' or 'aesthetical' obsolescence, which merely focuses on fashion. Different kinds of desire for novelty can lead to psychological obsolescence, which depends on the product as well as on the consumer profile.

121. Example: obsolescence due to aesthetics, fashion and style – A first reason why products could become psychologically obsolete relates to aesthetics, fashion and style.[475] Appearance plays a great role in the premature obsolescence of products. In our society, products serve to illustrate our identity and aspirations whilst defining us existentially.[476] When the user considers that the product no longer reflects their personality, he may decide to replace and discard it. This is especially true for "*products used closer to our bodies*", like clothing.[477] The obsolescence of products based on aesthetic grounds may be accelerated due to fashion and style. There are many products subject to annual, seasonal or social changes for which fashion and style carry substantial significance in design, without necessarily adding new functionalities. This type of premature obsolescence especially affects objects of fashion and so-called 'up-to-date products', defined as products that consumers tended to discard when they were considered 'out of date'.[478] Different marketing strategies can reinforce this consumption behaviour, including through advertising on social media.[479] Psychological obsolescence can also be boosted by regulations, like the right of withdrawal, which appears to encourage impulsive consumption and results in additional transport, a possible new purchase, and the risk that returned goods cannot be resold or repurposed.[480]

122. Example: obsolescence due to technological trends – Closely linked to aesthetic obsolescence, some products become obsolete due to technological trends. Technological advances can prompt consumers (especially tech-savvy ones) to replace their product with its latest version, even when

---

475 See also B. Burns, 'Re-evaluating obsolescence and planning for it', in T. Cooper, *Longer lasting products: Alternatives to the throwaway society* (Gower 2010) pp. 45–46.

476 J. Chapman, 'Subject/object relationships and emotionally durable design', in T. Cooper, *Longer lasting products: Alternatives to the throwaway society* (Gower 2010) p. 63.

477 B. Burns, 'Re-evaluating obsolescence and planning for it', in T. Cooper, *Longer lasting products: Alternatives to the throwaway society* (Gower 2010) p. 45.

478 Brook Lyndhurst, *Public understanding of product lifetimes and durability* (DEFRA 2011) p. 26.

479 See e.g. W. Ozuem, Y. Azemi, *Digital Marketing Strategies for Fashion and Luxury Brands* (IGI Global 2018); Y. Liu, T. Zhang, 'Research on Digital Marketing Strategies of Fast Fashion Clothing Brands Based on Big Data', in *34rd Youth Academic Annual Conference of Chinese Association of Automation – Conference proceedings* (IEEE 2019) p. 552 at p. 556; A. Cabigiosu, *Digitalization in the Luxury Fashion Industry* (Springer 2020).

480 E. Terryn, E. Van Gool, 'The Role of European Consumer Contract Law in Shaping the Environmental Impact of E-commerce', 10 *EuCML* (2021) p. 89 at p. 100. For further details on the right of withdrawal, see Chapter IV on the use stage, and more specifically n° 645.

the differences between the two products (including their functionalities) are minor. Through this new purchase, the consumer wants only to stay up-to-date.[481] For example, the 2016 German study issued by the *Umweltbundesamt* showed that *"over 60% of the still fully functional flat screen TVs were replaced in 2012 because their owners desired a better device"*, including larger screen size and better picture quality.[482] Business models can influence consumer needs, desires and the perceived loss in value of the owned product, and thus stimulate the psychological obsolescence of products. One of these commercial practices consists in continuously introducing new products and models onto the market. The short product development times drive obsolescence by making consumers feel outdated and by depreciating the resale value of existing products. Such a strategy was adopted in the 1920s by *General Motors*, with the yearly style change for its cars.[483] A more recent example of this strategy can be found in the smartphone sector, where manufacturers successively launch a new flagship model on the market, sometimes every year.[484] The successive introduction of new products can be accompanied by intensive advertising campaigns, sharpening the perception of inferior quality or performance of the owned product compared to new models. Claims have already been (successfully) brought against such advertising practices.[485] While the majority of consumers might not follow these technological trends, such practices could still influence their perception of their products and cause their premature obsolescence.[486]

123. Example: social obsolescence – Social pressures and status-seeking can also cause the premature obsolescence of products.[487] Some consumers believe that their identity, social acceptance, and status depend on materialistic

---

481 These cases of premature obsolescence are closely linked to functional and indirect obsolescence.

482 S. Prakash et al., *Einfluss der Nutzungsdauer von Produkten auf ihre Umweltwirkung – Schaffung einer Informationsgrundlage und Entwicklung von Strategien gegen "Obsoleszenz"* (Umweltbundesamt Study 2016) p. 45.

483 G. Slade, *Made to break – technology and obsolescence in America* (Harvard University Press 2006) p. 33. See n° 46.

484 H. Wieser, N. Tröger, 'Exploring the inner loops of the circular economy: Replacement, repair, and reuse of mobile phones in Austria', 172 *J. Clean. Prod.* (2018) p. 3043.

485 See e.g. HOP, 'Obsolescence esthétique: le Jury de déontologie publicitaire donne raison à HOP contre Microsoft', 29 July 2020, available on: <https://www.halteobsolescence.org/obsolescence-esthetique-le-jury-de-deontologie-publicitaire-donne-raison-a-hop-contre-microsoft/>; HOP, 'Obsolescence culturelle: le JDP juge fondée la plainte de HOP contre Chromebook (Google)', 5 janvier 2021, available on: <https://www.halteobsolescence.org/obsolescence-culturelle-le-jury-de-deontologie-publicitaire-juge-fondee-la-plainte-de-hop-contre-chromebook-google/>.

486 J. Guiltinan, 'Creative destruction and Destructive Creations: Environmental Ethics and Planned Obsolescence', 89 *Journal of Business Ethics* (2009) p. 22.

487 See also B. Burns, 'Re-evaluating obsolescence and planning for it', in T. Cooper, *Longer lasting products: Alternatives to the throwaway society* (Gower 2010) p. 46 at p. 48.

possessions,[488] which is reinforced by the discourse held by influencers on social media. Some cases of social obsolescence are closely linked to fashion. A phone can be perceived as obsolete when it makes its owner feel outdated or when it no longer performs the functions necessary to continue the social practices that are important to him.[489] Similar practices are used in the videogame sector, especially for games that can be played online. Producers distinguish between players who bought the latest version of the game and those who did not, creating a constant pull for the latter to join the community. Other cases of social obsolescence are due to a social response that appears suddenly, for example after a period of pressure for change related to safety or environmental concerns.[490] The social response related to environmental awareness has been called 'ecological obsolescence' in the literature.[491] Green trends have significantly grown over the last few years, with the support of regulations, including ecodesign requirements and voluntary standards, which influence the EU market and promote the shift towards greener products. Consumers are more and more willing to buy green. The energy-efficiency argument is often raised to justify the replacement of some products. Being aware of these green consumption trends, certain companies overuse this argument to urge consumers to purchase new and greener products. Practices of greenwashing, which are green claims that are not true or cannot be verified, are increasingly used in that regard, causing the premature obsolescence of still functioning products.[492]

c) *Causes of premature obsolescence*

(1) On the business side

124. Five main causes of premature obsolescence on the business side – Products can become prematurely obsolete due to (a combination of) different causes. Some of these causes can be associated with the business side. The premature obsolescence of products can be caused by the development and

---

[488] S.I. Becher, A.-L. Sibony, 'Confronting Product Obsolescence', 27 *Colum. J. Eur. L.* (2021) p. 104.

[489] H. Wieser, N. Tröger, 'Exploring the inner loops of the circular economy: Replacement, repair, and reuse of mobile phones in Austria', 172 *J. Clean. Prod.* (2018) p. 3046.

[490] M. Gladwell, *The Tipping Point: How Little Things Can Make a Big Difference* (Abacus 2002) pp. 12–13.

[491] See e.g. Centre Européen de la Consommation, *L'obsolescence programmée ou les dérives de la société de consommation* (2013) pp. 6–7; C. Déméné, A. Marchand, 'L'obsolescence des produits électroniques: des responsabilités partagées', 10 *The Ethics Forum* (2015) p. 13.

[492] The rise of greenwashing was observed by the EC and the national consumer authorities during the 2020 sweep, a screening of websites organised and coordinated by the EC. See the press release issued by the EC, 'Screening of websites for 'greenwashing': half of green claims lack evidence', 28 January 2021, available on: <https://ec.europa.eu/commission/presscorner/detail/en/ip_21_269>.

production conditions, and more specifically by (1) cost pressure, (2) the lack of economic incentives and (3) time pressure, as well as by other factors, including (4) asymmetrical information and (5) the different interpretation given to the customer's voice. All these causes are linked to the fact that products are seen as a value creation source by businesses.

125. Product as value creation source – The current economic model is based on profit-oriented market rules. Since products are considered as value creation sources, the strategy for increasing profits is to sell more products. Consequently, companies strive to maintain high rates of sales growth, sometimes with the use of pervasive advertising and promotional strategies.[493] The problem occurs when these strategies are too successful, causing overproduction and quick market saturation. This issue started with the development of mass production technology, which resulted in large quantities of unsold goods remaining in the warehouses. In such an economy, products with limited life spans and shortened launch times are preferred as they allow ensuring high rates of sales growth, and thus competing with other companies and satisfying shareholders, by (1) stimulating revenues through faster product replacement, (2) reducing competition against second-hand markets and (3) increasing prices for the replacement product by virtue of making used or owned goods less competitive.[494] This is known as the 'time-inconsistency problem'.[495]

126. First cause: cost pressure – The current economic model has led to cost pressure with shrinking product prices which is exacerbated by fierce global competition between firms.[496] Product prices are calculated top-down, meaning that they are the first to be fixed (by comparing product prices on the market),

---

493 B. Burns, 'Re-evaluating obsolescence and planning for it', in T. Cooper, *Longer lasting products: Alternatives to the throwaway society* (Gower 2010) p. 43.

494 J. Guiltinan, 'Creative destruction and Destructive Creations: Environmental Ethics and Planned Obsolescence', 89 *Journal of Business Ethics* (2009) p. 21.

495 It should be noted that no link should be established between competition and product quality. There are cases where horizontal agreements restrict innovation, limit product choice or degrade existing quality. In other cases, certain types of less obviously restrictive horizontal co-operation between competition firms may be acknowledged as generating efficiencies in the form of product quality benefits, for example, where the co-operation leads to product innovation or improved product performance. Moreover, some vertical restraints lead to higher quality products. See OECD Policy Roundtables of 28 October 2013 on the Role and Measurement of Quality in Competition Analysis, DAF/COMP(2013)17, p. 8.

496 See J. Guiltinan, 'Creative destruction and Destructive Creations: Environmental Ethics and Planned Obsolescence', 89 *Journal of Business Ethics* (2009) p. 21; J. Longmuss and E. Poppe, 'Planned obsolescence: who are those planners?', in C. Bakker and R. Mugge (eds.), *Product Lifetimes And The Environment 2017 – Conference Proceedings* (IOS Press 2017) pp. 219–220; E. Poppe, J. Longmuß, 'Zu Begriff und Theorie der geplanten Obsoleszenz', in E. Poppe, J. Longmuß (eds.), *Geplante Obsoleszenz Hinter den Kulissen der Produktentwicklung* (Transcript 2019) p. 49 at p. 51; J. Bachér et al., *Electronic products and obsolescence in a*

before any decision is taken on the component prices and manufacturing costs.[497] Since profit margins are based on the difference between the market price of products and their production costs, the strategy for increasing profits is to keep production costs as low as possible.[498] Cost efficiency drives the optimisation of global production chains by minimising the costs of resources, materials, product design, labour and transport.[499] Product testing, which also involves costs, is restricted to an absolute minimum.[500] All these development and production conditions can adversely impact product quality and hinder the production of sustainable products and innovations in that sense, leading to cases of material obsolescence.[501]

127. Second cause: lack of economic incentives for the development of sustainable products – In addition, businesses lack incentives to provide durable and reparable goods and take the end-of-life phase of their products into account. While some producers will never be influenced by moral arguments when dealing with business, the pro-environmental ones may also be forced to take environmentally harmful decisions after having struck the balance between environmental protection and other values – mostly economic.[502] Designing and producing sustainable products might require some costs and investments in the research and developments sector. Yet these costs and investments may result in increased product price which, even though only differing by a few cents, may represent a great deal from the company perspective because of low margins and fierce competition in some product sectors.[503] Similar reasoning can be applied to maintenance and repair, for which costs and investments are also required (e.g. costs to stock and manage spare parts). It may be deemed more profitable to sell new products than to repair old ones. This lack of incentives can trigger

circular economy (European Topic Centre Waste and Materials in a Green Economy 2020) p. 3.

497 J. Longmuss and E. Poppe, 'Planned obsolescence: who are those planners?', in C. Bakker and R. Mugge (eds.), *Product Lifetimes And The Environment 2017 – Conference Proceedings* (IOS Press 2017) p. 220.

498 EEA, *Circular by design: Products in the circular economy* (European Union 2017) p. 14.

499 This includes decisions to relocate parts, if not all, of the production chain in other countries outside the EU.

500 See S. Prakash et al., *Einfluss der Nutzungsdauer von Produkten auf ihre Umweltwirkung – Schaffung einer Informationsgrundlage und Entwicklung von Strategien gegen "Obsoleszenz"* (Umweltbundesamt Study 2016) p. 50; J. Longmuss and E. Poppe, 'Planned obsolescence: who are those planners?', in C. Bakker and R. Mugge (eds.), *Product Lifetimes And The Environment 2017 – Conference Proceedings* (IOS Press 2017) p. 219.

501 See *infra* on the product design trends and their impacts on product lifetime (n° 165–167).

502 Other values can tilt the balance against environmental protection, including health or safety. See E. Maitre-Ekern, 'The Choice of Regulatory Instruments for a Circular Economy', in Klaus Mathis and Bruce R. Huber (eds.), *Environmental Law and Economics* (Springer 2017) p. 313.

503 D. Jepsen, L. Spengler, L. Augsberg, *Delivering resource-efficient products – How Ecodesign can drive a circular economy in Europe* (European Environmental Bureau 2015) p. 54.

products with a limited lifetime, especially material obsolescence, economic and indirect obsolescence.

128. THIRD CAUSE: TIME PRESSURE – The current economic model also exerts time pressure on companies, leading to fast-changing technology.[504] In other words, companies' interests lie in the next generation of goods. As rightly explained by J. Guiltinan, "*[t]hrough the use of flexible, modular, and faster design software and production equipment, concurrent product development processes, and information technology, firms have reduced both the length of the production process and the time required to adapt production to demand and competitive actions.* This results in "*rapid execution of orders and delivery, faster implementation of new product concepts* (including new features to existing products and new innovative products), *and reduced capital, inventory, and unit costs*".[505] Artificial intelligence technology could further speed up and support the design and product development process for consumer electronics.[506] The speed of innovation cycles also means less time is dedicated to the practical application of product lifetime tests, with sometimes only the most important functions being subjected to review.[507] To ensure high profitability, companies resort to strategies of brand loyalty, e.g. by repeatedly offering free upgrades, allowing them to facilitate migration of their customers to their own version of the next technological advance rather than risk losing them to competitors.[508] In principle, technological and technical progress, and the resulting product obsolescence, is not a problem in itself but actually inherent in any human society. Product innovation is even embraced by policymakers and stimulated by means of policies.[509] It would thus make no sense to automatically sanction producers or sellers who place products on the market that have some technological progress in comparison with older versions.[510] Yet, today's rapidly

504 E. Giaretta, 'Ethical product innovation: in praise of slowness', 17 *TQM magazine* (2005) p. 161 at p. 167; J. Bachér et al., *Electronic products and obsolescence in a circular economy* (European Topic Centre Waste and Materials in a Green Economy 2020) p. 3.

505 J. Guiltinan, 'Creative destruction and Destructive Creations: Environmental Ethics and Planned Obsolescence', 89 *Journal of Business Ethics* (2009) p. 21.

506 Indeed, algorithms are capable of rapidly generating large quantities of design alternatives, optimising for multiple variables, as well as other design features. See Ellen MacArthur Foundation, *Artificial Intelligence and the Circular Economy* (2019) p. 27.

507 S. Prakash et al., *Einfluss der Nutzungsdauer von Produkten auf ihre Umweltwirkung – Schaffung einer Informationsgrundlage und Entwicklung von Strategien gegen "Obsoleszenz"* (Umweltbundesamt Study 2016) p. 50.

508 J. Guiltinan, 'Creative destruction and Destructive Creations: Environmental Ethics and Planned Obsolescence', 89 *Journal of Business Ethics* (2009) p. 22. In its paper, J. Guiltinan refers to the cellular phone service competition in which free phone upgrades are offered every two years as incentives to consumers to renew cellular service contracts.

509 EEA, *Circular by design: Products in the circular economy* (European Union 2017) p. 16; L. Bisschop, Y. Hendlin, J. Jaspers, 'Designed to break: planned obsolescence as corporate environmental crime', 78 *Crime, Law and Social Change* (2022) p. 280.

510 A. Hamann, 'Obsolescence programmée: le droit en panne?', 102 *D.C.C.R.* (2014) p. 43.

growing pace of technological innovation has been identified as the core driver for shorter product lifecycles and their premature obsolescence (including functional, indirect, psychological and material obsolescence).[511]

129. Fourth cause: information asymmetries – Beyond development and production conditions, some producers may place too little emphasis on the sustainability of their products due to information asymmetries. In fact, companies are generally reluctant and have no incentive to disclose information on the characteristics of their products, including those related to product sustainability aspects. First, it is difficult to convince consumers that a product is durable as durability is not visible at the time of purchase. Consequently, consumers lack the guarantee that the product will be cost-effective over its lifetime. Second, the results of the efforts devoted to product sustainability are only visible years later when it comes to recycling materials. As rightly explained in a study carried out by the Swedish Environmental Research Institute (*IVL*), "*[t]he business potential is not primarily related to an increased order stock due to the environmental management system, but rather a result of the management system being a tool for increased efficiency and reduced resource use, which in turn leads to lowering costs*".[512] Therefore, on the contrary, producers are tempted to take advantage of information asymmetry.[513] As G. Akerlof highlighted[514], the lack of transparency allows companies to pretend that their products are of high quality. The protection of intellectual property rights exacerbates this issue, triggering protective design measures that ultimately create barriers to repair.[515]

130. Fifth cause: different interpretations of the customer's voice – The customer's voice may be interpreted differently in a company, depending on the ability among staff members to understand and interpret facts in various contexts. For example, while product developers would generally perceive customers as economic and rational human beings, members of the corporate communications department may regard them as environmentally concerned

511 See J. Guiltinan, 'Creative destruction and Destructive Creations: Environmental Ethics and Planned Obsolescence', 89 *Journal of Business Ethics* (2009) p. 21 at p. 23; A. Girard et al., 'Obsolescence of Home Appliances and Electronics: What Is the Role of the Consumer?', *Équiterre* (2018) p. 13.

512 IVL, *Det lönsamma miljöarbetet – Miljöstrategier och resultat i småföretag – Rapport* (2004), as cited in A.-K. Jönbrink, H. Eric Melin, *How central authorities can support ecodesign – Company perspectives* (TemaNord 2008) p. 19.

513 R. Kurz, 'Quality, obsolescence and unsustainable innovation', 28 *Ekonomski vjesnik* (2015) p. 513.

514 G. Akerlof, 'The Market for Lemons: Quality Uncertainty and the Market Mechanism', 84 *Q. J. Econ.* (1970) p. 488 at p. 500.

515 EEA, *Circular by design: Products in the circular economy* (European Union 2017) p. 14. See also S. Svensson, J.L. Richter, E. Maitre-Ekern, T. Pihlajarinne, A. Maigret, C. Dalhammar, *The Emerging 'Right to Repair' legislation in the EU and the U.S.*, Paper presented at Going Green Care Innovation (Vienna 2018).

and interested.[516] These different understandings and interpretations can explain the lack of support of certain sustainable projects. Lower costs, comfort of use or better product performance may be favoured over improved product sustainability.

(2) On the consumer side

131. Eight causes of premature obsolescence on the consumer side – In addition to the causes associated with the business side, products also become prematurely obsolete due to causes associated with the consumer side. These causes included (1) lack of knowledge and sense of responsibility, (2) lack of information, (3) confusion, misinformation and mistrust, (4) other behavioural biases, (5) haphazard approach and myopic behaviour, with the desire for novelty, the locked-in feeling and the prices as main influencing factors, (6) lack of skills and incentive to care and repair and (7) disposal and storage habits. All these causes stem from the peculiar consumer-object relationships that exist in today's society.

132. Peculiar consumer-object relationships – Nowadays, products occupy a prominent place in consumers' daily lives. Electrical and electronic equipment, for example, can be found in nearly every EU household, and new appliances are regularly bought by consumers.[517] The use of mobile, wireless and connected products has significantly increased. Owning certain products, like home appliances, is no longer regarded as a luxury, but as the normal way to fulfil needs. These products are "*closely connected with the personal well-being and with the surrounding environment of the home*".[518] Furthermore, products also fulfil consumers' needs of social approval and have a value expressive function.[519] The continual evolution of the self-actualizing user and social norms poses therefore a significant challenge to old or outmoded possessions that are perceived as no longer representative of the self.[520] This phenomenon

---

516 E. Rex, *Produktens eller samhällets miljöproblem? Om miljöfrågans hanter-ing och kommunikation inom Volvo Lastvagnar* (Chalmers University of Technology 2007), as cited in A.-K. Jönbrink, H. Eric Melin, *How central authorities can support ecodesign – Company perspectives* (TemaNord 2008) p. 22.

517 A. Girard et al., 'Obsolescence of Home Appliances and Electronics: What Is the Role of the Consumer?', *Équiterre* (2018) p. 11; J. Bachér et al., *Electronic products and obsolescence in a circular economy* (European Topic Centre Waste and Materials in a Green Economy 2020) p. 7.

518 CECED, *Material flows of the home appliance industry. European Committee of Domestic Equipment Manufacturers* (2017) p. 20.

519 R. Grewal, 'The Timing of Repeat Purchase of Consumer Durable Goods: The Role of Functional Bases of Consumer Attitudes', 41 *Journal of Marketing Research* (2004) pp. 104–105.

520 J. Chapman, 'Subject/object relationships and emotionally durable design', in T. Cooper, *Longer lasting products: Alternatives to the throwaway society* (Gower 2010) p. 64.

has been exacerbated with the shift towards an information society, in which the hardware and software of a product stimulate the creation of a personal bond between the user and equipment.[521] All in all, the increasing number of products surrounding us, coupled with the rapid development of new products and technologies, has led to accelerating product consumption. Products, like electrical and electronic equipment, become outdated more rapidly and, as such, less desirable to repair.[522] Short-lived and disposable products have become the norm.

133. First cause: lack of knowledge and sense of responsibility – Among the major issues that contribute to premature obsolescence, there is the fact that some consumers are not aware or have little understanding of the environmental footprints of the products they purchase, use and discard and seldom recognize the environmental benefits of long-lasting products.[523] Since they do not know or understand the link between their consumption and the environmental issues, these consumers do not change their attitudes towards product sustainability.[524] Consumers may also take a passive stance, meaning that they do not feel responsible, but only victims of producers' and designers' strategies and/or of the capitalist system. The system is indeed made in a way that consumers wear blinkers about the consequences of their actions.

134. Second cause: lack of information on products – Consumer ignorance may stem from the lack of (reliable and relevant) information on products. Studies have revealed that, for the large majority of goods, there is no information related to product lifespan[525], or information on known aspects of products that could make them fail significantly earlier.[526] In other cases, such information is difficult to find, as reported by the 2018 behavioural study

---

521 This product attachment can be noted in E. Robinot, F. Durif, D. Kréziak, I. Prim-Allaz, *"Fifty ways to leave your cell phone": Product obsolescence, product replacement and product attachment* (European Marketing Association Conference 2014), where 85 students were asked to write a letter to their old phone with the objective of exploring how product attachment remains or is expressed at the time of the replacement.

522 J. Bachér et al., *Electronic products and obsolescence in a circular economy* (European Topic Centre Waste and Materials in a Green Economy 2020) p. 10.

523 J.D. Abbey, M.G. Meloy, V.D.R. Guide Jr., S. Atalay, 'Remanufactured products in closed-loop supply chains for consumer goods', 24 *Production and Operations Management* (2015) p. 488 at p. 503.

524 See J. Cox, S. Griffith, S. Giorgi, G. King, 'Consumer understanding of product lifetimes', 79 *Resources, Conservation and Recycling* (2013) p. 25.

525 According to the 2013 Eurobarometer, over 90% of citizens asked for clear labelling indicating product lifespan. See TNS Political & Social, *Flash Eurobarometer 367 – Attitudes of Europeans towards building the single market for green products* (European Commission 2013) p. 106.

526 See for ex. T. Cooper and K. Christer, 'Marketing durability', in T. Cooper, *Longer lasting products: Alternatives to the throwaway society* (Gower 2010) p. 282.

issued by the EC.[527] Yet, product sustainability can seldom be observed directly. If no explicit information is provided, consumers have to use intrinsic cues, namely the product's physical characteristics, and extrinsic cues, such as the product price, brand or online reviews, to infer the lifespan of the product.[528] However, these proxy indicators do not necessarily signal product quality and sustainability. For example, concerning the price, which is the most important driver and simultaneously barrier for consumers willing to buy sustainable goods, expensive products are not necessarily sustainable.[529] In other words, the price of products does not reflect their real environmental costs to society. As regards brands, premium brands are not necessarily the most reliable and within a particular brand, some products are better than others.[530] There are even situations where the manufacturer keeps selling a product under a trademark associated with certain material credence attributes of the product, while degrading its quality.[531] Regarding second-hand goods in particular, the lack of information can deter consumers from buying them. An overwhelming majority of consumers have already expressed their desire for more information on product lifetime[532], and more generally on product environmental information[533], to guide their choices at the time of purchase. As a consequence, imperfectly informed buyers, who are unable to establish the level of product quality and identify sustainable goods, will not opt for the product that is the

527 In the study, 82% of the participants agreed that it is difficult to find information on how long a product will last and 82% also stated the same for reparability information. See LE Europe, VVA Europe, Ipsos, ConPolicy, Trinomics, *Behavioural study on consumers' engagement in the circular economy* (European Commission 2018) p. 82.

528 T. Cooper and K. Christer, 'Marketing durability', in T. Cooper, *Longer lasting products: Alternatives to the throwaway society* (Gower 2010) p. 276 at p. 280; T. Knight, G. King, S. Herren, J. Cox (Brook Lyndhurst), *Electrical and electronic product design: product lifetime* (WRAP 2013) pp. 36–37.

529 See for ex. A.R. Roa, 'The quality of price as a quality cue', XLII *Journal of Marketing Research* (2005) p. 401 at p. 405.

530 T. Cooper and K. Christer, 'Marketing durability', in T. Cooper, *Longer lasting products: Alternatives to the throwaway society* (Gower 2010) p. 280.

531 A. Katz, 'Beyond search costs: the linguistic and trust functions of trademarks', 5 *Brigham Young University Law Review* (2010) p. 1605 at p. 1607, referring to J. S. Dillbary, 'Getting the Word Out: The Informational Function of Trademarks', 40 *Arizona State Law Journal* (2009) pp. 1026–1027.

532 According to the 2013 Eurobarometer, over 90% of citizens asked for clear labelling indicating product useful lifespan. See TNS Political & Social, *Flash Eurobarometer 367 – Attitudes of Europeans towards building the single market for green products* (European Commission 2013) p. 106. See also T. Cooper, 'Inadequate Life? Evidence of Consumer Attitudes to Product Obsolescence', 27 *J. Consum. Policy* (2004) p. 421 at p. 449.

533 According to the 2013 Eurobarometer, 81% of the respondents would like to find the environmental information about a product on its label. See TNS Political & Social, *Flash Eurobarometer 367 – Attitudes of Europeans towards building the single market for green products* (European Commission 2013) p. 77. See also GfK Belgium, time.lex, Milieu Ltd, BIO IS and the Ecologic Institute, *Consumer market study on environmental claims for non-food products* (European Commission 2014) p. 88.

most cost-effective over its lifetime and will not be willing to pay an adequate price for higher quality, making the market for good quality collapse.

135. Third cause: confusion, misinformation and mistrust – When information is provided, consumers have to contend with commercial practices which cause confusion and misinformation, or breed mistrust and dampen their interest in purchasing sustainable products. Along with the growing awareness and sensitivity of consumers to environmental concerns,[534] there has been a proliferation of green claims on both product packaging and in advertising in recent years. According to a 2014 Consumer Market Study on environmental claims, 76% of all the products assessed in shops contained an environmental claim, whether explicit or implicit, voluntary or mandatory.[535] Some of these claims are part of a wider marketing strategy aiming to urge consumers to buy new and greener products (ecological obsolescence).[536] The profusion of green claims goes hand in hand with an increasing number of complaints about vague, misleading or unfounded claims.[537] It becomes particularly difficult for consumers to understand, interpret, differentiate and verify the variety of sustainability logos, labels, trust marks, quality marks, claims and online tools (e.g. mobile applications comparing the carbon footprints of selected products).[538]It has been shown, for example, that some consumers make no distinction between non-certified (self-declarations) and third-party certified labels.[539]

136. Fourth cause: behavioural biases – Even if they receive information on products, several behavioural biases may prevent information recipients from taking sustainable decisions. There is, first of all, the fact that the human brain has limited capacity for perceptual stimuli and consumers' visual attention. Consumers

---

534 See for ex. Kantar, *Special Eurobarometer 501 - Attitudes of European citizens towards the Environment* (European Commission 2020).

535 GfK Belgium, time.lex, Milieu Ltd, BIO IS and the Ecologic Institute, *Consumer market study on environmental claims for non-food products* (European Commission 2014) p. 54.

536 Cases of so-called 'ecological obsolescence' pertain to psychological obsolescence, as explained *supra* (n° 123).

537 See TNS Political & Social, *Flash Eurobarometer 367 – Attitudes of Europeans towards building the single market for green products* (European Commission 2013) p. 80; GfK Belgium, time.lex, Milieu Ltd, BIO IS and the Ecologic Institute, *Consumer market study on environmental claims for non-food products* (2014 European Commission) p. 33.

538 61% of consumers state that they find it difficult to understand which products are truly environmentally friendly, either because they cannot make their way through the large number of environmental claims or because they find these claims unclear and 44% indicate that they do not trust this type of information. See GfK Belgium, time.lex, Milieu Ltd, BIO IS and the Ecologic Institute, *Consumer market study on environmental claims for non-food products* (European Commission 2014) p. 76. See also Ecorys, GFK and Tilburg University, *Study on the effects on consumer behaviour of online sustainability information displays – Final report* (Consumer Programme 2014).

539 GfK Belgium, time.lex, Milieu Ltd, BIO IS and the Ecologic Institute, *Consumer market study on environmental claims for non-food products* (2014 European Commission) p. 84.

are thus limited by the boundaries of their own perceptual capacity when searching for a particular product or brand in a grocery store.[540] Secondly, consumers are limited by the finite amount of time they have to make a decision. Seeking and processing information can take time and energy, and not all consumers are ready to make the effort in that regard.[541] These two biases can be exacerbated if consumers are overwhelmed with information. In certain cases, information overload can lead consumers to ignore certain information. Beyond these two biases, some consumers may avoid information *"to remain optimistic, reduce potential anxiety, prevent dissonance (with pro-environmental values), and avoid experiencing regret"*.[542] Biased and negative perception of reused, remanufactured and reparable products may even cause consumers to avoid labelled products altogether as they assume that these products are of lesser quality or would break more often than their new counterparts.[543] Other biases, like the present bias and the motivated reasoning and confirmation bias, influence consumer behaviour in the wrong direction, although consumers are well-informed.[544] All these biases can significantly diminish, or even reverse, the intended effects of information disclosure in changing purchasing norms and habits.[545]

137. Fifth cause: haphazard approach and myopic behaviour – Irrespective of whether they are informed or not, it has been observed that product lifetime and sustainability are generally not among the front-of-mind considerations for consumers when purchasing a product.[546] Even when they are aware of and concerned about the environmental impacts of products, it seems

---

540 J. Clement, T. Kristensen, K. Grønhaug, 'Understanding consumers' in-store visual perception: The influence of package design features on visual attention', 20 *Journal of Retailing and Consumer Services* (2013) p. 234 at p. 239.

541 G. Howells, 'The Potential and Limits of Consumer Empowerment by Information', 32 *Journal of law and society* (2005) pp. 356–357.

542 See S.I. Becher, A.-L. Sibony, 'Confronting Product Obsolescence', 27 *Colum. J. Eur. L.* (2021) p. 116, referring to T.L. Webb, B.P.I. Chang, Y. Benn, '"The Ostrich Problem': Motivated Avoidance or Rejection of Information about Goal Progress', 7 *Social and Personality Psychology Compass* (2013) p. 794 at p. 807; R. Golman, D. Hagmann, G. Loewenstein, 'Information Avoidance', 55 *Journal of Economic Literature* 96 (2017) p. 96 at p. 135.

543 See also I. Gåvertsson, L. Milios, C. Dalhammar, 'Quality Labelling for Re-used ICT Equipment to Support Consumer Choice in the Circular Economy', 43 *J. Consum. Policy* (2020) p. 353 at p. 377; V. Swaen, *Labelling the durability/reparability of a product* (EESC Conference on Tackling premature obsolescence in Europe 2018).

544 G. Howells, 'The Potential and Limits of Consumer Empowerment by Information', 32 *Journal of law and society* (2005) p. 358 at p. 362; S.I. Becher, A.-L. Sibony, 'Confronting Product Obsolescence', 27 *Colum. J. Eur. L.* (2021) p. 114.

545 G. Loewenstein, C. R. Sunstein, R. Golman, 'Disclosure: Psychology Changes Everything', 6 *Annual Review of Economic* (2014) p. 391 at p. 419.

546 T. Cooper, "Inadequate life? Evidence of consumer attitudes to product obsolescence", 27 *J. Consum. Policy* (2004) p. 442; T. Knight et al. (Brook Lyndhurst), *Electrical and electronic product design: product lifetime* (WRAP 2013) p. 39.

that their actions do not follow their speech and convictions.[547] On the contrary, consumers rarely evaluate their needs and existing possessions or make a critical assessment of product quality based on independent reviews prior to purchase.[548] Although it depends on their profile[549], consumers generally think in the short term when buying a product, wearing blinkers regarding environmental damage and opting for either the newest or the cheapest version of a product.

138. Three factors linked to this haphazard approach and myopic behaviour – A consumer purchase is essentially influenced by three factors. There is, first, their desire for novelty. Many former luxury goods are now regarded as necessities in the game of identity formation and status display.[550] Social pressure strengthens this desire, urging consumers to keep pace with fashion and technological advances. For instance, it has been shown that parents are sometimes put under direct pressure from their children to replace their phones.[551] Other explanations lie in structural issues, such as work life conditions, which favour a work-and-spend lifestyle, the conditions of urban living, cultural trends, the influence of mainstream markets, or the effects of pervasive marketing.[552] The desire for novelty is boosted by the fact that cheap, fashionable and up-to-date products are constantly advertised and put at consumers' disposal, including online.

The second factor that can influence consumer purchasing decisions is their feeling of being locked-in a throwaway culture. Rapid replacement cycles have become the norm and consumers express feeling 'locked-in' to wasteful consumption patterns.[553] Low expectations are developed from the consumers'

---

547 F. Echegaray, 'Consumers' reactions to product obsolescence in emerging markets: the case of Brazil', 134 *J. Clean. Prod.* (2016) p. 194; I. Gåvertsson, L. Milios, C. Dalhammar, 'Quality Labelling for Re-used ICT Equipment to Support Consumer Choice in the Circular Economy', 43 *J. Consum. Policy* (2020) p. 359. See also A.-L. Sibony, 'Data and arguments: Empirical research in consumer law', 2 *CeDIE Working Papers* (2018) p. 19.

548 S. Evans, T. Cooper, 'Consumer influences on product life-spans', in T. Cooper, *Longer lasting products: Alternatives to the throwaway society* (Gower 2010) p. 341.

549 C. Campbell distinguishes between three consumer profiles that desire new products: the 'pristinians', the technophiles and those who are first to respond to fashion. See C. Campbell, 'The desire for the new: Its nature and social location as presented in theories of fashion and modern consumerism', in R. Silverstone and E. Hirsch (eds.), *Consuming Technologies: Media and information in domestic spaces* (Routledge 1992) p. 48 at p. 63, and especially pp. 55–56. For other analysis based on consumer profiles, see S. Evans, T. Cooper, 'Consumer influences on product life-spans', in T. Cooper, *Longer lasting products: Alternatives to the throwaway society* (Gower 2010) p. 329; A. Girard et al., 'Obsolescence of Home Appliances and Electronics: What Is the Role of the Consumer?', *Équiterre* (2018) p. 20 at p. 26.

550 N. Maycroft, *Consumption, planned obsolescence and waste* (Lincoln School of Art and Design 2009) p. 7 and p. 30–31.

551 H. Wieser, N. Tröger, 'Exploring the inner loops of the circular economy: Replacement, repair, and reuse of mobile phones in Austria', 172 *J. Clean. Prod.* (2018) p. 3048.

552 C. Sanne, 'Willing consumers – or locked-in? Policies for a sustainable consumption', 42 *Ecological Economics* (2002) p. 273 at p. 287.

553 C. Bakker, C. Schuit, *The long view – Exploring product lifetime extension* (United Nations Environment Programme 2017) p. 5.

perceptions about the product[554], which might depend on the product type[555], as well as on consumers.[556] At the time of purchase, because they do not expect premium quality models to last longer, many consumers – although willing to have longer-lasting products – see little reason for paying higher prices for premium products and thus rather purchase low-quality products, at the expense of the environment.[557] The same reasoning can be held for second-hand products, which are seen as less attractive.[558]

Third, the easy affordability of certain new products makes it even more tempting for consumers to buy cheap products and not to repair old ones.[559] Bounded rationality leads consumers to focus on the purchase price rather than the use cost. Consumers can now afford products that were considered luxury products in the past, not only because the price of many products has sharply declined[560], but also due to increasing disposable incomes. Purchasing a new washing machine, for example, cost 59 working hours in 2004 but dropped to just 39 hours in 2014.[561] Moreover, the negative environmental externalities generated by short-lived products (e.g. resources used from raw materials and production processes, waste management) are generally not internalized by producers so that the price of these products remains low. By contrast, consumers may lack funds and certainty about future prices to buy premium range products.[562]

These consumer preferences can lead to the earlier replacement of functioning products. The replaced products are accumulated or discarded prior to failure (psychological obsolescence), whereas the new products are generally of low-quality and attract fewer emotions and thus might be more quickly outdated, hard to repair and made of less robust materials (material and

---

554 G. Kenyon, K. Sen, 'A Model for Assessing Consumer Perceptions of Quality', 4 *International Journal of Quality and Service Sciences* (2012) p. 175 at p. 188.

555 See e.g. the study conducted by the UK Environmental Agency, which distinguishes, between workhorse, up-to-date and investment products: Brook Lyndhurst, *Public understanding of product lifetimes and durability* (DEFRA 2011).

556 T. Cooper, 'Inadequate life? Evidence of consumer attitudes to product obsolescence', 27 *J. Consum. Policy* (2004) pp. 438–439.

557 H. Wieser, N. Tröger and R. Hübner, 'The consumers' desired and expected product lifetimes', in T. Cooper, N. Braithwaite, M. Moreno and G. Salvia (eds.), *Product Lifetimes and the Environment (PLATE) Conference proceedings* (Nottingham Trent University: CADBE 2015) p. 391.

558 *Ibid.*

559 N. Maycroft, *Consumption, planned obsolescence and waste* (Lincoln School of Art and Design 2009) p. 6; J. Bachér et al., *Electronic products and obsolescence in a circular economy* (European Topic Centre Waste and Materials in a Green Economy 2020) p. 10.

560 See *supra* on the causes of premature obsolescence on the business side (n° 133).

561 CECED, *Material flows of the home appliance industry. European Committee of Domestic Equipment Manufacturers* (2017) p. 27.

562 B. Keirsbilck, S. Rousseau, 'The Marketing Stage: Fostering Sustainable Consumption Choices in a "Circular" and "Functional" Economy', in B. Keirsbilck, E. Terryn (eds.), *Consumer Protection in a Circular Economy* (Intersentia 2019) p. 99.

psychological obsolescence). Worse, these impulsive purchases may send the signal to suppliers that they should produce more short-lived products.[563]

139. Sixth cause: lack of skills and incentives to care and repair – Another consumer behaviour that can cause or at least contribute to the premature obsolescence of products, and more specifically to their material obsolescence, is the way consumers use and look after their products. The life spans of products may considerably vary depending on its user.[564]

Concerning product care, studies have shown that many products are not properly and carefully used and maintained by consumers, even in spite of the presence of the manufacturer's instructions.[565] This is especially true for certain categories of products, like everyday footwear, for which the majority of consumers are indifferent to product care during use.[566] This lack of care can be explained by the fact that consumers find it too demanding, as such tasks require time, money, physical and cognitive effort and are not part of their routine.[567] Product obsolescence could occur even more prematurely if the product is of poor quality.

Concerning product repair, consumers are generally not keen on and/or skilled at repairing. A survey of over 800 households conducted in the UK in the 2000s revealed that about one-third of the surveyed householders 'rarely' or 'never' had their appliances repaired.[568] The 2018 behavioural study on consumer engagement in the circular economy obtained similar results, with 36% of participants indicating that they did not repair products, though this varied considerably between Member States.[569] Beyond legal guarantee, repair is often considered too expensive compared with product replacement, whereas DIY repair is seen as requiring too much time and effort, especially with the complex and protective design of most products. Repair has become an optional, sometimes expensive hobby, less an exercise in thrift.[570] What is more, the repair

---

563 S. Evans, T. Cooper, 'Consumer influences on product life-spans', in T. Cooper, *Longer lasting products: Alternatives to the throwaway society* (Gower 2010) p. 342.

564 See e.g. N. Gregson, A. Metcalfe, L. Crewe, 'Practices of object maintenance and repair: How consumers attend to consumer objects within the home', 9 *Journal of Consumer Culture* (2009) p. 248 at p. 272.

565 See e.g. S. Evans, T. Cooper, 'Consumer influences on product life-spans', in T. Cooper, *Longer lasting products: Alternatives to the throwaway society* (Gower 2010) p. 326 at p. 330.

566 *Ibid.*, p. 327.

567 L. Ackermann, R. Mugge, J. Schoormans, 'Consumers' perspective on product care: An exploratory study of motivators, ability factors, and triggers', 183 *J. Clean. Prod.* (2018) p. 381.

568 See T. Cooper, 'Inadequate life? Evidence of consumer attitudes to product obsolescence', 27 *J. Consum. Policy* (2004) p. 437.

569 LE Europe, VVA Europe, Ipsos, ConPolicy, Trinomics, *Behavioural study on consumers' engagement in the circular economy* (European Commission 2018) p. 83.

570 F. Trentmann, *Empire of things: How We Became a World of Consumers, from the Fifteenth Century to the Twenty-First* (Harper 2016) p. 772.

industry within the EU is in decline, meaning fewer repairers are available.[571] Last but not least, consumers tend to exclusively focus on negative past experiences with repair, fuelling their reluctance to repair.[572]

140. Seventh cause: disposal and storage habits – Different motives can shape consumer decisions to replace a product[573], although it varies greatly depending on the type of product.[574] Premature obsolescence can occur when consumers decide to discard products prior to failure, because of improved utility, improved expression and new desires. Low expectations may also be used as justification for replacing products before their technical end-of-life.[575] This is called the 'perceived obsolescence' of products. In those cases, products are discarded not because of technical failure, but rather because of their perceived inability to meet identity aspirations, to confer social status, and to communicate this to other individuals.[576] Unlike cases of material obsolescence, this type of psychological obsolescence is not imposed on consumers but rather chosen by them.[577] Although the product has not reached material obsolescence yet, it is replaced on technological, economical or emotional grounds. Once a product lifespan has met consumer expectations, it is 'mentally written off'.[578] In other words, consumer mindsets seem to be a limiting factor for product lifetime. This behaviour is reinforced by "*inadequate knowledge about the waste implications, a lack of concern or sense of personal responsibility, the perceived acceptability of [recycling or] passing on products to others for reuse and a desire to minimize risks associated with product failure*".[579]

When replaced, the product is not necessarily discarded, but can 'hibernate' in the consumer's drawer.[580] For example, it has been reported that 54–113

571 RREUSE, *Improving product reparability: Policy options at EU level* (2015) p. 2–3.

572 LE Europe, VVA Europe, Ipsos, ConPolicy, Trinomics, *Behavioural study on consumers' engagement in the circular economy* (European Commission 2018) p. 79.

573 N. van Nes, J. Cramer, 'Product lifetime optimization: a challenging strategy towards more sustainable consumption patterns', 14 *J. Clean. Prod.* (2006) p. 1307 at p. 1318.

574 J. Cox et al., 'Consumer understanding of product lifetimes', 79 *Resources, Conservation and Recycling* (2013) pp. 25–26.

575 H. Wieser, N. Tröger and R. Hübner, 'The consumers' desired and expected product lifetimes', in T. Cooper, N. Braithwaite, M. Moreno and G. Salvia (eds.), *Product Lifetimes and the Environment (PLATE) Conference proceedings* (Nottingham Trent University: CADBE 2015) p. 392.

576 A study carried out in Brazil showed that this was the case for nearly half of discarded products. See F. Echegaray, 'Consumers' reactions to product obsolescence in emerging markets: the case of Brazil', 134 *J. Clean. Prod.* (2016) p. 197.

577 D. Kreziak, I. Prim-Allaz and E. Robinot, *Des tiroirs pleins de téléphones remplacés: consommateurs et objets à obsolescence perçue* (ADEME 2017), especially p. 42.

578 L. Hennies, R. Stamminger, 'An empirical survey on the obsolescence of appliances in German households', 112 *Resources, Conservation and Recycling* (2016) p. 73 at p. 82.

579 S. Evans, T. Cooper, 'Consumer influences on product life-spans', in T. Cooper, *Longer lasting products: Alternatives to the throwaway society* (Gower 2010) p. 343.

580 See *infra* on the concept of hibernating products (n° 168).

million old mobile phones are hibernating in French households, of which more than 2/3 are still functioning.[581] This problem, however, is not confined to mobile phones. Some products, which are no longer used by households, never enter the reuse or waste stream and are stored at the consumer's place, like in their garage.[582] It seems that consumers feel "*the urge to collect and preserve old stuff, be it for a sense of physical security, status or immortality*".[583] Some replaced products also stay in consumers' drawers because of a residual sentimental value.[584] Concerns about data privacy and the lack of knowledge about where and how to dispose of certain products are other key reasons leading consumers to keep hold of their unused devices.[585] Consequently, "*[c]onsumer homes have turned into veritable mines of untapped materials*".[586]

D. RESISTING, POSTPONING AND REVERSING PREMATURE OBSOLESCENCE: RELEVANT CONCEPTS

1. STRATEGIES AGAINST PREMATURE OBSOLESCENCE AND ASSOCIATED CONCEPTS

141. Four types of strategies and their associated concepts – Beyond the concepts related to product lifetime[587], other concepts relate to the strategies that contribute to curbing practices of premature obsolescence and reaching

---

581 Sofies, Bio Innovation Service, *Étude du marché et parc de téléphones portables français en vue d'augmenter durablement leur taux de collecte – Synthèse* (2019) p. 8.

582 F. Trentmann, *Empire of things: How We Became a World of Consumers, from the Fifteenth Century to the Twenty-First* (Harper 2016) p. 775, referring to J. E. Arnold and U. A. Lang, 'Changing American Home Life: Trends in Domestic Leisure and Storage among Middle-class Families', 28 *J. Fam. Econ. Issues* (2007) p. 23 at p. 48.

583 F. Trentmann, *Empire of things: How We Became a World of Consumers, from the Fifteenth Century to the Twenty-First* (Harper 2016) p. 774.

584 See for example the case of phones: E. Robinot, F. Durif, D. Kréziak, I. Prim-Allaz, "*Fifty ways to leave your cell phone*"*: Product obsolescence, product replacement and product attachment* (European Marketing Association Conference 2014); G.T. Wilson, G. Smalley, J.R. Suckling, D. Lilley, J. Lee, R. Mawle, 'The hibernating mobile phone: dead storage as a barrier to efficient electronic waste recovery', 60 *Waste Management* (2017) p. 530.

585 V. Rizos, J. Bryhn, M. Alessi, A. Campmas, A. Zarra, *Identifying the impact of the circular economy on the Fast-Moving Consumer Goods Industry – Opportunities and challenges for businesses, workers and consumers – mobile phones as an example* (EESC 2019) p. 7 and p. 49. See also Kantar, *Special Eurobarometer 503 – Attitudes towards the impact of digitalisation on daily lives* (European Commission 2020) p. 27, which showed that 41% of the respondents would be willing to recycle their old digital devices if they were sure that it did not pose any potential privacy risks.

586 F. Trentmann, *Empire of things: How We Became a World of Consumers, from the Fifteenth Century to the Twenty-First* (Harper 2016) p. 775.

587 See *supra* on the concepts of product lifetime and product use cycle (n° 46), as well as of optimal product lifetime (n° 103).

the 'optimal product lifetime'. As rightly pointed out by M.C. Den Hollander, C.A. Bakker and H.J. Hultink, there are strategies to resist, postpone and reverse product obsolescence.[588] In addition to these three strategies, a fourth strategy aims to reduce the environmental impact of products when these reach the end of their lifetime. Each of these strategies corresponds to a wide array of concepts, namely durability, maintenance, upgrades, reuse, repair, refurbishment, remanufacturing and recycling. These concepts are of particular importance to complete the definition of premature obsolescence.

142. Emergence of the concepts in laws and policies – The concepts of durability, maintenance, upgrades, reuse, repair, refurbishment, remanufacturing and recycling already permeate laws and policies at EU and national levels. Product sustainability topics have become partly more political in recent years, especially with the revival of interest in product lifetime and premature obsolescence. These concepts are often grouped under the umbrella term of 'material efficiency' and/or 'resource efficiency'.[589] The new standards on material efficiency developed by CEN and CENELEC harmonise concepts and nomenclatures related to material efficiency aspects of energy-related products. Among these standards, the standard on definitions related to material efficiency provides a list of relevant terms corresponding to most of the concepts abovementioned, such as product durability, the ability to remanufacture, repair, reuse and upgrade products, product recyclability and recoverability, and many others, like 'normal use', 'part', 'component', 'end-of-life' and 'waste'. This list of definitions can be complemented by the UN glossary, which also provides further clarity on terms relevant for the study of premature obsolescence.[590] These concepts will be discussed in greater detail below under the umbrella of these four strategies.

2. RESISTING OBSOLESCENCE THROUGH DURABILITY

143. Resisting obsolescence – As explained in the 2017 study carried out within the framework of the UN Environment Programme[591], extending the lifetime of products can be achieved, first, by simply using the product for a longer period of time and thus by resisting obsolescence. This first strategy

[588] M.C. Den Hollander, C.A. Bakker, H.J. Hultink, 'Product design in a circular economy; development of a typology of key concepts and terms', 21 *Journal of Industrial Ecology* (2017) p. 521 at p. 523.

[589] As defined by the EC on its website, *"[r]esource efficiency means using the Earth's limited resources in a sustainable manner while minimising impacts on the environment"*. See <https://ec.europa.eu/environment/resource_efficiency/index_en.htm>.

[590] United Nations, Revised glossary of terms adopted by the Open-ended Working Group of the Basel Convention of 18 March 2016, UNEP/CHW/OEWG.10/INF/10.

[591] See C. Bakker, C. Schuit, *The long view – Exploring product lifetime extension* (United Nations Environment Programme 2017) p. 5.

corresponds to the concept of 'slower consumption' as coined by T. Cooper.[592] Through this strategy, the use cycles are prolonged through product durability.[593]

144. DURABILITY – As shown in a study commissioned by the EC in 2015, numerous definitions, emanating from policies and literature, have been given to the concept of product durability.[594] In this book, product durability will be understood in its strict sense, as defined in the European standard on definitions related to material efficiency. This standard defines 'product durability' as the "*ability to function as required, under defined conditions of use, maintenance and repair, until a limiting state is reached*".[595] The more durable the product, the longer it will perform its function and thus the longer consumers will be able to use it. A limiting state is reached when a primary or secondary function of the product is no longer delivered. This could either happen during the first or any subsequent use cycles of the product, due to failure, wear-out failure and/or other socio-economic conditions.[596]

145. PHYSICAL DURABILITY – Product durability comprises, first, the physical durability of the product and its parts (including hardware, firmware and software).[597] The physical durability of products has already been at the centre of extensive research.[598] One can determine the physical durability of a product by its robustness, meaning its resistance to the stress imposed in normal use and its ability to withstand wear, pressure or damage (effects of mechanisms such as fatigue or corrosion) and by its reliability, meaning its ability to remain functional without uneconomic maintenance or repair and early or planned failures. Two elements are important when determining the physical durability of a product: the durability of the materials and the durability of the engineering work.[599] In addition, products will be physically more durable depending on

---

592 T. Cooper, 'Slower Consumption: Reflections on Product Life Spans and the "Throwaway Society"', 9 *Journal of Industrial Ecology* (2005) p. 51 at p. 67.

593 *See* n° 92 on the concept of use cycles.

594 S. Boulos et al. (Ricardo-AEA), *The durability of products – Standards assessment for the circular economy under the Eco-Innovation Action Plan* (EC 2015) p. 32 at p. 42.

595 CEN-CENELEC TC10, Definitions related to material efficiency, EN 45550:2020, p. 5.

596 CEN-CENELEC TC10, Definitions related to material efficiency, EN 45550:2020, p. 6. In this standard, 'wear-out failure' is defined as "*failure due to cumulative deterioration caused by the stresses imposed in normal use*".

597 See the definition of 'part' in CEN-CENELEC TC10, Definitions related to material efficiency, EN 45550:2020, p. 8.

598 See e.g. S. Boulos et al. (Ricardo-AEA), *The durability of products – Standards assessment for the circular economy under the Eco-Innovation Action Plan* (EC 2015); P. Tecchio, F. Ardente, F. Mathieux, *Analysis of durability, reusability and reparability: Application to dishwashers and washing machines – JRC Technical Report* (European Commission 2016); F. Alfieri, M. Cordella R. Stamminger, A. Bues, *Durability assessment of products: analysis and testing of washing machines – JRC Technical Report* (European Commission 2018).

599 E.P. Mora, 'Life cycle, sustainability and the transcendent quality of building materials', 42 *Building and Environment* (2007) p. 1329 at p. 1334.

their compatibility with other products and their interoperability, meaning their *"ability (...) to function with hardware or software different from those with which goods of the same type are normally used"*.[600] Concerning the durability of software and firmware parts, it is determined by updates and the overall supporting period. This kind of durability prevents material, functional and indirect obsolescence.

146. Emotional durability – The second aspect of product durability concerns the emotional durability of the product. This kind of durability can also prevent the premature obsolescence of products. On the one hand, as rightly pointed out by S. Carlsson and A. Mallalieu, *"if the [consumer] associates the product with an own significant value or feeling, it can increase the consciousness of responsibility and obligation to take care of the product"*.[601] Consequently, it contributes to curbing the material obsolescence of the product. On the other hand, emotional bonding is likely to prevent the psychological obsolescence of the product as it is harder to dispose of the product when one feels attached to it (e.g. when the product is unique, personalised, or carries memories). In the absence of such attachment, the failed relationship between the consumer and the product can lead him to throw it away.[602] Yet, emotional attachment entails the risk that a product, when obsolete, remains in the consumer's possession for a longer period, when in fact the replacement of the product would be beneficial from a resource efficiency point of view.[603] Product attachment and emotional durability are influenced by many factors.[604] However, far less research has been carried out on this durability aspect.[605]

3. POSTPONING OBSOLESCENCE THROUGH MAINTENANCE AND UPGRADES

147. Postponing obsolescence – The second strategy to prolong the use cycles of a product consists in postponing its obsolescence. This can be done through (1) product maintenance (including product care) and (2) product upgrades.

600 This definition can be found in Article 2(10) and recital 27 SGD.

601 S. Carlsson, A. Mallalieu, *Design for Longevity – A Framework to Support Product Developers in Identifying Products' Optimal Lifetimes, Master's Thesis in Product Development* (Chalmers University of Technology 2021) p. 37.

602 This issue has for example been identified for clothes. See C. Morais, G. Montagna, 'Customized Wardrobe: Clothing according to user', 3 *Procedia Manufacturing* (2015) p. 5814 at p. 5821.

603 See *infra* on the notion of hibernating product (n° 157).

604 T. Page, 'Product attachment and replacement: Implications for sustainable design', 2 *International Journal of Sustainable Design* (2014) p. 256 at p. 282.

605 M.C. Den Hollander, C.A. Bakker, H.J. Hultink, 'Product design in a circular economy; development of a typology of key concepts and terms', 21 *Journal of Industrial Ecology* (2017) p. 521.

Indeed, early failures can be avoided, and the lifetime of products extended, if consumers properly and carefully use, maintain and upgrade their products.[606]

148. Maintenance – According to the European standard on definitions related to material efficiency, 'maintenance' is "*an action carried out to retain a product in a condition where it is able to function as required*".[607] In other words, it is "*the combination of all technical, administrative and managerial actions during the lifecycle of an item intended to retain or restore it to a state in which it can perform its required function*".[608] As examples of maintenance, the European standard mentions *inter alia* inspection, adjustments, cleaning, testing, software update and replacement of wear parts.[609] Similar to repair and upgrading[610], maintenance often requires disassembly and reassembly of the product for the purpose of parts inspection or replacement.[611] Maintenance activities differ depending on the product group. For most household products, such actions can be performed by users themselves in accordance with the manufacturer's instructions provided with the product. This includes, for example, cleaning the filter of a washing machine or a dishwasher or replacing the bag of a vacuum cleaner. In other cases, maintenance needs to be carried out by a professional, for example in the case of boilers.[612] Regular maintenance of a product in accordance with the manufacturer's instructions has a positive impact on the product's lifetime and postpones its obsolescence.

149. Upgrades – In the European standard on definitions related to material efficiency, 'upgrading a product' means "*enhancing the functionality, performance, capacity or aesthetics of a product*".[613] This process may concern the product software, firmware and/or hardware.[614] The changes made to the product through upgrades should however not be substantial.[615] Some products are more

---

606 Unfortunately, many products are not properly and carefully used and maintained by consumers. See *supra*, n° 139.

607 CEN-CENELEC TC10, Definitions related to material efficiency, EN 45550:2020, p. 7.

608 This definition is given on the website of the European Federation of National Maintenance Societies: see <https://www.efnms.eu/about-us/what-does-efnms-stand-for/>.

609 CEN-CENELEC TC10, Definitions related to material efficiency, EN 45550:2020, p. 7.

610 See *infra*.

611 'Disassembly' is "*the process by which a product can be separated into its parts in a non-destructive way*" and should be distinguished from 'dismantling', which entails the destruction of the product. See E. Bracquené, J. Brusselaers, Y. Dams, J. Peeters, K. De Schepper, J. Duflou, W. Dewulf., *Repairability criteria for energy related products – Study in the BeNeLux context to evaluate the options to extend the product life time* (KU Leuven, Vito, BeNeLux 2018) p. 18; M. Cordella, F. Alfieri, J. Sanfelix, S. Donatello, R. Kaps, O. Wolf, 'Improving material efficiency in the life cycle of products: a review of EU Ecolabel criteria', 25 *The International Journal of Life Cycle Assessment volume* (2020) p. 925.

612 S. Boulos et al. (Ricardo-AEA), *The durability of products – Standards assessment for the circular economy under the Eco-Innovation Action Plan* (EC 2015) pp. 40–41.

613 CEN-CENELEC TC10, Definitions related to material efficiency, EN 45550:2020, p. 9.

614 *Ibid.*

615 C. Bakker, M.C. den Hollander, E. van Hinte, Y. Zijlstra, *Products that last: Product design for circular business models* (BIS Publishers 2019) p. 115.

upgradable than others, meaning that they allow all or some of their parts to be separately replaced and upgraded without having to replace the entire product.[616] Different factors influence the upgradability of a product. These factors include *inter alia* skill level, working environment, disassembly depth, tools, fasteners and connectors.[617] For example, a product is deemed more easily upgradable if upgrades can be made by the user himself, without the need of special tools and technical skills. Upgrading a product may postpone its obsolescence as the product continues to be useful while its quality, value, effectiveness and/or performance has been improved. This is especially true for products that are subject to rapid technological changes or changes in use profiles over the use phase.[618] What is more, upgradable products are more easily reused.[619]

4. REVERSING OBSOLESCENCE THROUGH DIRECT REUSE, REPAIR, REFURBISHMENT AND REMANUFACTURING

150. Reversing obsolescence – Third, product lifetime can be extended by reversing the obsolescence of products through a recovery operation (see Figure 4).[620] As previously highlighted[621], product obsolescence is not always irreversible and can punctuate the lifetime of the product. There are four scenarios where the obsolescence of products (or parts) is reversed: (1) direct reuse, (2) repair, (3) refurbishment, and (4) remanufacturing. In the first three scenarios, the obsolete product that is discarded by the user is reused by someone else, either directly or after being repaired or refurbished, whereas in the last scenario, only some of its parts or components are recovered through remanufacturing. It should be noted that repair may also be used by the user to reverse the obsolescence of products that he did not discard, with a view to using them longer. In these four scenarios, the lifetime of the product (or its parts or components) continues. This is why these options have also been called the 'value-retention processes'.[622]

---

616 CEN-CENELEC TC10, Material Efficiency Aspects for Ecodesign, Secretary Enquiry (new work item 65685/prEN 45554), EN 45554:2017, CEN-CLC TC10/Sec/135/DC, p. 7.

617 See Annex A to CEN-CENELEC TC10, General methods for the assessment of the ability to repair, reuse and upgrade energy-related products, EN 45554:2020.

618 CEN-CENELEC TC10, General methods for the assessment of the ability to repair, reuse and upgrade energy-related products, EN 45554:2020, p. 9.

619 CEN-CENELEC TC10, General methods for the assessment of the ability to repair, reuse and upgrade energy-related products, EN 45554:2020, p. 11.

620 See *supra* on the concept of 'product lifetime' and related concepts (n° 46). See also M.C. Den Hollander, C.A. Bakker, H.J. Hultink, 'Product design in a circular economy; development of a typology of key concepts and terms', 21 *Journal of Industrial Ecology* (2017) p. 519.

621 See *supra* on the different types of premature obsolescence (n° 106–131).

622 See International Resource Panel, *Redefining Value – The Manufacturing Revolution. Remanufacturing, Refurbishment, Repair and Direct Reuse in the Circular Economy* (United

Figure 4. Product lifetime and the different scenarios reversing product obsolescence

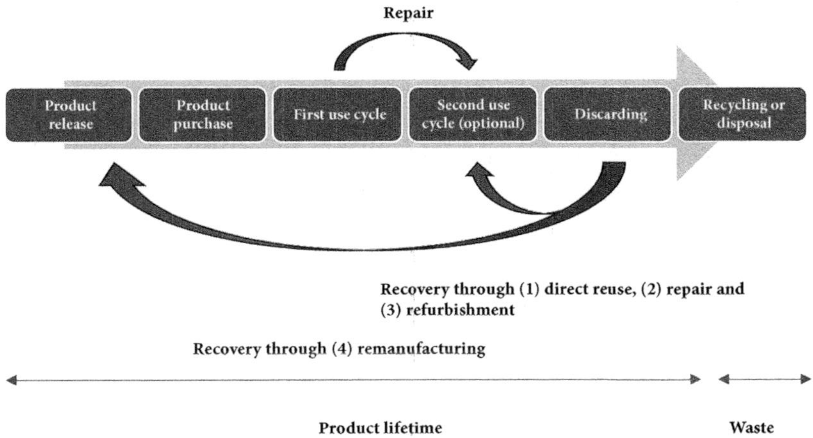

151. Direct reuse – The term 'reuse' can be defined as "*[t]he use of a product again for the same purpose in its original form or with little enhancement or change*".[623] A product can be directly reused if it does not need any preparation for reuse (including repair or refurbishment), except for minimal cleaning and adjustments that can be performed by the user himself.[624] The more adaptable the product[625], the easier it is to directly reuse it. Consumers who no longer use their product can decide to give or sell it to a relative, a friend or someone else.[626] M.C. Den Hollander, C.A. Bakker and H.J. Hultink describe this scenario with the term 'recontextualising' as the obsolete product is reused without any remedial action, in a different context than it was originally designed for.[627]

Nations Environment Programme 2018) p. 6.

623 See Ellen MacArthur Foundation, *Towards the circular economy: Economic and business rationale for an accelerated transition* (2013) p. 25. This definition corresponds almost verbatim to the one enshrined in CEN-CENELEC TC10, Definitions related to material efficiency, EN 45550:2020, p. 8, where 'reuse' is defined as "*the process by which a product or its parts, having reached the end of their first [or subsequent] use, are used for the same purpose for which they were conceived*".

624 See CEN-CENELEC TC10, Material Efficiency Aspects for Ecodesign, Secretary Enquiry (new work item 65684prEN 45550), EN 45550:2018, CEN-CLC TC10/Sec/137/DC, p. 7. See also United Nations, Revised glossary of terms adopted by the Open-ended Working Group of the Basel Convention of 18 March 2016, UNEP/CHW/OEWG.10/INF/10, p. 10.

625 'Product adaptability' can be defined as its ability to adjust to new conditions. See Oxford English Dictionary 2006 (3rd ed.).

626 See e.g. Gartner, *Reused, Resold, Recycled – Where Do Old Smartphones Go* (2015), available on: <https://www.gartner.com/en/newsroom/press-releases/2015–02–18-gartner-says-worldwide-market-for-refurbished-smartphones-to-reach-120-million-units-by-2017>, which reported that 41% of used smartphones in the U.S. and in Germany find new owners via private sales or trade-ins.

627 M.C. Den Hollander, C.A. Bakker, H.J. Hultink, 'Product design in a circular economy; development of a typology of key concepts and terms', 21 *Journal of Industrial Ecology* (2017)

Products subject to direct reuse are also called 'second-hand products'. In a broad sense, direct reuse also encompasses alternative models that pertain to the functional economy, like models with no transfer of ownership, such as product-lease and product-as-a-service[628], and to the collaborative economy, where individuals give, swap, borrow, trade, rent, and share products and services for a fee.[629] Such models may contribute to prolonging utilisation of products, and thus reducing the speed of resource flow, although they are not necessarily a catalyst for sustainability.[630]

152. Repair – An obsolete product can also be reused after being repaired.[631] 'Repair' means the "*process of returning a faulty product to a condition where it can fulfil its [originally] intended use*"[632], by fixing a specified fault and/or replacing defective components.[633] It encompasses a complex and fragmented set of activities that can involve consumers, original equipment manufacturers, retailers, independent or certified repairers, insurance companies (who manage guarantees), and even third sector organisations (e.g. *Repair Café's, iFixit*).[634] Repair activities typically include bonding, sealing and adjusting or replacing worn or defective parts. Repair does not necessarily mean exact restoration of the product to its past condition, but can act as a source of variation, improvisation and innovation. Yet, as highlighted by T. Cooper and G. Salvia, if a material or component that is of superior quality compared to the original is used, the practice should rather be considered as upgrading.[635] The distinction between repair and maintenance may also become blurred if maintenance is not carried out frequently enough as the performance or utility provided by a product may cross a threshold beyond which it is considered faulty.[636] The level of repair

---

p. 522.

628 For some examples, see H. Slachmuylders, 'Building back better after Covid-19 – the role of circular business models', CCM blog, 10 June 2021, available on: <https://law.kuleuven.be/ccm/blog/?p=162>.

629 See <https://www.investopedia.com/terms/c/collaborative-economy.asp>.

630 See e.g. A. Tukker, 'Eight types of product-service-system: Eight ways to sustainability? Experiences from Suspronet', *Business Strategy and the Environment* (2004) p. 246 at p. 260.

631 There are however various barriers to repair, as explained above (n° 139).

632 CEN-CENELEC TC10, Definitions related to material efficiency, EN 45550:2020, p. 9.

633 United Nations, Revised glossary of terms adopted by the Open-ended Working Group of the Basel Convention of 18 March 2016, UNEP/CHW/OEWG.10/INF/10, p. 8.

634 E. Bracquené et al., *Repairability criteria for energy related products – Study in the BeNeLux context to evaluate the options to extend the product life time* (KU Leuven, Vito, BeNeLux 2018) pp. 12–13.

635 T. Cooper, G. Salvia, 'Fix it: barriers to repair and opportunities for change', in R. Crocker (ed.), *Reuse in an Accelerated World: Mining the Past to Reshape the Future* (Routledge 2017) pp. 150–151.

636 T. Cooper, G. Salvia, 'Fix it: barriers to repair and opportunities for change', in R. Crocker (ed.), *Reuse in an Accelerated World: Mining the Past to Reshape the Future* (Routledge 2017) p. 150.

can vary widely, depending on product reparability.[637] A product is deemed 'reparable' if it "*allows all or some of its parts to be separately repaired or replaced without having to replace the entire product*"[638], and more particularly, if its parts can be "*brought back to working condition after failure in a reasonable amount of time for reasonable price*".[639] Product reparability is influenced by the same factors as upgradability, namely skill level, working environment, disassembly depth, tools, fasteners and connectors. In the Benelux study from 2018, product reparability is rated according to the provision of information (e.g. failure diagnostic guides or disassembly instructions), product design (e.g. easy access to parts, part interchangeability), and service (e.g. technical support, spare parts supply).[640] It should be noted that reparable products are not necessarily durable as certain low-quality easily breakable products could be reparable.

153. REFURBISHMENT – Regrettably, the standards developed by CEN and CENELEC give no definition of 'refurbishment' (also called 'reconditioning'). A satisfactory definition is provided by the Ellen McArthur Foundation, which defines it as the process of returning an obsolete product to a satisfactory working and/or cosmetic condition, that may be inferior to the original specification, by replacing and repairing all major components that are faulty, markedly damaged or close to failure, and by making cosmetic changes to update the appearance of a product, such as cleaning, changing the fabric, painting or refinishing.[641] These changes on the product are however not significant.[642] Along the same line, M. Cordella et al. define 'refurbishment' as a "*treatment or a modification of a product, or parts of a product, to increase or restore its performance and/or functionality or to meet applicable technical standards or regulatory requirements, with the result of making a fully functional product to be used for a purpose that is at least the one that was originally intended*".[643] The refurbishment process can result in second-hand goods that are resold. Some producers, retailers and

---

637 S. Boulos et al. (Ricardo-AEA), *The durability of products – Standards assessment for the circular economy under the Eco-Innovation Action Plan* (EC 2015) p. 41.

638 CEN-CENELEC TC10, Material Efficiency Aspects for Ecodesign, Secretary Enquiry (new work item 65685/prEN 45554), EN 45554:2017, CEN-CLC TC10/Sec/135/DC, p. 7.

639 E. Bracquené et al., *Repairability criteria for energy related products – Study in the BeNeLux context to evaluate the options to extend the product life time* (KU Leuven, Vito, BeNeLux 2018) p. 16.

640 *Ibid.*, p. 37.

641 Ellen MacArthur Foundation, *Towards the circular economy: Economic and business rationale for an accelerated transition* (2013) p. 25. See also M.C. Den Hollander, C.A. Bakker, H.J. Hultink, 'Product design in a circular economy; development of a typology of key concepts and terms', 21 *Journal of Industrial Ecology* (2017) p. 522.

642 See the note in CEN-CENELEC TC10, Definitions related to material efficiency, EN 45550:2020, p. 8.

643 See M. Cordella, F. Alfieri, J. Sanfelix, S. Donatello, R. Kaps, O. Wolf, 'Improving material efficiency in the life cycle of products: a review of EU Ecolabel criteria', 25 *The International Journal of Life Cycle Assessment volume* (2020) p. 925. Their definition draw great inspiration from the UN glossary. See United Nations, Revised glossary of terms adopted by the Open-

service providers even offer certified refurbished goods by organising voluntary take-back/buy-back of devices.[644]

154. Remanufacturing – The fourth scenario is when the product is "*obsolete beyond recovery at product level*"[645] and only its parts and components can be recovered through remanufacturing. 'Remanufacturing' is an industrial process that inspects, disassembles, cleans, reprocesses, stores, reassembles, tests and recovers a product at the subassembly or component level.[646] During this process, functioning, reusable parts are taken out of a used product and rebuilt into a new product, in such a manner that the product is in a condition equal to a newly manufactured product. This new product generally combines components originating from different used products with as few as possible new parts.[647] Remanufacturing includes quality assurance and potential enhancements or changes to the components which influence the safety, original performance, purpose or type of the product.[648] It is noteworthy that by contrast with direct reuse, repair and refurbishment, which allow for the continuation of the product lifetime, remanufacturing recovers only parts or components of the product and thus starts a new product lifetime.

5. REDUCING PRODUCT ENVIRONMENTAL IMPACTS THROUGH RECYCLING

155. Reducing environmental impacts of product end-of-life – In addition to strategies that prolong the lifetime of products, another strategy aims to reduce their environmental impact when the products reach the end of their lifetime and become waste. This scenario occurs when the state of obsolescence is irreversible. In that scenario, the product is either recycled or destroyed without being recycled, while sometimes used for energy recovery.[649] Because

---

ended Working Group of the Basel Convention of 18 March 2016, UNEP/CHW/OEWG.10/INF/10, p. 8.

644 D. Watson et al., *Circular Business Models in the Mobile Phone Industry* (TemaNord 2017) p. 30.

645 See *supra* on the concept of 'product lifetime' (n° 46).

646 See Ellen MacArthur Foundation, *Towards the circular economy: Economic and business rationale for an accelerated transition* (2013) p. 25, as well as CEN-CENELEC TC10, Definitions related to material efficiency, EN 45550:2020, p. 8.

647 M.C. Den Hollander, C.A. Bakker, H.J. Hultink, 'Product design in a circular economy; development of a typology of key concepts and terms', 21 *Journal of Industrial Ecology* (2017) p. 523.

648 Ellen MacArthur Foundation, *Towards the circular economy: Economic and business rationale for an accelerated transition* (2013) p. 25.

649 'Energy recovery' is defined as the "*production of useful energy through direct and controlled combustion or other processing of waste*", according to CEN-CENELEC TC10, Definitions related to material efficiency, EN 45550:2020, p. 9.

these operations occur at the end of the product lifetime and inevitably lead to the loss of product integrity, they do not constitute the primary focus of this study. These strategies will only be mentioned when they have an indirect impact on the product lifetime.[650]

156. Recycling – 'Recycling' consists in *"[recovering the resources] at the expense of permanently destroying product integrity"*.[651] This excludes energy production and the reprocessing into materials that are to be used as fuels or for backfilling operations.[652] If recycled, the product and its constituent components are dismantled and disintegrated.[653] The materials of the product are subsequently reprocessed into products, materials or substances, leading to new materials of lesser quality and/or reduced functionality ('downcycling'), new materials of higher quality and/or increased functionality ('upcycling'). Recycling can also consist in recovering the materials for the original purpose or other purposes, excluding energy recovery ('functional recycling').[654] Hence, the recycling process allows to recover some materials, but the product as a whole is inevitably destroyed. In other words, recycling prevents and reverses obsolescence at a material level only.[655]

157. Hibernating products – It is noteworthy that, in some cases, the obsolete product is not directly discarded by the user, but rather kept as a spare and stored at the user's place.[656] In other words, there are cases where, although still functioning or reusable, the product is no longer used but not discarded either. In this fourth scenario, the product is said to be 'hibernating'.[657] Such a scenario has, for example, been identified in the smartphone sector. Smartphones remain sometimes for years in the consumers' drawer once replaced.[658] This

650 For further details, see Chapter V on the end-of-life stage.

651 M.C. Den Hollander, C.A. Bakker, H.J. Hultink, 'Product design in a circular economy; development of a typology of key concepts and terms', 21 *Journal of Industrial Ecology* (2017) p. 519.

652 CEN-CENELEC TC10, Definitions related to material efficiency, EN 45550:2020, p. 10.

653 M.C. Den Hollander, C.A. Bakker, H.J. Hultink, 'Product design in a circular economy; development of a typology of key concepts and terms', 21 *Journal of Industrial Ecology* (2017) p. 519.

654 Ellen MacArthur Foundation, *Towards the circular economy: Economic and business rationale for an accelerated transition* (2013) p. 25.

655 M.C. Den Hollander, C.A. Bakker, H.J. Hultink, 'Product design in a circular economy; development of a typology of key concepts and terms', 21 *Journal of Industrial Ecology* (2017) p. 521.

656 See *supra*, n° 140.

657 I. Oswald, A. Reller, 'E-waste: A story of trashing, trading, and valuable resources', 20 *GAIA* (2011) p. 43.

658 V. Rizos et al., *Identifying the impact of the circular economy on the Fast-Moving Consumer Goods Industry – Opportunities and challenges for businesses, workers and consumers – mobile phones as an example* (EESC 2019) p. 49; D. Zhilyaeva, C. Cimpana, Z. Caoa, G. Liua, S. Askegaardb, H. Wenzela, 'The Living, the Dead, and the Obsolete: A Characterization of

particular case is situated between the use cycle and the moment when the product is discarded by the user, as indicated on Figure 5. In that case, the lifetime of the product is somehow 'suspended'. Hence, the obsolescence of the product and its subsequent replacement does not automatically imply that the obsolete product is discarded. In that sense, 'product replacement' actually means replacing the primary role of a product, and not necessarily the product itself.[659]

Figure 5. Product lifetime and the different scenarios of obsolescence

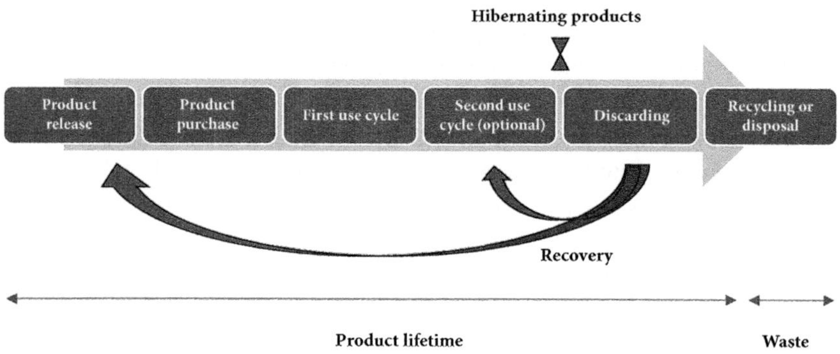

E. CONCLUSION

158. FIRST STEP: FROM PLANNED TO PREMATURE OBSOLESCENCE – The first section of this first chapter described the context in which the concept of 'planned obsolescence' emerged and was theorized. The literature review revealed timid discussions on the topic during the 20th century, which were mainly fed by economic and socio-political arguments, before attracting the interest of several other academic disciplines and becoming a buzzword in the media and popular discourses over the last few years. References to 'planned obsolescence' were also spotted in documents issued by policymakers, both at EU and national levels, as well as in studies they commissioned. It was noted that the law has long been ignoring the issue altogether. Although the EU and its Member States are becoming more and more proactive in the field, only France has adopted specific legislation on the topic so far. The first section ended with a critical analysis of the concept of planned obsolescence and concluded that the

Lifetime and Stock of ICT Products in Denmark', 164 *Resources, Conservation & Recycling* (2021) p. 2.

659 C.A. Roster, M. Richins, 'Ambivalence and attitudes in consumer replacement decisions', 19 *Journal of Consumer Psychology* (2009) p. 48 at p. 61.

concept of 'premature obsolescence', which is more neutral and general, should be preferred.

159. Second step: defining product lifetime and premature obsolescence – In view of the lack of a commonly accepted definition and understanding of the issue of premature obsolescence, it was deemed necessary to provide a comprehensive definition and description of the phenomenon. To this end, the second section of this chapter started by defining the concept of 'product lifetime', together with related concepts, namely 'product use cycle', 'product obsolescence', 'waste', 'recovery', 'optimal product lifetime' and 'product sustainability'. Based on this conceptual foundation, the definition of premature obsolescence was elaborated: 'premature obsolescence' means *"all practices that reduce product lifetime so that the product does not reach its optimal lifetime (from an environmental point of view), without it being the result of normal wear and tear"*. A description of the different types and causes of premature obsolescence was then provided. It was found that consumer products can, nowadays, become obsolete on material, functional, indirect, economic, or psychological grounds. These types of obsolescence exist due to different causes that can be related to business or consumer trends.

160. Third step: strategies to resist, postpone and reverse premature obsolescence – The third and last section of the chapter completed the definition of premature obsolescence by detailing concepts related to strategies that allow resisting, postponing, and reversing premature obsolescence, as well as those that allow reducing the environmental impact of products at their end-of-life. Definitions, explanations and comments were given for the concepts of durability, maintenance, upgrades, direct reuse, repair, refurbishment, remanufacturing and recycling.

161. The crucial importance of using appropriate concepts and definitions – The most important lesson to take away from this chapter is the neutral and general definition of premature obsolescence, which will not only serve as a basis for this book but should also be considered by law makers when regulating the issue. Law makers should refrain from using words that are shrouded in controversy, like the concept of 'planned obsolescence'. Even if they exist, cases of 'planned obsolescence' do not reflect the complexity of the phenomenon and represent only a small subset of problematic cases of premature obsolescence. Therefore, adopting this term exposes the legislature to the risk of making under-inclusive rules. Regarding the objective to protect the environment, the decisive point is that the lifetime of products does not live up to what is possible and desirable. What is important is to consider and stop all practices and behaviours that shorten product lifetime, whether these are intentional or not. Only with such a conceptual basis will the law makers be able

to adopt rules that are necessary, effective, coherent and consistent to cope with premature obsolescence, while avoiding overlaps, conflicts and gaps between the different legal instruments. Only contextualised approaches can lead to effective long-term solutions that strike the right balance between the different interests at stake, namely reduced environmental impact, consumer satisfaction, emerging technological evolution, and optimized product lifetime to mutual benefits. And considering the causes of premature obsolescence, the issue should be dealt with by social, technological, but also legal changes.[660] What is more, using more neutral concepts, such as 'premature obsolescence', 'durability' or 'repair', will help gather actors and stakeholders around the same table.

162. A LEGAL ANALYSIS OF EVERY STAGE OF PRODUCT LIFETIME – When legislating on the issue of premature obsolescence, the whole lifecycle of products must be looked at, involving all actors and stakeholders (producers, designers, consumers, sellers, repairers). As J. Cox rightly explained, "*improving product durability (through the design and manufacturing) alone is unlikely to deliver a step-change in sustainable consumption, because [it is] unlikely to overcome the very significant psychological, emotional and social factors which underpin the rapid churn of products in the modern throwaway society*".[661] Therefore, the next chapters of this book will identify and analyse EU and national measures that contribute to prolonging product lifetime, following a product lifecycle approach, from the design and production stage to the end-of-life stage of products.

---

660 See also J. Guiltinan, 'Creative destruction and Destructive Creations: Environmental Ethics and Planned Obsolescence', 89 *Journal of Business Ethics* (2009) p. 25; R. Lawlor, 'Delaying obsolescence', 21 *Science and Engineering Ethics* (2015) p. 423 at p. 425.

661 n>J. Cox et al., 'Consumer understanding of product lifetimes', 79 *Resources, Conservation and Recycling* (2013) p. 27.

CHAPTER II
THE DESIGN AND PRODUCTION STAGE: SHAPING THE DESIGN OF PRODUCTS TOWARDS MORE SUSTAINABILITY

A. INTRODUCTION

163. Ecodesign requirements – Among the rules that can tackle the premature obsolescence of products, some promote product sustainability at the design and production stage. This stage is a decisive moment in the lifetime of a product as many decisions taken at this stage can determine whether the product will become prematurely obsolete or not. A wide array of ecodesigned products can be found on the EU market. While some ecodesign approaches are voluntarily adopted by the manufacturers, others are imposed by mandatory rules. The major set of rules in this field consists of ecodesign regulations, which impose ecodesign requirements on producers of certain categories of energy-related products. Every business willing to sell products on the EU market has to adhere to these ecodesign requirements. These rules oblige producers to comply with requirements related to product sustainability when they conceive and produce products, including requirements on product durability, reparability and upgradability among others. With these ecodesign regulations, the product market is shaped towards products that are more sustainable and thus less prone to premature obsolescence.

164. Overview of the second chapter – This chapter will be dedicated to these ecodesign rules. The first section will explain the key role of product design in the fight against premature obsolescence, describing the current product trends and the different ways towards sustainable product design. After this introductory section, the second section of the chapter will examine the Ecodesign Directive and its implementing rules.[662] The section will describe

[662] Directive 2009/125/EC of the European Parliament and of the Council of 21 October 2009 establishing a framework for the setting of ecodesign requirements for energy-related products, OJ L 285, 31.10.2009, p. 10–35 (hereafter 'Ecodesign Directive').

the main provisions of this Directive and identify the existing implementing measures that are relevant for this book, before analysing and recommending possible improvements and future implementing measures, taking the most recent texts adopted by EU institutions and other organisations into account. Within this section, references will be made to other sector-specific regulations imposing ecodesign requirements, like the legislation on cars and plastic products.

B. MAPPING KEYS ELEMENTS OF PRODUCT ECODESIGN

1. PRODUCT DESIGN TRENDS AND THEIR IMPACTS ON PRODUCT LIFETIME

165. Four recent product design trends – Product design has considerably evolved over the last decades.[663] First of all, in comparison with the past, today's products have more varied and sophisticated designs. Products are generally composed of an increasing number of materials and additives, with smaller amounts of each specific material.[664] This evolution is conspicuous in the case of light bulbs, where LED technology is more energy-efficient, but also made of more complex materials than halogen lamps. Secondly, a wide array of products has become multifunctional and technology-intensive with increasing electronic systems in place, especially with the birth of new technologies and services like the Internet of Things[665], Smart devices[666], Artificial Intelligence[667], and many more. There is, thirdly, a trend towards the miniaturisation of products. Fourthly, and by contrast with ecodesign trends, a flood of poorly designed products has entered the EU market. For example, it has been reported that the construction of certain products moved from systems that use replaceable screws and bolts to adhesive bindings that cannot be removed quickly.[668] An increasing number of electronic devices can hardly be opened, some of their key components are invisible, glued and/or are assembled in units and cannot

663 Several market failures, imperfections, and other factors, including the cost and time pressure on the business side, influence these product design trends. See *supra*, n° 124 *et seq.*

664 EEA, *Circular by design: Products in the circular economy* (European Union 2017) p. 16.

665 See *supra*, n° 54, footnote n° 202.

666 *Ibid.*

667 See *supra*, n° 42, footnote n° 133.

668 Technopolis Group (in consortium with Fraunhofer ISI, Thinkstep and Wuppertal Institute), *Regulatory barriers for the Circular Economy – Lessons from ten cases studies* (European Commission 2016) p. 39.

be reached or replaced component-wise.[669] The smartphone sector perfectly illustrates these four trends.[670]

166. Coupled with a lack of knowledge – These four product design trends go hand in hand with a serious lack of knowledge among all economic actors about products. This lack of knowledge concerns not only the technical functioning of products, but also the ways of maintaining, upgrading, caring for and repairing them.[671] Modern production processes form a complex web of dispersed actions, and this systematically produces opacity, which is passed on to consumers, repairers and reuse centres. This opacity is one of the main characteristics of a linear economy. The lack of knowledge about products is compounded by the (mis)use of intellectual property rights, which can act as an impediment to the sharing of know-how and product information to external third parties (including consumers).[672] This leads to a paradoxical situation, where *"[a]lthough the relationship is so close that people and electronics almost become hybrids in the course of their everyday practices, they live like strangers"*.[673]

167. The significant impact of product design on product lifetime – The recent product design trends[674], combined with the lack of knowledge on products[675], have an impact on the lifetime of products and contribute, to some extent, to their premature obsolescence. Admittedly, some features of these newly designed products are eco-friendly. Certain innovations allow, for example, the reduction of energy or water consumption of products or optimise

669 M. Jaeger-Erben, M. Proske, 'What's hot what's not: the social construction of product obsolescence and its relevance for strategies to increase functionality', in C. Bakker and R. Mugge (eds.), *Product Lifetimes And The Environment 2017 – Conference Proceedings* (IOS Press 2017) p. 183.

670 C. Clemm, A. Berwald, C. Prewitz, N.F. Nissen, M. Schneider-Ramelow, 'Market Trends in Smartphone Design and Reliability Testing', in *Electronics Goes Green 2020+ – Conference Proceedings* (Fraunhofer IZM 2020) pp. 174–175.

671 M. Jaeger-Erben, M. Proske, 'What's hot what's not: the social construction of product obsolescence and its relevance for strategies to increase functionality', in C. Bakker and R. Mugge (eds.), *Product Lifetimes And The Environment 2017 – Conference Proceedings* (IOS Press 2017) pp. 183–184.

672 E. Eppinger, A. Jain, P. Vimalnath, A. Gurtoo, F. Tietze, R. Hernandez Chea, 'Sustainability transitions in manufacturing: the role of intellectual property', 49 *Current Opinion in Environmental Sustainability* (2021) pp. 121–122.

673 M. Jaeger-Erben, M. Proske, 'What's hot what's not: the social construction of product obsolescence and its relevance for strategies to increase functionality', in C. Bakker and R. Mugge (eds.), *Product Lifetimes And The Environment 2017 – Conference Proceedings* (IOS Press 2017) p. 184.

674 See *supra*, n° 165.

675 See *supra*, n° 166.

product use.[676] Moreover, products with multiple functions lower the number of resources and the amount of energy, waste, and emissions during the whole product lifecycle (production and packaging, transport and distribution, use, end-of-life) compared to cases where the same functions are provided by several single-function products.[677] However, the complexity, connectivity, multifunctionality, miniaturisation and poor design of products may increase product failure rates and reduce the potential for direct reuse, repair, refurbishment, remanufacturing and recycling, thus shortening product lifetime (or part/component lifetime) and going against the circular economy target.[678]

2. TACKLING PREMATURE OBSOLESCENCE THROUGH PRODUCT ECODESIGN

168. Product ecodesign as a remedy against premature obsolescence – Most of the environmental impact and performance of products is determined during the early phases of their development, and more specifically at the design and production stage. When designing a product, decisions are taken on the type and number of materials to be integrated into the product, its durability, ease of repair, upgrade and maintenance, as well as the recyclability of its components.[679] Afterwards, "*once a product is put on the market, there is relatively little that can be done to improve its environmental characteristics*".[680] Integrating environmental considerations at the design and production stage through 'ecodesign' is thus crucial in preventing premature obsolescence and the associated impacts on the environment.

169. Five main ecodesign strategies – Various ecodesign approaches and methods have been developed to mitigate environmental impacts caused by premature obsolescence.[681] Some strategies allow creating long-lasting

676 See for ex. cloud computing, which can contribute to prolonging the use of electronic devices by dematerialising and transferring capabilities from consumer hardware to the cloud. This allows a more optimal use of storage space and computing power since the operators of cloud services will make better use of resources than individuals' hardware. See Ellen MacArthur Foundation, *Circular consumer electronics: an initial exploration* (2018) p. 9.

677 A. Barsan, L. Barsan, A. Leu, L. Zafiu, '*Multi-functional Products – A Way to Decrease the Products Environmental Impact*', in I. Visa and A. Duta (eds.), *Nearly Zero Energy Communities* (CSE Springer 2017) p. 711 at p. 719.

678 EEA, *Circular by design: Products in the circular economy* (European Union 2017) p. 16.

679 D. Jepsen et al., *Delivering resource-efficient products – How Ecodesign can drive a circular economy in Europe* (European Environmental Bureau 2015) p. 6.

680 Green paper of the European Commission of 7 February 2001 on Integrated Product Policy, COM(2001) 68 final, p. 3.

681 For some examples of ecodesign approaches and methods, see M. Zallio, D. Berry, 'Design and Planned Obsolescence. Theories and Approaches for Designing Enabling Technologies', 20 *The Design Journal* (2017) S3756 at S3758.

products, while others contribute to extending product lifetime once in use.[682] After having reviewed the existing literature[683], it seems that ecodesign strategies can be categorised into 5 different types: (1) design for robustness and reliability, (2) design for attachment and trust, (3) design for standardization and compatibility, (4) design for ease of maintenance and repair, (5) design for upgradability and adaptability. These strategies allow to resist, postpone and reverse product obsolescence.[684] It is nevertheless worth noting that not all strategies are suitable for all products as products can aim to provide very different functions. In that regard, the three categories of products identified by the UK Department for Environment, Food and Rural Affairs (DEFRA), which distinguishes between 'up-to-date'[685], 'workhorse'[686], and 'investment'[687] products, are of particular relevance.[688] These five ecodesign strategies should therefore be implemented reasonably by producers, which need to analyse and understand the context surrounding their products.[689]

170. First ecodesign strategy: design for robustness and reliability – Product lifetime can, first, be prolonged by a design that enhances the robustness and reliability of the product, thus resisting obsolescence by making

682 N. M. P. Bocken, I. de Pauw, C. Bakker, B. van der Grinten, 'Product design and business model strategies for a circular economy', 33 *Journal of Industrial and Production Engineering* (2016) p. 310.

683 See among others N. van Nes and J. Cramer, 'Influencing product lifetime through product design', 14 *Business Strategy and Environment* (2005) pp. 295–296; R. Mugge, J.P.L. Schoormans, H.N.J. Schifferstein, 'Design Strategies to Postpone Consumers' Product Replacement: The Value of a Strong Person-Product Relationship', 8 *The Design Journal* (2005) p. 38 at p. 48; N. M. P. Bocken, I. de Pauw, C. Bakker, B. van der Grinten, 'Product design and business model strategies for a circular economy', 33 *Journal of Industrial and Production Engineering* (2016) pp. 310–311; C.A. Bakker, M.C. den Hollander, E. van Hinte, Y. Zijlstra, *Products That Last – product design for circular business models* (BIS Publishers 2019).

684 See *supra*, n° 141 *et seq*.

685 'Up-to-date' products are "*products which [consumers tend] to discard when they [are] considered 'out of date'*". See Brook Lyndhurst, *Public understanding of product lifetimes and durability* (DEFRA 2011) p. 26.

686 'Workhorse' products are products "*purchased primarily on the basis of their function*" and "*tend to be discarded only when they broke, rather than when their look needed updating*". See Brook Lyndhurst, *Public understanding of product lifetimes and durability* (DEFRA 2011) p. 54.

687 'Investment' products are "*in some way special*" and are expected to last long due to financial investment, emotional value or other similar factors. See Brook Lyndhurst, *Public understanding of product lifetimes and durability* (DEFRA 2011) p. 79.

688 Brook Lyndhurst, *Public understanding of product lifetimes and durability* (DEFRA 2011). See also J. Cox et al., 'Consumer understanding of product lifetimes', 79 *Resources, Conservation and Recycling* (2013).

689 S. Carlsson, A. Mallalieu, *Design for Longevity – A Framework to Support Product Developers in Identifying Products' Optimal Lifetimes, Master's Thesis in Product Development* (Chalmers University of Technology 2021) p. 37.

the product physically durable.[690] Material selection is an important part of the design process to increase product durability.[691] The design process is, however, far from being simple as products and parts are exposed to various amounts of stress and wear during their lifetime. It should be noted that the design for robustness and reliability is eco-friendly only if consumers do not dispose of the product too early but keep it as long as it performs its function(s). However, designing products that can perform their function(s) over a period of time that largely exceeds their actual lifetime can result in a waste of effort, energy, and resources (as it generally takes more effort, energy, and resources to make durable and reliable products).[692] As a consequence, design for robustness and reliability is not really suitable for up-to-date products that are replaced due to technology development with a high rate of innovation (e.g. mobile phones) or due to changing fashions (e.g. textiles). By contrast, requirements on robustness and reliability seem fully appropriate for workhorse products as they have expected longevity and are usually only replaced when they break down or are no longer fit for use.[693] Some opportunities have also been identified for certain investment products that are valued more for their functionality than fashion.[694]

171. Second ecodesign strategy: design for attachment and trust – A product may also resist obsolescence if its design promotes emotional durability.[695] This strategy consists of designing the product to generate emotional attachment and trust between the consumer and the product. Such emotional bonding is likely to extend the lifetime of the product by strengthening the consumer-product relationship – preventing or at least postponing its psychological obsolescence – and by creating and sharpening consumers' sense of responsibility to take care of the product – preventing its material obsolescence.[696] Various strategies can be followed to help build and develop more emotionally engaging product experiences, like creating a sense of nostalgia or giving the product a personality.[697] This category also includes the design for product variability, as identified by N. van Nes and J. Cramer, where

---

690 See *supra*, n° 145.

691 N. M. P. Bocken, I. de Pauw, C. Bakker, B. van der Grinten, 'Product design and business model strategies for a circular economy', 33 *Journal of Industrial and Production Engineering* (2016) p. 310.

692 S. Carlsson, A. Mallalieu, *Design for Longevity – A Framework to Support Product Developers in Identifying Products' Optimal Lifetimes, Master's Thesis in Product Development* (Chalmers University of Technology 2021) pp. 37–38.

693 S. Boulos et al. (Ricardo-AEA), *The durability of products – Standard assessment for the circular economy under the Eco-Innovation Action Plan* (European Union 2015) p. 23.

694 J. Cox et al., 'Consumer understanding of product lifetimes', 79 *Resources, Conservation and Recycling* (2013).

695 J. Chapman, *Emotionally Durable Design; Objects, Experiences and Empathy* (Earthscan Publishing 2005).

696 See *supra*, n° 146.

697 M. Haines-Gadd, J. Chapman, P. Lloyd, J. Mason and D. Aliakseyeu, 'Emotional Durability Design Nine – A Tool for Product Longevity', 10 *Sustainability* (2018) p. 12 at p. 15.

a more enduring interest in the product is achieved through a design that offers variation to the user without the need for additional parts.[698] Along the same line, K. Harmer evaluated how psychological obsolescence could be mitigated by the customization of products enabled through design for disassembly, which creates a unique and satisfying material culture that promotes product attachment and the management of psychological obsolescence.[699] By contrast, it is interesting to note that unemotional design has been advocated as a strategy towards product sustainability. Unemotional design would remove the emotional aspects linked to conspicuous consumption and consequently, consumers would acquire emotional detachment to products and in turn more sustainable consumption patterns.[700]

172. Third ecodesign strategy: design for standardisation and compatibility – In a third ecodesign strategy, the emphasis is on the implementation of standards in product design. This design strategy increases the compatibility of the product with other products and parts or interfaces that fit these other products, allowing resistance to obsolescence.[701] The level of compatibility of the product influences its ability to interact with other products and facilitates the replacement of worn and defective components. In other words, the higher the level of standardisation and compatibility, the longer the lifetime of the product is likely to last. Since standards are constantly evolving and established depending on the industry and technological progress, it is nonetheless crucial to assess whether it is worth changing the design of the product according to standards (if a choice is possible). As rightly pointed out by S. Carlsson and A. Mallalieu, "*products designed with outdated compatible standards could obtain a reduced customer value because of a decreased usefulness, affecting the product's lifetime*".[702]

173. Fourth ecodesign strategy: design for maintenance and repair – A fourth ecodesign strategy consists of designing the product to simplify

---

698 N. van Nes and J. Cramer, 'Influencing product lifetime through product design', 14 *Business Strategy and Environment* (2005) p. 296. For example, one could think of a game with different levels of difficulty or scenarios.

699 K. Harmer, 'Design for disassembly: Potential for durability', in *4th International Symposium on Environmentally Conscious Design & Inverse Manufacturing, Eco Design – Conference Proceedings* (IEEE 2005) p. 962 at p. 964.

700 C. Thornquist, C. Thornquist, 'Unemotional design: an alternative approach to sustainable design', 33 *Design Issues* (2017) p. 83 at p. 91. By contrast with fashion-related consumer goods, which may be prematurely discarded (psychological obsolescence), emotional detachment may help consumers to have lower expectations and thus perceive products in a favourable way because of the lack in emotional demand or expectation.

701 See *supra*, n° 145.

702 S. Carlsson, A. Mallalieu, *Design for Longevity – A Framework to Support Product Developers in Identifying Products' Optimal Lifetimes, Master's Thesis in Product Development* (Chalmers University of Technology 2021) p. 38.

or reduce the need for maintenance and repair, especially for its essential components, to postpone and reverse the obsolescence of the product.[703] This can be done, for example, by simplifying repair to the replacement of modules that can be performed with as little knowledge as possible so that consumers themselves can perform the replacement of the module.[704] With such a design for disassembly and reassembly, the performance and functionality of the product can be more easily maintained, which allows satisfying consumers' expectations regarding the product and reducing the risk of the product becoming materially and indirectly obsolete too early. The *Fairphone* is a characteristic example of such a modular design.[705] Furthermore, designers and product design can incentivise changes in consumer behaviour. For instance, equipping refrigerators with a transparent door can have an energy-saving effect as the user would directly take the goods that he needs instead of opening the door and then start looking for them.[706] Inspiration could be drawn from this case to design products in a way that encourages consumers to take care of their products. The Internet of Things could bolster this design strategy as it enables products to be tracked for location, status and quality, and to be remotely controlled in unprecedented ways.[707] One could imagine designing the product with a button that sends a signal on the connected mobile phone when a defect occurs. Such connectivity would not only facilitate repair but also stimulate circular behaviour as users who receive support are encouraged and more inclined to solve the problem than replace the defective product.[708] Moreover, user data could be gathered, enabling a virtuous circle where users would, as a result of data gathering, receive more customized support based on consumer segmentation.[709]

174. Fifth ecodesign strategy: design for upgradability and adaptability – A fifth ecodesign strategy consists of "*designing products to allow for future expansion and modification*"[710], for example, when updates with newer technologies are released, when new trends emerge or in case of direct reuse by another user. Designing products in a way that they are easily

703 See *supra*, n° 148 and 152.

704 N. van Nes and J. Cramer, 'Influencing product lifetime through product design', 14 *Business Strategy and Environment* (2005) p. 295.

705 See <https://www.fairphone.com/en/>.

706 LE Europe, VVA Europe, Ipsos, ConPolicy, Trinomics, *Behavioural study on consumers' engagement in the circular economy* (European Commission 2018) p. 69.

707 EEA, *Circular by design: Products in the circular economy* (European Union 2017) p. 24.

708 It would also be interesting, from a sustainability perspective, to implement such product design in Product-as-a-Service contracts.

709 J. Bouma, *Design for customer engagement in the transition to a circular economy: A case study in Senseo coffee machines* (TU Delft 2019).

710 N. M. P. Bocken, I. de Pauw, C. Bakker, B. van der Grinten, 'Product design and business model strategies for a circular economy', 33 *Journal of Industrial and Production Engineering* (2016) p. 311.

upgradeable and adaptable allows postponing and reversing obsolescence[711], especially if these changes can be made by the consumers themselves. Such a design strategy is particularly relevant to extend the lifetime of up-to-date products that are subject to frequent updates. A case study conducted by W. Sun and P. Sun, which analysed the design of the Ricoh R-series digital camera, confirmed that a flexible design process, which allows gradual upgrading of the product in terms of technology, function and appearance, could contribute to helping companies and society to create more wealth, but most importantly, to extending product lifetime.[712] Indeed, such a design enables consumers to customize the product according to their needs and desires and to maintain a performance standard.[713] Consequently, upgradable and adaptable products are less likely to become prematurely obsolete on psychological and functional grounds. Design for upgradability and adaptability includes design for modularity, which allows replacing only the parts that are outdated and prevents the redesign of the whole product (including the production equipment involved).[714] Likely positive effects can be expected through upgrades of modular products (e.g. replacement of defective modules or batteries, possible configuration of the product according to consumer needs), if this is moderately embraced by consumers, and if the upgrade is the alternative to the purchase of a new device.[715] Another interesting design strategy for upgradability and adaptability is the strategy of 'piggybacking', which enables renewed functionality of a technologically obsolete product through the integration or add-on of a secondary device or component.[716] Designing products that are upgradable for and adaptable to new technologies and trends may, however, be difficult as there is no certainty about future developments and evolution.[717] Design for standardisation and compatibility could reduce these difficulties.[718]

---

711 See *supra*, n° 149 and 151.

712 W. Sun, P. Sun, 'Post Planned Obsolescence', in *Proceedings of the 9th International Conference on Computer-Aided Industrial Design and Conceptual Design: Multicultural Creation and Design* (CAIDCD 2008) p. 1009 at p. 1011.

713 S. Carlsson, A. Mallalieu, *Design for Longevity – A Framework to Support Product Developers in Identifying Products' Optimal Lifetimes, Master's Thesis in Product Development* (Chalmers University of Technology 2021) p. 38.

714 N. van Nes and J. Cramer, 'Influencing product lifetime through product design', 14 *Business Strategy and Environment* (2005) p. 295.

715 For a good summary of the environmental impact of modularity, taking the case of smartphones as an example, see K. Schischke, *Eco-design of Mobile Devices – Project sustainablySMART* (European Union 2018).

716 R. Rai, J. Terpenny, 'Principles for Managing Technological Product Obsolescence', 31 *IEEE Transactions on Components, Packaging, and Manufacturing Technology* (2008) p. 880 at p. 889.

717 S. Carlsson, A. Mallalieu, *Design for Longevity – A Framework to Support Product Developers in Identifying Products' Optimal Lifetimes, Master's Thesis in Product Development* (Chalmers University of Technology 2021) p. 38.

718 N. van Nes and J. Cramer, 'Influencing product lifetime through product design', 14 *Business Strategy and Environment* (2005) p. 296.

C. ECODESIGN RULES, WITH A PARTICULAR FOCUS ON THE ECODESIGN DIRECTIVE

1. PRODUCT-SPECIFIC REQUIREMENTS THAT PRODUCTS MUST MEET TO CIRCULATE ON THE EU MARKET

175. A FRAMEWORK DIRECTIVE, 29 IMPLEMENTING MEASURES AND 3 SELF-REGULATIONS – The Ecodesign Directive is a framework legislation that enshrines general principles and criteria for the establishment of binding ecodesign requirements on energy efficiency or other environmental impacts for specific product groups. Based on this Directive, the EC adopts mandatory ecodesign requirements, which set the minimum thresholds that products must reach in order to be placed on the EU market.[719] There is currently a wide range of implementing measures that supplement the Ecodesign Directive. In total, the ecodesign framework comprises 29 implementing measures shaping the design of various energy-related products, such as computers and dishwashers[720], and establishing requirements on energy efficiency and sustainability aspects, such as durability, upgradability and reparability. Alternatively, some ecodesign requirements are contained in self-regulations that can be recognised by the EC within the framework of the Ecodesign Directive.[721] So far, three product categories are covered by such self-regulation, namely complex set-top boxes, imaging equipment[722], and games consoles.[723] At the time of writing, a Proposal for a Sustainable Products Regulation[724], which seeks to revise the ecodesign legislation, is being discussed within the Council of the European Union.[725] As

---

719 Conforming with ecodesign requirements is thus a precondition for entering the EU market, for both manufacturers from inside and outside the EU, as explained *infra* (n° 177 *et seq.*).

720 The list of the product categories covered by these 29 implementing measures is available on: <https://ec.europa.eu/growth/single-market/european-standards/harmonised-standards/ecodesign_en>.

721 Art. 17 of the Ecodesign Directive. For further details on the recognised place of self-regulation, see n° 205–210.

722 It should be noted that imaging equipment will soon no longer be regulated by self-regulation since the EC recently decided not to endorse the revised draft of the Voluntary Agreement proposed by representatives of the sector. See *infra*, n° 193.

723 The list of recognised voluntary agreements under the ecodesign legislation is available on: <https://ec.europa.eu/info/energy-climate-change-environment/standards-tools-and-labels/products-labelling-rules-and-requirements/energy-label-and-ecodesign/energy-efficient-products/voluntary-agreements-under-eco-design-legislation_en>.

724 Proposal for a Regulation of the European Parliament and of the Council establishing a framework for setting ecodesign requirements for sustainable products and repealing Directive 2009/125/EC, COM(2022) 142 final (hereafter 'Proposal for a Sustainable Products Regulation').

725 The EESC has already given its opinion on the Proposal for a Sustainable Products Regulation. See Opinion of the EESC of 19 July 2022 on the Sustainable products initiative, including Ecodesign Directive, NAT/851.

the proposal is still under consideration, this chapter will be based mainly on the Ecodesign Directive, while making reference to the above-mentioned proposal where relevant.

176. A SPECIFIC (AND LENGTHY) ADOPTION PROCEDURE FOR IMPLEMENTING MEASURES – The implementing measures are adopted separately following a specific procedure. First of all, the EC establishes a working plan for the following three years with an indicative list of priority products.[726] After the working plan has been issued, preparatory studies are carried out with the contribution of scientists, following a specific methodology.[727] Based on the preparatory studies, a draft implementing measure is submitted for consultation of stakeholders, gathering Member State representatives and all interested parties concerned with the product group in question, such as industry, trade unions, traders, retailers, importers, environmental protection groups and consumer organisations.[728] The fourth step consists of an impact assessment to evaluate the environmental, economic and social impacts of the proposed implementing measure. The proposal is then subject to the vote of the regulatory committee with Member States' representatives.[729] After the vote, the implementing measure is scrutinized by the EP and the Council (comitology procedure), before being finally adopted by the EC. With all these steps, a standard regulatory process for a product group (i.e. from the beginning of the preparatory study to the publication of the implementing act in the Official Journal) takes on average around three and a half years, according to the EC's estimates.[730] Sometimes, the actual regulatory process is even twice as long, as reported by the European Court of Auditors.[731] This lengthy period is one of the biggest shortcomings of the ecodesign regulations and is particularly problematic with regard to the fight against premature obsolescence of product categories with rapid technological progress. However, the importance of designing appropriate product requirements and proceeding carefully and stepwise in the process should not be neglected. It is indeed sound, as emphasized by C. Dalhammar, to avoid ecodesign rules that may have big unforeseen effects, leading to setbacks.[732]

---

726 Art. 16 of the Ecodesign Directive.

727 See *infra*, n° 211 *et seq.*

728 Art. 18 of the Ecodesign Directive.

729 Art. 19 of the Ecodesign Directive.

730 C. Canevari, *Energy Efficient Product Policy in the European Union- Slides* (European Commission 2017) p. 21. See also EC, 'New energy efficiency labels explained', 11 March 2019, available on: <https://ec.europa.eu/commission/presscorner/detail/en/MEMO_19_1596>.

731 European Court of Auditors, *EU action on Ecodesign and Energy Labelling: important contribution to greater energy efficiency reduced by significant delays and non-compliance – Special Report* (European Union 2020) p. 19.

732 C. Dalhammar, E. Machacek, A. Bundgaard, K. Overgaard Zacho, A. Remmen, *Addressing resource efficiency through the Ecodesign Directive* (TemaNord 2014) p. 25.

177. A PRECONDITION FOR ENTERING THE EU MARKET – The outcome of this long process is a product-specific regulation, directly applicable in all Member States. In other words, once the ecodesign implementing measure is adopted, every manufacturer who produces or imports and sells products within the EU boundaries has to comply with all mandatory requirements it contains. This reflects the overall objective of the Ecodesign Directive, which is to ensure that products which move freely within EU boundaries satisfy environmental and energy-related requirements.[733] With these ecodesign regulations, the Directive creates a level playing field where all producers – even those from outside the EU – are subject to the same rules. Barriers to trade and distortion of competition within the EU are avoided.[734] But more than that, unlike other EU policies in general, mandatory ecodesign requirements tend to be taken up in other jurisdictions, which want to ensure the competitiveness of their industries on the global market.[735] This extra-territorial effect is also called the 'Brussels effect'.[736] If non-complying products circulate within the EU, their manufacturers can be subject to public and private sanctions.[737] Similar effects can be noted concerning ecodesign self-regulations that are recognised and monitored by the EC, although these measures are initially agreed on a voluntary basis.

178. A COMPONENT OF THE EU ENVIRONMENTAL STRATEGY – The establishment of the ecodesign legal framework took place within the context of the 'Integrated Product Policy', which emerged in the early 2000s as a new EU environmental strategy. The aim was to minimise the environmental impacts of products and services throughout their lifecycles with a view to promoting sustainable and greener development of the market.[738] Alongside the Integrated Product Policy, the EU developed its own sustainable consumption and production policy, with a view to "*improving the overall environmental performance of products throughout their life-cycle, promoting and stimulating the demand of better products and production technologies and helping consumers to*

733 Proposal for a Directive of the European Parliament and of the Council establishing a framework for the setting of ecodesign requirements for energy related products, COM(2008) 399 final, p. 2 and pp. 5–6.

734 Otherwise, national ecodesign requirements would create barriers to trade and distortion of competition and could consequently hinder the shift towards a circular economy. See Recital 2 of the Ecodesign Directive.

735 C. Dalhammar et al., *Addressing resource efficiency through the Ecodesign Directive* (TemaNord 2014) p. 94.

736 For an in-depth analysis on the Brussels effect, see A. Bradford, *The Brussels Effect – How the European Union Rules the World* (Oxford University Press 2020).

737 For further details on the compliance (or not) with ecodesign requirements, see n° 288 *et seq.*

738 See the Green paper of the European Commission of 7 February 2001 on Integrated Product Policy, COM(2001) 68 final, as well as Communication from the Commission of 18 June 2003 to the Council and the European Parliament on Integrated Product Policy – Building on Environmental Life-Cycle Thinking, COM(2003) 302 final.

make better choices through a more coherent and simplified labelling".[739] Several policies were already in place, including on the climate package, industrial emissions, waste, ambient air quality, eco-labelling and energy. However, some market failures and imperfections remained unsolved. Because market forces were deemed to be failing to evolve in the right direction at an acceptable speed and because little or no voluntary initiative was undertaken – at least for certain products, the EU decided to take the lead and adopted a 'command-and-control approach' through the Ecodesign Directive.[740] Together with the Energy Labelling Regulation[741], these rules provide the legal support to alleviate the negative impacts of products on the environment, influencing the way products are made, used and disposed of. The Ecodesign Directive 'pushes' the market towards greener products by banning the worst-performing ones, while the Energy Labelling Regulation 'pulls' the market towards more energy-efficient products by encouraging and empowering consumers to buy such efficient products based on useful information.[742]

2. EXISTING AND FUTURE PRODUCT CATEGORIES COVERED BY ECODESIGN RULES

a) A scope confined to new or imported energy-related products

179. FROM 'ENERGY-USING' TO 'ENERGY-RELATED' PRODUCTS – With the recast of the former Ecodesign Directive[743] in 2009, the scope of application of the ecodesign legislation was extended from 'energy-using products'[744] to all

739 Communication from the Commission of 16 July 2008 to the European Parliament, the Council, the European Economic and Social Committee and the Committee of the Regions on Sustainable Consumption and Production and Sustainable Industrial Policy Action Plan, COM (2008) 397 final. The Action Plan was endorsed by the Council: see the Council conclusions of 5 December 2008 on Sustainable Consumption and Production and Sustainable Industrial Policy Action Plan, 16914/08, annex. Union institutions have also adopted more general sustainable development policies.

740 The term 'command-and-control approach' is used in E. Maitre-Ekern, 'The Choice of Regulatory Instruments for a Circular Economy', in Klaus Mathis and Bruce R. Huber (eds.), *Environmental Law and Economics* (Springer 2017) p. 317.

741 Regulation (EU) 2017/1369 of the European Parliament and of the Council of 4 July 2017 setting a framework for energy labelling and repealing Directive 2010/30/EU, OJ L 198, 28.7.2017, p. 1–23. This Regulation is analysed in the following chapter of this book (n° 512 *et seq.*).

742 Staff Working Document of the European Commission of 15 July 2015 on the Evaluation of the Energy Labelling and Ecodesign Directives, SWD(2015) 143 final, p. 3.

743 Directive 2005/32/EC of the European Parliament and of the Council of 6 July 2005 establishing a framework for the setting of ecodesign requirements for energy-using products and amending Council Directive 92/42/EEC and Directives 96/57/EC and 2000/55/EC of the European Parliament and of the Council, OJ L 191, 22.7.2005, p. 29–58.

744 Art. 2(1) of the former Ecodesign Directive (2005/32/EC) defined 'energy-using products' as products dependent on energy input (electricity, fossil fuels and renewable energy sources)

'energy-related products'. According to Article 2 of the Directive, 'energy-related products' means any good placed on the market and/or put into service that has an impact on energy consumption during its use. The notion covers (1) energy-using products that use, generate, transfer or measure energy (electricity, gas, fossil fuel) and (2) other energy-related products, which do not use energy but have an impact on energy consumption. The scope also includes parts intended to be incorporated into energy-related products which are placed on the market and/or put into service as individual parts for end-users and of which the environmental performance can be assessed independently. The extension of the Directive's scope was aimed at expanding the number of energy-efficient and eco-friendly products available on the EU market. As outlined in Recital 3 of the 2009 Ecodesign Directive, energy-related products "*account for a large proportion of the consumption of natural resources and energy*" in the EU and require the use of rare materials and manufacturing processes of high quality.[745] Ecodesign requirements can thus be imposed on any of these types of products or parts.

180. No application to means of transport – Some energy-related products remain nonetheless out of the scope of the Ecodesign Directive, the main category being the means of transport for persons or goods.[746] The reason for this exclusion is that these products are already subject to a wide range of regulatory and voluntary measures that, in addition to safety and other aspects, also address environmental performance.[747]

---

to work as intended, or products for the generation, transfer and measurement of such energy (including parts of these products). Energy-using products were deemed to have a particularly important impact on the environment compared to other products (see Proposal for a Directive of the European Parliament and of the Council on establishing a framework for the setting of Eco-design requirements for Energy-Using Products and amending Council Directive 92/42/EEC, COM(2003) 453 final, p. 2–3).

745 The narrower scope of the former Ecodesign Directive was considered as an important restriction on the contribution of the Ecodesign rules to the EU Integrated Product Policy (see Proposal for a Directive of the European Parliament and of the Council establishing a framework for the setting of ecodesign requirements for energy related products, COM(2008) 399 final, p. 5). Indeed, a study commissioned by the EC revealed that energy-using products were only responsible for 31–36% of the environmental impacts, while energy-related products also have an important environmental impact and high potential for improvement (see BIO Intelligence Service and O2 France, *Study on external environmental effects related to the lifecycle of products and services – Final Report* (European Commission 2003).

746 Article 1(3) of the Ecodesign Directive.

747 For example, the environmental impacts of cars is already regulated by many regulations that establish stringent ecodesign requirements, including the Directive 2000/53/EC of the European Parliament and of the Council of 18 September 2000 on end-of life vehicles – Commission Statements, OJ L 269, 21.10.2000, p. 34–43; Directive 2005/64/EC of the European Parliament and of the Council of 26 October 2005 on the type-approval of motor vehicles with regard to their reusability, recyclability and recoverability and amending Council Directive 70/156/EEC, OJ L 310, 25.11.2005, p. 10–27; Regulation (EC) No 715/2007 of the European Parliament and of the Council of 20 June 2007 on type approval of motor vehicles with respect to emissions from light passenger and commercial vehicles (Euro 5 and Euro 6) and on access to vehicle repair and maintenance information, OJ L 171, 29.6.2007,

181. Only new and imported products placed on the market – As explained in the Blue Guide issued by the EC in 2016 and reviewed in 2022[748], the Ecodesign Directive applies to finished and newly manufactured products which are intended to be placed (or put into service) on the market. Once these products reach the end-user, they are no longer considered as new, and the Ecodesign Directive no longer applies. Used and second-hand products (including products resulting from the preparation for re-use of electrical or electronic waste)[749] only fall under obligations of the Directive if they are imported from a third country when they enter the EU market for the first time. Otherwise, they fall outside of the scope.[750] Yet, if the product has been subject to important changes or overhauls aiming to modify its original performance, purpose or type, the same Blue Guide states that it may be considered as a new product.[751] This has to be assessed on a case-by-case basis. If this is the case, the person who carried out the changes becomes the manufacturer, with the corresponding obligations.[752] Remanufactured products, which are neither new nor used, should in principle be seen as products which "*have been subject to important changes or overhauls*". Hence, remanufactured and new products should in principle be treated equally as regards ecodesign rules. Similar requirements could be imposed on 'fully refurbished' products, as is done under medical devices legislation.[753] The application of ecodesign rules to refurbished goods is however subject to more debate, especially when the refurbished products have been subject to minor changes.[754]

p. 1–16; Regulation (EC) No 595/2009 of the European Parliament and of the Council of 18 June 2009 on type-approval of motor vehicles and engines with respect to emissions from heavy duty vehicles (Euro VI) and on access to vehicle repair and maintenance information and amending Regulation (EC) No 715/2007 and Directive 2007/46/EC and repealing Directives 80/1269/EEC, 2005/55/EC and 2005/78/EC,OJ L 188, 18.7.2009, p. 1–13.

748 Commission Notice – The 'Blue Guide' on the implementation of EU products rules 2022, OJ C 247, 29.06.2022 (hereafter 'Blue Guide'), p. 15.

749 The Blue Guide, p. 16.

750 The Blue Guide, p. 15.

751 According to the Blue Guide, "*a product, which has been subject to important changes or overhaul after it has been put into service must be considered as a new product if: i) its original performance, purpose or type is modified, without this being foreseen in the initial risk assessment; ii) the nature of the hazard has changed or the level of risk has increased in relation to the relevant Union harmonisation legislation; and iii) the product is made available (or put into service if the applicable legislation also covers putting into service within its scope)*". See the Blue Guide, pp. 17–18.

752 The Blue Guide, p. 15 and p. 18.

753 See Art. 2(31) of the Regulation (EU) 2017/745 of the European Parliament and of the Council of 5 April 2017 on medical devices, amending Directive 2001/83/EC, Regulation (EC) No 178/2002 and Regulation (EC) No 1223/2009 and repealing Council Directives 90/385/EEC and 93/42/EEC, OJ L 117, 5.5.2017, p. 1–175. According to this provision, fully refurbishing a device means "*the complete rebuilding of a device already placed on the market or put into service, or the making of a new device from used devices, to bring it into conformity with this Regulation, combined with the assignment of a new lifetime to the refurbished device*".

754 See *infra*, n° 187–188.

182. Product groups covered by ecodesign rules – There are currently 32 product groups covered by ecodesign rules, be it implementing or self-regulatory measures.[755] These product groups all concern energy-using products, ranging from fridges and washing machines to vacuum cleaners and electronic displays.[756] Some of these rules focus on specific parts of energy-using products, like electric motors and water pumps. It is intriguing to note that no implementing measure has been adopted on energy-related products other than energy-using products (i.e. windows, insulation material or shower heads) since the extension of the scope of application of the Ecodesign Directive in 2009. This is mainly due to the fact that some of these products are already covered by the ecodesign rules on buildings and construction products.[757]

b) *The possible and upcoming extension of the scope to non-energy-related products*

183. A possibility provided for in the Ecodesign Directive – Concerning other non-energy-related products, Article 21 of the Ecodesign Directive refers to the possibility of broadening the scope of application to these products in the future. Although the extension of the scope remains possible, a study commissioned by the EC in 2012 has already been carried out on the basis of this Article and concluded that although the use of ecodesign requirements could bring substantial improvements to an important number of non-energy-related products, no extension was needed.[758] In this study, it was considered that (1) there was still insufficient experience within the current scope (which had been extended to energy-related products a few years earlier), (2) significant progress needed to be made in the implementation of the existing Ecodesign

755 The complete list of product groups covered by ecodesign regulations is available on: <https://ec.europa.eu/info/energy-climate-change-environment/standards-tools-and-labels/products-labelling-rules-and-requirements/energy-label-and-ecodesign/energy-efficient-products_en>.

756 It should be noted that some products belonging to these groups are explicitly exempted from the requirements set out in these ecodesign regulations. See e.g. Annex III to the Commission Regulation (EU) 2019/2020 of 1 October 2019 laying down ecodesign requirements for light sources and separate control gears pursuant to Directive 2009/125/EC of the European Parliament and of the Council and repealing Commission Regulations (EC) No 244/2009, (EC) No 245/2009 and (EU) No 1194/2012, OJ L 315, 5.12.2019, p. 209–240 (hereafter 'Ecodesign regulation on light sources and separate control gears').

757 See Directive 2010/31/EU of the European Parliament and of the Council of 19 May 2010 on the energy performance of buildings, OJ L 153, 18.6.2010, p. 13–35, as well as Regulation (EU) No 305/2011 of the European Parliament and of the Council of 9 March 2011 laying down harmonised conditions for the marketing of construction products and repealing Council Directive 89/106/EEC, OJ L 88, 4.4.2011, p. 5–43. See also the Proposal for a Regulation of the European Parliament and of the Council laying down harmonised conditions for the marketing of construction products, amending Regulation (EU) 2019/1020 and repealing Regulation (EU) 305/2011, COM(2022) 144 final.

758 Centre for Strategy & Evaluation Services (CSES), *Evaluation of the Ecodesign Directive (2009/125/EC) – Final Report* (European Commission 2012), especially p. 159 at p. 220.

Directive prior to any possible extension, (3) a different approach was required for non-energy-related products, (4) it would be difficult to establish ecodesign requirements for such products and (5) the possibility of applying self-regulatory initiatives and other alternatives should first be examined. Therefore, although an extension of the scope remains possible, the framework Directive is so far restricted to energy-related products.

184. An idea under debate... – In spite of the conclusions reached by the 2012 impact assessment study, the idea of extending the scope of the Ecodesign Directive remains under debate. In its Resolution of July 2015 on resource efficiency[759], as well as in its Resolution of May 2018[760], the EP asked the EC to evaluate the possibility of using the current ecodesign methodology for other product categories in addition to energy-related products, and thus broadening its scope to cover all main product groups. The same suggestion was expressed by the EESC in its Opinion on the Circular Economy Package, where it stated that ecodesign principles should be applied across all sectors, mainly because mobility, housing and food have been identified as being responsible for 70–80% of the adverse environmental impact.[761]

185. ... embodied in the Proposal for a Sustainable Products Regulation – In its 2020 Circular Economy Action Plan[762], as well as in its 2020 Consumer Agenda[763], the EC acknowledged the possibility of widening the scope of the Ecodesign Directive beyond energy-related products through the Sustainable Products Initiative to make the ecodesign framework applicable to the broadest possible range of products and make it deliver on circularity and sustainability. This idea is now embodied in Articles 1(2) and 2(1) of the Proposal for a Sustainable Products Regulation. Nonetheless, this provision extends the scope to 'physical goods' and consequently excludes 'non-physical' goods, like application software products, for which ecodesign requirements would also be welcome.[764]

---

759 European Parliament Resolution of 9 July 2015 on resource efficiency: moving towards a circular economy, (2014/2208(INI)), pt. 24.

760 European Parliament Resolution of 31 May 2018 on the implementation of the Ecodesign Directive (2009/125/EC), (2017/2087(INI)), pt. 30.

761 Opinion of the EESC of 27 April 2016 on the Communication from the Commission to the European Parliament, the Council, the European Economic and Social Committee and the Committee of the Regions: Closing the loop – An EU action plan for the circular economy – COM(2015) 614 final, NAT/676, pt. 4.1.2.

762 Communication from the Commission of 11 March 2020 to the European Parliament, the Council, the European Economic and Social Committee and the Committee of the Regions on A new Circular Economy Action Plan – For a cleaner and more competitive Europe, COM(2020) 98 final, p. 4.

763 Communication from the Commission of 13 November 2020 to the European Parliament and the Council and the Council on New Consumer Agenda – Strengthening consumer resilience for sustainable recovery, COM(2020) 696 final, p. 6.

764 See *infra*, n° 194.

186. THE NEED FOR REGULATING (ALL) NON-ENERGY-RELATED PRODUCTS – As non-energy-related products are as prone to premature obsolescence as energy-related products, they should be covered by ecodesign requirements. This could be achieved by extending the scope of the Ecodesign Directive to non-energy-related products (see #1), as suggested in the Proposal for a Sustainable Products Regulation, though without excluding 'non-physical' goods. Should that option be chosen, the current method for adopting implementing measures within the ecodesign framework should be adapted to fit with such products. Alternatively, one could imagine adopting a twin Ecodesign Directive specifically dedicated to non-energy-related products, with a specific methodology (see #2). This alternative would however require more effort for its implementation compared to the first option and would add another piece to the legislative jigsaw. The first option should therefore be preferred.

Proposed review of the Ecodesign Directive:

#1 All references to 'energy-related products' should be replaced with 'products'.

Example:

Article 1
Subject matter and scope

1. This Directive establishes a framework for the setting of Community ecodesign requirements for ~~energy-related~~ products with the aim of ensuring the free movement of ~~such~~ products within the internal market.

(...)

Article 2
Definitions

For the purposes of this Directive, the following definitions shall apply:

1. '~~Energy-related~~ Product', ~~(a 'product'),~~ means any good ~~that has an impact on energy consumption during use~~ which is placed on the market and/or put into service, and includes parts intended to be incorporated into ~~energy-related~~ products covered by this Directive which are placed on the market and/or put into service as individual parts for end-users and of which the environmental performance can be assessed independently;

(...)

OR

Policy recommendation:

#2 A twin Ecodesign Directive should be adopted for non-energy-related products.

c) *Extending the scope to products refurbished within the EU?*

187. The particular case of refurbished goods – As previously explained[765], the Ecodesign Directive only applies to used and second-hand products in two cases: (1) if they are imported from a third country when they enter the EU market for the first time or (2) if they are considered as new products after having been subject to important changes or overhauls aiming to modify their original performance, purpose or type. Refurbished products that do not belong to these two categories fall outside the scope of the Directive. This poses some issues concerning their compliance with ecodesign requirements. A 2019 study commissioned by the EESC pointed out the lack of clarity of ecodesign requirements on refurbished products that already bear the CE marking when new. In this study, it has been suggested that for refurbished mobile phones that have undergone only minor modifications that do not change their performance, companies should not be subject to a new declaration of conformity, even if they are imported from non-EU countries.[766]

188. The need for specific ecodesign requirements – Although the non-application of ecodesign requirements to refurbished products facilitates and thus promotes product refurbishment on the business side, it may raise concerns about the quality and even safety of refurbished products on the consumer side. There is the need to ensure product quality and restore consumer trust in these products.[767] It would, however, be inappropriate to apply the requirements imposed on new products to refurbished product as these two product categories are not comparable in terms of performance. Moreover, refurbished products do not always comply with the latest version of product regulations, especially products with a long average lifespan (e.g. workhorse products).[768]

765 See *supra*, n° 181.

766 V. Rizos et al., *Identifying the impact of the circular economy on the Fast-Moving Consumer Goods Industry – Opportunities and challenges for businesses, workers and consumers – mobile phones as an example* (EESC 2019) p. 20.

767 T.S. Wallner, L. Magnier, R. Mugge, 'Buying new or refurbished? The influence of the product's durability and attractiveness, contamination risk and consumers' environmental concern on purchase intentions of refurbished and new products', in C. Fitzpatrick (eds.), *4th international Product Lifetimes and the Environment (PLATE) conference proceedings* (Limerick 2021) p. 653 at p. 659.

768 Such a conclusion was reached by E. Worrell and M. Reuter, who had noticed the potential issue of reusing products containing hazardous substances. On the one hand, the WFD is

Therefore, it would be preferrable to adopt specific ecodesign requirements for refurbished goods and distinct from those imposed on new goods, as suggested in the following paragraph of this chapter.[769] The Blue Guide should be amended accordingly (see #3). If adopting and imposing specific requirements for refurbished products is ultimately considered as too complex to implement in practice, it may be wiser to promote product refurbishment through other legal instruments, such as information and guarantee rules.[770]

> *Proposed amendment to the Blue Guide:*
>
> *#3*
>
> 2. WHEN DOES UNION HARMONISATION LEGISLATION ON PRODUCTS APPLY?
>
> 2.1. PRODUCT COVERAGE
>
> (...)
>
> The Union harmonisation legislation applies to newly manufactured products but also to used and second-hand products imported from a third country when they enter the Union market for the first time.
>
> **<u>The Union harmonisation legislation may also provide for specific requirements for refurbished products.*</u>**
>
> (...)
>
> ---
>
> * **<u>'Refurbished products' can be defined as products that are returned to a satisfactory working and/or cosmetic condition, that may be inferior to the original specification, by replacing and repairing all major components that are faulty, markedly damaged or close to failure, and by making cosmetic changes to update the appearance of a product, such as cleaning, changing the fabric, painting or refinishing.</u>**

d) A wide range of possible implementing measures-to-be

189. Products envisaged for future implementing measures – Studies are ongoing to scrutinize and identify the remaining gaps and opportunities

---

pushing for the reuse of waste as the preferred option. On the other hand, regulations such as REACH currently restrict the use of certain substances, including a ban on substances previously largely used in products available on the market and now approaching the end of their lives. See E. Worrell, M. Reuter, *Handbook of recycling – State-of-the-art for practitioners, analysts, and scientists* (Elsevier 2014).

769 See *supra*, n° 196. These requirements applicable to refurbished products are complementary to but must be distinguished from product-specific requirements related to the refurbishment process which apply before the product is refurbished (n° 276–281).

770 See Chapters III and IV of this book.

and assess the necessity of adopting new ecodesign implementing measures for other (non-)energy-related products. The preparatory study initiated in 2020 for the Ecodesign and Energy Labelling Working Plan mapped energy-related products not yet regulated[771], and recommended a range of product groups for future ecodesign implementing measures, including energy-using products (e.g. professional cooking appliances and swimming pool heaters) as well as energy-related products (e.g. low-temperature emitters).[772] Other products were set aside because they are already covered by other regulations.[773] The findings of this preparatory study show that a wide array of products could (and should) be covered by ecodesign regulations.

190. Electronics and ICT – In its new Circular Economy Action Plan from March 2020, the EC announced the adoption of a 'Circular Electronics Initiative', with the aim of promoting a longer lifetime for electronics and ICT through regulatory measures under the Ecodesign Directive, among others.[774] This separate track for ICT products had been suggested in the Working Plan 2016–2019[775],

---

771 Viegand Maagøe, VHK and Oeko-Institut, *Preparatory study for the Ecodesign and Energy Labelling Working Plan 2020–2024 – Task 2 Identification of product groups and horizontal initiatives – Final* (European Commission 2021); Viegand Maagøe, VHK and Oeko-Institut, *Preparatory study for the Ecodesign and Energy Labelling Working Plan 2020–2024 – Task 3 Preliminary analysis of product groups and horizontal initiatives – Final* (European Commission 2021).

772 Viegand Maagøe, Oeko-Institut, VHK, *Preparatory study for the Ecodesign and Energy Labelling Working Plan 2020–2024 – Task 4 Complementary analyses and recommendations for the Ecodesign and Energy Labelling Working Plan 2020–2024 – Final* (European Commission 2021), especially p. 63.

773 This is the case of windows, for which efficiency requirements have been established by Member States' implementation of the Energy Performance of Buildings Directive, as explained *supra* (n° 182). See Viegand Maagøe, VHK and Oeko-Institut, *Preparatory study for the Ecodesign and Energy Labelling Working Plan 2020–2024 – Task 2 Identification of product groups and horizontal measures to be considered for inclusion in the Ecodesign and Energy Labelling Working Plan 2020–2024 – Draft report* (European Commission 2020) p. 18.

774 Communication from the Commission of 11 March 2020 to the European Parliament, the Council, the European Economic and Social Committee and the Committee of the Regions on A new Circular Economy Action Plan – For a cleaner and more competitive Europe, COM(2020) 98 final, p. 7.

775 Communication from the Commission of 30 November 2016 on Ecodesign Working Plan 2016–2019, COM(2016) 773 final, p. 8. Several reasons were given to justify this separate track. First, it was deemed difficult to make a reliable estimate of their energy savings potential, given the uncertainty about future market developments. Second, there were doubts on the suitability of the ecodesign and energy labelling process (which takes on average around four years for establishing minimum energy and resource efficiency criteria) for the fast-moving ICT product sectors. Third, it was acknowledged that the voluntary agreements that were recognised for some electronic product groups (i.e. imaging equipment, game consoles, and complex set-top boxes) as alternatives to regulatory measures, had not always proven to be faster in achieving the objectives of ecodesign. Fourth, the EU-US Energy Star Agreement, under which both jurisdictions set the same voluntary efficiency requirements for office equipment, had to be reviewed prior to its expiry in 2018. Fifth, the increased connectivity of products – whether in the home or the industry – and the advent of smart appliances as well as their impact on overall system efficiency, required careful consideration.

though not without criticism.[776] The results of the 2020 ICT study confirm that various ICT products could be included in the long list of product groups covered by ecodesign regulations, such as data centres, telecommunication networks, personal ICT equipment, imaging equipment, home and office equipment, and ICT in public spaces.[777] Although some of these products are already regulated, such as electronic displays[778] and servers[779], legislation remains limited. Adopting regulatory measures for these products, as confirmed in the Ecodesign and Energy Labelling Working Plan 2022–2024[780], would therefore be welcome.

191. Mobile phones and tablets – In addition to the Circular Electronics Initiative, the EC launched a specific initiative on the environmental impact of mobile phones and tablets.[781] The EC considers that these products, which are produced and sold in large numbers, replaced frequently and causing a growing amount of electronic waste, present a clear potential for improvement, not only in terms of energy efficiency but also concerning the recycling of rare metals, product design, and removable batteries.[782] Within the framework of this initiative, the EC recently issued a draft regulation laying down resource efficiency requirements for mobile phones, cordless phones and slate tablets.[783]

776 The suggestion of a separate track for ICT products was mainly criticised due to the fear of delayed adoption of implementing measures. See BEUC Policy Paper of 5 December 2017 on Greener, better, faster, stronger Ecodesign – Consumer organisations' views on the implementation and enforcement of the Ecodesign Directive, BEUC-X-2017–146, p. 6; European Parliament Report of 7 May 2018 on the implementation of the Ecodesign Directive (2009/125/EC), (2017/2087(INI)); European Parliament Resolution of 31 May 2018 on the implementation of the Ecodesign Directive (2009/125/EC), (2017/2087(INI)), pt. 28; Coolproducts Open letter of 26 March 2018 to President Juncker on Regulate smartphones through Ecodesign, available on: <https://www.coolproducts.eu/policy/letter-to-the-european-commission-regulate-smartphones-through-ecodesign/>.

777 VHK and Viegand Maagøe, *ICT Impact study – Final Report* (European Commission 2020).

778 Commission Regulation (EU) 2019/2021 of 1 October 2019 laying down ecodesign requirements for electronic displays pursuant to Directive 2009/125/EC of the European Parliament and of the Council, amending Commission Regulation (EC) No 1275/2008 and repealing Commission Regulation (EC) No 642/2009, OJ L 315, 5.12.2019, p. 241–266.

779 Commission Regulation (EU) No 617/2013 of 26 June 2013 implementing Directive 2009/125/EC of the European Parliament and of the Council with regard to ecodesign requirements for computers and computer servers, OJ L 175, 27.6.2013, p. 13–33.

780 Communication from the Commission Ecodesign and Energy Labelling Working Plan 2022–2024, OJ C 182, 4.5.2022, p. 5.

781 Inception Impact Assessment from the European Commission of 23 December 2020 on Environmental impact of mobile phones and tablets, Ares(2020)7893117.

782 For further details on the criteria taken into account for the adoption of the implementing measures, see n° 211 *et seq*.

783 The Draft Commission Regulation of 31 August 2022 laying down ecodesign requirements for mobile phones, cordless phones and slate tablets pursuant to Directive 2009/125/EC of the European Parliament and of the Council, Ares(2022)6031498, as well as its Annex, are available on: <https://ec.europa.eu/info/law/better-regulation/have-your-say/initiatives/12797-Designing-mobile-phones-and-tablets-to-be-sustainable-ecodesign_en>. For a closer analysis of the ecodesign and information requirements contained in this draft regulation, see *infra* (n° 231 *et seq*.).

This draft regulation addresses the demand of European citizens for longer-lasting digital devices.[784] Several studies have already examined the potential of ecodesign requirements for mobile phones, smartphones and tablets.[785] As phones and tablets are prone to premature obsolescence, the prospect of having ecodesign regulations covering these products is very welcomed and the draft regulation should therefore be praised.

192. Mobile phone chargers and similar electronic devices – Legislative actions are also envisaged for mobile phone chargers and similar devices. Although chargers are already covered by ecodesign regulations on external power supplies[786], the EC announced its intention to introduce a common charger, improve the durability of charging cables and provide incentives to decouple the purchase of chargers from the purchase of new devices.[787] Following the expiry of the Memorandum of Understanding (MoU) in 2014[788], many manufacturers (*Apple*, *Google*, *Lenovo*, *LG*, *Motorola*, *Samsung*, and *Sony*) signed a new MoU12 committing new smartphone models to be chargeable through a USB Type-C connector or cable assembly.[789] However, the EC was not satisfied with this proposal from the industry and decided to initiate preparatory steps for regulatory actions with a view to establishing a common charging solution for all relevant devices.[790] After an

784 Kantar, *Special Eurobarometer 503 – Attitudes towards the impact of digitalisation on daily lives* (European Commission 2020) p. 12.

785 M. Cordella, F. Alfieri, J. Sanfelix, *Guidance for the Assessment of Material Efficiency: Application to Smartphones – JRC Technical Report* (European Commission 2020); Fraunhofer IZM, Fraunhofer ISI, VITO, *Ecodesign preparatory study on mobile phones, smartphones and tablets – Final Report* (European Commission 2021).

786 Commission Regulation (EU) 2019/1782 of 1 October 2019 laying down ecodesign requirements for external power supplies pursuant to Directive 2009/125/EC of the European Parliament and of the Council and repealing Commission Regulation (EC) No 278/2009, OJ L 272, 25.10.2019, p. 95–106.

787 Communication from the Commission of 11 March 2020 to the European Parliament, the Council, the European Economic and Social Committee and the Committee of the Regions on A new Circular Economy Action Plan – For a cleaner and more competitive Europe, COM(2020) 98 final, p. 7.

788 Memorandum of Understanding of 5 June 2009 regarding Harmonisation of a charging capability for mobile phones, available on: <https://ec.europa.eu/docsroom/documents/2417/attachments/1/translations/en/renditions/native>.

789 Memorandum of Understanding of 20 March 2018 on the future common charging solution for smartphones, available on: <https://www.digitaleurope.org/wp/wp-content/uploads/2019/01/2018.03.20-MoU%20on%20the%20future%20of%20Common%20Charging%20Solutions%20(1)%20(1)%202.pdf>.

790 The EC stated that it did not "*guarantee full interoperability between mobile phones (…) as proprietary solutions were proposed together with the previous USB 2.0 Micro B and the new USB Type C solutions*". See Inception Impact Assessment from the European Commission of 15 December 2018 on Common chargers for mobile telephones and other compatible devices, Ares(2018)6473169, pp. 1–2.

impact assessment study was carried out[791], the EC issued a proposal for a revised Radio Equipment Directive in September 2021.[792] In addition, the EC is planning to review the Regulation laying down the ecodesign requirements of external power supplies.[793] These new rules will harmonise charging port and fast charging technology, unbundle the sale of a charger from the sale of the electronic device and improve information for consumers.[794] Interesting suggestions have already been made concerning this envisaged legislative proposal on common chargers. It was, for example, suggested that the EC adopt measures standardising the marking of chargers and cables and requiring efficient wireless alternatives.[795] All these actions could play a significant role in curbing the material obsolescence of chargers and the indirect obsolescence of products using these chargers.

193. Imaging equipment – The EC has also confirmed in its Ecodesign and Energy Labelling Working Plan 2022–2024 that it will prepare regulatory measures for imaging equipment[796], thus rejecting the revised draft of the voluntary agreement proposed by representatives of the sector.[797] The draft voluntary agreement on imaging equipment was deemed not ambitious enough, in particular regarding the possible re-use of consumables.[798] It seems therefore preferable to establish mandatory ecodesign regulations for this product category. Such reasoning could similarly be applied to the video game sector, where the recent complaints against *Nintendo* have shown the lack of ambitious commitments taken by the producers of games consoles.[799]

194. Application software products – Although non-tangible products were not considered at the time the Ecodesign Directive was adopted[800], the

---

791 Ipsos and Trinomics, *Impact Assessment Study on Common Chargers of Portable Devices* (European Commission 2019).

792 Proposal for a Directive of the European Parliament and of the Council amending Directive 2014/53/EU on the harmonisation of the laws of the Member States relating to the making available on the market of radio equipment, COM(2021) 547 final.

793 See the press release issued by the EC, 'Pulling the plug on consumer frustration and e-waste: Commission proposes a common charger for electronic devices', 23 September 2021, as well as the factsheet on the Commission's proposal on a common charging solution for electronic devices (2022), both available on: <https://ec.europa.eu/commission/presscorner/detail/en/IP_21_4613>.

794 *Ibid.*

795 See C. McAlister, E. Oldyrevas, *One charger to fit them all – Using ecodesign to deliver an ambitious common charger initiative* (Ecos 2020).

796 Communication from the Commission Ecodesign and Energy Labelling Working Plan 2022–2024, OJ C 182, 4.5.2022, p. 5.

797 Draft Industry voluntary agreement of 9 April 2021 to improve the environmental performance of imaging equipment placed on the European market, FY20 v. 5, available on: <https://www.eurovaprint.eu/pages/voluntary-agreement/>.

798 Communication from the Commission Ecodesign and Energy Labelling Working Plan 2022–2024, OJ C 182, 4.5.2022, p. 7.

799 See n° 72 and n° 435.

800 In fact, no clear examples of non-tangible goods were widespread in the market.

definition of 'energy-related products' should be interpreted as covering such products[801], especially those related to new technological developments like application software products.[802] In fact, application software products, which can be placed on the market as standalone products, can have significant environmental impacts.[803] They can generate large energy and resource flows as they determine which hardware capacities are made available and how much electric energy is used by end-user devices, networks, and data centres.[804] But software products can also cause the functional obsolescence of products.[805] A study issued by the *Umweltbundesamt* demonstrated that software application products with the same functionality can markedly differ in terms of energy consumption and hardware efficiency (i.e. their impact on processor utilisation, working memory, permanent storage, and bandwidth for network access).[806] It is on the basis of such reasoning that France adopted legislation providing for the establishment of sustainable design criteria for digital services.[807] It is however preferable to introduce ecodesign regulations on this product category at EU level, as recommended in the Preparatory study for Ecodesign and Energy Labelling Working Plan.[808] Potential ecodesign, labelling and information requirements could be derived from *The Blue Angel* ecolabel for resource and energy-efficient software products.[809]

---

801 See *supra*, n° 184.

802 The same reasoning was made for the Product Liability Directive. See Art. 4(1) of the Proposal for a Directive on liability for defective products (COM(2022) 495 final), which states that 'product' includes software. See also the Commission Staff Working Document of 7 May 2018 on the Evaluation of Council Directive 85/374/EEC of 25 July 1985 on the approximation of the laws, regulations and administrative provisions of the Member States concerning liability for defective products, SWD(2018) 157 final, pp. 53–54.

803 See L. Hilty, S. Behrendt, K. Fichter, *Green Software: Establishing and exploiting potentials for environmental protection in information and communication technology* (Umweltbundesamt 2015); R. Liu, P. Gailhofer, C.-O. Gensch, A. Köhler, F. Wolff, *Impacts of the digital transformation on the environment and sustainability* (European Commission 2019), as cited in Viegand Maagøe, VHK and Oeko-Institut, *Preparatory study for the Ecodesign and Energy Labelling Working Plan 2020–2024 – Task 3 Preliminary analysis of product groups and horizontal initiatives – Final* (European Commission 2021) p. 633.

804 Viegand Maagøe, VHK and Oeko-Institut, *Preparatory study for the Ecodesign and Energy Labelling Working Plan 2020–2024 – Task 3 Preliminary analysis of product groups and horizontal initiatives – Final* (European Commission 2021) p. 655.

805 See *supra* on the concept of functional obsolescence (n° 106–111).

806 See J. Gröger, A. Köhler, S. Naumann, A. Filler, A. Guldner, E. Kern, L.M. Hilty, Y.V. Maksimov, *Entwicklung und Anwendung von Bewertungsgrundlagen für ressourceneffiziente Software unter Berücksichtigung bestehender Methodik* (Umweltbundesamt 2018), especially p. 24.

807 Art. 25 of the Law on the Environmental Footprint of Digital Technology.

808 Viegand Maagøe, Oeko-Institut, VHK, *Preparatory study for the Ecodesign and Energy Labelling Working Plan 2020–2024 – Task 4 Complementary analyses and recommendations for the Ecodesign and Energy Labelling Working Plan 2020–2024 – Final* (European Commission 2021) p. 60.

809 Basic Award Criteria of the German Ecolabel Blue Angel from January 2020 for resource and energy-efficient software products, DE-UZ 215, available on: <https://www.blauer-engel.de/en/products/electric-devices/resources-and-energy-efficient-software-products>. For example, a

195. Textiles and furniture – Textiles and furniture should also be covered by ecodesign regulations. These non-energy-related products have an important environmental impact and are prone to premature obsolescence too. For example, it has been shown that the number of times a garment is worn before it ceases to be used has decreased.[810] Besides the low level of 'emotional durability' of textile products, failures in quality such as colour fastness, tear strength or the quality of zippers and seams are among the main reasons for consumers to discard textiles.[811] The increasingly disposable nature of clothes aggravates the environmental impacts of textiles, which are already significant (i.e. resource use, land use, climate change and releases of pollutants).[812] This could partly be avoided if the design of these products was improved. The possibility of applying ecodesign requirements to textiles and furniture has already been examined.[813] Actions should now be taken in that sense. Inspiration could be drawn from existing durability requirements set out by the EU Ecolabel scheme[814], as well as other national voluntary schemes like *The Blue Angel*.[815] Concerning textiles, the EC has already stated that it should apply "*the new sustainable product framework to textiles, including developing ecodesign measures to ensure that textile products are fit for circularity*".[816] The EC confirmed its plan in the 2022 EU Strategy for Sustainable and Circular Textiles, announcing the adoption of binding product-specific ecodesign requirements on sustainability aspects (e.g. durability, reusability, reparability, fibre-to-fibre, recyclability and mandatory recycled fibre content) and starting with products with the highest potential and impacts in terms of environmental sustainability (e.g. personal and household textiles, carpets and mattresses).[817]

---

software product with a Blue Angel ecolabel must deliver its functions with a minimal use of resources and a minimal energy demand. For further information, see Chapter III on the marketing and pre-contractual stage, and more specifically n° 595.

810 Ellen MacArthur Foundation, *A New Textiles Economy: Redesigning fashion's future* (2017) p. 77.

811 ECOS, *Durable, repairable and mainstream – How ecodesign can make our textiles circular* (2021) p. 13.

812 EEA, *Briefing on Textiles in Europe's circular economy* (2019), available on: <https://www.eea.europa.eu/publications/textiles-in-europes-circular-economy>.

813 See e.g. B. Bauer, D. Watson, A. Gylling, A. Remmen, M. Hauris Lysemose, C. Hohenthal, A.-K. Jönbrink, *Potential Ecodesign Requirements for Textiles and Furniture* (TemaNord 2018).

814 See *infra*, n° 601 *et seq.*

815 Basic Award Criteria of the German Ecolabel Blue Angel from July 2017 for textiles, DE-UZ 154, available on: <https://www.blauer-engel.de/en/productworld/textiles>.

816 Communication from the Commission of 11 March 2020 to the European Parliament, the Council, the European Economic and Social Committee and the Committee of the Regions on A new Circular Economy Action Plan – For a cleaner and more competitive Europe, COM(2020) 98 final, p. 10.

817 Communication from the Commission of 30 March 2022 to the European Parliament, the Council, the European Economic and Social Committee and the Committee of the Regions on the EU Strategy for Sustainable and Circular Textiles, COM(2022) 141 final, pp. 3–4.

196. Horizontal measures on 'durability' – In addition to this vertical approach (i.e. product-specific, or related to a defined product group), where requirements depend on the features of the product group (i.e. materials, key components, design approaches), research has been carried out and is still ongoing on the possibility of elaborating implementing measures that would apply more horizontally across different product categories, including categories already regulated and those not yet covered by implementing measures. The preparatory study for the Working Plan 2022–2024 recommended, for example, the adoption of such horizontal implementing measures on 'product durability'.[818] One could imagine having horizontal durability requirements for all battery-operated products.[819] Such an approach has already been followed for standby, off mode electric power consumption of electrical and electronic household and office equipment.[820] Horizontal durability requirements for clusters of product groups could also be envisaged for refurbished products. R. Mugge, B. Jockina and N. Bockena found that "*[m]ost of the highest scoring incentives for purchasing refurbished smartphones were product-related and included improved battery life, guaranteed software updates, and upgraded performance, indicating a need for continued performance*".[821] However, as the preparatory study highlighted, it would not be realistic to envisage horizontal durability requirements covering all product categories as not all of them might face problems with shorter lifetimes or benefit from durability measures. Therefore, it was suggested that exemptions or more stringent durability performance requirements could be adopted for certain product categories.[822]

---

818 In this study, 'product durability' is understood in its broad sense, encompassing the "*reliability, maintenance, repair, upgrade and reuse of products*". See Viegand Maagøe, Oeko-Institut, VHK, *Preparatory study for the Ecodesign and Energy Labelling Working Plan 2020–2024 – Task 4 Complementary analyses and recommendations for the Ecodesign and Energy Labelling Working Plan 2020–2024 – Final* (European Commission 2021) p. 56.

819 Viegand Maagøe, VHK and Oeko-Institut, *Preparatory study for the Ecodesign and Energy Labelling Working Plan 2020–2024 – Task 3 Preliminary analysis of product groups and horizontal initiatives – Durability – Draft report* (European Commission 2020) p. 7.

820 Commission Regulation (EC) No 1275/2008 of 17 December 2008 implementing Directive 2005/32/EC of the European Parliament and of the Council with regard to ecodesign requirements for standby and off mode electric power consumption of electrical and electronic household and office equipment, OJ L 339, 18.12.2008, p. 45–52; Commission Regulation (EU) No 801/2013 of 22 August 2013 amending Regulation (EC) No 1275/2008 with regard to ecodesign requirements for standby, off mode electric power consumption of electrical and electronic household and office equipment, and amending Regulation (EC) No 642/2009 with regard to ecodesign requirements for televisions, OJ L 225, 23.8.2013, p. 1–12.

821 R. Mugge, B. Jockina, N. Bockena, 'How to sell refurbished smartphones? An investigation of different customer groups and appropriate incentives', 147 *J. Clean. Prod.* (2017) p. 284 at p. 296.

822 Viegand Maagøe, Oeko-Institut, VHK, *Preparatory study for the Ecodesign and Energy Labelling Working Plan 2020–2024 – Task 4 Complementary analyses and recommendations for the Ecodesign and Energy Labelling Working Plan 2020–2024 – Final* (European Commission 2021) p. 57.

197. More products should be covered by implementing measures – The previous paragraphs revealed that some important product categories – where substantial resource savings may still exist – remain unregulated. Among the categories that should be considered for new implementing measures, ICT products (including mobile phones and tablets), chargers, imaging equipment, software products, textiles and furniture should be prioritised (see #4). In addition, horizontal measures on product durability should be envisaged, including for refurbished goods (see #4).[823] This list is far from being exhaustive and could be extended if additional priority products prone to premature obsolescence were to be found, including products with short or decreasing lifetimes or a wide range of innovation cycles, with high failure rates or with key functions with a relatively high dependence on software, and in turn, regular software updates.[824] To avoid a lengthy regulatory process[825], these new implementing measures should be adopted when they are ready, rather than when a package is complete, as recommended by the European Court of Auditors.[826]

Proposed ecodesign implementing measures: #4

- *Commission Regulation implementing Directive 2009/125/EC with regard to ecodesign requirements for electronics and information and communication technologies*

NB: Because electronics and information and communication technologies cover a very wide range of products, distinct and specific regulations should be adopted for the different product categories encompassed within this product group (e.g. mobile phones and tablets).

- *Commission Regulation implementing Directive 2009/125/EC with regard to imaging equipment*

- *Commission Regulation implementing Directive 2009/125/EC with regard to ecodesign requirements for software products*

823 For further comments on durability requirements, see *infra*, n° 237 *et seq*.

824 These product categories were suggested in Viegand Maagøe, VHK and Oeko-Institut, *Preparatory study for the Ecodesign and Energy Labelling Working Plan 2020–2024 – Task 3 Preliminary analysis of product groups and horizontal initiatives – Durability – Draft report* (European Commission 2020) p. 6. The preparatory study also suggested focussing or prioritising "*product categories with comparably higher impacts in the manufacturing phase compared to the use phase throughout the lifecycle*".

825 See *supra*, n° 176.

826 European Court of Auditors, *EU action on Ecodesign and Energy Labelling: important contribution to greater energy efficiency reduced by significant delays and non-compliance – Special Report* (European Union 2020) p. 39.

- *Commission Regulation implementing Directive 2009/125/EC with regard to ecodesign requirements for textiles*
- *Commission Regulation implementing Directive 2009/125/EC with regard to ecodesign requirements for furniture*

NB: Because textiles and furniture cover a very wide range of products, distinct and specific regulations should be adopted for the different product categories encompassed within this product group (e.g. garments with fasteners)

- *Commission Regulation implementing Directive 2009/125/EC with regard to durability requirements*

e) *The (too strict) criteria for the development of new implementing measures*

198. Three criteria for the eligibility of products – When establishing the working plan, the EC defines the scope of the product categories to be investigated, indicating whether existing product-specific measures will be reviewed or whether additional product groups will be further examined. Article 15(2) of the Ecodesign Directive lays down criteria that govern the choice of products for the adoption of new implementing measures.[827] Pursuant to this provision, products shall be covered by an implementing measure if:

(a) they have a volume of sales that exceeds 200,000 units per year throughout the internal European market;
(b) they have a significant environmental impact; and
(c) they present significant potential for improvement in environmental impact without entailing excessive costs, taking into account in particular the absence of other relevant EU legislation, the existence of a market failure, and a wide disparity amongst similar products in terms of environmental performance.

These three criteria are implemented following the Methodology for Ecodesign of Energy-related Products (MEErP)[828], which provides guidance for the preparatory study by evaluating whether and to which extent energy-related

[827] The same criteria are applicable in case of self-regulation measures. See *infra*, n° 205.
[828] The MEErP follows a specific structure, starting by (1) the definition of the product category and the identification of the relevant standards and legislation, (2) an economic and market analysis, (3) an analysis of consumer behaviour and the social, cultural and infrastructural context, (4) a technical analysis of current products on the EU market and ending with (5) an assessment of base case, (6) improvement potential and (7) policy, scenario, impact and sensitivity analysis. For more details on the MEErP structure, see COWI Belgium, VHK, *Methodology for ecodesign of energy-related products (MEErP 2011) – Methodology report. Part 1, Methods* (European Commission 2011) p. 23 at p. 161.

products fulfil the criteria that make them eligible for implementing measures.[829] If the products are deemed to fulfil the criteria set out in Article 15, they may be covered by an implementing measure. Concerning the products that do not meet these criteria, it is interesting to note that those could still fall under Article 11, which requires information on components and sub-assemblies of products covered by implementing measures.

199. The notion of 'environmental impact' – Annexes I and II to the Ecodesign Directive provide some guidance on what should be understood under the notion of 'environmental impact' mentioned in the second and third criteria of Article 15(2). According to Part 1 of Annex I, the environmental impacts of energy-related products include consumption of materials, of energy and other resources, emissions to air, water or soil, pollution through physical effects such as noise, vibration, radiation, electromagnetic fields, generation of waste material, and possibilities for reuse, recycling and recovery of materials and/or of energy, that can occur at any phase of the product lifecycle. Annex I also provides parameters on which the potential for reducing the environmental impacts should be evaluated, including *inter alia* the extension of lifetime (as expressed through minimum guaranteed lifetime, minimum time for availability of spare parts, modularity, upgradeability, reparability), the quantity and nature of consumables needed for proper use and maintenance, the ease for reuse (e.g. time and complexity of tools necessary for disassembly) and the incorporation of used components.[830] The link can easily be made between these parameters and the three strategies against premature obsolescence.[831] In other words, product groups that have an environmental impact due to their premature obsolescence and that present potential for improvement could meet the criteria of Article 15(2).

200. The degree of significance of the environmental impact and potential – Whereas the first condition of Article 15(2) raises no problems in itself[832], this statement cannot be made for the second and third criteria. The vagueness of the terms used in these two criteria, especially due to the word 'significant', has already been pointed out as problematic.[833] These criteria leave indeed great latitude in the implementation of the Ecodesign Directive. Admittedly, aspects related to product sustainability are taken into consideration

---

829 European Commission, *Ecodesign: your future – How ecodesign can help the environment by making products smarter* (European Union 2012) p. 3.

830 See Annex I part 1.3. to the Ecodesign Directive.

831 See *supra*, n° 141 *et seq.*

832 The words 'significant volume' and 'indicatively' used in Art. 15(2)(a) indicate some flexibility on the part of the EC in electing product groups and designing measures.

833 See R. Malcolm, 'Ecodesign Laws and the Environmental Impact of our Consumption of Products', 23 *Journal of Environmental Law* (2011) p. 497.

when assessing the environmental impacts of energy-related products and their potential for improvement. However, as can be seen in the preparatory study of the previous Ecodesign Working Plan 2015–2017[834], the significance of environmental impact and potential for improvement cannot easily be measured when it concerns aspects that relate to the consumption of resources other than energy, especially due to a lack of information. This may create a barrier to the selection of certain product categories prone to premature obsolescence as well as second-hand products, for which the environmental impact and the potential for improvement may be considered as not being 'significant' enough. Yet every little step towards a longer product lifetime should be taken when possible.

201. The word 'significant' should be removed – From the perspective of product sustainability, it seems desirable to remove the word 'significant' from Article 15(2) of the Ecodesign Directive (see #5). This amendment should be seen as 'proportionate' as it is "*necessary to achieve the objectives of the Treaties*"[835], namely the protection of the environment.[836] Other safeguards still prevent the EU from going too far, like the one precluding improvements in environmental impact that would entail excessive costs and the one requiring the existence of a market failure, both described in the following paragraphs.[837] Alternatively, some clarification should at least be given on this term in Annex I to the Directive (see #6). For example, Annex I could specify that the potential for improvement in environmental impact should be considered as significant if the product can be designed in a more durable, repairable or reusable way, comparing poor and good product designs available on the market and taking the best available technologies into consideration.[838] The EU Product Environmental Footprint (PEF) methodology, which aims to provide a common way of measuring the environmental performance of products, may be of great help in this regard.[839]

---

834 BIO by Deloitte, Oeko-Institut and ERA Technology, *Preparatory Study to establish the Ecodesign Working Plan 2015–2017 implementing Directive 2009/125/EC – Task 3 Final Report* (European Commission 2014) p. 19 at p. 21.

835 Art. 5(4) TEU.

836 Art. 191 TFEU.

837 See *infra*, n° 202–203.

838 This would fit with the wording of Article 15(2)(c), which requires that "*the wide disparity amongst similar products in terms of environmental performance*" should be taken into account.

839 The PEF methodology is still in a testing phase. See <https://ec.europa.eu/environment/eussd/smgp/ef_pilots.htm>. See also Commission Recommendation (EU) 2021/2279 of 15 December 2021 on the use of the Environmental Footprint methods to measure and communicate the life cycle environmental performance of products and organisations, OJ L 471, 30.12.2021, p. 1–396; Corrigendum to Commission Recommendation (EU) 2021/2279 of 15 December 2021 on the use of the Environmental Footprint methods to measure and communicate the life cycle environmental performance of products and organisations (Official Journal of the European Union L 471 of 30 December 2021), OJ L 144, 23.5.2022, p. 1–384.

202. Without entailing excessive costs – The third criteria laid down in Article 15(2)(c) of the Directive adds another condition to the adoption of implementing measures for new products, namely that the improvement in environmental impact should not entail excessive costs.[840] Consequently, even if the environmental impact and the potential are both significant for a product category, ecodesign regulations (including on product sustainability) may not be adopted if it is estimated that the improvement options present excessive costs. The cost calculation is mainly based on a product life cycle costs analysis. For example, if the envisaged ecodesign requirements are likely to lead to products with life cycle costs that significantly exceed the current life cycle costs and/ or with a higher purchase price (from the consumer point of view)[841], these products may be deemed not eligible for ecodesign regulations. Yet even though ecodesigned products may incur higher costs for consumers[842], they generally generate consumer savings, at least in the long term. While consumers might feel the price difference in their wallet when purchasing ecodesigned products, these are also of better quality, more energy- and resource-efficient and longer-lasting. The transition from halogen lamps to LEDs aptly illustrates this point.[843]

203. The existence of a market failure – Article 15(2)(c)(i) states that, in the evaluation of the potential for improvement in environmental impact, consideration should be given to the existence of a market failure. Ecodesign regulations are particularly needed in sectors where the different actors in the product lifecycle are not incentivised to improve the product's environmental aspects due to the existence of general market failures, like asymmetrical information, split incentives or environmental externalities.[844] In other sectors,

---

840 See also recital 3 of the Ecodesign Directive.

841 BIO by Deloitte, Oeko-Institut and ERA Technology, *Preparatory Study to establish the Ecodesign Working Plan 2015–2017 implementing Directive 2009/125/EC – Task 3 Final Report* (European Commission 2014) p. 21.

842 It should be noted that there is no firm evidence that resource-related requirements lead to more costly products, especially as the ecodesign requirements may entail no or little additional development and production costs. Most requirements can be met with existing technical solutions, at relatively little additional cost if at all any. Moreover, ecodesign requirements are gradual and flexible (n° 219 and 213), which facilitates the introduction of the necessary changes into the product design.

843 While halogen lamps are individually cheaper than LEDs, purchasing the first instead of the second constitutes 'false economy' as halogen lamps use far more power (five times higher) and have a shorter lifespan (up to ten times shorter) than LEDs.

844 See for ex. Commission Staff Working Document – Impact Assessment of 1 October 2019 accompanying the document COMMISSION REGULATION (EU) …/… laying down ecodesign requirements for household washing machines and household washer-dryers pursuant to Directive 2009/125/EC of the European Parliament and of the Council, amending Commission Regulation (EC) No 1275/2008 and repealing Commission Regulation (EU) No 1015/2010 and COMMISSION DELEGATED REGULATION (EU) …/… supplementing Regulation (EU) 2017/1369 of the European Parliament and of the Council with regard to energy labelling of household washing machines and household washer-dryers and repealing

the regulatory push may not be necessary if other drivers, namely technology push and market pull, stimulate the shift towards product ecodesign.[845] Technology push corresponds to the case where product ecodesign is driven by technological progress. These technological developments may occur due to external factors. For example, the scarcity of resources, associated with a constant increase of material costs, may spur companies to develop new technologies and lead, for example, to include recycled materials in the design of their products.[846] Market pull constitutes the second important driver that can influence the market forces in place towards product ecodesign. For example, some manufacturers may voluntarily seek to make products more repairable and upgradable because the demand for such products increases. This is exactly what is happening nowadays: the development of product reparability and upgradability caters to an existing trend.[847] Such a driver can be reinforced through public procurement as public authorities are major consumers and can thus stimulate a decisive mass of demand for more sustainable goods.[848] Hence, if one of these drivers is present, it may lead to the conception and production of ecodesigned products, without the need for public authorities to legislate. Ecodesign regulations may still be adopted in this case if the positive effects of the technological and/or market trends, which point in the direction of material efficiency, are deemed not substantial enough.[849]

204. The absence of legislation and self-regulation – Article 15(2)(c)(i) also requires taking "*the absence of other relevant Community legislation*" into account when assessing the potential for improvement in the environmental impact of the considered products. Article 15(3) adds that the EC must take into account "*Community environmental priorities*"[850], as well as relevant

---

Commission Delegated Regulation (EU) No 1061/2010 and Commission Directive 96/60/EC, SWD(2019) 347 final, p. 15.

845 K. Rennings, 'Redefining innovation – eco-innovation research and the contribution from ecological economics', 32 *Ecological Economics* (2000) p. 319 at p. 332, and especially p. 326; J. Horbach, C. Rammer, K. Rennings, 'Determinants of eco-innovations by type of environmental impact – The role of regulatory push/pull, technology push and market pull', 78 *Ecological Economics* (2012) p. 112 at p. 122.

846 For concrete examples, see S. Gibbs, 'How we are changing the way we rate sustainability of consumer electronics', *The Guardian*, 29 December 2020, available on: <https://www.theguardian.com/technology/2020/dec/29/how-we-are-changing-the-way-we-rate-sustainability-of-consumer-electronics>.

847 N. van Nes and J. Cramer, 'Influencing product lifetime through product design', 14 *Business Strategy and Environment* (2005) p. 295.

848 See the EU GPP criteria developed to facilitate the inclusion of green requirements in public tender documents, available on: <https://ec.europa.eu/environment/gpp/eu_gpp_criteria_en.htm>.

849 See for ex. the analysis of the 'no action' option for mobile phones, smartphones and tablets in Fraunhofer IZM, Fraunhofer ISI, VITO, *Ecodesign preparatory study on mobile phones, smartphones and tablets – Final Report* (European Commission 2021) pp. 471–472.

850 Article 15(3)(a) of the Ecodesign Directive.

"Community legislation and self-regulation, such as voluntary agreements".[851] These provisions emphasize the fact that during the adoption process of new ecodesign regulations, attention should be paid to the scope of the existing and proposed ecodesign regulations, as well as to self-regulation measures, and their articulation. This helps decide whether mandatory ecodesign requirements are necessary and appropriate to trigger product sustainability.[852] Such an approach allows the avoidance of double regulation and contradictions between applicable rules but also contributes to the adoption of the most adequate measures for the concerned products.[853]

Proposed review of the Ecodesign Directive:

#5

Article 15
Implementing measures

(...)

2. The criteria referred to in paragraph 1 are as follows:

(a) the product shall represent a significant volume of sales and trade, indicatively more than 200,000 units a year within the Community according to the most recently available figures;

(b) the product shall, considering the quantities placed on the market and/or put into service, have a **significant** environmental impact within the Community, as specified in the Community strategic priorities as set out in Decision No 1600/2002/EC; and

(c) the product shall present ~~**significant**~~ potential for improvement in terms of its environmental impact without entailing excessive costs, taking into account in particular:

(i) the absence of other relevant Community legislation or failure of market forces to address the issue properly; and

(ii) a wide disparity in the environmental performance of products available on the market with equivalent functionality.

OR #6

851 Article 15(3)(b) of the Ecodesign Directive.

852 In some cases, self-regulation may be more appropriate. See *infra*, n° 206.

853 This provision does not preclude or exclude the possibility to adopt or maintaining complementary rules (e.g. product-specific ecodesign rules and general guarantee rules).

> ANNEX I
>
> **Part 1. Ecodesign parameters for products**
>
> 1.4. The potential for improvement in environmental impact should be considered as significant if the product can be designed in a more durable, reparable or reusable way, comparing poor and good product designs available on the market and taking the best available technologies into consideration.

f) The recognised place of self-regulation

205. Self-regulation as an alternative – As previously mentioned, the Ecodesign Directive raises voluntary agreements and other self-regulation measures as an alternative to implementing measures to set ecodesign requirements.[854] Self-regulation implies an agreement between different actors of the industry.[855] There are currently 3 recognised voluntary agreements. These agreements concern complex set-top boxes, imaging equipment (i.e. copy, print and scanner equipment) and games consoles.

206. Distinction between self-regulation and implementing measures – As rightly stated in Recital 19 of the Ecodesign Directive, self-regulation offers advantages compared to mandatory regulations: self-regulation can enable quick progress due to rapid and cost-effective implementation and allow for flexible and appropriate adaptations to technological options and market sensitivities. As opposed to the adoption of implementing measures where they are mere stakeholders, producers have the power to control the process of self-regulation measures and decide on their content. Moreover, self-regulation allows producers to avoid being subject to additional regulatory obligations, which lightens the legislative burden on the state at the same time. The procedure for controlling and sanctioning the non-compliance with ecodesign requirements contained in self-regulation also differs from the one applicable to implementing measures.[856] The distinction between legislation and self-regulation is nonetheless more than procedural. As pointed out by A.M. Bundgaard, whereas implementing measures are aimed at removing the worst-

---

854 Article 15(1) and (3)(b), 17 and Annex VIII to the Ecodesign Directive. The same approach is followed within the framework of the Energy labelling rules, which acknowledge voluntary energy labels such as the *Green Star*. See Chapter III on marketing and pre-contractual stages.

855 It is interesting to note that voluntary agreements are a permissible form of cooperation allowed under competition law.

856 For further comments, see *infra* (n° 288 *et seq.*).

performing products from the market, self-regulation strives to pull part of the market in a more environmentally sound direction.[857]

207. Washing machines as an example – One of the best examples that illustrates the distinction between self-regulation and implementing measures is the household washing machines. These products were firstly covered by voluntary ecodesign commitments from 1997 to 2008.[858] It has led to phasing out the least efficient household washing machines and improving their energy efficiency by 24% in the last 10 years. However, mandatory ecodesign requirements were finally adopted instead for two reasons.[859] On the one hand, there was a market failure. As over 90% of household washing machines were in the energy label's highest efficiency class, there was no incentive to further improve their energy efficiency. On the other hand, given the growing share of imports from non-EU-based manufacturers, the EU industry association feared that important actors would not join voluntary agreements and foresaw difficulties in avoiding free-riders. Hence, the case of washing machines demonstrates that mandatory ecodesign requirements may sometimes be preferable to self-regulation measures.

208. Recognition of self-regulations – When existing or proposed self-regulation measures concern product groups that are under analysis for further ecodesign requirements, the EC can recognise these self-regulation measures and refrain from adopting new implementing measures.[860] Self-regulation can thus be prioritised to promote ecodesigned products in some cases if it is in line with the policy objectives of the Ecodesign Directive. The Directive nonetheless requires such regulations to respect strict criteria established in an indicative list in its Annex VIII, in addition to the basic legal requirements.[861] These criteria include the openness of the participation of third-country operators; added value in terms of the improved overall environmental performance of the product; the representativeness of a large majority of the relevant economic sector;

---

857 A.M. Bundgaard, M.A. Mosgaard, A. Remmen, 'From energy efficiency towards resource efficiency within the Ecodesign Directive', 144 *J. Clean. Prod.* (2017) p. 371.

858 See the Voluntary Commitment of the CECED of 24 September 1997 on reducing energy consumption of domestic washing machines; Voluntary Commitment II of the CECED of 31 August 2002 on reducing energy consumption of domestic washing machines (2002–2008).

859 Impact assessment accompanying document to the Draft Commission Regulation implementing Directive 2009/125/EC of the European Parliament and of the Council with regard to ecodesign requirements for household washing machines, SEC(2010) 1354, pp. 6–7 and pp. 15–16.

860 This means that the product groups covered by recognised voluntary agreements also fulfil the criteria enshrined in Article 15(2) of the Ecodesign Directive, as emphasized in Article 15(1).

861 As recalled in Annex VIII to the Ecodesign Directive, self-regulatory initiatives must comply with all provisions of the Treaty (in particular internal market and competition rules), as well as with the international engagements of the Community.

quantified and staged objectives; the involvement of civil society; a well-designed monitoring and reporting system; the cost-effectiveness of administering a self-regulatory initiative; sustainability and incentive compatibility. A recommendation for self-regulation issued by the EC provides guidelines on these criteria.[862] Through all these requirements, the EC controls and monitors self-regulation measures.

209. Criticisms and concerns about self-regulation – The majority of Member States and European organisations (especially environmental groups) do not find self-regulatory measures appropriate to deal with product ecodesign.[863] According to these opponents, voluntary agreements tend not to set sufficiently stringent ecodesign requirements compared to the business-as-usual scenario and do not bring better or quicker results compared to implementing measures. The transparency of the procedures for initiating and establishing voluntary agreements has also been criticised. Moreover, criticisms and questions have been raised on the appropriateness, monitoring and transparency of the verification and compliance procedures established under voluntary agreements. Therefore, according to these stakeholders, self-regulation should only be used to complement legislation, especially in cases where issues and aspects cannot effectively be addressed by implementing measures. In the words of the consumer organisation BEUC, "*self-regulatory measures should not take precedence over regulatory measures*".[864] Industry representatives seem more positive about self-regulation, appreciating its flexibility, although concerns have been expressed about the capacity to reach agreements and enforce them.[865]

210. Self-regulation, an important alternative for the adoption of ecodesign requirements – There is no doubt that self-regulatory

---

862 Commission Recommendation (EU) 2016/2125 of 30 November 2016 on guidelines for self-regulation measures concluded by industry under Directive 2009/125/EC of the European Parliament and of the Council, C/2016/7770, OJ L 329, 3.12.2016, p. 109–117.

863 Centre for Strategy & Evaluation Services (CSES), *Evaluation of the Ecodesign Directive (2009/125/EC) – Final Report* (European Commission 2012) p. 148. See also the reactions concerning the voluntary agreement on imaging equipment: Position of Ecos, Coolproducts, EEB, iFixit Europe, Right to repair of 18 December 2020 on the Proposed Update to the Voluntary Agreement on Imaging Equipment, available on: <https://www.coolproducts.eu/wp-content/uploads/2021/06/ECOS-eNGO-Comments-on-Imaging-Equipment-December-2020.pdf>; Comments of EuRIC of 18 December 2020 on the Industry Voluntary Agreement to improve environmental performance of imaging equipment placed on the European market, available on: <https://www.euric-aisbl.eu/position-papers/item/464-euric-comments-on-the-industry-voluntary-agreement-to-improve-environmental-performance-of-imaging-equipment-placed-on-the-european-market>.

864 BEUC Policy Paper of 5 December 2017 on Greener, better, faster, stronger Ecodesign – Consumer organisations' views on the implementation and enforcement of the Ecodesign Directive, BEUC-X-2017–146, p. 8.

865 Centre for Strategy & Evaluation Services (CSES), *Evaluation of the Ecodesign Directive (2009/125/EC) – Final Report* (European Commission 2012) p. 148.

measures have a role to play in tackling premature obsolescence. As they follow different procedures and have different goals than implementing measures, self-regulation measures have features that make them complementary to implementing measures. On one hand, self-regulatory measures can be precursors of mandatory rules and pave the way to the adoption of ecodesign requirements, as shown by the example of washing machines. In order words, they can pull the market towards ecodesigned products. On the other hand, self-regulation can cover important parts of the market that are not (yet) covered by ecodesign implementing measures and bring substantial results. Voluntary agreements may be a particularly useful alternative option in cases where issues and aspects cannot effectively be addressed by implementing measures (i.e. complex products).[866] Hence, it may sometimes be preferable for certain product categories to (first) have voluntary agreements with minimum ecodesign requirements – within or outside the scope of the Ecodesign Directive, together with other appropriate measures (i.e. voluntary labelling).

3. ECODESIGN REQUIREMENTS BETWEEN PAST AND FUTURE

a) *The development of ecodesign requirements for eligible products*

211. Criteria for ecodesign requirements – When a product meets the three criteria enumerated in Article 15(2) of the Ecodesign Directive[867], it can be subject to ecodesign requirements. Article 15(3) to 15(10) further delineates the limits within which implementing measures can be adopted and sets out the legal basis for preparing ecodesign draft implementing measures. Article 15(5) imposes the following additional criteria on implementing measures:

(a) there shall be no significant negative impact on the functionality of the product, from the perspective of the user;
(b) health, safety and the environment shall not be adversely affected;
(c) there shall be no significant negative impact on consumers in particular as regards the affordability and the life cycle cost of the product;
(d) there shall be no significant negative impact on industry competitiveness;
(e) in principle, the setting of an ecodesign requirement shall not have the consequence of imposing proprietary technology on manufacturers; and
(f) no excessive administrative burden shall be imposed on manufacturers.

---

866 As they remove low performing products from the market, mandatory ecodesign requirements also require the greatest certainty of net benefit prior to their introduction. Such degree of certainty may be difficult to reach for some products, like complex products.

867 See *supra*, n° 198.

Article 15(4)(b) completes this provision by requiring the EC to carry out impact assessments to evaluate the impact on the environment, but also on consumers and manufacturers, including SMEs, in terms of competitiveness, innovation, market access, and costs and benefits.

212. A BALANCE OF INTERESTS – While the Ecodesign Directive aims to increase the level of environmental protection through a product-oriented approach[868], Article 15 shows that the environmental interest is far from being the only one taken into account when developing ecodesign requirements. This provision emphasizes the importance of satisfying consumers' interests, by guaranteeing the good functionality of the product and by ensuring health, safety, and product affordability while protecting the industry's competitiveness and manufacturers' technological and economic interests. In other words, these criteria allow conciliating all the interests at stake when adopting implementing measures. Striking a fair balance between consumers' and manufacturers' interests is crucial as these actors should feel involved and respected to actively participate in the fight against premature obsolescence.[869] Conflicts of interest are mostly avoided by the fact that implementing measures are ultimately defined by experts in a technology-independent way. The words 'significant' and 'excessive' used in Article 15(5) act as safeguards so that only 'significant negative impact' or 'excessive administrative burden' can hamper the adoption of mandatory ecodesign requirements that prolong product lifetime.

213. FLEXIBLE REQUIREMENTS – Ecodesign requirements are intended to remain flexible so that they allow for a swift improvement of environmental product performance.[870] In other words, requirements must set efficiency targets but not prescribe technical solutions in order to stimulate new options and adapt to technical progress.[871] Through this approach, ecodesign rules aim at progressively removing from the market the worst-performing products in terms of eco-efficiency, without entering the difficult area of identification and selection of the very best performing products.[872] The prime rationale of the Ecodesign Directive is not to promote the development of new technologies, although it incidentally does so by providing the necessary framework conditions, a clear timetable, and legal certainty to producers.

868 Article 1(2) of the Ecodesign Directive.

869 See *infra*, n° 214.

870 Recital 17 of the Ecodesign Directive.

871 Communication from the European Commission of 2 December 2015 to the European Parliament, the Council, the European Economic and Social Committee and the Committee of the Regions on Closing the loop – An EU action plan for the circular economy, COM(2015) 614 final, p. 3; CECED, *Let's close the loop through innovation & competition* (European Union 2015) pp. 1–2.

872 D. Jepsen et al., *Delivering resource-efficient products – How Ecodesign can drive a circular economy in Europe* (European Environmental Bureau 2015) p. 55.

214. The importance of stakeholders' participation and cooperation – Market actors along the value/supply chain are involved in the law-making process, from the industries supporting the provision of materials to suppliers, end-product industries, distributors, the repair and remanufacturing sectors, consumers, recyclers, etc. and their representatives.[873] The active participation and cooperation of these stakeholders are of utmost importance, especially for the adoption of ecodesign requirements tackling premature obsolescence, as they can cover the whole product lifecycle and thus involve the various actors in the chain. This involvement not only ensures the transparency and legitimacy of the mandatory rules[874] but also helps overcome the challenges related to the methodology, the new data requirements and the more complex, long and costly preparatory or revision studies.[875] Moreover, the involvement of economic actors allows anticipating and preventing potential adverse impacts and trade-offs through information and support. To improve this aspect of the law-making process, environmental protection associations should also be invited to take part in these discussions.[876]

215. Integration of resource and material efficiency aspects in the MEErP – The MEErP provides guidance not only for choosing the products that are eligible for implementing measures[877], but also for assessing whether and which ecodesign requirements are appropriate for a given product.[878] The methodology has been revised and complemented twice: first, in 2011, to extend its scope from energy-using to energy-related products, and second, in 2013, to include resource and material efficiency aspects.[879] This last review had been planned in Article 21(a) of the Ecodesign Directive. Together with the development of the new horizontal standards on material efficiency[880], the

---

873 See for ex. all the feedbacks given on the Draft Regulation on electronic displays (available on: <https://ec.europa.eu/info/law/better-regulation/initiatives/ares-2016-7108187/feedback_en?p_id=8483), which shows how challenging it can be to adopt ecodesign requirements>.

874 C. Devaux, 'Towards a legal theory of capture', 24 *E.L.J.* (2018) p. 458 at p. 473.

875 Viegand Maagøe, VHK and Oeko-Institut, *Preparatory study for the Ecodesign and Energy Labelling Working Plan 2020–2024 – Task 3 Preliminary analysis of product groups and horizontal initiatives – Durability – Draft report* (European Commission 2020) pp. 27–28.

876 This was highlighted in a former German legislative proposal: Antrag vom 09.01.2020 "Elektroschrott reduzieren – Recht auf Reparatur", BT-Drucks. 19/16419, p. 6.

877 See *supra*, n° 198.

878 European Commission, *Ecodesign: your future – How ecodesign can help the environment by making products smarter* (European Union 2012) p. 3.

879 BIO Intelligence Service, *Material-efficiency Ecodesign Report and Module to the Methodology for the Ecodesign of Energy-related Products (MEErP), Part 2 – Enhancing MEErP for Ecodesign* (European Commission 2013).

880 CEN-CENELEC TC10, Definitions related to material efficiency, EN 45550:2020; CEN-CENELEC TC10, General method for the assessment of the durability of energy-related products, EN 45552:2020; CEN-CENELEC TC10, General method for the assessment of the ability to re-manufacture energy-related products, EN 45553:2020; CEN-CENELEC TC10, General methods for the assessment of the ability to repair, reuse and upgrade energy-

revised methodology is of particular importance in the fight against premature obsolescence as it is better suited to examine the wider resource and material efficiency impacts of energy-related products, and thus facilitates the shift towards more sustainable products through ecodesign regulations. However, a standardised method, which would allow assessing the impact on resource and material efficiency across multiple product groups and carrying out systematic in-depth analyses of sustainability potential during preparatory studies, is still missing.[881] The MEErP is expected to be reviewed and updated in the near future.[882] Some comments have already been made with the view of improving the methodology so that product sustainability aspects are more easily included in ecodesign implementing measures.[883]

216. A LIFECYCLE ASSESSMENT (LCA) – When adopting ecodesign requirements for the selected products, the full product lifecycle has to be taken into account, as highlighted in Article 15(4)(a), as well as in Recitals 7 and 13 of the Ecodesign Directive. The assessment applies lifecycle thinking to cope with the multiple dimensions of environmental protection and to achieve absolute reductions of environmental damage. According to this approach, the environmental impacts of products across their whole lifecycle are evaluated, from the selection and use of raw materials, the product manufacturing, packaging, transport and distribution, installation and maintenance, use,

---

related products, EN 45554:2020; CEN-CENELEC TC10, General methods for assessing the recyclability and recoverability of energy-related products, EN 45555:2019; CEN-CENELEC TC10, General method for assessing the proportion of re-used components in an energy-related product, EN 45556:2019; CEN-CENELEC TC10, General method for assessing the proportion of recycled content in an energy-related product, EN 45557:2020; CEN-CENELEC TC10, General method to declare the use of critical raw materials in energy-related products, EN 45558:2019; CEN-CENELEC TC10, Methods for providing information relating to material efficiency aspects of energy-related products, EN 45559:2019.

881 See European Court of Auditors, *EU action on Ecodesign and Energy Labelling: important contribution to greater energy efficiency reduced by significant delays and non-compliance – Special Report* (European Union 2020) p. 23.

882 Viegand Maagøe, VHK and Oeko-Institut, *Preparatory study for the Ecodesign and Energy Labelling Working Plan 2020–2024 – Task 2 Identification of product groups and horizontal measures to be considered for inclusion in the Ecodesign and Energy Labelling Working Plan 2020–2024 – Draft report* (European Commission 2020) p. 10.

883 See e.g. ECOS, Coolproducts, EEB, iFixit and Rreuse comments of 2 July 2019 on The Future of the MEErP – Reinforcement of circular economy aspects in the methodology, p. 2. These organisations suggest (1) making it possible to model the majority of potential ecodesign material efficiency requirements with the MEErP EcoReport tool, (2) linking the Product Environmental Footprint (PEF) data and approach with the MEErP EcoReport tool (wherever possible), (3) using the new standards to develop the material aspects of MEErP and their systematic application, and (4) following a more holistic approach to life cycle costing that encompasses the costs to society as a whole (including environmental costs). See also Comments of Ecos, Coolproducts, EEB, Right to repair of 19 July 2021 on the review of the MEErP – Methodology for Ecodesign of Energy-related Products (Tasks 1 & 2), available on: <https://www.coolproducts.eu/wp-content/uploads/2021/07/07.2021-ECOS-MEErP-revision-comments-on-Tasks-1-2.pdf>.

and to the product end-of-life. The lifecycle assessment (LCA)[884] is a key tool for understanding which design options can be more beneficial from an environmental perspective and for identifying the potentially relevant trade-offs. It allows preventing environmental impacts to be merely transferred from one phase of the life cycle to another. Article 15(4)(a) nonetheless underlines that the adoption of ecodesign requirements on significant environmental aspects of a product should not be unduly delayed by uncertainties regarding any potential environmental damage. The aim of considering environmental impacts at the design stage is to facilitate improved environmental performance in a cost-effective way, including in terms of resource and material efficiency.[885] In this respect, the lifecycle approach has been considered as the "*prerequisite of any sound sustainability assessment*".[886]

217. A BALANCE BETWEEN ENVIRONMENTAL ASPECTS – In addition, Article 15(10) requires implementing measures to include provisions on the balancing of various environmental aspects.[887] Along the same lines, Annex I requires manufacturers to "*achieve a reasonable balance between the various environmental aspects and between environmental aspects and other relevant considerations, such as safety and health, technical requirements for functionality, quality, and performance, and economic aspects, including manufacturing costs and marketability, while complying with all relevant legislation*".[888] In fact, environmental aspects are sometimes conflicting. Although improving product resource and material efficiency can generally be perceived as being associated with environmental benefits, some aspects should not always be prioritised when adopting ecodesign requirements as they may have negative side effects. This means that, although durability requirements are generally beneficial for the environment, trade-off analyses may be needed for a fair balance between durability and other environmental aspects.[889] Requirements on product durability should, for example, not be

---

[884] Lifecycle assessment (LCA) is "*a cradle-to-grave or cradle-to-cradle analysis technique to assess environmental impacts associated with all the stages of a product's life, which is from raw material extraction through materials processing, manufacture, distribution, and use*". See I.V. Muralikrishna, V. Manickam, *Environmental Management* (Science and Engineering for Industry 2017) p. 57 at p. 75.

[885] Recital 13 of the Ecodesign Directive.

[886] W. Klöpffer, 'Life-Cycle Based Methods for Sustainable Product Development', 8 *The International Journal of Life Cycle Assessment* (2003) p. 158.

[887] As already mentioned, products' environmental aspects range from consumption of materials, of energy and other resources to emissions to air, water or soil, pollution through physical effects such as noise, vibration, radiation, electromagnetic fields, generation of waste material, and possibilities for reuse, recycling and recovery of materials and/or of energy (see n° 199).

[888] Annex I part 3 pt. 2 to the Ecodesign Directive.

[889] See ECOS, Coolproducts, EEB, iFixit and Rreuse comments of 2 July 2019 on The Future of the MEErP – Reinforcement of circular economy aspects in the methodology, p. 6; M. Cordella, F. Alfieri, J. Sanfelix, *Guidance for the Assessment of Material Efficiency: Application to Smartphones – JRC Technical Report* (European Commission 2020) pp. 90–91; Viegand Maagøe, VHK and Oeko-Institut, *Preparatory study for the Ecodesign and Energy Labelling*

adopted if the market evolution analysis indicates that it is less harmful to the environment to replace the product with a new and more efficient one.[890] A durable design might also interfere with design strategies for lightweight design, modularity, reparability, or recyclability (i.e. integrated vs. modular design). Moreover, design for durability might require additional material and resource consumption, with higher energy content requirements. Similar reasoning applies to other material efficiency requirements.[891]

218. Analyses should be performed with the help of a guidance to identify negative side-effects and trade-offs – When adopting implementing measures with requirements on product sustainability, systematic in-depth analyses should be carried out to avoid – or at least to balance – potential negative side-effects and to evaluate possible trade-offs.[892] A similar assessment must then be carried out by manufacturers who are faced with a choice between alternative design solutions to comply with these requirements. Regarding this, as already highlighted by the international NGO ECOS and other organisations[893], guidance should be provided to manufacturers on "*how to handle the trade-offs and complexities of addressing each material efficiency aspect*" (see #7).

Proposed amendment to the Ecodesign Directive:

#7

Article 15
Implementing measures

4. In preparing a draft implementing measure the Commission shall:

(...)

Working Plan 2020–2024 – Task 3 Preliminary analysis of product groups and horizontal initiatives – Durability – Draft report (European Commission 2020) pp. 31–32.

890 In this case, the positive impacts associated with the reduced environmental impacts of the new product compared to the decreasing efficiency of the worn-out product outweigh the ones of using the old product longer and thus postponing impacts related to the manufacturing and disposal of the product.

891 For example, design for disassembly, which influences the placement and connection of components, and material selection could affect the product's architecture and likely increases its own complexity and failure rate, although improving the product reparability and upgradability.

892 See also Viegand Maagøe, VHK and Oeko-Institut, *Preparatory study for the Ecodesign and Energy Labelling Working Plan 2020–2024 – Task 3 Preliminary analysis of product groups and horizontal initiatives – Durability – Draft report* (European Commission 2020) p. 27.

893 ECOS, Coolproducts, EEB, iFixit and Rreuse comments of 2 July 2019 on The Future of the MEErP – Reinforcement of circular economy aspects in the methodology, p. 6.

> (b) carry out an assessment, which shall consider the impact on the environment, consumers and manufacturers, including SMEs, in terms of competitiveness – including in relation to markets outside the Community – innovation, market access and costs and benefits;
>
> (...)
>
> 11. **<u>The Commission shall provide guidance to manufacturers on how to handle the trade-offs and complexities of addressing each material efficiency aspect when adopting implementing measures.</u>**

b) *The end result: ecodesign requirements and advanced benchmarks*

219. Ecodesign requirements – Once developed, ecodesign requirements are embodied in the implementing measure. Every implementing measure defines the type of products covered, the ecodesign requirements that apply to them, the transitional period for their implementation, and the date for their evaluation and possible revision.[894] The ecodesign requirements contained in these implementing measures are gradual and not retroactive[895], which is essential from a technological and financial but also from a legal point of view. Ecodesign requirements are furthermore regularly reviewed[896], so as to ensure that minimum requirements (and the associated advanced benchmarks)[897] remain relevant over time and provide businesses with a long-term perspective of future ecodesign regulations.

220. Generic and specific requirements – Ecodesign requirements exist in two types, either generic or specific. As defined in Article 2(25) of the Ecodesign Directive, generic requirements address important issues without quantitative targets being set. They can for example oblige producers to make batteries easily removable from their products or inform consumers and recyclers about waste disposal, disassembly and recycling. These generic requirements contribute to the achievement of the information requirements enshrined in Article 14 of the Directive. By contrast, specific requirements set numerical targets, for instance on maximum energy use during operation.[898] Annex I provides the methodology for setting these generic requirements, whereas Annex II provides the one for specific requirements. Until now, implementing measures almost exclusively contain specific requirements,

---

894 Annex VII to the Ecodesign Directive.
895 Art. 15(4)(f) of the Ecodesign Directive.
896 Art. 21 of the Ecodesign Directive.
897 See *infra*, n° 221.
898 Art. 2(26) of the Ecodesign Directive.

except for some generic ecodesign requirements relating to the supply of information.[899]

221. Advanced benchmarks – In addition to these minimum requirements, implementing measures identify advanced benchmarks of the environmental performance of the concerned products. These correspond to the level achieved by the top-performing products available on the market. Attaining such benchmarks is voluntary for the industry.[900] More than giving inspiration to producers, advanced benchmarks may become future mandatory ecodesign requirements. This clear mid-term orientation on future requirements is of particular importance for producers (and especially SMEs) as it ensures the necessary stability and reliability for product innovation. It enables producers to better take long-term strategic aspects into consideration when investigating the sustainability of their business models and product portfolio.[901] Discussions on using these best practices in legislation have already taken place. More than questioning the incentives of these advanced benchmarks for progressive firms, it was argued that weak ecodesign rules provide legitimacy to laggards. In other words, some companies would claim that their products are sustainable for the sole reason that they comply with the requirements adopted within the framework of the Ecodesign Directive.[902] Advancing this argument, an increasing number of stakeholders seem to view stringent standards as a potential source of competitive advantage for EU industries and advocate higher mandatory thresholds based on advanced benchmarks, as pointed out by C. Dalhammar et al.[903]

222. The need for more generic and updated requirements, together with new benchmarks – The characteristics of ecodesign requirements, including the fact that they are gradual, not retroactive, regularly reviewed, and flexible, make them perfectly able to tackle premature obsolescence. Concerning possible improvements, market data should be more regularly assessed (see #8), in particular for products based on fast-moving technologies such as ICT, so as to ensure that ecodesign requirements that are no longer relevant are swiftly

899 Viegand Maagøe, VHK and Oeko-Institut, *Preparatory study for the Ecodesign and Energy Labelling Working Plan 2020–2024 – Task 2 Identification of product groups and horizontal initiatives – Final* (European Commission 2021) p. 31.

900 Communication from the European Commission to the European Parliament, the Council, the European Economic and Social Committee of the Regions on the Sustainable Consumption and Production and Sustainable Industrial Policy Action Plan, COM(2008) 397 final, pp. 4–5.

901 D. Jepsen et al., *Delivering resource-efficient products – How Ecodesign can drive a circular economy in Europe* (European Environmental Bureau 2015) p. 54.

902 See A.-K. Jönbrink and H.E. Melin, *How central authorities can support ecodesign. Company perspectives.* (TemaNord 2008) p. 54.

903 C. Dalhammar et al., *Addressing resource efficiency through the Ecodesign Directive* (TemaNord 2014) p. 101.

updated.[904] Moreover, as suggested in the preparatory study for the Ecodesign Working Plan 2022–2024, it should be made possible to set generic ecodesign requirements in cases where the setting of specific ecodesign requirements is not possible (see #9).[905] Although generic requirements are more flexible than specific requirements, they may capture, value and encourage (future) product-specific innovations towards sustainability. Concerning advanced benchmarks, their role in pushing the market towards sustainable products should be better emphasized (see #10). For example, it should be considered making these advanced benchmarks correspond to the requirements established within the EU ecolabel framework.[906]

Policy recommendations:

#8 Market data should be more regularly assessed to ensure up-to-date ecodesign requirements.

#9 More generic ecodesign requirements should be adopted, especially when the setting of specific requirements is not possible.

#10 Advanced benchmarks should correspond to the requirements established within the EU Ecolabel framework.

c) An initial focus on energy efficiency requirements

223. An almost exclusive focus on energy efficiency for the first generation of ecodesign regulations – In spite of a methodology based on a lifecycle and multidimensional approach[907], the main focus of the existing ecodesign implementing measures has until recently been on setting energy efficiency improvements.[908] Through a 2009 report prepared for the European Environmental Bureau (EEB)[909], it was noted that implementing measures

---

904 See also European Court of Auditors, *EU action on Ecodesign and Energy Labelling: important contribution to greater energy efficiency reduced by significant delays and non-compliance – Special Report* (European Union 2020) p. 39.

905 Viegand Maagøe, VHK and Oeko-Institut, *Preparatory study for the Ecodesign and Energy Labelling Working Plan 2020–2024 – Task 3 Preliminary analysis of product groups and horizontal initiatives – Durability – Draft report* (European Commission 2020) p. 27; Viegand Maagøe, Oeko-Institut, VHK, *Preparatory study for the Ecodesign and Energy Labelling Working Plan 2020–2024 – Task 4 Complementary analyses and recommendations for the Ecodesign and Energy Labelling Working Plan 2020–2024 – Final* (European Commission 2021) p. 67.

906 See Chapter III on the marketing and pre-contractual stage, especially n° 593 *et seq.*

907 See *supra*, n° 216–217.

908 Over the last few years, the focus of ecodesign regulations has shifted from energy efficiency to resource and material efficiency, as further discussed below (see n° 229 *et seq.*).

909 C. Van Rossem, C. Dalhammar, E. Toulouse, *Designing Greener Electronic Products: Building Synergies between EU Product Policy Instruments or Simply Passing the Buck?* (EEB 2009).

included a wide scope of environmental issues at an early stage of the adoption procedure, before applying only to a few selected issues, mainly energy efficiency in the use phase.

224. THREE MAIN REASONS FOR THIS FOCUS – According to the same 2009 report, read in conjunction with the study issued by Defra in 2011[910], several reasons explain the focus on energy efficiency.[911] The first main reason lies in the interpretation of Article 15 of the Ecodesign Directive, and more particularly its second paragraph requiring "*a significant environmental impact*" and "*significant potential for improvement*". As was explained above[912], it seems more difficult to assess whether these two criteria are met when dealing with other parameters than energy, especially due to a lack of information. The 'significance' of energy in the use phase was furthermore overestimated by the consultants working on the preparatory studies for the development of ecodesign implementing measures. Secondly, the focus on energy efficiency finds its roots in the chosen methodology and adoption procedure. Due to the absence of the necessary data, no suitable measurement methods or testing standards were available for the development of requirements relating to other environmental aspects. This should change with the newly adopted standards on material efficiency and the revised MEErP, which facilitate the integration of product sustainability aspects.[913] Still concerning the procedure, the fact that ecodesign has been under the jurisdiction of DG Enterprise and DG Energy also contributed to this narrow focus.[914] The third barrier to more resource and material efficiency requirements is the necessary compliance with other legal instruments, such as the REACH Regulation[915], the WEEE Directive, and the RoHS Directive.[916] The report detected a 'passing the buck' strategy through reference to other environmental legislative measures, impeding the adoption of some ecodesign requirements.

---

910 D. Maxwell, K. Schischke, O. White, L. McAndrew, L. Stobbe, W. Sheate, *Review of EuP Preparatory Study Evidence: Does it support development of non-energy related implementing measures?* (DEFRA 2011).

911 C. Van Rossem et al., *Designing Greener Electronic Products: Building Synergies between EU Product Policy Instruments or Simply Passing the Buck?* (EEB 2009) p. 24.

912 See *supra*, n° 200.

913 See *supra*, n° 215.

914 While DG Energy mainly focuses on energy consumption in the use phase, DG Enterprise primarily focuses on the production phase and the extraction of raw materials.

915 Regulation (EC) No 1907/2006 of the European Parliament and of the Council of 18 December 2006 concerning the Registration, Evaluation, Authorisation and Restriction of Chemicals (REACH), establishing a European Chemicals Agency, amending Directive 1999/45/EC and repealing Council Regulation (EEC) No 793/93 and Commission Regulation (EC) No 1488/94 as well as Council Directive 76/769/EEC and Commission Directives 91/155/EEC, 93/67/EEC, 93/105/EC and 2000/21/EC, OJ L 396, 30.12.2006, p. 1–849 (hereafter 'REACH Regulation').

916 Directive 2011/65/EU of the European Parliament and of the Council of 8 June 2011 on the restriction of the use of certain hazardous substances in electrical and electronic equipment, OJ L 174, 1.7.2011, p. 88–110 (hereafter 'RoHS Directive').

225. Ban on certain products – Energy efficiency requirements have had an influence on the array of products available on the market. While products become more energy-efficient, others are simply banned from the EU market. An illustrative example concerns the inefficient halogen light bulbs, which were phased out on 1 September 2018.[917] Exceptions exist for bulbs that are difficult to replace by others or integrated into the products (e.g. ovens). These exceptions were made to empty the existing luminaire stock, to prevent undue costs on consumers, and to give manufacturers time to develop luminaires dedicated to more efficient lighting technologies.[918] It should also be noted that the regulation does not apply to products that are already on the shelves in stores, nor in consumers' houses, but only to new products being offered for sale.[919]

226. Positive impacts on energy efficiency... – Thanks to the existing implementing measures, there have been great reductions in energy use within the EU. The environment is the first to benefit from these improvements. It was estimated that by 2020 the ecodesign framework would result in energy savings of more than the annual primary energy consumption of Italy.[920] Energy efficiency improvements contribute to the achievement of the greenhouse gas emission targets, considered as a priority environmental goal by the Ecodesign Directive.[921] More importantly, when the Union's electricity 'fuel mix' becomes less dependent on fossil fuels, improved energy efficiency is also beneficial for consumers and businesses, who save on their energy and utilities bills.[922] Furthermore, ecodesign rules allow increasing security of supply and reducing import dependency, as highlighted in Recital 6 of the Ecodesign Directive.

227. ... but not on product lifetime – However, energy efficiency requirements do not play any role in preventing the premature obsolescence of products. It can even lead to shortened product lifetime by promoting the replacement of products with more energy-efficient ones. Moreover, imposing energy requirements on products may constitute a major obstacle to the development of the market for remanufactured products. Yet, although some remanufactured products consume a higher amount of energy during the use

917 Art. 3 of the Commission Regulation (EC) No 244/2009 of 18 March 2009 implementing Directive 2005/32/EC of the European Parliament and of the Council with regard to ecodesign requirements for non-directional household lamps, OJ L 76, 24.3.2009, p. 3–16 (hereafter 'Ecodesign regulation on non-directional household lamps').

918 Recital 21 of the Ecodesign regulation on non-directional household lamps.

919 Recital 4 of the Ecodesign regulation on non-directional household lamps.

920 Communication from the Commission of 30 November 2016 on Ecodesign Working Plan 2016–2019, COM(2016) 773 final, p. 2.

921 See Recital 14 of the Ecodesign Directive.

922 Communication from the Commission of 30 November 2016 on Ecodesign Working Plan 2016–2019, COM(2016) 773 final, p. 2.

phase compared to new products, they can achieve significant energy savings and carbon emissions reduction thanks to their reduced consumption of energy in the production phase.[923]

228. The focus on energy efficiency under criticism – The focus on energy efficiency has been highly criticized, whereas the need to go beyond energy considerations has been frequently emphasized. According to the EESC, "*there is a need to have a focus on the full lifecycle of products*" (i.e. their durability, ease of maintenance and repair, the potential for sharing and digitisation, reuse, upgradeability, recyclability, and actual uptake after use) so as to drive "*change in behaviour through the supply chains of goods and services at a pace that would permit the achievement of the Circular Economy Action Plan*".[924] The EP repeatedly called on the EC to gradually include all relevant resource efficiency features in the mandatory requirements for product design and introduce a mandatory product passport based on these requirements.[925] Along the same line, the consumer associations BEUC and ANEC stressed the importance of ambitious requirements for material efficiency, including a minimum product lifetime, the availability of spare parts at a reasonable cost, the availability of software updates, the limited use of hazardous chemicals, and better waste management.[926] For these new requirements, the EP emphasized the importance of having criteria well specified and defined clearly and objectively, while being easily measurable and achievable at a proportionate cost.[927] Closely linked to this lifecycle approach, the idea of horizontal requirements on, *inter alia*, durability, reparability, reusability and recyclability was also put forward.[928]

229. From energy to resource and material efficiency – The EC has increased the focus on resource and material efficiency over the last few years. Valuable research, commissioned by the EC, has been conducted in this

923 Centre for Strategy & Evaluation Services (CSES), *Evaluation of the Ecodesign Directive (2009/125/EC) – Final Report* (European Commission 2012) p. 23.

924 Opinion of the EESC of 5 July 2017 on the 'Communication from the Commission Ecodesign Working Plan 2016–2019' (COM(2016) 773 final), OJ C 345, 13.10.2017, p. 97–101, pt. 1.1. and pt. 1.2.

925 European Parliament Resolution of 9 July 2015 on resource efficiency: moving towards a circular economy, (2014/2208(INI)), pt. 24; European Parliament Resolution of 4 July 2017 on a longer lifetime for products: benefits for consumers and companies, 2016/2272(INI); European Parliament Resolution of 7 April 2022 on the right to repair, 2022/2515(RSP), pts 4–10.

926 BEUC Policy Paper of 5 December 2017 on Greener, better, faster, stronger Ecodesign – Consumer organisations' views on the implementation and enforcement of the Ecodesign Directive, BEUC-X-2017–146.

927 European Parliament Resolution of 31 May 2018 on the implementation of the Ecodesign Directive (2009/125/EC), (2017/2087(INI)), pt. 18.

928 European Parliament Resolution of 9 July 2015 on resource efficiency: moving towards a circular economy, (2014/2208(INI)), pt. 24.

respect.[929] The shift of focus is also visible in recent documents issued by the EC, like the new Circular Economy Action Plan.[930] In this action plan, the EC announced the adoption of initiatives that would lead to more resource and material efficiency requirements. Among them, there is the Sustainable Products Initiative[931], the Circular Electronics Initiative[932], and the EU Strategy for Textiles.[933] All these initiatives aim to mobilise existing and new instruments (including ecodesign regulations) in line with the policy framework for sustainable products to ensure that products are designed for durability, maintenance, dismantling, reuse and recycling. These initiatives, and their associated ecodesign requirements, could be major steps forward in the fight against premature obsolescence.[934]

230. Product sustainability should be given prominence – The provisions of the Ecodesign Directive should put the shift of focus from energy to resource and material efficiency under the spotlight. To this end, two amendments to the Ecodesign Directive should be made. First, Article 1 should highlight the sustainability aim of the Directive (see #11). This amendment would consist of adding references to product environmental sustainability in the two existing paragraphs of the provision, without necessarily specifying what is meant by 'sustainability'. This contrasts with Article 1(1) of the Proposal for a Sustainable Products Regulation, which explicitly enumerates the parameters on which ecodesign requirements are and will be elaborated (including those relating to sustainability). Instead, and this is the second

---

929 See e.g. P. Tecchio, F. Ardente, F. Mathieux, *Analysis of durability, reusability and reparability: Application to dishwashers and washing machines – JRC Technical Report* (European Commission 2016); J. Sanfelix, M. Cordella, F. Alfieri, *Methods for the Assessment of the Reparability and Upgradability of Energy-related Products: Application to TVs – JRC Technical Report* (European Commission 2019); M. Cordella, F. Alfieri, J. Sanfelix, *Guidance for the Assessment of Material Efficiency: Application to Smartphones – JRC Technical Report* (European Commission 2020). Some ideas contained in these studies are analysed in the following paragraphs.

930 Communication from the Commission of 11 March 2020 to the European Parliament, the Council, the European Economic and Social Committee and the Committee of the Regions on A new Circular Economy Action Plan – For a cleaner and more competitive Europe, COM(2020) 98 final, pp. 3–4.

931 See the Inception impact assessment from the European Commission of 11 September 2020 on Sustainable Products Initiative, Ares(2020)4754440.

932 See Inception Impact Assessment from the European Commission of 23 December 2020 on Environmental impact of mobile phones and tablets, Ares(2020)7893117.

933 See Communication from the Commission of 30 March 2022 to the European Parliament, the Council, the European Economic and Social Committee and the Committee of the Regions on the EU Strategy for Sustainable and Circular Textiles, COM(2022) 141 final.

934 See also the Proposal for a Directive of the European Parliament and of the Council on Corporate Sustainability Due Diligence and amending Directive (EU) 2019/1937, COM(2022) 71 final. This legislation would support the ecodesign legislation by laying down environmental due diligence rules for companies.

amendment, sustainability parameters would appear in the definition of 'sustainability' that would be introduced in Article 2 of the Ecodesign Directive (see #12). These amendments would allow the text to remain precise and concise while underlying the importance of product sustainability.

Proposed review of the Ecodesign Directive:

#11

Article 1
Subject matter and scope

1. This Directive establishes a framework for the setting of Community ecodesign requirements for energy-related products with the aim of **improving the environmental sustainability of products and** ensuring the free movement of such products within the internal market.

2. This Directive provides for the setting of requirements which the energy-related products covered by implementing measures must fulfil in order to be placed on the market and/or put into service. It contributes to sustainable development by increasing **resource and material efficiency,** energy efficiency and the level of protection of the environment, while at the same time increasing the security of the energy supply.

(...)

AND

#12

Article 2
Definitions

For the purposes of this Directive, the following definitions shall apply:

(...)

10a. 'Sustainability' means the ability of a product to reach its optimal lifetime, which depends among others on its durability, ease of maintenance, upgradability, reparability, refurbishment and remanufacturing.

(...)

d) *Requirements on durability*

(1) De lege lata

231. Ecodesign requirements on durability – In addition to energy efficiency, some ecodesign requirements deal with the durability of certain energy-related products or critical components (including consumables). These requirements shape the design of these specific products or components in a way that makes them more robust and reliable[935], as well as more compatible with other products or components[936], thus improving their physical durability and allowing them to resist premature obsolescence.[937] So far, only a few ecodesign rules support the durability of products. The focus is generally on components that are most prone to failure due to consumer misuse or other external cause. The first products to be affected by such requirements are vacuum cleaners.[938] According to the current ecodesign regulation, the hose of vacuum cleaners must be considered useable after 40,000 oscillations under strain[939], and the operational lifetime of their motor should last a minimum of 500 hours.[940] Since 1st March 2023, the battery for cordless vacuum cleaners have to last at least 600 cycles while maintaining 70% capacity.[941] The second category of products covered by durability requirements comprises lamps. Models of LED- and OLED- light sources must undergo endurance testing to verify their lumen maintenance and survival factor (e.g. number of switching cycles before failure), as defined in Annex V of the 2019 Regulation on light sources and separate control gears.[942]

---

935 See *supra* on the design for robustness and reliability (n° 170).

936 See *supra* on the design for standardisation and compatibility (n° 172).

937 See *supra* on the concept of durability described in Chapter I, and more specifically n° 145.

938 It should be noted that the EC aims to propose new rules for vacuum cleaners. See the Call for evidence for an impact assessment within the framework of the EC's initiative on Energy efficiency – ecodesign and energy labelling requirements for vacuum cleaners, available on: <https://ec.europa.eu/info/law/better-regulation/have-your-say/initiatives/12832-Energy-efficiency-ecodesign-requirements-for-vacuum-cleaners-review-_en>.

939 See Annex II, pt. 7 to the Commission Regulation (EU) No 666/2013 of 8 July 2013 implementing Directive 2009/125/EC of the European Parliament and of the Council with regard to ecodesign requirements for vacuum cleaners, OJ L 192, 13.7.2013, p. 24–34 (hereafter 'Ecodesign regulation on vacuum cleaners').

940 See Annex II, pt. 8 to the Ecodesign regulation on vacuum cleaners. It is envisaged to raise this minimum to 550 hours in the new ecodesign rules. See Annex II, pt. 2(9) to the Draft revised Ecodesign Regulation on vacuum cleaners, p. 10, available on: <https://www.eceee.org/static/media/uploads/site-2/ecodesign/products/Vacuum%20cleaners%20ENER%20Lot%2017/forslag-ekodesign-dammsugare_190930.pdf>.

941 See Annex II, pt. 2(11) to the Draft revised Ecodesign Regulation on vacuum cleaners, p. 11, available on: <https://www.eceee.org/static/media/uploads/site-2/ecodesign/products/Vacuum%20cleaners%20ENER%20Lot%2017/forslag-ekodesign-dammsugare_190930.pdf>.

942 See Annex II, pt. 2, and Annex V to the Commission Regulation (EU) 2019/2020 of 1 October 2019 laying down ecodesign requirements for light sources and separate control gears pursuant to Directive 2009/125/EC of the European Parliament and of the Council and repealing Commission Regulations (EC) No 244/2009, (EC) No 245/2009 and (EU) No

232. PROPOSED DURABILITY REQUIREMENTS FOR MOBILE PHONES, CORDLESS PHONES AND TABLETS – It is worth noting that, in the Draft Regulation of August 2022 on mobile phones, cordless phones and slate tablets, the EC proposed a wide array of durability requirements, including on resistance to accidental drops, scratch resistance, protection from dust and water, battery endurance in cycles and battery management.[943] If adopted, these requirements should have a decisive role in postponing the obsolescence of these devices.

233. DURABILITY REQUIREMENTS IN SELF-REGULATION – Besides these mandatory requirements, one durability requirement has been established in the voluntary agreement on imaging equipment and concerns the interoperability of cartridges.[944] The signatories of this agreement are required to design their machines in a way that does not prevent the use of cartridges other than those made by them.[945] This requirement prevents the indirect obsolescence of imaging equipment due to a lack of (compatible) consumables.[946]

234. INFORMATION REQUIREMENTS ON DURABILITY – Closely linked to requirements on physical durability, some implementing measures require manufacturers to give information relating to product durability. For example, the regulation on light sources and separate control gears establishes an obligation to inform end-users on the lifetime of light sources placed on the market (not in a containing product) in the hours prior to purchase.[947] This information must be clearly and prominently displayed on the packaging. Concerning vacuum cleaners, the technical documentation, booklet of instructions, and free access websites of manufacturers must contain a short title or reference to the measurement and calculation methods used to establish compliance with the durability requirements described above.[948] Similar requirements exist for notebook computers, for which manufacturers are obliged to inform, in the technical documentation and on free-access websites, on the minimum number of loading cycles that the batteries can withstand, as well as

1194/2012, OJ L 315, 5.12.2019, p. 209–240 (hereafter 'Ecodesign regulation on light sources and separate control gears').

943 Annex II A pt. 1.2., B pt. 1.2., C pt. 2.1. and D pt. 1.2. to Draft Commission Regulation of 31 August 2022 laying down ecodesign requirements for mobile phones, cordless phones and slate tablets pursuant to Directive 2009/125/EC of the European Parliament and of the Council, Ares(2022)6031498.

944 Industry voluntary agreement of April 2015 to improve the environmental performance of imaging equipment placed on the European market, VA v.5.2 (hereafter 'Voluntary agreement on imaging equipment').

945 See pt. 5.4.2. of the Voluntary agreement on imaging equipment, p. 11.

946 See *supra*, n° 113.

947 See Annex II, pt. 3 to the Ecodesign regulation on light sources and separate control gears.

948 Annex I, pt. 2(a) to the Ecodesign regulation on vacuum cleaners.

on the measurement methodology used to determine this information.[949] Since March 2020, manufacturers are also under obligation to provide information about the tests carried out on servers and online data storage products in order to verify that they function within the boundaries (such as temperature and humidity) of the declared operating condition class. This information must be provided in the technical documentation[950], as well as in the instruction manuals for installers and end-users, and on the free-access websites of manufacturers, their authorised representatives and importers from the time a product model is placed on the market until at least eight years after the placing on the market of the last product of a certain product model.[951] These pieces of information not only assist consumers in making informed choices on the quality of their products but also incentivise manufacturers to make more durable products.

235. Information requirements related to product durability – In the voluntary agreement on game consoles, the signatories are required to provide information to end-users "*to support product life extension*".[952] Such information includes, among others, an explanation on how to keep the game consoles in good working condition. For example, end-users can be informed on how to keep the product dust-free, how to install system updates, or how to remove trapped disks. These pieces of information can be conveyed either with the console, onscreen, in hardcopy or online. Similar (general) information obligations have been established under French law, which obliges distributors of computer equipment to give consumers alerts and advice on the use, maintenance and cleaning operations of their products at no cost in order to optimize their performance (in particular memory and storage management), with the aim of extending the lifespan of the devices.[953]

236. Standards and testing methods – In addition to the specific measurement methods contained in certain ecodesign regulations[954], EU and

949 Annex II, pt. 7 to the Commission Regulation (EU) No 617/2013 of 26 June 2013 implementing Directive 2009/125/EC of the European Parliament and of the Council with regard to ecodesign requirements for computers and computer servers, OJ L 175, 27.6.2013, p. 13–33 (hereafter 'Ecodesign regulation on computers and computer servers').

950 Annex II, pt. 3.4. to the Commission Regulation (EU) 2019/424 of 15 March 2019 laying down ecodesign requirements for servers and data storage products pursuant to Directive 2009/125/EC of the European Parliament and of the Council and amending Commission Regulation (EU) No 617/2013, OJ L 74, 18.3.2019, p. 46–66 (hereafter 'Ecodesign regulation on servers and data storage products').

951 Annex II, pt. 3.1. (k) and 3.2. (g) to the Ecodesign regulation on servers and data storage products.

952 Self-Regulatory Initiative of June 2021 to further improve the energy efficiency of Games Consoles, Version 4.0, p. 16 (hereafter 'Self-Regulatory Initiative on Game Consoles').

953 Art. L. 541-9-3-1 of the French Environmental Code, as introduced in 2021 by Art. 22 of the Law on the Environmental Footprint of Digital Technology.

954 See for example Annex V to the Ecodesign regulation on light sources and separate control gears.

international standards provide support to these durability requirements. The new EU standard related to durability[955], developed under the standardisation mandate M/543, defines a set of parameters and methods for assessing the durability of energy-related products. This standard provides examples for their assessment methods including details on accelerated tests to reduce testing time. Several international standards are also relevant, like IEC 60529[956], which classifies and rates the degree of protection provided by mechanical casings and electrical enclosures against intrusion, dust, accidental contact, and water, or IEC 60068[957], which provides methods to assess the ability of electronic equipment, components and electromechanical products to perform and survive under conditions such as transportation, storage, operational environments, extreme cold and heat. In addition to these standards, durability testing methods have been developed and performed by consumer organisations to assess and inform consumers about the different performance aspects and durability of their products. These tests assess, for example, the battery performance of smartphones, as well as their resistance to specific stresses like rain, water submersion, scratches or shocks.[958] Various studies have also been carried out on the notions, methods and parameters for the assessment of product durability.[959]

(2) De lege ferenda

237. The need for further durability requirements – Durability requirements play a major role in the fight against premature obsolescence as they compel manufacturers to put only products that comply with these standards on the EU market. More durability requirements should thus be adopted in future ecodesign regulations, as the EU legislature has well

955 CEN-CENELEC TC10, General method for the assessment of the durability of energy-related products, EN 45552:2020, available on: <https://www.cenelec.eu/dyn/www/f?p=104:110:861514833540201::::FSP_ORG_ID,FSP_PROJECT,FSP_LANG_ID:2240017,65712,25>.

956 IEC 60529:1989/AMD2:2013/COR1:2019, Degrees of protection provided by enclosures (IP Code), TC 70.

957 IEC 60068-2:2021 SER, Environmental conditions, classification and methods of test, TC 104.

958 For some examples of durability tests carried out by consumer testing organisations, see M. Cordella, F. Alfieri, J. Sanfelix, *Guidance for the Assessment of Material Efficiency: Application to Smartphones – JRC Technical Report* (European Commission 2020) p. 18; Fraunhofer IZM, Fraunhofer ISI, VITO, *Ecodesign preparatory study on mobile phones, smartphones and tablets – Final Report* (European Commission 2021) pp. 72–73.

959 See e.g. P. Tecchio, F. Ardente, F. Mathieux, *Analysis of durability, reusability and reparability: Application to dishwashers and washing machines – JRC Technical Report* (European Commission 2016); F. Alfieri et al., *Durability assessment of products: analysis and testing of washing machines – JRC Technical Report* (European Commission 2018); F. Alfieri, M. Cordella, J. Sanfelix, N. Dodd, 'An approach to the assessment of durability of energy-related products', 69 *Procedia CIRP* (2018) p. 878 at p. 881; M. Cordella, F. Alfieri, J. Sanfelix, *Guidance for the Assessment of Material Efficiency: Application to Smartphones – JRC Technical Report* (European Commission 2020).

understood.[960] In that respect, the preparatory study commissioned within the framework of the Ecodesign Working Plan 2022–2024 recommended, on one hand, to set horizontal minimum requirements on durability for all energy-related products, while defining exemptions to the application of specific aspects (e.g. by excluding product categories with long lifetimes, low failure rates, low manufacturing stage impacts, etc.). On the other hand, beyond horizontal minimum requirements, more stringent durability performance requirements could apply at a product-specific level for selected priority product groups (including reviews and new product groups).[961] Inspiration could be drawn from durability requirements that already exist, such as the ones applicable to vacuum cleaners[962], or the ones established within the framework of voluntary labels[963], as well as from durability tests developed by consumer organisations or by studies.[964] These additional durability requirements should be supported by corresponding legal definitions that should be introduced in Article 2 of the Ecodesign Directive, in accordance with existing definitions contained in standards or other legal instruments, like the SGD and the DCD (see #13).[965]

238. Durable design of materials and key components – Further ecodesign requirements should be established to increase the physical durability of product materials (see #14). These requirements could consist of making materials, components and construction more robust (i.e. water and dust proofing as well as corrosion-resistant housings, screen protectors and protective cases), ensuring that key components are well-secured against shock and vibrations, introducing sensors or electronic controls to reduce vibrations and wear, protecting parts against potential internal leaks, using clips to hold wires in place, making handheld products with slip-resistant design.[966] Ecodesign

---

960 See Communication from the Commission of 11 March 2020 to the European Parliament, the Council, the European Economic and Social Committee and the Committee of the Regions on A new Circular Economy Action Plan – For a cleaner and more competitive Europe, COM(2020) 98 final, p. 4; Communication from the Commission on the Ecodesign and Energy Labelling Working Plan 2022–2024, OJ C 182, 4.5.2022, p. 7.

961 Viegand Maagøe, Oeko-Institut, VHK, *Preparatory study for the Ecodesign and Energy Labelling Working Plan 2020–2024 – Task 4 Complementary analyses and recommendations for the Ecodesign and Energy Labelling Working Plan 2020–2024 – Final* (European Commission 2021), especially pp. 67–68.

962 See *supra*, n° 231. See also S. Bobba, F. Ardente, F. Mathieux, *Technical support for Environmental Footprinting, material efficiency in product policy and the European Platform on LCA: Durability assessment of vacuum cleaners – JRC Science and Policy Report* (European Commission 2015).

963 See Chapter III on the marketing and pre-contractual stage, and more specifically n° 591 *et seq*.

964 See *supra*, n° 236.

965 See e.g. Art. 2(10) of the SGD and Art. 2(12) of the DCD, which define 'interoperability' and 'compatibility'.

966 M. Cordella, F. Alfieri, J. Sanfelix, *Guidance for the Assessment of Material Efficiency: Application to Smartphones – JRC Technical Report* (European Commission 2020) pp. 72–73; Viegand Maagøe, VHK and Oeko-Institut, *Preparatory study for the Ecodesign and Energy*

requirements could, for example, require manufacturers to abide by existing laptop durability standards, which encompass standards related to shock resistance, vibration, drop tests, temperature stress, screen resilience, water spill ingress, keyboard lifespan, and screen hinge lifespan.[967] Similar rugged ecodesign requirements could apply to mobile and smartphones.[968] Moreover, the compatibility and interoperability of key components could be ensured by requiring standardised features. This is particularly important for IoT devices, for which the lack of interoperability has already been highlighted.[969] One could also imagine setting out requirements for product design that accepts spare parts made by non-original equipment manufacturers, under certain conditions. Although all these options for future material and component durability requirements are promising, it is important to set design requirements that are not too vague but also offer sufficient technological flexibility.[970]

239. Durable batteries – Other ecodesign requirements should be set out to increase the quality and durability of batteries (see #15), especially having regard to the increasing number of battery-operated products on the market. The performance of batteries is very important for the durability of these products, especially because they require more and more energy and thus long-lasting batteries.[971] One aspect concerns battery endurance. For example, a 2021 study suggested the adoption of a minimum requirement stating that phone and tablet batteries shall retain at least 90% of their initial capacity after 300 full charge/discharge cycles, measured in accordance with IEC/EN 61960.[972] Requirements on battery endurance are now contained in the Draft Regulation on mobile phones, cordless phones and slate tablets.[973] A similar suggestion was made for computer batteries.[974] Another aspect concerns battery lifetime optimisation. Battery-operated products could be equipped with a pre-installed

Labelling Working Plan 2020–2024 – Task 3 Preliminary analysis of product groups and horizontal initiatives – Durability – Draft report (European Commission 2020) p. 22.

967 E. Oldyrevas, C. McAlister, *Long live the machine – How ecodesign & energy labelling can prevent premature obsolescence of laptops* (Ecos 2020) p. 20.

968 Fraunhofer IZM, Fraunhofer ISI, VITO, *Ecodesign preparatory study on mobile phones, smartphones and tablets – Final Report* (European Commission 2021) p. 407 at p. 417.

969 Commission Staff Working Document of 9 June 2021 on Preliminary Report – Sector inquiry into consumer internet of things, SWD(2021) 144 final, p. 121.

970 See *supra*, n° 213.

971 M. Cordella, F. Alfieri, J. Sanfelix, *Guidance for the Assessment of Material Efficiency: Application to Smartphones – JRC Technical Report* (European Commission 2020) p. 73.

972 Fraunhofer IZM, Fraunhofer ISI, VITO, *Ecodesign preparatory study on mobile phones, smartphones and tablets – Final Report* (European Commission 2021) p. 412.

973 See Annex II A pt. 1.1. and 1.2., B pt. 1.1. and 1.2., C pt. 2.1. and D pt. 1.1. and 1.2. to Draft Commission Regulation of 31 August 2022 laying down ecodesign requirements for mobile phones, cordless phones and slate tablets pursuant to Directive 2009/125/EC of the European Parliament and of the Council, Ares(2022)6031498.

974 E. Oldyrevas, C. McAlister, *Long live the machine – How ecodesign & energy labelling can prevent premature obsolescence of laptops* (Ecos 2020) p. 23.

battery management software, which tackles accelerated battery ageing by preventing the battery remaining in trickle charge mode for extended periods of time after the charging process is complete or by allowing the user to select the charging rate instead of setting the fast charging mode as a default setting.[975] Such a requirement on battery lifetime optimisation had been proposed in the analysis on material efficiency aspects for computers (though it was regrettably not adopted in the end)[976] and is now enshrined in Article 14 of the Proposal for a new Batteries Regulation.[977] These requirements on battery durability could have a horizontal focus and apply to batteries of all battery-operated products.[978]

240. Durable design of accessories – Not only the product in itself but also its accessories should be more durable (see #16). As already explained[979], regulatory measures on chargers for mobile phones and similar devices, such as tablets, laptops and headphones, are being proposed. If adopted, manufacturers would be obliged to use USB-C type for the external power supply connector and to comply with at least the USB 3.1 standard (with backward interoperability) for the power supplies shipped with the product. Such requirements would ensure the interoperability of all chargers (i.e. capable of charging any corresponding portable product), and thus increase their potential for reuse. In these new ecodesign rules, reference could be made to relevant EU standards[980], but also international standards and guidelines.[981] Other requirements could aim

975 M. Cordella, F. Alfieri, J. Sanfelix, *Guidance for the Assessment of Material Efficiency: Application to Smartphones – JRC Technical Report* (European Commission 2020) p. 74; E. Oldyrevas, C. McAlister, *Long live the machine – How ecodesign & energy labelling can prevent premature obsolescence of laptops* (Ecos 2020) p. 23; Fraunhofer IZM, Fraunhofer ISI, VITO, *Ecodesign preparatory study on mobile phones, smartphones and tablets – Final Report* (European Commission 2021) pp. 414–415.

976 P. Tecchio, F. Ardente, M. Marwede, C. Christian, G. Dimitrova, F. Mathieux, *Analysis of material efficiency aspects of personal computers product group* (European Union 2018) p. 83 at p. 85, as well as Viegand Maagøe and VITO, *Preparatory study on the Review of Regulation 617/2013 (Lot 3) Computers and Computer Servers – Task 7 report – Policy measures and scenario analyses – Final version* (European Union 2018) p. 82.

977 Proposal for a Regulation of the European Parliament and of the Council concerning batteries and waste batteries, repealing Directive 2006/66/EC and amending Regulation (EU) No 2019/1020, COM(2020) 798 final (hereafter 'Proposal for a new Batteries Regulation'). For a more detailed analysis of this legislation, see Chapter V on the end-of-life stage.

978 See also Viegand Maagøe, VHK and Oeko-Institut, *Preparatory study for the Ecodesign and Energy Labelling Working Plan 2020–2024 – Task 3 Preliminary analysis of product groups and horizontal initiatives – Durability – Draft report* (European Commission 2020) p. 7.

979 See *supra*, n° 192.

980 IEC 62684:2018, Interoperability specifications of common external power supply (EPS) for use with data-enabled mobile telephones, TC 100/TA 18.

981 E.g. IEC 63002:2021, Interoperability specifications and communication method for external power supplies used with computing and consumer electronics devices, TC 100/TA 18; IEC 62680-1-3:2021, Universal serial bus interfaces for data and power – Part 1-3: Common components – USB Type-C® Cable and Connector Specification, TC 100/TA 18; IEC 62684:2018, Interoperability specifications of common external power supply (EPS) for use with data-enabled mobile telephones, TC 100/TA 18.

to increase the durability of charging cables and promote alternative design solutions, like wireless charging for physical ports.[982] Concerning other accessories, the provision of additional protection accessories with the product could be envisaged. For example, the mandatory provision of a protective shell has been suggested for mobile phones, smartphones and tablets.[983]

241. Additional information on product or component lifetime – More information requirements on the lifetime of specific products or their components should be adopted (see #17). This information would be available to consumers, repairers, manufacturers as well as actors from the recycling sector. Such a specific information requirement would complement the general information obligation on product durability and other related information established in horizontal consumer legislation, like the CRD and the UCPD, which are currently under review[984], or serve as an alternative if such information obligations were not clearly established under consumer law.[985]

Such a specific information requirement was envisaged in the recent ecodesign preparatory study on mobile phones, smartphones and tablets, which examined a potential requirement on the ability of batteries to track and report their own state of health.[986] Access to battery health data (i.e. nominal battery capacity, remaining battery capacity, number of charging cycles performed) could be beneficial for product lifetime as it could positively influence consumer behaviour and increase trust in used devices.[987] Yet, battery status reporting can also have drawbacks, for example by eliciting psychological obsolescence with the observable degradation of battery or by leading to premature disposal of used batteries during repair or refurbishment if battery health is below a certain threshold.[988] Therefore, 'fool-proof' and default solutions should sometimes be preferred to such information requirements, which highly depend on consumer cognitive capacity.

---

982 C. McAlister, E. Oldyrevas, *One charger to fit them all – Using ecodesign to deliver an ambitious common charger initiative* (Ecos 2020) p. 14.

983 Fraunhofer IZM, Fraunhofer ISI, VITO, *Ecodesign preparatory study on mobile phones, smartphones and tablets – Final Report* (European Commission 2021) p. 474.

984 See the EC's initiative 'Empowering the consumer for the green transition' and the Proposal for a Directive of the European Parliament and of the Council amending Directives 2005/29/EC and 2011/83/EU as regards empowering consumers for the green transition through better protection against unfair practices and better information, COM(2022) 143 final.

985 For further comments on general information obligations under consumer law, see Chapter III on marketing and pre-contractual stage.

986 Fraunhofer IZM, Fraunhofer ISI, VITO, *Ecodesign preparatory study on mobile phones, smartphones and tablets – Final Report* (European Commission 2021) pp. 416–417.

987 Such information requirements are proposed in Art. 13 and Annex VI to the Proposal for a Regulation on batteries and waste batteries.

988 C. Clemm, J. Emmerich, K. Schischke, N.F. Nissen, K.-D. Lang, 'Benefits and Pitfalls of Better Lifetime Data – The Case of Batteries in Mobile Electronic Equipment', in N.F. Nissen, M. Jaeger-Erben (eds.), *3rd international Product Lifetimes and the Environment (PLATE) conference proceedings* (Berlin 2019).

242. Additional consumer information related to product durability – The provision of additional information on durability targeting consumers should be required through ecodesign regulations (see #18).[989] For example, predetermined breaking points and wearing parts should be clearly identifiable and consumers should be informed on the conditions under which these breaking points and wearing parts fail or on the intervals (time, use cycles or limit values) in which maintenance should be carried out.[990] Consumers should also be informed on the correct use of products or on best practices for sustainable product use.[991] For example, it has been shown that consumers lack knowledge of phone sensitivity to changes in temperature, resistance to water and humidity and other potential causes of damage, resulting in misuse and early failures.[992] Consumers' lack of knowledge extends to the effect of charging patterns on batteries, which could be solved by providing information on the most appropriate charging patterns and/or information about the battery lifespan under a defined set of charging regimes.[993] It could furthermore be required to inform consumers on use restrictions for specific products (e.g. short-term use of hand mixers).[994] These pieces of information could positively influence user behaviours that are beneficial for the product lifespan.

243. Automated sensor system and use meters – Information could be given through other means, including automated sensor system and use meters (see #19). For example, the problem of clogged ventilation slits in a notebook could be dealt with by an automated sensor system (e.g. temperature sensor, or by time or number of circulation cycles), with an electronic indication that

---

989 Similar suggestions have also been made by the EC within the framework of its initiative 'Empowering the consumer for the green transition'. See the Proposal for a Directive of the European Parliament and of the Council amending Directives 2005/29/EC and 2011/83/EU as regards empowering consumers for the green transition through better protection against unfair practices and better information, COM(2022) 143 final.

990 S. Prakash et al., *Einfluss der Nutzungsdauer von Produkten auf ihre Umweltwirkung – Schaffung einer Informationsgrundlage und Entwicklung von Strategien gegen "Obsoleszenz"* (Umweltbundesamt Study 2016) p. 280.

991 One illustrative example is clothing where small behavioural changes such as reducing washing temperature, washing at full load, avoiding tumble-drying whenever possible, purchasing eco-friendly fibres, and donating clothes not used anymore can be achieved by improving user awareness about these issues. See E. Molenbroek, M. Smith, H. Groenenberg, P. Waide, S. Attali, C. Fischer, J. Krivošik, P. Fonseca, B. Santos, J. Fong, *Evaluation of the Energy Labelling Directive and specific aspects of the Ecodesign Directive – Final technical report* (Ecofys 2014) p. 66.

992 D. Watson et al., *Circular Business Models in the Mobile Phone Industry* (TemaNord 2017) p. 59.

993 K. Schischke, *Eco-design of Mobile Devices – Project sustainablySMART* (European Union 2018) p. 2.

994 S. Prakash et al., *Einfluss der Nutzungsdauer von Produkten auf ihre Umweltwirkung – Schaffung einer Informationsgrundlage und Entwicklung von Strategien gegen "Obsoleszenz"* (Umweltbundesamt Study 2016) p. 280.

maintenance is due.[995] Along the same lines, one could imagine mandatory incorporation of use meters combined with a default detection device, which would include consumer feedback mechanisms regarding optimised use and maintenance and warns the end-user about the need for maintenance practices.[996] Such odometers are already used in the automotive sector, where they provide information on product lifetime and remaining value of the vehicle. The idea of applying such a system to large household appliances and IT and telecommunications equipment was proposed in the draft version of the French Anti-Waste Law.[997]

According to the proponents of this idea, that kind of device could help prevent the early failure of products due to poor maintenance.[998] These meters and loggers could also be used for data collection on product use, which could serve as an input for future ecodesign requirements, standards and other legislation (e.g. guarantee rules), while fully respecting EU data protection rules.[999] This would be less complex and expensive compared to requirements based on accelerated tests. However, there are limits to how far the idea can be taken. One should not overlook the fact that extra meters and digital functionalities are costly, may make a product more rapidly obsolete or fragile and might be ineffective for behavioural reasons. Hence, it should always be carefully assessed whether requiring such solutions is warranted and whether the same goal cannot be achieved through different means (e.g. use instructions/ warnings, alternative design, etc.).

---

995 S. Prakash et al., *Einfluss der Nutzungsdauer von Produkten auf ihre Umweltwirkung – Schaffung einer Informationsgrundlage und Entwicklung von Strategien gegen "Obsoleszenz"* (Umweltbundesamt Study 2016) p. 280.

996 See the feedback of HOP on the Inception Impact Assessment Empowering the consumer for the green transition, available on: <https://ec.europa.eu/info/law/better-regulation/have-your-say/initiatives/12467-Empowering-the-consumer-for-the-green-transition/F539600>. See also extracts from the debate at the European Parliament on 23 November 2020 on the right to repair, available on: <https://multimedia.europarl.europa.eu/en/right-to-repair-debate-vote_I199181-V_v>.

997 Large household appliances and IT and telecommunications equipment (which belong to the first and third categories of WEEE Directive) should have been equipped with a device visible to the consumer that records the cumulative use of the product in number of units (number of hours, cycles, uses or others). A government report was planned in January 2022 at the latest to assess the ecological, sociological and economic impacts of such a measure as well as the possibility to extend this requirement to other product categories. See Article 4*ter* of Projet de loi relatif à la lutte contre le gaspillage et à l'économie circulaire, adopted by the Sénat on 30 September 2019, n° 2274.

998 N. Cases i Sampere, *Making more durable and reparable products – Building a rating system to inform consumers and trigger business innovation* (EEB 2015) p. 9; E. Fangeat, C. Chauvin, *Allongement de la durée de vie des produits* (ADEME 2016) p. 45.

999 Viegand Maagøe, VHK and Oeko-Institut, *Preparatory study for the Ecodesign and Energy Labelling Working Plan 2020–2024 – Task 3 Preliminary analysis of product groups and horizontal initiatives – Durability – Draft report* (European Commission 2020) p. 26.

244. Improved methodology – Although standards and testing methods already exist, the methodology needs to be improved and further developed for durability requirements (see #20), in addition to more general methodological improvements.[1000] In this regard, one should consider the recommendations made in the preparatory study for the Ecodesign and Energy Labelling Working Plan 2022–2024, which propose methodological developments, that is (1) further methodological analysis regarding the use and benefits of statistical parameters on reliability/failure rates, (2) better facilitating systematic assessment of durability and trade-off analyses and (3) further methodological analysis regarding minimum lifetimes for the purpose of setting information requirements.[1001] When assessing product durability, one should also take into account the practicalities of accelerated testing and ensure tests that are practical whilst at the same time representative of the real world.[1002] These suggested measures may not be easy to implement. While studies acknowledge that product lifetime is one of the parameters taken into account at the design and production stage, they also stress the difficulty of objectively defining the method and criteria for assessing product lifetime, the costs in terms of time and resources that this measurement would entail, as well as the need to verify *a posteriori* that the stated product lifetime has been respected.[1003]

Proposed amendment to the Ecodesign Directive:

#13

Article 2
Definitions

For the purposes of this Directive, the following definitions shall apply:

(...)

13a. 'Maintenance' means the action carried out to retain a product in a condition where it is able to function as required, as defined in the European standard EN 45550:2020;

1000 See *supra*, n° 215.

1001 Viegand Maagøe, VHK and Oeko-Institut, *Preparatory study for the Ecodesign and Energy Labelling Working Plan 2020–2024 – Task 3 Preliminary analysis of product groups and horizontal initiatives – Durability – Draft report* (European Commission 2020) p. 27.

1002 Concerning the differences between European harmonized test standards and tests conditions that are more representative of real life, see CLASP, ECOS, EEB and Topten, *Closing the 'Reality Gap' – Ensuring a Fair Energy Label for Consumers* (2017), available on: <https://eeb.org/closing-the-reality-gap/>.

1003 See RDC Environment, *L'obsolescence programmée: politiques et mesures belges de protection du consommateur* (2017); I. Oehme, A. Jacob, *Strategies against obsolescence. Ensuring a minimum product lifetime and improving product service life as well as consumer information* (Umweltbundesamt 2017).

13b. 'Durability' means the ability of a product to function as required, under defined conditions of use, maintenance and repair, until a limiting state is reached, as defined in the European standard EN 45550:2020;

13c. 'Interoperability' means the ability of a product to function with hardware or software different from those with which products of the same type are normally used;

13d. 'Compatibility' means the ability of a product to function with hardware or software with which products of the same type are normally used, without the need to convert it;

(...)

AND

Proposed requirements on product durability:

> *#14 Further ecodesign requirements should be established to make the design of materials and key components more durable, such as:*

Manufacturers shall abide by [existing durability standards, which relate to shock resistance, vibration, drop tests, temperature stress, screen resilience, water spill ingress and impose minimum lifespan for key components].

Manufacturers shall use standardised features to ensure the compatibility and interoperability of [key components].

Manufacturers are forbidden to design [the concerned product] in a way that prevents the use of spare parts made by non-original equipment manufacturers.

> *#15 Further ecodesign requirements should be established to make the batteries more durable, such as:*

Batteries shall retain at least x% of their initial capacity after x full charge/discharge cycles, measured in accordance with [existing standards].

Manufacturers shall equip [battery-operated products] with a pre-installed battery management software that prevents the battery to remain in trickle charge mode for extended periods of time after the charging process is complete OR that allows the user to select the charging rate instead of setting the fast-charging mode as a default setting.

> *#16 Further ecodesign requirements should be established to make the design of accessories more durable, such as:*

Manufacturers shall use USB-C type for the external power supply connector and comply with at least the USB 3.1 standard (with backward interoperability) for the power supplies shipped with the product.

Manufacturers shall provide [additional protection accessories] with [the product].

> *#17 Additional information on product or component lifetime should be required, such as:*

Manufacturers shall provide information to consumers, repairers and actors from the recycling sector on the number of hours or cycles that [a product or component] last.

> *#18 Additional consumer information related to product durability should be required, such as:*

Manufacturers shall provide in the technical documentation and make publicly available on free-access websites the following information: (a) the predetermined breaking points and wearing parts; (b) the conditions under which these breaking points and wearing parts fail or on the intervals (time, use cycles or limit values) in which maintenance should be carried out.

Manufacturers shall provide consumers with information on the correct use of [products] or on best practices for sustainable [product] use.

> *#19 Automated sensor and use meters should be integrated in the design of certain products.*

Manufacturers shall incorporate use meters combined with a default detection device, which include consumer feedback mechanisms regarding optimised use and maintenance and warns the end-user about the need for maintenance practices.

> *#20 The methodology for durability requirements needs to be improved and further developed.*

This would require, for example, (1) further methodological analysis regarding the use and benefits of statistical parameters on reliability/failure rates, (2) better facilitating systematic assessment of durability and trade-off analyses and (3) further methodological analysis regarding minimum lifetimes for the purpose of setting information requirements.

e) *Requirements on operating system, software and firmware*

(1) De lege lata

245. Requirements on software support and updates – Certain ecodesign requirements relate to the operating system, software and firmware, and more specifically to software support and the availability of updates. These requirements contribute to avoiding or at least postponing the functional obsolescence of the concerned products.[1004] A lack of support or updates might indeed render the device obsolete while its components are still fully functioning. In other words, the extended provision of software support for functionality (operating system) and safety (security updates) and the availability of software and firmware updates are as important as the maintenance of the physical elements of a product (hardware) in ensuring a longer lifetime and reducing its replacement rates.[1005]

While access to relevant software for independent operators was already regulated for cars a decade ago[1006], requirements on the availability of software and firmware updates have only recently been introduced for servers and data storage products[1007], likewise for electronic displays.[1008] Since 1 March 2021, the latest available version of the firmware must be made available for a minimum period of eight years after the placing on the market of the last unit of a certain product model, free of charge or at a fair, transparent and non-discriminatory cost. The latest available security update to the firmware must be made available from the time a product model is placed on the market until at least eight years after the placing on the market of the last product of a certain product model, free of charge. Washing machines and dishwashers are subject to similar requirements. Software and firmware (including reset software) must be available to professional repairers for a minimum period of 10 years after placing the last unit of the model on the market.[1009] In contrast to the regulations on servers and electronic displays, no mention is made of the cost. Mobile phones, cordless phones and slate tablets will soon follow suit.[1010]

1004 See *supra* on functional obsolescence (n° 106 *et seq.*).

1005 D. Watson et al., *Circular Business Models in the Mobile Phone Industry* (TemaNord 2017) p. 68.

1006 Art. 6 of the Regulation (EC) No 595/2009 on type-approval of motor vehicles and engines, which requires manufacturers to "*provide unrestricted and standardised access to vehicle OBD information, diagnostic and other equipment, tools including any relevant software and vehicle repair and maintenance information to independent operators*".

1007 Annex II 1.2.3. to the Ecodesign regulation on servers and data storage products.

1008 Annex II E.1.(a) to the Ecodesign regulation on electronic displays.

1009 See Annex II pt. 8(1)(a) to the Commission Regulation (EU) 2019/2023 of 1 October 2019 laying down ecodesign requirements for household washing machines and household washer-dryers pursuant to Directive 2009/125/EC of the European Parliament and of the Council, amending Commission Regulation (EC) No 1275/2008 and repealing Commission Regulation (EU) No 1015/2010, OJ L 315, 5.12.2019, p. 285–312 (hereafter 'Ecodesign regulation on household washing machines and household washer-dryers'); Annex II pt. 5(1)(a) to the Commission Regulation (EU) 2019/2022 of 1 October 2019 laying down ecodesign requirements for household dishwashers pursuant to Directive 2009/125/EC of the European Parliament and of the Council amending Commission Regulation (EC) No 1275/2008 and repealing Commission Regulation (EU) No 1016/2010, OJ L 315, 5.12.2019, p. 267–284 (hereafter 'Ecodesign regulation on household dishwashers').

1010 Annex II A pt. 1.2.(6), B pt. 1.2.(6) and D pt. 1.2.(5) to Draft Commission Regulation of 31 August 2022 laying down ecodesign requirements for mobile phones, cordless phones

246. Requirements on the impact of software updates – The Ecodesign Omnibus Regulation has recently added requirements on the impact of software updates applicable to electronic displays, refrigerating appliances, light sources and separate control gears, household dishwashers, household washing machines and household washer-dryers.[1011] According to the amended provisions, "*the energy consumption of the product and any of the other declared parameters shall not deteriorate after a software or firmware update when measured with the same test standard originally used for the declaration of conformity except with explicit consent of the end-user prior to the update. No performance change shall occur as result of rejecting the update. A software update shall never have the effect of changing the product's performance in a way that makes it non-compliant with the ecodesign requirements applicable for the declaration of conformity.*"[1012] Although these amendments should be praised, some flaws need to be fixed. Among them is the fact that the deterioration of the energy consumption of the product and any of the other declared parameters is still allowed – in case the end-user agrees.[1013] It remains unclear how detailed the information will be in practice about the possible implications on decreasing energy and/or resource efficiency of the product, and thus how well-informed the consumers will be before giving their consent.

247. Information requirements on software and firmware updates – The ecodesign regulation on electronic displays also sets out an information requirement on software and firmware updates.[1014] Since 1 March 2021, the manufacturer, importer or authorised representative is obliged to provide information on the minimum guaranteed availability of software and firmware updates and product support when placing on the market the first unit of a model or an equivalent model. This information must be indicated in the

---

and slate tablets pursuant to Directive 2009/125/EC of the European Parliament and of the Council, Ares(2022)6031498.

1011 Commission Regulation (EU) 2021/341 of 23 February 2021 amending Regulations (EU) 2019/424, (EU) 2019/1781, (EU) 2019/2019, (EU) 2019/2020, (EU) 2019/2021, (EU) 2019/2022, (EU) 2019/2023 and (EU) 2019/2024 with regard to ecodesign requirements for servers and data storage products, electric motors and variable speed drives, refrigerating appliances, light sources and separate control gears, electronic displays, household dishwashers, household washing machines and household washer-dryers and refrigerating appliances with a direct sales function, OJ L 68, 26.2.2021, p. 108–148.

1012 Art. 6 paragraph 2 and 3 of the Commission Regulation (EU) 2019/2021 of 1 October 2019 laying down ecodesign requirements for electronic displays pursuant to Directive 2009/125/EC of the European Parliament and of the Council, amending Commission Regulation (EC) No 1275/2008 and repealing Commission Regulation (EC) No 642/2009, OJ L 315, 5.12.2019, p. 241–266 (hereafter 'Ecodesign regulation on electronic displays').

1013 Viegand Maagøe, VHK and Oeko-Institut, *Preparatory study for the Ecodesign and Energy Labelling Working Plan 2020–2024 – Task 3 Preliminary analysis of product groups and horizontal initiatives – Final* (European Commission 2021) p. 646.

1014 Annex II E.1.(b) to the Ecodesign regulation on electronic displays.

product information sheet and be given free of charge to third parties dealing with professional repair and reuse of electronic displays.

(2) De lege ferenda

248. The need for further requirements on OS, software and firmware – Because the durability of the OS, software and firmware is as crucial as the physical durability of products, further requirements need to be fulfilled to prevent cases of functional obsolescence. The preparatory study commissioned within the framework of the Ecodesign and Energy Labelling Working Plan 2022–2024 sets the right tone in this regard as it includes firmware and software in the cross-cutting aspects relevant for a significant number of reviews and new product groups.[1015] In this same study, it is recommended, first, to set horizontal minimum requirements on firmware and software for all energy-related products, and second, to include and further specify requirements on software updates horizontally or as pre-requisite in all product-specific Ecodesign and Energy Labelling regulations to reduce the risk of deteriorating energy and resource efficiency of products after updates. Moreover, it is recommended to initiate a feasibility study on the possibility of setting energy and resource efficiency measures on application software.[1016]

249. More requirements on the availability of updates – Requirements on the availability of software and firmware updates (including security updates and updated support of OS) and/or upgrades for free for a minimum period of time after placing the last unit of the model on the market should be considered for more energy-related products to keep them secure and functional for a longer period of time (see #21). The wording of the corresponding provision contained in the regulations on servers and data storage products and on electronic displays could be transposed to other regulations. Extending the availability of these updates for a longer period should also be considered, especially corrective updates. Software updates could, for example, be provided for the full expected lifetime of the product, as suggested by the Finnish Competition and Consumer Agency, or for at least the duration of the minimum legal guarantee period[1017], as suggested by the Danish Consumer Complaints Board.[1018]

1015 Viegand Maagøe, Oeko-Institut, VHK, *Preparatory study for the Ecodesign and Energy Labelling Working Plan 2020–2024 – Task 4 Complementary analyses and recommendations for the Ecodesign and Energy Labelling Working Plan 2020–2024 – Final* (European Commission 2021), especially pp. 67–68.

1016 *Ibid.*

1017 See Chapter IV on the use stage, which describes the rules on guarantees in detail (n° 657 *et seq.*).

1018 D. Watson et al., *Circular Business Models in the Mobile Phone Industry* (TemaNord 2017) p. 68.

250. Further requirements on the installation of updates – Users should have the option of refusing updates, especially if these updates may have a detrimental effect on the device's performance (see #22). Therefore, the option not to install updates should be made mandatory. In other words, the consumer's informed consent should be obtained before the installation of upgrades. Alternatively, one could imagine tailored versions of updates being offered to the user, who would be able to choose to install only security updates or also other (e.g. functional) updates.[1019] This would allow optimising the performance for the particular model and satisfy user needs. However, doubts remain on the feasibility of such a requirement from a technical and commercial point of view (e.g. incompatibilities between software's plus additional costs necessary to verify all combinations).[1020]

251. Reversibility of software updates – Sometimes OS upgrades do not lead to the expected performance improvement and instead drain more quickly a battery and/or slow down a device, which limits its functionality. Consumers were facing some of these problems in the *Apple* and *Samsung* cases.[1021] In these cases, the best option might be to downgrade back to the former OS version. Frequently, such an option is not supported by OS and phone providers. Imposing reversible software updates through ecodesign regulations could solve this issue. If OS upgrades have a negative impact on the device performance and/or if consumers are not satisfied with new features, they should be able to go back to the original software version and restore the original functionality of their smartphones.[1022] Further research needs to be undertaken to assess whether uninstalling or reverting an update would be feasible from a memory capacity and performance point of view (as the previous version of the software needs to remain stored in the device) (see #23).

252. Information requirements on the characteristics of updates – Manufacturers should be under obligation to give more information on software

1019 For this requirement, a distinction could be made between critical, relevant and non-critical updates.

1020 Viegand Maagøe, VHK and Oeko-Institut, *Preparatory study for the Ecodesign and Energy Labelling Working Plan 2020–2024 – Task 3 Preliminary analysis of product groups and horizontal initiatives – Final* (European Commission 2021) pp. 652–653.

1021 Autorita Garante della Concorrenza e del Mercato, 25 September 2018, Apple; Autorita Garante della Concorrenza e del Mercato, 25 September 2018, Samsung. For further comments on these cases, see n° 359 and 399.

1022 See Consumer organizations views of 16 October 2017 on Ecodesign and Energy Labelling for Electronic Displays, BEUC-X-2017–112, p. 9; T. Libaert, *Pour une consommation plus durable en phase avec les enjeux européens* (2018) p. 53. See also HOP's feedback on the Inception Impact Assessment Empowering the consumer for the green transition: HOP, *Consumer policy: Strengthening the role of consumers in the green transition* (2020), available on: <https://ec.europa.eu/info/law/better-regulation/have-your-say/initiatives/12467-Empowering-the-consumer-for-the-green-transition/F539600>.

and firmware updates (see #24). Information requirements could, for example, be envisaged on the impact of these updates on the performance of the device, the frequency of updates, the conditions under which updates are available (e.g. price) or on the best version of the OS, system settings and storage regime for the device. These pieces of information could be conveyed on a website, via an app or a free service provided at the service centre.

253. Requirements that should be discarded – It should be noted that, in the preparatory study on mobile phones, smartphones and tablets, certain requirements were considered as not necessary or appropriate. For example, it has been recommended not to oblige manufacturers to equip new models of mobile and smartphones with the most recent OS as hardware in the market is not always compatible with the latest OS versions nor does the intended use require all latest OS features.[1023] Imposing a higher kind of 'future-proof' hardware in terms of memory (RAM) and storage (Flash), as mentioned in the JRC material efficiency study[1024], was also dismissed as it was deemed that just providing more memory and storage does not guarantee an upwards compatibility with future OS versions as other parts and hardware components need to be compatible too.[1025]

254. Articulation with consumer legislation – Existing and future ecodesign requirements on the OS, software and firmware should be considered in conjunction with the corresponding information and conformity obligations imposed by EU consumer law. A link should, first, be made with the general information obligations on the functionality, compatibility and interoperability established by the Consumer Rights Directive.[1026] Second, ecodesign regulations should be linked with the general obligation introduced by the Sale of Goods Directive and the Digital Content Directive to inform on and supply updates for all sales of goods with digital elements.[1027] With these provisions of consumer law, producers and sellers are still under obligation to provide updates and information about them in cases where the product is not covered by a product-

1023 Fraunhofer IZM, Fraunhofer ISI, VITO, *Ecodesign preparatory study on mobile phones, smartphones and tablets – Final Report* (European Commission 2021) p. 418.

1024 M. Cordella, F. Alfieri, J. Sanfelix, *Guidance for the Assessment of Material Efficiency: Application to Smartphones – JRC Technical Report* (European Commission 2020) p. 118.

1025 Fraunhofer IZM, Fraunhofer ISI, VITO, *Ecodesign preparatory study on mobile phones, smartphones and tablets – Final Report* (European Commission 2021) p. 420.

1026 See Chapter III on the marketing and pre-contractual stage, and more specifically n° 492–501.

1027 Articles 6(d), 7(3) and 10(2) of the SGD and Articles 7(d), 8(2) and 11(2) and (3) of the DCD oblige the seller to inform on and supply the consumer with security and other updates which are necessary to maintain conformity, during the period which the consumer may reasonably expect this or, if a continuous supply of digital content and services is agreed, during the legal guarantee period or an agreed longer period of continuous supply. See also recitals 28–31 of the SGD and recitals 44 and 47 of the DCD. For further comments on these provisions, see Chapter IV on the use stage, and more specifically n° 691 and 700.

specific regulation.[1028] Amending these consumer law directives, as proposed in the following chapters of this book, could be another option worth considering to impose general obligations on updates.

Proposed requirements on the operating system, software and firmware:

> *#21 Requirements on the availability of software and firmware updates (including security updates and updated support of OS) and/or upgrades for free for a minimum period of time should be considered for more energy-related products, such as:*

The latest available version of the firmware shall be made available from x years after the placing on the market of the first [product] of a certain [product] model for a minimum period of x years after the placing on the market of the last [product] of a certain [product] model, free of charge or at a fair, transparent and non-discriminatory cost.

The latest available security update to the firmware shall be made available from the time a [product] model is placed on the market until at least x years after the placing on the market of the last [product] of a certain [product] model, free of charge.

> *#22 Requirements on the possibility of not installing updates should be adopted, especially if these updates may have a detrimental effect on the product's performance, such as:*

Users shall be able to decide whether or not to install updates.

> *#23 Further scientific research should be undertaken to assess whether uninstalling or reverting an update would be feasible from a memory capacity and performance point of view.*

> *#24 Information requirements should be adopted on the impact of software and firmware updates on the product performance, the frequency of updates, the conditions under which updates are available (e.g. price) or on the best version of the OS, system settings and storage regime for the device.*

f) Requirements on reparability and upgradability

(1) De lege lata

255. Ecodesign requirements on disassembly – Some ecodesign regulations contain requirements for product disassembly. These requirements ensure and improve product reparability and upgradeability by facilitating

[1028] The connections between these legal instruments should be made in the (more general) consumer rules, as recommended in Chapter III on the marketing and pre-contractual stage (n° 501) and in Chapter IV on the use stage (n° 702).

the opening of the product, its disassembly and reassembly, and the removal and replacement of priority parts in a non-destructive way.[1029] Repair is fully optimised and individual components of the product can be easily upgraded, thus postponing and reversing obsolescence.[1030] Furthermore, ecodesign requirements on disassembly are also essential for reuse and recyclability, as emphasized by waste rules.[1031]

Such material efficiency requirements apply to computers and computer servers. Since 1 March 2020, manufacturers of these products must ensure that joining, fastening or sealing techniques do not prevent the disassembly for repair or reuse purposes of certain key components, such as the memory, the motherboard and batteries.[1032] Similar requirements apply to electronic displays. Since 1 March 2021, it is prohibited to weld or glue batteries or internal power supplies.[1033] Instead, these components should be easy to remove with commonly available tools.[1034] It is interesting to note that these requirements were the subject of great controversy. The request had been made to remove them from the implementing measure as it would arguably impede manufacturers in their ability to design products and hamper innovation, whereas the evidence that these fastening techniques inhibit component removability was deemed not concrete enough.[1035]

Ecodesign requirements facilitating the disassembly of spare parts have also been introduced for refrigerators, televisions, dishwashers and washing machines. Since 1 March 2021, the spare parts of these products must be replaceable with the use of commonly available tools and without permanent damage to the appliance.[1036] Manufacturers and importers of products containing one or more light sources (e.g. luminaire or furniture) are also targeted by similar requirements. Since 1 September 2021, they must ensure that light sources and separate control gears can be replaced with the use of commonly available tools and without permanent damage to the containing

1029 N. Cases i Sampere, *Making more durable and reparable products – Building a rating system to inform consumers and trigger business innovation* (EEB 2015) pp. 10–11.

1030 See *supra* on the strategies against premature obsolescence, and more specifically n° 149 (upgrades) and n° 152 (repair).

1031 Annex VII pt. 1 to the WEEE Directive and Art. 11 of the Batteries Directive.

1032 Annex II 1.2.1. to the Ecodesign regulation on servers and data storage products.

1033 See Annex II D.1. to the Ecodesign regulation on electronic displays.

1034 *Ibid.*

1035 See DigitalEurope's comments of 3 February 2017 on the Draft Ecodesign Regulation on Electronic Displays, as well as the Joint Industry Paper from DigitalEurope et al. of 3 July 2017 on the Draft Ecodesign Regulation on Electronic Displays.

1036 Annex II pt. 3(a)(3) to the Commission Regulation (EU) 2019/2019 of 1 October 2019 laying down ecodesign requirements for refrigerating appliances pursuant to Directive 2009/125/EC of the European Parliament and of the Council and repealing Commission Regulation (EC) No 643/2009, OJ L 315, 5.12.2019, p. 187–208 (hereafter 'Ecodesign regulation on refrigerating appliances'); Annex II D. pt. 5(a)(3) to the Ecodesign regulation on electronic displays; Annex II pt. 5(1)(c) to the Ecodesign regulation on household dishwashers; Annex II pt. 8(1)(c) to the Ecodesign regulation on household washing machines and household washer-dryers.

product, unless a technical justification related to the functionality of the containing product is provided in the technical documentation explaining why the replacement of light sources and separate control gear is not appropriate.[1037]

256. Proposed requirements for mobile phones, cordless phones and tablets – A wide array of disassembly requirements will soon be applicable to mobile phones, cordless phones and slate tablets. The Draft Regulation requires, for example, that (1) fasteners are removable or reusable, (2) the process for replacement is feasible with no tool or tools that are commercially available or supplied with the product and (3) able to be carried out in a workshop environment, (4) by a generalist or a layman.[1038]

257. Similar requirements on product disassembly in self-regulation – Besides these mandatory requirements, ecodesign requirements on product disassembly are set out in the voluntary agreement on imaging equipment. Through this self-regulation, the signatories committed to making products with commonly used fasteners for joining components, subassemblies, chassis and enclosures and to avoiding the use of non-separable connections between different materials, for example through weld or glue, unless they are technically or legally required.[1039] Game consoles are subject to similar requirements. Their maintenance and refurbishment must be possible by non-destructive disassembly of key components, such as the motherboard, hard disk drive, optical drive, and internal power supply.[1040] Moreover, joining or sealing techniques should not prevent the removal of the components listed in point 1 of Annex VII of the WEEE Directive (2012/19/EU), when applicable, except for user safety or quality reasons.[1041] Requirements on product disassembly have also been established by the voluntary agreement on set top boxes so that authorised operators can easily repair, replace and reuse key components and recycle the product with commonly available tools or by hand, except for safety or anti-theft reasons.[1042]

258. Information requirements on the possibility of disassembly – In addition to these ecodesign requirements, some regulations require information on the possibility of disassembling the product. For example, if a notebook

1037 Art. 4(1) of the Ecodesign regulation on light sources and separate control gears.
1038 Annex II A pt. 1.1.(5), B pt. 1.1.(5), C pt. 2.1.(6) and D pt. 1.1.(5) to Draft Commission Regulation of 31 August 2022 laying down ecodesign requirements for mobile phones, cordless phones and slate tablets pursuant to Directive 2009/125/EC of the European Parliament and of the Council, Ares(2022)6031498.
1039 See pt. 5.2. of the Voluntary agreement on imaging equipment, p. 10.
1040 Self-Regulatory Initiative on Game Consoles, pp. 15–16.
1041 *Ibid.*, p. 16.
1042 Voluntary Industry Agreement of 2 April 2018 to improve the energy consumption of Complex Set Top Boxes within the EU, Version 6.0, p. 27.

computer is equipped with a battery that cannot be accessed and replaced by a non-professional user, manufacturers must provide in the technical documentation, and make available on free-access websites and on the external packaging of the notebook computer, in a clearly visible and legible way, the following information: "*The batteries in this product cannot be easily replaced by users themselves*".[1043] Similar requirements have recently been added for light sources and separate control gears. According to Article 4(2) of this regulation, manufacturers, importers or authorised representatives of containing products must also provide information about the replaceability or non-replaceability of light sources and control gears by end-users or qualified persons without permanent damage to the containing product. This information must be available on a free-access website and, for products sold directly to end-users, on the packaging, at least in the form of a pictogram, as well as in the user instructions.[1044] The provision of such information ensures informed choices by consumers when purchasing a product.

259. Information requirements on how to disassemble and repair – When product disassembly is possible, other information requirements support repair and upgrade operations by obliging manufacturers to provide information on how to disassemble the product. Concerning vacuum cleaners, it is required that the technical documentation and the part for professionals of the free access websites of manufacturers contain information relevant for non-destructive disassembly for maintenance purposes, in particular in relation to the hose, suction inlet, motor, casing and cable.[1045] Similar information requirements can be found in the regulation on servers and data storage products.[1046] From 1 March 2020, manufacturers, their authorised representatives and importers of servers and data storage products are required to give instructions on the disassembly operations, including the type of operation, the type and number of fastening technique(s) to be unlocked and the tool(s) required. This product information must be made available from the time a product model is placed on the market until at least eight years after the placing on the market of the last product of a certain product model free of charge to third parties dealing with maintenance, repair, reuse, recycling and upgrading of servers (including brokers, spare parts repairers, spare parts providers, recyclers and third party maintenance) upon registration by the interested third party on a website provided. Such information requirements also exist for game consoles. Technical documentation must be made available to authorised repair centres, while end-users must be informed about out-of-warranty repair options, on whether

1043 See Annex II pt. 7.2. to the Ecodesign regulation on computers and computer servers.
1044 Art. 4(2) of the Ecodesign regulation on light sources and separate control gears.
1045 Annex I, pt. 2(b) to the Ecodesign regulation on vacuum cleaners.
1046 Annex II 3.3. of the Ecodesign regulation on servers and data storage products.

repair is possible with tools commercially available to repairers or specialized proprietary tools, and whether diagnostics for repair can be undertaken by any repairers or only authorised experts using a proprietary interface.[1047] Moreover, detailed information on disassembly operations must be included in the product disassembly instructions.[1048]

260. Requirements on the availability and delivery of spare parts – Several existing ecodesign regulations regulate the context surrounding repair. Some requirements concern the availability of spare parts and their quick delivery, which is essential to counter cases of premature obsolescence. On one hand, it urges producers to think about the design and the future of their products, thus preventing their material and indirect obsolescence. On the other, such requirements encourage consumers to keep their products as long as possible and postpone their replacement, thus preventing products' psychological and economic obsolescence. Since 1 March 2021, manufacturers and importers of refrigerators, televisions, dishwashers and washing machines must make spare parts available for a longer period of time after placing the last unit of the model on the market[1049], i.e. 7 years minimum for spare parts of refrigerating appliances (except door gaskets for which it is 10 years)[1050], 7 years minimum for spare parts of televisions[1051], 10 years minimum for spare parts of dishwashers (except for some parts for which access can be restricted to professional repairers for which it is 7 years)[1052] and 10 years minimum for spare parts of washing machines and washer-dryers.[1053] During that period, the manufacturer or importer must ensure the delivery of the spare parts within 15 working days after receiving the order. The list of the spare parts concerned by these obligations is provided in each regulation.[1054] Some parts are only available to professional repairers, whereas others are available to both professional repairers and end-users. No mention is made of the costs of these spare parts and after-sales services.

1047 Self-Regulatory Initiative on Game Consoles, p. 17.

1048 *Ibid.*, p. 18.

1049 If we refer to the case law related to the Product Liability Directive, a product is 'put into circulation' when it is taken out of the manufacturing process and enters a marketing process through which it is offered to the public to be used and consumed (see ECJ 9 February 2006, Case C-127/2004, *O'Byrne, EU:C:2006:93*). This period starts from the day on which the product was put into circulation by the producer and not by the retailer (see ECJ 16 January 2014, Case C-45/13, *Kainz, EU:C:2014:7*).

1050 Annex II pt. 3(a)(1) and (2) to the Ecodesign regulation on refrigerating appliances.

1051 Annex II D. pt. 5(a)(1) and (2) to the Ecodesign regulation on electronic displays.

1052 Annex II pt. 5(1)(a) and (b) to the Ecodesign regulation on household dishwashers.

1053 Annex II pt. 8(1)(a) and (b) to the Ecodesign regulation on household washing machines and household washer-dryers.

1054 In these regulations, 'spare parts' is defined as "*a separate part that can replace a part with the same or similar function in a product*". See for ex. Annex I pt. 15 to the Ecodesign regulation on household dishwashers.

261. Proposed requirements for mobile phones, cordless phones and tablets – Similar requirements on spare parts have recently been proposed for mobile phones, cordless phones and tablets.[1055] If the Draft Regulation is adopted, manufacturers, importers or authorised representatives will be required to make several spare parts available to repairers or end-users or both for five years after the date of end of placement on the market. It is interesting to note that if the battery cannot be made available for repair and reuse, the Draft Regulation imposes durability requirements on the battery of these devices. Also noteworthy is that manufacturers, importers or authorised representatives will be obliged to indicate an expected maximum pre-tax price at least in euros for certain spare parts.[1056]

262. Similar requirements in self-regulation – Similar requirements on the availability and delivery of spare parts exist in the recognised voluntary agreements. Concerning imaging equipment, spare parts should be made available for a minimum period of time after the end of product manufacturing (from 3 to 5 years depending on the model).[1057] In this voluntary agreement, 'spare parts' means "*those parts which it is reasonably anticipated by the manufacturer of a model as being likely to fail during the typical use of the product. In contrast, those parts whose life cycle usually exceeds the usual life of the product do not have to be made available as spare parts.*" Through this provision, the signatories committed to offering spare parts for sale through their usual spare part distribution channels. They comply with this obligation if they have, at the end of product manufacturing, "*established a sufficient stock of spare parts to meet reasonably anticipated demand during the specified period but that stock has been exhausted*" or if the non-availability of spare parts is due to a *force majeure* event. The provision also states that spare parts should be accessible and exchangeable by professionals in repair centres. Spare parts that can be exchanged by end-users should be available for customers for purchase. For spare parts that are offered to end-users, replacement instructions are to be made available either online or on the product manual.[1058]

From January 2022, game consoles will be subject to similar requirements. While hard disk drives and external power supply must be made available to professional repairers and end-users for a period of two years after placing the

---

1055 See Annex II A pt. 1.1., B pt. 1.1., C pt. 2.1. and D pt. 1.1. to Draft Commission Regulation of 31 August 2022 laying down ecodesign requirements for mobile phones, cordless phones and slate tablets pursuant to Directive 2009/125/EC of the European Parliament and of the Council, Ares(2022)6031498.

1056 See Annex II A pt. 1.1.(4), B pt. 1.1.(4), C pt. 2.1.(5) and D pt. 1.1.(4) to Draft Commission Regulation of 31 August 2022 laying down ecodesign requirements for mobile phones, cordless phones and slate tablets pursuant to Directive 2009/125/EC of the European Parliament and of the Council, Ares(2022)6031498.

1057 See pt. 6.2. of the Voluntary agreement on imaging equipment, p. 13.

1058 *Ibid.*

last unit of the console on the market, other key components (e.g. optical drive, motherboard) that are required for repair by authorised repair or refurbishment centres must be made available to them for a minimum period of two years after placing the last unit of the console on the market.[1059] This restriction to authorised centres is justified by safety and quality reasons).

263. Information requirement on spare parts – Information requirements were also adopted for the four product groups, for which requirements on the availability of spare parts are applicable, namely dishwashers, refrigerators, televisions, washing machines. For these products, the list of spare parts and the procedure for ordering them, as well as the repair instructions, must be publicly available on the free access website, at the latest two years after placing on the market.[1060] Moreover, these four product groups are subject to a requirement on the availability of repair and maintenance information.[1061]

Following a period of two years after the placing on the market and until the end of the availability period, manufacturers or importers must provide access to the appliance repair and maintenance information to registered professional repairers.[1062] They may charge reasonable and proportionate fees for access to information or for receiving regular updates. Once registered, a professional repairer must have access, within one working day after requesting it, to the requested repair and maintenance information (e.g. exploded view, list of the necessary repair and test equipment, etc.).

End-users have only access to maintenance and repair instructions, which must be freely accessible on the website of manufacturers, importers or authorised representatives.[1063] These user instructions must include *inter alia* instructions for the correct maintenance of the product, on how to access professional repair, on the identification and meaning of errors, on any

1059 Self-Regulatory Initiative on Game Consoles, p. 15.

1060 Annex II pt. 3(a)(4) and (5) to the Ecodesign regulation on refrigerating appliances; Annex II D. pt. 5(a)(4) and (5) to the Ecodesign regulation on electronic displays; Annex II pt. 5(1)(d) and (e) to the Ecodesign regulation on household dishwashers; Annex II pt. 8(1)(d) and (e) to the Ecodesign regulation on household washing machines and household washer-dryers.

1061 Annex II pt. 3(b) to the Ecodesign regulation on refrigerating appliances; Annex II D. pt. 5(b) to the Ecodesign regulation on electronic displays; Annex II pt. 5(3) to the Ecodesign regulation on household dishwashers; Annex II pt. 8(3) to the Ecodesign regulation on household washing machines and household washer-dryers.

1062 Concerning the registration process, manufacturers, importers or authorised representatives may require the professional repairer to demonstrate that: (i) he/she has the technical competence to repair the concerned product and complies with the applicable regulations for repairers of electrical equipment in the Member States where he/she operates, and (ii) he/she is covered by insurance covering liabilities resulting from its activity. The manufacturers, importers or authorised representatives can accept or refuse the registration within five working days from the date of the request.

1063 Annex II pt. 4 to the Ecodesign regulation on refrigerating appliances; Annex II pt. 6 to the Ecodesign regulation on household dishwashers; Annex II pt. 9 to the Ecodesign regulation on household washing machines and household washer-dryers.

implications of self-repair or non-professional repair for the safety of the end-user and the guarantee, on the minimum period during which spare parts are available. Other information requirements exist for game consoles. End-users must be informed if spare parts are available to all repairers or only authorised repair service providers and if an out-of-warranty repair service is provided.[1064]

264. National initiatives on spare parts availability – In addition to these EU ecodesign requirements, a general obligation on the availability of spare parts has been established in Article L. 111–4 of the French Consumer Code. This provision obliges, on one hand, manufacturers and importers to inform about the (non-)availability period of essential spare parts. This information must be provided to sellers, who must then pass it on to consumers. On the other hand, if available, spare parts must be provided within 15 working days to the professional seller or to the repairer (authorised or not) who requested them.[1065] Similar provisions are contained in the three existing Belgian legislative proposals.[1066] For example, it is being proposed to include a minimum period of availability of spare parts that equals the expected lifespan.[1067] This lifetime must not be shorter than 10 years in case of products sold at a price which exceeds 30% of the Belgian social law 'living wage'.[1068] Interestingly, many of the suggested measures were approved by the business sector.[1069] Such purely national initiatives are encouraged by Article 9(1)(e) of the recently amended WFD, which requires Member States to take measures to prevent waste generation, including on the availability of spare parts. These national initiatives are also compatible with EU ecodesign legislation as they may be seen as complementary to these rules.[1070] Yet questions could be raised on the compatibility of French rules

---

1064 Self-Regulatory Initiative on Game Consoles, p. 17.

1065 For further details on these obligations under French law, see Chapter III on the marketing and pre-contractual stage (n° 469–472).

1066 See for ex. Art. 4 and 6 Proposition de loi visant à lutter contre l'obsolescence programmée et à soutenir l'économie de la réparation, *Doc. Parl.*, Ch., 2019, 19 juillet 2019, n° 0193/001; Art. 4 and 11 Proposition de loi modifiant le Code civil et le Code de droit économique, visant à lutter contre l'obsolescence programmée et l'obsolescence prématurée et à augmenter les possibilités de réparation, *Doc. Parl.*, Ch., 2019–2020, 19 novembre 2019, n° 0771/001; Art. 23 Proposition de loi visant à lutter contre l'obsolescence organisée et à soutenir l'économie circulaire, *Doc. parl.*, Ch., 2019–2020, 7 janvier 2020, n° 0914/001. For more details on the Belgian legislative proposals suggesting measures to improve repair, see Chapter III on the marketing and pre-contractual stage (n° 476–479) and Chapter IV on the use stage (n° 793 and n° 796).

1067 Art. 23 Proposition de loi visant à lutter contre l'obsolescence organisée et à soutenir l'économie circulaire, *Doc. parl.*, Ch., 2019–2020, 7 janvier 2020, n° 0914/001.

1068 *Ibid.*

1069 See l'Avis du Conseil Supérieur des Indépendants et des PME du 18 février 2020 concernant les propositions de loi relatives à l'obsolescence, F PRAT COM – Obsolescence A1, pp. 5–6.

1070 See by analogy point 2.1. of the explanatory memorandum to the Proposal for a Regulation of the European Parliament and of the Council setting a framework for energy efficiency labelling and repealing Directive 2010/30/EU, COM(2015) 341 final, pp. 2–3.

with internal market rules. For example, there could be a breach of Article 34 of the TFEU if domestic manufacturers are in a better position to provide spare parts and information about them, as it would increase retailer and/or customer loyalty to domestic brands (except if justified on the basis of Article 36 of the TFEU).[1071] Similarly, these French measures rules may be problematic from a competition point of view as they create obligations to French producers.[1072]

(2) De lege ferenda

265. The need for further reparability and upgradeability requirements – Requirements improving product reparability and upgradability are of the utmost importance in the fight against premature obsolescence as they allow preventing cases of material, indirect, psychological and economic obsolescence. Extra requirements should thus be adopted, as acknowledged by the EC in its new Circular Economy Action Plan.[1073] The reparability scoring system, which was developed after the first Circular Economy Action Plan[1074], as well as other studies, like the Benelux study on reparability, which evaluated and quantified the ease of repair for energy-related products considering the economic impact from a consumer perspective[1075], could be used as a technical reference for the adoption of reparability requirements under the ecodesign framework. An additional insight could be gained from existing rules applicable to other sectors (e.g. cars) or in some Member States, as well as self-regulations (e.g. the Austrian Durability Mark for Electrical and Electronic appliances ONR 192102 or the German voluntary certification (*The Blue Angel*) and private initiatives (e.g. the *iFixit* reparability rate).[1076] It should be noted that requirements on product reparability and upgradability unveil their full potential only if combined. For example, better information is of limited effect if the repair process is still too complicated and if

1071 See E. Maitre-Ekern and C. Dalhammar,'Regulating planned obsolescence: a review of legal approaches to increase product durability and reparability in Europe', 25 *Review of European Community & International Environmental Law* (2016) pp. 392–393. For further analysis, see *infra*, n° 290.

1072 Rapport d'information fait au nom de la commission des affaires européennes (1) portant observations sur la transposition du droit européen par le projet de loi relatif à la lutte contre le gaspillage et à l'économie circulaire, 18 July 2019, n° 682, p. 39.

1073 Communication from the Commission of 11 March 2020 to the European Parliament, the Council, the European Economic and Social Committee and the Committee of the Regions on A new Circular Economy Action Plan – For a cleaner and more competitive Europe, COM(2020) 98 final, p. 4 and p. 7.

1074 M. Cordella, F. Alfieri, J. Sanfelix, *Analysis and development of a scoring system for repair and upgrade of products – Final Report* (European Commission 2019).

1075 E. Bracquené et al., *Repairability criteria for energy related products – Study in the BeNeLux context to evaluate the options to extend the product life time* (KU Leuven, Vito, BeNeLux 2018).

1076 For further details on these voluntary labels and standards, see Chapter III on the marketing and pre-contractual stage.

no spare parts are available. Like for durability requirements, these requirements should be supported by corresponding legal definitions in Article 2 of the Ecodesign Directive (see #25). These definitions should be aligned with those established by other legal instruments.[1077]

266. Further ecodesign requirements on product disassembly – So far, there is still a lack of design for the repair and upgrade of certain products.[1078] Further requirements on product disassembly should thus be adopted (see #26). As already highlighted by the Ellen MacArthur Foundation[1079], there are various possible avenues to improve product design in this sense. First, products should be entirely assembled by reversible (and reusable) means such as screws instead of glue, rivets or non-reversible snap locks.[1080] Second, the use of proprietary fasteners should be avoided. Standard fasteners should be preferred, and their number reduced.[1081] This goes along with the requirement that consists of requiring the easy removal and replacement of parts using basic or no repair tools.[1082] Third, as suggested in the Proposal for a new Batteries Regulation[1083], batteries should be easily removable during the lifetime of the appliance (if the batteries have a shorter lifetime than the appliance) or at the latest at the end-of-life stage of the appliance, preferably without the use of any tools, and should thus not be glued or soldered to a product. This recommendation was made for mobile and smartphones and tablets, not only for their batteries but also for the glass back covers and displays.[1084] Fourth, components should not be integrated to such a degree as to make individual replacement of functional components impossible. In addition, or alternatively, it could be envisaged to set a generic requirement on a maximum proxy-based time for product disassembly

---

1077 See e.g. Art. 3(15) of the Regulation (EC) No 715/2007, which defines 'independent operator'.

1078 This is the case for smartphones. See D. Watson et al., *Circular Business Models in the Mobile Phone Industry* (TemaNord 2017) p. 11.

1079 Ellen MacArthur Foundation, *Empowering repair* (2016) p. 12.

1080 Some joining techniques with reversible adhesive bonds were provided for smartphone and tablet batteries in Fraunhofer IZM, Fraunhofer ISI, VITO, *Ecodesign preparatory study on mobile phones, smartphones and tablets – Final Report* (European Commission 2021) pp. 420–421.

1081 See N. Cases i Sampere, *Making more durable and reparable products – Building a rating system to inform consumers and trigger business innovation* (EEB 2015) p. 11, referring to the Austrian Durability Mark for Electrical and Electronic appliances (ONR 192102).

1082 For a list of commonly available tools and their reference standards, see Annex A to the CEN-CENELEC TC10, General methods for the assessment of the ability to repair, reuse and upgrade energy-related products, EN 45554:2020.

1083 Art. 11 of the Proposal for a new Batteries Regulation.

1084 Fraunhofer IZM, Fraunhofer ISI, VITO, *Ecodesign preparatory study on mobile phones, smartphones and tablets – Final Report* (European Commission 2021) p. 422 at p. 426. See also the suggestions on the removability and replaceability of integrated batteries made for consumer electronics and light electric vehicles in the International Institute for Industrial Environmental Economics (IIIEE) and EEB, *Removable, replaceable and repairable batteries report* (2021), available on: <https://eeb.org/library/battery-repair-report/>.

(calculated on the basis of standards), which would combine all the parameters influencing the disassembly process.[1085] *iFixit* already provides indications about the time necessary to disassemble parts of certain devices in its repair guides.[1086] Attention should nonetheless be paid not to set too vague design requirements.[1087]

All these requirements would not only prevent material and psychological obsolescence by facilitating repair and upgrade, but also economic obsolescence as repair costs are reduced when repair operations are undertaken by the consumers themselves or take less time for professional repairers. However, it goes without saying that these requirements should not be automatically applied together and to all product categories. A product-specific assessment must be carried out on the basis of the criteria previously described.[1088]

267. Further requirements on the availability of spare parts – The importance of available spare parts had already been highlighted in the 1993 Green Paper issued by the EC.[1089] Therefore, as more recently emphasized by German scholars[1090], measures should be taken "*to ensure more effective implementation of the Ecodesign Directive regarding repairs*" (see #27). First, the availability of spare parts (in years) should at least be based on the expected lifetime of products. A similar idea has been suggested by the Ellen MacArthur Foundation, which suggested a requirement that all priority parts be available as spare parts to all interested parties, including independent operators and consumers, for a minimum number of years after placing the last unit of the model on the market (for a period after manufacturing that reflects the potential product life).[1091] Such requirements could be extended to repair services that are certified by manufacturers and/or retailers which would be available for the same period of time. Second, the (maximum) delivery time for spare parts should be shorter than the current 15 working days provided in existing

---

1085 M. Cordella, F. Alfieri, J. Sanfelix, *Analysis and development of a scoring system for repair and upgrade of products – Final Report* (European Commission 2019) p. 29.

1086 See <https://www.ifixit.com/Guide>.

1087 Technopolis Group (in consortium with Fraunhofer ISI, Thinkstep and Wuppertal Institute), *Regulatory barriers for the Circular Economy – Lessons from ten cases studies* (European Commission 2016) p. 39.

1088 See *supra*, n° 211 *et seq.*

1089 The Green Paper gave three solutions to improve after-sales services: (1) impose a standard obligation on manufacturers to stock the necessary spare parts during a certain period, which should correspond to the normal lifespan of the merchandise in question, (2) seek commitments on the part of industrial sectors to respect certain minimum conditions relating to the availability of spare parts on a purely voluntary basis and (3) require stating on the product label the period during which the manufacturer commits to stocking spare parts. See Green Paper from the European Commission of 15 November 1993 on Guarantees for Consumer Goods and After-sales Services, COM(93) 509 final, p. 100.

1090 F. Keimeyer et al., *Weiterentwicklung von Strategien gegen Obsoleszenz einschließlich rechtlicher Instrumente – Abschlussbericht* (Umweltbundesamt 2020) pp. 39–40.

1091 Ellen MacArthur Foundation, *Empowering repair* (2016) p. 12.

ecodesign regulations. This reduced time limit would ensure that consumers are not discouraged by the waiting time for repair.

268. Requirements on the price of spare parts? – In addition to these requirements, a cap on the price of spare parts and repair services (e.g. call-out charges, labour costs) has been suggested. Naturally, even when products are more easily repairable, consumers might still be reluctant to repair their products if repair costs are deemed too high.[1092] Requirements that would set a maximum repair price could influence consumers in repair decisions as it would change the ratio of the price to repair compared to the price to replace.[1093] Manufacturers could be required to guarantee a maximum (pre-tax) price for spare parts during the period of their mandatory availability.[1094] This information would be disclosed with other product information so that manufacturers are incentivised to set a price that reasonably reflect the production costs of spare parts. Such a requirement would allow the avoidance of cases of economic obsolescence. Doubts could be raised however on the feasibility of such requirements, as well as on the balance of interests at stake as it may result in higher costs on the business side.

269. Mandatory information provided to 'professional repairers' – According to the existing requirements contained in the ecodesign regulations on refrigerators, televisions, dishwashers and washing machines, maintenance and repair information must only be provided to registered professional repairers, but not to independent unregistered repairers. This is mainly due to the reluctancy of manufacturers to facilitate repair outside their authorized network because of quality and safety concerns[1095], liability issues[1096] or IP rights

---

1092 According to a 2012 Eurobarometer, almost half of consumers would decide not to have defective products repaired because of too high repair costs. See TNS Political & Social, *Flash Eurobarometer 367 – Attitudes of Europeans towards building the single market for green products* (European Commission 2013) p. 112. See also

1093 LE Europe, VVA Europe, Ipsos, ConPolicy, Trinomics, *Behavioural study on consumers' engagement in the circular economy* (European Commission 2018) p. 186.

1094 Fraunhofer IZM, Fraunhofer ISI, VITO, *Ecodesign preparatory study on mobile phones, smartphones and tablets – Final Report* (European Commission 2021) p. 478.

1095 Consumers and independent repairers may not have the proper experience or expertise to repair the product. Safety concerns also include cybersecurity which could be put at risk as the provision of some information entails the risk of creating a gateway into the electronic network of the device owner, increasing vulnerability against hackers and loss of sensitive personal, financial or professional information.

1096 The question on the identity of the 'producer' within the meaning of the product liability legislation in case of repair was raised in the Report from the Commission of 7 May 2018 to the European Parliament, the Council and the European Economic and Social Committee on the Application of the Council Directive on the approximation of the laws, regulations, and administrative provisions of the Member States concerning liability for defective products (85/374/EEC), COM(2018) 246 final, p. 9. Recital 29 of the Proposal for a Directive on liability for defective products (COM(2022) 495 final) states that *"[e]conomic operators that carry out repairs or other operations that do not involve substantial modifications should not be subject to liability under this Directive"*.

and other confidential proprietary knowledge.[1097] This is particularly salient in the voluntary agreement on game consoles.[1098] However, the restricted access to authorised professionals for certain maintenance and repair information is questionable, especially as regards the issue of premature obsolescence, as it limits the repair options available to consumers (e.g. consumers cannot do it themselves or go to an, often cheaper, independent repairer or repair café), may lead to higher repair costs for them, and create competition concerns (professional/authorized repairers are being 'favoured' over certain retailers and distributors of spare parts).[1099] Access to certain maintenance and repair information should be given to all professional repairers (see #28), including authorised and 'independent operators'[1100], for a certain period of time (e.g. 5 years after the placement of the last unit on the market). Interestingly, such access is already guaranteed in the automotive sector.[1101] Although the context in the car sector was particular[1102], some ideas could be transposed to household products. To avoid possible discrimination against independent repairers, an independent registration system of professional repairers should be developed in all Member States, as suggested by a 2020 study commissioned by the *Umweltbundesamt*.[1103] In this system, the assessment of repairers' technical competence (as legally required by ecodesign regulations for registration) would be carried out by an independent body and not by the manufacturers. Once registered, repairers should have access to information, updates, troubleshooting

---

1097 For more information, see E. Terryn, 'A Right to Repair: Towards Sustainable Remedies in Consumer Law', *E.R.P.L.* (2019) p. 864 at p. 867; H. Hartwig, 'Spare Parts Under European Design and Trade Mark Law', 11 *Journal of intellectual property law & practice* (2016) p. 121.

1098 Self-Regulatory Initiative of June 2021 to further improve the energy efficiency of Games Consoles, Version 4.0, p. 15 at p. 17.

1099 See ECOS, CoolProducts, TopTen, iFixit, EEB, RREUSE recommendations of November 2018 on the final Ecodesign and Energy Labelling proposals for washing machines and washer-dryers, p. 3, available on: <https://www.coolproducts.eu/s/Final-recommendations-on-Washing-Machines-Nov-2018.pdf>.

1100 This notion is already used in the legislation on cars, which defines it as "*undertakings other than authorised dealers and repairers which are directly or indirectly involved in the repair and maintenance of motor vehicles (…)*". See Art. 3(15) of the Regulation (EC) No 715/2007 of the European Parliament and of the Council of 20 June 2007 on type approval of motor vehicles with respect to emissions from light passenger and commercial vehicles (Euro 5 and Euro 6) and on access to vehicle repair and maintenance information, OJ L 171, 29.6.2007, p. 1–16.

1101 Car manufacturers must provide to independent operators (1) access to vehicle repair and maintenance information, training material and tools on the same basis as for authorised dealers and repairers and (2) a standardised, secure and remote facility to enable them to complete operations that involve access to the vehicle security system. See Art. 6 of the Regulation (EC) No 715/2007 on type approval of motor vehicles; Art. 6 of the Regulation (EC) No 595/2009 on type-approval of motor vehicles and engines; Art. 61 of the Regulation (EU) 2018/858 on the approval and market surveillance of motor vehicles and their trailers.

1102 Car legislation was originally implemented because of a lack of competitiveness on the repair market and not because of the difficulty to repair. See Deloitte, *Study on socioeconomic impacts of increased reparability – Final Report* (European Union 2016) p. 15.

1103 F. Keimeyer et al., *Weiterentwicklung von Strategien gegen Obsoleszenz einschließlich rechtlicher Instrumente – Abschlussbericht* (Umweltbundesamt 2020) p. 40.

and training under the same condition as authorised repairers. Concerning the fees that manufacturers may charge for such access, some clarifications should be given on the definition of "*reasonable and proportionate fees*".[1104] The ECJ may do so in *ADPA and Gesamtverband Autoteile-Handel*[1105], whereby the *Landgericht Köln* requested a preliminary ruling on these terms for the corresponding car legislation.[1106]

270. Mandatory information provided to consumers – So far, access to repair and maintenance information is mainly restricted to professionals. More information requirements should be directed towards consumers, while taking care not to create information overload (see #29).[1107] A distinction should nonetheless be made between information provided to professional repairers and consumers.[1108] Whereas it could for example be required to make the exploded diagram of the product, the sequence of disassembly steps for priority parts or information on the price of spare parts publicly available and comprehensible, other (more technical) information, such as information on component and diagnosis or wiring and connection diagrams, could be restricted to repairers.[1109] Certain pieces of information could also be accessible to both, though limited to basic repair activities for consumers (e.g. battery replacement or other minor defects).[1110] Information could be given on the internet or in the repair manuals and for free or on fair and reasonable terms.[1111] The provision of such information could ensure quality and safety and thus

1104 See also F. Keimeyer et al., *Weiterentwicklung von Strategien gegen Obsoleszenz einschließlich rechtlicher Instrumente – Abschlussbericht* (Umweltbundesamt 2020) p. 40.

1105 See the Request for a preliminary ruling from the Landgericht Köln (Germany) lodged on 25 June 2021, Case C-390/21, ADPA European Independent Automotive Data Publishers Association international not-for-profit association and Belgian law and Gesamtverband Autoteile-Handel e.V. v. Automobiles PEUGEOT SA and PSA Automobiles SA, OJ C 368, 13.9.2021, p. 7–8.

1106 Art. 7 of the Regulation (EC) No 715/2007 on type approval of motor vehicles; Art. 6 of the Regulation 595/2009 on type-approval of motor vehicles and engines; Art. 63 of the Regulation (EU) 2018/858 on the approval and market surveillance of motor vehicles and their trailers.

1107 On the risks of information overload, see *infra* (n° 339).

1108 For further comments on the importance of distinguishing between targeted audiences when adopting information requirements, see Chapter III, and more specifically n° 337.

1109 For other examples of information requirements, see the table n° 24 in M. Cordella, F. Alfieri, J. Sanfelix, *Guidance for the Assessment of Material Efficiency: Application to Smartphones – JRC Technical Report* (European Commission 2020) p. 80.

1110 LE Europe, VVA Europe, Ipsos, ConPolicy, Trinomics, *Behavioural study on consumers' engagement in the circular economy* (European Commission 2018) p. 187; M. Cordella, F. Alfieri, J. Sanfelix, *Guidance for the Assessment of Material Efficiency: Application to Smartphones – JRC Technical Report* (European Commission 2020) p. 80.

1111 Such a requirement already exists in the Right to Repair bills of more than 20 states of the U.S. See S. Svensson, J.L. Richter, E. Maitre-Ekern, T. Pihlajarinne, A. Maigret, C. Dalhammar, *The Emerging 'Right to Repair' legislation in the EU and the U.S.*, Paper presented at Going Green Care Innovation (Vienna 2018).

reassure manufacturers' concerns when maintenance and repair operations are carried out by operators outside their network. In any case, as highlighted in the preparatory study commissioned within the framework of the Ecodesign Working Plan 2022–2024, product information requirements should take closely into account the developments of a Digital Product Passport under the Sustainable Product Policy Initiative in order to ensure interlinkages to other product information systems, such as the EPREL database[1112], and the concept of a 'battery passport' (and database) introduced throughout the review of the existing Battery Directive or others.[1113]

271. Horizontal requirements on reparability and upgradability – More products, including non-energy-related products, should be subject to ecodesign and information requirements improving their reparability and upgradability. Some of these requirements could apply horizontally. For example, requirements could be adopted for all electrical and electronic products, as defined by the WEEE Directive.[1114] Such general obligations are already established by other legal instruments, like the CRD, which imposes information on the main product characteristics.[1115] Specific ecodesign and information requirements could complement these general rules by imposing more specific obligations on certain aspects for specific products or, in the absence of general rules, they could be used as an alternative to regulate product reparability and upgradability and at least fill the gap for certain product groups.

Proposed amendment to the Ecodesign Directive:

#25

Article 2
Definitions

For the purposes of this Directive, the following definitions shall apply:

(...)

13e. 'Repair' means the process of returning a faulty product to a condition where it can fulfil its originally intended use, as defined in the European standard EN 45550:2020;

1112 See Chapter III on the marketing and pre-contractual stage (n° 570-572).

1113 Viegand Maagøe, VHK and Oeko-Institut, *Preparatory study for the Ecodesign and Energy Labelling Working Plan 2020–2024 – Task 3 Preliminary analysis of product groups and horizontal initiatives – Durability – Draft report* (European Commission 2020) p. 27.

1114 F. Keimeyer et al., *Weiterentwicklung von Strategien gegen Obsoleszenz einschließlich rechtlicher Instrumente – Abschlussbericht* (Umweltbundesamt 2020) p. 40.

1115 See Chapter III on the marketing and pre-contractual stage (n° 467 *et seq.*).

13f. 'Reparability' means the ability of a product to have all or some of its parts separately repaired or replaced without having to replace the entire product;

13g. 'Spare part' means a separate part that can replace a part with the same or similar function in a product;

13h. 'Independent operator' means undertaking other than authorised dealers and repairers which are directly or indirectly involved in the repair and maintenance of products;

13i. 'Upgradability' means the ability of a product to have its functionality, performance, capacity or aesthetics enhanced;

(...)

AND

Proposed requirements on product reparability and upgradability:

> *#26 Further ecodesign requirements should be established to facilitate product disassembly, such as:*

Manufacturers shall ensure that joining, fastening or sealing techniques do not prevent the disassembly for repair or reuse purposes of [the concerned components], using commonly available or no tools.

Manufacturers shall ensure that [the concerned spare parts] can be replaced with the use of commonly available tools and without permanent damage to the appliance.

> *#27 Further ecodesign requirements should be established on the availability of spare parts and repair service, with a period that reflects the expected product lifetime and a shorter delivery time of spare parts.*

> *#28 Information requirements should give access to certain maintenance and repair information to all professional repairers, including authorised and 'independent operators', for a certain period of time.*

> *#29 More information requirements should be directed towards consumers.*

g) *Requirements on reuse, refurbishment and remanufacturing*

(1) De lege lata

272. Requirements on reuse, refurbishment and remanufacturing – Some ecodesign requirements apply at the end of product lifetime so that products are easily reused, refurbished and remanufactured, allowing their

added value to be kept for as long as possible and minimizing waste. Some of these requirements have already been described in the previous paragraphs of this section. Among them, there are for example ecodesign and information requirements facilitating product disassembly and availability of spare parts, which ensure the easy replacement of defective parts, or the suggested requirement on access to battery health data, which could reassure consumers about the state of second-hand products. Yet, other requirements on reuse, refurbishment and remanufacturing exist.

273. Ecodesign requirements on reuse – In the voluntary agreement on imaging equipment, the signatories made the commitment that "*[a]ny cartridge produced by or recommended by the [original equipment manufacturers] for use in the product shall not be designed to prevent its reuse and recycling*".[1116] Requirements on reuse were also recently established in France, where traders who repair and maintain electrical and electronic equipment have to offer their customers the possibility of choosing spare parts derived from circular economy instead of new spare parts.[1117]

274. Requirements in the automotive sector – The legislation on cars provides for the almost total reuse and recovery of end-of-life vehicles.[1118] Car components and materials are made easily accessible so that it is easier to recover components and resources from the product and use them for the next generation of products. These ecodesign requirements applicable to cars may be used as a source of inspiration for future ecodesign requirements for other categories of products.

275. Requirements on secure data deletion – For products to be reused, it is important that the transfer of ownership can take place without the transfer of any personal data. A too complicated transfer or deletion of data and the inability to reset a password and restore factory settings on a product can pose a major barrier to reuse.[1119] Moreover, as was reported in the first chapter of this book, some products hibernate in consumer's drawers, including due to concerns about data privacy.[1120] Easily accessible data transfer and deletion tools, together with the associated information, may help overcome these barriers and contribute to the reuse of hibernating products by enabling greater confidence

1116 See pt. 5.4.1. of the Voluntary agreement on imaging equipment, p. 11.

1117 Art. L. 224-109 of the French Consumer Code, introduced by Art. 19 II of the Anti-Waste Law. For further details, see *infra* (n° 801).

1118 Art. 7 of the Directive 2000/53/EC on end-of life vehicles. For further comments, see Chapter V on the end-of-life stage.

1119 CEN-CENELEC TC10, General methods for the assessment of the ability to repair, reuse and upgrade energy-related products, EN 45554:2020, pp. 27–28.

1120 See *supra*, n° 140 and n° 157.

in data sanitisation and increasing user willingness to pass products onto the second-hand market.

Such requirements apply since 1 March 2020 to all data storage devices, for which functionality for secure data deletion must be made available for the secure deletion of data contained in them.[1121] According to this regulation, 'secure data deletion' means "*the effective erasure of all traces of existing data from a data storage device, overwriting the data completely in such a way that access to the original data, or parts of them, becomes infeasible for a given level of effort*".[1122] Manufacturers are also under obligation to give information on the data deletion functionality, including instructions on how to use it, the techniques used and the supported secure data deletion standard(s).[1123] This information must be provided in the instruction manuals for installers and end-users (when present with the product), and on the free-access websites of manufacturers, their authorised representatives and importers from the time a product model is placed on the market until at least eight years after the placing on the market of the last product of a certain product model.[1124] Similar information requirements have been introduced for game consoles, for which end-users must receive explanations on how to delete personal data.[1125]

(2) De lege ferenda

276. The need for further requirements on reuse, refurbishment and remanufacturing – Reusing, refurbishing and remanufacturing products contribute to prolonging their lifetime. More of these requirements should therefore be adopted. This would consist, first, of extending existing requirements relating to reuse, refurbishment and remanufacturing to a wider range of products. For example, requirements on secure data deletion should be envisaged for mobile and smartphones to reduce their 'hibernation' in consumers' households.[1126] Second, additional ecodesign and information requirements facilitating these value-retention processes should be adopted[1127], as described below. To underpin the adoption of such requirements, the definitions of 'refurbishment' and 'remanufacturing' should be introduced in Article 2 of the Ecodesign Directive (see #30).

1121 Annex II 1.2.2. to the Ecodesign regulation on servers and data storage products.

1122 Annex I pt. 35 to the Ecodesign regulation on servers and data storage products.

1123 Annex II 3.1.(n) to the Ecodesign regulation on servers and data storage products.

1124 *Ibid.*

1125 Self-Regulatory Initiative on Game Consoles, p. 16.

1126 D. Kreziak, I. Prim-Allaz and E. Robinot, *Des tiroirs pleins de téléphones remplacés: consommateurs et objets à obsolescence perçue* (ADEME 2017) p. 48; V. Rizos et al., *Identifying the impact of the circular economy on the Fast-Moving Consumer Goods Industry – Opportunities and challenges for businesses, workers and consumers – mobile phones as an example* (EESC 2019).

1127 For an explanation of the notion of 'value-retention process', see n° 150.

277. Further requirements on data erasure and transfer – Ecodesign regulations could prohibit software settings that can only be removed by the original owner and that hinder the complete removal of personal information from phones, sending the otherwise-reusable phones for recycling (see #31).[1128] In addition to these requirements on data erasure, one could also imagine a requirement facilitating data transfer from an old to a new product via installed or downloadable tools or cloud-based services.[1129] Regarding this, it should be noted that guidance on data erasure has been developed under the project SustainabilitySMART and could serve as a basis for the adoption of such requirements.[1130]

278. Diagnostic tools – Manufacturers could also be required to provide easy access to diagnostic tools with the product (see #32), like a software tool on computers, to enable automatic evaluation of hardware status in terms of memory errors, battery cycle status, water damage and impact shocks.[1131] As rightly pointed out by E. Oldyrevas and C. McAlister, such a requirement would "*reduce the cost of checking the status of second-hand laptops and increase confidence in the quality of second-hand devices*".[1132]

279. Provision of products without external power supplies and other accessories – If products are sold without external power supplies or other accessories by default (e.g. headsets), this could contribute to reusing external power supplies and other accessories that consumers already own, especially if they are standardised and compatible (see #33). Consumers will continue to use the charger with their new device. Only a limited share of consumers would be expected to purchase a separate external power supply. Such a requirement of decoupling the sale of chargers from phones was analysed in the 2019 Impact Assessment Study on Common Chargers of Portable Devices.[1133] In summary, the study concluded that "*the higher the decoupling rates, the greater the environmental benefits cost savings for consumers, as well as the convenience benefits for the large number of consumers who feel they have too many chargers taking up space in their home and/or workplace. However, the higher decoupling scenarios would also be likely to lead to a certain growth in the*

[1128] D. Watson et al., *Circular Business Models in the Mobile Phone Industry* (TemaNord 2017) p. 49.

[1129] Fraunhofer IZM, Fraunhofer ISI, VITO, *Ecodesign preparatory study on mobile phones, smartphones and tablets – Final Report* (European Commission 2021) pp. 438–439.

[1130] J. Pörhönen, *Solid state memory data erasure – Guidance* (Project sustainablySMART 2018).

[1131] E. Oldyrevas, C. McAlister, *Long live the machine – How ecodesign & energy labelling can prevent premature obsolescence of laptops* (Ecos 2020) p. 26.

[1132] *Ibid.*, p. 17.

[1133] Ipsos and Trinomics, *Impact Assessment Study on Common Chargers of Portable Devices* (European Union 2020). The analysis was however confined to evaluating to what extent the initiative on common charger could help facilitate voluntary decoupling.

market for standalone chargers and, by extension, in the sales of unsafe and/or counterfeit chargers".[1134] As already highlighted[1135], the EC is planning to review the ecodesign regulation on external power supplies in the sense of decoupling the sale of chargers from electronic devices.[1136]

280. Incorporation of reused, refurbished and remanufactured parts and components – Reused, refurbished and remanufactured parts and components should be integrated into new or repaired products, whenever possible and desirable (see #34). To this end, there should be, on the one hand, an evaluation of part or component value so that it is possible to apportion 'bonus' points to the real, validated incorporation of such reused, refurbished and remanufactured parts or components in the new product placed on the market.[1137] The standard on the general method for assessing the proportion of reused components in energy-related products can be used to calculate the proportion of reused components.[1138] On the other, concerning products that have already been purchased and need to be repaired, it should be possible to repair them with reused, refurbished and remanufactured parts. In other words, users should be able to request spare parts derived from the circular economy, as it is the case in France.[1139] This horizontal obligation on traders could be established in ecodesign regulations or in another (consumer) legislation. For both cases, quality standards should be adopted for these reused, refurbished and remanufactured parts and components.[1140]

281. Information requirements on reuse, refurbishment and remanufacturing, including through product digital passports – To ensure the quality of reuse, refurbishment and remanufacturing, there is a need for traceable and reliable information (see #35), e.g. at the bill of material level for the product and/or in the supply chain, in order to identify and trace the previous use cycle(s) of the product, part or component as well as the different

1134 Ipsos and Trinomics, *Impact Assessment Study on Common Chargers of Portable Devices* (European Union 2020) pp. 140–141.

1135 See *supra*, n° 192 and n° 240.

1136 See the press release issued by the EC, 'Pulling the plug on consumer frustration and e-waste: Commission proposes a common charger for electronic devices', 23 September 2021, as well as the factsheet on the Commission's proposal on a common charging solution for electronic devices, both available on: <https://ec.europa.eu/commission/presscorner/detail/en/IP_21_4613>.

1137 Viegand Maagøe, VHK and Oeko-Institut, *Preparatory study for the Ecodesign and Energy Labelling Working Plan 2020–2024 – Task 3 Preliminary analysis of product groups and horizontal initiatives – Durability – Draft report* (European Commission 2020) p. 27.

1138 CEN-CENELEC TC10, General method for assessing the proportion of reused components in energy-related products, EN 45556:2019.

1139 See *supra*, n° 273.

1140 E. Oldyrevas, C. McAlister, *Long live the machine – How ecodesign & energy labelling can prevent premature obsolescence of laptops* (Ecos 2020) p. 18.

value-retention processes they went through. Digital product passports, as proposed in the Proposal for a Sustainable Products Regulation,[1141] could be of great help in this regard.

Proposed amendment to the Ecodesign Directive:

#30

Article 2
Definitions

For the purposes of this Directive, the following definitions shall apply:

(...)

13j. 'Refurbishment' means the process of returning a product to a satisfactory working and/or cosmetic condition, that may be inferior to the original specification, by replacing and repairing all major components that are faulty, markedly damaged or close to failure, and by making cosmetic changes to update the appearance of a product, such as cleaning, changing the fabric, painting or refinishing;

13k. 'Remanufacturing' means industrial process that inspects, disassembles, cleans, reprocesses, stores, reassembles, tests and recovers a product at the subassembly or component level, as defined in the European standard EN 45550:2020.

(...)

AND

Proposed requirements on reuse, refurbishment and remanufacturing:

> *#31 Requirements on secure data erasure and transfer should be envisaged for other products (e.g. mobile and smartphones).*
>
> *#32 Requirements should be adopted on the easy access to diagnosis tools for certain products.*
>
> *#33 The requirement of decoupling the sale of chargers from phones should be envisaged.*
>
> *#34 Requirements on the incorporation of reused, refurbished and remanufactured parts and components should be introduced.*
>
> *#35 Information on reuse, refurbishment and remanufacturing should be required and disclosed, including through digital product passports.*

[1141] Art. 8-13 of the Proposal for a Sustainable Products Regulation.

h) *Requirements on other environmental aspects, including recyclability*

(1) De lege lata

282. Requirements on other environmental aspects – In addition to these energy and resource efficiency requirements, requirements on other environmental aspects have been adopted. This type of requirement is varied, depending on the characteristics of the product concerned. There are ecodesign requirements that limit the consumption of other resources. For example, the ecodesign requirements contained in the implementing measure on domestic washing machines limit their water consumption. The implementing measure also imposes on producers the design of their washing machines with the possibility for the end-users of a cycle at 20 °C.

283. Ecodesign requirements on product recyclability – Some ecodesign regulations contain requirements on product recyclability. Such requirements can be found in the regulation on light sources and separate control gears. Manufacturers, importers or authorised representatives of products containing one or more light sources or separate control gears must ensure that these light sources and separate control gears can be dismantled from the products at end-of-life.[1142] Requirements for dismantling for material recovery and recycling have also been established for refrigerators, televisions, dishwashers and washing machines.[1143] For example, it is required that these products are designed in such a way that the materials and components referred to in Annex VII to Directive 2012/19/EU can be removed with the use of commonly available tools. Similar requirements have been imposed in the voluntary agreement on games consoles, for which any external plastic enclosure components weighing more than 100g must be removable using tools commercially available to recyclers.[1144] Commitments on design for recycling have also been made in the imaging sector. According to the voluntary agreement, the product must utilise commonly used fasteners for joining components, subassemblies, chassis and enclosures, and non-separable connections (e.g. glued or welded) between different materials must be avoided unless they are technically or legally required.[1145]

1142 Art. 4(3) of the Ecodesign regulation on light sources and separate control gears.

1143 Annex II pt. 3(d) to the Ecodesign regulation on refrigerating appliances; Annex II D. pt. 1 to the Ecodesign regulation on electronic displays; Annex II pt. 5(5) to the Ecodesign regulation on household dishwashers; Annex II pt. 8(5) to the Ecodesign regulation on household washing machines and household washer-dryers.

1144 Self-Regulatory Initiative of June 2021 to further improve the energy efficiency of Games Consoles, Version 4.0, p. 16.

1145 Voluntary agreement on imaging equipment, p. 10.

284. Information requirements on product recyclability – Accompanying these ecodesign requirements, there are information obligations on product recyclability. For example, it is required that instructions for dismantling light sources and separate control gears must be available on a free access website.[1146] Similarly, the technical documentation and the professional part of the free access websites of manufacturers, their authorised representatives, or importers of vacuum cleaners must contain information relevant for dismantling, in particular in relation to the motor and any batteries, recycling, recovery and disposal at end-of-life.[1147] Concerning electronic displays, it is required to make, on a free-access website, dismantling information available, which must include the sequence of dismantling operations, tools or technologies needed to access the targeted components referred to in point 1 of Annex VII of the WEEE Directive (e.g. external electric cables, cathode ray tubes).[1148] This information must be kept available for at least 15 years after the placing on the market of the last unit of a product model.[1149]

285. Requirements on recycled content – So far, no ecodesign regulation contains requirements on minimum recycled material content in new products. Such requirements only exist on paper as a proposed measure.[1150] The only requirement on recycled content at EU level can be found in the voluntary agreement on imaging equipment, which imposes an obligation to inform customers on the minimum percentage of post-consumer recycled plastic content. Interestingly, requirements on recycled content have been established by the French Anti-Waste Law. According to Article 13 of this law, producers and importers of waste-generating products are under obligation to inform consumers, by marking, labelling, displaying or any other appropriate process, of the environmental qualities and characteristics of these products, including the incorporation of recycled material and recyclability. The same provision states that when the recycled nature of a product is mentioned, the percentage of recycled material actually incorporated is specified. In its Article 61 II, the French Anti-Waste Law also states that "*the placing on the market of certain categories of products and materials may be subject to compliance with a minimum rate of incorporation of recycled material in these products and materials, with the exception of materials from renewable raw materials, provided that the life cycle analysis of this obligation is positive.*" Although this provision was initially aimed at implementing the Single-Use

1146 Art. 4(3) of the Ecodesign regulation on light sources and separate control gears.

1147 Annex I pt. 2(b) to the Ecodesign regulation on vacuum cleaners.

1148 Annex II D.1. to the Ecodesign regulation on electronic displays.

1149 *Ibid.*

1150 See European Parliament Resolution of 9 July 2015 on resource efficiency: moving towards a circular economy, (2014/2208(INI)), pt. 25.

Plastics Directive[1151], and thus concerns single-use plastic products[1152], its general terms could lead to a broader scope of application.

286. Requirements on circumvention – For electronic displays, refrigerating appliances, light sources and separate control gears, household dishwashers, household washing machines and household washer-dryers, the manufacturer, authorised representative or importer must not place on the market products designed to be able to detect they are being tested (e.g. by recognising the test conditions or test cycle), and to react specifically by automatically altering their performance during the test with the aim of reaching a more favourable level for any of the parameters declared by the manufacturer, importer or authorised representative in the technical documentation or included in any documentation provided.[1153] The Annexes on 'Verification procedure for market surveillance purposes' of all these ecodesign regulations state that when such product design is noted, *"the model and all equivalent models shall be considered not compliant"*.

(2) De lege ferenda

287. More ecodesign and information requirements on product recyclability – More ecodesign and information requirements on product recyclability should be envisaged (see #36). Design-related criteria affecting recyclability have been listed in the standard for assessing the recyclability and recoverability of energy-related products and could give rise to new ecodesign requirements on these aspects.[1154] These ecodesign requirements should be adopted in coherence with other rules, like chemical rules. For example, if no coherence is established when requirements on recycled content are adopted, manufacturers could be hesitant to use recycled materials if they fear that they

1151 Directive (EU) 2019/904 of the European Parliament and of the Council of 5 June 2019 on the reduction of the impact of certain plastic products on the environment, OJ L 155, 12.6.2019, p. 1–19 (hereafter 'Single-Use Plastics Directive').

1152 The initial goal of Article 61 II of the French Anti-Waste is explained in Rapport fait au nom de la Commission de l'aménagement du territoire et du développement durable (1) sur le projet de loi (PROCÉDURE ACCÉLÉRÉE) relatif à la lutte contre le gaspillage et à l'économie circulaire, 17 Septembre 2019, n° 727, p. 45.

1153 Commission Regulation (EU) 2021/341 of 23 February 2021 amending Regulations (EU) 2019/424, (EU) 2019/1781, (EU) 2019/2019, (EU) 2019/2020, (EU) 2019/2021, (EU) 2019/2022, (EU) 2019/2023 and (EU) 2019/2024 with regard to ecodesign requirements for servers and data storage products, electric motors and variable speed drives, refrigerating appliances, light sources and separate control gears, electronic displays, household dishwashers, household washing machines and household washer-dryers and refrigerating appliances with a direct sales function, OJ L 68, 26.2.2021, p. 108–148.

1154 CEN-CENELEC TC10, General method for assessing the recyclability and recoverability of energy-related products, EN 45555:2019.

contain toxics.[1155] In addition to these ecodesign requirements, other mandatory information on how and where to dispose of specific products could help avoid hibernating products.

> *Proposed requirements on product recyclability:*
>
> *#36 More ecodesign and information requirements on product recyclability should be envisaged, such as:*
>
> *Manufacturers, importers or authorised representatives shall ensure that [the concerned products] are designed in such a way that [the specified materials and components] can be removed with the use of commonly available tools.*

4. THE NECESSARY COMPLIANCE WITH AND ENFORCEMENT OF ECODESIGN REQUIREMENTS

a) *Conforming and proving the conformity*

288. The CE marking as passport for compliant products – If the product complies with the requirements, it can bear the CE marking and freely move within EU boundaries[1156], or more precisely within the EEA and Turkish market.[1157] Member States cannot restrict the movement of compliant products on the EU market. The free movement of goods requires them to allow onto their market any product legally manufactured and marketed in another Member State[1158], unless one of the grounds listed in Article 36 TFEU or mandatory requirements (e.g. protection of the environment) can be invoked. It should be noted that these derogations are narrowly interpreted by the ECJ, and even if one of the grounds is successfully invoked, the Member State must demonstrate that the measure is proportionate and suitable to reach the goal.[1159] Consequently, it seems difficult to imagine movement restrictions on products on grounds relating to premature obsolescence if they comply with all applicable ecodesign requirements.

289. A ban for non-compliant products – By contrast, if the product does not conform to ecodesign requirements, it cannot be placed on the

[1155] C. Dalhammar, 'Industry attitudes towards ecodesign standards for improved resource efficiency', 123 *J. Clean. Prod.* (2016) p. 159.
[1156] See Art. 5 and 6 of the Ecodesign Directive, as well as Annex III.
[1157] The Blue Guide, p. 64.
[1158] ECJ 11 July 1974, Case C-8/74, *Dassonville, EU:C:1974:82*; ECJ 20 February 1979, Case C-120/78, *Rewe* v *Bundesmonopolverwaltung für Branntwein, EU:C:1979:42.*
[1159] See for ex. ECJ 20 September 1988, Case C-302/86, *Commission* v *Denmark, EU:C:1988:421.*

EU market.[1160] Such a ban has already been imposed through ecodesign regulations, the most illustrative example being the ban on halogen lamps.[1161] Similar bans occurred due to the adoption of other specific legislation, like the Single-Use Plastics Directive, which prohibits the use of single-use plastic products, including cutlery, plates and straws.[1162] In Paris, since 1 July 2019, the most polluting cars can no longer drive.[1163] If more requirements on product sustainability were adopted in the future, one could imagine certain 'inherently unsustainable' products being barred or having restricted access.[1164]

290. Additional national requirements, barriers to free movement of goods? – Doubts remain concerning the compatibility with internal market rules of ecodesign requirements that are imposed by Member States in relation to a product or a sustainable aspect that is not covered by ecodesign regulations, like the French rules on the availability of spare parts.[1165] Such rules that lay down requirements to be met by goods certainly fall within the scope of Article 34 TFEU, as opposed to selling arrangements, which are associated with the marketing of goods rather than with their characteristics.[1166] The Ecodesign Directive only mentions, in its recital 11, that national provisions can be maintained "*on grounds of overriding needs relating to the protection of the environment*" or introduced "*based on new scientific evidence relating to the protection of the environment on grounds of a problem specific to that Member State that arises after the adoption of the applicable implementing measure*". These national provisions must then be notified to and approved by the EC, as required by Article 114(4), (5) and (6) TFEU. Such restrictive measures, although indistinctly applicable to all traders, are in principle prohibited by Article 34 TFEU as they are in practice more burdensome for foreign traders who have to comply with two sets of rules, namely the ones imposed by the originating State and by the importing State. National measures will escape prohibition only if they are (i) justified by mandatory requirements as set out in Article 36 TFEU or developed by ECJ case law (e.g. protection of the environment), (ii) proportionate and (iii) suitable to reach the goal. The EC seems however

1160 Article 7 of the Ecodesign Directive.

1161 See *supra*, n° 225.

1162 See Art. 5 of the Single-Use Plastics Directive, which refers to part B of the Annex.

1163 For further information on this restriction, see <https://www.gouvernement.fr/la-circulation-des-vehicules-polluants-restreinte-dans-le-grand-paris>.

1164 See also E. Maitre-Ekern, C. Dalhammar, 'Towards a hierarchy of consumption behaviour in the circular economy', 26 *Maastricht Journal of European and Comparative Law* (2019) p. 403.

1165 See *supra*, n° 264.

1166 ECJ 24 November 1993, Joined Cases C-267/91 and C-268/91, *Keck and Mithouard*, *EU:C:1993:905*. See also Commission Notice of 23 March 2021 on Guide on Articles 34–36 of the Treaty on the Functioning of the European Union (TFEU), 2021/C 100/03, pp. 48–49.

more lenient concerning national rules when they may complement EU rules, like those complementing EU ecodesign regulations.[1167]

291. Burden of proof on manufacturers – Manufacturers bear the burden of proof, meaning that they have to prove the compliance of their products with the applicable ecodesign requirements. The conformity assessment is based on self-assessment. As explained in Article 8(2) of Ecodesign Directive, implementing measures leave the choice between two procedures to assess product conformity, namely an internal design control or an appropriate management system. In this procedure, the methods used must be reliable, accurate and reproducible, take the generally recognised state of the art into account and produce results deemed to be of low uncertainty.

292. Conformity testing and tolerances – It is then for the authorities to assess the claims made by the manufacturers. These authorities are entitled to apply a margin for error (i.e. 'tolerance') to allow for variations that emerge in the measurements taken during verification tests.[1168] However, these tolerances pose some practical issues. It has been reported that some manufacturers use tolerances to achieve compliance with ecodesign requirements or to communicate better performance than has actually been measured and calculated. They do so by adding the value of tolerances on top of the measured values. As pointed out by ECOS and ANEC, this may result in products being less efficient than the regulations permit and above the uncontrollable 'uncertainty' value.[1169]

b) Products that are presumed to be compliant

293. Presumption of conformity – There are four particular cases where the product is presumed to conform to the applicable ecodesign requirements. These cases are enumerated in Article 9(1) to (4) of the Ecodesign Directive. Pursuant to these provisions, products shall be presumed to comply with the ecodesign requirements if they bear the CE marking (Article 9(1)), but also if

---

1167 See point 2.1. of the explanatory memorandum to the Proposal for a Regulation of the European Parliament and of the Council setting a framework for energy efficiency labelling and repealing Directive 2010/30/EU, COM(2015) 341 final, pp. 2–3.

1168 Commission Regulation (EU) 2016/2282 of 30 November 2016 amending Regulations (EC) No 1275/2008, (EC) No 107/2009, (EC) No 278/2009, (EC) No 640/2009, (EC) No 641/2009, (EC) No 642/2009, (EC) No 643/2009, (EU) No 1015/2010, (EU) No 1016/2010, (EU) No 327/2011, (EU) No 206/2012, (EU) No 547/2012, (EU) No 932/2012, (EU) No 617/2013, (EU) No 666/2013, (EU) No 813/2013, (EU) No 814/2013, (EU) No 66/2014, (EU) No 548/2014, (EU) No 1253/2014, (EU) 2015/1095, (EU) 2015/1185, (EU) 2015/1188, (EU) 2015/1189 and (EU) 2016/2281 with regard to the use of tolerances in verification procedures, C/2016/7767, OJ L 346, 20.12.2016, p. 51–110.

1169 ECOS/ANEC Position Paper of 11 February 2015 on measurement uncertainty and verification tolerances under Ecodesign and Energy Labelling Regulations.

harmonised standards have been applied (Article 9(2)) or if the products have been awarded the EU Ecolabel (Article 9(3)) or any other ecolabel that fulfils equivalent conditions (Article 9(4)). Further details are provided on the three last cases in the following paragraphs.

294. PRODUCTS BEARING THE CE MARKING – CE-marked products are the first product category which can be presumed compliant with legislative requirements. The CE marking provides the first indication that the necessary controls can be assumed to have been carried out before the product in question is placed on the market. The CE marking, which consists of the initials 'CE', is affixed by the manufacturer (established inside or outside the EU), or by their authorised representative established within the EU.[1170] By affixing the CE Marking, the manufacturer declares on their sole responsibility that the product conforms to all applicable Union legislative requirements, and that the appropriate conformity assessment procedures have been successfully completed.[1171] ANEC has already cautioned that the CE marking cannot be considered a safety or quality mark for consumers, especially since CE-marked products can be placed on the market subject only to an internal control by the manufacturer, with no independent confirmation of the conformity of the product with EU legislation.[1172] Moreover, the EC has acknowledged that the CE marking, like any other mark, may be misused.[1173] For example, the CE marking may be affixed to products which do not fulfil the requirements and conditions for its affixing or products for which the affixing is not foreseen. This may confuse consumers and reduce their confidence in the CE marking as well as in products compliant with ecodesign requirements. It is therefore crucial to invest in public enforcement, as argued below[1174], so that Member States identify non-compliant products bearing the EC marking and withdraw them from the market.[1175]

295. PRODUCTS SUBJECT TO HARMONISED STANDARDS, INCLUDING ON MATERIAL EFFICIENCY – Apart from the presumption of conformity conferred

1170 The definition, the format and the general principles governing the CE marking can be found in Regulation (EC) No 765/2008 of the European Parliament and of the Council of 9 July 2008 setting out the requirements for accreditation and market surveillance relating to the marketing of products and repealing Regulation (EEC) No 339/93, OJ L 218, 13.8.2008, p. 30–47. See also Decision No 768/2008/EC of the European Parliament and of the Council of 9 July 2008 on a common framework for the marketing of products, and repealing Council Decision 93/465/EEC, OJ L 218, 13.8.2008, p. 82–128.

1171 The Blue Guide, p. 65.

1172 ANEC Position Paper on CE marking – "Caveat Emptor – Buyer Beware" (2012), ANEC-SC-2012-G-026final.

1173 See Answer of 9 January 2008 on China Export (CE) mark given by Mr Verheugen on behalf of the Commission, replying to parliamentary question P-5938/2007.

1174 See *infra*, n° 299–301.

1175 For further comments on sanctions in these cases, see *infra*, n° 302 *et seq.*

to products with the CE marking, the second case of presumption concerns products for which harmonised standards developed by the European standardization bodies have been applied.[1176] Standards are being developed on the basis of Regulation (EU) 1025/2012 on European standardisation.[1177] Around 40 standardisation mandates were launched for the product groups covered by ecodesign implementing measures.[1178] These standards provide requirements and guidelines for testing and for result assessment, measurements and verification, which help producers make products conform to ecodesign requirements laid down in implementing measures.[1179] In addition to these product-specific standards, there is the series of generic standards on material efficiency that define and provide parameters and methods for assessing product durability, reparability, reusability, recyclability, ability to remanufacture, as well as documentation and/or marking relating to material efficiency of the product. The need for harmonised standards is determined at the time of developing implementing measures for specific products. Once adopted, their use remains voluntary.

296. More standards on material efficiency should be adopted – More than for the conformity assessment with ecodesign requirements, standards are of utmost importance for the transition towards product sustainability as they can "*create intra-firm and inter-firm efficiencies, facilitate economies of scale in manufacturing and promote interoperability between complementary products*".[1180] The new series of standards on material efficiency is thus a major step forward towards a longer product lifetime., To date, however, as pointed out by the European consumer association ANEC[1181], there is still a lack of standards on material efficiency despite the existence of the standardisation mandate M/543. Whenever relevant, new ecodesign requirements should be supported by standards (i.e. measurement standards, test standards and verification methods). More standards should therefore be adopted (see #38).

1176 Art. 9(2) Ecodesign Directive.

1177 Regulation (EU) No 1025/2012 of the European Parliament and of the Council of 25 October 2012 on European standardisation, amending Council Directives 89/686/EEC and 93/15/EEC and Directives 94/9/EC, 94/25/EC, 95/16/EC, 97/23/EC, 98/34/EC, 2004/22/EC, 2007/23/EC, 2009/23/EC and 2009/105/EC of the European Parliament and of the Council and repealing Council Decision 87/95/EEC and Decision No 1673/2006/EC of the European Parliament and of the Council, OJ L 316, 14.11.2012, p. 12–33.

1178 The complete list of harmonised standards, which have been published in the Official Journal under the ecodesign and energy labelling implementing measures, is available on: <https://ec.europa.eu/growth/single-market/european-standards/harmonised-standards_en>.

1179 P. Tecchio, C. McAlister, F. Mathieux, F. Ardente, 'In search of standards to support circularity in product policies', 168 *J. Clean. Prod.* (2017) p. 1534.

1180 A. Russell, 'Standardization in History: A Review Essay with an Eye to the Future', in S. Bolin (ed.), *The Standards Edge: Future Generations* (Sheridan Press 2005) p. 249.

1181 ANEC's preliminary views of July 2020 on the draft Annual Union Work Programme for European Standardisation for 2021, ANEC-WP1-2020-G-030, p. 3.

For example, standards should be developed for refurbished goods.[1182] The EC has acknowledged the need to write new standardisation requests for most if not all new or revised regulations under development within the framework of the Ecodesign and Energy Labelling Working Plan 2022–2024.[1183] When developing these standards, particular attention should be given on material efficiency aspects.

297. The European standardisation system should be improved – Improvements should moreover be made to enhance the effectiveness of the European standardisation system (see #39). A 2017 study issued by four environmental organisations identified several shortcomings of this system, including the difference between the prescribed testing conditions and the real-life use and the risk of outdated and useless test standards due to the fast pace of technological progress.[1184] Another shortcoming is the possibility for manufacturers to exploit loopholes in standards, use circumvention techniques (e.g. 'cheating devices') or obtain better ratings or falsely claim compliance with ecodesign requirements.[1185] Several policy recommendations could be made to remedy these major shortcomings. First, as recommended in the 2017 study[1186], the representativeness of standards should be seen as a key criterion when formulating test methodologies with a view to better reflecting product features and consumer behaviour. Second, as previously suggested for ecodesign requirements[1187], standards should be frequently reviewed to remain up to date.[1188] Third, improvements should be made to the system of market surveillance to ensure better enforcement.[1189] Hopefully, the 2022 EU Strategy

---

1182 D. Watson et al., *Circular Business Models in the Mobile Phone Industry* (TemaNord 2017) p. 74.

1183 Communication from the Commission on the Ecodesign and Energy Labelling Working Plan 2022–2024, OJ C 182, 4.5.2022, p. 7.

1184 CLASP, ECOS, EEB and Topten, *Closing the 'Reality Gap' – Ensuring a Fair Energy Label for Consumers* (2017) p. 4.

1185 See for example in the automotive sector: ECJ 17 December 2020, C-693/18, *CLCV and Others, EU:C:2020:1040.* In this case, the manufacturer had installed a defeat device that systematically improved, during approval procedures, the performance of the vehicle emission control system and thus obtained approval of the vehicle. For a detailed analysis on the potential of software in the context of circumvention, see Viegand Maagøe, VHK and Oeko-Institut, *Preparatory study for the Ecodesign and Energy Labelling Working Plan 2020–2024 – Task 3 Preliminary analysis of product groups and horizontal initiatives – Final* (European Commission 2021) p. 643 at p. 646.

1186 CLASP, ECOS, EEB and Topten, *Closing the 'Reality Gap' – Ensuring a Fair Energy Label for Consumers* (2017) p. 29.

1187 See *supra*, n° 222.

1188 CLASP, ECOS, EEB and Topten, *Closing the 'Reality Gap' – Ensuring a Fair Energy Label for Consumers* (2017) p. 29.

1189 The same argument is advanced (in greater detail) for the enforcement of ecodesign requirements. See *infra*, n° 301.

on Standardisation[1190], which proposes a set of actions to respond to the challenges encountered by the European standardisation system, will live up to its ambitious goals.

298. Products awarded the EU ecolabel or other ecolabels – The third and fourth presumption provided for in Article 9 covers products that have been awarded an EU Ecolabel[1191], or another ecolabel that fulfils equivalent conditions[1192], in so far as the applicable ecodesign requirements are met by the ecolabel. The extension of the presumption to other ecolabels is made on a case-by-case basis. Since the criteria on which ecolabels are awarded integrate more and more product sustainability aspects, such presumption may be used more and more often.[1193]

Policy recommendations:

#38 More standards should be adopted to support new ecodesign requirements, including on material efficiency aspects.

#39 The European standardisation system should be improved to ensure that standards reflect real-life usage patterns and conditions, are keeping up with technological evolution of appliances and are not easily circumvented by manufacturers.

c) *The difficult task of verifying compliance*

299. Verification by the national market surveillance authorities – The compliance with ecodesign requirements is then verified by the national market surveillance authorities, as prescribed in Article 3 of the Ecodesign Directive.[1194] The verification can be established directly on the product or on the basis of the technical documentation, depending on the implementing

1190 Communication from the Commission to the European Parliament, the Council, the European Economic and Social Committee and the Committee of the Regions on an EU Strategy on Standardisation Setting global standards in support of a resilient, green and digital EU single market, COM(2022) 31 final.

1191 Article 9(3) of the Ecodesign Directive.

1192 Article 9(4) of the Ecodesign Directive.

1193 For further details, see Chapter III on the marketing and pre-contractual stage, and more specifically Section D on the EU Ecolabel Regulation.

1194 The list of national market surveillance authorities by country is available on: <https://ec.europa.eu/docsroom/documents/46814>. In Belgium, the responsibility for market surveillance concerning ecodesign lies with the Federal Public Service Health, Food Chain Safety and Environment. In France, this responsibility lies with the Ministère de la transition écologique. In Germany, it is the responsibility of the various Länder to check the compliance of products with ecodesign requirements.

measure.[1195] The CE marking facilitates verification. It is for Member States to organise such controls and find the balance while controlling the design of products. Information on the results of the market surveillance is then passed on to the EC. Authorities can upload their inspections and laboratory test results on an Information and Communication System on Market Surveillance (ICSMS) to avoid duplication of work within the EU. Administrative Cooperation groups on ecodesign are also organised to share experience and knowledge between national authorities. The Market Surveillance Regulation[1196], which was recently amended by Regulation (EU) 2019/1020[1197], provides the framework for the Members States to organise their market surveillance.

300. Lack of control and coordination – Control and market surveillance are of utmost importance for effective enforcement of the ecodesign rules. As R. Malcolm stated, "*the enforcement of the Directive and its implementing regulations and their control of products, their energy use and environmental impact, is only as good as the enforcement mechanisms accompanying it*".[1198] However, the EC estimated that between 10 and 25% of products covered by the Directive do not satisfy the ecodesign and energy labelling requirements.[1199] In a 2017 study gathering stakeholder interviews[1200], the inadequate market surveillance was pointed out as one of the main obstacles to full implementation of ecodesign legislation, together with the lack of clear political support and direction and the slow pace of the regulatory process.[1201] The root of the problem is twofold. First, the level of activities undertaken by most Member states' market surveillance authorities in the field of ecodesign is moderate to low, especially due to a lack of financial resources, lack of human capacities and other

1195 Article 15(7) of the Ecodesign Directive.

1196 Regulation (EC) No 765/2008 of the European Parliament and of the Council of 9 July 2008 setting out the requirements for accreditation and market surveillance relating to the marketing of products and repealing Regulation (EEC) No 339/93, OJ L 218, 13.8.2008, p. 30–47.

1197 Regulation (EU) 2019/1020 of the European Parliament and of the Council of 20 June 2019 on market surveillance and compliance of products and amending Directive 2004/42/EC and Regulations (EC) No 765/2008 and (EU) No 305/2011, PE/45/2019/REV/1, OJ L 169, 25.6.2019, p. 1–44.

1198 R. Malcolm, 'Ecodesign Laws and the Environmental Impact of our Consumption of Products', 23 *Journal of Environmental Law* (2011) p. 503.

1199 Communication from the Commission of 30 November 2016 on Ecodesign Working Plan 2016–2019, COM(2016) 773 final, p. 9. The EC more recently confirmed that non-compliance was still an issue, based on the results of the EU projects and additional data from Member States. See EC, 'New energy efficiency labels explained', 11 March 2019, available on: <https://ec.europa.eu/commission/presscorner/detail/en/MEMO_19_1596>.

1200 C. Egenhofer et al., *1. Stakeholders views on the Ecodesign Directive: An assessment of the successes and shortcomings – Briefing paper* (European Union 2017).

1201 Recital K of the European Parliament Resolution of 31 May 2018 on the implementation of the Ecodesign Directive (2009/125/EC), (2017/2087(INI)).

priorities on food and safety.[1202] This does not violate the Regulation on market surveillance, which does not specify what level of market surveillance activities is required, but merely that authorities should perform "*appropriate checks*" on an "*adequate scale*".[1203] Second, there is a lack of cooperation and exchange of information between national market surveillance authorities, with great variations in compliance records throughout the EU. To alleviate these issues, several projects were funded by the EC.[1204] However, it seems that these projects "*provide a temporary solution for a recurring need*" as no improvement of market surveillance activities performed outside EU projects has been noticed.[1205] These concerns on the enforcement of ecodesign rules could grow if more material efficiency requirements were adopted, especially due to the lack of suitable methods to support enforcement of a lifecycle ecodesign approach in and beyond EU boundaries.

301. STEPPING-UP ENFORCEMENT – Effective control and enforcement is a cornerstone of the ecodesign legal framework, without which adopting further ecodesign requirements would be pointless. Several recommendations have already been made to solve this enforcement problem, which is far from being new.[1206] Yet it does not necessarily mean that the competence for controlling the market should be transferred from Member States to the EC, only that more could be done to promote controls and coordination between national authorities.[1207] As claimed by the EP in its 2015 Resolution on resource efficiency[1208], an emphasis should be given to the implementation of self-monitoring and third-party auditing to ensure that products comply with these standards (see #40). Self-monitoring and third-party auditing are potential tools to support compliance of (complex) products with ecodesign requirements, especially since market surveillance is expensive and not straightforward.[1209]

1202 J. Krivošík, S. Attali, *Market surveillance of Energy Labelling and Ecodesign product requirements – Overview of challenges and opportunities* (ADEME 2014) p. 11 at p. 13.

1203 Art. 11(3) of the Regulation (EU) 2019/1020 on market surveillance and compliance of products.

1204 See for ex. the European Eco-design Compliance Project (Ecopliant) and the Anti-circumvention of Standards for Better Market Surveillance (ANTICSS).

1205 European Court of Auditors, *EU action on Ecodesign and Energy Labelling: important contribution to greater energy efficiency reduced by significant delays and non-compliance – Special Report* (European Union 2020) p. 37.

1206 J. Krivošík, S. Attali, *Market surveillance of Energy Labelling and Ecodesign product requirements – Overview of challenges and opportunities* (ADEME 2014) p. 39 at p. 45.

1207 CLASP, ECOS, EEB and Topten, *Closing the 'Reality Gap' – Ensuring a Fair Energy Label for Consumers* (2017) p. 31.

1208 European Parliament Resolution of 9 July 2015 on resource efficiency: moving towards a circular economy, (2014/2208(INI)), pt. 24.

1209 For more detailed arguments in favour of private and polycentric enforcement of rules in other sectors, see e.g. C. P. Spreng, B.K. Sovacool, D. Spreng, 'All hands on deck: polycentric governance for climate change insurance', 139 *Climatic Change* (2016) p. 129 at p. 140; B. Dupont, 'Bots, cops, and corporations: on the limits of enforcement and the promise of

The 2018 EP Report gave two additional suggestions, which should be given particular attention, to tighten up coordination between the national authorities. First, best practices established by Member States should be shared (see #41). Sharing testing costs, results and best experience among national authorities would indeed make the best use of resources. To trigger such cooperation, participation in the Ecodesign and Energy Labelling Administrative Cooperative (ADCO) could be mandatory, and funding could be provided to ensure more systematic coordination and sharing of test results at EU level.[1210] Second, rapid screening methods should be implemented in cooperation with industry experts to detect the products that are most likely to be non-compliant (see #42).[1211] The well-functioning RAPEX system, which is used for public monitoring and verification of product safety, could serve as inspiration, as suggested in one of the Belgian legislative proposal against 'organised obsolescence'.[1212] The digital product passport, which would be introduced across different instruments[1213], could also be of use in this regard.

Policy recommendations:

> *#40 An emphasis should be given to the implementation of self-monitoring and third-party auditing to ensure that products comply with these standards.*
>
> *#41 Best practices established by Member States should be shared.*
>
> *#42 Rapid screening methods should be implemented in cooperation with industry experts to detect non-compliant products.*

d) *Sanctions in case of non-compliance*

302. Possible sanctions by public authorities – When Member States notice that non-complying products circulate within the EU, sanctions can be imposed on the responsible person. These sanctions must be effective, proportionate and dissuasive, depending on the extent of non-compliance and the number of units of non-complying products.[1214] In Belgium, these sanctions include among others imprisonment, fines, withdrawal of the non-

polycentric regulation as a way to control large-scale cybercrime', 67 *Crime, Law, and Social Change* (2017) p. 97 at p. 116.

1210 CLASP, ECOS, EEB and Topten, *Closing the 'Reality Gap' – Ensuring a Fair Energy Label for Consumers* (2017) p. 5.

1211 Report of the European Parliament of 7 May 2018 on the implementation of the Ecodesign Directive (2009/125/EC), (2017/2087(INI)), pp. 5–6.

1212 Art. 10 to 21 Proposition de loi visant à lutter contre l'obsolescence organisée et à soutenir l'économie circulaire, *Doc. parl.*, Ch., 2019–2020, 7 janvier 2020, n° 0914/001.

1213 Among these instruments, there is the Energy Labelling Regulation. See *infra*, n° 572.

1214 Article 20 of the Ecodesign Directive. See also the Blue Guide, p. 69.

complying products from the market, the publication of the judgement and/or the temporary or permanent closure of establishments that have been used to commit the infringement.[1215]

303. Private law sanctions – In addition to the sanctions imposed by the public authorities, companies that violate ecodesign regulations could be sanctioned under private law, and more specifically on the basis of the provisions contained in the UCPD.[1216] In this regard, the UCPD "*complements [the Ecodesign Directive] as a 'safety net' ensuring that a high common level of consumer protection against unfair commercial practices is maintained in all sectors*".[1217] Since ecodesign implementing measures are product-specific regulations, directly applicable in all EU countries, they have a direct effect and may be invoked by consumers and competitors against producers of consumer products. This allows consumers to get compensation when products are found to be non-compliant, even when it falls outside of the legal guarantee period. The interplay between the Ecodesign Directive and the UCPD should be made clearer by adding a concrete example in the corresponding section of the UCPD Guidance (#43).

304. The need for effective sanctions – To improve compliance with ecodesign rules, effective sanctions are needed. As highlighted by the EP, dissuasive measures should be taken to improve compliance with ecodesign requirements.[1218] Member States should thus adopt higher sanctions. Nonetheless, the effectiveness of negative publicity – compared to fines – should not be neglected. Thus, enforcement authorities should consider publicising grievous cases of non-compliance and circumvention of test standards. For the rest, it may be useful to establish criteria to be taken into account when imposing penalties, as was done for consumer rules with the adoption of the Enforcement and Modernisation Directive.[1219] Such criteria would ensure a certain degree of effectiveness and consistency in the penalties imposed by national authorities. Article 20 of the Ecodesign Directive could be amended in that sense (see #44).

1215 See Art. 17–18 Loi du 21 décembre 1998 relative aux normes produits ayant pour but la promotion de modes et de consommation durables et la protection de l'environnement et de la santé, *M.B.*, 11 février 1999, p. 3986.

1216 See *infra* on the UCPD, and more specifically n° 444 *et seq.* on enforcement and sanctions.

1217 UCPD Guidance, p. 74.

1218 Report of the European Parliament of 7 May 2018 on the implementation of the Ecodesign Directive (2009/125/EC), (2017/2087(INI)), pp. 5–6.

1219 Directive (EU) 2019/2161 of the European Parliament and of the Council of 27 November 2019 amending Council Directive 93/13/EEC and Directives 98/6/EC, 2005/29/EC and 2011/83/EU of the European Parliament and of the Council as regards the better enforcement and modernisation of Union consumer protection rules, OJ L 328, 18.12.2019, p. 7–28.

Suggested amendment to the UCPD Guidance:

#43

4.1.1.1. Interplay with other EU legislation on environmental claims

Article 3(4) and Recital 10 set out the principle that the UCPD complements other EU legislation as a 'safety net' ensuring that a high common level of consumer protection against unfair commercial practices is maintained in all sectors. In the area of environmental claims, UCPD complements instruments such as:

(...)

- Directive 2009/125/EC establishing a framework for the setting of ecodesign requirements for energy-related products [287];

(...)

Here are a few examples of the interplay between the UCPD and specific EU legislation concerning environmental claims.

For example:

- (...)
- **According to Regulation (EU) 2019/424 laying down ecodesign requirements for servers and data storage products, computer manufacturers must ensure that joining, fastening or sealing techniques do not prevent the disassembly for repair or reuse purposes of the memory, the motherboard and batteries. If a computer does not comply with this requirement, such practice could be regarded as misleading.**

(...)

AND

Suggested amendment to the Ecodesign Directive:

#44

Article 20
Penalties

1. The Member States shall lay down the rules applicable to infringements of the national provisions adopted pursuant to this Directive and shall take all measures necessary to ensure that they are implemented. The penalties provided for shall be effective, proportionate and dissuasive, taking into account the extent of non-

compliance and the number of units of non-complying products placed on the Community market. The Member States shall notify those provisions to the Commission by 20 November 2010 and shall notify it without delay of any subsequent amendment affecting them.

2. Member States shall ensure that the following non-exhaustive and indicative criteria are taken into account for the imposition of penalties, where appropriate:

(a) the nature, gravity, scale and duration of the infringement;

(b) any action taken by the trader to mitigate or remedy the non-compliance with the implementing measure;

(c) any previous infringements by the trader;

(d) the financial benefits gained or losses avoided by the trader due to the infringement, if the relevant data are available;

(e) penalties imposed on the trader for the same infringement in other Member States in cross-border cases;

(f) any other aggravating or mitigating factors applicable to the circumstances of the case.

e) Compliance with self-regulation

305. Verification by an independent inspector – Compliance with ecodesign requirements contained in voluntary agreements is generally monitored by an independent inspector.[1220] This inspector is selected by the signatories of the voluntary agreement and appointed in agreement with the EC. Completed product compliance reports are regularly submitted by the signatories to the inspector. Inspections may also start after the submission by a third party of an appropriately substantiated allegation of possible non-compliance with the voluntary agreement. The inspector verifies the compliance by checking the documentation provided by the signatories, testing products, and inspecting the signatories' premises. On the basis of these pieces of information, the inspector makes an inspection report, which is provided to the EC and the signatory concerned.

[1220] Voluntary agreement on imaging equipment, p. 15; Voluntary Industry Agreement of 2 April 2018 to improve the energy consumption of Complex Set Top Boxes within the EU, Version 6.0, p. 5; Self-Regulatory Initiative of June 2021 to further improve the energy efficiency of Games Consoles, Version 4.0, pp. 20–21.

306. Possible sanctions – In case of non-compliance, different actions and sanctions against the signatory concerned are possible. There are, first, measures provided for in the voluntary agreements. In general, a signatory who fails to meet its commitments must take corrective actions. Non-compliance that continues for a certain period after the identification of the non-compliance by the independent inspector, can lead to immediate exclusion of the signatory from the voluntary agreement. In addition to these sanctions, manufacturers may also be sanctioned on the basis of the UCPD, and more specifically on its Article 6(1)(c), which prohibits traders from misleading consumers on the extent and nature of their commitment.[1221]

D. CONCLUSION

307. Product design and premature obsolescence – The design of products has a considerable influence on product lifetimes. The intrinsic properties of the product influence the length of product use cycles and product lifetime and, by the same token, on the occurrence of premature obsolescence. When a product is durable, easily reparable, and upgradable, it will in principle last longer. In other words, ecodesign counters the different types of premature obsolescence, namely material, functional, indirect, economic, and psychological obsolescence. Integrating environmental considerations at the design and production stage through 'ecodesign' is thus crucial to prevent premature obsolescence and the associated impacts on the environment. The shift towards ecodesign may be fostered by technology push or market pull but can also be imposed to some extent by regulations. The EU is a forerunner in this regard with its Ecodesign Directive and its implementing measures. This legislation curbs premature obsolescence from a product-oriented perspective by imposing mandatory ecodesign requirements on product sustainability aspects for specific product groups.

308. The irreplaceable advantages of the ecodesign legal framework – The ecodesign legislation is undoubtedly one of the most useful legal tools in addressing premature obsolescence. While other legal instruments and self-regulatory measures, such as information disclosure and financial incentives, can encourage ecodesign solutions among producers, the ecodesign legal framework has distinct and irreplaceable advantages.[1222] On the environmental side, producers have no choice but to observe the mandatory ecodesign

1221 For further comments on this provision, see Chapter III, Section C on the UCPD, and more specifically n° 422.

1222 See in a concurring opinion, N. Sachs, 'Can we regulate our way to Energy Efficiency? Products standards as climate policy', 25 *Vanderbilt Law Review* (2012) p. 1631.

requirements as non-complying products could be banned from the EU market. Moreover, ecodesign requirements are tested and approved by official scientific methods and specifically adapted for the products concerned, which ensure that they enhance the protection of the environment with no or limited rebound effects. On the producer side, the Ecodesign Directive creates a level playing field where all producers – including those from outside the EU – are subject to the same rules. Consequently, producers are protected from competition from low-quality and inefficient imported products. Stringent ecodesign requirements are furthermore a potential source of competitive advantage, triggering quality products, innovation, energy and resource savings and new business models. Although some requirements might increase the costs for manufacturers in the short term, it makes a good return on investment in the longer term (i.e. less virgin material extracted, lower price volatilities and supply risks, less energy embedded, less waste generated). On the consumer side, ecodesign rules guarantee quality products with reliable and accessible information. Admittedly, consumers' freedom of choice is reduced by the fact that some products are phased out of the EU market.[1223] However, it is still possible for them to choose between a variety of best-performing products that correspond to their needs, including new technologies and models that were brought to the market following the adoption of ecodesign rules.[1224] Furthermore, rules banning non-eco-friendly products generally generate consumer savings, at least in the long term, as products are of better quality, more energy- and resource-efficient and have a longer lifespan.

309. Three types of recommendations – The contribution of the ecodesign rules in the fight against premature obsolescence could be even stronger. Three types of recommendations can be made to this end, following the structure of this chapter: recommendations (1) on the scope of the ecodesign legislation; (2) on ecodesign and information requirements contained in product-specific regulations; and (3) on the verification procedure and sanctions in case of non-compliance.

310. First: more products should be covered by ecodesign regulations – First of all, concerning the scope of the ecodesign legislation, more products should be covered by ecodesign requirements. It seems that market forces and external factors hinder the development of ecodesign for certain product categories, as shown by the recent product design trends.[1225] Public intervention

[1223] See in that regard examples of reactions to the ban on halogen lightbulbs: A. Nelsen, 'Europe to ban halogen lightbulbs', *The Guardian*, 23 August 2018, available on: <https://www.theguardian.com/environment/2018/aug/23/europe-to-ban-halogen-lightbulbs>.

[1224] D. Jepsen et al., *Delivering resource-efficient products – How Ecodesign can drive a circular economy in Europe* (European Environmental Bureau 2015) p. 57.

[1225] See *supra*, n° 165–167.

through ecodesign regulations seems necessary to shape the design of these products towards more sustainability and prevent their premature obsolescence. Otherwise, the absence of legislative measures may encourage the pursuit of business-as-usual and resistance to change, except in the case of ongoing or looming crises. Two kinds of measures should be taken in that regard. First, non-energy related products should be covered. This can be done either by an extension of the scope of the current Ecodesign Directive, as envisaged in the Proposal for a Sustainable Products Regulation, or by the adoption of a twin Directive for non-energy related products. Second, more implementing measures should be adopted, as is now also envisaged in the Proposal for a Sustainable Products Regulation. Product-specific requirements should be adopted for ICT products, software products, textiles and furniture. For the selection of these new product groups, it is recommended not to interpret the criteria set out in Article 15 of the Ecodesign Directive too strictly. In addition to these product-specific regulations, horizontal implementing measures on durability and on firmware and software should be envisaged. Further work and debate are already underway to include other products within this legal framework, with the question of whether ecodesign rules should be extended to all products. Meanwhile, voluntary agreements could be used to cover certain categories of non-energy-related products.

311. Second: ecodesign requirements should go beyond energy efficiency and cover product sustainability aspects – The development of requirements on sustainability aspects is still in its infancy. Admittedly, the focus on energy efficiency allows for a great reduction of the energy consumption of the covered products and, therefore, requirements on energy efficiency should still be developed. Nevertheless, the greater environmental impact of products is now shifting to resources and materials. Constant calls are being made to adopt a range of non-energy in use improvements. These calls should be heeded as only horizontal and product-specific ecodesign requirements on material and resource efficiency aspects will make a substantial contribution to prolonging the lifetime of consumer products. It is therefore time to devote effort to the development of such requirements, as the Commission stressed in its Proposal for a Sustainable Products Regulation. This chapter provided suggestions on improvements and possible future requirements on durability, reparability, upgradability, reuse, refurbishment and remanufacturing and on other sustainable aspects. Such requirements would prevent all types of premature obsolescence. For the development of these new requirements, inspiration could be drawn from existing legislation (e.g. on cars), self-regulatory measures (e.g. *The Blue Angel*) and private initiatives (e.g. *iFixit* reparability score).

312. Better sustainability information through digital product passports – In addition to ecodesign requirements, more product-specific information on product sustainability aspects should be made available to end-users, repairers, intermediaries, treatment facilities involved at the product end-of-life, but also to enforcement authorities. In this regard, further research is required to explore the adequacy of intellectual property rights (e.g. patents, design rights, trade secrets), and how they should be addressed in product regulations to foster product sustainability instead of hindering it. Digital product passports, which are among the key measures contained in Proposal for a Sustainable Products Regulation,[1226] could be used to enhance the disclosure of such information. These passports would complement information provided by product instruction and repair manuals and mandatory labels, such as those imposed by the Energy Labelling Regulation, which applies in parallel to the ecodesign legislation.[1227] Access to the pieces of information contained in the digital product passport would vary, depending on the target audience and based on access rights defined in each product regulation. Having access to such information, including through digital product passports, would help and encourage consumers to make sustainable choices, allow repairers and reuse centres to prolong product lifetime and enhance the enforcement of ecodesign requirements by the public authorities.

313. Third: the verification procedure and the sanctions should be more effective –Improvements are also desirable as regards the verification procedure and the sanctions imposed by national authorities. It is to be regretted that such measures are absent from the Proposal for a Sustainable Products Regulation as the enforcement of ecodesign rules is as crucial as their substance to ensure their effectiveness. Concerning the verification procedure, three recommendations can be made. First, an emphasis should be given to the implementation of self-monitoring and third-party auditing to ensure that products comply with these standards. Second, best practices established by Member States should be shared. Three, rapid screening methods should be implemented in cooperation with industry experts to detect non-compliant products. In addition to these policy recommendations, it should be noted that verification would be easier if more standards on material efficiency aspects were to be adopted. Concerning the sanctions in case of non-compliance, Member States currently enjoy a wide margin of discretion. It may be useful to establish criteria to be considered when imposing penalties. Such criteria would ensure a certain degree of effectiveness and consistency of the penalties imposed by the national authorities.

1226 Art. 8-13 of the Proposal for a Sustainable Products Regulation.

1227 For further information on the Energy Labelling Regulation and the delegated acts adopted on its basis, see Chapter III on the marketing and pre-contractual stage, and more specifically n° 512 *et seq*.

314. The legislative train is already on track – Many ideas that go in the same direction as these recommendations are already on the table. The EC has repeatedly underlined the substantial contribution of the Ecodesign Directive in the transition towards sustainable products, not only in its answers to parliamentary questions[1228], but also in its two action plans on circular economy.[1229] The importance of this legal instrument will grow as the EC committed to strive for more circular economy aspects in future product requirements under the Ecodesign Directive.[1230] In the Ecodesign Working Plan 2016–2019[1231], the EC indicated that it would explore the possibility of establishing more product-specific and/or horizontal requirements in areas such as durability, reparability, upgradeability, design for disassembly (e.g. easy removal of key components), information (e.g. marking of plastic parts) and ease of reuse and recycling (e.g. avoiding incompatible plastics) for existing and new products regulated under the Ecodesign Directive. The Ecodesign and Energy Labelling Working Plan 2022–2024 follow the same track.[1232] In addition to this working plan, the Sustainable Products Initiative is ongoing, as embodied by the Proposal for a Sustainable Products Regulation. Its aim is to revise the Ecodesign Directive and propose additional legislative measures to make products placed on the EU market more durable, reusable, repairable, recyclable, and energy-efficient for the benefit of consumers and the environment. This initiative goes

1228 See for ex. Answer of 16 February 2016 on planned obsolescence given by Mr Vella on behalf of the Commission, replying to parliamentary question E-015113/2015.

1229 Communication from the Commission to the European Parliament, the Council, the European Economic and Social Committee and the Committee of the Regions on Closing the loop – An EU action plan for the circular economy, COM(2015) 614 final, pp. 3–4; Communication from the Commission of 11 March 2020 to the European Parliament, the Council, the European Economic and Social Committee and the Committee of the Regions on A new Circular Economy Action Plan – For a cleaner and more competitive Europe, COM(2020) 98 final, pp. 4–5.

1230 See Annex to the first Circular Economy Action Plan, as well as the Report from the Commission of 26 January 2017 to the European Parliament, the Council, the European Economic and Social Committee and the Committee of the Regions on the implementation of the Circular Economy Action Plan, COM(2017) 33.

1231 Communication from the Commission of 30 November 2016 on Ecodesign Working Plan 2016–2019, COM(2016) 773 final.

1232 Communication from the Commission on the Ecodesign and Energy Labelling Working Plan 2022–2024, OJ C 182, 4.5.2022, p. 1–12. See also the preparatory study: Viegand Maagøe, VHK and Oeko-Institut, *Preparatory study for the Ecodesign and Energy Labelling Working Plan 2020–2024 – Task 1 Background, methodology and stakeholder consultation – Final* (European Commission 2021); Viegand Maagøe, VHK and Oeko-Institut, *Preparatory study for the Ecodesign and Energy Labelling Working Plan 2020–2024 – Task 2 Identification of product groups and horizontal initiatives – Final* (European Commission 2021); Viegand Maagøe, VHK and Oeko-Institut, *Preparatory study for the Ecodesign and Energy Labelling Working Plan 2020–2024 – Task 3 Preliminary analysis of product groups and horizontal initiatives – Final* (European Commission 2021); Viegand Maagøe, Oeko-Institut, VHK, *Preparatory study for the Ecodesign and Energy Labelling Working Plan 2020–2024 – Task 4 Complementary analyses and recommendations for the Ecodesign and Energy Labelling Working Plan 2020–2024 – Final* (European Commission 2021).

hand in hand with the Circular Electronics Initiative[1233] and the EU Strategy for Textiles.[1234]

315. One piece of the puzzle – Although the Ecodesign Directive has proven to be an effective tool towards ecodesigned and thus sustainable products, its effectiveness depends on synergies with other instruments. As rightly highlighted by the EP, the Ecodesign Directive is '*part of a larger toolbox*'.[1235] It is no alternative, but a complement to other legal instruments, such as the ones analysed in the following chapters of this book. If the focus was exclusively on ecodesign rules, there would be a risk of seeing the improvement achieved by these technical regulations partially offset by rebound mechanisms. Such mechanisms could consist of a reduced care by consumers, more confident of the stress resistance of their devices.[1236] However, as longer-lasting products often need more energy and resource input to be produced, their impacts on the environment would be much bigger if they were not bought or prematurely thrown away by consumers. It is thus of utmost importance to consider the whole puzzle of rules when dealing with premature obsolescence. Law makers should not only focus on products, but also on solutions to engage and address all stakeholders, including consumers, so that they all act responsibly at every stage of the product lifetime. The following chapters of this book provide some lines of thought concerning these other legal instruments and their articulation with ecodesign rules.

1233 The Circular Electronics Initiative was announced in the European Green Deal. See Communication from the Commission of 11 December 2019 to the European Parliament, the European Council, the Council, the European Economic and Social Committee and the Committee of the Regions on The European Green Deal, COM(2019) 640 final, p. 7. See also the Legislative Train Schedule issued by the EP, available on: <https://www.europarl.europa.eu/legislative-train/theme-a-european-green-deal/file-circular-electronics>.

1234 Communication from the Commission of 30 March 2022 to the European Parliament, the Council, the European Economic and Social Committee and the Committee of the Regions on the EU Strategy for Sustainable and Circular Textiles, COM(2022) 141 final.

1235 European Parliament Resolution of 31 May 2018 on the implementation of the Ecodesign Directive (2009/125/EC), (2017/2087(INI)), pt. 6.

1236 M. Cordella, F. Alfieri, J. Sanfelix, *Guidance for the Assessment of Material Efficiency: Application to Smartphones – JRC Technical Report* (European Commission 2020) p. 118.

CHAPTER III

THE MARKETING AND PRE-CONTRACTUAL STAGE: INCENTIVISING AND EMPOWERING CONSUMERS TO MAKE SUSTAINABLE CHOICES AT THE TIME OF PURCHASE

A. INTRODUCTION

316. Ecodesign rules are necessary, but not sufficient – While product lifetime can be prolonged at the design and production stage through ecodesign requirements imposed on producers, another important strategy consists in incentivising and empowering consumers to make sustainable choices at the time of purchase through the provision of product sustainability information. This strategy focuses on the information that is provided to consumers before they purchase a product. At this stage, product sustainability information includes information on product durability, upgradability and reparability. If well-informed, consumers may favour longer-lasting quality products over short-lived inferior products, repairable products over non-repairable products, etc. Providing information on product sustainability aspects to consumers can serve as a strong enabler of sustainable consumption. Labelling rules, pre-contractual information duties and other information law mechanisms can be valuable tools to curb premature obsolescence, defined in Chapter I as *"all practices that reduce product lifetime so that the product does not reach its optimal lifetime (from an environmental point of view), without it being the result of normal wear and tear"*.

317. The information paradigm is central in EU and national law – The rules regulating consumer information at the marketing and pre-contractual stage are scattered across four main EU instruments. There is, first, the Unfair Commercial Practices Directive ('UCPD')[1237], which contains informational duties and curbs a broad range of unfair commercial practices,

[1237] Directive 2005/29/EC of the European Parliament and of the Council of 11 May 2005 concerning unfair business-to-consumer commercial practices in the internal market and amending Council Directive 84/450/EEC, Directives 97/7/EC, 98/27/EC and 2002/65/EC

including untruthful information to consumers and aggressive marketing techniques to influence their choices. Second, pre-contractual information obligations are imposed by the Consumer Rights Directive ('CRD').[1238] The third major instrument is the Energy Labelling Regulation[1239], which requires the provision of product-specific information through a uniform label displayed on energy-related products at the point of sale. Finally, the EU Ecolabel Regulation[1240] establishes a voluntary label of environmental excellence that is awarded to the most environment-friendly products and services on the market. It is noteworthy that – on top of these four main instruments – other EU rules are also of particular relevance in encouraging and/or obliging businesses to inform consumers on products, including the rules on consumer sales[1241] and the product safety legislation.[1242] Beyond the implementation of the relevant EU rules, some Member States, including Belgium, France and Germany, have undertaken purely national initiatives to complement and reinforce information given to consumers.

318. Overview of the third chapter – The purpose of this chapter is threefold: first, to map the relevant rules dealing with information on product sustainability aspects provided to consumers; second, to evaluate the extent of the contribution of labelling rules, pre-contractual information duties and other information law mechanisms to foster sustainable consumption and combat premature obsolescence; and third, to investigate possible normative adjustments to the existing legal framework. The chapter will start by explaining the prominent role of consumer information, with a description of the different types of information, the role of consumer information in tackling premature obsolescence, the barriers that may impede consumers' sustainable choices, and the various challenges that law makers face when imposing information requirements and/or monitoring the voluntary provision of information by

of the European Parliament and of the Council and Regulation (EC) No 2006/2004 of the European Parliament and of the Council, OJ L 149, 11.6.2005, p. 22–39.

1238 Directive 2011/83/EU of the European Parliament and of the Council of 25 October 2011 on consumer rights, amending Council Directive 93/13/EEC and Directive 1999/44/EC of the European Parliament and of the Council and repealing Council Directive 85/577/EEC and Directive 97/7/EC of the European Parliament and of the Council, OJ L 304, 22.11.2011, p. 64–88.

1239 Regulation (EU) 2017/1369 of the European Parliament and of the Council of 4 July 2017 setting a framework for energy labelling and repealing Directive 2010/30/EU, OJ L 198, 28.7.2017, p. 1–23.

1240 Regulation (EC) No 66/2010 of the European Parliament and of the Council of 25 November 2009 on the EU Ecolabel, OJ L 27, 30.1.2010, p. 1–19.

1241 See Chapter IV on the use stage.

1242 The product safety legislation includes the Product Safety Directive (2001/95/EC), but also product-specific legislation, such as the Regulation on cosmetic products ((EC) No 1223/2009) and the Directive on pyrotechnic articles (2013/29/EU). This legislation falls however outside the scope of this book, as previously explained (n° 42).

market participants. This first section will be followed by an in-depth analysis of the most relevant EU and national consumer information rules concerning product sustainability. The relevant provisions will be described and evaluated from a sustainability perspective, taking recent developments and proposals into account. Alongside the analysis of these EU and national rules, policy recommendations will be made.

B. MAPPING KEY ELEMENTS OF PRODUCT SUSTAINABILITY INFORMATION

1. DIFFERENT TYPES OF INFORMATION ON PRODUCT SUSTAINABILITY

319. A PROFUSION OF INFORMATION, INCLUDING ON PRODUCT SUSTAINABILITY – Nowadays, consumers are faced with a profusion of information at the point of sale, lining shelves or available online.[1243] Some of this information relates to product sustainability aspects. The disclosure of some items at the marketing stage is imposed by EU and national rules. In addition, more and more businesses and other operators decide to go beyond mandatory information requirements and voluntarily provide additional information on their products, including on environmental aspects.[1244] For example, five of Europe's leading telecommunication network operators recently launched a new pan-industry eco-rating labelling scheme for mobile phones, which assesses devices' different environmental indicators (e.g. carbon footprint or resource depletion) and material efficiency criteria.[1245] To assert their claims, businesses can decide to apply for an ecolabel awarded by an independent third party. They can also make green claims outside the framework of ecolabels.[1246] Some brands have even developed their own label.[1247] Rating schemes have also been developed by other actors.[1248] Beyond the marketing stage, consumers can also get information on

1243 G.P. Gruere, 'An analysis of the growth in environmental labelling and information schemes', 38 *J. Consum. Policy* (2015) p. 1 at p. 18.

1244 It is staggering to note that there are currently 456 voluntary environmental labels worldwide (see <www.ecolabelindex.com/>, visited on 1st October 2020) and even more environmental claims.

1245 See <https://www.ecoratingdevices.com/>.

1246 See for ex. the environmental impact assessments published by Apple for its main products (<https://www.apple.com/environment/>), the product environmental reports issued by Google (<https://store.google.com/gb/magazine/sustainability>) and the product eco profiles made by Microsoft (<https://www.microsoft.com/en-us/download/details.aspx?id=55974>).

1247 See for ex. the French brand SEB, one of the leaders of household appliances manufacture, which launched a logo stating that the product will be repairable for ten years. For further details, see: <https://www.seb.fr/produits-reparables>.

1248 See for ex. the standalone consumer technology reviews written by S. Gibbs, consumer technology editor of *The Guardian*, available on: <https://www.theguardian.com/profile/

their products at the pre-contractual stage. Retailers occupy a key position at both stages as they can inform consumers about the products on their shelves and provide them with contact points if further information is needed.[1249]

320. 'Product sustainability information' – what's in a name? – Building on the definition of 'product sustainability' in Chapter I[1250], 'product sustainability information' is defined as "*information relating to the ability of a product to reach its optimal lifetime*". Information on product sustainability at the time of purchase translates into three main categories of information, which correspond to the three strategies to resist, postpone and reverse premature obsolescence.[1251] These items of information allow consumers to get an idea of how long they can expect the product to last.

321. Information on durability (resisting premature obsolescence) – The first category is information that gives an indication of the (physical) durability of the product prior to purchase. As was defined in the first chapter of this book, 'product durability' is the "*ability to function as required, under defined conditions of use, maintenance and repair, until a limiting state is reached*".[1252] Consequently, information on product durability encompasses information on the average or minimum lifespan (e.g. expected lifespan of the product or its key components), the existence of commercial guarantees, the risks of early failures, the availability of software and firmware updates and the overall support period, as well as information on product interoperability and compatibility with other versions of accessories and updates.

322. Information on maintenance and upgradability (postponing premature obsolescence) – Second, in addition to information on durability, consumers can be incentivised and empowered to make sustainable choices through the provision of information on maintenance and upgradability. The availability of maintenance instructions can help consumers lengthen the lifespan of the product. Information on product upgradability and, for products with digital content, on software upgrades can influence consumers towards sustainable goods. Such information can consist of information on how long, what frequency and under which conditions (e.g. price) the good will receive software updates to guarantee its appropriate and safe functioning.

---

samuel-gibbs+tone/reviews>. See also the comparators and calculators established by the Belgian consumer organisation *Test-Achats*, available on: <https://www.test-achats.be/explorer?type=comparators-and-calculators>.

1249 For more information on the key role played by retailers in sustainable consumption, see International Trade Centre, *The European Union Market for Sustainable Products – The retail perspective on sourcing policies and consumer demand* (ITC and European Commission 2019).

1250 See *infra*, n° 93.

1251 See Section D of Chapter I on the strategies against premature obsolescence, and more specifically n° 141.

1252 See *infra*, n° 144.

323. Information on reparability, refurbishment and remanufacturing (reversing premature obsolescence) – The third category of information that signals the sustainable nature of products encompasses information on their reparability and/or refurbished or remanufactured nature. Information on reparability relates to the availability of spare parts, like how long spare parts will be available after purchase, the maximum number of days that it will take to deliver spare parts and the maximum price of spare parts. It also includes information on available (recommended) repair service (e.g. website or phone number) in the specific country or region. Moreover, it can be useful for consumers to have access to all necessary details concerning repair, like repair manuals and instructions, information on product disassembly as well as on the type of and access to repair tools, to ensure good maintenance by consumers and to facilitate self-repair when possible.

324. Various forms possible – Information on product sustainability can be conveyed through different vehicles of communication, depending on whether the pieces of information are given separately to consumers or serve as qualitative and quantitative parameters for an index on the sustainable aspects. As rightly explained by the OECD Committee on Consumer Policy, "*[e]nvironmental claims can appear on a label, on product packaging, in related literature or advertising material, as well as in promotional and point-of-sales material, and other forms of marketing. Claims can take the form of words, symbols, emblems, logos, graphics, colours and product brand names. They can be transmitted through the written media, including newspapers and magazines, electronic media such as television and radio, and digital media such as the internet*".[1253] Other information on products can be found in technical documents, product documentation, like user or repair manuals (available online or in physical form with the product), websites, databases, QR codes, declarations and information materials.

2. BARRIERS THAT HAMPER THE TRANSITION TOWARDS SUSTAINABLE CONSUMPTION PATTERNS

325. Several barriers to consumers' sustainable choice – Despite the information already made available to consumers and their willingness to engage in sustainable consumption[1254], it has been shown that their environmental

1253 OECD, *Environmental Claims – Findings and Conclusions of the OECD Committee on Consumer Policy* (2011) p. 3.

1254 See for ex. The Gallup Organisation, *Flash Eurobarometer 256 – Europeans' attitudes towards the issue of sustainable consumption and production* (European Commission 2009); TNS political & social, *Flash Eurobarometer 367 – Attitudes of Europeans towards building the*

concerns are not always reflected in their consumption behaviour.[1255] Several barriers impede consumer eco-friendly behaviour at the time of purchase.[1256] Besides barriers relating to the limited availability of sustainable products[1257] and product prices[1258], others relate to the (non-)disclosure and processing of information, as described already to some extent in the first chapter of this book.[1259]

326. Barriers due to information asymmetries – Some barriers are linked to the asymmetries of information between consumers and businesses concerning the attributes of products. There is, first of all, a lack of (reliable and relevant) information on (certain aspects of) product sustainability. Proxy indicators, such as the product's physical characteristics, price and brand, do not help overcome information gaps as they do not necessarily indicate that the product is sustainable. Secondly, when information is provided, consumers have to contend with commercial practices that create confusion and misinformation, fuel mistrust and dampen their interest in buying sustainable goods. Other practices create the desire for novelty in consumers' minds. These practices are due to the fact that businesses are not incentivised to provide information on their products.[1260]

327. Barriers linked to consumer psychology – Finally, the provision of relevant, reliable, comparable and verifiable information does not necessarily lead consumers to change their attitudes, and even when it does, the change does not always translate into sustainable behaviour change. This is due to diverse biases and preferences that influence consumer behaviour, even when well-informed. Other side-effects of information disclosure may create barriers. For example, labels indicating the expected or minimum lifetime of products could result in a slower decrease of the value of the product in consumers' minds and

---

single market for green products (European Commission 2013); TNS political & social, *Special Eurobarometer 468 – Attitudes of European citizens towards the environment* (European Commission 2017); Kantar, *Special Eurobarometer 501 – Attitudes of European citizens towards the Environment* (European Commission 2020).

1255 See LE Europe, VVA Europe, Ipsos, ConPolicy, Trinomics, *Behavioural study on consumers' engagement in the circular economy* (European Commission 2018); K.A. Whalen, 'Three circular business models that extend product value and their contribution to resource efficiency', 226 *J. Clean. Prod.* (2019) p. 1128 at p. 1137.

1256 See also B. Keirsbilck, S. Rousseau, 'The Marketing Stage: Fostering Sustainable Consumption Choices in a "Circular" and "Functional" Economy', in B. Keirsbilck, E. Terryn (eds.), *Consumer Protection in a Circular Economy* (Intersentia 2019) p. 93 at p. 126.

1257 See *supra*, n° 124 *et seq.*

1258 Externalities are not necessarily reflected in market prices (see n° 138). In this regard, fiscal measures could incentivise consumers to take sustainable aspects into due consideration and base their consumption decisions on long-term costs.

1259 See *supra* on the causes of premature obsolescence, and more specifically n° 133–138.

1260 See *supra*, n° 129.

thus to its psychological obsolescence. Once the indicated period has elapsed, consumers could become negligent in the way they look after their products or even decide to dispose of them prematurely if the defects are deemed too substantial.[1261]

328. The negative impacts of these barriers on product lifetime – All in all, these barriers have negative consequences on the transition towards more sustainable consumption patterns and consequently on product lifetime. As the EC highlighted in its 2015 Action Plan, "*the choices made by millions of consumers can support or hamper the circular economy.*[1262] The lack of information and trust, misinformation and confusion, combined with behavioural biases and consumers' preferences, may result in consumers impulsively buying products that are of low quality. Consequently, there may not be sufficient incentives for traders to communicate the quality standards of their products[1263], or worse, to provide sustainable goods at all.

3. TACKLING PREMATURE OBSOLESCENCE THROUGH CONSUMER INFORMATION

329. Consumer information on product sustainability as a remedy against premature obsolescence – As already mentioned, providing information on product sustainability aspects to consumers can serve as a strong enabler of sustainable consumption and help tackle premature obsolescence. However, it is important to note that the mandatory or voluntary provision of information on product sustainability does not only influence consumer behaviour but indirectly also business practices.[1264] Both aspects will be discussed hereafter.

330. Fostering sustainable consumption choices – On the consumer side, information disclosure has three main impacts. The presence of reliable, comparable and verifiable information on products' environmental aspects can, first, steer consumer purchasing choices in favour of sustainable products, facilitating the transition towards a more environmental-friendly

1261 See also C. Bakker, C. Schuit, *The long view – Exploring product lifetime extension* (United Nations Environment Programme 2017) p. 45.

1262 Communication from the Commission of 2 December 2015 to the European Parliament, the Council, the European Economic and Social Committee and the Committee of the Regions on Closing the loop – EU action plan for circular economy, COM(2015) 614 final, p. 6.

1263 C. Twigg-Flesner, *Consumer Product Guarantees* (Routledge 2016) p. 55.

1264 See also B. Keirsbilck, E. Terryn, 'Informatieverplichtingen in het consumenten- en ondernemingsrecht', in *Informatie en recht* (Intersentia 2021) p. 117 at p. 163, and more specifically p. 119 at p. 122.

lifestyle.[1265] Giving consumers access to such information enables them to make sustainable choices and enhances their trust. Indeed, consumers can only take informed, autonomous and responsible decisions if they are aware which products are ecodesigned and sustainable and if they are reassured about their quality, especially concerning second-hand, refurbished and remanufactured goods.[1266] Bringing such information to the consumers' attention can induce them to purchase sustainable goods. Studies have shown that sustainability is generally not a front-of-mind issue for consumers.[1267] The disclosure of reliable, comparable and verifiable information on the environmental impacts and characteristics of products triggers sustainable consumer behaviour at the time of purchase, as demonstrated by the literature review, stakeholder interviews and behavioural experiments.[1268] Similar findings on the effects of information on consumer behaviour have been observed online.[1269] The findings of these studies are sometimes less marked, but in general, it has been observed that this information has an influence on purchasing decisions and perceived quality in favour of products with longer lifespans.

331. Combating psychological obsolescence – Second, consumer information contributes to sustainable consumption by slowing down the consumption pace and preventing impulsive purchases. Some advertising and marketing strategies encourage consumers to buy low-quality, short-lived, single-use and unnecessary products and/or prematurely replace their products with brand new ones.[1270] Through these strategies, companies strive to maintain high rates of sales growth.[1271] Marketing and promotional strategies

---

1265 K. Tonner, 'Sustainable consumption, consumer policy and the law', in C. Verdure (ed.), *Environmental law and consumer protection* (Larcier 2011) p. 15.

1266 D. Guiot, D. Roux, 'A second-hand shoppers' motivation scale: Antecedents, consequences, and implications for retailers', 86 *Journal of Retailing* (2010) p. 368.

1267 T. Knight et al. (Brook Lyndhurst), *Electrical and electronic product design: product lifetime* (WRAP 2013).

1268 See for ex. SIRCOME agency, the University of South Brittany and the University of South Bohemia, *The Influence of Lifespan Labelling on Consumers – ILLC study* (EESC 2016); GfK Belgium, *Consumer market study to support the fitness check of EU consumer and marketing law* (European Commission 2017) p. 416 *et seq.*; LE Europe, VVA Europe, Ipsos, ConPolicy, Trinomics, *Behavioural study on consumers' engagement in the circular economy* (European Commission 2018); V. Swaen, *Labelling the durability/reparability of a product* (EESC Conference on Tackling premature obsolescence in Europe 2018); L. Ackermann, R. Mugge, J. Schoormans, 'Consumers' perspective on product care: An exploratory study of motivators, ability factors, and triggers', 183 *J. Clean. Prod.* (2018) p. 388.

1269 Ecorys, GFK and Tilburg University, *Study on the effects on consumer behaviour of online sustainability information displays – Final report* (Consumer Programme 2014) p. 93.

1270 Such cases of psychological obsolescence have been identified for vacuum cleaners. See L. Harmer, T. Cooper, T. Fisher, G. Salvia, C. Barr, 'The joy of vacuuming? How the user experience affects vacuum cleaner longevity', in T. Cooper, N. Braithwaite, M. Moreno and G. Salvia (eds.), *Product Lifetimes and the Environment (PLATE) Conference proceedings* (Nottingham Trent University: CADBE 2015) p. 138 at p. 145.

1271 See *supra*, n° 133.

can heighten the value of the new product, which can lead consumers to decide that the relative value of the new product in comparison to the owned product is worth the financial investment, resulting in replacement.[1272] By prohibiting and sanctioning certain claims and practices, the legislation on consumer information combats and prevents these cases of psychological obsolescence.[1273]

332. Fostering sustainable use and disposal of products – Third, the provision of information on product sustainability at the marketing and pre-contractual stage may influence consumers' behaviour at the later stages of product lifetime. If well-informed, consumers may better take care of their products and repair them (more easily) when needed, which would consequently mitigate certain causes of premature obsolescence.[1274] Some information may also encourage consumers to enable their obsolete products to enter the reuse or waste stream.[1275]

333. Rewarding and encouraging the production and promotion of sustainable goods – More than influencing consumer behaviour, a more indirect impact that is often overlooked is the one on business practices. Information requirements on product sustainability also provide incentives to businesses to consider these features when designing and marketing products.[1276] First, it throws a spotlight on sustainable products and thus rewards businesses that design, produce, import and sell them. Second, it encourages other businesses, for who product sustainability is (still) not a priority, to bring sustainable aspects of their products to the fore. Generally, businesses prefer devoting their efforts on other features, such as production costs, visual appearance, performance, except if there is a competitive advantage to focus on product durability and reparability.[1277] If they are forced to give information on aspects relating to the sustainability of their products though, businesses will do their best to improve these aspects so that their image and reputation

---

1272 R. Van den Berg, L. Magnier, and R. Mugge, 'Too good to go? Consumers' replacement behaviour and potential strategies for stimulating product retention', 39 *Current opinion in psychology* (2021) p. 67.

1273 A fuller discussion of how helpful legislation can be to tackle psychological obsolescence is provided in the section dedicated to the UCPD (n° 340 *et seq.*).

1274 See *supra*, n° 149–151.

1275 K. Kianpour, A. Jusoh, A. Mardani, D. Streimikiene, F. Cavallaro, K. Md. Nor, E. Kazimieras Zavadskas, 'Factors Influencing Consumers' Intention to Return the End of Life Electronic Products through Reverse Supply Chain Management for Reuse, Repair and Recycling', 9 *Sustainability* (2017) p. 1657 at p. 1680.

1276 See G. Loewenstein, C. R. Sunstein, R. Golman, 'Disclosure: Psychology Changes Everything', 6 *Annual Review of Economic* (2014) p. 391 at p. 419; O. Bar-Gill, D. Schkade, C. R. Sunstein, 'Drawing false inferences from mandated disclosures', 3 *Behavioural Public Policy* (2018) p. 209 at p. 227.

1277 E. Maitre-Ekern, C. Dalhammar, 'Towards a hierarchy of consumption behaviour in the circular economy', 26 *Maastricht Journal of European and Comparative Law* (2019) p. 415.

are not harmed in the eyes of the public. In other words, the disclosure makes information salient and consequently elevates sustainability to a dimension in which businesses can compete. It then becomes a 'competition' parameter, just like price. Hence, even in the event that the direct impact of information disclosure on consumer decision-making is not tremendous[1278], information requirements remain valuable in the promotion of more sustainable goods for this influence on businesses.

334. A LIGHTENED BURDEN OF PROOF IN CASE OF PREMATURE OBSOLESCENCE – In addition to these important effects, another major added value of information availability is that it may lighten the burden of proof in cases of premature obsolescence. Information obligations can determine liability under eventually concluded contracts. Information given by the seller can qualify as a subjective conformity requirement under Article 6 of the SGD, while information communicated by producers can qualify as public statements by supply chain actors according to Article 7(1)(d) of the same Directive. If the product does not correspond to the information provided, consumers and public authorities can more easily demonstrate the lack of conformity.[1279] It will also be easier for them to invoke Articles 6, 7 and 12 of the UCPD and prove misleading practices such as those limiting product lifetime if the product does not reach the lifetime indicated by the trader at the marketing and/or pre-contractual stage(s).[1280] This is to be welcomed as adducing evidence of the shortened product lifetime can be particularly difficult.

4. THE CHALLENGES OF CONSUMER INFORMATION

335. FOUR MAIN CHALLENGES – Before analysing the relevant EU and national consumer information rules, it is noteworthy to mention four of the major challenges that policymakers face when regulating product sustainability information. Among these challenges, there is (1) the need to adapt information to the types of products as well as (2) to the target audience, (3) to acknowledge the various consumer profiles and (4) to avoid the risks of information overload. These challenges interact with each other, meaning that, for example, trade-offs concerning the risks of information overload may be different depending on the product group or the consumer profile.

1278 Information requirements do not automatically lead to more sustainable consumption patterns, especially due to behavioural biases, attitudes and preferences on the consumer side. See *infra* on the barriers to sustainable choice (n° 346) as well as *supra* on the causes of premature obsolescence (n° 145–148).

1279 See Chapter IV on the use stage, and more specifically n° 692 and n° 702.

1280 See *infra*, n° 394 *et seq*.

336. First: a diversity of products – Empirical studies have revealed that the degree of influence of durability and reparability information on consumer purchasing decisions vary depending on the type of product.[1281] This stems from the fact that consumers think differently about diverse categories of consumer goods.[1282] In this regard, reference can be made to the three categories of products identified by DEFRA, namely workhorse, up-to-date and investment products.[1283] For example, information on durability may be less relevant – and thus consumers may not pay attention to such information – when purchasing up-to-date products, by contrast with workhorse and investment products. Along the same lines, while the provision of information on product sustainable aspects generally induces consumer sustainable behaviour, effects of certain information may be stronger for certain product categories. For instance, the presence of durability information increases the choice for products with high durability more for washing machines than for televisions.[1284]

337. Second: the target audience – Information requirements must also be adopted taking the target audience into account. Not only the content but also the methods, timing and location of the information provided are essential. Compared to information useful for professionals (e.g. sellers, repairers or recyclers) and market surveillance authorities[1285], consumer information must meet specific characteristics. As regards content, the important points are simplicity, clarity and comparability in the label design.[1286] Symbols may be used to replace or support the use of long and complex texts, global aggregated notes that allow for easy comparison amongst products, as well as ranking systems with colours and letters to facilitate quicker understanding of the information.[1287] As regards the methods to measure and assess product sustainability aspects, the workability and veracity of parameters play a crucial role, especially for the credibility of the information conveyed.[1288] In this regard,

---

1281 See e.g. SIRCOME agency, the University of South Brittany and the University of South Bohemia, *The Influence of Lifespan Labelling on Consumers – ULC study* (EESC 2016) pp. 84–85.

1282 BIO Intelligence Service, *Study on different options for communicating environmental information for products – Final report* (European Commission 2012).

1283 Brook Lyndhurst, *Public understanding of product lifetimes and durability* (DEFRA 2011). See also J. Cox et al., 'Consumer understanding of product lifetimes', 79 *Resources, Conservation and Recycling* (2013).

1284 GfK Belgium, *Consumer market study to support the fitness check of EU consumer and marketing law* (European Commission 2017) p. 431.

1285 Ecodesign regulations impose the disclosure of some of these pieces of information to professionals and market surveillance authorities. See Chapter II on the design and production stage.

1286 E. Molenbroek et al., *Evaluation of the Energy Labelling Directive and specific aspects of the Ecodesign Directive – Final technical report* (Ecofys 2014) p. 87.

1287 BIO Intelligence Service, *Study on different options for communicating environmental information for products – Final report* (European Commission 2012).

1288 *Ibid.*

consumers prefer information verified by an independent party.[1289] As regards the most suitable timing and location, it depends on the information addressed to consumers, although it should, in any case, be visible, readable and easily accessible at the consumers' point of decision.[1290] Information that is intended to support consumers in a purchasing decision is best placed close to the exhibited product, meaning in locations where consumers collect information about products, such as on websites or at point of sale (e.g. on the product or shelf). Smartphones and websites can be useful places to present supporting information (e.g. methodology used, explanation of the indicators), that would seek to increase consumer understanding and trust in the label.[1291] Maintenance and repair information for consumers could be made available on designated websites or in the product documentation.[1292] In this regard, digitalisation offers opportunities to improve the accessibility of product information so that consumers can get access to it at any time.

338. Third: a diversity of consumer profiles – The third challenge relates to consumers themselves. The difficulty stems from the diversity of consumer profiles, which can vary depending on personal and social/situational characteristics.[1293] Some consumers are more aware of and receptive to environmental considerations than others when making decisions. In other words, the extent of the effects of labels – and other environmental claims – on consumer behaviour depends on consumer profile.[1294] To deal with all these profiles when drafting and applying protective rules, the 'average consumer' has been used as the yardstick of the rational consumer. This European standard corresponds to "*a reasonably well informed and reasonably observant and circumspect consumer, taking into account social, cultural and linguistic*

1289 R.E. Horne, 'Limits to labels: The role of eco-labels in the assessment of product sustainability and routes to sustainable consumption', 33 *International Journal of Consumer Studies* (2009) p. 175 at p. 182; BIO Intelligence Service, *Study on different options for communicating environmental information for products – Final report* (European Commission 2012) pp. 19–20.

1290 See CEN-CENELEC TC10, Methods for providing information relating to material efficiency aspects of energy-related products, EN 45559:2019, available on: <https://www.cenelec.eu/dyn/www/f?p=104:110:861514833540201::::FSP_ORG_ID,FSP_PROJECT,FSP_LANG_ID:2240017,65688,25>; BIO Intelligence Service, *Study on different options for communicating environmental information for products – Final report* (European Commission 2012) p. 38.

1291 BIO Intelligence Service, *Study on different options for communicating environmental information for products – Final report* (European Commission 2012) pp. 38–39.

1292 By contrast, information for professionals might be best provided through databases, websites or upon request.

1293 S. Evans, T. Cooper, 'Consumer influences on product life-spans', in T. Cooper, *Longer lasting products: Alternatives to the throwaway society* (Gower 2010) p. 330 at p. 337. See also A. Girard et al., 'Obsolescence of Home Appliances and Electronics: What Is the Role of the Consumer?', *Équiterre* (2018) p. 20 at p. 26.

1294 SIRCOME agency, the University of South Brittany and the University of South Bohemia, *The Influence of Lifespan Labelling on Consumers – ILLC study* (EESC 2016) pp. 85–86.

factors".[1295] This consumer standard is, however, increasingly criticised as being unrealistically high and not corresponding to reality.[1296]

339. Fourth: the risks of information overload – The fourth major challenge concerns the risks of information overload through additional mandatory information. It is well known that consumers can become easily confused by the amount and diversity of information.[1297] Consequently, adopting additional information requirements entails the risk of disinforming consumers rather than informing them. This is why mandatory disclosure of information, regardless of the field of law, has increasingly become the subject of criticism.[1298] There is general agreement in the research literature and among stakeholders on the need to display a reasonable amount of information.[1299] If extra information requirements were disclosed, it should not dilute existing information and should be beneficial for consumers, while avoiding an overload of information. Therefore, a balancing exercise has to be carried out before adopting information requirements. In that respect, there is a need for more consumer research to determine and optimise trade-offs and properly assess the effectiveness of the information disclosure. Inspiration could be drawn from the financial services and e-commerce sectors, where the legislature is experimenting with different forms of summary disclosures.[1300]

1295 See ECJ 16 July 1998, Case C-210/96, *Gut Springenheide and Tusky* v *Oberkreisdirektor des Kreises Steinfurt, EU:C:1998:369*, para 31; ECJ 13 January 2000, Case C-220/98, *Estée Lauder, EU:C:2000:8*, para 29. See also recital 18 UCPD.

1296 See for ex. G. Howells, 'The Potential and Limits of Consumer Empowerment by Information', 32 *Journal of law and society* (2005) p. 358 at p. 362; A.-L. Sibony, 'Can EU consumer law benefit from behavioural insights? An analysis of the unfair practices directive', 22 *E.R.P.L.* (2014) p. 901 at p. 942; B. Duivenvoorde, *The Consumer Benchmarks in the Unfair Commercial Practices Directive* (Springer 2015); T. Piazzon, 'L'information et la désinformation des consommateurs: Rapport français', in G. Straetmans (ed.), *Information Obligations and Disinformation of Consumers* (Springer International Publishing 2019) p. 157 at p. 204; K.P. Purnhagen, H. Schebesta, 'Island or Ocean: Empirical Evidence on the Average Consumer Concept in the UCPD', 28 *E.R.P.L.* (2020) p. 293 at p. 310.

1297 See for ex. G.A. Miller, 'The magical number seven, plus or minus two: Some limits on our capacity for processing information', 63 *Psychological Review* (1956) p. 81 at p. 97; J. Salzman, 'Informing the green consumer. The debate over the use and abuse of environmental labels', 1 *Journal of Industrial Ecology* (1997) p. 11 at p. 21.

1298 See for ex. B Wendlandt, 'EC Directives for Self-Employed Commercial Agents and on Time-Sharing and for self-employed commercial agents – Apples, Oranges and the Core of the Information Overload Problem', in G. Howells, A. Janssen, R. Schulze (eds.), *Information Rights and Obligations: A Challenge for Party Autonomy and Transactional Fairness* (Ashgate 2005) p. 67 at p. 92.

1299 For an in-depth and comparative analysis, see G. Straetmans, *Information Obligations and Disinformation of Consumers* (Springer International Publishing 2019). Concerning the stakeholders' opinion, see E. Molenbroek et al., *Evaluation of the Energy Labelling Directive and specific aspects of the Ecodesign Directive – Final technical report* (Ecofys 2014) p. 99.

1300 G. Straetmans, *Information Obligations and Disinformation of Consumers* (Springer International Publishing 2019) p. 447 *et seq.*

C. THE LEGISLATION ON UNFAIR COMMERCIAL PRACTICES

1. A THREE-TIERED 'CASCADE SYSTEM' THAT PROHIBITS UNFAIR COMMERCIAL PRACTICES

340. The Unfair Commercial Practices Directive – The Unfair Commercial Practices Directive ('UCPD')[1301] establishes a regulatory framework that prohibits unfair business-to-consumer commercial practices, thereby harmonising a previously fragmented field of law. The goal of this Directive is twofold, as reflected in its Article 1. It aims to promote and maintain the smooth functioning of the EU market while achieving a high level of consumer protection. Such a combination is not surprising as rules protecting consumers enhance their trust in the internal market, which in turn is expected to be an important factor for the completion and smooth functioning of the internal market.[1302] In this Directive, the protective purpose consists in strengthening freedom of decision-making, market transparency and information.[1303] When consumers face unfair practices affecting the protection conferred by this legislation, they can rely on its provisions against the concerned trader. Such legislation also has positive repercussions on legitimate competitors who are indirectly protected and further encouraged to adopt fair behaviour, which includes producing and promoting sustainable goods.[1304] The provisions of the UCPD are currently under review within the framework of its initiative 'Empowering the consumer for the green transition', with a view to strengthening the role of this legislation in the transition towards more sustainable production and consumption patterns.[1305]

1301 Directive 2005/29/EC of the European Parliament and of the Council of 11 May 2005 concerning unfair business-to-consumer commercial practices in the internal market and amending Council Directive 84/450/EEC, Directives 97/7/EC, 98/27/EC and 2002/65/EC of the European Parliament and of the Council and Regulation (EC) No 2006/2004 of the European Parliament and of the Council, OJ L 149, 11.6.2005, p. 22–39 (hereafter 'UCPD').

1302 B. Keirsbilck, *The new European law of unfair commercial practices and competition law* (Hart Publishing, 2011) p. 107.

1303 H.-W. Micklitz, 'Unfair commercial practices and misleading advertising', in N. Reich et al. (eds.), *European Consumer Law – Ius Commutatis V* (Intersentia 2014) pp. 77–78.

1304 Recital 6 UCPD.

1305 See Inception impact assessment from the European Commission of 23 June 2020 on Empowering the consumer for the green transition, Ares(2020)3256804. See also the Proposal for a Directive of the European Parliament and of the Council amending Directives 2005/29/EC and 2011/83/EU as regards empowering consumers for the green transition through better protection against unfair practices and better information, COM(2022) 143 final (hereafter 'Proposal for a Directive on empowering consumers for the green transition'), and more specifically Article 1.

341. The three-tiered 'cascade system' – To determine the unfairness of a practice, Article 5 of the UCPD establishes a three-tiered 'cascade system'.[1306] Firstly, the practice is deemed unfair if it corresponds to one of the 35 practices mentioned in Annex I of the Directive.[1307] Those practices are *per se* unfair, meaning that they are prohibited in all circumstances, without any further examination. If the practice is not included in this blacklist, the second step consists in checking whether it constitutes a misleading or aggressive practice as defined in Articles 6 to 9 of the UCPD ('small general clauses'). A practice that does not fulfil any of these previous tests can still be considered unfair through the definition given by Article 5(2) of the Directive ('grand general clause'), provided that (1) it is contrary to the requirements of professional diligence and (2) it materially distorts or is likely to materially distort the economic behaviour of the average consumer. The practice at hand will be prohibited if it fulfils one of these tests.[1308] The small general clauses are the most relevant provisions of the UCPD for combating premature obsolescence as they contain and reinforce information obligations on product sustainability, ban some practices that accelerate product replacement and help ensure that traders do not present green claims in ways that are unfair to consumers ('greenwashing').

342. Belgian implementing provisions – The Belgian legislature has scattered the provisions implementing the UCPD across the different books of the Economic Law Code (*Code de droit économique*). Book I contains general definitions of legal concepts of economic law in Article I.1, as well as definitions specific to the legislation on unfair commercial practices in Article I.8. The core provisions can be found in Article VI.92 to Article VI.103 of the Economic Law Code, which transpose the UCPD provisions with their exact wording.[1309] The

1306 These three degrees of unfairness are perfectly illustrated by the flowchart contained in the Commission Guidance on the UCPD. See Commission Notice of 17 December 2021 on Guidance on the interpretation and application of Directive 2005/29/EC of the European Parliament and of the Council concerning unfair business-to-consumer commercial practices in the internal market (hereafter 'UCPD Guidance'), p. 26. See also Opinion of Advocate General Trstenjak, delivered on 21 October 2008 in Joined Cases VTB-VAB, C-261/07 and C-299/07, *EU:C:2008:581*, pt. 79.

1307 It should be noted that the list of practices contained in Annex I to the UCPD was amended in 2019 to include 4 new practices. See Art. 3 of the Directive (EU) 2019/2161 of the European Parliament and of the Council of 27 November 2019 amending Council Directive 93/13/EEC and Directives 98/6/EC, 2005/29/EC and 2011/83/EU of the European Parliament and of the Council as regards the better enforcement and modernisation of Union consumer protection rules, OJ L 328, 18.12.2019, p. 7–28 (hereafter 'Enforcement and Modernisation Directive').

1308 For further explanation, see J. Goddaer and E. Terryn, 'Unfair commercial practices in B2C relations', in G. Straetmans and J. Stuyck (eds.), *Commercial Practices* (Larcier 2014) p. 48 at p. 50.

1309 Loi du 21 décembre 2013 portant insertion du Livre VI "Pratiques du marché et protection du consommateur" dans le Code de droit économique et portant insertion des définitions propres au Livre VI, et des dispositions d'application au Livre VI, dans les Livres Ier et XV du Code de droit économique, *M.B.*, 30 décembre 2013, p. 103506.

associated sanctions are detailed in Book XV of the Economic Law Code, and more specifically in Article XV.83 to Article XV.86.

343. French implementing provisions – Since the re-codification of the French Consumer Code in 2016[1310], the provisions related to unfair commercial practices can be found in Articles L. 120–1 to L. 122–23 of the Consumer Code (*Code de la consommation*).[1311] Sanctions are regulated under Articles L. 132–1 to L. 132–28, in accordance with the general structure of the Consumer Code.[1312] In addition to these provisions, other unfair commercial practices are banned under French law. These prohibitions can be found in other sections of the French Consumer Code, like the prohibition of 'planned obsolescence' established under Article L. 441–2, as well as in the French Environmental Code (*Code de l'environnement*), which for example forbids any advertising or commercial communication action inciting degradation of products under normal operating conditions and preventing their direct reuse or refurbishment.[1313] However, the compatibility of these prohibitions with the (fully harmonised) UCPD can be doubted.[1314]

344. German implementing provisions – In Germany, the UCPD is implemented in the German Act against Unfair Competition (*Gesetz gegen den unlauteren Wettbewerb* or *UWG*). It prohibits unfair commercial practices (§3 I UWG). The detailed blacklist of unacceptable practices is in Annex to §3 III UWG. Further general categories are amongst others breach of law (§3a UWG), aggressive (§4a UWG) and misleading commercial practices, which include misleading actions (§5 UWG) and omissions (§5a UWG). Against unfair practices, it is possible to bring claims for rectification or omission (§8 UWG), which may be raised by competitors and qualified organisations (including those whose purpose is to protect consumers). By contrast, §9 UWG provides claims for damages only for competitors, not for consumers. Consequently, most

1310 Ordonnance n° 2016–301, 14 mars 2016 relative à la partie législative du code de la consommation, JORF 16 mars 2016, n° 64.

1311 Although the structure of the French Consumer Code is clearer since 2016, questions remain as to the necessity of dedicating specific provisions to some unfair commercial practices (e.g. the refusal to sell and attaching preconditions to a sale in Article L. 121–11) as these practices are subject to the ordinary rules on unfair commercial practices. See H. Aubry, 'Pratiques commerciales interdites', in D. Fenouillet (ed.), *Droit de la consommation 2021/22 – Droit interne et européen* (Dalloz 2020) p. 240.

1312 For a detailed analysis of these provisions, see L. Vogel and J. Vogel, *Droit de la consommation – Traité de droit économique (tome 3)* (Lawlex/Bruylant 2017); H. Aubry, 'Pratiques commerciales interdites', in D. Fenouillet (ed.), *Droit de la consommation 2021/22 – Droit interne et européen* (Dalloz 2020) p. 237 at p. 312.

1313 Article L. 541–15–9 of the French Environmental Code.

1314 For further comments on the compatibility of certain total bans established under French law, see *infra*, n° 375.

scholars deny consumer claims for damages in tort law (§823 II BGB) solely based on violation of §3 UWG.[1315]

2. SCOPE OF APPLICATION AND LEVEL OF HARMONISATION

a) *A wide scope of application*

345. Ratione personae – As regards the scope *ratione personae*, Article 3(1) provides that the UCPD applies to unfair business-to-consumer commercial practices, before, during and after a commercial transaction in relation to a product.[1316] Consumers can invoke these protective rules against SMEs or big businesses, sellers or producers.[1317] The Directive also covers situations of 'hidden B2C' sales, meaning *"situations where individuals who appear to be consumers selling products to other consumers could in fact be either traders themselves or acting on behalf of traders"*.[1318] In principle, B2B relationships are out of the Directive's scope. Member States are nonetheless allowed to extend the scope of application to these relationships.[1319] Some Member States, such as France[1320], decided to enlarge the scope of the consumer protection legislation to transactions between professionals. Others, like Belgium[1321], have adopted similar specific provisions for B2B transactions. Such national measures are to be welcomed as extending the scope to B2B relationships allows professionals facing unfair commercial practices, including cases of premature obsolescence, to rely on rules on unfair commercial practices if national law provides them.

1315 B. Schinkels, 'Information Obligations and Disinformation of Consumers: German Law Report', in G. Straetmans (ed.), *Information Obligations and Disinformation of Consumers* (Springer International Publishing 2019) pp. 141–142.

1316 'Product' is defined as *"any goods or service including immovable property, rights and obligations"*. See Art. 2(c) UCPD.

1317 See Art. 2(b) UCPD, which defines 'trader' as *"any natural or legal person who, in commercial practices covered by this Directive, is acting for purposes relating to his trade, business, craft or profession and anyone acting in the name of or on behalf of a trader"*.

1318 UCPD Guidance, p. 27.

1319 Recital 6 UCPD.

1320 In France, two spill-overs of the UCPD standards has been expanded to B2B relations, namely the new general prohibition of misleading actions and the new blacklist of misleading commercial practices (Articles L. 442-1 to L. 442-11 of the French Commercial Code). For further details, see B. Keirsbilck, *The New European Law of Unfair Commercial Practices and Competition Law* (Hart Publishing 2011) p. 256.

1321 In Belgium, the protection against unfair commercial practices has been extended to professionals (Art. VI.105 *et seq.* of the Economic Law Code). The implementation of the UCPD resulted in two parallel regimes, one covering B2C practices and another covering B2B practices. For further details, see B. Keirsbilck, *The New European Law of Unfair Commercial Practices and Competition Law* (Hart Publishing 2011) p. 256.

346. Ratione materiae – Concerning its scope *ratione materiae*, the UCPD covers "*any act, omission, course of conduct or representation, commercial communication including advertising and marketing, by a trader, directly connected with the promotion, sale or supply of a product to consumers*".[1322] The wording is particularly broad[1323], encompassing any practice originating from traders and aiming to influence a transactional decision taken by the consumer on a product, without necessarily being repetitive or implying an intention from the producer.[1324] The notion of transactional decision is defined in Article 2(k) as "*any decision taken by a consumer concerning whether, how and on what terms to purchase, make payment in whole or in part for, retain or dispose of a product or to exercise a contractual right in relation to the product, whether the consumer decides to act or to refrain from acting*".

347. Covering practices of premature obsolescence – When they shorten the lifetime of their products or mislead consumers on that point, producers adopt commercial practices "*directly related to influencing consumers' transactional decisions in relation to products*".[1325] These commercial practices influence consumers by preventing them from using their products until the latter reach their optimal lifetime and/or urging or compelling them to purchase new and short-lived products.[1326] The wide definition of 'commercial practice' allows encompassing the different types of premature obsolescence, namely material, technological, economic and psychological obsolescence. The UCPD provisions apply to all forms of claims on the environmental attributes of goods or services made in the context of B2C relationships, including, according to circumstances, all types of statements, information, symbols, logos, graphics and brand names, and their interplay with colours, on the packaging, labelling, advertising, in all media (including websites) and made by any organisation, if it qualifies as a 'trader' and engages in commercial practices towards consumers.[1327] Since strategies of premature obsolescence fall within the definition of 'commercial practices' as given by Article 2(d), their (un)fairness

---

1322 Article 2(d) UCPD.

1323 ECJ 14 January 2010, Case C-304/08, *Plus Warenhandelsgesellschaft, EU:C:2010:12*, para 39; ECJ 9 November 2010, Case C-540/08, *Mediaprint, EU:C:2010:660*, para 21; ECJ 17 October 2013, Case C-391/12, *RLvS, EU:C:2013:669*, para 37.

1324 See ECJ 16 April 2015, Case C-388/13, *UPC Magyarország, EU:C:2015:225*, paras 47–48 and para 58. According to the Court, "*due account could [nonetheless] be taken of factors such as the frequency of the practice complained of, whether or not it is intentional, and the degree of harm caused to the consumer*" when applying sanctions so that the principle of proportionality is respected. For further comments on that point, see also L. Vogel and J. Vogel, *Droit de la consommation – Traité de droit économique (tome 3)* (Lawlex/Bruylant 2017) p. 245.

1325 Recital 7 UCPD.

1326 For concrete examples of such practices, see *infra*.

1327 UCPD Guidance, p. 72.

can be assessed through the three-tiered test established in the UCPD. If they are considered unfair, those practices will be banned from the EU market.

348. A HORIZONTAL FRAMEWORK DIRECTIVE – The scope of the UCPD allows for adaptations. As highlighted in the UCPD Guidance[1328], and the 2017 Fitness Check Report[1329], the Directive is, on the one hand, technology-neutral, meaning that it applies regardless of the channel, medium or device used to implement a business-to-consumer commercial practice. On the other hand, the UCPD has principle-based provisions that address a wide range of practices and are sufficiently broad to catch fast-evolving products, services and sales methods. Those characteristics enable the Directive not to become quickly outdated and retain the flexibility needed, which may be particularly useful in dealing with the different scenarios of premature obsolescence that may occur in future. The guidance document provides further information on its implementation, including in specific sectors.[1330] If technological developments bring new unfair commercial practices, they can be caught by the UCPD blacklist. If not, use can be made of the other stages of the cascade system, where individual assessment is needed.[1331] This is where the grand general clause could be the most useful.[1332]

b) Full harmonisation

349. FULL AND COMPLETE HARMONISATION – According to Article 4 and recitals 14 and 15 of the UCPD, the Directive aims to achieve 'full and complete harmonisation'.[1333] In other words, Member States cannot introduce or retain more stringent or lenient rules on unfair commercial practices and cannot adopt additional rules falling within the scope of the UCPD as the field of law on unfair commercial practices is entirely regulated by this Directive.[1334] The standard set by the Directive must be copy-pasted into national legislation (regulation), while national provisions that go further must be amended or repealed (deregulation).[1335] The maximum harmonisation approach finds its justification in the EU internal market, which requires eliminating distortions of competition and obstacles to cross-border activities.[1336]

1328 UCPD Guidance, p. 5 and p. 86.

1329 Commission Staff Working Document of 23 May 2017 on Report of the Fitness Check of consumer and marketing law (REFIT), SWD(2017) 209 final, p. 88.

1330 See UCPD Guidance, p. 72 *et seq.*

1331 See *supra* on the three-tiered 'cascade system' (n° 341).

1332 See *infra*, n° 440–443.

1333 See C. Verdure, 'La directive 2005/29/CE: base légale et degré d'harmonisation', *R.E.D.C.* (2013) p. 158.

1334 *Ibid.*

1335 B. Keirsbilck, *The new European law of unfair commercial practices and competition law* (Hart Publishing, 2011) p. 183.

1336 Art. 4 as well as recital 5 UCPD.

350. Situations within the scope – In addition to the personal and material scope[1337], the Directive confines itself to situations that harm the collective economic interests of market participants. This is due to the fact that the UCPD aims to protect consumer economic interests (as well as the economic interests of legitimate businesses in an indirect way).[1338] Consequently, national rules that aim to protect consumers' economic interests fall within the scope of the Directive and are thus subject to full harmonisation.

351. Situations out of the scope – Conversely, national rules on commercial practices that are issued to protect non-economic interests (such as health, safety and environment) fall outside the scope of the UCPD.[1339] In other words, these rules are no transposition or implementation of the UCPD, meaning that a new regime of controls and sanctions is needed. National rules setting requirements related to 'taste and decency' (e.g. ban on commercial solicitation in the streets) are also not covered by the UCPD.[1340] In all these cases where the national measures do not fall within the scope of the Directive, Member States are allowed to adopt such rules and thus add information requirements or ban certain commercial practices within their territory, even where such practices do not limit consumers' freedom of choice. In other words, Member States retain their freedom to regulate, provided that they do so within the boundaries of free movement of goods and other EU law principles. Problems may arise if Member States use these situations as a gateway to adopt additional *per se* prohibitions and escape the full harmonisation of the UCPD, claiming that the national measure falls outside the scope of the UCPD.[1341]

352. Ambiguous situations – The delineation of the scope is less clear when it comes to measures based on non-economic interests which regulate or restrict commercial practices affecting both economic and non-economic interests. In principle, national rules that aim to protect the economic interest of consumers, in conjunction with other interests, do fall within the scope of the UCPD.[1342] But what if the national rule is only explicitly aimed to protect non-economic interests, but also protect economic interests? Even if based on non-economic objectives, such measures in effect also provide overprotection of the economic interests at stake.[1343] When adopting such rules, Member States go beyond the maximum level of protection allowed by the UCPD. Such a compatibility issue

1337 See *supra*, n° 357–359.

1338 See Art. 1 as well as recital 8 UCPD.

1339 See Art. 3(3) UCPD.

1340 Recital 7 UCPD.

1341 This would jeopardize the objective of the full harmonisation approach as it would open the door to disparities between the Member States.

1342 UCPD Guidance, p. 7.

1343 B. Keirsbilck, *The new European law of unfair commercial practices and competition law* (Hart Publishing, 2011) pp. 263–264.

arises with the French legislation outlawing 'planned obsolescence'[1344], as well as with lots of other national measures currently being adopted. This compatibility issue is problematic as it could hinder the adoption of national rules that tackle practices of premature obsolescence. Therefore, this fundamental problem should no longer be ignored. To this end, Article 3 of the UCPD should be amended to exclude national rules that aim to protect the environment from the scope of application of the UCPD and its fully harmonised provisions (see #1). This amendment would remove the legislative barrier that currently outlaws national measures designed to curb premature obsolescence.

353. Exceptions – Besides rules that fall outside the scope of the UCPD, the Directive explicitly mentions exceptions to its maximum harmonisation character. Among these exceptions, there is the one contained in recital 14, which states that "*[t]he full harmonisation approach adopted in [the UCPD] does not preclude the Member States from specifying in national law the main characteristics of particular products.*" As an example, it cites collector items and electrical goods. This exception allows Member States to classify durability and reparability as main characteristics of products about which consumers should be informed. Failure to provide such information would then qualify as misleading omissions under the UCPD. Such information obligation has been established in France with the adoption of the Anti-Waste Law. Since 1st January 2022, producers and importers of waste-generating products are required, pursuant to Article 13, to inform consumers on the environmental qualities and characteristics of their products, including among others the incorporation of recycled material, durability, reparability, reusability, recyclability and the presence of hazardous substances.[1345] Moreover, Article 25 of the Anti-Waste Law makes clear that reparability must be considered as one of the main product characteristics, although it solely refers to the provisions implementing the Consumer Rights Directive. This exception on "*the main characteristics of particular products*" established by the UCPD is also in line with the new Sale of Goods Directive, which explicitly introduces the notion of 'durability' within the objective requirements.[1346]

1344 See *infra*, n° 375.

1345 It should be noted that similar information requirements are also imposed at EU level. See Regulation (EC) No 1907/2006 of the European Parliament and of the Council of 18 December 2006 concerning the Registration, Evaluation, Authorisation and Restriction of Chemicals (REACH), establishing a European Chemicals Agency, amending Directive 1999/45/EC and repealing Council Regulation (EEC) No 793/93 and Commission Regulation (EC) No 1488/94 as well as Council Directive 76/769/EEC and Commission Directives 91/155/EEC, 93/67/EEC, 93/105/EC and 2000/21/EC, OJ L 396, 30.12.2006, p. 1–849 (hereafter 'REACH Regulation').

1346 For further details on the provisions of the Sale of Goods Directive, see Chapter IV on the use stage.

Proposed review of the UCPD

#1

Article 3
Scope

1. This Directive shall apply to unfair business-to-consumer commercial practices, as laid down in Article 5, before, during and after a commercial transaction in relation to a product.

2. This Directive is without prejudice to contract law and, in particular, to the rules on the validity, formation or effect of a contract.

3. This Directive is without prejudice to Community or national rules relating to the health and safety aspects of products.

3a. This Directive does not prevent Member States from adopting rules regulating commercial practices for reasons of environmental protection. National rules that aim to protect the environment, even if it is in conjunction with consumers' economic interests, fall outside its scope.

(...)

c) *Interplay with other legal instruments*

354. INTERPLAY WITH SPECIFIC RULES – The very large scope of the Directive also creates risks of overlaps and inconsistencies with other general or sector-specific EU legislation. In this regard, some provisions of the Directive give clarifications on the interplay between the UCPD and these other EU instruments. Among them, Article 3(4), read in conjunction with recital 10, provides that the UCPD complements other EU legislation that regulates specific aspects of unfair commercial practices. In other words, the UCPD applies only in so far as no specific Community law provisions regulate specific aspects of unfair commercial practices, such as information requirements and rules on the way information is presented to the consumer. In case of conflict between legal provisions, Article 3(4) provides that the *lex specialis* must prevail.[1347] This topic was touched upon in the *Dyson* case, where the Court confirmed that where a conflict occurs between the UCPD and rules governing specific aspects of unfair commercial practices, like the (former) Directive 2010/30 on energy labelling

[1347] It should be noted that only national rules that exactly replicate sector-specific EU rules are allowed. If national measures are only allowed by minimum harmonisation of other EU rules, these measures cannot be adopted or maintained. See B. Keirsbilck, *The new European law of unfair commercial practices and competition law* (Hart Publishing 2011) p. 187 at p. 191.

and the (former) Delegated Regulation No 665/2013 on the energy labelling of vacuum cleaners, it is those latter provisions which must be applied.[1348] As stated in the UCPD Guidance, "*the UCPD works as a 'safety net' ensuring that a high common level of consumer protection against unfair commercial practices can be maintained in all sectors, including by complementing and filling gaps in other EU law*".[1349] This emphasizes the importance of the UCPD in the promotion of product sustainability as not all products are covered by energy labelling or ecodesign regulations.[1350]

355. Interplay with contract law – Article 3(2) adds that the UCPD "*is without prejudice to contract law and, in particular, to the rules on the validity, formation or effect of a contract*". According to recital 15, Member States can "*retain or add information requirements relating to contract law where this is allowed by the minimum clauses in the existing [EU] law instruments*". Recital 15 also explains that "*[w]here Member States have introduced information requirements over and above what is specified in [EU] law, on the basis of minimum clauses, the omission of that extra information will not constitute a misleading omission under [the UCPD]. By contrast Member States will be able, when allowed by the minimum clauses in [EU] law, to maintain or introduce more stringent provisions in conformity with [EU] law so as to ensure a higher level of protection of consumers' individual contractual rights.*" Hence, Member States are allowed to establish stringent information requirements, including on product sustainability, if allowed by EU law, but the violation of these additional requirements will not be sanctioned under the UCPD.[1351]

3. BLACKLISTED PRACTICES RELATED TO PREMATURE OBSOLESCENCE

356. First step: the blacklist – The first step in assessing the unfairness of a commercial practice under the UCPD is to check the blacklist set out in its Annex I. If the case at hand corresponds to a practice mentioned in the list, the practice is in all circumstances considered as unfair and can thus be sanctioned without having to apply a case-by-case test. In other words, there is no need for national enforcers to assess the (likely) influence of the practice on the average consumer's economic behaviour. The practice must be prohibited without any further analysis or conditions. This blacklist not only facilitates the enforcement

1348 ECJ 25 July 2018, Case C-632/16, *Dyson* v *BSH, EU:C:2018:599*, paras 33–34.

1349 UCPD Guidance, p. 8.

1350 Other provisions give clarifications on the interplay between the UCPD and other EU instruments (e.g. Art. 7(5) UCPD on information requirements established by EU rules). These provisions are identified and analysed in the following paragraphs where relevant.

1351 For a detailed analysis of that point, see *infra* n° 405.

of the UCPD by national authorities, but also increases legal certainty and awareness among traders and consumers.[1352]

a) *Confronting the blacklist with the concept of premature obsolescence*

357. No explicit reference to premature obsolescence – The UCPD blacklist makes no explicit reference to premature obsolescence. Quoting the EC in its most recent UCPD Guidance, the Directive "*does not have provisions specifically addressing obsolescence*".[1353] According to the Guidance, obsolescence is deemed 'early' if "*goods last less than their normal "lifespan" should be according to consumers' reasonable expectations*".[1354] In this Guidance, the EC focuses on 'planned obsolescence' or 'built-in obsolescence in industrial design', defined as "*a commercial policy involving deliberately planning or designing a product with a limited useful life so that it will become obsolete or non-functional after a certain period of time*".[1355] This definition corresponds to cases of 'material obsolescence' only, as described in the first chapter of this book dedicated to the concept of premature obsolescence.[1356] Interestingly, the 2021 UCPD Guidance added a reference to "*commercial practices which occur after the transaction has been made*", including those that reduce the functionality or slow down the operation of smart and connected goods through software updates without a valid reason.[1357] Although this amendment gives a fuller picture of the issue, the EC still overlooks other types of premature obsolescence, which are caused by functional, indirect, economic and psychological factors.[1358]

358. Product falsely described as free – Yet some practices mentioned in the UCPD blacklist could fall within these categories of premature obsolescence as they (indirectly) contribute to shortening product lifetime. The first example of such blacklisted practices corresponds to cases where a product has been falsely described as free.[1359] Combined offers can be banned under the UCPD if the price of the paid-for items has been inflated to recover the cost of supplying the free item.[1360] This kind of misleading practice has been identified in the smartphone sector when operators sell phone subscriptions with a 'free'

1352 Commission Staff Working Document of 23 May 2017 on Report of the Fitness Check of consumer and marketing law (REFIT), SWD(2017) 209 final, p. 87.

1353 UCPD Guidance, p. 84.

1354 *Ibid.*

1355 *Ibid.*

1356 See *supra*, n° 101 *et seq.*

1357 UCPD Guidance, p. 84.

1358 See *supra*, n° 106 *et seq.*

1359 Point 20 of the Annex I to the UCPD: "*Describing a product as 'gratis', 'free', 'without charge' or similar if the consumer has to pay anything other than the unavoidable cost of responding to the commercial practice and collecting or paying for delivery of the item*".

1360 UCPD Guidance, p. 67.

phone and hide the purchase price of the smartphone in monthly overall contract costs.[1361] New 'free' phones may also be offered during the phone subscription.[1362] Such misleading practices provoke consumers to prematurely replace their still functioning phone with a new device when taking out a phone subscription. In other words, the practice can make phones economically and psychologically obsolete. Studies have reported this consumer behaviour in practice, although in a minority of cases.[1363] Consequently, banning such practices helps avoid the rapid replacement of some products.

359. Persistent and unwanted solicitations – A second blacklisted practice that could indirectly lead to the premature obsolescence of products is the one referring to *"persistent and unwanted solicitations by telephone, fax, e-mail or other remote media"*.[1364] This practice is only allowed in respect of subscribers who have given their prior consent, as stated in Article 6(1)(a) of the General Data Protection Regulation[1365] and in Article 13(1) of the e-Privacy Directive.[1366] Under Belgian law, the prohibition has been extended to other communication techniques, taking into account the evolution of such techniques.[1367] Such persistent solicitations can happen within the context of software updates. At first sight, this practice could be seen as contributing to prolonging the lifetime of some products (especially 'up-to-date products')[1368] as ensuring continued software support allows maintaining the functionalities and security of these products.[1369] However, insistent solicitations on updates can be qualified as aggressive commercial practices, especially if these updates affect

1361 Such unfair practice has already been sanctioned under the UCPD provisions. See for ex. Joint Judgments Dnr B 2/11 and B 3/11 by Marknadsdomstolen, 11 May 2012, as mentioned in the UCPD Guidance, p. 67.

1362 See e.g. <https://www.modephone.com/>, where the trader offers *"a brand new device every 12 months with the latest features"* with the phone subscription.

1363 See H. Wieser, 'Beyond Planned Obsolescence: Product Lifespans and the Challenges to a Circular Economy', 25 *GAIA* (2016) p. 157; H. Wieser, N. Tröger, 'Exploring the inner loops of the circular economy: Replacement, repair, and reuse of mobile phones in Austria', 172 *J. Clean. Prod.* (2018) p. 3046.

1364 Point 26 of the Annex I to the UCPD.

1365 Regulation (EU) 2016/679 of the European Parliament and of the Council of 27 April 2016 on the protection of natural persons with regard to the processing of personal data and on the free movement of such data, and repealing Directive 95/46/EC, OJ L 119, 4.5.2016, p. 1–88.

1366 Directive 2002/58/EC of the European Parliament and of the Council of 12 July 2002 concerning the processing of personal data and the protection of privacy in the electronic communications sector (Directive on privacy and electronic communications), OJ L 201, 31.7.2002, p. 37–47.

1367 Art. VI.103 and VI.110–115 Economic Law Code. J. Stuyck, A.-M. Vandromme, 'Aggressive B2C Commercial Practices', in G. Straetmans and J. Stuyck (eds.), *Commercial Practices* (Intersentia 2016) p. 98 at p. 101.

1368 'Up-to-date products' are *"products which [consumers tend] to discard when they [are] considered 'out of date'"*. This distinction between products was made in Brook Lyndhurst, *Public understanding of product lifetimes and durability* (DEFRA 2011) p. 26.

1369 EEA, *Circular by design: Products in the circular economy* (European Union 2017) p. 44.

the performance of the device, leading to its premature replacement. The Italian Competition Authority (*Autorita Garante della Concorrenza e del Mercato*) applied this reasoning against *Apple*[1370] and *Samsung*.[1371] The two firms had pressed their customers to install software updates, without (sufficiently) informing them of the features, risks and issues associated with these updates, as well as the battery's features (e.g. its high correlation with smartphone performance, how to keep it in good condition and the need for occasional battery replacement). Interestingly, the companies were finally sanctioned on the basis of Articles 20, 21, 22 and 24 of the Italian Consumer Code, which transpose Articles 5 to 8 of the UCPD, instead of the UCPD blacklist.[1372]

360. Lack of access to after-sale service – Thirdly, the UCPD blacklist prohibits other practices that hinder consumer access to after-sale service and thus prevent them from extending the lifetime of their products. There is, first of all, the prohibition to "*[u]ndertake to provide after-sales service to consumers with whom the trader has communicated prior to a transaction in a language which is not an official language of the Member State where the trader is located and then making such service available only in another language without clearly disclosing this to the consumer before the consumer is committed to the transaction*".[1373] It is also forbidden for traders to "*[c]reate the false impression that after-sales service in relation to a product is available in a Member State other than the one in which the product is sold*".[1374] Such practices could indeed strongly discourage and prevent consumers from maintaining and repairing their products and thus lead to their premature obsolescence.

361. Inaccurate claims concerning the nature and extent of the risk to the personal security – Fourthly, as rightly pointed out by A. Perzanowski,[1375] another blacklisted practice could be of use to tackle repair restrictions and prolong product lifetime, that is the one that prohibits "*[m]aking a materially inaccurate claim concerning the nature and extent of the risk to the personal security of the consumer or his family if the consumer does not purchase the product*".[1376] As already highlighted, manufacturers often invoke quality and safety concerns to justify their reluctancy to facilitate repair outside their authorized network.[1377] Similar claims are made on refurbished devices

---

1370 Autorita Garante della Concorrenza e del Mercato, 25 September 2018, *Apple*, para 160.

1371 Autorita Garante della Concorrenza e del Mercato, 25 September 2018, *Samsung*, para 146.

1372 For further details on these two cases, see the section on misleading omissions (n° 399) and on aggressive practices (n° 436).

1373 Point 8 of the Annex I to the UCPD.

1374 Point 23 of the Annex I to the UCPD.

1375 A. Perzanowski, *The Right to Repair: Reclaiming the Things We Own* (Cambridge University Press 2022) p. 213.

1376 Point 12 of the Annex I to the UCPD.

1377 See *supra*, n° 269.

and spare parts made by non-original equipment manufacturers. Before making such claims, producers should be able to substantiate them. Otherwise, these claims should be considered as misleading.

362. BLACKLISTED GREEN CLAIMS – The UCPD blacklist also contributes to combating practices of 'greenwashing', that is green claims that are not true or cannot be verified. Greenwashing is closely linked to premature obsolescence as it can hinder the transition towards more sustainable patterns of production and consumption. Greenwashing may indeed result in consumers purchasing products of low quality and in traders lacking incentives to communicate and work on the quality standards of their products.[1378] There are no specific rules on greenwashing within the UCPD. However, the UCPD Guidance document dedicates a specific section to environmental claims.[1379] This document mentions several blacklisted practices that are relevant to green claims.[1380] They include practices that consist in falsely claiming to be a signatory of a code of conduct (including on the environmental performance of the product)[1381], that a code of conduct has been endorsed by a public or private body[1382] and that a trader (including their commercial practices) or a product has been approved, endorsed or authorised by a public or private body.[1383]Another blacklisted practice relevant to green claims concerns the display of a trust mark, quality mark or equivalent without having obtained the necessary authorisation.[1384] This would be the case if the trader was using any EU or national label, like the EU Ecolabel, the *Nordic Swan* Label or the *Blue Angel* logo, without authorisation. The blacklist also bans practices where the rights conferred on consumers by the law are presented as a distinctive feature of the trader's offer.[1385] In other words, "*traders should not mislead consumers by unduly emphasising attributes that come from regulatory requirements*".[1386] This provision aims at helping consumers make a clear distinction between commercial and legal guarantee rights as well as between advertising and information requirements.

363. AN EXHAUSTIVE LIST – Besides practices that accelerate product replacement and greenwashing, there is no practice on the blacklist that is directly linked to premature obsolescence and product sustainability. Due to the maximum harmonising character of the Directive, the blacklist provided

1378 C. Twigg-Flesner, *Consumer Product Guarantees* (Routledge 2016) p. 55.
1379 UCPD Guidance, p. 72 at p. 84.
1380 See UCPD Guidance, pp. 82–83.
1381 Point 1 of Annex I to the UCPD.
1382 Point 3 of Annex I to the UCPD.
1383 Point 4 of Annex I to the UCPD.
1384 Point 2 of Annex I to the UCPD.
1385 Point 10 of Annex I to the UCPD.
1386 UCPD Guidance, p. 83.

in its Annex I is exhaustive. As emphasized by Article 5(5), "*[t]he same single list shall apply in all Member States and may only be modified by revision of this Directive*".[1387] The blacklist cannot be applied *a contrario* or by analogy. This implies that for B2C transactions, Member States can no longer prohibit *per se* or regulate *in abstracto* the use of commercial practices that are not blacklisted by the UCPD, without giving the judge the power to appraise *in concreto* whether they are unfair towards consumers. Only the 35 practices mentioned in Annex I can be deemed unfair without a case-by-case assessment. Practices that are not blacklisted can be prohibited only *in concreto*, if the case-by-case assessment shows that they are misleading, aggressive or unfair within the meaning of the UCPD's general clauses.[1388] This principle, and the restricted room for manoeuvre that it entails for Member States, has been confirmed by the Court of Justice on numerous occasions.[1389] Yet the exhaustiveness of the UCPD blacklist has not prevented France from adopting additional bans on certain commercial practices, as discussed in the following paragraphs.

b) The French bans on 'planned obsolescence' and other related practices

364. A TOTAL BAN ON 'PLANNED OBSOLESCENCE' – In addition to the UCPD blacklist, other commercial practices are prohibited in France. This is the case of practices of 'planned obsolescence', which have been banned by Article L. 441–2 of the French Consumer Code since the adoption of the Energy Transition Act in 2015.[1390] This prohibition was introduced in the chapter on fraud (*fraude*), and more specifically to deception (*tromperie*).[1391] As described in Article L. 441–1 of the Consumer Code, fraud is when a person, either among the contracting parties or not, misleads one contracting party (or attempts to do so) on the product, including on its nature or essential qualities, and this by any means whatsoever.[1392] By deliberately reducing the lifetime of their products, producers

1387 See also recital 17 UCPD.

1388 B. Keirsbilck, *The new European law of unfair commercial practices and competition law* (Hart Publishing, 2011) pp. 234–235.

1389 Several Member States have already been condemned for this kind of violation of EU law. See for ex. ECJ 23 April 2009, Joined cases C-261/07 and C-299/07, *VTB-VAB, EU:C:2009:244*; ECJ 9 November 2010, C-540/08, *Mediaprint, EU:C:2010:660*; ECJ, 17 January 2013, Case C-206/11, *Köck, EU:C:2013:14.*

1390 Article L. 441–2 of the French Consumer Code defines 'planned obsolescence' as "*the set of techniques, including software-related ones, by which the person responsible for placing the product on the market seeks to deliberately reduce the lifetime of this product*". See *supra*, n° 70 *et seq.*

1391 Avis n° 244 (2014–2015) de L. NÈGRE, fait au nom de la commission du développement durable, déposé le 21 janvier 2015; Rapport n° 2736 de E. BAREIGTS, M.-N. BATTISTEL, S. BUIS, D. BAUPIN et P. PLISSON, fait au nom de la commission spéciale, déposé le 16 avril 2015.

1392 Article L. 441–1 of the French Consumer Code: "*Il est interdit pour toute personne, partie ou non au contrat, de tromper ou tenter de tromper le contractant, par quelque moyen ou procédé que ce soit, même par l'intermédiaire d'un tiers:*

mislead the other contractual party on product quality and sustainability (which can be considered as 'essential qualities').[1393] Consequently, Article L. 441-2 of the French Consumer Code extended the list of forbidden misleading practices to practices of planned obsolescence. It is interesting to note that Article L. 441-1 on deception also applies to professionals and B2B relations.[1394] However, an analogue extension to B2B transactions for Article L. 441-2 could hardly be considered, especially since it does not seem to be the intent of the French legislature.

365. A SET OF TECHNIQUES, INCLUDING SOFTWARE-RELATED ONES – The definition contained in Article L. 441-2 of the French Consumer Code can be deconstructed into three different elements.[1395] First, 'planned obsolescence' consists of a "*set of techniques*". Whereas no doubt taking action to reduce product lifetime falls within the definition, uncertainties remain concerning practices of planned obsolescence that would be implemented through omissions. Refraining from acting could indeed constitute a set of techniques that could be used to reduce product lifetime. For example, producers could deliberately omit to inform consumers of the risks associated with new OS updates or could decide not to provide spare parts. Hence, it is not clear from the wording of Article L. 441-2 of the French Consumer Code whether the definition of 'planned obsolescence' covers and prohibits both actions and omissions or only actions.[1396]

366. THE RESPONSIBLE PERSON – Second, the definition targets the "*person responsible for placing the product on the market*". No further details are provided in the law, which makes it difficult to identify the targeted person. Under

---

1° Soit sur la nature, l'espèce, l'origine, les qualités substantielles, la composition ou la teneur en principes utiles de toutes marchandises;

2° Soit sur la quantité des choses livrées ou sur leur identité par la livraison d'une marchandise autre que la chose déterminée qui a fait l'objet du contrat;

3° Soit sur l'aptitude à l'emploi, les risques inhérents à l'utilisation du produit, les contrôles effectués, les modes d'emploi ou les précautions à prendre.

Les dispositions du présent article sont également applicables aux prestations de services."

[1393] N. Jeanne, ""Prêt à jeter?" – A propos du délit d'obsolescence programmée", in *Mélanges en l'honneur de Geneviève Giudicelli-Delage* (Dalloz 2016) p. 611. Concerning the qualification of durability as an 'essential quality', the author refers to a case where it was considered that essential qualities could concern the number of kilometres during the sale of a second-hand vehicle for which the owner had concealed the number of kilometres driven (Crim. 21 juill. 1977, *Bull. Crim.* n° 240).

[1394] See e.g. Crim. 4 nov. 2008, *Bull. Crim.* n° 223.

[1395] The deconstruction of the French legal definition of 'planned obsolescence' corresponds to a combination of grammatical and technical interpretation as defined in L. Kestemont, *Methods for traditional legal research* (KU Leuven – University of Tilburg 2015).

[1396] N. Jeanne, ""Prêt à jeter?" – A propos du délit d'obsolescence programmée", in J. Alix et al. (eds.), *Humanisme et justice: Mélanges en l'honneur de Geneviève Giudicelli-Delage* (Dalloz 2016) p. 613.

French environmental law, these terms encompass manufacturers, importers, assembling or instructing persons and sellers. Yet, in practice, the person who decides to shorten product lifetime is not necessarily the one "*responsible for placing the product on the market*". The person who places the product on the market is sometimes not aware of the existence of planned obsolescence. Considering the purpose of the law, it would be more logical that Article L. 441-2 of the French Consumer Code uses the catch-all term 'responsible person' in order to target the truly responsible person, which may vary from case to case.

367. The intent of reducing product lifetime – Third, Article L. 441-2 requires that the person "*seeks to deliberately reduce the lifetime of this product*". The use of the verb 'seek' suggests that there is no need for results or damages. The mere fact that the 'planner' aims to reduce the lifetime of their products seems enough to sanction him on the basis of Article L. 441-2. Consequently, attempts to shorten product lifetime, even if not successful or stopped before affecting consumers, could be sanctioned.[1397] The word 'deliberately' suggests, however, a scope restricted to cases of intentional obsolescence.[1398] As regards the notion of product lifetime, a legal definition is also missing. The French Government brought some clarifications on that notion afterwards, borrowing the terminology established in the ADEME study from 2012.[1399] Based on this terminology, planned obsolescence in the sense of Article L. 441-2 consists in seeking to limit the useful lifetime of the product from its conception. The use of 'product lifetime' (*durée de vie*) implies that the reduction should be evaluated *in concreto* by the consumer, by contrast with the 'durability' (*durabilité*) of the product which has to be evaluated *in abstracto* against the product characteristics.[1400]

368. Sanctions – Due to its introduction in the chapter on fraud, the ban on planned obsolescence is accompanied by sanctions comparable to the ones provided for fraud cases. Pursuant to Article L. 454-6 of the Consumer Code, if someone is caught pursuing a strategy falling within the definition set out in Article L. 441-2, he could be held guilty of a criminal offence, reaching two years of imprisonment and € 300,000 fine or up to 5% of the average annual turnover

---

1397 N. Jeanne, ""Prêt à jeter?" – A propos du délit d'obsolescence programmée", in J. Alix et al. (eds.), *Humanisme et justice: Mélanges en l'honneur de Geneviève Giudicelli-Delage* (Dalloz 2016) p. 614.

1398 See also Rapport du Gouvernement au Parlement sur l'obsolescence programmée, sa définition juridique et ses enjeux économiques, en application de l'article 8 de la loi du 17 mars 2014 relative à la consommation, avril 2017, p. 11.

1399 Rapport du Gouvernement au Parlement sur l'obsolescence programmée, sa définition juridique et ses enjeux économiques, en application de l'article 8 de la loi du 17 mars 2014 relative à la consommation, avril 2017, pp. 13–14.

1400 Avis du Conseil National de la Consommation sur la durabilité des produits, 12 May 2015, N° NOR: EINC1511471V, p. 1.

(calculated on the last three annual turnovers known at the time of the events).[1401] These sanctions, and especially the threat of imprisonment[1402], may be dissuasive for companies that contemplate the idea of planning premature obsolescence of their products.[1403] Both undertakings and individuals can be held responsible for fraud cases. Additional sanctions could be taken against the undertaking or individuals involved through the undertaking. For example, individuals could be compelled to stop working as the head of the company.[1404] Damages could also be claimed by consumers who are victims of practices qualified as planned obsolescence, provided they successfully bring proof of the causal link between the fraud and their damages. However, they have to bring their claim before civil courts if they want the contract to be declared null and void.[1405]

369. Other prohibited practices – In addition to the blanket ban on 'planned obsolescence', French law prohibits other practices that contribute to the premature obsolescence of products. These prohibitions were introduced by the Anti-Waste Law of 2020. Article 13 of this Law prohibits green claims based on vague and general statements of environmental benefits such as 'environmentally friendly'.[1406] Article 25 introduced two prohibitions of fraudulent cases of premature obsolescence in the French Consumer Code. On the one hand, it bans "*any technique, including software, by which the person responsible for placing the product on the market seeks to make it impossible to repair or repackage a device outside its approved circuits*".[1407] A decree will define the list of products and the legitimate reasons, in particular the safety or health of users, for which the prohibition could be lifted. On the other hand, Article 25 outlaws "*any agreement or practice aimed at limiting professional repairers' or reusers' access to spare parts, instructions, technical information or any other instrument, equipment or software allowing repair*".[1408] The violation of these two prohibitions will be subject to the same sanctions as those imposed in case of planned obsolescence, reaching two years of imprisonment and € 300,000 fine or up to 5% of the average annual turnover.[1409] In its Article 50, the Anti-

[1401] Art. L. 454-6 §1-2 of the French Consumer Code. The initial legislative proposal imposed a fine reaching up to 10% of the average annual turnover but was deemed disproportionate and difficult to implement in some cases. See Rapport fait au nom de la Commission spéciale pour l'examen du projet de loi, 15 April 2015, n° 2736, p. 326 at p. 328.

[1402] People generally value their freedom more than their money. See OECD Policy roundtables from 10 January 2005 on Cartels: Sanctions against individuals, DAF/COMP(2004)39, p. 105.

[1403] See the similar reasoning followed for cartels in OECD Policy roundtables from 10 January 2005 on Cartels: Sanctions against individuals, DAF/COMP(2004)39.

[1404] Article L. 454-6 §3 of the French Consumer Code.

[1405] Y. Picod, N. Picod, E. Chevrier, *Code de la consommation 2018, annoté et commenté* (Dalloz 2017) p. 604-605.

[1406] Article L. 541-9-1 of the French Environmental Code.

[1407] Article L. 441-3 of the French Consumer Code.

[1408] Article L. 441-4 of the French Consumer Code.

[1409] Article L. 454-6 of the French Consumer Code.

Waste Law also forbids any advertising or commercial communication action encouraging degrading products in normal operating conditions and preventing their direct reuse or refurbishment.[1410] The provision adds that "*any advertising or commercial communication action aimed at promoting the scrapping of products must contain information encouraging reuse or recycling*".[1411] Such marketing practices have already been reported in practice, like the controversial promotional campaign organised by the French e-commerce website *Cdiscount*[1412], although no sanctions were finally issued.[1413] This new provision of the French Environmental Code can contribute to tackling excessive consumption and psychological obsolescence. Other practices may be prohibited in the near future. As an example, the Legislative proposal of April 2021 suggests introducing a ban on advertising or commercial communication that directly or indirectly encourages degradation, discard or replace prematurely products whose main function is still functional.[1414]

370. Coercive and preventive effects – These prohibitions undoubtedly contribute to the fight against the premature replacement of consumer goods in several respects. First, if its conditions of application are met, such legislation allows the sanctioning and elimination of practices that limit product lifespan. In the long term, this could help restore consumer confidence in the market. Second, and this is their biggest advantage, the French legislation has raised and continues to raise general awareness of the importance of product sustainability. It stirred up the debate on the topic at EU level and in the other Member States, but most importantly, it influences the behaviour of economic actors. On the consumer side, consumers are stimulated to think more deeply about the quality and sustainability of the products they 'consume'. On the producer side,

---

1410 Article L. 541-15-9 of the French Environmental Code. The French version of the provision uses the words '*réemploi*' et '*réutilisation*'.

1411 *Ibid.*

1412 The advertising visuals used by *Cdiscount* urged consumers to purchase a new laptop computer while "*my old computer still works*" and a large new television screen even if "*I don't need such a big screen*".

1413 See the open letter written by ADEME in October 2018, available on: <https://presse.ademe.fr/2018/10/lettre-ouverte-au-jury-de-deontologie-publicitaire-sur-une-campagne-cdiscount-consoresponsable.html>, as well as the press release 'L'industrie de la publicité refuse de reconnaître les incitations à la surconsommation de Cdiscount', 2 October 2018, available on: <https://presse.ademe.fr/wp-content/uploads/2018/10/CP-C-DISCOUNT-VF.pdf>.

1414 Art. 4 of the Proposition de loi n° 4054 visant à lutter contre l'obsolescence programmée: passer de la société du jetable à celle du durable, déposée à l'Assemblée Nationale le 7 avril 2021: "*Est interdite toute forme de publicité ou action de communication commerciale qui inciterait directement ou indirectement à dégrader, abandonner ou remplacer prématurément des produits dont la fonction principale est encore fonctionnelle. Est notamment considéré comme tel, tout contenu publicitaire, quel que soit son support, incitant au rachat à neuf de biens en état de marche, incitant au non-entretien ou au mésusage des produits, incitant à l'achat en vue de la revente et non en vue de l'utilisation durable ou valorisant les produits jetables au détriment des produits réutilisables.*"

producers are deterred from developing strategies stimulating overconsumption and encouraged to improve the quality of their products. While the criminal and civil sanctions have a deterrent effect in themselves, producers are mostly fearful of reputational risks.[1415] Being sued before the courts on the basis of allegations of planned obsolescence could indeed ruin their reputation with their customers, their trade partners and even with society as a whole. Hence, beyond its coercive nature, the French legislation also has preventive effects on premature obsolescence (in its broad sense).[1416]

371. Lack of legal certainty – The coercive and preventive effects of the French legislation on planned obsolescence could nonetheless be diluted in practice due to three main issues. First, uncertainties surround the definition of 'planned obsolescence' and the scope of Article L. 441-2 of the Consumer Code.[1417] It is not clear whether the prohibition covers all types of obsolescence, namely material, functional, indirect, economic and psychological obsolescence.[1418] This lack of legal certainty can impair the effectiveness of French law by confusing producers and hindering consumers from relying on this provision. Ambiguity on the scope of application of Article L. 441-2 could have been avoided, or at least mitigated, if the provision had incorporated an illustrative and non-exhaustive list of practices falling within the definition of 'planned obsolescence'.[1419] The French National Assembly had initially proposed a definition with a second paragraph listing techniques that amount to 'planned obsolescence': "*the voluntary introduction of a defect, a weakness, a planned or premature outage, a technical limitation, an inability to repair, or an incompatibility*".[1420] Later in the process, the provision even

---

1415 Y. Picod et al., *Code de la consommation 2018, annoté et commenté* (Dalloz 2017) p. 597.

1416 See also F. Keimeyer et al., *Weiterentwicklung von Strategien gegen Obsoleszenz einschließlich rechtlicher Instrumente – Abschlussbericht* (Umweltbundesamt 2020) p. 50. The preventive effect exerted by criminal sanctions has already been used in other areas of law. See for ex. Commission Staff Working Paper – Impact Assessment of 20 October 2011 accompanying the proposal for a Regulation on insider dealing market manipulation (market abuse) and the proposal for a Directive on criminal sanctions for insider dealing and market manipulation, SEC(2011) 1217 final, p. 52.

1417 Risks of misinterpretations had yet been acknowledged in the Waste Prevention Programme 2014–2020. See Ministère de l'Écologie, du Développement durable et de l'Énergie, *Programme national de prévention des déchets 2014–2020* (République Française 2014) p. 38.

1418 See also N. Jeanne, ""Prêt à jeter?" – A propos du délit d'obsolescence programmée", in J. Alix et al. (eds.), *Humanisme et justice: Mélanges en l'honneur de Geneviève Giudicelli-Delage* (Dalloz 2016) p. 614.

1419 See also E. Maitre-Ekern and C. Dalhammar,'Regulating planned obsolescence: a review of legal approaches to increase product durability and reparability in Europe', 25 *Review of European Community & International Environmental Law* (2016) p. 387.

1420 Article 22*ter* A (*nouveau*) of the draft law on energy transition for green growth, as adopted by the Assemblée Nationale on 14 October 2014, TA n° 412, which introduced Art. L. 213-4-1 in the French Consumer Code, stating that: "*II. – Ces techniques peuvent notamment inclure l'introduction volontaire d'une défectuosité, d'une fragilité, d'un arrêt programmé*

included specification of what the 'inability to repair' could consist of, namely "*the fact that a product cannot be dismantled or that spare parts necessary to its functioning are missing*".[1421] Instead, it was decided not to include such a list. Based on its wording, its origins, its objective and its place in the Consumer Code[1422], one could think that Article L. 441-2 is restricted to practices deliberately implemented by businesses.[1423] The recent amendment to the provision, which added "*software-related techniques*" to the definition[1424], brings some clarifications in this regard. Another legislative proposal suggests adding strategies that make repair impossible.[1425] Besides, the bans contained in Articles 25 and 50 of the Anti-Waste Law allow filling the gap and covering other practices related to premature obsolescence that could have been included in Article L. 441-2. Judicial decisions will be crucial to shed light on the concrete application of Article L. 441-2 and its articulation with these other provisions. Meanwhile, fog still covers Article L. 441-2 of the French Consumer Code.

372. A heavy burden of proof – Second, in addition to this legal certainty issue, the wording of Article L. 441-2 poses serious problems in terms of proof, which could jeopardize its effectiveness. To successfully claim the prohibition of planned obsolescence, the consumer must prove two elements: (1) a reduced product lifespan and (2) the professional's intent. The evidential burden has

ou prématuré, d'une limitation technique, d'une impossibilité de réparer ou d'une non-compatibilité." (free translation).

1421 Article 22*ter* of the draft law on energy transition for green growth, as adopted by the Assemblée Nationale on 26 May 2015, TA n° 519, which introduced Art. L. 213-4-1 in the French Consumer Code, stating that: "*I. – L'obsolescence programmée désigne l'ensemble des techniques par lesquelles un metteur sur le marché vise, notamment par la conception du produit, à raccourcir délibérément la durée de vie ou d'utilisation potentielle de ce produit afin d'en augmenter le taux de remplacement.*
Ces techniques peuvent inclure l'introduction volontaire d'une défectuosité, d'une fragilité, d'un arrêt programmé ou prématuré, d'une limitation technique, d'une impossibilité de réparer, en raison du caractère indémontable de l'appareil ou de l'absence de pièces détachées essentielles au fonctionnement de ce dernier, ou d'une incompatibilité." (free translation).

1422 See also *supra* on the French legislation on 'planned obsolescence' (n° 70-71). This adds systematic, teleological and legal-historical aspects to the interpretation of the legal definition, as defined in L. Kestemont, *Methods for traditional legal research* (KU Leuven – University of Tilburg 2015).

1423 It is interesting to note that, during the legislative process on the French Energy Transition Act, the Commission on Economic Affairs (*Commission des affaires économiques*) had suggested a broader definition of 'planned obsolescence', with no mention of intent nor emphasis on the business side: "*all practices that shorten the lifetime or potential use of a product from the time of its design, thus causing it to depreciate before normal material wear and tear and increasing its replacement rate*". See Amendment n° COM-30 of the Commission des affaires économiques du Sénat to the draft law on energy transition for green growth, as submitted by the Assemblée Nationale on 27 May 2015, n° 466.

1424 Art. 6 of the Law on the Environmental Footprint of Digital Technology.

1425 Art. 3 of the Proposition de loi n° 4054 visant à lutter contre l'obsolescence programmée: passer de la société du jetable à celle du durable, déposée à l'Assemblée Nationale le 7 avril 2021.

been somewhat lightened by the Law of November 2021 aimed at reducing the environmental footprint of digitalisation, which removed the need to prove the aim of stimulating the replacement rate of products.[1426] The two elements are cumulative, meaning that only the combination of them makes it possible to convict an individual or a company for planned obsolescence. The demonstration of these intentional and material elements may constitute a heavy burden on consumers and consumer associations' shoulders, which is exacerbated by the criminalisation of the practice.[1427]

373. PROVING THE REDUCED PRODUCT LIFETIME – Proving the reduced product lifetime is far from easy, especially when the violation is not due to blatant material obsolescence, but for example to incompatibility issues.[1428] To achieve this, the first necessary step is to objectively determine the (average) lifetime of products of the same types before comparing it to the actual lifetime of the concerned product.[1429] However, consumers generally have no access to the relevant information. This issue should soon be solved, at least for electrical and electronic equipment, with the introduction of the durability index as of 1st January 2024. Article 16 of the Anti-Waste Law creates the obligation for the producers of these goods to display the lifetime of their products.[1430] As a result, consumers facing premature obsolescence will simply need to demonstrate that the actual lifetime of their product was shorter than the one indicated by the producer on the durability index. It will be interesting to see how the two legislations will interact in practice. For goods that are not covered by the durability index, consumers will still experience serious difficulties in proving reduced product lifetime. Further legislation could prove useful in that respect. Better links should be established between the law on planned obsolescence and rules requiring product durability (see #2), like those set out in EU ecodesign regulations[1431] or by EU Ecolabel criteria[1432], so that consumers can rely on these rules to prove the reduced product lifetime. In the absence of such rules, the law could regulate and facilitate the intervention of product-specific experts, who

---

1426 Art. 5 of the Law on the Environmental Footprint of Digital Technology.

1427 Indeed, under criminal law, standards of proof are higher, bad faith cannot be presumed and there is the right against self-incrimination. See OECD Policy roundtables from 10 January 2005 on Cartels: Sanctions against individuals, DAF/COMP(2004)39, p. 21.

1428 A.-C. Martin, *Le délit d'obsolescence programmée* (Recueil Dalloz 2017).

1429 In this regard, reference could be made to the terminology used in the study commissioned by ADEME: S. Mugdal *et al.* (BIO Intelligence Service S.A.S.), *Etude sur la durée de vie des équipements électriques et électroniques* (ADEME 2012) pp. 11–12. In this study, the 'useful product lifetime' is the period during which consumers use the product from the moment it is acquired until it is no longer used. This period could be compared to the 'normative product lifetime', which refers to the average product lifetime as measured in specific test conditions established by standards or, failing that, by clear, transparent and recognized methods.

1430 See *infra*, n° 561–563.

1431 See *supra*, n° 231 *et seq.*

1432 See *infra*, n° 601–605.

would consider comparable products (regardless of product series and producers) and define the average lifetime of the sum on a case-by-case basis (see #3).[1433] Besides this issue, another question arises with regard to the statutory limitation periods (*délai de prescription*) as, in practice, the techniques could be applied way before the damages occur, and thus after the limitation period expires.[1434]

374. Proving the intent or the negligence – With regard to the second element of the legal test, consumers must demonstrate that unlike them, the person responsible for placing the product on the market was aware of the poor quality of the product. Article L. 441–2 of the Consumer Code requires thus a special intent or negligence on the part of the trader. One way of adducing this evidence is to prove that the producer did not properly control or check product quality. This behaviour is considered fraudulent under French law.[1435] Nevertheless, apart from this possibility, proving that the trader *deliberately* reduced product lifetime (or sought to do so) is particularly difficult. In most cases, it will suffice for producers to allege that their decisions as to the design of the product were dictated by economic, technical, safety or aesthetic reasons – all credible to justify the practice being criticised.[1436] While these rationales may not always be inaccurate, they may cover less worthy objectives.[1437] Hence, actions or omissions limiting product lifetime will remain unpunished if the person responsible for placing the product on the market proves that they did not intend to reduce the lifetime of products, but that it was only the result of their strategy.[1438] It is worth knowing however, that in practice, judges often presume the existence of special intent and it is then for the defendant to rebut the presumption.[1439] When assessing justifications, judges could state that the reasons invoked (whatever they are) may not justify the practice of limiting product lifetime, as it is the case in competition law.[1440]

1433 For a similar reasoning, see S. Wrbka, 'Warranty law in cases of planned obsolescence – The Austrian situation', 6 *EuCML* (2017) p. 67 at p. 76.

1434 N. Jeanne, ""Prêt à jeter?" – A propos du délit d'obsolescence programmée", in J. Alix et al. (eds.), *Humanisme et justice: Mélanges en l'honneur de Geneviève Giudicelli-Delage* (Dalloz 2016) p. 614.

1435 See C. Ambroise-Castérot, 'Consommation: Chapitre 3 – Protection pénale du consommateur contre les fraudes et falsifications', in Y. Mayaud (ed.), *Répertoire de droit pénal et de procédure pénale* (Paris Dalloz 2016) n° 357.

1436 For concrete examples of such allegations in cases of material obsolescence, see *supra*, n° 114.

1437 E. Maitre-Ekern and C. Dalhammar,'Regulating planned obsolescence: a review of legal approaches to increase product durability and reparability in Europe', 25 *Review of European Community & International Environmental Law* (2016) p. 387.

1438 It is interesting to note that this issue had already been raised during the adoption process of this legislation. See Rapport n°2230 de E. Bareigts, M.-N. Battistel, S. Buis, D. Baupin et P. Plisson, fait au nom de la commission spéciale, déposé le 27 septembre 2014, amendement CS1840.

1439 N. Jeanne, ""Prêt à jeter?" – A propos du délit d'obsolescence programmée", in J. Alix et al. (eds.), *Humanisme et justice: Mélanges en l'honneur de Geneviève Giudicelli-Delage* (Dalloz 2016) pp. 616–617.

1440 For example, in *Hilti* case, the Commission argued and the Court concluded that an undertaking cannot invoke safety reasons to justify abusive practices which seek to eliminate

375. Incompatibility issues – Third, for all the bans introduced under French law, doubts arise as to their compatibility with the exhaustive UCPD blacklist.[1441] Notwithstanding their initial objective of preventing waste, these provisions still fall within the scope of the UCPD, as the concerned practices are 'commercial practices' within the meaning of Article 2(d) of the Directive.[1442] The overlap between these legislations is particularly obvious in the claims brought by HOP against *Epson* and *Apple*.[1443] However, the general ban on planned obsolescence and those introduced by the Anti-Waste Law run counter to the provisions of the UCPD as the maximum harmonisation precludes Member States from adding forbidden practices to the UCPD blacklist, even to achieve a higher level of consumer protection.[1444] As they are not listed in Annex I to the UCPD, these practices cannot be prohibited in all circumstances, but only following a specific assessment against the criteria set out in Articles 5 to 9 of the Directive allowing the unfairness of those practices to be established. To avoid the compatibility issue, some scholars have interpreted the prohibition of planned obsolescence as not covering cases where producers give false information on product lifetime as such cases are already dealt with by the rules on misleading commercial practices and the rules on hidden defects guarantee.[1445] But this reasoning is not very convincing. Last but not least, these compatibility issues also raise the question of the necessity of adopting such specific legislation, taking into account all the existing rules that already contribute to combating premature obsolescence.[1446] To solve this problem, one should seriously consider amending the scope of the UCPD, as previously argued[1447], so that it no longer hinders the adoption of national rules tackling premature obsolescence.

---

those products from the market in order to protect its commercial position. See ECJ 12 December 1991, Case T-30/89, *Hilti v Commission, EU:T:1991:70*, paras 20 and 115–119.

1441 This compatibility question had already been asked for the prohibition of planned obsolescence. See C. Ambroise-Castérot, 'Consommation: Chapitre 3 – Protection pénale du consommateur contre les fraudes et falsifications', in Y. Mayaud (ed.), *Répertoire de droit pénal et de procédure pénale* (Paris Dalloz 2016) n° 357.

1442 Along the same lines, see ECJ 14 January 2010, Case C-304/08, *Plus Warenhandelsgesellschaft, EU:C:2010:12*, para 38; ECJ 9 November 2010, Case C-540/08, *Mediaprint, EU:C:2010:660*, paras 26–28.

1443 In these claims, HOP invokes the provisions transposing the UCPD in the alternative, referring directly to the arguments developed for the alleged violation of Article L. 441-2 of the Consumer Code. See Tribunal de grande instance de Nanterre 17 septembre 2017, Plainte au Procureur de la République, *HOP* v *X*, p. 14–15; Tribunal de grande instance de Paris 27 décembre 2017, Plainte au Procureur de la République, *HOP* v *Apple France*, p. 6–7.

1444 ECJ 9 November 2010, Case C-540/08, *Mediaprint, EU:C:2010:660*, para 30.

1445 A.-C. Martin, *Le délit d'obsolescence programmée* (Recueil Dalloz 2015) p. 1944.

1446 See also E. La Rosa, 'Planned Obsolescence and Criminal Law: A Problematic Relationship?', in V. Mauerhofer, D. Rupo, L. Tarquinio (eds.), *Sustainability and Law* (2020) p. 227 at p. 229.

1447 See *supra*, n° 352.

Policy recommendations to improve French legislation on planned obsolescence:

#2 Better links should be established between the law on planned obsolescence and rules requiring product durability (e.g. EU ecodesign regulations, EU Ecolabel criteria).

#3 In absence of such rules, the intervention of product-specific experts should be regulated and facilitated to define product lifetime.

c) *Belgian legislative proposals on planned obsolescence*

376. Three legislative proposals on planned obsolescence – As already mentioned[1448], three legislative proposals aimed to curb premature obsolescence are currently pending in Belgium. All these proposals suggest legally prohibiting practices that shorten product lifetime, though through different approaches.

377. Proposal I – In the Proposal from July 2019[1449], it is suggested introducing the criminal offence of 'planned obsolescence' (*obsolescence programmée*), defined as "*a set of techniques by which a producer deliberately reduces the lifetime of a product, without any benefits for the user, with the aim of stimulating the replacement rate of that product*".[1450] This provision is a glaring example of the French influence as the proposed definition is virtually identical to the definition contained in Article L. 441-2 of the French Consumer Code. This definition would be added to the list of definitions enshrined in Article I.8 of the Belgian Economic Law Code (*Code de droit économique*). Pursuant to Article 3 of Proposal I, practices falling within the definition of planned obsolescence should be considered as 'misleading commercial practices' within the meaning of the UCPD as implemented in Belgian law.[1451] In support of this idea, reference is made to the Italian decisions against *Samsung* and *Apple* from 2018.[1452] The objective is to make clear that practices of planned obsolescence fall within the scope of the legislation on unfair commercial practices.[1453] The explanatory memorandum to Proposal I explains that not all cases of obsolescence are planned nor detrimental to consumers and the

1448 See *supra*, n° 75.

1449 Proposition de loi visant à lutter contre l'obsolescence programmée et à soutenir l'économie de la réparation, *Doc. parl.*, Ch., 2019, 19 juillet 2019, n° 0193/001 (hereafter 'Proposal I').

1450 Art. 2 Proposal I: "*ensemble de techniques par lesquelles un producteur réduit délibérément la durée de vie d'un produit, sans avantage pour l'utilisateur, pour en augmenter le taux de remplacement*". (free translation).

1451 Art. VI.97–100 and XV.16 Economic Law Code.

1452 See the explanatory memorandum to Proposition de loi visant à lutter contre l'obsolescence programmée et à soutenir l'économie de la réparation, *Doc. Parl.*, Ch., 2019, 19 juillet 2019, n° 0193/001, p. 7.

1453 *Ibid.*

environment.[1454] This is the case of product obsolescence due to technological progress and fashion, as well as single-use products where consumers are aware of the product's limited lifetime. Except in these cases, planned obsolescence, when detrimental to consumers and the environment, should be considered as fraud. The legislative proposal provides a list of practices that fall within the concept of 'planned obsolescence':

- *a manufacturer who makes their product unusable after a certain period of time or a certain amount of use;*
- *a manufacturer who introduces into their product a device that makes any repair impossible or too expensive, e.g. by using non-standard screws or by ensuring that batteries cannot be replaced;*
- *a manufacturer who creates products that are incompatible with previous versions of the same product or with those of competitors;*
- *a manufacturer who reduces the lifetime of their products by choosing certain materials or assembling components in a particular way.*[1455]

In case of a breach of the proposed prohibition, Article 8 of Proposal I provides for the most severe sanction imposed by the Economic Law Code (level 6), which corresponds to a fine from € 500 to € 100,000 and one to five years imprisonment.[1456]

378. Proposal II – The approach followed by the second legislative proposal from November 2019[1457] is a bit different, distinguishing between 'planned obsolescence' (*obsolescence programmée*), defined as "*a set of techniques by which a producer seeks to deliberately reduce the lifetime of a product, with the aim of stimulating the replacement rate of that product*"[1458], and of 'premature

1454 *Ibid.*, p. 3.

1455 Proposal I, p. 4: "*[L'obsolescence programmée] peut prendre les formes suivantes:*
- *un fabricant qui rend son produit inutilisable après une certaine durée ou un certain nombre d'utilisations;*
- *un fabricant qui introduit dans son produit un dispositif qui rend toute réparation impossible ou anormalement chère, par exemple en utilisant des vis au format non standard ou en faisant en sorte que les batteries ne puissent pas être remplacées;*
- *un fabricant qui crée des produits incompatibles avec les versions antérieures du même produit ou avec ceux des concurrents;*
- *un fabricant qui réduit la durée de vie de ses produits par le choix de certains matériaux ou un assemblage particulier des composants.*" (free translation).

1456 Art. XV. 70 Economic Law Code.

1457 Art. 3, 10 and 14 Proposition de loi modifiant le Code civil et le Code de droit économique, visant à lutter contre l'obsolescence programmée et l'obsolescence prématurée et à augmenter les possibilités de réparation, *Doc. Parl.*, Ch., 2019–2020, 19 novembre 2019, n° 0771/001 (hereafter 'Proposal II').

1458 Art. 3 Proposal II: "*ensemble des techniques par lesquelles un producteur vise à réduire délibérément la durée de vie d'un produit pour en augmenter le taux de remplacement*". (free translation).

obsolescence' (*obsolescence prématurée*), defined as "*putting a product on the market having a lifetime that is shorter than the conformity period communicated by the producer*" (which cannot be below two years).[1459] Planned obsolescence is totally banned, whereas practices of premature obsolescence are only prohibited when they are systematically adopted by the producer. The logic behind this distinction lies in the intent on the part of the producer.[1460] The distinction between planned and premature obsolescence is reflected in the regime of sanctions. While the most severe sanction (level 6) is applicable to practices of planned obsolescence, cases of premature obsolescence would only be subject to a sanction of level 4 consisting of a fine from € 26 to € 50,000.

379. PROPOSAL III – The third and most recent legislative proposal from January 2020[1461], which is based on the former proposal from April 2016[1462], refers to 'organised obsolescence', defined as "*any practice by which the producer artificially reduces the potential lifetime or use time of a product from its design stage onwards, and in a manifest manner, with the aim of increasing the replacement rate of the product without any benefits for the consumer or the environment*".[1463] The wording 'organised obsolescence' was chosen to encompass practices that accelerate product obsolescence without being 'planned' *per se*.[1464] In that sense, Proposal III stands in contrast to the French legal definition as it prohibits not only planned obsolescence *stricto sensu*, but also less blatant cases of obsolescence, like product incompatibilities or products that are (almost) impossible to repair. Article 2 of Proposal III supplements this definition with a non-exhaustive list of four key types of organised obsolescence, including cases where the product is designed (1) with an electronic device that makes it stop working after a certain period of use, (2) in a way that makes repair impossible or too expensive, (3) with batteries and accumulators that cannot be easily removed or replaced or (4) in a way that, on the basis of tests and analyses set up by law, a defect occurs during the expected period of use in more than 10% of the cases.[1465] More cases of 'organised obsolescence' are listed in the explanatory memorandum to the proposal.[1466] In some less blatant cases,

---

1459 Art. 3 Proposal II: "*mise sur le marché de produits dont la durée de vie est inférieure à celle annoncée en vertu de l'article 1649 quater, §1er, du Code civil*". (free translation).

1460 See the explanatory memorandum to Proposal II, p. 7.

1461 Proposition de loi visant à lutter contre l'obsolescence organisée et à soutenir l'économie circulaire, *Doc. parl.*, Ch., 2019–2020, 7 janvier 2020, n° 0914/001 (hereafter 'Proposal III').

1462 Proposition de loi relative à la lutte contre l'obsolescence organisée et au soutien à l'économie circulaire, *Doc. parl.*, Ch., 2015–2016, 11 avril 2016, n° 1749/001.

1463 Art. 2 Proposal III: "*toute pratique par laquelle la durée de vie ou d'utilisation potentielle d'un produit, tel que défini à l'article I.1, 4°, est réduite artificiellement dès sa conception, de manière manifeste, par le producteur tel que défini à l'article I.10, 8°, afin d'en augmenter le taux de remplacement sans avantage pour le consommateur ou l'environnement*". (free translation).

1464 See the explanatory memorandum to Proposal III, p. 18.

1465 Art. 2 and 10–25 Proposal III.

1466 See the explanatory memorandum to Proposal III, pp. 18–19.

a subjective evaluation would be carried out, with a technical analysis of the concerned product.[1467] Article 8 of Proposal III suggests making a link between the ban on organised obsolescence and the provisions on the legal guarantee, although its wording and consequences remain unclear.[1468] This legislative proposal also stands apart from the two other proposals by adding sanctions and mechanisms to prevent practices of organised obsolescence. In addition to level 6 sanctions, Article 24 allows for the possibility of raising the fine to 5% of the average annual turnover of the company when the profits obtained from the breach are high, and 10% in the event of recidivism. In addition, Article 25 suggests specific civil sanctions in case of organised obsolescence: the sales contract would be deemed null and void, allowing the buyer to be fully reimbursed without having to prove any suffered damage. Another interesting suggestion contained in Proposal III consists in extending mechanisms provided for product safety to cases of (potential) organised obsolescence, including the product analysis and examination procedures, product withdrawal procedures, and the contact point.[1469]

380. A critical review of the Council of State – The three proposals have been critically reviewed by the Council of State.[1470] Its opinion unveiled the lack of clarity of many points of law contained in these proposals, including their legal definitions of 'planned', 'premature' and 'organised' obsolescence.[1471] Given this lack of clarity, the Council of State underlined that, should it be decided to introduce a definition of product obsolescence, its wording should be clear enough to allow sanctions on this basis. This criticism echoes what has previously been pointed out for the French legislation on planned obsolescence,

1467 See the explanatory memorandum to Proposal III, p. 20.

1468 See also Avis du Conseil d'Etat du 21 février 2020 sur la Proposition de loi visant à lutter contre l'obsolescence organisée et à soutenir l'économie circulaire (n° 0914/001), n° 66.910/1, p. 11, pt. 20.

1469 Art. 10–21 Proposition de loi n° 0914/001.

1470 Avis du Conseil d'Etat du 21 février 2020 sur la Proposition de loi modifiant le Code civil et le Code de droit économique, visant à lutter contre l'obsolescence programmée et l'obsolescence prématurée et à augmenter les possibilités de réparation (n° 0771/001), n° 66.908/1; Avis du Conseil d'Etat du 21 février 2020 sur la Proposition de loi visant à lutter contre l'obsolescence programmée et à soutenir l'économie de la réparation (n° 0913/001), n° 66.909/1; Avis du Conseil d'Etat du 21 février 2020 sur la Proposition de loi visant à lutter contre l'obsolescence organisée et à soutenir l'économie circulaire (n° 0914/001), n° 66.910/1.

1471 See Avis du Conseil d'Etat du 21 février 2020 sur la Proposition de loi modifiant le Code civil et le Code de droit économique, visant à lutter contre l'obsolescence programmée et l'obsolescence prématurée et à augmenter les possibilités de réparation (n° 0771/001), n° 66.908/1, p. 6; Avis du Conseil d'Etat du 21 février 2020 sur la Proposition de loi visant à lutter contre l'obsolescence programmée et à soutenir l'économie de la réparation (n° 0913/001), n° 66.909/1, pp. 5–6; Avis du Conseil d'Etat du 21 février 2020 sur la Proposition de loi visant à lutter contre l'obsolescence organisée et à soutenir l'économie circulaire (n° 0914/001), no 66.910/1, p. 8.

for which the lack of clarity led to legal uncertainty and consequently impairs the effectiveness of the law.[1472]

381. French law, a good example? – In addition to the lack of clarity, serious doubts can be raised as to the necessity and effectiveness of some proposed provisions. This is particularly the case for the suggested prohibitions of 'planned obsolescence' or 'organised obsolescence', which are inspired by French law. Although a total ban on these practices could contribute to the fight against the premature replacement of consumer goods, one should be careful not to reproduce the same mistakes as in France as to the burden of proof and the compatibility with EU law.[1473] Confusion also seems to exist in Belgium as to the leeway left by EU law and the compatibility of any proposal with EU law.[1474] The fog would be lifted if the scope of application of the UCPD was amended, as previously argued in this book.[1475] Once this scope is reviewed, one could envisage adopting additional prohibitions (including on premature obsolescence) on the basis of the legislation on unfair commercial practices, as has been proposed in Proposal I.

d) Promoting product sustainability through the UCPD blacklist

382. The need for an updated blacklist – Although the following paragraphs of this section reveal that practices that limit product lifetime can be sanctioned on the basis of the other steps of the UCPD cascade system, an update of the blacklist should be considered to further promote product sustainability at EU level. Some practices should indeed avoid the case-by-case assessment required by Articles 6 to 9 of the UCPD. This would leave less margin of appreciation to national enforcers, ensure legal certainty and raise awareness among public authorities and stakeholders about premature obsolescence.[1476]

1472 See *supra*, n° 371.

1473 See *supra*, n° 372–375.

1474 This confusion can be identified in the adoption process of the 2012 Senate Resolution. See the meeting minutes of 24 January 2012 contained in the Proposition de résolution en vue de lutter contre l'obsolescence programmée des produits liés à l'énergie, *Doc. lég.*, Sénat, 2011–2012, 1er février 2012, n° 5 – 1251/3, pp. 3–4. Moreover, discussions on the role of the UCPD took place at the Belgian Parliament after the adoption of the Italian decisions against Apple and Samsung. See Compte rendu intégral de la Commission de l'Economie, de la Politique scientifique, de l'Education, des institutions scientifiques et culturelles nationales, des Classes moyennes et de l'Agriculture, Doc. parl., Ch., 2018–2019, 13 novembre 2018, CRIV 54 COM 997, p. 43 at p. 46.

1475 See *supra*, n° 352 and n° 375.

1476 In this regard, we fully agree with the Belgian *Conseil d'Etat.* See Avis du Conseil d'Etat du 21 février 2020 sur la Proposition de loi visant à lutter contre l'obsolescence programmée et à soutenir l'économie de la réparation (n° 0193/001), n° 66.909/1, p. 7: "*la pratique pourrait donc d'ores et déjà être considérée comme trompeuse, mais il n'en demeure pas moins que la sécurité juridique et la clarté de l'ordonnancement juridique y gagneraient si l'assimilation de l'obsolescence programmée aux pratiques commerciales trompeuses est explicitée dans la proposition de loi soumise pour avis*". The lack of clarity is also visible in the literature: see

Furthermore, adding practices linked to sustainability aspects within the UCPD blacklist could better underline the importance of these aspects when assessing similar practices on the basis of Articles 6 to 9 of the UCPD. As the UCPD blacklist is of full harmonisation, such amendments will necessitate a review of the Directive itself, as stated in Article 5(5).

383. Re-emergence of the idea – Amendments to the UCPD blacklist have already been suggested in the past. For example, in its 2013 Opinion, the EESC called for a total ban on products with built-in defects deliberately designed to end product lifetime, referring to printers with prematurely limited lifetime as an illustrative example.[1477] In 2017, during the consultation within the context of the REFIT, several stakeholders put forward ideas for the possible updating of the UCPD blacklist. However, these suggestions showed a great diversity of views that did not converge on any specific priorities. Therefore, it was concluded that "*there does not appear any clear candidate for possible additional inclusion in the UCPD blacklist*".[1478] In other words, it was considered that there was no need to add more practices to the list, including those related to premature obsolescence. This reluctance to amend the UCPD blacklist seems to have disappeared, as demonstrated by the adoption of the Enforcement and Modernisation Directive, which introduced four new unfair commercial practices in the blacklist.[1479] Such amendments may soon be reiterated if the Proposal for a Directive on empowering consumers for the green transition is adopted. This proposal responds to the previous call of the EP for the Commission to "*tackle the premature obsolescence of products by considering adding to the list set out in Annex I to Directive 2005/29/EC practices which effectively shorten the lifetime of a product to increase its replacement rate and unduly constrain the reparability of products, including software*".[1480]

384. The proposed amendments to the UCPD blacklist – Article 1(4) of the Proposal for a Directive on empowering consumers for the green transition introduces certain flagrant cases of premature obsolescence in the UCPD blacklist.[1481] Among them are practices whereby the trader omits to inform the

---

for ex. A. Hamann, 'Obsolescence programmée: le droit en panne?', 102 *D.C.C.R.* (2014); D. Raes, "L'obsolescence programmée à l'épreuve de l'obligation d'information du vendeur, de la notion de conformité et de la garantie des vices cachés" in *Liber Amicorum François Glansdorf et Pierre Legros* (Bruylant 2014).

1477 See Opinion of the European Economic and Social Committee of 17 October 2013 on Towards more sustainable consumption: industrial product lifetimes and restoring trust through consumer information, CCMI/112, pt. 1.2.

1478 Commission Staff Working Document of 23 May 2017 on Report of the Fitness Check of consumer and marketing law (REFIT), SWD(2017) 209 final, p. 77.

1479 See Art. 3 of the Enforcement and Modernisation Directive.

1480 European Parliament Resolution of 25 November 2020 on Towards a more sustainable single market for business and consumers, 2020/2021(INI), pt. 6(g).

1481 The introduction of a blanket ban on 'planned obsolescence' or 'premature obsolescence' has also been considered within the framework of this initiative, though these options

consumer that a software update will negatively impact the use of goods (...)[1482], omits to inform about the existence of a feature of a good introduced to limit its durability[1483], claims that a good has a certain durability in terms of usage time or intensity when it does not[1484], presents goods as allowing repair when they do not (...)[1485], induces the consumer into replacing the consumables of a good earlier than for technical reasons is necessary[1486], omits to inform that a good is designed to limit its functionality when using consumables, spare parts or accessories that are not provided by the original producer.[1487] The Council has already suggested some changes to this proposed UCPD blacklist and proposed instead to amend Article 6(2) of the UCPD so that it would prohibit "*any marketing of a good when the trader is aware or may reasonably be aware that such good contains a feature that was incorporated to limit its durability*".[1488]

385. No general ban on 'planned obsolescence' should be introduced at EU level either – Whereas cases of intentional material obsolescence should undoubtedly be prevented and sanctioned, serious doubts exist as to the effectiveness of introducing a general ban of planned or built-in obsolescence within the UCPD blacklist. The French legislation on 'planned obsolescence' has revealed these flaws. Although the French law contributes to curbing certain cases of premature obsolescence, such a prohibition encounters the obstacles posed by the lack of legal certainty and the heavy burden of proof, which would lie with consumers and authorities, especially as it requires proving the intent to shorten product lifetime.[1489] Blacklisting planned obsolescence does therefore not seem appropriate.

386. Blacklisting violations of requirements on product sustainability imposed by EU law – Instead, the UCPD blacklist should

---

were finally not pursued by the EC. See the explanatory memorandum to the Proposal for a Directive of the European Parliament and of the Council amending Directives 2005/29/EC and 2011/83/EU as regards empowering consumers for the green transition through better protection against unfair practices and better information, COM(2022) 143 final, p. 11.

1482 See pt. 23d of the Annex to the Proposal for a Directive on empowering consumers for the green transition.

1483 See pt. 23e of the Annex to the Proposal for a Directive on empowering consumers for the green transition.

1484 See pt. 23f of the Annex to the Proposal for a Directive on empowering consumers for the green transition.

1485 See pt. 23g of the Annex to the Proposal for a Directive on empowering consumers for the green transition.

1486 See pt. 23h of the Annex to the Proposal for a Directive on empowering consumers for the green transition.

1487 See pt. 23i of the Annex to the Proposal for a Directive on empowering consumers for the green transition.

1488 This idea has raised many questions among the Member States, including questions about the practicalities of such a prohibition (e.g. how would this work in practice?; would traders be required to carry out tests prior to the sale?).

1489 For further comments, see *supra*, n° 384–391.

include practices of premature obsolescence that are related to the provision of information or other obligations imposed by EU law (see #6).[1490] By doing so, the blacklist would build a bridge with EU rules that impose ecodesign and information requirements on product sustainability. For example, if a television producer does not provide spare parts required under the ecodesign implementing measures, it should be seen as an illegal practice *per se*. Another example would be a computer battery which, contrary to what is required under the ecodesign legislation, cannot be easily removed and replaced without damage. The same reasoning should be held if the trader does not comply with information requirements on product lifetime or the availability period of spare parts.[1491] One of the biggest advantages of such an amendment is the lightened burden of proof. Instead of having to prove the intentional and material elements as required by the French legislation[1492], consumers (and authorities) would only need to demonstrate the non-compliance of the trader with EU rules. Nonetheless, this new protection would only be effective if consumers are well informed about these obligations imposed by EU law.

387. Blacklisting blatant cases causing premature obsolescence – Furthermore, the blacklist should mention practices that are regularly sanctioned in practice. One should consider for example including practices that consist of urging consumers to install software updates that negatively impact the performance of the device (see #7), as condemned in the two Italian cases against *Samsung* and *Apple*.[1493] A reference to such a situation could be made within the text of the blacklisted practice referring to "*persistent and unwanted solicitations*" established under Point 26 of Annex I to the UCPD. This idea was taken up in the Proposal for a Directive on empowering consumers for the green transition, though it is suggested to add a distinct blacklisted practice specifically dedicated to this situation.[1494] Another practice blacklisted by the Proposal is worth considering, that is the one targeting the trader who "*omit[s] to inform that a good is designed to limit its functionality when using consumables, spare parts or accessories that are not provided by the original producer*".[1495] Inspiration could, moreover, be drawn from other bans existing under national law, like the bans established

1490 This would increase the importance of the prohibition already established under Art. 7(5) UCPD. See *infra*, n° 403–408.

1491 For more example of ecodesign requirements, see Chapter II on the design and production stage.

1492 See *supra*, n° 372–374.

1493 Autorita Garante della Concorrenza e del Mercato, 25 septembre 2018, *Apple*; Autorita Garante della Concorrenza e del Mercato, 25 septembre 2018, *Samsung*.

1494 See pt. 23d in the Annex to the Proposal for a Directive on empowering consumers for the green transition, which targets traders who "*[omit] to inform the consumer that a software update will negatively impact the use of goods with digital elements or certain features of those goods even if the software update improves the functioning of other features.*"

1495 See pt. 23i in the Annex to the Proposal for a Directive on empowering consumers for the green transition. Such practices may, for example, occur in the printer sector.

by the French Anti-Waste Law on practices limiting professional repairers' or reusers' access to spare parts, instructions, technical information or any other instrument, equipment or software allowing repair (see #8), practices making it impossible, including through software technique, to repair or repackage a device outside its approved circuits (see #9) as well as practices encouraging degradation of products under normal operating condition and preventing their direct reuse or refurbishment through advertising or commercial communication (see #10).[1496]

388. Blacklisting practices of greenwashing – Certain practices of greenwashing should also be included in the UCPD blacklist.[1497] As a first example, practices whereby the trader presents product sustainability aspects that are legally required (e.g. by ecodesign rules) as a distinctive feature of their offer should be prohibited in all circumstances (see #5).[1498] Second, one could envisage a blanket ban on the use of the word 'sustainable' (here understood in its broad sense)[1499] for companies, brands and sectors that are known as being not eco-friendly (see #4). This ban would require that the law defines what is meant by 'not eco-friendly' and gives the criteria on which such qualification is based. Inspiration could be drawn from the new EU Taxonomy Regulation[1500], which establishes the criteria for determining whether an economic activity qualifies as environmentally sustainable for the purposes of establishing the degree to which an investment is environmentally sustainable. However, an option that should be disregarded is the French approach, which prohibits vague statements, such as 'environmentally friendly', 'ecological', 'green', 'sustainable', etc., in all circumstances. Such prohibition should indeed be lifted if the 'environmental excellence' of the product has been substantiated (e.g. via the EU Ecolabel or other recognised ISO-type I ecolabels, the PEF method or other lifecycle assessment (LCA) studies proving the product's positive environmental performance) and if the claim clearly and prominently qualifies the specific environmental benefit(s) of the product (compared to other products).[1501] That way, traders willing to communicate the environmental performance of their products to consumers can still do so

[1496] See *supra*, n° 369.

[1497] B. Keirsbilck, E. Terryn, A. Michel and I. Alogna, *Sustainable Consumption and Consumer Protection Legislation* (European Parliament 2020) p. 14.

[1498] This amendment is proposed in the Annex to the Proposal for a Directive on empowering consumers for the green transition (see pt. 10a).

[1499] In its broad sense, the word 'sustainable' defines something that allows "*meet[ing] the needs of the present without compromising the ability of future generations to meet their own needs*" (UN World Commission on Environment and Development, *Our Common Future* (1987) p. 41). See *infra*, n° 52.

[1500] Regulation (EU) 2020/852 of the European Parliament and of the Council of 18 June 2020 on the establishment of a framework to facilitate sustainable investment, and amending Regulation (EU) 2019/2088, OJ L 198, 22.6.2020, p. 13–43.

[1501] See *infra*, n° 417.

through such claims. The EC has proposed amending Annex I of the UCPD to combat greenwashing.[1502] Hopefully, some of these ideas will be taken into account.

Proposed review of Annex I (UCPD blacklist)

ANNEX I

COMMERCIAL PRACTICES WHICH ARE IN ALL CIRCUMSTANCES CONSIDERED UNFAIR

Misleading commercial practices

4a. Using the term 'sustainable' in a claim when the trader, brand or sector in question can be qualified as being not eco-friendly. #4

(…)

10a. Presenting product sustainability aspects that are legally required as a distinctive feature of the trader's offer. #5

(…)

23a. Violating requirements imposed by implementing rules adopted within the framework of the Ecodesign Directive. #6

Aggressive commercial practices

26. Making persistent and unwanted solicitations by telephone, fax, e-mail or other remote media, including to urge consumers to install software updates, except in circumstances and to the extent justified under national law to enforce a contractual obligation. This includes cases This is without prejudice to Article 10 of Directive 97/7/EC and Directives 95/46/EC (2) and 2002/58/EC. #7

31a. Limiting professional repairers' or reusers' access to spare parts, instructions, technical information or any other instrument, equipment or software allowing repair. #8

31b. Making it impossible, including through software technique, to repair or repackage a device outside its approved circuits. #9

31c. Inciting to degrade products in normal operating condition and to prevent their direct reuse or refurbishment through advertising or commercial communication. #10

1502 See Art. 1(4) of the Proposal for a Directive on empowering consumers for the green transition, as well as pts. (1) and (2) of its Annex.

e) *Defining 'premature obsolescence' and 'greenwashing' in the UCPD and in the Guidance*

389. The need for an EU-wide definition – Besides amendments to the UCPD blacklist, the EC should further elaborate on an EU-level definition of 'premature obsolescence'. An EU-wide definition of premature obsolescence would allow having a commonly shared definition between all Member States and, consequently, help tackle the issue in a coherent and harmonised way. The EESC had already emphasised the absence of a definitive consensus between the various definitions of 'planned obsolescence' and the need to find an overarching one.[1503] The EP floated the same idea, calling on the EC *"to propose, in consultation with consumer organisations, producers and other stakeholders, an EU-level definition of planned obsolescence for tangible goods and software"*.[1504] The idea of an objective and common definition of 'premature obsolescence' was reiterated in the 2020 EP Resolution.[1505] Some scholars expressed their agreement on that point.[1506] E. Maitre-Ekern, M. Taylor and M. van der Velden went one step further by proposing the adoption of a Product Framework Directive, which would contain a legal definition of 'premature obsolescence' and refer to all legal instruments relevant to tackle the issue.[1507] Such a horizontal approach is strongly encouraged by P. Durant, a member of the EP, who proposed the adoption of a directive on premature obsolescence with a view to facilitating the discussions on amendments to the various regulations involved.[1508]

390. From planned obsolescence... – So far, the UCPD Guidance focuses on the concept of 'planned obsolescence', with a definition similar to the one used in Article L. 441–2 of the French Consumer Code. While the French law aims to prohibit specific practices and can thus focus solely on the practices that should be prohibited, the UCPD Guidance aims to facilitate the proper application of the Directive. The concepts and definitions used by this Guidance should thus provide a clear and comprehensive view of the phenomenon to assist consumers, traders and public authorities in the application of the UCPD, including when

---

1503 Opinion of the EESC of 17 October 2013 on Towards more sustainable consumption: industrial product lifetimes and restoring trust through consumer information, CCMI/112, pt. 2.5. See *supra*, n° 68.

1504 See European Parliament Resolution of 4 July 2017 on a longer lifetime for products: benefits for consumers and companies, (2016/2272(INI)), pt. 30.

1505 European Parliament Resolution of 25 November 2020 on Towards a more sustainable single market for business and consumers, 2020/2021(INI), pt. 6(g).

1506 See e.g. E. Ober, B. Dell'Anno, J.-R. Drèze, L. Herrmann, A. Luciano, R. Maltry, I. Oehme, B. Schmon and J.-P. Ventère, 'Planned obsolescence: the government's choice?', in C. Bakker and R. Mugge (eds.), *Product Lifetimes And The Environment 2017 – Conference Proceedings* (IOS Press 2017) p. 318.

1507 See E. Maitre-Ekern, M. Taylor and M. van der Velden, 'Towards a Sustainable Circular Economy: SMART reform proposals', 12 *University of Oslo Faculty of Law Legal Studies Research Paper Series* (2020).

1508 See the speech of P. Durant at the EESC conference on premature obsolescence on 30 November 2018.

they face cases of premature obsolescence. The recent amendment to the UCPD Guidance has brought some improvements in that sense, but the current definition of 'planned obsolescence' given in the document is still restrictive and biased compared to the phenomenon of premature obsolescence.[1509] Therefore, it seems necessary to amend the UCPD and its Guidance so that it is no longer confined to the narrow concept of planned obsolescence but takes the different types of premature obsolescence into consideration.

391. ... TO PREMATURE OBSOLESCENCE – To fully exploit the potential of the UCPD in tackling premature obsolescence, it is necessary to use the concept of 'premature obsolescence' (instead of 'planned obsolescence')[1510] and associate it with the definition suggested in the first chapter of this book (see #11 and #14).[1511] Such amendments to Article 2 and the UCPD Guidance would contribute not only to facilitating the proper application of the Directive but also to reframing the debate on premature obsolescence.[1512] The recharacterization of the debate could pave the way for constructive and fruitful discussions with the business side and raise consumers' awareness of their role in influencing product obsolescence. In other words, replacing the controversial term 'planned obsolescence' with other general and neutral terms, like premature obsolescence and product sustainability, would circumvent the difficulties of legislating on the issue.[1513] Such an approach had been followed by the EESC, which had changed the title of its first opinion on the topic from 'For a European fight against planned obsolescence' to 'Towards more sustainable consumption: industrial product lifetimes and restoring trust through consumer information'.[1514]

392. A LIST OF EXAMPLES NEEDED? – Concerning the definition of premature obsolescence, one could wonder about the need to include within the definition a list of practices – exhaustive or illustrative – that amount to premature obsolescence. The establishment of such a list has the advantage of mitigating the indeterminacy and bringing clarity and thus legal certainty on the legislation, allowing companies, consumers and public authorities to better identify practices that should be avoided.[1515] However, specifying exhaustively or not cases

1509 See *supra*, n° 80–84.

1510 See *supra*, n° 78–90.

1511 See *supra*, n° 97. In this book, 'premature obsolescence' is defined as "*all practices that reduce product lifetime so that the product does not reach its optimal lifetime (from an environmental point of view), without it being the result of normal wear and tear*".

1512 See also T. Libaert, 'Consommation et controverse: le cas de l'obsolescence programmée', 73 *Hermès, La Revue* (2015) p. 156.

1513 For a theoretical approach on this issue, see D. Walton, F. Macagno., 'The importance and trickiness of definition strategies in legal and political argumentation', 137 *Journal of Politics and Law* (2015) p. 141.

1514 T. Libaert, 'Consommation et controverse: le cas de l'obsolescence programmée', 73 *Hermès, La Revue* (2015) pp. 155–156.

1515 For example, the lack of clarity made the Italian authorities take their decisions on the basis of Articles 7 and 8 of the UCPD in the *Apple* and *Samsung* cases, although they could have

contemplated by the law in great detail may lead to the risk of excluding other related situations which may not fit the legal definition.[1516] The right balance has to be struck between vagueness and precision to formulate a satisfactory definition of premature obsolescence. This hard choice on whether to include a list or not could exacerbate the difficulty of reaching an agreement on a legal definition of premature obsolescence. One thing that mitigates the difficulty of the choice is the influence that judicial authorities can have when interpreting the definition, although their room for manoeuvre will be limited the more the law is precise.

393. A LEGAL DEFINITION OF GREENWASHING – In addition to a definition of 'premature obsolescence', a definition of 'greenwashing' should be introduced in Article 2 of the UCPD as well as in the UCPD Guidance. The concept of greenwashing is already used in existing EU legislation. For example, the Regulation on the establishment of a framework to facilitate sustainable investment defines 'greenwashing' as "*practice of gaining an unfair competitive advantage by marketing a financial product as environmentally friendly, when in fact basic environmental standards have not been met*".[1517] Yet it seems more appropriate to use the words of the UCPD Guidance, and more specifically the definition of 'environmental claims' (or 'green claims'), copy-paste it in Article 2 of the UCPD (see #12) and take it as a basis for the definition of 'greenwashing' (see #13).

Proposed review of the UCPD:

Article 2
Definitions

For the purposes of this Directive:

(...)

(o) 'premature obsolescence' means all practices that reduce product lifetime, without it being the result of normal wear and tear. #11

(p) 'environmental claim' means practice of suggesting or otherwise creating the impression (in commercial communication, marketing or advertising) that a good or a service has a positive or no impact on the environment or is less damaging to the environment than competing goods or services. #12

---

used the blacklist as the condemned practices correspond to the invitation to install updates that slow down devices (see n° 372). This could have been avoided if a list of practices of premature obsolescence had been given in the UCPD Guidance.

1516 P. Anesa, 'Defining legal vagueness: a contradiction in terms?', 8 *Polemos* (2014) p. 201.

1517 See recital 11 of the Regulation (EU) 2020/852 of the European Parliament and of the Council of 18 June 2020 on the establishment of a framework to facilitate sustainable investment, and amending Regulation (EU) 2019/2088, OJ L 198, 22.6.2020, p. 13–43.

(q) 'greenwashing' means the practice of using misleading environmental claim. #13

AND/OR

Proposed review of the UCPD Guidance: #14

4. Application of the UCPD to specific fields

4.1. Sustainability

4.1.1. Environmental claims

The expressions 'environmental claims' and 'green claims' refer to the practice of suggesting or otherwise creating the impression (in commercial communication, marketing or advertising) that a good or a service has a positive or no impact on the environment or is less damaging to the environment than competing goods or services. This may be due to its composition, how it has been manufactured, how it can be disposed of and the reduction in energy or pollution expected from its use. When such claims are not true or cannot be verified, this practice is ~~often~~ called 'greenwashing'. The coordinated screening of websites ("sweep") that the Commission and national consumer authorities carried out in 2020 confirmed the prevalence of vague, exaggerated, false or deceptive green claims.

'Greenwashing' can relate to all forms of business-to-consumer commercial practices concerning the environmental attributes of products.

(…)

4.1.2. ~~Planned~~ Premature obsolescence

~~**Consumers can encounter early obsolescence practices whereby goods last less than their normal "lifespan" should be according to consumers' reasonable expectations. In particular, the premature failure of the goods can be due to planned obsolescence, or built-in obsolescence in industrial design, which is a commercial policy involving deliberately planning or designing a product with a limited useful life so that it will become obsolete or non-functional after a certain period of time.**~~

Premature obsolescence means all practices that reduce product lifetime, without it being the result of normal wear and tear.

There are different types of premature obsolescence, namely:

- **Material obsolescence, which encompasses practices that have a direct influence on product quality (e.g. obsolescence due to specific wear parts or manufacturing techniques);**

- Functional obsolescence, which is caused by the introduction onto the market of a product with additional and/or improved functionalities (e.g. obsolescence due to new software or OS updates, discontinued firmware or OS updates);
- Indirect obsolescence, which is caused by factors surrounding the product in question, rather than by its design, quality or performance (e.g. obsolescence due to unavailable consumables, (compatible) accessories, spare parts and repair and maintenance services);
- Economic obsolescence, whereby the product is perceived as economically worthless or not worth repairing, especially when compared to the purchase price of a new product (e.g. obsolescence due to the costs of use, maintenance and repair);
- Psychological obsolescence, whereby the product, though still fully functioning, is no longer attractive or satisfying in consumers' eyes, resulting in the purchase of a new product (e.g. obsolescence due to aesthetics, fashion and style, technological and social trends).

UCPD does not have provisions specifically addressing premature obsolescence. However, the Directive tackles some practices that are – directly or indirectly – related to premature obsolescence.

Where the trader, including manufacturer, engages in commercial practices towards the consumer, its failure to inform the consumer that a product has been designed with a limited lifetime might, subject to a case-by case assessment, be considered as omission of material information under Article 7 UCPD. Furthermore, such practices may also be contrary to the requirements of professional diligence under Article 5(2) UCPD if they are likely to materially distort the economic behaviour of the average consumer.

As explained under 2.3.1 above, the UCPD also covers commercial practices which occur after the transaction has been made. Regarding smart and connected goods, such commercial practices after the purchase can consist of reducing the functionality or slowing down the operation of the goods through software updates without a valid reason.

Other practices of premature obsolescence can be considered as unfair, including those that make repair technically impossible or unaffordable as well as those that make spare parts or software updates unavailable.

For example:

- Omitting information that a smartphone's battery (which is subject to particular wear and tear) cannot be replaced or that a printer ink cartridges are programmed so that their replacement is needed before they are actually used up could be in breach of Article 7 of the UCPD, even if there may be technical justifications for designing the good in this way.
- A national consumer protection authority fined a printer producer for misleading and aggressive practices, including not adequately highlighting the limitations on the use of non-original printer ink cartridges on sales packages.

- National consumer protection authorities took action concerning the premature obsolescence of smartphones. Certain smartphone models were negatively affected by the installation of a new operating system and subsequent updates, leading to reduced battery life and slowed down performance. Consumers were not adequately informed about the purpose of the updates and their consequences on the performance of the product under Article 7 UCPD.

(...)

4. MISLEADING AND AGGRESSIVE PRACTICES RELATED TO PREMATURE OBSOLESCENCE

394. SECOND STEP: THE SPECIAL GENERAL CLAUSES – The next important building block of the UCPD comprises Articles 6 to 9 of the UCPD, which constitute special general clauses. If not mentioned in the blacklist, the practice can then be assessed in the light of the criteria laid down in these provisions on misleading and aggressive practices. While the UCPD Guidance exclusively focuses on Article 7 on misleading omissions when dealing with 'planned obsolescence'[1518], it is important to note that premature obsolescence can be tackled by the other special general clauses too. Article 6 prohibits misleading actions, including those that reduce product lifetime. Moreover, Articles 6, 7 and 12 of the UCPD regulate green claims (or 'environmental claims'). These are voluntarily used by traders to suggest or create the impression that a good or a service has a positive or no impact on the environment or is less damaging to the environment than competing goods or services.[1519] Environmental claims can display information on environmental characteristics, environmental consequences and production principles and processes.[1520] By regulating those, the UCPD helps traders "*invest in the environmental performance of their products by enabling them to communicate these efforts to consumers transparently and by preventing competitors from presenting misleading environmental claims*".[1521] Best practices can even inspire ecolabels. On the other hand, consumers also benefit from these rules, which ensure the quality of green claims and could, in the long term, restore consumer trust in these claims. Finally, Articles 8 and 9 on aggressive practices can be of use combatting certain practices causing the premature obsolescence of products.

1518 UCPD Guidance, p. 84.

1519 This may be due to its production process, composition and design, energy consumption or pollution during use, durability, reparability, recyclability, etc. See UCPD Guidance, p. 72.

1520 M. Klintman, *A Review of Public Policies relating to the Use of Environmental Labelling and Information Schemes (ELIS) – OECD Environment Working Papers No.105* (OECD Publishing 2016).

1521 UCPD Guidance, p. 73.

a) *Misleading omissions of material product sustainability information*

(1) A general duty to disclose material information

395. Misleading omissions – Article 7 of the UCPD prohibits two kinds of 'misleading omissions'. There is, first of all, the case where the trader omits material information that the average consumer needs to take an informed transactional decision, as described in Article 7(1). The second prohibited practice can be found in Article 7(2) and concerns the case where the trader hides or provides material information in an unclear, incomprehensible, ambiguous or untimely manner. These omissions will be deemed misleading if they cause or are likely to cause the average consumer to take a transactional decision that he would not have taken otherwise.[1522] Through these prohibitions, Article 7 imposes "*a positive obligation on traders to provide all the information which the average consumer needs to make an informed purchasing decision*".[1523]

396. Product sustainability information as material information – The UCPD does not clearly define the terms 'material information', except in case of an invitation to purchase.[1524] Article 7(1) and (3) only provide decisive elements that national authorities and courts must take into account, in addition to the average consumer benchmark, to assess whether the consumer needs certain information to make an informed transactional decision and qualify this information as material. These elements include the factual context of the given practice, its features and circumstances and the limitations of the communication medium. Hence, it is not clear whether information on product lifetime or any other information in relation to product sustainability can be considered as "*material information that the average consumer needs to take an informed transactional decision*". The answer to this question is subject to a case-by-case assessment. Nonetheless, as empirical studies and surveys show that consumers are generally becoming increasingly aware of and sensitive to the environmental impact of products,[1525] it is safe to say information related to product sustainability will, on many occasions, be regarded as material.[1526]

[1522] The Court of Justice has interpreted the average consumer as a reasonably well informed and reasonably observant and circumspect consumer, taking into account social, cultural and linguistic factors. See ECJ 16 July 1998, Case C-210/96, *Gut Springenheide and Tusky* v *Oberkreisdirektor des Kreises Steinfurt, EU:C:1998:369*, para 31; ECJ 13 January 2000, Case C-220/98, *Estée Lauder, EU:C:2000:8*, para 29. This average consumer benchmark used by the Court has already caused much ink to flow in the literature. See *supra*, n° 338.

[1523] UCPD Guidance, p. 50.

[1524] See Article 7(4) UCPD. For further comments, see n° 400.

[1525] See for ex. Kantar, *Special Eurobarometer 501 – Attitudes of European citizens towards the Environment* (European Commission 2020).

[1526] B. Keirsbilck, S. Rousseau, 'The Marketing Stage: Fostering Sustainable Consumption Choices in a "Circular" and "Functional" Economy', in B. Keirsbilck, E. Terryn (eds.), *Consumer*

Consequently, where information on product sustainability must be provided, but is not, and where this omission is likely to cause the average consumer to take a different transactional decision, this constitutes a breach of Article 7 of the UCPD. Such reasoning is in line with the SGD, which includes durability as one of the main criteria to assess the conformity of the good.[1527]

397. 'Planned obsolescence' *sensu stricto* as misleading omission – In addition to the indications contained in Article 7, further clarifications can be found in the UCPD Guidance in its section specifically dedicated to 'planned obsolescence'. Pursuant to its wording, a trader might be considered to have omitted to provide material information as required by Article 7 if he fails *"to inform the consumer that a product has been designed with a limited lifetime"*, according to the specific circumstances of the individual case.[1528] Indeed, consumers might not have purchased the product if aware of the limited product lifetime. The Guidance provides two concrete examples of such practices of planned obsolescence.[1529] The first example relates to the case whereby the trader omits to inform that a smartphone's battery (which is subject to particular wear and tear) cannot be replaced. As for the second example, the Guidance refers to the case whereby printer ink cartridges are programmed so that their replacement is needed before they are actually used up, even if there may be technical justifications for designing the good in this way.[1530] Although consumers may be faced with such practices, these are particularly difficult to prove. Other legal instruments seem therefore more appropriate to tackle this kind of practice, like the EU legislation on ecodesign, which imposes mandatory requirements on producers concerning the design of their products.[1531]

398. Lack of information on the limitations on the use of non-original printer ink cartridges – Other practices of premature obsolescence could be qualified as misleading omissions under Article 7 of the UCPD. Two examples of such practices were recently added in the amended UCPD Guidance.[1532] There

---

Protection in a Circular Economy (Intersentia 2019) p. 102. See also A. Perzanowski, *The Right to Repair: Reclaiming the Things We Own* (Cambridge University Press 2022) p. 208 at p. 210, who argues that reparability should be considered as material information. As rightly highlighted by the author, *"if consumers knew that they would face hurdles to repairing their devices, they would make different choices"*.

1527 See *infra*, Chapter IV on the use stage (n° 698).

1528 UCPD Guidance, p. 84.

1529 See the first indent of the box in UCPD Guidance, p. 85.

1530 Interestingly, the former UCPD Guidance from 2016 provided two other examples (p. 83), namely where the producer omits to inform that (1) washing machines are designed with a weak drum suspension to 'make sure' that these break after a number of washing cycles and (2) the functional lifetime of a refrigerator is planned to be significantly shorter than for comparable products.

1531 See Chapter II on the design and production stage.

1532 See the second and third indents of the box in UCPD Guidance, p. 85.

is, first, the case whereby a printer producer does not adequately highlight the limitations on the use of non-original printer ink cartridges on sales packages. This example refers to the *HP* case from November 2020[1533], where the Italian Competition Authority fined *HP* € 10 million for misleading and aggressive commercial practices. The first practice concerned the withholding of information regarding the limitations on the use of non-genuine printer cartridges. In particular, *HP* only warned that the use of non-genuine cartridges could decrease the printing quality, whereas the use of such cartridges was prevented by the printer using an authentication system connected with an electronic circuit on the cartridge, capable of detecting a non-genuine cartridge, and disabling the printer from functioning in its presence.[1534] The second practice concerned the recording of the consumption data and data regarding the use of genuine and non-genuine cartridges, without providing prior information to the consumers, in order to refuse the free assistance for the printers that had non-original cartridges inserted. Moreover, *HP* refused to acknowledge the existence of a causal link between printer malfunction and the use of non-original cartridges, in respect of the assistance requests from retailers who provided the legal guarantee of conformity to their clients. In this regard, the Italian Competition Authority specified that, contrary to what *HP* argued, the findings of the proceedings did not reveal that the consumer had given their consent to such data collection. *Euroconsumers*[1535] has recently reached a settlement agreement with *HP* for the same kind of practices.[1536]

399. Lack of information on updates – The second and last example given in the UCPD Guidance refers to the Italian decisions against *Apple* and *Samsung*.[1537] As was explained above[1538], the two firms had omitted to inform

---

1533 Autorita Garante della Concorrenza e del Mercato, 17 November 2020, *HP*, available on: <https://agcm.it/dotcmsCustom/tc/2026/2/getDominoAttach?urlStr=192.168.14.10:8080/C12560D000291394/0/029F2043AE218669C12586760051FA81/$File/p28515.pdf>. See also the press release issued by Autorita Garante della Concorrenza e del Mercato (AGCM), 'HP fined 10 million Euros for misleading and aggressive commercial practices', 9 December 2020, available on: <https://en.agcm.it/en/media/press-releases/2020/12/PS11144>.

1534 This is a case of software doping by discrimination, as described *supra* (n° 113).

1535 *Euroconsumers* is a consumer's rights organisation, which gathers the Italian, Belgian, Spanish, Portuguese and Brazilian consumer organisations.

1536 Euroconsumers alleged that consumers were not properly informed that the technology used by *HP* ('Dynamic Security') would cause printers to reject certain non-HP replacement ink cartridges equipped with non-original chips or electronic circuitry. Under the settlement agreement, *HP* has agreed to establish a fund for payment of compensation to certain HP printer owners for losses allegedly suffered as a consequence of this lack of information. See Euroconsumers, 'HP and Euroconsumers settle on Dynamic Security', 7 September 2022, available on: <https://www.euroconsumers.org/activities/hp-and-euroconsumers-reach-a-settlement-on-dynamic-security-dispute>.

1537 Autorita Garante della Concorrenza e del Mercato, 25 September 2018, *Apple*; Autorita Garante della Concorrenza e del Mercato, 25 September 2018, *Samsung*.

1538 See *supra*, n° 359.

their customers of the greater energy demand of the new OS and possible malfunctions (including sudden shutdowns) that the new software updates could cause. Moreover, *Apple* was accused of not adequately informing consumers about the characteristics of lithium batteries, nor about the correct procedures to maintain, verify and replace them to preserve the full functionality of the device. The Italian Competition Authority concluded that the practice was misleading, not only due to these omissions, but also after having considered the commercial practice as a whole. For *Apple*, the easy transferability of content between all *Apple* devices encouraged consumers facing a defective product to buy a later model of the same brand.[1539] *Samsung* granted a 25% discount for the online purchase of a new product on its website to customers who did not accept the repair conditions of a defective product.[1540] All in all, these practices had (or were likely to have) distorted consumers' economic behaviour, accelerating the process of replacing devices with new ones.[1541] After investigation, the French authorities came to the same conclusion a few years later and *Apple* settled over € 25 million with them.[1542] The Belgian consumer organisation *Test-Achats* followed suit and initiated a class action against *Apple* before the Commercial Court of Brussels.[1543]

400. Invitation to purchase – Concerning cases where there is an invitation to purchase[1544]; Article 7(4) specifies a concise (albeit purely illustrative) list of information that must be regarded as material. Unless it is apparent from the context, these pieces of information must be disclosed in an intelligible and unambiguous manner before the conclusion of the contract so that the average consumer can take an informed transactional decision. As aptly put by H. Micklitz, "*the informational*

[1539] Autorita Garante della Concorrenza e del Mercato, 25 September 2018, *Apple*, para 67.

[1540] Autorita Garante della Concorrenza e del Mercato, 25 September 2018, *Samsung*, para 87.

[1541] Despite the lack of explicit reference to 'premature obsolescence' or any of its variants in its decisions, the Italian Authority acknowledges the necessity for companies to pursue strategies accelerating product replacement. According to it, "*the process of replacing old smartphones assumes an absolute and ever-increasing importance for sales volumes, given that increased competition, lower technological innovation and maturity of the market make it extremely difficult to acquire new consumers*". See Autorita Garante della Concorrenza e del Mercato, 25 September 2018, *Apple*, para 149.

[1542] See *Transaction pénale* agreed by French public prosecutor, DGCCRF and Apple, communicated on 7 Feb. 2020, <economie.gouv.fr/dgccrf/transaction-avec-le-groupe-apple-pour-pratique-commerciale-trompeuse>.

[1543] See the press release issued by Test Achats, 'Test Achats lance une action collective contre Apple pour obsolescence programmée', 2 December 2020, available on: <https://www.test-achats.be/hightech/gsm/presse/class-action-apple>. Consumers facing problems with their Iphones can register on: <https://www.test-achats.be/apple>. See also Test Achats, 'Action collective contre Apple: les premières plaidoiries ont débuté', 10 October 2022, available on: <https://www.test-achats.be/hightech/gsm/news/action-collective-apple>.

[1544] An 'invitation to purchase' means "*a commercial communication which indicates characteristics of the product and the price in a way appropriate to the means of the commercial communication used and thereby enables the consumer to make a purchase*" (Art. 2(i) of the UCPD). See also the examples mentioned in points 5, 6 and 28 of the Annex I to the UCPD, which provide further guidance on this notion.

obligations imposed on the trader increase within the narrower phase of contractual conclusion".[1545] The aim of Article 7(4) is to ensure a high level of protection for consumers when they are faced with a commercial offer.[1546] Among the key items of information to be provided, Article 7(4) cites "*the main characteristics of the product*".[1547] The open wording of Article 7(4)(a) may also encompass many types of information on product sustainability, including product durability, reparability, energy efficiency, availability of spare parts or other environmental impacts.[1548] Yet information requirements based on this provision are not static, but depend on the context of the invitation to purchase, on the product concerned and on the medium used by the trader to make the commercial communication.[1549] Even when key items of information do not feature on the list of Article 7(4) of the UCPD, they can still constitute material information if the consumer needs them to make an informed transactional decision.[1550] This case-by-case approach has been decided to avoid placing unnecessary or disproportionate information burdens on traders.[1551]

401. Article 7 should clearly include product sustainability information – Considering its wording, the corresponding sections of the UCPD Guidance and the existing case law, Article 7 of the UCPD can be seen as a key provision to establish information requirements on product sustainability. So far, such information is only implicitly included within the wording of the provision and can only be considered as material following a case-by-case assessment. Although Article 7 as it currently stands can serve as a basis to impose information requirements on product sustainability, it would be even more effective if not only a new definition of 'premature obsolescence' was given in the UCPD Guidance[1552], but also if it was made clearer that 'material information' can include the various types of product sustainability information, such as information on product environmental impact, durability, repairability, availability and cost of spare

1545 H.-W. Micklitz, 'Unfair commercial practices and misleading advertising', in N. Reich et al. (eds.), *European Consumer Law – Ius Commutatis V* (Intersentia 2014) p. 102.

1546 UCPD Guidance, p. 54.

1547 See Art. 7(4)(a) UCPD.

1548 For example, the Maltese Consumer Tribunal held on 6 December 2010 (Case CCT 2/10, Kenneth Ciangura v AR Tech Limited) that not providing information on the expected product lifetime constitutes a misleading omission. The plaintiff had purchased a solar water heater system. After a certain period of time, some parts of the water tank began to rust, and leaks were established. According to the plaintiff, the defendant had not informed the plaintiff on the relatively quick worsening of the water tank's state. It was ruled by the Tribunal that the information on the expected lifetime of a product is essential information. Next, the defendant could not prove such information was communicated to the plaintiff. As a result, the plaintiff had not been provided with all relevant information in order to make an informed transactional decision. Hence, the defendant had breached the prohibition of misleading omissions as established under Article 7 of the UCPD.

1549 Art. 7(4)(a) UCPD.

1550 ECJ 7 September 2016, Case C-310/15, *Sony*, para 48. See also recital 14 UCPD.

1551 UCPD Guidance, p. 54.

1552 See *supra*, n° 391.

parts, etc.[1553] Omitting material information on product sustainability would be seen as misleading and sanctioned on the basis of Article 7 of the UCPD. Conversely, if consumers were made aware of the reduced lifetime of certain products, including short-lived, disposable and single-use products (e.g. pens or razors) before purchase, they would be precluded from claiming any misleading omission.[1554] In that respect, information disclosure acts as a 'double-edged sword'. The information obligation imposed by Article 7 would still apply "*to an extent appropriate to the medium and the product*" and thus not require the trader to provide information on all sustainability aspects, otherwise leading to information overload. To mitigate the issue of legal uncertainty as regards the information to be considered as material, the UCPD Guidance could specify that sustainability aspects covered by ecodesign regulations should be seen as 'material information' and/or provide additional guidance for specific product categories.

402. Two possible amendments – The clarity of Article 7 could be enhanced in two ways: (1) by detailing 'material information' and 'main characteristics' in the provision itself and by adding a definition of 'product sustainability' in Article 2 (see #15) and/or (2) by amending the UCPD guidance document (see #16). Whereas the first option requires reviewing the Directive, the second option would be easier to implement, though not legally binding but informative for businesses and practitioners alike. Such amendments would better emphasize the importance of these pieces of information and ensure legal certainty for all stakeholders. The clarity of Article 7 of the UCPD would be even more strengthened if the general information requirements contained in the CRD and the UCPD were integrated.[1555] The EC has recently proposed to amend Article 7 of the UCPD, but confines itself to adding an information obligation on traders who provide a service that compares products.[1556] In case Article 7 remains unchanged, or in the meantime, Member States are entitled to specify the main characteristics of particular products in their national law.[1557] This is an important exception to the full harmonisation approach of the UCPD that could be used to trigger product sustainability.

1553 See also A. Michel, 'La directive 1999/44/CE sur la garantie des biens de consommation: un remède efficace contre l'obsolescence programmée?', *R.E.D.C.* (2018) pp. 234–235.

1554 However, this does not preclude consumers invoking other provisions of the UCPD. For example, if information is voluntarily given and is not true, consumers could invoke Article 6 and 12 of the UCPD. See *infra*, n° 415 *et seq*.

1555 See the following section on the Consumer Rights Directive (n° 457 *et seq*.).

1556 See Art. 1 of the Proposal for a Directive of the European Parliament and of the Council amending Directives 2005/29/EC and 2011/83/EU as regards empowering consumers for the green transition through better protection against unfair practices and better information, COM(2022) 143 final.

1557 See recital 14 UCPD, as already pointed out above (n° 353).

Proposed review of the Unfair Commercial Practices Directive:

#15

Article 2
Definitions

For the purposes of this Directive:

(…)

(r) 'product sustainability' means the ability of a product to reach its optimal lifetime, which depends among others on its durability, ease of maintenance, upgradability, reparability, refurbishment and remanufacturing.

Article 7
Misleading omissions

1. A commercial practice shall be regarded as misleading if, in its factual context, taking account of all its features and circumstances and the limitations of the communication medium, it omits material information that the average consumer needs, according to the context, to take an informed transactional decision and thereby causes or is likely to cause the average consumer to take a transactional decision that he would not have taken otherwise. **The following information shall be regarded as material, if not already apparent from the context:**

(a) the main characteristics of the product, including characteristics related to its sustainability, to an extent appropriate to the medium and the product;

(…)

2. It shall also be regarded as a misleading omission when, taking account of the matters described in paragraph 1, a trader hides or provides in an unclear, unintelligible, ambiguous or untimely manner such material information as referred to in that paragraph or fails to identify the commercial intent of the commercial practice if not already apparent from the context, and where, in either case, this causes or is likely to cause the average consumer to take a transactional decision that he would not have taken otherwise.

(…)

4. In the case of an invitation to purchase, the following information shall be regarded as material, if not already apparent from the context:

(a) the main characteristics of the product, **including characteristics related to its sustainability,** to an extent appropriate to the medium and the product;

(…)

AND/OR

Proposed review of the UCPD Guidance: #16

2.9.1 Material information

Articles 7(1) and (2) establish in very general terms a positive obligation on traders to provide all the information which the average consumer needs to make an informed purchasing decision. This is what is called 'material information' in Article 7.

The UCPD does not define 'material information', except for in the specific case of an 'invitation to purchase', which is dealt with in Article 7(4) (see section 2.9.5). In addition, Article 7(5) UCPD clarifies that 'information requirements established by EU law in relation to commercial communication, including advertising', shall be regarded as material (see section 1.2.2). **'Material information' may include, to an extent appropriate to the medium and the product, information related to product sustainability aspects, such as information on its durability, ease of maintenance, upgradability, reparability, refurbishment and remanufacturing. In this regard, product sustainability aspects that are subject to ecodesign regulations should in any case be seen as material information.**

In contrast, as explained in recital 15, where Member States have introduced information requirements over and above what is specified in Community law, on the basis of minimum clauses, the omission of that extra information will not constitute a misleading omission under this Directive.

In order to assess on a case-by-case basis whether material information has been omitted, national authorities and courts need to take into account all features and circumstances of a given commercial practice, including the limitations of the medium used to communicate it.

(…)

2.9.5 Material information in invitations to purchase – Article 7(4)

(…)

Material information

Article 7(4) lists a number of information requirements which are considered material. This is to ensure the maximum amount of legal certainty for consumers at this critical point. The aim of Article 7(4) is to ensure that, whenever traders make commercial offers, they make available simultaneously, in an intelligible and unambiguous manner, enough information to enable the consumer to take an informed decision to purchase, unless that information is already apparent from the context.

Product sustainability aspects may, subject to a case-by-case assessment, constitute a main characteristic of a product within the meaning of Article 7(4). These aspects encompass, among others, aspects that relate to product durability, ease of maintenance, upgradability, reparability, refurbishment and remanufacturing.

(2) Misleading omissions through the violations of information requirements contained in EU specific laws

403. The failure to provide required information – Article 7 does not only establish an indirect duty to disclose essential information to consumers.[1558] This provision also sanctions the failure to provide the information required by EU law. Article 7(5) states that "*information requirements established by EU law in relation to commercial communication including advertising or marketing (…) shall be regarded as material*". In other words, omitting to provide, hiding or providing such information in an unclear, incomprehensible, ambiguous or untimely manner, should be considered misleading.[1559] As a result, it can be said that Article 7 of the UCPD lays down the basis for the development of genuine consumer information rights.

404. Enforcing various information requirements – Article 7(5) refers to Annex II of the UCPD, which consists of a non-exhaustive list of EU legal instruments with an extremely wide scope. The information obligations contained in these instruments are pre-contractual as well as post-contractual. Among these rules, there are information requirements on product sustainability from sector-specific legislation[1560], like the Ecodesign Directive[1561] as well as the Energy Labelling Regulation.[1562] Also sanctionable under Article 7(5) is the failure to comply with the general information requirements on updates as established under Article 6(d) and 7(3) of the SGD.[1563]

405. Under EU law, but not national law – Only violations of information obligations established at EU level can be qualified as misleading on the basis of Article 7(5). Pursuant to recital 15, "*[w]here Member States have introduced*

1558 See also B. Keirsbilck, S. Rousseau, 'The Marketing Stage: Fostering Sustainable Consumption Choices in a "Circular" and "Functional" Economy', in B. Keirsbilck, E. Terryn (eds.), *Consumer Protection in a Circular Economy* (Intersentia 2019) p. 101.

1559 Such claims have already been raised in practice. See ECJ 25 July 2018, Case C-632/16, *Dyson, EU:C:2018:599*, where Dyson alleged that BSH had misled consumers by not providing them with information as required by the former Delegated Regulation No 665/2013 with regard to energy labelling of vacuum cleaners.

1560 UCPD Guidance, pp. 10–11.

1561 See Chapter II on the design and production stage.

1562 See *infra*, n° 512 *et seq.*

1563 See Chapter IV on the use stage.

information requirements over and above what is specified in Community law, on the basis of minimum clauses, the omission of that extra information will not constitute a misleading omission under this Directive. By contrast Member States will be able, when allowed by the minimum clauses in Community law, to maintain or introduce more stringent provisions in conformity with Community law so as to ensure a higher level of protection of consumers' individual contractual rights." If consumers are confronted with a breach of an information requirement established under national law[1564], they are not entitled to rely on unfair commercial practices legislation, except if it is considered as 'material information' based on a case-by-case assessment as provided for in Article 7(1) and (2).

406. A crucial link between EU rules – The link forged by Article 7(5) between unfair commercial practices legislation and information requirements established by EU law is a major gateway towards product sustainability. Existing information requirements on product sustainability, like the ones established within the framework of the ecodesign, energy labelling and consumer sales rules, are strengthened by such a provision as non-compliance with them can automatically lead to concrete sanctions.[1565]

407. A lack of link with national law – Regrettably, information requirements imposed by the Member States are excluded from the scope of Article 7(5), including those in relation to product sustainability that complement information requirements established by EU law. If such a link existed between Article 7 and national rules, one could imagine, for example, sellers being sanctioned if the reparability index imposed by the French Anti-Waste law was not affixed on the products.[1566] In absence of such a direct link, national requirements related to reparability or durability index can only be considered misleading if they are qualified as 'material information', which is a more flexible notion. Otherwise, consumers are only protected by contractual means. Hence, this exclusion of national information requirements creates a gap between unfair commercial practices law and contract law at national level.

408. Harmonising information requirements at EU level – Two options can be envisaged to close the gap between information requirements and unfair commercial practices at national level. The first option is to amend Article 7(5) and withdraw the exception. However, this amendment would go against the full harmonisation approach of the Directive as it would reinforce disparities

[1564] See for example the information requirements established under French law (n° 469 *et seq.* and n° 495 *et seq.*).

[1565] This is even more important knowing that controls and sanctions in the field of ecodesign regulations are very limited (see n° 299-300).

[1566] For more details on this reparability index, see n° 554–564.

between Member States. Moreover, one could wonder whether it is the role of EU law to reinforce national law. The second option, which should be preferred, is to harmonise national information requirements at EU level so that Article 7(5) of the UCPD applies to them (see #17). In this regard, it could be said that Article 7(5) creates pressure to build upon advanced information requirements existing at national level and expand them EU-wide.[1567] Meanwhile, sanctions could be provided at national level.

> *Policy recommendation:*
>
> *#17 Adopt more information requirements at EU level, drawing inspiration from existing national information requirements.*

b) *Misleading actions on product sustainability*

409. Misleading actions – In addition to rules on misleading omissions, the UCPD contains a general prohibition of 'misleading actions' in its Article 6.[1568] According to this provision, a practice can be deemed misleading if it "*contains false information and is therefore untruthful*" or if it "*in any way, including overall presentation, deceives or is likely to deceive the average consumer, even if the information is factually correct*".[1569] It should be noted that a deceptive claim does not necessarily require intent to deceive.[1570] The untruthful and deceptive nature of the commercial practice must relate to one or more of the elements exhaustively listed in Article 6(1)(a) to (g).[1571] Like for misleading omissions[1572], the misleading nature of actions is evaluated on a case-by-case basis by reviewing the practice as a whole, the content and presentation of the claim and its (likely)

1567 See along the same line, H.-W. Micklitz, 'Unfair commercial practices and misleading advertising', in N. Reich et al. (eds.), *European Consumer Law – Ius Commutatis V* (Intersentia 2014) p. 103.

1568 In practice, it can be difficult to draw a line in the sand between misleading actions and omissions. Many practices that are not positively untruthful but are likely to deceive consumers are built on combinations on information that is given but that is insufficient, and relevant information that is omitted. See B. Keirsbilck, *The New European Law of Unfair Commercial Practices and Competition Law* (Hart Publishing 2011) p. 339.

1569 For further details on the notions of untruthfulness and deceptiveness, see B. Keirsbilck, *The New European Law of Unfair Commercial Practices and Competition Law* (Hart Publishing 2011) p. 313 at p. 330; J. Stuyck and A.-M. Vandromme, 'Aggressive Commercial Practices', in G. Straetmans and J. Stuyck (eds.), *Commercial Practices* (Larcier 2014) pp. 76–77.

1570 As rightly pointed out by J. Stuyck and A.-M. Vandromme, "*not every lie is held to be deceiving and the truth can also deceive, as well as suggestions*". See J. Stuyck and A.-M. Vandromme, 'Agressive Commercial Practices', in G. Straetmans and J. Stuyck (eds.), *Commercial Practices* (Larcier 2014) pp. 76–77.

1571 If the commercial practice is misleading in relation to another element not listed in Article 6, its unfairness must be assessed against the general clause contained in Article 5 of the UCPD.

1572 See *supra*, n° 396.

impact on the average consumer's economic behaviour. In this assessment, national courts and administrative authorities are encouraged to take the most recent findings on behavioural economics into account.[1573] In practice, the line between misleading and accepted advertising and marketing practices can be very fine.[1574]

410. Misleading as regards products' nature or main characteristics – Among the elements contained in the list of Article 6(1), some are of particular importance as regards product sustainability. First and foremost, Article 6 prohibits traders from misleading consumers on "*the existence or nature of the product*" (Article 6(1)(a)) and on "*the main characteristics of the product*" (Article 6(1)(b)). Compared to Article 7 on misleading omissions, the notion of a product's main characteristics is much more elaborated, covering *inter alia* its availability, benefits, risks, composition, accessories, after-sale customer assistance and complaint handling, method and date of manufacture or provision, fitness for purpose, usage, the results to be expected from its use, or the results and material features of tests or checks carried out on the product. One point in common with Article 7 is that Article 6 does not explicitly mention product sustainable aspects, such as durability and reparability, as main characteristics of the product.[1575]

411. Some illustrative examples – Even though the notion of 'main characteristics' could be clearer, Article 6(1)(a) and (b) are still of great use against premature obsolescence. The provision can combat practices whereby the trader misleads consumers on the lifetime of its products (or the products' components) or other aspects directly related to it. Some examples of misleading actions given by the UCPD Guidance fall within this category, like when traders indicate a storage capacity or memory of IT products, such as mobile phones and tablets, that significantly differs from reality.[1576] Such a misleading practice can contribute to the functional obsolescence of the product.[1577] Other examples of misleading actions have been seen in practice. In France, the association HOP

1573 UCPD Guidance, p. 39.

1574 Recital 6 of the UCPD stipulates that the Directive "*does not affect accepted advertising and marketing practices, such as legitimate product placement, brand differentiation or the offering of incentives which may legitimately affect consumers' perceptions of products and influence their behaviour without impairing the consumer's ability to make an informed decision*". As regards premature obsolescence, this recital means that some practices causing the psychological obsolescence of products which strongly depends on consumers' decisions and behaviour is left out of the scope of the Directive.

1575 See *supra*, n° 396.

1576 UCPD Guidance, p. 39. The Guidance makes reference to the action taken by the Italian Competition Authority against Samsung on 19 December 2014 (See the press release available on: <https://en.agcm.it/en/media/press-releases/2014/12/alias-2175>).

1577 See *supra* on the concept of 'functional obsolescence' (n° 106 *et seq.*).

accuses *Epson* of misleading practice (in addition to its claim based on the French prohibition of 'planned obsolescence').[1578] According to HOP, *Epson* misleads consumers on the composition and the usage of its printers by giving false information on the lifetime of ink cartridges and printer absorber pads. Similar practices have also been observed in the automotive sector, where some traders mislead consumers on the lifetime and remaining value of second-hand cars by reducing the number of kilometres on the odometer.[1579] Other practices contributing to the premature obsolescence of products can be addressed by Article 6(1)(b), including those where the trader gives erroneous information on the availability of spare parts and accessories or on the availability period of updates.[1580]

412. Article 6 should clearly include product sustainability information – Admittedly, Article 6(1)(a) and (b) of the UCPD already plays a valuable role in tackling cases of premature obsolescence. Yet its effectiveness could be enhanced if the notion of 'main characteristics' explicitly mentioned product sustainability.[1581] Hence, here too[1582], amending Article 6, together with a definition of 'product sustainability' in Article 2, should be envisaged (see #18).[1583] The UCPD Guidance should also be reviewed in that sense and its section dedicated to the topic of premature obsolescence should highlight the importance of Article 6 of the UCPD (see #19). Such review has been suggested by the EC, which proposes to add 'environmental or social impact', 'durability' and 'reparability' to the list of product characteristics about which a trader should not deceive a consumer.[1584] Using a more comprehensive term like 'sustainability' should however be preferred to embrace the various aspects that are essential to prolong product lifetime (e.g. compatibility, upgradability, etc).

1578 Tribunal de grande instance de Nanterre 17 September 2017, Plainte au Procureur de la République, *HOP* v. *X*, pp. 14–15.

1579 DGCCRF, *Vente de voitures d'occasion, gare aux tromperies!*, 13 May 2020, available on: <https://www.economie.gouv.fr/dgccrf/vente-de-voitures-doccasion-gare-aux-tromperies#_ftnref3>. In order to effectively combat these unfair practices, the Belgian legislature has introduced the car-pass system. All sellers of used cars, whether private individuals or professionals, are obliged to hand over a car pass – an official certificate certifying the mileage – to the buyer, if the latter is a private individual. See Loi du 28 novembre 2018 modifiant la loi du 11 juin 2004 réprimant la fraude relative au kilométrage des véhicules, *M.B.*, 6 décembre 2018, p. 95970.

1580 Such practices could still be sanctioned on the basis of Article 6 if these pieces of information were to become mandatory requirements.

1581 See also A. Michel, 'La directive 1999/44/CE sur la garantie des biens de consommation: un remède efficace contre l'obsolescence programmée?', *R.E.D.C.* (2018) pp. 234–235.

1582 See *supra*, n° 401–402.

1583 It should be noted that such an amendment should especially be envisaged if Article 7 of the UCPD and Articles 5(1)(a) and 6(a)(1) of the CRD were to be amended in that sense, for the sake of coherence within and between legal instruments.

1584 Art. 1(2) of the Proposal for a Directive on empowering consumers for the green transition.

413. Misleading as regards price – Other elements listed in Article 6(1) can relate to practices of premature obsolescence. There is the prohibition to mislead consumers on the price or the manner in which the price is calculated, as mentioned in Article 6(1)(d). Practices leading to the economic obsolescence of products could be caught by this provision. The trader could, for instance, give false information or a false impression on the repair price by using an unreasonably high or otherwise misleading recommended or reference price for the purpose of price comparisons between repair and replacement. Such information could give consumers the impression that it is significantly more advantageous to purchase a new product than what is really the case. As a result, consumers could be discouraged to repair their actual product and encouraged to buy a brand new one. Along the same lines, the Italian Competition Authority has decided to assess Samsung's commercial promotions offering customers the opportunity to trade their old devices in at advantageous prices. The Italian Authority is of the opinion that "*the information provided is inadequate and unclear and that the consumer is not able to understand that a complex sale process is implied and the advertised sale price is merely an estimate*".[1585]

414. Misleading as regards services or consumer rights – Closely linked to this prohibition, Article 6(1)(e) forbids misleading claims in relation to the need for service, part, replacement or repair, whereas Article 6(1)(g) forbids those in relation to consumer rights, including the rights afforded under the Sale of Goods Directive.[1586] Pursuant to Article 6(1)(g), traders are, for example, forbidden to give false information on the two-year legal guarantee period.[1587] If not countered, such misleading actions could lead to the indirect obsolescence of the product.[1588]

1585 See the press release issued by the Italian Competition Authority (*Autorita Garante della Concorrenza e del Mercato*), 'The Italian Competition Authority has commenced an investigation against Samsung for alleged misleading and aggressive conduct', 27 July 2022, available on: <https://en.agcm.it/en/media/press-releases/2022/7/PS12373>.

1586 See Chapter IV on the use stage.

1587 Such practice has already been sanctioned on the basis of this provision in practice. See for ex. Autorità Garante della Concorrenza e del Mercato (AGCM), 21 December 2011, *Apple*, n° 23155 (English summary available on: <www.agcm.it/component/joomdoc/allegati-news/IP151_sintesi_Inglese.pdf/download.html>). In this case, Apple was providing consumers with false information and omitting to inform consumers both in its selling places throughout Italy and on its web pages about their statutory rights on legal guarantees that are valid for two years in accordance with the Consumer Sales Directive. The case led to a pan-European action against Apple throughout the EU. For further comments on this case, see M. Djurovic, 'The Apple Case: The Commencement of Pan-European Battle Against Unfair Commercial Practices', 9 *Eur. Rev. Contract Law* (2013) p. 253 at p. 266.

1588 See *supra*, n° 121 *et seq.*

Proposed review of the Unfair Commercial Practices Directive:

[Apart from the introduction of the definition of 'product sustainability' in Article 2 as proposed by #58][1589]

#18

Article 6
Misleading actions

1. A commercial practice shall be regarded as misleading if it contains false information and is therefore untruthful or in any way, including overall presentation, deceives or is likely to deceive the average consumer, even if the information is factually correct, in relation to one or more of the following elements, and in either case causes or is likely to cause him to take a transactional decision that he would not have taken otherwise:

(a) the existence or nature of the product;

(b) the main characteristics of the product, such as its **sustainability,** availability, benefits, risks, execution, composition, accessories, after-sale customer assistance and complaint handling, method and date of manufacture or provision, delivery, fitness for purpose, usage, quantity, specification, geographical or commercial origin or the results to be expected from its use, or the results and material features of tests or checks carried out on the product;

(...)

AND/OR

Proposed review of the UCPD Guidance: #19

2.8. Article 6 – misleading actions

(...)

2.8.1. General misleading information

Article 6(1)(a) to (g) prohibit misleading actions which are capable of deceiving the average consumer on a wide range of elements, including:

- the existence of the product;
- its main characteristics (e.g. its composition, method of manufacture, geographical or
- commercial origin, the risks and results to be expected from its use);
- the price or the manner in which it is calculated or the existence of a specific price advantage;
- the nature, attributes and rights of the trader.

[1589] See *supra*, n° 402.

Article 6 clearly covers any commercial practice which 'contains false information and is therefore untruthful'.

Information about the product's 'main characteristics' must be provided in an invitation to purchase in accordance with Article 7(4) UCPD and before the conclusion of the contract in accordance with the Consumer Rights Directive. Article 6(1)(b) UCPD prohibits providing incorrect information about the main characteristics of a product if it is likely to cause the average consumer to take a transactional decision they would not have taken otherwise. **Product sustainability aspects may, subject to a case-by-case assessment, constitute a main characteristic of a product within the meaning of Article 6. These aspects encompass, among others, aspects that relate to product durability, ease of maintenance, upgradability, reparability, refurbishment and remanufacturing.**

(...)

4.1.2. ~~Planned~~ Premature obsolescence

(...)

UCPD does not have provisions specifically addressing obsolescence. However, **its provisions can help curb some practices related to premature obsolescence. For example,** where the trader, including manufacturer, engages in commercial practices towards the consumer, its failure to inform the consumer that a product has been designed with a limited lifetime might, subject to a case-by-case assessment, be considered as omission of material information under Article 7 UCPD. **Article 6 can combat practices whereby the trader misleads consumers on the lifetime of its products or on other aspects directly related to it. (...)**[1590] Furthermore, ~~such~~ practices **of premature obsolescence** may also be contrary to the requirements of professional diligence under Article 5(2) UCPD if they are likely to materially distort the economic behaviour of the average consumer.

(...)

c) *Misleading green claims*

415. Misleading green claims – As clarified in the UCPD Guidance, the application of the UCPD to environmental claims can be summarised in two main principles relating to their form and their content.[1591] First, environmental claims must be truthful, not contain false information and be presented in a clear, specific, accurate and unambiguous manner, as required by Articles 6

[1590] It is also suggested to clarify the role played by Articles 8 and 9 of the UCPD against premature obsolescence in the UCPD Guidance. See *infra* on the aggressive practices of premature obsolescence (n° 433–439).

[1591] UCPD Guidance, p. 75.

and 7 of the UCPD. Second, they must be supported by scientific evidence that could be provided in an understandable way in case the claim is challenged. This second principle corresponds to Article 12 of the UCPD. If a green claim does not satisfy these cumulative conditions, it should be deemed misleading towards consumers and prohibited by competent national authorities on the basis of a case-by-case application of the UCPD.

(1) The obligation to present truthful claims in a specific, accurate and unambiguous manner

416. Misleading green claims on products' nature or main characteristics – Article 6(1)(a) and (b) prohibit green claims that suggest or create the impression that, due to its nature or main characteristics, a product is environmentally friendly or less damaging to the environment than competing goods.[1592] The most blatant cases of misleading green claims are those containing false information on the product's nature or main characteristics. For example, in Germany[1593], *Galeria Kaufhof* was sentenced for making false advertising statements such as 'particularly environmentally friendly and/or socially acceptable' for certain products in online trade[1594], whereas *Amazon* was sentenced on the same basis for having used the term 'biodegradable' for reusable bamboo cups.[1595] Other illustrative examples of this kind of misleading claims are provided in the UCPD Guidance.[1596] As regards cases of premature obsolescence, traders could for example mislead consumers by falsely claiming that a product is durable or reparable, although it is not. A claim will also be deemed misleading if "*it deceives or is likely to deceive the average consumer, even if the information is factually correct*".[1597] Accordingly, green claims should relate to aspects that are significant in terms of product sustainability and not overstate or highlight just one of the several environmental benefits of the product.[1598]

417. Green claims based on vague and general statements – Green claims can also be misleading if based on vague and general statements of environmental benefits. This includes green claims using words like 'environmentally friendly', 'green', 'nature's friend', 'ecological', 'sustainable', 'environmentally correct', 'climate friendly', 'gentle on the environment',

---

1592 To make it more explicit, BEUC has already proposed amending the UCPD Guidance "*so as to cover not only misleading green claims, but also e.g. misleading durability claims*". See BEUC Policy Paper of 18 August 2015 on Durable goods: More sustainable products, better consumer rights, BEUC-X-2015-069, p. 12.

1593 C. Meller-Hannich and E. Krausbeck, 'Sustainability, the Circular Economy and Consumer Law in Germany', 9 *EuCML* (2020) p. 170.

1594 LG Köln, 05.03.2018 – 31 O 379/17.

1595 LG München I, 02.07.2019 – 17 HK 6043/19.

1596 UCPD Guidance, p. 76.

1597 Article 6(1) UCPD.

1598 UCPD Guidance, p. 78.

'pollutant free' and even the broader claims of 'conscious' and 'responsible'.[1599] It is confusing that the 2021 UCPD Guidance does not mention 'sustainable' as an example of vague and general statements, as opposed to the former version of the UCPD Guidance.[1600] But the words 'such as' seem to imply that these are non-exhaustive examples and, in our opinion, this omission should not be interpreted as a deliberate exclusion by the EC.[1601] Indeed, all these claims may give consumers the (misleading) impression that a product or an activity of a trader has no or insignificant negative impact or only a positive impact on the environment.[1602] However, such products or activities are quite rare, if not inexistent. In fact, these claims generally concern only one or several sustainable aspect(s) and/or make a comparison with former or competing products. Therefore, claims that make those statements should be supplemented by prominent specifications or explanatory statements on the product's environmental impact, for example by limiting the claim to specific environmental benefits or by specifying the comparison.[1603] Similarly, traders who wish to make green claims on product lifetime are encouraged to "*provide any necessary information that the consumer may need in order to obtain the extended life characteristics*".[1604] The use of a general benefit claim may also be justified for products with excellent environmental performance and subject to detailed and ambitious rules.[1605] This encompasses products that are covered by a license to use the ecolabel of a publicly run ecolabel scheme (e.g. the Nordic Ecolabel 'the Swan', the German Ecolabel 'the Blue Angel' or the EU Ecolabel 'the Flower') or other robust and reputable labelling schemes subject to third party verification.[1606] This could also be the case if the LCA studies of the product (e.g. based on the PEF method) have proven its excellent environmental performance.[1607] For such products, traders should nevertheless ensure transparency concerning the relevant environmental aspects, and make sure that such information is easily available to consumers, including by displaying the relevant logo.[1608]

1599 UCPD Guidance, p. 76.

1600 2016 UCPD Guidance, p. 99.

1601 Moreover, it is interesting to note that the translation of the word 'sustainable' appears in the Dutch version ('duurzaam').

1602 UCPD Guidance, p. 77.

1603 UCPD Guidance, p. 79. For example, claims stating that a product is "*more environmentally friendly than another product*", while specifying the difference between the products and its importance (e.g. x% less x emissions than x; x times more durable than x), could be accepted, provided that these claims are duly substantiated.

1604 See J. R. Palerm, *Guidelines for Making and Assessing Environmental Claims* (European Commission 2000) p. 17.

1605 UCPD Guidance, pp. 80–81.

1606 This includes ecolabel schemes that meet the conditions set out by the international standard ISO 14024:2018 on Type I environmental labelling.

1607 For further comments on the obligation to substantiate green claims, see *infra*, n° 425–431.

1608 UCPD Guidance, p. 81, as well as Multi-stakeholder Dialogue on Environmental claims, *Multi-stakeholder advice to support the implementation/application of the Unfair Commercial*

418. Divergent interpretation of 'misleading' green claims by national courts – Since 'greenwashing' is not (yet)[1609] included in the UCPD blacklist, the national competent authorities have a wide discretion when assessing whether a green claim is misleading or not. In this regard, it should be noted that some national courts have a restrictive interpretation of 'misleading green claims' and have high expectations of the average consumer.[1610] For example, a Belgian court deemed that the claim 'ecological and more effective' for a detergent was not misleading, asserting that consumers are capable of critically assessing such claims and recognise when those are exaggerated.[1611] Such a decision seems to encourage traders to using vague claims without substantiating them.[1612]

419. The French definition of 'reconditioned' products – An interesting approach regarding vague and ambiguous claims is the one followed by France, which provides a legal framework for the use of the terms 'reconditioned' and 'reconditioned product'.[1613] The DGCCRF had pointed out the lack of homogenous controls of reconditioned products, the lack of information on their actual state and the increasing number of misleading practices.[1614] Through the adoption of Article L. 122–21–1, the aim was to protect consumers from operators who offer reconditioned products without having performed the necessary tests to verify that the product is in working order and does not pose any safety problems. This consumer protection was deemed even more necessary as the market for reconditioned products is developing significantly, given that these products are less expensive than new products.[1615] This trend towards reconditioned products was given further impetus by the French legislation, which obliges traders to inform consumers on the possibility of buying reconditioned goods instead of new ones.[1616]

Practices Directive 2005/29/EC on Compliance Criteria on Environmental Claims – Helping consumers make informed green choices and ensuring a level playing field for business (2016) p. 8 (hereafter 'Compliance Criteria on Environmental Claims').

1609 See Art. 1(4) of the Proposal for a Directive on empowering consumers for the green transition, as well as its Annex, especially pts (1) and (2).

1610 See E. Terryn, 'Lutter contre l'écoblanchissement est nécessaire mais ne suffit pas pour atteindre une consommation responsable', 47 *Revue juridique de l'environnement* (2022) p. 74.

1611 Prés. Trib. de Commerce Anvers 7 novembre 2013, *Annuaire pratiques du marché*, p. 512–521.

1612 E. Terryn, 'Lutter contre l'écoblanchissement est nécessaire mais ne suffit pas pour atteindre une consommation responsable', 47 *Revue juridique de l'environnement* (2022) p. 74.

1613 See Article L. 122–21–1 of the French Consumer Code. This provision was introduced by Art. 37 of the Anti-Waste Law.

1614 DGCCRF, *Produits électroniques reconditionnés, une alternative possible au neuf?*, 13 May 2020, available on: <https://www.economie.gouv.fr/dgccrf/produits-electroniques-reconditionnes-une-alternative-possible-au-neuf>.

1615 See explanatory memorandum to the Draft Implementing Decree, available on: <https://ec.europa.eu/growth/tools-databases/tris/fr/search/?trisaction=search.detail&year=2021&num=30>.

1616 Article L. 122–25 of the French Consumer Code.

The Implementing Decree[1617] restricts the use of these terms for second-hand products and spare parts and specifies the conditions under which they may be used, with regard to the performance of tests and the requirement of one or more technical interventions, to ensure the safety and functionality of the product.[1618] Furthermore, to prevent consumers from being misled as to the characteristics of a reconditioned product, this Decree prohibits any reference to a new product and restricts the use of the words 'reconditioned in France' for reconditioning operations that are carried out entirely on national territory.[1619]

Although this national initiative should be welcomed from a sustainability perspective, questions could be raised on its necessity, especially when taking into account the envisaged ecodesign rules at EU level[1620], as well as on its compatibility with the principle of free movement of goods as established under Article 34 of the TFEU, as it imposes obligations on businesses that may not be proportionate to the objective pursued (i.e. consumer protection).[1621] Such observations were made by the EC when analysing the Draft Implementing Decree within the framework of the notification procedure[1622], which leads us to believe that such an approach should rather be taken at EU level.

420. Comparisons between products' nature or main characteristics – Where those green claims on the product's nature or main characteristics are based on comparisons, they must also meet the requirements applicable to comparative claims as set out in Directive 2006/114/EU on misleading and comparative advertising.[1623] For example, comparisons should only be made with products within the same product category. In addition, the method used to produce the information should be the same, applied in a consistent manner (i.e. the same methodological choices and rules are applied, results are reproducible), and allow meaningful comparisons.[1624]

421. Misleading use of labels – Traders may also mislead consumers on the product's nature and characteristics by the misleading use of labels. Misleading practices can relate to EU labels, as illustrated by a couple of practical examples

---

1617 Décret n° 2022–190 du 17 février 2022 relatif aux conditions d'utilisation des termes "reconditionné" et "produit reconditionné", JORF n°0041 du 18 février 2022.

1618 Art. R. 122–4 of the French Consumer Code.

1619 See Art. R. 122–5 and 6 of the French Consumer Code.

1620 See e.g. the Sustainable Products Initiative and the Circular Electronics Initiative. See *supra*, n° 193 *et seq*.

1621 ECJ 22 January 2002, Case C-390/99, *Canal Satélite Digital, EU:C:2002:34*, para 33; ECJ 7 June 2007, Case C-254/05, *Commission v Belgium, EU:C:2007:319*, para. 33. See also Commission Notice of 5 March 2021 on the Guide on Articles 34–36 of the Treaty on the Functioning of the European Union (TFEU), C(2021) 1457 final, p. 52 at p. 54.

1622 See Communication from the Commission of 11 May 2021 within the framework of the Directive (UE) 2015/1535, TRIS/(2021) 01480, Ares(2021)3140907.

1623 Directive 2006/114/EC of the European Parliament and of the Council of 12 December 2006 concerning misleading and comparative advertising, OJ L 376, 27.12.2006, p. 21–27.

1624 UCPD Guidance, pp. 83–84. For further details on claim substantiation, see *infra*.

given in the UCPD Guidance.[1625] A self-declared label that resembles too closely the official EU label can be qualified as misleading.[1626] Analogous reasoning can be held for traders who obtain the EU energy label, but use it with additional labels, marks, symbols or inscriptions that are likely to mislead or confuse customers[1627], although forbidden by the Energy Labelling Regulation itself.[1628] The use of labels can also be misleading if the conditions for awarding the label are not actually met, as emphasized by the German Federal Court of Justice (BGH) for the ecolabel *The Blue Angel*.[1629]

422. Misleading green claims on commitments – Closely linked to labels, another relevant prohibition contained in Article 6(1) in relation to green claims is the one that forbids traders to mislead consumers on the extent and nature of their commitment.[1630] This prohibition can be linked to Article 6(2)(b), which qualifies practices as misleading if they involve non-compliance by the trader with commitments contained in codes of conduct by which the trader has undertaken to be bound. Codes of conduct may include general or product-specific commitments in relation to the environmental impact of a product and often materialize into a logo, ecolabel, symbol or certificate by the code signatory.[1631] Consumers expect code signatories to sell products that comply with that code and they expect products bearing the logo, ecolabel or any other marks to meet the commitments of the code.[1632] If a business has committed to such a code and indicates in a commercial practice that he did so (e.g. by using the code's logo), non-compliance with the code can constitute a breach of Article 6(2)(b), provided that those commitments are firm and are capable of being verified and provided that the economic behaviour of consumers is likely to be distorted. This would be the case if the printer producers do not comply with the commitments contained in the voluntary agreement on imaging equipment.[1633] For example, *HP* could be sanctioned on the basis of Article 6

1625 UCPD Guidance, pp. 74–75.

1626 The case at hand concerned a label affixed to tyres, which gave the misleading impression that they satisfied the testing and classification demands required by the EU tyre label. Market Court of Finland 30 March 2013, *Finnish Consumer Ombudsman v. Nokian Tyres*, MAO:185/13.

1627 In the case at hand, the use of the slogan 'very energy saving' for a refrigerator/freezer in energy efficiency class 'A' was considered as misleading by the German court as 308 out of 543 appliances on the German market at the time belonged to class 'A+' and 17% of all available appliances belonged even to energy efficiency class 'A++'.

1628 See recital 23 of the Energy Labelling Regulation.

1629 C. Meller-Hannich and E. Krausbeck, 'Sustainability, the Circular Economy and Consumer Law in Germany', 9 *EuCML* (2020) p. 170.

1630 Art. 6(1)(c) UCPD.

1631 UCPD Guidance, p. 79.

1632 *Ibid.*

1633 Industry voluntary agreement of April 2015 to improve the environmental performance of imaging equipment placed on the European market, VA v.5.2. For more details on these voluntary agreements, see Chapter II on the design and production stage (n° 231).

of the UCPD if, as claimed by *Euroconsumers*, its printers were not compatible with third-party cartridges.[1634] Also, such labels must not be capable of being confused with other labels, including, for example, labels of publicly run labelling schemes or schemes of competitors.[1635] Otherwise, it could constitute a misleading action within the meaning of Article 6(2)(b).[1636]

423. Green claims presented in an unclear, unintelligible, ambiguous or untimely manner – An environmental claim can be misleading under Article 7(2) of the UCPD if it is presented in an unclear, unintelligible, ambiguous or untimely manner. On the basis of a case-by-case assessment, this could be the case if the scope and boundaries of the claim are not made clear. A green claim will be sanctioned on the basis of Article 7 if it is not clear whether it covers the whole product or only one of its components, or the company's overall environmental performance or only certain of its activities or which environmental impact or process the claim refers to.[1637] If traders choose to use their own labelling schemes, symbols or certificates for marketing purposes, these labels must only be applied to the products/services or traders which meet the criteria set to qualify for use.[1638] The same reasoning can be held for claims focusing on a product's environmental impacts that are not the most significant over its lifecycle and ignoring the most relevant environmental issues. If businesses do not know the most significant environmental aspects of a product, they could perform a lifecycle assessment, or simply refrain from making environmental claims.[1639] A green claim will also breach Article 7(2) of the UCPD if the consumer cannot distinguish between the actual environmental impact of a specific product and the more general environmental claims regarding the trader, its practices and sustainability policies.[1640] Furthermore, claims should be reviewed and updated regularly to ensure that they remain relevant. The emergence of comparable products, technological development or other circumstances may indeed affect the accuracy or currentness of the claim.[1641]

1634 See the press release issued by Euroconsumers, 'Printergate: Euroconsumers asks HP to compensate printer owners up to € 150 each for unlawfully blocking 3rd party cartridges by pushing firmware update', 3 May 2021, available on: <https://assets.ctfassets.net/iapmw8ie3ije/6QK8BTorxlIqOMdmdLTWQt/9a67549a5b8bde96eef799e3887c2d00/HP_press_release_3_May_2021.docx.pdf>. See also the press release issued by Test Achats, 'Test Achats met HP en demeure pour le blocage de cartouches d'encre génériques', 3 May 2021, available on: <https://www.test-achats.be/hightech/imprimantes/presse/hp-printergate>. A settlement was ultimately reached between *HP* and the consumer organisations (see n° 398).

1635 Compliance Criteria on Environmental Claims, p. 9.

1636 See also B. Keirsbilck, S. Rousseau, 'The Marketing Stage: Fostering Sustainable Consumption Choices in a "Circular" and "Functional" Economy', in B. Keirsbilck, E. Terryn (eds.), *Consumer Protection in a Circular Economy* (Intersentia 2019) p. 102.

1637 UCPD Guidance, p. 81.

1638 Compliance Criteria on Environmental Claims, p. 9.

1639 For further details on claim substantiation, see *infra*.

1640 UCPD Guidance, p. 81.

1641 Compliance Criteria on Environmental Claims, p. 10, as well as UCPD Guidance, p. 77.

424. No total ban, but a case-by-case assessment of vague and ambiguous claims – In its initiative 'Empowering the consumer for the green transition', the EC had considered blacklisting unfounded generic or vague environmental claims.[1642] Although it would contribute to addressing the issue of information overload, it seems more appropriate to maintain a case-by-case assessment of these claims by the national authorities. A vague and ambiguous claim is indeed less likely to mislead consumers if the 'environmental excellence' of the product in question has been substantiated (e.g. via the EU Ecolabel or other ISO-type I ecolabels, the PEF method or other lifecycle assessment studies) and if the claim is supplemented by clear and prominent specifications or explanatory statements on the product's environmental impact and benefit(s). Yet making a distinction between different statements could be envisaged. For example, the use of the word 'sustainable' could be more restricted than the use of the word 'ecological' as the first is further reaching.[1643] Interestingly, the UCPD Guidance already makes a distinction when green claims are made by highly polluting industries.[1644] Hence, green claims using vague and general statements should rather be legally regulated than totally banned. The UCPD Guidance should provide a clear framework on that point (see #20). Otherwise, it could lead to fragmentation in national case law, as it is currently the case.

Proposed review of the UCPD Guidance: #20

4.1.1.3. Application of Article 6 of the UCPD to environmental claims

(...)

Environmental claims are likely to be misleading if they consist of vague and general statements of environmental benefits without appropriate substantiation of the benefit and without indication of the relevant aspect of the product the claim refers to. Examples of such claims are 'environmentally friendly', 'eco-friendly', 'eco', 'green', 'nature's friend', 'ecological', 'environmentally correct', 'climate friendly', 'gentle on the environment', 'pollutant free', 'biodegradable', 'zero emissions', 'carbon friendly', 'reduced CO_2 emissions' 'carbon neutral', 'climate neutral' and even the broader claims of 'conscious' and 'responsible'.

1642 See the explanatory memorandum to the Proposal for a Directive of the European Parliament and of the Council amending Directives 2005/29/EC and 2011/83/EU as regards empowering consumers for the green transition through better protection against unfair practices and better information, COM(2022) 143 final, p. 11.

1643 Whereas 'ecological' is defined as "*causing minimal damage to the environment*" (Oxford English Dictionary 2006 (3rd ed.)), 'sustainable' refers to "*the needs of the present*" and to "*the ability of future generations to meet their own needs*" (UN World Commission on Environment and Development, *Our Common Future* (1987) p. 41).

1644 The UCPD Guidance recommends highly polluting industries to ensure that their environmental claims are accurate in a sense of being relative, e.g. 'less harmful for the environment' instead of 'environmentally friendly'. This enables the average consumer to better understand the relative impact of the product. See UCPD Guidance, p. 78.

> Such unsubstantiated claims are likely to, in some cases, convey the impression to the consumers that a product or an activity of a trader has no negative impact or only a positive impact on the environment. They could fall under Article 6(1)(a) and 6(1)(b) UCPD if they are likely to deceive the average consumers and to cause them to take a transactional decision they would not have taken otherwise. **Therefore, making such vague and general statements should be prohibited, unless the 'environmental excellence' of the product has been substantiated (e.g. via the EU Ecolabel or other ISO-type I ecolabels, the PEF method or other LCA studies) and the claim clearly and prominently qualify the specific environmental benefit(s) of the product (possibly by means of a comparison with former or competing products within the same product category).**
>
> (...)

(2) The obligation to substantiate green claims

425. SUBSTANTIATION REQUIREMENTS – Pursuant to Article 12 of the UCPD, traders must have tangible evidence to support their claims, including environmental claims. Two consequent obligations derive from this obligation to substantiate green claims. First, traders must be ready to provide evidence to competent enforcement authorities in an understandable way if the claim is challenged so that the authorities can verify the concerned claim.[1645] The courts and administrative authorities must be enabled to require traders to produce all relevant documentation pertaining to the accuracy of factual claims (including confidential business information)[1646] and to consider factual claims as inaccurate if the evidence demanded is not furnished or is deemed insufficient. Second, traders should be transparent in making relevant information available to the public to support their claims. To assist consumers eager to find out further information about the basis of a claim, traders should consider disclosing further information on their websites which can be helpful in substantiating claims.[1647] The documentation or supporting evidence to be provided should however not be as elaborated as for the authorities.

426. THE NEED FOR APPROPRIATE EVIDENCE – As emphasized by the UCPD Guidance, "*claims should be based on robust, independent, verifiable and generally recognised evidence which takes into account updated scientific findings and methods*".[1648] To ensure that environmental claims are substantiated, traders should either have the evidence necessary to support their claims from

1645 See Article 12 and recital 21 UCPD.
1646 The competent body is required to treat confidential business information confidentially.
1647 For example, the website could mention the criteria underlying the claim or the results from third-party verification. See Compliance Criteria on Environmental Claims, p. 11.
1648 UCPD Guidance, p. 81.

the time the claims are put into use or be certain that this evidence can be obtained and presented upon request. Independent third-party testing should be made available for the competent bodies if the claim is challenged. If expert studies give rise to significant disagreement or doubt over environmental impacts, the trader should refrain from the claim altogether. Traders should also make sure that documentation for claims is up to date for as long as the claims remain in use in marketing. In fact, a claim may be correct and relevant to a product when the claim is first made, but it could become less meaningful with time.[1649] The content and scope of the documentation will depend on the specific content of the statement as well as on the complexity of the product.[1650]

427. No positive rules, but standards and guidelines – There are currently no detailed positive rules on the substantiation of environmental claims. Minimum requirements can only be found in standards.[1651] Traders who are willing to make green claims are further assisted by the document on Compliance Criteria on Environmental Claims, which gives advice to formulate environmental claims in compliance with the UCPD and to improve the transparency of these claims for the benefit of consumers.[1652] Other guidelines for making effective, trustworthy claims to consumers on product-related sustainability information have been issued at national, EU and international levels over the past few years.[1653] The recommendations on claim substantiation

---

1649 UCPD Guidance, p. 82.

1650 UCPD Guidance, p. 82, as well as Compliance Criteria on Environmental Claims, p. 10.

1651 The International Standards Office (ISO) has developed standards on environmental labels and declarations, and more specifically on general principles (ISO 14020:2000), on self-declared environmental claims (ISO 14021:2016), on claims based on life-cycle impacts (ISO 14025:2006) and on principles, requirements and guidelines for communication of footprint information (ISO 14026:2017).

1652 Multi-stakeholder Dialogue on Environmental claims, *Multi-stakeholder advice to support the implementation/application of the Unfair Commercial Practices Directive 2005/29/EC on Compliance Criteria on Environmental Claims – Helping consumers make informed green choices and ensuring a level playing field for business* (2016).

1653 At national level, see for ex. in Belgium: Avis du Conseil Central de l'Economie du 28 septembre 2018 sur la Guidance à destination des entreprises concernant des allégations environnementales loyales, CCE 2018–2280; SPF Economie, *Bonnes pratiques en matière d'allégations environnementales* (2021), available on: <https://economie.fgov.be/fr/themes/entreprises/guidance>; in France: DGCCRF, *Guide pratique des allégations environnementales à l'usage des professionnels et des consommateurs* (2012 République française); ADEME, *Guide anti-greenwashing* (2012), available on: <https://presse.ademe.fr/wp-content/uploads/2012/09/ademe_greenwashing_guide-2.pdf>; and in Germany: BMU, *Environmental Information for Products and Services Requirements – Tools – Examples* (2019). See also the detailed guidelines on sustainability claims issued by the Dutch authorities (ACM), available on: <https://www.acm.nl/sites/default/files/documents/guidelines-suistainability-claims.pdf>. For more examples of national guidelines, see the Report from the Multi-Stakeholder Dialogue on Environmental Claims – Helping consumers make informed green choices and ensuring a level playing field for business (European Consumer Summit 2013) p. 22 at p. 24. At EU level, see J. R. Palerm, *Guidelines for Making and Assessing Environmental Claims* (European Commission 2000). At the international level, see M. Barthel et al., *Guidelines*

contained in these soft law instruments can be summarized in two main points. First, the claim should be based on appropriate methods and standards and underpinned by a generally accepted methodology in the relevant scientific field(s). If expert studies give rise to significant disagreement or doubt over environmental impacts, the trader should refrain from marketing the message altogether.[1654] Second, the criteria for communicating product characteristics and claims should be verified by an independent and competent third party.

428. Emergence and development of various methods – The absence of positive rules on claim substantiation has led to the emergence and development of various methods to measure and assess product environmental impacts, which can be problematic. The different methods currently used for measuring and benchmarking the environmental performance of products vary and give different results when applied to the same product or organisation. Indeed, due to the number of methodological choices left to the discretion of the user, even results obtained with the same method are often not comparable. The existence of multiple schemes and the lack of harmonised criteria and standards can generate significant costs for businesses that can deter them from giving information on environmental impacts (e.g. if they need to use different methods or if they have to comply with labelling and verification requirements for different countries and retailers) and create obstacles to free movement of goods.[1655] Moreover, these methods are not always recognised by national courts.[1656]

429. The proposed common criteria against greenwashing and misleading environmental claims – To solve this issue and stimulate the use of green claims, the EC recently adopted a Proposal for a Directive on Green Claims, which sets minimum requirements on how companies substantiate voluntary green claims and labelling and how they communicate them to consumers.[1657] As regards the substantiation of green claims, Article 3 of the Proposal requires traders to carry out an assessment that meets minimum criteria to prevent misleading

for Providing Product Sustainability Information – Global guidance on making effective environmental, social and economic claims, to empower and enable consumer choice (United Nations Environment Programme 2017).

1654 Compliance Criteria on Environmental Claims, p. 10.

1655 Communication from the Commission of 9 April 2013 to the European Parliament and the Council on Building the Single Market for Green Products – Facilitating better information on the environmental performance of products and organisations, COM(2013) 196 final, p. 4 at p. 6.

1656 See for ex. the textile industry's labelling scheme Higg Material Sustainability Index, which was considered as misleading marketing by the Norwegian Consumer Authority: Naturvernforbundet, 'Textile industry's labelling scheme is misleading marketing, the Norwegian Consumer Authority rules', 17 June 2022, available on: <https://naturvernforbundet.no/sustainable-living/textile-industry-s-labelling-scheme-is-misleading-marketing-the-norwegian-consumer-authority-rules-article43213–995.html>.

1657 Art. 1 of the Proposal for a Green Claims Directive.

claims,[1658] whereas Article 4 imposes further requirements for comparative claims. Most of these requirements embody the recommendations contained in the UCPD Guidance. It should be noted that the Proposal does not prescribe a single method (i.e. a full lifecycle analysis for each type of claim) but establishes different levels of substantiation depending on the type of claims. As regards the communication of green claims, Articles 5 and 6 lay down requirements to ensure that claims offer environmental benefits as compared to common practice. Article 7 of the Proposal extends these substantiation and communication requirements to labels.

430. Using the (PEF) method for the substantiation and verification of environmental claims – Within the framework of the Proposal for a Green Claims Directive, the EC considered prescribing the use of common measurement and assessment tools, such as the PEF method, for the verification and substantiation of claims related to the environmental performance of products.[1659] Following this approach, traders who would wish to make environmental claims on products would be obliged to use these LCA methods of excellence to substantiate their claim. However, as explained in the previous paragraph, the EC finally decided not to pursue the option of one standard methodology to substantiate green claims and preferred a more flexible approach. Several reasons were given to justify this decision, including the fact that the PEF method do not yet cover all relevant impact categories for all product types and that many claims are made on environmental aspects for which this method is not suited.[1660] This is regrettable given the effectiveness of information based on the PEF method in guiding choices towards more environmentally friendly alternatives.[1661] On the trader side, LCA methods would enable them to make reliable, reproducible and comparable environmental claims, but also avoid undue transfer of impacts, that is the creation or increase of significant negative environmental impacts at other stages of the product's lifecycle. Therefore, the PEF method could, in the first instance, be strongly recommended to traders for the substantiation of their green claims (through the UCPD Guidance)(see #21), before becoming compulsory (with an explicit mention in Article 12 of the UCPD)(see #22).[1662]

1658 For example, the assessment must (a) specify if the claim is related to the whole product, part of a product or certain aspects of a product and (b) rely on widely recognised scientific evidence, use accurate information and take into account relevant international standards. See Art. 3 of the Proposal for a Green Claims Directive for further details.

1659 Inception impact assessment from the European Commission of 20 July 2020 on Legislative proposal on substantiating green claims, Ares(2020)3820384.

1660 See the explanatory memorandum to the Proposal for a Directive of the European Parliament and of the Council on substantiation and communication of explicit environmental claims (Green Claims Directive), COM(2023) 166 final, pp. 12-13.

1661 CentERdata, Ipsos, *Consumer testing of alternatives for communicating the Environmental Footprint profile of products – Final report* (European Commission 2019).

1662 Such a recommendation is in line with the Commission Recommendation of 15 December 2021 on the use of the Environmental Footprint methods to measure and communicate the life cycle environmental performance of products and organisations, C(2021) 9332 final;

431. Minimum requirements for transparent and reliable claims – Alternatively, or as an intermediary step, minimum requirements should be established for the transparency and/or reliability of all voluntary sustainability claims/labels/schemes/logos and all sustainability information tools (see #23), as proposed in the Proposal for a Directive on Green Claims.[1663] The disclosure of compliance with these criteria could then be ensured through self-statement, pre-endorsement or a specific website or online tool. To establish these criteria, examples could be taken from the existing guidelines and standards on green claims[1664], but also on guidelines from other sectors, like the voluntary certification schemes for agricultural products and foodstuffs[1665], and from national initiatives.[1666] If these requirements are not satisfied, the green claim could be banned on the basis of Articles 6 and 7 of the UCPD or on the basis of an amended blacklist that would specifically mention this case (see #24). Such reflection is taking place in Belgium, where efforts are being made to simplify and unify the procedures for assessing misleading green claims.[1667]

432. As a last resort option, establishing an authorisation scheme like for nutrition and health claims – If the abovementioned suggestions are implemented but do not yield satisfactory results against greenwashing, one should envisage adopting a more stringent approach requiring traders to get authorisation before being allowed to use green claims in the labelling, presentation and advertising of products placed on the market (see #25). Specific and general conditions could be established and, if fulfilled, the claim would be permitted. These conditions could relate to the content, the form and the substantiation of the claims. Such a 'command and control' approach already exists in the nutrition and health sector, where claims can only be made if certain conditions are fulfilled.[1668] For example, nutrition and health claims are only permitted if "*the presence, absence or reduced content in a food (...) of a nutrient (...) in respect of which the claim is made has been shown to have a*

Corrigendum to Commission Recommendation (EU) 2021/2279 of 15 December 2021 on the use of the Environmental Footprint methods to measure and communicate the life cycle environmental performance of products and organisations (Official Journal of the European Union L 471 of 30 December 2021), OJ L 144, 23.5.2022, p. 1–384.

1663 See *supra*, n° 429.

1664 See *supra*, n° 427.

1665 Communication from the Commission of 16 December 2010 on EU best practice guidelines for voluntary certification schemes for agricultural products and foodstuffs, OJ C 341, p. 5–11.

1666 See for ex. the German online portal ranking the labels existing in Germany: <https://label-online.de/unsere-bewertung/>.

1667 B. Keirsbilck, 'Sustainability, the Circular Economy and Consumer Law in Belgium' 9 *EuCML* (2020) p. 165.

1668 Regulation (EC) No 1924/2006 of the European Parliament and of the Council of 20 December 2006 on nutrition and health claims made on foods, OJ L 404, 30.12.2006, p. 9–25 (hereafter 'Regulation on nutrition and health claims').

beneficial nutritional or physiological effect".[1669] When the food product complies with these conditions, the food business operator can apply for authorisation and, if successful, use the claim.[1670] A Community Register of nutrition and health claims includes the nutrition claims and the conditions applying to them, restrictions, the authorised health claims and the conditions applying to them, as well as a list of rejected health claims and the reasons for their rejection.[1671]

Proposed review of the UCPD Guidance:

IN THE FIRST INSTANCE #21

4.1.1.5. Application of Article 12 of the UCPD to environmental claims

(...)

Article 12 of the UCPD clarifies that any claim (including environmental claims) should be based on evidence which can be verified by the relevant competent authorities. Traders must be able to substantiate environmental claims with appropriate evidence. Consequently, claims should be based on robust, independent, verifiable and generally recognised evidence which takes into account updated scientific findings and methods. There is no equivalent obligation in the UCPD for the trader to provide documentation or other supporting evidence to consumers.

The burden of proof regarding the accuracy of the claim rests on the trader. Article 12(a) of the UCPD provides that enforcement authorities should have the power 'to require the trader to furnish evidence as to the accuracy of factual claims in relation to a commercial practice'.

When furnishing the evidence supporting the claim related to the environmental performance of a product, the trader should preferably use the Product Environmental Footprint (PEF) method.* The substantiation of environmental claims should be presumed appropriate if the PEF method has been followed by the trader.

* See the Commission Recommendation (EU) 2021/2279 of 15 December 2021 on the use of the Environmental Footprint methods to measure and communicate the life cycle environmental performance of products and organisations, OJ L 471, 30.12.2021, p. 1–396.

1669 Art. 5 Regulation on nutrition and health claims.
1670 Art. 15–19 Regulation on nutrition and health claims.
1671 Art. 20 Regulation on nutrition and health claims.

(...)

IN THE SECOND INSTANCE #22

Proposed review of the UCPD

Article 12
Courts and administrative authorities: substantiation of claims

1. Member States shall confer upon the courts or administrative authorities powers enabling them in the civil or administrative proceedings provided for in Article 11:

(a) to require the trader to furnish evidence as to the accuracy of factual claims in relation to a commercial practice if, taking into account the legitimate interest of the trader and any other party to the proceedings, such a requirement appears appropriate on the basis of the circumstances of the particular case;

and

(b) to consider factual claims as inaccurate if the evidence demanded in accordance with (a) is not furnished or is deemed insufficient by the court or administrative authority.

2. Environmental claims shall be substantiated following the Product Environmental Footprint (PEF) method, as recommended in the Commission Recommendation (EU) 2021/2279 (*).

(*) Commission Recommendation (EU) 2021/2279 of 15 December 2021 on the use of the Environmental Footprint methods to measure and communicate the life cycle environmental performance of products and organisations, OJ L 471, 30.12.2021, p. 1–396.

IN THE ALTERNATIVE, OR AS AN INTERMEDIARY STEP:

#23 Minimum requirements should be established for the transparency and/or reliability of all voluntary sustainability claims/labels/schemes/logos and all sustainability information tools.

#24 The UCPD blacklist should be amended so that it prohibits green claims that do not fulfil these requirements.

#25 If none of these measures yield satisfactory results, an authorisation scheme similar to the one existing for nutrition and health claims should be established.

d) *Aggressive practices of premature obsolescence*

433. Aggressive practices – Beyond misleading actions and omissions, the UCPD prohibits 'aggressive commercial practices' through its Articles 8 and 9. Although these provisions may be less frequently used against premature obsolescence, some practices limiting product lifetime can fall within this category. Articles 8 and 9 should therefore also be mentioned in the section on 'premature obsolescence' of the UCPD Guidance (see #26). According to Article 8, a commercial practice must be deemed aggressive "*if, in its factual context, taking account of all its features and circumstances, by harassment, coercion, including the use of physical force, or undue influence, it significantly impairs or is likely to significantly impair the average consumer's freedom of choice or conduct with regard to the product and thereby causes him or is likely to cause him to take a transactional decision that he would not have taken otherwise.*" By contrast with Articles 6 and 7 on misleading practices, Article 8 requires a *significant* impairment of the average consumer's freedom of choice or conduct, which restricts its application in practice.

434. Harassment, coercion, physical force or undue influence – Aggressive commercial practices are those whereby the trader makes use of harassment, coercion, physical force or undue influence. As highlighted in the UCPD Guidance, aggressive practices encompass behaviour at the marketing stage, but also practices that occur during or after a transaction has taken place.[1672] Article 2 of the UCPD only provides a definition for 'undue influence', which is defined as "*exploiting a position of power in relation to the consumer so as to apply pressure, even without using or threatening to use physical force, in a way which significantly limits the consumer's ability to make an informed decision*".[1673] The 'position of power' can relate to both economic and intellectual domination and can derive out of many social ties besides the purely professional.[1674] As emphasized by Advocate General Campos Sanchez-Bordona in *Orange Polska* case, "*undue influence is not necessarily impermissible influence but influence which, without prejudice to its lawfulness, actively entails, through the application of a certain degree of pressure, the forced conditioning of the consumer's will*".[1675] In cases of premature obsolescence, aggressive practices mostly consist of coercion or undue influence on consumers to accelerate product replacement, as illustrated by the following paragraphs.

435. Factors to be taken into account – Article 9 lists a series of factors to be taken into consideration when assessing the aggressive nature of the

1672 UCPD Guidance, p. 59.

1673 Article 2(j) of the UCPD.

1674 B. Keirsbilck, *The New European Law of Unfair Commercial Practices and Competition Law* (Hart Publishing 2011) p. 373.

1675 Opinion of Advocate General Campos Sanchez-Bordona delivered on 30 January 2019 in ECJ 12 June 2019, Case C-628/17, *Orange Polska, EU:C:2019:480*, pt. 45.

practice. These include its timing, location, nature or persistence, the use of threatening or abusive language or behaviour, the exploitation by the trader of any specific misfortune or circumstance of such gravity as to impair the consumer's judgement, any onerous or disproportionate non-contractual barriers imposed by the trader where a consumer wishes to exercise rights under the contract, any threat to take any action that cannot legally be taken. Among the non-contractual barriers that impair consumers' freedom of choice, there is the one that prevents them from switching to another product or another trader ('consumer lock-in').[1676] This is the case when consumers buy applications and IoT products that are only interoperable with the mobile phone they bought. In such a situation, consumers who experience a loss of quality of their mobile phone find themselves limited in their choice as moving to another mobile phone ecosystem may entail financial loss, loss of time and loss of data. This barrier helps traders gain benefits from practices accelerating the replacement of old devices.[1677] Disproportionate barriers to repair could also be taken into account when assessing whether a commercial practice is aggressive within the meaning of Article 8 of the UCPD.[1678]

436. Premature obsolescence caused by the undue influence of Apple and Samsung – Cases of premature obsolescence through undue influence have already been observed in practice. Here too, the Italian cases can be taken as an illustrative example. As previously pointed out[1679], the Italian authorities sanctioned *Apple* and *Samsung* on the basis of Article 24 of the Italian Consumer Code which implements Article 8 of the UCPD. In the cases at hand, once updates were available, both traders would repeatedly send messages to their customers on the need to download and install these updates, restricting their choice between installing updates or postponing the installation. No clear and adequate information on updates was provided.[1680] This information asymmetry forced consumers to place their trust in the companies as regards the usefulness and benefits of updates. Once the updates were installed, *Apple* and *Samsung* did not allow consumers to restore the original functionality of their smartphones afterwards. The aggressive nature of the practices also stemmed from the fact that the companies hindered the repair and replacement of the defective smartphones and their batteries. Moreover, *Apple* and *Samsung* significantly and unduly influenced consumers not to switch to another trader. Whereas the easy transferability of content between all *Apple* devices provoked

1676 UCPD Guidance, pp. 106–107.
1677 Other examples are provided by the UCPD Guidance. See UCPD Guidance, p. 106.
1678 See also A. Perzanowski, *The Right to Repair: Reclaiming the Things We Own* (Cambridge University Press 2022) p. 208.
1679 See *supra*, n° 359.
1680 Such information, like information on the terms and consequences of a contract, is of utmost importance and should be provided to consumers beforehand. See ECJ 13 September 2018, Joined Cases C-54/17 and C-55/17, *Wind Tre and Vodafone Italia, EU:C:2018:710*, para 46.

consumers facing a defective product to buy a later model of the same brand[1681], *Samsung* granted a 25% discount for the online purchase of a new product on its website to customers who did not accept the repair conditions of a defective product.[1682] Altogether, those practices were considered as undue pressure on the consumers' freedom of choice as they restricted consumer ability to make free decisions on the use and functionality of their equipment and impelled them to make a transactional decision that they would not have taken otherwise.

437. BEUC COMPLAINT AGAINST NINTENDO FOR AGGRESSIVE PRACTICES OF PREMATURE OBSOLESCENCE – In 2021, BEUC launched an EU-wide complaint against *Nintendo* for 'premature obsolescence'.[1683] The practice in question relates to the *Nintendo* Switch and the recurring technical problem with its game controllers (commonly known as the 'Joy-Con Drift'), which had already been pointed out by the French consumer association *UFC-Que choisir*.[1684] According to BEUC, the practice pursued by *Nintendo* should be considered aggressive for several reasons. First, *Nintendo* did not inform consumers on the restricted lifetime of the game controllers and thus exploits its (intellectual) position of power that stems from the additional knowledge it has on the (mal) functioning of (part of) its product. Second, *Nintendo* exploits its position of power that stems from the lock-in effect. As accessories and games can only be used with the *Nintendo* ecosystem, the lack of interoperability makes it more difficult for consumers to switch to another brand. When facing a defective game controller, they have no choice but to buy a new device from *Nintendo* to continue playing on the same console with the same games. Third, the aggressive nature of this practice is exacerbated by the repair and guarantee policy of *Nintendo*, which can be seen as an 'onerous or disproportionate non-contractual barrier imposed by the trader' (e.g. excessive repair and replacement costs). Following this alert from BEUC, the European Commission and EU consumer authorities contacted *Nintendo*, which has agreed to offer all consumers the right to repair for affected game controllers free of charge, even beyond the legal guarantee.[1685]

1681 Autorita Garante della Concorrenza e del Mercato, 25 September 2018, *Apple*, para 67.

1682 Autorita Garante della Concorrenza e del Mercato, 25 September 2018, *Samsung*, para 87.

1683 See the press release issued by BEUC on 27 January 2021, 'BEUC launches Europe-wide complaint against Nintendo for premature obsolescence', BEUC-PR-2021-002, available on: <https://www.beuc.eu/publications/beuc-pr-2021-002_beuc_launches_europe-wide_complaint_against_nintendo_for_premature_obsolescence.pdf>.

1684 See *supra*, n° 72.

1685 See the press release issued by the European Commission on 4 April 2023, 'Consumer protection: Nintendo agrees to offer free repairs of irresponsive Nintendo Switch controllers', available on: <https://ec.europa.eu/commission/presscorner/detail/en/ip_23_2106>.

438. Material, functional and indirect obsolescence as aggressive practices – Other cases of material, functional and indirect obsolescence could be qualified as 'material coercion' or undue influence.[1686] Indeed, through these practices, traders force consumers to make decisions that they would not have taken otherwise and highly limit consumers' ability to make an informed decision. These include among others cases of material obsolescence whereby smart chip technology makes the product stop functioning, where batteries are not removable and cases where consumables (e.g. printer ink cartridges) are programmed with reduced lifetimes.[1687] The two cases of misleading omissions cited by the former 2016 UCPD Guidance also fall within this category as the products concerned (i.e. fridges and washing machines) are designed to have a limited lifetime.[1688] Similar reasoning can be held for practices of indirect and functional obsolescence, whereby for example the use of consumables[1689], accessories or software's from another brand is hindered.[1690]

439. Undue influence through economic obsolescence – Cases of economic obsolescence could also be seen as significantly influencing consumers through the exertion of undue influence. For example, a trader who sets an unreasonably high price for spare parts and repair service compared to the purchasing price of the product could be sanctioned on the basis of Articles 8 and 9 of the UCPD. Such commercial practice creates onerous non-contractual barriers that may prevent consumers from exercising their right to repair, as described in Article 9(d). Combined with other practices, this strategy could influence consumers to prematurely replace their product. The Italian authorities have condemned such practices followed by *Samsung*, which was asking for high repair costs for out-of-warranty repairs connected to malfunctions that were caused by the installation of updates that the firm had insistently suggested to its customers.[1691] The class action brought by *Test-Achats* against *Proximus* is another illustrative example of undue influence by economic means.[1692] *Proximus* had been accused of having forced its customers who had bought a decoder between 2008 and 2013 to get rid of it and rent a new one. *Proximus* had offered a free 12-month rental if customers responded before 25 June 2016. Customers who would not do so would lose access to the Proximus

1686 See also A. Hamann, 'Obsolescence programmée: le droit en panne?', 102 *D.C.C.R.* (2014) p. 59.

1687 The two last examples can be found in the UCPD Guidance, p. 85.

1688 See 2016 UCPD Guidance, p. 83.

1689 The UCPD Guidance gives the example of the incompatibility limitations on the use of non-original printer ink cartridges. See UCPD Guidance, p. 85.

1690 It should be noted that these incompatibilities can also be sanctioned on the basis of competition law as they can constitute an abuse of dominant position. See e.g. ECJ 17 September 2007, Case T-201/04, *Microsoft v Commission, EU:T:2007:289.*

1691 Autorita Garante della Concorrenza e del Mercato, 25 September 2018, *Samsung*, para 62.

1692 Bruxelles, 30 janvier 2019, *Proximus* v *Test-Achats, M.B.* 20 février 2019.

TV service. Although the appeal was ultimately considered unfounded, this case, which led to the obsolescence of decoders, could have been seen as aggressive.[1693]

> *Proposed review of the UCPD Guidance:*
>
> *#26*
>
> *4.1.2. ~~Planned~~ Premature obsolescence*
>
> (...)
>
> UCPD does not have provisions specifically addressing obsolescence. However, **its provisions can help curb some practices related to premature obsolescence. For example,** where the trader, including manufacturer, engages in commercial practices towards the consumer, its failure to inform the consumer that a product has been designed with a limited lifetime might, subject to a case-by-case assessment, be considered as omission of material information under Article 7 UCPD. **(...)**[1694] **Articles 8 and 9 may also be useful in tackling practices of premature obsolescence whereby the trader makes use of coercion or undue influence.** Furthermore, ~~such~~ practices **of premature obsolescence** may also be contrary to the requirements of professional diligence under Article 5(2) UCPD if they are likely to materially distort the economic behaviour of the average consumer.
>
> (...)

5. THE GENERAL CLAUSE PROHIBITING UNFAIR COMMERCIAL PRACTICES

440. Third step: the general clause – Although the blacklist and the provisions on misleading and aggressive practices may capture the vast majority of cases of premature obsolescence, those that do not fall within these provisions could still be caught by the grand general clause enshrined in Article 5 of the UCPD. This residual provision prohibits 'unfair commercial practices', meaning practices that (a) are contrary to the requirements of professional diligence and (b) materially distort or are likely to materially distort economic behaviour with regard to the product of the average consumer who it reaches or to whom it is

---

1693 The European Court of Justice already highlighted that such cases, whereby the consumer would risk the trader suspending the service in the event of the contract being amended, may fall within the category of aggressive practices. See ECJ 12 June 2019, Case C-628/17, *Orange Polska*, *EU:C:2019:480*, para 48.

1694 This suggested amendment to the UCPD Guidance is to be read in conjunction with the amendment related to Article 6 of the UCPD on misleading actions and its role against premature obsolescence. See *supra*, n° 409–414.

addressed, or of the average member of the group when a commercial practice is directed at a particular group of consumers.[1695] Commercial practices can only be prohibited on the basis of the general clause if they meet these two cumulative conditions.[1696] When applying the general clause, full account should be taken of the context of the individual case concerned.

441. A SAFETY NET PROVISION – This last resort provision can be used as a safety net to sanction unfair commercial practices that limit product lifetime and that do not correspond to blacklisted practices or the definitions of misleading and aggressive practices.[1697] The general clause was meant to deal with practices judged unfair even if they were not misleading or aggressive, as well as allowing enforcers to deal with innovative practices. The general prohibition was furthermore meant to help ensure that the UCPD can adapt to changing technologies and market developments.[1698]

442. IN CONTRADICTION TO PROFESSIONAL DILIGENCE – Concerning the first condition for the application of the general clause, Article 2(h) of the UCPD defines 'professional diligence' as "*the standard of special skill and care which a trader may reasonably be expected to exercise towards consumers, commensurate with honest market practice and/or the general principle of good faith in the trader's field of activity*". This condition is aimed at ensuring that normal business practices, which conform to custom and usage, are not caught out by the Directive even if they are capable of influencing consumers' economic behaviour.[1699] There is no European conception of this notion, which leaves a wide margin of discretion to national courts concerning its interpretation.[1700] Codes of conduct could help establish special standards of skill and care that can be expected in a specific sector, as highlighted by recital 20 of the UCPD. Regrettably, no codes have yet been adopted. Yet the European Court of Justice shed some light on the interpretation of the notion. As an example, in *Sony*, the Court held that the requirements of honest market practices or of the principle of good faith in the field of the manufacturing of computer equipment was likely to

---

1695 Art. 5(1) UCPD.

1696 ECJ 9 November 2010, Case C-540/08, *Mediaprint*, para 45–47.

1697 For further details on the relationship between the comprehensive general clause and the special general clauses, see H.-W. Micklitz, 'Unfair commercial practices and misleading advertising', in N. Reich et al. (eds.), *European Consumer Law – Ius Commutatis V* (Intersentia 2014) p. 95.

1698 Proposal for a Directive of the European Parliament and of the Council concerning unfair business-to-consumer commercial practices in the Internal Market and amending directives 84/450/EEC, 97/7/EC and 98/27/EC, COM (2003) 356 final, p. 12, pt. 50.

1699 Proposal for a Directive of the European Parliament and of the Council concerning unfair business-to-consumer commercial practices in the Internal Market and amending directives 84/450/EEC, 97/7/EC and 98/27/EC, COM (2003) 356 final, p. 12, pt. 53.

1700 B. Keirsbilck, *The New European Law of Unfair Commercial Practices and Competition Law* (Hart Publishing 2011) p. 273.

be fulfilled if "*the consumer was correctly informed, (..) the combined offer met the expectations of a significant proportion of consumers and (..) it was possible for the consumer to accept all the elements of that offer or to cancel the sale*".[1701] Following this reasoning, a trader would not meet the required standard of duty and care if they does not correctly inform consumers on the poor quality and reduced lifetime of their product and if the consumers were expecting the product to last longer. Hence, although the notion of 'professional diligence' remains vague, one could deduce that in the majority of cases, traders pursuing practices of premature obsolescence contravene the obligation of professional diligence.[1702]

443. Distortion of consumer behaviour – Concerning the second condition, it encompasses two important elements. First, the practice must materially distort consumers' behaviour. Pursuant to Article 2(e) of the Directive, it means "*using a commercial practice to appreciably impair the consumer's ability to make an informed decision, thereby causing the consumer to take a transactional decision that he would not have taken otherwise*". This implies two sub-conditions: (1) the impairment must be appreciable and (2) the practice must cause a transactional decision that would not otherwise have been taken. The commercial practice must have a significant enough effect to change, or be likely to change, the consumers' behaviour by causing them to take a transactional decision that they would not otherwise have taken, and it must have this effect by impairing the consumer's ability to make an informed decision. The consumer must be able to make a choice in full knowledge of the facts to make sure the choice meets their preferences.[1703] One could easily imagine that this information obligation is not fulfilled when the consumer has not been informed of the reduced product lifetime. The addition of 'likely' makes its scope very wide as it makes the proof of mere potential damage to the consumers' interest sufficient. Second, it must distort the behaviour of the average consumer. As stated in recital 18 of the Directive, this notion must be understood as a consumer who is "*reasonably well informed and reasonably observant and circumspect, taking into account social, cultural and linguistic factors*". The average consumer test is not a statistical test. National courts and authorities have to exercise their own faculty of judgement, having regard to the case law of the Court of Justice, to determine the typical reaction of the average consumer in a given case. In its case law, the Court has already ruled that when a consumer has been duly informed on the product characteristics (e.g. on the pre-installed software) prior to the purchase, the ability of that consumer to make an informed transactional decision should not be considered as appreciably impaired.[1704]

1701 ECJ 7 September 2016, Case C-310/15, *Sony*, para 37.

1702 As now explicitly mentioned in the 2021 UCPD Guidance. See UCPD Guidance, p. 84.

1703 J. Goddaer and E. Terryn, 'Unfair commercial practices in B2C relations', in G. Straetmans and J. Stuyck (eds.), *Commercial Practices* (Larcier 2014) p. 55.

1704 ECJ 7 September 2016, Case C-310/15, *Sony, EU:C:2016:633*, para 41.

6. ENFORCEMENT AND SANCTIONS

444. Enforcement and sanctions at national level – It is for Member States to enforce the provisions of the UCPD and apply sanctions in case of a breach. The enforcement of the UCPD and the accompanying sanctions are regulated by Articles 11, 12 and 13 of the Directive. These provisions have been amended by the Enforcement and Modernisation Directive (also known as the 'Omnibus Directive'), and more specifically by its Article 3. The amendments contained in Article 3 of the Enforcement and Modernisation Directive were adopted following the conclusions of several studies, which pointed out the room for improvement as regards the enforcement of the legislation on unfair commercial practices. A 2014 Consumer Market Study revealed that, as regards environmental claims, proactive surveillance or inspections are rather limited, and, in some cases, inspectors have limited knowledge about how to correctly interpret the UCPD with reference to environmental claims.[1705] The same study also observed the lack of exchange of information and the lack of alignment between enforcement authorities.[1706] In 2017, the Fitness Check Report reiterated those observations, emphasizing the need for more effective and consistent enforcement of EU consumer law.[1707]

445. Adequate and effective means – The first provision regulating the enforcement of the UCPD is Article 11. Pursuant to Article 11(1), Member States must ensure that there are adequate and effective means available in their national law to combat unfair commercial practices. In that respect, the Directive specifically requires that persons or organisations who have a legitimate interest under national law (including competitors), are granted the possibility of taking legal action against unfair commercial practices and/or bringing the case before an administrative authority competent either to decide on complaints or to initiate appropriate legal proceedings.[1708]

446. Right of access to proportionate and effective remedies – The Enforcement and Modernisation Directive has further strengthened consumer rights by inserting a new Article 11a in the UCPD, which grants consumers harmed by unfair commercial practices, the right to have access to proportionate and effective remedies, including compensation for damage suffered by the consumer and, where relevant, a price reduction or the termination of the

---

1705 GfK Belgium, time.lex, Milieu Ltd, BIO IS and the Ecologic Institute, *Consumer market study on environmental claims for non-food products* (2014 European Commission) p. 155 at p. 159.

1706 *Ibid.*

1707 Commission Staff Working Document of 23 May 2017 on Report of the Fitness Check of consumer and marketing law (REFIT), SWD(2017) 209 final, p. 26 at p. 31.

1708 Art. 11(1) and recital 21 UCPD.

contract.[1709] The new provision leaves discretion to Member States with respect to the conditions for the application and effects of those remedies as well as with respect to the assessment and relevance of certain circumstances, such as the gravity and nature of the unfair commercial practice and the damage suffered by the consumer. Article 11a finally underlines that those remedies must be without prejudice to the application of other remedies available to consumers under Union or national law. Through this new Article 11a, the Enforcement and Modernisation Directive seeks to ensure that consumers have the right to individual remedies. Such amendment was suggested in the 2017 Fitness Check Report. According to this report, such a right would strengthen the overall effectiveness of the UCPD and could also contribute to specific aspects of consumer-related policies, such as sustainable consumption and circular economy in line with the Commission's Circular Economy Action Plan.[1710]

447. In conjunction with other instruments – Article 11(1) and Article 11a must be read in conjunction with provisions from other EU instruments, which guarantee that consumers can enforce their rights. Among these instruments, there is the Regulation establishing a European small claims procedure[1711], which offers consumers and small businesses an inexpensive and citizen-friendly solution to settling cross-border payment claims worth up to € 5,000. Consumers have also access, across the whole EU, to out-of-court dispute resolution procedures for resolving their disputes with EU traders in a fast, fair and inexpensive way, thanks to the Directive on consumer alternative dispute resolution.[1712] If they opt for an alternative dispute resolution, consumers can submit their disputes over online purchases of goods and services online through the online dispute resolution platform provided for by Regulation on consumer online dispute resolution.[1713] Finally, the new Directive on representative actions may facilitate consumers' access to justice.[1714]

1709 Art. 3 Enforcement and Modernisation Directive.

1710 Commission Staff Working Document of 23 May 2017 on Report of the Fitness Check of consumer and marketing law (REFIT), SWD(2017) 209 final, p. 86.

1711 Regulation (EU) 2015/2421 of the European Parliament and of the Council of 16 December 2015 amending Regulation (EC) No 861/2007 establishing a European Small Claims Procedure and Regulation (EC) No 1896/2006 creating a European order for payment procedure, OJ L 341, 24.12.2015, p. 1–13.

1712 Directive 2013/11/EU of the European Parliament and of the Council of 21 May 2013 on alternative dispute resolution for consumer disputes and amending Regulation (EC) No 2006/2004 and Directive 2009/22/EC (Directive on consumer ADR), OJ L 165, 18.6.2013, p. 63–79.

1713 Regulation (EU) No 524/2013 of the European Parliament and of the Council of 21 May 2013 on online dispute resolution for consumer disputes and amending Regulation (EC) No 2006/2004 and Directive 2009/22/EC (Regulation on consumer ODR), OJ L 165, 18.6.2013, p. 1–12.

1714 Directive (EU) 2020/1828 of the European Parliament and of the Council of 25 November 2020 on representative actions for the protection of the collective interests of consumers and repealing Directive 2009/22/EC, OJ L 409 du 4.12.2020, p. 1–27.

448. Powers of courts and administrative authorities – In addition to these rights, Article 11 of the UCPD requires the courts or administrative authorities to be empowered, where such measures are necessary, to order the cessation of unfair commercial practices or to institute appropriate legal proceedings for such order, as well as to order the prohibition of unfair commercial practices or to institute appropriate legal proceedings for such order if those practices have not yet been carried out but are imminent, even without proof of actual loss or damage or intention or negligence on the part of the trader.[1715] In Belgium, producers who misleadingly fail to give information on essential characteristics of products (e.g. on their lifetime) could be asked to submit their products to a quality check at their own cost and might have to withdraw them from the market, together with a fine from € 26 to 10,000.[1716] Moreover, Member States are allowed to confer powers upon the courts or administrative authorities enabling them, with a view to eliminating the continuing effects of unfair commercial practices the cessation of which has been ordered by a final decision, to require the publication of that decision and a corrective statement.[1717] Article 12 of the UCPD adds that courts and administrative authorities must also have the powers enabling them in the civil or administrative proceedings to assess claim substantiation. All these powers can prove particularly relevant to curb practices of premature obsolescence.

449. Penalties as imposed by Member States – Penalties for infringements of the UCPD provisions are left to the discretion of Member States, as stated in Article 13 of the UCPD. Before the adoption of the Enforcement and Modernisation Directive, this discretion was particularly wide as the sole condition laid down in Article 13 was that the penalties must be effective, proportionate and dissuasive. As a result, the penalties currently available to the consumer enforcement authorities vary enormously across the EU, which can have a negative impact on the degree of deterrence of the rules.[1718] For example, in France, practices of 'planned obsolescence' have been criminalised. The threat of imprisonment for individuals might create a watchdog for companies that contemplate the idea of accelerating the obsolescence of products, although it then implies adequate certainty and protection of the rights of individuals. However, as for the French law outlawing 'planned obsolescence', the amount of 'if' makes the prospect of sanctions quite unlikely, especially when taking into account the possibilities of settlements.

1715 Art. 11(2) subparagraph 1 UCPD.
1716 See Art. XV.16/1 and Art. XV.16/2 of the Belgian Economic Law Code.
1717 Art. 11(2) subparagraph 3 UCPD.
1718 Commission Staff Working Document of 23 May 2017 on Report of the Fitness Check of consumer and marketing law (REFIT), SWD(2017) 209 final, p. 31. For some examples of penalties imposed at national level, see footnote 51 of the Report.

450. Criteria to be taken into account – Article 3 of the Enforcement and Modernisation Directive complements Article 13 of the UCPD. The new Article 13(2) provides for criteria to be taken into account when imposing penalties. The list of criteria includes (a) the nature, gravity, scale and duration of the infringement, (b) any action taken by the trader to mitigate or remedy the damage suffered by consumers, (c) any previous infringements by the trader, (d) the financial benefits gained or losses avoided by the trader due to the infringement, (e) penalties imposed on the trader for the same infringement in other Member States in cross-border cases and (f) any other aggravating or mitigating factors. Some of these criteria are of great relevance for cases of premature obsolescence. For example, particular attention should be paid to criterion (d) as sanctions meeting this criterion can mean the difference between viewing premature obsolescence on a cost/benefits basis as a reasonable risk-taking exercise and serious deterrence that prevents unlawful conducts.[1719] Criterion (e) reinforces the cooperation between national authorities responsible for the enforcement of the UCPD, which is of critical importance when confronted to unfair practices of premature obsolescence as they are generally widespread infringements. In the absence of cooperation, widespread infringements are treated in parallel and not in a coordinated manner, creating unnecessary duplication of enforcement efforts and inconsistencies in how EU consumer law is actually applied.[1720] The cooperation between national authorities in cross-border cases is further ensured by the Consumer Protection Cooperation (CPC) Regulation[1721], though it still does not allow generation of an efficient EU-level response.

451. Specific fines for major cross-border infringements – Furthermore, Article 13(3) of the UCPD, which was also introduced by the Enforcement and Modernisation Directive, requires EU countries to impose fines of up to at least 4% of the trader's turnover when national authorities of several countries are working together on major cross-border infringements affecting consumers in several EU countries. The fine can reach € 2 million when information about the trader's turnover is not available, as stated in Article 13(4). These additional paragraphs may increase the deterrent effect of the penalties imposed on the basis of the legislation on unfair commercial practices.

1719 See the similar reasoning followed for cartels in OECD Policy roundtables of 10 January 2005 on Cartels: Sanctions against individuals, DAF/COMP(2004)39, p. 19.

1720 The Apple and Samsung cases from September 2018 on smartphones updates are an illustrative example of widespread infringements where there was a lack of cooperation between the national authorities, leading to distinct investigations, legal proceedings and sanctions in Italy, France and Belgium.

1721 Regulation (EU) 2017/2394 of the European Parliament and of the Council of 12 December 2017 on cooperation between national authorities responsible for the enforcement of consumer protection laws and repealing Regulation (EC) No 2006/2004, OJ L 345, 27.12.2017, p. 1–26.

7. INTERMEDIATE CONCLUSION

452. A KEY INSTRUMENT AGAINST PREMATURE OBSOLESCENCE – Although the UCPD does not explicitly mention the notion of 'premature obsolescence' (or any of its variants), this legal instrument is one of the cornerstones in fighting these practices. The importance of the UCPD against premature obsolescence has not only been repeatedly underlined by the EC[1722], but also shown on several occasions in case law. As premature obsolescence affects consumer's interests protected under this directive, traders who engage in strategies that result in shortening of product lifetime expose themselves to lawsuits on the basis of national provisions transposing the UCPD. Through its wide scope and its three-tier cascade system, the UCPD tackles all five types of premature obsolescence (i.e. material, functional, indirect, economic and psychological obsolescence). Its provisions contain and reinforce information obligations on product sustainability, ban some practices that accelerate product replacement and help prevent greenwashing. Yet, the effectiveness of the UCPD against premature obsolescence could be improved, as suggested throughout this section and summarized below.

453. NEW PRACTICES SHOULD BE BLACKLISTED – A first recommendation is to amend the blacklist contained in Annex I to the UCPD. The UCPD already bans commercial practices that accelerate product replacement and that may increase consumer confusion and loss of confidence in the market. Yet some practices are of such a nature that they should be prohibited in all circumstances. This would facilitate enforcement of the directive against these practices and increase awareness and legal certainty among enforcers, businesses and consumers. It does not, however, seem appropriate to draft blacklist items using broad concepts, such as 'planned obsolescence' or 'greenwashing'. Although the French ban on 'planned obsolescence' has some positive effects on the promotion of sustainable products, it is not recommended to include a similar prohibition in the UCPD blacklist. Instead, other practices relating to the premature obsolescence of products should be blacklisted, like those limiting professional repairers' or reusers' access to spare parts, instructions, technical information or any other instrument, equipment or software allowing repair, those making it impossible, including through software technique, to repair or repackage a

1722 See for ex. Joint answer of 8 July 2011 given by J. Potočnik on the behalf of the Commission, replying to written parliamentary questions E-001284/11 and E-002875/11, as well as in Answer of 3 October 2011, replying to parliamentary questions E-007148/2011. See also the Proposal for a Directive of the European Parliament and of the Council amending Council Directive 93/13/EEC of 5 April 1993, Directive 98/6/EC of the European Parliament and of the Council, Directive 2005/29/EC of the European Parliament and of the Council and Directive 2011/83/EU of the European Parliament and of the Council as regards better enforcement and modernisation of EU consumer protection rules, COM(2018) 185 final, p. 7.

device outside its approved circuits and those inciting degradation of products in normal operating condition and to prevent their direct reuse or refurbishment through advertising or commercial communication. The UCPD blacklist could also include practices of premature obsolescence that violate other EU rules (e.g. ecodesign rules) or that are regularly sanctioned in practice (e.g. persistent and unwanted solicitations to urge consumers to install software updates that have a negative effect on the performance of the device). Moreover, prohibiting green claims using the term 'sustainable' for traders, brands and sectors that can be qualified as being not eco-friendly should be envisaged.

454. A NECESSARY AMENDMENT TO THE SECTION ON 'PLANNED OBSOLESCENCE' OF THE UCPD GUIDANCE – As it currently stands, the UCPD Guidance does not reflect the complexity and various facets of premature obsolescence. The title, as well as the content of its specific section on 'planned obsolescence', should be amended to assist consumers, traders and public authorities in the application of the UCPD when they face cases of premature obsolescence.

455. PRODUCT SUSTAINABILITY INFORMATION SHOULD BE MATERIAL INFORMATION – The UCPD provisions should clearly oblige traders to provide information in relation to the sustainability of their products. It should be clear that product sustainability aspects are to be regarded as 'material information' that traders should not omit to provide to consumers in the sense of Article 7, and that should not be untruthful within the meaning of Article 6. This could be done by amending Articles 6 and 7 and/or by updating the corresponding text of the UCPD Guidance. In any case, a new definition of 'product sustainability' should be introduced in Article 2 of the UCPD.

456. BETTER FRAMING VAGUE AND AMBIGUOUS GREEN CLAIMS – Concerning green claims, the UCPD Guidance should clarify that vague and general statements are prohibited, unless the 'environmental excellence' of the product has been substantiated (e.g. via the EU Ecolabel or other ISO-type I ecolabels, the PEF method or other LCA studies) and the claim clearly and prominently qualify the specific environmental benefit(s) of the product (possibly by means of a comparison with former or competing products within the same product category). Moreover, clarifications and recommendations should be made in the UCPD Guidance on the substantiation of green claims. Traders who substantiate their claims with the Product Environmental Footprint (PEF) method would benefit from a presumption that the claim has been appropriately substantiated. This amendment to the UCPD Guidance could be followed by an amendment of Article 12 of the UCPD, which would establish an obligation to use the PEF method to substantiate green claims. Alternatively, or as an intermediary step, minimum requirements should be established for the transparency and/or reliability of all voluntary sustainability labels/schemes/

logos and all sustainability information tools. Possibly, the UCPD blacklist could be amended so that it prohibits green claims that do not fulfil these requirements.

D. PRE-CONTRACTUAL INFORMATION OBLIGATIONS IMPOSED BY THE CONSUMER RIGHTS DIRECTIVE AND NATIONAL LAW

1. HORIZONTAL INFORMATION REQUIREMENTS PRIOR TO THE CONCLUSION OF THE CONTRACT

457. THE CONSUMER RIGHTS DIRECTIVE – The Consumer Rights Directive ('CRD')[1723] provides a single set of core rules for contracts concluded between consumers and traders, with the aim of strengthening consumer protection and contributing to the proper functioning of the internal market.[1724] To this end, its provisions introduce *inter alia* stricter pre-contractual information requirements[1725] as well as a uniform right of withdrawal period.[1726] Concerning more particularly information requirements on product sustainability, the CRD imposes on traders the obligation to provide, in a clear and comprehensible manner and prior to the conclusion of the contract, sufficient information regarding the main characteristics of the goods or services, the existence of guarantees of conformity for goods, after-sales service and the functionality of digital content and any interoperability of digital content with other hardware and software. It is for the trader to prove that the pre-contractual information was provided to consumers.[1727] As is the case for the UCPD, the EC has proposed amendments to the CRD to reinforce and extend the obligations to inform consumers on product sustainability at the point of sale.[1728]

1723 Directive 2011/83/EU of the European Parliament and of the Council of 25 October 2011 on consumer rights, amending Council Directive 93/13/EEC and Directive 1999/44/EC of the European Parliament and of the Council and repealing Council Directive 85/577/EEC and Directive 97/7/EC of the European Parliament and of the Council, OJ L 304, 22.11.2011, p. 64–88 (hereafter 'CRD').

1724 Art. 1 CRD.

1725 See Art. 5 to 8 CRD.

1726 Art. 9 CRD.

1727 Standard clauses where the consumer acknowledges that the trader's pre-contractual obligations have been fully and correctly performed cannot circumvent information obligations. See ECJ 18 December 2014, Case C-449/13, *CA Consumer Finance SA*, paras 30–31.

1728 See Art. 2 of the Proposal for a Directive on empowering consumers for the green transition. See also Inception impact assessment from the European Commission of 23 June 2020 on Empowering the consumer for the green transition, Ares(2020)3256804, especially p. 3.

458. Belgian implementing provisions – In Belgium, the main provisions on consumer information are contained in the Belgian Civil Code as well as in the Economic Law Code. Civil law rules comprise among others the general principle of good faith, which can be found in Article 1134, subparagraph 3 of the Civil Code. This principle encompasses the duty for traders to provide consumers with information that influences their consent. This duty to inform only exists if three conditions are met, namely that (1) the information is known by the trader, (2) the trader knows the importance of this information, and that (3) the consumer cannot be aware of this information. The three conditions will generally be fulfilled concerning the information relating to product sustainability, especially if the product has a shorter lifespan.[1729] In addition to civil law rules, the Economic Law Code contains provisions implementing the CRD. Among them, Article VI.2 regulates information obligations for contracts other than distance or off-premises contracts, whereas Articles VI.45-VI.46 and Articles VI.64-VI.65 cover distance or off-premises contracts. If information should have been given, but is not, consumers are entitled to ask for the annulment of the contract, as well as damages on the basis of Article 1382 of the Belgian Civil Code (*culpa in contrahendo*).

459. French implementing provisions – The French approach is one of the most advanced approaches in Europe in terms of consumer information on product sustainability.[1730] As explained by T. Piazzon, "*French consumer law resorts to two complementary techniques to improve consumer information*".[1731] On the one hand, it seeks to secure market transparency and emphasizes the free circulation of information. On the other hand, French consumer law demands that traders disclose information which they owe to consumers under certain circumstances or when consumers seem to be in a particularly weak position.[1732] Pre-contractual and general information obligations are enshrined in Article L. 111-1 *et seq.* of the French Consumer Code. The information duties imposed by the provisions of the Consumer Code are reinforced by the Civil Code. Article 1112-1 of the Civil Code states that "*the party who knows information which is of decisive importance for the consent of the other, must inform him of it where the latter legitimately*

1729 See also D. Raes, "L'obsolescence programmée à l'épreuve de l'obligation d'information du vendeur, de la notion de conformité et de la garantie des vices cachés", in *Liber Amicorum François Glansdorf et Pierre Legros* (Bruylant 2014) pp. 253–254.

1730 See *infra* on the mandatory information on the availability of spare parts (n° 469–472) or on the reparability and durability indexes (n° 554–563).

1731 T. Piazzon, 'L'information et la désinformation des consommateurs: Rapport français', in G. Straetmans (ed.), *Information Obligations and Disinformation of Consumers* (Springer International Publishing 2019) p. 157.

1732 *Ibid.*

does not know the information or relies on the contracting party".[1733] Along the same lines, the French legislation imposes a duty on the trader to be informed of the consumers' needs so that they can better advise and inform consumers.[1734] A person who claims that information was due to them, bears the burden of proving that the other party was under the obligation to provide it. It is then for the other party to demonstrate that they complied with their informational duties.[1735] Interestingly, the Court of Cassation has already sanctioned the conduct of diluting information required by law into a flood of secondary information that a contractor believes should be added to it.[1736] The failure to fulfil information obligations may lead to the annulment of the contract.[1737]

460. German implementing provisions – In Germany, pre-contractual information duties can be found especially in Article 246 *et seq.* of the Introductory Act to the Civil Code (*Einführungsgesetz zum BGB, EGBGB*). §312a II BGB and Article 246 EGBGB cover information obligations for consumer contracts in general. Articles 246a and b EGBGB address contracts concluded outside business premises and distance marketing. These rules transpose the CRD into German law. If information about the good is lacking or untrue prior to the conclusion of the contract, a defect may be presumed, allowing the buyer to ask for the respective remedies.[1738] This may include a claim for dissolution of a detrimental contract subsequently entered into. In addition, the buyer may be entitled to claim damages on the basis of *culpa in contrahendo* (§§280 I, 241 II, 311 II No. 1 BGB).[1739]

2. SCOPE OF APPLICATION AND LEVEL OF HARMONISATION

a) A wide scope of application

461. B2C contracts – According to Article 3(1) of the CRD, the Directive applies to any contract concluded between a trader and a consumer, under the conditions and to the extent set out in its provisions. As highlighted in the CRD

1733 D. Bazin-Beust, *L'essentiel du Droit de la consommation* (Gualino 2017) p. 34.
1734 See for ex. Cass. 1re civ., 28 oct. 2010, n° 09-16913; Cass. 1re civ. 3 déc. 2014, n° 13-27202.
1735 Art. 1112-1 subparagraph 4 of the French Civil Code. For a practical example, see Cass. 1re civ., 11 oct. 2017, n° 16-24.594.
1736 Cass. 3e civ., 26 janvier 1991, n° 89-21.325 (in the field of rural lease).
1737 Art. 1112-1 subparagraph 6 of the French Civil Code.
1738 B. Schinkels, 'Information Obligations and Disinformation of Consumers: German Law Report', in G. Straetmans (ed.), *Information Obligations and Disinformation of Consumers* (Springer International Publishing 2019) p. 137.
1739 *Ibid.*

Guidance[1740], the structure of the Directive is divided into three categories of contracts, namely (1) off-premises contracts[1741], (2) distance contracts[1742], and (3) contracts other than distance or off-premises contracts ('on-premises' contracts). Although the CRD sets out pre-contractual information requirements for all types of contracts, the bulk of the Directive deals with distance and off-premises contracts.[1743] Member States can extend the application of the Directive to other contracts, including B2B contracts.[1744] Some have decided to do so, like Germany, which gives a broader definition of consumers and thus extends the protection of the CRD to employees concluding contracts for professional purposes.[1745] The CRD is a law of general application. In case of conflicts between the provisions of the CRD and provisions of sector-specific legislation (e.g. the energy labelling rules), the *lex specialis* prevails, as provided for in Article 3(2).

462. Out of the scope – Article 3 formulates several exceptions to the scope of application of the CRD. Besides the list of exceptions provided by Article 3(3), Article 3(4) allows the Member States not to apply the CRD or not to maintain or introduce corresponding national provisions to off-premises contracts for which the payment to be made by the consumer does not exceed € 50. Member States are even allowed to define a lower value in their national legislation. Most Member States have made use of this regulatory choice.[1746] Such exception restricts the application of rules contained in the CRD, including information requirements, although it may be precisely in those situations that the Directive would be the most needed to promote sustainable consumption. Cheap products are indeed generally the ones that are of lower quality, less durable and difficult to repair. Setting information requirements on the (non-)sustainability of such products may help raise awareness among consumers and dissuade them to buy those, but also encourage producers to improve the quality of their products. Therefore, it would be desirable to remove the fourth paragraph of Article 3 of the CRD (see #1).

1740 Commission Notice of 17 December 2021 on Guidance on the interpretation and application of Directive 2011/83/EU of the European Parliament and of the Council on consumer rights, OJ C 525, 29.12.2021, p. 1–85 (hereafter 'CRD Guidance'), and more specifically p. 8.

1741 As defined in Art. 2(8) CRD.

1742 As defined in Art. 2(7) CRD.

1743 See art. 6–16 CRD.

1744 See recital 13 CRD.

1745 J. Ellenberger, *Bürgerliches Gesetzbuch – §13 BGB para 3* (Palandt 2014).

1746 See Commission Staff Working Document of 23 May 2017 on the Evaluation of the Consumer Rights Directive, SWD(2017) 169 final, p. 16, as well as RPA, CSES, EPRD, *Study on the application of the Consumer Rights Directive 2011/83/EU – Final Report* (European Commission 2017) p. 191 *et seq*.

Proposed review of the CRD:

#1

Article 3
Scope

(...)

~~**4. Member States may decide not to apply this Directive or not to maintain or introduce corresponding national provisions to off-premises contracts for which the payment to be made by the consumer does not exceed EUR 50. Member States may define a lower value in their national legislation.**~~

(...)

b) *A 'full targeted' harmonisation*

463. Full harmonisation – The level of harmonisation of the CRD is peculiar. In principle, the Directive is of full harmonisation.[1747] The full harmonisation approach applies to distance and off-premises contracts on aspects such as consumer information and the right of withdrawal.[1748] This harmonisation level was deemed necessary for the promotion of a real consumer internal market striking the right balance between a high level of consumer protection and the competitiveness of enterprises.[1749]

464. With some exceptions – In spite of the full harmonisation character of the Directive, some of its provisions are based on minimum harmonisation. As an example, Article 5(4) allows Member States to adopt or maintain additional pre-contractual information requirements for contracts other than distance or off-premises contracts. Since no corresponding provision exists in Article 6 of the CRD, the minimum harmonisation only concerns contracts other than distance or off-premises contracts and no additional information requirements can be taken for off-premises and distance contracts due to the full harmonisation. The latter are only subject to the exhaustive list of information requirements set out in the CRD.[1750] Some Member States made use of this possibility to impose additional pre-contractual information requirements for contracts other than distance or off-premises contracts, including on product sustainability. This is the case in France, where manufacturers and importers of

1747 Art. 4 CRD.
1748 See recital 5 CRD.
1749 Recital 4 CRD.
1750 See CRD Guidance, p. 24.

movable goods must inform professional sellers about the period of availability of essential spare parts. Sellers must then pass on the information to the final consumers.[1751]

465. Room for manoeuvre for stricter national requirements – The result of such an approach is a directive based on a so-called 'full targeted' harmonisation. While it could be regrettable not having a fully harmonised approach concerning information requirements, it is also interesting to leave room for manoeuvre to Member States so that they are free to adopt stricter measures to promote sustainable products, from which inspiration could be drawn at EU level. Nonetheless, the fact that the minimum harmonisation only concerns certain types of contracts, like Article 5(4) of the CRD with the 'on-premises' contracts, may be problematic as Member States, which decide to strengthen information obligations, may also generate a legal fragmentation within their national law.

466. There should be no distinction between contracts as regards harmonisation – Although the idea of a 'full targeted' harmonisation is not problematic *per se*, the harmonisation character of the CRD should not differ depending on the nature of the contracts. This can result in a legal maze, where some contracts are subject to stringent national information requirements, whereas others are not, and consequently lead to confusion and legal uncertainty. Because of that, and to avoid too many disparities between Member States, removing the fourth paragraph of Article 5 of the CRD should be envisaged (see #2).

Proposed review of the CRD:

#2

Article 5
Information requirements for contracts other than distance or off-premises contracts

(...)

~~**4. Member States may adopt or maintain additional pre-contractual information requirements for contracts to which this Article applies.**~~

[1751] See *infra*, n° 469–472.

3. OBLIGATION TO PROVIDE INFORMATION ABOUT THE MAIN PRODUCT CHARACTERISTICS

a) *Existing obligations at EU level*

467. Information on products' main characteristics – The first information requirement set out in the CRD, which is relevant within the context of premature obsolescence, obliges traders to provide information on the main characteristics of the goods and services.[1752] In this regard, a clear parallel can be drawn with the information requirement imposed by Article 7(4)(a) of the UCPD, in the case of an invitation to purchase.[1753] This general pre-contractual duty on the main product characteristics applies for both distance and off-premises contracts (Article 6(1)(a)) and other contracts (Article 5(1)(a)). Both provisions specify that account should be taken of the medium and the goods or services. Yet, for on-premises contracts only, Article 5(1) exempts traders from the obligation to give information if it is already apparent from the context. This means, for example, that the information obligation could be waived if the main product characteristics are apparent from looking at the product.[1754] However, this is generally not the case for product sustainability aspects, like product lifetime.

468. No explicit mention of sustainability aspects – Articles 5 and 6 of the CRD do not expressly require information on product sustainability (e.g. product durability, lifespan or reparability). Yet, the notion of 'main characteristics' can, like the corresponding provision from the UCPD[1755], cover many types of information on product sustainability, including on the durable and reparable design of the product, availability of spare parts or other sustainable aspects.

b) *The French law on the availability of spare parts*

469. Information and supply obligations on spare parts – The adoption of the Hamon Law (also called '*Loi consommation*')[1756] in 2014 marks an important milestone with regard to consumer information on product

---

1752 Art. 5(1)(a) and Art. 6(1)(a) CRD. This information requirement also applies to online digital content by virtue of Art. 5(2) and 6(2) CRD.

1753 CRD Guidance, p. 22 and p. 26. See *supra* on the invitation to purchase (n° 400).

1754 This was explicitly stated in the 2014 CRD Guidance. See European Commission Guidance from June 2014 concerning Directive 2011/83/EU of the European Parliament and of the Council of 25 October 2011 on consumer rights, amending Council Directive 93/13/EEC and Directive 1999/44/EC of the European Parliament and of the Council and repealing Council Directive 85/577/EEC and Directive 97/7/EC of the European Parliament and of the Council, p. 17.

1755 Namely Art. 7(4) UCPD. For more details on misleading omissions and information requirements, see *supra* (n° 395 *et seq.*).

1756 Loi n° 2014-344 du 17 mars 2014 relative à la consommation, JORF n°0065 du 18 mars 2014, p. 5400 (hereafter 'Hamon Law'). See also its implementing Decree: Décret n°2014-1482 du 9 Décembre 2014 relatif aux obligations d'information et de fourniture concernant les

sustainability. This French Law introduced Article L. 111–4 into the French Consumer Code, which requires information on the (non-)availability period of essential spare parts to be brought to the consumer's attention, and if such spare parts are said to be available, imposes supply obligations on the manufacturers and importers. The goal was to improve product reparability and encourage repair to promote responsible consumption and generate local employment.[1757] Since then, Article L. 111–4 has been subject to several amendments by the Anti-Waste Law, which has improved its clarity and effectiveness.[1758]

470. Obligation for manufacturers and importers to inform sellers – Article L.111–4 of the French Consumer Code establishes a twofold information obligation. First, it obliges manufacturers or importers to inform sellers about the availability, but also the non-availability, of spare parts. The information requirement on the non-availability of spare parts is a novelty of the Anti-Waste Law.[1759] Since 1st January 2022[1760], manufacturers or importers of movable goods who do not provide any spare parts are also under the obligation to give information on the non-availability of spare parts. If they remain silent on this matter, at least with regard to electrical and electronic equipment and furniture, the Anti-Waste Law has introduced a presumption of non-availability of spare parts.[1761] This amendment aims, on one hand, to solve the problem of the previous legislation which deterred producers from providing this information, especially if the availability of spare parts is low or inexistent.[1762] On the other hand, the new version of Article L.111–4 allows eliminating any confusion for consumers, who could not know whether the absence of information meant that spare parts were not available or if it was a mere lack of information, which consequently hindered their ability to compare products.[1763] Some consumers

---

pièces détachées indispensables à l'utilisation d'un bien, JORF n°0286 du 11 décembre 2014, p. 20707.

1757 See explanatory memorandum to the Hamon Law, available on: <https://www.legifrance.gouv.fr/dossierlegislatif/JORFDOLE000027383756/?detailType=EXPOSE_MOTIFS&detailId=>. See also Communiqué de presse en Conseil des ministres, 2 May 2013, available on: <http://archives.gouvernement.fr/ayrault/gouvernement/consommation.html>.

1758 Despite its protective aim, the Hamon Law was under criticism, which mainly deplored the lack of clarity and precision. See N. Dupont, 'Durabilité des produits et disponibilité des pièces détachées: où en est-on?', 1 *La Semaine Juridique Entreprise et Affaires* (2016) p. 34 at p. 38.

1759 Art. 19 Anti-Waste Law. Interestingly, this idea was initially present in the draft Hamon Law (see Projet de loi relatif à la consommation, submitted at the Assemblée nationale on 2 May 2013, n° 1015), but had been abandoned in the final version of the text and its implementing decree.

1760 Art. 130 Anti-Waste Law.

1761 Art. 19 Anti-Waste Law.

1762 See the arguments developed by the French association HOP in its claim for annulment brought before the Council of State on 27 March 2017, available on: <https://www.halteobsolescence.org/wp-content/uploads/2017/03/REP-CE-pi%C3%A8ces-d%C3%A9tach%C3%A9es-V4.pdf>.

1763 See Rapport fait au nom de la Commission de l'aménagement du territoire et du développement durable (1) sur le projet de loi (PROCÉDURE ACCÉLÉRÉE) relatif à la lutte

would even not notice missing information, which benefited producers who do not provide spare parts.[1764]

If spare parts are made available, Article D. 111–4 leaves manufacturers and importers the choice of indicating the period during which or the date until which spare parts will be available on the market.[1765] The obligation only concerns spare parts that are *"essential for the use of the goods"*. French law gives no precise details regarding the notion of 'essential spare parts', except for electrical and electronic equipment for which manufacturers or importers are required, since 1st January 2022, to inform sellers and professional repairers about their commitment relating to the availability of spare parts, if requested.[1766] Information on spare parts availability must be disclosed on any commercial document or durable medium accompanying the sale of goods.[1767] While a paper or an e-mail is considered a durable medium, the mere disclosure of the availability period on the product packaging is not sufficient.[1768] The consequent obligation that stems from the provision of this information implies that manufacturers and importers must respect their commitment and provide spare parts within 15 working days to sellers or repairers.[1769]

471. Obligation for sellers to inform consumers – Second, Article L.111–4 obliges sellers to pass on the information they receive from manufacturers and importers to consumers, including information on the duration of the availability period and the spare parts concerned. This information must be clearly visible and legible and must be given, first, on an appropriate medium before the conclusion of the contract and, second, it must appear on the order form or any other durable medium establishing or accompanying the sale.[1770] The wording of Article D. 111–4 gives greater latitude to sellers to satisfy the pre-contractual information obligation. Concerning information that must be provided at the time of purchase, the notion of

contre le gaspillage et à l'économie circulaire, 17 September 2019, n° 727, p. 29. This flaw had been pointed out earlier in Rapport d'information déposé par la Commission des affaires économiques sur la mise en application de la loi n°2014–344 du 17mars 2014 relative à la consommation, 19 octobre 2016, n°4139.

1764 This oblivion bias is called 'WYSIATI' by D. Kahneman. See D. Kahneman, *Thinking, Fast and Slow* (2011) p. 85 at p.88, as cited in S.I. Becher, A.-L. Sibony, 'Confronting Product Obsolescence', 27 *Colum. J. Eur. L.* (2021) p. 140.

1765 Art. 19 I of the Anti-Waste Law has restricted this choice for producers of household appliances, small IT and telecommunication equipment, screens and monitors, for which the availability period of spare parts will be fixed by decree and will not be less than five years from the date of placing the last unit of the model on the market.

1766 Art. 19 I Anti-Waste Law.

1767 Article D. 111–4 of the French Consumer Code.

1768 See the answer given the during the parliamentary debates on 24 January 2017 (Rép. min. n° 716: JOAN Q, 24 janv. 2017, p. 553, available on: <http://questions.assemblee-nationale.fr/static/14/questions/jo/jo_anq_201704.pdf>.

1769 The obligation to provide spare parts is further discussed below. See n° 472.

1770 Article D. 111–4 of the French Consumer Code.

'durable medium' excludes information on the product packaging, provided by a hyperlink or an SMS, but includes mediums like the receipt, an e-mail and an invoice.[1771] One could also imagine having information displayed on the product itself.[1772] As regards the beginning of the availability period, no indication is provided in the legislation.[1773] The guidance document issued by the DGCCRF plugs this legal loophole by clarifying that the period should start after the purchase of the product.[1774] It is for the seller to adapt the information received from the manufacturer or the importer to make it easily understandable and relevant to the consumer.[1775]

472. Combined with an obligation for manufacturers and importers to provide spare parts – According to the same provision, manufacturers and importers, who inform consumers on the availability period of spare parts, are under obligation to provide these spare parts within 15 working days to the professional seller or the repairer (authorised or not) who request them.[1776] This short period[1777] was aimed to ensure more coherence with the 30-day period imposed upon the seller by Article L. 217–10 of the French Consumer Code to repair or replace the defective product under guarantee.[1778] For household appliances, small IT and telecommunication equipment, screens and monitors, the availability period of spare parts should be fixed by decree and would not be less than five years from the date of placing the last unit of the model on the market.[1779] The list of products and parts concerned should also be established in the same decree.[1780] It remains to be seen how this provision will be concretely implemented. Article L. 111–4 also highlights the potential of three-dimensional printing technologies in the context of repair. When a spare part can be manufactured using a three-dimensional printing process and is no longer available on the market, the manufacturer or importer must, subject to respect for

1771 S. Castagné, 'Information du consommateur sur la disponibilité des pièces détachées – Quels supports durables assurent l'information?', *Contrats Concurrence Consommation* (2017) p. 38.

1772 *Ibid.*

1773 This flaw was pointed out in Rapport d'information déposé par la Commission des affaires économiques sur la mise en application de la loi n°2014–344 du 17mars 2014 relative à la consommation, 19 octobre 2016, n°4139.

1774 DGCCRF, *Les pièces détachées – fiches pratiques* (République française 2018) p. 2, <https://www.economie.gouv.fr/dgccrf/Publications/Vie-pratique/Fiches-pratiques/pieces-detachees>. According to the DGCCRF, this starting point is the only one that makes sense to consumers.

1775 *Ibid.*

1776 Such supporting measures are also allowed by the SGD (see recital 33), though it is deplorable that this aspect has not been harmonised at EU level.

1777 Art. 19 I of the Anti-Waste Law drastically shortened this period, which initially lasted two months.

1778 Rapport fait au nom de la Commission de l'aménagement du territoire et du développement durable (1) sur le projet de loi (PROCÉDURE ACCÉLÉRÉE) relatif à la lutte contre le gaspillage et à l'économie circulaire, 17 Septembre 2019, n° 727, p. 30.

1779 Art. 19 I of the Anti-Waste Law.

1780 *Ibid.*

intellectual property rights and in particular subject to the consent of the holder of the intellectual property, provide professional sellers or repairers requesting it with the drawing for manufacturing the spare part by a three-dimensional printing means or the technical information useful for its elaboration.

c) *The French information obligation on the environmental qualities and characteristics of products*

473. Information the environmental qualities and characteristics of waste-generating products – In addition to those obligations on the availability of spare parts, Article 13 of the French Anti-Waste Law introduced an information obligation on the environmental qualities and characteristics of products. Since 1st January 2022, Article L. 541–9–1 of the Environmental Code requires producers and importers of (new) waste-generating products to inform consumers about "*the characteristics aimed to inform the consumer on the conditions relating to better prevention and management of waste*".[1781] This information includes among others the incorporation of recycled material, the use of renewable resources, durability, compostability, reparability, reusability, recyclability and the presence of hazardous substances. Consumers must also be informed about the bonus and malus paid to eco-organisations.[1782] Such information can be disclosed through marking, labelling, posting or any other appropriate means, and must be visible or accessible by the consumer at the time of purchase.[1783] These provisions were introduced into the French Environmental Code as it is deemed to be a waste prevention measure that is part of the French Waste Prevention Programme as required by Article 29 of the Waste Framework Directive.[1784]

474. With details given in an implementing decree – Articles R. 541–220 to Art. R. 541–222 of the Environmental Code, which were introduced in 2022[1785], fix the methods of application of Article L. 541–9–1, the methods of establishment of these characteristics, the product categories concerned as well as the methods used to inform consumers. Article R. 541–221.-I refers, for example, to the mandatory reparability index applicable to electrical and

[1781] Art. R. 541–220 of the French Environmental Code.

[1782] For further information on the bonus and malus paid to eco-organisations, see Chapter V on the end-of-life stage, and more specifically n° 949.

[1783] In this regard, Article 13 adds that "*the producer or importer is responsible for making the data relating to the above qualities and characteristics available to the public by electronic means*".

[1784] See Rapport d'information fait au nom de la Commission des affaires européennes (1) portant observations sur la transposition du droit européen par le projet de loi relatif à la lutte contre le gaspillage et à l'économie circulaire, 18 July 2019, n° 682, p. 19.

[1785] Art. 1 Décret n° 2022–748 du 29 avril 2022 relatif à l'information du consommateur sur les qualités et caractéristiques environnementales des produits générateurs de déchets, JORF n°0101 du 30 avril 2022.

electronic equipment.[1786] Article 13 of the Anti-Waste Law emphasizes that the product environmental qualities and characteristics must be established by favouring an analysis of the entire lifecycle of the product. This statement is in line with the approach followed by the EU product policy. Within its text, Article 13 also underlines the importance of being implemented in coherence with EU law. This reference was made to avoid the situation encountered by Article 90 of the Energy Transition Act, which was also aimed at curbing greenwashing and substantiating environmental claims.[1787] No measure was finally taken on the basis of that provision as it was deemed too general but also problematic in terms of compatibility with EU law.[1788]

475. Fair criticisms expressed on the business side – The effectiveness of Article L. 541–9–1 of the Environmental Code and its compatibility with EU law will highly depend on the content of this implementing decree. However, no matter the content of the implementing decree, it can already be said that this legislation can be criticised on many counts. First, these national information requirements create barriers to the free movement of goods within the EU single market. Second, there are many uncertainties concerning the wording of Article L. 541–9–1 and the measurement methods of some criteria contained in the provision. Third, the deadline for fulfilling these additional requirements is deemed too short and should be extended significantly to allow companies to comply in time and create legal certainty for them. Fourth, the added value of this legislation, as well as its compatibility with EU law, has been questioned as similar requirements are already imposed under the REACH Regulation.[1789] These various concerns have also been raised by many business associations.[1790]

1786 For further details on this reparability index, see *infra*, n° 554–564.

1787 This provision required producers who would voluntarily make an environmental communication or claim about their products to make the main environmental characteristics of these products available to the public.

1788 Rapport fait au nom de la Commission de l'aménagement du territoire et du développement durable (1) sur le projet de loi (PROCÉDURE ACCÉLÉRÉE) relatif à la lutte contre le gaspillage et à l'économie circulaire, 17 Septembre 2019, n° 727, p. 20.

1789 See Regulation (EC) No 1907/2006 of the European Parliament and of the Council of 18 December 2006 concerning the Registration, Evaluation, Authorisation and Restriction of Chemicals (REACH), establishing a European Chemicals Agency, amending Directive 1999/45/EC and repealing Council Regulation (EEC) No 793/93 and Commission Regulation (EC) No 1488/94 as well as Council Directive 76/769/EEC and Commission Directives 91/155/EEC, 93/67/EEC, 93/105/EC and 2000/21/EC, OJ L 396, 30.12.2006, p. 1–849 (hereafter 'REACH Regulation'). This REACH Regulation requires manufacturers and importers to gather information on the properties of their chemical substances, which will allow their safe handling, and to register the information in a public database accessible to consumers and professionals.

1790 https://ec.europa.eu/growth/tools-databases/tris/fr/search/?trisaction=search.detail&year=2021&num=644.

d) Belgian legislative proposals on information requirements on product lifetime, reparability and spare parts availability

476. Three legislative proposals – Belgian law makers, who were to some extent inspired by French law, proposed several amendments to the existing pre-contractual information obligations.[1791] Along with measures criminalizing practices of premature obsolescence, the currently pending legislative proposals contain three main ideas in the field of consumer information. They suggest better informing consumers on (1) product lifetime, (2) product reparability and (3) the availability of spare parts. These suggestions are in line with the earlier government proposal[1792], as well as the Parliament Resolution from 2018, which requested to "*provide better information to the consumer on the lifespan of a product as well as on its repair possibilities*".[1793] Yet the legislative proposals diverge in several respects, including in the way these ideas are to be implemented and the criteria to be taken into consideration.

477. Proposal I – Proposal I suggests imposing on producers the disclosure of information on product lifetime, product reparability as well as the availability of spare parts via a product passport accessible online or affixed directly to the product packaging.[1794] It would be for the King to determine how to implement these new labelling rules. In addition to this new informational obligation, Article 6 of Proposal I grants the power to the King to require producers or importers, for specified product categories, to deliver to professional sellers or to repairers who request so, at least (1) the spare parts which are essential for the use of the sold products, (2) the tools that are necessary to repair the products, (3) the drawings and models of the products that are necessary to safely repair the products without damaging them, (4) the diagnostic instruments. It also grants the power to the King to determine the period of availability of spare parts for each specified product category taking into account their average lifetime.

478. Proposal II – In Proposal II, an amendment to the provision implementing Article 5 of the CRD is being proposed so as to include information on product reparability in the list of mandatory information

[1791] It should be noted that, under Belgian law, stricter information requirements are already imposed in the automobile sector. Information is required on the state of the vehicle, its spare parts and components when it is of a second-hand nature. See Art. 5 Arrêté royal du 5 avril 2019 relatif aux contrats de vente de véhicules automoteurs, *M.B.*, 8 mai 2019, p. 44214.

[1792] K. Peeters and M.C. Marghem, *Ensemble, faisons tourner l'économie en développant l'économie circulaire en Belgique* (Cabinet de l'Énergie, de l'Environnement et du Développement durable 2016), measures 12 and 13, available on: <https://www.health.belgium.be/sites/default/files/uploads/fields/fpshealth_theme_file/econ-circ-fr-light.pdf>.

[1793] Proposition de résolution visant le développement de l'économie circulaire et la lutte contre l'obsolescence programmée, *Doc. lég.*, Ch., 2017–2018, 11 janvier 2018, n° 2884/001, p. 14.

[1794] Art. 4 Proposition de loi n° 0193/001.

requirements.[1795] Prior to the conclusion of a contract other than a distance or off-premises contract, the business must provide the consumer, in a clear and comprehensible manner, with information on the reparable nature of the product as well as the period during which its spare parts are available. Moreover, pursuant to the provisions of this legislative proposal, products must, before being sold, bear a label that indicates their lifetime (expressed in number of hours, months, years or cycles of use) and their reparability.[1796] In case of non-compliance with the information obligation, a fine from € 26 to € 10.000 (sanction of level 2) could be imposed.[1797]

479. Proposal III – Proposal III makes similar suggestions to those contained in Proposal II. However, the list of mandatory information requirements comprises a wider range of new elements. As regards the amendment of the provision implementing Article 5 of the CRD, Article 3 of Proposal III imposes the pre-contractual obligation to inform consumers on (1) the normal period of use of the product (expressed in number of hours, months, years, kilometres or cycles of use), (2) the availability period of spare parts and accessories at a reasonable cost, (3) the product price per estimated year of life, (4) a notice detailing the possibilities of repair at a reasonable cost and the repair instructions, (5) the production price of spare parts, the delivery time of these parts, the persons or companies which provide them and the countries where they are available. As regards labelling and marketing rules, Articles 4 to 6 of Proposal III mandate the disclosure of the three first pieces of information required in Article 3, namely on product lifetime, the availability period of spare parts and the product price per estimated year of life.

e) Clarifying information obligations at the EU level

480. Prioritising rules at EU level – While the ideas developed in France and Belgium are welcomed from a sustainability perspective, these measures should rather be promoted and implemented at EU level. Otherwise, these additional national information requirements may be regarded as barriers to the smooth functioning of the EU internal market.[1798] By contrast, if such measures were harmonised at EU level, not only would they increase consumer protection and trigger product sustainability, but they would also be in line with the free

---

1795 Art. 4 Proposition de loi n° 0771/001.

1796 Art. 5–8 Proposition de loi n° 0771/001.

1797 See the explanatory memorandum to Proposition de loi n° 0771/001.

1798 Doubts have indeed been raised in literature on the compatibility of the French information requirement on spare parts availability with the free movements of goods and services and the prohibition of quantitative restriction, as enshrined in Art. 34 TFEU. See E. Maitre-Ekern and C. Dalhammar,'Regulating planned obsolescence: a review of legal approaches to increase product durability and reparability in Europe', 25 *Review of European Community & International Environmental Law* (2016) pp. 392–393.

movement of goods and services as they would reduce cross-border barriers and promote a level-playing field between traders.

481. With national law as a source of inspiration – Still, national rules could provide food for thought to improve information rules at EU level. Article L. 111–4 of the French Consumer Code has already piqued the interests of the EU legislature, to the satisfaction of the French Government, which hopes to strengthen those French information requirements.[1799] The EP had proposed the introduction of a similar provision into the SGD during its adoption procedure.[1800]

482. The proposed information obligation on the availability of spare parts – Since then, the idea of adopting such measures at EU level has gained ground and is now included in the EC's Proposal for a Directive on empowering consumers for the green transition.[1801] If adopted, the amended Articles 5 and 6 of the CRD would require the trader to provide the consumer with information made available by the producer about the availability of spare parts, including the procedure of ordering them, and about the availability of a user and repair manual. This information obligation would only apply if no reparability score was established for the product concerned. The Proposal also contains additional information obligations on the commercial guarantee of durability and the availability period of software updates, as further discussed in this section.[1802]

483. Product sustainability should be mentioned in Articles 5 and 6 – As pointed out by the EC within the framework of its initiative on 'Empowering consumers for the green transition', notwithstanding the existing possibilities given by Article 5(1)(a) and Article 6(1)(a) of the CRD, the role of this Directive to promote sustainable products would be greatly bolstered if the elements related to product sustainability explicitly appeared on the list of main characteristics. This could be done either by adding them in the provisions (see #3) and/or by updating the CRD Guidance (see #5).[1803] Such amendments would

---

1799 Ministère de la Transition Ecologique et Solidaire, *Feuille de route économie circulaire: 50 mesures pour une économie 100% circulaire* (République française 2018) p. 19, pt. 9.

1800 See amendment 117 of the Report on the amended proposal for a directive of the European Parliament and of the Council on certain aspects concerning contracts for the sales of goods, amending Regulation (EC) No 2006/2004 of the European Parliament and of the Council and Directive 2009/22/EC of the European Parliament and of the Council and repealing Directive 1999/44/EC of the European Parliament and of the Council, COM(2017) 637, p. 53.

1801 Art. 2(2)(b) and (3)(b) of the Proposal for a Directive on empowering consumers for the green transition.

1802 See n° 487 *et seq.*

1803 Along the same line, see A. Michel, 'La directive 1999/44/CE sur la garantie des biens de consommation: un remède efficace contre l'obsolescence programmée?', *R.E.D.C.* (2018)

enhance the clarity and legal certainty of Articles 5 and 6 by making it crystal clear that product sustainability aspects, such as the availability of spare parts, are to be considered as main product characteristics. This kind of clarification can already be found in French law, where Article 25 of the Anti-Waste Law explicitly qualifies reparability as an essential characteristic of the product. A similar amendment to the provision implementing Article 5 of the CRD is being proposed in Belgium.[1804] Such clarification would also dispel doubts as to the precise application of additional national information requirements on product sustainability which would apply both to distance and off-premises contracts and to contracts other than distance or off-premises contracts.

484. Specific information requirements on product sustainability aspects – Alternatively, or in addition to that, information obligations on specific product characteristics could be added to the list provided in Articles 5 and 6 of the CRD as a distinct information requirement (see #6). For example, these provisions could explicitly include an information obligation on the availability of spare parts, as proposed in the Proposal for a Directive on empowering consumers for the green transition.[1805] Inspiration could be drawn from French law.[1806] Traders could also be required to inform consumers about any known aspects in the design of the product (hardware, firmware and software) that can cause it to fail significantly earlier than could be reasonably expected or than the majority of products from the same group.[1807] Such amendments would establish more stringent information obligations on specific sustainability aspects for which the mandatory nature would no longer depend on the circumstances of the case at hand. If such amendments were to be adopted, particular attention would have to be paid to the risk of overloading consumers with information. For example, it should be questioned whether the

---

pp. 234–235; B. Keirsbilck, E. Terryn, A. Michel and I. Alogna, *Sustainable Consumption and Consumer Protection Legislation* (European Parliament 2020) p. 15; BEUC's view of 26 March 2020 on the European Green Deal – Consumers at the centre of the drive to sustainability, BEUC-X-2020-012, p. 7.

1804 See Art. 3 Proposition de loi visant à lutter contre l'obsolescence organisée et à soutenir l'économie circulaire, *Doc. parl.*, Ch., 2019–2020, 7 janvier 2020, n° 0914/001; Art. 4 Proposition de loi modifiant le Code civil et le Code de droit économique, visant à lutter contre l'obsolescence programmée et l'obsolescence prématurée et à augmenter les possibilités de réparation, *Doc. Parl.*, Ch., 2019–2020, 19 novembre 2019, n° 0771/001.

1805 See *supra*, n° 482.

1806 See *supra*, n° 469–472.

1807 Inspiration has been drawn from the 2012 Belgian legislative proposal aimed at preventing obsolescence. See Art. 2 Proposition de loi visant à lutter contre l'obsolescence organisée et à soutenir l'économie circulaire, *Doc. parl.*, Ch., 2019–2020, 7 janvier 2020, n° 0914/001. See also the former legislative proposals suggesting the same provision: Art. 3 Proposition de loi modifiant la loi du 9 février 1994 relative à la sécurité des produits et des services, visant la prévention de l'obsolescence, *Doc. Parl.*, Ch., 2011–2012, 14 février 2012, n° 2061/001; Art. 2 Proposition de loi relative à la lutte contre l'obsolescence organisée et au soutien à l'économie circulaire, *Doc. parl.*, Ch., 2015–2016, 11 avril 2016, n° 1749/001.

consumer really needs information on the production price of spare parts, as proposed in Belgium.[1808] In this regard, it should be noted that an experiment carried out within the framework of the 2017 Fitness Check showed that the provision of information on the average costs of spare parts increased choices of reparable products significantly less and even had a negative effect on consumers' willingness-to-pay for products with high as well as low costs of spare parts.[1809]

485. Articulation with other consumer rules – If information requirements on product sustainability were to be adopted through the CRD, consideration should be given to other existing legislative instruments dealing with similar requirements to ensure a coherent and consistent legal framework. The importance of following an integrated approach taking the CRD and the UCPD provisions into account has already been acknowledged by the EC.[1810] Similar reasoning should be held in relation to the SGD. This newly adopted Directive qualifies durability as an objective requirement that products must fulfil to be in conformity with the contract. Since the SDG complements the CRD[1811], its objective requirements could be considered as main product characteristics about which consumers should be informed. Inversely, information requirements could be used as a benchmark to assess whether the product satisfies objective and subjective requirements established by the SGD.[1812] The link between both instruments could be further fostered if the information requirements of Articles 5 and 6 of the CRD were connected to commercial guarantee rights as regulated by Article 17 of the SGD. Producers could be obliged to indicate the durability of their products, sellers would pass on this information to consumers and, if the product is less durable than indicated, consumers could invoke the commercial guarantee.[1813] The relevance of such measure would be even greater if the product concerned was not covered by any ecodesign requirements.[1814]

1808 See Proposal III (n° 479). See also Avis du Conseil d'Etat du 21 février 2020 sur la Proposition de loi visant à lutter contre l'obsolescence organisée et à soutenir l'économie circulaire (n° 0914/001), n° 66.909/1, p. 9, pt. 12.

1809 GfK Belgium, *Consumer market study to support the fitness check of EU consumer and marketing law* (European Commission 2017) p. 424.

1810 See Inception impact assessment from the European Commission of 23 June 2020 on Empowering the consumer for the green transition, Ares(2020)3256804, p. 3.

1811 Recital 11 Sale of Goods Directive.

1812 See Chapter IV on the use stage.

1813 Along the same line, see K. Tonner, R. Malcolm, *How an EU lifespan guarantee model could be implemented across the European Union (study)* (European Parliament 2017); I. Oehme, A. Jacob, *Strategies against obsolescence Ensuring a minimum product lifetime and improving product service life as well as consumer information* (Umweltbundesamt 2017). For further details, see Chapter IV on the use stage.

1814 If specific durability requirements are applicable to the concerned product, consumers should rather be entitled to rely on legal guarantee rights. For further comments, see Chapter IV on the use stage.

486. Articulation with product regulations – Beyond consumer law rules, links should also be made between the CRD and other legal instruments. One could imagine connecting the CRD to ecodesign rules, especially those requiring information on product sustainability.[1815] For example, information requirements on the availability period of spare parts established under the Ecodesign regulation on electronic displays could constitute information on the main characteristics of the goods that should be provided on the basis of the CRD too. The link between those rules could be embodied through references to this product regulation in the provisions of the CRD itself and/or in the CRD Guidance (see #4). Inspiration could be drawn from Article 7(5) of the UCPD, which already builds a bridge between consumer law and product regulation.[1816] In addition to this interplay, product regulations could also fill the potential gaps left by the provisions of the CRD in absence of general information requirements on product sustainability. In this scenario, information requirements could be developed on a product-specific basis within the framework of the ecodesign and energy labelling regulations.[1817]

Proposed review of the Consumer Rights Directive:

#3

Article 2
Definitions

For the purpose of this Directive, the following definitions shall apply:

(...)

<u>(22) 'product sustainability' means the ability of a product to reach its optimal lifetime, which depends among others on its durability, ease of maintenance, upgradability, reparability, refurbishment and remanufacturing.</u>

Article 5
Information requirements for contracts other than distance or off-premises contracts

1. Before the consumer is bound by a contract other than a distance or an off-premises contract, or any corresponding offer, the trader shall provide the consumer with the following information in a clear and comprehensible manner, if that information is not already apparent from the context:

1815 For more details on the existing ecodesign requirements, see Chapter II on the design and production stage, and more specifically n° 231 *et seq.*

1816 See *supra*, n° 403 *et seq.*

1817 For more details on information requirements imposed by ecodesign regulations, see Chapter II on the design and production stage, and more specifically n° 231 *et seq.* Energy labelling regulations are further discussed in this chapter (see n° 515 *et seq.*).

(a) the main characteristics of the goods or services, **including characteristics related to sustainability,** to the extent appropriate to the medium and to the goods or services;

(…)

10. **Information requirements established by EU, a non-exhaustive list of which is contained in Annex III, shall be regarded as information that must be provided on the basis of this Directive.** #4

Article 6
Information requirements for distance and off-premises contracts

1. Before the consumer is bound by a distance or off-premises contract, or any corresponding offer, the trader shall provide the consumer with the following information in a clear and comprehensible manner:

(a) the main characteristics of the goods or services, **including characteristics related to sustainability,** to the extent appropriate to the medium and to the goods or services;

(…)

5. Information requirements established by EU, a non-exhaustive list of which is contained in Annex III, shall be regarded as information that must be provided on the basis of this Directive. #4

AND *#4*

ANNEX III
LAW PROVISIONS SETTING OUT INFORMATION REQUIREMENTS

Energy Labelling Directive

Ecodesign Directive

(…)

AND/OR *#4 and #5*

Proposed review of the CRD Guidance

3.2. Common requirements for on-premises and distance / off-premises contracts

3.2.1. Main characteristics

(…)

The same obligation is imposed by Article 7(4) of the UCPD that lays down the information requirements for the 'invitation to purchase'. Accordingly, for choosing the main characteristics to be communicated to the consumer, the traders should apply the same approach as for the purposes of the UCPD, i.e. provide information about those characteristics that consumers need to make an informed purchasing decisions. Information about the main characteristics for goods may be available from their packaging or labelling that the consumer can consult. More complex goods may require the communication of additional information to establish their main characteristics.

Product sustainability aspects may, subject to a case-by-case assessment, constitute a main characteristic of a product within the meaning of Article 5(1)(a) and 6(1)(a). These aspects encompass among others aspects that relate to product durability, ease of maintenance, upgradability, reparability, refurbishment and remanufacturing. Product sustainability aspects may include aspects that are required under other EU legal instruments, like ecodesign regulations. Objective requirements established under Article 7 of the Sale of Goods Directive should also be considered as main product characteristics about which consumers should get informed.

(...)

ALTERNATIVELY, OR IN ADDITION TO THAT #6

Article 5
Information requirements for contracts other than distance or off-premises contracts

1. Before the consumer is bound by a contract other than a distance or an off-premises contract, or any corresponding offer, the trader shall provide the consumer with the following information in a clear and comprehensible manner, if that information is not already apparent from the context:

(...)

(ea) the (non-)availability period of essential spare parts;

(...)

Article 6
Information requirements for distance and off-premises contracts

1. Before the consumer is bound by a distance or off-premises contract, or any corresponding offer, the trader shall provide the consumer with the following information in a clear and comprehensible manner:

(...)

(ma) the (non-)availability period of essential spare parts;

(...)

4. OBLIGATION TO PROVIDE INFORMATION ON AFTER-SALES SERVICES AND GUARANTEES

487. Information on the legal guarantee – The CRD also obliges traders to inform consumers about the existence and conditions of after-sales service and of the legal and commercial guarantees.[1818] With regard to information about the legal guarantee, Articles 5(1)(e) and 6(1)(l) require traders to provide a reminder of the existence of a legal guarantee of conformity for goods. These provisions must be read in conjunction with Article 6(1)(g) of the UCPD and Article 17(2) of the SGD, which further develop this information requirement.[1819] Whereas Article 6(1)(g) of the UCPD (together with Article 3 and Annex to the Unfair Contract Terms Directive)[1820] sanctions cases of misleading information on legal guarantee rights, Article 17(2) of the SGD establishes the obligation to provide information about these rights only when a commercial guarantee is offered by the trader. Because consumers do not (properly) know their rights and traders often misunderstand their legal obligations, it is to be regretted that the obligation established under the CRD does not require the provision of information on the content of the legal guarantee[1821], as required for the right of withdrawal.[1822] It should nonetheless be noted that Article 5 of the Enforcement and Modernisation Directive reinforces consumer information by requiring the EC to ensure that citizens seeking information on their rights benefit from an online entry point, through the single digital gateway established by Regulation (EU) 2018/1724.[1823]

488. Information on commercial guarantees and after-sales service – Furthermore, Article 5(1)(e) and Article 6(1)(m) of the CRD lay down information requirements on the existence and conditions of after-sales service and commercial guarantees.[1824] According to the CRD Guidance, information

1818 Article 21 of the CRD also states that consumers who use the telephone helpline of the trader to obtain information in relation to the contract, should not be bound to pay more than the basic rate. The aim of this provision is to ensure that consumers are not discouraged from seeking information or from asserting their rights relating to, *inter alia*, a guarantee. See ECJ 2 March 2017, C-568/15, *Zentrale zur Bekämpfung unlauteren Wettbewerbs Frankfurt am Main, EU:C:2017:154*, para 29.

1819 See also CRD Guidance, p. 33.

1820 Council Directive 93/13/EEC of 5 April 1993 on unfair terms in consumer contracts, OJ L 95, 21.4.1993, p. 29–34 (hereafter 'UCTD').

1821 For further comments, see Chapter IV on the use stage.

1822 As regards the right of withdrawal, information obligations are much more elaborated. See Art. 6(1)(h) to (k) as well as Art. 10 CRD.

1823 See Regulation (EU) 2018/1724 of the European Parliament and of the Council of 2 October 2018 establishing a single digital gateway to provide access to information, to procedures and to assistance and problem-solving services and amending Regulation (EU) No 1024/2012, OJ L 295, 21.11.2018, p. 1–38.

1824 Providing this information in accordance with the CRD is sufficient to also comply with the requirements of the Service Directive, which obliges providers to make information on the

about after-sales services should in particular explain where the service will be carried out and who bears the cost of transport.[1825] Other items of information about after-sales services and commercial guarantees are of particular relevance in terms of product sustainability, such as the length of the commercial guarantee period, the defects covered and the available remedies. Not only can such information help consumers extend the lifetime of their products once purchased, but it can also signal the durability and reliability of products and thus influence consumer choice prior to the purchase. Nonetheless, the provision of these pieces of information is mandatory only if the respective additional benefits are actually offered.[1826] Moreover, the ECJ recently ruled that "*the information requirement imposed on the trader does not arise from the mere fact that that guarantee exists, but only where the consumer has a legitimate interest in obtaining information concerning that guarantee in order to decide whether to enter into a contractual relationship with the trader*".[1827]

489. Proposed information obligation on the existence of a longer commercial guarantee of durability – The EC has proposed to reinforce the obligations set out in Articles 5(1)(e) and 6(1)(m) of the CRD by imposing information on the existence of a commercial guarantee of durability of more than two years.[1828] First, traders would be under obligation to pass on the information they receive from producers on the commercial guarantee of durability and its duration in units of time, where that guarantee covers the entire good and has a duration of more than two years. Second, if the producer does not make this information available for 'energy-using goods', the trader would be obliged to inform the consumer on this absence of information. This amendment aims to incentivise producers to provide such guarantees to consumers.[1829] Article 2 of the Proposal adds that "*[t]his information shall be at least as prominent as any other information about the existence and the conditions of after-sales services and commercial guarantees*". For both cases, the Council proposes a Union harmonised graphic format.[1830] Two comments can be made on these proposed amendments. First, it is surprising to find the term 'energy-using products', which was abandoned in favour of 'energy-related products'

main features of the service available to the recipient. See Art. 22 j) of the Directive 2006/123/EC of the European Parliament and of the Council of 12 December 2006 on services in the internal market, OJ L 376, 27.12.2006, p. 36–68.

1825 CRD Guidance, p. 33.

1826 *Ibid.*

1827 See ECJ 5 May 2022, Case C-179/21, *Victorinox, EU:C:2022:353.*

1828 Art. 2(2)(a) and (3)(a) of the Proposal for a Directive on empowering consumers for the green transition.

1829 See the explanatory memorandum to the Proposal for a Directive on empowering consumers for the green transition, p. 2.

1830 See Council's comments of 27 September 2022 on the Proposal for a Directive on empowering consumers for the green transition, 10937/2/22 REV 2, p. 28 and p. 30.

in product regulations since the recast of the former Ecodesign Directive in 2009.[1831] One could wonder why restricting the scope of application of this obligation to these products. Second, it is peculiar to require information on the lack of information, and not on the lack of guarantee itself.

490. Information on repair and maintenance service – For off-premises contracts, Article 7(4) sets an additional information requirement in cases where consumers explicitly request the services of traders for the purpose of carrying out repairs or maintenance. This required information includes information about the main characteristics of the service and the price or the manner in which the price is to be calculated together with an estimate of the total price. These pieces of information can be provided on paper, on another durable medium or orally, if the consumer agrees.[1832] This informational obligation applies only where the trader and the consumer immediately perform their contractual obligations and where the service requested does not require the payment of more than € 200 by the consumer. The provision allows the Member States not to apply this paragraph. Consequently, several Member States opted for a simplified information regime for off-premises contracts concerning repair or maintenance works not exceeding € 200 explicitly requested by the consumer.[1833] This is regrettable as having such information allows transparency on the price of maintenance and repair operations, which consequently reassures consumers who consider these options.

491. Better informing consumers on their rights – Three recommendations can be made to improve the role of these provisions in prolonging product lifetime. First, informing consumers on the non-existence of a commercial guarantee and after-sales services could also be made mandatory (see #7), as proposed by the Proposal for the commercial guarantee of durability.[1834] Some scholars have already proposed to make information on the existence and the length of commercial guarantees mandatory in all circumstances and thus oblige traders to make a 'zero statement' in absence of a commercial guarantee or after-sales service.[1835] As this idea is deemed very promising, its implementation should be considered by the EU law makers not only for commercial guarantees but also for after-sales services. Such

---

1831 See *supra*, n° 179.

1832 Art. 7(4)(a) CRD.

1833 Commission Staff Working Document of 23 May 2017 on the Evaluation of the Consumer Rights Directive, SWD(2017) 169 final, p. 16.

1834 See *infra*, n° 489.

1835 See K. Tonner, R. Malcolm, *How an EU lifespan guarantee model could be implemented across the European Union (study)* (European Parliament 2017) pp. 54–55; I. Oehme, A. Jacob, *Strategies against obsolescence – Ensuring a minimum product lifetime and improving product service life as well as consumer information* (Umweltbundesamt 2017) pp. 12–13. For further details, see Chapter IV on the use stage.

information would make it easier for consumers to differentiate products on the basis of these sustainability aspects. Second, to ensure that consumers are properly informed about their rights under the legal guarantee, traders should also be obliged to provide information on the content of the legal guarantee (see #7). Third, the information obligation imposed by Article 7(4) on repair and maintenance services should be of full harmonisation (see #8).

Proposed review of the CRD:

#7

Article 5
Information requirements for contracts other than distance or off-premises contracts

1. Before the consumer is bound by a contract other than a distance or an off-premises contract, or any corresponding offer, the trader shall provide the consumer with the following information in a clear and comprehensible manner, if that information is not already apparent from the context:

(...)

(e) in addition to a reminder of the existence **and the content** of ~~a~~**the** legal guarantee of conformity for goods, the **(non-)**existence of after-sales services and commercial guarantees, **as well as on their conditions, where applicable**;

Article 6
Information requirements for distance and off-premises contracts

1. Before the consumer is bound by a distance or off-premises contract, or any corresponding offer, the trader shall provide the consumer with the following information in a clear and comprehensible manner:

(...)

(l) a reminder of the existence **and the content** of ~~a~~**the** legal guarantee of conformity for goods;

(m) ~~where applicable,~~ the **(non-)**existence ~~and the conditions~~ of after sale customer assistance, after-sales services and commercial guarantees, **as well as their conditions, where applicable**;

(...)

AND *#8*

Article 7
Formal requirements for off-premises contracts

(...)

4. With respect to off-premises contracts where the consumer has explicitly requested the services of the trader for the purpose of carrying out repairs or maintenance for which the trader and the consumer immediately perform their contractual obligations and where the payment to be made by the consumer does not exceed EUR 200:

(a) the trader shall provide the consumer with the information referred to in points (b) and (c) of Article 6(1) and information about the price or the manner in which the price is to be calculated together with an estimate of the total price, on paper or, if the consumer agrees, on another durable medium. The trader shall provide the information referred to in points (a), (h) and (k) of Article 6(1), but may choose not to provide it on paper or another durable medium if the consumer expressly agrees;

(b) the confirmation of the contract provided in accordance with paragraph 2 of this Article shall contain the information provided for in Article 6(1).

~~**Member States may decide not to apply this paragraph.**~~

(...)

5. OBLIGATION TO PROVIDE INFORMATION ABOUT THE FUNCTIONALITY, COMPATIBILITY AND INTEROPERABILITY OF DIGITAL CONTENT

a) *Existing obligations at EU level*

492. Information on functionality, compatibility and interoperability – In addition to these general information obligations, Articles 5 and 6 of the CRD add specific information requirements for products with digital content that could help to prevent their functional obsolescence. These provisions have been amended by the Enforcement and Modernisation Directive, which refers to the definitions given in the Digital Content Directive. Pursuant to Articles 5(1)(g) and 6(1)(r) of the CRD, traders must, on one hand, provide information on the functionality of digital content. The notion of 'functionality' corresponds to "*the ability of the digital content or digital* *service to perform its functions having regard to its purpose"*.[1836] On the other hand, traders are required by Articles 5(1)(h) and 6(1)(s) to inform consumers about the compatibility and interoperability of digital content. 'Compatibility' is defined as *"the ability of the digital content or digital service to function with hardware or software with which digital content or digital services of the same type are normally used, without the need to convert the digital content or digital service"*[1837], while 'interoperability' means *"the ability of the digital content or digital service to function with hardware or software different from those with which digital content or digital services of the same type are normally used"*.[1838]

493. Depending on the product – Given the considerable diversity of digital products, it is not possible to have a single list of functionality and interoperability parameters that would apply to all digital products. It is thus for the traders to examine the need to disclose such information according to the product and its characteristics.[1839] To assist traders in their assessment, the CRD Guidance gives a non-exhaustive list of parameters for functionality and interoperability.[1840] The need to provide information on the functionality of digital content may depend *inter alia* on whether there is a commitment by the trader or a third party to maintain or update the product, whether there is a need for other users to have specific software installed or whether functionalities are conditional on additional purchases (e.g. additional hardware or software). Concerning information on interoperability, it corresponds to information on devices that the digital content can be used with. For example, it can include information about the necessary OS and additional software (e.g. the version number) and hardware (e.g. processor speed and graphics card features).

494. An indicator of product lifetime – These items of information can serve as indications of product durability and upgradability on which consumers could rely to take a sustainable purchasing decision. Prior to the conclusion of the purchase agreement, consumers must be clearly and sufficiently informed about the functionalities and lifecycle of the product, and particularly that those functionalities or that lifecycle may have been or could be manipulated through the use of (remotely operated) software. As regards interoperability

1836 Art. 2(20) CRD, referring to Art. 2(11) DCD. This definition supplements the one contained in recital 19 CRD, which defines 'functionality' as *"the ways in which digital content can be used"*.

1837 Art. 2(19) CRD, referring to Art. 2(10) DCD.

1838 Art. 2(21) CRD, referring to Art. 2(12) DCD. This definition supplements the one contained in recital 19 CRD, which defines 'interoperability' as *"the standard hardware and software environment with which the digital content is compatible, for instance the operating system, the necessary version and certain hardware features"*.

1839 CRD Guidance, p. 35.

1840 *Ibid.*

information, it can help consumers identify and thus avoid lock-in situations.[1841] Since information on the compatibility and interoperability of digital content with hardware and software may be quite technical for the man in the street, it is important that traders provide it in a simple and understandable way.[1842]

b) The French mandatory information on updates

495. Explicit information obligations on updates – In addition to those extra obligations on the availability of spare parts, Article L. 111–6 of the French Consumer Code imposes mandatory information on updates. This obligation was initially introduced by Article 27 of the Anti-Waste Law in the section dedicated to guarantee rules, before being moved to its current section. Article L. 111–6 can be divided into two informational obligations in relation to software updates for goods with digital elements. Manufacturers are under obligation to give information (1) on the period during which updates will remain compatible with the product and (2) on their essential characteristics. Some of these obligations are applicable since 1st January 2021.

496. Information on the availability period of compatible updates – First, manufacturers of goods containing digital elements must inform sellers of the period during which updates to the software supplied during the purchase of the goods remain compatible with the functionality of the device. Sellers must then pass on this information to consumers. With this information, consumers get indications on the period of time during which the performance and functionality of the device will remain unaffected by the successive updates and during which they will be able to make normal use of the product. In that way, they are guided in their choice at the time of purchase in favour of sustainable products. It remains to be seen how this provision will be concretely applied.[1843]

497. Information on the essential characteristics of updates – Second, manufacturers are obliged to inform consumers, in a clear and comprehensible manner, of the essential characteristics of each update of the digital elements of the good, in particular the storage space it requires, its impact on the performance of the good and the changes in functionality it involves. The disclosure of such information can help prevent misleading omissions linked to the lack of information on updates.[1844]

1841 UCPD Guidance, p. 106.

1842 See *supra*, n° 352.

1843 The methods of application of this provision are to be specified by decree, which has not been adopted yet.

1844 See *supra*, n° 399.

c) Bringing coherence between the legal instruments

498. THE PROPOSED INFORMATION OBLIGATION ON THE AVAILABILITY PERIOD OF SOFTWARE UPDATES – It is worth noting that the Proposal for a Directive on empowering consumers for the green transition contains amendments to the CRD which aim to introduce mandatory information on the availability period of software updates.[1845] If adopted, Article 5(1) and Article 6(1) of the CRD would additionally impose pre-contractual information on the existence and length of the period during which the producer commits to providing software updates for goods with digital elements. Such amendments would constitute a major step forward in the fight against functional obsolescence, but also remove the doubts on the compatibility of the French rules with the CRD.

499. SPECIFIC INFORMATION REQUIREMENTS ON SOFTWARE AND FIRMWARE UPDATES – The amendments proposed by the EC are to be welcomed. Yet these information obligations should not be limited to the availability period of software updates but should apply to firmware updates and include information on the main characteristics of updates (e.g. the storage space they require, their impact on the performance of the goods and the changes in functionality they involve). In this regard, French law could serve as a source of inspiration.[1846] There are two ways of introducing such update obligations within the framework of the CRD. The first option would consist in amending the CRD Guidance to clarify the scope of Article 5(1)(g) and (h) and Article 6(1)(r) and (s) and explain that these provisions require traders to provide information on the availability period of updates and their main characteristics (see #10). The second option would be to add software and firmware updates specifically and explicitly to the list of mandatory information imposed by Articles 5 and 6, next to the specific information requirements on the functionality, compatibility and interoperability of digital content (see #9). This more stringent option would highlight the existence and importance of these update obligations. The first option could also be seen as an intermediary step, with a view to adopting the second option at a later stage.

500. COMPLEMENTARY TO THE UPDATE OBLIGATION ESTABLISHED UNDER THE SGD – Pre-contractual information obligations on updates go hand in hand with the new obligations established under the SGD, which require the seller to ensure that the consumer is informed of and supplied with 'necessary'

[1845] See Art. 2(2)(a) and (3)(a) of the Proposal for a Directive on empowering consumers for the green transition.

[1846] See *supra*, n° 495–497.

updates.[1847] More than informing consumers on the lifetime they can expect for the product before purchasing it, Articles 5 and 6 of the CRD also protect them against lack of conformity when combined with the provisions of the SGD, and more specifically with the subjective and objective conformity requirements.[1848] These information requirements are also closely linked to the new 'update obligations' established in Article 7(3) of the SGD and Article 8(2) of the DCD.[1849] Because these links between the CRD and the SGD are essential, they should be made more obvious. Inspiration could be drawn from Article L. 111–1 of the French Consumer Code where those links have been made more obvious with the terms referring to "*the existence of any software installation restrictions*", as introduced by Article 28 of the Anti-Waste Law. Without necessarily having to review Articles 5 and 6 of the Directive, references to the relevant provisions of the SGD should be introduced in the CRD Guidance (see #11).

501. Articulation with product regulations – As highlighted in the previous chapter of this book, requirements on the operating system, software and firmware have been established for specific products in several ecodesign regulations.[1850] These regulations impose requirements on the availability of software and firmware updates, the impacts of these updates as well as corresponding information requirements. Future requirements are and should be envisaged for a wider range of products and on additional aspects, such as the possibility of not installing updates, the reversibility of software updates and information relating to the frequency of updates, the conditions under which updates are available and the differences between the versions of OS, system settings and the storage regime.[1851] These existing and future requirements concern the functionality, compatibility and interoperability of digital content about which consumers should be informed according to the CRD provisions. Therefore, it is also recommended to make the links between these rules more explicit by adding references to product regulations in the CRD Guidance (see #11). This would improve the coherence and consistency between all the rules tackling premature obsolescence.

1847 See Chapter IV on the use stage, especially n° 691 and n° 700–701.
1848 See Art. 6(a) and 7(1)(d) SGD. See *infra*, Chapter IV on the use stage.
1849 For further comments on this 'update obligation', see Chapter IV on the use stage.
1850 See *supra*, n° 245–247.
1851 See *supra*, n° 248–252.

Proposed review of the CRD:

#9

Article 5
Information requirements for contracts other than distance or off-premises contracts

1. Before the consumer is bound by a contract other than a distance or an off-premises contract, or any corresponding offer, the trader shall provide the consumer with the following information in a clear and comprehensible manner, if that information is not already apparent from the context:

(...)

(i) the availability period of software and firmware updates as well as their main characteristics;

(...)

Article 6
Information requirements for distance and off-premises contracts

1. Before the consumer is bound by a distance or off-premises contract, or any corresponding offer, the trader shall provide the consumer with the following information in a clear and comprehensible manner:

(...)

(sa) the availability period of software and firmware updates as well as their main characteristics;

(...)

IN THE ALTERNATIVE, OR AS AN INTERMEDIARY STEP:

#10

Proposed review of the CRD Guidance

3.2.8. Functionality, compatibility and interoperability

(...)

The trader should assess the need to provide information about the features of the goods with digital elements, digital content or digital service according to their particular characteristics. The following indicative and non-exhaustive list of elements, covering also aspects of functionality, compatibility and interoperability, may be used as a checklist when deciding what information is to be provided about a specific good with digital elements, digital content or digital service (see also section 3.2.1 regarding information about the main characteristics):

The trader should assess the need to provide information about the features of the goods with digital elements, digital content or digital service according to their particular characteristics. The following indicative and non-exhaustive list of elements, covering also aspects of functionality, compatibility and interoperability, may be used as a checklist when deciding what information is to be provided about a specific good with digital elements, digital content or digital service (see also section 3.2.1 regarding information about the main characteristics):

(…)

(5) Whether there is a commitment or no commitment by the trader or a third party to maintain or update the goods with digital elements, digital content or service;

(5a) the availability period of software and firmware updates as well as their main characteristics, such as the storage space they require, their impact on the performance of the goods and the changes in functionality they involve;

(…)

AND *#11*

Proposed review of the CRD Guidance

3.2.8. Functionality, compatibility and interoperability

(…)

The notions of functionality, compatibility and interoperability are defined in Article 2 of the Digital Content Directive ('DCD').

'Goods with digital elements' (i.e. 'smart' devices) are a sub-category in the updated definition of 'goods' in the Sale of Goods Directive ('SGD'), which also applies in the context of the CRD. Recital 14 of the SGD explains that 'goods with digital elements' incorporate or are inter-connected with digital content or digital service in such a way that the absence of that digital content or digital service would prevent the goods from performing their functions. Digital content that is incorporated in or inter-connected with a good can be any data which are produced and supplied in digital form, such as operating systems, applications and any other software. Digital content can be pre-installed at the moment of the conclusion of the sales contract or, where that contract so provides, can be installed subsequently. Digital services interconnected with a good can include services which allow the creation, processing or storage of data in digital form, or access thereto, such as software-as-a-service offered in the cloud computing environment, the continuous supply of traffic data in a navigation system, or the continuous supply of individually adapted training plans in the case of a smart watch.

> These information requirements on the functionality, compatibility and interoperability of digital elements should be read in conjunction with Articles 6(a) and 7(1)(d) and (3) of the SGD as well as with Article 8(2) of the DCD.
>
> Furthermore, requirements on the functionality, compatibility and interoperability of digital content which are imposed by other sector-specific EU legislation, like the ecodesign regulations, are also part of the information that should be provided to consumers on the basis of Articles 5 and 6 of the CRD.
>
> (...)

6. ENFORCEMENT AND SANCTIONS

502. Enforcement and sanctions at national level – Like most of the EU consumer law instruments, the CRD leaves matters of enforcement and sanctions to a large extent for Member States to decide. Apart from a few explicit provisions[1852], Articles 23 and 24 of the Directive only require Member States to ensure adequate and effective means of enforcement and to provide for effective, proportionate and dissuasive sanctions. The Enforcement and Modernisation Directive has nonetheless amended Article 24 by adding a list of non-exhaustive and indicative criteria to be taken into account for the imposition of penalties.[1853] These criteria include the nature, gravity, scale and duration of the infringement, any action taken by the trader to mitigate or remedy the damage suffered by consumers, any previous infringements by the trader, the financial benefits gained or losses avoided by the trader due to the infringement, penalties imposed on the trader for the same infringement in other Member States in cross-border cases, any other aggravating or mitigating factors.

503. Various existing sanctions – This freedom has led to a variety of sanctions in Member States, which established either specific sanctions or sanctions derived from general rules of private law. In France, when consumers are not informed about the product's essential characteristics, the contract can be annulled.[1854] Failing to comply with one of the pre-contractual and contractual obligations on spare parts may result in an administrative fine not exceeding € 3,000 for a natural person and € 15,000 for a legal person.[1855] A breach of those obligations may also be considered as fraud or an unfair commercial practice and therefore be subject to the corresponding sanctions, namely two years

[1852] See for ex. Art. 18(2) and (3) and Art. 22 CRD.
[1853] Art. 4 Enforcement and Modernisation Directive.
[1854] See CA Amiens (1re ch. civ.), 11 December 2018, n° 17/00571.
[1855] Art. L. 131-2 of the French Consumer Code.

imprisonment and a € 300,000 fine. Civil sanctions, like contract cancellation and/or damages, can also be taken against the trader who would not have fulfilled their duties.[1856] In the event of a dispute concerning these obligations, it is for the trader to prove that they performed their obligations.[1857] In Germany, a violation of the information requirements contained in the CRD may give rise to claims for damages by consumers under the doctrine of *culpa in contrahendo*.[1858] Additionally, a breach of pre-contractual information duties laid down in the CRD can also be sanctioned on the basis of the UCPD. In addition to these sanctions, the Enforcement and Modernisation Directive stipulates that national authorities will have the power to impose a fine of up to 4% of the trader's turnover, or up to € 2 million when information on turnover is not available. Member States are free to keep or introduce higher maximum fines.[1859]

504. The need for cooperation – The cooperation between the different national authorities is important in this regard, as emphasized in the CPC Regulation.[1860] The EC coordinates the cooperation between these authorities to ensure that consumer law is consistently applied and enforced within the EU territory. It can alert the CPC network and coordinate EU-wide enforcement action to curb practices that affect a large majority of EU consumers. Authorities can acknowledge commitments from the traders concerned, which commit to correcting their practices, providing remedies and compensating affected consumers. With the entry into force of the Enforcement and Modernisation Directive[1861], the sanction could reach at least 4% of the turnover of the businesses in the Member States concerned.

7. INTERMEDIATE CONCLUSION

505. The power of information obligations through the CRD – The information requirements laid down in the CRD are of particular relevance from a sustainability perspective. Pursuant to its provisions, prior to the conclusion of the purchase agreement, consumers must be clearly and

1856 D. Bazin-Beust, *L'essentiel du Droit de la consommation* (Gualino 2017) pp. 39–40.
1857 Art. L. 111-5 of the French Consumer Code.
1858 §280 Sec 1, §311 Sec 2 BGB.
1859 Art. 4 Enforcement and Modernisation Directive.
1860 Regulation (EU) 2017/2394 of the European Parliament and of the Council of 12 December 2017 on cooperation between national authorities responsible for the enforcement of consumer protection laws and repealing Regulation (EC) No 2006/2004, OJ L 345, 27.12.2017, p. 1–26 (hereafter 'CPC Regulation').
1861 Directive (EU) 2019/2161 of the European Parliament and of the Council of 27 November 2019 amending Council Directive 93/13/EEC and Directives 98/6/EC, 2005/29/EC and 2011/83/EU of the European Parliament and of the Council as regards the better enforcement and modernisation of Union consumer protection rules, OJ L 328, 18.12.2019, p. 7–28.

sufficiently informed about aspects relating to the sustainability of the product, such as product lifetime, reparability and upgradability. Its role in triggering product sustainability could be even more prominent if greater importance was given to these aspects within its text. The CRD was at the centre of discussions with the adoption of the New Deal for Consumers and the subsequent adoption of the Enforcement and Modernisation Directive. However, those amendments brought to the CRD within that context make only a very small contribution to sustainable consumption.

506. An explicit obligation to give information about product sustainability – As was argued for the UCPD, sustainability aspects should be mentioned in the list of mandatory pre-contractual information contained in Articles 5 and 6 of the CRD. This could be done by amending these two provisions and/or by updating the CRD Guidance. In any case, these clarifications should be made in parallel for the UCPD and the CRD so that the information obligations imposed by both instruments are aligned. Cross-references could possibly be added in both directives to emphasize the close interplay between their provisions. The general obligations to disclose information on sustainability aspects are particularly beneficial for products that are exempted from specific information requirements under product-specific legislation, like the ecodesign rules and energy labelling. In this regard, it complements the tailored approach followed by the Energy Labelling Regulation and EU Ecolabel Regulation for specific products.

507. More information on after-sales services and guarantees should be provided – The information obligation established by the CRD concerning after-sales service and guarantees could be improved on three fronts. First, consumers should be informed about the non-existence of a commercial guarantee and after-sales services. Such information would make it easier for consumers to differentiate products on the basis of these sustainability aspects. Second, to ensure that consumers are properly informed about their rights under the legal guarantee, traders should be obliged to provide information on the content of the legal guarantee. Third, the information obligation imposed by Article 7(4) on the price of maintenance and repair operations should be of full harmonisation. These improvements would guide consumers towards sustainable choices and help them prolong the lifetime of their products.

508. Specific information requirements on software and firmware updates should be imposed – Article 5(1) and Article 6(1) of the CRD should explicitly impose pre-contractual information on the existence and length of the period during which the producer commits to providing software and firmware updates for goods with digital elements as well as on the main characteristics of updates (e.g. the storage space they require, their impact on the performance of the goods and the changes in functionality they involve). There are two ways of introducing such update obligations within the framework of the CRD. The first option would consist in amending the CRD Guidance to clarify the scope of Article 5(1)(g) and (h) and Article 6(1)(r) and (s) and explain that these provisions require traders to provide information on the availability period of updates and their main characteristics. The second option would be to add software and firmware updates specifically and explicitly to the list of mandatory information imposed by Articles 5 and 6, next to the specific information requirements on the functionality, compatibility and interoperability of digital content. This more stringent option would highlight the existence and importance of these update obligations. The first option could also be seen as an intermediary step, with a view to adopting the second option at a later stage.

509. More explicit references to SGD and DCD should be made – Various links exist between the provisions of the CRD and those contained in the SGD and the DCD. While these links have been clarified in the CRD Guidance concerning the information on after-sales services and guarantees, this cannot be said of other provisions. No reference is made, for instance, to the objective conformity requirement on durability or to the update obligation established under the SGD. To underline these links, explicit references to the SGD and the DCD should be added to the CRD Guidance in the corresponding sections dedicated to the information on the main product characteristics and on the functionality, compatibility, and interoperability of digital content.

510. Connecting CRD with product regulations – Besides consumer law rules, this section of the book also revealed the close links between the provisions of the CRD and the requirements imposed by product regulations. This is especially true for the ecodesign regulations requiring information on some product sustainability aspects. For example, information requirements on the availability period of spare parts established under the Ecodesign regulation on electronic displays constitute information on the main characteristics of the goods that should be provided to consumers on the basis of the CRD. Other requirements that shape the design of products could also be linked to the information obligations imposed by the CRD. For instance, the information obligation on functionality, compatibility and interoperability established by the CRD can cover ecodesign requirements on these aspects. This would enhance the effectiveness of ecodesign requirements by informing consumers and raising their awareness about product sustainability aspects. The connections between the CRD and product regulations should therefore be clear and sufficiently conspicuous. Such links could be embodied through references to these product regulations in the provisions or recitals of the CRD itself or in the CRD Guidance. To this end, inspiration could be drawn from Article 7(5) of the UCPD, which builds a bridge between consumer law and product regulation.

511. National information requirements should be harmonised – National legislation have played a role as regulatory sandboxes when it comes to sustainability information. The French information obligations relating to the availability of spare parts is a notable step forward in promoting product sustainability and fighting against premature obsolescence. Likewise, some ideas contained in the Belgian legislative proposals are laudable. This is a good thing. Yet, at some point, it would be better to introduce these measures at EU level. Otherwise, such legal fragmentation may undermine the smooth functioning of the internal market and lead to a legal maze for consumers and businesses.

E. THE EU ENERGY LABELLING RULES AND THE (FUTURE) LABEL ON PRODUCT SUSTAINABILITY

1. PRODUCT-SPECIFIC MANDATORY LABELS DISPLAYED AT THE POINT OF SALE

512. The Energy Labelling Regulation and its delegated acts – The main EU legal instrument imposing product-specific information requirements at the marketing stage is undoubtedly the Energy Labelling Regulation.[1862] This Regulation provides for a uniform label that energy-related products must display at the point of sale to be put on the EU market and benefit from free movement.[1863] Delegated acts supplement the Regulation by setting out detailed requirements for the label of specific product groups. Products are labelled on a scale A–G (with A being the best) according to their energy efficiency. The classification is derived from the result of a standardized test and the calculation of a ranking order. The scale was reviewed in 2019 for dishwashers, washing machines and washer-driers, refrigerators, lamps and electronic displays due to the development of more energy efficient products and because the difference between A++ and A+++ became less obvious to consumers. In addition to the energy efficiency scale, the label also contains information on product characteristics, environmental impact and performance.[1864]

513. A component of the EU policy on energy – This framework regulation is part of the Union policy on energy. Based on Article 194(2) TFEU, it aims to contribute to the proper functioning of the internal market

1862 Regulation (EU) 2017/1369 of the European Parliament and of the Council of 4 July 2017 setting a framework for energy labelling and repealing Directive 2010/30/EU, OJ L 198, 28.7.2017, p. 1–23.

1863 Art. 1 of the Energy Labelling Regulation.

1864 Art. 1 of the Energy Labelling Regulation.

and to preserve and improve the environment. The label was first introduced for a number of household appliances in 1994[1865], after the second oil crisis raised doubts about the security of oil supplies.[1866] Together with the Ecodesign Directive, they are core elements of the transformation of the EU market. Whereas the Ecodesign Directive 'pushes' the market towards greener products by banning the worst-performing ones, the Energy Labelling Regulation 'pulls' the market towards more energy-efficient products.[1867] It is also interesting to note that the EU energy label is used by many non-EU countries, generating impacts beyond EU boundaries.[1868] As already mentioned in the analysis of the Ecodesign Directive[1869], this phenomenon is called the 'Brussels effect'.[1870]

514. Towards an EU labelling of product sustainability – Although the label established under the Energy Labelling Regulation currently focuses on energy efficiency, it could be used to convey information on product sustainability aspects. Labels displaying such information would underline the importance of these product characteristics and raise awareness among consumers and businesses, as they already do for energy-efficient products. The idea has already been examined and suggested at EU level and is now on the table, as shown by the 2020 Circular Economy Action Plan[1871], as well as the Preparatory study for the Ecodesign and Energy Labelling Working Plan 2022–2024.[1872] This section provides some comments and recommendations concerning this idea and its implementation.

1865 Commission Directive 94/2/EC of 21 January 1994 implementing Council Directive 92/75/EEC with regard to energy labelling of household electric refrigerators, freezers and their combinations, OJ L 45, 17.2.1994, p. 1–22.

1866 Waide Strategic Efficiency, Ecofys, Tait Consulting, ISR University of Coimbra, Consumer Research Associates, *Impacts of the EU's Ecodesign and Energy/Tyre Labelling Legislation on Third Jurisdictions* (European Commission 2014) p. 13.

1867 Staff Working Document of the European Commission of 15 July 2015 on the Evaluation of the Energy Labelling and Ecodesign Directives, SWD(2015) 143 final, p. 3.

1868 Waide Strategic Efficiency, Ecofys, Tait Consulting, ISR University of Coimbra, Consumer Research Associates, *Impacts of the EU's Ecodesign and Energy/Tyre Labelling Legislation on Third Jurisdictions* (European Commission 2014).

1869 See *supra*, n° 177.

1870 For an in-depth analysis on the Brussels effect, see A. Bradford, *The Brussels Effect – How the European Union Rules the World* (Oxford University Press 2020).

1871 Communication from the Commission of 11 March 2020 to the European Parliament, the Council, the European Economic and Social Committee and the Committee of the Regions on A new Circular Economy Action Plan – For a cleaner and more competitive Europe, COM(2020) 98 final, p. 5.

1872 Viegand Maagøe, Oeko-Institut, VHK, *Preparatory study for the Ecodesign and Energy Labelling Working Plan 2020–2024 – Task 4 Complementary analyses and recommendations for the Ecodesign and Energy Labelling Working Plan 2020–2024 – Final* (European Commission 2021) p. 67.

2. SCOPE OF APPLICATION AND LEVEL OF HARMONISATION

a) *A scope limited to energy-related products*

515. Current scope of application and exclusions – The scope of the Energy Labelling Regulation is similar to the one of the Ecodesign Directive, meaning that it only applies to 'energy-related products'.[1873] Like the Ecodesign Directive[1874], the Regulation excludes means of transport for persons or goods from its scope. This has led to separate labelling schemes for cars[1875], and tyres[1876], adding pieces to this already complex jigsaw. Suggestions have already been made to integrate tyre labelling into the more general energy labelling rules.[1877] Another exception concerns second-hand products, which also fall outside the scope of the Regulation, except those imported from a third country which are placed on the EU market for the first time.[1878] The Regulation does not define 'second-hand good' in its provisions. However, the document on frequently asked questions issued by the EC, though not legally binding, provides some indications on that notion.[1879] For example, repaired and refurbished products are to be considered second-hand products unless they have undergone significant changes and come with a new warranty period. By contrast, products returned after cancellation of contract or withdrawal rights as well as products held in stock and sold as 'phase-out-model' should be considered as new if they have not been used or sold before.

1873 Art. 1 of the Energy Labelling Regulation. Article 2(1) of the Regulation defines 'energy-related product' as "*good or system with an impact on energy consumption during use which is placed on the market or put into service, including parts with an impact on energy consumption during use which are placed on the market or put into service for customers and that are intended to be incorporated into products*". For further details on this notion, see *supra*, n° 179.

1874 See *supra*, n° 180.

1875 Directive 1999/94/EC of the European Parliament and of the Council of 13 December 1999 relating to the availability of consumer information on fuel economy and CO_2 emissions in respect of the marketing of new passenger cars, OJ L 12, 18.1.2000, p. 16–23. This Directive enables Member States to introduce car energy labels. Various EU countries have introduced (national versions of) an energy label, with a format different from one country to another.

1876 Regulation (EU) 2020/740 of the European Parliament and of the Council of 25 May 2020 on the labelling of tyres with respect to fuel efficiency and other parameters, amending Regulation (EU) 2017/1369 and repealing Regulation (EC) No 1222/2009, PE/3/2020/INIT, OJ L 177, 5.6.2020, p. 1–31.

1877 See E. Molenbroek et al., *Evaluation of the Energy Labelling Directive and specific aspects of the Ecodesign Directive – Final technical report* (Ecofys 2014) p. 49. See also the following Staff Working Document of the European Commission of 15 July 2015 on the Evaluation of the Energy Labelling and Ecodesign Directives, SWD(2015) 143 final, p. 24.

1878 Art. 1(2)(a) and recital 5 of the Energy Labelling Regulation.

1879 Frequently Asked Questions (FAQ) on the Energy Labelling Regulation EU 2017/1369 of 4 July 2017 setting a framework for energy labelling and repealing Directive 2010/30/EU and its delegated acts, p. 4, available on: <https://ec.europa.eu/energy/sites/ener/files/documents/ec_faq_el_2015-1.pdf>.

516. Products sold in B2B and B2C relationships – The Regulation uses the term 'customer' instead of 'consumer'.[1880] This means that energy labels can be affixed on products sold in B2B and B2C relationships. Professionals are also customers, so the products they purchase are not *a priori* excluded from energy label legislation. The existing labelling regulations have different approaches in this regard. Each regulation contains specific provisions in which case labels must be provided. As opposed to 'customer', the Regulation refers to the 'supplier', who is the manufacturer or their authorized representative who "*places a product on the Union market*"[1881], and the 'dealer', who is the "*retailer or other natural or legal person who offers for sale, hire, or hire purchase, or displays products to customers or installers in the course of a commercial activity, whether or not in return for payment*".[1882] Both must abide by their obligations under the Energy Labelling Regulation.[1883]

517. Four criteria for the eligibility of products – Article 16(2) of the Regulation details the criteria that products should satisfy to be covered by a delegated act. These criteria are almost identical to the ones established under Article 15 of the Ecodesign Directive and so draw the same comments.[1884] First of all, the product group must have significant potential for saving energy and other resources. The assessment is made according to the most recently available figures and considering the quantities placed on the EU market. It is interesting to note that resources other than energy are considered when envisaging the adoption of delegated acts. As already explained in the previous chapter dedicated to the Ecodesign Directive[1885], this first criterion may be problematic for the development of labels if interpreted too strictly. The second criterion requires significant differences in performance levels between models within product groups with equivalent functionality. In the absence of noticeable differences between products, the label would lose its relevance. Thirdly, there must be no significant negative impact as regards the affordability and the lifecycle cost of the product group. The fourth and final criterion requires that "*the introduction of energy labelling requirements for a product group [must] not have a significant negative impact on the functionality of the product during use*". In practice, the product groups chosen for energy labelling are generally those for which it was decided to develop ecodesign requirements. The link between the EU energy label and the ecodesign regulations has been strengthened with the upcoming common working plan for these instruments. Such an integrated

[1880] Art. 2(16) of the Energy Labelling Regulation.
[1881] Art. 2(14) of the Energy Labelling Regulation.
[1882] Art. 2(13) of the Energy Labelling Regulation.
[1883] See *infra*, n° 565 *et seq.*
[1884] See Chapter II on the design and production stage, especially n° 198–204.
[1885] See *supra*, n° 200.

approach, with common preparatory studies, allows for the creation of a unified evidence base.

518. Products covered by existing delegated acts – So far, 15 product groups require an energy label, all of which are subject to ecodesign regulations. Since March 2021, an additional product group is covered by the label, namely refrigerating appliances with a direct sales function.[1886] In spite of the extension of the scope to energy-related products[1887], delegated acts taken based on the Energy Labelling Regulation are still limited to energy-using products such as fridges, washing machines, televisions or lighting products.[1888]

519. The exclusion of second-hand products should be removed – It is regrettable that the Energy Labelling Regulation excludes 'second-hand products' from its scope, except those that are imported from a third country. It should be possible to establish mandatory labels for second-hand products, at least for certain 'workhorse products'.[1889] Labels would reassure consumers about the quality of second-hand products and encourage them to buy such products. The exclusion established under Article 1(2)(a) of the Regulation should therefore be removed (see #2). This would allow extending the application of some delegated acts to second-hand products, which contrary to what might sometimes be believed, can be as sustainable as new products.

520. The scope should be extended to non-energy-related products – Although the current focus of the Regulation on energy efficiency does not allow widening the scope to non-energy-related products (e.g. textiles and furniture), enlarging this labelling scheme to these products should be considered (see #1), especially if the label gives more information on product sustainability aspects

---

1886 Commission Delegated Regulation (EU) 2019/2018 of 11 March 2019 supplementing Regulation (EU) 2017/1369 of the European Parliament and of the Council with regard to energy labelling of refrigerating appliances with a direct sales function, OJ L 315, 5.12.2019, p. 155–186.

1887 The scope has been extended to energy-related products since the adoption of the previous Energy Labelling Directive (Directive 2010/30/EU of the European Parliament and of the Council of 19 May 2010 on the indication by labelling and standard product information of the consumption of energy and other resources by energy-related products, OJ L 153, 18.6.2010, p. 1–12).

1888 It should also be noted that some products belonging to these product groups are explicitly excluded from the scope of application of energy labelling rules. See e.g. Art. 1(2) of the Commission Delegated Regulation (EU) 2019/2013 of 11 March 2019 supplementing Regulation (EU) 2017/1369 of the European Parliament and of the Council with regard to energy labelling of electronic displays and repealing Commission Delegated Regulation (EU) No 1062/2010, OJ L 315, 5.12.2019, p. 1–28.

1889 'Workhorse' products are products "*purchased primarily on the basis of their function*" and "*tend to be discarded only when they broke, rather than when their look needed updating*". See Brook Lyndhurst, *Public understanding of product lifetimes and durability* (DEFRA 2011) p. 54. See *supra*, n° 169.

such as durability or reparability.[1890] A 2014 technical report on the Energy Labelling Directive recommended postponing the extension of the scope until a number of methodological obstacles were overcome, and subsequently assessing potential extensions on a case-by-case basis.[1891] In any case, it seems worthwhile to make the scope of the Energy Labelling Regulation correspond to the one of the Ecodesign Directive as both instruments are closely intertwined in their development.[1892] Alternatively, a new EU mandatory label could be created for non-energy-related products (see #4). In the meantime, this limited scope of application and the great number of products still uncovered by specific labelling rules highlight the need for general information requirements covering all products, like the one contained in the CRD and the UCPD.[1893]

521. Additional delegated acts should be adopted – As it was suggested for the ecodesign scheme[1894], additional delegated acts should be adopted for a wider range of products, which also have a significant environmental impact and present significant potential for improvement in environmental impact (see #2). Studies have already made suggestions on the extension of the energy labelling rules to other product categories. The study carried out for the Working Plan 2022–2024 reaches conclusions and provides recommendations that apply both to the Ecodesign and Energy Labelling regulations. In this study, it is recommended to extend mandatory labels to products such as professional cooking appliances and low-temperature emitters.[1895] In addition to these products, the ICT Impact study of 2020 recommends the adoption of energy labelling rules for ICT products[1896], such as smart industrial sensors.[1897] It would also be useful for consumers to have information on smartphones and their components (e.g. batteries).[1898] Furthermore, labels should be envisaged

1890 See *infra* on the Possible future labelling on product sustainability aspects (n° 543 *et seq.*).

1891 E. Molenbroek et al., *Evaluation of the Energy Labelling Directive and specific aspects of the Ecodesign Directive – Final technical report* (Ecofys 2014) p. 102 at p. 104.

1892 See n° 508 and n° 521 *et seq.* See also Staff Working Document of the European Commission of 15 July 2015 on the Evaluation of the Energy Labelling and Ecodesign Directives, SWD(2015) 143 final, pp. 23–24.

1893 See *supra* in this chapter.

1894 See Chapter II on design and production stage, especially n° 197.

1895 Viegand Maagøe, Oeko-Institut, VHK, *Preparatory study for the Ecodesign and Energy Labelling Working Plan 2020–2024 – Task 4 Complementary analyses and recommendations for the Ecodesign and Energy Labelling Working Plan 2020–2024 – Final* (European Commission 2021), especially p. 63.

1896 VHK, Viegand Maagøe, *ICT Impact study – Final Report* (European Commission 2020).

1897 'Smart industrial sensors' are "*electronic packages added to new and existing electrical motors, fans, pumps and compressors to lower running costs (energy, auxiliaries), optimise maintenance (lower costs and down-time), increase product life and integrate systems across platforms.*" See VHK, Viegand Maagøe, *ICT Impact study – Final Report* (European Commission 2020) p. 177.

1898 The lack of information on batteries has already contributed to the premature obsolescence of certain smartphones. See Autorita Garante della Concorrenza e del Mercato, 25 September 2018, Apple, para 8, point B).

for software products. The German ecolabel *The Blue Angel*, which introduced award criteria for 'Resource and Energy-Efficient Software Products'[1899], could serve as an inspiration in this regard.

Proposed review of the Energy Labelling Regulation:

#1 All references to 'energy-related products' should be replaced with 'products'.

Example:

Article 1
Subject-matter and scope

1. This Regulation lays down a framework that applies to ~~**energy-related**~~ products ~~**('products')**~~ placed on the market or put into service. (…)

2. This Regulation does not apply to:

~~**(a) second-hand products, unless they are imported from a third country;**~~ #2

(…)

AND *#3*

Proposed delegated acts:

- *Commission Delegated Regulation supplementing Regulation (EU) 2017/1369 with regard to energy labelling of electronics and information and communication technologies*

NB: Because electronics and information and communication technologies cover a very wide range of products, distinct and specific regulations should be adopted for the different product categories encompassed within this product group (e.g. mobile phones and tablets).

- *Commission Delegated Regulation supplementing Regulation (EU) 2017/1369 with regard to energy labelling of software products*
- *Commission Delegated Regulation supplementing Regulation (EU) 2017/1369 with regard to energy labelling of textiles*
- *Commission Delegated Regulation supplementing Regulation (EU) 2017/1369 with regard to energy labelling of furniture*

[1899] Basic Award Criteria of the German Ecolabel Blue Angel from January 2020 for resource and energy-efficient software products, DE-UZ 215, available on: <https://www.blauer-engel.de/en/products/electric-devices/resources-and-energy-efficient-software-products>.

NB: Because textiles and furniture cover a very wide range of products, distinct and specific regulations could be adopted for the different product categories encompassed within this product group.

OR

#4 Alternatively, a new EU mandatory label for non-energy-related products should be developed.

b) A fully harmonised approach

522. The choice for regulation – Through its delegated acts, the Energy Labelling Regulation harmonises energy labels and their application across the EU for specific product groups. The choice for regulation was justified by the objective of "*simplify[ing] the regulatory environment for the Member States and economic operators*" and by the need "*to ensure a uniform application and implementation throughout the Union*".[1900] The Regulation and the delegated acts adopted on its basis impose clear and detailed rules, precluding divergent transposition by Member States. As a result, the costs for manufacturers are reduced, and the level playing field and free movement of goods are ensured.[1901] Furthermore, full harmonisation allows increasing familiarity, understanding and trust in the information, therefore making the Energy Labelling Regulation a source of inspiration for other legislation.[1902] The legal basis of the Regulation, its objectives and the choice of legal instrument seems to indicate that full harmonization of labelling is aimed for, at least for the products, environmental aspects and issues regulated under the Regulation.[1903] In other words, Member States are precluded from adopting labels falling within the scope of the Regulation.

523. Room left for national labelling schemes? – The full harmonisation character of the Energy Labelling Regulation nonetheless raises serious questions on the room for manoeuvre left to Member States as regards labels. Where energy-related products are exempted from delegated acts, recital 23 of the Regulation clearly states that Member States are entitled to maintain or introduce new national schemes for the labelling of these products. The answer

1900 Point 2.4. of the explanatory memorandum to the Proposal for a Regulation of the European Parliament and of the Council setting a framework for energy efficiency labelling and repealing Directive 2010/30/EU, COM(2015) 341 final, p. 3.

1901 Recital 6 of the Energy Labelling Regulation.

1902 See for ex. C. Brannigan, S. Amaral, I. Sikora, M. Zabalo, N. Hill, I. Skinner, J. Lawrence, J. Farrington, C. Reiner, T. Loke, *Technical analysis of measures to improve consumer awareness of emissions and fuel consumption of vehicles* (European Union 2021) p. 134.

1903 See also E. Maitre-Ekern and C. Dalhammar,'Regulating planned obsolescence: a review of legal approaches to increase product durability and reparability in Europe', 25 *Review of European Community & International Environmental Law* (2016) p. 392.

is less obvious concerning products that are covered by delegated acts. The current EU labelling legislation confines itself to energy efficiency, consumption of energy and other resources by products during use.[1904] Hence, it could be argued that Member States are still allowed to adopt mandatory labels on other information, including on product sustainability aspects. Such reasoning is supported by the explanatory memorandum of the Regulation that was issued at its proposal stage, where the EC underlined that Article 114 TFEU (establishment and functioning of the internal market) should not be chosen as a legal basis as "*there is a risk that this could unintentionally limit Member States legislating on provision of information on energy-related products that may be complementary to the energy label*".[1905] The French law imposing information on the availability of spare parts is given as an example of such legislation. The French reparability index, for which no compatibility issue was raised during the adoption process of the Anti-Waste Law, could be seen as a further proof of the room for manoeuvre left to Member States.[1906] Even if national labels were seen as limiting the free movement of goods, it may be possible to justify these on grounds of protection of the environment, which has been recognised by the ECJ as constituting an overriding mandatory requirement, provided that the national measures in question are proportionate and suitable to reach the goal.[1907]

524. Clarifications needed on the articulation between EU and national labels – To dispel the doubts on the room for manoeuvre left to the Member States as regards labels, recital 23 of the Regulation should better clarify the articulation between the Energy Labelling Regulation and national schemes for the labelling of such products (see #5). As additional labelling rules may contribute to promoting sustainable products, Member States should be allowed to adopt such rules for products or aspects that are not covered by delegated acts. As these rules could be considered as 'technical regulation' in accordance with the Directive (EU) 2015/1535, the notification procedure established under the Technical Regulations Information System (TRIS) could serve as a watchdog to ascertain whether the national labelling rule does not create barriers to the free movement of goods, the free provision of Information Society services, or to EU secondary legislation.[1908]

1904 See *infra*, n° 528 *et seq*.

1905 See Point 2.1. of the explanatory memorandum to the Proposal for a Regulation of the European Parliament and of the Council setting a framework for energy efficiency labelling and repealing Directive 2010/30/EU, COM(2015) 341 final, pp. 2–3.

1906 See Rapport d'information fait au nom de la Commission des affaires européennes (1) portant observations sur la transposition du droit européen par le projet de loi relatif à la lutte contre le gaspillage et à l'économie circulaire, 18 July 2019, n° 682, p. 19, pt. 10.

1907 See ECJ 20 September 1988, Case C-302/86, *Commission* v *Denmark, EU:C:1988:421*, para 8.

1908 Art. 5 of the Directive (EU) 2015/1535 of the European Parliament and of the Council of 9 September 2015 laying down a procedure for the provision of information in the field of

Proposed review of the Energy Labelling Regulation:

#5

Whereas:

(...)

(23) In order for customers to retain confidence in the energy label, other labels that mimic the energy label should not be allowed to be used for energy-related products and non-energy-related products. Where energy-related products **or sustainability aspects** are not covered by delegated acts, Member States should be able to maintain or introduce new national schemes for the labelling of such products. Additional labels, marks, symbols or inscriptions that are likely to mislead or confuse customers with respect to the consumption of energy for the product concerned should not be allowed for the same reason. Labels provided for pursuant to Union law, such as the labelling of tyres with respect to fuel efficiency and other environmental parameters, and additional labels such as the EU Energy Star and EU Ecolabel should not be considered to be misleading or confusing.

(...)

3. EXISTING LABELLING REQUIREMENTS

a) *The development of delegated acts*

525. Several steps – When a product group meets the criteria, the procedure to adopt a delegated act described in Article 11 of the Energy Labelling Regulation can be launched.[1909] This procedure is very similar to the procedure established within the framework of the Ecodesign Directive. It starts with a working plan, which sets out an indicative list of product groups which are considered to be priorities for the adoption of delegated acts as well as plans for the revision and rescaling of existing labels.[1910] After the preparatory study has been conducted, the product-specific regulation is drafted detailing the energy label for the concerned product group. The draft delegated act is then presented to the Consultation Forum which invites Member States' representatives and all interested parties concerned to comment on the results of the preparatory study

technical regulations and of rules on Information Society services, OJ L 241, 17.9.2015, p. 1–15.

[1909] For a detailed analysis of this procedure, see E. Molenbroek et al., *Evaluation of the Energy Labelling Directive and specific aspects of the Ecodesign Directive – Final technical report* (Ecofys 2014) pp. 119–120.

[1910] Article 15 of the Energy Labelling Regulation.

and the proposed delegated act.[1911] In practice, ecodesign and energy labelling regulations have always been developed together using the Ecodesign Directive's working plan and stakeholder forum as a basis. Only the final stage of the procedure differs from the Ecodesign procedure as Member States are not asked for a formal vote. Instead, a Member States Experts Group advises on a proposed act, but the final decision lies with the EC. The EP and the Council can exercise a right of objection to the act after the EC has adopted it. The delegated act is only published if no objection is raised.[1912]

526. A LENGTHY PROCEDURE – Like for the adoption of implementing measures under the Ecodesign Directive[1913], the adoption process of energy labelling regulations may be quite lengthy and exceed the theoretical time.[1914] Several reasons can explain delays and difficulties in adopting and developing labelling regulations, including the thorough preparatory study and availability of sufficient quality data, the technical complexity of some products or potential conflicts resulting from the involvement of stakeholders with opposed interests.[1915] Problems can also appear after the adoption of delegated acts. One illustrative example is the *Dyson* case and the related energy labelling rules for vacuum cleaners.[1916] The case led to the annulment of the Delegated Regulation No 665/2013[1917] by the EC because the method adopted by the EC to calculate the energy performance of vacuum cleaners was based on an empty receptacle and thus did not reflect normal conditions of use as required by Article 10 of the former Energy Labelling Directive (2010/30). As a result, the label misled consumers about the energy efficiency of vacuum cleaners. Following this case, *Dyson* brought a second claim to obtain damages from the EC.[1918] The *Dyson* case shows the difficulties in establishing labels. This case also resulted in delays

---

1911 See also Article 14 of the Energy Labelling Regulation.

1912 This is because delegated acts are adopted on the basis of Art. 290 TFEU, by contrast with ecodesign implementing measures which are adopted on the basis of Art. 291 TFEU.

1913 See *supra*, n° 176.

1914 The actual regulatory process is sometimes twice as long as the theoretical process. See European Court of Auditors, *EU action on Ecodesign and Energy Labelling: important contribution to greater energy efficiency reduced by significant delays and non-compliance – Special Report* (European Union 2020) p. 19.

1915 Staff Working Document of the European Commission of 15 July 2015 on the Evaluation of the Energy Labelling and Ecodesign Directives, SWD(2015) 143 final, pp. 19–20.

1916 See ECJ 8 November 2018, Case T-544/13 RENV, *Dyson* v *Commission, EU:T:2018:761.*

1917 Commission Delegated Regulation (EU) No 665/2013 of 3 May 2013 supplementing Directive 2010/30/EU of the European Parliament and of the Council with regard to energy labelling of vacuum cleaners, OJ L 192, 13.7.2013, p. 1–23 (*no longer in force*).

1918 See ECJ 21 February 2019, Case T-127/19, *Dyson and Others* v *Commission, EU:T:2021:870.* In its claim, Dyson argued that the Commission exceeded its legal competence, breached the principle of equal treatment, the principle of sound administration and/or its duty to act diligently, as well as the applicant's fundamental right to pursue a trade or business (see <https://op.europa.eu/en/publication-detail/-/publication/10e0fc40-7254-11e9-9f05-01aa75ed71a1/language-en/format-HTML/source-120578711>).

as the EC decided to freeze temporarily the regulatory process to review the adequacy of the policy as a whole. Long delays can lead to a reduced impact of the policy as technological progress may make labelling requirements outdated. Admittedly, the introduction of information on product sustainability in the energy label might exacerbate these delays and issues. This is however no reason to exclude the idea.

527. THE ROLE OF STANDARDS – Harmonised standards can play a key role in the adoption process of delegated acts. Harmonised standards provide *inter alia* methods to measure and test the environmental parameters of energy-related products. If taken into account in the preparatory study, they can facilitate and fasten the process. Inversely, their absence can constitute an obstacle to the smooth drafting and adoption of regulations. Harmonised standards are also particularly useful after the adoption of a delegated act as they help complying with the measurement and calculation requirements of the delegated act.[1919]

b) A main focus on energy efficiency and energy consumption

528. REQUIREMENTS ON ENERGY EFFICIENCY AT THE USE PHASE – The existing delegated acts establish energy labelling requirements for a wide range of consumer products. To date, the emphasis has been laid on the energy efficiency of products at the use phase. This focus on energy efficiency can be explained by the fact that labels are in practice developed together with ecodesign requirements, which still mainly focus on energy efficiency.[1920]

529. A FOCUS ON ENERGY EFFICIENCY VISIBLE ON THE LABEL – The emphasis on energy efficiency is also clearly visible on the label design. As described in Article 2(19) of the Energy Labelling Regulation, the label consists of "*a graphic diagram, either in printed or electronic form, including a closed scale using only letters from A to G, each letter representing a class and each class corresponding to energy savings, in seven different colours from dark green to red*". The scale is reinforced by the different lengths of arrows, which correspond to the different levels of energy efficiency (see Figure 6). As stated by the ECJ, the harmonisation of the design, the references contained on the energy label, as well as its simple and concise nature, are aimed at ensuring better legibility and comparability of the information contained on it for the benefit of the end-user.[1921] This goal seems to have been reached as several studies and surveys show that the

1919 Art. 13 Energy Labelling Regulation. See *infra*.
1920 See *supra*, n° 223.
1921 ECJ 25 July 2018, Case C-632/16, *Dyson* v *BSH*, *EU:C:2018:599*, para 37. See also recital 10 of the Energy Labelling Regulation.

energy label is a clear sign that is understood by most consumers and taken into consideration in purchasing decisions.[1922]

Figure 6. Examples of existing energy labels

Washing machines | Refrigerators | Electronic displays

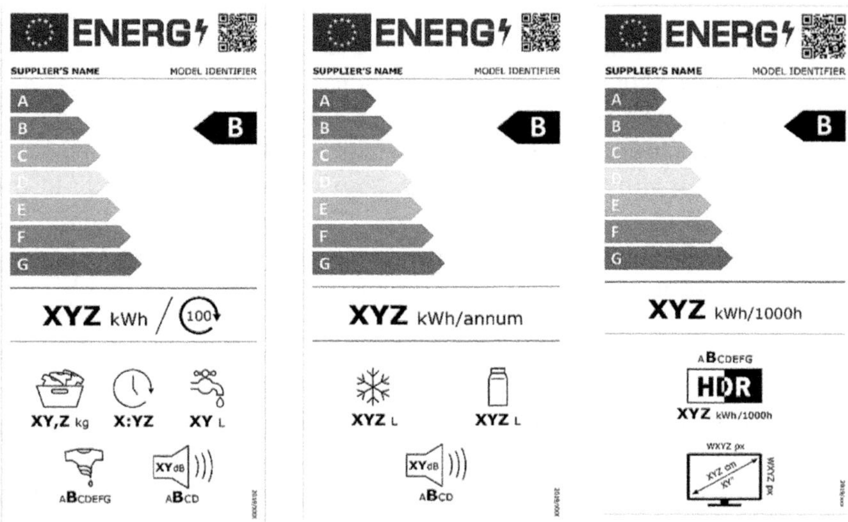

530. The energy efficiency scale – As highlighted in Article 16(3)(b), the A to G steps of the classification must correspond to significant energy and cost savings and appropriate product differentiation from the customer's perspective. The delegated act specifies how the A to G steps of the classification are displayed[1923], as well as the measurement and calculation methods to be used to determine label and product information sheet information, including the definition of the energy efficiency index or equivalent parameter.[1924] A rule of thumb when developing the energy label of a specific product group is not to show energy classes below the ecodesign minimum requirements. In situations where products no longer fall into class 'E', 'F' or 'G' because of ecodesign

[1922] According to a 2019 Eurobarometer, nearly 80% of the respondents recognise energy labelling and say the label had an influence on their choice of purchase. See also K. van den Akker, M. Elsen, *Study on consumer understanding of the energy label for air conditioners and heat pumps ≤ 12 kW – Draft final report* (European Commission 2018); M. Elshout, M. Elsen, *Study on the impact on consumer understanding and purchase decisions of energy labels for lighting products – Final report* (European Commission 2018); London Economics, *Study on the impact of the energy label – and potential changes to it – on consumer understanding and on purchase decisions* (European Commission 2014); P. Waide et al., *The new energy label: assessing consumer comprehension and effectiveness as a market transformation tool* (ECEEE 2013).

[1923] Art. 16(3)(b) Energy Labelling Regulation.

[1924] Art. 16(3)(k) Energy Labelling Regulation.

measures, recital 11 of the Regulation indicates that those classes should be shown on the label in grey. There may also be cases where a lower class might be needed for products that are not subject to ecodesign requirements but still labelled. However, as explained in a 2014 technical report evaluating the energy labelling rules, "*this should be envisaged only if there is a significant number of such products with significant market share and should be restricted to one or maximum two classes. In general, the benefits of showing the poor performance of these products are limited compared to the negative effects of many (almost) empty classes at the bottom on consumer understanding – especially given the fact that these products would be in the lowest class anyway*".[1925]

531. With information on energy consumption – To supplement the energy efficiency scale, the label of certain products also indicates, in a prominent position[1926], the absolute energy consumption so that "*customers can predict the direct impact of their choices on their energy bills*".[1927] The provision of this information is also aimed at avoiding the promotion of large appliances that reach higher label classes but do not correspond to consumer needs.[1928] Certain energy labels could indeed give consumers the wrong perception that an A label television with large screen diameter is as 'good' as a television with a smaller screen size, whereas it consumes considerably more energy.[1929] Labels could also lead consumers to buy a large washing machine when they would not use it at its full capacity. Despite its laudable goal, it appears that this more complex information on energy consumption is not well understood and thus disregarded by consumers.[1930] Besides information on energy consumption, it has been recommended to adopt stricter labelling requirements for products with bigger capacity.[1931]

532. Positive impacts on energy efficiency – The EU energy labelling legislation has proven to be an effective tool for energy efficiency. Since the adoption of energy labelling rules, the energy efficiency of regulated products has

---

1925 E. Molenbroek et al., *Evaluation of the Energy Labelling Directive and specific aspects of the Ecodesign Directive – Final technical report* (Ecofys 2014) p. 51.

1926 Art. 16(3)(b) of the Energy Labelling Regulation.

1927 Recital 10 of the Energy Labelling Regulation.

1928 Report from the Commission of 15 July 2015 to the European Parliament and the Council on the Review of Directive 2010/30/EU of the European Parliament and of the Council of 19 May 2010 on the indication of labelling and standard product information of the consumption of energy and other resources by energy-related products, COM(2015) 345 final, p. 3.

1929 E. Molenbroek et al., *Evaluation of the Energy Labelling Directive and specific aspects of the Ecodesign Directive – Final technical report* (Ecofys 2014) p. 134.

1930 S. Waechter, B. Sütterlin, M. Siegrist, 'Desired and undesired effects of energy labels – An eyetracking study', 10 *PLoS One* (2015) p. 1 at p. 26.

1931 See BEUC and ANEC paper of 25 June 2015 on Simplifying the EU Energy Label – Restoring the successful and well-understood closed A to G scheme, BEUC-X-2015-065, p. 12.

increased, leading to the need for rescaled labels for some product categories.[1932] While this increase could be explained by ongoing market trends in energy efficiency improvement independent of the policy, the case of vacuum cleaners clearly demonstrates the contribution of the Energy Labelling Regulation to product energy efficiency.[1933]

533. ... BUT NOT ON PRODUCT LIFETIME – As already highlighted in the previous chapter on ecodesign rules[1934], energy efficiency allows reducing the energy used by the products but has no role in tackling their premature obsolescence. It can even lead to shortening product lifetime by promoting the replacement of products with more energy-efficient ones. Moreover, imposing energy efficiency labelling on products may constitute a major obstacle to the development of the market for remanufactured products. However, although some remanufactured products consume a higher amount of energy during the use phase compared to new products, they can achieve significant energy savings and carbon emissions reduction thanks to their reduced consumption of energy in the production phase.[1935]

c) *Supplementary information on non-energy efficiency aspects*

534. SUPPLEMENTARY INFORMATION CONTAINED ON THE LABEL – In addition to the diagram on energy efficiency and information on energy consumption, Article 16(3)(c) of the Energy Labelling Regulation states that delegated acts related to specific product groups can specify, where appropriate, the use of other resources and supplementary information concerning the product. According to Article 2(24), 'supplementary information' means "*information, as specified in a delegated act, on the functional and environmental performance of a product*". Article 16(3)(c) of the Regulation lays down conditions that supplementary information must fulfil to be added to the label. The information must be unambiguous and with no negative impact on the clear intelligibility and effectiveness of the label towards customers. This issue relates to the risk of confusing and bombarding consumers with too much information. Moreover, information must be based on data relating to physical product characteristics that are measurable and verifiable by market surveillance authorities.

1932 The increase in energy efficiency is particularly visible on the television market. See the Staff Working Document of the European Commission of 1st October 2018 on Impact assessment accompanying the document Draft Commission Regulation laying down ecodesign requirements for electronic displays, SWD(2019) 354 final, p. 10.

1933 Before being regulated, energy use of vacuum cleaners was increasing rather than decreasing. See AEA Energy & Environment, *Work on Preparatory Studies for Eco-Design Requirements of EuPs – Lot 17 Vacuum Cleaners* (European Commission 2008).

1934 See *supra*, n° 226.

1935 Centre for Strategy & Evaluation Services (CSES), *Evaluation of the Ecodesign Directive (2009/125/EC) – Final Report* (European Commission 2012) p. 23.

535. THE USE OF PICTOGRAMS – Many existing labels display supplementary energy and non-energy information through pictograms (see Figure 6). This includes, for example, information about water used per washing cycle, storage capacity or noise emitted during the use of the product. These pieces of information are nonetheless less prominent than the energy scale on the label, as required by Article 16(3)(c). Moreover, they are sometimes given as absolute values only, without a comparative scale, even if this may well be possible. They are therefore less likely to guide consumers' choices than the energy efficiency scale.[1936] Studies have also reported that some icons were unclear or misunderstood by consumers, like the dish-drying performance icon or the on/off icon on the television label.[1937] All in all, the features of the pictograms may make the provision of supplementary information useless.

536. INFORMATION ON THE EU ECOLABEL – Other pieces of information can be conveyed by the label. Suppliers can add a copy of the EU Ecolabel awarded to their products on the energy label if the delegated act provides so. This was the case of the annulled delegated act on vacuum cleaners.[1938] Because some EU Ecolabels require products to meet certain requirements on product sustainability[1939], this additional information could give further indications on the product to consumers.

537. QR CODES AND OTHER MEANS OF INFORMATION – Consumers can also get additional information on products by scanning the QR code featured on the new energy labels with a common smartphone. Data is inserted by suppliers into the European Product Database for Energy Labelling (EPREL).[1940] So far, the database contains supplementary information on fridges, freezers, dishwashers, washing machines and electronic displays[1941], as well as on tyres[1942], and on

---

[1936] E. Molenbroek et al., *Evaluation of the Energy Labelling Directive and specific aspects of the Ecodesign Directive – Final technical report* (Ecofys 2014) p. 30.

[1937] E. Molenbroek et al., *Evaluation of the Energy Labelling Directive and specific aspects of the Ecodesign Directive – Final technical report* (Ecofys 2014) p. 82.

[1938] See Annex II to Commission Delegated Regulation (EU) No 665/2013 of 3 May 2013 supplementing Directive 2010/30/EU of the European Parliament and of the Council with regard to energy labelling of vacuum cleaners, OJ L 192, 13.7.2013, p. 1–23 (*no longer in force*).

[1939] See *infra*, n° 601 *et seq.*

[1940] See *infra* on the Obligation to register in a public database (n° 570–572).

[1941] See Commission Delegated Regulation (EU) 2021/340 of 17 December 2020 amending Delegated Regulations (EU) 2019/2013, (EU) 2019/2014, (EU) 2019/2015, (EU) 2019/2016, (EU) 2019/2017 and (EU) 2019/2018 with regard to energy labelling requirements for electronic displays, household washing machines and household washer-dryers, light sources, refrigerating appliances, household dishwashers, and refrigerating appliances with a direct sales function, OJ L 68, 26.2.2021, p. 62–107 (also called 'Energy Labelling Omnibus Regulation').

[1942] Art. 5 of the Regulation (EU) 2020/740 of the European Parliament and of the Council of 25 May 2020 on the labelling of tyres with respect to fuel efficiency and other parameters, amending Regulation (EU) 2017/1369 and repealing Regulation (EC) No 1222/2009, OJ L 177, 5.6.2020, p. 1–31.

lamps.[1943] For example, consumers can get information on the minimum guaranteed availability of spare parts as well as software and firmware updates (from the date of end of the placement on the market) for electronic displays. This information tool seems very promising as it allows consumers eager to get more detailed information on their products to easily access this information. In addition to the QR code, the private sector and different NGOs are developing apps that could further assist consumers in their purchase choice (e.g. by helping to calculate the return costs and compare different products). These technological solutions enable the communication of large amounts of data in small format with the advantage of giving access to further information to those interested while leaving the label simple and clear for others.

d) No existing supplementary information on product sustainability

538. No supplementary information on product sustainability, though possible – No existing delegated acts refer to product sustainability aspects, such as durability or reparability. Yet, as highlighted by the EC, it is possible to adopt such specific information requirements under the Energy Labelling Regulation as supplementary information.[1944] Although the initial proposal of the Regulation was clearer on that point[1945], the possibility of considering product durability as supplementary information is confirmed by recital 36, which explicitly refers to durability as supplementary information. Even if no such reference is made for product reparability or any other sustainability aspects, it is safe to say that the broad definition of 'supplementary information' also encompasses these notions as they allow for maintaining the product function. Hence, specific information requirements on product sustainability can be envisaged under this Regulation, provided that they meet the conditions set out in Article 16(3)(c).

539. A (growing) divergence with ecodesign regulations – The current absence of information on product sustainability makes the Energy Labelling Regulation and its delegated acts deviate from the requirements established within the framework of the Ecodesign Directive. While some ecodesign requirements concern among others product durability (e.g. minimum operational motor

[1943] Art. 3 of the Commission Delegated Regulation (EU) 2019/2015 of 11 March 2019 supplementing Regulation (EU) 2017/1369 of the European Parliament and of the Council with regard to energy labelling of light sources and repealing Commission Delegated Regulation (EU) No 874/2012, OJ L 315, 5.12.2019, p. 68–101.

[1944] See the Communication from the European Commission of 2 December 2015 to the European Parliament, the Council, the European Economic and Social Committee and the Committee of the Regions on Closing the loop – An EU action plan for the circular economy, COM(2015) 614 final, p. 6.

[1945] See Art. 2(20) of the Proposal for a Regulation of the European Parliament and of the Council setting a framework for energy efficiency labelling and repealing Directive 2010/30/EU, COM(2015) 341 final.

lifetime of vacuum cleaners) and product reparability (e.g. availability of spare parts of dishwashers)[1946], these requirements have not been integrated into the mandatory energy labels. One of the main reasons for focusing on energy performance seems to be the fear of diluting the energy performance information and bombarding consumers with too much information.[1947] Although this reason may be valid, it seems unreasonable to exclude the introduction of information on product sustainability on those grounds.

540. Towards an EU labelling of product sustainability – Interestingly, the EC already suggested in 1993 that "*a final solution (...) would be to require stating, on the product label, the period during which the manufacturer commits himself to stocking spare parts. The advantage here would be to ensure market transparency and giving free rein to competition without requiring manufacturers to respect specific time limits*".[1948] In its first Circular Economy Action Plan, the EC stated that "*it will specifically consider durability information in future Energy Labelling measures*".[1949] Such an idea was reiterated in the 2020 Circular Economy Action Plan, where the EC confirmed that it will consider "*setting minimum requirements for sustainability labels/logos and for information tools*".[1950] The Preparatory study for the Ecodesign and Energy Labelling Working Plan 2022–2024 goes in that direction, recommending the introduction of labelling requirements on durability (in its broader sense).[1951] Furthermore, the idea of an EU-wide reparability score has recently been embodied in the Proposal for a Directive on empowering consumers for the green transition.[1952] Finally, it is interesting to note that the mandatory label of textiles, which is

---

1946 For more examples of such ecodesign requirements, see Chapter II on the design and production stage, and more specifically n° 231 *et seq*.

1947 For more details, see E. Molenbroek et al., *Evaluation of the Energy Labelling Directive and specific aspects of the Ecodesign Directive – Final technical report* (Ecofys 2014) p. 99.

1948 See Green Paper from the European Commission of 15 November 1993 on Guarantees for Consumer Goods and After-sales Services, COM(93) 509 final, p. 100.

1949 Communication from the European Commission of 2 December 2015 to the European Parliament, the Council, the European Economic and Social Committee and the Committee of the Regions on Closing the loop – An EU action plan for the circular economy, COM(2015) 614 final, p. 8.

1950 Communication from the Commission of 11 March 2020 to the European Parliament, the Council, the European Economic and Social Committee and the Committee of the Regions on A new Circular Economy Action Plan – For a cleaner and more competitive Europe, COM(2020) 98 final, p. 5.

1951 Viegand Maagøe, Oeko-Institut, VHK, *Preparatory study for the Ecodesign and Energy Labelling Working Plan 2020–2024 – Task 4 Complementary analyses and recommendations for the Ecodesign and Energy Labelling Working Plan 2020–2024 – Final* (European Commission 2021) p. 67. In this study, 'product durability' is understood as encompassing the "*reliability, maintenance, repair, upgrade and reuse of products*". See Viegand Maagøe, Oeko-Institut, VHK, *Preparatory study for the Ecodesign and Energy Labelling Working Plan 2020–2024 – Task 4 Complementary analyses and recommendations for the Ecodesign and Energy Labelling Working Plan 2020–2024 – Final* (European Commission 2021) p. 56.

1952 See Art. 2(2)(b) and (3)(b) of the Proposal for a Directive on empowering consumers for the green transition.

regulated by Regulation (EU) No 1007/2011[1953], should also be reviewed in the near future.[1954]

541. An EU mandatory label on product sustainability should be developed – As previously highlighted in this chapter, the disclosure of information on product sustainability (including aspects related to the three strategies of resisting, postponing and reversing premature obsolescence)[1955] through product labelling can make a substantial contribution to the promotion of sustainable products at the time of purchase. Several studies have already examined the influence of labels with information on durability and reparability on consumer purchasing decisions and the perceived quality of products. Although some side effects were observed for reparability labels[1956], these studies confirmed that, albeit to different extents[1957], both durability and reparability labels effectively guide consumers' choices towards more sustainable products. A 2016 ILLC study on lifespan labelling showed that, on average, sales of products with a label showing a longer lifespan than competing products increased by 13.8%.[1958] More than influencing consumer behaviour and decisions, such a labelling scheme would also encourage businesses to provide more sustainable products.[1959] Since the Energy Labelling Regulation allows for information on

1953 Regulation (EU) No 1007/2011 of the European Parliament and of the Council of 27 September 2011 on textile fibre names and related labelling and marking of the fibre composition of textile products and repealing Council Directive 73/44/EEC and Directives 96/73/EC and 2008/121/EC of the European Parliament and of the Council, OJ L 272, 18.10.2011, p. 1–64.

1954 Communication from the Commission of 30 March 2022 to the European Parliament, the Council, the European Economic and Social Committee and the Committee of the Regions on the EU Strategy for Sustainable and Circular Textiles, COM(2022) 141 final, p. 5.

1955 See *supra* on the Different types of information on product sustainability (n° 320–323).

1956 Reparability labels are sometimes perceived in a negative way as some consumers thought that the product would break more often. See R. van den Berge, L. Magnier, R. Mugge, 'A poorly educated guess: consumers' lifetime estimations, attitudes towards repairability, and a product lifetime label', in C. Fitzpatrick (eds.), *4th international Product Lifetimes and the Environment (PLATE) conference proceedings* (Limerick 2021) p. 641 at p. 646.

1957 The extent of the effects of labels on consumer behaviour depends on various factors, including the product concerned, its price, its brand, the consumer profile and the form of the label.

1958 See SIRCOME agency, the University of South Brittany and the University of South Bohemia, *The Influence of Lifespan Labelling on Consumers – ILLC study* (EESC 2016). See also B. Dupont, V. Swaen, J. Vanhamme, *Labelling the durability of a product through the lens of intertemporal choices theory* (European Marketing Academy Conference 2015); V. Swaen, *Labelling the durability/reparability of a product* (EESC Conference on Tackling premature obsolescence in Europe 2018); P. Munten, J. Vanhamme, 'Fighting Planned Obsolescence Practices and Excessive Consumption: The Positive Effect of Pre-Purchase Product Reparability Communication on Consumers' Attitude', 47 *Advances in Consumer Research* (2019) p. 776; M. Elsen, K. van den Akker, R. van Giesen, T. Meeusen, S. Davidson, D. Anné, T. van der Linden, R. van de Meulengraaf, *Consumer study on the impact of reparability information formats on consumer understanding and purchase decisions – Final report* (European Union 2021) p. 57.

1959 See *supra* on the barriers that hamper the transition towards sustainable consumption patterns (n° 325–328).

product sustainability to be included in the energy label of specific products, the development of such labelling requirements should be envisaged through this existing scheme (see #6). This is, however, not the only option to establish an EU mandatory label on product sustainability, as shown by the following paragraphs of this section.[1960]

542. In coordination with the ecodesign legislation – In any case, the labelling of product sustainability information should be made in coordination with the ecodesign legislation, for which gradually including requirements on resource and material efficiency is envisaged.[1961] There are two ways of coordinating the energy labelling and ecodesign scheme (see #7).[1962] The first option would consist in setting minimum requirements on product sustainability under the ecodesign regulations, whereas labelling criteria would allow consumers to choose among legally compliant products according to their sustainable characteristics. The second option would be to consider labelling as an alternative when it is not appropriate or too complex to set mandatory requirements related to product sustainability through ecodesign regulations. Although mandatory labelling requirements alone are less restrictive than mandatory ecodesign requirements, the former are still binding on producers, who are obliged to comply with what is indicated on the label. These options are not mutually exclusive but complementary. The choice between the two options may depend on the product categories and the sustainability aspects. The combination of these two options can be particularly powerful against premature obsolescence as it allows regulating a wider range of products.

Policy recommendations:

> *#6 Information on product sustainability should be conveyed through an EU mandatory label.*
>
> *#7 If possible, this EU mandatory label on product sustainability should correspond to the minimum requirements on product sustainability under the ecodesign regulations. If no ecodesign regulations covers the specific product group or the sustainability aspect in question, the label could be adopted as an alternative.*

1960 See *infra* on the possible future labelling on product sustainability (n° 543).

1961 See Chapter II on the design and production stage, and more specifically n° 229 *et seq.*

1962 These two options were identified in E. Maitre-Ekern and C. Dalhammar, 'Regulating planned obsolescence: a review of legal approaches to increase product durability and reparability in Europe', 25 *Review of European Community & International Environmental Law* (2016) p. 386.

4. POSSIBLE FUTURE LABELLING ON PRODUCT SUSTAINABILITY ASPECTS

a) *Different ways of labelling product sustainability*

543. As supplementary information, on a distinct label or through an extension of the energy label – Three options can be envisaged for product sustainability labelling. The first option is to convey the pieces of information on EU energy labels as supplementary information. The Environmental Coalition on Standards (ECOS) put this idea forward with its project called 'Energy labelling should go circular'. According to this project, the label on energy efficiency could be complemented by a durability indicator (based on software updates, expected lifetime of the product or its parts, years of warranty), a reparability score (based on availability of spare parts, instructions) and other pieces of information (e.g. water consumption, noise, green-house gases, toxicity).[1963] As for the second option, it would consist in developing a distinct EU mandatory label on product sustainability, like a distinct reparability scoring index. The third option is a compromise option, which would consist in reviewing the Energy Labelling Regulation so that it no longer focuses primarily on energy efficiency but broadens the focus to include product sustainability. This option corresponds to the suggestion made by E. Maitre-Ekern, M. B. Taylor, M. van der Velden, which is to go beyond the mere integration of product durability and reparability information as supplementary information on the EU energy label and replace the current Energy Labelling Regulation by a 'Sustainable Labelling Regulation' that would apply to all products.[1964]

544. An extension of the EU energy label to product sustainability should be preferred – Although the three options are worth considering, the compromise option, which corresponds to the review of the Energy Labelling Regulation, should be preferred (see #8). First, it would be easier to implement as it is based on an already existing framework. Second, adding supplementary information on product sustainability to the energy labels is less likely to create information overload for consumers compared to the introduction of another label on products. Third, giving the same weight to energy efficiency and product sustainability on the label would raise greater public awareness on the importance of product durability, reparability and other sustainable aspects. The first option, which suggests the integration of product sustainability information on the EU energy label as supplementary information, could be implemented

---

1963 See the ECOS postcard, available on: <https://ecostandard.org/wp-content/uploads/Energy-Label-should-go-circular.pdf>.

1964 E. Maitre-Ekern, M. B. Taylor, M. van der Velden, 'Towards a Sustainable Circular Economy: SMART reform proposals', 12 *University of Oslo Faculty of Law Research Paper* (2020) p. 33.

as an intermediary step (see #9). This could be done, first, for products already covered by delegated acts.

Proposed review of the Energy Labelling Regulation:

> *#8 The focus of the Energy Labelling Regulation should be broadened from 'energy' labelling to 'sustainability' labelling.*

Example:

REGULATION (EU) XXXX/XXXX OF THE EUROPEAN PARLIAMENT AND OF THE COUNCIL

of X/X/X

setting a framework for ~~energy~~ **sustainability** labelling and repealing Regulation (EU) 2017/1369

(...)

Article 1
Subject-matter and scope

1. This Regulation (...) provides for the labelling of those products and the provision of standard product information regarding **sustainability**, energy efficiency, the consumption of energy and of other resources by products during use and supplementary information concerning products, thereby enabling customers to choose more **sustainable and** efficient products in order to reduce their ~~energy consumption~~ **environmental impact**.

(...)

Article 2
Definitions

For the purposes of this Regulation the following definitions apply:

(...)

(16a) 'sustainability' means the ability of a product to reach its optimal lifetime, which depends among others on its durability, ease of maintenance, upgradability, reparability, refurbishment and remanufacturing.

(...)

AS AN INTERMEDIARY STEP

> *#9 Product sustainability information should be integrated on the EU energy label as supplementary information.*

545. Directly disclosed or through indexes – When disclosed through labels, items of information related to product sustainability could either be selected to appear separately on the label or they could be combined and serve as parameters for indexes on product durability and reparability, like in France.[1965] It had been suggested, for example, to include a more global aggregated environmental index, such as the Product Environmental Footprint (PEF), on the energy label.[1966] The 2020 draft report dedicated to 'durability' and issued within the context of the Working Plan 2022–2024, provides a list of "*potential durability measures related to consumer information/labelling*", including the introduction of a reparability scoring index, the product-specific labelling of minimum lifetime and the average statistical parameters on reliability/failure rates.[1967] The project 'Energy label should go circular' issued by ECOS combines some of these ideas.[1968]

546. Pictograms and scales – Concerning their forms, these new items of information can be conveyed by pictograms, together with absolute values or a comparative scale. Comparing these different forms of labels, the ILLC study on lifespan labelling demonstrated that consumers' purchasing decisions were particularly influenced by the lifespan labels with a scale from A to G (20,4%) and displaying the minimum useful lifetime (14,1%) compared to other labels (+ 11.4% for the label displaying the cost per year and + 9% for the label displaying the minimum lifespan in years). The same conclusion on the effectiveness of comparative scales was reached for indications on product reparability.[1969] Such a conclusion supports the approach followed by the French legislature with its reparability index.[1970] These studies nonetheless reported that an additional colour-coded scale was also likely to bring confusion among consumers with the existing colour-coded energy efficiency scale.[1971]

1965 *See infra*, n° 554–563.

1966 E. Molenbroek et al., *Evaluation of the Energy Labelling Directive and specific aspects of the Ecodesign Directive – Final technical report* (Ecofys 2014) p. 33.

1967 Viegand Maagøe, VHK and Oeko-Institut, *Preparatory study for the Ecodesign and Energy Labelling Working Plan 2020–2024 – Task 3 Preliminary analysis of product groups and horizontal initiatives – Durability – Draft report* (European Commission 2020) pp. 26–27. See also the Communication from the Commission on the Ecodesign and Energy Labelling Working Plan 2022–2024, OJ C 182, 4.5.2022, p. 7.

1968 See *supra*, n° 543.

1969 M. Elsen, K. van den Akker, R. van Giesen, T. Meeusen, S. Davidson, D. Anné, T. van der Linden, R. van de Meulengraaf, *Consumer study on the impact of reparability information formats on consumer understanding and purchase decisions – Final report* (European Union 2021) p. 57.

1970 See *infra*, n° 554 *et seq.*

1971 SIRCOME agency, the University of South Brittany and the University of South Bohemia, *The Influence of Lifespan Labelling on Consumers – ILLC study* (EESC 2016) p. 76; M. Elsen et al., *Consumer study on the impact of reparability information formats on consumer understanding and purchase decisions – Final report* (European Union 2021) p. 8.

547. GLOBAL INDEXES WITH A COMPARATIVE SCALE AND STRONG VISUAL SHOULD BE PREFERRED – Global indexes with a comparative scale and strong visual emphasizing these new pieces of information on product sustainability seem very promising and should therefore be preferred (see #10).[1972] As an alternative, or as an intermediary step, information related to product sustainability could be selected to appear directly on the label (see #11). If using indexes, the different environmental impacts and criteria used for the scoring matrix should be transparent and indicate the factors included in the labelling criteria. The QR code could be used to provide more detail to information-hungry consumers. This would avoid diluting the energy performance information and overwhelming consumers with information. To exploit the full potential of these additional pieces of information, the EC should carry out studies on consumer understanding, perceptions and behaviours, before adopting or reviewing energy labels, as it did for heaters.[1973] Labels on sustainability aspects should be understandable and straightforward, like the one conveying information on energy efficiency.[1974] This would ensure that consumers consider this information when buying a product. In any case, it is crucial to accompany the introduction of such labels by educational and promotional information campaigns, as already emphasized in Article 7(3) of the Energy Labelling Regulation.[1975]

548. PROVIDED TOGETHER OR ALTERNATIVELY, DEPENDING ON THE PRODUCT – Information on product sustainability aspects should not necessarily appear on all existing and future labels. Some of these pieces of information may be required only for certain types of products, whereas others can apply horizontally. In this regard, similar reasoning can be held as for product design, for which a distinction could be made between workhorse, investment and up-to-date products.[1976] For instance, durability labels would be less appropriate for products that are replaced due to technological development with a high rate of innovation (e.g. mobile phones) or due to changing fashions (e.g. video games).[1977] A durability index could also be envisaged for product parts, like laptop batteries or for software support.[1978] The adoption of specific

[1972] Such a suggestion had already been made in E. Molenbroek et al., *Evaluation of the Energy Labelling Directive and specific aspects of the Ecodesign Directive – Final technical report* (Ecofys 2014) p. 33.

[1973] K. van den Akker, M. Elsen, *Study on consumer understanding of the energy label for air conditioners and heat pumps ≤ 12 kW – Draft final report* (European Commission 2019).

[1974] See *supra*, n° 529.

[1975] See also M. Elsen et al., *Consumer study on the impact of reparability information formats on consumer understanding and purchase decisions – Final report* (European Union 2021) p. 58.

[1976] See *supra*, n° 169.

[1977] See also SIRCOME agency, the University of South Brittany and the University of South Bohemia, *The Influence of Lifespan Labelling on Consumers – ILLC study* (EESC 2016) pp. 84–85.

[1978] For example, the EU energy label could include ratings for battery life based on the number of cycles at which 80% of initial capacity is still achieved. See E. Oldyrevas, C. McAlister, *Long*

information requirements on product sustainability could also be restricted to certain (categories of) products before widening (or not) their scope of application to other products. This approach has been followed in France, where the reparability index has been introduced only for electrical and electronic equipment, starting with washing machines, smartphones, laptops, televisions and lawn mowers.[1979]

549. A PRODUCT-SPECIFIC ANALYSIS NEEDS TO BE CARRIED OUT – A product-specific analysis needs to be conducted within the framework of future preparatory studies to determine which product categories should be prioritised (including those not yet covered by the energy labelling scheme) and which product sustainability aspects should be indicated on the label of these specific products (see #12). The studies conducted within the framework of the Working Plan 2022–2024, as well as other studies like the ICT Impact study[1980], provide valuable insight on this. The labelling of product sustainability could be developed in parallel with ecodesign requirements, starting with products that are already subject to ecodesign requirements on product sustainability, although labels could also be affixed to products that are not covered by ecodesign regulations.

Policy recommendations

#10 Information on product sustainability should preferably be conveyed through global indexes with a comparative scale and strong visual.

#11 As an alternative or as an intermediary step, information related to product sustainability could be selected to appear directly on the label.

#12 A product-specific analysis should be conducted to determine:

- *which product categories should be prioritised (including those not yet covered by the energy labelling scheme);*
- *which product sustainability aspects should be indicated on the label of these specific products.*

b) Methods for assessing product sustainability aspects

550. THREE MAIN METHODOLOGICAL CHALLENGES – It is critical that law makers impose the methods to assess product sustainability aspects, such as product

live the machine – How ecodesign & energy labelling can prevent premature obsolescence of laptops (Ecos 2020) pp. 24–25.

1979 Art. 16 of the Anti-Waste Law. For further details, see *infra*, n° 560.

1980 See *supra*, n° 521.

durability and reparability. Otherwise, information may be prone to confusion, not transparent and difficult to compare for businesses and consumers.[1981] In comparison with the energy efficiency index and its quantitative method[1982], the measurement and calculation methods to determine product sustainability is more complex to develop. Three main challenges occur in the establishment of an objective, reliable, comparable and verifiable tool to assess and determine the environmental performance of products. The first challenge relates to the increasing complexity and variety of product design. Although some criteria can be used for all products, the methodology should be adapted to the specificities of any product on the market. Secondly, assessing product sustainability aspects such as durability and reparability may be tricky as it may depend on parameters that cannot be tested in laboratories (e.g. availability of spare parts). The third major challenge for durability labels stems from the variations in how consumers look after their products which can result in considerable differences in product lifespan depending on the household.[1983] This issue could affect the credibility of the durability label in consumers' eyes as they may not trust or identify the method used to calculate product durability. The definition of the methodology would be more challenging if indexes were favoured over the mere display of certain information, like information on the time of storing spare parts, which can easily be determined and communicated on the market.

551. Methods proposed in EU standards – As was already reported in the previous chapter, a wide array of possible methodologies exists for measuring product sustainability aspects.[1984] First, many methodologies have been developed in the series of new horizontal standards on material efficiency. More specifically, the standard on information relating to material efficiency aspects proposes a methodology intended to support the determination of strategies to communicate information on these aspects.[1985] This standard is to be read in conjunction with the standards on durability[1986] and the one on the ability to repair, reuse and upgrade[1987], which give among others harmonised test

1981 See also RDC Environment, *L'obsolescence programmée: politiques et mesures belges de protection du consommateur* (2017) pp. 129–130 and pp. 151–152.

1982 Quantitative methods use measurable data to calculate an index or metric. See Bracquené et al., *Repairability criteria for energy related products – Study in the BeNeLux context to evaluate the options to extend the product life time* (KU Leuven, Vito, BeNeLux 2018) p. 20.

1983 J. Cox et al., 'Consumer understanding of product lifetimes', 79 *Resources, Conservation and Recycling* (2013) p. 27.

1984 See *supra*, n° 236 and 244 on the methods for assessing product durability and n° 265 on those for assessing product reparability.

1985 CEN-CENELEC TC10, Methods for providing information relating to material efficiency aspects of energy-related products, EN 45559:2019.

1986 CEN-CENELEC TC10, General method for the assessment of the durability of energy-related products, EN 45552:2020.

1987 CEN-CENELEC TC10, General methods for the assessment of the ability to repair, reuse and upgrade energy-related products, EN 45554:2020.

standards and calculation methodologies to assess and validate the 'technical' lifetime and reparability of specific energy-related products. For example, the standard related to product repair explains that *"assessments of reparability can take place at three levels, at part level, at product level and in terms of the service that accompanies the product"*.[1988] An example of a scoring system that assesses the ability of a product to be repaired, reused and/or upgraded can be found in Annex A to the standard on the ability to repair, reuse and upgrade.[1989] According to this scoring system, products may be classified for example on the basis of their disassembly depth, the availability of information, tools and spare parts, their diagnostic support and interfaces and the existence of return options. Together, these standards can be used to develop a scoring system on product sustainability aspects.

552. Methods developed in studies – Besides these standards, a second important support can be found in studies, some of which focused on specific products.[1990] These studies define notions and parameters that could be useful when determining product durability and reparability. Interesting studies on the methodology can also be found at national level.[1991] Concerning more particularly product reparability, a 2019 EU study specifically analysed and developed a possible scoring system to rate and provide information about the

---

[1988] For further details, see CEN-CENELEC TC10, General methods for the assessment of the ability to repair, reuse and upgrade energy related products, EN 45554:2019, p. 9.

[1989] See pt. A.4 of the Annex A to CEN-CENELEC TC10, General methods for the assessment of the ability to repair, reuse and upgrade energy related products, EN 45554:2019, p. 14 at p. 29.

[1990] See for ex. S. Boulos et al. (Ricardo-AEA), *The durability of products – Standard assessment for the circular economy under the Eco-Innovation Action Plan* (European Union 2015); S. Bobba, F. Ardente, F. Mathieux, *Technical support for Environmental Footprinting, material efficiency in product policy and the European Platform on LCA: Durability assessment of vacuum cleaners – JRC Science and Policy Report* (European Commission 2015); P. Tecchio, F. Ardente, F. Mathieux, *Analysis of durability, reusability and reparability: Application to dishwashers and washing machines – JRC Technical Report* (European Commission 2016); F. Alfieri et al., *Durability assessment of products: analysis and testing of washing machines – JRC Technical Report* (European Commission 2018); J. Sanfelix, M. Cordella, F. Alfieri, *Methods for the Assessment of the Reparability and Upgradability of Energy-related Products: Application to TVs – JRC Technical Report* (European Commission 2019); M. Cordella, F. Alfieri, J. Sanfelix, *Guidance for the Assessment of Material Efficiency: Application to Smartphones – JRC Technical Report* (European Commission 2020).

[1991] See e.g. in Belgium: Bracquené et al., *Repairability criteria for energy related products – Study in the BeNeLux context to evaluate the options to extend the product life time* (KU Leuven, Vito, BeNeLux 2018). In France, see the studies conducted within the framework of the new French voluntary label on environmental characteristics: ADEME, RDC Environment, *Modélisation et évaluation environnementale de produits de consommation et biens d'équipement* (2019); ADEME, *Mise en œuvre de l'affichage environnemental des produits et services* (République française 2020). In Germany, see: F. Keimeyer et al., *Weiterentwicklung von Strategien gegen Obsoleszenz einschließlich rechtlicher Instrumente – Abschlussbericht* (Umweltbundesamt 2020).

ability to repair and upgrade products.[1992] The existing ecodesign requirements on product sustainability aspects that were developed on the basis of some of these studies may serve as a benchmark for the development of sustainability labels.

553. Inspiration from existing labels – Third, experience could be drawn from existing labels related to product sustainability, such as the French reparability and durability indexes[1993], the *iFixit* scorecard standard[1994], and the Austrian standard ONR 192102 developed for household appliances and consumer electronics.[1995] For example, the *iFixit* score takes into account the difficulty of opening the device, the types of fasteners, the degree of complexity of the replacement of major components, the availability of service manuals, the use of non-proprietary tools and component modularity. Labels from other sectors could serve as additional sources of inspiration. For example, one could imagine calculating product durability or reparability using a scientifically validated algorithm, like for the French Nutri-score affixed to food products.[1996] This front-of-pack label follows an 'across-the-board' approach, whereby all foods are considered using the same criteria. Specific criteria are used in specific food groups (i.e. cheese, added fat, and beverages) where the original algorithm did not accurately reflect the observed variability in nutritional values within these groups. It should be noted though that it may be more difficult to calculate product sustainability, which encompasses some hypotheses (e.g. product failure rates), compared to the nutritional composition of food products, which can be accurately measured based on data in laboratories.[1997] In addition to this Nutri-score, the Eco-score, which measures the environmental impact of food based

1992 M. Cordella, F. Alfieri, J. Sanfelix, *Analysis and development of a scoring system for repair and upgrade of products – Final Report* (European Commission 2019).

1993 See *infra*, n° 554 *et seq.*

1994 See <https://www.ifixit.com/>. For example, repairability scores have been developed for smartphones (https://www.ifixit.com/smartphone-repairability) and laptop (https://www.ifixit.com/laptop-repairability).

1995 The Austrian standard awards points to products that can be easily repaired, resulting in a 'good', 'very good' or 'excellent' score.

1996 See <https://www.santepubliquefrance.fr/determinants-de-sante/nutrition-et-activite-physique/articles/nutri-score>. Many studies confirmed the effectiveness of the Nutri-score algorithm. See for ex. C. Julia, C. Méjean, M. Touvier, S. Péneau, C. Lassale, P. Ducrot, S. Hercberg, E. Kesse-Guyot, 'Validation of the FSA nutrient profiling system dietary index in French adults – findings from SUVIMAX study', 55 *European Journal of Nutrition* (2016) p. 1901 at p. 1910; C. Romero Ferreiro, D. Lora Pablos, A. Gómez de la Cámara, 'Two Dimensions of Nutritional Value: Nutri-Score and NOVA', 13 *Nutrients* (2021) 2783. All the relevant studies are available on: <https://solidarites-sante.gouv.fr/prevention-en-sante/preserver-sa-sante/nutrition/nutri-score/etudes-et-rapports-scientifiques/article/etudes-sur-la-validation-de-l-algorithme-du-nutri-score-en-france>.

1997 N. Bériot, L. Farrant, 'L'information des consommateurs sur l'impact environnemental des produits: le cas des industries agroalimentaires', 73 *Annales des Mines- Responsabilité et Environnement* (2014) p. 37.

on an LCA approach, could also be inspiring.[1998] Conversely, certain labels show negative experience that should not be followed, like the Directive on the CO_2 emission label for cars, which shows the need to establish a common methodology, otherwise resulting in a variety of classification approaches (absolute, relative, no classification), which in some cases undermines consumer understanding.[1999]

c) *Drawing inspiration from the French reparability and durability indexes*

554. The French reparability and durability indexes – When developing the EU mandatory label on product sustainability, inspiration could be drawn from French law, which already imposes such labels. Article 16 of the Anti-Waste Law amended the French Environmental Code to introduce, in the first instance, a reparability index and, in the second instance, a durability index.[2000]

555. First step: a reparability index for electrical and electronic equipment – Since 1st January 2021, producers, importers, distributors or other marketers of electrical and electronic equipment must communicate without charge to sellers of their products and to any person who requests it the index of reparability of the equipment as well as the criteria used to establish it. Sellers of electrical and electronic equipment as well as those using a website, platform or any other online distribution channel in the context of their commercial activity in France, must inform consumers of this reparability index at the time of purchase.[2001] The provision of this information to consumers must be made free of charge and through marking, labelling, posting or any other appropriate means, based on the same mechanism as energy labelling.[2002] This information must also be provided by producers or importers within 15 days at anyone's request for a period of at least two years after the last unit of an equipment model has been placed on the market.[2003] The objective is to prolong useful product lifetime and limit the extraction of new resources.[2004] The value

1998 Art. 7 Loi n° 2021-1104 du 22 août 2021 portant lutte contre le dérèglement climatique et renforcement de la résilience face à ses effets, JORF n°0196 du 24 août 2021.

1999 Commission Staff Working Document of 20 July 2016 on the Evaluation of Directive 1999/94/EC relating to the availability of consumer information on fuel economy and CO_2 emissions in respect of the marketing of new passenger cars ('car labelling Directive'), SWD(2016) 270 final, p. 17; C. Brannigan et al., *Technical analysis of measures to improve consumer awareness of emissions and fuel consumption of vehicles* (European Union 2021) p. 134.

2000 See Art. L. 541-9-2 Code de l'environnement.

2001 The detail of the index must be made available to the consumer by the seller at the time of purchase and by the manufacturer on request, for each model concerned.

2002 The digitalisation of information, like via QR code, can be seen as an 'appropriate means'.

2003 Art. R. 541-212.-V Code de l'environnement.

2004 See the explanatory memorandum related to Projet de loi relatif à la lutte contre le gaspillage et à l'économie circulaire, adopted by the Sénat on 30 September 2019, n° 2274.

of the reparability label was fostered by the 2021 Law that aims to reduce the environmental footprint of digital technology, which requires public authorities to take the label into account in public procurements.[2005]

556. An idea dating back to the Energy Transition Act – This idea had already been developed during the adoption process of the Energy Transition Act in 2014. The French legislature wanted to make information on product lifetime compulsory for any product with a value equivalent to 30% of the growth-indexed minimum wage (with an assessment method provided by the law).[2006] The final version of the text was less ambitious, merely encouraging professionals to carry out, on a voluntary basis, experiments on giving information on product lifetime to consumers to foster longer use of products.[2007] Afterwards, studies showed the difficulties of measuring and labelling product lifetime and favoured the concept of reparability instead, which was already used by some companies.[2008] Consequently, the Roadmap (*Feuille de route*) from 2018 which listed measures to foster circular economy, focused on information on product reparability.[2009] This *Feuille de route* served as a basis for the adoption of Article 16 of the Anti-Waste Law.

557. A calculation based on five criteria – The implementing decree defines the criteria and the method of calculation retained for the establishment of the reparability index. According to Article R. 541–210 and Article R. 541–214.-I of the Environmental Code, electrical and electronic equipment are marked out of ten (see Figure 7) on the basis of five criteria: (1) the availability period of technical documentation and advice on use and maintenance (for professionals and consumers), (2) the ease of product disassembly, which refers to the number of steps necessary to have access to components and parts and to the characteristics of the tools and fasteners, (3) the availability period of spare parts and the delivery time (for professionals and consumers), (4) the ratio between the selling price of spare parts and the selling price of the product and (5) other criteria specific to the product category concerned.[2010] More practical details

[2005] Art. 15 of the Law on the Environmental Footprint of Digital Technology.

[2006] Art. 19 II 1° Projet de loi relatif à la transition énergétique pour la croissance verte, adopted by the Assemblée Nationale on 14 October 2014, TA n° 412.

[2007] Art. L. 541–1 I 2° Code de l'environnement.

[2008] Rapport fait au nom de la Commission de l'aménagement du territoire et du développement durable (1) sur le projet de loi (PROCÉDURE ACCÉLÉRÉE) relatif à la lutte contre le gaspillage et à l'économie circulaire, 17 Septembre 2019, n° 727, p. 23.

[2009] Ministère de la Transition Ecologique et Solidaire, *Feuille de route économie circulaire: 50 mesures pour une économie 100% circulaire* (République française 2018) p. 19.

[2010] These criteria correspond to those initially proposed in Rapport fait au nom de la Commission de l'aménagement du territoire et du développement durable (1) sur le projet de loi (PROCÉDURE ACCÉLÉRÉE) relatif à la lutte contre le gaspillage et à l'économie circulaire, 17 Septembre 2019, n° 727, pp. 23–24.

on these criteria are provided in the implementing decree.[2011] The reparability index is obtained by adding the five scores obtained (which are calculated out of twenty) and then by dividing the total by ten to express a synthetic score on a scale from 1 to 10.[2012] In addition to these criteria, Article L. 541–9–2.-I of the Environmental Code states that the presence of a usage meter visible to the consumer must also serve as a criterion for developing the reparability index, whenever relevant.

Figure 7. Label relating to the reparability index

558. Specifically defined for each product category – For every category of electrical and electronic equipment covered, an implementing decree (*arrêté des ministres*) specifies all criteria and sub-criteria, including category-specific criteria, and how the reparability index is calculated.[2013] Work has been organised per product category and per sector working group with participants from manufacturers, retailers, business associations, environmental NGOs, consumer organisations, repair sector organisations, remanufacturing organisations and administrations. The objective was to identify shared standards between companies of the same sector. The first product categories subject to the reparability index are washing machines[2014], smartphones[2015], laptops[2016], televisions[2017], and lawn mowers.[2018] It should be noted that the

---

2011 Arrêté du 29 décembre 2020 relatif aux modalités d'affichage, à la signalétique et aux paramètres généraux de calcul de l'indice de réparabilité, JORF n°0316 du 31 décembre 2020.

2012 Art. R. 541–214.-II Code de l'environnement.

2013 Art. R. 541–214.- III Code de l'environnement.

2014 Arrêté du 29 décembre 2020 relatif aux critères, aux sous-critères et au système de notation pour le calcul et l'affichage de l'indice de réparabilité des lave-linges ménagers à chargement frontal, JORF n°0316 du 31 décembre 2020.

2015 Arrêté du 29 décembre 2020 relatif aux critères, aux sous-critères et au système de notation pour le calcul et l'affichage de l'indice de réparabilité des téléphones mobiles multifonctions, JORF n°0316 du 31 décembre 2020.

2016 Arrêté du 29 décembre 2020 relatif aux critères, aux sous-critères et au système de notation pour le calcul et l'affichage de l'indice de réparabilité des ordinateurs portables, JORF n°0316 du 31 décembre 2020.

2017 Arrêté du 29 décembre 2020 relatif aux critères, aux sous-critères et au système de notation pour le calcul et l'affichage de l'indice de réparabilité des téléviseurs, JORF n°0316 du 31 décembre 2020.

2018 Arrêté du 29 décembre 2020 relatif aux critères, aux sous-critères et au système de notation pour le calcul et l'affichage de l'indice de réparabilité des tondeuses à gazon électriques filaires, JORF n°0316 du 31 décembre 2020; Arrêté du 29 décembre 2020 relatif aux critères, aux sous-critères et au système de notation pour le calcul et l'affichage de l'indice de réparabilité des tondeuses électriques batteries, JORF n°0316 du 31 décembre 2020; Arrêté du 29 décembre 2020 relatif aux critères, aux sous-critères et au système de notation pour le

index is only mandatory for new electrical and electronic equipment.[2019] The index relates to each model of the equipment concerned.[2020] 'Model' means "*an equipment version of which all units share the same technical characteristics relevant to the calculation of the reparability index*".[2021] A website dedicated to the reparability index lists the reparability indexes assigned to products covered by this legislation and provides details on the calculation and the scores obtained per criterion.[2022]

559. VARIOUS SUPPORT AT BUSINESSES' DISPOSAL – Additional support documents have been made available to professionals as well as to the public to accustom all the economic actors to this new mandatory index.[2023] These support documents include among others an instruction manual (accompanying regulatory texts and aiming to provide additional and practical information for calculating the index), a graphic chart (for a uniform display easily recognizable and understandable for the consumer) and an automatic calculation grid (allowing an 'automatic' calculation of the index by entering the different criteria and sub-criteria scores).[2024] Furthermore, personalised help can be provided to the businesses if needed.[2025] Businesses can even register for an online training module of four hours on the reparability index.[2026] Businesses have one year to prepare for the implementation of this new legislation. Afterwards, controls will be organised by the DGCCRF and sanctions will be applied in cases of non-compliance.

560. DIVERGENT VIEWS ON THE REPARABILITY LABEL – The business side seems quite favourable to the introduction of the reparability index, although some voices requested postponing the implementation deadline.[2027] Additional comments were made by *DigitalEurope*, the European organisation representing

calcul et l'affichage de l'indice de réparabilité des tondeuses électriques robot, JORF n°0316 du 31 décembre 2020.

2019 Art. R. 541-210 Code de l'environnement.

2020 *Ibid.*

2021 Art. R. 541-211 6° Code de l'environnement.

2022 See the website dedicated to the reparability index: <https://www.indicereparabilite.fr/>.

2023 See Direction interministérielle de la transformation publique, The Behavioural Insights Team, Commissariat général au développement durable, *Appliquer les sciences comportementales pour accompagner la mise en place d'un indice de réparabilité des ordinateurs portables* (Gouvernement français 2020) pp. 42–43.

2024 These support documents are available on: <https://www.ecologie.gouv.fr/indice-reparabilite>.

2025 See <https://www.indicereparabilite.fr/nous-contacter/>.

2026 For more information on this training, see: <https://www.eventbrite.fr/e/inscription-formation-tout-savoir-sur-lindice-de-reparabilite-139442130165>.

2027 See the comments made during the public consultation, available on: <www.consultations-publiques.developpement-durable.gouv.fr/indice-de-reparabilite-pour-les-produits-a2178.html>. A clear and concise summary of the public consultation is provided on the same webpage.

the digital technology industry, which expressed concerns on the "*risk of fragmentation of the internal market by the proliferation of national scoring and labelling requirements*" and the "*increased regulatory, technical, financial and administrative burdens for businesses when introducing products onto the French market*".[2028]

561. Second step: a durability index – In addition to the reparability index, Article 16 of the Anti-Waste Law lays the foundation for the establishment of a durability index in the same Article L. 541–9–2 of the French Environmental Code. The wording of this paragraph is similar to the one dedicated to the reparability index, except for the deadline, which is extended to 1st January 2024. Manufacturers and importers will have to inform sellers and consumers about the durability of their products, as well as the criteria on which this index is based. Sellers must inform consumers through marking, labelling, posting or any other appropriate means, including a QR code.

562. Articulation with the reparability index – Compared to the reparability index, the durability index will include new criteria, such as the reliability and robustness of the product. The work on the reparability index will contribute to making progress on the establishment of the durability index. Concerning the interplay between the reparability index and the durability index, Article 16 states that the durability index will complement or replace the reparability index.

563. Many questions remain unanswered – The durability index raises many question marks, some of which might disappear gradually with the implementation of the reparability index. For the rest, it would be worthwhile to draw support, or at least inspiration, from existing EU ecodesign regulations and standards for the implementation of such an index.

564. Replacing these national indexes by an EU-wide label on product sustainability – Although these French rules can be seen as a critical stepping stone towards labels on product sustainability aspects, the reparability and durability indexes they established should be replaced by an EU-wide label, as previously argued.[2029] These French rules could indeed be regarded as barriers to market access and integration as they create financial and administrative burdens for producers (who then pass on the costs to final consumers) and as they exacerbate the legal fragmentation issue, creating legal uncertainty for consumers and businesses. The introduction of a mandatory

2028 DigitalEurope's contribution of 5 October 2020 to TRIS notification 2020/468–473/F (French proposed repairability index for electronic equipment).

2029 See *supra*, n° 541.

label at EU level would not only solve these internal market issues, but also allow avoiding discussions on the room for manoeuvre left to Member States and on the compatibility of national labelling schemes with EU law.[2030] The French Government shares this idea and has already expressed its support for the harmonisation of the obligation imposing information on product reparability.[2031]

5. COMPLIANCE WITH ENERGY LABELLING REQUIREMENTS

a) Obligation to display accurate and clear information

565. Mandatory labels and product information sheets – Once products are covered by a delegated act, manufacturers are obligated to submit new appliances to extended testing to determine the energy efficiency class of the device, as well as any other parameter required on the label. This information subsequently needs to be displayed on the product via an EU Energy Label before it is put on the market. Pursuant to Article 3(1) of the Energy Labelling Regulation, suppliers of products covered by a delegated act must ensure that each individual unit of these products, when placed on the market, is accompanied, free of charge, with accurate printed labels and with product information sheets. The labels and product information sheets are delivered to dealers, as required by Article 3(2) of the Regulation. Dealers must then display, in a visible manner, including for online distance selling, the label provided by the supplier, and make available to customers the product information sheet, including, upon request, in physical form at the point of sale.[2032] The energy efficiency class of the product and the range of the efficiency classes available on the label can also appear in visual advertisements or technical promotional material.[2033]

566. Form of the label – According to the definition laid down in Article 2(19) of the Regulation, the label can be either in printed or electronic form, depending on what is provided in the delegated act. Article 16(3)(e) gives more details on the different possible locations where the label may be displayed. Pursuant to this provision, the label may be attached to the product unit where no damage is caused to it, printed on the packaging, provided in electronic format or displayed online. The energy labelling rules have been adapted

2030 See *supra*, n° 524.
2031 Ministère de la Transition Ecologique et Solidaire, *Feuille de route économie circulaire: 50 mesures pour une économie 100% circulaire* (République française 2018) p. 19, pt. 9.
2032 Art. 5(1) of the Energy Labelling Regulation.
2033 Art. 6(a) of the Energy Labelling Regulation.

to ensure that the energy label is shown on products sold via the internet.[2034] The EC acknowledged that a shift from physical labels to digital provision of information should be envisaged.[2035]

567. The challenges posed by the digitalisation of labels – The digitalisation of labels may prove beneficial for consumers, but also for the introduction of labels on product sustainability. This is because the label would convey more data in a targeted way, the information contained in the label would be easier to update and consumers would be able to check and compare product information before going to shops.[2036] However, an online environment demands a different strategy than a traditional retail environment. The development of online labels must take into account the limited amount of space and possible misinterpretations due to the limited amount of information that smaller labels can communicate.[2037] In other words, labels need to be designed specifically for the internet channel and not just mimic the off-line environment.

568. Obligations and prohibitions in relation to the accuracy of information – Not only does Article 3 impose an obligation on suppliers to display information, but it also requires them to ensure the accuracy of the labels and product information sheets.[2038] Suppliers are, moreover, under the obligation to produce technical documentation sufficient to enable the accuracy to be assessed. Still concerning the accuracy of information, Article 3(5) of the Regulation adds a ban on defeat devices. Defeat devices have been designed so that the performance of a model is automatically altered in test conditions to reach a more favourable level for any of the parameters specified in the relevant delegated act or included in any of the documentation provided with the product. This provision makes implicit reference to the *Dieselgate* cases[2039],

2034 Commission Delegated Regulation (EU) No 518/2014 of 5 March 2014 amending Commission Delegated Regulations (EU) No 1059/2010, (EU) No 1060/2010, (EU) No 1061/2010, (EU) No 1062/2010, (EU) No 626/2011, (EU) No 392/2012, (EU) No 874/2012, (EU) No 665/2013, (EU) No 811/2013 and (EU) No 812/2013 with regard to labelling of energy-related products on the internet, OJ L 147, 17.5.2014, p. 1–28.

2035 Commission Staff Working Document of 4 March 2019 on Sustainable Products in a Circular Economy – Towards an EU Product Policy Framework contributing to the Circular Economy, SWD(2019) 91 final, p. 60.

2036 See the feedback of DigitalEurope on the Inception Impact Assessment Empowering the consumer for the green transition, p. 4, available on: <https://ec.europa.eu/info/law/better-regulation/have-your-say/initiatives/12467-Empowering-the-consumer-for-the-green-transition/F539442>.

2037 Ecorys, GFK and Tilburg University, *Study on the effects on consumer behaviour of online sustainability information displays – Final report* (Consumer Programme 2014).

2038 Art. 3(3) of the Energy Labelling Regulation.

2039 See for ex. ECJ 17 December 2020, Case C-693/18, *CLCV and Others, EU:C:2020:1040*. See also ECJ 14 July 2022, Case C-128/20, *GSMB Invest, EU:C:2022:570*; ECJ 14 July 2022, Case C-134/20, *Volkswagen, EU:C:2022:571*; ECJ 14 July 2022, Case C-145/20, *Porsche Inter Auto and Volkswagen, EU:C:2022:572*. For a national example, see the German case law relating

where certain car manufacturers equipped several vehicle models with software built into diesel engines that was able to recognise when a vehicle underwent emission tests to change the emissions accordingly to achieve better test results ('software doping by switching').[2040]

569. No information overload or confusion – When displaying the label on products covered by delegated acts, Article 6(c) requires suppliers and dealers not to provide or display other labels, marks, symbols or inscriptions which do not comply with the requirements of the Regulation and the relevant delegated acts, if doing so would be likely to mislead or confuse customers with respect to the consumption of energy or other resources during use. It remains possible however to add information on other places than the energy label.[2041] Article 6(d) and (e) adds that for products not covered by delegated acts, as well as for non-energy related products, suppliers and dealers should not supply or display labels which mimic the labels provided for under the Energy Labelling Regulation and the relevant delegated acts. Violation of these provisions could lead to sanctions based on the horizontal legislation on unfair commercial practices.[2042] The last sentence of Article 6 clarifies that the prohibition laid down in its point (d) does not affect labels provided for in national law, unless those labels are provided for in delegated acts. These provisions aim at avoiding information overload and confusion, although certain exceptions make them less effective in this regard.

b) Obligation to register in a public database

570. The European Product Database for Energy Labelling – Since January 2019, suppliers need to register their appliances covered by a delegated act in the European Product Database for Energy Labelling (EPREL) before selling them on the EU market.[2043] The database consists of two parts, a consumer-oriented public part and a compliance part, both based on the same product information but presented differently.[2044] As highlighted in Article 12(2) of the Regulation, the aim of this database is threefold: (1) to support market surveillance authorities in carrying out their tasks under the Energy Labelling

---

to the Dieselgate: LG Bad Kreuznach, 05.10.2018 – 2 O 250/17; OLG Koblenz, 12.06.2019 – 5 U 1318/18; BGH, Urteil v. 25.05.2020 – VI ZR 252/19. For a good summary of the German case law, see <https://www.bundesgerichtshof.de/SharedDocs/Pressemitteilungen/DE/2020/2020063.html>.

2040 G. Barthe, P.R. D'Argenio, B. Finkbeiner, H. Hermanns, 'Facets of Software Doping', in T. Margaria, B. Steffen (eds), *Leveraging Applications of Formal Methods, Verification and Validation: Discussion, Dissemination, Applications. ISoLA 2016. Lecture Notes in Computer Science* (Springer 2016) pp. 605–606.

2041 ECJ 25 July 2018, Case C-632/16, *Dyson* v *BSH, EU:C:2018:599,* para 42.

2042 UCPD Guidance, pp. 106–107. See also ECJ 25 July 2018, Case C-632/16, *Dyson* v *BSH, EU:C:2018:599.*

2043 Art. 4 of the Energy Labelling Regulation.

2044 Art. 2(25) of the Energy Labelling Regulation.

Regulation and the relevant delegated acts, including enforcement thereof; (2) to provide the public with information about products placed on the market and their energy labels, and product information sheets; (3) to provide the EC with up-to-date energy efficiency information for products for reviewing energy labels. Regarding more specifically the information in the public part of the database, it shall not be deleted, even after the final unit of a model has been placed on the market.[2045]

571. A MEANS FOR COMMUNICATING ADDITIONAL AND UPDATED INFORMATION – The EPREL database will not only serve as an alternative to printed labels and information sheets, as described in Article 3(1) subparagraph 2 of the Regulation. First, through this database, suppliers will be able or even required to insert additional, official (non-commercial) information on products and link the database with product tags on the product label. The initial focus for the database could be on information that suppliers are legally required to produce, including under the ecodesign regulations. This would bring coherence between the different legal instruments. The database could then be used to add and link information on the environmental performance of products, possibly on a voluntary basis at first, as argued by EEB.[2046] Second, it is important to note that the database will not remain static, but rather be a dynamic, real-time digital-information sharing system, allowing suppliers and other operators to add information on the same product at a later stage.

572. ADDED VALUE OF THE EPREL DATABASE – More than improving information transparency and restoring consumer trust in the market[2047], the EPREL database has other positive impacts from a sustainability perspective. First, it can discourage future 'Phoebus cartels' if the suppliers are obliged to provide detailed information on the durability of their products. Second, since product information will be more easily accessible and usable in the supply chain, it will "*facilitate[e] efficient material flows and encourage[e] the creation of value in the circular economy*".[2048] This could even result in the development of more sustainable products. Ultimately, the database could serve as a basis to create a digital product passport, used at every stage of the product lifecycle.[2049] Such an EU harmonised product information system would reduce administrative costs for businesses according to the principle of 'report once and use several

---

2045 Art. 4(6) of the Energy Labelling Regulation.

2046 EEB, *Towards an EU Product Policy Framework contributing to the Circular Economy* (Brussels 2018) p. 8.

2047 See *supra*, n° 537.

2048 European Resource Efficiency Platform (EREP), *Manifesto & Policy Recommendations – Action for a resource efficient Europe* (2013) p. 7.

2049 See Art. 8-13 of the Proposal for a Sustainable Products Regulation.

times'.[2050] Standardising technical and environmental information on product characteristics could build on the experiences with existing voluntary schemes, such as cradle-to-cradle® certification, environmental product declarations, chemicals or recycling passports.

c) *Obligation related to updates*

573. Review of the label – It remains possible to review the label afterwards, in case of software updates. In that case, Article 4(4) of the Regulation clarifies that "*a product for which changes are made that are relevant for the label or the product information sheet shall be considered to be a new model*". It is then for the supplier to indicate in the database when it no longer places units of a model on the market. As emphasized in the document on frequently asked questions issued by the EC[2051], if a software update which changes information contained on the label is provided by the supplier and installed by the dealer before selling the product to the end-user, the supplier is the one responsible for the provision of a new label. The only obligation for the dealer is to display this new label. The dealer is not at fault if the supplier did not actively communicate that the update is connected to a change of the label.

574. Information obligation on updates – If software or firmware updates are done after the products have been placed on the market and put into use, Article 3(4) of the Regulation also requires suppliers to inform consumers about the objective of these updates and the changes caused on the energy efficiency and other product parameters indicated on the energy label.[2052] Although such updates are typically intended to improve product performance, consumers must be informed about changes made to their products, especially if it is to the detriment of what is indicated on the label. Furthermore, the supplier is under the obligation to request explicit consent from customers regarding any changes that would be detrimental to the parameters of the label, as set out in the relevant delegated act. For a period proportionate to the average lifespan of the product, customers should be given the option of refusing the update without avoidable loss of functionality, as provided for in Article 3(4) and recital 24 of the Regulation.[2053] This provision is of particular relevance against functional

---

2050 EEB, *Towards an EU Product Policy Framework contributing to the Circular Economy* (Brussels 2018) p. 8.

2051 Frequently Asked Questions (FAQ) on the Energy Labelling Regulation EU 2017/1369 of 4 July 2017 setting a framework for energy labelling and repealing Directive 2010/30/EU and its delegated acts, p. 7, available on: <https://ec.europa.eu/energy/sites/ener/files/documents/ec_faq_el_2015-1.pdf>.

2052 See also recital 24 of the Energy Labelling Regulation.

2053 Frequently Asked Questions (FAQ) on the Energy Labelling Regulation EU 2017/1369 of 4 July 2017 setting a framework for energy labelling and repealing Directive 2010/30/EU and its delegated acts, p. 7.

obsolescence, especially if the future label includes information related to product lifetime.

6. VERIFICATION AND SANCTIONS

a) Verification and sanctions by the market surveillance authorities

575. Enforcement by national market surveillance authorities – Market surveillance is an exclusive competence of Member States. Consequently, market surveillance authorities, which are responsible for ensuring the compliance of manufacturers and retailers with the legislation when selling products on the EU market, are established at national level.[2054] The Market Surveillance Regulation[2055], which was amended by Regulation (EU) 2019/1020[2056], provides the framework for Members States to organise their market surveillance. To ensure a common interpretation in enforcing the requirements and using tolerances[2057], and to organise market surveillance efficiently across the EU, Member States' market surveillance authorities exchange information through Administrative Cooperation groups (ADCO). This is particularly important as divergent interpretation could weaken the impact of the label.

576. The proof of compliance – Companies must be able to provide evidence supporting product information that features on the label. This can include proof of actions by people and machines, documents such as certificates, and collecting or importing data from production systems. Some

---

2054 The list of national market surveillance authorities by country is available on: <https://ec.europa.eu/docsroom/documents/46814>. In Belgium, the responsibility for market surveillance concerning energy labelling lies with the Federal Public Service Economy, S.M.E.s, Self-employed and Energy. In France, this responsibility lies with the Ministère de l'Économie, des Finances et de la Relance. In Germany, it is the responsibility of the various Länder.

2055 Regulation (EC) No 765/2008 of the European Parliament and of the Council of 9 July 2008 setting out the requirements for accreditation and market surveillance relating to the marketing of products and repealing Regulation (EEC) No 339/93, OJ L 218, 13.8.2008, p. 30–47.

2056 Regulation (EU) 2019/1020 of the European Parliament and of the Council of 20 June 2019 on market surveillance and compliance of products and amending Directive 2004/42/EC and Regulations (EC) No 765/2008 and (EU) No 305/2011, PE/45/2019/REV/1, OJ L 169, 25.6.2019, p. 1–44.

2057 Like for ecodesign requirements, Member States can use verification tolerances when verifying compliance with the requirements. Article 2(26) defines verification tolerances as the maximum admissible deviation of the measurement and calculation results of the verification tests performed by, or on behalf of, market surveillance authorities, compared to the values of the declared or published parameters, reflecting deviation arising from interlaboratory variation.

pieces of information are more easily proven, but also more easily sanctioned if omitted or false. Article 4(1) of the Regulation obliges the supplier to register information in the compliance part of the product database. This information must remain in the database for 15 years after the final unit of a model has been placed on the market, unless a shorter retention period is more appropriate having regard to the average lifespan of the product.[2058] Pursuant to Article 13 of the Regulation, a product will be presumed to comply with the relevant provisions of the applicable delegated act if it complies with the measurement and calculation methods set out in the relevant harmonised standard. In the absence of a harmonised standard, older standards, international standards or other relevant methods can be used to measure energy consumption or other parameters, but this can lead to different results, and the legislation becomes difficult to apply and enforce. This is why it is important to develop harmonised standards, which are reliable, accurate, reproducible, and representative of real-life use.[2059]

577. A CONDITION FOR CIRCULATING ON THE EU MARKET – If the product complies with the Energy Labelling Regulation and the applicable delegated acts, Article 7(1) of the Regulation precludes Member States from impeding the placing on the market or putting into service of the product within their territories. By contrast, when market surveillance authorities face a case of non-compliance, they must without delay order the supplier (or the dealer) to take all appropriate corrective action to bring the product into compliance with the requirements. They can also require to withdraw the product from the market or recall it within a reasonable period, commensurate with the nature of the risk.[2060] Article 6(b) requests supplier and dealer to cooperate with market surveillance authorities and take immediate action to remedy the non-compliance. If the supplier or the dealer does not take all appropriate corrective action within a reasonable period, the market surveillance authorities must take all appropriate provisional measures to prohibit or restrict the availability of the product on their national market, to withdraw the product from that market, or to recall it.[2061] The market surveillance authorities must then pass on information on the measures taken to the EC and the other Member States.

2058 Art. 4(6) of the Energy Labelling Regulation.

2059 European Court of Auditors, *EU action on Ecodesign and Energy Labelling: important contribution to greater energy efficiency reduced by significant delays and non-compliance – Special Report* (European Union 2020) p. 28.

2060 Art. 9(2) of the Energy Labelling Regulation.

2061 Art. 9(5) of the Energy Labelling Regulation.

578. Compliance issues – Based on the results of EU projects and additional data from Member States[2062], experts estimate that 10–25% of products on the market do not fully comply with energy efficiency labelling regulations and that around 10% of potential energy savings are lost due to non-compliance.[2063] This can consequently lead to a lack of trust in labels. These compliance issues are partly due to difficult enforcement by national market surveillance authorities because of lengthy controls. In practice, the number of tests organised by the national market authorities remains very limited. Industry representatives have called for better enforcement of the regulation.[2064] The new product database may facilitate the enforcement of labelling rules by national market authorities as it makes information more easily accessible. For the rest, studies have shown that market surveillance and testing could be done in a more systematic, effective and cost-efficient way.[2065]

579. The need for effective sanctions – In case of non-compliance, Article 7(4) of the Regulation also requires Member States to provide for effective, proportionate and dissuasive penalties. This leaves a wide margin of discretion to the Member States. In Belgium, for example, the provisions implementing the Energy Labelling Regulation explicitly refer to the national provisions implementing the UCPD.[2066] As suggested for the Ecodesign Directive[2067], it may be useful to establish criteria to be taken into account when imposing penalties (see #13), as was done for consumer rules with the adoption of the Enforcement and Modernisation Directive.[2068] Such criteria would ensure a certain degree of effectiveness and consistency of the penalties imposed by national authorities. Amendment to Article 7 of the Energy Labelling Regulation could be made in that sense.

2062 For a summary of the relevant projects and literature on market surveillance, see J. Krivošík, S. Attali, *Market surveillance of Energy Labelling and Ecodesign product requirements – Overview of challenges and opportunities* (ADEME 2014).

2063 E. Molenbroek et al., *Evaluation of the Energy Labelling Directive and specific aspects of the Ecodesign Directive – Final technical report* (Ecofys 2014) p. 159.

2064 Joint Industry letter of 31 May 2018 from APPLiA, EHI, EHPA, EPEE, EUnited Cleaning and LightingEurope to the Commission on Ecodesign, available on: <https://www.applia-europe.eu/images/Advancing-Sustainable-Lifestyles/Joint-Industry-letter-on-Ecodesign---May-2018.pdf>.

2065 A. Ricci, S. Proietti, M. Gualdi, *ATLETE I – Appliance Testing for Energy Label Evaluation* (Intelligent Energy Europe 2011); S. Faberi, *ATLETE II – Appliance Testing for Washing Machines Energy Label & Ecodesign Evaluation* (Intelligent Energy Europe 2014).

2066 Art. 18 Arrêté royal du 13 août 2011 concernant l'indication, par voie d'étiquetage et d'informations uniformes relatives aux produits, de la consommation en énergie et en autres ressources des produits liés à l'énergie, *M.B.*, 5 septembre 2011, p. 56361.

2067 See *supra*, n° 304.

2068 Directive (EU) 2019/2161 of the European Parliament and of the Council of 27 November 2019 amending Council Directive 93/13/EEC and Directives 98/6/EC, 2005/29/EC and 2011/83/EU of the European Parliament and of the Council as regards the better enforcement and modernisation of Union consumer protection rules, OJ L 328, 18.12.2019, p. 7–28.

Proposed review of the Energy Labelling Regulation:

#13

Article 7
Obligations of Member States

4. Member States shall lay down the rules on penalties and enforcement mechanisms applicable to infringements of this Regulation and the delegated acts, and shall take all measures necessary to ensure that they are implemented. The penalties provided for shall be effective, proportionate and dissuasive. Rules which fulfil the requirements of Article 15 of Directive 2010/30/EU shall be considered to fulfil the requirements of this paragraph as regards penalties.

Member States shall, by 1 August 2017, notify the Commission of the rules referred to in the first subparagraph that have not previously been notified to the Commission, and shall notify the Commission, without delay, of any subsequent amendment affecting them.

Member States shall ensure that the following non-exhaustive and indicative criteria are taken into account for the imposition of penalties, where appropriate:
(a) the nature, gravity, scale and duration of the infringement;
(b) any action taken by the trader to mitigate or remedy the non-compliance with the implementing measure;
(c) any previous infringements by the trader;
(d) the financial benefits gained or losses avoided by the trader due to the infringement, if the relevant data are available;
(e) penalties imposed on the trader for the same infringement in other Member States in cross-border cases;
(f) any other aggravating or mitigating factors applicable to the circumstances of the case.

b) Private law sanctions

580. Possible private sanctions – In addition to tests and sanctions taken by national market surveillance authorities, businesses and consumers can call for sanctions against producers who do not respect energy labelling rules. These sanctions are the result of the combination of the energy labelling rules with other EU legal instruments, like the UCPD and the SGD. These latter rules give civil law effect to product-specific labelling rules in case of a breach.

581. Businesses' investigations – Due to the sometimes fierce competition between brands, some companies decide to do tests on competing products by themselves and verify their competitors compliance with the labelling regulations. If these tests finally reveal non-compliance, it can lead to a claim before the competent court and, if the claim is deemed well-founded, to sanctions. The *Dyson* case[2069] perfectly illustrates the link between energy labelling rules and EU liability mechanisms, and more specifically the UCPD.[2070] In this case, *Dyson* criticised, *inter alia*, *BSH* for misleading consumers through the label affixed to its vacuum cleaners and claimed that *BSH*'s labelling practices were unfair. In its judgment, the ECJ confirmed that labelling forms a 'commercial practice' within the meaning of Article 2(d) of the UCPD.[2071] It also clarified that (1) withholding information regarding testing conditions, used for determining the vacuum cleaner's energy classification, does not necessarily constitute a misleading omission pursuant to Article 7 of the UCPD[2072], and (2) displaying additional labels and symbols was prohibited by the delegated act if this was likely to mislead or confuse end-users.[2073] Following this case, the supplementing act with regard to energy labelling of vacuum cleaners was annulled.[2074]

582. Consumer complaints – Consumers can also report cases of breach of the energy labelling rules. They have different EU legislation at their disposal to this end. They can, first, invoke the legislation on unfair commercial practices. As previously mentioned[2075], consumers can, for example, rely on Article 6 of the UCPD if a self-declared label resembles too closely the EU energy label, or if the trader, who obtained the EU energy label, uses it with additional labels, marks, symbols or inscriptions that are likely to mislead or confuse customers. There is also Article 7(5) of the UCPD, which sanctions misleading omissions relating to existing EU information requirements, such as those imposed by the energy labelling legislation.[2076] The second set of rules that are of particular relevance for sanctioning breaches of energy labelling rules is the consumer sales legislation. Consumers can rely on Article 6 and 7 of the SGD and claim that the omitted or false information on the product characteristics constitute a lack of conformity with the contract.[2077] This possibility is of tremendous importance from the perspective of sustainable consumption. If the label contained information on product sustainability, consumers could more easily demonstrate the premature obsolescence of their products. They would only

2069 ECJ 25 July 2018, Case C-632/16, *Dyson* v *BSH*, *EU:C:2018:599*.

2070 For a critical analysis of this case law, see C. Koolen, 'Vacuum Cleaner Energy Labels and Misleading Commercial Practices: EU Consumers Left in the Dust?', 8 *EuCML* (2019) p. 82 at p. 88.

2071 ECJ 25 July 2018, Case C-632/16, *Dyson* v *BSH*, *EU:C:2018:599*, para 29.

2072 ECJ 25 July 2018, Case C-632/16, *Dyson* v *BSH*, *EU:C:2018:599*, para 46.

2073 ECJ 25 July 2018, Case C-632/16, *Dyson* v *BSH*, *EU:C:2018:599*, para 58.

2074 ECJ 8 November 2018, Case T-544/13 RENV, *Dyson* v *Commission*, *EU:T:2018:761*.

2075 See *supra*, n° 416.

2076 See *supra*, n° 403–408.

2077 See also F. Keimeyer et al., *Weiterentwicklung von Strategien gegen Obsoleszenz einschließlich rechtlicher Instrumente – Abschlussbericht* (Umweltbundesamt 2020) p. 42 at p. 44.

need to base their arguments on the fact that the product does not comply with the information indicated on the label.[2078]

583. THE NEED FOR MAKING LINKS BETWEEN PRODUCT AND CONSUMER LAW – Private law sanctions can play a key role in ensuring compliance with energy labelling rules. On one hand, consumers can be reassured about the accuracy and veracity of longer claimed product lifetime and of other environmental claims, thus restoring their trust and encouraging them to purchase more sustainable products.[2079] On the other hand, producers have another compelling reason to think about the sustainability of their products, in fear of contractual liability. In the absence of such a link between these legislations, producers may be tempted to disclose mandatory information required by the delegated act and not comply with its content. As a consequence, these private law enforcement mechanisms supplement the enforcement actions taken by market surveillance authorities and can thus help mitigate the lack of controls on labelled products. Nevertheless, the effectiveness of private enforcement depends on the articulation between the specific information requirements imposed by the energy labelling legislation on one hand, and the UCPD and the consumer sales legislation on the other. The connection between these EU legal instruments should therefore be made clearer, including through cross-references in the relevant provisions, as already argued in the previous sections of this chapter.[2080]

7. INTERMEDIATE CONCLUSION

584. A LABEL WITH GREAT POTENTIAL FOR THE PROMOTION OF SUSTAINABLE PRODUCTS – The Energy Labelling Regulation has proven to be an effective tool for energy efficiency. On one hand, it empowers and encourages consumers to choose more energy-efficient products by providing accurate, relevant, and comparable information on products at the point of sale.[2081] A 2019 Eurobarometer survey revealed that the EU energy label is recognised by 93% of consumers, while 79% consider it when they are buying products.[2082] On the other hand, it drives innovation and investment in energy efficiency

2078 For further comments, see Chapter IV on the use stage.

2079 T. Knight et al. (Brook Lyndhurst), *Electrical and electronic product design: product lifetime* (WRAP 2013).

2080 See *supra*, n° 404 and n° 486.

2081 In this regard, the Energy Labelling Regulation also contributes to consumer protection. See ECJ 25 July 2018, Case C-632/16, *Dyson* v *BSH, EU:C:2018:599*, para 33.

2082 Kantar Belgium, *Special Eurobarometer 492 – European's attitudes on EU energy policy* (European Commission 2019). The results of this survey show how much environmental concerns among consumers have increased compared to the former survey ten years ago, where only 37% of consumers said they often consider the energy efficiency of products and 40% said they always take this into account when they make purchasing decisions. See Gallup

on the business side. Beyond its prominent role in the EU energy policy, the system established under the Energy Labelling Regulation offers tremendous opportunities to promote sustainable products. Although initially dedicated to energy efficiency, the label could be used to convey information on product sustainability aspects. Access to the EU market would be conditional upon the full availability of the requested information. Labels displaying such information would stress the importance of these product features for consumers and businesses, as they already do for energy efficiency. Consumers would be better informed when purchasing products, whereas businesses would be encouraged to think more carefully about product sustainability and embrace labels as an important feature that can differentiate their products.

585. A WIDE RANGE OF PRODUCTS SHOULD BE COVERED BY THE LABEL ON PRODUCT SUSTAINABILITY – The EU energy label should be affixed to a broader range of products, especially if the label gave more information on product sustainability aspects. Sustainability labels should be introduced for products that are covered by the energy label, but also for other products. Information on sustainability aspects should be conveyed on the label of products already covered by delegated acts. More than that, a wider range of products should be covered by these labelling rules. First, the exclusions of second-hand products from the scope of the Energy Labelling Regulation should be removed. Labelling second-hand products would reassure consumers about the quality of these products and encourage them to buy such products. Second, mandatory labels should be established for non-energy-related products. This could be done by extending the scope of the Energy Labelling Regulation to non-energy related products or by adopting a twin legal instrument for these products. Third, whether the scope is extended or not, more delegated acts should be adopted.

586. FROM EU ENERGY LABEL TO EU SUSTAINABILITY LABEL – The focus of the labelling scheme should shift from energy efficiency to product sustainability so that the EU energy label would become the EU sustainability label. As an intermediary step, product sustainability information could be integrated into the EU energy label as supplementary information, without being the main focus of the label. Products that are already covered by delegated acts should be the first ones for which an enhanced label should be made mandatory. Adding information on product sustainability aspects on the label would constitute the vehicle of choice for those measures on product sustainability that cannot be included in horizontal legislation. In other words, such labels would complement the general information obligations imposed by the UCPD and the CRD. Furthermore, this would restore the broken link between the energy labelling

Organisation, *Flash Eurobarometer 256 – Europeans' attitudes towards the issue of sustainable consumption and production* (European Commission 2009).

and the ecodesign schemes as the labels would convey information relating to ecodesign requirements. Alternatively, and depending on the products, these sustainability labels could be used when it is not appropriate or too complex to set mandatory requirements related to product sustainability through ecodesign regulations.

587. Global indexes with a comparative scale and strong visual should be preferred – Such revision of the EU energy label should however be carefully and thoroughly thought out, especially concerning the form and methodology to be adopted. It is indeed important that the label remains understandable and trustworthy. For these new sustainability labels, it is preferable to use global indexes with a comparative scale and strong visuals emphasizing these new pieces of information on product sustainability. As an alternative or as an intermediary step, selected pieces of information could appear directly on the label. A product-specific analysis needs to be conducted within the framework of future preparatory studies to determine which product categories should be prioritised (including those not yet covered by the energy labelling scheme) and which product sustainability aspects should be indicated on the label of these specific products. A wide array of possible methodologies exists for measuring product sustainability aspects. The framework established by the Ecodesign Directive and the horizontal standards on material efficiency offers a robust basis in this respect. Inspiration could also be drawn from numerous studies and existing labels, including the French mandatory labels on product reparability and durability.

588. Sanctions for non-compliance should be effective – Member States enjoy a wide margin of discretion is left to concerning sanctions in case of non-compliance. The Energy Labelling Regulation only states that penalties should be effective, proportionate and dissuasive. To increase compliance with the labelling rules, it may be useful to establish criteria to be considered when imposing penalties, as was done for consumer rules with the adoption of the Enforcement and Modernisation Directive. Such criteria would ensure a certain degree of effectiveness and consistency in the penalties imposed by the national authorities. Article 7 of the Energy Labelling Regulation could be amended in that sense. The effectiveness of private enforcement should also be improved by clarifying the connection between specific information requirements imposed by the energy labelling legislation on one hand, and the UCPD and consumer sales legislation on the other. This would entail cross-referencing the relevant provisions in each of these directive and national transposition legislation.

589. The articulation between EU and national labels should be clarified – There are doubts about the room for manoeuvre left to Member States as regards labels. Therefore, recital 23 of the Energy Labelling Regulation

should better clarify the articulation between EU and national labelling schemes. Since additional labelling rules may contribute to promoting sustainable products, Member States should be allowed to adopt such rules for products or aspects that are not covered by delegated acts. As these rules could be considered as 'technical regulation' in accordance with the Directive (EU) 2015/1535, the notification procedure established under the Technical Regulations Information System (TRIS) could serve as a watchdog to ascertain whether the national labelling rule does not create barriers to the free movement of goods, the free provision of Information Society services, or to EU secondary legislation.

590. Mandatory rather than voluntary labels – Compared to voluntary labels, establishing mandatory labels for all products of specific categories has some advantages. Behavioural studies have indeed shown that even when facing products with voluntary labels, some consumers still buy products without labels.[2083] Only if introducing these new pieces of mandatory information takes too much time or if it does not seem possible, then there is still the possibility of stimulating voluntary labels on product sustainability aspects. This may be appropriate for product groups undergoing rapid technological progress.

F. THE EU ECOLABEL REGULATION

1. VOLUNTARY LABELS AWARDED TO THE MOST ENVIRONMENT-FRIENDLY PRODUCTS

591. The Ecolabel Regulation – Regulation (EC) No 66/2010 on EU Ecolabel[2084] lays down rules for the establishment and application of the EU Ecolabel, which is a voluntary label of environmental excellence that is awarded to the most environment-friendly products and services on the market. To carry the ecolabel, products have to satisfy clear and specific criteria, developed by experts, in consultation with main stakeholders and awarded by an independent third party. Among the criteria established under the EU Ecolabel legislation, operators are required to abide by product durability and reparability standards. Like the ecodesign requirements[2085], the ecolabel scheme is based on the principle of product lifecycle thinking and various environmental parameters

[2083] See Direction interministérielle de la transformation publique, The Behavioural Insights Team, Commissariat général au développement durable, *Appliquer les sciences comportementales pour accompagner la mise en place d'un indice de réparabilité des ordinateurs portables* (Gouvernement français 2020) p. 41.

[2084] Regulation (EC) No 66/2010 of the European Parliament and of the Council of 25 November 2009 on the EU Ecolabel, OJ L 27, 30.1.2010, p. 1–19 (hereafter 'Ecolabel Regulation').

[2085] See *supra*, n° 216–217.

are taken into account. Access to the EU Ecolabel is open to any 'operator'[2086] who is willing to get it and is conforming to the requirements. The criteria established under the EU Ecolabel scheme are regularly reviewed to reflect technical innovation.[2087]

592. Promoting sustainable production and consumption through the voluntary EU ecolabel – The EU Ecolabel scheme was established as part of the 2008 Sustainable Consumption and Production and Sustainable Industrial Policy Action Plan.[2088] Based on the former Article 175 TEC[2089], the aim is to reduce the negative impact of consumption and production on the environment, health, climate and natural resources.[2090] The Ecolabel scheme promotes sustainable products on two fronts. On the one hand, the EU Ecolabel gives support to producers who decide to go beyond what is legally required to design, produce and put on the market quality and sustainable goods. On the other, it helps consumers identify such products thanks to accurate, non-deceptive and science-based information, and encourages them to purchase sustainable goods.[2091] Retailers play a pre-eminent role in the application and promotion of the Ecolabel legislation. Not only can they ecolabel products sold under their own brand name, but they can also influence both consumer and producer behaviours by strongly encouraging or requesting suppliers to apply for the EU Ecolabel, by favouring ecolabelled products on the shelves and placing them in prominent places to attract the shopper's attention, as well as by providing consumers with information on the EU Ecolabel through marketing campaigns and in the shops so they can take sustainable decisions. For all these reasons, the EU Ecolabel is seen as a key instrument for the transition towards the circular economy by the EC.[2092]

2086 According to Article 3(2), 'operator' means "*any producer, manufacturer, importer, service provider, wholesaler or retailer.*"

2087 The EU Ecolabel meets all the conditions set out by the international standard ISO 14024:2018.

2088 Communication from the Commission of 16 July 2008 to the European Parliament, the Council, the European Economic and Social Committee and the Committee of the Regions on the Sustainable Consumption and Production and Sustainable Industrial Policy Action Plan, COM(2008) 397 final.

2089 Now Article 192 TEU.

2090 Recital 5 of the EU Ecolabel Regulation.

2091 Some improvements could however be made in this regard as only 49% of European consumers who have seen the EU Ecolabel before, know that the EU Ecolabel means that a product is amongst the most environmentally friendly in its category. GfK Belgium, time.lex, Milieu Ltd, BIO IS and the Ecologic Institute, *Consumer market study on environmental claims for non-food products* (2014 European Commission) p. 80.

2092 Communication from the Commission of 2 December 2015 to the European Parliament, the Council, the European Economic and Social Committee and the Committee of the Regions on Closing the loop – EU action plan for circular economy, COM(2015) 614 final, p. 6.

2. A WIDE SCOPE OF APPLICATION, WITH UNEVEN UPTAKE

593. An ecolabel for all types of products – The EU Ecolabel offers a reference point of environmental excellence in a wide range of product and service groups for B2C and B2B transactions. Whilst the Ecodesign and the Energy Labelling Directives are limited to 'energy-related products'[2093], the scope of the EU Ecolabel scheme extends to all types of products. According to Article 2, the EU Ecolabel Regulation applies to "*any goods or services which are supplied for distribution, consumption or use on the Community market whether in return for payment or free of charge*". This wide scope is particularly valuable as it contributes to increasing the sustainability of a broader range of products, including those that are not covered by other EU mandatory legal instruments. However, as ecolabelling is only suited for product groups for which differences in environmental performance can be distinguished, certain products are not suitable for ecolabelling.[2094] So far, more than thirty product categories have been covered by the EU Ecolabel legislation, including wooden furniture, televisions and bed mattresses.[2095] The only services covered by the Ecolabel system concerns tourist accommodation services.[2096]

594. With uneven uptake – The uptake has been very uneven, including at geographical level, ranging from zero licences to hundreds of licences[2097], depending on the country and the product categories.[2098] A steady increase in the number of products awarded the EU Ecolabel has been observed for the majority of product groups.[2099] This may continue, especially for office equipment (e.g. computers, displays) that formerly fell within the scope of the Energy Star Programme[2100] as the EU ecolabel could be seen as an alternative.[2101] Yet, there

2093 See *supra*, n° 179 on the scope of the Ecodesign Directive and n° 515 on the scope of the Energy Labelling Directive.

2094 A. Thidell, *Influences, effects and changes from interventions by eco-labelling schemes: What a Swan can do?* (IIIEE Dissertations 2009) pp. 42–43.

2095 European Commission and EUEB, EU Ecolabel Work Plan for 2016 – 2018, p. 11. See also Table 1 in Annex I of this Work Plan (p. 23), which presents the product groups with EU Ecolabel criteria.

2096 Commission Decision (EU) 2017/175 of 25 January 2017 on establishing EU Ecolabel criteria for tourist accommodation, OJ L 28, 2.2.2017, p. 9–43.

2097 One license is an EU Ecolabel contract including one or several awarded products in a same product group.

2098 See the EU Ecolabel facts and figures from September 2020, available on: <https://ec.europa.eu/environment/ecolabel/facts-and-figures.html>.

2099 *Ibid.*

2100 Regulation (EU) No 174/2013 of the European Parliament and of the Council of 5 February 2013 amending Regulation (EC) No 106/2008 on a Community energy-efficiency labelling programme for office equipment, OJ L 63, 6.3.2013, p. 1–4.

2101 The EU-US Agreement was signed in 2001 and started to be operational from 2003, for 5 years. It has been renewed twice for 5 years and finally expired on 20 February 2018. For

are still barriers that impede businesses from applying for the EU ecolabel, such as lack of recognition and rewards by public institutions, consumers and retailers, high costs of implementation and licensing and lack of economic incentives (including funding).[2102] In 2017, the Fitness Check indicated that, in order to fully exploit the potential of the Ecolabel scheme, efforts needed to be made to enhance its uptake.[2103]A study has been launched by the EC to identify opportunities to increase uptake of the EU Ecolabel by focusing on the most promising product and service groups.[2104]

595. Developing an EU ecolabel for software products – In spite of its already broad scope and growing uptake, the EU Ecolabel scheme still has a great deal of potential for improvements to further promote sustainable production and consumption patterns. In this regard, it is recommended that an EU ecolabel be developed for software products (see #1).[2105] These products have indeed important impacts on the environment, as already pointed out in the second chapter of this book.[2106] Inspiration could be drawn from the German ecolabel *The Blue Angel*, which introduced award criteria for 'resource and energy-efficient software products' at the beginning of 2020.[2107] The *Blue Angel* ecolabel requires, among others, that software products deliver their functions with a minimal use of resources and a minimal energy demand, do not contribute to the early replacement of existing hardware with more powerful hardware, and ensure user autonomy with respect to the product (e.g. transparency, uninstallabillity, continuity, offline capability, modularity).

596. Developing an EU ecolabel for services – An extension of the system to services merits further investigation in light of the emerging 'servitisation' of the economy (see #1). Although not all 'servitisation' automatically leads to increased

further details, see <https://ec.europa.eu/energy/topics/energy-efficiency/energy-efficient-products/energy-star_en#archive>.

2102 F. Iraldo, M. Barberio, 'Drivers, Barriers and Benefits of the EU Ecolabel in European Companies' Perception', 9 *Sustainability* (2017) p. 754 and p. 760 at p. 763.

2103 Report from the Commission of 30 June 2017 to the European Parliament and the Council on the review of implementation of Regulation (EC)No 122/2009 of the European Parliament and of the Council on 25 November 2009 on the voluntary participation by organisations in a Community eco-management and audit scheme (EMAS) and the Regulation (EC) No 66/2010 of the parliament and of the Council of 25 November 2009 on the EU Ecolabel, COM(2017) 355 final, p. 5.

2104 See <https://circulareconomy.europa.eu/platform/fr/node/1422>.

2105 J. Gröger, A. Köhler, S. Naumann, A. Filler, A. Guldner, E. Kern, L.M. Hilty, Y.V. Maksimov, *Entwicklung und Anwendung von Bewertungsgrundlagen für ressourceneffiziente Software unter Berücksichtigung bestehender Methodik* (Umweltbundesamt 2018).

2106 See *supra*, n° 193.

2107 Basic Award Criteria of the German Ecolabel Blue Angel from January 2020 for resource and energy-efficient software products, DE-UZ 215, available on: <https://www.blauer-engel.de/en/products/electric-devices/resources-and-energy-efficient-software-products>.

sustainability[2108], purchasing a service instead of a product can be an effective way of encouraging sustainable consumption patterns. Service-oriented consumption could increase incentives to prolong the lifetime of products and thus contribute to breaking the link between profit and production volume. EU ecolabels should be envisaged for repair services, refurbishment and reuse of goods and leasing of second-hand goods aimed at ensuring the durability and more intense use of products (e.g. computers, clothing, toys).[2109] The development of EU Ecolabel criteria for services was envisaged by the EC in the 2017 Fitness Check[2110], though it emphasized the importance to pay attention to the potential confusion and synergies with EMAS.[2111] It also seems important to avoid ecolabelling services which can have a rebound effect and trigger higher consumption of new goods as the objective should be minimising material consumption.[2112] Interestingly, the idea of developing a voluntary European quality standard for repair services is now contained in the Proposal for a Directive on common rules promoting repair.[2113]

Policy recommendation

> *#1 The development of additional EU ecolabels, including for software products and services, should be envisaged.*

3. EXISTING EU ECOLABEL CRITERIA

a) *The development of EU Ecolabel criteria*

597. PRODUCT-SPECIFIC ENVIRONMENTAL PERFORMANCE AS A BASIS – As stated in Article 6(1) of the Ecolabel Regulation, the ecolabel is awarded based on the environmental performance of products, in consideration of "*the latest strategic objectives of the Community in the field of the environment*". To bear the EU Ecolabel, products must fulfil environmental requirements set out by the EU Ecolabel criteria, which are tailored to address the specific and unique

2108 See A. Tukker, 'Eight types of product-service-system: Eight ways to sustainability? Experiences from Suspronet', *Business Strategy and the Environment* (2004) p. 246 at p. 260.

2109 See also EEB and BEUC comments of 13 December 2018 to the Study "identification of elements for a future Strategy of the EU Ecolabel", p. 3.

2110 Commission Staff Working Document of 30 June 2017 on Fitness Check of the Eco-Management and Audit Scheme (EMAS) and the EU Ecolabel Scheme, SWD(2017) 253 final, p. 62.

2111 EMAS is the EU Eco-Management and Audit Scheme which allows all types of organizations to improve their environmental performance and achieve recognition for doing so.

2112 EEB and BEUC comments of 13 December 2018 to the Study "identification of elements for a future Strategy of the EU Ecolabel", p. 4.

2113 See recital 27 of the Proposal for a Directive of the European Parliament and of the Council on common rules promoting the repair of goods and amending Regulation (EU) 2017/2394, Directives (EU) 2019/771 and (EU) 2020/1828, COM(2023) 155 final.

characteristics of each product group. These criteria are developed by experts, in consultation with main stakeholders, and revised regularly to follow technological evolution such as the evolution of materials, production processes or in emission reduction and changes in the market.[2114] They are determined on a scientific basis, considering the whole lifecycle of products and taking various environmental parameters into account. The best products available on the EU market in terms of environmental performance throughout the lifecycle are taken as a benchmark.[2115]

598. Various environmental parameters taken into account – Concerning the environmental parameters taken into account when determining the EU Ecolabel criteria, they are conducive to the adoption of criteria based on product sustainability. In other words, product requirements can be imposed via ecolabels so that only sustainable products can get the ecolabel. Article 6(3) of the Regulation cites, first, "*the most significant environmental impacts*" associated with the products.[2116] Another relevant parameter mentioned by the same provision is "*the potential to reduce environmental impacts due to durability and reusability of products*".[2117] Article 6(3)(f) also mentions that criteria established for other environmental labels, particularly officially recognised, nationally or regionally, should be taken into account. This parameter is particularly interesting when considering national labelling schemes like *The Blue Angel* where criteria on product sustainability aspects have been developed for a wide range of products.[2118] The following paragraph of Article 6 states that EU Ecolabel criteria must include "*requirements intended to ensure that the products bearing the EU Ecolabel function adequately in accordance with their intended use*".[2119] As a result, compared to ecodesign and energy labelling requirements, those established under the Ecolabel scheme can be more varied and thus tackle aspects that are not tackled under these mandatory legal instruments.

599. A methodology to be reviewed – The methodology used to develop the EU Ecolabel criteria and assess the compliance of products with them is also of utmost importance. The 2017 Fitness Check Study found that "*the existing process ensures that criteria are set at a level that reflects the best performing products on the single market*", but that "*it is impossible to say if the target of identifying the 10–20% best performing products in terms of environmental performance is being met*".[2120] This stems from the lack of data and methodology

2114 The procedure for the development and revision of EU Ecolabel criteria is detailed in Annex I to the EU Ecolabel Regulation.
2115 Point A.2. of the Annex I to the Ecolabel Regulation.
2116 Art. 6(3)(a) of the Ecolabel Regulation.
2117 Art. 6(3)(c) of the Ecolabel Regulation.
2118 For further details on *The Blue Angel*, see n° 615–618.
2119 Art. 6(4) of the Ecolabel Regulation.
2120 Commission Staff Working Document of 30 June 2017 on Fitness Check of the Eco-Management and Audit Scheme (EMAS) and the EU Ecolabel Scheme, SWD(2017) 253 final, p. 30.

for quantification and benchmarking and the complexity involved with multi-criteria labelling and the life cycle stages covered.[2121] To solve this issue, the EC announced in its new Circular Economy Action Plan that it will "*test the integration of [the Product/Organisation Environmental Footprint ('PEF'/'OEF')] methods in the EU Ecolabel*".[2122] These harmonised methods for the calculation of the environmental footprint of products have been developed by the EC on the basis of existing LCA approaches and international standards[2123], following a request from the Council of the European Union.[2124] Studies should be undertaken to analyse how this method can be used within the framework of the EU Ecolabel framework (e.g. if these methods should be mandatory or voluntary). The ongoing initiative 'Substantiating green claims' may offer an answer to that question.[2125]

600. The need for coherence and coordination with other product legislation – When reviewing the methodology of the EU Ecolabel scheme, it is important to ensure coherence and coordination with other product legislation, like the ecodesign and energy labelling rules (see #2).[2126] At present, the EU Ecolabel scheme uses methods for some products and parameters that are different than the ones used within the ecodesign and energy labelling frameworks. This is regrettable in terms of coherence and effectiveness. The ecodesign, energy label and ecolabel requirements should be developed simultaneously for the specific product groups, especially if more requirements related to product sustainability are adopted. An approach could be tested to apply the same metrics for building different ambition levels for the worst and best products.[2127] Besides the 'PEF' and 'OEF' methods, the new standards on material efficiency could be useful in this regard. The use of these standards could lead to a symbiotic relationship between the different instruments as they harmonise concepts, methods and nomenclatures to apply in the assessment of material efficiency aspects of energy-related products. As rightly pointed out by M. Cordella et al., regulatory and standardisation frameworks can offer a

2121 *Ibid.*

2122 Communication from the Commission of 11 March 2020 to the European Parliament, the Council, the European Economic and Social Committee and the Committee of the Regions on A new Circular Economy Action Plan – For a cleaner and more competitive Europe, COM(2020) 98 final, p. 8.

2123 For more details, see <https://ec.europa.eu/environment/eussd/smgp/dev_methods.htm>.

2124 See the Council conclusions of 20 December 2010 on Sustainable materials management and sustainable production and consumption, 3 061st Environment Council meeting, where the Council invited the Commission "*to develop a common method on the quantitative assessment of environmental impacts of products, throughout their life-cycle*".

2125 Inception impact assessment from the European Commission of 20 July 2020 on Legislative proposal on substantiating green claims, Ares(2020)3820384.

2126 See recital 4 of the Ecolabel Regulation.

2127 EEB and BEUC comments of 13 December 2018 to the Study "identification of elements for a future Strategy of the EU Ecolabel", p. 4.

robust basis for justifying the integration of material efficiency aspects in the EU Ecolabel, while the EU Ecolabel can explore and promote approaches targeted at frontrunners acting voluntarily towards product sustainability.[2128]

Policy recommendation

> *#2 The methodology used to develop the EU Ecolabel criteria and assess the compliance of products with them should be reviewed, in a way that ensures coherence and coordination with other product legislation, especially with the ecodesign and energy labelling rules.*

b) Existing criteria for product durability

601. Criteria on product resistance – Different EU Ecolabel criteria relate to product durability. There are, first of all, criteria that concern product resistance to stresses with references to durability parameters and tests. To get the award of the ecolabel, some furniture must be resistant to fire, cold liquids, wet and dry heat, scratching, pilling and abrasion.[2129] Clothes are subject to criteria on the dimensional changes during washing and drying, colour fastness, resistance to pilling and abrasion, as well as on the durability of repellency, easy care and flame retardancy functions.[2130] Floor coverings must be resistant to indentation, wear and impact.[2131] Similar requirements (which are currently under review)[2132] have also been established for notebook computers, which must pass tests to certify their resistance to shock, vibration, accidental dropping, temperature stress and water spill ingress.[2133] Screen resilience is also tested.[2134] Concerning the data storage drives of these computers, they must have a minimum failure rate and be specified to protect both the drive and data

2128 M. Cordella, F. Alfieri, J. Sanfelix, S. Donatello, R. Kaps, O. Wolf, 'Improving material efficiency in the life cycle of products: a review of EU Ecolabel criteria', 25 *The International Journal of Life Cycle Assessment volume* (2020) p. 921 at p. 935.

2129 Annex to the Commission Decision (EU) 2016/1332 of 28 July 2016 establishing the ecological criteria for the award of the EU Ecolabel for furniture, OJ L 210, 4.8.2016, p. 100–149.

2130 See criterion 17 to 25 of the annex to the Commission Decision 2014/350/EU of 5 June 2014 establishing the ecological criteria for the award of the EU Ecolabel for textile products, OJ L 174, 13.6.2014, p. 45–83.

2131 Criterion 8 of the annex to the Commission Decision (EU) 2017/176 of 25 January 2017 on establishing EU Ecolabel criteria for wood-, cork- and bamboo-based floor coverings, OJ L 28, 2.2.2017, p. 44–68.

2132 See N. Dodd, C. Vidal-Abarca and O. Wolf, *Revision of the European Ecolabel Criteria for Personal, Notebook and Tablet Computers – JRC Science and Policy Reports* (European Commission 2019).

2133 Criterion 3(a) of the annex to the Commission Decision (EU) 2016/1371 of 10 August 2016 establishing the ecological criteria for the award of the EU Ecolabel for personal, notebook and tablet computers, OJ L 217, 12.8.2016, p. 9–37.

2134 *Ibid.*

from shock and vibration.[2135] The resistance to stress required by these criteria guarantees a longer lifetime for the concerned products.

602. Minimum thresholds on endurance and reliability – In addition to requirements on resistance, some criteria set minimum thresholds on endurance and reliability over the lifetime of the product. Nonetheless, only a limited number of product groups are subject to such criteria. There are, for example, bed mattresses which are required not to lose height and firmness over the years[2136], and be equipped with a durable flame retardant function.[2137] Furniture moving parts must pass a strength and durability test after which the components should not be damaged and should still function as intended.[2138] But the most advanced requirements on product lifetime extension have been developed for computers and laptops. The keyboard and screen hinge must successfully undergo a durability test. The stability and hinge integrity must remain intact after the screen was fully opened and then closed 20 000 times. Rechargeable batteries must have an operating life of 7 hours minimum and maintain a high percentage of their declared minimum initial capacity after a certain number of charging cycles.[2139]

603. Other durability requirements – Without mentioning and testing product lifetime, other Ecolabel criteria directly influence the durability of products. This is the case of imaging equipment, which must be designed with reused and remanufactured toner and ink cartridges in mind. Moreover, the design of the cartridge recommended by the manufacturer ('OEM')[2140] for use in the product must promote its durability. Devices and practices that would prevent its reutilisation (sometimes referred to as anti-reutilisation devices/practises) must not be present or applied.[2141] When considering this criterion,

---

2135 Criterion 3(c) of the annex to the Commission Decision (EU) 2016/1371 of 10 August 2016 establishing the ecological criteria for the award of the EU Ecolabel for personal, notebook and tablet computers, OJ L 217, 12.8.2016, p. 9–37.

2136 Criterion 12 of the annex to the Commission Decision 2014/391/EU of 23 June 2014 establishing the ecological criteria for the award of the EU Ecolabel for bed mattresses, OJ L 184, 25.6.2014, p. 18–48.

2137 Criterion 5.10. of the annex to the Commission Decision 2014/391/EU of 23 June 2014 establishing the ecological criteria for the award of the EU Ecolabel for bed mattresses, OJ L 184, 25.6.2014, p. 18–48.

2138 Criterion 9 of the annex to the Commission Decision (EU) 2016/1332 of 28 July 2016 establishing the ecological criteria for the award of the EU Ecolabel for furniture, OJ L 210, 4.8.2016, p. 100–149.

2139 Criterion 3 of the annex to the Commission Decision (EU) 2016/1371 of 10 August 2016 establishing the ecological criteria for the award of the EU Ecolabel for personal, notebook and tablet computers, OJ L 217, 12.8.2016, p. 9–37.

2140 'OEM' means original equipment manufacturer.

2141 Criterion 10 of the annex to the Commission Decision of 17 December 2013 establishing the ecological criteria for the award of the EU Ecolabel for imaging equipment, OJ L 353, 28.12.2013, p. 53–63.

it is hard not to make the link with blatant cases of material obsolescence where printer manufacturers were accused of similar practices.[2142] The adoption of such criterion allows avoiding such criticism for Ecolabelled printers.

604. A MINIMUM GUARANTEE PERIOD AT NO ADDITIONAL COST – Closely related to lifetime extension requirements, EU Ecolabel legislation also obliges applicants to offer a minimum guarantee period at no additional cost to ensure that the product will function for a minimum period of time from the date of delivery to the customer. The duration of the guarantee period depends on the product groups. Batteries in notebook computers must be guaranteed for two years[2143], computers for three years[2144], televisions for three years[2145], furniture for five years[2146], imaging equipment for five years[2147] and mattresses for ten years.[2148] These extended product guarantees are commercial guarantees, meaning that their terms and conditions are determined by the guarantor. Hence, if a defect occurs during the guarantee period, consumers will not necessarily be offered the possibility to repair the defective good. Other options could be proposed instead, including the replacement of the product, which is far from extending product lifetime.[2149] If not satisfied with the proposed remedies, consumers can still invoke their right to repair granted by EU law, provided that the good is still covered under the two-year legal guarantee.[2150] In this regard, it

2142 See for ex. Tribunal de grande instance de Nanterre 17 September 2017, Plainte au Procureur de la République, *HOP* v. *X*.

2143 See criteria 3(b) of the annex to the Commission Decision (EU) 2016/1371 of 10 August 2016 establishing the ecological criteria for the award of the EU Ecolabel for personal, notebook and tablet computers, OJ L 217, 12.8.2016, p. 9–37. The Commission Decision (EU) 2016/1371 indicates that 'defects' include failure to charge and to detect the battery's connection, but do not encompass a progressive reduction in the battery's capacity due to usage unless it is covered by a specific warranty provision.

2144 Criterion 3(d) of the annex to the Commission Decision (EU) 2016/1371 of 10 August 2016 establishing the ecological criteria for the award of the EU Ecolabel for personal, notebook and tablet computers, OJ L 217, 12.8.2016, p. 9–37.

2145 See criterion 3(e) of the annex to the Commission Decision (EU) 2020/1804 of 27 November 2020 establishing the EU Ecolabel criteria for electronic displays, OJ L 402, 1.12.2020, p. 73–88. This provision also requires the applicant to offer this guarantee with a service agreement with pick-up and return for cases where repair in not done on-site.

2146 See criterion 9.2. of the annex to the Commission Decision (EU) 2016/1332 of 28 July 2016 establishing the ecological criteria for the award of the EU Ecolabel for furniture, OJ L 210, 4.8.2016, p. 100–149.

2147 Criterion 14 of the annex to the Commission Decision of 17 December 2013 establishing the ecological criteria for the award of the EU Ecolabel for imaging equipment, OJ L 353, 28.12.2013, p. 53–63.

2148 Criterion 12.3. of the annex to the Commission Decision 2014/391/EU of 23 June 2014 establishing the ecological criteria for the award of the EU Ecolabel for bed mattresses, OJ L 184, 25.6.2014, p. 18–48.

2149 For a more detailed analysis of this remedy, see Chapter IV on the use stage, and more specifically n° 646.

2150 Consumer guarantee rights are more thoroughly discussed in Chapter IV on the use stage (see n° 657 *et seq.*).

is surprising to note that some minimum guarantee periods required under EU Ecolabel law last two years when one knows that a two-year guarantee is already provided for by the Sale of Goods Directive for all consumer goods.

605. Information requirements on the use, maintenance and disposal of products – Finally, EU Ecolabel legislation requires applicants to provide information on how to use, maintain and dispose of their products. For example, a list of recommendations on how to use, maintain and dispose of ecolabelled bed mattresses must be reported in the warranty documentation.[2151] Similar recommendations for the use, cleaning and maintenance of floor coverings are required.[2152] For computers, information must be provided about known factors influencing the lifetime of rechargeable batteries, as well as instructions on how the user can prolong battery life. This information must be included in factory-installed energy management software, written user instructions and posted on the manufacturer's website. Computer users must also be informed that extension of computer lifetime reduces the product's overall environmental impacts and must receive indications on how to prolong computer lifetimes.[2153]

c) *Existing criteria for product reparability*

606. Criteria on the ease of disassembly – EU Ecolabel criteria on product reparability are mainly a combination of three elements. First of all, products are required to be designed with features that ensure their easy disassembly. As an example, imaging equipment must be easily disassembled by professionally trained personnel using the tools usually available to them, for the purpose of repairs and replacements of worn-out parts and upgrading older or obsolete parts.[2154] Spare parts of electronic displays, such as screen assembly and LED backlight, must be accessible and exchangeable by the use of commercially available tools.[2155] Moreover, the Ecolabel criteria for electronic displays forbid the use of adhesives which need to be removed with heat or chemicals to fix the back cover of the product as well as casing parts designed with electronic

---

2151 Criterion 12 and 15 of the annex to the Commission Decision 2014/391/EU of 23 June 2014 establishing the ecological criteria for the award of the EU Ecolabel for bed mattresses, OJ L 184, 25.6.2014, p. 18–48.

2152 Criterion 10 of the annex to the Commission Decision (EU) 2017/176 of 25 January 2017 on establishing EU Ecolabel criteria for wood-, cork- and bamboo-based floor coverings, OJ L 28, 2.2.2017, p. 44–68.

2153 Criterion 3 of the annex to the Commission Decision (EU) 2016/1371 of 10 August 2016 establishing the ecological criteria for the award of the EU Ecolabel for personal, notebook and tablet computers, OJ L 217, 12.8.2016, p. 9–37.

2154 Criterion 9 of the annex to the Commission Decision of 17 December 2013 establishing the ecological criteria for the award of the EU Ecolabel for imaging equipment, OJ L 353, 28.12.2013, p. 53–63.

2155 Criterion 3(a)(i) of the annex to the Commission Decision (EU) 2020/1804 of 27 November 2020 establishing the EU Ecolabel criteria for electronic displays, OJ L 402, 1.12.2020, p. 73–88.

assemblies which cannot be removed with use of commercially available tools.[2156] Concerning furniture consisting of multiple component parts or materials, it must be designed for disassembly to facilitate repair, reuse and recycling. Moreover, disassembly and replacement operations must be capable of being carried out using common and basic manual tools and unskilled labour.[2157] Similar criteria exist for bed mattresses[2158] and floor coverings that are not glued down.[2159]

More advanced requirements have been adopted for computers.[2160] First, computer design must allow major components (e.g. memory and cooling fan assemblies) to be easily accessible, exchangeable and upgradeable by the end-user using universal tools. Second, rechargeable battery packs must be easy to extract by one person (either a non-professional user or a professional repair service provider) without tools or with common tools with a maximum of three or four steps, with the help of simple instructions accessible on the website or in a manual. Third, batteries must not be glued or soldered into a product and there should be no metal tapes, adhesive strips or cables that prevent access to extract the battery.

607. Criteria related to spare parts – Secondly, there are some EU Ecolabel criteria on spare parts, which must be available publicly, at a reasonable cost and for a minimum period of time after the end of production of the product. The availability period varies between products, lasting eight years for electronic displays[2161] and five years for furniture[2162], imaging equipment[2163] and computers (including rechargeable batteries).[2164] Interestingly, an exception

---

2156 Criterion 3(a)(ii) and (iii) of the annex to the Commission Decision (EU) 2020/1804 of 27 November 2020 establishing the EU Ecolabel criteria for electronic displays, OJ L 402, 1.12.2020, p. 73–88.

2157 Criterion 9.4. of the annex to the Commission Decision (EU) 2016/1332 of 28 July 2016 establishing the ecological criteria for the award of the EU Ecolabel for furniture, OJ L 210, 4.8.2016, p. 100–149.

2158 Criterion 13 of the annex to the Commission Decision 2014/391/EU of 23 June 2014 establishing the ecological criteria for the award of the EU Ecolabel for bed mattresses, OJ L 184, 25.6.2014, p. 18–48.

2159 Criterion 9 of the annex to the Commission Decision (EU) 2017/176 of 25 January 2017 on establishing EU Ecolabel criteria for wood-, cork- and bamboo-based floor coverings, OJ L 28, 2.2.2017, p. 44–68.

2160 Commission Decision (EU) 2016/1371 of 10 August 2016 establishing the ecological criteria for the award of the EU Ecolabel for personal, notebook and tablet computers, OJ L 217, 12.8.2016, p. 9–37.

2161 Criterion 3(d) of the annex to the Commission Decision (EU) 2020/1804 of 27 November 2020 establishing the EU Ecolabel criteria for electronic displays, OJ L 402, 1.12.2020, p. 73–88.

2162 Criterion 9.3. of the annex to the Commission Decision (EU) 2016/1332 of 28 July 2016 establishing the ecological criteria for the award of the EU Ecolabel for furniture, OJ L 210, 4.8.2016, p. 100–149.

2163 Criterion 14 of the annex to the Commission Decision of 17 December 2013 establishing the ecological criteria for the award of the EU Ecolabel for imaging equipment, OJ L 353, 28.12.2013, p. 53–63.

2164 Commission Decision (EU) 2016/1371 of 10 August 2016 establishing the ecological criteria for the award of the EU Ecolabel for personal, notebook and tablet computers, OJ L 217, 12.8.2016, p. 9–37.

is provided for imaging equipment if there are "*unavoidable and temporary circumstances that are beyond manufacturer's control such as a natural disaster*".[2165] Nonetheless, cost and time of delivery of these spare parts are not specified in any detail. The only indications in this regard can be found in the Ecolabel criteria for furniture, where the cost (if any) of spare parts must be proportional to the total cost of the furniture product.[2166]

608. Criteria related to the provision of disassembly and repair instructions and contact details – Thirdly, some reparability requirements related to the provision of disassembly and repair instructions and contact details. Simple and illustrated instructions regarding the disassembly and replacement of damaged component parts/materials must be provided for furniture[2167], floor covering[2168] and electronic displays.[2169] For labelled computers, traders must also provide a diagram showing the location of the components to the end-user to enable basic repairs to be undertaken.[2170] In addition to information on repair and disassembly, contact details must be provided to let the user know who is qualified to repair, where to go to obtain professional repairs and arrange the delivery of spare parts.[2171] The Ecolabel criteria for electronic displays also require information on the recommended

2165 Criterion 14 of the annex to the Commission Decision of 17 December 2013 establishing the ecological criteria for the award of the EU Ecolabel for imaging equipment, OJ L 353, 28.12.2013, p. 53–63.

2166 Criterion 9.3. of the annex to the Commission Decision (EU) 2016/1332 of 28 July 2016 establishing the ecological criteria for the award of the EU Ecolabel for furniture, OJ L 210, 4.8.2016, p. 100–149.

2167 Criterion 9.4. of the annex to the Commission Decision (EU) 2016/1332 of 28 July 2016 establishing the ecological criteria for the award of the EU Ecolabel for furniture, OJ L 210, 4.8.2016, p. 100–149.

2168 Criterion 9 of the annex to the Commission Decision (EU) 2017/176 of 25 January 2017 on establishing EU Ecolabel criteria for wood-, cork- and bamboo-based floor coverings, OJ L 28, 2.2.2017, p. 44–68.

2169 Criterion 3(b) and 6.1.(e) and (f) of the annex to the Commission Decision (EU) 2020/1804 of 27 November 2020 establishing the EU Ecolabel criteria for electronic displays, OJ L 402, 1.12.2020, p. 73–88.

2170 Commission Decision (EU) 2016/1371 of 10 August 2016 establishing the ecological criteria for the award of the EU Ecolabel for personal, notebook and tablet computers, OJ L 217, 12.8.2016, p. 9–37.

2171 See criterion 9.3. of the annex to the Commission Decision (EU) 2016/1332 of 28 July 2016 establishing the ecological criteria for the award of the EU Ecolabel for furniture, OJ L 210, 4.8.2016, p. 100–149; Criterion 3(c) of the annex to the Commission Decision (EU) 2020/1804 of 27 November 2020 establishing the EU Ecolabel criteria for electronic displays, OJ L 402, 1.12.2020, p. 73–88; Criterion 6(a) Commission Decision (EU) 2016/1371 of 10 August 2016 establishing the ecological criteria for the award of the EU Ecolabel for personal, notebook and tablet computers, OJ L 217, 12.8.2016, p. 9–37. The ecolabel rules on electronic displays adds that the applicant may only provide information on its authorized service providers during the commercial guarantee period.

manufacturer price of spare parts.[2172] These pieces of information must generally be disclosed in the user instructions as well as on the manufacturer's website. Restriction of access to information is allowed for computers, allowing this information to be limited to the applicant's authorised service providers during the commercial guarantee period.[2173]

d) *Existing criteria on reuse, recycling and end-of-life management*

609. Criteria on the ease of dismantling – Some EU Ecolabel criteria facilitate the dismantling of (obsolete) products at the end-of-life stage. As already explained in the first chapter of this book[2174], products and their constituent components are dismantled and disintegrated when recycled.[2175] Dismantling can also help to reuse obsolete products. Electronic displays are subject to such criteria. For example, plastic enclosures of ecolabelled televisions should not contain moulded-in or glue-on metal unless the metal inserts can be removed with commercially available tools.[2176] Applicant are also under obligation to make available to professional operators of the waste sector, in a website and free of charge, information relevant for the dismantling and recovery of electronic displays.[2177] Similar criteria apply to ecolabelled imaging equipment, which must be easily dismantled for recycling or reuse by professionally trained personnel using the tools usually available to them.[2178] These requirements are complementary to those set out by waste rules for specific product categories, such as electrical and electronic equipment, batteries and vehicles.[2179]

610. Criteria on the design for recycling and reuse of toner and ink cartridges – Ecolabel rules on imaging equipment also regulate the design of

2172 Criterion 3(c) of the annex to the Commission Decision (EU) 2020/1804 of 27 November 2020 establishing the EU Ecolabel criteria for electronic displays, OJ L 402, 1.12.2020, p. 73–88.

2173 Commission Decision (EU) 2016/1371 of 10 August 2016 establishing the ecological criteria for the award of the EU Ecolabel for personal, notebook and tablet computers, OJ L 217, 12.8.2016, p. 9–37.

2174 See *supra*, n° 156.

2175 In this regard, 'dismantling' should be distinguished from 'disassembly', which is "*the process by which a product can be separated into its parts in a non-destructive way*" (n° 148).

2176 Criterion 4.1.(a)(iii) of the annex to the Commission Decision (EU) 2020/1804 of 27 November 2020 establishing the EU Ecolabel criteria for electronic displays, OJ L 402, 1.12.2020, p. 73–88.

2177 Criterion 4.1.(b)(2) of the annex to the Commission Decision (EU) 2020/1804 of 27 November 2020 establishing the EU Ecolabel criteria for electronic displays, OJ L 402, 1.12.2020, p. 73–88.

2178 Criterion 9 of the annex to the Commission Decision of 17 December 2013 establishing the ecological criteria for the award of the EU Ecolabel for imaging equipment, OJ L 353, 28.12.2013, p. 53–63.

2179 See Chapter V on the waste stage, and more specifically n° 956.

toner and ink cartridges in a way that makes them easier to recycle and reuse.[2180] Ecolabelled printers must accept remanufactured toner and/or ink cartridges and be designed taking reuse of toner and/or ink cartridge into consideration. Anti-reutilisation devices and practices, which prevent the reutilisation of cartridges, is prohibited. In addition, manufacturers are required to include the following message in the instruction manual of the product: "*The cartridges of this equipment are designed for reuse. It is recommended to reuse the cartridge as this is saving resource.*".[2181] These criteria help counter cases of indirect obsolescence, which are due to a lack of consumables.[2182]

611. Toner and ink cartridge take-back requirement – To facilitate the reuse and recycling of consumables, printer manufacturers who apply for the EU Ecolabel are also obliged to offer to users a take-back system for the return of toner and ink cartridges that are supplied or recommended for use in the product.[2183] Toner and ink modules and containers can be channelled in person or by shipment and must be taken back free of charge by the return facility named by the applicant. Detailed information on the return system must be included in the product documents. Manufacturers may ask third parties to perform this task. In this case, they must provide them with instructions for proper handling of residual toner. If recycling is not possible, non-recyclable product parts must be properly disposed.[2184]

612. Information requirements on the disposal of the product – Finally, some EU Ecolabel criteria contribute to raising consumer awareness on and draw their attention to the importance of discarding their (obsolete) products.[2185] For example, electronic display manufacturers who apply for an EU Ecolabel must provide end-of-life instructions for the proper disposal of the product at civic amenity sites or through retailer take-back schemes as applicable.[2186] These instructions must comply with the provisions of the WEEE Directive.[2187]

2180 Criterion 10 of the annex to the Commission Decision of 17 December 2013 establishing the ecological criteria for the award of the EU Ecolabel for imaging equipment, OJ L 353, 28.12.2013, p. 53–63.

2181 Criterion 15(c) of the annex to the Commission Decision of 17 December 2013 establishing the ecological criteria for the award of the EU Ecolabel for imaging equipment, OJ L 353, 28.12.2013, p. 53–63.

2182 See *supra*, n° 113.

2183 Criterion 11 of the annex to the Commission Decision of 17 December 2013 establishing the ecological criteria for the award of the EU Ecolabel for imaging equipment, OJ L 353, 28.12.2013, p. 53–63.

2184 Similar take-back obligations exist for specific waste streams, such as batteries. See Chapter V on the waste stage, and more specifically n° 951.

2185 Similar information obligations are imposed for batteries. See *infra*, n° 961.

2186 Criterion 6.1.(g) of the annex to the Commission Decision (EU) 2020/1804 of 27 November 2020 establishing the EU Ecolabel criteria for electronic displays, OJ L 402, 1.12.2020, p. 73–88.

2187 For further details on the WEEE Directive, see Chapter V on the waste stage.

4. POSSIBLE FUTURE EU ECOLABEL CRITERIA ON PRODUCT SUSTAINABILITY ASPECTS

a) *Integrating more criteria on product sustainability*

613. The need for more EU Ecolabel criteria on product sustainability – Having regard to the existing EU Ecolabel criteria, it can be observed that a broad range of durability and reparability aspects have been integrated into the EU Ecolabel criteria. Yet, the potential of the EU Ecolabel scheme to promote product sustainability should be further exploited. The main criteria should be reviewed to make sure that it fits neatly within the 2019 EU Circular Economy Action Plan (see #3).[2188] If consumers (including public institutions) know that Ecolabelled products are synonymous with sustainable goods, the demand for them may grow and consequently stimulate EU Ecolabel uptake. The development of new Ecolabel criteria on product sustainability is even more important as it could be seen as an alternative while waiting for the adoption of mandatory ecodesign and labelling requirements on these aspects. Of course, this should be thoroughly thought through as imposing more restrictive conditions on voluntary ecolabels may deter producers from opting for such labels in the first place.[2189] Therefore, as opposed to the suggestion made in the EU Ecolabel Work Plan[2190], improving the uptake of existing criteria should not have priority over, but be done in combination with, the development of new criteria.

614. Various possible criteria on product sustainability – A wide array of requirements on material efficiency could be integrated into the EU Ecolabel criteria.[2191] For example, applicants for the EU Ecolabel could be required to inform consumers about predetermined breaking points and wearing parts as well as about the conditions under which these fail or at which intervals (time, use cycles or limit values) maintenance should be carried out. This also includes information on use restrictions, like the need to use hand mixers only for a short period of time.[2192] Moreover, requirements on the availability of software and firmware updates, as well as on the deletion and transfer of personal data, could

[2188] B. Keirsbilck, E. Terryn, A. Michel and I. Alogna, *Sustainable Consumption and Consumer Protection Legislation* (European Parliament 2020) p. 14.

[2189] This is for example the case with textiles. See Wendy, 'What Is BCI Cotton and Is It Sustainable, Ethical or Organic?', *Moral Fibres*, 13 September 2021, available on: <https://moralfibres.co.uk/what-is-bci-cotton-and-is-it-sustainable-ethical-or-organic/>.

[2190] European Commission and EUEB, EU Ecolabel Work Plan for 2016 – 2018, p. 11.

[2191] See also M. Cordella, F. Alfieri, J. Sanfelix, S. Donatello, R. Kaps, O. Wolf, 'Improving material efficiency in the life cycle of products: a review of EU Ecolabel criteria', 25 *The International Journal of Life Cycle Assessment volume* (2020) p. 921 at p. 935.

[2192] S. Prakash et al., *Einfluss der Nutzungsdauer von Produkten auf ihre Umweltwirkung – Schaffung einer Informationsgrundlage und Entwicklung von Strategien gegen "Obsoleszenz"* (Umweltbundesamt Study 2016) p. 280.

be adopted. These criteria would allow avoiding or delaying the obsolescence of products with digital content, support the promotion of second-hand markets and prolong product lifetimes.[2193] This is increasingly important because the expanding 'Internet of Things' increases the number of those goods and because electronics have a significant impact on sustainable development. The lifecycle assessment (LCA)[2194] could help select the most appropriate criteria for the products concerned. For example, the technical analysis of LCA studies revealed that for computers, especially those with short lifetimes (e.g. notebooks and tablets), the manufacturing phase has more significant environmental impacts compared to the use phase.[2195] Consequently, new criteria on lifetime extension have been developed for computers, including criteria on durability, reparability and upgradability. Similar analysis should be undertaken for other products.

> *Policy recommendation:*
>
> *#3 More sustainability aspects should be integrated into the EU Ecolabel criteria.*

b) Drawing inspiration from the German Blue Angel ecolabel

615. The Blue Angel ecolabel – In addition to the EU Ecolabel Regulation, other voluntary ecolabels have been developed within the Member States. Among these national ecolabels, there is the German Blue Angel certification scheme, which awards the *Blue Angel* ecolabel to products that meet specific criteria on product sustainability, including on durability and reparability. Hence, the *Blue Angel* ecolabel provides environmental information on products and services which guides consumers at the time of purchase towards products and services that have a reduced environmental impact throughout their lifetime. The label is owned by the German authorities and is verified by the certification company RAL gGmbH. The label is awarded based on a specific set of requirements and criteria developed by the independent Environmental Label Jury[2196], in cooperation with the German Government and the Federal Environment Agency (*Umweltbundesamt*). The continuous development and update of the

---

[2193] M. Cordella, F. Alfieri, J. Sanfelix, S. Donatello, R. Kaps, O. Wolf, 'Improving material efficiency in the life cycle of products: a review of EU Ecolabel criteria', 25 *The International Journal of Life Cycle Assessment volume* (2020) p. 928.

[2194] For further details on the LCA, see Chapter II on the design and production stage, and more specifically n° 216.

[2195] N. Dodd, C. Vidal-Abarca and O. Wolf, *Revision of the European Ecolabel Criteria for Personal, Notebook and Tablet Computers – JRC Science and Policy Reports* (European Commission 2019) p. 11.

[2196] The Environmental Label Jury includes representatives from environmental and consumer associations, trade unions, industry, the trade, crafts, local authorities, academia, the media, churches, young people and the German federal states.

criteria is supported by environmental and consumer organizations as well as manufacturers.

616. Requirements on product durability and reparability – Among the requirements that manufacturers must satisfy to get the *Blue Angel* label on their products, there are requirements on product durability and reparability. For certain products, the label certifies a product design that enables ease of repair and ensures a long lifespan, but it also ensures guarantees that go beyond legal requirements and the availability of spare parts after the end of sale. Such requirements are particularly well-advanced for mobile phones. The label *The Blue Angel* will only be awarded to mobile phones that have a battery which meets particularly high-quality standards (e.g. achieve a minimum of 500 full charge cycles) and which can be replaced by the user without special expert knowledge and without damaging the phone. Mobile phones must be designed to enable qualified specialist workshops to replace, with reasonable effort, spare parts which typically break down within the scope of the ordinary use of a product (e.g. batteries, displays and front glasses). These spare parts must be available for at least 3 years from the time that production ceases and must be offered at reasonable prices by the manufacturer itself or by a third party. There are also requirements on software updates that impose the availability of security updates for the operating system of the mobile phone for at least 4 years from the time that production ceases. Another key requirement for labelled mobile phones is that the user must be able to delete all personal data completely and securely without the help of pay software. This requirement should reassure consumers who are reluctant to give or sell their mobile phone for second-hand use.[2197] Similar durability and reparability requirements were set up for other electric devices, like computers[2198], vacuum cleaners.[2199] Requirements have also been established for software products[2200], on which the lifetime of many devices depends.

617. Making the label more visible and internationally recognised – A 2014 study commissioned by the EC revealed that an overwhelming majority

[2197] Basic Award Criteria of the German Ecolabel Blue Angel from July 2017 for mobile phones, DE-UZ 106, available on: <https://www.blauer-engel.de/en/products/electric-devices/mobile-phones>.

[2198] Basic Award Criteria of the German Ecolabel Blue Angel from January 2017 for computers and keyboards, RAL-UZ 78, available on: <https://www.blauer-engel.de/en/products/electric-devices/computers-and-keyboards>.

[2199] Basic Award Criteria of the German Ecolabel Blue Angel from January 2020 for vacuum cleaners, DE-UZ 188, available on: <https://www.blauer-engel.de/en/products/electric-devices/vakuum-cleaners-new>.

[2200] Basic Award Criteria of the German Ecolabel Blue Angel from January 2020 for resource and energy-efficient software products, DE-UZ 215, available on: <https://www.blauer-engel.de/en/products/electric-devices/resources-and-energy-efficient-software-products>.

of German consumers understand and trust the logo Blue Angel.[2201] Still, empirical surveys showed that the *Blue Angel* label was no longer perceived as quite contemporary, particularly among younger target groups. A study was therefore launched with the view of modernizing the label.[2202] The objective was to increase the visibility and conciseness of the label while maintaining the recognition value and long-established trust. In addition to this project, a 2013 study funded by the German Environment Ministry evaluated the possibility for the *Blue Angel* label to function internationally and promote sustainable consumption beyond Germany.[2203] The results showed that a targeted internationalisation strategy is needed to ensure the medium- to long-term success of the label in foreign markets. Key elements of such a strategy are the development of Common Core Criteria with national ecolabels that have already established an international position, and the mutual recognition and certification of ecolabels among each other.

618. A SOURCE OF INSPIRATION FOR THE EU ECOLABEL – With its high recognition value among the vast majority of consumers and its well-established scheme, the *Blue Angel* certification is an inspiring example of initiatives that contribute to the promotion of sustainable products. Inspiration should be drawn from this national ecolabel not only because of its requirements and reputation but also because of the constant search for improvement. *The Blue Angel* proves that self-regulatory norms can deal with the shortening lifespans of products. The importance of voluntary instruments and the involvement of manufacturers in the fight against premature obsolescence has already been emphasized in German policy documents and literature.[2204] As rightly pointed out by T. Cooper, "*a voluntary approach may suffice when there is a broad social consensus that a particular course of action is appropriate*".[2205]

2201 According to the study, 8 out of 10 German consumers showed a partial understanding of the logo Blue Angel (83%) and 11% no understanding at all. Only 6% demonstrated a full understanding (with no wrong answers). 81% of respondents trust the label Blue Angel. See GfK Belgium, time.lex, Milieu Ltd, BIO IS and the Ecologic Institute, *Consumer market study on environmental claims for non-food products* (2014 European Commission) p. 82 and p. 86.

2202 K. Götz, B. Birzle-Harder, *Modernisierung des Blauen Engel* (Umweltbundesamt 2018).

2203 S. Prakash, J. Gröger, M. Lichtl, *Stärkung der internationalen Nutzung des Blauen Engels als Klimaschutzzeichen – Vorhaben im Rahmen der nationalen Klimaschutzinitiative* (2013).

2204 See for ex. S. Prakash et al., *Einfluss der Nutzungsdauer von Produkten auf ihre Umweltwirkung – Schaffung einer Informationsgrundlage und Entwicklung von Strategien gegen "Obsoleszenz"* (Umweltbundesamt 2016); J. Longmuss and E. Poppe, 'Planned obsolescence: who are those planners?', in C. Bakker and R. Mugge (eds.), *Product Lifetimes And The Environment 2017 – Conference Proceedings* (IOS Press 2017) p. 217 at p. 221.

2205 T. Cooper, 'Policies for longevity', in T. Cooper (ed.), *Longer lasting products: Alternatives to the throwaway society* (Gower 2010) p. 225.

5. AWARD AND USE OF EU ECOLABELS, COMPLIANCE MONITORING AND SANCTIONS

619. Award procedure – To be awarded the label, operators must submit an application to one or more EU countries[2206], which sends it to the competent national body designated by Member States, as required by Article 4 of the Regulation.[2207] After having received the application dossier with the relevant declarations, data sheets and test results, the competent body verifies that all submitted information is accurate and substantiated and carries out further tests if necessary. The effectiveness of these assessments is highly dependent on the methodology established under the EU Ecolabel scheme and may be improved by the adoption of the initiative on 'Substantiating green claims'.[2208] If the product complies with the ecolabel criteria, the competent body concludes a contract with the operator, establishing the terms of use and withdrawal of the label.[2209] The use of the label is subject to payment of a fee when the application is made, and an annual fee.

620. Use of the label – Once the EU Ecolabel has been awarded, operators are entitled to place the label on the product and communicate on their EU Ecolabel products. Operators are advised to take full advantage of the EU Ecolabel and make their environmental and quality commitment via the EU Ecolabel visible on various channels. They can, first, display the EU Ecolabel logo and their licence number on the product and on all related promotional material, as emphasized in Article 9(11) of the Regulation.[2210] Second, they can present the EU Ecolabel logo and licence number on the homepage of their website in a visible way, along with a dedicated page on their environmental commitment. Third, they can use social media to multiply communication about their EU Ecolabel logo. Finally, for greater visibility, they can register their products on the EU Ecolabel Product Catalogue.[2211]

2206 If the product is made within the European Economic Area, the application must be submitted to the country in which the product originates. If the product is made outside the European Economic Area, the application must be submitted to the countries where the product is marketed or will be placed on the market.

2207 In this regard, a distinction must be made between the responsibility for establishing and revising the criteria which lies mainly with 'Lead' Competent Bodies and the European Commission, and the award of the label to products which is solely a matter for the national Competent Bodies.

2208 See the previous section on the development procedure of EU ecolabel criteria (n° 597 *et seq.*).

2209 A template of the standard contract covering the terms of use of the EU Ecolabel can be found in Annex IV to the Ecolabel Regulation.

2210 Operators can get more information on how to correctly use the logo in the EU Ecolabel Logo Guidelines, available on: <https://ec.europa.eu/environment/ecolabel/documents/Logo%20Guidelines_June%202020.pdf>.

2211 The EU Ecolabel Product Catalogue is available on: <http://ec.europa.eu/ecat/>.

621. Compliance monitoring – It is for the operators to ensure compliance with criteria throughout the entire validity of their licence(s). In that respect, they must conduct test samples of their products and keep a journal of all tests conducted along with their results. This documentation should always be available and may be requested by the competent body. Pursuant to Article 10(2) of the Regulation, the competent body may also decide to carry out factory inspections and product tests, including upon complaint, to monitor on-going compliance with the EU Ecolabel criteria and the rules on its use. Article 10(3) and (4) require the user of the EU Ecolabel to allow the competent body to undertake all necessary investigations and access to the premises on which the product concerned is produced if the competent body requests so. All these verifications must be undertaken regularly. The aim is to ensure that environmental excellence is maintained.

622. Different sanctions in case of non-compliance – Article 10 of the Regulation provides for different sanctions in case of non-compliance with EU Ecolabel legislation. According to Article 10(5), if the competent body receives evidence that a product no longer complies with the criteria during the validity period, it can request an immediate corrective action plan or prohibit the use of the EU Ecolabel on that product. If the EU Ecolabel has been awarded by another competent body, it must inform that competent body. The competent body must without delay inform all other competent bodies and the EC of that prohibition. Besides these cases of non-compliance, Article 10(1) also prohibits cases whereby false or misleading advertising or use of any label or logo leads to confusion with the EU Ecolabel. Although the provision does not mention the sanctions accompanying this prohibition, its wording can be easily linked to Article 6 of the UCPD and to point 2 of the UCPD blacklist, which allows for private sanctions.

6. INTERMEDIATE CONCLUSION

623. The limited impact of voluntary ecolabels as a sole measure – Ecolabels target the best-performing products and services available on the EU market. The share of ecolabelled products in the mass market is inevitably small. As ecolabels internalize the external environmental costs, ecolabelled products and services are generally sold at a premium price to consumers. Price-sensitive consumers are unlikely to consider ecolabels in their purchase decisions. Consequently, voluntary labelling schemes on their own, do not have a large-scale direct market effect and hence have limited potential in moving markets towards greater sustainability.

624. A HIGHER IMPACT IF INTEGRATED IN A MIX OF LEGAL INSTRUMENTS – However, when integrated into a mix of instruments within a product policy framework, ecolabels can achieve a higher impact. They complement ecodesign mandatory requirements on three counts. First, while ecodesign rules phase-out the worst-performing products from the EU market, ecolabels set incentives for producers to go beyond these mandatory minimum requirements. The periodical revisions of the EU Ecolabel criteria lead to a stepwise push towards product sustainability. Second, the EU Ecolabel scheme indirectly sets standards that can be used for future mandatory ecodesign regulations. As a voluntary tool targeting frontrunners, the EU Ecolabel scheme can provide a reference base and a potential benchmark for design, communication and policy activities aimed at promoting material efficiency.[2212] Third, the EU Ecolabel can be seen as an alternative if no mandatory requirements can be adopted for specific products.

625. EU ECOLABELS SHOULD BE DEVELOPED FOR A BROADER RANGE OF PRODUCTS – At present, some products cannot be awarded the EU Ecolabel. An extension of the EU Ecolabel scheme to other product categories should thus be envisaged, especially if more criteria on product sustainability are to be adopted. Ecolabels should, for example, be envisaged for software products. Inspiration could be drawn from the German ecolabel *The Blue Angel*, which introduced award criteria for 'resource and energy-efficient software products'. Ecolabels should also be developed for services that contribute to prolonging the lifetime of products. These services encompass ancillary services such as after-sale, maintenance and repair services, and models without transfer of ownership such as product-lease or product-as-a-service.

626. MORE SUSTAINABILITY ASPECTS SHOULD BE INTEGRATED INTO THE EU ECOLABEL CRITERIA – Although applicants for the EU Ecolabel are already obliged to meet product durability and reparability requirements for certain product categories, more requirements of this kind should be introduced. Such Ecolabel criteria would spur the production of sustainable goods. Frontrunners would be further rewarded if these EU Ecolabel criteria become mandatory conditions to access the market. Moreover, such criteria would contribute to improving the recognition value of the EU Ecolabel, resulting in an increased uptake of it. Indeed, if the EU Ecolabel reflects the sustainable nature of products, consumers who are becoming increasingly aware of and sensitive to these aspects, may pay more attention to and favour Ecolabelled products. The growing demand for Ecolabelled products may then incentivise businesses to opt for the EU Ecolabel. Green public procurement and economic instruments may play a decisive role in this respect. Of course, a balancing exercise needs to be

[2212] M. Cordella, F. Alfieri, J. Sanfelix, S. Donatello, R. Kaps, O. Wolf, 'Improving material efficiency in the life cycle of products: a review of EU Ecolabel criteria', 25 *The International Journal of Life Cycle Assessment volume* (2020) p. 923.

carried out when imposing more stringent conditions on voluntary ecolabels as they may erect barriers that hinder and deter producers from choosing such a label in the first place.

627. The methodology should be reviewed – At present, the EU Ecolabel scheme uses methods for some products and parameters that are different from the ones used within the ecodesign and energy labelling frameworks. This is regrettable in terms of coherence and effectiveness. The ecodesign, energy label and ecolabel requirements should be developed simultaneously for the specific product groups. An approach could be tested to apply the same metrics for building different ambition levels for the worst and best products. The 'PEF' and 'OEF' methods, as well as the horizontal standards on material efficiency, could be useful in this regard.

628. The EU Ecolabel should be preferred over national voluntary labels – Although ecolabels remain voluntary and thus dependent on the choice of operators, the EU Ecolabel should be made more attractive to them so that only a limited number of ecolabels would exist within the EU market. As highlighted in the former Proposal for the EU Ecolabel Regulation, "*within a single market, a single set of guidelines benchmarking the environmental credibility of products is the logical way forward, as opposed to having different benchmarks in each Member State. An EU-wide scheme makes it easier for businesses wishing to market more 'environmentally friendly' products within the EU and it means consumers can purchase so-called 'greener' products, wherever they are, safe in the knowledge that these products share common environmental credentials. The EU Ecolabel is the only formal scheme for the entire internal market – existing national or regional ecolabel schemes cover it only in part.*"[2213] The demand for Ecolabelled products may grow, and consequently stimulate EU Ecolabel uptake, if consumers associate Ecolabelled products with sustainable goods. Developing new Ecolabel criteria on product sustainability aspects for a wider range of products is crucial in this regard. As for the national voluntary labels, it would be pointless and inappropriate to try to eliminate them. A close watch should nonetheless be kept on the compliance of these ecolabels with the legislation on unfair commercial practices.

G. CONCLUSION

629. Information on product sustainability is (already) available – Nowadays, consumers already have access to some information about the sustainability of products at the marketing and pre-contractual stage. Beyond

[2213] Proposal for a Regulation of the European Parliament and of the Council on a Community Ecolabel scheme, COM(2008) 401 final, p. 3.

the CE marking which attests conformity of the product with the applicable ecodesign requirements and the information requirements established under the Ecodesign Directive[2214], additional information is given either voluntarily by businesses and other actors or in accordance with information requirements set out in the law. EU and national rules regulate the mandatory and voluntary provision of this information and thus contribute, in one way or another, to the fight against premature obsolescence.

630. Four main EU legal instruments regulate consumer information – When it comes to making information available to consumers, different pieces of EU secondary law are concerned. These instruments embody consumers' subjective right to information enshrined in Article 169 TFEU. First, there is the UCPD, which prohibits misleading information, regulates voluntary claims related to product sustainability, imposes mandatory general information requirements and sanctions non-compliance with EU information requirements. The second relevant instrument is the CRD, which establishes additional pre-contractual information duties which cover sustainable aspects of products. Thirdly, specific information requirements are imposed under the Energy Labelling rules, which regulate the marketing stage of certain products. Consumers can rely on the energy label to get not only energy-related information but also extra information on specific products. Fourthly, consumers can identify products that have a reduced environmental impact throughout their lifecycle thanks to the label established by the EU Ecolabel Regulation.

631. National initiatives – At national level, some Member States, including Belgium, France and Germany, have decided or envisage going beyond the mere implementation of these EU rules and strengthening consumer information. France is undoubtedly the most proactive of the three Member States in this area of law, with, among others, its pioneering initiatives establishing a total ban on 'planned obsolescence', a reparability index and a duty to inform consumers on the availability of spare parts. Inspired by its French neighbour, Belgian law makers are currently considering and studying several amendments to Belgian law, though it is still at the stage of legislative proposals. Several legislative proposals were also put on the table in Germany, but none of them were finally adopted. Germany is also known for its strong base of research excellence, including on the topic of premature obsolescence, and for the voluntary ecolabel *The Blue Angel*.

632. Change is needed – However, in spite of the information already disclosed and consumers' strong intentions to adopt a sustainable lifestyle,

[2214] For more details, see *supra*, chapter on the design and production stage.

studies have revealed that there are still barriers that hamper sustainable consumption. In the light of these findings, it seems essential to review the current legal framework on consumer information. This, however, does not necessarily mean that new legal instruments or labels specifically dedicated to product sustainability should be adopted, quite the contrary. Although it could wipe the slate clean and raise awareness about the importance of product sustainability, embarking on such an ambitious enterprise would involve a tremendous workload, but also risks of increasing the complexity of the already complex network of rules.[2215] Adding more product labels could also make information overload worse for consumers. The existing rules only need some adjustments to unleash their untapped potential to serve as a key driver for sustainable consumption.[2216] These adjustments can be summarised in five main points.

633. First: explicit references to premature obsolescence and product sustainability in horizontal consumer legislation – Premature obsolescence and product sustainability should appear more clearly in general consumer legislation. On the one hand, the UCPD should explicitly ban practices of premature obsolescence. On the other, the UCPD and the CRD should clearly oblige traders to provide information on product sustainability aspects. Whereas it should be clear that product durability and reparability are to be regarded as 'material information' that traders should not omit to provide to consumers in the sense of Article 7 of the UCPD, these sustainable aspects should also be mentioned in the list of mandatory pre-contractual information contained in Articles 5 and 6 of the CRD. This could be done by amending the concerned provisions of both directives and/or by updating their respective guidance document. In any case, these clarifications should be made in parallel so that the information obligations of both legal instruments are aligned. Cross-references could be added in both directives to emphasize the close interplay of their provisions. These obligations are particularly beneficial for products that are exempted from specific information requirements under product-specific legislation, such as the energy labelling and ecodesign rules. In this regard, it complements the tailored approach followed by the Energy Labelling Regulation and EU Ecolabel Regulation for specific products. In the absence of these general

2215 *A contrario*, see E. Maitre-Ekern, C. Dalhammar, 'Towards a hierarchy of consumption behaviour in the circular economy', 26 *Maastricht Journal of European and Comparative Law* (2019) p. 415; E. Maitre-Ekern, M. Taylor and M. van der Velden, 'Towards a Sustainable Circular Economy: SMART reform proposals', 12 *University of Oslo Faculty of Law Legal Studies Research Paper Series* (2020) p. 10 at p. 32.

2216 These adjustments could possibly be accompanied by a more general adjustment. In this regard, some propose a right to know which would allow anyone to ask any company about the sustainability of products. See E. Maitre-Ekern, M. Taylor and M. van der Velden, 'Towards a Sustainable Circular Economy: SMART reform proposals', 12 *University of Oslo Faculty of Law Legal Studies Research Paper Series* (2020) pp. 30–31.

obligations, the development of product-specific requirements through the existing mandatory and voluntary labels would be even more welcome.

634. SECOND: MORE PRODUCT-SPECIFIC REQUIREMENTS ON PRODUCT SUSTAINABILITY FOR A WIDER RANGE OF PRODUCTS AND SERVICES – At present, some products and services fall outside the scope of product-specific rules and are thus exempted from the specific information requirements imposed by the Energy Labelling rules and/or cannot be awarded the EU Ecolabel. Yet, affixing mandatory or voluntary labels to some of these products and services would contribute to helping and encouraging consumers to take eco-friendly purchasing decisions and incentivising businesses to consider sustainability aspects when designing and marketing products. Therefore, more product-specific requirements on product sustainability aspects should be adopted for a wider range of products and services.

635. THIRD: A SINGLE, ROBUST AND EU-WIDE METHODOLOGY – A single, robust and EU-wide methodology should be developed to assess and verify environmental claims and the environmental labelling of products. The use of this methodology could be widespread. For example, it could be used within the framework of the EU Ecolabel scheme and help substantiate green claims. Further research should be undertaken to examine whether the 'PEF' and 'OEF' methods, which were developed by the EC to measure and benchmark the environmental performance of products, could fill this gap. When developing such a methodology, particular attention should be given to the need for the alignment and coherence between the definitions of terms (e.g. 'durability', 'product lifetime', 'spare parts', etc.) used in the different EU product, consumer and waste policies. The new standards on material efficiency developed by CEN and CENELEC could be of great use in this regard as they harmonise concepts, methods and nomenclatures to apply in the assessment of material efficiency aspects of energy-related products. If successful, the adoption and implementation of such common methods would increase coherence and effectiveness between the EU instruments involved. It would prevent consumers' confusion and loss of confidence in labels and claims, legal fragmentation in that area of law and unfair competition between businesses. Moreover, these methods would facilitate control mechanisms concerning information requirements.

636. FOURTH: REGULATING ENFORCEMENT AND SANCTIONS AT EU LEVEL – The enforcement of consumer information legislation and the accompanying sanctions could be improved. EU rules generally leave the Member States with considerable leeway in that regard. Even so, some adjustments could be made at EU level, especially to tackle infringements that produce effects beyond national boundaries. EU law should strengthen the cooperation between the national public authorities and could set minimum requirements, like the

Omnibus Directive or other legal rules from other sectors.[2217] In that respect, it is important to improve both control and ex-post mechanisms. At national level, different civil or criminal sanctions are imposed to punish companies which breach the law. These sanctions should have a deterrent effect and be appropriate considering the level of harm to competitors and consumers.

637. Fifth: bringing coherence between legal instruments – As repeatedly underlined throughout this third chapter, links should be made not only between the four main instruments regulating consumer information (i.e. UCPD, CRD, Energy Labelling Regulation and EU Ecolabel Regulation), but also with other legal rules, including those identified and analysed in the other chapters of this book. One way to strengthen these links would be to introduce a digital product passport, as proposed in the Proposal for Ecodesign for Sustainable Products Regulation. Such a passport would allow using and updating information on product sustainability over the whole lifecycle of products and prevent information overload. With this information, parties engaged in repair could, for example, estimate what it might cost to repair the device in-house or have it repaired, or what profit could be made from selling the device as a whole or as individual components. This would require manufacturers, collection schemes, recyclers, knowledge providers and sales platforms to work together to share relevant information and facilitate the sales of second-hand or harvested components.[2218]

638. The central role of product sustainability information to influence consumer purchasing decisions – With all the proposed adjustments, consumer information rules could occupy an even more central role in triggering sustainable products and tackling practices of premature obsolescence. Notwithstanding the challenges and limitations inherent in consumer information[2219], the provision of reliable, comparable, and verifiable information on product sustainability can enable and incentivise consumers to take more enlightened and eco-friendly decisions concerning their products at the point of sale.[2220] To maximize the potential influence of these rules on consumer behaviour, educational and awareness campaigns should be conducted.[2221]

2217 See for ex. Directive (EU) 2017/1371 of the European Parliament and of the Council of 5 July 2017 on the fight against fraud to the Union's financial interests by means of criminal law, OJ L 198, 28.7.2017, p. 29–41.

2218 Ellen MacArthur Foundation, *Empowering repair* (2016) p. 10.

2219 See the first section of this chapter (n° 335–339), which touched upon four main challenges of consumer information, namely (1) the need to adapt information to the types of products as well as (2) to the target audience, (3) to acknowledge the various consumer profiles and (4) to avoid the risks of information overload.

2220 Along the same lines, see O'Rourke and Ringer, 'The Impact of Sustainability Information on Consumer Decision Making', *Journal of Industrial Ecology* (2015) p. 882 at p. 892.

2221 Such educational and awareness campaigns were suggested in S. Prakash et al., *Einfluss der Nutzungsdauer von Produkten auf ihre Umweltwirkung – Schaffung einer*

639. With positive effects in other stages of the product lifetime – It is important to note that the positive effects of information disclosure are not restricted to the marketing and pre-contractual stage but can expand to the whole lifecycle of the product, if complemented and combined with other policies.[2222] Hence, even if there are uncertainties on the impact of these rules on consumer behaviour, there are supplementary reasons to regulate consumer information from a sustainability perspective. Making information on product sustainability available to consumers can help them maintain and properly use products, but also invoke their guarantee rights and lodge liability claims against producers and sellers when confronted with a prematurely obsolete product.[2223] If consumers know that they are better protected through information, they may pay more attention to information on product sustainability. Furthermore, information disclosure encourages professionals to design, produce, import and sell sustainable goods. They are encouraged and supported to bring sustainable products and practices to the fore and compete on sustainable aspects of products. At the same time, they are deterred from limiting the lifetime of their products for fear of reputational losses, especially if their liability may be engaged. Finally, some pieces of information, although addressed to consumers, can be used at the end-of-life stage of the product. Consequently, other strategies need to be considered alongside a strategy of information disclosure.

640. A necessity already known by national and EU law makers – This third chapter has demonstrated that the legislation mandating the disclosure of general and specific information on product sustainability and regulating voluntary claims and ecolabels occupies an important place in the network of rules tackling premature obsolescence. Given the recent developments, studies and initiatives, it seems that EU and national law makers are aware of the necessity to improve consumer information. At EU level, the EC has repeatedly emphasised the important part played by reliable, comparable and verifiable information in enabling consumers to make more sustainable decisions, including in its Green Deal[2224], but also more recently in its new Circular

Informationsgrundlage und Entwicklung von Strategien gegen "Obsoleszenz" (Umweltbundesamt Study 2016) pp. 280–281. These campaigns would inform consumers on the environmental impact of short-lived products, the product lifecycle costing (LCC), products' resource consumption, etc. See also the recommendations made for the Consumer Information Programme of the 10 Year Framework of Programmes for Sustainable Consumption and Production in C. Bakker, C. Schuit, *The long view – Exploring product lifetime extension* (United Nations Environment Programme 2017) p. 10.

2222 See also G. Howells, 'The Potential and Limits of Consumer Empowerment by Information', 32 *Journal of law and society* (2005) p. 362.

2223 For further details, see Chapter IV on the use stage.

2224 Communication from the Commission of 11 December 2019 to the European Parliament, the European Council, the Council, the European Economic and Social Committee and the Committee of the Regions on The European Green Deal, COM(2019) 640 final, p. 8.

Economy Action Plan.[2225] In this Action Plan, the EC even announced "*a revision of EU consumer law to ensure that consumers receive trustworthy and relevant information on products at the point of sale, including on their lifespan and on the availability of repair services, spare parts and repair manuals*". The EC also planned to "*consider further strengthening consumer protection against green washing and premature obsolescence, setting minimum requirements for sustainability labels/logos and for information tools*".[2226] Since then, key legislative proposals were adopted, including on 'Empowering consumers for the green transition',[2227] on 'Sustainable Products',[2228] on 'Substantiating green claims'[2229] and on 'Promoting the repair of goods'[2230]). At national level, efforts are also expended in this area of law, giving rise to various legislative proposals and studies on the topic. It remains to be seen whether the measures that are planned at both levels will be as ambitious as needed.

2225 Communication from the Commission of 11 March 2020 to the European Parliament, the Council, the European Economic and Social Committee and the Committee of the Regions on A new Circular Economy Action Plan – For a cleaner and more competitive Europe, COM(2020) 98 final, p. 5.

2226 *Ibid.*, p. 5.

2227 Proposal for a Directive of the European Parliament and of the Council amending Directives 2005/29/EC and 2011/83/EU as regards empowering consumers for the green transition through better protection against unfair practices and better information, COM(2022) 143 final.

2228 Proposal for a Regulation of the European Parliament and of the Council establishing a framework for setting ecodesign requirements for sustainable products and repealing Directive 2009/125/EC, COM(2022) 142 final.

2229 Proposal for a Directive of the European Parliament and of the Council on substantiation and communication of explicit environmental claims (Green Claims Directive), COM(2023) 166 final.

2230 Proposal for a Directive of the European Parliament and of the Council on common rules promoting the repair of goods and amending Regulation (EU) 2017/2394, Directives (EU) 2019/771 and (EU) 2020/1828, COM(2023) 155 final.

CHAPTER IV

THE USE STAGE: EXTENDING THE LIFETIME OF PRODUCTS ONCE PURCHASED

A. INTRODUCTION

641. Influencing product lifetime after purchase – Once a product has been purchased, several instruments of consumer law can have an impact on its lifetime. Some rules contribute to prolonging the lifetime of products, whereas others provide the wrong incentive and lead to the premature obsolescence of certain goods.

642. The remedies offered by EU and national consumer law – There are different remedies that protect consumers when the product does not live up to their expectations or when a defect occurs. First of all, consumers who are dissatisfied with the quality of a product bought online or away from business premises can invoke the right of withdrawal granted by Article 9 of the CRD. Once the withdrawal period has expired, the legal guarantee established under the 2019 Sale of Goods Directive ('SGD')[2231] offers consumers the possibility of having their defective products brought into conformity with the sale. Among the remedies available, the consumer is entitled to request repairs from the seller. Besides the legal guarantee, the SGD regulates commercial guarantees that are voluntarily offered to the consumer by the seller or the producer. In cases of lack of supply or conformity of the digital content or digital service, the 2019 Digital Content Directive ('DCD')[2232] grants consumers the right to call upon the trader to supply the conformed digital content or digital service. In addition to these EU legal instruments, some national contractual rules give consumers additional

---

2231 Directive (EU) 2019/771 of the European Parliament and of the Council of 20 May 2019 on certain aspects concerning contracts for the sale of goods, amending Regulation (EU) 2017/2394 and Directive 2009/22/EC, and repealing Directive 1999/44/EC, OJ L 136, 22.5.2019, p. 28–50.

2232 Directive (EU) 2019/770 of the European Parliament and of the Council of 20 May 2019 on certain aspects concerning contracts for the supply of digital content and digital services, OJ L 136, 22.5.2019, p. 1–27.

rights which they can rely on when their products are prematurely obsolete, like the guarantee against hidden defects.

643. Overview of the fourth chapter – In its first section, the fourth chapter of this book will start by enumerating the different remedies available to consumers who are dissatisfied with the quality of their product or confronted with a defective product, and by explaining the influence of these remedies on product lifetime. The first section will also pinpoint and describe several barriers that hinder consumers' sustainable choices at the use stage. The following sections of this chapter will identify and analyse the relevant provisions of the above-mentioned directives, with particular focus on the SGD, and the national implementing measures as well as purely national initiatives. Recommendations will be made when the contribution of these rules in the fight against premature obsolescence could be stronger.

B. MAPPING THE REMEDIES AVAILABLE TO CONSUMERS

1. DIFFERENT REMEDIES AND THEIR IMPACTS ON PRODUCT LIFETIME AND THE ENVIRONMENT

644. Various remedies at consumer's disposal – Before exploring the panoply of rules regulating the use stage, it is worth examining and comparing the remedies available to consumers once they purchase a product of unsatisfactory quality or which becomes defective. Some of these remedies are provided and regulated by the law in certain circumstances. If dissatisfied, consumers can, first of all, invoke the right of withdrawal for the first 14 days (at least) as established by Article 9 of the CRD and, in Ireland, the right to reject.[2233] Once these remedies of first resort are no longer possible, consumers who are confronted with a defect (e.g. due to an accident, improper use, weak parts or unavailable updates) have other remedies, which are regulated by the provisions of the SGD, namely replacement, repair, the appropriate reduction of the price or the termination of the contract. These remedies may however depend on the product type, the nature of the defect, but also on the existence of guarantee rights. If the defective product is covered by the legal guarantee and/or by a commercial guarantee offered by the seller or producer on a voluntary basis, consumers may be entitled to choose between repair, replacement, an appropriate reduction of the price or the termination of the contract.[2234] If the

[2233] See the Sale of Goods Act 1893, Section 53. It should be noted that the right to reject also exists in the UK: see the 2015 Consumer Rights Act, Section 19 *et seq.*

[2234] See *infra* (n° 657 *et seq.*).

defective product is not covered by such guarantees, consumers can still opt for repair through different avenues, including DIY initiatives and independent or authorised repair networks, or decide to replace the defective product with a substitute one. Among the variety of options, some are more sustainable than others.

645. The right of withdrawal and the right to reject – The first possibility for the consumer discontent with a product purchased online or away from business premises is to return the product to the trader within a short period of time after the delivery of the product.[2235] This period lasts 14 days from the physical possession of the goods for the right of withdrawal, whereas it can extend to 30 days for the right to reject. When this option is chosen, this marks the end of the use cycle of the returned product. The exercise and abuse of the right of withdrawal and the right to reject are particularly polluting, especially because of additional kilometres driven, the need for cleaning and repackaging, the (potential) diminished use or destruction of the returned products, and the waste produced during these operations.[2236] This problem is exacerbated by the ever-increasing number of returned products.[2237] The environmental impacts of these remedies may be offset if transportation and logistics are greened, if modular installation techniques are chosen and if returned goods are reused by being resold or donated.[2238] Interestingly, some national initiatives have already been undertaken to make e-commerce more environmentally friendly.[2239]

2235 These remedies concern a significant number of European consumers as online transactions are increasingly used, reaching 73% of internet users in 2020. See the E-commerce statistics for individuals published by Eurostat, showing the percentage of internet users in the EU who bought or ordered goods or services for private use in the previous 12 months by age group, from 2010 to 2020, available on: <https://ec.europa.eu/eurostat/statistics-explained/index.php/E-commerce_statistics_for_individuals>.

2236 See J. Schiffer, 'The unsustainable cost of free returns', *Vogue Business*, 30 July 2019, available on: <https://www.voguebusiness.com/consumers/returns-rising-costs-retail-environmental>, as well as R. De Bruyn, 'Vente en ligne: quel impact sur l'environnement?', *Ecoconso*, 13 December 2019, available on: <https://www.ecoconso.be/fr/content/vente-en-ligne-quel-impact-sur-lenvironnement>.

2237 S. Dennis, 'The Ticking Time Bomb of E-commerce Returns', *Forbes*, 14 February 2018, available on: <forbes.com/sites/stevendennis/2018/02/14/the-ticking-time-bomb-of-e-commerce-returns/?sh=77bcfabd4c7f>.

2238 For a detailed analysis of the possibilities of greening the right of withdrawal, see E. Terryn, E. Van Gool, 'Kunnen we e-commerce vergroenen door het consumentencontractenrecht te herzien?', *TvC* (2021) p. 15 at p. 28. See also E. Terryn, E. Van Gool, 'The Role of European Consumer Regulation in Shaping the Environmental Impact of E-Commerce', 10 *EuCML* (2021) p. 89 at p. 101.

2239 In Belgium, the *Conseil Central de l'Economie* has formulated several recommendations to make e-commerce, and especially the last mile, more sustainable. These recommendations include the use of price differentiation between sustainable (e.g. pick-up point) and less sustainable last mile delivery options and additional information to increase transparency on the environmental impact of home delivery. See Rapport du Conseil Central de l'Economie, Vision d'experts d'entreprises concernant le futur des livraisons e-commerce: A sustainable

646. Replacement – When a defect occurs, consumers can decide to replace the defective good. Replacement can have huge environmental impacts, especially if the replacement good is made of new materials (as it creates negative externalities due to resource extraction, production and transport) and if the replaced good is immediately discarded.[2240] The environmental impacts of replacement may be even worse if the product was designed to last as long-lasting products generally require more energy and resources to be produced. Product replacement is less damaging for the environment when the defective product is replaced by a reused, refurbished or remanufactured good ('circular replacement')[2241] and when the replaced product is given a new use cycle through direct reuse, repair, refurbishment or when its components are recovered through remanufacturing.[2242]

647. Repair – Consumers can also choose to repair the defective product. Through this remedy, consumers seek to retain or restore products to a desired level of performance so they can continue using them[2243], thus reversing product obsolescence.[2244] If successful, repair prolongs the lifespan of the product and consequently "*slows resource loops*"[2245] as consumers keep their good and do not buy a new one. This is why repair, with its lower materials consumption and, ultimately, less waste, is the most environmentally sustainable remedy.[2246] Repair is more sustainable than replacement, especially replacement by new goods, as it creates fewer negative externalities, by avoiding the resource extraction, production and transport required for a newly manufactured product and the likely disposal of the replaced good. Repair is also more sustainable than other circular strategies, such as recycling, as it preserves resource value and energy

---

last mile parcel delivery market, CCE 2019–2298, available on: <https://www.ccecrb.fgov.be/p/fr/725/vision-d-experts-d-entreprises-sur-le-futur-des-livraisons-e-commerce>. In France, since 1 January 2022, the destruction of new non-food products is prohibited. Producers, importers and distributors of new non-food products intended for sale are required to reuse (including by donation to charity organisations) or recycle their unsold goods. See Art. 35 Anti-Waste Law.

2240 E. Van Gool and A. Michel, 'The New Consumer Sales Directive 2019/771 and Sustainable Consumption: A Critical Analysis', 10 *EuCML* (2021) pp. 144–145.

2241 *Ibid*., p. 145.

2242 For further details on the different possible scenarios at the end of the product use cycle, see *infra* n° 909-913.

2243 E. Maitre-Ekern, C. Dalhammar, 'Towards a hierarchy of consumption behaviour in the circular economy', 26 *Maastricht Journal of European and Comparative Law* (2019) p. 404.

2244 See *supra*, n° 150 and 152.

2245 N.M.P. Bocken, I. de Pauw, C. Bakker and B. van der Grinten, 'Product design and business model strategies for a circular economy', *Journal of Industrial and Production Engineering* (2016) p. 309.

2246 See E. Maitre-Ekern, C. Dalhammar, 'Towards a hierarchy of consumption behaviour in the circular economy', 26 *Maastricht Journal of European and Comparative Law* (2019) p. 419; E. Terryn, 'A right to repair: Towards Sustainable Remedies in Consumer Law', 27 *E.R.P.L.* (2019) pp. 853–854; Ellen MacArthur Foundation, *Empowering repair* (2016), pp. 5–6.

more efficiently.[2247] Furthermore, repair is generally considered preferable to reconditioning or remanufacturing because less energy is needed and virtually all material is kept in use. Repair is even more sustainable if completed with refurbished and remanufactured components. Additionally, repair offers social and economic benefits as it creates local skilled-labour jobs instead of resource extraction and production activities that often take place in other parts of the world.[2248]

648. Appropriate reduction of the price – Instead of repair and replacement, consumers may be entitled to ask for an appropriate reduction of the price, provided that the conditions under the legal guarantee are fulfilled or that the commercial guarantee provides for such a remedy. The appropriate reduction of the price can be seen as contributing to prolonging product lifetime as the consumer keeps the defective good. However, such remedies create the possibility that consumers subsequently buy alternative goods, which cause new transaction and product lifecycle externalities. In that case, there is an increased risk that the original goods are not properly collected for circular purposes or waste processing.[2249] Yet, it is also likely that consumers do not buy alternative goods after price reduction, especially when goods lack full conformity but still offer one or more functionalities.

649. Termination of the contract – In some cases, consumers can also opt for the termination of the contract. It can be assumed that this remedy creates substantial externalities. First, terminating the contract requires restitution efforts, which depend on distance, the nature of goods and their possible installation. Second, the termination of the contract causes the risk of diminished use or destruction of the returned goods, like for the right of withdrawal and the right to reject.[2250] Third, like the appropriate reduction of the price[2251], consumers who terminate the contract could be tempted to subsequently buy alternative goods, which again cause new transaction and product lifecycle externalities. Nevertheless, the termination of the contract is not necessarily followed by alternative purchases. This scenario refers to the

---

2247 Ellen MacArthur Foundation, *Empowering repair* (2016) p. 6; N. Nasr, J.D. Russell, *Redefining Value – The Manufacturing Revolution. Remanufacturing, Refurbishment, Repair and Direct Reuse in the Circular Economy. A Report of the International Resource Panel* (United Nations Environment Programme 2018) p. 6; Material Economics, *Retaining Value in the Swedish Materials System. Material Economics* (2018).

2248 See Deloitte, *Study on Socioeconomic impacts of increased reparability – Final Report* (European Commission 2016) p. 14.

2249 E. Van Gool and A. Michel, 'The New Consumer Sales Directive 2019/771 and Sustainable Consumption: A Critical Analysis', 10 *EuCML* (2021) p. 146.

2250 See *supra*, n° 645.

2251 See *supra*, n° 648.

first circular strategy called 'refuse'.[2252] Furthermore, if alternative goods are purchased, the externalities associated with this purchase could, like for the other remedies, be countered by implementing circular strategies (i.e. reuse, repair, refurbishment and remanufacturing), by greening transportation and logistics and by developing modular installation techniques.

650. Supply of conformed digital content or digital service – Concerning goods that incorporate or are inter-connected with digital content or a digital service, consumers can request the supply of conformed digital content or digital service if the trader failed to do so. This remedy helps consumers keep their goods with digital elements for a longer period of time, avoiding the externalities attached to product replacement.

2. BARRIERS THAT HINDER THE PROLONGED USE OF PRODUCTS

651. Five main barriers to sustainable remedies – Despite these possibilities of remedying the defect in a (more) sustainable way, several technical, legal, economic and psychological barriers impede the choice of consumers opting for more sustainable remedies, i.e. repair, 'circular replacement' or a greener termination of the contract. Some of these barriers reduce the propensity and hinder the ability of consumers to repair their own goods ('DIY-repair') or to have them repaired at a reasonable price and speed by either third-party repair service providers ('independent repair') or by the original manufacturers and traders ('original repair').[2253]

652. First: barriers linked to product design – First, as already highlighted in the second chapter of this book, product design can greatly influence the lifetime of products. Consumers and independent repairers face increasingly complex products, which often have embedded software and might be designed in ways that discourage repair.[2254] For example, some products are particularly difficult or even impossible to repair as they cannot be (easily) disassembled – and the defective parts removed and replaced – without risking breaking the products. This includes products with mechanisms of authentication, which prevent products from functioning with third party parts or equipment and thus prevent repair outside the authorized repair

[2252] E. Maitre-Ekern, C. Dalhammar, 'Towards a hierarchy of consumption behaviour in the circular economy', 26 *Maastricht Journal of European and Comparative Law* (2019) p. 403.

[2253] E. Van Gool, 'A European 'right to repair': Yes! But how (far)?', *CCM Blog*, 25 April 2021, available on: <https://law.kuleuven.be/ccm/blog/?p=68>.

[2254] See *supra*, n° 165–167.

network.[2255] In a 2020 survey requested by the EC, 79% of respondents "*think that manufacturers should be required to make it easier to repair digital devices or replace their individual parts*".[2256] Repair may also be impeded by the lack of compatibility with other products and parts or interfaces (including software) that fit these other products as well as by the lack of product upgradability and adaptability. Consequently, when a defect occurs for those products, the consumer is forced to replace the whole product. These cases pertain to material and functional obsolescence.[2257]

653. SECOND: LACK OF CONSUMABLES, ACCESSORIES, SPARE PARTS, UPDATES AND REQUIRED TOOLS – The second barrier to sustainable remedies is the lack of access to consumables, accessories, spare parts, software and firmware updates and the (sometimes proprietary) tools required for repair. These items may simply not be made available to the public or may be deemed too expensive when compared to the remaining value of the defective product and the price of a new one. The few consumers and independent repairers who would try to find creative alternatives to overcome such a lack may face fundamental legal barriers.[2258] First, by using non-OEM consumables, accessories, spare parts and updates, they risk violating intellectual property rights (including copyrights, patent rights, trademark rights) as well as certain contractual terms (including commercial guarantee terms). The unauthorized replication of patented spare parts or tools also constitutes direct patent infringement. Moreover, it is forbidden to sell or import refurbished spare parts bearing trademark in a way that causes confusion.[2259] This second category of barriers can cause the indirect and economic obsolescence of products.[2260]

654. THIRD: LACK OF INFORMATION ON PRODUCTS AND CONSUMER RIGHTS – The third major barrier is the lack of crucial information that would enable consumers and independent repairers to prolong product lifetime after a defect occurs. There is, first, a lack of information on products. This lack of information has already been spotted at the marketing and pre-contractual stage of products,

2255 For concrete examples of such mechanisms, See *supra* n° 116.

2256 Kantar, *Special Eurobarometer 503 – Attitudes towards the impact of digitalisation on daily lives* (European Commission 2020) p. 23.

2257 See Chapter I on the concepts of material obsolescence (n° 101–105) and functional obsolescence (n° 106–111).

2258 S. Svensson, J.L. Richter, E. Maitre-Ekern, T. Pihlajarinne, A. Maigret, C. Dalhammar, *The Emerging 'Right to Repair' legislation in the EU and the U.S.* (Going Green Care Innovation 2018) pp. 6–7.

2259 See e.g. ECJ 17 March 2005, Case C-228/03, *Gillette Company and Gillette Group Finland, EU:C:2005:177*, especially para 49; ECJ 14 July 2011, Case C-46/10, *Viking Gas, EU:C:2011:485*, especially para 40.

2260 See Chapter I on the concepts of indirect obsolescence (n° 112–116) and economic obsolescence (n° 117–119).

as shown in the previous chapter of this book.[2261] For example, it may be particularly difficult for consumers and independent repairers to repair the defective product if no (easy and free) access to repair guides was provided by the manufacturer. Some free repair guides are provided by independent online platforms, but it is challenging for the community to crowdsource enough repair guides to keep up with the flood of products entering the EU market every year.[2262] Yet, access to such information is of critical importance for enabling repair, especially for repairs performed by relatively inexperienced people. Other information may be necessary to repair goods, like passwords without which repair attempts will be blocked.[2263] The second type of information that is lacking concerns consumers' guarantee rights. The vast majority of consumers are not aware of or barely know the existence and content of legal and commercial guarantees as well as the distinction and articulation between the two.[2264] This lack of information is exacerbated by traders' misunderstanding and misinformation.[2265] For example, misleading information on legal guarantees may consist in stipulating that they no longer apply if the product is repaired by an unauthorised third party of if the consumer tries to disassemble the device himself.[2266]

655. Fourth: barriers linked to the conditions of after-sales support – Fourth, the choice of consumers facing a defect may deviate towards less sustainable options due to the conditions of after-sales support, which make repair and other more sustainable remedies difficult to access and conduct. Among the factors that deter consumers from choosing these remedies is the fact that the services related to them frequently prove difficult to access, time-consuming and/or expensive. Concerning repair, in addition to costly spare parts, repair costs can be high due to sophisticated product design, the need for special tools, and the labour-intensive work involved in the repair services, which require more and more skills to follow technological breakthroughs. Repair services offered by (unauthorised) third-parties, which may be more convenient than original repair services in terms of access, time and money, can be deemed forbidden under contract, patent and copyright law. For example,

---

2261 See Chapter III on the marketing and pre-contractual stage, and more specifically n° 326. See also n° 134.

2262 Ellen MacArthur Foundation, *Empowering repair* (2016) pp. 8–9.

2263 S. Svensson, J.L. Richter, E. Maitre-Ekern, T. Pihlajarinne, A. Maigret, C. Dalhammar, *The Emerging 'Right to Repair' legislation in the EU and the U.S.* (Going Green Care Innovation 2018) p. 6.

2264 For more details on this lack of information, see *infra* (n° 858).

2265 For further comments on this issue, see *infra* (n° 859).

2266 S. Svensson, J.L. Richter, E. Maitre-Ekern, T. Pihlajarinne, A. Maigret, C. Dalhammar, *The Emerging 'Right to Repair' legislation in the EU and the U.S.* (Going Green Care Innovation 2018) p. 5.

unauthorized circumvention of digital rights management ('DRM')[2267] on copyrighted software constitutes a violation of intellectual property rights.[2268] Similar barriers can be identified for 'circular replacements' and the greener termination of the contract. Therefore, replacement by a new good is generally considered the more attractive consumer sales remedy. In other words, the premature replacement of the defective good is in these cases due to its indirect and economic obsolescence.

656. Fifth: consumer preferences and attitudes not favouring repair or other sustainable remedies – Finally, there are barriers that relate to consumer preferences and attitudes.[2269] Research has shown that 31% of washing machines, 66% of vacuum cleaners, 56% of TVs and 69% of smartphones are replaced for other reasons than being broken 'beyond' repair.[2270] Notwithstanding the right to repair and the asserted willingness of consumers to adopt a sustainable behaviour[2271], consumer choice is guided by a wide range of factors, which will, most of the time, tilt the balance in favour of replacement with new goods.[2272] Besides the conditions of after-sales support, other inconveniences may arise from repair and other sustainable remedies. First, these remedies generally require more time and effort from consumers.[2273] Second, consumers may give more weight to cost saving than to the environment and thus favour the most economically advantageous remedy,

---

2267 'Digital rights management' is "*the control or protection of digital rights using various technologies to prevent unauthorized access, copying, etc.*" (Oxford English Dictionary 2006 (3rd ed.)).

2268 S. Svensson, J.L. Richter, E. Maitre-Ekern, T. Pihlajarinne, A. Maigret, C. Dalhammar, *The Emerging 'Right to Repair' legislation in the EU and the U.S.* (Going Green Care Innovation 2018) pp. 6–7.

2269 See also Chapter I on the causes of premature obsolescence on the consumer side (n° 131–140).

2270 H. Wieser, N. Tröger, 'Exploring the inner loops of the circular economy: Replacement, repair, and reuse of mobile phones in Austria', 172 *J. Clean. Prod.* (2018) p. 3042 at p. 3055; L. Harmer, T. Cooper, T. Fisher, G. Salvia, C. Barr, 'Design, dirt and disposal: influences on the maintenance of vacuum cleaners', 228 *J. Clean. Prod.* (2019) p. 1176 at p. 1186; L. Hennies, R. Stamminger, 'An empirical survey on the obsolescence of appliances in German households', 112 *Resources, Conservation & Recycling* (2016) p.73 at p. 82.

2271 See LE Europe, VVA Europe, Ipsos, ConPolicy, Trinomics, *Behavioural study on consumers' engagement in the circular economy* (European Commission 2018); Kantar, *Special Eurobarometer 503 – Attitudes towards the impact of digitalisation on daily lives* (European Commission 2020) p. 23.

2272 J. McCollough, 'Consumer Discount Rates and the Decision to Repair or Replace a Durable Product: A Sustainable Consumption Issue', 44 *Journal of Economic Issues* (2010) p. 183 at p. 204; T. Cooper, G. Salvia, 'Fix it: barriers to repair and opportunities for change', in R. Crocker (ed.), *Reuse in an Accelerated World: Mining the Past to Reshape the Future* (Routledge 2017) p. 147 at p. 165; V. Perez-Belis, M. Braulio-Gonzalo, P. Juan, M.D. Bovea, 'Consumer attitude towards the repair and the second-hand purchase of small household electrical and electronic equipment. A Spanish case study', 158 *J. Clean. Prod.* (2017) p. 261 at p. 275.

2273 See *supra*, n° 139.

namely replacement.[2274] Third, consumers may have quality concerns about DIY repair if they do not feel confident enough in their own repair knowledge. Consumers may express similar concerns for services provided by repairers and manufacturers, and more generally about repaired, reused, refurbished and remanufactured goods.[2275] Such concerns are far from being addressed by certain case law, like in France, where the courts held that there is no obligation of results for repairers, who are not obliged to know the factors causing the defect before repair, and that consumers have to pay repair costs even when the good is still defective.[2276] Concerns about data security may also deter consumers from making use of repair services.[2277] The influence of all these factors on consumers can greatly differ, depending on consumer perceptions, expectations and profiles as well as on the concerned product. Similarly, the perception of what constitutes a defect also varies between individuals.[2278] For instance, some consumers may purchase a new device because the performance of the old but still functioning device has significantly deteriorated.[2279] Consumers may disregard those drawbacks if they have a strong emotional attachment to the product ('emotional durability')[2280] or if the product is of high price.[2281] Besides these two particular cases, replacement mostly prevails. By contrast with repair, replacement is often completed simultaneously with the handover of the replaced good. Furthermore, consumers' choice for replacement is 'rewarded' by a brand-new good with a reset lifespan. If a replaced good is no longer produced, has become technologically obsolete or when this is opportune from a reputational perspective, a seller may even offer improved replacement models.[2282] One should also note the wrong signal sent by some legal mechanisms, like the withdrawal right, which overprotects consumers and encourages them to take unsustainable decisions.

2274 T. Cooper, "Inadequate life? Evidence of consumer attitudes to product obsolescence", 27 *J. Consum. Policy* (2004) p. 442; T. Knight et al. (Brook Lyndhurst), *Electrical and electronic product design: product lifetime* (WRAP 2013) p. 39. This reasoning may also lead to the premature replacement of the defective good and thus to its economic obsolescence (n° 118).

2275 I. Gåvertsson, L. Milios, C. Dalhammar, 'Quality Labelling for Re-used ICT Equipment to Support Consumer Choice in the Circular Economy', 43 *J. Consum. Policy* (2020) p. 356.

2276 The case at hand concerned a second-hand car. See <https://www.lemonde.fr/idees/article/2019/02/16/le-garagiste-et-le-cout-de-la-panne_5424218_3232.html>.

2277 K. Hobsona, N. Lynchb, D. Lilleyc, G. Smalleyc, 'Systems of practice and the Circular Economy: Transforming mobile phone product service systems', 26 *Environmental Innovation and Societal Transitions* (2018) p. 147 at p. 157.

2278 E.L. Dewberry, L. Saca, M. Moreno, L. Sheldrick, M. Sinclair, C. Makatsoris, M. Charter, 'A landscape of repair', in C. Martin (ed.), *Proceedings of the Sustainable innovation 2016: circular economy innovation & design: towards sustainable product design: 21st international conference* (University for the Creative Arts 2016) p. 80.

2279 Kantar, *Special Eurobarometer 503 – Attitudes towards the impact of digitalisation on daily lives* (European Commission 2020) p. 18.

2280 See *supra*, n° 146.

2281 L. Ackermann, R. Mugge, J. Schoormans, 'Consumers' perspective on product care: An exploratory study of motivators, ability factors, and triggers', 183 *J. Clean. Prod.* (2018) p. 380 at p. 391.

2282 E. Van Gool and A. Michel, 'The New Consumer Sales Directive 2019/771 and Sustainable Consumption: A Critical Analysis', 10 *EuCML* (2021) p. 144.

Hence, on the basis of these considerations, most consumers may not consider sustainable remedies as valuable options.

C. THE GUARANTEE RIGHTS UNDER CONSUMER SALES RULES

1. HORIZONTAL RULES ALLOWING CONSUMERS TO BRING GOODS INTO CONFORMITY

657. The Directives on consumer sales – Consumers who are faced with a defective product – including due to strategies of premature obsolescence – can rely on guarantee rights established at EU level. These rights were enshrined in the 1999 Consumer Sales Directive ('CSD')[2283], which was replaced in May 2019 by the SGD, which applies to sales contracts concluded after 1 January 2022.[2284] Both instruments introduce common rules on the conformity of goods, remedies in the event of a lack of conformity and modalities for their exercise.[2285] The provisions of the CSD and the SGD also regulate some aspects of commercial guarantees, especially on its binding nature and on the information that must be given to consumers. These rules are mandatory, although sellers are allowed to offer the consumer contractual arrangements that go beyond the protection provided for in these directives.[2286]

658. Four possible remedies, including repair – According to these consumer sales rules, when a product becomes defective, consumers are entitled, for (at least) two years from the delivery of the product, to claim different remedies against the seller, under the conditions and modalities established by the directives. If the good is not in conformity with the contract, consumers can ask for the good to be repaired, replaced or, alternatively, for a reduction in price or the termination of the contract.[2287] This mechanism is based on core principles of contract law under which a seller who does not deliver a good in conformity with the sales contract fails to fulfil their contractual duty and must bring the good into conformity. While the CSD and the SGD aim at contributing to the proper functioning of the internal market and providing for a high level of consumer protection[2288], they can also play an important role in the protection

[2283] Directive 1999/44/EC of the European Parliament and of the Council of 25 May 1999 on certain aspects of the sale of consumer goods and associated guarantees, OJ L 171, 7.7.1999, p. 12–16.

[2284] Article 24(2) SGD. For sales contracts concluded before this period of time, the CSD will still be of application.

[2285] See recital 11 SGD.

[2286] See Art. 21 SGD, which replaces Art. 7 CSD.

[2287] Art. 13 of the SGD.

[2288] Recital 2 SGD.

of the environment and in the fight against premature obsolescence. Not only do legal and commercial guarantees provide an incentive for sellers (and indirectly producers) to offer goods with longer lifetimes, but they also further increase the chance that such goods are repaired, postponing the purchase of a replacement good.[2289] That is why the EC refers to the legal guarantee system as a key element in the transition towards a greener and circular economy.[2290]

659. A FUTURE DIRECTIVE ON THE RIGHT TO REPAIR? – To fully exploit the potential of these rules in the green transition, the EC recently adopted the Proposal for a Directive on common rules promoting repair.[2291] This Proposal introduces a new 'right to repair' for consumers, both within and beyond the legal guarantee. Reference to this Proposal will be made throughout the chapter where relevant.

660. BELGIAN IMPLEMENTING PROVISIONS – Different kinds of guarantees are provided or regulated under Belgian law. The first type of guarantees that consumers can invoke in cases of premature obsolescence is the legal guarantee of conformity for goods. The relevant provisions related to the legal guarantee can be found in Articles 1649*bis* to 1649*octies* of the Belgian Civil Code.[2292] In these provisions, the Belgian Civil Code also regulates commercial guarantees that can be offered by traders. These provisions were recently amended to transpose the SGD into Belgian law.[2293] In addition to these two guarantees, Articles 1641 to 1649 of the Belgian Civil Code establish a third guarantee, namely the guarantee against hidden defects (*garantie des vices cachés*). This guarantee covers cases where the product, although complying with the contract, has hidden defects that hamper its use. Finally,

---

2289 M. Loos, 'Not good but certainly not content: the proposals for European harmonisation of online and distance selling of goods and the supply of digital content', in E. Terryn, I. Claeys (eds.), *Digital content & distance sales* (Intersentia 2017) p. 21.

2290 See e.g. Communication from the Commission of 2 December 2015 to the European Parliament, the Council, the European Economic and Social Committee and the Committee of the Regions on Closing the loop – EU action plan for circular economy, COM(2015) 614 final, pp. 6–7.

2291 Proposal for a Directive of the European Parliament and of the Council on common rules promoting the repair of goods and amending Regulation (EU) 2017/2394, Directives (EU) 2019/771 and (EU) 2020/1828, COM(2023) 155 final.

2292 During the transposition process of the SGD, it had been proposed to integrate the provisions on guarantee rules in the Economic Law Code: see Avis du Conseil Central de l'Economie du 3 septembre 2019 sur la transposition de directives européennes concernant la vente aux consommateurs tant de biens que de contenus et services numériques, CCE 2019-1660, p. 4, available on: <https://www.ccecrb.fgov.be/dpics/fichiers/2019-09-19-03-21-55_CCE20191660transpositiondirectives..pdf>. See also Art. 4 Proposition de loi relative à la protection des consommateurs en cas de vente de biens de consommation, *Doc. parl.*, Ch., 2019-2020, 5 novembre 2019, n° 0693/001.

2293 See Loi du 20 mars 2022 modifiant les dispositions de l'ancien Code civil relatives aux ventes à des consommateurs, insérant un nouveau titre VI*bis* dans le livre III de l'ancien Code civil et modifiant le Code de droit économique, *M.B.*, 31 mars 2022, p. 26223, which enters into force on 1st June 2022. Belgium has lagged behind in the transposition of the SGD, which should have been transposed into national law by 1st July 2021 at the latest, as required in its Art. 24(1).

consumers have the possibility to rely on the Belgian general sale of goods legislation when a product becomes obsolete, if they successfully prove a lack of consent. All these guarantees are closely intertwined and form together a legal network that helps protect consumers against a broad range of cases of premature obsolescence.

661. French implementing provisions – Under French law, the provisions on the legal guarantee of conformity for goods can be found in Articles L. 217-7 to L. 217-14 of the French Consumer Code. The SGD has been transposed through several legal acts, including the Anti-Waste Law.[2294] In this area of law, it is worth noting that France has taken the lead in promoting (sustainable) repair by complementing and departing to some extent from the content of the Eu legislation. Commercial guarantees are regulated by Article L. 217-15 of the French Consumer Code. Like in Belgium, consumers can also invoke the guarantee against hidden defects (*garantie des vices cachés*), which is enshrined in Article 1641 of the French Civil Code. These guarantees interact with each other and help protect consumers against defective products. In addition to these guarantees, the French general sale of goods legislation enables consumers to cancel the contract where there is a lack of consent.

662. German implementing provisions – Most of the consumer sales rules are to be found in §13-14 and in §433 to §477 of the German Civil Code (*BGB*), except for the concept of 'producer', which is regulated in §4 I,II of the German Product Liability Act (*Produkthaftungsgesetz*). The SGD was transposed in June 2021 via a single act into the German Civil Code, namely the German Act regulating the sale of goods with digital elements and other aspects of the contract of sale.[2295] The German legislation faithfully transposes the rules on the remedies, granting consumers the right to repair or replacement within a reasonable time frame as first remedies (§439 BGB), except if this is impossible for the seller (§275 BGB) or only possible at a disproportionate expense (§439(3) BGB). While German law previously departed on some points from the CSD, some of these discrepancies were eliminated by the SGD.[2296]

2294 See also Loi n° 2020-1508 du 3 décembre 2020 portant diverses dispositions d'adaptation au droit de l'Union européenne en matière économique et financière, JORF n°0293 du 4 décembre 2020; Ordonnance n° 2021-1247 du 29 septembre 2021 relative à la garantie légale de conformité pour les biens, les contenus numériques et les services numériques, JORF n°0228 du 30 septembre 2021.

2295 Gesetz zur Regelung des Verkaufs von Sachen mit digitalen Elementen und anderer Aspekte des Kaufvertrags vom 25.06.2021 (BGBl. I S. 2133).

2296 See for example the obligation to deliver the good to the buyer "*free from material and legal defects*" (§433 BGB), which has been echoed in Art. 9 and recital 35 of the new SGD.

2. LEVEL OF HARMONIZATION AND SCOPE OF APPLICATION

a) *A directive of maximum but targeted harmonisation*

(1) The choice for maximum harmonisation

663. From minimum to maximum harmonisation – As opposed to the CSD, which was based on minimum harmonization[2297], the 2019 SGD provides for maximum harmonization.[2298] This means that Member States can no longer maintain or introduce provisions diverging from those laid down in the SGD, including more, or less, stringent provisions to ensure a different level of consumer protection, unless otherwise provided for in this Directive. Both directives leave nonetheless the Member States free to decide how to transpose the provisions into national law. There were heated debates on the level of harmonisation of the SGD during its adoption process, involving EU institutions, scholars, stakeholders and Members States.[2299] The full harmonisation approach finally prevailed. With the adoption of the SGD, new elements of consumer law have been fully harmonised. One example concerns the remedies available to consumers for lack of conformity of goods, the conditions under which they can be exercised and the hierarchy between them.[2300]

664. With the aim of avoiding disparities between Member States – The choice for maximum harmonisation was justified by the promotion of the internal market and the related so-called 'consumer confidence' argument.[2301] The minimum

2297 See Art. 8(2) as well as recitals 5 and 24 CSD.

2298 Article 4 as well as recitals 6 and 10 SGD.

2299 As regards the position adopted by the EU institutions, see e.g. Opinion of the EESC on the 'Proposal for a directive of the European Parliament and of the Council on certain aspects concerning contracts for the supply of digital content' (COM(2015) 634 final) and the 'Proposal for a directive of the European Parliament and of the Council on certain aspects concerning contracts for the online and other distance sales of goods' (COM(2015) 635 final), OJ C 264, 20.7.2016, especially pts 1.6., 3.2. and 4.2.2. In favor of full harmonization, see the explanatory memorandum to the Report on the amended proposal for a directive of the European Parliament and of the Council on certain aspects concerning contracts for the sales of goods, amending Regulation (EC) No 2006/2004 of the European Parliament and of the Council and Directive 2009/22/EC of the European Parliament and of the Council and repealing Directive 1999/44/EC of the European Parliament and of the Council, COM(2017) 637, p. 57 at p. 59. As regards the position adopted by some scholars, see e.g. Statement of the European Law Institute on the European Commission's Proposed Directive on the Supply of Digital Content to Consumers (COM (2015) 634 final) (2016), p. 1 and p. 8. For more details on the debate and its evolution, see E. Terryn, 'Nieuw kooprecht en nieuw recht voor digitale inhoud en digitale diensten in context', in E. Terryn, I. Claeys (eds.), *Nieuw recht inzake koop & digitale inhoud en diensten* (Intersentia 2020) p. 4 at p. 6.

2300 Recitals 10 and 47 SGD. For more information on remedies, see *infra*, n° 767 *et seq.*

2301 C. Twigg-Flesner, '"Good-bye harmonisation by directives, hello cross-border only regulation?" A way forward for EU consumer contract law', 7 *Eur. Rev. Contract Law* (2011) p. 240.

harmonising nature of the 1999 CSD was deemed to lead to enormous disparities between Member States' legislation, sometimes on essential elements. Several studies reported on the various approaches followed by EU Member States, as well as by the European Economic Area (EEA) countries to which the CSD also applied.[2302] These divergences consequently created contract law-related obstacles to cross-border trade, which translated into higher prices[2303], and confusion among consumers and traders. Therefore, the EC advocated for maximum harmonisation to ensure that "*whether domestically or cross-border, online or offline, consumers enjoy the same high level of consumer protection across the European Union and traders can sell to consumers in all Member States based on the same contractual terms.*"[2304] Through full harmonisation, the 2019 SGD would respect the principles of subsidiarity, as those obstacles cannot be removed at national level, and of proportionality, as fully harmonised rules allow reaching the directive's objectives.[2305]

665. The pitfalls of maximum harmonisation – Mitigating the divergences between Member States is certainly a laudable objective, but maximum harmonisation is not always the ideal solution, especially from a sustainability perspective. Since it precludes Member States from maintaining or introducing additional rules, including rules that are more sustainable, this approach necessitates thoughtful choice about the content of the directive. In the present case, some provisions of the SGD could have been arguably more sustainable, like the available remedies.[2306] Furthermore, maximum harmonisation has always been subjected to considerable criticisms. Some scholars hold the view that national laboratories can have added value, that non-contractual factors constitute more important internal market obstacles, that parallel national rules will continue to exist, and that maximum harmonization should remain limited to cross-border consumer issues.[2307] Such reasoning can

---

2302 See for ex. ICF, *Study on the costs and benefits of extending certain rights under the Consumer Sales and Guarantees Directive 1999/44/CE* (European Commission 2017) p. 12 at p. 20; K. Tonner, R. Malcolm, *How an EU lifespan guarantee model could be implemented across the European Union (study)* (European Parliament 2017) p. 16 at p. 34. See also the country fiches undertaken within the framework of the study Ipsos-London Economics-Deloitte consortium, *Consumer market study on the functioning of legal and commercial guarantees for consumers in the EU* (European Union 2015), available on: <ec.europa.eu/consumers/consumer_evidence/market_studies/guarantees/index_en.htm>.

2303 Companies, forced to comply with rules that differ from one country to another, face additional financial and administrative costs, which they then pass on to the final consumer.

2304 Commission Staff Working Document of 31 October 2017 on the Impacts of fully harmonised rules on contracts for the sales of goods supplementing the impact assessment accompanying the proposal for a Directive of the European Parliament and of the Council on certain aspects concerning contracts for the online and other distance sales of goods, SWD(2017) 354 final, p. 11.

2305 Recital 70 SGD.

2306 See *infra*, n° 767 *et seq.*

2307 See M. Faure, 'Towards a maximum harmonization of consumer contract law?!?', *Maastricht Journal of European and Comparative Law* (2008) pp. 437–439; G. Howells, C. Twigg-Flesner and T. Wilhelmsson, *Rethinking EU Consumer Law* (Routledge 2018) p. 4, 21, 170 and 209.

equally be held for the SGD. As a result, the new fully harmonised directive is in some regards more harmful to sustainable consumption than its predecessor.[2308]

(2) Exceptions to maximum harmonisation

666. Various exceptions to maximum harmonisation – Despite the full harmonisation character of the SGD, many of its provisions give some degree of latitude to Member States. This contrasts with the initial proposal made by the EC, where the full harmonisation approach was stricter.[2309] Some of these exceptions allow Member States to increase consumer protection, including against cases of premature obsolescence, and to trigger sustainable consumption. A first noteworthy exception to the maximum harmonisation principle is the possibility for Member States to prolong the legal guarantee period beyond two years.[2310] Member States are also entitled to maintain or introduce a presumption period of two years (instead of one year).[2311] However, the Directive also allows Member States to take less sustainable choices. For instance, national legislation can provide for a reduced liability period for second-hand goods.[2312]

667. Many aspects left unregulated – Other important aspects, though closely linked to the rules on guarantees, are not regulated by the Directive and thus left to the discretion of Member States.[2313] As an example, Article 3(6) leaves Member States free to regulate aspects of general contract law, such as rules on the formation, validity, nullity or effects of contracts, but also rules regarding the withholding of payment by the consumer and the right to damages.[2314] Moreover, Member States are allowed to further develop aspects regarding repair and replacement under their national laws, such as by introducing or maintaining an obligation to make spare parts available and to inform consumers about it.[2315] It is also possible for Member States to introduce or maintain other remedies falling outside the scope of the Directive and

2308 See E. Van Gool and A. Michel, 'The New Consumer Sales Directive 2019/771 and Sustainable Consumption: A Critical Analysis', 10 *EuCML* (2021) p. 137.

2309 See Amended proposal for a Directive of the European Parliament and of the Council on certain aspects concerning contracts for the online and other distance sales of goods, amending Regulation (EC) No 2006/2004 of the European Parliament and of the Council and Directive 2009/22/EC of the European Parliament and of the Council and repealing Directive 1999/44/EC of the European Parliament and of the Council, COM(2017) 637 final, p. 20.

2310 Art. 10(3) and recital 41 SGD. See *infra*, n° 730.

2311 Art. 11(2) SGD. See *infra*, n° 759.

2312 Art. 10(6) SGD. See *infra*, n° 742 *et seq.*

2313 In that regard, it could be said that the directive is of full but not complete harmonisation. The distinction between maximum and complete harmonisation was advocated in C. Verdure, 'La directive 2005/29/CE: base légale et degré d'harmonisation', *R.E.D.C.* (2013) p. 158 at p. 162, building on the ECJ's case law.

2314 See also recital 18 SGD.

2315 See recital 18 in conjunction with recital 33 SGD. Such legislation exists in France (see *supra* n° 469–472).

supplementing its established hierarchy.[2316] Finally, there are some notions and elements that are not regulated by the Directive and must be defined in national law, such as the word 'delivery'[2317] or the place where the delivery or repair and replacement have to be undertaken.[2318] Such leeway could give rise to legislation triggering or curtailing sustainable consumption.

668. Disguised minimum harmonisation – After having taken note of these numerous exceptions, it appears that the maximum harmonisation initially envisaged for the SGD has given way to a disguised minimum harmonisation approach. Rules that are fully harmonised are scarce. On many aspects, Member States enjoy a certain degree of freedom, although national legislation should not make it impossible or excessively difficult for consumers to exercise the rights they derive from the Directive.[2319] This degree of freedom offers the opportunity for Member States to further promote product sustainability. The aforementioned drawbacks of maximum harmonisation are consequently avoided for most provisions.

669. A missed opportunity to harmonise rules at EU level – It is regrettable that the EU legislature did not use the SGD to take the lead towards more sustainable guarantee rules, as envisaged by the EC in its new Circular Economy Action Plan.[2320] It could have built on inspiring national practices, which were allowed by the minimum harmonising character of the former CSD, and set a higher threshold at EU level for a wider range of aspects related to guarantees. One of the most significant missed opportunities is undoubtedly the lack of fully harmonised rules on the availability of spare parts. Instead, the Directive leaves the choice to Member States, risking at the same time ineffectiveness and distortions of competition or barriers to trade by imposing stringent obligations at national level.

2316 Recital 18 SGD. Among these extra remedies, the SGD implicitly refers to the right to reject existing under UK law (Art. 3(7) and recital 19) and the guarantee against hidden defects existing under Belgian and French law (recital 18). For further details on these remedies, see *infra*, n° 819–820 (right to reject) and n° 868–875 (guarantee against hidden defects). Recital 18 also mentions the possibility to establish non-contractual remedies against manufacturers under national law.

2317 Recital 38 SGD.

2318 Recital 56 SGD.

2319 See ECJ 4 June 2015, Case C-497/13, *Faber, EU:C:2015:357*, para 64. This condition could be problematic to some extent for the Member States willing to adopt more sustainable guarantee rules. For instance, it could preclude them from restricting consumers' right to replace in favour of repair (which is inherently more sustainable).

2320 Communication from the Commission of 11 March 2020 to the European Parliament, the Council, the European Economic and Social Committee and the Committee of the Regions on A new Circular Economy Action Plan – For a cleaner and more competitive Europe, COM(2020) 98 final, p. 5.

b) *Scope of application*

(1) Personal scope

670. B2C CONTRACTS – As indicated in its Article 3(1), the SGD applies to sales contracts between consumers and sellers. Pursuant to Article 2(2), the notion of 'consumer' must be understood as "*any natural person who, in relation to contracts covered by this Directive, is acting for purposes which are outside that person's trade, business, craft or profession*". This notion is not to be interpreted too widely under EU law. In fact, the ECJ has consistently held that legal persons (including those with a non-business character)[2321] are not consumers.[2322] Member States are nonetheless allowed to extend the scope of application of the Directive to B2B transactions.[2323] Legal persons could thus benefit from these protective rules of consumer law if so provided by national law. In the case of dual-purpose contracts[2324], the Directive leaves it to the Member States to determine whether the person should be considered a consumer.[2325] Extending the protection given by the SGD at national level to persons other than consumers and to cases of mixed transactions should be encouraged as it would allow covering a greater number of cases of premature obsolescence under this legislation. As regards the notion of 'seller', Article 2(3) of the SGD defines it as "*any natural person or any legal person, irrespective of whether privately or publicly owned, that is acting, including through any other person acting in that natural or legal person's name or on that person's behalf, for purposes relating to that person's trade, business, craft or profession, in relation to contracts covered by this Directive*". Like for the similar notion of 'trader'[2326], the meaning and scope of the concept of 'seller' should be determined in relation to the concept of 'consumer'.[2327] To

2321 This category of legal persons includes, for example, non-profit associations.

2322 See ECJ 2 April 2020, Case C-329/19, *Condominio di Milano, via Meda, EU:C:2020:263*, para 25; ECJ 22 November 2001, Case C-541/99 and Case-542/99, *Cape and Idealservice MN RE, EU:C:2001:625*, para 16; ECJ 14 March 1991, Case C-361/89, *Di Pinto, EU:C:1991:118*, paras 15–19.

2323 Recital 21 SGD. This extension of the scope could be done through different approaches: see J.M. Carvalho, 'Sale of Goods and Supply of Digital Content and Digital Services – Overview of Directives 2019/770 and 2019/771', 5 *EuCML* (2019) p. 196. In Belgium, scholars foresee no extension of the scope to professionals, who will have to rely on Belgian general law. See R. Steennot, S. Geiregat, 'Consumentenkoop en digitale inhoud: toepassingsgebied en afbakening', in E. Terryn, I. Claeys (eds.), *Nieuw recht inzake koop & digitale inhoud en diensten* (Intersentia 2020) pp. 32–33.

2324 This kind of contracts especially occurs in the case of self-employed persons who purchase dual-use products such as a computer or car.

2325 Recital 22 SGD. Different approaches can be followed by the Member States on that point. For further details, see R. Manko, *The notion of 'consumer' in EU law – Library briefing* (European Parliament 2013) p. 2.

2326 The notion of 'trader' is used in other EU consumer law instruments, like the UCPD.

2327 ECJ 3 October 2013, Case C-59/12, *Zentrale zur Bekämpfung unlauteren Wettbewerbs, EU:C:2013:634*, para 33.

complement this definition, the ECJ gave a non-exhaustive list of criteria that can be taken into account when assessing whether a person should be qualified as 'trader'.[2328] These same elements could also be used to define the contours of the notion of 'seller'.[2329]

671. Including platform providers – The SGD acknowledges that platform providers could be held liable as 'sellers' for a lack of conformity "*if they act for purposes relating to their own business and as the direct contractual partner of the consumer for the sale of goods*".[2330] In other words, the liability could be established on the part of online platforms where consumers have purchased goods through an online marketplace.[2331] Member States can even decide to extend the scope of application of the Directive to all platform providers, regardless of whether they fulfil these conditions.[2332] Such an amendment is to be welcomed, having regard to the increasing number of online transactions. Yet, it raises a more fundamental question as to whether the current notion of 'seller' still fits with the type of responsibilities that may arise in new systems encompassing software and open ecosystems, which involve new actors in the value chain, such as software producers, users and third parties. In this respect, there may be a need to further adapt the notion of 'seller'.[2333]

672. No C2C contracts, except when traders act as intermediaries – *A contrario*, sales contracts concluded between two consumers do not fall within the scope of the Directive. However, if a trader acts as an intermediary on behalf

2328 See ECJ 4 October 2018, Case C-105/17, *Kamenova*, *EU:C:2018:808*, para 38. The ECJ suggested verifying *inter alia* whether the sale was intended to generate profit, whether the seller had technical information and expertise relating to the products which he offered for sale which the consumer did not necessarily have or whether the seller had a legal status which enabled him to engage in commercial activities.

2329 R. Steennot, S. Geiregat, 'Consumentenkoop en digitale inhoud: toepassingsgebied en afbakening', in E. Terryn, I. Claeys (eds.), *Nieuw recht inzake koop & digitale inhoud en diensten* (Intersentia 2020) p. 38.

2330 Recital 23 SGD.

2331 The Belgian law makers have decided not to extend the obligations established by the SGD to platform providers when they act solely as intermediaries as consumers are in any case protected by the legal guarantee they have against the seller. See the explanatory memorandum to the Projet de loi modifiant les dispositions de l'ancien Code civil relatives aux ventes à des consommateurs, insérant un nouveau titre VIbis dans le livre 3 de l'ancien Code civil et modifiant le Code de droit économique, *Doc. parl.*, Ch., 2021–2022, 7 décembre 2021, n° 2355/001, p. 10.

2332 Recital 23 SGD.

2333 Such a discussion is currently taking place with the review of the Product Liability Directive (COM(2022) 495 final) and the Proposal for a Digital Services Act (COM(2020) 825 final). See also the Commission Staff Working Document of 7 May 2018 on the Evaluation of Council Directive 85/374/EEC of 25 July 1985 on the approximation of the laws, regulations and administrative provisions of the Member States concerning liability for defective products, SWD(2018) 157 final, p. 54. This issue could also be addressed by strengthening the sellers' right of redress (see *infra*, n° 821 *et seq.*).

of a private individual to sell the good and fails to duly inform the consumer that he is not the owner of the good in question, the seller's liability regime established under the SGD can apply to the intermediary.[2334] It is interesting to note that in Belgium, marketplaces are under obligation to inform consumers about the quality of the seller.[2335] In any of these cases, it should be underlined that guarantee rights are transferable from one consumer to another. In other words, a consumer who bought a second-hand good from another consumer can claim the remedies granted by the legal guarantee against the initial seller for the remaining guarantee period in case of defect.

(2) Material scope

673. Sales contracts of goods – Concerning the scope *ratione materiae*, the SGD applies to sales contracts of goods, regardless of the sales channels.[2336] Sales contracts are defined in Article 2(1) as "*any contract under which the seller transfers or undertakes to transfer ownership of goods to a consumer, and the consumer pays or undertakes to pay the price thereof*". The words of this definition entail two important elements that the sales contract must comprise to fall within the scope of the Directive: (1) the transfer of ownership and (2) the payment of the price.

674. The transfer of ownership of a good (first condition) – The first condition of a sales contract is the transfer of ownership of a good. According to Article 2(5) of Directive, the notion of 'goods' covers "*any tangible movable items*" as well as "*goods with digital elements*".[2337] The last category has been added by the SGD, which defines them as "*any tangible movable items that incorporate or are inter-connected with digital content or a digital service in such a way that the absence of that digital content or digital service would prevent the goods from performing their functions*".[2338] The Directive applies therefore to goods as well as to digital content and digital services which are incorporated in or inter-connected with goods and are provided under the sales contract.[2339] Recitals 14 and 15 of the Directive provide some examples of such goods, like smartphones, smart TVs or smart watches. By contrast, new alternatives with no

2334 ECJ 9 November 2016, Case C-149/15, *Wathelet, EU:C:2016:840*, para.

2335 Art. VI.45/1 of the Belgian Economic Law Code. If the seller is a consumer, the marketplace has to inform consumers that the rules on guarantees do not apply. See R. Steennoot 'Het toepassingsgebied van nieuwe garantieregelingen voor goederen, digitale inhoud en digitale diensten', in *Nieuw consumentenrecht: omzetting richtlijnen koop en digitale inhoud en digitale diensten, omzetting "omnibus"-richtlijn, omzetting richtlijn representatieve vorderingen* (Larcier Intersentia 2022) pp. 7–8.

2336 Recital 9 SGD.

2337 Some provisions of the Directive are specifically dedicated to goods with digital elements. See for ex. Art. 7(3), Art. 10(2) or Art. 11(3) SGD.

2338 Article 5(2)(b) SGD.

2339 Art. 3(3) SGD.

transfer of ownership, such as servitisation (e.g. product-lease and product-as-a-service) and collaborative economy (e.g. platforms to share and resale goods), which increasingly replace sales of consumers goods, do not fall within the scope of the SGD.[2340] Consequently, consumers using those alternatives only benefit from the (limited) protection of general contract law, including in case of premature obsolescence.[2341]

675. Excluding contracts for the supply of digital content or digital services – *A contrario*, if the absence of digital content or digital service does not prevent the goods from performing their functions, or if the consumer concludes a contract for the supply of digital content or a digital service which does not form part of the contract concerning the sale of goods with digital elements[2342], that contract should be considered to be separate from the contract for the sale of the goods, even if the seller acts as an intermediary of that second contract with the third-party supplier.[2343] The SGD does not apply to such contracts[2344], nor to contracts whereby a tangible medium serves exclusively as a carrier for digital content.[2345] These contracts will rather fall within the scope of the DCD if the conditions of that Directive are satisfied.[2346] In this respect, the two directives complement each other.[2347]

676. A distinction somewhat blurred in practice – It remains to be seen how these contracts will be distinguished from each other and how to interpret the necessity of the digital content or service.[2348] For example, GPS integrated within a car or bought fall within the scope of the SGD, whereas later uploads

---

2340 E. Van Gool and A. Michel, 'The New Consumer Sales Directive 2019/771 and Sustainable Consumption: A Critical Analysis', 10 *EuCML* (2021) p. 137.

2341 Regarding implications for consumer protection, see B. Keirsbilck, E. Terryn, E. Van Gool, 'Consumentenbescherming bij servitisation en product-dienst-systemen (PDS)', 56 *T.P.R.* (2019) p. 817 at p. 899; F. Zoll, 'From a Product-Based Economy to Services: Legal Aspects of an Economy in Transition', in B. Keirsbilck, E. Terryn (eds.), *Consumer Protection in a Circular Economy* (Intersentia 2019) p. 149 at p. 158.

2342 In the event of doubt, Art. 3(3) last sentence of the SGD states that the digital content or digital service is presumed to be covered by the sales contract.

2343 Recital 16 SGD.

2344 Article 3(3) SGD.

2345 Article 3(4) SGD.

2346 For further comments on the scope of application of the DCD, see S. Geiregat, R. Steennot, 'Proposal for a Directive on Digital Content. Scope of Application and Liability for a Lack of Conformity', in I. Claeys, E. Terryn (eds.), *Digital Content & Distance Sales* (Intersentia 2017) p. 100 at p. 117; K. Sein, G. Spindler, 'The New Directive on Contracts for the Supply of Digital Content and Digital Services Scope of Application and Trader's Obligation to Supply', 15 *Eur. Rev. Contract Law* (2019) p. 260 at p. 269.

2347 Recital 13 SGD.

2348 R. Steennot, S. Geiregat, 'Consumentenkoop en digitale inhoud: toepassingsgebied en afbakening', in E. Terryn, I. Claeys (eds.), *Nieuw recht inzake koop & digitale inhoud en diensten* (Intersentia 2020) p. 73.

of maps fall within the DCD.[2349] It will sometimes be hard to know which of the two Directives applies.[2350] It will depend on whether the digital content or service is necessary for the functioning of the goods as well as on what the consumers can expect from the functioning of the good.[2351] But these two notions might lead to interpretation issues, which could finally have an impact on the rights given to consumers as the level of protection of the two directives is different.[2352]

677. Possible exclusion of second-hand goods sold at public auction – In addition, Member States may exclude contracts for the sale of second-hand goods at public auction from the scope of application of this Directive.[2353] This exception already existed under the CSD[2354], with the only difference that there was no explicit mention of the obligation to inform consumers about its existence. Consumers who buy second-hand goods in such a context will thus remain outside the protection afforded by the Directive, although more and more consumers are involved.[2355] The justification of this exclusion appears to be the limited knowledge of auctioneers regarding auctioned products. But this equally applies to new auctioned goods.[2356] If this provision is considered in conjunction with Article 10(6) of the SGD, which allows for a reduced guarantee period for second-hand goods[2357], it seems that a special regime has been established by the SGD for second-hand goods. This special regime creates major issues related

2349 For more practical examples, see R. Steennot, S. Geiregat, 'Consumentenkoop en digitale inhoud: toepassingsgebied en afbakening', in E. Terryn, I. Claeys (eds.), *Nieuw recht inzake koop & digitale inhoud en diensten* (Intersentia 2020) p. 77 at p. 79; J.M. Carvalho, 'Sale of Goods and Supply of Digital Content and Digital Services – Overview of Directives 2019/770 and 2019/771', 5 *EuCML* (2019) p. 197.

2350 K. Sein, G. Splinder, 'The new Directive on Contracts for the Supply of Digital Content and Digital Services – Scope of Application and Trader's Obligation to Supply – Part 1', 15 *Eur. Rev. Contract Law* (2019) p. 273.

2351 Consumer expectations are also taken into account in order to assess the lack of conformity. See *infra*, n° 699.

2352 For example, instead of the hierarchy of remedies established under the SGD, the DCD only affords consumers the right to call upon the trader to supply the digital content or digital service (Art. 13(1) DCD).

2353 Art. 3(5)(a) SGD. This possibility of excluding second-hand goods sold at public auction has been implemented in France (Article L217–2 2° Code de la consommation) and in Germany ((§474(2) BGB). In Belgium, no distinction has been made between new and second-hand goods: all goods sold at public auction are excluded from the scope of guarantee rules (Art. 1649*bis* §2 3° of the Belgian Civil Code).

2354 Art. 1(3) CSD.

2355 For detailed figures, see for ex. the graph made by Statista on the sales volume of second-hand goods in Great Britain from the first quarter of 2015 to the fourth quarter of 2019, available on: <https://www.statista.com/statistics/523343/second-hand-goods-retail-sales-volume-quarterly-index-in-great-britain/>.

2356 E. Van Gool and A. Michel, 'The New Consumer Sales Directive 2019/771 and Sustainable Consumption: A Critical Analysis', 10 *EuCML* (2021) p. 138.

2357 See *infra*, n° 742 *et seq.*

to product sustainability as it promotes the erroneous idea that all second-hand goods have low value and limited durability and that their buyers do not merit equal legal protection.[2358] Moreover, the lack of definition of 'second-hand goods' may result in an interpretation other than that intended and possibly to the exclusion of a wider range of products.

678. THE PAYMENT OF THE PRICE (SECOND CONDITION) – Secondly, the SGD only applies in the case of sales, which means that consumers must have paid a price. However, if consumers receive a 'free' smartphone when buying a phone subscription or 'free' options when purchasing a new car, it constitutes a joint offer, which means that the legal guarantee applies to these products too.[2359] This is positive from a sustainability point of view as it provides an incentive for sellers (and indirectly producers) who adopt such practices to offer goods with a minimum quality and durability.

679. EXCLUDING ANCILLARY SALES CONTRACTS – It should nonetheless be noted that the SGD does not apply to sales contracts if they are merely ancillary by comparison with the provision of services, which is the principal subject of the contract. The Directive only applies to contracts of sale *sensu stricto* as well as contracts for the supply of consumer goods to be manufactured or produced and contracts providing for the installation of such goods linked to the sale if the supply of services is ancillary to the sale.[2360] The exclusion of ancillary sales contracts from the scope of the Directive is problematic as goods that become prematurely obsolete in those cases are no longer covered by guarantee rules.

680. THE POSSIBILITY OF EXCLUDING SECOND-HAND GOODS SHOULD BE REMOVED – The exclusion provided for in Article 3(5)(a) of the SGD goes against the European goal of transitioning to a more sustainable and circular economy, in which maintenance, repair and reuse are primary strategies. A tailored conformity assessment is a more appropriate and sufficient way of dealing with second-hand goods.[2361] This exclusion should therefore be removed by means of an amendment to the SGD (see #2). The corresponding recitals should also be amended. If no amendment were to be made at EU level, it is recommended to Member States not to use the possibility left by Article 3(5)(a) of the SGD if

2358 E. Van Gool and A. Michel, 'The New Consumer Sales Directive 2019/771 and Sustainable Consumption: A Critical Analysis', 10 *EuCML* (2021) p. 138.

2359 SPF Economie, *Guidance sur la garantie* (2019) p. 3, available on: <https://economie.fgov.be/sites/default/files/Files/Entreprises/guidance-garantie-fr.pdf>.

2360 ECJ 7 September 2017, Case C-247/16, *Schottelius*, *EU:C:2017:638*, paras 37–38.

2361 See also E. Van Gool and A. Michel, 'The New Consumer Sales Directive 2019/771 and Sustainable Consumption: A Critical Analysis', 10 *EuCML* (2021) p. 138.

they want to fully encourage sustainable consumption. Interestingly, such an approach is already envisaged in Belgium.[2362]

681. The notion of 'second-hand goods' should be defined – In addition to these amendments, the SGD should contain or make reference to an EU-wide definition of 'second-hand goods' to address the current lack of clarity surrounding the concept (see #1). The definition of 'second-hand goods' previously proposed in the first chapter of this book could be introduced into the SGD, that is "*goods that are used again for the same purpose in their original form or with little enhancement or change*".[2363] Alternatively, the definition could be borrowed or at least inspired by existing EU legislation or standards. For example, the Directive 2006/112/EC[2364] defines 'second-hand goods' as "*means movable tangible property that is suitable for further use as it is or after repair, other than works of art, collectors' items or antiques and* other *than precious metals or precious stones*".[2365] It is worth noting that under EU product regulation, repaired and refurbished products are to be considered as second-hand products unless they have undergone significant changes and come with a new warranty period.[2366] By contrast, products returned after cancellation of contract or withdrawal rights as well as products held in stock and sold as 'phase-out-model' should be considered as new if they have not been used or sold before.[2367] If the product has been subject to important changes or overhauls aimed at modifying its original performance, purpose or type, it may be considered as a new product.[2368] This has to be assessed on a case-by-case basis. If this is the case, the person who carried out the changes becomes the manufacturer, with the corresponding obligations. Remanufactured products, which are neither new nor used, should in principle be seen as products which "*have been subject to important changes or overhauls*".

682. A legal gap should be filled in – As explained in the previous paragraphs, the SGD only applies to sales contracts of goods (except if ancillary), thus excluding alternative consumption models pertaining to functional and

---

2362 Art. 3 Projet de loi modifiant les dispositions de l'ancien Code civil relatives aux ventes à des consommateurs, insérant un nouveau titre VI*bis* dans le livre 3 de l'ancien Code civil et modifiant le Code de droit économique, *Doc. parl.*, Ch., 2021–2022, 7 décembre 2021, n° 2355/001.

2363 This definition is based on the definition of the concept of 'direct reuse' (see *supra*, n° 151).

2364 Council Directive 2006/112/EC of 28 November 2006 on the common system of value added tax, OJ L 347, 11.12.2006, p. 1–118 (hereafter 'VAT Directive').

2365 Art. 311 of the VAT Directive.

2366 See *supra*, n° 181.

2367 It is interesting to note that France adopted a different standpoint by considering that 'reconditioned products' are second-hand products. See Art. R. 122-4 of the French Consumer Code. See also *supra*, n° 419.

2368 The Blue Guide, p. 15 at p. 18.

collaborative economies. The major problem is the legal gap in this field.[2369] Indeed, consumers opting for these alternatives also need legal protection as they could equally be confronted with defective products, including due to premature obsolescence. The current limited consumer protection and lack of harmonisation outside the scope of the SGD is an emerging issue, which can negatively impact new sustainable consumption models.[2370] European law makers should thus roll up their sleeves to fill in this legal gap, either by extending the scope of application of existing legal instruments (such as the SGD) or by adopting a distinct legal instrument specifically dedicated to this area of law.

Proposed amendments to the SGD:

#1

Article 2
Definitions

For the purposes of this Directive, the following definitions apply:

(…)

(5a) 'second-hand goods' means goods that are used again for the same purpose in their original form or with little enhancement or change.

AND *#2*

Article 3
Scope

(…)

5. Member States may exclude from the scope of this Directive contracts for the sale of:

~~**(a) second-hand goods sold at public auction; and**~~

(b) living animals.

(…)

2369 See B. Keirsbilck, E. Terryn, E. Van Gool, 'Consumentenbescherming bij servitisation en product-dienst-systemen (PDS)', 56 *T.P.R.* (2019) p. 817 at p. 899.

2370 E. Van Gool and A. Michel, 'The New Consumer Sales Directive 2019/771 and Sustainable Consumption: A Critical Analysis', 10 *EuCML* (2021) pp. 137–138.

3. SELLER LIABILITY CONDITIONS FOR LEGAL GUARANTEE

683. Three cumulative conditions – If the consumer is confronted with a defective good, EU consumer law grants him the right to complain to the seller about it.[2371] According to Article 10(1) of the SGD, there are three cumulative conditions to trigger the seller's liability: (a) a lack of conformity, (b) occurring within two years of the delivery and (c) existing prior to the delivery of the good. While those conditions were already present in the CSD[2372], several changes have been made with the adoption of the SGD, including in regard to product sustainability.

a) A lack of conformity

684. Objective requirements, subjective requirements and incorrect installation – First of all, the good must be *affected by a lack of conformity.* The question is then whether practices of premature obsolescence could be considered as a lack of conformity within the meaning of EU consumer sales law. This could be answered affirmatively for the 1999 CSD and its conformity requirements enshrined in its Article 2(2).[2373] Under its general terms, this provision encompassed more specific requirements linked to product sustainability.[2374] Under the new SGD, the conformity requirements, which can be found in Articles 6 to 8, have been detailed. The Directive provides a list of subjective requirements (Article 6) and objective requirements (Article 7) which must be satisfied in order for the product to be in conformity with the contract.[2375] Subjective requirements refer to those mentioned in the sales contract, whereas objective requirements correspond to consumers' reasonable expectations. This combination of conformity criteria was suggested "*to*

2371 The seller has then the possibility to pursue remedies against the person or persons liable, as allowed by the right of redress enshrined in Art. 4 of the CSD and Art. 18 of the SGD. See *infra*, n° 821 *et seq.*

2372 See Article 3 in conjunction with Article 5 CSD.

2373 A. Michel, 'La directive 1999/44/CE sur la garantie des biens de consommation: un remède efficace contre l'obsolescence programmée?', *R.E.D.C.* (2018) p. 207 at p. 236; T. Brönneke, 'Premature Obsolescence: Suggestions for Legislative Counter-measures in German and European Sales & Consumer Law', 14 *Journal for European Environmental & Planning Law* (2017) pp. 364–365.

2374 Some Member States explicitly detailed the conformity requirements set out in the Consumer Sales Directive to include specific requirements like the availability of spare and accessories or a reasonable durability. See Annex I to the study Ipsos-London Economics-Deloitte consortium, *Consumer market study on the functioning of legal and commercial guarantees for consumers in the EU* (European Union 2015) pp. 25–26.

2375 A similar structure can be found in Article 6 of the DCD concerning the conformity requirements applicable to digital content or digital service.

safeguard legitimate interests of both parties to a sales contract".[2376] In addition to these requirements, there is also the lack of conformity related to the incorrect installation of the goods set out in Article 8 of the SGD. Consumers can invoke the violation of one or more of these requirements to prove the lack of conformity, as was already the case under the CSD regime.[2377]

(1) Subjective requirements

685. Four subjective requirements – Article 6 of the SGD mentions different subjective requirements that the product must meet when delivered by the seller. These requirements depend on the content of the sales contract. Products will be considered in conformity with the contract if they are:

(a) of the description, type, quantity and quality, and possesses the functionality, compatibility, interoperability and other features, as required by the sales contract;
(b) fit for any particular purpose for which the consumer requires them and which the consumer made known to the seller at the latest at the time of the conclusion of the sales contract, and in respect of which the seller has given acceptance;
(c) delivered with all accessories and instructions, including on installation, as stipulated by the sales contract; and
(d) supplied with updates as stipulated by the sales contract.

686. Applicable to cases of premature obsolescence – Products that become prematurely obsolete could be considered as not corresponding to what was promised in the contract and thus not fulfilling one of the subjective requirements contained in Article 6 of the SGD. Consumers could then rely on this provision to invoke their guarantee rights. It is noteworthy that when something is agreed by both parties, it becomes automatically part of the sales contract, even if not explicitly written in Article 6 of the SGD. This principle has been used by some scholars to question the necessity of having such detailed conformity requirements.[2378]

687. Subjective requirement under Article 6(a) – The first requirement set out in Article 6(a) is particularly useful for consumers confronted with cases

---

2376 Proposal for a Directive of the European Parliament and of the Council on certain aspects concerning contracts for the online and other distance sales of goods, COM(2015) 635 final, p. 14.

2377 C. Delforge et Y. Ninane, 'La garantie de conformité des biens de consommation', in P. Wéry (ed.), *Théorie générale des obligations et contrats spéciaux* (Larcier 2016) p. 379 at p. 381.

2378 See J.M. Carvalho, 'Sale of Goods and Supply of Digital Content and Digital Services – Overview of Directives 2019/770 and 2019/771', 5 *EuCML* (2019) p. 198.

of premature obsolescence. While consumers could expect a certain quality level from elements implicitly agreed with the seller[2379], the contractual parties could explicitly define product features in the contract.[2380] These features can pertain to functionality[2381], compatibility[2382] and interoperability[2383], but other features that are not explicitly mentioned by the provision could also be included, such as durability.[2384] Products prematurely obsolete could then be considered as not reaching the quality level required by the sales contract or possessing the required functionality, compatibility or interoperability. For goods with digital elements, such requirement would be satisfied only if the digital content or service, which forms part of the contract, is supplied.[2385] Recital 27 adds that "*successful functioning could include, for instance, the ability of the goods to exchange information with such other software or hardware and to use the information exchanged.*"

688. Functionality, compatibility and interoperability – The notions of functionality, compatibility and interoperability have been added by the 2019 SGD. All these concepts are inextricably linked to product sustainability since good quality products which remain functional, compatible and interoperable with accessories and competitors' products last longer. Altogether, those criteria complement each other to tackle all types of premature obsolescence. Whereas products satisfying criteria of functionality, compatibility and interoperability are particularly less likely to become functionally or indirectly obsolete, the quality criterion could be used to combat cases of material obsolescence. Some of these notions are not new but were already used in other legal instruments.[2386] The links between them still have to be determined by the courts and tribunals, which could be different depending on cases. For example, a smartphone which is no longer compatible with the operating system developed by the producer loses its functionality and thus its conformity with the contract. Article 6(a)

2379 See *infra* on objective conformity requirements (n° 693 *et seq.*).

2380 Y. Ninane, O. Gilard, 'Section 3: La garantie des biens de consommation', in C. Delforge (ed.), *Vente. Commentaire pratique* (Kluwer 2009) p. 28.

2381 Article 2(9) defines 'functionality' as "*the ways in which the goods can perform their functions having regard to their purpose.*"

2382 Article 2(8) defines 'compatibility' as "*the ability of the goods to function with hardware or software with which goods of the same type are normally used, without the need to convert the goods, hardware or software.*"

2383 Article 2(10) defines 'interoperability' as "*the ability of the goods to function with hardware or software different from those with which goods of the same type are normally used.*" In other words, "*whether and to what extent the goods are able to function with hardware or software that is different from those with which goods of the same type are normally used*" (recital 27).

2384 The non-exhaustive character of the list is confirmed by the words 'other features'.

2385 See recital 15 SGD.

2386 See for ex. Art. 5(g) and 6(r) of the CRD on 'functionality' and Art. 5(h) and 6(s) of the same Directive on 'interoperability'. Since then, the definitions of 'compatibility', 'functionality' and interoperability' have been introduced in the CRD by the Enforcement and Modernisation Directive (see *supra*, n° 492).

could also serve as a basis when the smartphone is no longer compatible with headphones, although this compatibility is required by the contract. It is noteworthy that these notions were already implicitly included in the more generally formulated conformity requirements of the CSD.[2387] For example, Article 2 of the CSD has been interpreted as including compatibility.[2388]

689. Subjective requirement under Article 6(b) – The second subjective requirement set out in Article 6(b) states that goods must "*be fit for any particular purpose for which the consumer requires them and which the consumer made known to the seller at the latest at the time of the conclusion of the sales contract, and in respect of which the seller has given acceptance*". This provision can tackle some particular cases of premature obsolescence. Consumers could, for example, rely on this provision if they bought a smartphone specifically for an application that no longer works on the device due to discontinued updates of the operating system, causing the functional obsolescence of the device.[2389]

690. Subjective requirement under Article 6(c) – Third, Article 6(c) of the SGD requires products to be delivered with all accessories and instructions, including on installation, if stipulated by the sales contract. Although this conformity requirement was not (explicitly) mentioned in the CSD, such requirements already existed in some national laws.[2390] Such a conformity requirement is of utmost importance to tackle premature obsolescence, especially as a preventive tool. The delivery of accessories allows consumers to keep their products longer as they get all the compatible accessories at their disposal, while they can maintain and repair their products more easily thanks to instructions. When a defect occurs, consumers are more able to identify and solve the problem and can thus avoid the premature obsolescence of their product. However, this subjective requirement can be a double-edged sword for consumers: the liability of the guarantor could be limited or excluded if the instructions have not been followed by the consumer.[2391]

2387 F. Van den Abeele, B. Tilleman, 'Conformiteit in de richtlijn consumentenkoop 2019: Heeft de berg een muis gebaard?', in E. Terryn, I. Claeys (eds.), *Nieuw recht inzake koop & digitale inhoud en diensten* (Intersentia 2020) p. 99.

2388 See for ex. in Belgium: Mons 5 juin 1990, *Pas*. 1990, II, (237) 239.

2389 See *supra*, n° 109.

2390 See for ex. Art. 1615 of the Belgian Civil Code: "*L'obligation de délivrer la chose comprend ses accessoires et tout ce qui a été destiné à son usage perpétuel*". For other examples, see Annex I to the study Ipsos-London Economics-Deloitte consortium, *Consumer market study on the functioning of legal and commercial guarantees for consumers in the EU* (European Union 2015) pp. 25–26.

2391 Such a rule existed under Dutch law on consumer sales implementing the previous CSD. See C. Twigg-Flesner, 'Consumer Goods Guarantees in the DCFR – 'Best Solution' or Grasping the Wrong Nettle?', 17 *E.R.P.L.* (2009) p. 649.

691. Subjective requirement under Article 6(d) – Finally, according to Article 6(d), a lack of conformity would exist if the product with digital elements was not supplied with updates as stipulated by the contract. This provision, together with Article 7(3) of the SGD[2392] and Articles 5 and 19 of the DCD[2393], is crucial in the fight against premature obsolescence as updates contribute to countering (or at least postponing) the functional obsolescence of products. Goods with digital elements are indeed subject to constant changes, some of them possibly leading to their rapid obsolescence. Updates constitute therefore *"a necessary tool in order to ensure that the goods able to function in the same way that it did at the time of delivery"*.[2394] Moreover, updates *"can improve and enhance the digital content or digital service element of goods, extend their functionalities, adapt them to technical developments, protect them against new security threats or serve other purposes"*.[2395] If, contrary to what is required by the sales contract, updates are not supplied or are defective or incomplete, it would be considered as a lack of conformity on which consumers could rely.[2396] This new conformity requirement places a greater obligation on traders as they have to comply with it after delivery. This goes beyond the traditional obligation to merely deliver a product which conform to the contract.[2397]

692. A necessary combination with information requirements – The effectiveness of these subjective requirements would be significantly strengthened if combined with information requirements. Information given by the seller, voluntarily or compulsorily, in the sales contract or as pre-contractual statements, can indeed be qualified as a subjective conformity requirement.[2398] Once information is given by the seller (including on product durability, reparability, the availability of accessories and instructions, the supply of updates, etc.), it forms an integral part of the contract.[2399] As a consequence, the seller can be held liable if it occurs that the good does not comply with the features promised in the pre-contractual statements and/or written in the sales contract. The consumer can thus rely on Article 6 of the SGD if the product does

---

2392 For a detailed analysis of this provision, see *infra* n° 700.

2393 These provisions oblige the trader to supply the digital content or digital service to the consumer without undue delay after the conclusion of the contract and modify the digital content or digital service beyond what is necessary to maintain the digital content or digital service in conformity.

2394 Recital 31 SGD.

2395 Recital 28 SGD.

2396 Recital 28 SGD.

2397 F. Van den Abeele, B. Tilleman, 'Conformiteit in de richtlijn consumentenkoop 2019: Heeft de berg een muis gebaard?', in E. Terryn, I. Claeys (eds.), *Nieuw recht inzake koop & digitale inhoud en diensten* (Intersentia 2020) p. 101.

2398 See recital 26 SGD.

2399 Recital 32 SGD. See also Art. 6(5) CRD.

not comply with the content of the information provided[2400], alternatively to the UCPD provisions that prohibit greenwashing and other untrue or unverifiable sustainability claims.[2401] The combination of information and guarantee rights is more effective if the seller is legally obliged to provide such information.[2402] Otherwise, the absence of information obligations could have adverse effects, the most problematic being that traders might be deterred from giving information to avoid being sued on the basis of the rules on guarantees. Mandatory information requirements are therefore of utmost importance.[2403] However, the third chapter of this book revealed that so far, information requirements remain scarce, though some Member States have undertaken initiatives to complement and reinforce information given to consumers.[2404] This paragraph stresses once more how important it is to adopt more general and product-specific information requirements on product sustainability, as was repeatedly argued in the third chapter[2405], as well as in the second chapter of this book.[2406] References to these rules should then be made in the SGD.[2407]

(2) Objective requirements

693. Four objective requirements – In addition to subjective requirements, Article 7(1) of the SGD enumerates objective requirements, which are based on consumers' reasonable expectations and on what is normal for goods of the same type. They impose on sellers the obligation to only deliver goods that are:

2400 Having such information available also lightens the burden of proof for the consumer to prove the lack of conformity, as discussed in the previous chapter of this book. See also n° 719.

2401 See Chapter III on the marketing and pre-contractual stage, and more specifically n° 409 *et seq*. The European consumer sales regime presents a very effective alternative instrument for consumers, especially due to the possible remedies and the modalities for their exercise.

2402 This argument has been developed in Chapter III on the marketing and pre-contractual stage. For a good summary, see n° 639.

2403 See also M. Schaub, 'How to Make the Best of Mandatory Information Requirements in Consumer Law', 25 *E.R.P.L.* (2017), p. 31 at p. 33 and pp. 43–44. This necessity has also been acknowledged by the EC. See Communication from the Commission of 13 November 2020 to the European Parliament and the Council and the Council on New Consumer Agenda – Strengthening consumer resilience for sustainable recovery, COM(2020) 696 final, pp. 7–8.

2404 A prominent example is new French legislation that imposes information obligations on producers of certain products regarding durability, repairability and environmental/social impact (n° 473–563).

2405 In the third chapter, amendments to the UCPD, CRD and labelling rules were proposed to make more information on product sustainability available to consumers. For more details, see Chapter III on the marketing and pre-contractual stage.

2406 In the second chapter, it was also recommended to adopt more product-specific information requirements within the framework of the Ecodesign Directive. For more details, see Chapter II on the design and production stage.

2407 The complementarity of product-specific legislation with the SGD is already acknowledged in its recital 32.

(a) fit for the purposes for which goods of the same type would normally be used, taking into account, where applicable, any existing Union and national law, technical standards or, in the absence of such technical standards, applicable sector-specific industry codes of conduct;
(b) where applicable, of the quality and correspond to the description of a sample or model that the seller made available to the consumer before the conclusion of the contract;
(c) where applicable, delivered along with such accessories, including packaging, installation instructions or other instructions, as the consumer may reasonably expect to receive; and
(d) of the quantity and possess the qualities and other features, including in relation to durability, functionality, compatibility and security normal for goods of the same type and which the consumer may reasonably expect given the nature of the goods and taking into account any public statement made by or on behalf of the seller, or other persons in previous links of the chain of transactions, including the producer, particularly in advertising or on labelling.

694. Applicable to cases of premature obsolescence – Objective requirements set out in Article 7(1)(a), (c) and (d) can be particularly useful in case of premature obsolescence, especially in the absence of explicit contractual terms specifying conformity criteria. In that sense, it could be said that Article 7 applies in a subsidiary manner, alternatively to Article 6 on subjective requirements. Therefore, when comparing both provisions, it is not surprising to find that they share many similarities. Their main difference, namely the fact that they depend on either contractual elements or consumer expectations, is however not negligible as it constitutes a decisive factor for consumers who bear the burden of proof regarding the lack of conformity.[2408] By contrast with the content of a contract, consumers' reasonable expectations are more nebulous and volatile. How long a consumer expects a specific product to last depends on a number of proxies, including prices, brand, online reviews and the length of the commercial guarantee.[2409] According to recital 24, "*the standard of reasonableness should be objectively ascertained, having regard to the nature and purpose of the contract, the circumstances of the case and to the usages and practices of the parties involved.*" Such margin of appreciation could variably tilt the balance in favour of one party or the other.

695. Objective requirement under Article 7(1)(a) – The first relevant objective requirement is enshrined in Article 7(1)(a). It requires goods to be

[2408] See *infra*, n° 715 *et seq.*
[2409] J. Cox et al., 'Consumer understanding of product lifetimes', 79 *Resources, Conservation and Recycling* (2013).

"fit for the purposes for which goods of the same type would normally be used". Various cases of premature obsolescence could be seen as infringing this provision. For example, a smartphone for which the producer stops developing the adapted operating system (OS) could be considered as not conforming to the contract. Indeed, without this OS, the smartphone becomes unsuitable for the use for which goods of the same type are normally used and for which the consumer acquired it.[2410] By contrast, cases of normal wear and tear resulting from the (normal) use of the product do not pertain to this category, though the good is no longer fit for the purposes for which goods of the same type would normally be used.[2411] While deriving from Article 2(2)(c) of the CSD, the provision has been further developed in the SGD. The new provision refers now to existing Union and national law, technical standards and codes of conduct as benchmarks against which the assessment of the fitness for normal use should be made. This covers for example durability and reparability requirements established by ecodesign regulations.[2412] These benchmarks, which are expected to expand in the following months[2413], will help draw the boundaries of this requirement and reinforce its effectiveness against premature obsolescence. If the product does not comply with these regulations, consumers could claim their guarantee rights on the basis of these product requirements[2414], like the Court held in *Porsche Inter Auto and Volkswagen* for cars fitted with a defeat device.[2415]

696. Objective requirement under Article 7(1)(c) – Article 7(1)(c) could also contribute to tackling premature obsolescence as it creates the obligation to supply accessories and instructions along with the product if consumers could have reasonably expected to receive them. This provision complements Article 6(c), allowing consumers to rely on it when they do not get these accessories and/or instructions, although it is not stipulated in the contract. Like Article 7(1)(a), the effectiveness of Article 7(1)(c) could be maximised if combined with other rules, especially ecodesign requirements. As an example, ecodesign requirements on electronic displays, which oblige producers to give

2410 This example had been given for Article 2(2)(c) CSD in A. Hamann, 'Obsolescence programmée: le droit en panne?', 102 *D.C.C.R.* (2014) pp. 68–69.

2411 Anvers, 28 avril 2014, *NjW*, 2014, liv. 308, p. 701, note R. Steennot.

2412 See Chapter II on the design and production stage, especially n° 231 *et seq*.

2413 See the numerous initiatives issued by the EC for the adoption of additional product requirements, as described in Chapter II on the design and production stage (n° 314).

2414 These product requirements may also lighten consumers' burden of proof. See *infra*, n° 719.

2415 See ECJ 14 July 2022, Case C-145/20, *Porsche Inter Auto and Volkswagen, EU:C:2022:572*. In this case, the Court ruled that the purchaser of a vehicle with a prohibited defeat device has a right under EU law to cancel the contract of sale because it does not show the quality which is normal in goods of the same type and which the consumer can reasonably expect. The Court also held that the lack of conformity with relevant vehicle standards was not a minor irregularity. Although this ruling relates to the conformity requirement now enshrined in Article 7(1)(d) of the SGD, it shows the potential for combining guarantee rules and product regulations.

dismantling instructions[2416], could confirm consumers' reasonable expectations for a television when delivered without such instructions, though nothing is mentioned in the contract. By contrast, consumers should not expect the delivery of accessories together with the product if ecodesign requirements decouple the sale of these accessories (e.g. headphones or chargers) from the concerned product category (e.g. laptops or smartphones).[2417] More than helping consumers to claim their rights, Article 7(1)(c) has a preventive effect on premature obsolescence too as it encourages producers to improve the reparability and interoperability of their products.

697. Objective requirement under Article 7(1)(d) – Last but not least, consumers could invoke Article 7(1)(d), which corresponds to the former Article 2(d) of the CSD, when the goods do not "*possess the qualities and other features normal for goods of the same type and which the consumer may reasonably expect*". This provision remains one of the most relevant requirements when dealing with cases of premature obsolescence. It works as a safety net when there is neither mention of features related to product sustainability in the sales contract nor legal obligation to do so. Compared to Article 2(d) of the CSD, the provision has been detailed, citing a range of features that the product should possess, including durability, functionality, compatibility and security. Surprisingly, the concept of 'interoperability' is not part of this second list of product features, by contrast with Article 6(a) on subjective requirements. This had led some scholars to argue that interoperability cannot be expected by consumers[2418], which shows the flaws of the more detailed provision of the new Directive. Article 7(1)(d) nonetheless refers to 'other features', implying the non-exhaustive character of the list.[2419] Among these other features and intrinsic qualities of the product, one could also include the availability of after-sales services, which also contribute to prolonging product lifetime.[2420]

698. Durability as a conformity requirement – In terms of premature obsolescence, one of the most crucial improvements in the SGD is the introduction of the durability criterion as a conformity requirement. 'Durability' is defined in Article 2(13) as the "*ability of the goods to maintain their required*

2416 Annex II D.1. to the Ecodesign regulation on electronic displays.

2417 Such requirements are envisaged for phone chargers. See *supra*, n° 279.

2418 See for ex. D. Staudenmayer, 'Les directives européennes sur les contrats numériques', 116 *Revue des contrats* (2019) p.135.

2419 E. Van Gool and A. Michel, 'The New Consumer Sales Directive 2019/771 and Sustainable Consumption: A Critical Analysis', 10 *EuCML* (2021) p. 138.

2420 As highlighted by the EC during the adoption process of the CSD, "*a product for which after-sales service is poor or non-existent cannot be used in line with the purchaser's legitimate expectations and may thus be considered defective under the terms of the legal guarantee.* See Green Paper from the European Commission of 15 November 1993 on Guarantees for Consumer Goods and After-sales Services, COM(93) 509 final, p. 50.

functions and performance through normal use".[2421] This change had been suggested by the EESC[2422], as well as in a study commissioned by the EP.[2423] Although consumers may struggle bringing proof of a lack of durability[2424], the new provision has the merit of lifting the fog on the scope of Article 7(1)(d), which was still obscure and discussed in the literature.[2425] Since the adoption of the SGD, it is now clear that a product should reach a certain durability threshold in order to show the quality of goods of the same type that consumers may reasonably expect and thus be in conformity with the contract.[2426] It remains to be seen how this new objective requirement will be construed and conciliated with the guarantee period.[2427] It is to be regretted that the definition of 'durability' was not made in coherence with EU standards, which also contains a definition of this concept.[2428] The definition given by Article 2(13)

2421 It is interesting to note that the EESC referred to the stock of replacement parts to define 'durability'. See Opinion of the European Economic and Social Committee on the 'Amended proposal for a Directive of the European Parliament and of the Council on certain aspects concerning contracts for the sales of goods, amending Regulation (EC) No 2006/2004 of the European Parliament and of the Council and Directive 2009/22/EC of the European Parliament and of the Council and repealing Directive 1999/44/EC of the European Parliament and of the Council' (COM(2017) 637 final), OJ C 227, 28.6.2018, p. 59, pt. 1.5. d).

2422 See Opinion of the EESC on the 'Proposal for a directive of the European Parliament and of the Council on certain aspects concerning contracts for the supply of digital content' (COM(2015) 634 final) and the 'Proposal for a directive of the European Parliament and of the Council on certain aspects concerning contracts for the online and other distance sales of goods' (COM(2015) 635 final), OJ C 264, 20.7.2016, p. 63, pt. 4.2.5.4. See also Opinion of the European Economic and Social Committee on the 'Amended proposal for a Directive of the European Parliament and of the Council on certain aspects concerning contracts for the sales of goods, amending Regulation (EC) No 2006/2004 of the European Parliament and of the Council and Directive 2009/22/EC of the European Parliament and of the Council and repealing Directive 1999/44/EC of the European Parliament and of the Council' (COM(2017) 637 final), OJ C 227, 28.6.2018, p. 59, pt. 1.5. d).

2423 K. Tonner, R. Malcolm, *Study on How an EU lifespan guarantee model could be implemented across the European Union* (European Parliament 2017), especially p. 54.

2424 See *infra*, n° 717.

2425 See for ex. A. Hamann, 'Obsolescence programmée: le droit en panne?', 102 *D.C.C.R.* (2014) pp. 68–69; D. Raes, "L'obsolescence programmée à l'épreuve de l'obligation d'information du vendeur, de la notion de conformité et de la garantie des vices cachés", in *Liber Amicorum François Glansdorf et Pierre Legros* (Bruylant 2014) p. 271 *et seq.*; M. Bianca, S. Grundmann, *EU Sales Directive* (Intersentia 2002) p. 158.

2426 This reflection had already taken place at the time of the adoption of Directive 1999/44/EC. See Green Paper from the European Commission of 15 November 1993 on Guarantees for Consumer Goods and After-sales Services, COM(93) 509 final, p. 48 at p. 50. This document indicates that "*the fact that certain consumer durables may not function properly after a lapse of time which is less than their 'durability expectation' may be considered as a defect*".

2427 The Commission guidance on the meaning of 'durability' as an objective conformity requirement could be useful in this regard. See the feedback of the Union Luxembourgeoise des consommateurs on the Inception Impact Assessment Empowering the consumer for the green transition, available on: <https://ec.europa.eu/info/law/better-regulation/have-your-say/initiatives/12467-Empowering-the-consumer-for-the-green-transition/F538921>.

2428 See CEN-CENELEC TC10, Definitions related to material efficiency, EN 45550:2020, p. 5, which defines 'durability' as the "*ability to function as required, under defined conditions of use, maintenance and repair, until a limiting state is reached*". See *supra*, n° 144.

of the SGD makes it uncertain whether 'durability' encompasses 'repairability', though it would be surprising if it did not. Repairability contributes to product durability and from the perspective of the Union's circular economy policy, standard 'repair' should indeed become part of the "*normal use*" of goods referred to in Article 2(13).[2429] Should the notion of 'durability' be interpreted in its strict sense, 'reparability' could in any event be encompassed within the 'other features'.

699. The assessment of consumer expectations – Article 7(d) specifies different factors that should be taken into account when assessing the compliance of the product with consumer expectations. The nature of the goods is the first factor that plays a role in this assessment, especially when goods are specific and need, for example, reasonable maintenance.[2430] In this regard, the Belgian courts have emphasized that the second-hand nature of a car does not prevent the consumer from reasonably expecting that he can drive it for a certain period of time without any significant technical problems.[2431] The second factor is public statements that would have been made by or on behalf of the seller, the producer or other persons in previous links of the chain of transactions, particularly in advertising or on labelling. In this regard, Article 7(d) also combats misleading claims prohibited under the UCPD.[2432] Article 7(2) of the SGD clarifies nonetheless that the seller is not bound by public statements if he shows that (1) he was not, and could not reasonably have been, aware of the public statement in question, (2) that by the time of conclusion of the contract, the public statement had been corrected in the same way as, or in a way comparable to how, it had been made, or (3) that the decision to buy the goods could not have been influenced by the public statement.[2433] These exceptions should be interpreted restrictively. In addition to these two factors, recital 32 adds that the assessment of consumer expectations should also be based on "*all other relevant circumstances, such as the price of the goods and the intensity or frequency of the use that the consumer makes of the goods*". Consumers can indeed expect no defect for a certain period of time if they paid a high price[2434], or if they have only been using the product occasionally for a few months.[2435] Otherwise, it may constitute abnormal wear and tear, which may be qualified

---

2429 E. Van Gool and A. Michel, 'The New Consumer Sales Directive 2019/771 and Sustainable Consumption: A Critical Analysis', 10 *EuCML* (2021) p. 138.

2430 Recital 32 SGD mentions the case of cars, which need regular inspection or changing of filters.

2431 Liège, 18 avril 2016, R.G. no 2015/RG/995; Civ. Bruxelles, 7 mai 2009, *J.T.*, 2009, pp. 737-738.

2432 See Chapter III on the marketing and pre-contractual stage, and more specifically n° 409 *et seq*.

2433 These exclusions can make direct producer liability more desirable, as argued below (n° 825 *et seq.*).

2434 Liège (3e ch. B), 17 mars 2015, R.G. no 2014/RG/663.

2435 Civ. Bruxelles, 7 mai 2009, J.T., 2009, pp. 737-738. In the case at hand, the second-hand cars had broken down less than two months after delivery.

as a lack of conformity. Finally, consumer expectations may also depend on the provisions of the contract, the presentation of the product, the brand, any information provided on the product and the purpose of the product or the laws and regulations concerning the product (e.g. ecodesign rules).[2436] The law could have an influence on all these factors and shape consumer expectations to make them higher[2437], not only by imposing product-specific sustainability requirements, but also by regulating misleading business practices.

700. THE SUPPLY OF UPDATES AS FIFTH OBJECTIVE REQUIREMENT – In addition to the three objective requirements described above, Article 7(3) of the SGD incorporates another objective requirement for its new category of goods with digital elements: the supply of updates. As already explained in the corresponding subjective requirement[2438], updates play a significant role in the fight against the premature obsolescence of products, and more specifically against functional obsolescence. Compared to Article 6 of the SGD, the introduction of this 'update obligation' in the objective conformity requirements is even more valuable for consumers, who can make a complaint against the seller if, contrary to what they expected, they were not informed of nor supplied with updates (other than the ones contractually agreed) that are necessary to keep their goods in conformity.[2439] The lack of definition of the term 'necessary' is regrettable as it leaves some uncertainties in its interpretation, which could restrict the effectiveness of this new obligation.[2440] The provision applies even if the goods were in conformity at the time of delivery.[2441] However, the consumer cannot hold the seller liable for such a lack of conformity if he failed to install the supplied updates within a reasonable time.[2442] This new 'update-obligation' echoes the issue raised in the recent *Apple* and *Samsung* decisions, where consumers had been pushed to install new firmware updates on their smartphone which had reduced the functionality of their device, without having received any (adequate) information on the characteristics, risks and

---

2436 These examples were given in the Green Paper from the European Commission of 15 November 1993 on Guarantees for Consumer Goods and After-sales Services, COM(93) 509 final, p. 86.

2437 Consumers' expectations might be low if they have no confidence in the product due to past experiences or if they believe that the product lifespan has been deliberately shortened with practices of planned obsolescence (See *supra*, n° 60). Consequently, the defect may not be considered as a lack of conformity if consumers' expectations are too low.

2438 See Art. 6(d) SGD (n° 691).

2439 Recital 30 SGD clarifies that *a contrario*, *"[u]nless the parties have contractually agreed otherwise, the seller should not be obliged to provide upgraded versions of the digital content or digital service of the goods or to improve or extend the functionalities of goods beyond the conformity requirements."*

2440 R. Steennot, S. Geiregat, 'Consumentenkoop en digitale inhoud: toepassingsgebied en afbakening', in E. Terryn, I. Claeys (eds.), *Nieuw recht inzake koop & digitale inhoud en diensten* (Intersentia 2020) p. 35.

2441 Recital 31 SGD.

2442 Art. 7(4) SGD. For further comments on this exception to the seller's liability, see n° 723.

solutions related to these updates.[2443] These practices were qualified as unfair within the meaning of the UCPD.[2444] Now such cases could be tackled by both instruments, increasing the chance of catching and sanctioning these practices. As previously argued, the effectiveness of this provision would be maximised if a twin information obligation on updates was introduced in the CRD[2445], taking inspiration from French law.[2446]

701. The supply of 'non-necessary' updates under French law – In addition to this new obligation, the French legislature decided to go one step further by introducing in Article L. 217–20 of the French Consumer Code four obligations for the seller who would supply updates "*that are not necessary to keep their goods in conformity*". First, the contract must allow the supply of such updates and provide a valid reason for them. Second, the seller must inform the consumer, in a clear and comprehensible manner, reasonably in advance and on a durable medium, of the planned update, specifying the date on which it will take place. Third, the update is carried out at no additional cost to the consumer. Fourth, the seller must inform the consumer that they have the right to refuse the update or, where appropriate, to uninstall it, if the update has a negative impact on their access to or use of the digital content or service. If the update has such a negative impact, Article L. 217–20 grants consumers the right to terminate the contract at no cost, within a maximum of thirty days, unless the update has only a minor impact on the consumer. The termination of the contract is only possible if no offer was made by the seller to keep the digital content or service unchanged, including by uninstalling the update, and if the update resulted in a lack of conformity of the digital content or service.

Several points can be made concerning this legislation. First, although the objective of these rules (i.e. curbing functional obsolescence) is laudable, one could wonder about the usefulness of some information in the eyes of the consumer (e.g. date of update installation) and the ensuing risks of information overload. Second, the provision on update costs should be more nuanced as certain non-necessary updates could be offered at a fair, transparent and non-discriminatory cost. Third, as for the implicit right to uninstall updates, further research first needs to be undertaken to assess whether uninstalling or reverting an update would be feasible from a memory capacity and performance point of

---

2443 See Autorita Garante della Concorrenza e del Mercato, 25 September 2018, *Apple*; Autorita Garante della Concorrenza e del Mercato, 25 September 2018, *Samsung*; *Transaction pénale* agreed by French public prosecutor, DGCCRF and Apple, communicated on 7 February 2020, <https://www.economie.gouv.fr/dgccrf/transaction-avec-le-groupe-apple-pour-pratique-commerciale-trompeuse>.

2444 See Chapter III on the marketing and pre-contractual stage, especially n° 359 and 399.

2445 For further comments on this proposed amendment to the CRD, see Chapter III on the marketing and pre-contractual stage (n° 498–501).

2446 For more details on the French mandatory obligation on updates, see Chapter III on the marketing and pre-contractual stage (n° 495–497).

view, as already pointed out in the second chapter of this book.[2447] Fourth, the last provision that grants consumers the right to terminate the contract weakens the hierarchy of remedies established under the SGD and is questionable from a sustainability point of view. If repair or price reduction is possible, these options should be preferred. Fifth, the CRD and the national rules implementing its provisions (i.e. Article L. 111–6 of the French Consumer Code) would be more appropriate to impose such information obligations.[2448] The only provision worth considering is the obligation to provide the consumer with the option not to install non-necessary updates. In this sense, Article 7 of the SGD should establish the obligation to obtain consumer's prior consent before the installation of these updates and oblige the seller to inform the consumer of this possibility (see #3). Such an amendment would strengthen future ecodesign requirements imposing the corresponding obligations on producers.[2449]

702. The great potential of objective conformity requirements against premature obsolescence – Objective requirements represent a powerful tool in the hands of consumers to cure defects of their products that occurred prematurely. Many cases of premature obsolescence are being tackled by these broad requirements, as was already the case under the CSD. The vague notion of 'consumer expectations' on which these objective requirements are based might nonetheless cause some difficulties for consumers in proving a lack of conformity of a product prematurely obsolete.[2450] This problem could be circumvented if the factors on which these objective requirements depend, namely what is normal for goods of the same type and what consumers may reasonably expect, were detailed and clarified. Here too, combinations with other legal instruments are worth considering. On one hand, ecodesign requirements on product sustainability aspects (e.g. durability, availability of accessories and instructions) could contribute to clarifying what is normal for goods of the same type.[2451] On the other hand, if producers are nudged or obliged to indicate product lifetime or other information through labelling, even for mere information purposes, it would give a benchmark which consumers could rely on and on which their level of expectations about the good could be evaluated.[2452] However, "*the sustainability merits of the conformity framework*

2447 For further comments, see *supra*, n° 251.

2448 Amendments to the CRD were proposed in relation to updates. See Chapter III on the marketing and pre-contractual stage, and more specifically n° 498–501.

2449 See *supra*, n° 250.

2450 See *infra*, n° 715 *et seq*.

2451 On the link between product regulations and guarantee rules, see ECJ 14 July 2022, Case C-145/20, *Porsche Inter Auto and Volkswagen, EU:C:2022:572.*

2452 Here too, making certain information disclosures mandatory may be preferable as producers might refrain from giving sustainability information, in fear of contractual liability (see *supra*, n° 692).

are nothing more than a potential".[2453] Once these conformity requirements are fulfilled, it is then crucial to have conditions that favour sustainable remedies, as emphasized in the following paragraphs of this section.

Proposed amendment to the SGD

#3

Article 7
Objective requirements for conformity

(...)

3. In the case of goods with digital elements, the seller shall ensure that the consumer is informed of and supplied with updates, including security updates, that are necessary to keep those goods in conformity, for the period of time:

(a) that the consumer may reasonably expect given the type and purpose of the goods and the digital elements, and taking into account the circumstances and nature of the contract, where the sales contract provides for a single act of supply of the digital content or digital service; or

(b) indicated in Article 10(2) or (5), as applicable, where the sales contract provides for a continuous supply of the digital content or digital service over a period of time.

3a. As for updates that are not necessary to keep those goods in conformity, the seller shall ensure that the consumer has the option of refusing these updates without avoidable loss of functionality and inform the consumer of this possibility.

4. Where the consumer fails to install within a reasonable time updates supplied in accordance with paragraph 3 **and 3a**, the seller shall not be liable for any lack of conformity resulting solely from the lack of the relevant update, provided that:

(a) the seller informed the consumer about the availability of the update and the consequences of the failure of the consumer to install it; and

(b) the failure of the consumer to install or the incorrect installation by the consumer of the update was not due to shortcomings in the installation instructions provided to the consumer.

(...)

[2453] E. Van Gool and A. Michel, 'The New Consumer Sales Directive 2019/771 and Sustainable Consumption: A Critical Analysis', 10 *EuCML* (2021) p. 139.

(3) Conformity requirement related to the installation of the goods

703. Incorrect installation of the goods as a lack of conformity – There is a third category of conformity requirements which relates to the correctness of provided installation services, instructions or software. According to Article 8, any lack of conformity resulting from the incorrect installation of the goods shall be regarded as lack of conformity of the goods, if:

(a) the installation forms part of the sales contract and was carried out by the seller or under the seller's responsibility; or
(b) the installation, intended to be carried out by the consumer, was done by the consumer and the incorrect installation was due to shortcomings in the installation instructions provided by the seller or, in the case of goods with digital elements, provided by the seller or by the supplier of the digital content or digital service.

704. An additional case of premature obsolescence tackled – This conformity criterion already existed in the former CSD, though not in a separate provision and without reference to goods with digital content.[2454] Since the adoption of the SGD, it has been made explicit that a lack of conformity can also result from the incorrect installation of digital content or digital service.[2455] Not only are producers obliged to supply updates as required by Article 7(3) of the Directive, but they also have to ensure their good installation on the goods. Recital 34 elaborates on this point, explaining that incomplete or unclear installation instructions which are difficult to use for the average consumer could lead to a lack of conformity. Hence, consumers can invoke guarantee rights in cases where the product becomes obsolete due to the fact that installation services, instructions or software were incorrectly provided. This is to be welcomed from a sustainable consumption perspective as it enables consumers to repair these obsolete products.

(4) A liability period of (at least) two years

705. Established with the adoption of the CSD – The two-year liability period has been established at EU level since the adoption of the CSD.[2456] During the adoption process of the CSD, some were in favour of a variable period depending on different factors, such as the estimated lifetime of the product, the ability of the parties to influence the risk of defect or the value of

2454 See Art. 2(5) CSD.
2455 See recital 34 SGD.
2456 Art. 5(1) CSD.

the good.[2457] A single two-year period will finally be chosen as the minimum protection threshold for greater legal certainty. The SGD maintains the two-year liability period, though with a possible different relevant time for assessing the conformity of the goods continuously supplied with digital elements[2458] and with a possible extension of the liability period for the latter goods.[2459] Although some European organisations still advocated for a longer guarantee period[2460], the EC concluded that, based on the available data[2461], the two-year guarantee period *"effectively caters for a very large proportion of the defects in goods discovered by consumers"*.[2462]

706. With some leeway left to the Member States – While the SGD provides for a two-year guarantee period, some leeway has (still) been left to Member States on the length of the liability period. According to Article 10(3), national law makers are allowed to *"maintain or introduce longer time limits"*.[2463] Hence, consumers could, if so provided by national law, be entitled to claim remedies under the legal guarantee for a period longer than two years. Several Member States have decided not to use this possibility and maintained the two-year minimum guarantee period, like Belgium[2464] and France.[2465] By contrast,

---

2457 S. Grundmann, F. Gomez, 'Introduction', in M.C. Bianca, S. Grundmann and S. Stijns (eds.), *La directive communautaire sur la vente – Commentaire* (Bruylant-L.G.D.J. 2004) p. 84; J. Stuyck, 'La notion de conformité et l'articulation des délais', in C. Biquet-Mathieu, P. Wéry (eds.), *La nouvelle garantie des biens de consommation et son environnement légal* (La Charte 2005) p. 121.

2458 See recitals 37 and 39 SGD.

2459 See Art. 10(1) and (2) SGD. For further comments, See *infra*, n° 739 *et seq*.

2460 See for ex. BEUC Policy Paper of 18 August 2015 on Durable goods: More sustainable products, better consumer rights, BEUC-X-2015-069, p. 12; Opinion of the EESC on the 'Proposal for a directive of the European Parliament and of the Council on certain aspects concerning contracts for the supply of digital content' (COM(2015) 634 final) and the 'Proposal for a directive of the European Parliament and of the Council on certain aspects concerning contracts for the online and other distance sales of goods' (COM(2015) 635 final), OJ C 264, 20.7.2016, pt. 4.2.5.11.

2461 A study commissioned by the Commission and based on self-reported data from consumers found that most of the defects occurred during the first two years. For further information, see ICF, *Study on the costs and benefits of extending certain rights under the Consumer Sales and Guarantees Directive 1999/44/CE* (European Commission 2017), especially p. 22 at p. 63.

2462 Commission Staff Working Document of 31 October 2017 on the Impacts of fully harmonised rules on contracts for the sales of goods supplementing the impact assessment accompanying the proposal for a Directive of the European Parliament and of the Council on certain aspects concerning contracts for the online and other distance sales of goods, SWD(2017) 354 final, p. 22 at p. 24.

2463 See also recital 41 SGD.

2464 See Art. 1649*quater* §1 subparagraph 1 of the Belgian Civil Code. It is interesting to note that before the adoption of the CSD, there was no time limit for the guarantee under Belgian law. Consumers could argue that the absence of durability constitutes a defect from the point of view of conformity with expectations. On that point, see the Green Paper from the European Commission of 15 November 1993 on Guarantees for Consumer Goods and After-sales Services, COM(93) 509 final, p. 50.

2465 Art. L. 217-12 of the French Consumer Code.

other Member States have decided to extend the guarantee period beyond two years.[2466] The first approach consists in extending the legal guarantee without making a distinction between products.[2467] The second approach is to establish differentiated but general guarantee periods depending on the type and expected lifetime of products.[2468] The third approach consists of fully differentiated guarantee periods that depend on the purchased good's expected lifespan.[2469] In other words, consumers may claim that non-conformity existed at the time of delivery as long this is not attributed to wear and tear due to expiration of the good's expected lifespan. For this third approach, the assessment of the expected lifespan is supported by soft law, which indicates expected lifespans for different product categories.[2470] The length of the liability period can thus greatly vary between the Member States. This is without mentioning other aspects left to the discretion of the Member States, like the meaning of 'delivery', which is the starting point of the guarantee period.[2471]

707. A TOO SHORT GUARANTEE PERIOD – Serious doubts remain on the adequacy of the current legal guarantee period as established by the SGD, especially with regard to the premature obsolescence of consumer goods. Aside from the longer period provided for digital content or service continuously supplied[2472], the two-year liability period seems too short, especially for goods with a longer expected lifetime (e.g. white goods). It is easy to imagine,

---

[2466] For more details on the various national approaches concerning the guarantee period, see for ex. ICF, *Study on the costs and benefits of extending certain rights under the Consumer Sales and Guarantees Directive 1999/44/CE* (European Commission 2017); K. Tonner, R. Malcolm, *Study on How an EU lifespan guarantee model could be implemented across the European Union* (European Parliament 2017). See also the various country fiches accompanying the study Ipsos-London Economics-Deloitte consortium, *Consumer market study on the functioning of legal and commercial guarantees for consumers in the EU* (European Commission 2015), available on: http://ec.europa.eu/consumers/consumer_evidence/market_studies/guarantees/index_en.htm.

[2467] Sweden is among them, providing a uniform three-year period for all products (§23 Konsumentköplag (1990:932)).

[2468] For example, in Norway, the legal guarantee is extended from two to five years for products which are deemed to last longer than two years (art. 27(2) Lög um neytendakaup 48/2003).

[2469] This approach is followed by the Netherlands, where the legal guarantee depends on the average expected lifespan of product categories as well as on the price (Art. 17(2) Burgerlijk Wetboek), as well as by Finland, where consumers can rely on legal guarantee rules when the product does not last as long as it can be ordinarily be expected (§16 Kuluttajansuojalaki (1978/38)).

[2470] In the Netherlands, a table has been established a Dutch industry group (see the UNETO-VNI table, available on: <www.uneto-vni.nl/onze-leden/waar-staan-onze-leden-voor/gebruiksduurverwachting>). In Finland, the expected lifespan of the good is established by non-binding decisions of the Finnish Consumer Dispute Board, which takes into account the expected lifespan of goods of the same category, the price and the usual frequency of use.

[2471] See recital 38 SGD. In this recital, reference is made to the CRD, which delineates the notion of 'delivery' in its Article 18.

[2472] See *infra*, n° 739–741.

for example, that a dishwasher would break down after two years of use, without this being due to normal wear and tear or improper use, but rather due to a defect attributable to the seller or the producer.[2473] This limited guarantee period is even more questionable when taking into consideration the new 'durability' requirement introduced by the SGD.[2474] Hence, at present, consumers are deprived of any protection under EU legislation after the two years.[2475] Admittedly, Member States may go beyond the minimum level of protection granted by the SGD and protect consumers in those cases. The SGD could nonetheless have been the opportunity to extend the liability period at EU level[2476], which would have prevented national disparities and their related drawbacks.[2477]

708. The positive effects of longer guarantee periods – Not only would an extension of the liability period at EU level satisfy the two main goals of the Directive (functioning of the internal market and consumer protection), but it would also protect the environment by fostering product sustainability. An extended guarantee period could indeed incite sellers (and indirectly producers) to offer goods with a longer lifetime to avoid any costs, time and energy incurred by guarantee claims. This constitutes the most beneficial effects of an extended guarantee period. Although a longer guarantee period may increase the price of products, as predicted by some studies (e.g. due to the necessary stock of large inventories of repair materials)[2478], the majority of consumers say that they are

---

2473 For example, it could be a defect caused by inherent weaknesses in its design, poor workmanship or the use of faulty materials in the manufacturing process, as mentioned by C. Twigg-Flesner in C. Twigg-Flesner, *Consumer Product Guarantees* (Routledge 2016) p. 5. See *infra* on the third condition, namely the existence of the lack of conformity prior to the delivery of the good.

2474 See *supra*, n° 698.

2475 See also J. Hijma, 'De Koopregeling in het Richtlijnvoorstel Consumentenrechten', in M.W. Hesselink and M.B.M. Loos (eds.), *Het Voorstel voor een Europese Richtlijn Consumentenrechten. Een Nederlands Perspectief* (Boom Juridische Uitgevers Den Haag 2009) p. 177; S. Van Camp, S. Bouyon, *Impact assessment of proposed substantial amendments introducing a commercial lifespan guarantee in the proposed online sales and digital content directive* (European Parliament 2017) p. 5.

2476 Such arguments have been raised in particular during the process of adopting the Consumer Rights Directive 2011/83. See for ex. Y. Ninane et O. Gilard, 'La garantie des biens de consommation', in C. Delforge, *Vente. Commentaire pratique*, Waterloo, Kluwer, 2009, p. 33; M. Loos, 'Consumer Sales Law in the Proposal for a Consumer Rights Directive', *E.R.P.L.* (2010) p. 15 at p. 55.

2477 Disparities obstruct cross-border transactions, not only because it creates financial and administrative burden on businesses, but also because consumers are consequently more reluctant to buy products in another Member State (especially for goods with an expected lifetime longer than two years).

2478 See E.H. Lauridsen and M.S. Jørgensen, 'Transitions in waste treatment as a driver for product life extension', in T. Cooper, N. Braithwaite, M. Moreno and G. Salvia (eds.), *Product Lifetimes and the Environment (PLATE) Conference proceedings* (Nottingham Trent University 2015) p. 187 at p. 193; ICF, *Study on the costs and benefits of extending*

prepared to pay more if it means that products will have longer lifespan.[2479] In any case, the price increase would arguably be offset in the long term by longer-lasting products and lower costs of repairs.

709. Three possible options – As shown by the national rules above[2480], three approaches could be followed to extend the liability period under the SGD. The liability period could be generally extended (first approach) or only for certain categories of products. In the latter case, the liability period could be fixed (second approach) or vary from product to product depending on their average lifetime or other criteria, such as the purchase price or the product characteristics (third approach). In a recent study commissioned by the EP, it was proposed to adopt the second approach – with differentiated but general guarantee periods – at EU level.[2481] By contrast, E. Maitre-Ekern and C. Dalhammar are in favour of fully differentiated guarantee periods – which corresponds to the third approach – and suggested guaranteeing products for their whole lifetime.[2482] In support of their idea, these scholars asserted that "*if consumers are made responsible, also economically, for normal maintenance and repair, the attractiveness of products with a longer lifetime might decrease accordingly*".[2483]

710. Fully differentiated guarantee periods (third approach) should be established at EU level – The three approaches of extended guarantee

certain rights under the Consumer Sales and Guarantees Directive 1999/44/CE (European Commission 2017) p. 28 *et seq.*; UFC Que Choisir, *Extension à 2 ans de la garantie légale: Une information du consommateur loin d'être garantie!* (May 2015), available on: <https://www.quechoisir.org/dossier-de-presse-extension-a-2-ans-de-la-garantie-legale-une-information-du-consommateur-loin-d-etre-garantie-n12641/>. A similar reasoning can also be found for commercial warranties: see N. Podolyakina, 'Estimation of the Relationship between the Products Reliability, Period of Their Warranty Service and the Value of the Enterprise Cost', 178 *Procedia Engineering* (2017) p. 558 at p. 568. By contrast, a German study argued that the potential initial price increase would be offset by competition in the long-term: see K. Bizer et al., *Die Okonomischen Auswirkungen einer Verbesserung des Deutschen Gewährleistungsrechts* (Verbraucherzentrale Bundesverband 2016).

2479 See TNS Political & Social, *Flash Eurobarometer 367 – Attitudes of Europeans towards building the single market for green products* (European Commission 2013); SIRCOME agency, the University of South Brittany and the University of South Bohemia, *The Influence of Lifespan Labelling on Consumers – ILLC study* (EESC 2016); LE Europe, VVA Europe, Ipsos, ConPolicy, Trinomics, *Behavioural study on consumers' engagement in the circular economy* (European Commission 2018).

2480 See *supra*, n° 730.

2481 This would consist of "*a basic limitation period of three years and an extension to five years for products with a lifespan of more than three years as an option for Member States*". See K. Tonner, R. Malcolm, *How an EU lifespan guarantee model could be implemented across the European Union (study)* (European Parliament 2017) p. 54.

2482 E. Maitre-Ekern, C. Dalhammar, 'Towards a hierarchy of consumption behaviour in the circular economy', 26 *Maastricht Journal of European and Comparative Law* (2019) p. 417 at p. 419.

2483 E. Maitre-Ekern, C. Dalhammar, 'Towards a hierarchy of consumption behaviour in the circular economy', 26 *Maastricht Journal of European and Comparative Law* (2019) p. 418.

periods have pros and cons that must be weighed while considering the interests at stake (businesses, consumers and the environment). The first and second approaches have the benefit of legal certainty. But with these approaches, the guaranteed goods may have a shorter or longer expected lifetime compared to the chosen guarantee period, which results in a cross-subsidy at the cost of consumers who buy more durable goods.[2484] The third Dutch-Finnish approach is more flexible (and thus future-proof) and allows maximizing the positive effects of an extended guarantee period.[2485] This option should therefore be preferred (see #6), especially in the light of the satisfactory experiences given by the current national laboratories.[2486] This reasoning is even more convincing when considering the possible combinations between the rules on guarantees and other EU rules, as shown in the following paragraphs.

711. A NECESSARY LINK BETWEEN GUARANTEE RULES AND PRODUCT REGULATIONS – The first worthwhile idea consists in linking the length of the guarantee period to ecodesign requirements, which impose a minimum lifetime for certain product categories or components (see #6).[2487] In other words, the guarantee period for products covered by ecodesign requirements as to their durability should not end after two years, but rather correspond to the minimum duration set by these ecodesign requirements. As an example, if a washing machine had to be designed for at least 10 years to access the European market, consumers should be entitled to claim that the machine is covered by the guarantee for this whole period. This could already apply to energy-related products that are subject to minimum durability requirements.[2488] It is noteworthy that suggestions to develop a holistic approach to product regulation had already been made before the recast of the CSD.[2489] Unfortunately, those suggestions were finally not followed, as demonstrated by the absence of any reference to these product-specific rules in Article 10 of the SGD. The only

2484 F. Gomez, 'Economic Analysis of the Directive', in M. Bianca, S. Grundmann (eds.), *EU Sales Directive: Commentary* (Intersentia 2002) p. 71.

2485 See *supra*, n° 732.

2486 B. Keirsbilck, E. Terryn, A. Michel and I. Alogna, *Sustainable Consumption and Consumer Protection Legislation* (European Parliament 2020) pp. 20–21; E. Van Gool and A. Michel, 'The New Consumer Sales Directive 2019/771 and Sustainable Consumption: A Critical Analysis', 10 *EuCML* (2021) p. 142.

2487 Such an idea must be accompanied by minimum information requirements so that consumers are well informed about the length of the legal guarantee period which, compared to a uniform guarantee period, would be more complex to grasp (see *infra*, n° 857–866).

2488 See for ex. ecodesign requirements applying to vacuum cleaners and lamps (see *supra*, n° 231).

2489 See B. Schmitz, 'Missing link ecodesign & sales guarantees', *European Parliament Conference on a longer lifetime for products: A win-win solution for European consumers and business* (European Parliament 2015), cited in C. Montalvo, D. Peck, E. Rietveld, *A Longer Lifetime for Products: Benefits for Consumers and Companies (study commissioned by the European Parliament)*(European Union 2016) pp. 54–55. See also K. Tonner, R. Malcolm, *How an EU lifespan guarantee model could be implemented across the European Union (study)* (European Parliament 2017); European Parliament Resolution of 4 July 2017 on a longer lifetime for products: benefits for consumers and companies, 2016/2272(INI), pt. 34.

reference to product regulations is contained in its recital 32, which specifies that "*the Directive should (...) be complementary to the objectives pursued in (...) Union product-specific legislation*", without mentioning the possibility of a longer guarantee period.

712. A LINK TO INFORMATION REQUIREMENTS OR SOFT LAW – In the absence of product regulations, information requirements and soft law could help set the duration of the guarantee period (see #8). This suggestion has already been put forward by the EP, who suggested at least considering assessing the impact of aligning durability information and lifespan labelling with the duration of the legal guarantee.[2490] This idea is simple: if producers were obliged to give information on the durability of their products, and if the minimum lifetime indicated was longer than two years, the guarantee period could then be equivalent to the indicated period. Consumers experiencing premature obsolescence could then easily prove that their product did not last as long as guaranteed by the producer and on that basis, claim their rights under legal guarantee rules. In the meantime, if nothing is indicated as regards product lifetime and no soft law exists, the two-year guarantee period could apply, provided that the conditions established under the SGD are fulfilled (see #7).[2491]

713. TOGETHER WITH OTHER MEASURES – If the guarantee period were to be extended, other provisions of the SGD should be adapted to conciliate all the interests at stake. Indeed, a longer guarantee would particularly affect the interests of the sellers and retailers. Among the measures that should be taken along with the extension of the guarantee period, two are of particular importance. First, repair should be prioritized over replacement in the hierarchy of remedies.[2492] This would prevent consumers from requesting the replacement of their product with a brand-new one after too many years of use. Second, the direct producer liability mechanism should be introduced within the SGD. That way, consumers can pin the liability upon those truly responsible for lack of durability.[2493]

714. POSSIBLE ALTERNATIVE MEASURES IF NO EXTENDED GUARANTEE PERIOD – If the EU legislature were ultimately to decide not to prolong the legal guarantee, it should be stressed that other (alternative) measures could at least be taken to trigger product sustainability after the two-year period.[2494] There is indeed a dearth of legislation regulating the period after the expiry of the legal guarantee, provoking the premature obsolescence of products where it could have been

---

2490 See European Parliament Resolution of 4 July 2017 on a longer lifetime for products: benefits for consumers and companies, 2016/2272(INI), pt. 27.

2491 Those conditions include, for example, the compatibility of the product with the two-year guarantee period or the unawareness of the consumer about the lack of conformity.

2492 See *infra*, n° 773.

2493 See *infra*, n° 825–833.

2494 See *infra*, n° 882 *et seq.*

avoided. Among possible measures, introducing an obligation on sellers to keep spare parts for a minimum period exceeding the two-year guarantee period could be suggested.[2495] Such measures could represent a good compromise, raising the level of protection for consumers who could more easily repair their products, while having lower (financial) impact and imposing fewer burdens on businesses compared to an extension of the legal guarantee.[2496] Furthermore, commercial guarantees, which sometimes cover defects beyond two years, could be better regulated.[2497]

Proposed amendments to the SGD:

#6

Article 10
Liability of the seller

1. The seller shall be liable to the consumer for any lack of conformity which exists at the time when the goods were delivered and which becomes apparent within the durability period imposed by EU law or, if not applicable, within the period during which no such lack of conformity should be expected by the consumer given the nature of the goods and taking into account any public statement made by or on behalf of the seller, or other persons in previous links of the chain of transactions, including the producer, particularly in advertising or on labelling ~~within two years of that time~~. Without prejudice to Article 7(3), this paragraph shall also apply to goods with digital elements.

(...)

AS AN INTERMEDIARY STEP

#7

Article 10
Liability of the seller

1. The seller shall be liable to the consumer for any lack of conformity which exists at the time when the goods were delivered and which becomes apparent within the durability period imposed by EU law or, if not applicable, within two years of that time. Without prejudice to Article 7(3), this paragraph shall also apply to goods with digital elements.

2495 See *infra*, n° 883. This would be in line with product-specific regulations, which already impose such obligations. See *supra*, n° 260–262.

2496 ICF, *Study on the costs and benefits of extending certain rights under the Consumer Sales and Guarantees Directive 1999/44/CE* (European Commission 2017) p. 54.

2497 See *infra*, n° 852–856.

(...)

AND

Policy recommendations

> *#8 A guidance document should be issued to assist consumers and traders in determining the period during which no lack of conformity should be expected by the consumer.*

(5) Burden of proof and obligation on consumers to notify

715. A (LIMITED) BURDEN OF PROOF ON CONSUMERS – It is for the consumers to prove that a lack of conformity exists.[2498] If they fail to do so, no lack of conformity will be deemed to exist, and the seller will not be held liable. Yet, when it comes to the lack of conformity, their burden of proof is restricted to this single piece of evidence. Consumers are under no obligation to prove the cause of that lack of conformity or to establish that its origin is attributable to the seller.[2499] The underlying justification for this limited burden of proof is the asymmetry of information between the contractual parties, with consumers remaining the weaker party after the conclusion of the contract.[2500]

716. INCLUDING IN CASE OF NOTIFICATION – This limited burden of proof also applies when the consumer is required, if so provided under national law, to notify the lack of conformity to the seller within a certain period after its discovery.[2501] This obligation of notification exists in Belgium. If the consumer notices a defect during the guarantee period, Article 1649*quater* §3 of the Belgian Civil Code gives him one year to report it to the seller to benefit from the legal guarantee. The contractual parties can agree that the consumer is required to notify the lack of conformity within two months (minimum) from the discovery of the defect.[2502] The concrete consequences of the absence or delay of notification are however not specified in the Belgian legislation, giving rise to debate in the literature and before the courts. Contrary to Article 12 of the SGD, it is therefore still unclear under Belgian law whether failure to comply with the notification period results in a loss of consumer rights. As regards the

2498 The SGD does not regulate certain aspects related to this burden of proof (e.g. the standard and the means of proof), leaving that to the discretion of Member States.

2499 ECJ 4 June 2015, Case C-497/13, *Faber, EU:C:2015:357*, para 70.

2500 Opinion of Advocate General Sharpston delivered on 27 November 2014 in ECJ 4 June 2015, Case C-497/13, *Faber, EU:C:2015:357*, pt. 66.

2501 Art. 12 SGD. The provision specifies that consumers should have at least two months from the date on which they detected the lack of conformity to notify it to the seller.

2502 Art. 1649*quater* §2 of the Belgian Civil Code.

content of that notification, the ECJ has already emphasized that "*the consumer cannot be required, at that stage, to furnish evidence that a lack of conformity actually adversely affects the goods that he has purchased*".[2503] The notification must only "*include a certain number of particulars – the degree of precision of which will necessarily vary depending on the specific circumstances of each case – relating to the nature of the goods in question, the wording of the contract of sale in respect of those goods and the way in which the alleged lack of conformity became apparent*".[2504]

717. Single evidence difficult to produce – The fact that consumers are only required to demonstrate the existence of the lack of conformity is appropriate for cases of premature obsolescence as consumers are generally not aware of the details related to the defect in those cases. However, they might still experience great difficulties to produce this only evidence, especially for products which do not satisfy objective requirements.[2505] One lack of conformity that might be particularly difficult to prove is the lack of durability of the delivered product.[2506] In fact, consumers willing to claim a lack of durability would need to demonstrate that the product in question did not last as long as products of the same type, as they may have legitimately expected.[2507] In other words, they would have to prove that it is not normal wear and tear, but rather a lack of conformity, for which they are entitled to claim legal guarantee rights. While some professionals voluntarily disclose information on the lifetime of their products, they are far from forming the majority. Even when such information is provided, doubts may arise as to their reliability. Hence, consumers generally do not know nor have access to (reliable) information on or related to product lifetime, placing a too heavy burden of proof on their shoulders for the assessment of whether and to what extent the good does not correspond with their reasonable expectations.[2508]

718. Reinforcing national procedural rules with measures at EU level – As the ECJ has already underlined, "*it is for the national legal order of each Member*

2503 ECJ 4 June 2015, Case C-497/13, *Faber, EU:C:2015:357*, para 63.

2504 *Ibid.*

2505 By contract with subjective requirements, which are based on the contract, objective requirements are based on more nebulous and volatile concepts, such as the reasonable consumer expectation. See *supra*, n° 697–699.

2506 S. Wrbka had already pointed out the issue related to the burden of proof on consumers for product durability. See S. Wrbka, 'Warranty Law in cases of planned obsolescence – The Austrian situation', 6 *EuCML* (2017) p. 69.

2507 This also applies to products with short lifespans for which consumers claim that no defect should have so prematurely occurred.

2508 The weak position of consumers in this regard was emphasized in Opinion of Advocate General Sharpston delivered on 27 November 2014 in ECJ 4 June 2015, Case C-497/13, *Faber, EU:C:2015:357*, pt. 66.

State to establish the ways in which evidence is to be elicited, what evidence is to be admissible before the appropriate national court, or the principles governing that court's assessment of the probative value of the evidence adduced before it and also the level of proof required".[2509] The case at hand concerned the burden of proof faced by patients who had suffered harm from a defective vaccine and who had brought a claim on the basis of the Product Liability Directive. According to this ruling, to ensure the effectiveness of the rights which individuals derive directly from EU law, procedural rules should not render practically impossible or excessively difficult the exercise of rights conferred by EU law.[2510] At the same time, Member States should not introduce unjustified presumptions to the detriment of the producer.[2511] A good way of striking a fair balance between those opposing interests would be to facilitate the task of proving the lack of conformity. Different measures could be adopted at EU level to minimize these difficulties.

719. LIGHTENING THE BURDEN OF PROOF THROUGH INFORMATION REQUIREMENTS – One measure would be to impose on every professional an obligation to give information on product expected lifespan, while regulating and controlling the methods and criteria to be used for the assessment. This would, on one hand, help determine the average lifetime of products and consumers' reasonable expectations.[2512] For example, if a refrigerator, described as lasting for more than ten years, breaks down after five, the consumer could more easily establish the lack of conformity.[2513] It would then be for the seller to prove, for example, that the consumer did not correctly use or maintain the good as recommended by the instruction manual. On the other hand, producers and sellers could derive advantages from this obligation. If consumers were

---

2509 ECJ 21 June 2017, Case C-621/15, *N. W and Others* v *Sanofi Pasteur MSD SNC and Others, EU:C:2017:484*, para 25.

2510 ECJ 21 June 2017, Case C-621/15, *N. W and Others* v *Sanofi Pasteur MSD SNC and Others, EU:C:2017:484*, paras 26 and 31. In the case at hand, the Court held that excluding any method of proof other than proof based on medical research would be inconsistent with the objectives of the Product Liability Directive as this could make it excessively difficult to establish producer liability in many situations. Consequently, evidence that is sufficiently serious, specific and consistent, such as the temporal proximity between the vaccination and the occurrence of a disease, the lack of personal and familiar history of that disease, together with the existence of other reported cases of the disease that occurred after such vaccines, could be received.

2511 ECJ 21 June 2017, Case C-621/15, *N. W and Others* v *Sanofi Pasteur MSD SNC and Others, EU:C:2017:484*, para 34. In the case at hand, the Court ruled out the use of automatic and irrefutable presumptions based on predetermined factual evidence as this would deprive the producer of the possibility of adducing facts and arguments to rebut that presumption.

2512 See also in that sense T. Brönneke, *Premature obsolescence and European law – Possibilities with regard to the Reform of the Consumer Sales Directive* (BEUC conference on sustainable consumption 2015) p. 4.

2513 This possibility is conditional on the extension of the legal guarantee period beyond two years, as put forward *infra* (n° 729 *et seq.*).

informed on the limited lifetime of the product prior to the conclusion of the contract, they would not be entitled to complain about this lack of durability, exempting professionals from their liability under the legal guarantee rules.[2514] The idea is gaining momentum at the EU and national levels.[2515] Yet, it is not immune to criticism. The main critical comments concern the questionable reliability of information given by professionals and the difficulty of verifying this information.[2516]

720. Determining the minimum or average expected product lifetime – Another key measure would consist in legally determining the minimum or average expected lifetime of certain products. Such an idea has been implemented in the Netherlands, though via soft law, with the UNETO-VNI table[2517] and could be developed in EU law. The first option would be to issue guidance on the SDG which would define criteria to determine product lifetime on a case-by-case basis (soft law). As for the second option, it would consist in using the EU ecodesign legal framework (hard law). Some ecodesign implementing measures already establish a minimum product lifetime for certain products or components, including vacuum cleaners and lamps.[2518] A product covered by such an implementing measure that would break down before the minimum period legally required could be considered as not conforming to the contract. While the second option may be the most effective, its main drawback lies in its product-specific nature as it would not cover all products.[2519]

721. Facilitating product-specific expertise – A third option to lighten the burden of proof on consumers is to facilitate the product-specific expertise provided on a case-by-case basis. This option is currently and will remain applicable, at least until one of the two abovementioned measures is implemented. A consumer seeking to argue that goods failed earlier than what could reasonably be expected can produce expert evidence to persuade, first, the

---

2514 See *infra*, n° 724.

2515 At EU level, see for ex. Opinion of the European Economic and Social Committee of 17 October 2013 on Towards more sustainable consumption: industrial product lifetimes and restoring trust through consumer information, CCMI/112, pt. 1.7. At national level, information obligation on product lifetime has been suggested in the Belgian legislative proposal from July 2019, as well as in the French legislative proposal from September 2019. For further details, see Chapter III on the marketing and pre-contractual stage.

2516 On the difficulty of verifying such technical information, see Chapter II on the design and production stage (n° 299–301).

2517 On a test basis, the UNETO-VNI table is an informal document which indicates the average lifetime to be expected for certain products under normal use conditions, taking their purchase price into account. The table is available on: <www.uneto-vni.nl/onze-leden/waar-staan-onze-leden-voor/gebruiksduurverwachting>.

2518 See *supra*, n° 231.

2519 For further comments on the advantages and shortcomings of ecodesign rules, see Chapter II on the design and production stage.

seller and, ultimately, the judge if the dispute reaches the court.[2520] Experts could be called upon to compare the lifetime of similar products (regardless of product series and producers) and define the average lifetime of the product category.[2521] Legislation could be adopted to enhance the procedure and mitigate the likely lack of legal certainty. For example, a list of criteria could be laid down in the law for the assessment of product lifetime, as previously argued.

(6) Exceptions to seller's liability

722. Three exceptions to seller's liability – Even when the good is affected by a lack of conformity, there are three cases where the seller may be discharged of their liability under the SGD: (1) where the consumer failed to install updates, (2) where the consumer was informed of the deviating product characteristic and (3) where the consumer contributed to the lack of conformity.[2522]

723. First: where the consumer failed to install updates – First of all, Article 7 of the SGD states, in its fourth paragraph, that "*where the consumer fails to install within a reasonable time updates supplied [as required by Article 7(3)], the seller shall not be liable for any lack of conformity resulting solely from the lack of the relevant update*". However, this exception only applies provided that (a) the seller informed the consumer about the availability of the update and the consequences of the failure of the consumer to install it; and (b) the failure of the consumer to install or the incorrect installation by the consumer of the update was not due to shortcomings in the installation instructions provided to the consumer. Hence, this provision imposes additional information obligations that the seller must respect if he does not want to be held liable when the consumer failed to install the supplied updates within a reasonable period of time. If these information obligations were fulfilled and the consumers, who remained free to choose whether to install the updates provided[2523], decided not to, those consumers should not expect such goods to remain in conformity.[2524]

724. Second: where the consumer was informed of the deviating product characteristic – Secondly, Article 7(5) exempts the seller from their

2520 C. Twigg-Flesner, 'The law on guarantees and repair work', in T. Cooper (ed.), *Longer lasting products – Alternatives to the throwaway society* (Gower Publishing Limited 2010) p. 197.

2521 S. Wrbka, 'Warranty law in cases of planned obsolescence – The Austrian situation', 6 *EuCML* (2017) p. 67 at p. 76.

2522 There are other exceptions to sellers' liability related to the two other conditions of this liability. See *infra*, n° 753–754 and n° 764–766.

2523 There is however no obligation for these updates to be reversible, despite the call made by the EP. See European Parliament Resolution of 4 July 2017 on a longer lifetime for products: benefits for consumers and companies, 2016/2272(INI), pt. 39.

2524 See recital 30 SGD.

liability if "*at the time of the conclusion of the sales contract, the consumer was specifically informed that a particular characteristic of the goods was deviating from the objective requirements for conformity (...) and the consumer expressly and separately accepted that deviation when concluding the sales contract.*" If national law provides so, this exemption can be extended to cases where the seller warns the consumer about certain characteristics of the good, the suitability of materials provided by the consumer or possible disadvantages resulting from specific requests of the consumer.[2525] Consequently, if a lack of conformity within the meaning of Article 7(1) or (3) occurs and the consumer had been informed, the lack of conformity will be deemed inexistent. This provision derives from Article 2(3) of the CSD, which absolved the seller of their liability "*if the consumer was aware, or could not reasonably be unaware of, the lack of conformity*" when the contract was concluded. The conditions laid down in Article 7(5) of the SGD are nonetheless stricter, restricting the application of this exception.[2526] Applied to cases of premature obsolescence, it means for example that the seller will not be held liable for a product that does not meet the durability requirement contained in Article 7(d) if he has informed the consumer on the limited lifetime of the product beforehand.

725. Without allowing sellers to deviate from mandatory requirements – Of course, one could presume that this exception was not intended to allow sellers (and indirectly producers) to deviate from mandatory requirements, such as durability requirements established by ecodesign rules. This should be made clear by adding a sentence in Article 7(5) of the SGD (see #4). The SGD also gives the example of second-hand goods, for which parties can deviate from these objective requirements.[2527] Nevertheless, such deviation is only possible under the conditions that (1) the consumer was specifically informed about it and (2) the consumer accepted it separately from other statements or agreements, and by way of active and unequivocal conduct.[2528] It remains however unclear how detailed the information will be in practice, and thus how well-informed the consumer will be before giving their consent.

726. Third: where the consumer contributed to the lack of conformity – Finally, another exception to the seller's liability relates to cases where the consumer contributed to the lack of conformity.[2529] For example, the

2525 See Recital 20 SGD, which gives the example of a request by the consumer to use a specific fabric for the tailoring of a ball gown.

2526 Some scholars argued that Article 2(3) of the CSD was weakening the conformity requirements. See S. Pelet, 'L'impact de la directive 99/44/EC relative à certains aspects de la vente et des garanties des biens de consommation sur le droit français', *R.E.D.C.* (2000) pp. 49–50.

2527 Recital 36 SGD.

2528 *Ibid.*

2529 This is when the consumer contributes to the occurrence of a lack of conformity that is inherent to the product. If the lack of conformity is completely due to the consumer, then the

lack of conformity due to wear of parts could be worsened by improper use. According to Article 13(7) of the SGD, consumers' right to remedies could be affected if they contributed to the lack of conformity. This provision finds its justification in the moral hazard created by consumers, who can mistreat goods and lower their remaining value without consequences once the liability of the seller is established.[2530] Article 13(7) leaves it to Member States to regulate that point in their legislation.

727. Some uncertainties should be resolved – The issue that could arise with this provision is linked to the way consumers' contribution to the lack of conformity is assessed and interpreted. First, it is uncertain whether negligence on the part of consumers should fall within the scope of this exception or whether it should only concern cases where they committed a fault which would not have been committed by the average consumer.[2531] In this regard, some scholars argue that "*normal wear and tear could be widened to include dropping a phone on to a hard surface and immersion in water*".[2532] Their main argument is that it would allow retailers to replace like with like and would thus remove the risk of consumers purposefully dropping phones to gain an upgrade.[2533] Recital 57 of the SGD could be of use in this regard as it outlines what should be considered as 'normal' use of the goods. According to its words, "*the use should be considered as normal if it is in accordance with the nature and purpose of the goods*". It remains nonetheless unclear whether the consumer, who notices the lack of conformity and continues to make normal use of the (defective) product, should be considered as contributing to the lack of conformity. Under Belgian law, the right to remedies may be affected if the consumer has aggravated the damage by using the goods after he noticed the lack of conformity or should have noticed it.[2534] This provision should however be clarified, otherwise it could lead to a high risk of abuses.[2535] Second, it may be fraught with difficulties to distinguish the influence of consumers' behaviour on the lack of conformity from the influence of producers' actions and decisions. To solve these difficulties, one could imagine excluding the application of this exception if the trader did

---

lack does not exist prior to the delivery of the good and the consumer cannot invoke the legal guarantee. See *infra*, n° 755.

2530 E. Van Gool and A. Michel, 'The New Consumer Sales Directive 2019/771 and Sustainable Consumption: A Critical Analysis', 10 *EuCML* (2021) p. 144.

2531 Such discussions took place in Belgium. See Avis du Conseil Central de l'Economie du 3 septembre 2019 sur la transposition de directives européennes concernant la vente aux consommateurs tant de biens que de contenus et services numériques, CCE 2019–1660, p. 14.

2532 D. Watson et al., *Circular Business Models in the Mobile Phone Industry* (TemaNord 2017) p. 76.

2533 *Ibid.*

2534 Art. 1649*quinquies* §1, subparagraph 2 of the Belgian Civil Code.

2535 Avis du Conseil Central de l'Economie du 3 septembre 2019 sur la transposition de directives européennes concernant la vente aux consommateurs tant de biens que de contenus et services numériques, CCE 2019–1660, p. 14.

not comply with certain EU rules, like ecodesign requirements or blacklisted practices (see #5). Although the assessment of this exception will strongly depend on the facts and circumstances of each individual case[2536], some guidance on that point (e.g. through criteria or practical examples) would have been welcomed in the SGD or in an SGD guidance document.

Proposed amendments to the SGD:

#4

Article 7
Objective requirements for conformity

(...)

5. There shall be no lack of conformity within the meaning of paragraph 1 or 3 if, at the time of the conclusion of the sales contract, the consumer was specifically informed that a particular characteristic of the goods was deviating from the objective requirements for conformity laid down in paragraph 1 or 3 and the consumer expressly and separately accepted that deviation when concluding the sales contract. **<u>This exception to the seller's liability should however not allow deviations from existing Union mandatory rules.</u>**

AND *#5*

Article 13
Remedies for lack of conformity

(...)

7. Member States may regulate whether and to what extent a contribution of the consumer to the lack of conformity affects the consumer's right to remedies. <u>Member States shall however ensure that such exception to the consumer's right to remedies does not apply if the lack of conformity is also due to a violation of Union mandatory law by the seller.</u>

b) Within two years of the delivery

728. A TWO-YEAR GUARANTEE PERIOD AS A GENERAL RULE – Among the cumulative conditions to trigger the seller's liability, there is, secondly, the fact that the lack of conformity must appear *within two years of delivery of the goods.*[2537] In other words, goods (including their components and accessories)

[2536] Many factors could be taken into account for this assessment, such as the availability and the clarity of instruction manuals for consumers.
[2537] Art. 10(1) SGD.

are guaranteed to be free from defects for (minimum) two years, provided that this period is compatible with their nature (including their expected lifetime) and that the lack of conformity is not merely due to normal wear and tear.[2538] This two-year period also applies to goods with digital elements, except where the contract provides for a continuous supply of digital content or digital service.[2539] In the latter case, the seller will be liable for any lack of conformity of the digital content or digital service that occurs or becomes apparent within this supply period.[2540] The SGD leaves nonetheless a wide discretion to the Member States that allows them to extend or shorten this liability period.

(1) A liability period of (at least) two years

729. Established with the adoption of the CSD – The two-year liability period has been established at EU level since the adoption of the CSD.[2541] During the adoption process of the CSD, some were in favour of a variable period depending on different factors, such as the estimated lifetime of the product, the ability of the parties to influence the risk of defect or the value of the good.[2542] A single two-year period will finally be chosen as the minimum protection threshold for greater legal certainty. The SGD maintains the two-year liability period, though with a possible different relevant time for assessing the conformity of the goods continuously supplied with digital elements[2543] and with a possible extension of the liability period for the latter goods.[2544] Although some European organisations still advocated for a longer guarantee period[2545], the EC concluded that, based on the available data[2546], the two-year guarantee

2538 See *infra*, n° 753–754.

2539 Art. 10(2) SGD.

2540 *Ibid.*

2541 Art. 5(1) CSD.

2542 S. Grundmann, F. Gomez, 'Introduction', in M.C. Bianca, S. Grundmann and S. Stijns (eds.), *La directive communautaire sur la vente – Commentaire* (Bruylant-L.G.D.J. 2004) p. 84; J. Stuyck, 'La notion de conformité et l'articulation des délais', in C. Biquet-Mathieu, P. Wéry (eds.), *La nouvelle garantie des biens de consommation et son environnement légal* (La Charte 2005) p. 121.

2543 See recitals 37 and 39 SGD.

2544 See Art. 10(1) and (2) SGD. For further comments, See *infra*, n° 739 *et seq.*

2545 See for ex. BEUC Policy Paper of 18 August 2015 on Durable goods: More sustainable products, better consumer rights, BEUC-X-2015-069, p. 12; Opinion of the EESC on the 'Proposal for a directive of the European Parliament and of the Council on certain aspects concerning contracts for the supply of digital content' (COM(2015) 634 final) and the 'Proposal for a directive of the European Parliament and of the Council on certain aspects concerning contracts for the online and other distance sales of goods' (COM(2015) 635 final), OJ C 264, 20.7.2016, pt. 4.2.5.11.

2546 A study commissioned by the Commission and based on self-reported data from consumers found that most of the defects occurred during the first two years. For further information, see ICF, *Study on the costs and benefits of extending certain rights under the Consumer Sales and Guarantees Directive 1999/44/CE* (European Commission 2017), especially p. 22 at p. 63.

period *"effectively caters for a very large proportion of the defects in goods discovered by consumers"*.[2547]

730. With some leeway left to the Member States – While the SGD provides for a two-year guarantee period, some leeway has (still) been left to Member States on the length of the liability period. According to Article 10(3), national law makers are allowed to *"maintain or introduce longer time limits"*.[2548] Hence, consumers could, if so provided by national law, be entitled to claim remedies under the legal guarantee for a period longer than two years. Several Member States have decided not to use this possibility and maintained the two-year minimum guarantee period, like Belgium[2549] and France.[2550] By contrast, other Member States have decided to extend the guarantee period beyond two years.[2551] The first approach consists in extending the legal guarantee without making a distinction between products.[2552] The second approach is to establish differentiated but general guarantee periods depending on the type and expected lifetime of products.[2553] The third approach consists of fully differentiated guarantee periods that depend on the purchased good's expected lifespan.[2554] In other words, consumers may claim that non-conformity existed at the time of delivery as long this is not attributed to wear and tear due to expiration of the

---

2547 Commission Staff Working Document of 31 October 2017 on the Impacts of fully harmonised rules on contracts for the sales of goods supplementing the impact assessment accompanying the proposal for a Directive of the European Parliament and of the Council on certain aspects concerning contracts for the online and other distance sales of goods, SWD(2017) 354 final, p. 22 at p. 24.

2548 See also recital 41 SGD.

2549 See Art. 1649*quater* §1 subparagraph 1 of the Belgian Civil Code. It is interesting to note that before the adoption of the CSD, there was no time limit for the guarantee under Belgian law. Consumers could argue that the absence of durability constitutes a defect from the point of view of conformity with expectations. On that point, see the Green Paper from the European Commission of 15 November 1993 on Guarantees for Consumer Goods and After-sales Services, COM(93) 509 final, p. 50.

2550 Art. L. 217–12 of the French Consumer Code.

2551 For more details on the various national approaches concerning the guarantee period, see for ex. ICF, *Study on the costs and benefits of extending certain rights under the Consumer Sales and Guarantees Directive 1999/44/CE* (European Commission 2017); K. Tonner, R. Malcolm, *Study on How an EU lifespan guarantee model could be implemented across the European Union* (European Parliament 2017). See also the various country fiches accompanying the study Ipsos-London Economics-Deloitte consortium, *Consumer market study on the functioning of legal and commercial guarantees for consumers in the EU* (European Commission 2015), available on: http://ec.europa.eu/consumers/consumer_evidence/market_studies/guarantees/index_en.htm.

2552 Sweden is among them, providing a uniform three-year period for all products (§23 Konsumentköplag (1990:932)).

2553 For example, in Norway, the legal guarantee is extended from two to five years for products which are deemed to last longer than two years (art. 27(2) Lög um neytendakaup 48/2003).

2554 This approach is followed by the Netherlands, where the legal guarantee depends on the average expected lifespan of product categories as well as on the price (Art. 17(2) Burgerlijk Wetboek), as well as by Finland, where consumers can rely on legal guarantee rules when the product does not last as long as it can be ordinarily be expected (§16 Kuluttajansuojalaki (1978/38)).

good's expected lifespan. For this third approach, the assessment of the expected lifespan is supported by soft law, which indicates expected lifespans for different product categories.[2555] The length of the liability period can thus greatly vary between the Member States. This is without mentioning other aspects left to the discretion of the Member States, like the meaning of 'delivery', which is the starting point of the guarantee period.[2556]

731. A TOO SHORT GUARANTEE PERIOD – Serious doubts remain on the adequacy of the current legal guarantee period as established by the SGD, especially with regard to the premature obsolescence of consumer goods. Aside from the longer period provided for digital content or service continuously supplied[2557], the two-year liability period seems too short, especially for goods with a longer expected lifetime (e.g. white goods). It is easy to imagine, for example, that a dishwasher would break down after two years of use, without this being due to normal wear and tear or improper use, but rather due to a defect attributable to the seller or the producer.[2558] This limited guarantee period is even more questionable when taking into consideration the new 'durability' requirement introduced by the SGD.[2559] Hence, at present, consumers are deprived of any protection under EU legislation after the two years.[2560] Admittedly, Member States may go beyond the minimum level of protection granted by the SGD and protect consumers in those cases. The SGD could nonetheless have been the opportunity to extend the liability period at EU level[2561], which would have prevented national disparities and their related drawbacks.[2562]

2555 In the Netherlands, a table has been established a Dutch industry group (see the UNETO-VNI table, available on: <www.uneto-vni.nl/onze-leden/waar-staan-onze-leden-voor/gebruiksduurverwachting>). In Finland, the expected lifespan of the good is established by non-binding decisions of the Finnish Consumer Dispute Board, which takes into account the expected lifespan of goods of the same category, the price and the usual frequency of use.

2556 See recital 38 SGD. In this recital, reference is made to the CRD, which delineates the notion of 'delivery' in its Article 18.

2557 See *infra*, n° 739–741.

2558 For example, it could be a defect caused by inherent weaknesses in its design, poor workmanship or the use of faulty materials in the manufacturing process, as mentioned by C. Twigg-Flesner in C. Twigg-Flesner, *Consumer Product Guarantees* (Routledge 2016) p. 5. See *infra* on the third condition, namely the existence of the lack of conformity prior to the delivery of the good.

2559 See *supra*, n° 698.

2560 See also J. Hijma, 'De Koopregeling in het Richtlijnvoorstel Consumentenrechten', in M.W. Hesselink and M.B.M. Loos (eds.), *Het Voorstel voor een Europese Richtlijn Consumentenrechten. Een Nederlands Perspectief* (Boom Juridische Uitgevers Den Haag 2009) p. 177; S. Van Camp, S. Bouyon, *Impact assessment of proposed substantial amendments introducing a commercial lifespan guarantee in the proposed online sales and digital content directive* (European Parliament 2017) p. 5.

2561 Such arguments have been raised in particular during the process of adopting the Consumer Rights Directive 2011/83. See for ex. Y. Ninane et O. Gilard, 'La garantie des biens de consommation', in C. Delforge, *Vente. Commentaire pratique*, Waterloo, Kluwer, 2009, p. 33; M. Loos, 'Consumer Sales Law in the Proposal for a Consumer Rights Directive', *E.R.P.L.* (2010) p. 15 at p. 55.

2562 Disparities obstruct cross-border transactions, not only because it creates financial and administrative burden on businesses, but also because consumers are consequently more

732. The positive effects of longer guarantee periods – Not only would an extension of the liability period at EU level satisfy the two main goals of the Directive (functioning of the internal market and consumer protection), but it would also protect the environment by fostering product sustainability. On the consumer side, an extended guarantee period would tackle psychological obsolescence by reflecting more accurately the lifetime of goods. On the business side, it could incite sellers (and indirectly producers) to offer goods with a longer lifetime to avoid any costs, time and energy incurred by guarantee claims. This constitutes the most beneficial effects of an extended guarantee period. Although a longer guarantee period may increase the price of products, as predicted by some studies (e.g. due to the necessary stock of large inventories of repair materials)[2563], the majority of consumers say that they are prepared to pay more if it means that products will have longer lifespan.[2564] In any case, the price increase would arguably be offset in the long term by longer-lasting products and lower costs of repairs.

733. Three possible options – As shown by the national rules above[2565], three approaches could be followed to extend the liability period under the SGD. The liability period could be generally extended (first approach) or only for certain categories of products. In the latter case, the liability period could be fixed (second approach) or vary from product to product depending on their average lifetime or other criteria, such as the purchase price or the product characteristics (third approach). In a recent study commissioned by the EP, it was proposed to adopt the second approach – with differentiated but general guarantee periods – at EU level.[2566] By contrast, E. Maitre-Ekern and

---

reluctant to buy products in another Member State (especially for goods with an expected lifetime longer than two years).

2563 See E.H. Lauridsen and M.S. Jørgensen, 'Transitions in waste treatment as a driver for product life extension', in T. Cooper, N. Braithwaite, M. Moreno and G. Salvia (eds.), *Product Lifetimes and the Environment (PLATE) Conference proceedings* (Nottingham Trent University 2015) p. 187 at p. 193; ICF, *Study on the costs and benefits of extending certain rights under the Consumer Sales and Guarantees Directive 1999/44/CE* (European Commission 2017) p. 28 *et seq.*; UFC Que Choisir, *Extension à 2 ans de la garantie légale: Une information du consommateur loin d'être garantie!* (May 2015), available on: <https://www.quechoisir.org/dossier-de-presse-extension-a-2-ans-de-la-garantie-legale-une-information-du-consommateur-loin-d-etre-garantie-n12641/>. A similar reasoning can also be found for commercial warranties: see N. Podolyakina, 'Estimation of the Relationship between the Products Reliability, Period of Their Warranty Service and the Value of the Enterprise Cost', 178 *Procedia Engineering* (2017) p. 558 at p. 568. By contrast, a German study argued that the potential initial price increase would be offset by competition in the long-term: see K. Bizer et al., *Die Okonomischen Auswirkungen einer Verbesserung des Deutschen Gewährleistungsrechts* (Verbraucherzentrale Bundesverband 2016).

2564 See TNS Political & Social, *Flash Eurobarometer 367 – Attitudes of Europeans towards building the single market for green products* (European Commission 2013); SIRCOME agency, the University of South Brittany and the University of South Bohemia, *The Influence of Lifespan Labelling on Consumers – ILLC study* (EESC 2016); LE Europe, VVA Europe, Ipsos, ConPolicy, Trinomics, *Behavioural study on consumers' engagement in the circular economy* (European Commission 2018).

2565 See *supra*, n° 730.

2566 This would consist of "*a basic limitation period of three years and an extension to five years for products with a lifespan of more than three years as an option for Member States*". See K.

C. Dalhammar are in favour of fully differentiated guarantee periods – which corresponds to the third approach – and suggested guaranteeing products for their whole lifetime.[2567] In support of their idea, these scholars asserted that "*if consumers are made responsible, also economically, for normal maintenance and repair, the attractiveness of products with a longer lifetime might decrease accordingly*".[2568]

734. FULLY DIFFERENTIATED GUARANTEE PERIODS (THIRD APPROACH) SHOULD BE ESTABLISHED AT EU LEVEL – The three approaches of extended guarantee periods have pros and cons that must be weighed while considering the interests at stake (businesses, consumers and the environment). The first and second approaches have the benefit of legal certainty. But with these approaches, the guaranteed goods may have a shorter or longer expected lifetime compared to the chosen guarantee period, which results in a cross-subsidy at the cost of consumers who buy more durable goods.[2569] The third Dutch-Finnish approach is more flexible (and thus future-proof) and allows maximizing the positive effects of an extended guarantee period.[2570] This option should therefore be preferred (see #6), especially in the light of the satisfactory experiences given by the current national laboratories.[2571] This reasoning is even more convincing when considering the possible combinations between the rules on guarantees and other EU rules, as shown in the following paragraphs.

735. A NECESSARY LINK BETWEEN GUARANTEE RULES AND PRODUCT REGULATIONS – The first worthwhile idea consists in linking the length of the guarantee period to ecodesign requirements, which impose a minimum lifetime for certain product categories or components (see #6).[2572] In other words, the guarantee period for products covered by ecodesign requirements as to their durability should not end after two years, but rather correspond to the minimum duration set by these ecodesign requirements. As an example, if a washing

---

Tonner, R. Malcolm, *How an EU lifespan guarantee model could be implemented across the European Union (study)* (European Parliament 2017) p. 54.

2567 E. Maitre-Ekern, C. Dalhammar, 'Towards a hierarchy of consumption behaviour in the circular economy', 26 *Maastricht Journal of European and Comparative Law* (2019) p. 417 at p. 419.

2568 E. Maitre-Ekern, C. Dalhammar, 'Towards a hierarchy of consumption behaviour in the circular economy', 26 *Maastricht Journal of European and Comparative Law* (2019) p. 418.

2569 F. Gomez, 'Economic Analysis of the Directive', in M. Bianca, S. Grundmann (eds.), *EU Sales Directive: Commentary* (Intersentia 2002) p. 71.

2570 See *supra*, n° 732.

2571 B. Keirsbilck, E. Terryn, A. Michel and I. Alogna, *Sustainable Consumption and Consumer Protection Legislation* (European Parliament 2020) pp. 20–21; E. Van Gool and A. Michel, 'The New Consumer Sales Directive 2019/771 and Sustainable Consumption: A Critical Analysis', 10 *EuCML* (2021) p. 142.

2572 Such an idea must be accompanied by minimum information requirements so that consumers are well informed about the length of the legal guarantee period which, compared to a uniform guarantee period, would be more complex to grasp (see *infra*, n° 857–866).

machine had to be designed for at least 10 years to access the European market, consumers should be entitled to claim that the machine is covered by the guarantee for this whole period. This could already apply to energy-related products that are subject to minimum durability requirements.[2573] It is noteworthy that suggestions to develop a holistic approach to product regulation had already been made before the recast of the CSD.[2574] Unfortunately, those suggestions were finally not followed, as demonstrated by the absence of any reference to these product-specific rules in Article 10 of the SGD. The only reference to product regulations is contained in its recital 32, which specifies that "*the Directive should (...) be complementary to the objectives pursued in (...) Union product-specific legislation*", without mentioning the possibility of a longer guarantee period.

736. A LINK TO INFORMATION REQUIREMENTS OR SOFT LAW – In the absence of product regulations, information requirements and soft law could help set the duration of the guarantee period (see #8). This suggestion has already been put forward by the EP, who suggested at least considering assessing the impact of aligning durability information and lifespan labelling with the duration of the legal guarantee.[2575] This idea is simple: if producers were obliged to give information on the durability of their products, and if the minimum lifetime indicated was longer than two years, the guarantee period could then be equivalent to the indicated period. Consumers experiencing premature obsolescence could then easily prove that their product did not last as long as guaranteed by the producer and on that basis, claim their rights under legal guarantee rules. In the meantime, if nothing is indicated as regards product lifetime and no soft law exists, the two-year guarantee period could apply, provided that the conditions established under the SGD are fulfilled (see #7).[2576]

737. TOGETHER WITH OTHER MEASURES – If the guarantee period were to be extended, other provisions of the SGD should be adapted to conciliate all the interests at stake. Indeed, a longer guarantee would particularly affect the interests of the sellers and retailers. Among the measures that should be taken along with the extension of the guarantee period, two are of particular importance. First,

---

2573 See for ex. ecodesign requirements applying to vacuum cleaners and lamps (see *supra*, n° 231).

2574 See B. Schmitz, 'Missing link ecodesign & sales guarantees', *European Parliament Conference on a longer lifetime for products: A win-win solution for European consumers and business* (European Parliament 2015), cited in C. Montalvo, D. Peck, E. Rietveld, *A Longer Lifetime for Products: Benefits for Consumers and Companies (study commissioned by the European Parliament)*(European Union 2016) pp. 54–55. See also K. Tonner, R. Malcolm, *How an EU lifespan guarantee model could be implemented across the European Union (study)* (European Parliament 2017); European Parliament Resolution of 4 July 2017 on a longer lifetime for products: benefits for consumers and companies, 2016/2272(INI), pt. 34.

2575 See European Parliament Resolution of 4 July 2017 on a longer lifetime for products: benefits for consumers and companies, 2016/2272(INI), pt. 27.

2576 Those conditions include, for example, the compatibility of the product with the two-year guarantee period or the unawareness of the consumer about the lack of conformity.

repair should be prioritized over replacement in the hierarchy of remedies.[2577] This would prevent consumers from requesting the replacement of their product with a brand-new one after too many years of use. Second, the direct producer liability mechanism should be introduced within the SGD. That way, consumers can pin the liability upon those truly responsible for lack of durability.[2578]

738. Possible alternative measures if no extended guarantee period – If the EU legislature were ultimately to decide not to prolong the legal guarantee, it should be stressed that other (alternative) measures could at least be taken to trigger product sustainability after the two-year period.[2579] There is indeed a dearth of legislation regulating the period after the expiry of the legal guarantee, provoking the premature obsolescence of products where it could have been avoided. Among possible measures, introducing an obligation on sellers to keep spare parts for a minimum period exceeding the two-year guarantee period could be suggested.[2580] Such measures could represent a good compromise, raising the level of protection for consumers who could more easily repair their products, while having lower (financial) impact and imposing fewer burdens on businesses compared to an extension of the legal guarantee.[2581] Furthermore, commercial guarantees, which sometimes cover defects beyond two years, could be better regulated.[2582]

Proposed amendments to the SGD:

#6

Article 10
Liability of the seller

1. The seller shall be liable to the consumer for any lack of conformity which exists at the time when the goods were delivered and which becomes apparent **within the durability period imposed by EU law or, if not applicable, within the period during which no such lack of conformity should be expected by the consumer given the nature of the goods and taking into account any public statement made by or on behalf of the seller, or other persons in previous links of the chain of transactions, including the producer, particularly in advertising or on labelling** ~~within two years of that time~~. Without prejudice to Article 7(3), this paragraph shall also apply to goods with digital elements.

2577 See *infra*, n° 773.

2578 See *infra*, n° 825–833.

2579 See *infra*, n° 882 *et seq.*

2580 See *infra*, n° 883. This would be in line with product-specific regulations, which already impose such obligations. See *supra*, n° 260–262.

2581 ICF, *Study on the costs and benefits of extending certain rights under the Consumer Sales and Guarantees Directive 1999/44/CE* (European Commission 2017) p. 54.

2582 See *infra*, n° 852–856.

(...)

AS AN INTERMEDIARY STEP

#7

Article 10
Liability of the seller

1.The seller shall be liable to the consumer for any lack of conformity which exists at the time when the goods were delivered and which becomes apparent **within the durability period imposed by EU law or, if not applicable, within two years of that time**. Without prejudice to Article 7(3), this paragraph shall also apply to goods with digital elements.

(...)

AND

Policy recommendations

#8 A guidance document should be issued to assist consumers and traders in determining the period during which no lack of conformity should be expected by the consumer.

(2) Longer guarantee period for goods with digital elements

739. Where the contract provides for a continuous supply of digital elements for more than two years – In addition to the two-year guarantee period, the SGD introduces a novelty for goods with digital elements. For those goods, Article 10(2) of the SGD provides for a longer liability period "*where the contract provides for a continuous supply for more than two years*". In that case, "*the seller shall be liable for any lack of conformity of the digital content or digital service that occurs or becomes apparent within the period of time during which the digital content or digital service is to be supplied under the sales contract*".[2583] The extended liability period only covers that digital content or digital service element.[2584]

740. Where updates must be supplied – This extended guarantee period goes hand in hand with the new subjective and objective conformity requirements on updates, which oblige sellers to ensure that the consumer

[2583] See also recital 41 SGD.
[2584] See recital 37 SGD.

receives updates for a period of time that can exceed two years.[2585] The period of time for the supply of updates depends on whether this supply is a simple act or has a continuous nature. Where it provides for a single act of supply of digital content or digital service, updates must be supplied for the period of time that the consumer may reasonably expect given the type and purpose of the goods and the digital elements and taking into account the circumstances and nature of the contract. As stated in recital 31, a consumer would normally expect to receive updates for at least as long as the period during which the seller is liable for a lack of conformity, while in some cases the consumer's reasonable expectation could extend beyond that period, as might be the case particularly with regard to security updates. In other cases, for instance as regards goods with digital elements the purpose of which is limited in time, the seller's obligation to provide updates would normally be limited to that time. Where the contract provides for a continuous supply of the digital content or digital service over a period of time, the supply of updates should last at least as long as this period, in accordance with Article 10(2) and (5). However, if an update provided by the seller or a third party causes a lack of conformity of the good, the seller would be liable for bringing the good into conformity again.[2586] Consequently, sellers might be liable for the lack of conformity linked to digital content and services, for which they have no control.[2587]

741. A MAJOR CONTRIBUTION TO DELAY FUNCTIONAL OBSOLESCENCE – These extended guarantee periods introduced by the SGD are a high added value in the fight against premature obsolescence as they contribute to delaying the functional obsolescence of some goods with digital elements. The development of the Internet of Things and smart products require a focus on the continuous good functioning of products, which must remain updated and connected throughout their lifespan.[2588] With these provisions, the SGD establishes a guarantee of 'good functioning' instead of a static non-conformity assessment at delivery.[2589]

(3) A possible reduced liability period for second-hand goods

742. THE POSSIBILITY FOR CONTRACTUAL PARTIES TO LIMIT LIABILITY FOR SECOND-HAND GOODS – Whereas Article 10 allows Member States to prolong the

---

[2585] See *supra*, n° 691 and n° 700.

[2586] Recital 30 SGD.

[2587] In those cases, sellers can exercise their right of redress against the liable person, though they may encounter some difficulties. See *infra*, n° 822–823.

[2588] S. Van Camp, S. Bouyon, *Impact assessment of proposed substantial amendments introducing a commercial lifespan guarantee in the proposed online sales and digital content directive* (European Parliament 2017) p. 6.

[2589] *Ibid.*

two-year liability period[2590], the same provision permits the contractual parties, if national law so provides, to include a clause limiting seller's liability to one year in the context of sales of second-hand goods.[2591] This exception already existed under the CSD.[2592] It has been introduced following the suggestion made by the EESC, which asserted that holding the seller liable for two years would be inappropriate in some cases because of the particular properties of the good purchased.[2593] With this exception, the objective sought to strike a fair balance of interests between the seller and the buyer.[2594] Following this reasoning, requiring the parties to satisfy all the requirements laid down in the Directive would hinder the development of the second-hand market as it would require more thorough checks and thus increase costs for businesses.[2595]

743. If national law so provides – This is only if national law so provides. Some Member States made use of the room for manoeuvre left by the CSD (and maintained in the SGD) to modulate this liability period. This is the case of Germany, which established this possibility in §475(2) BGB. In Belgium, Article 1649*quater* §1, subparagraph 3 of the Civil Code also allows the seller and the consumer, in the case of second-hand goods, to agree on a period of less than two years but not less than one year.[2596] However, if they do so, Belgian law requires them to indicate the new guarantee period in the terms of the sales contract. Otherwise, the two-year period applies.[2597] By contrast, French law makes no distinction between new and second-hand goods concerning the duration of the legal guarantee period. This does not prevent the nature of second-hand goods from being taken into account in the conformity assessment. In this regard, the French approach fits neatly within the long-term goal of transitioning towards a more circular economy and should thus be applied at EU level.

2590 See *supra*, n° 730.

2591 Art. 10(6) SGD. This provision states that the limitation period, within which consumers can exercise their rights, could also be reduced to one year.

2592 Art. 7(1), subparagraph 2, as well as recital 16 of the CSD.

2593 Opinion of the Economic and Social Committee on the 'Proposal for a European Parliament and Council Directive on the sale of consumer goods and guarantees', OJ C 66, 3.3.1997, pt. 3.10. and pt. 5.1.

2594 Opinion of Advocate General Szpunar delivered on 6 April 2017 in ECJ 13 July 2017, Case C-133/16, *Ferenschild*, pt. 81.

2595 Opinion of Advocate General Szpunar delivered on 6 April 2017 in ECJ 13 July 2017, Case C-133/16, *Ferenschild*, pt. 82.

2596 This provision was under discussion within the framework of the transposition of the new SGD. See Avis du Conseil Central de l'Economie du 3 septembre 2019 sur la transposition de directives européennes concernant la vente aux consommateurs tant de biens que de contenus et services numériques, CCE 2019–1660, p. 9.

2597 See C. Delforge, Y. Ninane, 'La garantie de conformité des biens de consommation', in P. Wéry (ed.), *La Théorie générale des obligations et contrats spéciaux* (2016) pp. 397–398.

744. A SIGNIFICANT EXCEPTION WITH UNDESIRABLE EFFECTS – Admittedly, the second-hand nature of a good should be taken into consideration when applying the rules on guarantees. However, Article 10(6) of the SGD constitutes a significant exception to the (already too short)[2598] guarantee period which could have undesirable effects with regard to product sustainability and more generally to sustainable consumption.[2599] Such limited period might discourage consumers from buying second-hand goods as they will be afforded a lower level of protection compared to consumers purchasing brand new goods. Studies have indeed shown that guarantees play an important role in reassuring consumers who may have concerns about the durability and performance of second-hand goods.[2600] The one-year liability period seems especially inadequate for products with a longer expected lifetime. Furthermore, a study commissioned by the EC on the market of second-hand cars pointed out the surprisingly large number of abuses with this exception, reporting that "*in more than one third of the cases, mystery shoppers were offered a legal guarantee of less than 1 year duration, in violation of the 1999 Directive on guarantees*".[2601] The one-year guarantee period and its related cases of abuse could not only dissuade consumers from opting for second-hand goods (and lead them to buy new products instead), but also create confusion in their minds. Consequently, this exception runs counter to the long-term target of shifting towards a more circular economy, in which consumers are encouraged to extend product lifetime by giving a second life to products previously used by an end user.

745. WORSENED BY THE LACK OF DEFINITION – The exception established by Article 10(6) of the SGD is even more problematic as there is no definition of 'second-hand goods' in the SGD.[2602] For example, one could wonder whether the notion includes refurbished goods.[2603] It remains also unclear which duration

---

2598 See *supra*, n° 731.

2599 Again, environmental protection should have been taken into account in the balancing of the interests at stake when adopting the SGD, as required by Art. 11 TFEU.

2600 D. Guiot, D. Roux, 'A second-hand shoppers' motivation scale: Antecedents, consequences, and implications for retailers', 86 *Journal of Retailing* (2010) pp. 368–369; S.S. Van Dam, C.A. Bakker, I. de Pauw and B. Van der Grinten, 'The circular pathfinder: development and evaluation of a practice-based tool for selecting circular design strategies', in C. Bakker and R. Mugge (eds.), *Product Lifetimes And The Environment 2017 – Conference Proceedings* (IOS Press 2017) p. 106.

2601 GFK, *Consumer market study on the functioning of the market for second-hand cars from a consumer perspective* (European Union 2015) p. 98.

2602 See *supra*, n° 677. See also E. Van Gool, 'De nieuwe richtlijn consumentenkoop en duurzame consumptie', in E. Terryn, I. Claeys (eds.), *Nieuw recht inzake koop & digitale inhoud en diensten* (Intersentia 2020) p. 315; Avis du Conseil Central de l'Economie du 3 septembre 2019 sur la transposition de directives européennes concernant la vente aux consommateurs tant de biens que de contenus et services numériques, CCE 2019–1660, p. 9.

2603 Avis du Conseil Central de l'Economie du 3 septembre 2019 sur la transposition de directives européennes concernant la vente aux consommateurs tant de biens que de contenus et services numériques, CCE 2019–1660, p. 9.

and intensity of prior use suffices in order to qualify goods as 'second-hand'.[2604] The lack of definition may be problematic if these terms are too broadly interpreted, although exceptions are in principle of strict interpretation.[2605] The limited guarantee period would consequently apply to a wider range of products, reducing consumer protection in a wider range of cases.

746. THE POSSIBILITY OF SHORTENING THE GUARANTEE PERIOD FOR SECOND-HAND GOODS SHOULD BE REMOVED – It is therefore supported to remove the transposition choice left to Member States which allow reduced guarantee periods for second-hand goods (see #9). There is no doubt that the second-hand nature of a good should be taken into account when evaluating conformity. Yet it does not require a reduction of the legal guarantee period.[2606] A reduced guarantee period seems even less appropriate when the sales involve long-lasting and high value products. Such a provision is in glaring contradiction to the long-term objective of transitioning towards circular economy as it penalizes and dissuades the consumption of second-hand goods, which contributes to preserving the value of products for as long as possible. An equal protection should therefore be granted to new and second-hand goods, together with a tailored conformity assessment.[2607] As aptly explained by Advocate General Szpunar, "*taking account of the specific nature of second-hand goods is not intended to deprive the consumer of the protection guaranteed to him, but merely to limit the list of rights which he enjoys*".[2608] This amendment should be made together with the introduction of a definition of 'second-hand goods', as previously put forward.[2609] While waiting for the necessary amendments in this sense at EU level, Member States should not introduce these rules if they want to fully engage in sustainable consumption.

2604 E. Van Gool and A. Michel, 'The New Consumer Sales Directive 2019/771 and Sustainable Consumption: A Critical Analysis', 10 *EuCML* (2021) p. 138.

2605 This principle has been established by European Court of Justice in a settled case law and has already been confirmed for this exception. See ECJ 13 July 2017, Case C-133/16, *Ferenschild, EU:C:2017:541*, para 46.

2606 See also S. Gomez, 'Economic Analysis of the Directive', in M.C. Bianca and S. Grundmann (eds.), *EU Sales Directive: Commentary* (Intersentia 2002), p. 71.

2607 E. Van Gool and A. Michel, 'The New Consumer Sales Directive 2019/771 and Sustainable Consumption: A Critical Analysis', 10 *EuCML* (2021) p. 138.

2608 Opinion of Advocate General Szpunar delivered on 6 April 2017 in ECJ 13 July 2017, Case C-133/16, *Ferenschild, EU:C:2017:541*, pt. 92.

2609 See *supra*, n° 681.

Proposed amendment to the SGD:

#9

Article 10
Liability of the seller

(...)

~~6. Member States may provide that, in the case of second-hand goods, the seller and the consumer can agree to contractual terms or agreements with a shorter liability or limitation period than those referred to in paragraphs 1, 2 and 5, provided that such shorter periods shall not be less than one year.~~

(4) Suspension and interruption of the liability period

747. THE POSSIBILITY OF SUSPENDING OR INTERRUPTING THE LIABILITY PERIOD – Along with the possibility of extending the liability period under national law, the SGD enables Member States to provide for the suspension or interruption of the liability period.[2610] Recital 44 cites three examples where the period could be suspended or interrupted, namely in the event of repair, replacement or negotiations between the parties. Suspension and renewal of the guarantee period constitute other key elements, which could be further developed to trigger product sustainability. First of all, they prolong the duration of the guarantee period, with all the benefits that it brings in terms of sustainability. But more than that, they can be used to prioritize repair over other remedies by counterbalancing the drawbacks associated with the (sometimes lengthy) repair procedure.

748. THREE DIFFERENT APPROACHES AT NATIONAL LEVEL – There are currently three main approaches followed by the Member States which made use of the room for manoeuvre left by the SGD. The first approach is to freeze the guarantee period when the product is being repaired or replaced. The suspension of the guarantee period exists under Belgian law[2611], as well as under French law.[2612] The second approach consists in renewing the guarantee period after repair and/or replacement. The renewal is sometimes applied, although not explicitly provided for by the law, like in Germany.[2613] In some Member States, the two-year guarantee period is fully reset, whereas in others, it is only

2610 Recital 44 SGD.
2611 Art. 1649*quater* §1, subparagraph 2 of the Belgian Civil Code.
2612 Art. L. 217-28 of the French Consumer Code.
2613 §438(1)3 BGB states that after a replacement of a defective good other than immovable property, consumers can claim legal guarantee rights for two years.

prolonged for a certain period of time.[2614] The renewed guarantee can cover the whole product or only concern the repaired or exchanged part.[2615] The third approach consists in extending the guarantee period by adding the time spent in the execution of the remedy or the claim process. Such an extension has been introduced by the French Anti-Waste Law. Since 1st January 2022, the two-year period is extended by six months after repair.[2616] Moreover, consumers who have chosen repair but where repair is not performed will be offered both a replacement and a renewal of the guarantee period.[2617]

749. AN IDEA UNDER DEBATE AT EU LEVEL – During the adoption process of the SGD, it has been repeatedly proposed to introduce a provision that would lead to reset or prolong the guarantee period in case of repair or replacement. In its Opinion, the EESC suggested providing for the suspension of the legal guarantee during the repair or replacement period, as well as during the period of mediation, arbitration and legal recourse, like it applies in most Member States (first approach).[2618] The EESC also advocated for a new and identical guarantee period for the replaced good as of the moment it is delivered (second approach).[2619] Similar ideas were shared by the EP. In its 2017 Resolution, it suggested that, in the event of a recurrent lack of conformity or a repair period in excess of one month, the guarantee period should be extended by a period equivalent to the time required to carry out repair (third approach).[2620] Its last

---

2614 See for ex. in Denmark, where there is a renewal of the guarantee, but with a maximum of three years in total.

2615 See for ex. in Germany or in Hungary, where the new guarantee only applies to the repaired or exchanged component.

2616 See Art. L. 217-13 of the French Consumer Code, which was introduced by Art. 22 of the Anti-Waste Law.

2617 *Ibid.*

2618 Opinion of the EESC on the 'Proposal for a directive of the European Parliament and of the Council on certain aspects concerning contracts for the supply of digital content' (COM(2015) 634 final) and the 'Proposal for a directive of the European Parliament and of the Council on certain aspects concerning contracts for the online and other distance sales of goods' (COM(2015) 635 final), OJ C 264, 20.7.2016, p. 64, pt. 4.2.5.8. See also Opinion of the European Economic and Social Committee on the 'Amended proposal for a Directive of the European Parliament and of the Council on certain aspects concerning contracts for the sales of goods, amending Regulation (EC) No 2006/2004 of the European Parliament and of the Council and Directive 2009/22/EC of the European Parliament and of the Council and repealing Directive 1999/44/EC of the European Parliament and of the Council' (COM(2017) 637 final), OJ C 227, 28.6.2018, p. 59, pt. 1.5. e).

2619 Opinion of the EESC on the 'Proposal for a directive of the European Parliament and of the Council on certain aspects concerning contracts for the supply of digital content' (COM(2015) 634 final) and the 'Proposal for a directive of the European Parliament and of the Council on certain aspects concerning contracts for the online and other distance sales of goods' (COM(2015) 635 final), OJ C 264, 20.7.2016, p. 64, pt. 4.2.5.8.

2620 European Parliament Resolution of 4 July 2017 on a longer lifetime for products: benefits for consumers and companies, 2016/2272(INI), pt. 9.

amendments related to the SGD reiterated this idea and recommended granting a two-year guarantee for the replaced good or for the component that has been replaced as part of the repair, starting from the reception of the repaired or replaced good (second approach).[2621] In its New Consumer Agenda, the EC especially considered the second approach, namely to restart a new liability period after repair.[2622]

750. The suspension of the guarantee period during the repair process should be harmonised – It is regrettable that the SGD does not harmonise this aspect of guarantee rules and leaves, once more, leeway to Member States on this point. Along with the extension of the guarantee period, it should be considered to establish the suspension, interruption or extension of the guarantee period in the SGD for new goods that consumers choose to repair instead of replacing them. Such a provision, if integrated within the SGD, would not only eliminate all disparities between Member States' rules, but also encourage consumers to opt for repair. Inspiration could be drawn from national experiences.[2623] Other interesting suggestions were made by scholars, like granting consumers a new guarantee period after replacement with refurbished or remanufactured goods.[2624] Between the three options, the suspension of the guarantee period during the repair process, which is the least drastic option, could be chosen as a first step (see #10). This proposal would only be truly effective in promoting product sustainability if repair is prioritized over replacement in the hierarchy of remedies. Otherwise, such a bonus extension could create a moral hazard for the seller to 'push' replacement. This could be especially counterproductive given that it is the seller who in current practice most often determines the remedy.[2625]

2621 See amendments 84 and 85 of the Report of 27 February 2018 on the amended proposal for a directive of the European Parliament and of the Council on certain aspects concerning contracts for the sales of goods, amending Regulation (EC) No 2006/2004 of the European Parliament and of the Council and Directive 2009/22/EC of the European Parliament and of the Council and repealing Directive 1999/44/EC of the European Parliament and of the Council, COM(2017) 637, C8-0379/2017, 2015/0288(COD), p. 42.

2622 Communication from the Commission of 13 November 2020 to the European Parliament and the Council and the Council on New Consumer Agenda – Strengthening consumer resilience for sustainable recovery, COM(2020) 696 final, p. 8.

2623 For example, T. Libaert suggests prioritizing repair over replacement by offering consumers the possibility to obtain an extra guarantee period of six months, like in France. See T. Libaert, *Pour une consommation plus durable en phase avec les enjeux européens* (2018) p. 55.

2624 See E. Terryn, 'A right to repair: Towards Sustainable Remedies in Consumer Law', 27 *E.R.P.L.* (2019) p. 861.

2625 E. Van Gool and A. Michel, 'The New Consumer Sales Directive 2019/771 and Sustainable Consumption: A Critical Analysis', 10 *EuCML* (2021) pp. 144–145.

Proposed amendment to the SGD:

#10

Article 10
Liability of the seller

(...)

1a. The guarantee period provided for in the first paragraph is suspended for the time necessary for the repair or replacement of the goods or in the event of negotiations between the seller and the consumer with a view to an amicable settlement.

(...)

(5) Burden of proof

751. A HEAVY BURDEN OF PROOF ON CONSUMERS – While the seller has to demonstrate that the lack of conformity did not exist during the liability period[2626], it is for the consumer to prove that the product still falls within the legal guarantee period. This could be a difficult task for consumers if they forget the exact date of purchase, and even more if the guarantee period was suspended or extended.[2627] If consumers lose the document providing evidence of the date of the purchase or on the suspension/extension period, it will be impossible for them to exercise the rights they enjoy under the legal guarantee regime. Consumer associations have already pointed out that the receipt is not sufficient to help consumers in this regard.[2628] To overcome this issue, some shops allow consumers to record data relating to their purchase (e.g. the date of purchase) on their ID card.[2629]

752. THE BURDEN OF PROOF ON CONSUMERS SHOULD BE LIGHTENED – For the guarantee rights to be effective, it should not be too difficult for the consumer to enforce them. This would involve the consumer providing evidence, without great difficulty, that the lack of conformity occurred within the guarantee period. The SGD should contribute to ensuring that the burden of proof does not render practically impossible or excessively difficult the exercise of rights

2626 Recital 45 SGD.
2627 See *supra*, n° 747–748.
2628 See e.g. L. Vasseur et al., *Livre blanc: 50 mesures pour une consommation et une production durables. Le guide des politiques publiques pour une société sans obsolescence accélérée* (HOP 2018) pp. 31–32.
2629 This practice is for example adopted by MediaMarkt (https://www.mediamarkt.be/fr/shop/faq/commande-paiement/factures-taxes.html).

conferred by EU law. For example, the proof of purchase could be simplified by linking the information on the guarantee to the goods rather than the purchaser and by further encouraging the introduction of e-receipts and digital guarantee schemes.[2630] Such recommendations could also be made in the recital accompanying the amended Articles 5(1)(e) and 6(1)(l) of the CRD requiring information on the content of the legal guarantee.[2631]

(6) Exceptions to the two-year guarantee period

753. THE INCOMPATIBLE NATURE OR SHORT LIFESPAN OF PRODUCTS AND COMPONENTS – It is noteworthy that not all products and components are being covered by the two-year legal guarantee established by the SGD. The nature, and more specifically the expected lifetime, of some products and components might be incompatible with the two-year guarantee period, such as perishable or single-use goods.[2632] For some goods and components, a defect might occur within a period of less than two years due to normal wear and tear. In this case, the legal guarantee does not apply.[2633] As rightly explained by J. Smits, "*the legal liability period is not a lifespan or durability guarantee: it does not require that all goods must have a lifespan of at least two years, but it only means that the seller's liability can be engaged if the non-conformity was present at the time of delivery and manifests itself within two years after the delivery*".[2634]

754. THE TRICKY CONCEPT OF 'NORMAL WEAR AND TEAR' – It is for the consumer to prove that the product of the component should be covered by the rules on guarantees. It might nonetheless be particularly difficult to evaluate the compatibility of certain products or components with the two-year guarantee period, especially when these products or components are not expected to last longer than two years. More importantly, it remains to be seen how to distinguish 'normal wear and tear' from a lack of conformity caused by actions and decisions of the producer. This question is central to the issue of premature obsolescence. If this exception to the two-year guarantee period were too broadly interpreted,

[2630] This recommendation has already been made by the EP, which called on the EC to "*[simplify] proof of purchase for the consumer by linking the guarantee to the goods rather than the purchaser, and by further encouraging the introduction of e-receipts and digital guarantee schemes across the board*". See European Parliament Resolution of 4 July 2017 on a longer lifetime for products: benefits for consumers and companies, 2016/2272(INI), pt. 34.

[2631] See *supra*, n° 491.

[2632] A similar reasoning has been followed for second-hand goods, leading to the possibility of a reduced guarantee period. See *supra*, n° 742.

[2633] Similar comments had been made on Article 2(3) CSD. See J. Stuyck, "La notion de conformité et l'articulation des délais", in C. Biquet-Mathieu et P. Wéry (eds.), *La nouvelle garantie des biens de consommation et son environnement légal* (la Charte 2005) p. 122.

[2634] J. Smits, *The new proposal for harmonised rules for the online sales of tangible goods: conformity, lack of conformity and remedies* (European Parliament 2016) p. 11.

many goods prematurely obsolete could fall outside the scope of application of the legal guarantee rules. So far, if there is a conflict between the contractual parties on this point and there is no legal information or from the producer on the expected lifetime, it is for the judge to evaluate whether the legal guarantee period is compatible with the nature of the concerned good.[2635] Therefore, as previously argued for the lack of durability[2636], a link should be made with other rules to improve consumer information on the expected product lifetime. This would help determine if the nature of the product or component is compatible with the two-year legal guarantee established by the SGD and thus delineate the scope of application of this exception

c) Prior to the delivery of the good

755. A DEFECT EXISTING PRIOR TO THE DELIVERY OF THE GOOD – In addition to the conditions on (a) the existence of a lack of conformity (b) which must occur within two years of the delivery[2637], the third condition to fall under the legal guarantee rules requires that the *defect exists prior to the delivery of the good.*[2638] For this third condition, the SGD provides for a presumption period during which consumers are exempted from the obligation to prove the prior existence of the defect if they succeed in demonstrating that (1) there is a lack of conformity (2) which appeared within the one-year presumption period.[2639]

(1) A defect existing prior to the delivery of the good

756. A CONDITION FULFILLED BY CASES OF MATERIAL OBSOLESCENCE – Not all lack of conformity occurring within the guarantee period are covered. Consumers will only benefit from the guarantee rules for those that existed prior to the delivery of the good. A broad range of cases of premature obsolescence undoubtedly meet this requirement. Smartphone batteries that no longer work and cannot be easily replaced, printers that stop working after a certain number of copies, etc. All these defects are inherent to the product and exist before it has been delivered.

757. BUT NOT FOR OTHER CASES OF PREMATURE OBSOLESCENCE? – However, questions remain in the case of other lack of conformity occurring after the delivery of the good. This includes the case whereby the trader stops supplying

2635 See Y. Ninane, "Le défaut de la chose vendue selon le régime de la garantie des biens de consommation", in C. Delforge and J. Van Zuylen (eds.), *Les défauts de la chose: Responsabilités contractuelle et extracontractuelle* (Anthemis 2015) p. 70.

2636 See *supra*, n° 719–721.

2637 See *supra*, n° 684 *et seq.* on the first condition (a lack of conformity) and n° 728 *et seq.* on the second condition (within two years of the delivery).

2638 Article 10(1) SGD.

2639 ECJ 4 June 2015, Case C-497/13, *Faber, EU:C:2015:357,* paras 68–72.

updates, as mentioned in Article 6(d) and 7(3) of the SGD.[2640] These new update obligations have partially outdated the notion of conformity as a static condition at the time of delivery of a product and raise the more general question of whether this third condition is still mandatory for the application of the guarantee rules.[2641]

(2) A presumption period of one year

758. A ONE-YEAR PRESUMPTION PERIOD AS A GENERAL RULE – It has been reported that the question on the prior existence of the defect is one of the most disputed points between parties.[2642] To lighten the burden of proof on consumers, who already have to prove certain elements to benefit from the guarantee rules[2643], Article 11(1) of the SGD provides that the lack of conformity is presumed to have existed at the time of delivery if it becomes apparent within the first year.[2644] In that case, consumers only have to prove that a lack of conformity exists and that it became (physically) apparent within the presumption period.[2645] It is for the seller to prove that, contrary to what is presumed, the lack of conformity did not exist at that time and was due, for example, to improper handling by the consumer. The logic behind this is that the occurrence of that lack of conformity within the first year makes it possible to assume that, although it became apparent after the delivery of the good, the lack of conformity already existed 'in embryonic form' at the time of delivery.[2646] On that aspect too, goods with digital elements are under a special regime as consumers can benefit from the presumption during the period of time for establishing conformity, which may be longer than one year.[2647] In any case, once the presumption period has elapsed, the burden of proof lies with consumers.

2640 See *supra*, n° 691 and n° 700.

2641 See also S. Van Camp, S. Bouyon, *Impact assessment of proposed substantial amendments introducing a commercial lifespan guarantee in the proposed online sales and digital content directive* (European Parliament 2017) p. 6.

2642 See for ex. Ombudsman du commerce, *Rapport annuel 2018*, p. 28, available on: <https://www.ombudsmanvoordehandel.be/asset/ombudsman-jaarverslag-2018-fr-lowres_2.pdf>.

2643 See *supra*, n° 715–717 and n° 751.

2644 The SGD strengthened consumer rights compared to the former CSD, which provided for a presumption period of six months (Article 5(3) CSD), although the initial proposal was more ambitious, suggesting a two-year presumption period (Article 8(3) of the Amended proposal for a Directive of the European Parliament and of the Council on certain aspects concerning contracts for the online and other distance sales of goods, amending Regulation (EC) No 2006/2004 of the European Parliament and of the Council and Directive 2009/22/EC of the European Parliament and of the Council and repealing Directive 1999/44/EC of the European Parliament and of the Council, COM(2017) 637 final).

2645 ECJ 4 June 2015, Case C-497/13, *Faber, EU:C:2015:357*, paras 69–71.

2646 See the explanatory memorandum to the Proposal for a European Parliament and Council Directive on the sale of consumer goods and associated guarantees, COM(95) 520 final, p. 12.

2647 See Art. 11(3) and recital 45 SGD.

759. With some leeway left to Member States – Like in the CSD[2648], Member States are allowed to maintain or introduce a longer presumption period, though no longer than two years.[2649] The French legislature exploited this possibility and prolonged the presumption period to two years.[2650] Belgium and Germany recently followed suit.[2651] Consequently, under these national laws, defects occurring during the whole guarantee period will be presumed as existing at the time of delivery, except if proved otherwise by the seller. Only second-hand goods are subject to a different regime: French and German law provides for a six-month presumption period[2652], while Belgian law states that the second-hand nature of a good should be taken into consideration when the exception to the presumption period is envisaged.[2653] The French Government had even suggested allowing the transfer of the two-year presumption period applicable to the initial buyer to the subsequent buyer, if the latter can provide the original invoice of the initial purchase.[2654] In other words, consumers who buy second-hand goods would enjoy a presumption period of two years from the initial delivery instead of one year from the date they purchased second-hand goods. If implemented, such a measure would completely remove the distinction between new and second-hand goods that currently exists under French law.

760. A rule of valuable help towards product sustainability – The reversal of the burden of proof for the first months of the guarantee period is valuable in the fight against premature obsolescence. On one hand, it makes it easier for consumers to claim their rights under the legal guarantee (including repair).[2655] Proving the prior existence of the defect mainly consists in establishing that the cause of that lack of conformity or its origin is attributable to the seller or the producer. This is particularly challenging for consumers, especially in cases of premature obsolescence, which is by nature difficult to distinguish from normal wear and tear. Moreover, they may face the cost of enlisting the assistance of a (potentially expensive) expert to support their position within an ADR mechanism or court. On the other hand, the presumption incites sellers and, indirectly, producers to ensure that the products

---

2648 See Article 8(2) CSD, which provided for minimum harmonisation.

2649 Art. 11(2) SGD.

2650 Art. L. 217-7 subparagraph 1 of the French Consumer Code.

2651 See Art. 1649*quater* §4 of the Belgian Civil Code (Belgium) and §476 (2) BGB (Germany).

2652 Art. L. 217-7 subparagraph 2 of the French Consumer Code (France) and §476 (2) BGB (Germany).

2653 Art. 1649*quater* §4 of the Belgian Civil Code. For further comments on the exception to the presumption period, see *infra* (n° 764-766).

2654 Rapport du Gouvernement au Parlement sur l'opportunité de l'extension de la durée de garantie légale de conformité de deux à cinq ans, voire à dix ans, pour certaines catégories ciblées de produits, April 2017, p. 6.

2655 See the explanatory memorandum to the Proposal for a European Parliament and Council Directive on the sale of consumer goods and associated guarantees, COM(95) 520 final, p. 12, as recalled in ECJ 4 June 2015, Case C-497/13, *Faber*, *EU:C:2015:357*, para 54.

that they make and sell, will not fail shortly after the delivery. Indeed, they want to avoid that non-conformities manifest themselves during this period, given the high risk of ensuing liability.[2656] The extended presumption period established under French law is more beneficial in this regard, though the dichotomy between new and second-hand goods is regrettable.

761. Though with a too short deadline – Following these considerations, it can be argued that even a one- or two-year presumption period is insufficient for many goods with longer lifespans, like washing machines and cars.[2657] Defects in such goods will often appear after a longer period and it will then be for the consumer to prove the prior existence of the defect. The seller can always deny consumers' allegations by arguing that the lack of conformity was caused by improper use or by external factors. And the more time goes by, the easier it becomes for the seller to do so. In these cases, consumers run into extreme difficulties to furnish evidence to the contrary and rebut this conclusion, especially due to the lack of knowledge and information on products.[2658] It is only when it goes before the court that the judge can examine the allegations and expertise, decide if another expert report is needed and settle the dispute. That is why it is important to ensure that expert reports, from both sides, are objective and clear on the cause of the defect.[2659] If too heavy, the burden of proof can constitute an insurmountable obstacle for consumers, who would then abstain from claiming their rights under the legal guarantee regime.

762. The presumption should apply during the whole guarantee period – The extension of the presumption period by the SGD from six months to one year is to be welcomed, especially because the lack of conformity appears mostly during the first year after the delivery of the good, as reported by some Belgian associations.[2660] However, the presumption period should be longer than one year, for reasons similar to those cited for the legal guarantee

2656 E. Van Gool and A. Michel, 'The New Consumer Sales Directive 2019/771 and Sustainable Consumption: A Critical Analysis', 10 *EuCML* (2021) p. 142.

2657 See also S. Van Camp, S. Bouyon, *Impact assessment of proposed substantial amendments introducing a commercial lifespan guarantee in the proposed online sales and digital content directive* (European Parliament 2017) p. 5.

2658 See for ex. Service de Médiation pour le Consommateur, *Rapport annuel 2018*, p. 30, available on: <https://mediationconsommateur.be/sites/default/files/content/download/files/cod-jaarverslag_2018-fr-lr.pdf>.

2659 In some Member States, there is a list of experts who are recognised as independent or a state body which can be approached. Additionally, in Malta, expert opinion is mandatory for the ADR mechanism and the expert will be appointed by the ADR. See Annex I to the study Ipsos-London Economics-Deloitte consortium, *Consumer market study on the functioning of legal and commercial guarantees for consumers in the EU* (European Commission 2015) p. 19.

2660 Avis du Conseil Central de l'Economie du 3 septembre 2019 sur la transposition de directives européennes concernant la vente aux consommateurs tant de biens que de contenus et services numériques, CCE 2019–1660, p. 10.

period.[2661] In other words, a lack of conformity occurring at any time during the (fully-differentiated) guarantee period should be presumed to have existed at the time of delivery, except if proved otherwise by the seller (see #11). In the meantime, the presumption period should be extended to two years (see #12). Heated debates on this aspect have taken place at national level since Member States are allowed by Article 11(2) of the SGD to extend the presumption period beyond one year.[2662] Yet, it would be better to harmonise the presumption period at EU level, as initially proposed by the EC.[2663]

763. Though a fair balance of interests remains important – Consumer protection and product sustainability must however be balanced with the interests of sellers, for whom a longer presumption period arguably constitutes a bigger burden than a longer legal guarantee period.[2664] Furthermore, extending presumption periods will result in increased prices, although this should be nuanced as the presumption remains rebuttable and sellers are generally in a better position to deliver the required proof than consumers.[2665] A possible sustainability disadvantage that should not be ignored is the risk that longer presumption periods invite consumers to use goods less carefully ('moral hazard').[2666] This provides an additional reason to the Member States to establish a proportional liability system for cases where consumers have contributed to the lack of conformity.[2667] In conclusion, both extending the presumption period and the legal guarantee towards the expected lifetime of a product type can potentially contribute to sustainability. But if combining both is unrealistic, then the extension of the latter should be considered as it would

2661 See *supra*, n° 732.

2662 See for ex. the debate that took place in Belgium before the adoption of the rules transposing the SGD into Belgian law: Avis du Conseil Central de l'Economie du 3 septembre 2019 sur la transposition de directives européennes concernant la vente aux consommateurs tant de biens que de contenus et services numériques, CCE 2019–1660, p. 10.

2663 See Art. 8 of the Proposal for a Directive of the European Parliament and of the Council on certain aspects concerning contracts for the online and other distance sales of goods, COM(2015) 635 final, where the EC proposed an harmonised two-year presumption period.

2664 Interestingly, a 2015 study commissioned by the EC reported that in practice, the reversal of proof was rarely applied by companies. See Ipsos-London Economics-Deloitte consortium, *Consumer market study on the functioning of legal and commercial guarantees for consumers in the EU* (European Commission 2015) p. 58.

2665 See D. Staudenmayer, 'The Directives on Digital Contracts: First Steps Towards the Private Law of the Digital economy', 28 *E.R.P.L.* (2020) p. 248, who argues that this asymmetry between parties is even greater for goods with digital elements.

2666 See S. Gomez, 'Economic Analysis of the Directive', in Bianca and Grundmann (eds.), *EU Sales Directive: Commentary* (Intersentia 2002) p. 59 at p. 61. See also in Belgium: Avis du Conseil Supérieur des Indépendants et des PME du 21 février 2017 sur des propositions visant à renforcer la garantie légale des biens de consommation, F PRAT COM – Garantie légale A1, pp. 3–4; Avis du Conseil Central de l'Economie du 3 septembre 2019 sur la transposition de directives européennes concernant la vente aux consommateurs tant de biens que de contenus et services numériques, CCE 2019–1660, pp. 10–11.

2667 See *supra*, n° 726.

allow consumers to claim their rights (including the right to repair)[2668] for a longer period, thus prolonging product lifetime. In this scenario, the burden of proof on consumers could still be lightened by other means and on other aspects, as previously underlined.[2669]

Proposed amendments to the SGD:

#11

Article 11
Burden of proof

1. Any lack of conformity which becomes apparent ~~within one year of the time when the goods were delivered~~ within the guarantee period referred to in Article 10(1) shall be presumed to have existed at the time when the goods were delivered, unless proved otherwise or unless this presumption is incompatible with the nature of the goods or with the nature of the lack of conformity. This paragraph shall also apply to goods with digital elements.

~~**2. Instead of the one-year period laid down in paragraph 1, Member States may maintain or introduce a period of two years from the time when the goods were delivered.**~~

3. In the case of goods with digital elements where the sales contract provides for the continuous supply of the digital content or digital service over a period of time, the burden of proof with regard to whether the digital content or digital service was in conformity within the period of time referred to in Article 10(2) shall be on the seller for a lack of conformity which becomes apparent within the period of time referred to in that Article.

AS AN INTERMEDIARY STEP

#12

Article 11
Burden of proof

1. Any lack of conformity which becomes apparent within ~~one year~~ two years of the time when the goods were delivered shall be presumed to have existed at the time when the goods were delivered, unless proved otherwise or unless this presumption is incompatible with the nature of the goods or with the nature of the lack of conformity. This paragraph shall also apply to goods with digital elements.

2668 For a thorough analysis of the right to repair, see *infra* (n° 770 *et seq.*).

2669 See *supra*, n° 715–721 and n° 751–752.

~~2. Instead of the one-year period laid down in paragraph 1, Member States may maintain or introduce a period of two years from the time when the goods were delivered.~~

(...)

(3) Exceptions to the presumption period

764. Two exceptions to the presumption period – Article 11 of the SGD mentions two major exceptions to the presumption it grants. These exceptions can deprive consumers from protection in a substantial number of cases (including cases of premature obsolescence), if too broadly interpreted.

765. When incompatible with the nature of the good – The first exception relates to the incompatibility of the presumption period with the nature of the concerned good.[2670] Recital 45 cites two illustrative examples, namely perishable and single-use products. While the exception seems justified for these specific and clear-cut categories of goods, the application of the same exception might be unclear for other goods.[2671] For example, it is not clear whether certain goods with short lifespans, such as light bulbs and earphones, should be considered as being incompatible with the one-year presumption period.[2672] If so, it would mean that consumers experiencing the premature obsolescence of such products would lose the presumption conferred by Article 11 of the SGD and would face the difficult task of proving the prior existence of the defect. This exception and its vague terms could thus seriously hinder consumers' ability to claim guarantee rights for certain products, which prematurely break down.

766. When incompatible with the nature of the lack of conformity – The second exception corresponds to cases where the presumption period is deemed incompatible with the nature of the lack of conformity.[2673] Recital 45 also provides an example for this exception, citing the case where the lack of conformity can only be a result of an action by the consumer or of an evident external cause, which occurred after the goods were delivered. More than losing the presumption, consumers could even lose their rights under the legal guarantee as those kinds of lack of conformity do not exist prior to the delivery of the good. In other words, the legal guarantee does not apply if the

2670 Article 11(1) SGD.

2671 It should be noted that the concept of 'perishable' and 'single-use' products might not be as clear-cut as they seem, leaving uncertainties too.

2672 This issue had been raised within the framework of the CSD in A. Hamann, 'Obsolescence programmée: le droit en panne?', 102 *D.C.C.R.* (2014) p. 70.

2673 Article 11(1) SGD.

lack of conformity was due to incorrect treatment, failure to comply with the instructions or other external causes.[2674] If their behaviour is not the sole cause, but only contributed to the lack of conformity, consumers could still enjoy their guarantee rights but might have a restricted choice of remedies, depending on what is provided for under national law.[2675]

4. CONSUMER REMEDIES

767. A TWO-TIERED HIERARCHY OF REMEDIES – When the three abovementioned conditions are met, consumers are entitled to seek remedies against the seller in accordance with the two-tiered hierarchy established under Article 13 of the SGD.[2676] In the first place, the consumer may require the seller to bring the defective goods into conformity, choosing between the repair or replacement of the defective good (performance in kind). If the good cannot be brought into conformity due to one of the circumstances enumerated in Article 13(4), the consumer may, alternatively, demand an appropriate reduction in the price or withdraw from the contract. These remedies and their conditions have been fully harmonised by the SGD[2677], although the harmonisation on this aspect is somewhat weakened by some provisions.[2678] The right to repair granted by the Directive constitutes a key tool in tackling the accelerating obsolescence of consumer goods.[2679] However, while repair is the most sustainable of the four remedies[2680], the current hierarchy and modalities do not stimulate, let alone require, consumers to repair their defective products. And other remedies are not as sustainable as they could be.

768. POSSIBLY COMBINED WITH THE RIGHT TO DAMAGES – Article 3(6) of the SGD leaves Member States free to allow a right to damages to consumers.

2674 See for ex. Prés. Commerce Francophone Bruxelles, 28 avril 2014, Cami SA v Mobistar SA.

2675 See Article 13(7) SGD, which leaves it for Member States to regulate whether and to what extent a contribution of the consumer to the lack of conformity affects the consumer's right to remedies. See *supra*, n° 726.

2676 According to Article 10(4) and (5) of the SGD, Member States may constrain consumers to exercise their rights within a certain period of time after they became aware of the lack of conformity, provided that this limitation period does not hinder consumers from exercising the remedies. Like the liability period, the limitation period can be reduced for second-hand goods (Art. 10(6)) as well as suspended or interrupted (recital 44).

2677 See recital 47 SGD. Member States can no longer offer a completely free choice of remedy to consumers, as allowed by the CSD, and must adopt this two-tier system. See Annex I to the study Ipsos-London Economics-Deloitte consortium, *Consumer market study on the functioning of legal and commercial guarantees for consumers in the EU* (European Commission 2015) p. 12.

2678 See *infra*.

2679 The importance of the right to repair is underlined in recital 48 of the SGD itself.

2680 See *supra*, n° 647.

Such freedom has been taken in some national law, like in Belgium[2681] and in France[2682], where consumers can claim damages in case of detriment. Although it is not its initial objective, the right to damages can also contribute to supporting sustainable consumption patterns. For example, this right could be used to sanction traders who would have caused significant inconvenience and delay when executing consumers request to repair.

769. Complemented by the remedies applicable to digital content and digital service – It should be noted that these remedies are complemented by those offered by the DCD[2683], which protects consumers in case of lack of supply or conformity of the digital content or the digital service.[2684] If the digital content or digital service has not been supplied, Article 13 gives consumers the right to call upon the trader to supply the conformed digital content or digital service. The same provision states that if the trader then fails to supply the digital content or digital service without undue delay, or within an additional period of time, as expressly agreed to by the parties, the consumer can terminate the contract. In case of lack of conformity of digital content and digital service, similar remedies as those provided for in the SGD can be found in Article 14 of the DCD. This provision allows consumers to ask for the digital content or the digital service to be brought into conformity free of charge, within reasonable time and without significant inconvenience. As subsidiary remedies, consumers can choose between a proportionate reduction of the price and the termination of the contract. In the event of the termination of the contract, Article 16(4) requires the trader, at the request of the consumer, to make available to the consumer any content other than personal data, which was provided or created by the consumer when using the digital content or digital service supplied by the trader. This avoids situations where consumers feel locked-in.[2685] Hence, the DCD affords an extra protection to consumers in case of premature obsolescence (and more specifically functional obsolescence), which contributes to prolonging product lifetime. Without such remedies, goods with digital elements may have shorter lifetimes if the lack of supply or conformity of the digital content or digital service prevents the goods from performing their functions.

2681 Art. 1649*quinquies* §1 of the Belgian Civil Code.

2682 Art. L. 217-11 and L. 217-13 of the French Consumer Code.

2683 For further details on the DCD, see K. Sein, G. Splinder, 'The new Directive on Contracts for Supply of Digital Content and Digital Services – Conformity Criteria, Remedies and Modifications – Part 2', 15 *Eur. Rev. Contract Law* (2019) p. 365 at p. 391.

2684 Concerning the scope of application of the DCD and its articulation with the SGD, See *supra*, n° 675–676.

2685 UCPD Guidance, p. 134.

a) A right to repair

(1) Repair as primary remedy

770. A FIRST RANK BASED ON TWO MAIN REASONS – The right to repair was established as a consumer right by the CSD.[2686] Repair was elevated to the rank of primary remedy in accordance with the logic of privileging the execution of the contract.[2687] As explained by advocate General Mazak, it allows "*the original synallagma under the contract of sale [to be] restored and the consumer [to obtain] the performance for which he contracted.*"[2688] The SGD emphasises another justification for this ranking based on sustainability. By promoting repair as one of the two primary remedies, the SGD intends to "*encourage sustainable consumption and (...) contribute to greater durability of products*".[2689]

771. NO LEGAL DEFINITION OF REPAIR – The SGD provides no definition of 'repair', by contrast with the CSD.[2690] However, scholars have argued that it suffices for the repaired good to be in a state that would have been acceptable originally compared to the contractual requirements.[2691] Such reasoning fits with the definition enshrined in the EU standards on material efficiency, which defines repair as the "*process of returning a faulty product to a condition where it can fulfil its [originally] intended use*".[2692] This definition echoes the one contained in the Basel Convention, where repair is defined as "*fixing a specified fault in an object that is a waste or a product and/or replacing defective components, in order to make the waste or product a fully functional product to be used for its originally intended purpose.*"[2693] In other words, as argued in the first chapter of this book[2694], repair should be understood as a means to remediate non-conformities, without necessarily bringing the good to a brand-new state.

2686 Before the CSD, repair was not an option left to consumers in some Member States. See the Green Paper from the European Commission of 15 November 1993 on Guarantees for Consumer Goods and After-sales Services, COM(93) 509 final, p. 32 at p. 38.

2687 ECJ 16 June 2011, Joined cases C-65/09 and C-87/09, *Weber and Putz, EU:C:2011:396*, para 72. See also G. Howells, C. Twigg-Flesner T. Wilhelmsson, *Rethinking Eu Consumer Law* (Routledge 2017) p. 186; H. Sivesand, *The Buyer's Remedies for Non-Conforming Goods* (Sellier, 2005).

2688 Opinion of Advocate General Mazak delivered on 18 May 2010 for Case C-65/09, *Weber*, in ECJ 16 June 2011, Joined cases C-65/09 and C-87/09, *Weber and Putz*, pt. 47.

2689 Recital 48 SGD.

2690 Article 1(2)(f) of the CSD defined 'repair' in its broad sense as "*bringing consumer goods into conformity with the contract of sale, in the event of lack of conformity*".

2691 See D. Staudenmayer, 'The Directive on the Sale of Consumer Goods and Associated Guarantees – a milestone in the European consumer and private law', 4 *E.R.P.L.* (2004) p. 555.

2692 CEN-CENELEC TC10, Definitions related to material efficiency, EN 45550:2020, p. 9.

2693 United Nations, Revised glossary of terms adopted by the Open-ended Working Group of the Basel Convention of 18 March 2016, UNEP/CHW/OEWG.10/INF/10, p. 8.

2694 See *supra*, n° 152.

This also means that the defective product could be repaired with refurbished and remanufactured parts, as provided for under French law.[2695]

772. Repair should be defined under the SGD – To avoid any misunderstanding and to clarify the concept, the SDG should include a definition of 'repair' in its Article 2 (see #13). Since it is particularly important to ensure coherence between the different EU instruments, the SDG should replicate the definition contained in the EU standards on material efficiency, that is the "*process of returning a faulty product to a condition where it can fulfil its [originally] intended use*".[2696] In addition to this new definition, the SGD could indicate in its recitals that repair should not necessarily consist in bringing the good into conformity with a brand-new state, but could also be carried out by using refurbished and remanufactured parts.

773. The hierarchy should be reviewed to prioritise repair over replacement – The hierarchy of remedies established under the SGD should not only "*serve the main interest of the parties to a contract*"[2697], but also fit with the objective of sustainable development as enshrined in Article 11 of the TFEU. The best way to reconcile these aims is to elevate repair as the only remedy at the top of the hierarchy and relegate replacement to a subsidiary rank (see #14).[2698] First of all, repair is an inherently more sustainable remedy.[2699] Secondly, repair, if it is carried out according to the conditions listed in Article 13(2) and Article 14 SGD, is a contractual remedy that satisfies both the consumer's contractual expectations and the seller's right to cure.[2700] Finally, although

2695 In France, professionals who maintain and repair certain goods (such as electrical and electronic appliances) are obliged to offer consumers the possibility to opt for spare parts coming from the circular economy. See *infra*, n° 801.

2696 CEN-CENELEC TC10, Definitions related to material efficiency, EN 45550:2020, p. 9.

2697 Opinion of Advocate General Mazak delivered on 18 May 2010 for Case C-65/09, *Weber*, in ECJ 16 June 2011, Joined cases C-65/09 and C-87/09, *Weber and Putz*, pt. 47.

2698 See also E. Terryn, 'A Right to Repair: Towards Sustainable Remedies in Consumer Law', *E.R.P.L.* (2019) p. 858; E. Maitre Ekern and C. Dalhammar, 'Towards a hierarchy of consumption behaviour in the circular economy', 26 *MJ* (2019) p. 419; A. Michel, 'La directive 1999/44/CE sur la garantie des biens de consommation: un remède efficace contre l'obsolescence programmée?', *R.E.D.C.* (2018) p. 228.

2699 See *supra*, n° 647.

2700 It has been argued that consumers should continue to have freedom of choice between repair and replacement because sometimes a repair would not meet the consumer's performance interest. K. Kryla-Cudna, 'Sales Contracts and the Circular Economy', 28 *E.R.P.L.* (2020) p. 1213. BEUC went one step further by advocating for a free choice of remedy for consumers (BEUC Position Paper of 3 June 2016 on the Proposal for a Directive on certain aspects concerning contracts for distance sales of goods, BEUC-X-2016–053, p. 11 at p. 13). This approach is misguided. First of all, repair as a remedy means that, although the repaired good should not be identical to a new good, it has to be brought back into compliance with all applicable conformity requirements (see D. Staudenmayer, 'The Directive on the Sale of Consumer Goods and Associate Guarantees: A Milestone in the European Consumer and Private Law', 8 *E.R.P.L.* (2000) p. 555). Secondly, the repair also needs to be carried out in

repair and replacement are theoretically equal remedies, repair is currently far less attractive in the eyes of the average consumer and the sellers.[2701] For these three main reasons, repair should be prioritised over replacement. Replacement would still be possible if repair is impossible or disproportionate.[2702]

774. A FIRST STEP TOWERDS A NEW HIERARCHY OF REMEDIES? – It is noteworthy that the EC has recently suggested the review of Article 13 of the SGD in its Proposal for a Directive on common rules promoting repair. While maintaining the hierarchy between the remedies of repair and replacement, Article 12 of the Proposal promotes repair over replacement by adapting the conditions under which the choice of consumers can be exercised. More specifically, Article 12 adds a sentence to Article 13(2) SGD, stating that "*where the costs for replacement are equal to or greater than the costs for repair, the seller shall repair the goods in order to bring those goods in conformity*". As a result, consumers may only choose replacement as a remedy when it is cheaper than repair.

775. TOGETHER WITH MEASURES DEVELOPING, STIMULATING AND FACILITATING REPAIR – It is nonetheless essential to further develop, stimulate and facilitate repair before establishing repair as the sole remedy in all circumstances.[2703] Otherwise, the effectiveness of these changes in the hierarchy might be compromised. On one hand, there is a risk that the consumer and the seller agree to disregard the hierarchy if they consider that their interests are not well served. On the other hand, even without such an agreement, it would lead to issues in terms of acceptance and effectiveness if, for example, repair leads to inappropriate waiting periods and costs.[2704] This is why other measures should first be taken to favour repair during the whole product lifecycle. These measures include repair-friendly Ecodesign regulation, access to spare parts and diagnostic information, imposing mandatory or soft law repair-related information and restricting other legal and technical obstacles to repair.[2705] Should it be decided to leave the hierarchy of remedies unchanged, these measures would still represent a good alternative.

---

accordance with the requirements stipulated in art. 14. Hence, the SGD's repair remedy meets the performance interest of the consumer.

2701 See *supra*, n° 651–656.

2702 These two exceptions should however be interpreted narrowly. See *infra*, n° 777–782.

2703 E. Terryn, 'A Right to Repair: Towards Sustainable Remedies in Consumer Law', *ERPL* (2019) p. 858.

2704 S. Schlacke, K. Tonner, E. Gawel, *Stärkung eines nachhaltigen Konsums im Bereich Produktnutzung durch Anpassungen im Zivil- und öffentlichen Recht* (Umweltbundesamt Study 2015) pp. 31–32.

2705 See the series of measures proposed in the previous chapters of this book, including among others n° 265–271, n° 543–553 and n° 613–614.

Proposed amendments to the SGD:

#13

Article 2
Definitions

For the purposes of this Directive, the following definitions apply:

(…)

(16) 'repair' means the process of returning a faulty product to a condition where it can fulfil its originally intended use, as defined by CEN-CENELEC TC10 EN 45550:2020.

AND *#14*

Article 13
Remedies for lack of conformity

(…)

2. In order to have the goods brought into conformity, the consumer may ~~choose between repair and replacement,~~ **request the seller to repair the goods, unless** the remedy chosen **this is impossible or, compared to** the other remedy **replacement, would impose costs on the seller that would be disproportionate,** taking into account all circumstances (…)

(2) Restrictions to the right to repair

776. Two major exceptions – Article 13(2) of the SGD prevents consumers from opting for repair if it "*would be impossible or, compared to the other remedy, would impose costs on the seller that would be disproportionate*". Different elements must be considered when determining the impossibility or disproportionality of the remedy, including (a) the value the goods would have if there were no lack of conformity, (b) the significance of the lack of conformity and (c) whether the alternative remedy could be provided without significant inconvenience to the consumer. It goes without saying that both exceptions severely restrict consumers' right to repair, especially because it is for the seller to assess whether in a certain, specific individual situation the exercise of this right is impossible or would impose disproportionate costs on him.[2706] Hence,

[2706] See in that sense the Opinion of the European Economic and Social Committee on the 'Amended proposal for a Directive of the European Parliament and of the Council on certain aspects concerning contracts for the sales of goods, amending Regulation (EC) No 2006/2004 of the European Parliament and of the Council and Directive 2009/22/EC of the European

even when consumers are willing to repair their defective products, they can face major obstacles.

(A) When repair is impossible

777. When premature obsolescence leads to impossible repair – The right to repair could first be denied if repair is deemed 'impossible'. The impossibility of repairing the good could stem from different causes. Besides cases where the lack of conformity is too severe, there are cases where the good is manufactured in such a way that it is physically impossible to repair, i.e. in cases of material obsolescence. Another scenario where repair is impossible is when spare parts are no longer available, i.e. in cases of indirect obsolescence. A lack of spare parts in the seller's stock or a lack of qualified staff should however not make repair impossible as long as other professionals (including independent repairers) could be approached.[2707] Consequently, where the producer makes the product materially or indirectly obsolete, the consumer has no choice but to replace the defective good. In *Weber and Putz*, the EC added that "*it is not excluded that in extreme cases, where the only possible remedy involves a cost which is highly disproportionate in relation to the interest of the consumer in being compensated, there is an instance of impossibility (…)*".[2708] According to this interpretation, impossibility would also encompass cases where repair is too costly, i.e. cases of economic obsolescence.[2709] It would, however, make more sense to classify these cases within the second exception relating to disproportionality.[2710] In addition to this 'factual impossibility', the SGD adds that the choice between repair and replacement could be limited where the option chosen would be legally impossible.[2711] Such an extensive interpretation increases the number of cases where the consumers' repair requests could be denied.

778. Restricting consumer choice of replacement – *A contrario*, it should be noted that this impossibility criterion can also preclude consumers from choosing to replace their defective products and constrain them to ask for repair.[2712] The CSD gave the example of 'second-hand goods', which have such a specific nature that it "*makes it generally impossible to replace them*".[2713] Although

Parliament and of the Council and repealing Directive 1999/44/EC of the European Parliament and of the Council' (COM(2017) 637 final), OJ C 227, 28.6.2018, p. 61, pt. 4.4.

2707 The contracting seller would then pay back the price of repair to the consumer. For further comments, see n° 800.

2708 ECJ 16 June 2011, Joined cases C-65/09 and C-87/09, *Weber and Putz*, *EU:C:2011:396*, para 65.

2709 The position adopted by the EC has not (yet) been endorsed by the ECJ.

2710 See *infra*, n° 780.

2711 Recital 48 SGD.

2712 This is true only if repair is not made impossible too. Otherwise, consumers will only be able to choose between the two subsidiarity remedies, that is the adequate reduction of the price and the termination of the contract. See *infra*, n° 811–817.

2713 Recital 16 CSD.

this was only a general statement of principle and not an outright exclusion of second-hand goods from the remedy of replacement, it gives some guidelines on the interpretation of this 'impossibility' exception. Another interesting example was given by C. Twigg-Flesner, who referred to the English case law *Alexander v Comet Group*[2714], where it was deemed impossible to replace the defective good because the particular model had been discontinued and the model that came closest to the concerned good was significantly more expensive.[2715] This case constitutes a paradox having regard to premature obsolescence as it would mean that functional obsolescence would induce repair. It would have been different if the product could have been obtained by the seller from another supplier.[2716]

779. Making the impossible possible – Besides a strict interpretation of the notion of 'impossibility'[2717], a series of rules promoting product reparability could reduce cases where repair is deemed impossible. For example, EU waste legislation requires producers to make laptops with removable batteries.[2718] Other rules compel producers and importers to ensure that essential spare parts are available, delivered and easy to replace during the expected lifespan of goods.[2719] Such legislation has been adopted at EU level through product-specific ecodesign regulations[2720], but can also be found as a general obligation at national level, including in France (Art. L. 111–4 of the Consumer Code)[2721] and in Germany (principle of good faith in the automotive sector).[2722] A general

2714 *Alexander v Comet Group plc* [1995] *Consumer Policy Review* 29.

2715 C. Twigg-Flesner, *Consumer Product Guarantees* (Routledge 2016) p. 12.

2716 G. Howells, C. Twigg-Flesner T. Wilhelmsson, *Rethinking Eu Consumer Law* (Routledge 2017) p. 189.

2717 As with any exception under EU law, Article 13(2) of the SGD is to be interpreted narrowly, as established by the settled case law of the ECJ. See for ex. ECJ 13 July 2017, Case C-133/16, *Ferenschild, EU:C:2017:541*, para 46. To further restrict the application of this exception and the margin of discretion left to sellers, the EESC suggested to use the terms 'technologically impossible' instead of 'impossible'. See Opinion of the European Economic and Social Committee on the 'Amended proposal for a Directive of the European Parliament and of the Council on certain aspects concerning contracts for the sales of goods, amending Regulation (EC) No 2006/2004 of the European Parliament and of the Council and Directive 2009/22/EC of the European Parliament and of the Council and repealing Directive 1999/44/EC of the European Parliament and of the Council' (COM(2017) 637 final), OJ C 227, 28.6.2018, p. 61, pt. 4.4.2.

2718 See Art. 11 of the Batteries Directive. For other examples of product requirements imposed by waste legislation, see Chapter V on the end-of-life stage.

2719 Such measures are encouraged by recital 33 SDG.

2720 For further details on these new ecodesign requirements, see *supra* n° 260.

2721 See *infra*, n° 264.

2722 In the automotive sector, the German courts have construed an obligation to provide spare parts for a certain period of time on the basis of the principle of good faith. The nature and scope of this contractual duty depend on the circumstances of the individual case and more particularly the sold good. The more durable and expensive the product, the longer the availability period of spare parts should be. For example, it has been considered that on average it should be around 10 years for cars. See ICF, *Study on the costs and benefits of extending certain rights under the Consumer Sales and Guarantees Directive 1999/44/CE* (European Commission 2017) p. 57.

obligation on the availability of spare parts merits further consideration in EU consumer protection law[2723], as already suggested by the EP[2724] and envisaged in 1993 by the EC.[2725] EU consumer law could also explicitly prohibit certain practices affecting repairers' rights, like French legislation which bans "*any technique, including software, by which the person responsible for placing the product on the market seeks to make it impossible to repair or repackage a device outside its approved circuits*" and "*any agreement or practice aimed at limiting professional repairers' access to spare parts, instructions, technical information or any other instrument, equipment or software allowing repair*".[2726] Hence, more EU legislation of this kind is needed. Such obligations could be established by the SGD or, if more appropriate, by other EU legal instruments. In the second scenario, references to these EU legal instruments should be added in the SGD.

(b) When repair is disproportionate

780. When premature obsolescence leads to disproportionate repair – The second situation that might hamper consumers' right to repair is when repair is regarded as disproportionate, i.e. when it would impose disproportionate costs on the seller, compared to replacement.[2727] In *Weber and Putz*, the ECJ described this proportionality rule as 'relative', emphasizing that it applies only between repair and replacement.[2728] Consequently, it is not possible for the seller to refuse the only primary remedy which allows the good to be brought into conformity with the contract if the other one is disproportionate. The proportionality test must be conducted by assessing whether the costs are considerably higher compared to the other primary remedy, taking into account the value of the good, the significance of the lack of conformity and the inconvenience that the alternative remedy could cause to consumers.[2729] An illustrative example of disproportionality is given by recital 48 of the SGD, which refers to the case where a consumer would require the replacement of the good because of minor scratches, whereas such replacement

---

2723 B. Keirsbilck, E. Terryn, A. Michel and I. Alogna, *Sustainable Consumption and Consumer Protection Legislation* (European Parliament 2020) p. 16.

2724 European Parliament Resolution of 4 July 2017 on a longer lifetime for products: benefits for consumers and companies, 2016/2272(INI), pt. 10.

2725 The EC had stated that "*[t]he most stringent solution would be to impose a standard obligation on manufacturers to stock the necessary spare parts during a certain period from the date they quit selling the products. This product-specific period should correspond to the normal lifespan of the merchandise in question and could be "fleshed out" through codes of conduct or through recourse to standardisation.* Green Paper from the European Commission of 15 November 1993 on Guarantees for Consumer Goods and After-sales Services, COM(93) 509 final, p. 100.

2726 These French prohibitions are more thoroughly analysed in the section dedicated to the UCPD in the third chapter of this book. See *supra*, n° 369.

2727 Article 13(2) SGD.

2728 ECJ 16 June 2011, Joined cases C-65/09 and C-87/09, *Weber and Putz*, *EU:C:2011:396*, para 68.

2729 Article 13(2) SGD.

would create significant costs and the scratch could easily be repaired.[2730] The majority of disproportionality cases will unfortunately be the opposite, favouring replacement over repair. Indeed, repair is generally more costly than replacement. For most products, repair costs, which comprise *inter alia* call-out charges, labour costs, costs of spare parts or infrastructure, are often higher compared to the price of a brand-new product, mostly produced in automated manufacturing or low-wage countries.[2731] The proportionality test constitutes thus a major obstacle to the right to repair and even fosters early replacement of products.

781. Limiting the only feasible remedy to a proportionate amount – The ECJ further accentuates this restriction in *Weber and Putz* by limiting the only feasible remedy in kind (in this case, replacement) to a proportionate amount.[2732] Thus, if the remaining remedy – repair or replacement – entails costs that are manifestly disproportionate for the seller, the consumer can either remain faithful to their initial claim or instead request one of the subsidiary remedies per equivalent, i.e. the appropriate reduction of the price or the termination of the contract.[2733] Applied to the case where only repair is available, this interpretation severely impedes the right to repair and encourages consumers to turn to subsidiary remedies. The ECJ justifies this 'absolute lack of proportionality' rule by the need to strike a fair balance between the interests of the two contracting parties.[2734] However, as previously argued[2735], this purely contractual perspective does not take into account the general interest of environmental protection, which seems contrary to the principle of consistency required by Article 7 of the TFEU.[2736]

782. The proportionality test should be reviewed – Whether the hierarchy of remedies remains unchanged or not[2737], the proportionality test should (at least) serve as a basis to foster repair. Several amendments should be made in that sense (see #15). First, the lists of elements to take into account for the assessment of proportionality could also refer to substantial technical difficulties, economic costs or other risks involving repair. The word 'substantial' would suggest that those difficulties, costs and risks need to be of considerable

2730 Replacement represents a loss for the seller, who gives the consumer a brand-new substitute product and keeps the defective good, which generally would not be resold at its full price.

2731 It has been shown that for some products, like vacuum cleaners and washing machines, repair was a more economical strategy than replacement as it resulted in a lower lifecycle cost (cost per annum). See E. Bracquené et al., *Repairability criteria for energy related products – Study in the BeNeLux context to evaluate the options to extend the product life time* (Benelux, VITO, KUL 2018) p. 127.

2732 ECJ 16 June 2011, Joined cases C-65/09 and C-87/09, *Weber and Putz*, *EU:C:2011:396*, para 74.

2733 *Ibid.*, para 77.

2734 *Ibid.*, para 75.

2735 See *supra*, n° 773.

2736 Indeed, this approach creates inconsistency between environmental protection (Art. 11 TFEU) and consumer protection (Art 12 TFEU).

2737 See *supra*, n° 773.

importance to restrict consumers' right to repair. The second amendment to the list of Article 13(2) would consist in adding the design of the relevant product components as well as the availability of indispensable spare parts, repair information or repair services. Since more and more obligations on these aspects are established at EU and national levels, this amendment should not pose any problem in the proportionality test, but on the contrary, would strengthen the obligations imposed by other legal instruments.[2738] Third, Article 13(2) should be completed by an explicit reference to the potential environmental impacts caused by the chosen remedy. Although such an element is already implicitly included within the non-exhaustive list of Article 13[2739], this amendment would underline the importance of environmental protection in the proportionality test and restrict exceptions to the right to repair.[2740] In addition to these amendments, all the elements cited in Article 13(2) should be interpreted in a way that is consistent with the objective of environmental protection. For example, if the lack of conformity is not significant as required by Article 13(2)(b), repair should be preferred. A similar approach should be followed as regards the significant inconvenience to the consumer required by Article 13(2)(c).[2741]

783. Reducing the costs of repair – Like for the first exception of Article 13(2) relating to the impossibility of repairing the good[2742], the proposed amendments should be accompanied by the adoption of other rules so that repair becomes less disproportionate and costly compared to replacement. Besides rules improving product reparability (e.g. availability of spare parts), economic and fiscal measures could help lower repair costs. Interestingly, the VAT Directive allows reduced VAT rates to be applied to services of "*minor repairing of bicycles, shoes and leather goods, clothing and household linen (including mending and alteration)*".[2743] It is nonetheless regrettable that this possibility of reduced VAT rates does not cover a wider range of goods and services. Amending the VAT Directive should be envisaged to broaden the lists of goods and services with reduced VAT rates.[2744] Other initiatives have been taken by some Member States, like in Sweden, which adopted a 50% tax break for the repair of shoes, clothes

2738 Such obligations are imposed by ecodesign regulations and information rules, as developed in the previous chapters of this book.

2739 It is interesting to note, as an example, that the Norwegian Supreme Court stressed the environmental impacts of replacement to justify repair. See E. Maitre-Ekern and C. Dalhammar, 'A Scandinavian perspective on the role of consumers in the circular economy', in B. Keirsbilck and E. Terryn (eds.), *Consumer Protection in a Circular Economy* (Intersentia 2019) p. 201 at p. 224.

2740 Along the same line, see E. Terryn, 'A Right to Repair: Towards Sustainable Remedies in Consumer Law', *ERPL* (2019) p. 856.

2741 See also n° 794–796.

2742 See *supra*, n° 779.

2743 See Art. 98 of the VAT Directive, as well as Annex III, pt. 19 to the same Directive.

2744 Similar suggestions were made in RREUSE, *Improving product reparability: Policy options at EU level* (2015) p. 9.

and bicycles and allows consumers to claim back half the labour cost of product repair from income tax.[2745] It seems however unrealistic to impose a price on spare parts, as suggested in a Belgian proposal, which proposes to impose the availability of spare parts at a reasonable price, without exceeding 25% of the original sales price.[2746] Such measures requiring reasonable costs would, among others, threaten to distort free competition.[2747]

Proposed amendments of the SGD:

#15

Article 13
Remedies for lack of conformity

(...)

2. In order to have the goods brought into conformity, the consumer may choose between repair and replacement, unless the remedy chosen would be impossible or, compared to the other remedy, would impose costs on the seller that would be disproportionate, taking into account all circumstances, including:

(a) the value the goods would have if there were no lack of conformity;

(b) the significance of the lack of conformity;

(c) whether the alternative remedy could be provided without significant inconvenience to the consumer;

(d) substantial technical difficulties, economic costs or other risks involving the repair;

(e) the design of the relevant product components as well as the availability of indispensable spare parts, repair information or repair services; and

(f) the potential environmental impact caused by the chosen remedy.

(...)

2745 See E. Maitre-Ekern and C. Dalhammar, 'A Scandinavian perspective on the role of consumers in the circular economy', in B. Keirsbilck and E. Terryn (eds.), *Consumer Protection in a Circular Economy* (Intersentia 2019) p. 180.

2746 See Art. 23 Proposition de loi visant à lutter contre l'obsolescence organisée et à soutenir l'économie circulaire, *Doc. parl.*, Ch., 2019–2020, 7 janvier 2020, n° 0914/001.

2747 Avis du Conseil d'Etat du 21 février 2020 sur la Proposition de loi visant à lutter contre l'obsolescence programmée et à soutenir l'économie de la réparation (n° 0193/001), n° 66.909/1, p. 9.

(3) Repair modalities

784. Free of charge, within a reasonable period of time and without any significant inconvenience – When the consumer is entitled to choose repair and decides to do so, the seller is then required to repair the defective goods in accordance with the conditions laid down in Article 14 of the SGD. According to this provision, repair must be carried out (1) free of charge, (2) within a reasonable period of time and (3) with no significant inconvenience to the consumer. The aim is to avoid discouraging consumers from exercising their rights and to effectively protect them.[2748] These three modalities must be applied and interpreted in accordance with the obligation of due diligence, which applies both to consumers[2749] and sellers.[2750]

785. A double-edged sword that should not be neglected – Although these three conditions could encourage consumers to choose repair, it should not be forgotten that the exact same conditions are applicable to replacement. Consequently, consumers could just as well be tempted to opt for replacement having regard to these supportive modalities. The temptation is even higher considering other modalities specifically dedicated to and favouring replacement.[2751] The modalities set out in Article 14 would be more effective in fostering repair if repair was made the only remedy at the top of the hierarchy.[2752] As for future amendments to Article 14, an important point to bear in mind is that the conditions laid down in this provision should not be too burdensome on sellers. Otherwise, sellers could be unable to meet these conditions, leaving consumers with little choice but to ask for a proportionate reduction of the price or the termination of the contract.[2753]

(A) Free of charge

786. All necessary costs borne by the seller – The first condition given by Article 14 is that the remedy has to be carried out 'free of charge'. Article 2(14) of the SGD indicates that these terms must be understood as "*free of the necessary costs incurred in order to bring the goods into conformity, particularly the cost of postage, carriage, labour or materials*". The list is not exhaustive but illustrative, as shown

2748 ECJ 17 April 2008, C-404/06, *Quelle, EU:C:2008:231*, para 35.

2749 See ECJ 23 May 2019, Case C-52/18, *Fülla, EU:C:2019:447*, para 65.

2750 See also the Proposal for a Directive of the European Parliament and of the Council on Corporate Sustainability Due Diligence and amending Directive (EU) 2019/1937, COM(2022) 71 final. The EU Corporate Sustainability Due Diligence Directive would foster sustainable and responsible corporate behaviour throughout global value chains. See also European Parliament Report of 11 February 2021 with recommendations to the Commission on corporate due diligence and corporate accountability, (2020/2129(INL)).

2751 See for ex. Art. 14(4) SGD, which states that "*consumer [is] not be liable to pay for normal use made of the replaced goods during the period prior to their replacement*". For further comments on this provision, see *infra*, n° 807.

2752 See *supra*, n° 773.

2753 See Art. 13(4)(d) SGD. For more details, see also n° 811–817.

by the use of 'particularly'.[2754] Consequently, all necessary costs accompanying repair and replacement must be borne by the seller. This applies even if the lack of conformity is not the seller's own fault.[2755] The 'free of charge' requirement could even impose on the seller, who must bring the good into conformity, to bear the transport costs to the seller's place of business, if the fact that the consumer must advance these costs constitutes such a burden as to deter them from asserting their rights.[2756] For some consumers, these transport costs are indeed considered as real investment in prolonging the lifetime of their products and could inhibit their incentive to repair if those costs are too high.[2757] The aim of this first condition is "*to protect consumers from the risk of financial burdens which (...) might dissuade them from asserting their rights in the absence of such protection*".[2758] While it seems to strongly tilt the balance in favour of consumers, it should be borne in mind, as recalled by the ECJ[2759], that the seller's financial interests are protected by other mechanisms, including the two-year time-limit[2760], the right to refuse if disproportionate[2761], as well as the right of redress.[2762]

787. Payment made in advance by consumers – It is noteworthy that the SGD does not mention whether the consumer should advance the money and then be reimbursed by the seller, which could discourage the consumer from taking action.[2763] The ECJ shed light on this matter in the recent *Fülla* case, where it states that the fact that consumers must pay in advance does not systematically constitute a significant inconvenience.[2764] In other words, this judgement suggests that it is not contrary to the SGD to require consumers to pay in advance. Such reasoning might raise problems, depending on how the 'significant inconvenience' will be interpreted in practice.

788. A crucial requirement fostering repair and curbing economic obsolescence – The 'free of charge' requirement was said to be "*an essential*

2754 See in that sense ECJ 17 April 2008, C-404/06, *Quelle, EU:C:2008:231*, para 31.
2755 This rule is justified by the fact that by delivering a good not in conformity, the seller has not correctly performed their contractual obligation. ECJ 16 June 2011, Joined cases C-65/09 and C-87/09, *Weber and Putz, EU:C:2011:396*, paras 56 and 57.
2756 ECJ 23 May 2019, C-52/18, *Fülla, EU:C:2019:447*, para 56.
2757 D. Roux, *Obsolescence: ce qu'en disent les consommateurs* (PICO Working paper 2016), p. 8.
2758 ECJ 17 April 2008, C-404/06, *Quelle, EU:C:2008:231*, paras 33 and 34. Along the same line, see also ECJ 2 March 2017, C-568/15, *Zentrale zur Bekämpfung unlauteren Wettbewerbs Frankfurt am Main, EU:C:2017:154*, para 29.
2759 ECJ 16 June 2011, Joined cases C-65/09 and C-87/09, *Weber and Putz, EU:C:2011:396*, para 58.
2760 See *supra*, n° 729.
2761 See *supra*, n° 780.
2762 See *infra*, n° 821.
2763 C. Twigg-Flesner, 'The law on guarantees and repair work', in T. Cooper (ed.), *Longer lasting products – Alternatives to the throwaway society* (Gower Publishing Limited 2010) p. 200.
2764 ECJ 23 May 2019, C-52/18, *Fülla, EU:C:2019:447*, para 55.

element of the protection afforded to consumers by [the] directive".[2765] This statement is even more accurate within the context of premature obsolescence. Since repair is free of charge, consumers are encouraged to choose this option and even protected from cases of economic obsolescence[2766], which would have flourished in the absence of such requirement.[2767] Moreover, this requirement indirectly deters sellers and producers from shortening the lifetime of their products, at least during the first two years, as it would entail costs for them to repair or replace the products that are not in conformity. Arguably, those costs could ultimately lead the seller to increase their prices, passing on the costs to consumers.[2768] Such scenarios could also presumably occur in case of an extension of the legal guarantee.[2769] However, these higher prices would be compensated for by the fact that products would be made more durable and could be repair free of charge for a longer period. It has already been demonstrated that consumers are prepared to purchase more expensive products for such reasons.[2770]

(b) A reasonable period of time

789. Repairing the good within the shortest possible time necessary – The second requirement enshrined in Article 14 of the SGD imposes on the seller the obligation to carry out repair within a reasonable period of time from the moment of being informed by the consumer about the lack of conformity.[2771] This condition stems from the EU law makers aim to resolve any issues between the consumer and the seller in a speedy and amicable way.[2772] Recital 55 of the SGD defines 'reasonable time' as "*the shortest possible time necessary, considering the nature and complexity of the goods, the nature and severity of the lack of conformity, and the effort needed*

2765 ECJ 23 May 2019, Case C-52/18, *Fülla*, *EU:C:2019:447*, para 46.
2766 See *supra*, n° 117–118.
2767 In fact, repair costs are often disproportionate compared to the purchase of a new product. Repair costs can be high due to the sophisticated product design, the insufficient availability of spare parts at a reasonable cost, the need for special tools, and the labour-intensive work involved (n° 118). If consumers had to pay these costs when invoking their guarantee rights, they would be even more inclined to replace the defective product.
2768 See Opinion of Advocate General Wahl delivered on 15 January 2019 in ECJ 23 May 2019, C-52/18, *Fülla*, *EU:C:2019:447*, pt. 56.
2769 See for ex. reactions of business stakeholders in ICF, *Study on the costs and benefits of extending certain rights under the Consumer Sales and Guarantees Directive 1999/44/CE* (European Commission 2017) p. 36 at p. 39.
2770 See TNS Political & Social, *Flash Eurobarometer 367 – Attitudes of Europeans towards building the single market for green products* (European Commission 2013); SIRCOME agency, the University of South Brittany and the University of South Bohemia, *The Influence of Lifespan Labelling on Consumers – ILLC study* (EESC 2016); LE Europe, VVA Europe, Ipsos, ConPolicy, Trinomics, *Behavioural study on consumers' engagement in the circular economy* (European Commission 2018).
2771 Art. 14(1)(b) SGD.
2772 Proposal for a European Parliament and Council Directive on the sale of consumer goods and associated guarantees, COM(95) 520 final, pp. 14–15.

to complete repair or replacement".[2773] Some guidelines for the interpretation of this notion were also given in *Fülla* case.[2774] The Court underlined that the seller does not comply with this obligation if "*[he] does not take any appropriate steps, at the very least, to inspect the goods not in conformity, including the obligation to inform the consumer, within a reasonable time, of the place where the goods not in conformity are to be made available to him to be brought into conformity*".[2775] Moreover, the Court emphasized the need for the consumer to make some efforts sometimes, for example by bringing the defective good to the seller at their place of business.[2776]

790. With the possibility of establishing a fixed period under national law – Member States are entitled to provide for a fixed period of time in their legislation.[2777] Several Member States made use of this possibility, with a timeframe varying from 15 days to one month or even 45 days.[2778] In France, Article L. 217–10 of the Consumer Code specifies a time-limit of one month within which repair (or replacement) is to be completed. This time-limit starts from the day following the consumer's claim. If the deadline cannot be met, the consumer is entitled to demand the termination of the contract or a proportionate reduction of the price. The Anti-Waste Law complemented this provision by offering consumers the possibility to request the replacement of the concerned product and additionally obtaining a renewed guarantee, if repair is not achieved within the time-limit or if the seller refuses to do so.[2779] Hence, consumers who would have favoured repair in the first place are granted a third attractive option if they encounter difficulties in implementing their first choice. Such legislation could admittedly encourage consumers to opt for repair, though the effectiveness of this provision in that sense greatly depends on its implementation, and more particularly on the fact that repair is not too easily abandoned. Otherwise, it would considerably facilitate replacement. By contrast, there is currently no time limit specified under Belgian and German law to achieve repair. Instead, contracting parties are recommended to fix a deadline and to move to a refund solution if the deadline is not met.

791. A crucial requirement for repair that could be improved – This second requirement is among the provisions of the SGD that (could) play an

[2773] This constitutes an improvement compared to the former CSD, which gave no definition of the notion, leaving considerable uncertainty for consumers. The issue had been raised in BEUC, Position Paper of 3 June 2016 on the Proposal for a Directive on certain aspects concerning contracts for distance sales of goods, BEUC-X-2016–053, p. 12.

[2774] ECJ 23 May 2019, Case C-52/18, *Fülla, EU:C:2019:447.*

[2775] *Ibid.*, para 66.

[2776] *Ibid.*, para 37.

[2777] See recital 55 SGD.

[2778] ICF, *Study on the costs and benefits of extending certain rights under the Consumer Sales and Guarantees Directive 1999/44/CE* (European Commission 2017) p. 18.

[2779] See Art. L. 217–13 of the French Consumer Code, which was introduced by Art. 22 of the Anti-Waste Law. See *supra*, n° 748.

essential role in promoting reparable and longer-lasting products. In fact, if consumers are guaranteed repair within reasonable time, they will be encouraged to choose this option in case of faulty goods.[2780] On the business side, traders are urged to improve the reparability of their products to satisfy this condition. Yet, the most serious weakness of this provision is the subjective nature of the notion of 'reasonable time', leaving significant room for discretion to the seller when no fixed period has been set out under national law. Such legal uncertainty might deter consumers from choosing repair. The fixed period established by some Member States solves this issue, though creating disparities between Member States.

792. A FIXED AND HARMONISED TIMEFRAME SHOULD BE PROVIDED AT EU LEVEL – To bring an end to this legal uncertainty and these national divergences, it would be preferable to go beyond a mere definition of 'reasonable time' and provide for a fixed and harmonised timeframe in the SGD. This idea was suggested during the adoption process of the Directive. Whereas the EESC proposed establishing a 15-day period as applied in some EU countries[2781], focusing especially on repair[2782], the EP held the view that repair[2783] as well as replacement[2784] should be completed within one month. It seems more reasonable – at least as a first step – to impose a one-month period for the completion of the remedy (see #16). Of course, this requirement should be interpreted in accordance with the principle of due diligence and good faith (e.g. in case of force majeure), as already highlighted. This would be coherent with ecodesign regulations, which oblige producers of certain products, like dishwashers and televisions, to ensure the delivery of the spare parts within 15 working days after having received the request of the professional seller or repairer.[2785]

2780 Indeed, it has been demonstrated that repair time constitutes one of factors causing dissatisfaction among consumers. See for ex. TNS Qual+, *Sales remedies – Qualitative Eurobarometer Study* (European Commission 2009) p. 56; Ellen MacArthur Foundation, *Empowering repair* (2016) p. 9.

2781 Opinion of the European Economic and Social Committee on the 'Proposal for a directive of the European Parliament and of the Council on certain aspects concerning contracts for the supply of digital content' (COM(2015) 634 final) and the 'Proposal for a directive of the European Parliament and of the Council on certain aspects concerning contracts for the online and other distance sales of goods' (COM(2015) 635 final, OJ C 264, 20.7.2016, p. 63, pt. 4.2.5.7, para 2.

2782 Opinion of the European Economic and Social Committee on the 'Amended proposal for a Directive of the European Parliament and of the Council on certain aspects concerning contracts for the sales of goods, amending Regulation (EC) No 2006/2004 of the European Parliament and of the Council and Directive 2009/22/EC of the European Parliament and of the Council and repealing Directive 1999/44/EC of the European Parliament and of the Council' (COM(2017) 637 final), OJ C 227, 28.6.2018, p. 61, pt. 3.4. c).

2783 Amendment 95 of the Report on the amended proposal for a directive of the European Parliament and of the Council on certain aspects concerning contracts for the sales of goods, amending Regulation (EC) No 2006/2004 of the European Parliament and of the Council and Directive 2009/22/EC of the European Parliament and of the Council and repealing Directive 1999/44/EC of the European Parliament and of the Council, COM(2017) 637, p. 45.

2784 *Ibid.*, p. 46, amendment 97.

2785 See *supra*, n° 260.

793. Together with other measures – Other accompanying measures should be adopted in support of this provision to ensure repair within a reasonable period of time. Otherwise, it could paradoxically produce adverse effects on repair. A too short timeframe might indeed be too difficult for the seller to comply with[2786], constraining consumers to instead claim one of the subsidiary remedies.[2787] As already underlined, a series of measures should be adopted to lessen the effort needed to complete repair. First, measures should be taken to reduce the complexity of consumer goods, which is one of the factors delaying the repair process. This could be done through ecodesign implementing measures[2788], or soft law, like labels, which could establish additional product and information requirements for specific product categories already covered by such rules, as well as for other products not yet covered.[2789] Second, rules should require the availability of spare parts, repair and product information as well as other necessary tools.[2790] Alongside these measures, the suspension of the guarantee period should be envisaged in order to counter repair waiting periods and reflect the circular value of a repaired good.[2791]

Proposed amendment to the SGD:

#16

Article 14
Repair or replacement of the goods

1. Repairs or replacements shall be carried out:

(...)

(b) within ~~a reasonable period of time~~ <u>one month</u> from the moment the seller has been informed by the consumer about the lack of conformity; and

(...)

2786 Especially when the faulty product must be passed on to the service centre of the producer (on which the seller has no control).

2787 See Art. 13(4) and recital 50 SGD.

2788 See *supra*, n° 265–271.

2789 See *supra*, n° III.F.4.a)-614.

2790 Certain Belgian legislative proposals suggest imposing obligations on producers and importers to provide indispensable software updates, repair information (including drawings and models of the products), necessary repair tools, diagnostic instruments and the like within a reasonable period (which can be determined by the King or equivalent to the conformity period communicated by the producer) and at a reasonable cost. See Art. 6 Proposition de loi visant à lutter contre l'obsolescence programmée et à soutenir l'économie de la réparation, *Doc. Parl.*, Ch., 2019, 19 juillet 2019, n° 0193/001; Art. 11 Proposition de loi modifiant le Code civil et le Code de droit économique, visant à lutter contre l'obsolescence programmée et l'obsolescence prématurée et à augmenter les possibilités de réparation, *Doc. Parl.*, Ch., 2019–2020, 19 novembre 2019, n° 0771/001.

2791 See *supra*, n° 750.

(c) No significant inconvenience

794. No inconvenience in general, including practical obstacles and financial inconvenience – Thirdly, Article 14 of the SGD requires the seller not to cause any significant inconvenience to the consumer when bringing the good into conformity.[2792] In *Weber and Putz*, the ECJ gave a broad interpretation to these terms, not restricting them to the delivery obligation.[2793] In this regard, the Court followed the view of its Advocate General in *Quelle*, who asserted that "*the terms 'significant inconvenience' covers not only practical obstacles to replacing goods but also inconvenience in general, and financial 'inconvenience' is an additional inconvenience which (...) can be even more significant than the practical obstacles*".[2794]

795. But not excluding insignificant or minor inconveniences – Nonetheless, it does not mean that there cannot be any inconvenience for consumers. As highlighted by the Advocate General in *Fülla*, consumers "*must (...) accept insignificant or minor inconveniences in having goods repaired or replaced*".[2795] Hence, consumers may be required to invest some time and effort in order to bring the good into conformity.[2796] The only condition is that the inconvenience cannot be 'significant', meaning that it would constitute a "*burden likely to deter the average consumer from asserting his rights*".[2797] According to Article 14(1)(c) of the SGD, the assessment of whether the inconvenience is 'significant' depends on the nature of the goods and the purpose for which the consumer required the goods. This assessment must be made based on the objective standard of the kind of burden that would dissuade the average consumer.[2798]

796. Minimizing inconveniences by providing for a substitute product – Whereas consumers should be prepared to deal with some inconvenience when choosing repair, these should be avoided, or at least minimized, as much as possible. Otherwise, it may discourage consumers from claiming repair. A measure that could contribute to making repair less inconvenient would be to entitle consumers to borrow a (potentially used) replacement good from

2792 Art. 14(1)(c) SGD.

2793 ECJ 16 June 2011, Joined cases C-65/09 and C-87/09, *Weber and Putz, EU:C:2011:396,* para 53. See also

2794 Opinion of Advocate General Trstenjak delivered on 15 November 2007 in ECJ 17 April 2008, C-404/06, *Quelle, EU:C:2008:231,* pt. 47.

2795 Opinion of Advocate General Wahl delivered on 15 January 2019 in ECJ 23 May 2019, Case C-52/18, *Fülla, EU:C:2019:447,* pt. 64.

2796 This can be considered as part of the duty of due diligence (n° 784).

2797 ECJ 23 May 2019, Case C-52/18, *Fülla, EU:C:2019:447,* para 40.

2798 Opinion of Advocate General Wahl delivered on 15 January 2019 in ECJ 23 May 2019, Case C-52/18, *Fülla, EU:C:2019:447,* pt. 68.

the seller or retailer during the repair process against deposit.[2799] One could easily imagine the inconvenience caused by the lack of certain products when they are sent somewhere for repair. Consumers could be deprived of goods that they really need in their daily life, such as mobile phones, washing machines or cars.[2800] Having access to a substitute product during the whole repair process could fill the gap left by the defect. Such a suggestion was made by the EESC during the adoption process of the SGD, stating that there should be a temporary replacement while waiting for the product to be repaired.[2801] This suggestion was ultimately not integrated into the provisions of the Directive. Interestingly, one of the three Belgian legislative proposals encourages professionals to provide for substitutes goods when the defective good is being repaired by prolonging the time-limit during which repair is to be completed (from seven days to two months).[2802] Following this idea, one could imagine having a fixed and harmonised one-month period for completing repair, with the possibility of prolonging it to two months if a substitute good is provided (see #17).[2803]

Proposed amendment to the SGD:

#17

Article 14
Repair or replacement of the goods

1. Repairs or replacements shall be carried out:

(…)

(b) within ~~a reasonable period of time~~ one month (or two months if a substitute good is provided to the consumer) from the moment the seller has been informed by the consumer about the lack of conformity; and

(…)

2799 See T. Libaert, *Pour une consommation plus durable en phase avec les enjeux européens* (2018) p. 56; Avis du Conseil Central de l'Economie du 3 septembre 2019 sur la transposition de directives européennes concernant la vente aux consommateurs tant de biens que de contenus et services numériques, CCE 2019-1660, p. 15.

2800 Consumers have already expressed their wish to be offered a temporary replacement product for the time that it takes to repair the defective item. See TNS Qual+, *Sales remedies – Qualitative Eurobarometer Study* (European Commission 2009) p. 54.

2801 *Ibid.*, pt. 4.2.5.7., p. 64, para 6.

2802 Art. 8 Proposition de loi visant à lutter contre l'obsolescence organisée et à soutenir l'économie circulaire, *Doc. parl.*, Ch., 2019–2020, 7 janvier 2020, n° 0914/001, p. 27.

2803 See *supra*, n° 792.

(d) Supplementary repair modalities

797. The location where consumers should make the good available – Article 14 of the SGD contains two additional rules that may direct consumer choice towards repair. First, according to Article 14(2), when implementing one of the primary remedies, the consumer has to make the goods available to the seller. And the seller has to take back the replaced goods at their expense. These operations have to satisfy the first modalities of Article 14, meaning that they should be free of charge, within a reasonable period of time and without significant inconvenience to the consumer. The location where consumers should make the good available is left to national law, provided that a high level of consumer protection is ensured, and the triple requirements established by Article 14(1) are fulfilled.[2804] This clarification is even more important for distance sales contracts, which was the case in *Fülla*. The nature of the product and its intended use by an average consumer must be considered in assessing whether the chosen place is suitable. It will therefore depends on the specific circumstances of each cases.[2805] For example, it might be significantly inconvenient to bring the defective good to the place of the seller if the good is heavy, large and fragile or has been installed at the consumer's place.[2806] To reduce cases with significant inconveniences and improve legal certainty, it has been suggested to oblige the seller to pick up the product and bring it back to consumers once repaired if the defect appears during the presumption period (especially for large household appliances).[2807] Questions remain on the feasibility of such an idea in the case of distance selling, especially when the good has been acquired on online marketplaces. Furthermore, obligations should not be too burdensome for sellers, otherwise repair could be seen as disproportionate (e.g. due to the distance or shipping costs incurred).[2808]

798. The removal of goods – Article 14(3) of the Directive establishes a second obligation that may foster repair, that is the removal of the defective goods by the seller. According to this provision, where a repair requires the removal of goods that had been installed in a manner consistent with their nature and purpose before the lack of conformity became apparent, or where such goods are to be replaced, the obligation to repair (or replace) the goods includes the removal of the non-conforming goods, and the installation of (replacement)

2804 Recital 56 SGD. See also ECJ 23 May 2019, Case C-52/18, *Fülla, EU:C:2019:447*, para 33.

2805 ECJ 23 May 2019, Case C-52/18, *Fülla, EU:C:2019:447*, para 45.

2806 ECJ 23 May 2019, Case C-52/18, *Fülla, EU:C:2019:447*, paras 43–44.

2807 See T. Libaert, *Pour une consommation plus durable en phase avec les enjeux européens* (2018) p. 54.

2808 See also on that sense G. Izquierdo Grau, 'Where should the consumer make goods available to the seller to bring them into conformity? An appraisal of Directive (EU) 2019/771', 1 *EuCML* (2020) p. 31 at p. 34.

or repaired goods, or bearing the costs of that removal and installation. That obligation on the seller exists regardless of whether they were obliged under the contract of sale to install the consumer goods originally purchased.[2809]

799. The consumer right to withhold payment – In addition to the modalities laid down in Article 14 of the SGD, Article 13(6) states that consumers should be entitled to withhold the payment of any outstanding part of the price or a part thereof until the seller has fulfilled their obligations. Such right could be used as means of pressure to bring the good into conformity through repair. It is for Member States to determine the conditions and modalities under which this right can be exercised. This consumer right could support and facilitate repair, though it depends on the way Member States regulate this aspect under national law.

800. The right to carry out repair by a person other than the seller – Recital 54 of the SGD also allows Member States to regulate the conditions under which the performance of the debtor can be fulfilled by another person. This includes the conditions under which the seller's obligation to repair a good can be performed by the consumer or a third party at the seller's expense. The right to repair would be facilitated if consumers and independent repairers could be more easily involved. This recital leaves many opportunities to further stimulate the independent repair industry and DIY repair initiatives. It is interesting to note that, for certain specific sectors, the legal guarantee rules on repair have been further developed at national level. For example, in Belgium, specific rules have been adopted for the automotive sector.[2810] When repair or maintenance of cars is made by a repairer outside the producer's network, Belgian law stresses that the legal guarantee should remain applicable.[2811] These provisions are to be combined with the provisions of the SGD. If these rules are inconsistent with each other, the legislation affording the highest degree of protection for consumers should prevail.[2812]

801. Making 'circular' spare parts available to consumers – In addition to these conditions explicitly mentioned in the SGD, the French Anti-Waste Law introduced an obligation for professionals who maintain and repair certain goods (such as electrical and electronic appliances) to offer consumers the possibility of opting for spare parts coming from the circular economy instead

2809 ECJ 16 June 2011, Joined cases C-65/09 and C-87/09, *Weber and Putz*.

2810 Arrêté royal du 5 avril 2019 relatif aux contrats de vente de véhicules automoteurs, *M.B.*, 8 mai 2019, p. 44214.

2811 Art. 6 §2, 11° Arrêté royal du 5 avril 2019 relatif aux contrats de vente de véhicules automoteurs, *M.B.*, 8 mai 2019, p. 44214.

2812 See Y. Van Couter et al., 'La vente aux consommateurs après la loi du 1er septembre 2004', 3 *Revue de la Faculté de droit de l'Université de Liège* (2005) p. 386.

of new parts.[2813] This provision extends the scope of Article L. 224–67 of the French Consumer Code which, since 2016, allows consumers to ask automobile professionals to repair or maintain their vehicles using second-hand rather than new spare parts, except for example when those spare parts are not (quickly) available or pose some risks.[2814] A list of the spare parts and products concerned has yet to be established by the Council of State, as well as the definition of 'parts coming from the circular economy' and the conditions under which professionals would be exempted from this obligation (e.g. unavailability or other legitimate reasons).[2815] Information obligations on this possibility should also be established, like in the legislation on cars[2816], though the decree has not been adopted yet. In the event of a dispute, Article L. 224–109 clarifies that it is for the professional to prove that they performed their obligations. Sanctions for traders not complying with Article L. 224–109 consist of an administrative fine not exceeding € 3000 for a natural person and € 15000 for a legal person.[2817] This new provision of the French Consumer Code makes repair even more sustainable, though its effectiveness will greatly depend on the implementing decree. Hence, before following suit at EU level, it is recommended first to observe and examine these measures once implemented and applied at the French level and then draw conclusions from the French experience.

b) Other (less sustainable) remedies

802. Three other remedies in the hierarchy – Besides repair, there are three other remedies provided for by the SDG, namely replacement, the adequate reduction of the price and the termination of the contract. As already highlighted, repair is the most sustainable remedy and should be privileged and facilitated in case of defect.[2818] Yet, repair does not have to be the sole remedy available to consumers. Other remedies may also contribute to product sustainability. It is therefore important to improve the sustainability of the three remaining remedies in case repair is not a valid option.[2819]

2813 Art. L. 224–109 of the French Consumer Code, which was introduced by Art. 19 II of the Anti-Waste Law.

2814 Art. R. 121–27 of Décret n° 2016–703 du 30 mai 2016 relatif à l'utilisation de pièces de rechange automobiles issues de l'économie circulaire, JORF n°0125 du 31 mai 2016.

2815 Art. L. 224–109 of the French Consumer Code.

2816 Arrêté du 8 octobre 2018 relatif à l'information du consommateur sur les prix et les conditions de vente des pièces issues de l'économie circulaire dans le cadre des prestations d'entretien ou de réparation des véhicules automobiles, JORF n°0236 du 12 octobre 2018.

2817 Article L. 242–46 of the French Consumer Code.

2818 See *supra*, n° 647 and n° 770 *et seq.*

2819 This can happen if the product cannot be repaired, if the repair costs are disproportionate for the seller or if this remedy is simply not chosen by the consumer (see *infra*).

(1) Replacement

803. The second primary remedy, next to repair – According to the current hierarchy, replacement is the second primary remedy that consumers could opt for. Consumers who are not willing to repair their defective product can thus require the seller to replace it instead – even when the good is repairable. It is interesting to note that it had been initially considered to offer replacement as an option only during the first year after the delivery of the good.[2820] This would have forced consumers to act as agents of change taking sustainable decisions but issues of non-acceptance, non-reasonableness and inefficiency could arise. Less radical measures are possible to discourage consumers from choosing replacement, as developed below.[2821]

804. Replacement accelerates product obsolescence, except if circular – The freedom of choice between repair and replacement does not solve the problem of products becoming prematurely obsolete, quite the contrary. As already emphasized, replacement can have huge environmental impacts, especially if the replacement good is made of new materials and if the replaced good is immediately disposed of.[2822] These impacts are significantly reduced if the good lacking conformity is replaced by a repaired, refurbished or remanufactured good that meets all conformity criteria. Moreover, if the replaced good itself is whenever possible subsequently repaired, refurbished or remanufactured, its resource and energy value is also preserved, and it can later be resold or reused in a similar 'circular replacement'. The 'circular replacement' remedy combines the sustainability benefits of a repair with the speed of a replacement.

805. The possibility of offering circular replacement allowed by the SGD – A 'circular replacement' is already possible based on the current provisions of the SGD.[2823] In light of the theoretical coherence of this Directive, replacement should be interpreted as akin to repair. Hence, the criterion is whether the replacement meets all contractually applicable conformity requirements. If a repaired, refurbished or remanufactured good satisfies these requirements and could initially have been delivered[2824], it should be possible

2820 Art. 3(4) of the Proposal for a European Parliament and Council Directive on the sale of consumer goods and associated guarantees, COM(95)520 final, OJ C 307, 16.10.1996, p. 8–11.

2821 See *infra*, n° 807–810.

2822 See *supra*, n° 646.

2823 E. Van Gool and A. Michel, 'The New Consumer Sales Directive 2019/771 and Sustainable Consumption: A Critical Analysis', 10 *EuCML* (2021) p. 146.

2824 This is especially likely for properly 'remanufactured' goods, which by definition aim to recreate goods as good as 'new goods' that are entirely manufactured based on new components and virgin resources. See G.D. Hatcher, W.L. Ijomah and J.F.C. Windmill,

to offer it as a replacement remedy. This interpretation is also supported by Article 11 TFEU.

806. The consumer right to replace with new goods – However, at present, circular replacement is far from being promoted, especially having regard to the case law of some Member States. A Dutch court has already twice held that consumers are entitled to replacement by a new good instead of a refurbished one.[2825] Along the same lines, in a Danish case *David Lysgaard v. Apple*, the Danish Consumer Complaints Board (*Forbrugerklagenævnet*) asserted that consumers have a right to a new replacement device rather than a refurbished one or to a full refund of the purchase price.[2826] No consideration was given to the environmental benefits of circular replacement. Instead, the decision was based on the fact that the economic value of a phone containing refurbished parts may be lower than the value of an entirely new phone, even if it has the same appearance, function and life expectancy.[2827] From a sustainability perspective, this is regrettable. Although quality concerns may be raised for certain refurbished goods[2828], rejecting circular replacements on the sole basis of the repaired, refurbished or remanufactured nature of the part or product is not the correct approach.

807. No compensation obligation for consumers in case of replacement – The ECJ had already indicated in *Quelle* that in the event of the right to replacement being exercised, consumers may not be required to pay compensation for using the defective good until its replacement with the new good.[2829] This principle is now enshrined in Article 14(4) of the SGD. Allowing sellers to do so would have been a problem for products which depreciate quickly in value, including due to functional obsolescence.[2830] However, although the decision of the ECJ in *Quelle* was well-intentioned from a consumer protection perspective, it disproportionately encourages replacement and is economically unfair to both sellers and consumers choosing repair.[2831]

'Design for remanufacture: a literature review and future research needs', 19 *J. Clean. Prod.* (2011) p. 2004.

2825 Rb Amsterdam 8 July 2016, *NL:RBAMS:2016:4197*, TvC 2017/4, 183 case note V. MAK; Rb Amsterdam 18 April 2017, *NL:RBAMS:2017:2519*.

2826 K. Kryla-Cudna, 'Sales Contracts and the Circular Economy', 28 *E.R.P.L.* (2020) p. 1223; D. Watson et al., *Circular Business Models in the Mobile Phone Industry* (TemaNord 2017) p. 58.

2827 *Ibid.*

2828 See e.g. a 2016 study by Test-Achats, which found that half of the (18) tested refurbished iPhones showed important defects, while only one phone (refurbished by Apple) was flawless: <www.test-aankoop.be/hightech/gsmsen-smartphones/nieuws/een-op-twee-refurbished-iphones-deugt-niet>.

2829 ECJ 17 April 2008, C-404/06, *Quelle, EU:C:2008:231*, para 43.

2830 See in this regard the Opinion of Advocate General Trstenjak delivered on 15 November 2007 in ECJ 17 April 2008, C-404/06, *Quelle, EU:C:2008:231*, pt. 49.

2831 E. Van Gool and A. Michel, 'The New Consumer Sales Directive 2019/771 and Sustainable Consumption: A Critical Analysis', 10 *EuCML* (2021) p. 145.

808. Replaced products should be correctly handled – Establishing replacement as the second primary remedy of the hierarchy would be less problematic if it was more sustainable, though it could hardly be as sustainable as repair. The first measure to be taken to improve replacement sustainability consists in requiring sellers to correctly handle replaced products. This could be done through the SGD or any other EU legislation.[2832] Such legislation would, at least to some extent, lessen the negative impacts of the limited lifetime of the replaced product on the environment. This kind of measure has been adopted in France where, since 1 January 2022, the destruction of new non-food products is prohibited. Producers, importers and distributors of new non-food products intended for sale are required to reuse (including by donation to charity organisations) or recycle their unsold goods.[2833]

809. Repaired, refurbished or remanufactured products should be promoted – Second, replacement by products that have been repaired, refurbished or remanufactured should figure prominently in the hierarchy of remedies.[2834] As there is no definition of 'replacement' in the SGD, nothing requires that replacement should involve identical products.[2835] Other EU legislation confirms this reasoning and emphasizes that defective products could be replaced by already used, repaired, refurbished or remanufactured good as long as these would have been initially acceptable according to the contractual conformity requirements.[2836] Hence, like for repair, the provisions of the SGD should make it clear that repaired, refurbished or remanufactured goods can be used to replace a defective product, provided that they have the same value as the replaced product (see #18). The value of these products could be determined through their compliance with ecodesign requirements that would be specifically dedicated to these products, as previously proposed in the second chapter of this book.[2837] Such clarifications regarding repaired,

---

2832 Such requirements could, for example, be set out in waste legislation if replaced products are deemed to fall within the definition of waste or in the UCPD through the introduction of a new prohibition in the blacklist.

2833 See Art. L. 541-15-8, which was introduced by Art. 35 of the Anti-Waste Law. For further comments, see Chapter V on the end-of-life stage (n° 939).

2834 E. Maitre-Ekern, C. Dalhammar, 'Towards a hierarchy of consumption behaviour in the circular economy', 26 *Maastricht Journal of European and Comparative Law* (2019) pp. 419–420.

2835 G. Howells, C. Twigg-Flesner T. Wilhelmsson, *Rethinking Eu Consumer Law* (Routledge 2017) p. 189.

2836 See Art. 2(31) of the Regulation (EU) 2017/745 of the European Parliament and of the Council of 5 April 2017 on medical devices, amending Directive 2001/83/EC, Regulation (EC) No 178/2002 and Regulation (EC) No 1223/2009 and repealing Council Directives 90/385/EEC and 93/42/EEC, OJ L 117, 5.5.2017, p. 1–175. According to this provision, fully refurbishing a device means "*the complete rebuilding of a device already placed on the market or put into service, or the making of a new device from used devices, to bring it into conformity with this Regulation, combined with the assignment of a new lifetime to the refurbished device*".

2837 See *supra*, n° 188.

refurbished or remanufactured goods would adjust national implementation of this legislation.[2838]

E. Terryn has also suggested – as a compromise solution that balances consumer protection interests and sustainability – to oblige sellers to give a new guarantee period in the case of replacement with a repaired, refurbished or remanufactured good.[2839] This idea merits further consideration at EU level, though less drastic measures (e.g. the suspension of the guarantee period during the repair process) should first be taken as an intermediary step.[2840] In any event, the renewal of the guarantee period should be accompanied by other measures to strike a fair balance with the interests of sellers (e.g. direct producer liability). Otherwise, such a bonus extension could create a moral hazard for the seller to avoid such replacement.

810. Consumers should be charged in case of replacement by a new good – In addition to these measures fostering sustainable replacement, it is also important to offset the imbalance between repair and replacement. Whereas replacement allows consumers to receive for free a good with an entirely reset lifespan, repair includes a quality risk and even high-quality repairs can result in goods with shorter remaining lifespans than newly produced goods.[2841] Because of these differences, repair is currently only attractive to a minority of consumers with strong environmental motivations or emotional attachment to certain goods. Even then, their choice may be restricted.[2842] Therefore, Article 14(4) of the SGD should be reversed: sellers should be entitled to charge consumers for prior use when offering new goods as replacements (see #19).[2843] This compensation could be calculated following the same reasoning as the one applicable to the right of withdrawal when consumers make use of goods acquired under a distance contract before returning.[2844] Logically, this charge for prior use would not be possible in case of a replacement by a repaired, refurbished or remanufactured instead of a new good, as discussed in the previous paragraph. Indeed, such replacements create no – or at least a smaller – imbalance with repair.

2838 See also D. Watson et al., *Circular Business Models in the Mobile Phone Industry* (TemaNord 2017) p. 74.

2839 See E. Terryn, 'A Right to Repair: Towards Sustainable Remedies in Consumer Law', *ERPL* (2019) p. 858.

2840 See *supra*, n° 750.

2841 E. Van Gool and A. Michel, 'The New Consumer Sales Directive 2019/771 and Sustainable Consumption: A Critical Analysis', 10 *EuCML* (2021) p. 144.

2842 See *supra*, n° 770 *et seq.*

2843 E. Van Gool and A. Michel, 'The New Consumer Sales Directive 2019/771 and Sustainable Consumption: A Critical Analysis', 10 *EuCML* (2021) p. 145.

2844 See Art. 14(2) CRD. See also ECJ 3 September 2009, Case C-489/07, *Pia Messner*, *EU:C:2009:502*.

Proposed amendments to the SGD:

#18

Article 2
Definitions

For the purposes of this Directive, the following definitions apply:

(...)

<u>(17) 'replacement' means the remediation by the seller of a lack of conformity by providing to the consumer a good, which can be a repaired, refurbished or remanufactured good, that conforms with the sales contract.</u>

AND *#19*

Article 14
Repair or replacement of the goods

(...)

4. The consumer shall_not be liable to<u> pay a fair compensation </u>for normal use made of the replaced goods during the period prior to their replacement.

(2) Subsidiary remedies

811. Two subsidiary remedies, favoured in four cases – The proportionate reduction of the price and the termination of the sales contract are relegated to a subsidiary rank in the hierarchy of remedies.[2845] These two remedies are characterized by a mutual surrender of the benefits of the contract.[2846] While price reduction consists in receiving a reduction in the price proportionate to the decrease in the value of the goods which were received by the consumer compared to the value the goods would have if they were in conformity[2847], the termination of the sales contract obliges the parties to return what they have received (the seller refunds the price received from the consumer and the consumer returns the good).[2848] Member States remain free to regulate

2845 Note that it is always possible for the contracting parties to derogate from this hierarchy if consumer and seller agree on a remedy.

2846 Opinion of Advocate General Mazak delivered on 18 May 2010 for Case C-65/09, *Weber*, in ECJ 16 June 2011, Joined cases C-65/09 and C-87/09, *Weber and Putz*, pt. 48; and et Opinion of Advocate General Mazak delivered on 18 May 2010 for Case et C-87/09, Putz in ECJ 16 June 2011, Joined cases C-65/09 and C-87/09, *Weber and Putz*, pt. 49.

2847 Art. 15 SGD.

2848 Art. 16 and recital 59 SGD.

the modalities for reimbursement of the price to the consumer (e.g. decrease in product value, costs and fees incurred, time limits, etc.).[2849] Nevertheless, the SGD facilitates the shift towards subsidiary remedies in four cases[2850], which are enumerated in Article 13(4) of the Directive.

812. First: where the seller has not attempted and refused to bring the good into conformity – There are, first, cases where the seller has not attempted and refused to bring the good into conformity, either because it was impossible, disproportionate or for any other reasons connected to him.[2851] The right to refuse includes the scenario whereby either repair or replacement is impossible and the alternative remedy would impose disproportionate costs on the seller.[2852] Recital 49 mentions also the case where goods are located in a place that is different from where they were originally delivered, which could incur disproportionate costs of postage and carriage for the seller. The fact that it is for the seller to assess and make a decision could be problematic in some cases as it could increase cases where the right to repair is denied.

813. Second: in case of recurrent defect – Second, the SGD offers consumers the possibility to opt for a subsidiary remedy when they are faced with 'recurrent defect', i.e. when the seller has taken action to bring the good into conformity, but a lack of conformity becomes apparent subsequently.[2853] The formulation seems to include cases where another new lack of conformity – different from the first one – appears.[2854] The rationale of this provision is that in these cases, the consumer has lost confidence that the trader/seller will still bring the products into conformity.[2855] When determining whether the consumer should accept further attempts by the seller to remedy the lack of conformity, all the circumstances should be taken into account, such as the type and the value of the goods, and the nature and the significance of the lack of conformity.[2856] For example, for expensive and complex products, it could be justified to allow the seller another attempt. By contrast, it should not be the case in situations where the same problem appears twice or where the lack of conformity is of such a serious nature. While Article 13(4)(b) is welcome from a consumer protection perspective, this provision also leads to reducing the number of cases

2849 Recital 60 SGD.

2850 See also D. Staudenmayer, 'The Directives on Digital Contracts: First Steps Towards the Private Law of the Digital economy', 28 *E.R.P.L.* (2020) pp. 244–245.

2851 Art. 13(4)(a) SGD. See also *supra*, n° 777–783.

2852 Recital 49 SGD.

2853 Art. 13(4)(b) SGD.

2854 This broad scope runs counter to what has been suggested by some scholars. See G. Howells, C. Twigg-Flesner T. Wilhelmsson, *Rethinking Eu Consumer Law* (Routledge 2017) p. 187.

2855 D. Staudenmayer, 'The Directives on Digital Contracts: First Steps Towards the Private Law of the Digital economy', 28 *E.R.P.L.* (2020) p. 246.

2856 Recital 52 SGD.

where the defective products will be repaired. Moreover, as highlighted by D. Staudenmayer, this provision is drafted in a rather vague manner and, despite the explanations and examples provided in recital 52, is likely to give raise to interpretation issues.[2857]

814. Third: in case of serious lack of conformity – Third, consumers are entitled to opt for a subsidiary remedy if the lack of conformity is of such a serious nature as to justify an immediate price reduction or the termination of the sales contract.[2858] There is, however, no indication on how to determine the seriousness of a lack of conformity. If these terms were too broadly interpreted, it could lead consumers to overlook their right to repair and directly turn to subsidiary remedies. As an example, one could think of cases of greenwashing, like the *Dieselgate* cases, where price reduction or the termination of the contract may be the only appropriate remedies. However, if repair is possible in such cases, this remedy should be preferred from a sustainability perspective.[2859]

815. By contrast with a minor lack of conformity – The consumer is however not entitled to terminate the contract when the lack of conformity is only minor, as stated in Article 13(5) of the SGD.[2860] It is for the seller to prove that the lack of conformity is minor.[2861] In that case, consumers may still benefit from the right to seek an appropriate reduction in the price of these goods.[2862] It is interesting to note that Germany has a formal approach to cases of minor defects. In a landmark case, the German Federal Court of Justice (*Bundesgerichtshof*) held that, as a general rule, a defect cannot be deemed 'minor' when remedying this defect would cost more than 5% of the purchase price of the good.[2863]

816. Fourth: in case of explicit or tacit declaration by the trader – Fourth, subsidiary remedies could be chosen instead of the primary remedies if there is an explicit or tacit declaration by the trader that he would not bring the goods into conformity within a reasonable time or without major inconvenience to the consumer.[2864] In *Fülla*, the ECJ underlined that the obligation on the seller

---

2857 D. Staudenmayer, 'The Directives on Digital Contracts: First Steps Towards the Private Law of the Digital economy', 28 *E.R.P.L.* (2020) p. 246.

2858 Art. 13(4)(c) SGD.

2859 E. Van Gool and A. Michel, 'The New Consumer Sales Directive 2019/771 and Sustainable Consumption: A Critical Analysis', 10 *EuCML* (2021) p. 139.

2860 See also recital 53 SGD.

2861 Art. 13(5) SGD.

2862 National courts could even grant their own motion of an appropriate reduction in the price of goods. See ECJ 3 October 2013, Case C-32/12, *Soledad Duarte Hueros, EU:C:2013:637.*

2863 BGH, Urteil v. 28.05.2014 – VIII ZR 94/13, available on: <https://openjur.de/u/701340.html>.

2864 Art. 13(4)(d) SGD.

to apply a remedy within a reasonable period of time is not satisfied if the seller does not take any appropriate steps.[2865]

817. Price reduction and termination should be made more sustainable – Whereas subsidiary remedies are generally less sustainable than repair and circular replacement, it would be wrong to assume that they are, in any case, unsustainable. In fact, as was explained above, these remedies do not necessarily lead to the purchase of an alternative product, and even if they do, measures to counter the negative environmental externalities could be taken.[2866] For instance, as with replaced products, products returned to sellers after the contract is terminated should also be correctly handled (e.g. reconditioned) and not destroyed.[2867] In some cases, subsidiary remedies could even be preferred to primary remedies. For example, when a good lacking conformity still clearly offers functionality and repair or 'circular replacement' are impossible, consumers should be entitled to ask for price reduction instead of replacement by a new good.[2868] This possibility should be explicitly mentioned in Article 13 of the SGD (see #20). To avoid alternative purchases in case of termination of the contract, the SGD could also give the right to consumers to receive cash instead of vouchers (see #21).[2869] Such an amendment would be in line with the first circular strategy, which is to avoid new consumption.[2870]

818. No priority should be given to price reduction – Admittedly, price reduction and the termination of the contract are not equally unsustainable.[2871] However, one should remain careful when envisaging the prioritization of price reduction over the termination of the contract in the hierarchy of remedies. There are two main arguments against the idea of depriving consumers of their right to choose between these two subsidiary remedies. First, price reduction is not always the most sustainable option. Some defective goods may remain unused in consumer's drawers after price reduction when they could have been returned, repaired and reused by another consumer. Hence, having regard to single cases, the right to choose is a means to solve the lack of conformity in the most efficient and appropriate manner. The second main argument in favour of preserving the consumer's freedom of choice relates to issues of non-acceptance. Forcing consumers to keep products with defects for sustainability reasons may cause them economic harm and dissatisfaction and, consequently, may unnecessarily oppose consumer interests to environmental interests. Instead,

2865 ECJ 23 May 2019, Case C-52/18, *Fülla*, *EU:C:2019:447*, para 66.
2866 See *supra*, n° 648–649.
2867 See *supra*, n° 808.
2868 E. Van Gool and A. Michel, 'The New Consumer Sales Directive 2019/771 and Sustainable Consumption: A Critical Analysis', 10 *EuCML* (2021) p. 146.
2869 In fact, vouchers encourage consumers to buy new products.
2870 See *supra*, n° 649.
2871 See *supra*, n° 649.

amendments to the SGD should aim at increasing incentives for sustainability. Such drastic amendments to the subsidiary level of the hierarchy should therefore not be considered.[2872]

Proposed amendments to the SGD:

#20

Article 13
Remedies for lack of conformity

(…)

<u>5a. The consumer shall be entitled to a proportionate reduction of the price if the goods lacking conformity still clearly offer functionality and if repair or 'circular replacement' are impossible.</u>

(…)

AND *#21*

Article 16
Termination of the sales contract

(…)

<u>4. Concerning the reimbursement, consumers should have the choice to receive either cash or vouchers.</u>

(3) Extra remedies, including the right to reject

819. A CONSUMER RIGHT TO REJECT ALLOWED BY THE SGD – Although the hierarchy of remedies established under the SGD is supposed to exhaustively list the remedies available to consumers, Article 3(7) of the Directive weakens this hierarchy by acknowledging other remedies offered by national law.[2873] According to this provision, Member States are free to allow consumers to reject the good if the lack of conformity becomes apparent shortly after its delivery. In this case, consumers could consider the contract as rescinded or ask for immediate replacement, within a specific short period of time after the delivery of the goods, which should not exceed 30 days.[2874] Consumers can reject the

[2872] See also S. Schlacke, K. Tonner, E. Gawel, *Stärkung eines nachhaltigen Konsums im Bereich Produktnutzung durch Anpassungen im Zivil- und öffentlichen Recht* (Umweltbundesamt Study 2015) pp. 31–32.

[2873] See also recital 19 SGD.

[2874] Such a remedy exists under Irish law. See Section 53 of the Irish Sale of Goods Act.

good only if they prove that they have not accepted it. After 30 days, the four remedies of the hierarchy apply. The right to reject is thus a remedy of first resort. In addition to the right to reject, Article 3(7) of the SGD states that national rules (not specific to consumer contracts) may also provide for specific remedies for certain types of defects that were not apparent at the time of conclusion of the sales contract.

820. The leeway left to Member States on the right to reject should be removed – Because these additional remedies – and more particularly the right to reject – far from encourage sustainable behaviour on the consumer side, it is recommended to restrict the leeway left to the Member States to specific remedies that national rules (not specific to consumer contracts) provide for (see #22). The possibility of granting the right to reject to consumers should be removed. In fact, the right to reject appears to encourage impulsive consumption and results in additional transports, a possible new purchase and the risk of returned goods not being resold or repurposed. In this regard, this right has environmental impacts comparable to the right of withdrawal granted by Article 9 of the CRD, though the latter has a stronger justification as it exists to counterbalance the fact that the consumer is deprived of their first impression or subject to a potential surprise element when buying online or outside the premises.[2875] If such right to reject was to be maintained, the environmental impacts should at least be made transparent to raise awareness among consumers.

Proposed amendments to the SGD:

#22

Article 3
Scope

(…)

7. This Directive ~~shall not affect the freedom of Member States to allow consumers to choose a specific remedy, if the lack of conformity of the goods becomes apparent within a period after delivery, not exceeding 30 days. In addition, this Directive~~ shall not affect national rules not specific to consumer contracts providing for specific remedies for certain types of defects that were not apparent at the time of conclusion of the sales contract.

[2875] Yet, even with such justification, the right of withdrawal could also be questioned from a sustainable consumption perspective. See E. Terryn, E. Van Gool, 'The Role of European Consumer Regulation in Shaping the Environmental Impact of E-Commerce', 10 *EuCML* (2021) p. 89 at p. 101.

5. RIGHT OF REDRESS AND PRODUCER LIABILITY

821. Seller's right of redress and its limitations – The legal guarantee mechanism makes the seller, namely the consumer's contractual partner and point of contact, liable for any lack of conformity falling within the conditions of the Directive. The SGD, like the CSD, provides no possibility for the consumer to claim their rights against another person, even if the seller is acting in good faith and has not committed any fault.[2876] The seller will be held liable even when the lack of conformity results from a manufacturing defect, from a public statement made by the producer or from the failure by a third party to supply updates.[2877] Yet that is true in most cases of premature obsolescence, where the lack of conformity is (mainly) due to a decision taken by the producer or the designer of the digital content.[2878] Whereas final sellers could also contribute to the lack of conformity[2879], they generally have no influence or knowledge of the production process or the release of updates and, in many cases, have not even unpacked the product. To restore the balance between the different liabilities, Article 18 of the SGD grants sellers the right of redress against the person or persons liable in the chain of transactions.[2880] This right of redress suffers nonetheless from a number of flaws which are particularly problematic within the context of premature obsolescence, leading to reconsider the introduction of an EU-wide direct producer liability.

a) *Seller's remedies*

822. A useful weapon against those truly responsible for premature obsolescence – When the seller is liable to the consumer because of a lack of conformity resulting from an act or omission by a person in previous links of the chain of transactions, he is entitled by Article 18 of the SGD to pursue remedies against the person or persons liable in the chain of transactions.[2881] As specified by this provision, 'omission' encompasses cases where updates have not been provided to goods with digital elements in accordance with Article 7(3). As regards the details for exercising that right, the SGD leaves Member States

---

2876 Such rule was previously unknown in many Member States. See M. Ebers, A. Janssen and O. Meyer, 'Comparative report', in M. Ebers, A. Janssen et O. Meyer (eds.), *European perspectives on producers' liability: direct producers' liability for non-conformity and the sellers' right of redress* (Sellier European Law Publishers 2009) p. 37.

2877 See *supra*, n° 693 *et seq*.

2878 This is especially true for cases of material obsolescence (n° 101–105), functional obsolescence (n°106–111) and indirect obsolescence (n° 112–116).

2879 For example, if the good does not conform to a public statement made by the seller or if the seller did not deliver the accessories as stipulated by the sales contract. See *supra*, n° 685 *et seq*.

2880 A similar right of redress has been established by Art. 20 of the DCD.

2881 See also recital 63 SGD.

with great freedom, allowing them to determine the person against whom the seller may pursue remedies as well as the relevant actions and conditions of exercise.[2882] Through the establishment of this right of redress, the EU legislature intended to enable sellers who are held liable, though the lack of conformity is not attributable to them, to "*recover the costs caused by defects which can be imputed to the liable person*".[2883] In other words, it leads to "*a series of actions along the contractual chain until liability arrives at the party responsible for the non-conformity*".[2884] The right of redress is a useful weapon in the fight against premature obsolescence as it allows pinning the liability upon those responsible for lack of conformity linked to product durability, i.e. the producer of the product, the designer of the digital content or the software producer (in most cases).

823. With its flaws – However, in practice, the producer of the good or the original designer of the digital content will generally remain out of reach. Indeed, various factors tend to interrupt the remission of liability to the source of non-conforming goods. Among them, there is the fact that rules on commercial sales are more restrictive than rules on consumer sales[2885], the potential insolvency of the upstream contracting parties and the presence of clauses limiting or removing liability in the contract between two sequential sellers.[2886] A striking example of flaws in the system is when producers only offer single year legal guarantees that sellers have to top up to meet the minimum legal guarantee period of two years.[2887] So far, there is no information within the Directive or the related case law of the ECJ to clarify whether there are

2882 Article 18 of the SGD does not compel the Member States to introduce a direct claim for the final seller against the responsible link in the contractual chain. As a result, in the majority of the Member States, it is only possible to pass back liability via the contractual chain. Only some Member States grant such right to the final seller, like in Belgium (see *supra*).

2883 Proposal for a European Parliament and Council Directive on the sale of consumer goods and associated guarantees, COM(95)520 final, OJ C 307, 16.10.1996, p. 14.

2884 M. Ebers, A. Janssen and O. Meyer, 'Comparative report', in M. Ebers, A. Janssen, O. Meyer (eds.), *European perspectives on producers' liability: direct producers' liability for non-conformity and the sellers' right of redress* (Sellier European Law Publishers 2009) p. 47. See also M. Bridge, 'Article 4: Right of redress', in M.C. Bianca and S. Grundmann (eds.), *EU Sales Directive, Commentary* (Intersentia 2002) pp. 184–185.

2885 The difficulty for the seller is even greater when the producer is established outside the European Union as Rome I (Regulation (EC) No 593/2008) does not apply to B2B relationships.
OJ L 177, 4.7.2008, p. 6–16.

2886 M. Ebers, A. Janssen and O. Meyer, 'Comparative report', in M. Ebers, A. Janssen et O. Meyer (eds.), *European perspectives on producers' liability: direct producers' liability for non-conformity and the sellers' right of redress* (Sellier European Law Publishers 2009) p. 38 *et seq.*; B. Keirsbilck, 'Right of redress', in I. Claeys and E. Terryn (eds.), *Digital Content & Distance Sales* (Intersentia 2017) pp. 273–274.

2887 D. Watson et al., *Circular Business Models in the Mobile Phone Industry* (TemaNord 2017) p. 76.

minimum requirements for the exercise of the seller's right of redress.[2888] Taken together, these practical obstacles and the lack of (clear) minimum requirements could lead to the assumption that the liability system established under the SGD is not the most suitable to effectively combat the premature obsolescence of products. The Directive fails in targeting those who shorten product lifetime, except in the rare cases where the seller successfully asserts their right of redress. As a consequence, the system loses its potential deterrent effects.[2889]

824. The need for an improved liability system – Based on this assumption, there have been calls to improve the right of sellers seeking redress against producers, suggesting for example the right to recover the full amount of the costs incurred.[2890] The burden on the sellers' shoulders would also be lightened if, for example, producers were compelled to provide spare parts.[2891] Inspiration could be gained from the legislation of some Member States.[2892] In addition to improving the seller's right of redress, consumers should be granted the right, under EU law, to directly claim remedies against the producer (or their regional representative), as argued in the following paragraphs.

b) Direct producer liability

825. No direct producer liability under the SGD – So far, the SGD provides no right of redress to consumers that would entitle them to directly claim against producers (including designers of digital content) under the rights they have within the framework of the legal guarantee. The sole reference to such right within the SGD, which is a notable novelty of this legislation, is found in its Article 17. This provision makes the producer directly liable to the consumer where a commercial guarantee of durability has been offered, for the entire period of the commercial guarantee.[2893] Besides this exceptional case, consumers are also entitled to claim

---

2888 M. Ebers, A. Janssen and O. Meyer, 'Comparative report', in M. Ebers, A. Janssen et O. Meyer (eds.), *European perspectives on producers' liability: direct producers' liability for non-conformity and the sellers' right of redress* (Sellier European Law Publishers 2009) p. 134.

2889 The only deterrent effects would be exerted on sellers, who could decide not to sell products from certain producers anymore. Such decision could then have repercussions on producers.

2890 See Opinion of the European Economic and Social Committee on the 'Proposal for a directive of the European Parliament and of the Council on certain aspects concerning contracts for the supply of digital content' (COM(2015) 634 final) and the 'Proposal for a directive of the European Parliament and of the Council on certain aspects concerning contracts for the online and other distance sales of goods' (COM(2015) 635 final), OJ C 264, 20.7.2016, p. 65, pt. 4.2.5.1.3.

2891 Avis du Conseil Central de l'Economie du 3 septembre 2019 sur la transposition de directives européennes concernant la vente aux consommateurs tant de biens que de contenus et services numériques, CCE 2019-1660, p. 18. Such measure has been adopted in France. See *supra*, n° 472.

2892 See *infra*, n° 828.

2893 See *infra*, n° 834 *et seq.*

rights granted by commercial guarantees against the guarantor, who may be the producer.[2894] In absence of commercial guarantees, recital 63 of the SGD states that "*the question as to whether the consumer can also raise a claim directly against a person in previous links of the chain of transactions should not be regulated by this Directive*". The issue is thus, once again, left to the discretion of Member States.

826. Though initially envisaged in the CSD – Originally, the EC had envisaged establishing direct producer liability for the legal guarantee, developing many arguments in that direction.[2895] It emphasised, *inter alia*, the relation of trust between the consumer and the producer (despite the absence of contractual link between them), the direct producer liability already existing under the Product Liability Directive[2896] and the greater solvency and accessibility of producer compared to sellers. Its idea was that where the fault lies with the producer, they could be asked by the consumer either to repair or replace the faulty good or provide reimbursement.[2897] In spite of the long list of arguments, no such liability system was introduced and no explanation was given for this sudden change of mind.[2898] The CSD only mentioned in its recital 23 that "*it may be necessary to envisage more far-reaching harmonisation, notably by providing for the producer's direct liability for defects for which he is responsible*". In its 2007 Green Paper on the review of the consumer acquis, the Commission acknowledged the various forms of direct liability of producers and pointed out the fact that an EU-wide rule would "*eliminate possible internal market barriers and would favour especially consumers buying cross-border*".[2899] In the end, the liability regime remains unchanged under the SGD, making the seller assume the liability for the legal guarantee.

827. The proposed producer's obligation to repair – Interestingly, Article 5 of the Proposal for a Directive on common rules promoting repair introduces an obligation for producers to repair defects outside the liability of the seller upon the request of consumers. This obligation only applies to "*goods for which and to the extent that reparability requirements are provided for by Union legal acts*",[2900] which includes product groups covered by reparability

2894 See Art. 17(1) first subparagraph as well as recital 63 SGD.

2895 See the Green Paper from the European Commission of 15 November 1993 on Guarantees for Consumer Goods and After-sales Services, COM(93) 509 final, pp. 86–87.

2896 Council Directive 85/374/EEC of 25 July 1985 on the approximation of the laws, regulations and administrative provisions of the Member States concerning liability for defective products, OJ L 210, 7.8.1985, p. 29–33.

2897 Green Paper from the European Commission of 15 November 1993 on Guarantees for Consumer Goods and After-sales Services, COM(93) 509 final, pp. 87–88.

2898 B. Keirsbilck, 'Right of redress', in I. Claeys and E. Terryn (eds.), *Digital Content & Distance Sales* (Intersentia 2017) p. 271.

2899 Green Paper from the European Commission of 8 February 2007 on the Review of the Consumer Acquis, COM(2006) 744 final, p. 28.

2900 Art. 5(1) of the Proposal for a Directive on common rules promoting repair.

requirements under the ecodesign framework.[2901] The producer may perform this obligation against a price or for free as part of a commercial guarantee, and may be exempted from it where repair is impossible. Article 5(2) of the Proposal specifies how to enforce this obligation where the producer is established outside the EU. Article 6 strengthens this obligation to repair by requiring producers to inform consumers of that obligation and provide information on the repair services. If adopted, these provisions would be an important step towards a more coherent legal framework: consumer sales rules would complement reparability requirements imposed at the design and production stage by allowing and encouraging consumers to directly claim repair against the producer at the use phase. However, this obligation to repair is limited by the scope of the reparability requirements and differs from a general direct producer liability system.

828. Developed by some Member States – In parallel, some Member States took the lead in developing their own direct producer liability.[2902] Belgium is among these jurisdictions. In this Member State, while the seller is the only person who can be held liable under the legal guarantee regime, consumers can sue the producer based on the legal guarantee against hidden defects. Concerning the seller's right of redress, Belgium follows the traditional model along the contractual chain in line with the approach of Article 18 of the SGD. Article 1649*sexies* of the Belgian Civil Code mentions the possibility for the final seller to claim against the immediate prior seller as well as against all previous sellers further up the chain (including the producer). The same provision goes nonetheless beyond the requirements set out in the Directive and strengthens the sellers' right of redress. First, Belgian law allows the seller to seek redress against every actor in the supply chain. This possibility of direct claim is based on the doctrine of qualitative rights as well as on Article 1649*sexies* of the Belgian Civil Code.[2903] It is regrettable to note, from a sustainability perspective, that in cases where the seller was requested by the consumer to repair or replace the defective good, they can only seek a price reduction or the termination of the contract with their own seller or claim damages in case of knowledge of the defect by the seller.[2904] Second, contractual clauses in this chain which limit or exclude liability cannot be invoked against him. Some amendments to the

2901 Among these product groups are washing machines, dishwashers, refrigerating appliances, electronic displays and vacuum cleaners. For a complete overview of existing and proposed reparability requirements and the products concerned, see *supra*, n° 255 *et seq.*

2902 For a good summary, see also ICF, *Study on the costs and benefits of extending certain rights under the Consumer Sales and Guarantees Directive 1999/44/CE* (European Commission 2017) pp. 66–67.

2903 Cass. (1re ch.), 5 décembre 1980, *Pas.*, 1980, I, p. 398. For further details, see B. Keirsbilck, 'Right of redress', in I. Claeys and E. Terryn (eds.), *Digital Content & Distance Sales* (Intersentia 2017) pp. 275–276, as well as all the cited sources.

2904 B. Keirsbilck, 'Right of redress', in I. Claeys and E. Terryn (eds.), *Digital Content & Distance Sales* (Intersentia 2017) p. 276.

current legislation have been suggested with the aim of further enhancing the seller's right of redress.[2905]

829. Many reasons for introducing direct producer liability at EU level – Although Member States are given the possibility to establish the direct producer liability under their own national law and fill the gap left by EU law, it would be preferable to regulate this issue at EU level.[2906] First, it would promote the proper functioning of the internal market by avoiding further fragmentation of the legal guarantee rules and, consequently, by decreasing transaction costs and increasing consumer confidence.[2907] Second, consumers would benefit from a higher level of protection as they get the opportunity to trigger the liability of another person in case of faulty goods. This would meet their expectations to be able to sue the responsible person, which constitute a third reason for the introduction of such a liability system. The fourth argument is the fairness towards the seller. As already highlighted[2908], in most cases of premature obsolescence, the seller had no influence on the lack of conformity, which is (mainly) due to a decision taken by the producer or the designer of the digital content. With joint liability, the balance of interests between the different actors in the product chain would thus be restored.[2909] Fifth, such legislation would fit not only with existing product liability rules, but also with the principle of extended producer responsibility introduced by the Waste Framework Directive. Since the producer is liable for injuries caused to individuals or other goods, as well as at the end-of-life of the product through the take-back obligation, it seems logical to make him liable in the middle of the product lifecycle for the legal guarantee. Last but not least, the introduction of a direct action against producers would be another opportunity to integrate sustainable aspects into the Directive. An EU system of direct producer liability could incentivize producers to bring more sustainable products to the market.[2910] As a consequence, consumer trust in producers and brands might be restored and enhanced in the long term.

830. Three possible options of joint liability – The system of direct producer liability should not be exclusive, but complementary to the liability

2905 See Art. 4 Proposition de loi n° 0693/001.

2906 For more details on all the good reasons for the introduction of an EU system of direct producer liability, see B. Keirsbilck, 'Verhaalsrechten', in I. Claeys and E. Terryn (eds.), *Nieuw recht inzake koop & digitale diensten* (Intersentia 2020) p. 261 at p. 302.

2907 This is one of the main goals of the SGD. See Art. 1 SGD.

2908 See *supra*, n° 821.

2909 K. Tonner, R. Malcolm, *How an EU lifespan guarantee model could be implemented across the European Union (study)* (European Parliament 2017) p. 16.

2910 C. Willet, 'Direct producer liability', in G. Howells, R. Schulze, *Modernising and Harmonising Consumer Contract Law* (Sellier 2009) p. 203.

of the seller.[2911] In this regard, three approaches could be followed for the implementation of this liability system and its articulation with seller's liability. The first approach is a joint and several liability, whereby both seller and producer can be held independently liable for any lack of conformity falling within the conditions of the SGD, regardless of their respective degrees of fault.[2912] The second approach is a joint and subsidiary liability, whereby the seller and the producer can be held liable only for the lack of conformity resulting from their own fault. The third approach, which is a midway solution between several and subsidiary liability, is a quasi-subsidiary joint liability.[2913] According to this option, the consumer is first required to resort to the remedies provided for by the legal guarantee rules against the seller. It is only if it is impossible or too onerous to do so that the consumer is entitled to sue the producer.

831. A QUASI-SUBSIDIARY JOINT LIABILITY SHOULD BE INTRODUCED – Between the three aforementioned approaches, the quasi-subsidiary joint liability (third approach) seems to be the option that would most effectively improve the protection granted to consumers in case of premature obsolescence. With the first option, there is a risk that sellers and producers adopt a 'passing the buck' strategy and deny any responsibility for the lack of conformity. The second approach does not seem appropriate either as it lessens the protection granted to consumers. By contrast, the third approach would allow having all the positive effects of the introduction of such a direct liability system, as listed above.[2914] Moreover, it would not bring too many changes to the current regime and should therefore not create a risk of confusion in the minds of consumers. The quasi-subsidiary joint liability should thus be preferred (see #23).

832. SUBJECT TO STRICT AND SPECIFIC CONDITIONS – The direct liability of the producer or any other liable person in the previous links of the supply

[2911] Joint liability is particularly necessary for cases where the consumer cannot reach the manufacturer, e.g. when manufacturers do not have interfaces to directly interact with consumers.

[2912] This option was proposed by the EESC: see Opinion of the EESC on the 'Proposal for a directive of the European Parliament and of the Council on certain aspects concerning contracts for the supply of digital content' (COM(2015) 634 final) and the 'Proposal for a directive of the European Parliament and of the Council on certain aspects concerning contracts for the online and other distance sales of goods' (COM(2015) 635 final), OJ C 264, 20.7.2016, p. 64, pt. 4.2.5.13.2. See also Opinion of the European Economic and Social Committee on the 'Amended proposal for a Directive of the European Parliament and of the Council on certain aspects concerning contracts for the sales of goods, amending Regulation (EC) No 2006/2004 of the European Parliament and of the Council and Directive 2009/22/EC of the European Parliament and of the Council and repealing Directive 1999/44/EC of the European Parliament and of the Council' (COM(2017) 637 final), OJ C 227, 28.6.2018, p. 61, pt. 3.4.(h).

[2913] This approach was suggested by the EC before the adoption of the CSD. See the Green Paper from the European Commission of 15 November 1993 on Guarantees for Consumer Goods and After-sales Services, COM(93) 509 final, p. 88.

[2914] See *supra*, n° 829.

chain could be subject to strict conditions. For example, direct producer liability could only apply to newly manufactured goods.[2915] By contrast, it should not be possible to hold the original producer liable for a lack of conformity of a refurbished good if he had no influence on the refurbishment of the good (see #23). Remedies granted within the framework of the producer liability system could also be limited compared to the ones provided for by Article 13 of the SGD for seller's liability, restricting the choice, for example, between repair and replacement only (performance in kind)(see #23). It would indeed make no sense to require the rescission of the contract as there is no contract between the consumer and the producer, or the reduction of the price as the price has been agreed with and paid to the seller.[2916]

833. Combined with representative actions – The system of direct producer liability would be even more effective against premature obsolescence if it was combined with class actions.[2917] In fact, in most cases of premature obsolescence, the defect affects products which are mass-produced. The direct producer liability mechanism would allow centralising all the related claims against the producer instead of bringing claims that concern the same problem separately against different sellers.

Policy recommendation:

#23 The quasi-subsidiary joint liability should be established at the EU level.

6. COMMERCIAL GUARANTEES

a) *The (unexploited) potential of commercial guarantees against premature obsolescence*

834. Five main functions of commercial guarantees – In addition to the legal guarantee, some undertakings (sellers and producers) voluntarily offer commercial guarantees to consumers.[2918] Commercial guarantees have various

---

2915 This restriction exists in Germany for the right to redress (§478 BGB).

2916 See the Green Paper from the European Commission of 15 November 1993 on Guarantees for Consumer Goods and After-sales Services, COM(93) 509 final, p. 88.

2917 See in this regard Directive (EU) 2020/1828 of the European Parliament and of the Council of 25 November 2020 on representative actions for the protection of the collective interests of consumers and repealing Directive 2009/22/EC, OJ L 409 du 4.12.2020, p. 1–27.

2918 Article 2(12) of the SGD defines 'commercial guarantee' as "*any undertaking by the seller or a producer (the guarantor) to the consumer, in addition to the seller's legal obligation relating to the guarantee of conformity, to reimburse the price paid or to replace, repair or service goods in any way if they do not meet the specifications or any other requirements not related to conformity set out in the guarantee statement or in the relevant advertising available at the time of, or before*

functions that could be particularly valuable within the context of premature obsolescence.[2919] On the consumer side, it has both (1) a *protective role* by providing remedies against early failures due to product design, manufacturing or quality problems during the guarantee period, and (2) an *informative role* by acting as an indicator of product quality and durability for consumers who are unable to evaluate the performance of complex and/or innovative products due to lack of knowledge, expertise or experience. On the guarantor side, it plays (3) a *protective role* by limiting their liability in case of failure due to the improper and careless use or abuse of product by the consumer. It also plays (4) a *promotional role* by signalling the quality and durability of products to the consumers.[2920] Finally, it acts as (5) an *incentive and a powerful advertising tool* for a manufacturer/dealer to compete effectively in the market on the sustainability of their products.[2921] New brands entering the market can establish a reputation for longer lasting products, while existing brands can strengthen their existing reputation in this area.[2922] These functions are even more accurate within the context of sales of second-hand goods.[2923]

835. A VERY LIMITED LEGAL FRAMEWORK – The current EU consumer sales regime hardly regulates commercial guarantees.[2924] The SGD, like its predecessor[2925], dedicates only one provision to commercial guarantees, namely Article 17. This provision mainly lays down information requirements and indicates the binding nature of commercial guarantees.[2926] With these limited obligations, guarantors are left with considerable freedom to draw up the terms of their commercial guarantee. Consequently, commercial guarantees

the conclusion of the contract". In Belgium, definitions of 'commercial guarantee' can be found in Article 1649*bis* §2, 5° of the Civil code and Article I.8, 37° of the Economic Law Code.

2919 These functions were described in A. Rahman, G. Chattopadhyay, *Long Term Warranty and After Sales Service – Concept, Policies and Cost Models* (Springer 2015) p. 4.

2920 This informational function of guarantees refers to the 'signalling theory', which was formulated in: M. Spence, 'Job Market Signalling', 87 *Q. J. Econ.* (1973) p. 355 at p. 374; S. J. Grossman, 'The Informational Role of Warranties and Private Disclosure about Product Quality', 24 *J.L. & Econ.* (1981) p. 461 at p. 483. This function must nonetheless be nuanced. See C. Twigg-Flesner, *Consumer Product Guarantees* (Routledge 2016) p. 54 at p. 70.

2921 S. Van Camp, S. Bouyon, *Impact assessment of proposed substantial amendments introducing a commercial lifespan guarantee in the proposed online sales and digital content directive* (European Parliament 2017) p. 6.

2922 T. Knight et al. (Brook Lyndhurst), *Electrical and electronic product design: product lifetime* (WRAP 2013) p. 60.

2923 A. Rahman, G. Chattopadhyay, *Long Term Warranty and After Sales Service – Concept, Policies and Cost Models* (Springer 2015) p. 42.

2924 The freedom left to guarantors has always been justified by the importance of competition between the traders. See M. Bianca, S. Grundmann, *EU Sales Directive* (Intersentia 2002) p. 221.

2925 See Art. 6 CSD.

2926 For further comments on the information requirements relating to commercial guarantees, see *infra*, n° 857 *et seq.*

may vary considerably from product to product and brand to brand.[2927] Much of the content is governed by the terms of the guarantee itself, including the guaranteed parts of the product, the defects covered, the available remedies and the conditions under which the guarantor can be held liable. Unfortunately, the freedom left to the guarantors is not necessarily used with the aim of prolonging product lifespan. Since there is no incentive for companies to take sustainability into account, the sustainability potential of commercial guarantees is not exploited. Some commercial guarantees are even harmful to sustainable consumption, restricting for example the choice of remedies between the termination of the contract or damages.[2928]

836. Commercial guarantees of durability – It should be noted that Article 17(1) of the SGD introduces additional obligations for producers who offer 'commercial guarantees of durability'. Although the added value of this provision is undeniable from a sustainability perspective, it is to be regretted that its scope has not been more clearly defined.[2929] The SGD provides no definition, except the one of 'durability' given in its Article 2(13). This may be problematic, on one hand, to know exactly what should be understood by 'durability' and its relationship with expected product lifespan and, on the other hand, to distinguish between 'commercial guarantees of durability' and other commercial guarantees.

b) Scope of application

837. A possible wider range of products – The scope of application of commercial guarantees may differ greatly from the one of legal guarantees. First, commercial guarantees may apply to second-hand goods. This can be particularly beneficial for consumers, especially if they bought their second-hand good at public auction, as those goods may be excluded from the scope of application of the SGD[2930], or if the second-hand good is subject to a reduced guarantee period due to a contractual clause limiting seller's liability to one year.[2931]

2927 The notion of 'guarantee' used in the CSD (and the SGD) should be understood in its broad sense, covering the various forms of commercial guarantees. See E. Van den Haute, *Contrats spéciaux* (Larcier 2018) p. 109.

2928 E. Terryn, 'A Right to Repair: Towards Sustainable Remedies in Consumer Law', *E.R.P.L.* (2019) p. 861 at p. 863; S. Van Camp, S. Bouyon, *Impact assessment of proposed substantial amendments introducing a commercial lifespan guarantee in the proposed online sales and digital content directive* (European Parliament 2017) p. 23. For further details, see *infra* (n° 837 *et seq.*).

2929 S. Vandemaele, *Commerciële garanties in de verschillende koopregimes: naar een uniforme regeling?* (PhD KU Leuven 2019) p. 125.

2930 See *supra*, n° 677.

2931 See *supra*, n° 742 *et seq.*

838. More or less defects covered than legal guarantees – Second, commercial guarantees can protect consumers against more or less types of defects than legal guarantees and cover all or only certain parts of the product.[2932] As an example, some commercial guarantees cover damages caused by consumers themselves, like failure to follow the instruction manual, water damage or accidental breakage. Other commercial guarantees promise the proper functioning of the good for a defined period and guarantee additional services, like preventive maintenance or a stock of available spare parts. An enlarged scope of application can have both positive and negative impacts on product lifetime. On one hand, commercial guarantees could cover cases of premature obsolescence which fall outside the scope of application of the legal guarantee. On the other hand, it might incite consumers to use goods less carefully and lead to their premature obsolescence ('moral hazard'). Therefore, if minimum standards were to be established on this aspect, the scope of application should be restrained to relieve the guarantor from their liability in some cases (of abuse) and avoid complete coverage of defects for the consumer.[2933]

c) Liability period

839. Duration mainly left to the discretion of the guarantor – There is no minimum period provided by the Directive, except for commercial guarantees of durability for which Article 17(1) of the SGD states that the producer is liable during the entire period of the commercial guarantee of durability. Some Member States decided to further regulate this aspect. For example, Article L. 217–16 of the French Consumer Code provides for the suspension of the commercial guarantee period for the duration of the repair when the good is out of use for repair for more than seven days. It is also interesting to note that, by contrast with the legal guarantees, the limitation period of commercial guarantees lasts five years.[2934] In other words, if a defect occurs during the period set by the commercial guarantee, the consumer has five years to bring a claim. Except for these few rules, the duration of the commercial guarantees is thus left at the discretion of the guarantors.

840. A possible longer liability period – In practice, the liability period provided by commercial guarantees often lasts longer than the one provided by the legal guarantee.[2935] The longer liability period is particularly beneficial to

2932 For a detailed list of exclusions from guarantee cover, see ECC-Net, *Commercial warranties – are they worth the money?* (2014) p. 79.

2933 S. Schlacke, K. Tonner, E. Gawel, *Stärkung eines nachhaltigen Konsums im Bereich Produktnutzung durch Anpassungen im Zivil- und öffentlichen Recht* (Umweltbundesamt Study 2015) pp. 32–33.

2934 Art. 110–4 of the French Commercial Code.

2935 Ipsos-London Economics-Deloitte consortium, *Consumer market study on the functioning of legal and commercial guarantees for consumers in the EU* (European Commission 2015) p. 92.

consumers in case a defect occurs after the expiry of the legal guarantee. In this regard, it is interesting to know that commercial guarantees can achieve what is still at a proposal stage for the legal guarantee, that is an extended liability period.[2936] The commercial guarantee prolongs the protection granted to consumers and helps fill the gap left by the legal guarantee for products for which the guarantee period seems too short.[2937] Whereas extending the legal guarantee in law may take some time, especially if specific liability periods are introduced per product categories, the commercial guarantees may be of help in tackling the premature obsolescence of products in the meantime.[2938]

841. THE DUTY TO ISSUE A GUARANTEE STATEMENT – Several ideas have already been put forward to further regulate the duration of commercial guarantees. A study commissioned by the EP suggested introducing a duty for producers to inform consumers of the product's expected lifetime as well as a duty to issue a guarantee statement, with a possibility of making a 'zero statement'.[2939] Producers would have the choice of either indicating a guaranteed lifetime (that they would determine) or indicating a 'zero' period and not offering guarantee cover. In the first scenario, the indicated period is binding on the producer, who must then cure defects which occur during this period. In the second scenario, it is merely a duty of disclosure for the producer. While commercial guarantees would lose their voluntary nature and become a mandatory instrument (or at least a mandatory negative declaration), producers would remain free to decide on the duration of the guarantee period.[2940] This measure was deemed to have one of the largest potentials to stimulate the offering of commercial lifespan guarantees compared to other approaches based on soft law and those imposing the supply of a lifespan commercial guarantee (on the basis of soft law or binding technical standards).[2941] The duty to inform consumers about not providing a guarantee would nudge producers to provide a guarantee and compete on this aspect, but also to invest further in the design of sustainable products.[2942] Moreover, such guarantees could

2936 S. Vandemaele, *Commerciële garanties in de verschillende koopregimes: naar een uniforme regeling?* (PhD KU Leuven 2019) p. 252.

2937 On the questionable adequacy of the length of the legal guarantee period, See *supra* (n° 731).

2938 S. Van Camp, S. Bouyon, *Impact assessment of proposed substantial amendments introducing a commercial lifespan guarantee in the proposed online sales and digital content directive* (European Parliament 2017) p. 6.

2939 K. Tonner, R. Malcolm, *How an EU lifespan guarantee model could be implemented across the European Union (study)* (European Parliament 2017) pp. 54–55.

2940 S. Van Camp, S. Bouyon, *Impact assessment of proposed substantial amendments introducing a commercial lifespan guarantee in the proposed online sales and digital content directive* (European Parliament 2017) p. 6.

2941 For further details on this comparison, see S. Van Camp, S. Bouyon, *Impact assessment of proposed substantial amendments introducing a commercial lifespan guarantee in the proposed online sales and digital content directive* (European Parliament 2017), especially p. 72 at p. 74.

2942 K. Tonner, R. Malcolm, *How an EU lifespan guarantee model could be implemented across the European Union (study)* (European Parliament 2017) p. 32 at p. 34 as well as p. 55; I. Oehme,

raise awareness among consumers, who may be prepared to pay more if they are apprised of product lifespan.[2943] The implementation of this option would also involve lower costs and take less time compared to measures imposing the supply of a lifespan commercial guarantee. Interestingly, the idea of a guarantee statement obligation was taken up by the German Federal Ministry of the Environment as of March 2020 with the Environmental Digital Agenda, where the ministry announced its intention of implementing this at EU level.[2944] A hint of this idea can now be found in Article 2(2)(a) and (3)(a) of the Proposal for a Directive on empowering consumers for the green transition, which obliges the trader to inform the consumer that the producer does not make available the information on the commercial guarantee of durability for 'energy-using goods'.[2945]

842. A minimum liability period for commercial guarantees – Besides the idea of a mandatory guarantee statement, it has been proposed to legally set a minimum liability period for commercial guarantees and prohibit those that do not last as long.[2946] However, such a measure is not without criticism, the main one being that it would deter companies from giving any commercial guarantee at all.[2947] A less drastic measure would be to provide for the suspension of the commercial guarantee period when the good is being repaired, as proposed for the legal guarantee[2948] and as already applies under French law.[2949]

d) Burden of proof

843. Another aspect determined by the guarantor – Guarantors also enjoy freedom to determine who carries the burden of proof and if there is any extension of the reversal of burden of proof. Yet, for most commercial guarantees, it is for the guarantor to prove that the defect has been caused by

A., Jacob, *Strategies against obsolescence Ensuring a minimum product lifetime and improving product service life as well as consumer information* (Umweltbundesamt 2017) p. 12; S. Vandemaele, *Commerciële guaranties* (PhD) (KU Leuven 2019).

2943 T. Knight et al. (Brook Lyndhurst), *Electrical and electronic product design: product lifetime* (WRAP 2013).

2944 BMU, 'Umweltpolitische Digitalagenda' (2 March 2020) p. 39, available on: <www.bmu.de/fileadmin/Daten_BMU/Download_PDF/Digitalisierung/digitalagenda_bf.pdf>.

2945 For further comments on these proposed amendments, see *supra* (n° 489).

2946 For example, T. Libaert proposes to prohibit commercial guarantees which last less than 24 months or which last 24 months if only partial. See T. Libaert, *Pour une consommation plus durable en phase avec les enjeux européens* (2018) p. 53.

2947 S. Schlacke, K. Tonner, E. Gawel, *Stärkung eines nachhaltigen Konsums im Bereich Produktnutzung durch Anpassungen im Zivil- und öffentlichen Recht* (Umweltbundesamt Study 2015) p. 32.

2948 See *supra*, n° 750.

2949 Art. L. 217-28 of the French Consumer Code. Interestingly, under the former Article L. 217-16 of the French Consumer Code, the commercial guarantee period was suspended only when the immobilisation of the defective good was longer than seven days. See also H. Temple, M. Dépincé, *Droit de la consommation* (Dalloz 2020) p. 273.

the consumer or external factors. This also represents a major advantage for consumers compared to the legal guarantee for which they bear the burden of proof after the presumption period has elapsed. Hence, if consumers deem the burden too heavy to invoke the rights granted by the legal guarantee regime, they can decide alternatively to rely on the commercial guarantee.

844. Filling the gap left open by the legal guarantee – The reasoning employed on the role of commercial guarantees as regards the extension of the guarantee period can be repeated for this aspect.[2950] The amendment proposed for the legal guarantee concerning the reversal of the burden of proof (i.e. a longer presumption period) can indeed be equally achieved through commercial guarantees.[2951]

e) Consumer remedies

845. No mandatory hierarchy of remedies – If, during the guaranteed period, the product fails to meet the features set out in the guarantee statement or in the advertising relating thereto, the consumer has several remedies against the guarantor, without these being necessarily equivalent to those provided for by the legal guarantee. Instead of the hierarchy established under Article 13 of the SGD, commercial guarantees can restrict the choice of remedies, sometimes between the termination of the contract or damages.[2952] It can also allow for the direct replacement of the item with no attempt to repair.[2953] The modalities of the remedies under commercial guarantee might also differ. For example, implementation of the remedies may not be free of charge for the consumer. The commercial warranty might also allow the consumer to get a replacement item during examination or repair as well as organise a procedure for return of items or repair at the consumer's home.[2954]

846. Except for commercial guarantees of durability – This freedom does not apply to commercial guarantees of durability for which producers are obliged to give consumers the choice between repair and replacement in accordance with Article 14 of the SGD, unless more favourable conditions apply. Yet, the additional obligations set out for this type of guarantee remain limited too.[2955]

2950 See *supra*, n° 840.

2951 S. Vandemaele, *Commerciële garanties in de verschillende koopregimes: naar een uniforme regeling?* (PhD KU Leuven 2019) p. 252.

2952 C. Twigg-Flesner, 'The law on guarantees and repair work', in T. Cooper (ed.), *Longer lasting products – Alternatives to the throwaway society*, Farnham, Gower Publishing Limited, 2010, p. 209.

2953 ECC-Net, *Commercial warranties – are they worth the money?* (2014) p. 76.

2954 ECC-Net, *Commercial warranties – are they worth the money?* (2014) p. 75.

2955 The EP had proposed stringent obligations on the producers, including a time-limit under which repair and replacement should be achieved. See Amendment 114 of the Report on the amended proposal for a directive of the European Parliament and of the Council on certain

847. The need for rules promoting a sustainable hierarchy – The arguments that were raised within the framework of rules on legal guarantee concerning the sustainability of remedies can be repeated for rules on commercial guarantees.[2956] For commercial guarantees too, there is a need to rethink the hierarchy of remedies to foster repair and integrate more sustainability into the other available remedies (see #24). Some guarantors use their contractual freedom in that sense, issuing sustainable commercial guarantees like 'all damage repair with temporary replacement good' or 'circular replacement'. However, there are also risks of unsustainable guarantee terms, especially for commercial guarantees other than the ones on durability, as the obligations imposed by the SGD on those guarantors are very limited. E. Terryn gives the example of companies offering commercial guarantees such as "*direct replacement, do not wait for repair*".[2957] If such guarantees (appear to) pertain to the consumer's rights under the legal guarantee, they breach Article 21 of the SGD and possibly also the legislation on unfair contract terms and commercial practices.[2958] Otherwise, they are completely legal.

Proposed amendment to the SGD:

#24

Article 17
Commercial guarantees

1. Any commercial guarantee shall be binding on the guarantor under the conditions laid down in the commercial guarantee statement and associated advertising available at the time, or before the conclusion, of the contract. Under the conditions laid down in this Article and without prejudice to any other applicable provisions of Union or national law, where a producer offers to the consumer a commercial guarantee of durability for certain goods for a certain period of time, the producer shall be liable directly to the consumer, during the entire period of the commercial guarantee of durability for repair **or, if impossible or disproportionate, for** replacement of the goods, in accordance with Article 14. The producer may offer to the consumer more favourable conditions in the commercial guarantee of durability statement.

(...)

aspects concerning contracts for the sales of goods, amending Regulation (EC) No 2006/2004 of the European Parliament and of the Council and Directive 2009/22/EC of the European Parliament and of the Council and repealing Directive 1999/44/EC of the European Parliament and of the Council, COM(2017) 637, p. 52.

2956 See *supra*, n° 767 *et seq.*

2957 E. Terryn, 'A Right to Repair: Towards Sustainable Remedies in Consumer Law', *E.R.P.L.* (2019) p. 862.

2958 E. Van Gool and A. Michel, 'The New Consumer Sales Directive 2019/771 and Sustainable Consumption: A Critical Analysis', 10 *EuCML* (2021) p. 147.

f) Guarantor liability

848. An extendable liability – According to Article 17(1) of the SGD, commercial guarantees are binding on the guarantor under the conditions laid down in the commercial guarantee statement and associated advertising available at the time, or before the conclusion, of the contract. The terms of the commercial guarantee may also be binding on the seller if he approved them and bound himself to the consumer.[2959] Hence, in case of defect, the consumer can claim the rights enshrined in the commercial guarantee against the guarantor or against the seller (if approved). The commercial guarantee may also bind the guarantor vis-à-vis subsequent buyers, if it provides so.[2960] In Belgium, it has been argued to introduce a prohibition of clauses that prevent the transferability of commercial guarantees.[2961] Such transferability could be particularly interesting in case of second-hand goods.[2962] Because commercial guarantees can be issued by sellers or producers, consumers can thus sue sellers and producers, as opposed to what the rules on legal guarantee allow. The possibility of holding the producer liable is also explicitly given by Article 17(1) of the SGD for commercial guarantees of durability. On this aspect, commercial guarantees are more effective in allocating liability for cases of premature obsolescence than legal guarantees as the producer can often be identified as responsible for the limited product lifetime.[2963]

849. Under the conditions imposed by the guarantor – Guarantor liability can only be invoked if the conditions set out in the commercial guarantee statement and associated advertising are met. However, the conditions under which the commercial guarantee is binding are imposed by the guarantor. Hence, the consumer still needs to be aware of the conditions and make sure that these are complied with.[2964] The conditions can be stricter and less advantageous than the legal guarantee, though

2959 Samoy, 'Garantie op transparentie? De conventionele garantie in het wetsontwerp tot omzetting van de Richtlijn Consumentenverkoop', 109 *Tijdschrift voor Belgisch handelsrecht* (2003) p. 383 at p. 390.

2960 In this regard, the commercial guarantee can be seen as an accessory to the item.

2961 Avis du Conseil Central de l'Economie du 3 septembre 2019 sur la transposition de directives européennes concernant la vente aux consommateurs tant de biens que de contenus et services numériques, CCE 2019–1660, p. 17.

2962 The initial proposal included the obligation to provide information on the transferability of commercial guarantees. See Art. 15(2)(b) of the Amended proposal for a Directive of the European Parliament and of the Council on certain aspects concerning contracts for the online and other distance sales of goods, amending Regulation (EC) No 2006/2004 of the European Parliament and of the Council and Directive 2009/22/EC of the European Parliament and of the Council and repealing Directive 1999/44/EC of the European Parliament and of the Council, COM(2017)637 final, 2015/0288 (COD).

2963 See *supra* on the right of redress and producer liability (n° 821 *et seq.*).

2964 C. Twigg-Flesner, *Consumer Product Guarantees* (Routledge 2016) p. 155 at p. 157.

it should not mislead consumers on their rights under the legal guarantee regime.[2965] If the conditions laid down in the commercial guarantee statement are less advantageous to the consumer than those laid down in the associated advertising, the conditions laid down in the advertising prevail, unless, before the conclusion of the contract, the concerned advertising was corrected in the same way or in a comparable way to that in which it was made.[2966]

850. With clauses limiting or removing liability – Commercial guarantees can also include liability restrictions. Among them, there are restrictions that are used to hinder independent repair or repair by the consumer themselves.[2967] For instance, some commercial guarantees restrict the guarantor's liability, and thus the consumer's right to remedies, if the consumer tried to repair the product himself or asked an independent repairer. Such clauses are used by the sellers and the producers to exclude the risk of a badly executed repair by a third party. However, as highlighted by E. Terryn, such widely formulated clauses hinder the development of a network of independent repair shops.[2968] Regrettably enough, these clauses, just as those restricting the remedies, are completely legal, provided that they do not (appear to) pertain to the consumer's rights under the legal guarantee.[2969] Beyond these restrictions, producers can also limit their liability in an unreasonable way. As an example, they could unreasonably exclude their liability in case the product was used in sub-zero temperatures.[2970]

851. Some liability restrictions should be banned by the SGD – Although some of these restrictions could be covered by the UCTD, amendments to the SGD should be envisaged to legally ban certain unreasonable liability restrictions. For example, the SGD could prohibit clauses removing liability due to repair by a third party if repair was carried out by a repairer registered on an official list of professional repairers (see #25).[2971]

2965 Otherwise, it could be considered as misleading within the meaning of Article 6 of the UCPD.

2966 Art. 17(1) second subparagraph SGD.

2967 E. Terryn, 'A Right to Repair: Towards Sustainable Remedies in Consumer Law', *E.R.P.L.* (2019) p. 862.

2968 *Ibid.*

2969 See for ex. in France, in the automotive sector: Cass., 1re civ., 20 mars 2013, n° 12–14.432. In this case, the French Court held that contractual terms preventing the consumer from repairing their car outside the authorised network were not unfair.

2970 D. Watson et al., *Circular Business Models in the Mobile Phone Industry* (TemaNord 2017) p. 76.

2971 Similar prohibitions already exist in the US, as explained in A. Perzanowski, *The Right to Repair: Reclaiming the Things We Own* (Cambridge University Press 2022) p. 218. The author refers to the Magnuson–Moss Warranty Act, which forbids manufacturers from conditioning warranty protections on consumers using particular brands of parts or services.

Proposed amendment to the SGD:

#25

Article 17
Commercial guarantees

(…)

<u>1a. Any clause restricting the guarantor's liability on the ground that repair was carried out by a third party shall not be binding on the consumer if repair was carried out by a repairer registered on an official list of professional repairers.</u>

(…)

g) *The need for a more developed legal framework*

852. Further regulation on commercial guarantees is needed – Commercial guarantees, although not initially linked to environmental concerns, can theoretically serve to promote product sustainability and sustainable consumption. Compared to the legal guarantee, they can apply to a wider range of products and parts (including second-hand goods) and provide extended coverage for a longer period of time, offer more sustainable remedies and involve additional liable parties, as discussed in the preceding paragraphs. However, this is rarely the case in practice. Producers may have no incentive for quality signals if such behaviour is not rewarded by the market.[2972] Moreover, there are concerns that commercial guarantees are often overpriced and may mislead consumers on their rights under the legal guarantee regime.[2973] Policymakers can address these complex challenges posed by commercial guarantees by creating a clearer legal framework for commercial guarantees and by supporting bottom-up initiatives.[2974]

853. The links between legal and commercial guarantees should be clarified and fully exploited – In addition to the specific amendments that were proposed in the previous paragraphs, more general comments could be made regarding the legal framework for commercial guarantees. First, the possible links

2972 S. Schlacke, K. Tonner, E. Gawel, *Stärkung eines nachhaltigen Konsums im Bereich Produktnutzung durch Anpassungen im Zivil- und öffentlichen Recht* (Umweltbundesamt Study 2015) pp. 32–33.

2973 L.A. DiMatteo, S. Wrbka, 'Planned Obsolescence and Consumer Protection: The Unregulated Extended Warranty and Service Contract Industry', 28 *Cornell Journal of Law and Public Policy* (2019) p. 518 at p. 520.

2974 See also S. Vandemaele, *Commerciële garanties in de verschillende koopregimes: naar een uniforme regeling?* (PhD KU Leuven 2019) pp. 253–254.

between legal and commercial guarantees should be clarified and fully exploited. The articulation between both guarantees had already been explored prior to the adoption of the CSD. In its 1993 Green Paper, the EC underlined that consumers should be entitled to claim both guarantees simultaneously (complementarity principle) as well as invoke the legal guarantee if their claim based on the commercial guarantee was unsuccessful (subsidiarity principle).[2975] This line of thought should be taken further. Not only is the commercial guarantee complementary to the legal guarantee and helps tackle cases of premature obsolescence that fall outside its scope, but it can also reach targets that are still being proposed for the legal guarantee and could serve as an experiment.[2976] Furthermore, commercial guarantees could be taken into account when assessing the compliance of the product with the objective conformity requirement related to product durability under the legal guarantee regime.[2977]

854. The main aspects of commercial guarantees should be standardised – A second measure that should be taken consists in standardising the main aspects of commercial guarantees, while their duration could still be determined by the guarantors.[2978] This would, on one hand, clear up confusion among consumers regarding the distinction between legal and commercial guarantees.[2979] On the other hand, the comparison between products would be facilitated and, consequently, competition between guarantors would be boosted. If consumers trust in commercial guarantees, they would more easily rely on them, which would encourage producers to compete on that aspect. As a consequence, commercial guarantees would be used as a competitive device for producers. Because offering more generous commercial guarantees may increase costs for guarantors, they would be encouraged to increase the quality and durability of their products.[2980] The standardisation of the content of commercial guarantees would make even more sense if the duty to issue a guarantee statement were to be adopted.[2981]

855. Rules should be adopted at EU level – As previously argued for many other rules, the legal gaps relating to commercial guarantees should preferably be filled at EU level. In this regard, it is noteworthy that recital 71

[2975] Green Paper from the European Commission of 15 November 1993 on Guarantees for Consumer Goods and After-sales Services, COM(93) 509 final, p. 88.

[2976] S. Vandemaele, *Commerciële garanties in de verschillende koopregimes: naar een uniforme regeling?* (PhD KU Leuven 2019) p. 252.

[2977] See *supra*, n° 697–699.

[2978] S. Schlacke, K. Tonner, E. Gawel, *Stärkung eines nachhaltigen Konsums im Bereich Produktnutzung durch Anpassungen im Zivil- und öffentlichen Recht* (Umweltbundesamt Study 2015) pp. 32–33.

[2979] Other measures could be taken with a view to improving consumers' awareness and understanding, as highlighted in n° 857 *et seq.*

[2980] C. Twigg-Flesner, *Consumer Product Guarantees* (Routledge 2016) pp. 67–68.

[2981] See *supra*, n° 841.

of the SGD mentions that a particular focus will be given on the producer's commercial guarantee of durability in the future review of the SGD. In the meantime, Member States can further regulate on commercial guarantees to exploit their full potential in terms of product sustainability, as long as the minimum protection of the Directive is preserved.[2982]

856. WHILE LEAVING SOME FREEDOM TO THE GUARANTOR – Policymakers should nonetheless remain cautious and bear in mind that commercial guarantees are voluntary acts. Imposing more restrictive conditions on commercial guarantees may indeed dissuade producers from offering such guarantees in the first place.[2983] This may already be the case for the new provision on commercial guarantees of durability as producers willing to offer such guarantee would have to satisfy stricter requirements compared to producers who do not provide any. Hence, legislation should not eliminate the advantages gained with the functions of the commercial guarantees[2984], especially its signalling function where commercial guarantees become a competition tool and are able to increase the quality of sustainability in the market permanently if the demand for quality on the market is communicated.

7. INFORMATION ON LEGAL AND COMMERCIAL GUARANTEES

857. THE CRUCIAL IMPORTANCE OF INFORMATION ON GUARANTEES – Guarantee rights and remedies will only be fully effective if consumers are aware and have a good understanding of them. The importance of informing consumers on guarantees had already been pinpointed as a priority issue prior to the adoption of the 1999 CSD.[2985] Yet, it has been observed that consumers still do not (properly) know their rights. The new regime established by the SGD and the DCD, which introduces new rules and nuances, may not help in this regard. This can create a barrier to repair.[2986] The SGD, like its predecessor, imposes some information obligations on legal and commercial guarantees. These obligations are to be found in its Article 17(2). However, this provision does not seem capable of solving the current lack of knowledge among consumers.

2982 Art. 17(4) and recital 62 SGD.

2983 E. Van Gool and A. Michel, 'The New Consumer Sales Directive 2019/771 and Sustainable Consumption: A Critical Analysis', 10 *EuCML* (2021) p. 147.

2984 On the five main functions of commercial guarantees, see *supra*, n° 834.

2985 Green Paper from the European Commission of 15 November 1993 on Guarantees for Consumer Goods and After-sales Services, COM(93) 509 final, pp. 88–89.

2986 See *supra*, n° 654.

a) *Lack of knowledge of guarantee rights*

858. A SERIOUS LACK OF KNOWLEDGE AMONG CONSUMERS – The consumers' lack of knowledge of guarantee rights has been a recurrent problem for many years, even after the adoption and the implementation of the CSD. According to a 2015 study commissioned by the EC, only 35% of consumers know the legal guarantee period that applies in their country.[2987] These findings were confirmed by a more recent study, which identified a significant lack of consumer awareness regarding the length of guarantee periods provided by the manufacturers and a general lack of knowledge of consumer protection rights.[2988] Moreover, some consumers do not know whether they should claim their legal guarantee rights against the seller or the producer. Some sellers take advantages of this lack of information and redirect the consumer to the producer of the defective good, stressing that the lack of conformity is linked to a manufacturing problem.[2989] There is also a large proportion of consumers for whom the distinction between legal and commercial guarantee is blurred.[2990] Consumers might be more tempted to rely on rights granted by a commercial guarantee, which are more accessible and clearer to them and more focused on the remedies that are made available.[2991]

859. EXACERBATED BY TRADERS' MISUNDERSTANDING AND MISINFORMATION – The consumers' lack of information is exacerbated by traders' misunderstanding and misinformation. Firstly, there are traders who misunderstand their legal obligations.[2992] Second, it was reported by several European Consumer Centres that sellers were well trained in setting out the advantages of a commercial warranty without making any reference to the legal guarantee.[2993] Third, there are still many cases whereby traders do not provide the required information on the legal guarantee or misinform consumers.[2994] Such lack of information and

[2987] Ipsos-London Economics-Deloitte consortium, *Consumer market study on the functioning of legal and commercial guarantees for consumers in the EU* (European Commission 2015) p. 38.

[2988] D. Watson et al., *Circular Business Models in the Mobile Phone Industry* (TemaNord 2017).

[2989] ECC-Net, *Commercial warranties – are they worth the money?* (2014) p. 13.

[2990] Ipsos-London Economics-Deloitte consortium, *Consumer market study on the functioning of legal and commercial guarantees for consumers in the EU* (European Commission 2015) p. 77.

[2991] C. Twigg-Flesner, *Consumer Product Guarantees* (Routledge 2016) p. 56.

[2992] This issue was raised in Belgium: see Avis du Conseil Central de l'Economie du 3 septembre 2019 sur la transposition de directives européennes concernant la vente aux consommateurs tant de biens que de contenus et services numériques, CCE 2019–1660, p. 4; Service de Médiation pour le Consommateur, *Rapport annuel 2018*, p. 31, available on: <https://mediationconsommateur.be/sites/default/files/content/download/files/cod-jaarverslag_2018-fr-lr.pdf>.

[2993] ECC-Net, *Commercial warranties – are they worth the money?* (2014) p. 69.

[2994] See Service de Médiation pour le Consommateur, *Rapport annuel 2018*, p. 7, available on: <https://mediationconsommateur.be/sites/default/files/content/download/files/cod-jaarverslag_2018-fr-lr.pdf>.

misinformation have consequences on consumers' understanding, leading to complaints from consumers who have been misled about their rights under the legal guarantee and also sometimes under commercial guarantees.[2995]

b) *Information obligations under the Sale of Goods Directive*

860. Information obligations as regards commercial guarantees – The SGD establishes a transparency obligation as regards commercial guarantees in its Article 17(2).[2996] Article 17(3) adds that the commercial guarantee is still binding if the guarantor does not comply with the information obligation provided for in Article 17(2). Besides formal requirements[2997], Article 17(2) sets out information requirements on the content of the commercial guarantee statement.[2998] Consumers should be informed with the name and address of the guarantor, the procedure to be followed to obtain the implementation of the commercial guarantee, the goods to which the commercial guarantee applies and the terms of the commercial guarantee. This provision has to be read in conjunction with Article 5(1)(e) and Article 6(1)(m) of the CRD, Article 6(1)(g) of the UCPD and Article 3 of the UCTD, which add and reinforce obligations on the information to be provided when offering a commercial guarantee.[2999] This duty to inform about the commercial guarantee can support sustainable consumption as it imposes duties on producers. Yet, the positive effects of these provisions would be magnified if the informational obligations were clearer. For example, producers could be explicitly obliged to provide information about the length of the commercial guarantee period and, if they do not offer any, about the non-existence of the commercial guarantee.[3000] Unfortunately, the ECJ case law does not strengthen consumer information on commercial guarantees, quite the contrary. In *Victorinox*, the Court ruled that "*the information requirement imposed on the trader does not arise from the mere fact that that guarantee exists,*

2995 See for ex. in Italy: Autorità Garante della Concorrenza e del Mercato (AGCM), 21 décembre 2011, *Apple*, n. 23155, for which an English summary is available on: <www.agcm.it/component/joomdoc/allegati-news/IP151_sintesi_Inglese.pdf/download.html>. The Belgian consumer association Test-Achats followed suit (see <https://belgium-iphone.lesoir.be/2013/01/14/test-achats-en-justice-contre-apple-pour-non-respect-du-droit-de-la-garantie/>), though a settlement was ultimately reached with Apple. In France, see HOP, 'Une plainte pénale contre Amazon pour pratiques commerciales trompeuses déposée par HOP', 19 décembre 2019, available on: <https://www.halteobsolescence.org/une-plainte-penale-contre-amazon-pour-pratiques-commerciales-trompeuses-deposee-par-hop/>.

2996 See also recital 62 SGD.

2997 Article 17(2) requires the commercial guarantee statement to "*be provided to the consumer on a durable medium at the latest at the time of the delivery of the goods*" and to "*be expressed in plain, intelligible language*".

2998 These information requirements were already imposed by Article 6(2) of the CSD, though with a different wording.

2999 See Chapter III on the marketing and pre-contractual stage, and more specifically n° 414 (Art. 6(1)(g) UCPD) and n° 488 (Art. 5(1)(e) and 6(1)(m) CRD).

3000 For further comments on this idea, see *supra* (n° 841).

but only where the consumer has a legitimate interest in obtaining information concerning that guarantee in order to decide whether to enter into a contractual relationship with the trader".[3001]

861. Information obligation on the existence of the legal guarantee – Article 17(2)(a) of the SGD also requires the commercial guarantee statement to include "*a clear statement that the consumer is entitled by law to remedies from the seller free of charge in the event of a lack of conformity of the goods and that those remedies are not affected by the commercial guarantee*". The aim is to avoid consumers being confused and ill-informed about the different types of guarantees. Although it is crucial to clarify the distinction between the legal and commercial guarantees, no such information obligation on the legal guarantee exists in the SGD, except when the producer or seller offers a commercial guarantee. The SGD establishes an obligation to provide information on the legal guarantee only in the case of the granting of a commercial guarantee. It requires informing consumers about the existence of their rights under the legal guarantee and of the fact that the commercial guarantee in no way alters their legal rights. The obligation to inform about the existence of the legal guarantee, even in the absence of any commercial guarantee, is provided for by two other instruments. On one hand, Articles 5(1)(e) and 6(1)(l) of the CRD explicitly mention this obligation in its list of pre-contractual information requirements.[3002] In this regard, the CRD and the SGD are said to be complementary.[3003] On the other hand, Article 6(1)(g) of the UCPD sanctions cases of misleading information on guarantee rights.[3004]

862. Additional information obligations under national law – According to Article 20 of the SGD, Member States are required to take appropriate measures to ensure that information on the rights of consumers under this Directive, as well as on the means to enforce those rights, are available to those consumers. In this sense, several Member States have established additional information obligations, including in the car sector. For example, Belgian law states that the sales conditions should inform the consumer that they do not lose their legal guarantee rights if the maintenance or repair of the vehicle is carried out outside the network of repairers approved by the manufacturer, provided that it is conducted in accordance with the instructions of that manufacturer.[3005] In France, the seller must inform consumers about the

3001 See ECJ 5 May 2022, Case C-179/21, *Victorinox, EU:C:2022:353*. See also *supra*, n° 488.
3002 See *supra*, n° 487.
3003 See recitals 6 and 11 SGD.
3004 See *supra*, n° 414.
3005 Article 6, 11° Arrêté royal du 5 avril 2019 relatif aux contrats de vente de véhicules automoteurs, *M.B.*, 8 mai 2019, p. 44214.

possibility of implementing the commercial guarantee for their vehicle outside the professional's network.[3006]

863. Reinforced by the Regulation establishing a single digital gateway – Consumer information on their Union consumer rights and on the way of enforcing them is reinforced by Regulation (EU) 2018/1724, which establishes a single digital gateway to ensure that citizens seeking information on their consumer rights or on out-of-court dispute resolution benefit from an online entry point. The aim is that consumers gain access to up-to-date information about their consumer rights in a clear, understandable and easily accessible manner and can submit a complaint through the online dispute resolution platform established under Regulation (EU) No 524/2013 and to the competent centre of the European Consumer Centres Network, depending on the parties involved. According to that Regulation on a single digital gateway, Member States are required to ensure that consumers are well informed. In Belgium, such information is given on the website of the Federal Public Service Economy.[3007] Moreover, the contact point established by the Belgian Federal Public Service Economy enables consumers to report their suspicions of premature obsolescence and to receive replies from competent services.[3008]

c) *Possible amendments to improve consumer information*

864. The SGD should explicitly establish an information obligation on the content of the legal guarantee – In addition to the information already required by the SGD and the CRD, it may be desirable to explicitly include in the SGD the general obligation for the trader to provide information on the content of the legal guarantee (see #26 and #27).[3009] First, it would ensure that consumers are well-informed, especially if the guarantee period is no longer uniform but varies from product to product[3010], and consequently provide incentives to firms to invest in product quality as they know that more consumers may ask for a new product once their old one breaks down in the warranty period.[3011] Second, such an amendment

---

3006 Article 1 de l'Arrêté du 26 mai 2014 modifiant l'arrêté du 28 juin 2000 relatif à l'information des consommateurs et à la publicité des prix des véhicules automobiles, JORF n°0129 du 5 juin 2014, p. 9404.

3007 See for ex. SPF Economie, Guidance sur la garantie (2019), available on: <https://economie.fgov.be/sites/default/files/Files/Entreprises/guidance-garantie-fr.pdf>.

3008 See <https://pointdecontact.belgique.be/meldpunt/fr/bienvenue>.

3009 The obligation to provide information on the content of the legal guarantee is already provided for in some national laws. See for ex. Art. L. 111-1 4° and Art. L. 211-2 1° of the French Consumer Code.

3010 See *supra* on the proposed fully differentiated guarantee periods (n° 734).

3011 R. F. Hartl, P. M. Kort, S. Wrzaczek, 'Reputation or warranty, what is more effective against planned obsolescence?', *International Journal of Production Research* (2022) p. 11.

would contribute to informing and raising awareness among professionals about the existence and importance of the legal guarantee, thus facilitating its implementation in a 'friendly' manner. Finally, this could put an end to the presence of certain unfair terms in the general conditions of sale.[3012] The EC has already expressed its reluctance on this subject, citing the negative effects that this could have on cross-border trade.[3013] However, its explicit inclusion in the SGD would increase its effectiveness. If the Proposal related to the SGD incorporated this obligation to make clear statements concerning the legal rights of the consumer in cases of the granting of a commercial guarantee[3014], it is regrettable that this amendment was not to be found in the final version of the text and that the opportunity has not been taken to do the same in cases of absence of commercial guarantees.[3015] Not only should the information on the content of the legal guarantee be automatically provided by professionals (before the conclusion of the contract but also before implementing the remedy), but once provided, it should also be clear, transparent and not misleading, which is unfortunately not always the case in practice.[3016]

865. As applied in France and proposed in Belgium – In France, Article L. 211-2 of the Consumer Code, which was introduced by the Hamon Law, requires information on guarantees, including on their content, to be mentioned in the general terms and conditions of the sales contract. Furthermore, since 1st January 2022, the billing document (i.e. sales receipt or invoice) delivered to the consumer must include, for certain categories of goods, a compulsory mention on the existence and duration of the two-year legal guarantee.[3017] In Belgium, car sellers are already obliged to

---

3012 See in that sense the Green Paper from the European Commission of 15 November 1993 on Guarantees for Consumer Goods and After-sales Services, COM(93) 509 final, pp. 88–89.

3013 See the Answer of 24 May 2012 given by Mrs Reding on behalf of the Commission, replying to the written parliamentary question E-003494/2012.

3014 See Art. 15(2)(a) of the Amended proposal for a Directive of the European Parliament and of the Council on certain aspects concerning contracts for the online and other distance sales of goods, amending Regulation (EC) No 2006/2004 of the European Parliament and of the Council and Directive 2009/22/EC of the European Parliament and of the Council and repealing Directive 1999/44/EC of the European Parliament and of the Council, COM(2017) 637 final.

3015 For more details on legislative developments in the field of commercial guarantees, see S. Vandemaele, E. Terryn, 'Commercial Guarantees in the Proposal for a Directive on Certain Aspects Concerning Contracts for the Online and Other Distance Sales of Goods', in I. Claeys and E. Terryn (eds.), *Digital Content & Distance Sales* (Intersentia 2017) p. 233 at p. 263.

3016 See for ex. Autorità Garante della Concorrenza e del Mercato (AGCM), 21 décembre 2011, *Apple*, n. 23155, for which an English summary is available on: <www.agcm.it/component/joomdoc/allegati-news/IP151_sintesi_Inglese.pdf/download.html>.

3017 Art. 20 Anti-Waste Law.

inform consumers on the length of the legal guarantee.[3018] Moreover, it has been suggested that a form containing information on the legal guarantee rights and scope should be signed by both parties when concluding the sales contract.[3019]

866. Information on guarantees should be standardised – The most effective way of improving consumer information on legal and commercial guarantees would be to adopt minimum standards for the disclosure of this information.[3020] This could take the form of a mandatory label on the products' packaging, which would indicate certain pieces of information, like the duration of the guarantee period.[3021] Another idea that deserves serious consideration is the introduction of a standardised information form for B2C transactions that would be provided before the conclusion of the sales contract, with information on the relation between legal and commercial guarantees as well as on the content of both of them (see #28).[3022] This would enable consumers to compare both guarantees. Interestingly, this idea of a form comparing the rights granted by legal and commercial guarantees was taken up in a Belgian legislative proposal.[3023] It is noteworthy that such a standardised contract was previously applicable in France for commercial guarantees and after-sale services.[3024] Under this contract, guarantors had to inform consumers on the duration of both guarantees, the remedies provided and the renewal of guarantee for replaced parts among others. Guarantors remained nonetheless free to decide on the content and conditions of the commercial guarantee when filling the gaps of the model contract.[3025] Inspiration could also be taken from the financial sector, where the creditor is already obliged to provide key information to consumers in a standardised format.[3026]

3018 Article 3, 12° Arrêté royal du 5 avril 2019 relatif aux contrats de vente de véhicules automoteurs, *M.B.*, 8 mai 2019, p. 44714

3019 Service de Médiation pour le Consommateur, *Rapport annuel 2018*, p. 32, available on: <https://mediationconsommateur.be/sites/default/files/content/download/files/cod-jaarverslag_2018-fr-lr.pdf>.

3020 See also S. Schlacke, K. Tonner, E. Gawel, *Stärkung eines nachhaltigen Konsums im Bereich Produktnutzung durch Anpassungen im Zivil- und öffentlichen Recht* (Umweltbundesamt Study 2015), p. 32.

3021 This could also be useful now as the length of the legal guarantee period may depend from one Member State to another. D. Watson et al., *Circular Business Models in the Mobile Phone Industry* (TemaNord 2017), p. 77.

3022 For further details on the concrete implementation of this idea, see S. Vandemaele, *Commerciële garanties in de verschillende koopregimes: naar een uniforme regeling?* (PhD KU Leuven 2019).

3023 See Proposition de loi relative à la protection des consommateurs en cas de vente de biens de consommation, *Doc. parl.*, Ch., 2019–2020, 5 novembre 2019, n° 0693/001, pp. 9–10.

3024 See Annex of the former Article R. 211-2 of the French Consumer Code.

3025 H. Temple, M. Dépincé, *Droit de la consommation* (Dalloz 2020) pp. 279–280.

3026 See the Standard European Consumer Credit Information form, available on: <https://ec.europa.eu/info/sites/info/files/standard_european_consumer_credit_information_en.pdf>.

Proposed amendments to the SGD:

#26

Article 17
Commercial guarantees

(...)

2. The commercial guarantee statement shall be provided to the consumer on a durable medium at the latest at the time of the delivery of the goods. The commercial guarantee statement shall be expressed in plain, intelligible language. It shall include the following:

(a) a clear statement that the consumer **has legal rights as provided for in this Directive** ~~**is entitled by law to remedies from the seller free of charge**~~ in the event of a lack of conformity of the goods and that those ~~**remedies**~~ **rights** are not affected by the commercial guarantee;

(...)

AND *#27*

Article 20
Consumer information

1. Before the conclusion of the sales contract, the seller shall inform the consumer on the existence and the content of the legal guarantee of conformity. The seller shall provide, at the same time, the standard information by means of the form set out in Annex x.

2. Member States shall take appropriate measures to ensure that information on the rights of consumers under this Directive, and on the means to enforce those rights, are available to consumers. **Member States shall ensure that, before the consumer is bound by any sales contract, the seller shall provide the consumer with the standard information by means of the relevant form as set out in Annex x.**

AND

> *#28 A standardised information form should be created and introduced in the Annexes of the SGD, with information on the relation between legal and commercial guarantees as well as on the content of both of them.*

8. LIABILITY BEYOND LEGAL AND COMMERCIAL GUARANTEES

867. Possibilities left once the legal and commercial guarantees are no longer applicable – If a defect occurs after the expiration of the legal guarantee, and if no commercial guarantee was voluntarily offered by the seller or the producer, the consumer is left unprotected by the SGD. Yet, consumers can be protected by mechanisms established under national law, like the guarantee against hidden defects or other mechanisms of general sales law. The same scenario unfolds if the product falls outside the scope of the legal guarantee and is not covered by the commercial guarantee. Besides these legal possibilities, consumers may also rely on their own repair skills or those of independent repairers to reverse the obsolescence of their products, provided that these non-legal remedies are not made impossible by technical, legal, economic and psychological obstacles.[3027]

a) Guarantee against hidden defects

868. A guarantee with other modalities, acknowledged by the SGD – The SGD acknowledges the existence of specific national rules, which create a liability system against hidden defects.[3028] The guarantee against hidden defects provides consumers with the right to remedies against the seller or the producer if a 'hidden defect' appears after the legal guarantee period has expired. Such a right allows consumers to return the good and ask for reimbursement or retain the good and demand a price reduction or the termination of the contract. This guarantee may be invoked when a defect existed at the time of the sale but could not be identified through a normal check of the product at the moment of delivery.

869. A possibility provided under Belgian and French law – Both Belgium and France offer this additional means of protection against premature obsolescence. The guarantee against hidden defects (*garantie des vices cachés*) is granted by Articles 1641 to 1649 of the Belgian Civil Code and by Articles 1641 to 1649 of the French Civil Code, which are almost identical. It should be noted that Belgium is currently undertaking a profound reform of its Civil Code[3029], which raises many questions as to the application of the guarantee against hidden defects and its articulation with the provisions of the SGD.[3030] These questions will only be answered once the new Book 7 of the Civil Code is adopted.

870. Scope of application – By contrast with the guarantee of conformity, which sanctions the difference between the promised good and the delivered

[3027] See also *supra*, n° 651–656.

[3028] Art. 3(7) and recital 18 SGD.

[3029] For an updated overview of this reform, see: <https://justice.belgium.be/fr/bwcc>.

[3030] See also F. Van den Abeele, B. Tilleman, 'Remedies in het nieuwe consumenten(koop)recht: een (her)nieuw(d) getrapt systeem', 135 *D.C.C.R.* (2022) p. 59 at p. 102.

good[3031], the guarantee against hidden defects covers other types of defects. Article 1641 of the Belgian and French Civil Codes lays down three conditions under which the guarantee applies.[3032] First, the defect must be of such a nature that the good is unfit for the use for which it is intended or that the use of the good is reduced so much that the buyer would not have purchased it, or would have paid only a lower price, if he had known. This threshold can be difficult to reach as it requires a certain degree of seriousness of the defect.[3033] The Belgian Court of Cassation held that the guarantee against hidden defects also covers defects that affect the functioning of the product, even though they do not intrinsically affect the product.[3034] Consequently, consumers can invoke the guarantee against hidden defects not only in cases of material obsolescence (*vices structurels*), but also in cases of functional obsolescence (*vices fonctionnels*).[3035] Second, the defect must have existed before the purchase of the product. Third, the defect must be 'hidden', meaning that it existed at the time of the conclusion of the sales contract, but could not be detected by the consumer through a normal check on the product at the time of delivery. If these conditions are met, which should be the case for most cases of premature obsolescence, the consumer can rely on this guarantee. Concerning the material scope of the guarantee against hidden defects, it is noteworthy that it applies to new and second-hand goods. As for its personal scope, the guarantee may be invoked against traders or individuals. A notable difference between the Belgian and French regimes is that under Belgian law, the guarantee against hidden defects also applies to B2B sales and thus protects both consumers and professionals in case of premature obsolescence.[3036]

871. Liability period and time-limits – As opposed to the legal guarantee of conformity, the starting point of the prescription period for the legal action based on the guarantee against hidden defects is the date on which the consumer

---

3031 The French Court of cassation clarified the distinction between the two guarantees in Cass. 1re civ., 5 mai 1993, n° 90-18.331, as cited in D. Chauchis, 'La protection de l'acquéreur d'un bien dans le droit interne de la vente', *Bulletin d'information de la Cour de Cassation*, 1 novembre 2010, p. 14.

3032 According to this provision: "*[l]e vendeur est tenu de la garantie à raison des défauts cachés de la chose vendue qui la rendent impropre à l'usage auquel on la destine, ou qui diminuent tellement cet usage, que l'acheteur ne l'aurait pas acquise, ou n'en aurait donné qu'un moindre prix, s'il les avait connus.*"

3033 See e.g. Antwerpen, 8 februari 2017, *NJW* 2017, 746–748. In this case, the court decided that the defect (i.e. the need to install specific software for the good functioning of the device) was not serious enough to invoke the guarantee against hidden defects.

3034 See Cass. (1re ch.), 18 novembre 1971, *Pas.*, 1971, I, p. 258: "*Le vice caché de la chose vendue, qui oblige le vendeur à garantie, peut être un vice qui, même s'il n'affecte pas intrinsèquement la chose, la rend impropre à l'usage auquel, à la connaissance du vendeur, l'acheteur la destinait*".

3035 This had already been raised in A. Hamann, 'Obsolescence programmée: le droit en panne?', 102 *D.C.C.R.* (2014) p. 74.

3036 D. Philippe, 'La garantie des vices cachés', 1 *Cahier du juriste* (2000) p. 2, citant notamment Mons, 10 juin 1985, *Entreprise et Droit*, 1990, p. 243.

discovers the defect, and not the date on which the product is delivered. In Belgium, consumers are entitled to invoke this guarantee for 10 years, starting from the moment they discover the defect.[3037] They must nonetheless do so within a short period of time after the discovery of the defect, as required by Article 1648 of the Belgian Civil Code.[3038] This requirement is of suppletive nature, meaning that contractual parties can agree on a fixed period or that the seller may eventually renounce it.[3039] In absence of such agreement or renunciation, it is for the court to determine the start and length of this period on a case-by-case basis, giving rise to great uncertainty.[3040] In France, consumers can rely on this subsidiary guarantee within a period of two years from the day on which they noticed the defect[3041], and until five years after the purchase of the product. This long period is what makes the guarantee against hidden defects particularly worthwhile for consumers who are confronted with the premature obsolescence of their product after the two-year period of the guarantee of conformity. The requirement to react within a short period of time might however hamper consumers from successfully obtaining remedies based on this guarantee. It is also noteworthy that consumers cannot invoke the guarantee against hidden defect before the expiration of the two-year guarantee period.[3042]

Still concerning the liability period, it is important to bear in mind that the guarantee against hidden defects is *propter rem*, meaning that the rights it entails should be considered as accessories to the good and are thus transferable to subsequent buyers. Consequently, if a hidden defect (e.g. specific wear parts) occurs after the good has been sold to another consumer, the new owner of the good could bring a claim on the basis of the regime of hidden defects against their seller, but also against previous sellers (including producer), provided that the hidden defect in question already existed at that time.

3037 See Article 2262*bis* §1 of the Belgian Civil Code, which applies to the guarantee against hidden defects.

3038 For further details on the relationship between the limitation period and the short delay, see B. Kohl, 'L'action en garanties des vices cachés doit-elle être initiée endéans le délai de prescription décennal?', in *Liber Amicorum François Glansdorf et Pierre Legros* (Bruylant 2013) p. 199 at p. 215. See also Cass. (1re ch.), 29 novembre 2013, R.G. n° C.12.443.F, p. 2591, which distinguishes the short delay and the limitation period.

3039 B. Goffaux, 'Le "bref délai" en matière de garantie des vices cachés: le temps de quelques réflexions', 174 *Forum de l'assurance* (2017) p. 102.

3040 B. Goffaux, 'Le "bref délai" en matière de garantie des vices cachés: le temps de quelques réflexions', 174 *Forum de l'assurance* (2017) p. 101 at p. 106.

3041 Article 1648 of the French Civil Code.

3042 See in this regard F. Glansdorff, 'Panorama des actions ouvertes à l'acheteur insatisfait', in *Actualités de quelques contrats spéciaux* (Bruylant 2005) p. 22; C. Delforge, Y. Ninane, 'La garantie de conformité des biens de consommation', in P. Wéry (ed.), *La Théorie générale des obligations et contrats spéciaux* (2016) pp. 351–352. See also Anvers (7e ch. B), 6 février 2018, *R.W.* 2019–20, liv. 28, p. 1107.

872. Burden of proof – It is for the consumer to prove that the abovementioned conditions are fulfilled to benefit from the protection granted by the guarantee against hidden defects. This task may nonetheless be particularly challenging for consumers, especially because there is no presumption in their favour, as opposed to the legal guarantee of conformity.[3043] Once the evidence of the hidden defect has been provided, the traders are in a less comfortable position. The seller and the producer are supposed to know their goods perfectly, including the defects they could have. Therefore, they should be treated like traders acting in bad faith if a defect occurs. They must prove their ignorance or the undetectable character of the defect to escape their liability under this regime.[3044]

873. Consumer remedies – On the basis of Article 1644 of the Belgian and French Civil Codes, consumers are (only) entitled to return the good and ask for reimbursement and terminate the contract or retain the good and ask for a price reduction.[3045] If consumers opt for reimbursement after having discovered a hidden defect, the seller must return the paid price without reduction. This contrasts with the legal guarantee of conformity, for which the reimbursement may be partial as the seller is allowed to apply a rate to take into consideration the use of the product by the consumer.[3046] The restricted choice between the termination of the contract and price reduction was under discussion in Belgium within the framework of the transposition of the SGD. Some are of the opinion that repair and replacement should also be made available to consumers, justifying this amendment for the sake of product sustainability.[3047] This idea should undoubtedly be further promoted. Interestingly, such a possibility formerly existed for car buyers, who were entitled to repair in case of a hidden defect.[3048] If repair was technically impossible, the parties had to agree on an

3043 See *supra*, n° 758.

3044 E. Montero, 'Les produits défectueux dans un écheveau de responsabilités – note sous Liège (3e ch.), 7 novembre 2005', 10 *R.G.D.C.* (2006) p. 627. See also case law in this regard: Cass. (1re ch.), 13 novembre 1959, *Pas.*, 1960, I, p. 313; Liège, 10 octobre 2007, *J.T.*, 2008, p. 177.

3045 In addition to these remedies, Article 1645 of the same Codes grants consumers the right to get damages if the seller knew about the existence of the defect and thus acted in bad faith.

3046 See in Belgium: Art. 1649*quinquies* §3 of the Civil Code. In France, see: Cass. 1re civ., 21 mars 2006, n° 03-16.075; Cass. 1re civ., 21 mars 2006, n° 03-16.307; Cass. 1re civ., 21 mars 2006, n° 03-16.407.

3047 Avis du Conseil Central de l'Economie du 3 septembre 2019 sur la transposition de directives européennes concernant la vente aux consommateurs tant de biens que de contenus et services numériques, CCE 2019-1660, p. 7. See also Art. 4 Proposition de loi relative à la protection des consommateurs en cas de vente de biens de consommation, *Doc. parl.*, Ch., 2019-2020, 5 novembre 2019, n° 0693/001.

3048 Arrêté royal du 9 juillet 2000 relatif aux informations essentielles et aux conditions générales de vente devant figurer sur le bon de commande des véhicules automobiles neufs, *M.B.*, 9 août 2000, p. 27300.

alternative remedy which was the most appropriate to cure the defect.[3049] It is regrettable that such provision has not been maintained under the new rules.[3050]

874. Liable persons – The Belgian and French law makers granted additional rights to the consumer through the guarantee against hidden defects. Under Belgian law, consumers are entitled to seek redress not only against the final seller, but also against all previous sellers further up the chain, including the producer, based on the doctrine of qualitative rights.[3051] Hence, in addition to the legal guarantee of conformity, consumers have the possibility to invoke the guarantee against hidden defects against the seller or the producer.[3052] As already argued, such direct producer liability is of particular relevance within the context of premature obsolescence as the limited product lifetime is often the result of decisions and actions taken by the producer.[3053] It is interesting to note that these means of action may be combined: consumers may bring a joint action against the seller (on the basis of the guarantee of conformity) and the producer (on the basis of hidden defects).[3054] In addition to the possible direct producer liability, Belgian law ensures that the liable person is not out of reach by regulating clauses limiting or excluding liability. Based on the same doctrine of qualitative rights, exoneration or limitation clauses contained in contracts between the seller and the producer (or wholesaler further up the contractual chain) are not opposable to consumers.[3055] In this regard, the Belgian Supreme Court (*Cour de Cassation*) has clarified that any seller may be called on to offer a complete guarantee to the consumer.[3056]

875. Filling the gaps left by the guarantee of conformity – As highlighted throughout this section, the guarantee against hidden defects can be of particular use for consumers, especially in cases of premature obsolescence falling outside the scope of the legal guarantee rules and where no commercial guarantee has been offered or may be invoked by consumers. The complementary nature of these guarantees was particularly conspicuous in the *Dieselgate* case, where the defect appeared after the legal guarantee period and could not have

3049 E. Terryn, 'A Right to Repair: Towards Sustainable Remedies in Consumer Law', *E.R.P.L.* (2019) p. 858.

3050 Arrêté royal du 5 avril 2019 relatif aux contrats de vente de véhicules automoteurs, *M.B.*, 8 mai 2019, p. 44214.

3051 See *supra*, n° 828.

3052 See E. Montero, 'Les produits défectueux dans un écheveau de responsabilités – note sous Liège (3e ch.), 7 novembre 2005', 10 *R.G.D.C.* (2006) p. 627.

3053 See *supra*, n° 829 *et seq.*

3054 See for ex. Liège, 5 novembre 2009, *D.C.C.R.*, 2010, vol. 87, p. 80, note M. Hostens.

3055 S. Stijns, I. Samoy, ' Le nouveau droit de la vente: la transposition en droit belge de la Directive europ é enne sur la vente des biens de consommation', 17 *R.G.D.C.* (2003), p. 29.

3056 Cass., 15 décembre 2006, *R.W.*, 2008–2009, p. 230.

been detected by consumers.[3057] The existence of the guarantee against hidden defects should however not prevent amendments that would enhance the legal guarantee rules towards more product sustainability. For example, some stakeholders – especially from the business community – have argued that the extension of the legal guarantee of conformity should not be envisaged since the guarantee against hidden defect can be used by consumers after the expiration of the two-year period.[3058] The reasoning supporting this argument seems rather flawed as the legal regimes of those guarantees are markedly different on essential aspects, such as burden of proof, available remedies and the possibility of seeking redress against the producer.

b) *The lack of consent under the general sales legislation*

876. Three other possible mechanisms of general sales law – In addition to these guarantees, the general sale of goods legislation may provide consumers with other redress mechanisms against the other contracting party in case of premature obsolescence at the use stage. Such mechanisms exist in the Belgian Civil Code.[3059] Under Belgian law, the cancellation of the sales contract can be based on lack of consent on the consumer side. There are two types of lack of consent that are relevant for cases of premature obsolescence, namely error (*erreur*)[3060] and deceit (*dol*).[3061] Besides these two scenarios, the third option consists of claiming that the cause of the contract is unlawful or erroneous based on the theory of the cause (*théorie de la cause*). These three mechanisms could be of use in certain cases of premature obsolescence, though consumer law rules strongly diminish the importance of these instruments.

877. In case of an error – The first argument that the consumer may advance to cancel the sales contract in case of premature obsolescence is to claim that there is an error on the essential qualities of the good.[3062] In other words, a claim can be made that the contract is based on an erroneous view of the good and that the buyer would not have concluded the contract if they had known the truth.

3057 J.M. Carvalho, K. Nemeth, '"Dieselgate" and Consumer Law: Repercussions of the Volkswagen scandal in the European Union', *EuCML* (2017), p. 35.

3058 Avis du Conseil Supérieur des Indépendants et des PME du 1er octobre 2019 sur la transposition de deux directives relatives au droit des consommateurs, F Droit des consommateurs 2019 A2, p. 4; Avis du Conseil Supérieur des Indépendants et des PME du 21 février 2017 sur des propositions visant à renforcer la garantie légale des biens de consommation, F PRAT COM – Garantie légale A1, p. 4.

3059 See also A. Hamann, 'Obsolescence programmée: le droit en panne?', 102 *D.C.C.R.* (2014) p. 41 at p. 82.

3060 Art. 1110 Civil Code.

3061 Art. 1116 Civil Code.

3062 S. Stijns, *Verbintenissenrecht* (Die Keure 2005) p. 80; D. Philippe, "À propos de la substance de l'erreur", note sous Cass., 24 septembre 2007, *R.G.D.C.*, 2009, p. 218.

Consequently, the consumer cannot invoke lack of consent if they were informed about the short product lifetime prior to the conclusion of the contract. There are two main conditions to use this argument. First, the error cannot be inexcusable, meaning that the lack of consent should not be the result of a mistake due to the consumer's imprudence or negligence. Second, the error had to exist at the conclusion of the contract. Error has already been invoked in cases that could qualify as premature obsolescence, though such cases would now fall within the legislation on unfair commercial practices.[3063]

878. In case of a deceit – Secondly, consumers may resort to deceit. If they successfully prove that the producer has materially and intentionally limited the lifetime of their product and intentionally hidden its limited lifetime (*réticence dolosive*), consumers may be entitled to ask for price reduction or the termination of the contract. This lack of consent is however difficult to invoke, especially due to the burden of proof. In fact, the consumer has to prove not only that they would not have bought the good (or with different terms and conditions), but also that there was intent on the part of the trader. This evidence is particularly difficult to furnish in cases of premature obsolescence as the defect may be due to negligence or justified based on various reasons, including economic, technical, safety, aesthetic, financial or IP reasons.[3064] Moreover, the cause of premature obsolescence generally stems from the actions, decisions or negligence of the manufacturer and thus not the contracting party with whom the consumer concluded the sales contract. In these cases, consumers will only be able to invoke the lack of consent against the seller if the latter knew about the deceit.[3065] In this regard, a Belgian court has already held that the failure to warn the buyer at the time of sale that the manufacturer is about to change its model does not constitute deceit.[3066] Here too, and as shown by this case law, close links can be pointed out between deceit and the UCPD provisions. Deceit can be the result of unfair commercial practice if it leads to the conclusion of a contract.[3067]

879. In cases of unlawful cause or error of cause – Thirdly, the theory of the cause (*théorie de la cause*) could be relevant in certain cases of premature

3063 See e.g. Bruxelles, 19 avril 1985, *J.T.*, 1986, p. 162, which concerned a computer which did not have a function described in the brochure that had convinced the buyer to purchase the device.

3064 See *supra*, n° 105.

3065 A. Hamann, 'Obsolescence programmée: le droit en panne?', 102 *D.C.C.R.* (2014) p. 72. For a similar reasoning, see also S. BAR, "Quand le compteur kilométrique trompe l'acheteur d'un véhicule d'occasion", note sous Anvers, 24 juin 2002, R.G.D.C., 2004, pp. 46 *et seq.*

3066 Bruxelles, 17 janvier 1973, réformant Comm. Bruxelles, 25 août 1971, *J.C.B.*, 1973, 295, as cited in A. Hamann, 'Obsolescence programmée: le droit en panne?', 102 *D.C.C.R.* (2014) p. 63.

3067 P. Van Ommeslaghe, *Droit des obligations – Tome I*, (Bruylant 2010) n° 152.

obsolescence.[3068] The cause can be defined as all the reasons that have led the parties to conclude the contracts.[3069] If the cause of the contract is unlawful or erroneous, the contractual parties can ask for the contract to be cancelled. The cause could, for example, be deemed unlawful if the product has been designed in a way that artificially and purposefully limits its lifetime, like cases of obsolescence by notification.[3070] Such practices could also be sanctioned on the basis of the UCPD, as discussed in the third chapter of this book.[3071] One could consider that there is an error of cause on the consumer side if the product lifetime is shorter than the normal product lifetime that could have been expected.[3072] This encompasses cases where the smartphone operating system is no longer developed or where spare parts are no longer produced. Both contractual options are interesting for consumers facing premature obsolescence as they provide protection that last longer than the guarantee period.

c) *Other non-legal remedies*

880. Other possible (sustainable) remedies as a last resort – Besides the remedies provided for by legal and commercial guarantees and by general sales law, consumers who are confronted with premature obsolescence still have some possibilities to remedy the defect and prolong the lifetime of their goods. On one hand, some manufacturers and sellers voluntarily provide for remedies ('original repair'). They have their own repair network and sometimes offer repair subscriptions.[3073] Consumers may thus turn to them to request repair against payment. On the other hand, if no such remedies are available, the consumer also has the possibility of repairing the good himself ('DIY-repair'), which can be done within the framework of *Repair cafés* or with the assistance of the networked learning platform *iFixit*[3074], or to have it repaired by an independent repairer ('independent repair').

881. A long and rocky road towards repair – However, as already discussed, a number of obstacles hinder the ability of consumers to repair their own goods or have them repaired at a reasonable price and speed by either third-

[3068] A. Hamann, 'Obsolescence programmée: le droit en panne?', 102 *D.C.C.R.* (2014) pp. 66–67 and pp. 72–73.

[3069] Cass. (1re ch.), 14 mars 2008, *Pas.*, 2008, I, p. 708.

[3070] See *supra*, n° 102.

[3071] See *supra*, n° 340.

[3072] On that point, the reasoning is very similar to the one followed when relying on the objective conformity requirements established by Article 7 of the SGD (n° 693 *et seq.*).

[3073] J. Rasking, 'Abonnement op herstelling', 23 January 2021, available on: <https://www.standaard.be/cnt/dmf20210122_98206055>.

[3074] See *supra*, n° 61. For other concrete examples of such initiatives, see Ellen MacArthur Foundation, *Empowering repair* (2016) pp. 7–8.

party repair service providers or by the original manufacturers and traders.[3075] Barriers to DIY and independent repairs are mainly due to the reluctancy of manufacturers to facilitate repair outside their authorized network because of quality and safety concerns[3076], liability issues[3077] or intellectual property rights and other confidential proprietary knowledge.[3078] Faced with such barriers, consumers may easily be tempted to replace their defective products instead. In comparison with the relatively high repair costs, the purchase price of a new product may seem economically more attractive.[3079] Moreover, consumers who choose replacement get a brand-new appliance, which usually incorporates new or up-to-date functionalities and is accompanied by at least the EU-wide minimum legal guarantee of two years. Taken together, the repair obstacles result in a significant tendency to discard the product too soon in favour of new products.

882. Further measures ensuring sustainable remedies beyond the legal guarantee period should be adopted – The protection granted by the SGD is restricted to cases where the legal and commercial guarantees apply. Nonetheless, as highlighted by the Council of the European Union[3080], it is important to ensure the right to repair beyond the liability period and at a reasonable cost. This does not only consist in ensuring repair in the original supply chain but also enable 'DIY' repair and independent repair. Rather than compelling sellers and producers to repair at reasonable prices beyond the legal

---

3075 These barriers are linked to (1) product design, (2) the lack of consumables, accessories, spare parts, updates and required tools (3) the lack of information (4) the conditions of after-sales support and (5) the consumer preferences and attitudes. See *supra*, n° 651–656.

3076 Consumers and independent repairers may not have the proper experience or expertise to repair the product. Safety concerns also include cybersecurity, which could be put at risk as the provision of some information entails the risk of creating a gateway into the electronic network of the device owner, increasing vulnerability against hackers and loss of sensitive personal, financial or professional information.

3077 The question on the identity of the 'producer' within the meaning of the product liability legislation in case of repair was raised in the Report from the Commission of 7 May 2018 to the European Parliament, the Council and the European Economic and Social Committee on the Application of the Council Directive on the approximation of the laws, regulations, and administrative provisions of the Member States concerning liability for defective products (85/374/EEC), COM(2018) 246 final, p. 9. Recital 29 of the Proposal for a Directive on liability for defective products (COM(2022) 495 final) states that "*[e]conomic operators that carry out repairs or other operations that do not involve substantial modifications should not be subject to liability under this Directive*".

3078 For more information, see E. Terryn, 'A Right to Repair: Towards Sustainable Remedies in Consumer Law', *E.R.P.L.* (2019) p. 864 at p. 867; H. Hartwig, 'Spare Parts Under European Design and Trade Mark Law', 11 *Journal of intellectual property law & practice* (2016) p. 121.

3079 According to a 2012 study, almost half of consumers give up on repairing the defective good because it is too expensive. See TNS Political & Social, *Flash Eurobarometer 367 – Attitudes of Europeans towards building the single market for green products*, Bruxelles, Commission européenne, 2013, p. 8.

3080 Council conclusions of 22 February 2021 on the New Consumer Agenda, 6364/21, pt. 11.

guarantee period, broader additional measures are necessary to tackle current obstacles to repair. As discussed in the previous chapters of this book, some existing rules already promote sustainable consumption to a certain extent. In addition to the measures already proposed in the previous chapters[3081], additional measures should be taken at EU level to facilitate sustainable remedies throughout the product lifetime.[3082]

883. SPARE PARTS SHOULD BE AVAILABLE FOR A LONGER PERIOD – First, measures should be adopted to ensure the accessibility of spare parts for both consumers and independent repairers. A system where the obligation on sellers would extend beyond the legal guarantee period means that while the faulty product is no longer covered by the guarantee, an obligation remains to assist consumers (and independent repairers) if they request such spare parts.[3083] Such a robust spare parts supply chain design would contribute to more consumer participation in repair and thus to longer product lifespan.[3084] Improving spare parts accessibility could consist in the obligation to keep spare parts for a minimum period and/or for certain types of goods.[3085] The minimum period could be determined according to the average lifespan of products or more general categorisation (e.g. white or brown goods) or only apply to certain products. 3D printing technology could be useful for the implementation of such legislation.[3086] Measures should also be taken to ensure that spare parts (and required tools) are available outside the authorised network. Such rules exist in EU competition law, as shown by Article 4 f) of the new Vertical Block Exemption Regulation.[3087] This provision aims to promote competition

---

3081 See Chapter II on the design and production stage, which recommends the adoption of ecodesign and information requirements on product reparability and upgradability, and Chapter III on the marketing and pre-contractual stage, which recommends improved information on repair to ensure informed consumer choices.

3082 The EC acknowledged the need to *"promot[e] new consumption concepts and behaviours, such as the sharing economy (...) or support for repairs through community and social economy organisations actions (e.g. repair cafés) and for second-hand markets"*. See Communication from the Commission of 13 November 2020 to the European Parliament and the Council on New Consumer Agenda – Strengthening consumer resilience for sustainable recovery, COM(2020) 696 final, p. 8.

3083 ICF, *Study on the costs and benefits of extending certain rights under the Consumer Sales and Guarantees Directive 1999/44/CE* (European Commission 2017) p. 54.

3084 A.R. Mashhadi, B. Esmaeilian, W. Cade, K. Wiens, S. Behdad, 'Mining consumer experiences of repairing electronics: Product design insights and business lessons learned', 137 *J. Clean. Prod.* (2016) p. 725.

3085 Such obligations have already been established for specific product categories under ecodesign regulations. See *supra*, n° 260.

3086 Instead of storing spare parts, it would suffice to produce them with 3D printing when necessary.

3087 Commission Regulation (EU) 2022/720 of 10 May 2022 on the application of Article 101(3) of the Treaty on the Functioning of the European Union to categories of vertical agreements and concerted practices, OJ L 134, 11.5.2022, p. 4–13.

on the aftersales market by facilitating the availability of spare parts outside the authorised network to end-users or to repairers.[3088] Complementary to this legislation, Article 5(a) and (b) of the Regulation on the application of Article 101(3) of the TFEU to categories of vertical agreements and concerted practices in the motor vehicle sector[3089] also restrict vertical agreements, which limit access to spare parts, repair tools or diagnostic or other equipment. Manufacturers are nonetheless allowed to impose the use of original spare parts supplied by them for repairs under guarantees, for free service and when recalling vehicles.[3090] The traceability of repair (including through ICT tools and the Internet of Things) could be used to solve liability issues in case a defect occurs due to improper repair. Another inspiring example comes from France, which established a network connecting manufacturers and repairers, where repairers can get a label.[3091]

884. Spare parts and repair services should remain affordable – Second, fiscal and economic measures should be adopted to make repair less costly and mitigate cases of economic obsolescence.[3092] Inspiration could be drawn from rules applicable in some Member States, like in Sweden, which introduced tax reductions for repair and remanufacturing activities. In the German state of Thuringia, consumers can be reimbursed up to a maximum of 100 euros for a repair carried out by independent repairers or the original manufacturers and traders.[3093] A similar measure has been implemented since 15 December 2022 in France, where consumers will have the possibility of being reimbursed for the repair of certain electrical and electronic appliances that are no longer covered by guarantees, provided that the repair is carried out by authorised repairers.[3094] At EU level, amending the VAT Directive and broaden the lists of goods and services for which reduced VAT rates can be applied should

3088 E. Dieny, 'Ententes – Exemption catégorielle – Article 101§3 TFUE', *in JurisClasseur Concurrence Consommation* (2016) p. 26, para 73.

3089 Commission Regulation (EU) No 461/2010 of 27 May 2010 on the application of Article 101(3) of the Treaty on the Functioning of the European Union to categories of vertical agreements and concerted practices in the motor vehicle sector, OJ L 129, 28.5.2010, p. 52–57.

3090 E. Dieny, *Ententes – Exemption catégorielle – Article 101§3 TFUE, in JurisClasseur Concurrence Consommation* (2016) p. 40, para 141.

3091 This project is called 'STAR' (*Stations Techniques Agréées en Réseau*). See <https://optigede.ademe.fr/fiche/accessibilite-des-pieces-detachees-le-reseau-star>.

3092 TNS Political & Social, *Flash Eurobarometer 367 – Attitudes of Europeans towards building the single market for green products* (European Commission 2013) p. 8.

3093 See <https://www.reparaturbonus-thueringen.de/so-funktioniert-der-reparaturbonus-thueringen>. See also <https://runder-tisch-reparatur.de/der-reparaturbonus-ein-ueberblick/>.

3094 See Art. L. 541-10-4 of the Environmental Code, as introduced by Art. 62 of the Anti-Waste Law. This 'repair bonus' varies from € 10 to € 45 according to the type of product (e.g. € 10 for a coffee machine). The repair fund is financed by producers who must pay financial contributions to producer responsibility organisations ('PROs') to handle products at the end of their lifecycle. For further details on the extended producer responsibility, see Chapter V and more specifically n° 950.

be envisaged.[3095] Another measure for making more spare parts available at competitive prices would be to harvest components from discarded devices.[3096]

885. Access to repair information should be ensured – Third, repair information should be made (more) easily accessible. Manufacturers should be obliged to make maintenance guides and repair instructions publicly available.[3097] At present, this gap is filled by information that is available online. While platforms provide access to repair instructions and videos, fixer community websites, forums and blogs offer advice and expert help. These initiatives for sharing repair information online should be encouraged, as the Ellen MacArthur Foundation emphasized.[3098] On the other hand, spreading existing repair information should not be penalized.[3099] Such bottom-up initiatives could be legally supported, for example, by obliging manufacturers to collaborate with existing platforms for repair information. In addition, Member States should consider providing information on the repairer network to consumers so that the latter would know where to go in case of defect. The Belgian *Conseil Central de l'Economie* made the suggestion of establishing an official list of professional repairers in order to assist consumers in the exercise of their right to repair.[3100] Some German cities and regions already offer an overview of local repair shops on their websites.[3101]

886. Interestingly, the Proposal for a Directive on common rules promoting repair proposes two measures in this sense. First, Article 4 of the Proposal establishes a European Repair Information Form, which consumers will be able to request from any repairer. Having standardised key information on repair services would bring transparency to repair conditions and price and make it easier for consumers to assess and compare repair offers. Second, Article 7 introduces an obligation for Member States to provide for at least one online national platform to connect consumers with repairers and sellers of refurbished goods in their area. The platform would enable searches by location and quality standards, helping consumers find attractive offers, and boosting visibility for repairers.

887. Some aspects of IP law should be reviewed – Last but not least, patent, copyright, design and trademark law, which hinders some types of

---

3095 Similar suggestions were made in RREUSE, *Improving product reparability: Policy options at EU level* (2015) p. 9.

3096 See Chapter V on the end-of-life stage.

3097 See also European Parliament Resolution of 4 July 2017 on a longer lifetime for products: benefits for consumers and companies, 2016/2272(INI), pt. 9.

3098 Ellen MacArthur Foundation, *Empowering repair* (2016) p. 11.

3099 *Ibid.*

3100 Avis conjoint du Conseil Central de l'Economie du 21 février 2020 sur l'économie circulaire, CCE 2019-1660, p. 8.

3101 See <https://runder-tisch-reparatur.de/wo-finde-ich-eine-werktstatt-in-der-naehe/>.

repair and the spreading of repair information[3102], should be reviewed. Among these legal barriers, there is the fact that a repair could be qualified as '(re) making' a patented product or applying a patented process and thus constitute an infringement under current patent law.[3103] Another barrier stems from the broad prohibition under copyright law on circulating means to circumvent technological protective measures, which might make it difficult to effectively repair consumer goods with embedded software.[3104] Several policy solutions have been formulated to remove or mitigate these barriers to repair. For example, a general copyright misuse clause to EU copyright could be adopted in order to avoid situations where manufacturers use protective measures that force the consumer to turn to their repair services.[3105]

D. CONCLUSION

888. The various strengths of guarantee rules – While, as explained in the previous chapters of this book, ecodesign measures and preventative measures linked to consumer information could go some way towards combatting premature obsolescence, guarantee rights also have an important role to play in a comprehensive strategy. As rightly emphasized by the EC, the SGD establishes 'horizontal material rights for consumers'.[3106] These rights include the right to repair, which helps extend the lifespan of products by reversing product obsolescence, thus avoiding products being (prematurely) discarded when a

---

3102 For a good summary of the major legal barriers to repair, see E. Van Gool, 'A European 'right to repair': Yes! But how (far)?', *CCM Blog*, 25 April 2021, available on: <https://law.kuleuven.be/ccm/blog/?p=68>. For a more detailed analysis on how device makers try to leverage intellectual property (IP) rights to restrict repair See also A. Perzanowski, *The Right to Repair: Reclaiming the Things We Own* (Cambridge University Press 2022) p. 110 at p. 166.

3103 R.M. Ballardini, M. Norrgård, T. Minssen, 'Enforcing patents in the era of 3D printing Get access Arrow', 10 *Journal of Intellectual Property Law & Practice* (2015) p. 852 at p. 856, as cited in E. Van Gool, 'A European 'right to repair': Yes! But how (far)?', *CCM Blog*, 25 April 2021, available on: <https://law.kuleuven.be/ccm/blog/?p=68>. See also A. Perzanowski, *The Right to Repair: Reclaiming the Things We Own* (Cambridge University Press 2022) p. 119 at p. 124.

3104 A.J.D. Rosborough, 'Unscrewing the Future: The Right to Repair and the Circumvention of Software TPMs in the EU', 11 *Journal of Intellectual Property, Information Technology and E-Commerce Law* (2020) p. 26 at p. 48, as cited in E. Van Gool, 'A European 'right to repair': Yes! But how (far)?', CCM Blog, 25 April 2021, available on: <https://law.kuleuven.be/ccm/blog/?p=68>.

3105 S. Svensson, J.L. Richter, E. Maitre-Ekern, T. Pihlajarinne, A. Maigret, C. Dalhammar, *The Emerging 'Right to Repair' legislation in the EU and the U.S.*, Paper presented at Going Green Care Innovation (Vienna 2018).

3106 See Communication from the Commission of 11 March 2020 to the European Parliament, the Council, the European Economic and Social Committee and the Committee of the Regions on A new Circular Economy Action Plan – For a cleaner and more competitive Europe, COM(2020) 98 final, p. 5.

defect occurs.[3107] The new 'update-obligation' imposed on sellers by the SGD also contributes to postponing the (functional) obsolescence of goods with digital elements. This makes an important difference in a context of the increased digitalisation of consumer goods. Thanks to the relatively open-ended conformity criteria set out by the SGD, consumers can invoke these provisions in a wide variety of cases of premature obsolescence. But the biggest strength of the SGD lies in the indirect effects of those rights and obligations on businesses and consumers. On the business side, the SGD provides an incentive to sellers (and indirectly to producers) to offer goods with a longer lifetime in fear of contractual liability and the ensuing economic and reputational consequences. On the consumer side, the guarantee rights help bring product lifetime to the front of consumers' minds and influence their purchasing decisions in favour of long-lasting and quality goods.[3108]

889. The complex interplay between consumer law and environmental concerns – Consumer sales rules, like the SGD, have always aimed at protecting the economic rights of consumers while finding a fair balance between the interests of contractual parties, without considering the more general interest of environmental protection. Consumer law is traditionally based on the paradigm that consumers should be protected so that they can 'consume' more. This is exemplified by the right to replace defective goods enshrined in the SGD or the right of withdrawal granted by the CRD. As rightly pointed out by the EESC, the rules on legal and commercial guarantees "*are designed to ensure consumers' money is well spent. Consumer goods, particularly durables, are investments which can only be shown to have 'paid off' in the buyer's household after years of use*".[3109] Hence, more than disregarding the environmental impact of consumer rights, the traditional focus of consumer law on economic and contractual interests is in conflict with the objective of environmental protection. This friction is also reflected in the attitude of consumers, who "*may advocate for a better environment, but they may advocate even more strongly in favour of the rights of the widest possible selection of goods at the cheapest price*".[3110]

890. Greening consumer law – As argued at the outset of this book[3111], preserving the environment is so fundamental that it should be reflected in all

3107 See also C. Twigg-Flesner, 'The law on guarantees and repair work', in T. Cooper (ed.), *Longer lasting products – Alternatives to the throwaway society* (Gower Publishing Limited 2010) pp. 195–196.

3108 GfK Belgium, *Consumer market study to support the fitness check of EU consumer and marketing law* (European Commission 2017) p. 42.

3109 Opinion of the Economic and Social Committee on the 'Proposal for a European Parliament and Council Directive on the sale of consumer goods and guarantees', OJ C 66, 3.3.1997, pt. 2.4.

3110 C. Kye, 'Environmental Law and the Consumer in the European Union', 7 *Journal of Environmental Law* (1995) p. 32 *et seq.*

3111 See *supra*, n° 34.

EU policies, including consumer policy. Therefore, consumer policy should contribute to this goal far more substantially than it currently does by integrating environmental concerns in its application and interpretation.[3112] This does not mean that environmental protection should undermine consumer protection.[3113] The two objectives, enshrined in Article 11 (sustainable development) and Article 12 (consumer protection) of the TFEU, need to be reconciled, and only in case of conflict, the first should prevail. Such a shift seems possible and even encouraged under primary EU Law, given the principle of consistency in Article 7 of the TFEU and the Union's goals and fundamental rights of Article 3(3) and (5) of the TEU and Article 37 of the Charter. This implies the need to enhance the idea of consumers, who should not be seen merely as the vulnerable party that needs to be protected[3114], but also as 'citizens' capable of adopting environmentally responsible behaviours with a long-term perspective, even at the cost of other interests attached to their own position in the marketplace.[3115]

891. Guarantee rules should apply to all consumer goods – The guarantee rules do not apply to all consumer goods. While some exclusions are justifiable, like when the nature of the goods is incompatible with the guarantee rules, other exclusions do not seem appropriate. This is the case of second-hand goods sold at public auction, which may be excluded from the scope of application of this legislation by Member States. Because this exclusion runs contrary to the European goal of transitioning to a more sustainable and circular economy, it should be removed by means of an amendment to the SGD. The corresponding recitals should also be amended. In addition to these amendments, the SGD should contain or refer to an EU-wide definition of 'second-hand goods' to address the current lack of clarity surrounding the concept. The definition of 'second-hand goods' previously proposed in the first chapter of this book could be introduced in the SGD, that is "*goods that are used again for the same purpose in their original form or with little enhancement or change*". Alternatively, the definition could be borrowed or at least inspired by existing EU legislation or standards.

3112 See also E. Terryn, 'A Right to Repair? Towards Sustainable Remedies in Consumer Law', 4 *E.R.P.L.* (2019) p. 853; H.-W. Micklitz, 'Squaring the Circle? Reconciling Consumer Law and the Circular Economy', 8 *EuCML* (2019) pp. 230–231; V. Mak, E. Terryn, 'Circular Economy and Consumer Protection: The Consumer as a Citizen and the Limits of Empowerment Through Consumer Law', 43 *J. Consum. Policy* (2020) p. 235 at p. 244.

3113 E. Maitre-Ekern, C. Dalhammar, 'Towards a hierarchy of consumption behaviour in the circular economy', 26 *Maastricht Journal of European and Comparative Law* (2019) p. 412.

3114 N. Jeanne, ""Prêt à jeter?" – A propos du délit d'obsolescence programmée", in *Mélanges en l'honneur de Geneviève Giudicelli-Delage* (Dalloz 2016) p. 612; E. Maitre-Ekern, C. Dalhammar, 'Towards a hierarchy of consumption behaviour in the circular economy', 26 *Maastricht Journal of European and Comparative Law* (2019) p. 398.

3115 T. Wilhelmsson, 'Consumer Law and the Environment: From Consumer to Citizen', 21 *J. Consum. Policy* (1998) p. 61; J. Lewis, S. Inthorn, K. Wahl-Jorgensen, *Citizens or Consumers? What the Media Tell Us About Political Participation* (Open University Press 2005); E. Terryn, 'A Right to Repair: Towards Sustainable Remedies in Consumer Law', *E.R.P.L.* (2019) p. 873.

892. Exceptions should not be allowed to circumvent mandatory rules of EU law – Defects other than wear and tear can occur due to different causes, including poor quality and/or the improper and careless use or abuse of the product by the consumer.[3116] To ensure a fair balance between the responsibility of consumers and sellers/producers, the SGD provides for exceptions to the seller's liability if the consumer was informed of the deviating product characteristic or if he contributed to the lack of conformity. However, these exceptions may be used by sellers to circumvent mandatory rules imposed by EU law. The application of these exceptions should therefore be explicitly excluded if the traders (including producers) did not comply with certain EU rules, like ecodesign requirements or blacklisted practices. In addition, some guidance should be given on the application and interpretation of these exceptions in practice. This could be done by the introduction of criteria and/or practical examples in the SGD or in an SGD guidance document.

893. The legal guarantee period should last longer – The SGD establishes a two-year liability period that applies to all goods, except where the contract provides for a continuous supply of the digital content or digital service. Once this period has elapsed, consumers are deprived of any protection under EU law and can only rely on commercial guarantees (if any) or on other national law mechanisms, which are generally more difficult to invoke and offer fewer remedies. Admittedly, Member States may go beyond the minimum level of protection granted by the SGD and provided for a longer liability period. This wide discretion creates nonetheless many disparities between the Member States which negatively impact cross-border transactions and contribute to confusing consumers on their rights. Three amendments to the SGD should be made to solve this issue. First, the guarantee period should be fully differentiated, meaning that it should vary from product to product depending on their average lifetime or other criteria, such as the purchase price or product characteristics. This approach, which is already followed by The Netherlands and Finland, is more flexible (and thus future-proof) and allows maximizing the positive effects of an extended guarantee period. This is particularly true when considering the possible combinations of the guarantee rules with other EU rules, like product regulations and information requirements. Second, the possibility of reducing the guarantee period to one year for second-hand goods should be removed as this exception runs counter to the long-term target of shifting towards a more circular economy, in which consumers are encouraged to extend product lifetime by giving a second life to used products. Third, establishing the suspension of the guarantee period in the SGD for new goods that consumers choose to repair instead of replacing them should be considered. This would not only eliminate all disparities between Member States' rules, but also encourage consumers to opt for repair.

[3116] F. Parisi, 'The harmonization of legal warranties in European Sales Law: An economic analysis', 52 *American Journal of Comparative Law* (2004) p. 413.

894. The presumption period should last as long as the guarantee period – Along with the extended guarantee period, the presumption period should also be extended, for the same reasons as explained above. Although this would constitute a bigger burden on the sellers compared to a longer legal guarantee period, they can always deny consumers' allegations by arguing that the lack of conformity was caused by improper use or by external factors. And the more time goes by, the easier it becomes for the sellers to do so. But if combining both extensions is unrealistic, then the extension of the guarantee period should be considered as a higher priority as this measure would be the most effective to prolong product lifetime.

895. The hierarchy of remedies should prioritise repair – As it currently stands, the hierarchy of remedies established by the SGD insufficiently triggers product sustainability. Repair and replacement of obsolete products should not be on an equal footing, but the former should be elevated to the rank of a preferred remedy. It is therefore necessary to rethink the priorities established under this Directive and prioritise repair over replacement, with a view to more effectively countering the premature obsolescence of consumer goods. The EC has recently moved towards this direction with the adoption of its Proposal for a Directive on common rules promoting repair, though the hierarchy established under Article 13 of the SGD could be more thoroughly reviewed.

896. Restrictions to the right to repair should be limited – Whether the hierarchy of remedies is reviewed or not, the exercise of the right to repair should at the very least be facilitated and subject to fewer legal and case law restrictions. While consumers are entitled by the SGD to request repair, they may have no choice but to abandon this sustainable option and turn to replacement or other methods of compensation – namely adequate price reduction or the termination of the contract – if repair is impossible or disproportionate. Such cases should be as limited as possible. Therefore, in addition to a restrictive interpretation of these exceptions to the right to repair, it is recommended to add three new elements to be considered for the proportionality test so that the balance tilts more easily towards repair. These elements include (1) substantial technical difficulties, economic costs or other risks involving the repair, (2) the design of the relevant product components as well as the availability of indispensable spare parts, repair information or repair services, and (3) the potential environmental impact caused by the chosen remedy. In addition to that, several measures should be adopted to lift obstacles to repair. Such measures may consist of adopting ecodesign requirements as to product reparability, imposing the availability of (essential) spare parts and lowering repair costs through economic and fiscal means.

897. Repair should be (further) developed, facilitated and stimulated – According to the SGD, repair must be carried out free of charge, within a reasonable period of time and without any significant inconvenience to the consumer. Although these modalities facilitate repair to a certain extent, the current legislation is not sufficient to nudge consumers towards this remedy. Additional rules may foster repair, without it becoming too burdensome for the sellers. Besides measures encouraging consumers to adopt sustainable behaviour[3117], other rules could improve the convenience of repair. For example, the SGD should provide repair to be carried out within one month, except if a substitute good is provided to the consumer. In this latter case, the timeframe could be prolonged to two months.

898. The imbalance between repair and the three other remedies should be offset – As already emphasized, the possibility of invoking replacement and the two subsidiary remedies should be restricted; repair should be favoured. Several amendments to the SGD could be made to offset the imbalance between repair and the three other remedies. For example, contrary to what the SGD currently provides, sellers should be entitled to charge consumers for prior use when offering new goods as replacements, except if these new goods are repaired, refurbished or remanufactured.

899. Remedies other than repair should be made more sustainable – In case repair is not a practicable option, it is also important to improve the sustainability of the three other remedies, namely replacement, price reduction and the termination of the contract. First, to foster sustainable replacement, it should be clear that repaired, refurbished or remanufactured goods can be used to replace a defective product provided that they have the same value as the replaced product. These clarifications should be given through a definition in the SGD to adjust national implementation of this legislation. Second, in case of termination of the contract, consumers should have the choice to receive either cash or vouchers as reimbursement. Third, as regards price reduction, the consumer should be entitled to a proportionate reduction of the price if the goods lacking conformity still clearly offer functionality and if repair or 'circular replacement' are impossible.

900. The right to reject should no longer be possible – Because the right to reject far from encourage sustainable behaviour on the consumer side, it is recommended to restrict the leeway left to the Member States to specific remedies that national rules (not specific to consumer contracts) provide for. The possibility of granting consumers the right to reject should be removed.

901. Producer liability mechanisms should be improved – In most cases of premature obsolescence, the lack of conformity is (mainly) due to a decision

3117 See Chapter III on the marketing and pre-contractual stage.

taken by the producer of the product, the software producer or the designer of the digital content. It is therefore important to pin the liability upon who is truly responsible for the lack of conformity linked to product durability. The seller's right of redress may be particularly useful in this regard, but due to various factors, the chances for the seller to successfully assert their right are quite low in practice. Consequently, the system loses its potential deterrent effects. Two kinds of measures should be taken to improve this liability system. First, the seller's right of redress should be strengthened by measures that lighten their burden, including measures on the availability of spare parts. Second, consumers should be granted the right, under EU law, to directly claim remedies against the producer (or their regional representative). The producers' obligation to repair introduced by Article 5 of the Proposal for a Directive on common rules promoting repair is an important step forward, though in the long term EU law makers should go one step further and establish a general direct producer liability system.

902. Commercial guarantees should be further regulated – Commercial guarantees, although not initially linked to environmental concerns, can serve to promote product sustainability and sustainable consumption. While they can reassure and protect consumers against early failures for a wider range of products and give them an indicator of product quality and durability, these guarantees also help traders to signal the sustainable features of their products and encourage them to compete effectively in the market on these aspects. However, the SGD hardly regulates commercial guarantees and the freedom left to the guarantors is not necessarily used with the aim of prolonging product lifespan. The SGD should therefore further regulate commercial guarantees. Among the possible amendments that could be made in this regard, there is a need to rethink the hierarchy of remedies to foster repair and integrate more sustainability into the other available remedies, as proposed for the legal guarantee. Amendments to the SGD should also be envisaged to legally ban unreasonable liability restrictions. For example, the SGD could prohibit clauses removing liability due to repair by a third party if repair was carried out by a repairer registered on an official list of professional repairers.

903. Information on guarantees should be clearer – Guarantee rights and remedies will only be fully effective if consumers are aware and have a good understanding of them. However, studies have revealed that this is far from being the case at present. As rightly pointed out by T. Knight et al., "*[t]his implies some form of advertising will be necessary – both as a means of ensuring lifetime is a conscious consideration at the start of the purchase process and increasing consumers' receptiveness to information on lifetimes they encounter during the process*".[3118] In this regard, it is recommended to explicitly include in the SGD

[3118] T. Knight et al., *Electrical and electronic product design: product lifetime* (WRAP 2013) p. 60.

the general obligation for the seller to provide information on the content of the legal guarantee, whether a commercial guarantee is granted or not. Moreover, minimum standards for the disclosure of this information should be adopted. This could take the form of a standardised information form that would be provided before the conclusion of the sales contract, with information on the relation between legal and commercial guarantees as well as on the content of both of them. This form would be included in the Annexes to the SGD.

904. Measures promoting sustainable remedies throughout the product lifetime – Amending the SGD must not remain an isolated intervention. In addition to the proposed amendments, parallel legislative initiatives should be taken at EU level to promote and facilitate sustainable remedies throughout the product lifetime. These measures include among others those that were proposed in the previous chapters of this book, such as ecodesign requirements, labels or obligations on spare parts, but also other measures, such as fiscal and economic measures. Only with the support of such measures can the potential of the SGD's conformity framework to foster more sustainable consumption choices be unleashed. These measures are also of crucial importance for cases that do not fall within the scope of the legal and commercial guarantees and where repair must be carried out by consumers themselves and independent repairers. For this combination of rules to be the most effective, a certain degree of consistency should be ensured between all references to product sustainability aspects (e.g. product lifetime, durability, reparability) as well as between all the established periods (e.g. guarantee periods, availability period of spare parts, information obligation on product lifetime).

905. Ambitious amendments are needed – The comprehensive analysis of the SGD revealed that it makes only a minor contribution to the achievement of the non-economic goal of sustainable consumption of goods. Admittedly, some businesses devote a great deal of effort to providing aftersales advice and services to consumers (and sometimes to independent repairers). However, minimal intervention and voluntary commitments do not seem appropriate to promote product sustainability. Only regulatory intervention will remove the barriers that hinder the prolonged use of products and allow the necessary shift towards a more sustainable and circular economy. The EC has acknowledged the need for amendments of the still very new SGD,[3119] as evidenced by the adoption of the Proposal for a Directive on common rules promoting repair. Hopefully, the SGD will be reviewed so that it no longer ignores sustainability aspects, while optimally interacting with the wider network of rules.

3119 Communication from the Commission of 13 November 2020 to the European Parliament and the Council on New Consumer Agenda – Strengthening consumer resilience for sustainable recovery, COM(2020) 696 final, p. 7 at p. 9 and especially action n°6.

CHAPTER V

THE END-OF-LIFE STAGE: PREVENTING PRODUCTS FROM BECOMING WASTE AND REDUCING THEIR ENVIRONMENTAL IMPACTS ONCE THEY ARE

A. INTRODUCTION

906. Beyond recycling – As previously discussed, when a product reaches the end of its lifetime and the state of obsolescence is irreversible, it becomes waste.[3120] In this scenario, the product can either be recycled or destroyed without being recycled, while some of its parts or components may be used for energy or other forms of recovery. However, before that waste stage, when products are not irreversibly obsolete, several operations may lengthen product lifetime. These are called 'value-retention processes' and include direct reuse, repair, refurbishment and remanufacturing.[3121] While recycling has been the main focus of the government and industry over recent decades, attention is now turning to these value-retention processes. These are particularly important in the fight against premature obsolescence as they allow this inevitable event to occur as late as possible, by prolonging or renewing the use cycle of products.

907. General and sectoral waste rules – Current EU waste law includes general rules and guidelines, like the Waste Framework Directive ('WFD')[3122], but also sector-oriented rules, such as the Waste Electrical and Electronic Equipment Directive ('WEEE')[3123], the Batteries Directives[3124], as well as the

[3120] See *supra*, n° 92.

[3121] See *supra*, n° 150.

[3122] Directive 2008/98/EC of the European Parliament and of the Council of 19 November 2008 on waste and repealing certain Directives, OJ L 312, 22.11.2008, p. 3–30.

[3123] Directive 2012/19/EU of the European Parliament and of the Council of 4 July 2012 on waste electrical and electronic equipment (WEEE), OJ L 197, 24.7.2012, p. 38–71.

[3124] Directive 2006/66/EC of the European Parliament and of the Council of 6 September 2006 on batteries and accumulators and waste batteries and accumulators and repealing Directive 91/157/EEC, OJ L 266, 26.9.2006, p. 1–14.

Directive on end-of life vehicles ('ELV').[3125] These legal instruments set among others targets on collection and recycling activities and promote repair, reuse and recycling. They impose minimum requirements for extended producer responsibility schemes and differentiate the contribution paid by producers based on the costs necessary to treat their products at the end-of-life stage. These EU rules generally leave a wide margin of discretion to the Member States, leading to very heterogenous approaches within the Member States.[3126] In addition, some of them, including Belgium, France and Germany, have adopted purely national initiatives to further prolong the lifetime of discarded products.

908. Overview of the fifth chapter – The fifth and last chapter of this book will be dedicated to the network of rules surrounding the end-of-life stage of consumer products. The first section will describe the three possible scenarios for discarded products, namely reuse, recycling and disposal, and examine them through the lens of product sustainability. The section will also discuss the barriers on the consumer and business side that prevent obsolete products from being reused or recycled. The second section of this chapter will delve into waste law, taking the WFD as a basis for the analysis of all the rules. Several recommendations will be made with a view to improving the contribution of these rules to product sustainability.

B. MAPPING KEY ELEMENTS OF PRODUCT'S END-OF-LIFE STAGE

1. SUSTAINABLE AND LESS SUSTAINABLE SCENARIOS AT THE END-OF-LIFE STAGE

909. Three possible paths – There are different possibilities to handle products that have reached the end of their use cycle. Besides recycling, two other options exist, namely reuse or disposal of the obsolete products. All the options that can be envisaged by businesses at the products' end-of-life stage can be put under the umbrella term of 'reverse logistics' (or 'reverse supply chain'), which means the process of moving goods from their typical final destination for the purpose of capturing value, or proper disposal.[3127] The choice between these options depends on the previous product use cycle(s) and how the product became obsolete. As previously discussed in this book, there are various types of

[3125] Directive 2000/53/EC of the European Parliament and of the Council of 18 September 2000 on end-of life vehicles, OJ L 269, 21.10.2000, p. 34–43.

[3126] The legal fragmentation is even more important in Belgium as waste policy is a regional competence. See Art. 39 of the Belgian Constitution as well as Art. 6 §1 II 2° of the Loi spéciale du 8 août 1980 de réformes institutionnelles, *M.B.*, 15 août 1980, p. 9434.

[3127] K. Hawks, 'What is Reverse Logistics?', *Reverse Logistics Magazine* (2006) p. 12.

obsolescence (i.e. material, functional, indirect, economic and psychological).[3128] In some cases, product obsolescence is reversible, whereas in others, products are obsolete beyond recovery at product level. In terms of sustainability, it is better to favour options that delay the moment when products become waste.

910. Prolonging product lifetime through reuse – The first possibility is to reuse products. This encompasses direct reuse, repair, refurbishment and remanufacturing.[3129] These 'value-retention processes' allow retaining the value of the products within the system through the extension of their lifetime.[3130] Reuse is only possible for products that are not irreversibly obsolete and is highly dependent on the design of the product.[3131] In the first three scenarios, the obsolete product that is discarded by the user is reused by someone else, either directly or after being repaired or refurbished, whereas in the last scenario, only some of its parts or components are recovered through remanufacturing. As already explained in the first chapter of this book, these options allow lengthening the lifetime of the product – or its parts or components in the case of remanufacturing. This shows, once again, how ecodesign is fundamental: the more ecodesigned the products, the greater their value at their end-of-life.

911. Reducing the environmental impacts of the end-of-life stage of the product through recycling – The second option is to recycle the product.[3132] This reduces the environmental impacts of products at the end-of-life stage. However, recycling obsolete products alone is not enough to retain the value lost in such a cycle. A 2018 study for the Swedish Recyclers' Association shows that when materials are recycled, three quarters of the value is lost after one use cycle.[3133] Moreover, in contrast with the general belief that recycling is intrinsically green, it is important to note that recycling activities, like any physical process, have an impact on the environment. As rightly summarised by T. Cooper, energy is consumed and pollution is caused when collecting, sorting, cleaning and separating waste products into their constituent materials, as well as when manufacturing and distributing the products made from recycled materials.[3134] Therefore, although recycling is better than landfilling

---

3128 See Chapter I, and more specifically n° 98 *et seq.*

3129 See *supra*, n° 150–154.

3130 See International Resource Panel, *Redefining Value – The Manufacturing Revolution. Remanufacturing, Refurbishment, Repair and Direct Reuse in the Circular Economy* (United Nations Environment Programme 2018) p. 6.

3131 This highlights once again how ecodesign is important to tackle premature obsolescence. See *supra*, n° 168–174.

3132 For further details on recycling, see *supra*, n° 155–156.

3133 Material Economics, *Retaining Value in the Swedish Materials System. Material Economics* (2018) p. 3.

3134 T. Cooper, *Beyond recycling – The longer life option* (The New Economics Foundation 1994) p. 1.

and incineration, it should still be a last resort option, especially when it implies 'downcycling' (i.e. when the materials of the product are subsequently reprocessed into products, materials or substances, leading to new materials of lesser quality and/or reduced functionality).[3135]

912. DESTROYING OBSOLETE PRODUCTS – When neither reuse nor recycling is possible or carried out, products are destroyed. The disposal of products can consist in landfilling or incinerating waste. Landfill means waste disposal sites for the deposit of waste onto or into land. Incineration is the process of burning waste to ashes. Some parts or components can also be used to produce energy or reprocessed into materials that are to be used as fuels or for backfilling operations. This third option is chosen by certain businesses, for example, right after the release of the product if it has not been bought by any consumer. This is also the case of some products that are returned by consumers who invoked their right of withdrawal, which are being incinerated.[3136]

913. Different degrees of sustainability – In terms of sustainability, products that are discarded must preferably recirculate. And "*the tighter the circles are, the larger the savings should be in the embedded costs in terms of material, labour, energy, capital and of the associated rucksack of externalities, such as GHG emissions, water, or toxic substances*".[3137] Following this 'inner circle' reasoning, consumers should refrain from discarding products they no longer want, but instead sell or pass them on for reuse, and as a last resort, explore the possibilities of returning them for remanufacturing or recycling.[3138] Indeed, as emphasized by E. Maitre-Ekern, "*[w]aste is a resource that has the potential to replace primary raw materials from traditional extractive resources*".[3139] Such reasoning shows that planning the obsolescence of products could be acceptable if the services provided at the end-of-life of products were better organised.[3140] In other words,

---

3135 See *supra*, n° 156.

3136 See J. Schiffer, 'The unsustainable cost of free returns', *Vogue Business*, 30 July 2019, available on: <https://www.voguebusiness.com/consumers/returns-rising-costs-retail-environmental>, as well as R. De Bruyn, 'Vente en ligne: quel impact sur l'environnement?', *Ecoconso*, 13 December 2019, available on: <https://www.ecoconso.be/fr/content/vente-en-ligne-quel-impact-sur-lenvironnement>. See *supra*, n° 645.

3137 Ellen MacArthur Foundation, *Towards the circular economy: Economic and business rationale for an accelerated transition* (2013) p. 30.

3138 E. Maitre-Ekern, C. Dalhammar, 'Towards a hierarchy of consumption behaviour in the circular economy', 26 *Maastricht Journal of European and Comparative Law* (2019) p. 405.

3139 E. Maitre-Ekern, 'Taking products out of waste law: a new legal framework for the circular economy', in Nils F. Nissen & Melanie Jaeger-Erben (eds.), *3rd international Product Lifetimes and the Environment (PLATE) conference* (Berlin 2019) p. 495.

3140 C. Montalvo et al., *A longer lifetime for products: benefits for consumers and companies* (European Union 2016) p. 17; A. Zeeuw van der Laan, M. Aurisicchio, 'Planned obsolescence in the circular economy', in C. Bakker and R. Mugge (eds.), *Product Lifetimes And The Environment 2017 – Conference Proceedings* (IOS Press 2017) p. 446 at p. 452. See also n° 7.

"[p]roducts that are part of a performance-based service can have shorter lifespans with fewer negative consequences if the product is remanufactured or recycled after the use phase".[3141]

2. BARRIERS THAT HINDER REVERSING PRODUCT OBSOLESCENCE

914. Several barriers on the consumer and business side – There are several barriers that prevent obsolete products from being reused or recycled. These barriers have already been identified as some of the main causes of premature obsolescence in the first chapter of this book.[3142] They can be assigned to two categories: the barriers associated with consumer behaviour and perception and those encountered by businesses.

915. Consumers' storage habits and lack of knowledge and trust – There are two main barriers on the consumer side. First, some products are stored in consumers' households.[3143] While some of these hibernating products are finally being either donated to charity or handed on to friends or family[3144], others remain in consumers' drawers, the main reasons for this being their concerns about the data stored, their willingness to keep their phones as back-ups or the lack of demand for used devices. This hamper still functioning products from being reused and recycled.[3145] Second, consumer lack knowledge and confidence in the quality of reused, refurbished and remanufactured goods. It should be clear that product quality is not weakened by the use of second-hand spare parts.

916. No incentives for producers – There are different barriers on the business side.[3146] First, there is a lack of economic incentives. Strategies to reverse obsolescence and recycle obsolete products require some costs and

---

3141 EEA, *Circular by design – Products in the circular economy* (European Union 2017) p. 21.

3142 See *supra* on the causes of premature obsolescence (n° 124 *et seq.*).

3143 For more details, see *supra* n° 140 and n° 157.

3144 See also H. Wieser, N. Tröger, 'Exploring the inner loops of the circular economy: Replacement, repair, and reuse of mobile phones in Austria', 172 *J. Clean. Prod.* (2018) p. 3044.

3145 G.T. Wilson, G. Smalley, J.R. Suckling, D. Lilley, J. Lee, R. Mawle, 'The hibernating mobile phone: dead storage as a barrier to efficient electronic waste recovery', 60 *Waste Management* (2017) p. 521 at p. 533.

3146 See also C. Bakker, C. Schuit, *The long view – Exploring product lifetime extension* (United Nations Environment Programme 2017) pp. 51–52. On the barriers encountered in remanufacturing, see K. Jansson, S. Vatanen, I. Karvonen, K. Behm, R. Waugh, D. Fitzsimons, E. Sundin, D. Parker, *Targeted Recommendations – A report by the partners of European Remanufacturing Network* (European Commission 2017), available on: <https://www.remanufacturing.eu/about-remanufacturing.php>.

investments in the research and developments sector. However, some businesses lack initial capital to invest in that area. Moreover, these costs and investments may result in increased product price which may represent a great deal from the company perspective because of low margins and fierce competition in some product sectors.[3147] Second, businesses may also lack the means to reuse and recycle products. They may have no experts at business management level, infrastructure and capacity. Today's product design does not make things easier. As already highlighted in the second chapter of this book, a wide array of products is becoming increasingly complex and technology-intensive, with increasing electronic systems in place.[3148] These product design trends are likely to pose more severe problems for independent operators that do not have a thorough knowledge of the product. Last but not least, the lack of certainty erects a major barrier to product sustainability at the end-of-life stage. Businesses may be uncertain about product returns in terms of quality, quantity and timing, causing an unpredictable flow and unclear potential financial benefits of reverse logistics.[3149]

C. EU WASTE RULES AND NATIONAL INITIATIVES

1. A FRAMEWORK LEGISLATION, THREE MAIN SECTOR-SPECIFIC DIRECTIVES AND A WIDE ROOM FOR MANOEUVRE FOR THE MEMBER STATES

917. The Waste Framework Directive – The Waste Framework Directive, which was amended by Directive (EU) 2018/851[3150], sets out a legal framework for the proper management of waste in the EU, with a view to protecting public health and the environment. The WFD defines key concepts related to waste management, such as the concept of 'waste'. It also establishes core principles, including the waste hierarchy, which promotes waste prevention and re-use over waste recovery and disposal, and extended producer responsibility, whereby the original waste producers bear financial (and sometimes organisational) responsibility for the management of the waste stage of their products. Moreover, the WFD sets targets for preparing for the reuse and recycling of

---

3147 See *supra*, n° 127.

3148 See *supra*, n° 165.

3149 C. Schuit, *The long view – Exploring product lifetime extension* (United Nations Environment Programme 2017) p. 51, referring to M. Starostka-Patyk, M. Zawada, A. Pabian, and M. Abed, *Barriers to reverse logistics implementation in enterprises* (International Conference on advanced Logistics and Transport 2013); M.R. Shaharudin, S. Zailani and K.C. Tan, 'Barriers to product returns and recovery management in a developing country: investigation using multiple methods', 96 *J. Clean. Prod.* (2015) p. 220 p. 232.

3150 Directive (EU) 2018/851 of the European Parliament and of the Council of 30 May 2018 amending Directive 2008/98/EC on waste, OJ L 150, 14.6.2018, p. 109–140.

household waste as well as construction and demolition waste to be achieved by 2025, 2030 and 2035. As emphasized by the recently amended Article 1 of the WFD, this Directive is crucial for the transition to a circular economy. Through its provisions, the WFD allows the mitigation of negative environmental effects of products at the end-of-life, but also to drive product design changes. By allocating the responsibility to producers for the take-back and recycling of their products, and by setting binding targets for preparing for reuse and recycling, it incentivises producers to make products more durable and easier to repair, upgrade, reuse and recycle. The EC is planning to reinforce the role of this legislation through a targeted revision of the Directive.[3151]

918. The WEEE Directive – In addition to this framework directive, several sectoral directives regulate specific streams of waste. They apply the general principles and rules contained in the WFD to various product categories. Among these sectoral directives, there is the WEEE Directive, which was amended by Directive (EU) 2018/849.[3152] The WEEE Directive seeks to prevent waste from electrical and electronic equipment and increase the rates of reuse, recycling and other forms of recovery of this fast-growing waste stream.[3153] This is essential from an environmental perspective on two main grounds. First, the Directive contributes to avoiding or at least minimizing the (significant) environmental and health problems that this type of waste could cause if not managed properly as EEE contains a complex mixture of materials, some of which are hazardous. Second, modern electrical and electronic equipment contains rare and expensive resources, which can be reused and recycled if the waste is effectively managed.

919. The Batteries Directives (soon to be repealed by Regulation?) – Sectoral waste legislation also exists for batteries. This legislation is embodied in the Batteries Directive, which was amended by Directive 2013/56/EU[3154] and

3151 For more information on the impact assessment carried out by the EC in preparation for the revision of the WFD, see <https://ec.europa.eu/info/law/better-regulation/have-your-say/initiatives/13225-Waste-Framework-review-to-reduce-waste-and-the-environmental-impact-of-waste-management_en>.

3152 Directive (EU) 2018/849 of the European Parliament and of the Council of 30 May 2018 amending Directives 2000/53/EC on end-of-life vehicles, 2006/66/EC on batteries and accumulators and waste batteries and accumulators, and 2012/19/EU on waste electrical and electronic equipment, OJ L 150, 14.6.2018, p. 93–99.

3153 According to Eurostat, from 2011 to 2019, the amount of EEE put on the market in the EU evolved from 7.6 million tonnes in 2011 to a new peak of 11.2 million tonnes in 2019. See Eurostat, *Waste statistics – electrical and electronic equipment* (European Union 2022), available on: <https://ec.europa.eu/eurostat/statistics-explained/index.php?title=Waste_statistics_-_electrical_and_electronic_equipment#Electronic_equipment_.28EEE.29_put_on_the_market_and_WEEE_processed_in_the_EU>.

3154 Directive 2013/56/EU of the European Parliament and of the Council of 20 November 2013 amending Directive 2006/66/EC of the European Parliament and of the Council on batteries and accumulators and waste batteries and accumulators as regards the placing on the market of portable batteries and accumulators containing cadmium intended for use in cordless

Directive (EU) 2018/849. This Directive aims at minimising the negative impacts of batteries and accumulators on the environment. To achieve this objective, it prohibits the marketing of batteries containing hazardous substances, defines measures to establish schemes aiming at high levels of collection and recycling, fixes targets for collection and recycling activities, sets out provisions on labelling of batteries and their removability from equipment, and makes producers responsible for the waste management of batteries and accumulators that they place on the market. The Batteries Directive may soon be repealed by a Regulation[3155], as proposed by the EC. The new regulatory framework would (1) establish requirements on recycled content, ensure the recovery of valuable materials and provide guidance to consumers, (2) address non-rechargeable batteries with a view to progressively phasing out their use where alternatives exists and (3) impose sustainability and transparency requirements for batteries taking account of, for instance, the carbon footprint of battery manufacturing, and facilitating reuse, repurposing and recycling.[3156] Such legislation would be a great step forward in the fight against premature obsolescence as batteries are key parts that greatly influence the length of product lifetime.

920. THE ELV DIRECTIVE – Like EEE and batteries, vehicles can cause significant negative environmental impacts if not properly managed at their end-of-life. The ELV Directive, which was also amended by Directive (EU) 2018/849, harmonises rules on end-of life vehicles, with a view to preventing waste from vehicles and promoting the reuse, recycling and recovery of end-of life vehicles and their components, as well as improving the environmental performance of all of the economic operators involved in the life cycle of vehicles. The evaluation of the ELV Directive in 2020 revealed that some improvements were possible, including on the contribution of the Directive to a more circular economy.[3157] The Directive is now under review, with the aim of ensuring that it neatly fits with the European Green Deal objectives and that it encourages the car industry to adopt a sustainable model for the design and production of cars.[3158]

---

power tools, and of button cells with low mercury content, and repealing Commission Decision 2009/603/EC, OJ L 329, 10.12.2013, p. 5–9.

3155 Proposal for a Regulation of the European Parliament and of the Council concerning batteries and waste batteries, repealing Directive 2006/66/EC and amending Regulation (EU) No 2019/1020, COM(2020) 798 final.

3156 Communication from the Commission of 11 March 2020 to the European Parliament, the Council, the European Economic and Social Committee and the Committee of the Regions on A new Circular Economy Action Plan – For a cleaner and more competitive Europe, COM(2020) 98 final, p. 8.

3157 Trinomics, Oeko-Institut, *Support for the Evaluation of the Directive 2000/53/EC on end-of-life vehicles – Final Report* (European Commission 2020).

3158 For more information on the revision of the ELV Directive, see <https://ec.europa.eu/info/law/better-regulation/have-your-say/initiatives/12633-End-of-life-vehicles-revision-of-EU-rules_en>.

921. Implemented by national plans and programmes – To reach the objectives given by these legal instruments, national authorities must establish waste-management plans and waste-prevention programmes.[3159] In these plans and programmes, Member States generally plan to adopt a wide array measures to encourage the design, manufacturing and use of products that are resource efficient, durable, reparable, reusable and capable of being upgraded. Annex IV to the WFD provides a detailed list of examples of waste prevention measures. On the basis of these provisions, Belgium, France and Germany have adopted their waste-management plans and waste-prevention programmes.[3160]

2. SCOPE OF APPLICATION AND LEVEL OF HARMONISATION

922. The (broad) concept of 'waste' – As highlighted by the WFD Guidance, the definition of 'waste' is one of the key concepts of the WFD as it determines whether the substance or object falls within the scope of the Directive[3161], but also whether or not it is subject to *"a mass of rules and regulations which can involve significant costs for various actors"*.[3162] Only certain types of waste are excluded from the scope, such as radioactive waste and waste waters.[3163] Article 3(1) of the WFD defines the notion of 'waste' as *"any substance*

[3159] See Art. 29 WFD, as amended by Directive (EU) 2018/851.

[3160] Concerning national waste-prevention programmes: in Belgium, see OVAM, *Uitvoeringsplan huishoudelijk afval en gelijkaardig bedrijfsafval* (2018), available on: <https://ovam.vlaanderen.be/uitvoeringsplan-huishoudelijk-gelijkaardig-bedrijfsafval>; Gouvernement Wallon, *Plan Wallon des Déchets-Ressources* (2018), available on: <http://environnement.wallonie.be/rapports/owd/pwd/PWDR_3.pdf>; Gouvernement de la Région de Bruxelles Capitale, *Plan de gestion des ressources et des déchets – Pour une consommation durable, sobre, locale et circulaire Pour une société zéro déchet* (2018), available on: <https://environnement.brussels/sites/default/files/user_files/pgrd_181122_fr.pdf>. In France, see Ministère de l'Écologie, du Développement durable et de l'Énergie, *Programme national de prévention des déchets 2014–2020* (République Française 2014), available on: < <https://www.ecologie.gouv.fr/sites/default/files/Programme_national_prevention_dechets_2014-2020.pdf>. The 2021–2017 French Waste Prevention Plan is now being finalised (https://www.ecologie.gouv.fr/cadre-general-prevention-des-dechets). In Germany, see BMU, *Wertschätzen statt Wegwerfen – Abfallvermeidungsprogramm des Bundes unter Beteiligung der Länder Fortschreibung* (2020), available on: <https://www.bmuv.de/fileadmin/Daten_BMU/Download_PDF/Abfallwirtschaft/fortschreibung_abfallvermeidungsprogramm_bund_laender_bf.pdf>. For a good summary of the measures contained in these plans, see the country profiles on waste prevention made by the EEA, available on: <https://www.eea.europa.eu/themes/waste/waste-prevention/countries>.

[3161] Guidance on the interpretation of key provisions of Directive 2008/98/EC on waste (hereafter 'WFD Guidance'), p. 9. See also recital 8 WFD.

[3162] N. Jones, G. Van Calster, 'Waste Regulation', in E. Lees and J. E. Viñuales (eds.), *The Oxford Handbook of Comparative Environmental Law* (Oxford University Press 2019) p. 613. The waste legislation imposes stringent obligations, such as permits and registration, inspections, requirements for cross-border shipments, in order to protect human health and the environment in waste collection, transport, treatment, storage and tipping.

[3163] See the list given in Article 2 of the WFD, which cites the exclusions from the scope of the Directive.

or object which the holder discards or intends or is required to discard". In other words, products become 'waste' when the holder discards (action or activity) or intends to discard (intention) or is required to discard (legal obligation).[3164] The term 'discard' is key in this definition and is meant to embody a comprehensive notion of waste, which may encompass any substance and object that undergoes a recovery or disposal operation.[3165] Whether a substance or object is being discarded has to be decided on a case-by-case basis and taking account of all the specific factual circumstances involved.[3166] For example, the fact that the good is not or is no longer of any use to its holder may constitute evidence that it has been discarded or of an intention or requirement to discard it.[3167] It should be noted that the concept of 'waste' has been broadly interpreted by the ECJ[3168], which mainly aims to avoid the harm caused to the environment by the dumping or uncontrolled disposal of goods. Interestingly, the ECJ clearly stated that the concept of 'waste' does not exclude substances or objects which are capable of economic reuse.[3169] Hence, obsolete products, which are not or no longer of any use to their holder, and which constitute a burden which the latter seeks to discard, are to be considered as waste, even if their state of obsolescence may be reversed.[3170]

923. As opposed to 'non-waste' – Despite this broad interpretation, the ECJ has also drawn a number of boundaries to the concept of waste. In *Shell*, the ECJ ruled that a client who returned the substance or object to the trader, with a view to obtaining a refund pursuant to the sale contract, cannot be

3164 WFD Guidance, p. 10.

3165 *Ibid.* See also ECJ 18 December 1997, Case C-129/96, *Inter-Environnement Wallonie v Région wallonne, EU:C:1997:628*, para 26; ECJ 15 June 2000, Joined cases C-418/97 and C-419/97, *ARCO Chemie Nederland and Others, EU:C:2000:318*, para 36.

3166 N. De Sadeleer, *Droit des déchets de l'UE: de l'élimination à l'économie circulaire* (Bruylant 2016) p. 130.

3167 ECJ 18 April 2002, Case C-9/00, *Palin Granit and Vehmassalon kansanterveystyön kuntayhtymän halitus, EU:C:2002:232*, para 37.

3168 See e.g. ECJ 25 June 1997, Joined cases C-304/94, C-330/94, C-342/94 and C-224/95, *Euro Tombesi, EU:C:1997:314*, para 54; ECJ 15 June 2000, Joined cases C-418/97 and C-419/97, *ARCO Chemie Nederland and Others, EU:C:2000:318*, paras 88 and 97; ECJ 7 September 2004, Case C-1/03, *Van de Walle, EU:C:2004:490*, para 61; ECJ 11 November 2004, Case C-457/02, *Niselli, EU:C:2004:707*, paras 40 and 53; ECJ 4 July 2019, C-624/17, *Tronex, EU:C:2019:564*, para 18.

3169 ECJ 28 March 1990, Joined cases C-206/88 and C-207/88, *Vessoso and Zanetti, EU:C:1990:145*, para 9; ECJ 24 June 2008, Case C-188/07, *Commune de Mesquer, EU:C:2008:359*, para 40; ECJ 3 October 2013, Case C-113/12, *Brady, EU:C:2013:627*, para 42; ECJ 14 October 2020, Case C-629/19, *Sappi Austria Produktion and Wasserverband "Region Gratkorn-Gratwein", EU:C:2020:824*, para 48.

3170 E. Maitre-Ekern gives the example of clothes, which are discarded in containers to be donated. See E. Maitre-Ekern, 'Taking products out of waste law: a new legal framework for the circular economy', in Nils F. Nissen & Melanie Jaeger-Erben (eds.), *3rd international Product Lifetimes and the Environment (PLATE) conference* (Berlin 2019) p. 497.

regarded as having intended to dispose of or recover the substance or object.[3171] This suggests that obsolete products which are returned to the seller when the consumer invokes their withdrawal or guarantee rights should not be considered as waste. Likewise, if it is highly probable that the product will be reused without a prior processing operation, this product "*must no longer be regarded as a burden which its holder seeks to 'discard', but as a genuine product*".[3172] The degree of probability that the product will be reused without a prior processing operation constitutes a criterion relevant for the assessment of whether or not it falls within the definition of 'waste' within the meaning of Article 3 of the WFD. The likelihood of such reuse will be considered high if, beyond the mere possibility of re-using the product in question, there is also a financial advantage for the holder in so doing.[3173] There is no explanation on what is meant by 'prior processing operation', but it can be assumed that reuse operations are not included and may thus be carried out as 'reuse' is defined as "*any operation by which products or components that are not waste are used again for the same purpose for which they were conceived*".[3174] The WFD Guidance gives the example of piece of clothing directly taken from the current owner with the intention of reusing it for the same purpose (even if some repairing is necessary). In this case, the WFD Guidance emphasizes that the material is not waste.[3175] Therefore, obsolete products that have a high probability of being reused (including after some repair) may not be considered as waste.

924. The concept of 'by-products'– Alongside the concept of waste, the WFD introduces the concepts of 'by-products' and 'end-of-waste', which are to be considered as 'non-waste'. Article 5 of the WFD provides the rules and conditions against which the Member States can establish criteria for by-products. This provision was further clarified in Directive (EU) 2018/851. By-products are production residues (i.e. materials that are not deliberately produced)[3176] for which the use is certain and lawful and which can be used directly without any further processing other than normal industrial practice and is produced as an integral part of a production process.[3177]

925. The concept of 'end-of-waste' – The concept of 'end-of-waste' is enshrined in Article 6 of the WFD. It can be used for substances or objects which meet the waste definition and which can reach a non-waste status, after

---

3171 ECJ 12 December 2013, Case C-241/12, *Shell Nederland and Belgian Shell, EU:C:2013:821*, para 46.
3172 ECJ 4 July 2019, Case C-624/17, *Tronex, EU:C:2019:564*, para 23.
3173 *Ibid.* See also ECJ 12 December 2013, Case C-241/12, *Shell Nederland and Belgian Shell, EU:C:2013:821*, para 53.
3174 Art. 3(13) WFD.
3175 WFD Guidance, p. 30.
3176 WFD Guidance, p. 15.
3177 Art. 5(1) WFD.

undergoing a recovery operation (including recycling).[3178] Here, recovery operations are to be distinguished from reuse operations whereby the product or component never becomes waste.[3179] This is also what distinguishes 'end-of-waste' from 'by-products'.[3180] A particular waste stream can cease to be waste if the substance or object is to be used for specific purposes, a market or demand exists for such a substance or object, the substance or object fulfils the technical requirements for the specific purposes and meets the existing legislation and standards applicable to products[3181], and the use of the substance or object will not lead to overall adverse environmental or human health impacts.[3182] If the conditions are met, the products fall outside the scope of the waste legislation.

926. The inappropriate definition of waste – The definition of waste given by the WFD and its broad interpretation is problematic in terms of product sustainability. Admittedly, the rationale underlying this broad interpretation is legitimate. The aim is to minimise the negative effects of waste generation and management on human health and the environment by ensuring that virtually all 'substances and objects' may fall within the scope of waste law and thus have to abide by its stringent rules.[3183] However, as a result, the definition encompasses products that, although they may have no further use for the holder, constitute valuable resources for another user or production process.[3184] The same applies to what the industry calls 'cores', which are product components that are destined to be remanufactured or refurbished but that legally speaking are often classified as waste.[3185] The classification of end-

---

3178 WFD Guidance, p. 22. According to Art. 3(15) WFD, 'recovery' means "*any operation the principal result of which is waste serving a useful purpose by replacing other materials which would otherwise have been used to fulfil a particular function, or waste being prepared to fulfil that function, in the plant or in the wider economy*". It should be noted that "*a recovery operation may be as simple as the checking of waste to verify that it fulfils the end-of-waste criteria*", as emphasized by recital 22 WFD. See also G. Van Calster, *EU Waste Law* (Oxford University Press 2014) pp. 18–19.

3179 For further explanation on this distinction, see *infra*, n° 933.

3180 N. de Sadeleer, 'Scrap Metal Intended for Metal Productions: The Thin Line between Waste and Products', 9 *Journal for European Environmental & Planning Law* (2012) pp. 162–163.

3181 This includes ecodesign requirements, as described in Chapter II on the design and production stage.

3182 Art. 6(1) WFD.

3183 See recital 6 WFD. See also N. de Sadeleer, 'Scrap Metal Intended for Metal Productions: The Thin Line between Waste and Products', 9 *Journal for European Environmental & Planning Law* (2012) pp. 162–163, which rightly points out that this regime seeks to stimulate the recycling market (especially for metal residues) and progressively to replace primary materials with secondary materials, thus triggering resource efficiency.

3184 See E. Maitre-Ekern, 'Taking products out of waste law: a new legal framework for the circular economy', in Nils F. Nissen & Melanie Jaeger-Erben (eds.), *3rd international Product Lifetimes and the Environment (PLATE) conference* (Berlin 2019) p. 496.

3185 European Commission, *Promoting Remanufacturing, Refurbishment, Repair, and Direct Reuse: as a contribution to the G7 alliance on resource efficiency 7–8 February 2017 Brussels, Belgium: workshop report* (European Union 2017) p. 37.

of-use or broken products or cores as waste has various legal, practical and psychological implications[3186], the most problematic one being that it leads to the premature obsolescence of products. Products and cores, which could have been reused, can be disadvantaged (e.g. due to heavy and lengthy procedural requirements to circulate across borders) or excluded from trade because they were classed as waste.[3187] This creates difficulties for reuse businesses to extend the lifetime of certain products. Furthermore, the distinction between waste and non-waste may be unclear in practice.[3188] Hence, the barriers that hinder the extension of product lifetime stem here from the rules themselves. This issue has been acknowledged in France where it has been planned to facilitate products that are waste to stop being waste.[3189]

927. A DISTINCTION SHOULD BE MADE BETWEEN 'WASTE' AND 'OBSOLETE PRODUCTS' – The definition of 'waste' should be fine-tuned and narrowed so that waste legislation is more compatible with the objectives of a circular economy and sustainable consumption. Waste legislation should only apply when no other more sustainable option is available (see #1). It is important to differentiate true 'waste' from "*products that have life left in them*".[3190] Bottom line would be that products at the end of their lifecycle that are now being considered as waste, for example because the probability of being reused is not high enough, would more often be considered as resources. Cores should be as far as possible considered as 'non-waste'. To this end, one could imagine introducing the intermediary concept of 'obsolete products' (see #2).[3191] Discarded products would first be qualified as 'obsolete products', and if after a preliminary assessment at the treatment facilities or by the seller, no reuse operation is possible, the product would be considered as waste. This assessment should be carefully carried out and based on objective and cumulative criteria, otherwise opening the floodgates

3186 For a more detailed description of these implications, see E. Maitre-Ekern, 'Re-Thinking Producer Responsibility for a Sustainable Circular Economy: From Extended Producer Responsibility to Pre-market Producer Responsibility', 286 *J. Clean. Prod.* (2021) p. 6.

3187 European Commission, *Promoting Remanufacturing, Refurbishment, Repair, and Direct Reuse: as a contribution to the G7 alliance on resource efficiency 7–8 February 2017 Brussels, Belgium: workshop report* (European Union 2017) p. 5. See also M.B. Taylor and M. van der Velden, 'Resistance to Regulation: Failing Sustainability in Product Lifecycles', 11 *Sustainability* (2019) p. 10.

3188 D. Watson et al., *Circular Business Models in the Mobile Phone Industry* (TemaNord 2017) p. 74.

3189 Ministère de la Transition Ecologique et Solidaire, *Feuille de route économie circulaire: 50 mesures pour une économie 100% circulaire* (République française 2018) p. 31, pt. 37.

3190 European Commission, *Promoting Remanufacturing, Refurbishment, Repair, and Direct Reuse: as a contribution to the G7 alliance on resource efficiency 7–8 February 2017 Brussels, Belgium: workshop report* (European Union 2017) p. 5.

3191 A similar idea was proposed by E. Maitre-Ekern through the concept of 'a priori non-waste'. See E. Maitre-Ekern, 'Taking products out of waste law: a new legal framework for the circular economy', in Nils F. Nissen & Melanie Jaeger-Erben (eds.), *3rd international Product Lifetimes and the Environment (PLATE) conference* (Berlin 2019) p. 498.

to abuses, i.e. dumping of waste under the guise of value-retention processes.[3192] Those criteria should be laid down by the WFD and could be similar to those established for the end-of-waste status. The introduction of a product passport, as envisaged with the Proposal for Ecodesign for Sustainable Products Regulation, could help obtain the necessary items of information for this assessment.

928. The too strict and fragmented end-of-waste criteria – In addition to introducing the concept of 'obsolete products', amendments should be envisaged concerning the 'end-of-waste' criteria introduced by Article 6 of the WFD. The current criteria are quite strict, preventing substances or objects from reaching a non-waste status. End-of-waste criteria are mostly in place for simple products, while a lot of new waste streams are composed of combined or composite waste streams.[3193] Moreover, the implementation of end-of-waste criteria varies significantly across Member States[3194], and even within the Member State in the case of Belgium.[3195] In some of them, the WFD has been interpreted in such a way that it is very difficult to reuse a product once it becomes waste.[3196] The lack of harmonisation creates legal uncertainty for waste management decisions and for the different actors dealing with specific waste streams.

929. The end-of-waste criteria should be less strictly applied and further harmonised – The end-of-waste status can play an important role in prolonging product lifetime by facilitating the reintroduction of waste flows into the market as raw materials in replacement of primary materials. To this end, two measures should be taken. First, the four criteria should be less strictly applied. For example, concerning the technical requirements and existing legislation and standards that substances or objects must fulfil to cease to be waste, distinct requirements for reused products should be adopted.[3197] End-of-waste criteria can promote the production of higher quality secondary products by defining technical and environmental minimum requirements to be fulfilled by the materials. This may increase user confidence on quality standards and encourage the use of secondary materials. Second, end-of-waste status should

3192 International Resource Panel, *Redefining Value – The Manufacturing Revolution. Remanufacturing, Refurbishment, Repair and Direct Reuse in the Circular Economy. A Report of the International Resource Panel* (UN Environment Programme 2018) p. 47.

3193 K. Van Acker et al., *Circular Economy – Position paper working group Metaforum* (KU Leuven Metaforum 2016) p. 26.

3194 See Umweltbundesamt GmbH and ARCADIS Belgium NV, *Study to assess member states (MS) practices on by-product (BP) and end-of waste (EoW) – Final report* (European Union 2020).

3195 In Belgium, the 'end-of-waste' criteria are established by the three regions (Brussels, Flanders, Wallonia), while product legislation is a federal competence.

3196 RREUSE, *Putting re-use and repair at the heart of the EU's circular economy package* (2015) p. 2.

3197 On the need for specific ecodesign requirements for refurbished products, see n° 188.

preferably be defined at EU level to help reduce legal uncertainties regarding waste treatment and different interpretations between Member States (see #3).[3198] This issue was acknowledged by the EC, which announced that it will "*assess the scope to develop further EU-wide end-of-waste criteria for certain waste streams based on monitoring Member States' application of the revised rules on end-of-waste status and by-products, and support cross-border initiatives for cooperation to harmonise national end-of-waste and by-product criteria.*"[3199]

Proposed review of the Waste Framework Directive:

Article 3
Definitions

For the purposes of this Directive, the following definitions shall apply:

1. 'waste' means any substance or object which the holder discards or intends or is required to discard **and which cannot be reused**; #1

(...)

4b. 'obsolete product' means any product which the holder discards or intends or is required to discard and which may be reused, according to the criteria established under this Directive; #2

(...)

AND #3

Article 6
End-of-waste status

(...)

2. The Commission shall ~~**monitor the development of national end-of-waste criteria in Member States, and assess the need to develop Union-wide criteria on this basis. To that end, and where appropriate, the Commission shall**~~ adopt implementing acts in order to establish detailed criteria on the uniform application of the conditions laid down in paragraph 1 to certain types of waste.

(...)

3198 Ecos, EEB, *Key recommendations for the development of further EU-wide end-of-waste (EoW) criteria* (2021).

3199 Communication from the Commission of 11 March 2020 to the European Parliament, the Council, the European Economic and Social Committee and the Committee of the Regions on A new Circular Economy Action Plan – For a cleaner and more competitive Europe, COM(2020) 98 final, p. 14.

3. A HIERARCHY RANKING WASTE PREVENTION AND MANAGEMENT OPTIONS

930. Five options within the waste hierarchy – Article 4 of the WFD establishes a 'waste hierarchy', which ranks the different options of waste prevention and management, based on assumed environmental impacts (see Figure 8). Disposal, which encompasses landfill, incineration, physico-chemical treatment and permanent storage[3200], is ranked as the least preferred option. This option is followed by waste recovery generating energy, heat or fuels[3201], and by recycling, which means "*any recovery operation by which waste materials are reprocessed into products, materials or substances whether for the original or other purposes*".[3202] At the top of this hierarchy, there is the prevention of waste, which corresponds to measures taken before a substance, material or product has become waste.[3203] The second prioritised option is preparation for reuse, defined as "*checking, cleaning or repairing recovery operations, by which products or components of products that have become waste are prepared so that they can be re-used without any other pre-processing*".[3204] These two preferred options are the most relevant in terms of product sustainability and are thus further described in the following paragraphs.[3205]

Figure 8. The waste hierarchy as established by Article 4 WFD

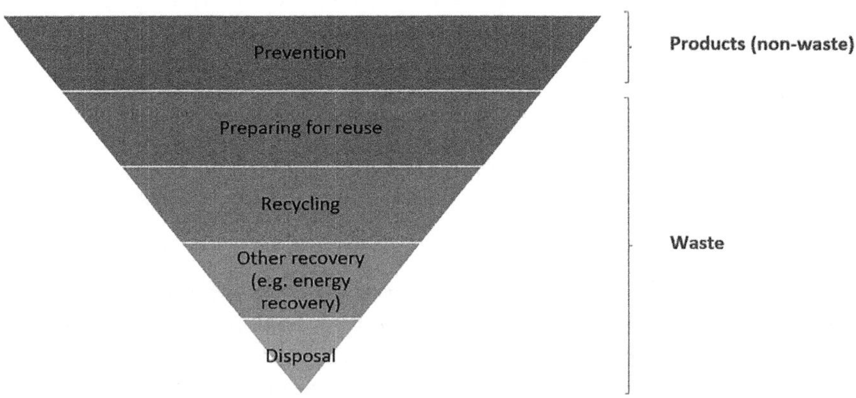

3200 See Art. 3(19) WFD, as well as the non-exhaustive list of disposal operations in Annex I to the WFD.
3201 Art. 15a WFD *a contrario*.
3202 Art. 3(17) WFD.
3203 Art. 3(12) WFD.
3204 Art. 3(16) WFD.
3205 See *infra*, n° 932–933.

931. Member States are responsible for applying the waste hierarchy – Before providing further explanation as to what is meant by 'prevention' and 'preparing for reuse', it should be noted that it is for the Member States to apply the waste hierarchy. Article 4(2) of the WFD states that "*Member States shall take measures to encourage the options that deliver the best overall environmental outcome*". The same provision allows Member States to depart from the hierarchy for specific waste streams where this is justified by lifecycle thinking on the overall impacts of the generation and management of such waste. When applying the waste hierarchy, Member States are required to take into account the general environmental protection principles of precaution and sustainability, technical feasibility and economic viability, protection of resources as well as the overall environmental, human health, economic and social impacts.[3206] The Directive (EU) 2018/851 provides examples of incentives to apply the waste hierarchy, such as landfill and incineration charges and pay-as-you-throw schemes. This responsibility also implies that Member States set a good example in their own waste prevention and management practices.[3207]

932. Primary option: preventing products from becoming waste – According to Article 3(12) of the WFD, 'prevention' means "*measures taken before a substance, material or product has become waste, that reduce the quantity of waste, including through the re-use of products or the extension of the life span of products, the adverse impacts of the generated waste on the environment and human health, or the content of hazardous substances in materials and products*". Article 9(1), which was amended by the Directive (EU) 2018/851, lists measures that Member States should take to prevent waste generation. Interestingly, this list includes measures that "*encourage the design, manufacturing and use of products that are resource-efficient, durable (including in terms of life span and absence of planned obsolescence), reparable, re-usable and upgradable*"[3208], that "*encourage the re-use of products and the setting up of systems promoting repair and re-use activities*"[3209], as well as those that "*encourage, as appropriate and without prejudice to intellectual property rights, the availability of spare parts, instruction manuals, technical information, or other instruments, equipment or software enabling the repair and re-use of products without compromising their quality and safety*".[3210] All these measures must be established in a national waste

3206 Art. 4(2) subparagraph 3 WFD.

3207 See e.g. French legislation, which requires public authorities to favour reuse when discarding computer equipment (Art. 16 of the Law on the Environmental Footprint of Digital Technology). In Germany, new requirements on product sustainability have been adopted for public procurement: sustainable products should be preferred, provided that it does not imply unreasonable additional costs (§45 Kreislaufwirtschaftsgesetz).

3208 Art. 9(1)(b) WFD.

3209 Art. 9(1)(d) WFD.

3210 Art. 9(1)(e) WFD.

prevention programme, as required by Article 29 of the WFD. A more detailed list of examples of such measures is given in Annex IV to the WFD and includes among others ecodesign, eco-labels and awareness campaigns among businesses and consumers and economic incentives. If taken, such measures can prevent waste by decreasing consumption, designing more sustainable products, using lesser resources in production and extending the lifetime of products through maintenance, repair and reuse. Various measures of this kind have been taken at national level, as revealed in the previous chapters of this book. Additional examples could be given, like in France, where goods that are still functioning but no longer used by the French authorities can be easily given to associations for free.[3211] This shows how waste prevention and the fight against premature obsolescence are closely intertwined.

933. Second preferred option: preparing for reuse – According to Article 3(16), 'preparing for reuse' is to be understood as "checking, cleaning or repairing recovery operations, by which products or components of products that have become waste are prepared so that they can be re-used without any other pre-processing". This concept has to be distinguished from 'reuse', which is defined by Article 3(13) as "any operation by which products or components that are not waste are used again for the same purpose for which they were conceived". While reuse concerns non-waste, the same cannot be said for the preparation for reuse. As illustrated by the WFD Guidance, preparing for re-use comprises for example "repairing bicycles, furniture, or electrical or electronic equipment which have been previously discarded by their owners".[3212] Article 11(2) sets targets for the Member States which impose an increase in the preparing for re-use and the recycling of municipal waste to a minimum of 55% by weight by 2025.[3213] Similar targets can be found in sectoral legislation.[3214] To reach these targets, Article 11(1) requires the Member States to set up separate collection at least for paper, metal, plastic and glass, and, by 1 January 2025, for textiles.

934. The waste hierarchy should be renamed – Since the hierarchy does not only concern waste but also the phase before products become waste, the name of the hierarchy should be reviewed. Such a proposal has already been made by several scholars. M. Gharfalkar, R. Court, C. Campbell, Z. Ali and G. Hillier proposed replacing the name 'waste hierarchy' with the 'hierarchy of

---

3211 See the website <https://dons.encheres-domaine.gouv.fr/>. This measure was part of the *Feuille de route* on Circular economy. See Ministère de la Transition Ecologique et Solidaire, *Feuille de route économie circulaire: 50 mesures pour une économie 100% circulaire* (République française 2018) p. 37, pt. 44.

3212 WFD Guidance, p. 30.

3213 The targets reach 60% by 2030 and 65% by 2035.

3214 See e.g. Art. 11 of the WEEE Directive and Annex V on recovery targets for WEEE.

resource use'.[3215] This denomination was subsequently approved by E. Maitre-Ekern, who considers that it would be more in line with the objective of the transition towards a circular economy.[3216] However, a less radical change could be made, which is to rename the 'waste hierarchy' as the 'waste prevention and management hierarchy'.

935. The hierarchy should further promote prevention and value-retention processes – As rightly pointed out by E. Maitre-Ekern, "*even if waste management must further increase and improve, the best way to mitigate pollution from waste is to prevent it from occurring altogether*".[3217] The hierarchy should therefore encourage options that prevent waste and offer the greatest value-retention potential, thus promoting prevention and value-retention processes to positions that take precedence over recycling, where appropriate. To bring product sustainability to the fore in the hierarchy, the terms 'prevention' and 'preparing for reuse' should be replaced by a wider range of more detailed and accurate terms (see Figure 9 as well as #13).[3218] This amendment would allow a clear understanding and differentiation between the different options of the hierarchy, which is currently lacking. The definitions of these different options would be given in Article 3 of the WFD and should be aligned with the definitions given by other existing legal instruments and standards (see #5 to #11). The other options that are envisaged after the products become waste, including recycling, should appear below as they should only be envisaged if no other options are possible. Hence, it is recommended to review the hierarchy established by the WFD to make sure that it is truly in line with the new EU Circular Economy Action Plan and the objective of product sustainability. The hierarchy should nonetheless not be too rigid but allow taking the specific circumstances into account as not all options are appropriate for all products. This proposal should be read in conjunction with the proposed definition of 'waste' and 'obsolete products'.[3219]

3215 M. Gharfalkar, R. Court, C. Campbell, Z.Ali, G. Hillier, 'Analysis of waste hierarchy in the European waste directive 2008/98/EC', 39 *Waste Management* (2015) p. 310.

3216 E. Maitre-Ekern, 'Taking products out of waste law: a new legal framework for the circular economy', in Nils F. Nissen & Melanie Jaeger-Erben (eds.), *3rd international Product Lifetimes and the Environment (PLATE) conference* (Berlin 2019) p. 498.

3217 E. Maitre-Ekern, 'Taking products out of waste law: a new legal framework for the circular economy', in Nils F. Nissen & Melanie Jaeger-Erben (eds.), *3rd international Product Lifetimes and the Environment (PLATE) conference* (Berlin 2019) p. 495.

3218 See also M. Gharfalkar, R. Court, C. Campbell, Z.Ali, G. Hillier, 'Analysis of waste hierarchy in the European waste directive 2008/98/EC', 39 *Waste Management* (2015), p. 305 at p. 313.

3219 See *supra*, n° 927.

Figure 9. Proposed alternative hierarchy

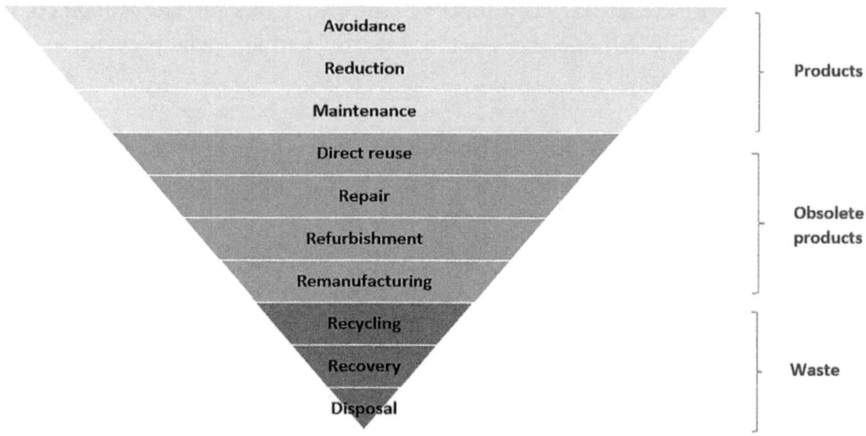

936. Prevention should be detailed into avoidance, reduction and maintenance – The word 'prevention' that currently appears as the preferred option of the hierarchy is too broad and vague. Instead, the different options preventing waste, that are implicitly included within the term 'prevention', should be explicitly integrated into the first ranks of the hierarchy. As advocated by E. Maitre-Ekern, 'prevention' should be detailed into three options, namely avoidance, reduction and maintenance.[3220] The definition of these terms could correspond to the elements contained in the current definition of 'prevention'. 'Avoidance' could be defined as "*the quantitative reduction in the amounts of products produced and consumed*" (see #5). 'Reduction', which is the second option, could be defined as "*the qualitative reduction of the environmental impacts of products*" (e.g. fewer materials, less harmful substances, more durability and reparability)(see #6). The third option, which is 'maintenance', could refer to the definition given in the European standard on definitions related to material efficiency, that is "*the action carried out to retain a product in a condition where it is able to function as required*" (see #7).[3221]

937. Preparing for reuse should be replaced by direct reuse, repair, refurbishment and remanufacturing – Strangely enough, preparing for reuse is currently ranked after reuse, which is implicitly included in the prevention of waste. The logical place for reuse would be after preparing for

3220 E. Maitre-Ekern, 'Taking products out of waste law: a new legal framework for the circular economy', in Nils F. Nissen & Melanie Jaeger-Erben (eds.), *3rd international Product Lifetimes and the Environment (PLATE) conference* (Berlin 2019) pp. 498–499.

3221 CEN-CENELEC TC10, Definitions related to material efficiency, EN 45550:2020, p. 7. See *supra*, n° 148.

reuse.[3222] Moreover, the term 'preparing for reuse' is not clear. The lack of clear definition of the process of 'preparation for use' results in legal uncertainty for businesses, as has already been reported for WEEE.[3223] Therefore, it is suggested to remove this term and replace it with direct reuse, repair, refurbishment and remanufacturing, which are the four strategies to reverse product obsolescence (see #8, #9, #10 and #11).[3224] All these options lead to the reuse of the products and thus divert them from waste at the end-of-life stage. Some of these options (repair and reuse) are currently included under the umbrella terms 'prevention' and 'preparing for reuse', which blurs the distinction between the two options. Some of the measures included in the list of 'prevention of waste' of Article 9 of the WFD should be removed from this provision and included in the provision specifically dedicated to reuse (see #14). In addition, distinct targets should be established for reuse (see #15).

938. The definition of 'recycling' should be amended – As explained in the first chapter of this book there are three types of recycling processes, namely downcycling, upcycling and functional recycling.[3225] These processes should be explicitly mentioned in the definition of 'recycling' established under Article 3 of the WFD (see #12). Moreover, the provision dedicated to recycling should be distinguished from the one on reuse (see #16).

939. The destruction of unsold durable goods should be banned – Although the disposal should be avoided by all means, it is not recommended to remove the term 'disposal' from the hierarchy.[3226] Admittedly, this is the less desirable option to manage waste, but it is still an option. Furthermore, this position in the hierarchy could be used to regulate and ban certain practices of disposal, with the aim of delaying the end-of-life of products and discouraging overproduction.

940. Drawing inspiration from French law – Such an approach was followed by France, which bans the destruction of new non food products that are already covered by an EPR since 1 January 2022.[3227] Article L. 541-15-8 of the French Environmental Code, which was introduced by Article 35 of the

3222 M. Gharfalkar et al., 'Analysis of waste hierarchy in the European waste directive 2008/98/EC', 39 *Waste Management* (2015), p. 308.

3223 D. Watson et al., *Circular Business Models in the Mobile Phone Industry* (TemaNord 2017) p. 66.

3224 See *supra*, n° 150–154.

3225 See *supra*, n° 156.

3226 See *a contrario* E. Maitre-Ekern, 'Taking products out of waste law: a new legal framework for the circular economy', in Nils F. Nissen & Melanie Jaeger-Erben (eds.), *3rd international Product Lifetimes and the Environment (PLATE) conference* (Berlin 2019) p. 499.

3227 For the products not covered by an EPR, the ban will enter into force no later than 31 December 2023. See Art. 35 VI of the Anti-Waste Law.

Anti-Waste Law, states that producers, importers and distributors of new non-food products intended for sale are under obligation to reuse (including by rebate sales to their employees or by donation to charity organisations) or recycle their unsold products.[3228] This obligation does not apply if the reuse or recycling of these products is illegal or if it entails significant safety or health risks and/or significant negative impacts for the environment. French law encourages the donation of unsold products by establishing a specific regime, under which the producer/importer/distributor can benefit from a tax incentive and be exempted from VAT for the donated products and may transfer the management of these products to an eco-organisation for free if donation is refused three times.[3229] However, questions remain as to the scope of this obligation. The legislation refers to 'new unsold goods' and seems to exclude products that were already used, including goods that were used and returned after consumers invoked their withdrawal or guarantee rights. Such an exclusion would be questionable as it would exclude a large majority of unsold goods.[3230]

941. The German duty of care – Along the same lines, Germany introduced a 'duty of care' (*Obhutspflicht*). This duty requires distributors to ensure that, in case of distance sales, the goods remain fit for use if returned by the customer (e.g. in case of withdrawal) instead of becoming waste.[3231] Based on the findings from a study on the destruction of returns in online trade, an amendment to the German Recycling Management Act is being planned.[3232] This new legislation will be accompanied by a 'transparency ordinance', which will force retailers to disclose their policy on how they treat returned goods (e.g. what portion of such products is resold, donated or destroyed). For a more precise definition of the duty of care, a legal regulation with reporting obligations for companies will be issued.[3233]

942. The Proposal for a Sustainable Products Regulation – Interestingly, the ideas of banning the destruction of unsold products and establishing a transparency obligation were echoed at EU level in the Proposal

---

3228 See also Décret n° 2020-1724 du 28 décembre 2020 relatif à l'interdiction d'élimination des invendus non alimentaires et à diverses dispositions de lutte contre le gaspillage, JORF n°0315 du 30 décembre 2020.

3229 Art. D. 541-320 and Art. R. 541-321 to 324 of the Environmental Code.

3230 See also C. Lepla, 'L'obligation de gestion des invendus non alimentaires', 47 *Revue juridique de l'environnement* (2022) p. 84.

3231 §23 Absatz 2 Nummer 11 Kreislaufwirtschaftsgesetz.

3232 See Referentenentwurf eines Gesetzes zur Umsetzung der Abfallrahmenrichtlinie der Europäischen Union (BMU, 3 February 2020) <www.bmu.de/fileadmin/Daten_BMU/Download_PDF/Glaeserne_Gesetze/19._Lp/krwg_entwurf/Entwurf/krwg_novelle_refe.pdf.

3233 C. Meller-Hannich and E. Krausbeck, 'Sustainability, the Circular Economy and Consumer Law in Germany', 9 *EuCML* (2020) p. 172.

for a Sustainable Products Regulation.[3234] The Proposal establishes, first, a general obligation of transparency for economic operators who discard unsold consumer products. These operators are required to publicly disclose the number of discarded products, the reasons for the discarding of products, and their further treatment in terms of preparing for reuse, recycling, incineration or landfilling. Second, the Proposal provides for the possibility to adopt delegated acts to prohibit economic operators from destroying unsold consumer products where the destruction has significant environmental impact. These delegated acts may contain exemptions to the general prohibition where it is appropriate in view of (a) health and safety concerns, (b) damage to products as a result of their handling or detected after a product has been returned by a consumer, (c) fitness of the product for the purpose for which it is intended, taking into account, where applicable, Union and national law and technical standards and (d) refusal of products for donation, preparing for re-use or remanufacturing.[3235] If such an exemption is used, economic operators still have to comply with the obligation of transparency. While health and safety concerns can be regarded as justified reasons for such an exemption, the three other reasons given in the Proposal are more questionable, especially because they could lead to abuses. Exemptions should therefore be clearly defined. For the rest, the provisions of the Proposal, including its definition of 'unsold products'[3236], are to be welcomed and could be introduced verbatim in Articles 3 and 12 of the WFD (see #4 and #17).

Proposed review of the Waste Framework Directive:

Article 3
Definitions

For the purposes of this Directive, the following definitions shall apply:

(...)

<u>4c. 'unsold product' means any consumer product that has not been sold or that has been returned by a consumer in view of their right of withdrawal in accordance with Article 9 of Directive (EU) 2011/83/EU; #4</u>

(...)

3234 See Art. 20 of the Proposal for a Regulation of the European Parliament and of the Council establishing a framework for setting ecodesign requirements for sustainable products and repealing Directive 2009/125/EC, COM(2022) 142 final.

3235 Art. 30(3) of the Proposal for a Sustainable Products Regulation.

3236 Art. 2(37) of the Proposal for a Sustainable Products Regulation.

12a. 'Avoidance' means the quantitative reduction in the amounts of substances and objects produced and consumed; #5

12b. 'Reduction' means the qualitative reduction of the environmental impacts of products; #6

12c. 'Maintenance' means the action carried out to retain a product in a condition where it is able to function as required, as defined in the European standard EN 45550:2020; #7

(…)

13a. 'Direct reuse' means the process by which a product or its parts, having reached the end of their first or subsequent use, are used for the same purpose for which they were conceived, as defined in the European standard EN 45550:2020; #8

13b. 'Repair' means the process of returning a faulty product to a condition where it can fulfil its originally intended use, as defined in the European standard EN 45550:2020; #9

13c. 'Refurbishment' means the process of returning a product to a satisfactory working and/or cosmetic condition, that may be inferior to the original specification, by replacing and repairing all major components that are faulty, markedly damaged or close to failure, and by making cosmetic changes to update the appearance of a product, such as cleaning, changing the fabric, painting or refinishing; #10

13d. 'Remanufacturing' means industrial process that inspects, disassembles, cleans, reprocesses, stores, reassembles, tests and recovers a product at the subassembly or component level, as defined in the European standard EN 45550:2020. #11

(…)

17. 'recycling' means any recovery operation by which waste materials are reprocessed into products, materials or substances whether for the original or other purposes. It includes the reprocessing of ~~organic material~~ waste materials into products, materials or substances of higher quality and/or increased functionality than the original ('upcycling'), the reprocessing of waste materials into products, materials or substances of lesser quality and/or reduced functionality than the original ('downcycling') or the recovery of products, materials or substances for the original purpose or other purposes ('functional recycling'). However, it ~~but~~ does not include energy recovery and the reprocessing into materials that are to be used as fuels or for backfilling operations; #12

(…)

AND #13

Article 4

Waste <u>prevention and management</u> hierarchy

1. The following waste <u>prevention and management</u> hierarchy shall apply as a priority order in waste prevention and management legislation and policy:

(a) ~~prevention;~~ <u>avoidance, reduction and maintenance</u>;
(b) ~~preparing for re-use~~ <u>direct reuse, repair, refurbishment and remanufacturing</u>;
(c) recycling;
(d) other recovery, e.g. energy recovery; and
(e) disposal.

AND #14

Article 9

~~Prevention of waste~~ <u>Avoidance, reduction and maintenance</u>

1. Member States shall take measures to prevent waste generation. Those measures shall, at least:

(…)

~~(d) encourage the re-use of products and the setting up of systems promoting repair and re-use activities, including in particular for electrical and electronic equipment, textiles and furniture, as well as packaging and construction materials and products;~~

(…)

AND #15

Article 11

~~Preparing for re-use and recycling~~ <u>Direct reuse, repair, refurbishment and remanufacturing</u>

1. Member States shall take measures to promote preparing for re-use activities, notably by encouraging the establishment of and support for preparing for re-use and repair networks, by facilitating, where compatible with proper waste management, their access to waste held by collection schemes or facilities that can be prepared for re-use but is not destined for preparing for re-use by those schemes or facilities, and by promoting the use of economic instruments, procurement criteria, quantitative objectives or other measures.

2. In order to comply with the objectives of this Directive, and move to a European circular economy with a high level of resource efficiency, Member States shall take the necessary measures designed to achieve the following targets:

[distinct targets for reuse]

AND #16

Article 11a
Recycling

1. Member States shall take measures to promote high-quality recycling and, to this end, subject to Article 10(2) and (3), shall set up separate collection of waste.

(...)

7. By 31 December 2028, the Commission shall review the target laid down in point (e) of paragraph 2. To that end, the Commission shall submit a report to the European Parliament and to the Council, accompanied, if appropriate, by a legislative proposal.

The Commission shall assess co-processing technology that allows the incorporation of minerals in the co-incineration process of municipal waste. Where a reliable methodology can be found, as part of this review, the Commission shall consider whether such minerals may be counted towards recycling targets.

AND #17

Article 12
Disposal

1. Member States shall ensure that, where recovery in accordance with Article 10(1) is not undertaken, waste undergoes safe disposal operations which meet the provisions of Article 13 on the protection of human health and the environment.

1a. Member States shall ensure that economic operators that discard unsold consumer products directly, or on behalf of another economic operator, disclose:

(a) the number of unsold consumer products discarded per year, differentiated pertype or category of products;

(b) the reasons for the discarding of products;

(c) the delivery of discarded products to preparing for re-use, remanufacturing, recycling, energy recovery and disposal operations in accordance with the waste hierarchy as defined by Article 4 of Directive 2008/98/EC.

The economic operator shall disclose that information on a freely accessible website or otherwise make it publicly available, until a delegated act adopted pursuant to paragraph 3 starts applying to the category of unsold consumer products discarded by the operator in question.

1b. The Commission may adopt implementing acts setting out the format for the disclosure of the information referred to in paragraph 1, including the type or category and how the information is to be verified.

Those implementing acts shall be adopted in accordance with the examination procedure referred to in Article 67(3).

1c. The Commission shall be empowered to adopt delegated acts in accordance with Article 66 to supplement this Regulation by prohibiting economic operators to destroy unsold consumer products in the Union, where the destruction of unsold consumer products falling within a certain product group has significant environmental impact.

In the delegated acts adopted pursuant to the first subparagraph, the Commission shall set out certain exemptions to those prohibitions where it is appropriate in view of:

(a) health and safety concerns;

(b) damage to products as a result of their handling or detected after a product has been returned by a consumer;

(c) fitness of the product for the purpose for which it is intended, taking into account, where applicable, Union and national law and technical standards;

(d) refusal of products for donation, preparing for re-use or remanufacturing.

1d. When preparing a delegated act adopted pursuant to paragraph 3, the Commission shall:

(a) assess the prevalence and environmental impact of the destruction of specific consumer products;

(b) take into account the information disclosed by economic operators pursuant to paragraph 1;

(c) carry out an impact assessment based on best available evidence and analyses, and on additional studies as necessary.

The Commission shall consult the Ecodesign Forum referred to in Article 17, and take account of its views on possible prohibitions of destruction of unsold consumer products referred to in paragraph 3, prior to the preparation of the delegated acts setting out those prohibitions.

1e. Where unsold consumer products are destroyed under an exemption referred to in paragraph 3, second subparagraph, the responsible economic operator shall disclose on a freely accessible website or otherwise make publicly available:

(a) the number of unsold consumer products destroyed;

(b) the reasons for their destruction, referring to the applicable exemption;

(c) the delivery of the products destroyed to recycling, energy recovery and disposal operations in accordance with the waste hierarchy as defined by Article 4 of Directive 2008/98/EC.

The details and format for the disclosure of information provided in the implementing act adopted pursuant to paragraph 2 shall apply to the information to be disclosed pursuant to this paragraph, unless the delegated act adopted pursuant to paragraph 3 provides otherwise.

1f. This Article shall not apply to SMEs. However, the Commission may, in the delegated acts adopted pursuant to paragraph 3, provide that the prohibition to destroy unsold consumer products referred to in paragraph 3 or the disclosure obligation referred to in paragraph 4 shall apply to:

(a) medium-sized enterprises, where there is sufficient evidence that they account for a substantial proportion of unsold consumer products being destroyed;

(b) microenterprises, small enterprises or medium-sized enterprises, where there is sufficient evidence that they may be used to circumvent the prohibition to destroy unsold consumer products referred to in paragraph 3 or the disclosure obligation referred to in paragraph 4.

2. By 31 December 2024, the Commission shall carry out an assessment of the disposal operations listed in Annex I, in particular in light of Article 13, and shall submit a report to the European Parliament and to the Council, accompanied, if appropriate, by a legislative proposal, with a view to regulating disposal operations, including through possible restrictions, and to consider a disposal reduction target, to ensure environmentally sound waste management.

4. THE EXTENDED PRODUCER RESPONSIBILITY

943. A LONG-TERM ENVIRONMENTAL RESPONSIBILITY ON PRODUCERS – To facilitate the implementation of the waste hierarchy, the WFD has established the 'extended producer responsibility' ('EPR'). Article 8 of this Directive, read in conjunction with Article 3(21), makes the producer of the product bear financial responsibility or financial and organisational responsibility for the management of the waste stage of a product's life cycle.[3237] As a result, the responsibility of the producer is extended to "*the post-consumer stage of a product's life cycle*".[3238] The EPR can be inscribed in the broader polluter-pays principle, extending the concept of polluter to the economic agent who can play a decisive role in avoiding pollution (i.e. the producer).[3239] It is an attempt to internalize the negative environmental externalities associated with the end-of-life of products so that they are no longer borne by local and regional authorities in the context of their waste collection activities and, consequently, by taxpayers.[3240] Germany was a pioneer of EPR, with the 1991 German Packaging Ordinance.[3241] The rationale underlying the establishment of EPR was twofold. First, it was expected to facilitate the collection and recycling of materials by closing the downstream loop of consumption and creating a reverse logistic system, and to improve overall efficiency.[3242] The second aim, which was the strongest argument in support of the EPR, was that it would induce manufacturers to incorporate waste considerations in their strategies, and therefore foster sustainable product design and waste prevention.[3243] With EPR, producers are encouraged to reduce the production of (waste-generating) products on one hand, and on the other hand, to change the design of their products towards more sustainability.[3244] This shows how EPR can play a pivotal role in the fight against premature obsolescence.[3245]

3237 The EPR is implemented by the sectoral directives for specific waste streams: see Art. 5 of the Directive on end-of life vehicles; Art. 16 of the 2006 Batteries Directive; Art. 12 WEEE Directive. EPR is also enshrined in Article 7 of the European Parliament and Council Directive 94/62/EC of 20 December 1994 on packaging and packaging waste, OJ L 365, 31.12.1994, p. 10–23.

3238 OECD, *Extended Producer Responsibility – A Guidance Manual for Governments* (2001) p. 9.

3239 BIO Intelligence Service, *Development of Guidance on Extended Producer Responsibility (EPR) – Final Report* (European Commission 2014) pp. 28–29.

3240 L. Krämer, *EU Environmental Law* (Sweet & Maxwell 2016).

3241 N. Jones, G. Van Calster, 'Waste Regulation', in E. Lees and J. E. Viñuales (eds.), *The Oxford Handbook of Comparative Environmental Law* (Oxford University Press 2019) p. 620.

3242 A. Massarutto, 'The long and winding road to resource efficiency – An interdisciplinary perspective on extended producer responsibility', 85 *Resources, Conservation and Recycling* (2014) p. 14.

3243 *Ibid.* See also recital 27 of the WFD.

3244 S.I. Becher, A.-L. Sibony, 'Confronting Product Obsolescence', 27 *Colum. J. Eur. L.* (2021) p. 132.

3245 The role of EPR in tackling premature obsolescence had first been pointed out by the EESC. See Opinion of the EESC of 17 October 2013 on Towards more sustainable consumption:

944. Implemented by the Member States – The WFD lays the foundations for the EPR schemes and enables Member States to establish EPR schemes.[3246] According to Article 8(1) subparagraph 2 of the WFD, national measures can consist in obliging producers to accept returned products and the waste that remains after those products have been used, to manage the waste and take financial responsibility for such activities or to provide publicly available information as to the extent to which the product is re-usable and recyclable. Article 8(3) places some limits to the margin for manoeuvre left to Member States by requesting them to "*take into account the technical feasibility and economic viability and the overall environmental, human health and social impacts, respecting the need to ensure the proper functioning of the internal market*". According to Article 8(4) of the Directive, Member States must also ensure that "*any original waste producer or other holder carries out the treatment of waste himself or has the treatment handled by a dealer or an establishment or undertaking which carries out waste treatment operations or arranged by a private or public waste collector*". In that regard, Member States may decide that the responsibility for arranging waste management is to be borne partly or wholly by the producer of the product from which the waste came and that distributors of such product may share this responsibility.[3247]

945. Mandatory for a variety of product categories – In the EU, EPR is mandatory within the context of the WEEE, Batteries, and ELV Directives. The producers of these three product categories are thus responsible for the end-of-life stage of their products. The Packaging Directive also indirectly enshrines the EPR principle as it requires Member States to establish and ensure the good functioning of the collection and recycling systems of packaging waste.[3248] Other waste streams are concerned by EPR rules within the EU territory, including construction and demolition waste, and tyres. Nonetheless, it should be noted that a much wider range of waste streams are subject to mandatory or voluntary producer responsibility schemes in some Member States, including furniture, farm plastics, medicines and medical waste, plastic bags, lamps and light bulbs. France is the Member State with the highest number of sectors covered by the EPR principle, with no less than 14 mandatory EPR regulations.[3249]

---

industrial product lifetimes and restoring trust through consumer information, CCMI/112, pt. 1.8.

3246 More detailed provisions were adopted in 2018 for the implementation of the EPR principle. See Article 8a of the WFD, as introduced by Directive (EU) 2018/851 of the European Parliament and of the Council of 30 May 2018 amending Directive 2008/98/EC on waste, OJ L 150, 14.6.2018, p. 109–140.

3247 See Art. 15(3) WFD.

3248 See Art. 7(1) of the European Parliament and Council Directive 94/62/EC of 20 December 1994 on packaging and packaging waste, OJ L 365, 31.12.1994, p. 10–23.

3249 The Anti-Waste Law extended the EPR to new sources of waste, such as toys, cigarettes, sanitary textiles (e.g. household wipes, disposable diapers, cotton), building construction

946. The broad notion of 'producer' – Article 8(1) of the WFD defines the 'producer of the product' as "*any natural or legal person who professionally develops, manufactures, processes, treats, sells or imports products*". The term 'producer' is deliberately broad so that there is always a responsible person. In case of an anonymous product, the seller can be held liable unless he discloses the identity of the manufacturer or the responsible person. It may be difficult in practice to know who owns the waste and who should be allowed to collect it. This differs highly between countries.[3250] Online sales add to the difficulty of implementing the EPR to producers as transactions are carried out through multi-seller online marketplaces where thousands of online sellers from all over the world operate.[3251] In France, Article L. 541–10–9 of the Environmental Code states that the EPR also applies to persons who facilitate distance selling by the use of platforms. This approach is based on the fact that since marketplace producers facilitate sales of products that fall within the EPR principle, they have to organise or contribute to waste prevention and management that derive from those products. Marketplace producers can be released from their responsibility if they obtained evidence that this obligation was fulfilled by the producer of the products.

947. Two ways to comply with EPR: individual and collective schemes – There are two ways for producers to meet their obligations related to EPR: either they do it individually and themselves or they make an agreement with other producers to create and finance producer responsibility organisations ('PROs'), which handle products at the end of their lifecycle.[3252] The first way is possible when the product market is concentrated and when it is possible for producers to take back their products (e.g. for specific devices produced in limited series for a specific industry).[3253] Producers can then reuse the products or directly sell them to recyclers. The second way consists in transferring their responsibility to a specific PRO, created for collecting and managing post-consumer products. Membership to the PRO can be compulsory or not, and if compulsory, producers can be given the choice between competing PROs or not. In practice, collective compliance schemes are much more common than individual schemes.[3254] France has gone one step further with the Anti-Waste

products and materials or even private cars, vans and motorized vehicles with 2 or 3 wheels, etc. See Rapport d'information fait au nom de la Commission des affaires européennes (1) portant observations sur la transposition du droit européen par le projet de loi relatif à la lutte contre le gaspillage et à l'économie circulaire, 18 July 2019, n° 682, p. 26.

3250 For some examples of national rules regulating this issue, see D. Watson et al., *Circular Business Models in the Mobile Phone Industry* (TemaNord 2017) p. 65.

3251 See OECD, *Extended producer responsibility and the impact of online sales* (OECD 2019) p. 9.

3252 Examples are the Duales System Deutschland in Germany and Eco-Emballages in France.

3253 BIO Intelligence Service, *Development of Guidance on Extended Producer Responsibility (EPR) – Final Report* (European Commission 2014) p. 78.

3254 For information on collective and individual compliance schemes in a particular Member State, see the national registers available on: <https://www.ewrn.org/national-registers/national-registers>.

Law by making the collective compliance scheme the common law scheme and the individual scheme a possible derogation under certain conditions.[3255]

948. The obligation to finance the end-of-life of products – To comply with their EPR obligations, producers must pay financial contributions that cover the costs of separate collection of waste and its subsequent transport and treatment, costs of providing adequate information to waste holders, costs of data gathering and reporting.[3256] The fact that the financial responsibility for waste management lies with producers was recently recalled and emphasized by the ECJ in *Vysocina Wind*.[3257] In Germany, producers must provide an insolvency-proof guarantee upon registration to ensure that e-waste is being properly treated and recovered even if the original producer is no longer in the market.[3258] In France, Article L. 541–10 VI of the Environmental Code offers the possibility to take back products derived from reuse and recovery activities free of charge.

949. Modulation of financial contributions to PROs, including on the basis of product sustainability – The WFD, as amended in 2018, requires Member States to "*take the necessary measures to ensure that the financial contributions paid by the producer (...) are modulated, where possible, for individual products or groups of similar products, notably by taking into account their durability, repairability, re-usability and recyclability (...)*".[3259] This only applies in the case of collective fulfilment of EPR obligations. Article 8a of the WFD also states that such a modulation must be implemented by taking a life-cycle approach and aligned with the requirements set by relevant EU law, and where available, based on harmonised criteria to ensure smooth functioning of the internal market. Such a modulation can play a role in curbing premature obsolescence.[3260] In France, Article L. 541–10–3 of the Environmental Code establishes a bonus/penalty system (based on the price of the product) depending on the compliance of products with environmental performance criteria, including durability, repairability, reusability and recyclability.[3261] Producers who design their products in a more sustainable way can benefit from a bonus on the contribution they pay to their eco-organisation for the management and

---

3255 Art. L. 541–10. – I of the French Environmental Code.

3256 Article 8a(4)(a) WFD.

3257 ECJ 25 January 2022, Case C-181/20, *VYSOČINA WIND, EU:C:2022:51.*

3258 M. Cordella, F. Alfieri, J. Sanfelix, *Guidance for the Assessment of Material Efficiency: Application to Smartphones – JRC Technical Report* (European Commission 2020) p. 21.

3259 Art. 8a(4)(b) WFD.

3260 It has already been shown that the introduction of a disposal fee can prompt producers to make sustainable choices in the design of their products. See H. Kinokuni, S. Ohori, Y. Tomoda, 'Optimal Waste Disposal Fees When Product Durability is Endogenous: Accounting for Planned Obsolescence', 73 *Environmental and Resource Economics* (2019) p. 33 at p. 50.

3261 As introduced by Art. 62 of the Anti-Waste Law.

end-of-life treatment of their products. Conversely, those who do not adopt such a sustainable design approach must pay a higher financial contribution. For example, washing machine manufacturers who provide parts essential for the use of their machines for 11 years will pay a 20% lower financial contribution, while refrigerator producers who do not give product technical documentation to repairers will have to pay a 20% higher contribution.[3262] Information on the bonus/malus applicable to products is made available to the public.[3263] These financial incentives are, however, weak for producers as eco-contributions are only a small fraction of product price.[3264]

950. Financing repair and reuse funds via PROs – In addition to this bonus/penalty system, France establishes the participation of PROs in funds financing repair and reuse costs. According to Articles L. 541-10-4 and L. 541-10-5 of the Environmental Code, the financial contributions collected by eco-organisations finance repair and reuse funds that can be used to mitigate repair and reuse costs for some products. The repair fund can only be used when repair is carried out by an authorised repairer. The objective is to reduce the cost of repair for consumers when they go to a certified repairer passing on this price reduction. This would encourage consumers to favour repair over replacement when the product is no longer covered by the legal guarantee.[3265] Repair costs may indeed constitute an obstacle when the product is no longer covered by the legal guarantee. Concerning the reuse funds, the law establishes the conditions under which operators can benefit. The beneficiaries of the fund are under obligation to report on the actions undertaken thanks to the funding received and the results achieved. The accompanying decree must still be adopted to determine the product categories to which this fund apply, the share of contributions to the funds, the terms of the funds' operation and management, consumer information, and repairer certification.

951. The obligation to take back waste – For certain specific waste streams, it is even compulsory for producers to organise the management of the waste stage of their products and take back the generated waste. This is the case of industrial batteries and accumulators, for which producers cannot refuse to take

[3262] Cahier des charges du 17 novembre 2014 annexé à l'arrêté du 2 décembre 2014 relatif à la procédure d'agrément et portant cahier des charges des éco-organismes de la filière des déchets d'équipements électriques et électroniques ménagers en application des articles R. 543-189 et R. 543-190 du code de l'environnement.

[3263] Art. L. 541-10-15 4° of the French Environmental Code.

[3264] Rapport fait au nom de la Commission de l'aménagement du territoire et du développement durable (1) sur le projet de loi (PROCÉDURE ACCÉLÉRÉE) relatif à la lutte contre le gaspillage et à l'économie circulaire, 17 September 2019, n° 727, p. 74.

[3265] Rapport fait au nom de la Commission de l'aménagement du territoire et du développement durable (1) sur le projet de loi (PROCÉDURE ACCÉLÉRÉE) relatif à la lutte contre le gaspillage et à l'économie circulaire, 17 September 2019, n° 727, p. 79.

back waste from end-users, regardless of chemical composition and origin.[3266] Similarly, producers of automotive batteries and accumulators set up schemes for the collection of waste automotive batteries and accumulators from end-users or from an accessible collection point in their vicinity, where collection is not carried out under the schemes referred to in Article 5(1) of the ELV Directive. In the case of automotive batteries and accumulators from private, non-commercial vehicles, the Batteries Directive states that such schemes shall not involve any charge to end-users when discarding waste batteries or accumulators.[3267] In France, Article L. 541–10–8 of the Environmental Code opens up the possibility to establish such an obligation for other waste streams. Based on this provision, the EPR has been extended to furniture and will apply to toys and sport items from 1st January 2023. It should be noted that some delivery services are already experimenting with taking back waste and reusable goods as part of the service offered when delivering new products – without a one-on-one take-back obligation.[3268]

952. A POTENTIAL POLICY TOOL FOR TRIGGERING PRODUCT SUSTAINABILITY – In view of the foregoing, the EPR, if properly implemented, can promote product sustainability and prevent the premature obsolescence of products. Assigning such a significant responsibility to producers may deter them from making products that generate a great amount of waste and encourage them to think carefully about the end-of-life of their products, including by designing longer-lasting products and using value-retention processes at the products' end-of-life.[3269] The principle of EPR can also serve as a basis to make available means for product maintenance to repairers or to (financially) support repair networks. Consequently, EPR tackles all forms of obsolescence; all discarded goods are affected, whatever the cause.[3270]

953. THOUGH WITH SOME WEAKNESSES – Despite its aim and potential to promote product sustainability, EPR has increased rates of waste collection but prompted no or limited change in product design.[3271] Five main reasons can

---

3266 Art. 8(3) of the 2006 Batteries Directive.

3267 Art. 8(4) of the 2006 Batteries Directive.

3268 EEA, *Circular by design: Products in the circular economy* (European Union 2017) p. 19.

3269 As rightly highlighted by the OECD, "*[o]ne of the key objectives of extended producer responsibility is to shift responsibility for end-of-life management to producers and therewith incentivise them to invest in design-for-environment in order to minimise waste management costs*". See OECD, *Extended producer responsibility – Updated guidance for efficient waste management* (OECD Publishing 2016) p. 161.

3270 S.I. Becher, A.-L. Sibony, 'Confronting Product Obsolescence', 27 *Colum. J. Eur. L.* (2021) p. 133.

3271 See N. Kunz, A. Atasu, K. Mayers, L. Van Wassenhove, *Extended producer responsibility: stakeholder concerns and future developments – Report for The INSEAD Social Innovation Centre* (2014). The same conclusion was reached for the packaging sector: see K. Pouikli,

explain this failure. First, the lack of incentives stems from the insignificant costs that producers must pay to manage the end-of-life of their products. The financial contributions represent only a very small share of sales price. What is more, a significant part of EPR costs is passed on to consumers through sale prices.[3272] Second, the potential benefits that producers can derive from waste management are uncertain. The price of recovered materials is subject to fluctuations. Moreover, there is no guarantee that consumers will do what is necessary so that producers get the product back at its end-of-life.[3273] The third important reason is the lack of individualised responsibility. Collective compliance schemes, which are the most commonly used in practice, entail the risks of 'averaging' the costs among producers and thereby deterring individual efforts. PROs may also lead to abuses of market power through excessive or opaque pricing or other anti-competitive practices, such as horizontal agreements among competing producers to establish one or more PROs, regulatory barriers to entering markets served by PROs or vertical agreements between PROs.[3274] Fourth, it is particularly difficult to implement EPR within the framework of marketplaces, leading to unfair competition problems. According to the OECD, free-riding that consists in not undertaking physical 'take-back' obligations leads to lower collection rates for end of life products, free-riding by not paying EPR fees results in financing problems for waste management activities, and free-riding by under-estimating the number of products placed on the market results in a potential over-estimation of national recycling rates.[3275] Finally, the margin of discretion left to Member States to implement EPR leads to legal fragmentation, which makes the assessment of the performance and effectiveness of EPR models rather challenging and complex.[3276]

954. Three possible improvements – Because it makes producers responsible during the entire lifecycle of the product, EPR has great potential for curbing premature obsolescence. However, the current system suffers from some weaknesses that lead to weak or non-existent incentives and thus affect its effectiveness. Several amendments to the existing mandatory EPR rules should

---

'Concretising The Role of Extended Producer Responsibility in European Union Waste Law and Policy Through the Lens of the Circular Economy', 20 *ERA FORUM* (2020) p. 501.

3272 E. Maitre-Ekern, M. Taylor and M. van der Velden, 'Towards a Sustainable Circular Economy: SMART reform proposals', 12 *University of Oslo Faculty of Law Legal Studies Research Paper Series* (2020) p. 43.

3273 E. Maitre-Ekern, M. Taylor and M. van der Velden, 'Towards a Sustainable Circular Economy: SMART reform proposals', 12 *University of Oslo Faculty of Law Legal Studies Research Paper Series* (2020) pp. 43–44.

3274 OECD, *The State of Play on Extended Producer Responsibility (EPR): Opportunities and Challenges* (2014) pp. 10–11.

3275 OECD, *Extended producer responsibility and the impact of online sales* (OECD 2019), p. 3.

3276 K. Pouikli, 'Concretising the role of extended producer responsibility in European Union waste law and policy through the lens of the circular economy', 20 *ERA Forum* (2020) p. 501.

be made to overcome or at least minimize these weaknesses.[3277] The following paragraphs provided three possible improvements.

955. Fees to PROs should be modulated on the basis of product sustainability aspects, with criteria established at EU level –First, the financial contribution paid by producers under EPR schemes should be differentiated on the basis of the environmental impact of their products (see #18). The modulated fees would create a direct economic incentive to design products that can be more easily recycled or reused, as highlighted by the EC.[3278] To enhance the impact of such modulated fees, the criteria used for this modulation should be established at EU level, drawing inspiration from the French bonus/penalty system and taking the criteria of other legal instruments into consideration (e.g. ecodesign rules). The focus should (first) be narrowed onto aspects with significant environmental gains to limit additional administrative costs incurred by the modulated fees.[3279]

956. Fees should be set high enough, including through improved cost internalisation – Second, whether modulated or not, the fees charged for the management of products at the end-of-life stage should be set high enough (see #19). The magnitude of the financial incentive is indeed decisive to drive product design changes.[3280] This could consist of internalising more costs related to the waste management of products via EPR, thus allocating more (if not all) of these costs to producers (e.g. costs for clean-up of litter, costs for enforcement and monitoring of the EPR scheme).

957. The scope of products covered by mandatory EPR schemes should be expanded – Third, mandatory EPR rules should be introduced for a broader range of product categories (see #20). Some Member States have already established EPR schemes for far more waste streams than those covered by EU law. However, the disparities between Member States weaken the impact of these EPR schemes, especially for consumer products that are designed for the global market. It is therefore preferrable to adopt (harmonised) EU rules for waste streams for which producer responsibility organisations have been most commonly identified within the EU.

3277 All these legal measures could be underpinned by new technology for the marking and tracking of products which open possibilities for reduced waste management costs and improved secondary materials handling. See Material Economics, *Retaining Value in the Swedish Materials System. Material Economics* (2018) p. 5.

3278 Communication from the Commission of 2 December 2015 to the European Parliament, the Council, the European Economic and Social Committee and the Committee of the Regions on Closing the loop – EU action plan for circular economy, COM(2015) 614 final, p. 4.

3279 Existing ecodesign requirements could be used to determine these priority aspects.

3280 OECD, *Extended producer responsibility – Updated guidance for efficient waste management* (OECD Publishing 2016) pp. 171–172.

Policy recommendations

#18 Fees paid by producers to PROs should be differentiated on the basis of product sustainability aspects, with criteria established at EU level.

#19 These fees should be set high enough, including through further internalisation of costs related to the waste management of products.

#20 EPR should be mandatory for a wider range of products at EU level.

5. SPECIFIC OBLIGATIONS ESTABLISHED BY SECTORAL WASTE RULES

958. THREE MAIN OBLIGATIONS THAT PROMOTE THE IMPLEMENTATION OF THE WASTE HIERARCHY – To implement the abovementioned hierarchy in accordance with extended producer responsibility, the sectoral directives have established specific obligations, including (1) ecodesign requirements, (2) information obligations and (3) obligations on the collection and separation of waste.

959. FIRST: ECODESIGN REQUIREMENTS FOR EEE, BATTERIES AND ELV – First, the sectoral directives contain specific ecodesign requirements. Article 4 of the WEEE requires producers to opt for specific design features or manufacturing processes that allow WEEE to be reused, dismantled or recovered, unless such specific design features or manufacturing processes present overriding advantages (e.g. with regard to the protection of the environment and/or safety requirements).[3281] This provision makes the link with implementing measures adopted on the basis of the Ecodesign Directive[3282], which put into practice the most important principles contained in this instrument.[3283] The same provision is to be found in the ELV Directive. According to its Article 4(1)(b) and (c), Member States should encourage the design and production of new vehicles which take into full account and facilitate the dismantling, reuse and recovery, in particular the recycling, of end-of life vehicles, their components and materials and which integrate an increasing quantity of recycled material in vehicles and other products. The ELV Directive even sets targets for the reuse and recovery of end-of life vehicles.[3284] Along the same line, Article 11 of the Batteries Directive

3281 R. Waugh, H. Symington, D. Parker, M. Kling, F. Zotz, *Study on the implementation of product design requirements set out in Article 4 of the WEEE Directive – The case of re-usability of printer cartridges – Final report* (European Union 2018).

3282 See also recital 11 of the WEEE Directive.

3283 D. Jepsen et al., *Delivering resource-efficient products – How Ecodesign can drive a circular economy in Europe* (European Environmental Bureau 2015) p. 43.

3284 Art. 7(2) of the ELV Directive.

establishes the obligation to equip laptops with removable battery. Since its recent amendment, Article 11 further states that "*[w]here they cannot be readily removed by the end-user, Member States shall ensure that manufacturers design appliances in such a way that waste batteries and accumulators can be readily removed by qualified professionals that are independent of the manufacturer.* Such ecodesign requirements are particularly important to tackle the premature obsolescence of battery-operated products as the durability of batteries that cannot be easily removed and replaced often dictates the lifespan of the products.

960. ECODESIGN REQUIREMENTS SHOULD BE MORE PRECISE AND CONCRETE – Nevertheless, some of these ecodesign requirements lack preciseness and concreteness. For example, the wording of Article 11 of the Batteries Directive leaves open the question of how 'readily removable' should be defined. As a result, in practice, the design of an increasing share of products and batteries makes it challenging for reuse centres to prepare products for reuse.[3285] Many of the centres think about stopping reuse activities with white goods and focus on smaller electric items (e.g. like smartphones, tablets, and laptops), which require less storage space.[3286] This leads to shortened product lifetime and thus a waste of raw materials and other natural resources. It should therefore be ensured that these ecodesign requirements are precise and concrete enough (see #22). There are two (cumulative) options to improve the preciseness and concreteness of those requirements. The first option consists of clarifying the (more general) ecodesign requirements contained in these sectoral waste directives by amending the relevant provisions of these instruments. The second option is to connect these rules with the corresponding implementing measures taken on the basis of the Ecodesign Directive, which complement these rules by establishing product-specific ecodesign requirements. References to these implementing measures should be made in waste rules, and vice versa. With regard to the particular case of batteries, for which no implementing measure exists (yet), Article 11 of the Batteries Directive should be amended to give a definition of the removability of waste batteries (see #21), as suggested in the recent Proposal for a Regulation on batteries, which adds that "*a battery is readily replaceable where, after its removal from an appliance, it can be substituted by a similar battery, without affecting the functioning or the performance of that appliance*".[3287]

961. SECOND: OBLIGATIONS TO INFORM USERS AND TREATMENT FACILITIES – Sectoral waste legislation also establishes information requirements that promote the implementation of the waste hierarchy. There is, first, information

3285 See *supra*, n° 165.

3286 Technopolis Group (in consortium with Fraunhofer ISI, Thinkstep and Wuppertal Institute), *Regulatory barriers for the Circular Economy – Lessons from ten cases studies* (European Commission 2016), p. 39.

3287 Art. 11 of the Proposal for a new Batteries Regulation.

requirements that contribute to raising consumer awareness on waste prevention and management. For example, Article 14 of the WEEE Directive requires Member States to ensure that users have information on the return and collection systems available to them, as well as on their role in contributing to re-use, recycling and other forms of recovery of WEEE. Article 20 of the Batteries Directive contains similar requirements to ensure that end-users are fully informed on the importance of collecting and recycling waste batteries. In addition, Article 21 of the same Directive provides the basis for a labelling system, which should provide end-users with transparent, reliable and clear information on batteries and accumulators and any heavy metals they contain. Concerning cars, Article 9 of the ELV Directive obliges producers to make information on the reuse, recycling and recovery of end-of life vehicles and their components accessible to prospective buyers. All these measures may overcome barriers on the consumer side that hinder reversing premature obsolescence, and more specifically consumers' storage habits and lack of knowledge.[3288] It should be noted that similar information requirements are imposed by some EU Ecolabel rules.[3289]

Second, sectoral waste legislation requires the provision of information that facilitates the maintenance and reuse of products at the end-of-life stage. For example, Article 15 of the WEEE Directive gives clear guidelines concerning information that producers should provide free of charge to treatment facilities (including reuse centres). Interestingly, this information obligation also applies the other way around in France. Article L. 541–10. III. of the French Environmental Code requires waste management organisations to provide producers with access to technical information so that it facilitates product ecodesign. Information requirements can also be found in Article 11 of the Batteries Directive, which states that "*[a]ppliances in which batteries and accumulators are incorporated shall be accompanied by instructions on how those batteries and accumulators can be safely removed by either the end-user or by independent qualified professionals. Where appropriate, the instructions shall also inform the end-user of the types of battery or accumulator incorporated into the appliance.*" Information obligations are also imposed on car producers and car components manufacturers on the basis of Article 8 of the ELV Directive. These operators are under obligation to provide information to treatment facilities on the dismantling of cars and their (reusable) components.

962. Information obligations should be detailed and strengthened at EU level – The sectoral legal instruments should be more specific on the basic information that producers should provide, such as labels, technical documentation and online, as well as on more specific information to end-users and economic operators who request it (see #23). In addition, schemes could

---

3288 See *supra*, n° 915.

3289 See Chapter III on the marketing and pre-contractual stage, and more specifically n° 612.

be established to encourage end-users to reuse and recycle their products. An interesting project is the CIRC4Life EU-funded project, which created and studied an innovative incentive scheme based on a mobile app that informed consumers about the negative environmental impacts of their purchases and offered them economic rewards for delivering their unused devices.[3290] Such measures can help educate consumers and raise their awareness about waste prevention.

963. A PRODUCT PASSPORT SHOULD BE INTRODUCED – Product-related information, which is at the moment scattered across various legislations, should be registered, processed and shared through a product passport, as previously argued (see #24).[3291] Such a passport would increase the traceability of raw materials from extraction to recycling and the transparency about the environmental impacts of different products. Information would be accessible via a QR code. This passport would be used at the product's end-of-life stage by reuse centres and recyclers that would unite the relevant pieces of information on the product and its components. More than that, the product passport would make producers responsible for the entire lifetime of their products and incentivise them to shift to more sustainable production patterns. As previously pointed out[3292], such an idea has been conveyed in the Sustainable Products Initiative[3293], and a 'battery passport' (and database) is also envisaged within the framework of the review of the Batteries Directive.[3294]

964. THIRD: OBLIGATIONS ON THE COLLECTION AND SEPARATION OF WASTE – To maximize preparing for reuse, the sectoral directives add obligations concerning the collection and separation of waste. The aim of these obligations is to avoid, whenever possible, consumers discarding products as residual, unsorted waste.[3295] Furthermore, such obligations allow avoiding products hibernating in consumers' households.[3296] The WEEE Directive establishes obligations on the collection and separation of waste in its Article 5 and 6. Article 5 requires among others the possibility for end-users to return the WEEE free of charge in collection facilities that are available and accessible, with no obligation to buy EEE of an equivalent type. In France, EEE producers and their eco-organisations are invited to carry out national collection operations

3290 For more information on this project, see <https://www.circ4life.eu/home>.

3291 See *supra*, n° 637.

3292 See *supra*, n° 270.

3293 Art. 8 to 13 of the Proposal for a Regulation of the European Parliament and of the Council establishing a framework for setting ecodesign requirements for sustainable products and repealing Directive 2009/125/EC, COM(2022) 142 final.

3294 Art. 65 of the Proposal for a new Batteries Regulation.

3295 E. Maitre-Ekern, C. Dalhammar, 'Towards a hierarchy of consumption behaviour in the circular economy', 26 *Maastricht Journal of European and Comparative Law* (2019) p. 405.

3296 See *supra*, n° 157.

each year during which individuals can get a bonus when they bring back the equipment they wish to get rid of.[3297] Regarding the access to waste streams, Article 6(2) of the WEEE Directive states that *"prior to any further transfer, collection schemes or facilities provide, where appropriate, for the separation at the collection points of WEEE that is to be prepared for reuse from other separately collected WEEE, in particular by granting access for personnel from reuse centres"*. Article 7 of the Batteries Directive adds an overarching objective for Member States to maximise the separate collection of waste batteries and accumulators and to minimise the disposal of batteries and accumulators as mixed municipal waste. The collection of end-of-life vehicles, which is regulated by Article 5 of the ELV Directive, differs from these other waste streams by requiring the presentation of a certificate of destruction for the deregistration and treatment of end-of life vehicles.

965. THE BARRIERS TO REUSE AT COLLECTION POINTS – In practice, the objectives of collecting and separating waste do not sufficiently promote reuse, if at all. The problem may stem from the distinction between reuse and preparing for reuse as well as the (inappropriate) legal definition of 'waste'.[3298] Since discarded products are almost automatically classified as waste, they are subject to stringent rules, which restrict the access of reuse organisations to materials available at collection points.[3299] For example, in some cases, organisations involved in reuse activities are required to get a license as waste management companies allowed to process waste, even though the organisations do not intend to process waste, but only to prepare the products for reuse. Such technical requirements are challenging and costly for often rather small companies, but also senseless for reuse activities that cause no direct harm to the environment or human health.[3300]

966. THE COLLECTION AND TREATMENT OF WASTE SHOULD BE FURTHER REGULATED BY EU LAW – The systems of separate collection and treatment of waste should be organised at EU level for certain waste streams (see #25), as proposed by the EC in the 2020 Circular Economy Action Plan.[3301] This idea of EU-wide take-back and return schemes is already being explored by the

3297 Art. L. 541-10-20 of the Environmental Law Code, as introduced by Art. 13 of the Law on the Environmental Footprint of Digital Technology.

3298 See *supra*, n° 922–927.

3299 See also P. Tecchio, F. Ardente, F. Mathieux, *Analysis of durability, reusability and reparability: Application to dishwashers and washing machines – JRC Technical Report* (European Commission 2016) p. 86.

3300 Technopolis Group (in consortium with Fraunhofer ISI, Thinkstep and Wuppertal Institute), *Regulatory barriers for the Circular Economy – Lessons from ten cases studies* (European Commission 2016), p. 38.

3301 Communication from the Commission of 11 March 2020 to the European Parliament, the Council, the European Economic and Social Committee and the Committee of the Regions

EC for small electronics like old mobile phones, tablets and chargers within the framework of the Circular Electronics Initiative. The aim is to improve the collection and treatment of e-waste and provide consumers with more information and options to return their used and waste electronics stored at home.[3302] More (specific) obligations could also be imposed by EU rules. This may include a command-and-control approach, but also information-sharing, eco-labelling, financial incentives and environmental-awareness raising (see #26). As an example, the Proposal for a Regulation on batteries suggest that "*producers are obliged to provide for the necessary practical arrangements for collection and transport of waste batteries from those collection point to ensure that the waste portable batteries are subsequently subject to treatment and recycling*".[3303] It could also be required to adapt infrastructure and programming in place to include diversion of products and components to secondary markets for reuse and value-retention processes production.[3304] Specific containers could for example be established at waste centres for products that are still functioning.

967. COOPERATION BETWEEN ACTORS SHOULD BE FURTHER PROMOTED – The collection, separation and reuse of harvested products, components and materials would also be facilitated by greater cooperation between manufacturers, sellers, collection schemes, reuse organisations and recyclers.[3305] In Belgium, access for reuse has been eased through the collaboration between reuse centres and take-back schemes. Reuse centres have better access to high quality products, which can be resold in their shops, while the take-back schemes reduce their costs for treatment.[3306] EU law could encourage such cooperation by introducing an explicit obligation to cooperate (see #27), as suggested in the Proposal for a Regulation on batteries, where producers are required to establish, free of charge for the end-user, a network of collection points in cooperation with other operators involved.[3307]

---

on A new Circular Economy Action Plan – For a cleaner and more competitive Europe, COM(2020) 98 final, p. 13.

3302 Communication from the Commission of 11 March 2020 to the European Parliament, the Council, the European Economic and Social Committee and the Committee of the Regions on A new Circular Economy Action Plan – For a cleaner and more competitive Europe, COM(2020) 98 final, p. 7; Communication from the Commission of 13 November 2020 to the European Parliament and the Council and the Council on New Consumer Agenda – Strengthening consumer resilience for sustainable recovery, COM(2020) 696 final, p. 7.

3303 Art. 48(1)(c) of the Proposal for a new Batteries Regulation.

3304 N. Nasr, J.D. Russell, *Redefining Value – The Manufacturing Revolution. Remanufacturing, Refurbishment, Repair and Direct Reuse in the Circular Economy* (United Nations Environment Programme 2018) p. 36.

3305 Ellen MacArthur Foundation, *Empowering repair* (2016) p. 12; D. Watson et al., *Circular Business Models in the Mobile Phone Industry* (TemaNord 2017) pp. 45–46.

3306 Technopolis Group (in consortium with Fraunhofer ISI, Thinkstep and Wuppertal Institute), *Regulatory barriers for the Circular Economy – Lessons from ten cases studies* (European Commission 2016), p. 39.

3307 Art. 48(2) of the Proposal for a new Batteries Regulation.

968. ECONOMIC INCENTIVES SHOULD BE USED – To bolster the collection and separation of waste, the waste legal framework should also contain economic incentives (see #27). On the business side, subsidy programs could be used to help offset the costs paid by producers to adopt value-retention processes as well as their efforts to improve the efficiency and accessibility of existing collection infrastructure and systems. An interesting idea implemented in Belgium consists of inviting e-waste recyclers to place bids on collected appliances. The winning bidder has a right to purchase 50% of the lot and others can purchase the rest by aligning with the winning price.[3308] On the consumer side, in a way similar to Art. L. 541–10–20 of the French Environmental Law Code[3309], one could imagine establishing a deposit that would economically incite consumers to return obsolete products at the end of their use cycle.[3310]

Proposed amendment to the Batteries Directive:

#21

Article 11
Removal of waste batteries and accumulators

<u>1.</u> Member States shall ensure that manufacturers design appliances in such a way that waste batteries and accumulators can be readily removed. Appliances into which batteries and accumulators are incorporated shall be accompanied by instructions showing how they can be removed safely and, where appropriate, informing the end-user of the type of the incorporated batteries and accumulators.

<u>A battery is readily replaceable where, after its removal from an appliance, it can be substituted by a similar battery, without affecting the functioning or the performance of that appliance.</u>

<u>2. The obligations set out in paragraph 1</u> shall not apply where, for safety, performance, medical or data integrity reasons, continuity of power supply is necessary and requires a permanent connection between the appliance and the battery or accumulator.

AND

3308 M. Cordella, F. Alfieri, J. Sanfelix, *Guidance for the Assessment of Material Efficiency: Application to Smartphones – JRC Technical Report* (European Commission 2020) p. 21.

3309 See *supra*, n° 964.

3310 Such an idea was proposed in a former German legislative proposal: Antrag vom 09.01.2020 "Elektroschrott – Wertstoffkreisläufe schließen", BT-Drucks. 19/16412. In this proposal, it was proposed to introduce a € 25 deposit on smartphones and tablets to create additional incentives for consumers to return their old devices.

Policy recommendations

#22 The (more general) ecodesign requirements contained of sectoral waste directives should be amended for more clarity. When appropriate, references to the corresponding implementing measures taken on the basis of the Ecodesign Directive should be made (and vice versa).

#23 The sectoral waste directives should be clearer on the basic and specific information that producers are required to provide to end-users and other economic operators (e.g. labels, technical documentation and online).

#24 Product-related information should be registered, processed and shared through a digital product passport.

#25 EU-wide take-back and return schemes should be introduced for specific waste streams.

#26 Measures related to information-sharing, eco-labelling, financial incentives and environmental-awareness raising should be taken at EU level.

#27 EU law should introduce an explicit obligation to cooperate and adopt other measures in that sense, such as subsidy programs.

D. CONCLUSION

969. Prolonging product lifetime as much as possible – When a product is prematurely obsolete, it does not automatically become waste. Three scenarios are possible at the end of the product use cycle: the obsolete product (or its parts and components) can be reused, recycled or disposed of. From a sustainability perspective, reusing the product though direct reuse, repair, refurbishment and remanufacturing should undoubtedly be the preferred option. Only these processes allow lengthening the lifetime of the product – or its parts or components in the case of remanufacturing. Recycling and disposal are far less sustainable and should be seen as last resort options.

970. A shift of focus from recycling to reuse – For many years, the focus of attention by government, industry and environmental campaigners was on recycling. The progress made in recycling in recent years is welcome, but as T. Cooper warned, "*it will prove an obstacle rather than a steppingstone if it detracts attention from the more fundamental changes that are now required to reduce the excessive throughput of energy and materials in our economy*".[3311] A wide array

[3311] T. Cooper, *Beyond recycling – The longer life option* (The New Economics Foundation 1994) p. 19.

of initiatives has been taken or proposed within the EU to divert products from recycling to reuse. These include practical initiatives, such as municipal reuse parks and public procurement of reused furniture and ICT products, but also legal initiatives, such as the obligation for producers, importers and distributors of new (non-food) products to reuse their unsold products, including by rebate sales to their employees or by donation to charity organisations.

971. Two sides of the same coin – The existing rules regulating the end-of-life stage of products can have both positive and negative impacts on product lifetime. On the one hand, they mitigate the negative impacts of products on the environment at their end-of-life and, most importantly, they indirectly prevent the premature obsolescence of products by deterring producers from making waste-generating products and by encouraging them to design longer-lasting products and favour value-retention processes at the products' end-of-life. This consequently promotes and facilitates product maintenance and reuse, allowing the postponement and reverse of premature obsolescence. On the other hand, several barriers to extended product lifetime can stem from the waste legislation itself, which is often complex, unclear and fragmented, thereby posing challenges for reuse businesses that need to comply with them.

972. Key concepts of waste law should be improved – The definitions of key concepts given in the WFD are among the causes of regulatory barriers to reuse. First, the concept of 'waste' is too broadly defined and interpreted. As a result, end-of-use or broken products or cores are often categorised as waste and thus subject to the stringent waste rules. This has various legal, practical and psychological implications, leading to the premature obsolescence of products. The definition of 'waste' should therefore be fine-tuned and narrowed so that waste legislation (and its strict obligations) only applies when no other more sustainable option is available. To this end, the intermediary concept of 'obsolete product' could be introduced. Discarded products would first be qualified as 'obsolete products', and if after a preliminary assessment, no reuse operation is possible, the product would be considered as waste. The criteria on which the assessment would be carried out could be established by the WFD and could be similar to those used for end-of-waste status. Second, the end-of-waste status defined in Article 6 of the WFD should be amended on two fronts. This would consist, firstly, of a less strictly application of the four criteria set out by this provision. For example, reused products should be subject to distinct technical requirements to cease to be waste. Secondly, end-of-waste status should preferably be defined at EU level to help reduce legal uncertainties regarding waste treatment and the disparities between Member States.

973. The waste hierarchy should be reviewed – Amendments should also be made to the waste hierarchy established by the WFD to further promote

waste prevention and value-retention processes, which allow extending product lifetime. First, the name of the 'waste hierarchy' should be changed to 'waste prevention and management hierarchy'. Second, to bring product sustainability to the fore in the hierarchy, the terms 'prevention' and 'preparing for reuse' should be replaced by a wider range of more detailed and accurate terms. 'Prevention' should be detailed into 'avoidance', 'reduction' and 'maintenance', while 'preparation for use' should be replaced with 'direct reuse', 'repair', 'refurbishment' and 'remanufacturing'. The definitions of these different options would be given in Article 3 of the WFD and should be aligned with the definitions given by other existing legal instruments and standards. Measures and targets that are mentioned in the WFD should be distinctly defined for these options. Third, the three types of recycling processes, namely downcycling, upcycling and functional recycling, should appear in the definition of 'recycling' established under Article 3 of the WFD. Finally, measures prohibiting the destruction of unsold products should be explicitly mentioned in Article 12 of the WFD dedicated to disposal.

974. The implementation of EPR should be enhanced – By assigning financial (and sometimes organisational) responsibility to producers for the management of the waste stage of their products, EPR can play a crucial role in tackling the five types of premature obsolescence. EPR can provide incentives to prevent waste at source, promote product sustainable design and support the achievement of public recycling and materials management goals. So far, electronic and electrical equipment products, batteries and accumulators, vehicles and packaging are covered by these rules, as required by the corresponding sectoral directives. In addition to implementing EPR schemes on these four waste streams, some Member States have extended this principle to other product categories, like furniture, lamps and toys. However, it seems that EPR currently falls short of its potential. There are different ways of improving the implementation of EPR so that it bolsters product sustainability. First, the financial contribution paid by producers under EPR schemes should be modulated on the basis of product sustainability aspects. The criteria used for this modulation should be established at EU level, drawing inspiration from the French bonus/penalty system and taking the criteria of other legal instruments into consideration (such as ecodesign rules). Second, the fees charged for the management of products at the end-of-life stage should be set high enough. This could consist of internalising more costs related to the waste management of products via EPR, thus allocating more (if not all) of these costs to producers. Third, mandatory EPR rules should be introduced at EU level for a broader range of product categories, starting with waste streams for which producer responsibility organisations have been most commonly identified within the EU.

975. Sectoral rules should be strengthened and linked to other instruments – Sectoral waste directives have established specific obligations to implement the waste hierarchy enshrined in the WFD. Among these obligations, there are, first, specific ecodesign requirements, which contribute to extending product lifetime. To improve the effectiveness of these requirements, they should be clarified and linked to the corresponding implementing measures taken on the basis of the Ecodesign Directive as described in the second chapter of this book. With regard to the particular case of batteries, for which no implementing measures exist (yet), Article 11 of the Batteries Directive should be amended to define what is meant by the 'removability of waste batteries'. Second, sectoral directives contain information requirements, which contribute to raising consumer awareness on waste prevention and management and facilitate the maintenance and reuse of products at the end-of-life stage. Yet, the basic and specific information that producers have to provide to end-users and other economic operators should be clearly specified in the relevant provisions. These information obligations should be coupled with the introduction of a digital product passport, which would register, process and share product-related information to the various stakeholders at EU level. Third, the obligations on the collection and separation of waste imposed by the sectoral directives should be reinforced at EU level by the introduction of EU-wide take-back and return schemes for specific waste streams and by the adoption and promotion of other measures related to information-sharing, eco-labelling, financial incentives, and environmental-awareness raising.

976. The potential and need for a sustainable end-of-life stage – Waste law is an (unexploited) tool for tackling all types of premature obsolescence. It enables the return of discarded products (or their parts and components) to our production and consumption systems, the reduction of product environmental impacts at their end-of life, but also a drive for sustainable product design. It is time to untap this potential and lift the barriers that hinder the extension of products' lifetime after their premature obsolescence. To this end, many amendments to waste legislation are needed, as discussed in this fifth chapter. One of the key takeaways of this chapter is that the EU should leave less discretion to the Member States and lead the way for the prevention and management of waste. This legislation should be underpinned by digitalisation and artificial intelligence technology, which can encourage on-demand custom manufacturing, help keep electronic products in use and handle materials more efficiently at their end-of-life (including returned products).[3312]

[3312] Artificial intelligence technology can, for example, help in managing reverse logistics and screening, testing, repairing, refurbishing and remanufacturing used devices. See the concrete examples given in See Ellen MacArthur Foundation, *Artificial Intelligence and the*

977. Many challenges, including a cultural one – Making these necessary legal amendments may be challenging. Enforcement of waste rules can be particularly difficult, especially given the variety of actors involved, including small and large traders, small refurbishing companies, and charity organisations.[3313] But the biggest challenge of all is cultural. Increasing reuse at the end of the product use cycle is partly a cultural challenge, dependent on a change in values, attitudes and behaviours among traders and end-users. While engineers must see ways to use second-hand parts, consumers must understand the value of repair and returning products.[3314] Such changes often need to be driven by legislation, for example, by raising consumer awareness through information or by stimulating design for reuse.

Circular Economy (2019) p. 30 at p. 32. See also Material Economics, *Retaining Value in the Swedish Materials System. Material Economics* (2018).

3313 J. Huisman et al., *Countering WEEE Illegal Trade – Summary Report, Market Assessment, Legal Analysis, Crime Analysis and Recommendations Roadmap* (CWIT 2015).

3314 As highlighted by L. Hennies, R. Stamminger, "*consumers are the link in the chain to extend the product lifecycle, because the reuse and deferred disposal can only be solved with their support*". See L. Hennies, R. Stamminger, 'An empirical survey on the obsolescence of appliances in German households', 112 *Resources, Conservation and Recycling* (2016) p. 73 at p. 82.

CHAPTER VI
GENERAL CONCLUSION AND POLICY RECOMMENDATIONS

978. A LONG JOURNEY DRIVEN BY ONE CENTRAL QUESTION – This book set out to answer one central question: How do EU and national legal rules tackle premature obsolescence, and if necessary, how could the legal framework be improved? To achieve this aim, the central question was split into four main components, which constitute the structure of this book: (i) define the concept of premature obsolescence; (ii) identify and describe the multiple legal rules addressing premature obsolescence; (iii) evaluate these multiple legal rules; and (iv) where necessary, propose policy recommendations. The first chapter of this book provided a comprehensive definition of premature obsolescence and related concepts, while the following chapters identified and examined the wide array of measures that tackles this issue at the different stages of the product lifecycle, starting from the design and production stage and ending with the end-of-life stage.

979. FROM PLANNED TO PREMATURE OBSOLESCENCE – As outlined above, the first chapter laid the conceptual foundations upon which this book is built. After a critical analysis of the concept of planned obsolescence, it was established that the concept of 'premature obsolescence' should be preferred as it is sufficiently neutral and general. The concept of planned obsolescence was integrated as a sub-category of the more fitting concept of premature obsolescence, which was defined as *"all practices that reduce product lifetime so that the product does not reach its optimal lifetime (from an environmental point of view), without it being the result of normal wear and tear"*. Five different yet inextricably linked types of premature obsolescence were identified, namely material, functional, indirect, economic, and psychological obsolescence. The study also found that premature obsolescence occurs due to (a combination of) various causes associated either with the business side or the consumer side. In addition to these findings, the first chapter established other complementary definitions, including those of 'product lifetime', 'product use cycle', 'product obsolescence', 'waste', 'recovery', 'optimal product lifetime' and 'product sustainability'. The analysis conducted in this first chapter does not only extend knowledge on premature obsolescence,

but also clarifies issues and offers concepts and definitions that law makers should use when regulating the issue.

980. STRATEGIES TO RESIST, POSTPONE AND REVERSE PREMATURE OBSOLESCENCE – The last section of the first chapter distinguished and described four strategies that contribute to curbing practices of premature obsolescence and reaching the 'optimal product lifetime'. Each of these strategies was associated with concepts that completed the definition of premature obsolescence. The first strategy consists of resisting obsolescence by making products physically or emotionally more durable. Second, product obsolescence can be postponed thanks to maintenance and upgrades. The third strategy is to reverse the obsolescence of products through recovery operations such as direct reuse, repair, refurbishment, and remanufacturing. Fourth, in addition to these three strategies that prolong product lifetime, it is also possible to reduce the environmental impacts of obsolete products at the end of their life through recycling. As with the concept of premature obsolescence, this wide array of concepts should also be considered by the law makers when designing strategies to fight premature obsolescence. The use of these terms makes measures more meaningful and encourages stakeholders to take positive actions in favour of product sustainability instead of banning certain practices. These concepts already appear in existing legal instruments but can have different meanings. Particular attention should thus be given to the need for alignment and coherence between the concepts used in product, consumer, and waste policies. The EU standards on material efficiency aspects and the UN glossary provide a solid conceptual basis that should be used to harmonise all these definitions.

981. SHAPING THE DESIGN OF PRODUCTS TOWARDS MORE SUSTAINABILITY – Chapters II to V of this book were dedicated to the legal rules implementing these four strategies curbing premature obsolescence and reducing its environmental impacts at the EU and national levels. The first types of measures that were analysed were those shaping the design and production stage of the product lifecycle. This second chapter showed how crucial ecodesign legislation is to address premature obsolescence. Ecodesign regulations directly influence the lifetime of specific product categories by imposing ecodesign and information requirements on product sustainability aspects. Those require, for example, to design vacuum cleaner motors with an operational lifetime of at least 500 hours, to make software and firmware updates for servers and data storage products available for a minimum period of eight years after placing the last unit of the model on the market and to supply some television spare parts for a minimum period of seven years. The focus of these regulations was initially on energy-using products and energy efficiency aspects. But recent years have seen a gradual shift in focus towards resource and material efficiency. A series of initiatives is now envisaged at EU level to further strengthen the role of ecodesign legislation in making products placed on the EU market more sustainable. To this end, three recommendations should be made: (1) adopting more ecodesign and information requirements on product sustainability aspects (2) for a wider range of products, (3) while improving the enforcement of this legislation.

982. Incentivising and empowering consumers to make sustainable choices at the time of purchase – The third chapter of this book revealed that rules regulating the disclosure of product sustainability information are also of utmost importance to combat premature obsolescence. The mandatory and voluntary provision of reliable, comparable, and verifiable information on product sustainability aspects steers consumer purchasing choices in favour of (more) sustainable products, contributes to combatting psychological obsolescence and fosters the sustainable use and disposal of products. Moreover, making such information available can lighten the burden of proof to enforce consumer rights in case of premature obsolescence. But most importantly, such rules indirectly influence business practices as they incentive producers and sellers to consider these features when designing and marketing products. Four instruments regulate the marketing and pre-contractual stage of product lifecycle at EU level, namely the UCPD, the CRD, the Energy Labelling Regulation and the EU Ecolabel Regulation. These EU rules are complemented and reinforced by purely national initiatives. This panoply of rules prohibits certain practices that accelerate product replacement, regulate voluntary environmental claims, and impose general and product-specific information on product sustainability aspects. However, despite the information already available to consumers and their strong intentions to adopt a sustainable lifestyle, there is still an intention-action gap. To overcome barriers that hamper sustainable consumption, several adjustments to existing rules should be made. These include (1) explicit references to premature obsolescence and product sustainability in horizontal consumer legislation, (2) more product-specific requirements on product sustainability for a wider range of products and services, (3) the development of a single, robust and EU-wide methodology to assess and verify environmental claims and labelling of products, (4) more effective enforcement and sanctions regulated at EU level, (5) the integration of national initiatives into EU information rules and (6) the creation of links between all these legal instruments, including through the introduction of digital product passports. Adopting these changes would unleash the untapped potential of existing rules to serve as a key driver for sustainable consumption.

983. Extending the lifetime of products once purchased – Once the product has been purchased, its lifetime can still be prolonged by certain remedies, some of which are provided and regulated by consumer law. The fourth chapter of this book focused on the protection granted by the SGD, and more specifically on the right to repair. The SGD offers consumers the possibility of requesting repairs from the seller of the concerned defective products for a period of (at least) two years. If this period has elapsed, or if the case falls outside the scope of the legal guarantee, consumers may reverse the premature obsolescence of their products by other means, including those granted by the commercial guarantee (if any) or by national contractual law mechanisms, like the guarantee against hidden defects established under Belgian and French law. The rules on guarantees laid down by the SGD also impose an 'update-obligation', which contributes to postponing the (functional) obsolescence of goods with digital elements. Consumers can make a complaint against the seller if, contrary to what they expected or to what was contractually agreed, they were not informed of nor supplied with updates that are necessary to keep their goods in conformity. But most importantly, guarantee rules help bring product lifetime to the front of consumers' and traders' minds and influence their decisions in favour of long-lasting and quality goods. Yet, several amendments to these rules should be made to further promote product sustainability, including for example by extending the legal guarantee period, facilitating repair, and allowing for a direct producer liability mechanism.

984. Preventing products from becoming waste and reducing their environmental impacts once they are – The fifth chapter of this book showed that product lifetime can also be prolonged once discarded by the user. Three scenarios are possible at the end of the product use cycle: the obsolete product (or its parts and components) can either be reused, recycled, or disposed of. From a sustainability perspective, reusing the product through value-retention processes (i.e. direct reuse, repair, refurbishment and remanufacturing) should be preferred. The main legislation in this field comprises the WFD and three sectoral instruments, namely the WEEE Directive, the Batteries Directive and the ELV Directive. Although the environmental strategy was based on recycling for many years, attention is now turning to the possibility of diverting products from recycling to reuse. This shift of focus is to be welcomed in the fight against premature obsolescence and should be supported by the adoption of four types of measures. First, the definition of 'waste' should be fine-tuned and narrowed so that waste legislation is more compatible with the objectives of a circular economy and sustainable consumption. Second, the hierarchy of waste prevention and management options should be reviewed to further promote waste prevention and value-retention processes. Third, EPR, which has great potential for curbing all types of premature obsolescence, should be strengthened, including through modulated fees and an expanded scope of application. Fourth, the specific obligations established by the sectoral directives, which encompass ecodesign requirements, information obligations and obligations on the collection and separation of waste, should be improved. Such amendments would turn 'waste' legislation from an obstacle to an asset for product sustainability.

985. A NETWORK OF RULES EXISTS TO TACKLE THE VARIOUS FORMS OF PREMATURE OBSOLESCENCE – This book has gone some way towards enhancing our understanding of premature obsolescence and the panoply of existing legal rules that can be used to tackle this phenomenon. As summarised in Figure 10, measures curbing premature obsolescence can be classified in the light of the five types of premature obsolescence, taking the different stages of the product lifetime into account. Every measure can be correlated with the four strategies against premature obsolescence and the related notions of product sustainability (i.e. durability, maintenance, upgrades, reuse, repair, refurbishment, remanufacturing and recycling). This patchwork of rules forms the legal framework tackling the issue.

Figure 10. Summary of existing and possible measures tackling the five types of premature obsolescence at the different stages of the product lifecycle

	Material obsolescence	Functional obsolescence	Indirect obsolescence	Economic obsolescence	Psychological obsolescence
Design and production stage	Requirements on durability (* and **) Requirements on product disassembly (** and ***) Requirements on reuse, refurbishment and remanufacturing (***)	Requirements on OS, software and firmware (* and **) Requirements on data deletion (***)	Requirements on the availability and delivery of spare parts (***)	Ecodesign and information requirements that (help) lower repair costs (***)	Information requirements that contribute to raising consumer awareness on product lifetime (*)
Marketing and pre-contractual stage	Durability and reparability labels (*) Indirect incentives through mandatory and voluntary information on durability (*) Ban or sanctions against practices that mislead consumers on product lifetime (* and **) Ban or sanctions against aggressive practices that shorten product lifetime (**)	Indirect incentives through mandatory and voluntary information on functionality, compatibility and interoperability (* and **) Ban or sanctions against practices that urge consumers to install software updates that negatively impact the performance of the device (**)	Reparability labels (***) General information on repair (***) Indirect incentives through mandatory and voluntary information on spare parts (***) Indirect incentives through ecolabel criteria on reuse of consumables (*) Ban or sanctions against aggressive practices (**)	Blacklisted practices whereby products are falsely described as free (*) Ban or sanctions against practices that mislead consumers on the price or the manner in which the price is calculated (***)	Ban or sanctions against marketing and advertising practices that directly or indirectly encourages degradation, discard or replace prematurely still-functioning products (*) Durability and reparab-ility labels (* and ***) Information on after-sales services and guarantees (* and ***)

	Material obsolescence	Functional obsolescence	Indirect obsolescence	Economic obsolescence	Psychological obsolescence
Use stage	Conformity criteria on durability (*)	Update obligation (* and **)	Measures promoting repair (***)	Measures that contribute to keeping repair costs as reasonable as possible (***)	Information on guarantees, including on the right to repair (* and ***)
	Guarantee against hidden defects (***)	Conformity criteria on functionality, compatibility and interoperability (* and **)			
		Guarantee against hidden defects (***)			
End-of-life stage	Waste prevention measures (*)	Data deletion (***)	/	Repair and reuse funds (***)	Ban on the destruction of returned goods (***)

* Resisting premature obsolescence
** Postponing premature obsolescence
*** Reversing premature obsolescence

986. Combatting premature obsolescence on different fronts – The most obvious finding to emerge from this study is that a wide web of legal instruments exists to combat premature obsolescence. This book proposed a set of policy recommendations for each of them so that the law does not impede but fosters sustainable production and consumption patterns. These recommendations should be seen as part of an overall comprehensive policy against premature obsolescence.[3315] It is indeed necessary to consider this panoply of rules (preventive/coercive, product-/consumer-oriented, self-regulatory/legislative measures) as a toolbox to deal with this complex issue, which involves many actors and covers many different types of products. For example, it would be pointless to require producers to design reparable and durable products, which may take more effort, energy and resource, if ultimately consumers do not buy them or take care of them. Product lifetime will only be effectively extended if actions addressing user behaviour are taken, such as informing and educating consumers about the proper use and maintenance of products, praising the advantages of repairing broken products and of purchasing second-hand or remanufactured products, and promoting the collection of unused products for the recovery of their residual value through second-hand markets or refurbishment and remanufacturing processes. In other words, product sustainability is determined not only by the intrinsic characteristics of products but also by the system of which they are a part.

987. Taking the appropriate rules – Concerning the choice of measures to be taken, T. Cooper rightly pointed out that "the ability and willingness of industry and consumers to take actions considered necessary by public authorities will influence decisions concerning which instruments to use".[3316] While it may be necessary to impose mandatory requirements on traders and prohibit certain practices, it may be just as essential to encourage economic actors to act through more indirect and preventive measures, such as ecolabels, guarantee rights and other liability mechanisms. The choice of rules may also vary depending on the product categories (i.e. workhorse, investment and up-to-date products), which may require a particular approach to prolong product lifetime. There is no one-size-fits-all solution, which is another reason why this combination of rules is of utmost importance.

988. Adopting a consistent and coherent approach – While identifying and exploring the various legal rules triggering product sustainability, this book

3315 The EC has already developed such an approach with the Integrated Product Policy, an initiative aimed at minimising the environmental impacts of products and services throughout their lifecycles. See Communication from the Commission of 18 June 2003 to the Council and the European Parliament on Integrated Product Policy – Building on Environmental Life-Cycle Thinking, COM(2003) 302 final.

3316 T. Cooper, 'Policies for longevity', in T. Cooper (ed.), *Longer lasting products: Alternatives to the throwaway society* (Gower 2010) p. 225.

also brought to light the fragmentation of the legal framework, with the risks of gaps, contradictions and overlaps between the different legal instruments. The most striking observation was that (transparent) connections are lacking between the different legal texts. Law makers should ensure consistency and coherence between the various legal instruments. This, however, does not mean that the legal instruments should be merged into a single law specifically dedicated to premature obsolescence. Although it could wipe the slate clean and raise awareness about the importance of product sustainability, embarking on such an ambitious enterprise would involve a tremendous workload, but also risks of increasing the complexity of the already complex network of rules. What is crucial is that existing rules and policies remain coherent, mutually supportive, with streamlined procedures and methods, and represent clear task sharing. This objective could be achieved by centralising all ideas and recommendations on the topic in comprehensive action plans and by making cross-references throughout the legal texts. Such strong links already exist between ecodesign regulations and energy labelling rules and should serve as an example.

989. Acting preferably at EU level – This book also confirmed the necessity of prioritising rules at EU level, in accordance with the principles of proportionality and subsidiarity. Harmonising rules at EU level has many advantages that satisfy all the interests at stake (i.e. consumers, businesses and the environment). First, EU rules prevent disparate national legislation from becoming obstacles to intra-EU trade. The obligation to comply with rules differing from one Member State to another creates a financial and administrative burden for producers, who may then pass on the costs to final consumers. The absence of harmonisation also exacerbates the fragmentation of the legal framework, constraining consumers and producers to deal with a tortuous legal maze. Second, the wider the level playing field, the more it influences economic actors beyond the EU boundaries ('Brussels effect'). This is already the case with mandatory ecodesign requirements, which tend to be taken up in other jurisdictions with the view to ensure the competitiveness of their industries on the global market. This is a major advantage as environmental issues are of a global or at least a cross-border nature.

990. While leaving some freedom to the Member States – Yet maximum harmonization may not always be the most appropriate approach to refine the legal framework on premature obsolescence as it prevents the Member States from taking measures to curb this phenomenon. Purely national initiatives may be welcomed, especially when considering the lengthy period that it may take to adopt EU rules. The margin for manoeuvre left to Member States should however not result in contradictions and overlaps between EU and national rules. In this regard, the notification procedure established by Directive (EU) 2015/1535 is of utmost importance.

991. Environmental protection should outweigh consumer and business interests – As underlined in the introduction of this book, environmental protection should be given priority in case of conflict of interests as preserving the environment is in the interest of both consumers and businesses.[3317] Only such a priority order will make the legal framework effective to combat premature obsolescence. Such an approach is in line with Article 11 of the TFEU, which requires integrating environmental protection requirements in the definition and implementation of the Union's policies and activities, in particular to promote sustainable development. However, this is far from being the case at present. For example, the fourth chapter of this book demonstrated that some rights enshrined in consumer law (e.g. the right of withdrawal, the right to replace defective goods) encourage consumers to buy more products, which might hinder the objective of sustainable goods. Some provisions contained in existing legal instruments should therefore be amended in favour of environmental protection. This does not mean that environmental protection should undermine consumer protection, but rather that consumers should be considered as citizens and not only as the vulnerable party that needs protection.[3318] To this end, the system of representative actions, as modernised by the Directive (EU) 2020/1828 on representative actions, can help individual consumers to secure their rights and be proactive in the fight against premature obsolescence. Hence, both consumers and businesses should be seen as agents of change, with their decisions and actions guided by the common long-term objective of environmental protection.

992. And beyond the law – The preceding paragraph highlighted the importance of involving all economic actors in the fight against premature obsolescence. This also constitutes one important limitation of this book, which is confined to exploring the issue from a legal perspective.[3319] In and of themselves, the recommendations offered in this book are not enough to trigger sustainable production and consumption patterns. To counter premature obsolescence, one should not neglect the need to move beyond a top-down approach that focuses solely on traditional sources of state power, such as the law, and consider bottom-up initiatives. This bottom-up approach requires to expand the notion of the law to include social and cultural norms, which are "*rules and standards that are understood by members of a group, and that guide and/or constrain social behaviour without the force of law*".[3320] These norms

[3317] See *supra*, n° 34.

[3318] See also E. Maitre-Ekern, C. Dalhammar, 'Towards a hierarchy of consumption behaviour in the circular economy', 26 *Maastricht Journal of European and Comparative Law* (2019) p. 393.

[3319] See *supra*, n° 17.

[3320] See K. Power, O. Mont, 'The role of formal and informal forces in shaping consumption and implications for sustainable society: Part II', 2 *Sustainability* (2010) p. 2587, as cited in M. Gorrie, 'Regulating our Consumer Culture: What Role Can the Law Play in Addressing

can have a crucial role in promoting sustainable production and consumption and act as a complement to legal rules, by influencing individuals where the law cannot or does not (yet) do so.[3321] Social and cultural norms could still be guided by public authorities through a 'lead-by-example' approach, for example by adopting sustainable public procurement practices and policies that raise awareness and stimulate demand for sustainable products.

993. On the right track towards changes – Over the years, I have witnessed the revival of interest in the topic of premature obsolescence. I am honoured to make my contribution to this wave of interest by enhancing our understanding of the phenomenon and proposing policy recommendations to tackle the issue. At the time of writing, a wide array of noteworthy initiatives is being proposed and discussed at national and EU levels, with many promises. This clearly demonstrates that law makers are willing to go the extra mile to promote product sustainability. Hopefully, these initiatives will materialise into hard law and live up to these promises.

> *"The more deliberate we are about both recognizing the inevitable obsolescence of all products and applying that recognition to appropriate planning for obsolescence, the better prepared our products will be at the time of their predictable demise".*[3322]

Excessive Consumption?', in V. Mauerhofer, D. Rupo, L. Tarquinio (eds.), *Sustainability and Law* (2020) p. 130.

3321 For convincing arguments on the role of social and cultural norms, see M. Gorrie, 'Regulating our Consumer Culture: What Role Can the Law Play in Addressing Excessive Consumption?', in V. Mauerhofer, D. Rupo, L. Tarquinio (eds.), *Sustainability and Law* (2020) p. 119 at p. 134.

3322 P. Boot et al., 'Up-front thinking for the optimization of product life', in B. Burns (ed.), *Ecosuss* (Carleton University Press 2008) p. 256.

SELECTED BIBLIOGRAPHY

A. BOOKS

G. Adamson, *Industrial Strength Design: How Brooks Stevens Shaped Your World* (MIT Press for the Milwaukee Art Museum 2003)

C. Bakker, M.C. den Hollander, E. van Hinte, Y. Zijlstra, *Products that last: Product design for circular business models* (BIS Publishers 2019)

J. Baudrillard, *La société de consommation* (Denoël 1970)

D. Bazin-Beust, *L'essentiel du Droit de la consommation* (Gualino 2017)

C. Behrends, *Consequences of Planned Obsolescence for Consumer Culture and the promotional self – Analysing ads* (GRIN Verlag 2004)

N. Benqué, C. du Tertre, P. Vuidel, *Trajectoire vers l'économie de fonctionnalité et de la coopération, dans une perspective de développement durable* (Atemis 2014)

A. Bradford, *The Brussels Effect – How the European Union Rules the World* (Oxford University Press 2020)

M. Braungart, W. McDonough, *Cradle to cradle: remaking the way we make the things* (North Point Press 2002)

T. Brönneke, A. Wechsler, *Obsoleszenz interdisziplinär – Vorzeitiger Verschleiß aus Sicht von Wissenschaft und Praxis* (Nomos 2015)

A. Cabigiosu, *Digitalization in the Luxury Fashion Industry* (Springer 2020)

I. Claeys, E. Terryn, *Digital Content & Distance Sales* (Intersentia 2017)

T. Cooper, *Beyond recycling – The longer life option* (The New Economics Foundation 1994)

T. Cooper, *Longer lasting products: Alternatives to the throwaway society* (Gower 2010)

C. Delforge and J. Van Zuylen, *Les défauts de la chose: Responsabilités contractuelle et extracontractuelle* (Anthemis 2015)

S. Eisenriegler, *The Circular Economy in the European Union – An Interim Review* (Springer 2020)

M. Gladwell, *The Tipping Point: How Little Things Can Make a Big Difference* (Abacus 2002)

B. Héger, *De l'obsolescence programmée, du recyclage insuffisant et de toutes ces sortes* (Altande 2020)

C. Hess, *Geplante Obsoleszenz – Rechtliche Zulässigkeit in der Lebensdauerplanung von technischen Gebrauchgütern* (Nomos 2018)

G. Howells, C. Twigg-Flesner and T. Wilhelmsson, *Rethinking EU Consumer Law* (Routledge 2018)

B. Keirsbilck, *The new European law of unfair commercial practices and competition law* (Hart Publishing, 2011)

B. Keirsbilck, E. Terryn, *Consumer Protection in a Circular Economy* (Intersentia 2019)

C. Kye, *EU environmental law and policy and EU consumer law: converging and diverging trends* (Story Scientia 1995)

S. Latouche, *Bon pour la casse: Les déraisons de l'obsolescence programmée* (Les liens qui libèrent 2012)

J. Lewis, S. Inthorn, K. Wahl-Jorgensen, *Citizens or Consumers? What the Media Tell Us About Political Participation* (Open University Press 2005).

T. Libaert, *Pour une consommation plus durable en phase avec les enjeux européens* (2018)

A.-C. Martin, *Le délit d'obsolescence programmée* (Recueil Dalloz 2017)

J. Newman, *Best before: Videogames, Supersession and Obsolescence* (Routledge 2012)

V. Packard, *The Waste Makers* (David MacKay 1960)

A. Perzanowski, *The Right to Repair: Reclaiming the Things We Own* (Cambridge University Press 2022)

Y. Picod, N. Picod, E. Chevrier, *Code de la consommation 2018, annoté et commenté* (Dalloz 2017)

K. Pope, *Understanding planned obsolescence – Unsustainability through production, consumption and waste generation* (Kogan Page 2017)

E. Poppe, J. Longmuß, *Geplante Obsoleszenz: Hinter den Kulissen der Produktentwicklung* (Transcript 2019)

A. Rahman, G. Chattopadhyay, *Long Term Warranty and After Sales Service – Concept, Policies and Cost Models* (Springer 2015)

J. Reuß, C. Dannoritzer, *Kaufen für die Müllhalde: Das Prinzip der Geplanten Obsoleszenz* (Orange-Press 2013)

E. Rex, *Produktens eller samhällets miljöproblem? Om miljöfrågans hanter-ing och kommunikation inom Volvo Lastvagnar* (Chalmers University of Technology 2007)

B. Röper, R. Marfeld, *Gibt es geplanten Verschleiss? Untersuchungen zur Obsoleszenzthese* (Schwartz Verlag 1976)

N. De Sadeleer, *Droit des déchets de l'UE: de l'élimination à l'économie circulaire* (Bruylant 2016)

G. Slade, *Made to break – technology and obsolescence in America* (Harvard University Press 2006)

S. Schridde, *Murks? Nein danke!: Was wir tun können, damit die Dinge besser werden* (Oekom 2014)

W. Stahel, *Circular economy* (Macmillan 2016)

W.R. Stahel, *The Circular Economy: A User's Guide* (Routledge 2019)

G. Straetmans, *Information Obligations and Disinformation of Consumers* (Springer International Publishing 2019)

H. Temple, M. Dépincé, *Droit de la consommation* (Dalloz 2020)

E. Terryn, I. Claeys, *Nieuw recht inzake koop & digitale inhoud en diensten* (Intersentia 2020)

F. Trentmann, *Empire of things: How We Became a World of Consumers, from the Fifteenth Century to the Twenty-First* (Harper 2016)

G. Van Calster, *EU Waste Law* (Oxford University Press 2014)

E. van Hinte, *Eternally Yours – Time in Design* (OIOpublishers 2004)

S. Vandemaele, *Commerciële garanties in de verschillende koopregimes: naar een uniforme regeling?* (PhD KU Leuven 2019)

T. Veblen, *The theory of the leisure class: An economic study in the evolution of institutions* (Macmillan 1899)
C. Vezzoli, E. Manzini, *Design for Environmental Sustainability* (Springer 2008)
L. Vogel and J. Vogel, *Droit de la consommation – Traité de droit économique (tome 3)* (Lawlex/Bruylant 2017)
E. Worrell, M. Reuter, *Handbook of recycling – State-of-the-art for practitioners, analysts, and scientists* (Elsevier 2014)

B. CHAPTERS IN BOOKS

C. Ambroise-Castérot, 'Consommation: Chapitre 3 – Protection pénale du consommateur contre les fraudes et falsifications', in Y. Mayaud (ed.), *Répertoire de droit pénal et de procédure pénale* (Paris Dalloz 2016) n° 357.
H. Aubry, 'Pratiques commerciales interdites', in D. Fenouillet (ed.), *Droit de la consommation 2021/22 – Droit interne et européen* (Dalloz 2020) p. 237 at p. 312.
A. Barsan, L. Barsan, A. Leu, L. Zafiu, *'Multi-functional Products – A Way to Decrease the Products Environmental Impact'*, in I. Visa and A. Duta (eds.), *Nearly Zero Energy Communities* (CSE Springer 2017) p. 711 at p. 719.
G. Barthe, P.R. D'Argenio, B. Finkbeiner, H. Hermanns, 'Facets of Software Doping', in T. Margaria, B. Steffen (eds), *Leveraging Applications of Formal Methods, Verification and Validation: Discussion, Dissemination, Applications. ISoLA 2016. Lecture Notes in Computer Science* (Springer 2016) p. 601 at p. 608.
P. Boot, A. Hare and R. Ho, 'Up-front thinking for the optimization of product life', in B. Burns (ed.), *EcoSuss* (Carleton University Press 2008)
T. Bourgoignie, 'Sustainable consumption and obsolescence of consumer products', in A. do Amaral Junior, L. de Almeida, L. Klein Vieira (eds.), *Sustainable Consumption – The Right to a Healthy Environment* (2020) p. 27 at p. 47.
C. Campbell, 'The desire for the new: Its nature and social location as presented in theories of fashion and modern consumerism', in R. Silverstone and E. Hirsch (eds.), *Consuming Technologies: Media and information in domestic spaces* (Routledge 1992) p. 48 at p. 63
C. Clemm, J. Emmerich, K. Schischke, N.F. Nissen, K.-D. Lang, 'Benefits and Pitfalls of Better Lifetime Data – The Case of Batteries in Mobile Electronic Equipment', in N.F. Nissen, M. Jaeger-Erben (eds.), *3rd international Product Lifetimes and the Environment (PLATE) conference proceedings* (Berlin 2019) p. 141 at p. 146.
C. Clemm, A. Berwald, C. Prewitz, N.F. Nissen, M. Schneider-Ramelow, 'Market Trends in Smartphone Design and Reliability Testing', in *Electronics Goes Green 2020+ – Conference Proceedings* (Fraunhofer IZM 2020) p. 171 at p. 178.
T. Cooper, G. Salvia, 'Fix it: barriers to repair and opportunities for change', in R. Crocker (ed.), *Reuse in an Accelerated World: Mining the Past to Reshape the Future* (Routledge 2017) p. 147 at p. 165.
S. Dangal, R. van den Berge, B. Pozo Arcos, J. Faludi, R. Balkenende, 'Perceived Capabilities and Barriers for Do-It-Yourself Repair', in C. Fitzpatrick et al. (eds.), *4th international Product Lifetimes and the Environment (PLATE) conference proceedings* (Limerick 2021) p. 132 at p. 137.

C. Delforge, Y. Ninane, 'La garantie de conformité des biens de consommation', in P. Wéry (ed.), *La Théorie générale des obligations et contrats spéciaux* (2016) p. 334 at p. 435.

E.L. Dewberry, L. Saca, M. Moreno, L. Sheldrick, M. Sinclair, C. Makatsoris, M. Charter, 'A landscape of repair', in C. Martin (ed.), *Proceedings of the Sustainable innovation 2016: circular economy innovation & design: towards sustainable product design: 21st international conference* (University for the Creative Arts 2016) p. 76 at p. 85.

W. Dewulf, J.R. Duflou, 'The environmentally optimised lifetime: a crucial concept in life cycle engineering', in G. Seliger et al. (eds.), *Proceedings of the global conference on sustainable product development and life cycle engineering* (Berlin Uni Edition 2004) p. 59 at p. 62

T. Dobs, D. Sánchez, K. Schischke, O. Wittler, M. Schneider-Ramelow, 'Assessment of the influencing parameters of the tumble test for robustness testing of smartphones', in *Electronics Goes Green 2020+ – Conference Proceedings* (Fraunhofer IZM 2020) p. 515 at p. 520

M. Ebers, A. Janssen and O. Meyer, 'Comparative report', in M. Ebers, A. Janssen et O. Meyer (eds.), *European perspectives on producers' liability: direct producers' liability for non-conformity and the sellers' right of redress* (Sellier European Law Publishers 2009) p. 3 at p. 76

P. Galindo da Fonseca, 'The Shift from Consumer Protection to Consumer Empowerment and the Consequences for Sustainable Consumption', in A. do Amaral Junior, L. de Almeida, L. Klein Vieira (eds.), *Sustainable Consumption – The Right to a Healthy Environment* (2020) p. 49 at p. 61.

F. Glansdorff, 'Panorama des actions ouvertes à l'acheteur insatisfait', in F. Glansdorff (ed.), *Actualités de quelques contrats spéciaux* (Bruylant 2005) p. 1 at p. 24.

M. Gorrie, 'Regulating our Consumer Culture: What Role Can the Law Play in Addressing Excessive Consumption?', in V. Mauerhofer, D. Rupo, L. Tarquinio (eds.), *Sustainability and Law* (2020) p. 119 at p. 134.

K. Harmer, 'Design for disassembly: Potential for durability', in *4th International Symposium on Environmentally Conscious Design & Inverse Manufacturing, Eco Design – Conference Proceedings* (IEEE 2005) p. 962 at p. 964

L. Harmer, T. Cooper, T. Fisher, G. Salvia, C. Barr, 'The joy of vacuuming? How the user experience affects vacuum cleaner longevity', in T. Cooper, N. Braithwaite, M. Moreno and G. Salvia (eds.), *Product Lifetimes and the Environment (PLATE) Conference proceedings* (Nottingham Trent University: CADBE 2015) p. 138 at p. 145

M. Jaeger-Erben, M. Proske, 'What's hot what's not: the social construction of product obsolescence and its relevance for strategies to increase functionality', in C. Bakker and R. Mugge (eds.), *Product Lifetimes And The Environment 2017 – Conference Proceedings* (IOS Press 2017) p. 181 at p. 185

N. Jeanne, ""Prêt à jeter?" – A propos du délit d'obsolescence programmée", in *Mélanges en l'honneur de Geneviève Giudicelli-Delage* (Dalloz 2016) p. 603 at p. 618

N. Jones, G. Van Calster, 'Waste Regulation', in E. Lees and J. E. Viñuales (eds.), *The Oxford Handbook of Comparative Environmental Law* (Oxford University Press 2019) p. 607 at p. 625

E. La Rosa, 'Planned Obsolescence and Criminal Law: A Problematic Relationship?', in V. Mauerhofer, D. Rupo, L. Tarquinio (eds.), *Sustainability and Law* (2020) p. 221 at p. 236

E.H. Lauridsen and M.S. Jørgensen, 'Transitions in waste treatment as a driver for product life extension', in T. Cooper, N. Braithwaite, M. Moreno and G. Salvia (eds.), *Product Lifetimes and the Environment (PLATE) Conference proceedings* (Nottingham Trent University 2015) p. 187 at p. 193

J. Longmuss and E. Poppe, 'Planned obsolescence: who are those planners?', in C. Bakker and R. Mugge (eds.), *Product Lifetimes And The Environment 2017 – Conference Proceedings* (IOS Press 2017) p. 217 at p. 221.

M. Loos, 'Not good but certainly not content: the proposals for European harmonisation of online and distance selling of goods and the supply of digital content', in E. Terryn, I. Claeys (eds.), *Digital content & distance sales* (Intersentia 2017) p. 3 at p. 53

E. Maitre-Ekern, 'The Choice of Regulatory Instruments for a Circular Economy', in Klaus Mathis and Bruce R. Huber (eds.), *Environmental Law and Economics* (Springer 2017) p. 305 at p. 334.

E. Maitre-Ekern, 'Taking products out of waste law: a new legal framework for the circular economy', in Nils F. Nissen & Melanie Jaeger-Erben (eds.), *3rd international Product Lifetimes and the Environment (PLATE) conference* (Berlin 2019) p. 495 at p. 502

A. Michel, 'Est-il pertinent de définir légalement et de pénaliser les pratiques d'obsolescence prématurée? – Analyse de la loi française au regard des récentes décisions italiennes contre Apple et Samsung', in A. Bailleux (ed.), *Le droit en transition. Les clés juridiques d'une prospérité sans croissance* (Presses de l'Université Saint-Louis 2020) p. 245 at p. 284

E. Ober, B. Dell'Anno, J.-R. Drèze, L. Herrmann, A. Luciano, R. Maltry, I. Oehme, B. Schmon and J.-P. Ventère, 'Planned obsolescence: the government's choice?', in C. Bakker and R. Mugge (eds.), *Product Lifetimes And The Environment 2017 – Conference Proceedings* (IOS Press 2017) p. 315 at p. 318.

T. Piazzon, 'L'information et la désinformation des consommateurs: Rapport français', in G. Straetmans (ed.), *Information Obligations and Disinformation of Consumers* (Springer International Publishing 2019) p. 157 at p. 204

D. Raes, "L'obsolescence programmée à l'épreuve de l'obligation d'information du vendeur, de la notion de conformité et de la garantie des vices cachés" in *Liber Amicorum François Glansdorf et Pierre Legros* (Bruylant 2014) p. 235 at p. 318

B. Schinkels, 'Information Obligations and Disinformation of Consumers: German Law Report', in G. Straetmans (ed.), *Information Obligations and Disinformation of Consumers* (Springer International Publishing 2019) p. 131 at p. 156

R. Steennoot 'Het toepassingsgebied van nieuwe garantieregelingen voor goederen, digitale inhoud en digitale diensten', in *Nieuw consumentenrecht: omzetting richtlijnen koop en digitale inhoud en digitale diensten, omzetting "omnibus"-richtlijn, omzetting richtlijn representatieve vorderingen* (Larcier Intersentia 2022) p. 3 at p. 23

W. Sun, P. Sun, 'Post Planned Obsolescence', in *Proceedings of the 9th International Conference on Computer-Aided Industrial Design and Conceptual Design: Multicultural Creation and Design* (CAIDCD 2008) p. 1009 at p. 1011

T. Thysen, A. Berwald, 'Consumers' experiences with premature obsolescence – Insights from seven EU countries', in C. Fitzpatrick et al. (eds.), *4th international Product Lifetimes and the Environnement (PLATE) conference proceedings* (Limerick 2021) p. 614 at p. 619.

K. Tonner, 'Sustainable consumption, consumer policy and the law', in C. Verdure (ed.), *Environmental law and consumer protection* (Larcier 2011) p. 9 at p. 24.

S.S. Van Dam, C.A. Bakker, I. de Pauw and B. Van der Grinten, 'The circular pathfinder: development and evaluation of a practice-based tool for selecting circular design strategies', in C. Bakker and R. Mugge (eds.), *Product Lifetimes And The Environment 2017 – Conference Proceedings* (IOS Press 2017) p. 102 at p. 107

R. van den Berge, L. Magnier, R. Mugge, 'A poorly educated guess: consumers' lifetime estimations, attitudes towards repairability, and a product lifetime label', in C. Fitzpatrick et al. (eds.), *4th international Product Lifetimes and the Environment (PLATE) conference proceedings* (Limerick 2021) p. 641 at p. 646.

T.S. Wallner, L. Magnier, R. Mugge, 'Buying new or refurbished? The influence of the product's durability and attractiveness, contamination risk and consumers' environmental concern on purchase intentions of refurbished and new products', in C. Fitzpatrick (eds.), *4th international Product Lifetimes and the Environment (PLATE) conference proceedings* (Limerick 2021) p. 653 at p. 659.

H. Wieser, N. Tröger and R. Hübner, 'The consumers' desired and expected product lifetimes', in T. Cooper, N. Braithwaite, M. Moreno and G. Salvia (eds.), *Product Lifetimes and the Environment (PLATE) Conference proceedings* (Nottingham Trent University: CADBE 2015) p. 388 at p. 392

C. Willet, 'Direct producer liability', in G. Howells, R. Schulze, *Modernising and Harmonising Consumer Contract Law* (Sellier 2009) p. 189 at p. 209

A. Zeeuw van der Laan, M. Aurisicchio, 'Planned obsolescence in the circular economy', in C. Bakker and R. Mugge (eds.), *Product Lifetimes And The Environment 2017 – Conference Proceedings* (IOS Press 2017) p. 446 at p. 452

C. ARTICLES IN ACADEMIC JOURNALS

J.D. Abbey, M.G. Meloy, V.D.R. Guide Jr., S. Atalay, 'Remanufactured products in closed-loop supply chains for consumer goods', 24 *Production and Operations Management* (2015) p. 488 at p. 503

L. Ackermann, R. Mugge, J. Schoormans, 'Consumers' perspective on product care: An exploratory study of motivators, ability factors, and triggers', 183 *J. Clean. Prod.* (2018) p. 380 at p. 391

V.V. Agrawal, S. Kavadias, L. B. Toktay, 'The Limits of Planned Obsolescence for Conspicuous Durable Goods', 18 *M&SOM* (2016) p. 216 at p. 226

G. Akerlof, 'The Market for Lemons: Quality Uncertainty and the Market Mechanism', 84 *Q. J. Econ.* (1970) p. 488 at p. 500

T. K. Aladeojebi, 'Planned obsolescence', 4 *International Journal of Scientific & Engineering Research* (2013) p. 1504 at p. 1508

F. Alfieri, M. Cordella, J. Sanfelix, N. Dodd, 'An approach to the assessment of durability of energy-related products', 69 *Procedia CIRP* (2018) p. 878 at p. 891

B.L. Bayus, 'Accelerating the Durable Replacement Cycle with Marketing Mix Variables', 5 *J. Prod. Innov. Manag.* (1988) p. 216 at p. 226

O. Bar-Gill, D. Schkade, C. R. Sunstein, 'Drawing false inferences from mandated disclosures', 3 *Behavioural Public Policy* (2018) p. 209 at p. 227

S.I. Becher, A.-L. Sibony, 'Confronting Product Obsolescence', 27 *Colum. J. Eur. L.* (2021) p. 97 at p. 150

N. Bériot, L. Farrant, 'L'information des consommateurs sur l'impact environnemental des produits: le cas des industries agroalimentaires', 73 *Annales des Mines-Responsabilité et Environnement* (2014) p. 35 at p. 39

L. Bisschop, Y. Hendlin, J. Jaspers, 'Designed to break: planned obsolescence as corporate environmental crime', 78 *Crime, Law and Social Change* (2022) p. 271 at p. 293

N.M.P. Bocken, I. de Pauw, C. Bakker, B. van der Grinten, 'Product design and business model strategies for a circular economy', 33 *Journal of Industrial and Production Engineering* (2016) p. 308 at p. 320

F. Bonciu, 'The European Economy: From a linear to a circular economy', 14 *Romanian Journal of European Affairs* (2014) 78–91

T. Brönneke, 'Premature Obsolescence: Suggestions for Legislative Counter-measures in German and European Sales & Consumer Law', 14 *Journal for European Environmental & Planning Law* (2017) p. 361 at p. 372

E. Brown, 'Time to Pull the Plug? Empowering Consumers to Make End-of-Life Decisions for Electronic Devices through Eco-Labels and Right to Repair', 1 *Journal of Law, Technology & Policy* (2020) p. 227 at p. 252

J. Bulow, 'An economic theory of planned obsolescence', 101 *Q. J. Econ.* (1986) p. 729 at p. 749

J.M. Carvalho, 'Sale of Goods and Supply of Digital Content and Digital Services – Overview of Directives 2019/770 and 2019/771', 5 *EuCML* (2019) p. 194 at p. 201

S. Castagné, 'Information du consommateur sur la disponibilité des pièces détachées – Quels supports durables assurent l'information?', *Contrats Concurrence Consommation* (2017) p. 1.

J.P. Choi, 'Network Externality, Compatibility Choice, and Planned Obsolescence', 42 *The Journal of Industrial Economics* (1994) p. 167 at p. 182

T. Cooper, 'Inadequate Life? Evidence of Consumer Attitudes to Product Obsolescence', 27 *J. Consum. Policy* (2004) p. 421 at p. 449

T. Cooper, 'Slower Consumption: Reflections on Product Life Spans and the "Throwaway Society"', 9 *Journal of Industrial Ecology* (2005) p. 51 at p. 67

M. Cordella, J. Sanfelix, F. Alfieri, 'Development of an approach for assessing the reparability and upgradability of energy-related products', 69 *Procedia CIRP* (2018) p. 888 at p. 892

M. Cordella, F. Alfieri, J. Sanfelix, S. Donatello, R. Kaps, O. Wolf, 'Improving material efficiency in the life cycle of products: a review of EU Ecolabel criteria', 25 *The International Journal of Life Cycle Assessment volume* (2020) p. 921 at p. 935

J. Cox, S. Griffith, S. Giorgi, G. King, 'Consumer understanding of product lifetimes', 79 *Resources, Conservation and Recycling* (2013) p. 21 at p. 29

C. Dalhammar, 'Industry attitudes towards ecodesign standards for improved resource efficiency', 123 *J. Clean. Prod.* (2016) p. 155 at p. 166

M. DeBell, R. Dardis, 'Extending Product Life: Technology Isn't the Only Issue', 6 *Advances in Consumer Research* (1979) p. 381 at p. 385

C. Déméné, A. Marchand, 'L'obsolescence des produits électroniques: des responsabilités partagées', 10 *The Ethics Forum* (2015) 4–32

M.C. Den Hollander, C.A. Bakker, H.J. Hultink, 'Product design in a circular economy; development of a typology of key concepts and terms', 21 *Journal of Industrial Ecology* (2017) p. 517 at p. 525.

L.A. DiMatteo, S. Wrbka, 'Planned Obsolescence and Consumer Protection: The Unregulated Extended Warranty and Service Contract Industry', 28 *Cornell Journal of Law and Public Policy* (2019) p. 483 at p. 544

M. Djurovic, 'The Apple Case: The Commencement of Pan-European Battle Against Unfair Commercial Practices', 9 *Eur. Rev. Contract Law* (2013) p. 253 at p. 266.

N. Dupont, 'Durabilité des produits et disponibilité des pièces détachées: où en est-on?', 1 *La Semaine Juridique Entreprise et Affaires* (2016) p. 34 at p. 38

F. Echegaray, 'Consumers' reactions to product obsolescence in emerging markets: the case of Brazil', 134 *J. Clean. Prod.* (2016) p. 191 at p. 203

E. Eppinger, A. Jain, P. Vimalnath, A. Gurtoo, F. Tietze, R. Hernandez Chea, 'Sustainability transitions in manufacturing: the role of intellectual property', 49 *Current Opinion in Environmental Sustainability* (2021) p. 118 at p. 126

A. Fishman N. Gandal, O. Shy, 'Planned obsolescence as an engine of technological progress', 141 *Journal of Industrial Economics* (1993) p. 361 at p. 370

I. Gåvertsson, L. Milios, C. Dalhammar, 'Quality Labelling for Re-used ICT Equipment to Support Consumer Choice in the Circular Economy', 43 *J. Consum. Policy* (2020) p. 353 at p. 377

E. Gawel, W. Bretschneider, 'Die Nutzungs- und Lebensdauer von Konsumprodukten als Gegenstand staatlicher Nachhaltigkeitssteuerung', 39 *Zeitschrift für Umweltpolitik und Umweltrecht* (2016) p. 1 at p. 36

M. Gharfalkar, R. Court, C. Campbell, Z. Ali, G. Hillier, 'Analysis of waste hierarchy in the European waste directive 2008/98/EC', 39 *Waste Management* (2015) p. 305 at p. 313

P. Ghisellini, C. Cialani, S. Ulgiati, 'A review on circular economy: the expected transition to a balanced interplay of environmental and economic systems', 114 *J. Clean. Prod.* (2016) p. 11 at p. 32

R. Golman, D. Hagmann, G. Loewenstein, 'Information Avoidance', 55 *Journal of Economic Literature* 96 (2017) p. 96 at p. 135

P.M. Gregory, 'A Theory of Purposeful Obsolescence', 14 *Southern Economic Journal* (1947) p. 24 at p. 45

N. Gregson, A. Metcalfe, L. Crewe, 'Practices of object maintenance and repair: How consumers attend to consumer objects within the home', 9 *Journal of Consumer Culture* (2009) p. 248 at p. 272

R. Grewal, 'The Timing of Repeat Purchase of Consumer Durable Goods: The Role of Functional Bases of Consumer Attitudes', 41 *Journal of Marketing Research* (2004) p. 101 at p. 115

S. J. Grossman, 'The Informational Role of Warranties and Private Disclosure about Product Quality', 24 *The Journal of Law and Economics* (1981) p. 461 at p. 483

P. A. Grout, I.-U. Park, 'Competitive Planned Obsolescence', 36 *The RAND Journal of Economics* (2005) p. 596 at p. 612

G.P. Gruere, 'An analysis of the growth in environmental labelling and information schemes', 38 *J. Consum. Policy* (2015) p. 1 at p. 18.

J. Guiltinan, 'Creative destruction and Destructive Creations: Environmental Ethics and Planned Obsolescence', 89 *Journal of Business Ethics* (2009) p. 19 at p. 28

D. Guiot, D. Roux, 'A second-hand shoppers' motivation scale: Antecedents, consequences, and implications for retailers', 86 *Journal of Retailing* (2010) p. 355 at p. 371.

M. Haines-Gadd, J. Chapman, P. Lloyd, J. Mason and D. Aliakseyeu, 'Emotional Durability Design Nine – A Tool for Product Longevity', 10 *Sustainability* (2018) p. 1 at p. 19

A. Hamann, 'Obsolescence programmée: le droit en panne?', 102 *D.C.C.R.* (2014) p. 41 at p. 82

A. Hamann, 'Obsolescence programmée: vers la fin de l'impunité?', 124 *D.C.C.R.*, (2019) p. 15 at p. 25

L. Harmer, T. Cooper, T. Fisher, G. Salvia, C. Barr, 'Design, dirt and disposal: influences on the maintenance of vacuum cleaners', 228 *J. Clean. Prod.* (2019) p. 1176 at p. 1186

G.D. Harrell, D.M. McConocha, 'Personal Factors Related to Consumer Product Disposal Tendencies', 26 *Journal of Consumer Affairs* (1992) p. 397 at 417

R. F. Hartl, P. M. Kort, S. Wrzaczek, 'Reputation or warranty, what is more effective against planned obsolescence?', *International Journal of Production Research* (2022) p. 1 at p. 16.

H. Hartwig, 'Spare Parts Under European Design and Trade Mark Law', 11 *Journal of intellectual property law & practice* (2016) p. 121 at p. 129

L. Hennies, R. Stamminger, 'An empirical survey on the obsolescence of appliances in German households', 112 *Resources, Conservation and Recycling* (2016) p. 73 at p. 82

K. Hobsona, N. Lynchb, D. Lilleyc, G. Smalleyc, 'Systems of practice and the Circular Economy: Transforming mobile phone product service systems', 26 *Environmental Innovation and Societal Transitions* (2018) p. 147 at p. 157

T. Hohmuth, ‚Murks? Nein, danke?! Rechtliche Aspekte zum Umgang mit dem Phänomen "geplante Obsoleszenz"', *Zeitschrift zum Innovations- und Technikrecht* (2014) p. 74 at p. 85

R.E. Horne, 'Limits to labels: The role of eco-labels in the assessment of product sustainability and routes to sustainable consumption', 33 *International Journal of Consumer Studies* (2009) p. 175 at p. 182

G. Howells, 'The Potential and Limits of Consumer Empowerment by Information', 32 *Journal of law and society* (2005) p. 349 at p. 370

F. Iraldo, M. Barberio, 'Drivers, Barriers and Benefits of the EU Ecolabel in European Companies' Perception', 9 *Sustainability* (2017) p. 751 at p.

C Jolls, C.R. Sustein, R.H. Thaler, 'A behavioral approach to law and economics', 50 *Stanford Law Review* (1998) p. 1471 at p. 1550

A. Katz, 'Beyond search costs: the linguistic and trust functions of trademarks', 5 *Brigham Young University Law Review* (2010) p. 1555 at p. 1608

B. Keirsbilck, E. Terryn, E. Van Gool, 'Consumentenbescherming bij servitisation en product-dienst-systemen (PDS)', 56 *T.P.R.* (2019) p. 817 at p. 899

B. Keirsbilck, 'Sustainability, the Circular Economy and Consumer Law in Belgium' 9 *EuCML* (2020) p. 165 at p. 168

G. Kenyon, K. Sen, 'A Model for Assessing Consumer Perceptions of Quality', 4 *International Journal of Quality and Service Sciences* (2012) p. 175 at p. 188

H. Kinokuni, S. Ohori, Y. Tomoda, 'Optimal Waste Disposal Fees When Product Durability is Endogenous: Accounting for Planned Obsolescence', 73 *Environmental and Resource Economics* (2019) p. 33 at p. 50

C. Koolen, 'Vacuum Cleaner Energy Labels and Misleading Commercial Practices: EU Consumers Left in the Dust?', 8 *EuCML* (2019) p. 82 at p. 88

K. Kryla-Cudna, 'Sales Contracts and the Circular Economy', 28 *E.R.P.L.* (2020) p. 1207 at p. 1230

R. Kurz, 'Quality, obsolescence and unsustainable innovation', 28 *Ekonomski vjesnik* (2015) p. 511 at p. 522.

M. Langhendries, Le coût de la panne: droit et obsolescence programmée, 71 *Revue du Droit des Technlogies de l'Information* (2018) p. 55 at p. 86

R. Lawlor, 'Delaying obsolescence', 21 *Science and Engineering Ethics* (2015) p. 401 at p. 427

C. Lepla, 'L'obligation de gestion des invendus non alimentaires', 47 *Revue juridique de l'environnement* (2022) p. 81 at p. 89

T. Libaert, 'Consommation et controverse: le cas de l'obsolescence programmée', 73 *Hermès, La Revue* (2015) p. 151 at p. 158

G. Loewenstein, C. R. Sunstein, R. Golman, 'Disclosure: Psychology Changes Everything', 6 *Annual Review of Economic* (2014) p. 391 at p. 419

G. Loiseau, 'Renforcement de la lutte contre l'obsolescence programmée d'un produit, étendue à l'obsolescence logicielle', 1 *Communication* (2022) pp. 1–2.

M. Maggiolino, 'Planned Obsolescence: A Strategy in Search of Legal Rules', 50 *International Review of Intellectual Property and Competition Law* (2019) p. 405 at p. 407

E. Maitre-Ekern and C. Dalhammar,'Regulating planned obsolescence: a review of legal approaches to increase product durability and reparability in Europe', 25 *Review of European Community & International Environmental Law* (2016) p. 378 at p. 394

E. Maitre-Ekern, C. Dalhammar, 'Towards a hierarchy of consumption behaviour in the circular economy', 26 *Maastricht Journal of European and Comparative Law* (2019) p. 394 at p. 420

E. Maitre-Ekern, 'Re-Thinking Producer Responsibility for a Sustainable Circular Economy: From Extended Producer Responsibility to Pre-market Producer Responsibility', 286 *J. Clean. Prod.* (2021) p. 1 at p. 25.

V. Mak, E. Terryn, 'Circular Economy and Consumer Protection: The Consumer as a Citizen and the Limits of Empowerment Through Consumer Law', 43 *J. Consum. Policy* (2020) p. 235 at p. 244

R. Malcolm, 'Ecodesign Laws and the Environmental Impact of our Consumption of Products', 23 *Journal of Environmental Law* (2011) p. 487 at p. 503

J. Malinauskaite, F.B. Erdem, 'Planned Obsolescence in the Context of a Holistic Legal Sphere and the Circular Economy', 41 *Oxford Journal of Legal Studies* (2021) p. 719 at p. 749

A.R. Mashhadi, B. Esmaeilian, W. Cade, K. Wiens, S. Behdad, 'Mining consumer experiences of repairing electronics: Product design insights and business lessons learned', 137 *J. Clean. Prod.* (2016) p. 716 at p. 727

A. Massarutto, 'The long and winding road to resource efficiency – An interdisciplinary perspective on extended producer responsibility', 85 *Resources, Conservation and Recycling* (2014) p. 11 at p. 21

M. Mayer, 'Planned obsolescence: Rx for tired markets?', 73 *Dun's Review and Modern Industry* (1959) p. 40 at p. 80

J. McCollough, 'Consumer Discount Rates and the Decision to Repair or Replace a Durable Product: A Sustainable Consumption Issue', 44 *Journal of Economic Issues* (2010) p. 183 at p. 204

C. Meller-Hannich and E. Krausbeck, 'Sustainability, the Circular Economy and Consumer Law in Germany', 9 *EuCML* (2020) p. 168 at p. 172

C.-H. Miao, 'Tying, Compatibility and Planned Obsolescence', 58 *The Journal of Industrial Economics* (2010) p. 579 at p. 606

A. Michel, 'La directive 1999/44/CE sur la garantie des biens de consommation: un remède efficace contre l'obsolescence programmée?', *R.E.D.C.* (2018) p. 207 at p. 236

H.-W. Micklitz, 'Squaring the Circle? Reconciling Consumer Law and the Circular Economy', 8 *EuCML* (2019) p. 229 at p. 237.

G.A. Miller, 'The magical number seven, plus or minus two: Some limits on our capacity for processing information', 63 *Psychological Review* (1956) p. 81 at p. 97

E. Montero, 'Les produits défectueux dans un écheveau de responsabilités – note sous Liège (3e ch.), 7 novembre 2005', 10 *R.G.D.C.* (2006) p. 624 at p. 628.

Morais, G. Montagna, 'Customized Wardrobe: Clothing according to user', 3 *Procedia Manufacturing* (2015) p. 5814 at p. 5821

R. Mugge, J.P.L. Schoormans, H.N.J. Schifferstein, 'Design Strategies to Postpone Consumers' Product Replacement: The Value of a Strong Person-Product Relationship', 8 *The Design Journal* (2005) p. 38 at p. 48

R. Mugge, B. Jockina, N. Bockena, 'How to sell refurbished smartphones? An investigation of different customer groups and appropriate incentives', 147 *J. Clean. Prod.* (2017) p. 284 at p. 296

P. Munten, J. Vanhamme, 'Fighting Planned Obsolescence Practices and Excessive Consumption: The Positive Effect of Pre-Purchase Product Reparability Communication on Consumers' Attitude', 47 *Advances in Consumer Research* (2019) p. 776.

P. Munten, J. Vanhamme, V. Swaen, 'Reducing obsolescence practices from a product-oriented PSS perspective: A research agenda', *Recherche et Applications en Marketing* (2021)

S. Murakami, H. Ohsugi, R. Murakami-Suzuki, A. Mukaida and H. Tsujimura, 'Average life span of mobile phones and in-use and hibernating stocks in Japan', 5 *Journal of Life Cycle Assessment, Japan* (2009) p. 138 at p. 144

I. Oswald, A. Reller, 'E-waste: A story of trashing, trading, and valuable resources', 20 *GAIA* (2011) p. 41 at p. 47

T. Page, 'Product attachment and replacement: Implications for sustainable design', 2 *International Journal of Sustainable Design* (2014) p. 256 at p. 282

V. Perez-Belis, M. Braulio-Gonzalo, P. Juan, M.D. Bovea, 'Consumer attitude towards the repair and the second-hand purchase of small household electrical and electronic equipment. A Spanish case study', 158 *J. Clean. Prod.* (2017) p. 261 at p. 275

N. Podolyakina, 'Estimation of the Relationship between the Products Reliability, Period of Their Warranty Service and the Value of the Enterprise Cost', 178 *Procedia Engineering* (2017) p. 558 at p. 568

K. Pouikli, 'Concretising the role of extended producer responsibility in European Union waste law and policy through the lens of the circular economy', 20 *ERA Forum* (2020) p. 491 at p. 508.

M. Proske, 'How to address obsolescence in LCA studies – Perspectives on product use-time for a smartphone case study', 376 *J. Clean. Prod.* (2022) 134283

K.P. Purnhagen, H. Schebesta, 'Island or Ocean: Empirical Evidence on the Average Consumer Concept in the UCPD', 28 *E.R.P.L.* (2020) p. 293 at p. 310

R. Rai, J. Terpenny, 'Principles for Managing Technological Product Obsolescence', 31 *IEEE Transactions on Components, Packaging, and Manufacturing Technology* (2008) p. 880 at p. 889

A. Rees, 'The Waste-Makers and the String-Savers', 34 *The Journal of Business* (1961) p. 367 at p. 373

J.L. Rivera, A. Lallmahomed, 'Environmental implications of planned obsolescence and product lifetime: a literature review', 9 *International Journal of Sustainable Engineering* (2016) p. 119 at p. 129

A.J.D. Rosborough, 'Unscrewing the Future: The Right to Repair and the Circumvention of Software TPMs in the EU', 11 *Journal of Intellectual Property, Information Technology and E-Commerce Law* (2020) p. 26 at p. 48

C.A. Roster, M. Richins, 'Ambivalence and attitudes in consumer replacement decisions', 19 *Journal of Consumer Psychology* (2009) p. 48 at p. 61

O'Rourke and Ringer, 'The Impact of Sustainability Information on Consumer Decision Making', *Journal of Industrial Ecology* (2015) p. 882 at p. 892

J. Salzman, 'Informing the green consumer. The debate over the use and abuse of environmental labels', 1 *Journal of Industrial Ecology* (1997) p. 11 at p. 21

C. Sanne, 'Willing consumers – or locked-in? Policies for a sustainable consumption', 42 *Ecological Economics* (2002) p. 273 at p. 287

M. Schaub, 'How to Make the Best of Mandatory Information Requirements in Consumer Law', 25 *E.R.P.L.* (2017), p. 25 at p. 44

G. Scholl, F. Rubik, H. Kalimo, K. Biedenkopf, Ó. Söebech, 'Policies to promote sustainable consumption: innovative approaches in Europe', 34 *Natural Resources Forum* (2010) p. 39 at p. 50

I. Schumacher, 'Ecolabeling, consumers' preferences and taxation', 69 *Ecological Economics* (2010) p. 2202 at p. 2212

K. Sein, G. Spindler, 'The New Directive on Contracts for the Supply of Digital Content and Digital Services Scope of Application and Trader's Obligation to Supply', 15 *Eur. Rev. Contract Law* (2019) p. 260 at p. 269

M.R. Shaharudin, S. Zailani and K.C. Tan, 'Barriers to product returns and recovery management in a developing country: investigation using multiple methods', 96 *J. Clean. Prod.* (2015) p. 220 at p. 232

A.-L. Sibony, 'Can EU consumer law benefit from behavioural insights? An analysis of the unfair practices directive', 22 *E.R.P.L.* (2014) p. 901 at p. 942

J. Spinney, K. Burningham, G. Cooper, N. Green and D. Uzzell, 'What I've found is that your related experiences tend to make you dissatisfied': Psychological obsolescence, consumer demand and the dynamics and environmental implications of de-stabilization in the laptop sector', 12 *Journal of Consumer Culture* (2012) p. 347 at p. 370

D. Staudenmayer, 'Les directives européennes sur les contrats numériques', 116 *Revue des contrats* (2019)

R. Strausz, 'Planned obsolescence as an incentive device for unobservable quality', 119 *The Economic Journal* (2009) p. 1405 at p. 1421

P.L. Swan, 'Optimum Durability, Second-Hand Markets, and Planned Obsolescence', 80 *Journal of Political Economy* (1972) p. 575 at p. 585

M.B. Taylor and M. van der Velden, 'Resistance to Regulation: Failing Sustainability in Product Lifecycles', 11 *Sustainability* (2019) 6526.

P. Tecchio, C. McAlister, F. Mathieux, F. Ardente, 'In search of standards to support circularity in product policies', 168 *J. Clean. Prod.* (2017) p. 1533 at p. 1546

E. Terryn, 'A Right to Repair: Towards Sustainable Remedies in Consumer Law', *E.R.P.L.* (2019) p. 851 at p. 874

E. Terryn, E. Van Gool, 'The Role of European Consumer Contract Law in Shaping the Environmental Impact of E-commerce', 10 *EuCML* (2021) p. 89 at p. 100

E. Terryn, E. Van Gool, 'Kunnen we e-commerce vergroenen door het consumentencontractenrecht te herzien?', *TvC* (2021) p. 15 at p. 28

E. Terryn, 'Lutter contre l'écoblanchissement est nécessaire mais ne suffit pas pour atteindre une consommation responsable', 47 *Revue juridique de l'environnement* (2022) p. 73 at p. 79.

C. Thornquist, 'Unemotional design: an alternative approach to sustainable design', 33 *Design Issues* (2017) p. 83 at p. 91

C. Tietje, 'The Concept of Coherence in the TEU and the CFSP', 2 *Eur. Foreign Aff. Rev.* (1997) p. 211 at p. 233.

K. Tonner, 'Consumer Protection and Environmental Protection: Contradictions and Suggested Steps Towards Integration', 23 *J. Consum. Policy* (2000) p. 63 at p. 78

F. Trentmann, 'The Long History of Contemporary Consumer Society – Chronologies, Practices, and Politics in Modern Europe', 49 *Archiv für Sozialgeschichte* (2009) p. 107 at p. 128.

A. Tukker, 'Eight types of product-service-system: Eight ways to sustainability? Experiences from Suspronet', *Business Strategy and the Environment* (2004) p. 246 at p. 260

J. Turiel, 'Consumer electronic right to repair laws: focusing on an environmental foundation', 45 *William & Mary Environmental Law and Policy Review* (2021) p. 579 at p. 599.

A. Utaka, 'Planned Obsolescence and Marketing Strategy', 21 *Managerial and Decision Economics* (2000) p. 339 at p. 344

F. Van den Abeele, B. Tilleman, 'Remedies in het nieuwe consumenten(koop)recht: een (her)nieuw(d) getrapt systeem', 135 *D.C.C.R.* (2022) p. 59 at p. 102.

R. Van den Berg, L. Magnier, and R. Mugge, 'Too good to go? Consumers' replacement behaviour and potential strategies for stimulating product retention', 39 *Current opinion in psychology* (2021) p. 66 at p. 71

E. Van Gool and A. Michel, 'The New Consumer Sales Directive 2019/771 and Sustainable Consumption: A Critical Analysis', 10 *EuCML* (2021) p. 136 at p. 148.

N. van Nes, J. Cramer, 'Influencing product lifetime through product design', 14 *Business Strategy and Environment* (2005) p. 286 at p. 299

N. van Nes, J. Cramer, 'Product lifetime optimization: a challenging strategy towards more sustainable consumption patterns', 14 *J. Clean. Prod.* (2006) p. 1307 at p. 1318

S. Waechter, B. Sütterlin, M. Siegrist, 'Desired and undesired effects of energy labels – An eyetracking study', 10 *PLoS One* (2015) p. 1 at p. 26

M. Waldman, 'A New Perspective on Planned Obsolescence', 108 *Q. J. Econ.* (1993) p. 273 at p. 283

M. Waldman, 'Planned Obsolescence and the R&D Decision', 27 *The RAND Journal of Economics* (1996) p. 583 at p. 595

F. Wang et al., 'Enhancing E-waste estimates: improving data quality by multivariate input/output analysis', 33 *Waste Manage* (2013) p. 2397 at p. 2407

T.L. Webb, B.P.I. Chang, Y. Benn, "The Ostrich Problem': Motivated Avoidance or Rejection of Information about Goal Progress', 7 *Social and Personality Psychology Compass* (2013) p. 794 at p. 807

K.A. Whalen, 'Three circular business models that extend product value and their contribution to resource efficiency', 226 *J. Clean. Prod.* (2019) p. 1128 at p. 1137

N. Whiteley, 'Toward a Throwaway Culture: Consumerism, "Style Obsolescence" and Cultural Theory in the 1950s and 1960s', 10 *Oxford Art Journal* (1987) p. 3 at p. 27

H. Wieser, 'Beyond Planned Obsolescence: Product Lifespans and the Challenges to a Circular Economy', 25 *GAIA* (2016) p. 156 at p. 160

H. Wieser, N. Tröger, 'Exploring the inner loops of the circular economy: Replacement, repair, and reuse of mobile phones in Austria', 172 *J. Clean. Prod.* (2018) p. 3042 at p. 3055

T. Wilhelmsson, 'Consumer law and the environment: from consumer to citizen', 21 *J. Consum. Policy* (1998) p. 45 at p. 70

G.T. Wilson, G. Smalley, J.R. Suckling, D. Lilley, J. Lee, R. Mawle, 'The hibernating mobile phone: dead storage as a barrier to efficient electronic waste recovery', 60 *Waste Management* (2017) p. 521 at p. 533

S. Wrbka, 'Warranty law in cases of planned obsolescence – The Austrian situation', 6 *EuCML* (2017) p. 67 at p. 76

M. Zallio, D. Berry, 'Design and Planned Obsolescence. Theories and Approaches for Designing Enabling Technologies', 20 *The Design Journal* (2017) S3749-S3761

D. Zhilyaeva, C. Cimpana, Z. Caoa, G. Liua, S. Askegaardb, H. Wenzela, 'The Living, the Dead, and the Obsolete: A Characterization of Lifetime and Stock of ICT Products in Denmark', 164 *Resources, Conservation & Recycling* (2021) 105117

D. REPORTS, STUDIES AND WORKING PAPERS

F. Alfieri, M. Cordella R. Stamminger, A. Bues, *Durability assessment of products: analysis and testing of washing machines – JRC Technical Report* (European Commission 2018)

J. Bachér et al., *Electronic products and obsolescence in a circular economy* (European Topic Centre Waste and Materials in a Green Economy 2020)

C. Bakker, C. Schuit, *The long view – Exploring product lifetime extension* (United Nations Environment Programme 2017)

B. Bauer, D. Watson, A. Gylling, A. Remmen, M. Hauris Lysemose, C. Hohenthal, A.-K. Jönbrink, *Potential Ecodesign Requirements for Textiles and Furniture* (TemaNord 2018)

S. Bobba, F. Ardente, F. Mathieux, *Technical support for Environmental Footprinting, material efficiency in product policy and the European Platform on LCA: Durability assessment of vacuum cleaners – JRC Science and Policy Report* (European Commission 2015)

S. Boulos, A. Sousanoglou, L. Evans, J. Lee, N. King, C. Facheris, F. Iraldo, B. Nucci, M. Donelli, *The durability of products – Standards assessment for the circular economy under the Eco-Innovation Action Plan* (European Commission 2015)

J. Bouma, *Design for customer engagement in the transition to a circular economy: A case study in Senseo coffee machines* (TU Delft 2019)

E. Bracquené, J. Brusselaers, Y. Dams, J. Peeters, K. De Schepper, J. Duflou, W. Dewulf., *Repairability criteria for energy related products – Study in the BeNeLux context to evaluate the options to extend the product life time* (KU Leuven, Vito, BeNeLux 2018)

C. Brannigan, S. Amaral, I. Sikora, M. Zabalo, N. Hill, I. Skinner, J. Lawrence, J. Farrington, C. Reiner, T. Loke, *Technical analysis of measures to improve consumer awareness of emissions and fuel consumption of vehicles* (European Union 2021)

T. Brönneke, 'Premature obsolescence and European law – Possibilities with regard to the Reform of the Consumer Sales Directive', in *Polytechnic Pforzheim Conference Proceedings* (Hochschule Pforzheim 2014), available on <www.beuc.eu/documents/files/FC/durablegoods/conference/presentations/Bronneke_SustainableConsumption_EN.pdf>

Brook Lyndhurst, *Public understanding of product lifetimes and durability* (DEFRA 2011)

S. Carlsson, A. Mallalieu, *Design for Longevity – A Framework to Support Product Developers in Identifying Products' Optimal Lifetimes, Master's Thesis in Product Development* (Chalmers University of Technology 2021)

N. Cases i Sampere, *Making more durable and reparable products – Building a rating system to inform consumers and trigger business innovation* (EEB 2015)

CECED, *Material flows of the home appliance industry. European Committee of Domestic Equipment Manufacturers* (2017)

Centre Européen de la Consommation, *L'obsolescence programmée ou les dérives de la société de consommation* (2013)

CLASP, ECOS, EEB and Topten, *Closing the 'Reality Gap' – Ensuring a Fair Energy Label for Consumers* (2017), available on: <https://eeb.org/closing-the-reality-gap/>.

M. Cordella, F. Alfieri, J. Sanfelix, *Analysis and development of a scoring system for repair and upgrade of products – Final Report* (European Commission 2019)

M. Cordella, F. Alfieri, J. Sanfelix, *Guidance for the Assessment of Material Efficiency: Application to Smartphones – JRC Technical Report* (European Commission 2020)

C. Dalhammar, E. Machacek, A. Bundgaard, K. Overgaard Zacho, A. Remmen, *Addressing resource efficiency through the Ecodesign Directive* (TemaNord 2014)

Deloitte, *Study on socioeconomic impacts of increased reparability – Final Report* (European Union 2016)

N. Dodd, C. Vidal-Abarca and O. Wolf, *Revision of the European Ecolabel Criteria for Personal, Notebook and Tablet Computers – JRC Science and Policy Reports* (European Commission 2019)

B. Dupont, V. Swaen, J. Vanhamme, *Labelling the durability of a product through the lens of intertemporal choices theory* (European Marketing Academy Conference 2015)

ECC-Net, *Commercial warranties – are they worth the money?* (2014)

Ecorys, GFK and Tilburg University, *Study on the effects on consumer behaviour of online sustainability information displays – Final report* (Consumer Programme 2014)

Ecos, EEB, *Key recommendations for the development of further EU-wide end-of-waste (EoW) criteria* (2021)

Ellen MacArthur Foundation, *Towards the circular economy: Economic and business rationale for an accelerated transition* (2013)

Ellen MacArthur Foundation, *A New Textiles Economy: Redesigning fashion's future* (2017)

Ellen MacArthur Foundation, *Artificial Intelligence and the Circular Economy* (2019)

M. Elsen, K. van den Akker, R. van Giesen, T. Meeusen, S. Davidson, D. Anné, T. van der Linden, R. van de Meulengraaf, *Consumer study on the impact of reparability information formats on consumer understanding and purchase decisions – Final report* (European Union 2021)

European Commission, *Promoting Remanufacturing, Refurbishment, Repair, and Direct Reuse: as a contribution to the G7 alliance on resource efficiency 7–8 February 2017 Brussels, Belgium: workshop report* (European Union 2017)

European Court of Auditors, *EU action on Ecodesign and Energy Labelling: important contribution to greater energy efficiency reduced by significant delays and non-compliance – Special Report* (European Union 2020)

European Environmental Agency, *Circular by design: Products in the circular economy* (European Union 2017)

European Environmental Bureau, *Coolproducts don't cost the earth – full report* (2019)

European Parliament, *Planned obsolescence: Exploring the issue* (European Union 2016)

M. Fabre, W. Winkler, *L'obsolescence programmée, symbole de la société du gaspillage – Le cas des produits électriques et électroniques* (Les Amis de la Terre 2010)

E. Fangeat, C. Chauvin, *Allongement de la durée de vie des produits* (ADEME 2016)

Fraunhofer IZM, Fraunhofer ISI, VITO, *Ecodesign preparatory study on mobile phones, smartphones and tablets – Final Report* (European Commission 2021).

Gartner, *Reused, Resold, Recycled – Where Do Old Smartphones Go* (2015), available on <https://www.gartner.com/en/newsroom/press-releases/2015–02–18-gartner-says-worldwide-market-for-refurbished-smartphones-to-reach-120-million-units-by-2017>

GfK Belgium, time.lex, Milieu Ltd, BIO IS and the Ecologic Institute, *Consumer market study on environmental claims for non-food products* (European Commission 2014)

A. Girard, C. Thorpe, F. Durif, E. Robinot, 'Obsolescence of Home Appliances and Electronics: What Is the Role of the Consumer?', *Équiterre* (2018)

B. Granberg, *The Quality Re-evaluation Process: Product Obsolescence in a Consumer-Producer Interaction Framework* (The Swedish Environmental Protection Agency 1997)

J. Gröger, A. Köhler, S. Naumann, A. Filler, A. Guldner, E. Kern, L.M. Hilty, Y.V. Maksimov, *Entwicklung und Anwendung von Bewertungsgrundlagen für ressourceneffiziente Software unter Berücksichtigung bestehender Methodik* (Umweltbundesamt 2018)

Halte à l'Obsolescence Programmée, *Imprimantes: cas d'école de l'obsolescence programmée* (September 2017)

Halte à l'Obsolescence Programmée, *Durabilité des produits – Le temps de l'action* (2020)

ICF, *Study on the costs and benefits of extending certain rights under the Consumer Sales and Guarantees Directive 1999/44/CE* (European Commission 2017)

IIIEE and EEB, *Removable, replaceable and repairable batteries report* (2021)

International Trade Centre, *The European Union Market for Sustainable Products – The retail perspective on sourcing policies and consumer demand* (ITC and European Commission 2019)

Ipsos-London Economics-Deloitte consortium, *Consumer market study on the functioning of legal and commercial guarantees for consumers in the EU* (European Commission 2015)

Ipsos and Trinomics, *Impact Assessment Study on Common Chargers of Portable Devices* (European Commission 2019)

D. Jepsen, L. Spengler, L. Augsberg, *Delivering resource-efficient products – How Ecodesign can drive a circular economy in Europe* (European Environmental Bureau 2015)

Kantar, *Special Eurobarometer 501 – Attitudes of European citizens towards the Environment* (European Commission 2020)

Kantar, *Special Eurobarometer 503 – Attitudes towards the impact of digitalisation on daily lives* (European Commission 2020)

F. Keimeyer, P. Gailhofer, M. Gsell, K. Graulich, S. Prakash, C.-S. Scherf, T. Brönneke, R. Gildeggen, R. Schmitt, *Weiterentwicklung von Strategien gegen Obsoleszenz einschließlich rechtlicher Instrumente – Abschlussbericht* (Umweltbundesamt 2020)

T. Knight, G. King, S. Herren, J. Cox (Brook Lyndhurst), *Electrical and electronic product design: product lifetime* (WRAP 2013)

M. Krajewski, *The Great Lighbulb Conspiracy* (IEEE Spectrum 2014)

D. Kreziak, I. Prim-Allaz and E. Robinot, *Des tiroirs pleins de téléphones remplacés: consommateurs et objets à obsolescence perçue* (ADEME 2017)

N. Kunz, A. Atasu, K. Mayers, L. Van Wassenhove, *Extended producer responsibility: stakeholder concerns and future developments – Report for The INSEAD Social Innovation Centre* (2014)

LE Europe, VVA Europe, Ipsos, ConPolicy, Trinomics, *Behavioural study on consumers' engagement in the circular economy* (European Commission 2018)

B. London, *Ending the depression through planned obsolescence* (1932)

M. McVeigh, C. Dalhammar, J. Richter, *Planned obsolescence. Built not to last* (European Liberal Forum 2019)

A. Manhart, M. Blepp, C. Fischer, K. Graulich, S. Prakash, R. Priess, T. Schleicher, M. Tür, *Resource Efficiency in the ICT Sector* (Greenpeace 2016)

J.S. Marcus, G. Zachmann, S. Gardner, S. Tagliapietra, E. Lykogianni, *Promoting product longevity – How can the EU product safety and compliance framework help promote product durability and tackle planned obsolescence, foster the production of more sustainable products, and achieve more transparent supply chains for consumers?* (European Parliament 2020)

N. Maycroft, *Consumption, planned obsolescence and waste* (Lincoln School of Art and Design 2009)

C. McAlister, E. Oldyrevas, *One charger to fit them all – Using ecodesign to deliver an ambitious common charger initiative* (Ecos 2020)

D.H. Meadows, D.L. Meadows, J. Randers, W.W. Behrens III, *The limits to growth* (Universe 1972)

E. Molenbroek, M. Smith, H. Groenenberg, P. Waide, S. Attali, C. Fischer, J. Krivošik, P. Fonseca, B. Santos, J. Fong, *Evaluation of the Energy Labelling Directive and specific aspects of the Ecodesign Directive – Final technical report* (Ecofys 2014)

C. Montalvo, D. Peck, E. Rietveld, *A longer lifetime for products: benefits for consumers and companies* (European Union 2016)

S. Mugdal, B. Tinetti, T. Faninger, S. Lockwood, G. Anderson, *Etude sur la durée de vie des équipements électriques et électroniques* (ADEME 2012)

N. Nasr, J.D. Russell, *Redefining Value – The Manufacturing Revolution. Remanufacturing, Refurbishment, Repair and Direct Reuse in the Circular Economy. A Report of the International Resource Panel* (United Nations Environment Programme 2018)

OECD, *Product Durability and Product Life Extension: Their Contribution to Solid Waste Management* (1982)

OECD, *Extended Producer Responsibility – A Guidance Manual for Governments* (2001)

OECD, *Environmental Claims – Findings and Conclusions of the OECD Committee on Consumer Policy* (2011)

OECD, *The State of Play on Extended Producer Responsibility (EPR): Opportunities and Challenges* (2014)

OECD, *Extended producer responsibility – Updated guidance for efficient waste management* (OECD Publishing 2016)

I. Oehme, A. Jacob, *Strategies against obsolescence. Ensuring a minimum product lifetime and improving product service life as well as consumer information* (Umweltbundesamt 2017)

E. Oldyrevas, C. McAlister, *Long live the machine – How ecodesign & energy labelling can prevent premature obsolescence of laptops* (Ecos 2020)

R. Postpischil, K. Jacob, H. Bär, A. Siemons, F. Keimeyer, K. Schumacher, *Ecological Steering with Value-Added Tax and Taxes on Consumption* (Freie Universität Berlin 2021)

S. Prakash, G. Dehoust, M. Gsell, T. Schleicher, R. Stamminger, *Einfluss der Nutzungsdauer von Produkten auf ihre Umweltwirkung – Schaffung einer Informationsgrundlage und Entwicklung von Strategien gegen "Obsoleszenz"* (Umweltbundesamt 2016)

S. Prakash, T. Schleicher, M. Michalscheck, *Barrier Analysis and Strategies for Ecolabels and Sustainable Public Procurement Implementation* (Deutsche Gesellschaft für Internationale Zusammenarbeit 2021)

RDC Environment, *L'obsolescence programmée: politiques et mesures belges de protection du consommateur* (2017).

L. Reisch, A. Oehler, T. Brönneke, K.-H. Fezer, J. Stellpflug, *Qualität statt vorzeitiger Verschleiß – Diskussionspapier zur eingebauten Obsoleszenz bei Konsumgütern* (Verbraucher Kommission 2014)

V. Rizos, J. Bryhn, M. Alessi, A. Campmas, A. Zarra, *Identifying the impact of the circular economy on the Fast-Moving Consumer Goods Industry – Opportunities and challenges for businesses, workers and consumers – mobile phones as an example* (EESC 2019)

E. Robinot, F. Durif, D. Kréziak, I. Prim-Allaz, *"Fifty ways to leave your cell phone": Product obsolescence, product replacement and product attachment* (European Marketing Association Conference 2014)

RREUSE, *Improving product reparability: Policy options at EU level* (2015)

RREUSE, *Putting re-use and repair at the heart of the EU's circular economy package* (2015)

I. Rüdenauer, C.O. Gensch, *Eco-efficiency analysis of washing machines. Refinement of task 4: further use versus substitution of washing machines in stock* (Oeko-Institut 2005)

S. Sala, A. Beylot, S. Corrado, E. Crenna, E. Sanyé-Mengual, M. Secchi, *Indicators and assessment of the environmental impact of EU consumption – JRC Science for Policy Report* (European Commission 2019).

J. Sanfelix, M. Cordella, F. Alfieri, *Methods for the Assessment of the Reparability and Upgradability of Energy-related Products: Application to TVs – JRC Technical Report* (European Commission 2019)

K. Schischke, *Eco-design of Mobile Devices – Project sustainablySMART* (European Union 2018)

S. Schlacke, K. Tonner, E. Gawel, *Stärkung eines nachhaltigen Konsums im Bereich Produktnutzung durch Anpassungen im Zivil- und öffentlichen Recht* (Umweltbundesamt Study 2015)

B. Schmitz, 'Missing link ecodesign & sales guarantees', *European Parliament Conference on a longer lifetime for products: A win-win solution for European consumers and business* (European Parliament 2015)

S. Schridde, C. Kreiss, J. Winter, *Geplante Obsoleszenz: Entstehungsursachen – Konkrete Beispiele – Schadensfolgen – Handlungsprogramm* (Arge Regio 2014)

SIRCOME agency, the University of South Brittany and the University of South Bohemia, *The Influence of Lifespan Labelling on Consumers – ILLC study* (EESC 2016)

Sofies, Bio Innovation Service, *Étude du marché et parc de téléphones portables français en vue d'augmenter durablement leur taux de collecte – Synthèse* (2019)

D. Staudenmayer, 'The Directives on Digital Contracts: First Steps Towards the Private Law of the Digital economy', 28 *E.R.P.L.* (2020) p. 219 at p. 250

S. Svensson, J.L. Richter, E. Maitre-Ekern, T. Pihlajarinne, A. Maigret, C. Dalhammar, *The Emerging 'Right to Repair' legislation in the EU and the U.S.*, Paper presented at Going Green Care Innovation (Vienna 2018)

V. Swaen, *Labelling the durability/reparability of a product* (EESC Conference on Tackling premature obsolescence in Europe 2018)

P. Tecchio, F. Ardente, F. Mathieux, *Analysis of durability, reusability and reparability: Application to dishwashers and washing machines – JRC Technical Report* (European Commission 2016)

P. Tecchio, F. Ardente, M. Marwede, C. Christian, G. Dimitrova, F. Mathieux, *Analysis of material efficiency aspects of personal computers product group* (European Union 2018).

Technopolis Group (in consortium with Fraunhofer ISI, Thinkstep and Wuppertal Institute), *Regulatory barriers for the Circular Economy – Lessons from ten cases studies* (European Commission 2016)

The Swedish Energy Agency, *Increasing the lifespan of products – Policies and consumer perspectives* (2021)

TNS Political & Social, *Flash Eurobarometer 367 – Attitudes of Europeans towards building the single market for green products* (European Commission 2013)

TNS political & social, *Special Eurobarometer 468 – Attitudes of European citizens towards the environment* (European Commission 2017)

K. Tonner, R. Malcolm, *How an EU lifespan guarantee model could be implemented across the European Union (study)* (European Parliament 2017)

Umweltbundesamt GmbH and ARCADIS Belgium NV, *Study to assess member states (MS) practices on by-product (BP) and end-of waste (EoW) – Final report* (European Union 2020)

S. Van Camp, S. Bouyon, *Impact assessment of proposed substantial amendments introducing a commercial lifespan guarantee in the proposed online sales and digital content directive* (European Parliament 2017)

R. van den Berge, T. Thysen, *State-of-the-art knowledge on user, market and legal issues related to premature obsolescence* (PROMPT 2020)

C. Van Rossem, C. Dalhammar, E. Toulouse, *Designing Greener Electronic Products: Building Synergies between EU Product Policy Instruments or Simply Passing the Buck?* (EEB 2009)

L. Vasseur et al. (HOP), *Livre blanc: 50 mesures pour une consommation et une production durables. Le guide des politiques publiques pour une société sans obsolescence accélérée* (HOP 2018)

VHK and Viegand Maagøe, *ICT Impact study – Final Report* (European Commission 2020)

D. Watson, C. Gylling, B. Bauer, N. Tojo, H. Throne-Holst, *Circular Business Models in the Mobile Phone Industry* (TemaNord 2017)

R. Waugh, H. Symington, D. Parker, M. Kling, F. Zotz, *Study on the implementation of product design requirements set out in Article 4 of the WEEE Directive – The case of re-usability of printer cartridges – Final report* (European Union 2018)

H. Wieser, N. Tröger, *Die Nutzungsdauer und Obsoleszenz von Gebrauchsgütern im Zeitalter der Beschleunigungs – Eine Empirische Untersuchung in Österreichischen Haushalten* (Arbeiterkammer Wien 2015)